DISCOVERING
FICTION

DISCOVERING FICTION

HANS P. GUTH

GABRIELE L. RICO

San Jose State University

A BLAIR PRESS BOOK

PRENTICE HALL, ENGLEWOOD CLIFFS, NJ 07632

Library of Congress Cataloging-in-Publication Data

Guth, Hans Paul
    Discovering fiction / Hans P. Guth and Gabriele L. Rico.
        p.   cm.
    "A Blair Press book."
    Includes index.
    ISBN 0-13-219858-4
    1. English language—Rhetoric.   2. Fiction—Collections.
3. College readers.   I. Rico, Gabriele L.   II. Title.
PE1417.G865   1993
    808.3—dc20   92-26687
                                                            CIP

Cover designer: Thomas Nery
Prepress buyer: Herb Klein
Manufacturing buyers: Robert Anderson and Patrice Fraccio
Photo researchers: Joelle Burrows and Lori Morris-Nantz
Cover art: Edward Hopper, *Nighthawks* (detail), 1942. Oil on canvas 76.2 × 144 cm. Friends of
American Art Collection, 1942. 51. Diego Rivera, *The Flower Vendor* (detail), 1949. Museo Es-
paniol de Arte Contemporaneo, Madrid.

Acknowledgments appear on pages 618–621, which constitute
a continuation of the copyright page.

Blair Press
The Statler Building
20 Park Plaza, Suite 1113
Boston, MA 02116-4399

© 1993 by Prentice Hall, Inc.
A Simon & Schuster Company
Englewood Cliffs, NJ 07632

Printed in the United States of America
10 9 8 7 6 5 4 3 2

ISBN 0-13-219858-4

Prentice-Hall International (UK) Limited, *London*
Prentice-Hall of Australia Pty. Limited, *Sydney*
Prentice-Hall Canada Inc., *Toronto*
Prentice-Hall Hispanoamericana, S.A., *Mexico*
Prentice-Hall of India Private Limited, *New Delhi*
Prentice-Hall of Japan, Inc., *Tokyo*
Simon & Schuster Asia Pte. Ltd., *Singapore*
Editora Prentice-Hall do Brasil, Ltda., *Rio de Janerio*

PREFACE
To the Instructor

Everything is new under the sun.
CZESLAW MILOSZ

Silence is the real crime against humanity.
NADYEZHDA MANDELSHTAM

The purpose of *Discovering Fiction* is to help today's students discover the life of the imagination and the power of literature. In this book we set out

✧ to help students (many of them non-readers) become active and responsive readers;

✧ to do justice to the emotional and imaginative as well as the intellectual dimensions of literature;

✧ to contribute to the task of redefining the canon, making works by women and by authors from culturally diverse backgrounds an integral part of the study of literature;

✧ to help students bring their own imagination and creativity into play;

✧ to talk to today's students in a lively, supportive, and accessible style designed to demystify traditional terms and categories;

✧ to provide more motivation, guidance, and student models for writing about literature than any comparable text.

REDEFINING THE CANON

Discovering Fiction provides balanced coverage of the rich diversity of our literary culture. We have aimed at a fruitful interaction of classics and moderns (and we have included many modern classics). We have aimed at a balance of women and men—for example, more than half of the selections are by women. We frequently juxtapose traditional or mainstream authors with writers from culturally diverse backgrounds.

Rediscovering the Hertitage   Classics are works that speak to readers across distances in time or place. Our reward as teachers comes when classics are rediscovered by a new generation of students. *Discovering Fiction* tries to make

v

students sense the enduring freshness and power of classic stories by Joyce, Welty, and Steinbeck. The book features fresh readings of authors like Flannery O'Connor and Franz Kafka.

Tomorrow's Classics   We take special pride in recognizing contemporary writers who write with integrity and passion. The book highlights short fiction by writers like Alice Walker and Bobbie Ann Mason.

Multicultural Literacy   A central aim of teaching literature is the broadening of imaginative sympathy. This book is rich in selections by authors who offer new perspectives—Third World writers like Chinua Achebe and Gabriel García Márquez as well as writers who dramatize the meeting of cultures, like Barahti Mukherjee.

Juxtapositions   Paired readings help students see the presence of the past or the continuity of perennial themes in works rooted in diverse cultural traditions. Often a classic is seen in a fresh light as it is juxtaposed with a modern story on the same theme. Often juxtapositions help students see the continuity between canonized traditional readings and newer voices—as when a short story by Sherwood Anderson is juxtaposed with one by Jamaica Kincaid.

Author Covered in Depth   The work of Flannery O'Connor is covered in depth with a variety of selections and a rich array of biographical and critical materials.

THE ACTIVE READER

The questions and activities following literary selections promote the ideal of the active, involved, empathetic reader. Several strands intermesh in the after-selection apparatus: "The Receptive Reader"—promoting close, attentive reading; "The Personal Response"—validating the personal connection that makes the literature meaningful for readers; and "The Creative Dimension"— fostering the creative participation that brings the readers' own imaginations into play and helps them enter imaginatively into a writer's world.

The Receptive Reader   This strand promotes close reading (and rereading) of a story, encouraging openness to the difficult and new. Questions and discussions focus on how details and formal elements serve the larger whole. (The questions encourage exploration not only of the what but also of the why and so what.)

The Personal Response   Questions and activities under this heading validate the reader's personal response, doing justice to the imaginative and emotional as well as the intellectual appeal of literature. Students are encouraged to find the personal connection, to relate what they read to their own experience.

The Creative Dimension   Creative activities following many selections bring the reader's imagination into play. Students are invited, for instance, to re-create a haunting image or dominant impression, to write a sequel to a classic story, to dramatize a key moment or scene, or to resee a story from the point of view of a different character.

A DYNAMIC CRITICAL PERSPECTIVE

This book owes a special debt to the dynamic variety of contemporary literary criticism and literary theory. We are indebted to provocative recent readings of authors like John Steinbeck and Flannery O'Connor; to probing rereadings of authors like Charlotte Perkins Gilman from a feminist perspective.

Updating the Critical Tradition   For decades, literature texts in the tradition of the New Criticism taught the elements of literature as if they were ends in themselves (contrary to the spirit of the best New Critics). The best current criticism has moved beyond a formalistic preoccupation with the technical workings of literature—without abandoning the tradition of close, faithful attention to the text that is the major legacy of the twentieth-century critical tradition. Throughout this book, we aim at the right balance of close reading, personal engagement, and creative participation.

Correlating Form and Meaning   In teaching students to respond to the formal elements of literature, we focus on how setting, character, point of view, symbol, or irony serves its larger human meaning. Setting, for instance, is more than a matter of physical location; when we study setting, we focus on the world a story creates, which may bring with it a characteristic history, set of assumptions, or way of life. Point of view is more than a technical concern; when we study point of view, we become aware of the window a story opens on the world.

The Range of Interpretation   As Pablo Neruda has said, it takes two poets to make a poem: The poet who wrote it and the poet-reader who brings the letters on the page to life in the theater of the mind. This book explores the range of both critics' reactions and students' responses to key works. Major critical trends are shown in exceptionally accessible critical excerpts representing the range of interpretation for selected authors.

A TEXT FOR TEACHERS AND LEARNERS

Our aim is to help teachers find *a way into* literature for their students —regardless of the students' previous experience or the preconceptions they bring to the reading. We have made it our special concern to help teachers overcome negative attitudes that students may bring with them from previous encounters with literature.

A Lively, Accessible Style To make key terms and categories come to life for today's students means initiating students who tend to be unschooled in mastering demanding concepts or new terms. We try not to give students technically correct "dictionary definitions" purporting to take care of key terms once and for all. Instead, we try to make students see the need for or the vital significance of a key term. We focus on essentials first, having students discover complications and finer points later. We provide the reinforcement needed if students are to make key concepts their own.

A Learning Sequence The organization of the book often leads students from the more accessible to the more challenging. Literal chronological sequence is one thing; the dynamics of learning and discovery are another.

Cross-References "Cross-references" for discussion or writing invite students to explore connections between selections related in theme or form—helping them discover recurrent patterns and illuminating contrasts, helping them see a familiar selection from a fresh perspective.

WRITING ABOUT LITERATURE

We have tried to provide more guidance, encouragement, and recognition for student writing than any comparable text. Guidelines for writing about literature and sample student papers do not appear in a one-size-fits-all writing chapter or as an afterthought in an appendix. Instead, they come with *each* chapter.

Writing Workshops The writing workshops following each chapter focus on the process that makes substantial, purposeful, live student writing take shape. Students repeatedly see sample assignments move from prewriting (journal writing, note-taking, clustering, brainstorming) to drafting and from there to instructor response and peer critique and then to revision and final editing.

The Imaginative Dimension As part of both after-selection apparatus and the writing workshops, imaginative writing opportunities enable students to give voice to their own experience and bring their own creativity into play.

Model Student Papers A wealth of motivated, well-developed student writing provides model papers for class discussion of writing strategies and for peer review. Emphasis is on the potential, the promise, of student writing. Peer editors are encouraged to help student writers build on their strengths as well as to correct their weaknesses.

Research and Documentation *Discovering Fiction* initiates students into library research and sets up an ample choice of research paper projects on literary topics. The text provides guidelines and a model of a documented paper. Pointed instructions elucidate for the student the mysteries of the current MLA documentation style, clarifying the rationale while giving a wealth of sample entries.

ACKNOWLEDGMENTS

Working on this book has been a privilege and a joy. We owe special thanks to Kathleen Evans, who did first-rate work while helping us with many editing and writing tasks. Nancy Perry of Blair Press had the vision to make this book possible, and she and Denise Wydra accomplished the impossible in coordinating the work of perceptive, dedicated reviewers and shepherding a complex enterprise. We owe a special debt to the admirable patience and competence of Julie Sullivan, who saw the book through production.

We are indebted to students whose intelligence, curiosity, and imagination have kept alive our faith in the power of literature and in the human enterprise. Of the many students from whose writing we have learned and who have allowed us to use or adapt their papers, we want to thank especially Debbie Nishimura, Andrea Sandke, Olivia Nunez, Francia Stephens, Mike DeAngelis, Dea Nelson, Kam Chieu, Greg Grewell, Johanna Wright, Merritt Ireland, Linda Spencer, Elizabeth Kerns, Conard Mangrum, Joyce Halenar, Marilyn Johnson, Michael Guth, John Newman, Judith Gardner, Pamela Cox, Rita Farkas, Barbara Hill, Melody Brune, Paul Francois, Ruth Randall, Katheryn Crayton-Shay, Dorothy Overstreet, Bill Irwin, Ruth Veerkamp, Martha Kell, Kevin McCabe, Thomas Perez-Jewell, Janelle Ciraulo, Irina Raicu, Joyce Sandoval, Catherine Hooper, Gail Bowman, Todd Marvin, and Catherine Russell.

Among the colleagues who pored over the manuscript and shared with us their enthusiasms and apprehensions, we want to thank especially Patricia E. Connors, Memphis State University; Carla Johnson, St. Mary's College; Bob Mayberry, University of Nevada at Las Vegas; Susan J. Miller, Santa Fe Community College; Patricia G. Morgan, Louisiana State University; and William E. Sheidley, University of Connecticut.

Working with colleagues from around the country has renewed our faith in our common task. As members of our profession, in spite of the political and theoretical allegiances that divide us, we share the love of learning, the love of language, and the love of literature. May this book give pleasure to those who teach and learn from it.

HANS P. GUTH
GABRIELE L. RICO

BRIEF CONTENTS

CONTENTS

WRITING ABOUT LITERATURE
Writing Workshops at a Glance

DISCOVERING FICTION

1 PREVIEW
The World of Fiction

Fiction . . . is like a spider's web, attached ever so lightly perhaps, but still attached to life at all four corners.
VIRGINIA WOOLF

Truth may be stranger than fiction, but fiction is truer.
FREDERIC RAPHAEL

Catching the very note and trick, the strange irregular rhythm of life, that is the attempt whose strenuous force keeps Fiction upon her feet.
HENRY JAMES

FOCUS ON FICTION

Listeners have been enchanted with the storyteller's art from time immemorial. The people who painted bison and horses on cave walls fifty thousand years ago very likely gathered around the fire on long winter nights to listen to the storyteller of the clan or tribe. The gift of "storying," of weaving stories, enabled human beings to find the connecting thread in the events of the past. It helped them find continuity and meaning in their lives.

Through the centuries, people have told and listened to stories—on long winter evenings on an isolated farm, in a country retreat while waiting out an epidemic ravaging the city, on the dusty road while on a pilgrimage to a famous shrine. What is the perennial appeal of a good story? The Greek writer Nikos Kazantzakis tells a story that is very short but has in it essential elements of the storyteller's art:

> There was a smell of fig trees in the air. A little old woman who was walking past stopped next to me. She lifted up some leaves covering a basket she was carrying. She picked out two of the figs in the basket and offered them to me. "Do you know me from somewhere, granny?" I asked. She looked at me, surprised. "No, my lad. Do I have to know you to give you something? You are a human being. So am I. Isn't that enough?"

3

This very short story does for us in miniature what other stories take longer to do for their readers. The story takes us on a flight of the imagination to a setting; it takes us to a time and a place. We come to know two characters, who become real to us as human beings. Something happens that is worth remembering, worth telling. As we imagine ourselves in the traveler's place, we are likely to be moved by what the old woman said. The figs become a symbol—they represent the nourishment that sustains life, but they are also a token of human solidarity, of the fellow feeling or bonding that helps us survive. What happened here, what the woman did and said, is likely to make us think. (Is the woman unlike other people? Or does she represent something that is part of human nature? Would we have acted similarly or differently in the same situation?) In the hurry and worry of everyday life, this incident stands out. It is complete and self-contained, with a meaning of its own. It makes a good story.

In the last hundred years, the writing of short stories has become a craft. Many of the same authors also write novels, but they approach the shorter form as a special challenge, where they can make every detail count. The test for the classics of the modern short story is that they become richer on second and third reading. They become more rewarding as we reread. A good storyteller has a lively imagination—the ability to create an imaginary world, to widen our horizons by taking us to an imaginary setting and having us accept the assumptions on which it operates. A good storyteller is an alert observer, sharpening our gifts of observation, helping us use our eyes. Much good storytelling probes personality, giving us a glimpse of a character's real motives, making us reexamine and rethink stereotypes. Effective storytelling makes us take pleasure in language more rich and expressive than everyday talk, carrying graphic details and shades of feeling, leaving us with haunting images that stay with us.

GUIDELINES FOR THE RECEPTIVE READER

The process of reading is not a half-sleep, but, in the highest sense, a gymnast's struggle. . . . The reader is to do something for himself, must be on the alert, must himself or herself construct indeed the poem, the argument, the history—the text furnishing the hints, the clue, the start or framework.

WALT WHITMAN

Receptive readers meet the author halfway. Storytelling is a cooperative enterprise—the writer provides the script, but the readers bring it to life by using their imagination. What can you do to get out of a story what the writer put in? Remember guidelines like the following:

✧ *Read with an open mind:* A story takes you into a world of its own, with values that may be different from yours. Try to be a receptive, responsive reader. Some readers are too quick to find fault with what is new and unfamiliar. They are too quick to judge writing that looks at the world through lenses different from their own. If you are too quick to judge, to reject, you may cut yourself off from much that good reading has to offer.

❖ *Read a story more than once:* A story is not like a note with a message that we take in before we crumple up the paper and throw it away. The "message" of a story is in the way it takes shape, the way it creates its own reality. The stories in this book offer rewards for the reader who lingers over them, who goes back to them for a closer look. Look for significant details that may have passed by too quickly. Be alert for revealing words, telling gestures.

❖ *Take notes as you read:* Highlight key passages or dramatic moments. Do a running commentary. Jot down quotable quotes. (If nothing else, write a few exclamation marks and question marks in the margin!)

❖ *Try to get a sense of the story as a whole:* As you look back over your notes, try to see whether an overall pattern has taken shape. Try to see what role details play in the larger context of the story.

❖ *Use your imagination:* Try to visualize the scenes, the people, the events. Learn to hear the dialogue with the mind's ear as if it were being read aloud. Try to see the world from the vantage point of the narrator, the person telling the story.

❖ *Allow your emotions to come into play:* Respond with your feelings as well as your analytical faculties. A short story does not present a case history for your diagnosis. Try to relate to the characters as people. Develop your capacity for empathy—for entering imaginatively into what others think and feel.

❖ *Think about your reactions:* Were you puzzled? appalled? frustrated when the story took a turn you did not expect? What standards and expectations did you bring to the story?

❖ *Talk with other readers:* Learn from their reactions, questions, and confusions. Explore your reading with others—one on one or in small groups. What did they see that you missed? What triggered reactions different from yours?

❖ *Do some unrequired reading:* Branch out. Discover on your own authors that mean something to you personally or other stories by a favorite author.

THE ART OF THE STORY

We are story-telling animals. As our primitive ancestors sat around the fire carving spearheads and eating blackberries, they told stories which in time were woven into a tapestry of myth and legend. These tales were the first encyclopedia of human knowledge.

SAM KEEN

Writing a story is one way of discovering sequence in experience. Connections slowly emerge. Like distant landmarks you are approaching, cause and effect begin to align themselves.

EUDORA WELTY

*A writer out of loneliness is trying to communicate like a
distant star sending signals. . . . We are lonely animals.
We spend all life trying to be less lonesome. One of our
ancient methods is to tell a story, begging the listener to
say—and to feel—"Yes, that the way it is, or at least the
way I feel it. You're not as alone as you thought."*
                                                    JOHN STEINBECK

Every story is different. It makes its own rules; it creates its own world.
Nevertheless, as readers, we become aware of questions that arise in our minds
again and again. We expect the storyteller to answer them in one way or another—not in so many words; rather, we expect the story as a whole to provide
the answers. Some of these questions loom larger in some stories than in others, and any one of them may seem beside the point in a given story. However,
together they make us more responsive to the elements of a short story—to
the dimensions that we need to respond to as readers, to the clues we need to
read if we are to take in the writer's meaning.

A preview of key questions that readers and critics ask about a story might
look like this:

SETTING: Where are we? Where is the story taking us? What kind of
world, what kind of reality, does it create for us? What
difference do the time and the place make to the story as
a whole?

CHARACTER: Who are these people? What is their history or their current situation? What are their real motives, needs, or desires? What explains the way they act?

PLOT: What happens in the story and why? What pattern, or
story line, gives shape to the story as a whole? Is there a
central conflict or a central problem, and how is it going
to be resolved? Do events build up to a high point? Is
there a turning point, a turning of the tide?

POINT OF VIEW: Who is telling the story? Through whose eyes do you see
the people and events? Through what window are you
looking at the world?

SYMBOL: What in the story has a meaning beyond itself? Do objects, people, or incidents acquire a symbolic meaning—
the way a handshake might symbolize brotherhood, or
the way a new shoot on a tree might stand for rebirth or
renewal?

THEME: Does the story make you think? What issues does it raise?
What ideas does it explore? Does it imply or act out an
idea about life or a point about human nature that you
can try to spell out?

STYLE: How does the author use language? Is the language graphic, rich in striking images? Does the story play down or play
up emotion? Is the tone mournful, bitter, happy, or ironic
—making us look at events with a wry smile?

Look at *short* short stories (or "short shorts") in which one or the other of these elements plays a major role.

Setting

Where Are We?   Whatever else storytellers do, they take us to a world of their creation. That world may share many features with our own, but it may also strike us as different or strange. The story takes us to a place, a time, a situation. Often the place becomes so vivid that we forget for the duration of a story that we are not in a real place but merely in an imagined setting, a country of the mind.

To become more aware of setting, you can ask yourself: Could this story be happening anywhere? You will be reading a different story depending on whether you watch white officials in a colonial situation in Africa, or tenant farmers scraping together a living in the backwoods, or a young woman growing up in an old-fashioned patriarchal family. Setting, in fiction as in reality, is a major player in the drama of life. It molds character; it helps make people what they are. It sets boundaries, limiting what people can strive for or aspire to. It sets up challenges. It limits or creates opportunities.

Sometimes a story is devoted almost entirely to creating a setting. Sandra Cisneros, a Mexican American writer, centers her story "The House on Mango Street" (1983) on the contrast between the dream house a family always wanted and the places in which they have to live. The house the parents talk about is a house of their own with a yard and trees, where the children could make noise without the landlord banging on the ceiling with a broom, where the water pipes would not break rusted through with age. It would be a house with a basement and several bathrooms, "so when we took a bath we wouldn't have to tell everybody."

But the house on Mango Street where the girl telling the story finds herself after one of the family's frequent moves is not the way the parents had described their ideal house at all:

> It's small and red with tight little steps in front and windows so small you'd think they were holding their breath. Bricks are crumbling in places, and the front door is so swollen you have to push hard to get in. There is no front yard . . . the house has only one washroom, very small. Everybody has to share a bedroom.

The story is in the contrast between how things should be and in how they are, and in the girl's determination not to settle for today's reality. She remembers when she pointed out another house where the family used to live to a nun from her school. The nun said, "You live *there?*" As the girl telling the story says at the end:

> I knew then I had to have a house. A real house. One I could point to. But this isn't it. The house on Mango Street isn't it. For the time being, Mama say. Temporary, says Papa. But I know how those things go.

Character

Who Are the People? In a traditional story, the storyteller places believable characters in a vividly imagined setting and then puts them in motion. How well do we get to know them? What is their history? What goes on behind the subdued public surface? What are their true needs, their true motives? Is what they do or say "in character"?

We come to know characters in fiction by reading a variety of clues. We may know them from what the author says about them (or, more exactly, from what the **narrator** says—the person telling the story). We may come to know them at least in part from what *other* characters in the story tell us. However, we also watch characters in action—reaching conclusions about their motives, their problems, their ambitions, their desires. Above all, we know them from listening to them. The following short short story by Grace Paley is in large part talk—it consists mostly of **dialogue.** The verbal exchange between the two people in the story is like a tennis match—except that instead of our eyes following the ball from one side of the net to the other, our ears turn alternately from one speaker to the other. At the same time, we listen in to the narrator mentally talking to herself, thinking to herself.

How much do you learn about the two people in this story? How much can you infer about these characters from listening to what one critic has called their "loud, energetic, quirky voices full of Paley's humor" (Kathleen A. Coppula)? For each, can you piece together a coherent person from the glimpses you get of their memories, regrets, resentments, apprehensions, or ambitions?

G R A C E   P A L E Y   (born 1922)

Wants   1974

I saw my ex-husband in the street. I was sitting on the steps of the new library.

Hello, my life, I said. We had once been married for twenty-seven years, so I felt justified.

He said, What? What life? No life of mine.

I said, O.K. I don't argue when there's real disagreement. I got up and went into the library to see how much I owed them.

The librarian said $32 even and you've owed it for eighteen years. I didn't deny anything. Because I don't understand how time passes. I have had those books. I have often thought of them. The library is only two blocks away.   5

My ex-husband followed me to the Books Returned desk. He interrupted the librarian, who had more to tell. In many ways, he said, as I look back, I attribute the dissolution of our marriage to the fact that you never invited the Bertrams to dinner.

That's possible, I said. But really, if you remember: first, my father was sick that Friday, then the children were born, then I had those Tuesday-night meetings, then the war began. Then we didn't seem to know them any more. But you're right. I should have had them to dinner.

I gave the librarian a check for $32. Immediately she trusted me, put my past behind her, wiped the record clean, which is just what most other municipal and/or state bureaucracies will *not* do.

I checked out the two Edith Wharton books I had just returned because I'd read them so long ago and they are more apropos now than ever. They were *The House of Mirth* and *The Children,* which is about how life in the United States in New York changed in twenty-seven years fifty years ago.

A nice thing I do remember is breakfast, my ex-husband said. I was surprised. All   10 we ever had was coffee. Then I remembered there was a hole in the back of the kitchen closet which opened into the apartment next door. There, they always ate sugar-cured smoked bacon. It gave us a very grand feeling about breakfast, but we never got stuffed and sluggish.

That was when we were poor, I said.

When were we ever rich? he asked.

Oh, as time went on, as our responsibilities increased, we didn't go in need. You took adequate financial care, I reminded him. The children went to camp four weeks a year and in decent ponchos with sleeping bags and boots, just like everyone else. They looked very nice. Our place was warm in winter, and we had nice red pillows and things.

I wanted a sailboat, he said. But you didn't want anything.

Don't be bitter, I said. It's never too late.   15

No, he said with a great deal of bitterness. I may get a sailboat. As a matter of fact I have money down on an eighteen-foot two-rigger. I'm doing well this year and can look forward to better. But as for you, it's too late. You'll always want nothing.

He had had a habit throughout the twenty-seven years of making a narrow remark which, like a plumber's snake, could work its way through the ear down the throat, halfway to my heart. He would then disappear, leaving me choking with equipment. What I mean is, I sat down on the library steps and he went away.

I looked through *The House of Mirth,* but lost interest. I felt extremely accused. Now, it's true, I'm short of requests and absolute requirements. But I do want *something*.

I want, for instance, to be a different person. I want to be the woman who brings these two books back in two weeks. I want to be the effective citizen who changes the school system and addresses the Board of Estimate on the troubles of this dear urban center.

I *had* promised my children to end the war before they grew up.   20

I wanted to have been married forever to one person, my ex-husband or my present one. Either has enough character for a whole life, which as it turns out is really not such a long time. You couldn't exhaust either man's qualities or get under the rock of his reasons in one short life.

Just this morning I looked out the window to watch the street for a while and saw that the little sycamores the city had dreamily planted a couple of years before the kids were born had come that day to the prime of their lives.

Well! I decided to bring those two books back to the library. Which proves that when a person or an event comes along to jolt or apprise me I *can* take some appropriate action, although I am better known for my hospitable remarks.

THE RECEPTIVE READER

1. What would you include in a brief *capsule portrait* of the narrator—the character doing most of the talking in this story? What do you think are her outstanding traits, and how are they shown? (Do they go together to make up a believable personality?)

2. What kind of person is the ex-husband? How does he serve as a *foil*—a character who brings out traits in the other character that otherwise might have lain dormant?

3. Do you think readers will care about these people one way or the other? Why or why not?

Plot

What Is Happening and Why?   What is the situation? What tensions simmer? What needs or wants create an unfinished agenda? What conflicts are coming to a head? What resentments are waiting to be acted out? Stories vary greatly in how much overt action they incorporate. Whatever development unfolds in a story may be taking place in a character's mind. (Note that the *failure* of something to happen, or the failure of a character to budge, can also make a story.)

The following African folktale shows the power of a good story line to create **suspense**, to hold the reader's attention. The tale is one of many retold by Chinua Achebe, a famous Nigerian novelist, in his *Things Fall Apart* (1958). His recreating of a traditional tale shows how a storyteller hooks us into a story. We need to know: How will it come out? In this story, as we see turtle best his friends, their—and our?—resentment builds. We are waiting for his comeuppance—and the story obliges; we are not disappointed. A good storyteller creates expectations and then fulfills them (or sometimes disappoints them on purpose).

CHINUA ACHEBE   (born 1930)
Why the Tortoise's Shell Is Not Smooth   1958

Low voices, broken now and again by singing, reached Okonkwo from his wives' huts as each woman and her children told folk stories. Ekwefi and her daughter, Ezinma, sat on a mat on the floor. It was Ekwefi's turn to tell a story.

"Once upon a time," she began, "all the birds were invited to a feast in the sky. They were very happy and began to prepare themselves for the great day. They painted their bodies with red cam wood and drew beautiful patterns on them with dye.

"Tortoise saw all these preparations and soon discovered what it all meant. Nothing that happened in the world of the animals ever escaped his notice; he was full of cunning. As soon as he heard of the great feast in the sky his throat began to itch at the very thought. There was a famine in those days and Tortoise had not eaten a good meal for two moons. His body rattled like a piece of dry stick in his empty shell. So he began to plan how he would go to the sky."

"But he had no wings," said Ezinma.

"Be patient," replied her mother. "That is the story. Tortoise had no wings, but he   5
went to the birds and asked to be allowed to go with them.

"'We know you too well,' said the birds when they had heard him. 'You are full of cunning and you are ungrateful. If we allow you to come with us you will soon begin your mischief.'

" 'You do not know me,' said Tortoise. 'I am a changed man. I have learned that a man who makes trouble for others is also making it for himself.'

"Tortoise had a sweet tongue, and within a short time all the birds agreed that he was a changed man, and they each gave him a feather, with which he made two wings.

"At last the great day came and Tortoise was the first to arrive at the meeting place. When all the birds had gathered together, they set off in a body. Tortoise was very happy as he flew among the birds, and he was soon chosen as the man to speak for the party because he was a great orator.

" 'There is one important thing which we must not forget,' he said as they flew on their way. 'When people are invited to a great feast like this, they take new names for the occasion. Our hosts in the sky will expect us to honor this age-old custom.'

"None of the birds had heard of this custom but they knew that Tortoise, in spite of his failings in other directions, was a widely traveled man who knew the customs of different peoples. And so they each took a new name. When they had all taken, Tortoise also took one. He was to be called *All of you*.

"At last the party arrived in the sky and their hosts were very happy to see them. Tortoise stood up in his many-colored plumage and thanked them for their invitation. His speech was so eloquent that all the birds were glad they had brought him, and nodded their heads in approval of all he said. Their hosts took him as the king of the birds, especially as he looked somewhat different from the others.

"After kola nuts had been presented and eaten, the people of the sky set before their guests the most delectable dishes Tortoise had even seen or dreamed of. The soup was brought out hot from the fire and in the very pot in which it had been cooked. It was full of meat and fish. Tortoise began to sniff aloud. There was pounded yam and also yam pottage cooked with palm oil and fresh fish. There were also pots of palm wine. When everything had been set before the guests, one of the people of the sky came forward and tasted a little from each pot. He then invited the birds to eat. But Tortoise jumped to his feet and asked: 'For whom have you prepared this feast?'

" 'For all of you,' replied the man.

"Tortoise turned to the birds and said: 'You remember that my name is *All of you*. The custom here is to serve the spokesman first and the others later. They will serve you when I have eaten.'

"He began to eat and the birds grumbled angrily. The people of the sky thought it must be their custom to leave all the food for their king. And so Tortoise ate the best part of the food and then drank two pots of palm wine, so that he was full of food and drink and his body grew fat enough to fill out his shell.

"The birds gathered round to eat what was left and to peck at the bones he had thrown all about the floor. Some of them were too angry to eat. They chose to fly home on an empty stomach. But before they left each took back the feather he had lent to Tortoise. And there he stood in his hard shell full of food and wine but without any wings to fly home. He asked the birds to take a message for his wife, but they all refused. In the end Parrot, who had felt more angry than the others, suddenly changed his mind and agreed to take the message.

" 'Tell my wife,' said Tortoise, 'to bring out all the soft things in my house and cover the compound with them so that I can jump down from the sky without very great danger.'

"Parrot promised to deliver the message, and then flew away. But when he reached Tortoise's house he told his wife to bring out all the hard things in the house. And so she brought out her husband's hoes, machetes, spears, guns, and even his cannon. Tortoise looked down from the sky and saw his wife bringing things out, but it was too far

10

15

to see what they were. When all seemed ready he let himself go. He fell and fell and fell until he began to fear that he would never stop falling. And then like the sound of his cannon he crashed on the compound."

"Did he die?" asked Ezinma.

20

"No," replied Ekwefi. "His shell broke into pieces. But there was a great medicine man in the neighborhood. Tortoise's wife sent for him and he gathered all the bits of shell and stuck them together. That is why Tortoise's shell is not smooth."

THE RECEPTIVE READER

1. What makes the characters and the story *believable?* (Do you think modern readers would be too sophisticated to be charmed by animals talking and acting like people?)

2. Do you feel a sneaking admiration for the cleverness of the turtle? Or do you mainly sympathize with his victims?

3. How did you expect the story to come out? When did you first guess what the ending would be?

4. Many traditional stories follow the pattern of a journey. How does this one?

5. Folklorists call this kind of tale a "tell-me-why" story (or *pourquoi* story, from the French word for *why*). Do you know any other stories of this type? (Tell it to your classmates.)

THE CREATIVE DIMENSION

Modern readers have often felt the urge to update proverbs or to rewrite folktales to bring them into harmony with the modern temper. Try your hand at a modern rewrite of this traditional tale or of a folktale likely to be familiar to your readers. (In rewriting this story, would you choose different and more familiar animals? Would you change the way the animals behave and the way readers—or listeners—are expected to react?)

Point of View

Through Whose Eyes Are We Looking at the World?   From what point of view? What is included, what left out? What special insights or privileged information are we able to share? What biases may cloud our vision? What blind spots do we need to take into account? The following story is told from the point of view of a white male. What difference does it make?

TOBIAS WOLFF   (born 1945)
Say Yes   1985

They were doing the dishes, his wife washing while he dried. He'd washed the night before. Unlike most men he knew, he really pitched in on the housework. A few months earlier he'd overheard a friend of his wife's congratulate her on having such a considerate husband, and he thought, *I try.* Helping out with the dishes was a way he had of showing how considerate he was.

They talked about different things and somehow got on the subject of whether white people should marry black people. He said that all things considered, he thought it was a bad idea.

"Why?" she asked.

Sometimes his wife got this look where she pinched her brows together and bit her lower lip and stared down at something. When he saw her like this he knew he should keep his mouth shut, but he never did. Actually it made him talk more. She had that look now.

"Why?" she asked again, and stood there with her hand inside a bowl, not washing it but just holding it above the water.

"Listen," he said, "I went to school with blacks, and I've worked with blacks and lived on the same street with blacks, and we've always gotten along just fine. I don't need you coming along now and implying that I'm a racist."

"I didn't imply anything," she said, and began washing the bowl again, turning it around in her hand as though she were shaping it. "I just don't see what's wrong with a white person marrying a black person, that's all."

"They don't come from the same culture as we do. Listen to them sometime— they even have their own language. That's okay with me, I *like* hearing them talk"—he did; for some reason it always made him feel happy—"but it's different. A person from their culture and a person from our culture could never really *know* each other."

"Like you know me?" his wife asked.

"Yes. Like I know you."

"But if they love each other," she said. She was washing faster now, not looking at him.

Oh boy, he thought. He said, "Don't take my word for it. Look at the statistics. Most of those marriages break up."

"Statistics." She was piling dishes on the drainboard at a terrific rate, just swiping at them with the cloth. Many of them were greasy, and there were flecks of food between the tines of the forks. "All right," she said, "what about foreigners? I suppose you think the same thing about two foreigners getting married."

"Yes," he said, "as a matter of fact I do. How can you understand someone who comes from a completely different background?"

"Different," said his wife. "Not the same, like us."

"Yes, different," he snapped, angry with her for resorting to this trick of repeating his words so that they sounded crass, or hypocritical. "These are dirty," he said, and dumped all the silverware back into the sink.

The water had gone flat and gray. She stared down at it, her lips pressed tight together, then plunged her hands under the surface. "Oh!" she cried, and jumped back. She took her right hand by the wrist and held it up. Her thumb was bleeding.

"Ann, don't move," he said. "Stay right there." He ran upstairs to the bathroom and rummaged in the medicine chest for alcohol, cotton, and a Band-Aid. When he came back down she was leaning against the refrigerator with her eyes closed, still holding her hand. He took the hand and dabbed at her thumb with the cotton. The bleeding had stopped. He squeezed it to see how deep the wound was and a single drop of blood welled up, trembling and bright, and fell to the floor. Over the thumb she stared at him accusingly. "It's shallow," he said. "Tomorrow you won't even know it's there." He hoped that she appreciated how quickly he had come to her aid. He'd acted out of concern for her, with no thought of getting anything in return, but now the thought occurred to him that it would be a nice gesture on her part not to start up that conversation again, as he was tired of it. "I'll finish up here," he said. "You go and relax."

"That's okay," she said. "I'll dry."

He began to wash the silverware again, giving a lot of attention to the forks.   20

"So," she said, "you wouldn't have married me if I'd been black."

"For Christ's sake, Ann!"

"Well, that's what you said, didn't you?"

"No, I did not. The whole question is ridiculous. If you had been black we probably wouldn't even have met. You would have had your friends and I would have had mine. The only black girl I ever really knew was my partner in the debating club, and I was already going out with you by then."

"But if we had met, and I'd been black?"   25

"Then you probably would have been going out with a black guy." He picked up the rinsing nozzle and sprayed the silverware. The water was so hot that the metal darkened to pale blue, then turned silver again.

"Let's say I wasn't," she said. "Let's say I am black and unattached and we meet and fall in love."

He glanced over at her. She was watching him and her eyes were bright. "Look," he said, taking a reasonable tone, "this is stupid. If you were black you wouldn't be you." As he said this he realized it was absolutely true. There was no possible way of arguing with the fact that she would not be herself if she were black. So he said it again: "If you were black you wouldn't be you."

"I know," she said, "but let's just say."

He took a deep breath. He had won the argument but he still felt cornered. "Say   30
what?" he asked.

"That I'm black, but still me, and we fall in love. Will you marry me?"

He thought about it.

"Well?" she said, and stepped close to him. Her eyes were even brighter. "Will you marry me?"

"I'm thinking," he said.

"You won't, I can tell. You're going to say no."   35

"Let's not move too fast on this," he said. "There are lots of things to consider. We don't want to do something we would regret for the rest of our lives."

"No more considering. Yes or no."

"Since you put it that way–"

"Yes or no."

"Jesus, Ann. All right. No."   40

She said. "Thank you," and walked from the kitchen into the living room. A moment later he heard her turning the pages of a magazine. He knew that she was too angry to be actually reading it, but she didn't snap through the pages the way he would have done. She turned them slowly, as if she were studying every word. She was demonstrating her indifference to him, and it had the effect he knew she wanted it to have. It hurt him.

He had no choice but to demonstrate his indifference to her. Quietly, thoroughly, he washed the rest of the dishes. Then he dried them and put them away. He wiped the counters and the stove and scoured the linoleum where the drop of blood had fallen. While he was at it, he decided, he might as well mop the whole floor. When he was done the kitchen looked new, the way it looked when they were first shown the house, before they had ever lived here.

He picked up the garbage pail and went outside. The night was clear and he could see a few stars to the west, where the light of the town didn't blur them out. On El Camino the traffic was steady and light, peaceful as a river. He felt ashamed that he had let his wife get him into a fight. In another thirty years or so they would both be dead. What would all that stuff matter then? He thought of the years they had spent together, and how close they were, and how well they knew each other, and his throat tightened so that he could hardly breathe. His face and neck began to tingle. Warmth flooded his chest. He stood there for a while, enjoying these sensations, then picked up the pail and went out the back gate.

The two mutts from down the street had pulled over the garbage can again. One of them was rolling around on his back and the other had something in her mouth. Growling, she tossed it into the air, leaped up and caught it, growled again and whipped her head from side to side. When they saw him coming they trotted away with short, mincing steps. Normally he would heave rocks at them, but this time he let them go.

The house was dark when he came back inside. She was in the bathroom. He   45
stood outside the door and called her name. He heard bottles clinking, but she didn't answer him. "Ann, I'm really sorry," he said. "I'll make it up to you, I promise."

"How?" she asked.

He wasn't expecting this. But from a sound in her voice, a level and definite note that was strange to him, he knew that he had come up with the right answer. He leaned against the door. "I'll marry you," he whispered.

"We'll see," she said. "Go on to bed. I'll be out in a minute."

He undressed and got under the covers. Finally he heard the bathroom door open and close.

"Turn off the light," she said from the hallway.   50

"What?"

"Turn off the light."

He reached over and pulled the chain on the bedside lamp. The room went dark. "All right," he said. He lay there, but nothing happened. "All right," he said again. Then he heard a movement across the room. He sat up, but he couldn't see a thing. The room was silent. His heart pounded the way it had on their first night together, the way it still did when he woke at a noise in the darkness and waited to hear it again—the sound of someone moving through the house, a stranger.

THE RECEPTIVE READER

1. How does the world look as we see it through the eyes of the white male narrator?

2. Do you find yourself taking sides in the argument between him and the woman? Would you call him a biased or prejudiced person? (How do you think he looks to readers who are not male or not white?)

3. How do you react to the way the story ends?

THE CREATIVE DIMENSION

How might the story read if it were retold from the point of view of the woman? Write a short alternative story as told by her; or write a part of her story.

Symbol

What in the Story Might Have a Meaning beyond Itself?   What objects, people, or incidents seem to have a **symbolic** significance beyond their literal meaning? A river, for instance, might begin to suggest the steady, slow flow of time, which can never be stopped or reversed. How do such symbolic elements acquire a meaning beyond themselves?

In the following short short, we focus on a single significant day in the life of a couple. We learn something about the setting of their lives, about them as people, about their relationship. But details of setting, character, and plot are almost crowded out by something the wife has brought home from the store: Halloween pumpkins. They are the first and last things we see in the story. The people work on them and talk about them for most of the story. They loom large. What do they mean? What role do they play?

MARY ROBISON   (born 1949)
Yours   1983

Allison struggled away from her white Renault, limping with the weight of the last of the pumpkins. She found Clark in the twilight on the twig-and-leaf-littered porch behind the house.

He wore a wool shawl. He was moving up and back in a padded glider, pushed by the ball of his slippered foot.

Allison lowered a big pumpkin, let it rest on the wide floorboards.

Clark was much older—seventy-eight to Allison's thirty-five. They were married. They were both quite tall and looked something alike in their facial features. Allison wore a natural-hair wig. It was a thick blond hood around her face. She was dressed in bright-dyed denims today. She wore durable clothes, usually, for she volunteered afternoons at a children's day-care center.

She put one of the smaller pumpkins on Clark's long lap. "Now, nothing surreal," she told him. "Carve just a *regular* face. These are for kids."   5

In the foyer, on the Hepplewhite desk, Allison found the maid's chore list with its cross-offs, which included Clark's supper. Allison went quickly through the day's mail: a garish coupon packet, a bill from Jamestown Liquors, November's pay-TV program guide, and the worst thing, the funniest, an already opened, extremely unkind letter from Clark's relations up North. "You're an old fool," Allison read, and, "You're being cruelly deceived." There was a gift check for Clark enclosed, but it was uncashable, signed, as it was, "Jesus H. Christ."

Late, late into this night, Allison and Clark gutted and carved the pumpkins together, at an old table set on the back porch, over newspaper after soggy newspaper, with paring knives and with spoons and with a Swiss Army knife Clark used for exact shaping of tooth and eye and nostril. Clark had been a doctor, an internist, but also a Sunday watercolorist. His four pumpkins were expressive and artful. Their carved features were suited to the sizes and shapes of the pumpkins. Two looked ferocious and jagged. One registered surprise. The last was serene and beaming.

Allison's four faces were less deftly drawn, with slits and areas of distortion. She had cut triangles for noses and eyes. The mouths she had made were just wedges—two turned up and two turned down.

By one in the morning they were finished. Clark, who had bent his long torso forward to work, moved back over to the glider and look out sleepily at nothing. All the lights were out across the ravine.

Clark stayed. For the season and time, the Virginia night was warm. Most leaves   10
had been blown away already, and the trees stood unbothered. The moon was round
above them.

Allison cleaned up the mess.

"Your jack-o'-lanterns are much, much better than mine," Clark said to her.

"Like hell," Allison said.

"Look at me," Clark said, and Allison did.

She was holding a squishy bundle of newspapers. The papers reeked sweetly with   15
the smell of pumpkin guts.

"Yours are *far* better," he said.

"You're wrong. You'll see when they're lit," Allison said.

She went inside, came back with yellow vigil candles. It took her a while to get
each candle settled, and then to line up the results in a row on the porch railing. She
went along and lit each candle and fixed the pumpkin lids over the little flames.

"See?" she said.

They sat together a moment and looked at the orange faces.   20

"We're exhausted. It's good night time," Allison said. "Don't blow out the candles. I'll put in new ones tomorrow."

That night, in their bedroom, a few weeks earlier in her life than had been predicted, Allison began to die. "Don't look at me if my wig comes off," she told Clark.
"Please."

Her pulse cords were fluttering under his fingers. She raised her knees and kicked
away the comforter. She said something to Clark about the garage being locked.

At the telephone, Clark had a clear view out back and down to the porch. He
wanted to get drunk with his wife once more. He wanted to tell her, from the
greater perspective he had, that to own only a little talent, like his, was an awful,
plaguing thing; that being only a little special meant you expected too much, most of
the time, and liked yourself too little. He wanted to assure her that she had missed
nothing.

He was speaking into the phone now. He watched the jack-o'-lanterns. The jack-   25
o'-lanterns watched him.

THE RECEPTIVE READER

1. How do you learn about the situation in which the two characters find themselves? What clues are especially important?

2. What role does the age difference between the two people play in the story? Is
it treated differently from what you might have expected? How?

3. When do you first suspect that the pumpkins have a special significance? (What
kind of fruit are they? What associations with them do you bring to the story?) What
role do they play in the story as a whole? Does it matter that they are carved differently?
What do you think they symbolize?

THE PERSONAL RESPONSE

This story deals with age, illness, and death. How does it treat these topics?
Do you think the story as a whole is affirmative toward life or disillusioned or depressing?

Theme

What Is the Meaning of the Story as a Whole?   A good storyteller makes us think. Even a short and lighthearted story is likely to say something about human nature; it may offer some comment on life. It is likely to have a point, although that point may not be spelled out in so many words. We call the implied point, the implied comment, the theme of the story. Most writers in our century have been wary of spelling out the **theme** of a story too directly— afraid that it would sound like a ready-made secondhand sentiment, a cliché. They want us to live through the experience of the story to discover what it has to say. What we witness raises questions to which the story as a whole suggests possible answers. The ideas implied slowly come into focus as we think about what we have read.

Many twentieth-century writers refuse to preach, to editorialize. Old-fashioned storytelling was often less shy about pointing out the moral of the tale. A case in point is the traditional **fable,** going back thousands of years to ancient Greece (many of the familiar traditional fables are attributed to Aesop). Traditionally, the fable ends by spelling out the advice the story was written to drive home. Even so, many of the fables would make their point even if the moral had been lost. Often the story speaks for itself. The following is a modern rendering of a fable that William Caxton had included in the fifteenth century in one of the first books printed in England. In this retelling, the moral has been left out. What to you is the idea acted out in the story?

A E S O P   (sixth century B.C.)

The Wolf and the Lamb   about 570 B.C.

The wolf and the lamb were both thirsty and went to the river to drink. It happened that the wolf drank a ways up the river and the lamb drank farther down. And as the wolf saw and perceived the lamb, he said in a loud voice: "Hah, knave, why has thou troubled and befouled my water that I should now drink?" "Alas, My Lord, God save Your Grace," said the lamb, "the water flows down the river from you towards me!" Then said the wolf to the lamb: "Hast thou no shame or dread to curse me?" And the lamb said "My Lord, I am sorry." And the wolf said again: "It is only six months ago that thy father wronged me in the same manner." And the lamb answered: "I was then not even born." And the wolf said again to him: "Thou hast killed and devoured my father!" And the lamb said: "But I have no teeth to eat meat!" Then said the wolf: "Thou art like your father, and for that sin and misdeed thou shalt die!" The wolf then seized the lamb and devoured him.

THE RECEPTIVE READER

1. What is the *moral?* What statement does the fable seem to make about human nature? Is it out-of-date, obsolete—or does the fable have a meaning for you as a modern reader?

2. Does this fable give us a *realistic* view of human nature? Or would you call it pessimistic? Would you call it cynical?

Style

How Does the Author Use Language?   What is the relation between what is said and how it is said? What we mean, what we communicate to others, is not just in what we say but also in how we say it. Language is not just words— it is also the knowing wink, the twinkle in the eye, the bitter tone, the exasperated gesture. Similarly, the style of a writer can make a passage seem passionate or low-key, eloquent or halting, conciliatory or bitter, assertive or diffident. Style is more than a matter of style—it makes a statement of its own.

The following story is written in an understated early modern style. Hemingway set the directions for the style of much modern fiction with his suspicion of cheap words, emotional outbursts, or stylistic embellishments. Most of what is important in the story we have to read between the lines. (Many of Hemingway's stories are set in a foreign country, such as Italy or Spain. In the following story, the Ebro is a river in Spain, and *reales* are Spanish coins.)

ERNEST HEMINGWAY   (1899–1961)

Hills like White Elephants   1927

The hills across the valley of the Ebro were long and white. On this side there was no shade and no trees and the station was between two lines of rails in the sun. Close against the side of the station there was the warm shadow of the building and a curtain, made of strings of bamboo beads, hung across the open door into the bar, to keep out flies. The American and the girl with him sat at a table in the shade, outside the building. It was very hot and the express from Barcelona would come in forty minutes. It stopped at this junction for two minutes and went on to Madrid.

"What should we drink?" the girl asked. She had taken off her hat and put it on the table.

"It's pretty hot," the man said.

"Let's drink beer."

"Dos cervezas," the man said into the curtain.   5

"Big ones?" a woman asked from the doorway.

"Yes. Two big ones."

The woman brought two glasses of beer and two felt pads. She put the felt pads and the beer glasses on the table and looked at the man and the girl. The girl was looking off at the line of hills. They were white in the sun and the country was brown and dry.

"They look like white elephants," she said.

"I've never seen one," the man drank his beer.   10

"No, you wouldn't have."

"I might have," the man said. "Just because you say I wouldn't have doesn't prove anything."

The girl looked at the bead curtain. "They've painted something on it," she said. "What does it say?"

"Anis del Toro. It's a drink."

"Could we try it?"   15

The man called "Listen" through the curtain. The woman came out from the bar.

"Four reales."

"We want two Anis del Toro."

"With water?"

"Do you want it with water?"   20

"I don't know," the girl said. "Is it good with water?"

"It's all right."

"You want them with water?" asked the woman.

"Yes, with water."

"It tastes like licorice," the girl said and put the glass down.   25

"That's the way with everything."

"Yes," said the girl. "Everything tastes of licorice. Especially all the things you've
waited so long for, like absinthe."

"Oh, cut it out."

"You started it," the girl said. "I was being amused. I was having a fine time."

"Well, let's try and have a fine time."   30

"All right. I was trying. I said the mountains looked like white elephants. Wasn't
that bright?"

"That was bright."

"I wanted to try this new drink. That's all we do, isn't it—look at things and try
new drinks?"

"I guess so."

The girl looked across at the hills.   35

"They're lovely hills," she said. "They don't really look like white elephants. I just
meant the coloring of their skin through the trees."

"Should we have another drink?"

"All right."

The warm wind blew the bead curtain against the table.

"The beer's nice and cool," the man said.   40

"It's lovely," the girl said.

"It's really an awfully simple operation, Jig," the man said. "It's not really an operation at all."

The girl looked at the ground the table legs rested on.

"I know you wouldn't mind it, Jig. It's really not anything. It's just to let the air
in."

The girl did not say anything.   45

"I'll go with you and I'll stay with you all the time. They just let the air in and
then it's all perfectly natural."

"Then what will we do afterward?"

"We'll be fine afterward. Just like we were before."

"What makes you think so?"

"That's the only thing that bothers us. It's the only thing that's made us unhappy."   50

The girl looked at the bead curtain, put her hand out and took hold of two of the
strings of beads.

"And you think then we'll be all right and be happy."

"I know we will. You don't have to be afraid. I've known lots of people that have
done it."

"So have I," said the girl. "And afterward they were all so happy."

"Well," the man said, "if you don't want to you don't have to. I wouldn't have   55
you do it if you didn't want to. But I know it's perfectly simple."

"And you really want to?"

"I think it's the best thing to do. But I don't want you to do it if you don't really
want to."

"And if I do it you'll be happy and things will be like they were and you'll love me?"

"I love you now. You know I love you."

"I know. But if I do it, then it will be nice again if I say things are like white ele-   60
phants, and you'll like it?"

"I'll love it. I love it now but I just can't think about it. You know how I get when
I worry."

"If I do it you won't ever worry?"

"I won't worry about that because it's perfectly simple."

"Then I'll do it. Because I don't care about me."

"What do you mean?"   65

"I don't care about me."

"Well, I care about you."

"Oh, yes. But I don't care about me. And I'll do it and then everything will be
fine."

"I don't want you to do it if you feel that way."

The girl stood up and walked to the end of the station. Across on the other side,   70
were fields of grain and trees along the banks of the Ebro. Far away, beyond the river,
were mountains. The shadow of a cloud moved across the field of grain and she saw the
river through the trees.

"And we could have all this," she said. "And we could have everything and every
day we make it more impossible."

"What did you say?"

"I said we could have everything."

"We can have everything."

"No, we can't."   75

"We can have the whole world."

"No, we can't"

"We can go everywhere."

"No, we can't. It isn't ours any more."

"It's ours."   80

"No, it isn't. And once they take it away, you never get it back."

"But they haven't taken it away."

"We'll wait and see."

"Come on back in the shade," he said. "You mustn't feel that way."

"I don't feel any way," the girl said. "I just know things."   85

"I don't want you to do anything that you don't want to do—"

"Nor that isn't good for me," she said. "I know. Could we have another beer?"

"All right. But you've got to realize—"

"I realize," the girl said. "Can't we maybe stop talking?"

They sat down at the table and the girl looked across at the hills on the dry side of   90
the valley and the man looked at her and at the table.

"You've got to realize," he said, "that I don't want you to do it if you don't want
to. I'm perfectly willing to go through with it if it means anything to you."

"Doesn't it mean anything to you? We could get along."

"Of course it does. But I don't want anybody but you. I don't want any one else. And I know it's perfectly simple."

"Yes, you know it's perfectly simple."

"It's all right for you to say that, but I do know it."   95

"Would you do something for me now?"

"I'd do anything for you."

"Would you please please please please please please please stop talking?"

He did not say anything but looked at the bags against the wall of the station. There were labels on them from all the hotels where they had spent nights.

"But I don't want you to," he said, "I don't care anything about it."   100

"I'll scream," the girl said.

The woman came out through the curtains with two glasses of beer and put them down on the damp felt pads. "The train comes in five minutes," she said.

"What did she say?" asked the girl.

"That the train is coming in five minutes."

The girl smiled brightly at the woman, to thank her.   105

"I'd better take the bags over to the other side of the station," the man said. She smiled at him.

"All right. Then come back and we'll finish the beer."

He picked up the two heavy bags and carried them around the station to the other tracks. He looked up the tracks but could not see the train. Coming back, he walked through the barroom, where people waiting for the train were drinking. He drank an Anis at the bar and looked at the people. They were all waiting reasonably for the train. He went out through the bead curtain. She was sitting at the table and smiled at him.

"Do you feel better?" he asked.

"I feel fine," she said. "There's nothing wrong with me. I feel fine."   110

THE RECEPTIVE READER

1. As you first listen to the conversation of the two characters in this story, what makes the *dialogue* seem trivial or empty? (How does their style of talking echo their life-style?)

2. The woman's comparing the hills to white elephants is touched on several times in the story. (And it gave the story its title.) Do the hills or other elements of the story have a *symbolic* significance?

3. When do you first realize that these two people are talking about an important *choice*? How does the man talk about it? (What does it mean to him?) How does the woman talk about it? (What does it mean to her?) How does the woman react to the man's attitude?

4. Hemingway, as one of the first great moderns, was wary of emotionalism and melodrama. Where in the story are you most aware of the emotions and tensions beneath the understated, "cool" surface?

5. Does this story reach a *conclusion*? Has anything changed or been accomplished by the end? (Where do you think these two people are headed? What is ahead for them?)

THE PERSONAL RESPONSE

Eloquent pleas for sympathy are not part of the Hemingway style. Do you find yourself taking sides? If so, how and why?

EXPLORATIONS

Setting Up Expectations

The following is the opening of a short story called "The Coming Triumph of the Free World" by Rick DeMarinis. What kind of setting do these opening paragraphs establish? What characters come into focus? What kind of story can you imagine taking place in this setting? Answer the questions that follow the excerpt. Then write a brief story that you can imagine as following these opening paragraphs.

The grizzled psychotic entered Safeway laughing. His laugh had the false heartiness of a department-store Santa Claus. He stood in front of the checkout lines, chuckling at some private observation that tickled him. He was full of expansive, arm-waving gestures. A young woman, on her way out, made the mistake of stopping near him to adjust the shoulder strap of her purse. He laughed out loud and opened his arms, inviting her to join his merry world. As his arm circled her neck, she pushed it deftly away, as if accustomed to handling the blunt familiarities of the insane. She was good-natured and not at all frightened. The man was at least six feet three and over two hundred pounds. His raggy clothes were stiff with grime.

I'd seen him before. He was not usually so happy. Most of the time he seemed stunned and bewildered. He'd stand, teetering on the balls of his feet, touching his face with trembling finger-tips as if trying to remember how it once looked. Or he would move, zombie-slow, through the aisles, perplexed by the rage of colors and shapes that gleamed like hallucinations from the shelves. Once I saw him marching fiercely to a Sousa piece on the Muzak, a large fresh salmon and a six-pack of toilet paper in his cart. I didn't know his name, but I called him Muni, after the 1930s movie actor, Paul Muni, whom the man resembled in some distorted way.

Muni followed the young woman out of the store and into the moonlit parking lot. A checkout clerk followed them to make sure Muni didn't try any rough stuff. I wheeled my cart after the clerk, thinking that neither one of us would be a match for Muni if he got it into his head to fight for love. Raquel, my wife, lagged at the checkout counter, squinting suspiciously at the receipt. "Are you coming?" I yelled. I was nervous and annoyed. Muni wasn't the only reason for getting out of Safeway quickly. They were out in droves that Monday night, even though the moon was not quite full . . . bag ladies, bikers, frayed winos fondling slim bottles of fortified Tokay.

THE RECEPTIVE READER

1. Does the setting seem strange or familiar to you? What striking details help bring it to life? What for you is the keynote or unifying prevailing mood?

2. How much do you learn about the characters? Do they become believable?

3. Is there a germ of a plot here? What do you think might happen in the rest of the story?

4. From whose point of view is the story told? What difference does it make?

5. Does anything here have possible symbolic significance?

6. What might be a possible theme? What statement might the story as a whole be making about the homeless mentally ill or about the cityscape in which many Americans live?

7. What is the *tone* of these paragraphs—what seems to be the attitude of the nar-

rator; what mood or what emotions seem to prevail? For instance, do these paragraphs sound angry, sentimental, humorous, or earnest? Does the style make the narrator seem passionate or detached? How does the writer steer our reactions toward Muni?

CLOSE READING AND THE PERSONAL RESPONSE

My writing expects, demands participatory reading, and that is what I think literature is supposed to do. It's not just about telling the story; it's about involving the reader. The reader supplies the emotions. The reader supplies even some of the color, some of the sound. My language has to have holes and spaces so that the reader can come into it.
TONI MORRISON

Reading imaginative literature is different from recording data or crunching numbers. It is more multidimensional. It brings not only our intelligence but also our imagination and our emotions into play. It involves us as complete human beings. When we respond fully to a story or a poem, we are living more alertly in the world. We are broadening our sympathies. We are educating the emotions.

You may want to think of your reading as involving three major dimensions:

The Receptive Reader   A receptive reader is on the writer's side. As a receptive reader, you make an extra effort of understanding; you give a difficult story the benefit of the doubt. You develop the habit of close, attentive reading (rather than skimming the page to get a "general idea"). In a well-crafted short story, details are not just there to fill the page. You are likely to notice striking details that make the author's world real for the reader. You should be alert to gestures or actions that provide a clue to a character's motives. You will need an eye for objects with symbolic overtones, an ear for revealing comments and shades of meaning. You will need to respond to patterns that give shape to the story as a whole.

The Personal Response   The stories and the writers we return to have some special personal meaning for us. The stories that move us powerfully do in some way touch our own lives, though the connection may not always be obvious. At some level, they engage with our own needs, desires, or apprehensions. The writer does not really expect us to read the story the way an electronic scanner would, retrieving data to be analyzed later. Our emotions as well as our intellect must be engaged if we are to understand what mattered to the author.

The following is one student's reaction to a short story classic. How did she make the personal connection? What mattered to her most in the story, and why?

"The Open Boat" by Stephen Crane is a story about men who were shipwrecked and forced to brave the open sea with very little protection and with little hope of survival. While I read this story, I felt much concern about the men who were trying to survive in a contest with nature that seemed bent on defeating them and had the power to destroy them. What struck me most in this story was the spirit of teamwork, of working together. They helped each other out in order to survive; they knew that was the only way to beat the sea. The cook bailed the water out of their tiny boat; the journalist and the engineer took turns rowing the boat ("Will you spell me for a little while?"), never complaining or saying they were dead tired when they were all on the brink of exhaustion. The captain, although he was injured and unable to do physical work, gave directions and moral support to the "crew." What if they had not been able to work as a team? What if they had started bickering, using abusive language, as many people would today? What if they had let the short fuse set off an explosion of stupid hostility and pride? They would all have drowned. At the end of the story, I found myself cheering them all on, and I was full of grief when one of the crew drowned. The surprising thing to me was that the one who drowned was the strongest of the four. It may not always be the "fittest" who survive.

The Creative Dimension   Fiction stimulates the reader's imagination. For instance, you may want to re-create an impression that lingered in your memory. You may want to evoke a haunting image that in some ways seems to sum up the story. Look at the following student-written response to Mary Robison's "Yours." Does it in any way add to or enhance your own reading of the story?

> Pumpkins in orange October,
>   their sweet soggy smell
>   rises from carved insides
>   on wet news
> Their fierce pumpkin faces, lit by candles,
>   glow till morning,
>   the live flame softening their shells
> Pumpkin, a child's toy,
>   not for May or December,
>   but for late October, ushering in
>   November and a Thanksgiving of sorts
> Pumpkins from the brittle vine
>   the last sweet
>   harvest

WRITING ABOUT LITERATURE

1. Keeping a Short Story Journal (Materials for Writing)

The Writing Workshop   Writing is more than a way of communicating what you already know. It is a way of learning, of understanding, of thinking through what you have learned. Writing about literature can make you a more attentive, a more thoughtful reader. When you keep a short story **journal**, you record your impressions and reactions as you read. You have a chance to register your questions, to record tentative conclusions, and to do some preliminary sorting out of your thinking. You try to formulate your personal responses, puzzling over contradictory or unexpected reactions on your part. You experiment with creative responses to what you have read, such as quickly sketched re-creations of a haunting image, a prevailing mood, a turning point in a story.

Writing weekly or biweekly entries in a reading journal or reading log gives you a chance to do some extensive prewriting for more structured papers, to accumulate a rich fund of materials for more formal writing tasks. Here are some possible kinds of entries for your journal:

Thinking about Previous Reading   In one of your first journal entries, you may want to look back over your previous experiences as a reader of fiction. What kind of reading has shaped your expectations as a reader? What kind of story made a lasting impression on you, and why? The story you write about may be a story you loved or admired, but it could also be a story that upset you or disturbed you. Perhaps you will choose a story that did not mean much at the time but that in retrospect has acquired a special meaning.

First Impressions   You will often find it helpful to record your initial impressions after your first reading of a story. Sort out and put into words your first reactions and your preliminary understanding of the story. Take time to gather your thoughts, to pull together what seems most significant. Include any questions the story may have raised in your mind. Here is one reader's first reaction to a story by the Canadian author Alice Munro:

> Alice Munro's "Boys and Girls" takes place in Canada where the head of a small family raises silver foxes for furs. Of the two children, the girl tells the story, making pertinent observations on life on the fox farm and on the other members of the family. Life is seen entirely through her eyes. Foxes are slaughtered and their skins prepared for sale. Old injured horses are killed for food for the foxes. What it means to be a boy and what it means to be a girl become major issues in the story. (Is it significant that both the foxes and the horses are given male and female names?) Gender roles flip-flop in the story as the narrator prides herself on doing "man's work" as her father's helper while her mother grumbles about not getting enough help from her in the kitchen. Stereotypes are constantly challenged, but in the end they seem to triumph as the girl realizes she is "only a girl."

Running Commentary   An excellent way to make the most of your reading is to prepare a running commentary. You jot down your observations, queries, and comments as you read along. You include striking details, quotable quotations, and puzzlers to be checked out later. What at first was a puzzling detail may acquire fuller meaning as the author sounds the same note again or follows up an earlier hint.

Your entry will be your record of how your understanding of a story took shape. Doing such a running commentary will alert you to the clues the author provides to the intention, overall pattern, or overall meaning of a story. However, it will also make sure you get involved in the detail of the story before you interpret, speculate, or editorialize. It will make you realize how much of the **texture** of a story—its web of revealing details, significant dialogue—can be missed in a quick reading.

The following running commentary traces one reader's growing understanding of Ernest Hemingway's "Hills like White Elephants." The story takes the reader into a world of thinking and feeling different from the macho world of bullfights, big-game hunting, and deep-sea fishing that for many readers is the stereotypical Hemingway setting.

A man and a woman (American) are at a railroad station somewhere in Spain. Everything is hot and dry. Very succinct and concrete images: "a curtain, made of strings of bamboo beads, hung across the open door into the bar, to keep out flies."

There seems to be some kind of communication problem, or a misunderstanding of some sort that is unresolved between them. The woman says the hills remind her of "white elephants" but later says that the man "wouldn't have" seen one, so he couldn't know what they look like. He doesn't have the spirit of adventure or the imagination?

Why does everything taste like licorice? The exotic drinks—Anis del Toro and absinthe—both taste like licorice to the woman: "the things you've waited so long for" taste like licorice. A note of bitterness, discontent?

There seems to be a pointlessness in their lives: "all we do" is "look at things and try new drinks."

They start talking about an operation. The man keeps saying it's "an awfully simple operation." The operation is "just to let the air in"—ha! The man pretends he wouldn't mind if the girl didn't go through with the abortion: "If you don't want to you don't have to." Actually, he sees it as very important: "the only thing that bothers us." She feels, "once they take it away, you never get it back." But she also knows that if she decides against the abortion he will not be happy.

The girl knows she really has no choice despite the man's words. He keeps saying, "I don't want you to, I don't care anything about it." But he is actually pushing her to have the abortion. She cannot listen to him anymore; she drives home the word PLEASE seven times when she tells him to stop talking. She says, "I'll scream."

She probably knows that either way they are at the end of their once carefree relationship. Nothing will be as before. "We could have everything and every day we make it more impossible." She sees the end of their lives, as they know them.

At the end, the woman says, "There's nothing wrong with me. I feel fine." But she is not fine. As in much of the story, we have to read her true feelings between the lines. The author doesn't waste words; as he shows in portraying the man in the story, words are cheap. The effect of the story emerges as much from what is not said in the story as from what is.

Possible symbolic overtones: The two lines of railroad track going in opposite directions may stand for the diverging lives of the two characters? The young woman's comparing the hills to elephants shows her affinity with living things—does it hint at her positive attitude toward the unborn child?

Is Hemingway passé? On the surface, the man acts concerned and reassuring: "I don't want anyone but you." But he is really selfish, deceiving, and pushy. This story is timely today. A young woman close to me and her boyfriend are going through the same thing now. He wants her to have an abortion, because that would be easy for him, but she doesn't want one. It is an age-old dilemma. Hemingway doesn't hit the reader over the head with it; there are no flowery descriptive phrases. He never mentions the word *abortion,* and he gives just barely enough facts. But the meaning emerges from the story cleanly, economically, and poignantly.

Clustering   Many writers use clustering to start and organize the flow of ideas. For a story to work, it has to engage with what we already know. What images and feeling does a story activate in the reader's mind? What associations with a central term does the reader bring to the story? **Clustering** is a prewriting technique that lets you explore a network of images, memories, or associations. With strands of ideas branching out from a central stimulus word, you can follow the different chains of associations the central idea brings into play. The idea is to sketch in freely, spontaneously, what a key word or key term brings to mind.

Clustering is a stimulus technique of double value to you if you are the kind of writer who might otherwise be staring at a blank sheet or screen. First, you call up from the memory bank of your mind much material that might potentially be relevant to a topic. You access thoughts and feelings; you map graphically what you are inclined to think and feel on a topic. At the same time, however, a pattern takes shape. You begin to see possible connections and relations. Some sorting, some shaping, is going on at the same time that you are taking stock of relevant memories, associations, and overtones.

In a story like Bernard Malamud's "The Magic Barrel" or Shirley Jackson's "The Lottery," tradition plays a central role—tradition and the way the characters in the story live up to it, or make it suit their purposes. A cluster like the one on the next page might map the network of associations that a reader brings to the story. Notice that in this cluster a pattern is taking shape: The cluster graphically shows thinking in progress. It shows the writer thinking about the two-sided nature of tradition, a force for good and evil.

The passage following the cluster lays out the material and traces the pattern that the cluster has generated.

SAMPLE CLUSTER

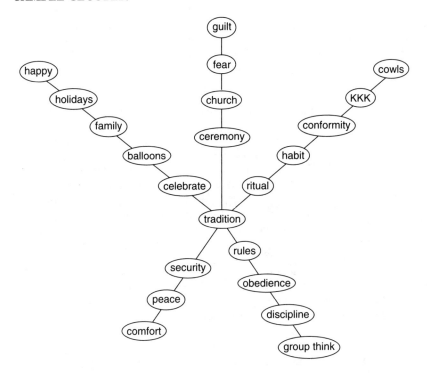

Tradition to many of us means first of all nostalgic memories of Christ-mas or Easter or Passover, happy hours spent with family and friends, birth-day celebrations with balloons and ice cream cake and candles. In the traditional family, there is a sense of security—of knowing what to do, of re-lying on the tried and true. However, we also feel the weight of tradition— feeling guilty about not going to mass, feeling fear of retribution for our sins and backslidings. The inherent danger in tradition is the reliance on group-think. Blind obedience to traditional rules and regulations can lead to un-questioned acceptance of cruel or idiotic practices. When we look at the dual nature of tradition, we see interlocking elements that can suddenly cover the face of love with a cowl of enmity and violence.

Focusing on Character In other journal entries, you may go beyond the note-taking stage to start to organize your thinking. For instance, in a **capsule portrait** of a character, you pull together traits illustrated in the incidents of the story. You integrate crucial hints about the character that may be scattered over quite a few pages. What kind of person does the author show you? What are key traits, and how are they related? Is there a trait that provides the clue to the character as a whole? Does the character change or grow in the course of the story? Here is a sample of such a character portrait:

The central character in Alice Munro's story "Boys and Girls" is struggling to adjust to the fact that she is slowly changing from a girl to a young woman. In the beginning, she is her Daddy's helper around the fox farm where her father raises foxes for their pelts. Oblivious to the stereotypical female gender role, she helps her father care for the animals, rakes up the grass or weeds he has cut, and does other traditional "male" chores. However, she begins to realize that as a female she is expected to do some things and not others; in particular, she is expected to help her mother in the kitchen, a place she detests. She rebels against her expected role, trying to stay out of the kitchen and close to the outdoors she loves. Her grandmother's comments, such as "Girls don't slam doors like that" or "Girls keep their knees together when they sit down," lead her to continue to slam doors and to sit as awkwardly as possible. Her rebellious behavior shows her strong will, stubbornness, and nonconformity, and, most of all, her spirit. Her spiritedness is mirrored in her daydreams of performing heroic rescues. She has a zest for constant excitement in life, and when her life doesn't supply it, she creates her own, as when she dares her three-year-old little brother to climb the barn ladder to the top beam. As she gets older, her old spirit carries over when she allows Flora, the horse scheduled to be shot for meat for the foxes, to escape through the gate. This scene shows her developing her own person, her own opinions, her own values. Despite the ending of the story, where she seems to be submitting herself to her expected gender roles, I believe that the strong spirit she has exhibited throughout the story will never leave her.

Focusing on Theme   You may frequently want to sum up for yourself the impact or meaning of a story as a whole. What idea or ideas stay with the reader at the end of the story? What seems to give the story its special quality or particular force? Here is a sample entry:

"The Open Boat," by Stephen Crane, is a late 19th to early 20th century story. Crew members and a newspaper correspondent in a lifeboat struggle for days in the stormy shark-infested sea, with their hopes for rescue or an easy landfall repeatedly dashed. In the end one of them drowns; the others make it to shore. This is an early modern view: There is no loving or benevolent nature. The shipwrecked sailors undergo a terrible ordeal, but they do not conclude that nature was out to punish them, nor do they feel that nature is loving or maternal. Birds were made to survive on the ocean; they are part of nature. The only way for human beings to survive is to work together—practice brotherhood. Since they are not at home in nature, they must make their home within it with the help of others. They need solidarity. Nature is alien and inhospitable; it couldn't care less.

For Class Interaction   You may want to share one or more early journal entries with your classmates. For instance, you might want to discuss with them what made a story especially meaningful to you, or what expectations you brought to it, or what made it difficult for you to read or enjoy.

2 SETTING
Landscapes of the Mind

Here I am, where I ought to be. A writer must have a place where he or she feels this, a place to love and be irritated with.

LOUISE ERDRICH

Once in their lives people ought to concentrate their minds upon the remembered earth. They ought to give themselves up to a particular landscape in their experience, looking at it from as many angles as they can, to wonder upon it, to dwell upon it.

N. SCOTT MOMADAY

FOCUS ON SETTING

A story creates its own world. It takes us to a **setting** in space and in time. In a successful story, that place becomes a small universe of its own, consistent in itself. The story creates a context whose assumptions we accept for the duration of the story. We enter into the world of the story the way we might honor customs, closing hours, and curfews when we spend time in another country. While a powerful story works its spell, we think and feel in the context of the story—somewhat the way organisms in a biosphere live on the terms of their self-contained environment.

Some writers sketch times and locations only in rough outline, leaving much to our imagination. But other writers painstakingly re-create or reenact a setting, a scene. They conjure up a place and take us there. They rely heavily on the setting to help them create the illusion of reality, so that we will accept characters and events as real also. Toward the beginning of his story "Araby," James Joyce takes us to the Dublin of his childhood, where the neighborhood boys played in a dead-end street during the short days of winter, when dusk fell early. What kind of world is beginning to take shape in the following passage?

When we met in the street the houses had grown somber. The space of sky above us was the color of ever-changing violet and toward it the lamps of the street lifted their feeble lanterns. The cold air stung us and we played till our bodies glowed. Our shouts echoed in the silent street. The career of our play brought us through the dark muddy lanes behind the houses where we ran the gauntlet of the rough tribes from the cottages, to the back doors of the dark dripping gardens where odors arose from the ashpits, to the dark odorous stables where a coachman smoothed and combed the horse or shook music from the buckled harness.

In creating this setting for us, the imaginative writer is our scout and interpreter. He is more alert and sensitive than ordinary people, more responsive to experience, taking in more of its sights and sounds and odors. Joyce recreates for us the shade of light, the feeble streetlights "lifting" their lanterns toward the sky, the odors from the ashpits and the stables. He registers what there is for an alert observer to see and hear and smell. The reality he re-creates for us is down-to-earth, with dark muddy alleys, danger from rough kids from a low-income neighborhood close by, and the decaying odor of ashes from old-style hearths and stoves. But the world created for us here is also laced with strange beauty—"the ever-changing violet of the sky," the jangling metal of the horse's harness sounding like music that the coachman "shook" from the gear.

The setting created in the opening paragraphs of this story is not just a backdrop against which any optional drama might be played out. It projects a **mood**—a somber if not gloomy mood, contrasting with the intense vitality of the shouting children, who played till their bodies "glowed." Subliminally, this contrast creates expectations; it steers our attention. Whatever shape the story may take, we do not expect a story in which frivolous characters will tiptoe through tulips. Nor do we expect a story in which burnt-out individuals play variations on a theme of "I-don't-care." Instead, we will not be surprised if we see an imaginative, intense character (or characters) in a setting that offers obstacles or limitations to the life of the imagination.

Becoming sensitive to setting will help you meet a story on its own terms. Often the setting will not just be geographical or physical; it will bring with it ways of thinking or feeling that come with the territory. It is likely to come with customs, assumptions, or collective memories that will play a role in the story. The story may in fact be about how a character discovers these, is shaped by them, rebels against them, or leaves them behind. The setting of a story is not just an external landscape; it is more often a landscape of the mind.

THE SETTING AND THE STORY

There are deserts in every life, and the desert must be depicted if we are to give a fair and complete idea of the country.

ANDRÉ MAUROIS

One of the first questions we ask of a story is, "Where is the story taking us?" By establishing the setting, a writer lets us know where we are, makes us realize what time it is. The setting may create a pervasive mood, felt not only by the reader but also by the characters in the story—decay, constraint, splendor, guilt, liberation. The setting may be exotic, with the story placing us in strange circumstances, requiring of us a major effort of the imagination. But the setting may also be totally ordinary, reacquainting us with what Marian Evans (whose pen name was George Eliot) called "the beauty of the commonplace." It may ask us to look at familiar surroundings as if we were seeing them for the first time.

Often the setting plays a major role in shaping the characters, the action, or the theme of a story. A *New York Times* reviewer said about the stories in Bobbie Ann Mason's *Shiloh and Other Stories* (1982),

> Mason's setting was Kentucky—not the old Kentucky of small towns and gracious farms, but that proud territory of the new South speckled with shopping malls and subdivisions, fast-food franchises and drive-in movies, a shiny new place, vacuumed clean of history and tradition. Reeling from the swiftness of the transition, Mason's characters all seemed to wander about in a fog, either spacing out in front of the television or passively drifting away from their families and friends, aware, however dimly, that they had misplaced something important along the way. (Michiko Kakutani)

Here are some major ways the setting may help give shape to a story as a whole.

The Setting as Mirror   The setting may mirror a prevailing mood. It may signal or reinforce prevailing emotions. An arid landscape, for instance, may mirror despair, spiritual desolation. Barren hills, scrubby vegetation, and dusty dirt roads may provide a fitting setting for emotionally dried-up characters. On the other hand, sultry weather and thunderstorms, like the mood music in a movie, may prepare you for pent-up passions and emotional upheavals.

However, we cannot always expect an obvious connection between the setting and the people who play their roles in it. The setting may be ironic. Our sense of **irony** makes us respond with a grim smile when things do not turn out the way we would like or expect, while a little voice in the back of our minds says: "I should have known!" Modern writers often have a highly developed sense of irony. Their characters are just as likely to be depressed as happy in a springtime setting. A modern story may show us people who are lonely in a crowd.

The Setting as Mold   The setting of a story often shapes character. It helps make people what they are. Someone growing up on a farm, with its endless chores, dependence on rain and sun, and closeness to living things, is likely to have a different outlook, a different definition of life, than someone growing up in a city neighborhood where the only open spaces are parking lots.

A story may show its characters as creatures of the setting, reflecting its mood, living out its mores or approved ways of acting and thinking. A familiar theme in serious modern fiction is that of invisible walls: Characters find themselves trapped in a restrictive environment. The story may show them discovering its limitations, coming up against invisible barriers that hem them in. Characters may find themselves trapped in the spiritual wasteland of suburbia, or in a small decaying town that becomes for them the graveyard of hope. (On the other hand, a story may show a character rebelling against a stifling environment, struggling to break free, to break out.)

The Setting as Challenge   A story may take people out of their usual setting, their daily routine, and put them to the test. An unusual setting may become a major player in the drama acted out in a story. In Jack London's classic "To Light a Fire," the extreme numbing cold of the frozen north becomes the mortal enemy of the traveler who finds himself unable to light the life-saving fire.

The Setting as Escape   Escape literature takes us to imaginary settings where we act out daydreams to which ordinary reality is not hospitable. The story may take us to a mansion in the pre–Civil War South to make us witness scenes of flaming passion. It may take us to ancient Rome to appall us with scenes of treachery and depravity. However, a faraway setting may not necessarily provide an escape; it may really be the destination of a journey of discovery, where we may encounter facets of our own personality denied an outlet in our ordinary world.

The Alien Setting   Much modern literature circles back to the loss of roots, the loss of home. You may find yourself in a setting that is inhospitable, like an alien planet. You may identify with the exile, the undesirable, the refugee. In the short stories of Ernest Hemingway and other writers of the twenties and thirties, you encounter the eternal tourist, the expatriate—the person in exile from his or her own country. In much of the fiction of Franz Kafka, you find yourself in a nightmare setting. As in a bad dream, you may struggle with an environment that defies your best efforts at getting control of the situation, at understanding what is going on.

A CLASSIC SHORT STORY: JOYCE'S "ARABY"

*"This race and this country and this life produced me," he
said. "I shall express myself as I am."*
    JAMES JOYCE, *A PORTRAIT OF THE ARTIST AS A YOUNG MAN*

James Joyce (1882–1941), one of the towering innovators in modern fiction, was one of the Irish writers that have helped shape twentieth-century literature. Like other artists, writers, and intellectuals of his time, Joyce worked most of his life in self-imposed exile from his native country, becoming one of the great expatriate authors of the century. Joyce was born in a suburb of

Dublin; he left Dublin at the age of twenty-two, and he was to return only twice for brief visits. However, the city of his birth and its people are in almost everything he wrote.

Joyce was the son of an outgoing but spendthrift father and a devoutly Catholic mother. At the age of six, he entered a school run by Jesuit priests; he later enrolled at the Jesuit order's Belvedere College in Dublin. (His mother wanted him as the oldest of her ten children to become a priest in the Roman Catholic church.) His work is steeped in the vocabulary, and in the ways of thinking and feeling, of centuries of religious tradition. However, he decided against entering the priesthood, fighting the narrowing of vision that he saw as the price of committing to a traditional creed. He similarly distanced himself from the passionate and often intolerant nationalism that was the legacy of his country's struggle for liberation from British colonial rule. Family, church, and country came to seem to him like nets thrown to contain and restrain the free exercise of the creative spirit. He came to see his native city as "a place too preoccupied with the past and too much in love with lost causes." As he said in his largely autobiographical first novel, *A Portrait of the Artist as a Young Man* (1916), "I will not serve that in which I no longer believe."

For almost a quarter of a century, Joyce barely survived by teaching English and doing clerical work, first in Zurich (Switzerland) and later in Trieste (Italy) and Paris. He wrote constantly, developing the narrative technique known as **stream of consciousness** that was to revolutionize much of modern fiction. Human beings do not think in complete sentences, carry on coherent logical conversations with themselves, or make rational decisions after lining up the pro and con. Instead, their mental world is a shifting sequence of sensations, thoughts, and feelings—a kaleidoscopic mix of fleeting images, bodily sensations, memories, half-finished trains of thought. To approximate the reality of what it feels like to be a feeling, thinking human being, a writer should transcribe this **interior monologue,** tracing the typical mixture of daydream and reality, pursuing chains of association. In Joyce's masterpiece, the novel *Ulysses* (1922), a thread of external events alternates with extended stretches of interior monologue immersing the readers in a stream of impressions, reminiscences, and half-formulated thoughts.

Since the mind dwells on basic emotional concerns without polite disguise, the treatment of sex in *Ulysses* was too explicit for the guardians of public morality, and the novel for many years had to be smuggled into the United States. At the same time, it made wide use of complex allusions and symbolic parallels to Greek mythology, with the daily round of Leopold Bloom, a Dublin salesman, paralleling the mythical journey of Ulysses. In his *Finnegan's Wake* (1939), Joyce developed a rich private language exploiting multileveled puns, allusions, and associations.

We call a work of literature a classic when readers and critics return to it again and again, when it survives changes in fashion. The following classic short story is from an early collection, *Dubliners* (1914), intended by Joyce as "a chapter of the moral history of Ireland." Compared with Joyce's later work, these stories have a straightforward, conventional story line. However, they anticipate his later work by focusing on the private thoughts, emotions, and daydreams of his characters.

J A M E S   J O Y C E   (1882–1941)
Araby   1914

[A few references in this story might puzzle today's reader. One of the books mentioned early told the life story of Vidocq, a legendary French detective. The Freemasons, members of private fraternal organizations, were viewed with suspicion by people with traditional religious views. The florin was a British silver coin worth two shillings. A Café Chantant was a French coffeehouse with musical entertainment.]

North Richmond Street, being blind, was a quiet street except at the hour when the Christian Brothers' School set the boys free. An uninhabited house of two stories stood at the blind end, detached from its neighbors in a square ground. The other houses of the street, conscious of decent lives within them, gazed at one another with brown imperturbable faces.

The former tenant of our house, a priest, had died in the back drawing-room. Air, musty from having been long enclosed, hung in all the rooms, and the waste room behind the kitchen was littered with old useless papers. Among these I found a few paper-covered books, the pages of which were curled and damp: *The Abbot,* by Walter Scott, *The Devout Communicant* and *The Memoirs of Vidocq.* I liked the last best because its leaves were yellow. The wild garden behind the house contained a central apple-tree and a few straggling bushes under one of which I found the late tenant's rusty bicycle-pump. He had been a very charitable priest; in his will he had left all his money to institutions and the furniture of his house to his sister.

When the short days of winter came dusk fell before we had well eaten our dinners. When we met in the street the houses had grown somber. The space of sky above us was the color of ever-changing violet and toward it the lamps of the street lifted their feeble lanterns. The cold air stung us and we played till our bodies glowed. Our shouts echoed in the silent street. The career of our play brought us through the dark muddy lanes behind the houses where we ran the gauntlet of the rough tribes from the cottages, to the back doors of the dark dripping gardens where odors arose from the ash-pits, to the dark odorous stables where a coachman smoothed and combed the horse or shook music from the buckled harness. When we returned to the street light from the kitchen windows had filled the areas. If my uncle was seen turning the corner we hid in the shadow until we had seen him safely housed. Of if Mangan's sister came out on the doorstep to call her brother in to his tea we watched her from our shadow peer up and down the street. We waited to see whether she would remain or go in and, if she remained, we left our shadow and walked up to Mangan's steps resignedly. She was waiting for us, her figure defined by the light from the half-opened door. Her brother always teased her before he obeyed and I stood by the railings looking at her. Her dress swung as she moved her body, and the soft rope of her hair tossed from side to side.

Every morning I lay on the floor in the front parlor watching her door. The blind was pulled down to within an inch of the sash so that I could not be seen. When she came out on the doorstep my heart leaped. I ran to the hall, seized my books and followed her. I kept her brown figure always in my eye and, when we came near the point at which our ways diverged, I quickened my pace and passed her. This happened morning after morning. I had never spoken to her, except for a few casual words, and yet her name was like a summons to all my foolish blood.

Her image accompanied me even in places the most hostile to romance. On Saturday evenings when my aunt went marketing I had to go to carry some of the parcels. We walked through the flaring streets, jostled by drunken men and bargaining women, amid the curses of laborers, the shrill litanies of shop-boys who stood on guard by the barrels of pigs' cheeks, the nasal chanting of street-singers, who sang a *come-all-you* about O'Donovan Rossa, or a ballad about the troubles in our native land. These noises converged in a single sensation of life for me: I imagined that I bore my chalice safely through a throng of foes. Her name sprang to my lips at moments in strange prayers and praises which I myself did not understand. My eyes were often full of tears (I could not tell why) and at times a flood from my heart seemed to pour itself out into my bosom. I thought little of the future. I did not know whether I would ever speak to her or not or, if I spoke to her, how I could tell her of my confused adoration. But my body was like a harp and her words and gestures were like fingers running upon the wires.

One evening I went into the back drawing-room in which the priest had died. It was a dark rainy evening and there was no sound in the house. Through one of the broken panes I heard the rain impinge upon the earth, the fine incessant needles of water playing in the sodden beds. Some distant lamp or lighted window gleamed below me. I was thankful that I could see so little. All my senses seemed to desire to veil themselves and, feeling that I was about to slip from them, I pressed the palms of my hands together until they trembled, murmuring: *"O love! O love!"* many times.

At last she spoke to me. When she addressed the first words to me I was so confused that I did not know what to answer. She asked me was I going to *Araby*. I forgot whether I answered yes or no. It would be a splendid bazaar, she said she would love to go.

"And why can't you?" I asked.

While she spoke she turned a silver bracelet round and round her wrist. She could not go, she said, because there would be a retreat that week in her convent. Her brother and two other boys were fighting for their caps and I was alone at the railings. She held one of the spikes, bowing her head towards me. The light from the lamp opposite our door caught the white curve of her neck, lit up her hair that rested there and, falling, lit up the hand upon the railing. It fell over one side of her dress and caught the white border of a petticoat, just visible as she stood at ease.

"It's well for you," she said.

"If I go," I said, "I will bring you something."

What innumerable follies laid waste my waking and sleeping thoughts after that evening! I wished to annihilate the tedious intervening days. I chafed against the work of school. At night in my bedroom and by day in the classroom her image came between me and the page I strove to read. The syllables of the word *Araby* were called to me through the silence in which my soul luxuriated and cast an Eastern enchantment over me. I asked for leave to go to the bazaar on Saturday night. My aunt was surprised and hoped it was not some Freemason affair. I answered few questions in class. I watched my master's face pass from amiability to sternness; he hoped I was not beginning to idle. I could not call my wandering thoughts together. I had hardly any patience with the serious work of life which, now that it stood between me and my desire, seemed to me child's play, ugly monotonous child's play.

On Saturday morning I reminded my uncle that I wished to go to the bazaar in the evening. He was fussing at the hallstand, looking for the hat-brush, and answered me curtly:

"Yes, boy, I know."

As he was in the hall I could not go into the front parlor and lie at the window. I felt the house in bad humor and walked slowly toward the school. The air was pitilessly raw and already my heart misgave me.

When I came home to dinner my uncle had not yet been home. Still it was early. I sat staring at the clock for some time and, when its ticking began to irritate me, I left the room. I mounted the staircase and gained the upper part of the house. The high cold empty gloomy rooms liberated me and I went from room to room singing. From the front window I saw my companions playing below in the street. Their cries reached me weakened and indistinct and, leaning my forehead against the cool glass, I looked over at the dark house where she lived. I may have stood there for an hour, seeing nothing but the brown-clad figure cast by my imagination, touched discreetly by the lamplight at the curved neck, at the hand upon the railings and at the border below the dress.

When I came downstairs again I found Mrs. Mercer sitting at the fire. She was an old garrulous woman, a pawn-broker's widow, who collected used stamps for some pious purpose. I had to endure the gossip of the tea-table. The meal was prolonged beyond an hour and still my uncle did not come. Mrs. Mercer stood up to go: she was sorry she couldn't wait any longer, but it was after eight o'clock and she did not like to be out late, as the night air was bad for her. When she had gone I began to walk up and down the room, clenching my fists. My aunt said:

"I'm afraid you may put off your bazaar for this night of Our Lord."

At nine o'clock I heard my uncle's latchkey in the halldoor. I heard him talking to himself and heard the hallstand rocking when it had received the weight of his overcoat. I could interpret these signs. When he was midway through his dinner I asked him to give me the money to go to the bazaar. He had forgotten.

"The people are in bed and after their first sleep now," he said.

I did not smile. My aunt said to him energetically:

"Can't you give him the money and let him go? You've kept him late enough as it is."

My uncle said he was very sorry he had forgotten. He said he believed in the old saying: "All work and no play makes Jack a dull boy." He asked me where I was going and, when I had told him a second time he asked me did I know *The Arab's Farewell to his Steed*. When I left the kitchen he was about to recite the opening lines of the piece to my aunt.

I held a florin tightly in my hand as I strode down Buckingham Street toward the station. The sight of the streets thronged with buyers and glaring with gas recalled to me the purpose of my journey. I took my seat in a third-class carriage of a deserted train. After an intolerable delay the train moved out of the station slowly. It crept onward among ruinous houses and over the twinkling river. At Westland Row Station a crowd of people pressed to the carriage doors; but the porters moved them back, saying that it was a special train for the bazaar. I remained alone in the bare carriage. In a few minutes the train drew up beside an improvised wooden platform. I passed out on to the road and saw by the lighted dial of a clock that it was ten minutes to ten. In front of me was a large building which displayed the magical name.

I could not find any sixpenny entrance and, fearing that the bazaar would be closed, I passed in quickly through a turnstile, handing a shilling to a weary-looking man. I found myself in a big hall girdled at half its height by a gallery. Nearly all the stalls were closed and the greater part of the hall was in darkness. I recognized a silence like that which pervades a church after a service. I walked into the center of the bazaar timidly. A few people were gathered about the stalls which were still open. Before a curtain, over which the words *Café Chantant* were written in colored lamps, two men were counting money on a salver. I listened to the fall of the coins.

Remembering with difficulty why I had come I went over to one of the stalls and examined porcelain vases and flowered tea-sets. At the door of the stall a young lady was talking and laughing with two young gentlemen. I remarked their English accents and listened vaguely to their conversation.

"O, I never said such a thing!"

"O, but you did!"

"O, but I didn't!"

"Didn't she say that?"   30

"Yes. I heard her."

"O, there's a . . . fib!"

Observing me the young lady came over and asked me did I wish to buy anything. The tone of her voice was not encouraging; she seemed to have spoken to me out of a sense of duty. I looked humbly at the great jars that stood like eastern guards at either side of the dark entrance to the stall and murmured:

"No, thank you."

The young lady changed the position of one of the vases and went back to the two   35
young men. They began to talk of the same subject. Once or twice the young lady glanced at me over her shoulder.

I lingered before her stall, though I knew my stay was useless, to make my interest in her wares seem the more real. Then I turned away slowly and walked down the middle of the bazaar. I allowed the two pennies to fall against the sixpence in my pocket. I heard a voice call from one end of the gallery that the light was out. The upper part of the hall was now completely dark.

Gazing up into the darkness I saw myself as a creature driven and derided by vanity; and my eyes burned with anguish and anger.

What might a responsive reader get from this story? There are probably at least two ways to look at the role of the setting in this story. (Which is closer to your own response as a reader?)

❖ Love surfaces in unlikely places—in the ordinary settings of uninteresting people and their dull lives. When we see the ordinary boys play in the muddy street, we do not expect an emotional attachment that has the intensity of religious devotion. However, the power of the imagination transfigures the dull, everyday reality of people's lives. We are not doomed to be unimaginative clods.

❖ The setting sets invisible limits. We have a capacity for love, for worship, for imagination far beyond what the ordinary reality of our lives can accommodate or bring to fruition. We are doomed to disappointment. Our yearnings create a dream of fulfillment that cannot possibly come true. The setting, the real world we live in, is hostile to our dreams.

THE RECEPTIVE READER

1. What striking details help the setting come to life for you? Which seem to set the tone or point forward to the rest of the story?

2. What striking images help you understand the boy's feelings? What images give his devotion a quasi-religious quality? (What are the associations of the word *chalice*; what feelings does it bring into play?)

3. Is the boy able to share his feelings with anyone? If not, why not?

4. What is the role of the uncle in the story?

5. Is it a coincidence that the climactic high point of the story takes place in a bazaar—a special annual event?

6. As we watch crucial scenes in the story, we at times have to sense the boy's feelings rather than having them explained in so many words by the author. What are some examples?

THE PERSONAL RESPONSE

Is the boy merely infatuated? Should he have known better? Is he acting "immature"?

THE CREATIVE DIMENSION

Writers sometimes describe how a short story took shape from a striking, teasing image in the writer's mind. Sometimes after we finish reading, what stays with us is a haunting image that seems to sum up something essential in the story. The following student-written passages re-create a key moment in Joyce's "Araby." What do they capture in the story? Write your own re-creation of a haunting image or key moment in Joyce's story or in another story in this chapter.

1.   We played in
      the cold, short winter evenings
      colored violet with dusk.
      We made a career
      of playing long in
      the streets
      and alleys with shadows
      our bodies small and cold
      and glowing.
      In the street the lamps
      lined up,
      illuminating
      a playmate's sister strolling
      towards us,
      soft smooth hair,
      swinging skirt.

2.   When I was eight, I would play till the night came on, the dusk slipping over the world in the sky above our heads and between the buildings. As the violet glowed stronger, the world would suddenly, for a flash, have sharp outlines, shapes of heavy black cut out against the coming night. I would be running hard. There were the times after the shouts had flown past me down

the streets, when the echoes of my feet clacked underneath me, and then I would pull up breathless at the front steps, my throat raw. Mangan's sister there, in the dim light, three years older than I, with her long rich brown hair. I would watch from the shadows. I watched the night come on. I felt its chill; I felt its warmth.

SETTINGS: THE SENSE OF PLACE

Some writers are especially effective at creating a compelling environment —a world that we can imaginatively enter and reenter. In reading the following stories, pay special attention to the role the setting plays in the story as a whole.

EUDORA WELTY   (born 1909)

What alone can instruct the heart is the experience of living, experience which can be vile; but what can never do it any good, what harms it more than vileness, are those tales, those legends . . . , those universal false dreams, the hopes, sentimental and ubiquitous, which are not on any account to be gone by.

EUDORA WELTY

Eudora Welty was born and has spent most of her life in Mississippi. Both as a writer and as a friendly critic of other writers' work, she helped make the modern short story a major contemporary literary form. Critics have identified as major themes in her work her love of the South, the pain of growing up, and the agony of loneliness. Her novels include *The Optimist's Daughter* (1972), for which she received the Pulitzer Prize in 1973.

Welty helped set the tone for much modern fiction by her refusal to indulge in "false dreams" and sentimental hopes. Katherine Anne Porter, another master of the modern short story, said of her that she had "an eye and an ear sharp, shrewd, and true as a tuning fork." Welty prided herself on what Porter called her "blistering humor" and "just cruelty." In the following story, Welty looks at both youth and age without sentimentality—without the rosy glow that comes from making reality more innocent, more heart-warming, or more reassuring than it is.

A Visit of Charity   1941

It was mid-morning—a very cold, bright day. Holding a potted plant before her, a girl of fourteen jumped off the bus in front of the Old Ladies' Home, on the outskirts of town. She wore a red coat, and her straight yellow hair was hanging down loose from the pointed white cap all the little girls were wearing that year. She stopped for a moment beside one of the prickly dark shrubs with which the city had beautified the Home, and then proceeded slowly toward the building, which was of whitewashed brick and reflected the winter sunlight like a block of ice. As she walked vaguely up the steps she shifted the small pot from hand to hand; then she had to set it down and remove her mittens before she could open the heavy door.

"I'm a Campfire girl. . . . I have to pay a visit to some old lady," she told the nurse at the desk. This was a woman in a white uniform who looked as if she were cold; she had close-cut hair which stood up on the very top of her head exactly like a sea wave. Marian, the little girl, did not tell her that this visit would give her a minimum of only three points in her score.

"Acquainted with any of our residents?" asked the nurse. She lifted one eyebrow and spoke like a man.

"With any old ladies? No—but—that is, any of them will do," Marian stammered. With her free hand she pushed her hair behind her ears, as she did when it was time to study Science.

The nurse shrugged and rose. "You have a nice *multiflora cineraria* there," she remarked as she walked ahead down the hall of closed doors to pick out an old lady.

There was loose, bulging linoleum on the floor. Marian felt as if she were walking on the waves, but the nurse paid no attention to it. There was a smell in the hall like the interior of a clock. Everything was silent until, behind one of the doors, an old lady of some kind cleared her throat like a sheep bleating. This decided the nurse. Stopping in her tracks, she first extended her arm, bent her elbow, and leaned forward from the hips—all to examine the watch strapped to her wrist; then she gave a loud double-rap on the door.

"There are two in each room," the nurse remarked over her shoulder.

"Two what?" asked Marian without thinking. The sound like a sheep's bleating almost made her turn around and run back.

One old woman was pulling the door open in short, gradual jerks, and when she saw the nurse a strange smile forced her old face dangerously awry. Marian, suddenly propelled by the strong, impatient arm of the nurse, saw next the side-face of another old woman, even older, who was lying flat in bed with a cap on and a counterpane drawn up to her chin.

"Visitor," said the nurse, and after one more shove she was off up the hall.

Marian stood tongue-tied; both hands held the potted plant. The old woman, still with that terrible, square smile (which was a smile of welcome) stamped on her bony face, was waiting. . . . Perhaps she said something. The old woman in bed said nothing at all, and she did not look around.

Suddenly Marian saw a hand, quick as a bird claw, reach up in the air and pluck the white cap off her head. At the same time, another claw to match drew her all the way into the room, and the next moment the door closed behind her.

"My, my, my," said the old lady at her side.

Marian stood enclosed by a bed, a washstand and a chair; the tiny room had altogether too much furniture. Everything smelled wet—even the bare floor. She held onto the back of the chair, which was wicker and felt soft and damp. Her heart beat more and more slowly, her hands got colder and colder, and she could not hear whether the old women were saying anything or not. She could not see them very clearly. How dark it was! The window shade was down, and the only door was shut. Marian looked at the ceiling. . . . It was like being caught in a robber's cave, just before one was murdered.

"Did you come to be our little girl for awhile?" the first robber asked.

Then something was snatched from Marian's hand—the little potted plant.

5

10

15

"Flowers!" screamed the old woman. She stood holding the pot in an undecided way. "Pretty flowers," she added.

Then the old woman in bed cleared her throat and spoke. "They are not pretty," she said, still without looking around, but very distinctly.

Marian suddenly pitched against the chair and sat down in it.

"Pretty flowers," the first old woman insisted. "Pretty—pretty. . . ." 20

Marian wished she had the little pot back for just a moment—she had forgotten to look at the plant herself before giving it away. What did it look like?

"Stinkweeds," said the other old woman sharply. She had a bunchy white forehead and red eyes like a sheep. Now she turned them toward Marian. The fogginess seemed to rise in her throat again, and she bleated, "Who—are—you?"

To her surprise, Marian could not remember her name. "I'm a Campfire Girl," she said finally.

"Watch out for the germs," said the old woman like a sheep, not addressing anyone.

"One came out last month to see us," said the first old woman. 25

A sheep or a germ? wondered Marian dreamily, holding onto the chair.

"Did not!" cried the other old woman.

"Did so! Read to us out of the Bible, and we enjoyed it!" screamed the first.

"Who enjoyed it!" said the woman in bed. Her mouth was unexpectedly small and sorrowful, like a pet's.

"We enjoyed it," insisted the other. "You enjoyed it—I enjoyed it." 30

"We all enjoyed it," said Marian, without realizing that she had said a word.

The first old woman had just finished putting the potted plant high, high on the top of the wardrobe, where it could hardly be seen from below. Marian wondered how she had ever succeeded in placing it there, how she could ever have reached so high.

"You mustn't pay any attention to old Addie," she now said to the little girl. "She's ailing today."

"Will you shut your mouth?" said the woman in bed. "I am not."

"You're a story." 35

"I can't stay but a minute—really, I can't," said Marian suddenly. She looked down at the wet floor and thought that if she were sick in here they would have to let her go.

With much to-do the first old woman sat down in a rocking chair—still another piece of furniture!—and began to rock. With the fingers on one hand she touched a very dirty cameo pin on her chest. "What do you do at school?" she asked.

"I don't know . . ." said Marian. She tried to think but she could not.

"Oh, but the flowers are beautiful," the old woman whispered. She seemed to rock faster and faster; Marian did not see how anyone could rock so fast.

"Ugly," said the woman in bed. 40

"If we bring flowers—" Marian began, and then fell silent. She had almost said that if Campfire Girls brought flowers to the Old Ladies' Home, the visit would count one extra point, and if they took a Bible with them on the bus and read it to the old ladies, it counted double. But the old woman had not listened, anyway; she was rocking and watching the other one, who watched back from the bed.

"Poor Addie is ailing. She has to take medicine—see?" she said, pointing a horny finger at a row of bottles on the table, and rocking so high that her black comfort shoes lifted off the floor like a little child's.

"I am no more sick than you are," said the woman in bed.

"Oh yes you are!"

"I just got more sense than you have, that's all," said the other old woman, nodding her head.

"That's only the contrary way she talks when *you all* come," said the first old lady
with sudden intimacy. She stopped the rocker with a neat pat of her feet and leaned toward Marian. Her hand reached over—it felt like a petunia leaf, clinging and just a little
sticky.

"Will you hush! Will you hush!" cried the other one.

Marian leaned back rigidly in her chair.

"When I was a little girl like you, I went to school and all," said the old woman in
the same intimate, menacing voice. "Not here—another town. . . . ."

"Hush!" said the sick woman. "You never went to school. You never came and
you never went. You never were anywhere—only here. You never were born! You don't
know anything. Your head is empty, your heart and hands and your old black purse are
all empty, even that little old box that you brought with you you brought empty—you
showed it to me. And yet you talk, talk, talk, talk, talk all the time until I think I'm losing my mind. Who are you? You're a stranger—a perfect stranger! Don't you know
you're a stranger? Is it possible that they have actually done a thing like this to anyone—sent them in a stranger to talk, and rock, and tell away her whole long rigmarole?
Do they seriously suppose that I'll be able to keep it up, day in, day out, night in, night
out, living in the same room with a terrible old woman—forever?"

Marian saw the old woman's eyes grow bright and turn toward her. This old
woman was looking at her with despair and calculation in her face. Her small lips suddenly dropped apart, and exposed a half circle of false teeth with tan gums.

"Come here, I want to tell you something," she whispered. "Come here!"

Marian was trembling, and her heart nearly stopped beating altogether for a moment.

"Now, now, Addie," said the first old woman. "That's not polite. Do you know
what's really the matter with old Addie today?" She, too, looked at Marian; one of her
eyelids drooped low.

"The matter?" the child repeated stupidly. "What's the matter with her?"

"Why, she's mad because it's her birthday!" said the first old woman, beginning to
rock again and giving a little crow as though she had answered her own riddle.

"It is not, it is not!" screamed the old woman in bed. "It is not my birthday, no
one knows when that is but myself, and will you please be quiet and say nothing more,
or I'll go straight out of my mind!" She turned her eyes toward Marian again, and
presently she said in the soft, foggy voice, "When the worst comes to the worst, I ring
this bell, and the nurse comes." One of her hands was drawn out from under the
patched counterpane—a thin little hand with enormous black freckles. With a finger
which would not hold still she pointed to a little bell on the table among the bottles.

"How old are you?" Marian breathed. Now she could see the old woman in bed
very closely and plainly, and very abruptly, from all sides, as in dreams. She wondered
about her—she wondered for a moment as though there was nothing else in the world
to wonder about. It was the first time such a thing had happened to Marian.

"I won't tell!"

The old face on the pillow, where Marian was bending over it, slowly gathered and
collapsed. Soft whimpers came out of the small open mouth. It was a sheep that she
sounded like—a little lamb. Marian's face drew very close, the yellow hair hung forward.

"She's crying!" She turned a bright, burning face up to the first old woman.

"That's Addie for you," the old woman said spitefully.

Marian jumped up and moved toward the door. For the second time, the claw almost touched her hair, but it was not quick enough. The little girl put her cap on.

"Well, it was a real visit," said the old woman, following Marian through the doorway and all the way out into the hall. Then from behind she suddenly clutched the child with her sharp little fingers. In an affected, high-pitched whine she cried, "Oh, little girl, have you a penny to spare for a poor old woman that's not got anything of her own? We don't have a thing in the world—not a penny for candy—not a thing! Little girl, just a nickel—a penny—"

Marian pulled violently against the old hands for a moment before she was free. 65
Then she ran down the hall, without looking behind her and without looking at the nurse, who was reading *Field & Stream* at her desk. The nurse, after another triple motion to consult her wrist watch, asked automatically the question put to visitors in all institutions: "Won't you stay and have dinner with *us?*"

Marian never replied. She pushed the heavy door open into the cold air and ran down the steps.

Under the prickly shrub she stooped and quickly, without being seen, retrieved a red apple she had hidden there.

Her yellow hair under the white cap, her scarlet coat, her bare knees all flashed in the sunlight as she ran to meet the big bus rocketing through the street.

"Wait for me!" she shouted. As though at an imperial command, the bus ground to stop.

She jumped on and took a big bite out of the apple. 70

THE RECEPTIVE READER

1. The *setting* of a story helps create expectations—it can precondition us to expect certain kinds of things (and not others) to happen there. What striking details early in the story help establish the mood? How do they make you feel about the institution? How do they guide your expectations?

2. What telling details shape your reaction to the nurse?

3. How does the author bring the two old women to life? (What are striking images?) How do the two women fit the setting in which they live?

4. What are the motives and feelings of the girl as the *major character*? Why is she there? How does she respond to finding herself transplanted to a strange new setting? How does she react to being "out of her element"?

5. Is the apple at the end of the story a *symbol*? What might it stand for or symbolize?

THE PERSONAL RESPONSE

How do you think the author expects you to feel toward the girl? toward the old women? How do *you* feel toward them? Do you think the girl should have acted more "mature"? Do you think the old women should be shown more compassion?

THE CREATIVE DIMENSION

How much of the way a setting strikes the reader is in the eye of the author? Do you think a more cheerful person (or, for that matter, an angrier person) would have seen the old folks' home and the staff there in a different light? Rewrite the opening paragraphs of the story as they might have been written by someone seeing the place and the personnel through different eyes.

BOBBIE ANN MASON   (born 1940)

Mason was part of a group of writers (informally called the literary "brat pack") who became known in the eighties. Their trademark was studied understatement and a determination to be true to the trivial, undramatic realities of ordinary life. The stories in her collection *Shiloh and Other Stories* (1982) are set in Paducah, in rural Kentucky, where she grew up. She takes her readers to a New South where the struggles with the North are ancient history. Her characters are part of a new working class of truck drivers, retail clerks, and Tupperware sales representatives, who bake zucchini bread and make casseroles from potatoes and mushroom soup, and who pass their free time building model log cabins from Lincoln Logs or making wall hangings of an Arizona sunset. These characters are steeped in American popular culture—talk shows, shopping malls, made-for-TV movies.

Against this setting, Mason plays off plots where, "with no decisive snap of the thread, human relationships become unraveled" (Francis King); where "restless women strain again the confines of marriage" (Robert Towers); and where the men are sometimes "silent and transient" (Anatole Broyard). As David Quammen said in the *New York Times Book Review*, Mason "examines in her various truck drivers and sales clerks the dawning recognition—in some cases only a vague worry—of having missed something, something important, some alternate life more fruitful than the life that's been led." What has struck reviewers of her stories is that she does not treat these "unremarkable" people with condescension but with "complete respect." They are capable of moments of insight or self-understanding; they try "so hard, and with such optimism, to keep up with change" (Anne Tyler).

Shiloh   1982

Leroy Moffitt's wife, Norma Jean, is working on her pectorals. She lifts three-pound dumbbells to warm up, then progresses to a twenty-pound barbell. Standing with her legs apart, she reminds Leroy of Wonder Woman.

"I'd give anything if I could just get these muscles to where they're real hard," says Norma Jean. "Feel this arm. It's not as hard as the other one."

"That's 'cause you're right-handed," says Leroy, dodging as she swings the barbell in an arc.

"Do you think so?"

"Sure."   5

Leroy is a truckdriver. He injured his leg in a highway accident four months ago, and his physical therapy, which involves weights and a pulley, prompted Norma Jean to try building herself up. Now she is attending a body-building class. Leroy has been collecting temporary disability since his tractor-trailer jackknifed in Missouri, badly twisting his left leg in its socket. He has a steel pin in his hip. He will probably not be able to drive his rig again. It sits in the backyard, like a gigantic bird that has flown home to roost. Leroy has been home in Kentucky for three months, and his leg is almost healed, but the accident frightened him and he does not want to drive any more long hauls. He is not sure what to do next. In the meantime, he makes things from craft kits. He started by building a miniature log cabin from notched Popsicle sticks. He varnished it and placed it on the TV set, where it remains. It reminds him of a rustic Nativity scene. Then he tried string art (sailing ships on black velvet), a macramé owl kit, a snap-together B-17 Flying Fortress, and a lamp made out of a model truck, with a light fixture screwed in the top of the cab. At first the kits were diversions, something to kill time, but now he is thinking about building a full-scale log house from a kit. It would be considerably cheaper than building a regular house, and besides, Leroy has grown to appreciate how things are put together. He has begun to realize that in all the years he was on the road he never took time to examine anything. He was always flying past scenery.

"They won't let you build a log cabin in any of the new subdivisions," Norma Jean tells him.

"They will if I tell them it's for you," he says, teasing her. Ever since they were married, he has promised Norma Jean he would build her a new home one day. They have always rented, and the house they live in is small and nondescript. It does not even feel like a home, Leroy realizes now.

Norma Jean works at the Rexall drugstore, and she has acquired an amazing amount of information about cosmetics. When she explains to Leroy the three stages of complexion care, involving creams, toners, and moisturizers, he thinks happily of other petroleum products—axle grease, diesel fuel. This is a connection between him and Norma Jean. Since he has been home, he has felt unusually tender about his wife and guilty over his long absences. But he can't tell what she feels about him. Norma Jean has never complained about his traveling; she has never made hurt remarks, like calling his truck a "widow-maker." He is reasonably certain she has been faithful to him, but he wishes she would celebrate his permanent homecoming more happily. Norma Jean is often startled to find Leroy at home, and he thinks she seems a little disappointed about it. Perhaps he reminds her too much of the early days of their marriage, before he went on the road. They had a child who died as an infant, years ago. They never speak about their memories of Randy, which have almost faded, but now that Leroy is home all the time, they sometimes feel awkward around each other, and Leroy wonders if one of them should mention the child. He has the feeling that they are waking up out of a dream together—that they must create a new marriage, start afresh. They are lucky they are still married. Leroy has read that for most people losing a child destroys the marriage—or else he heard this on *Donahue*. He can't always remember where he learns things anymore.

At Christmas, Leroy bought an electric organ for Norma Jean. She used to play   10
the piano when she was in high school. "It don't leave you," she told him once. "It's like riding a bicycle."

The new instrument had so many keys and buttons that she was bewildered by it at first. She touched the keys tentatively, pushed some buttons, then pecked out "Chopsticks." It came out in an amplified fox-trot rhythm, with marimba sounds.

"It's an orchestra!" she cried.

The organ had a pecan-look finish and eighteen preset chords, with optional flute, violin, trumpet, clarinet, and banjo accompaniments. Norma Jean mastered the organ almost immediately. At first she played Christmas songs. Then she bought *The Sixties Songbook* and learned every tune in it, adding variations to each with the rows of brightly colored buttons.

"I didn't like these old songs back then," she said. "But I have this crazy feeling I missed something."

"You didn't miss a thing," said Leroy.   15

Leroy likes to lie on the couch and smoke a joint and listen to Norma Jean play "Can't Take My Eyes Off You" and "I'll Be Back." He is back again. After fifteen years on the road, he is finally settling down with the woman he loves. She is still pretty. Her skin is flawless. Her frosted curls resemble pencil trimmings.

Now that Leroy has come home to stay, he notices how much the town has changed. Subdivisions are spreading across western Kentucky like an oil slick. The sign at the edge of town says "Pop: 11,500"—only seven hundred more than it said twenty years before. Leroy can't figure out who is living in all the new houses. The farmers who used to gather around the courthouse square on Saturday afternoons to play checkers and spit tobacco juice have gone. It has been years since Leroy has thought about the farmers, and they have disappeared without his noticing.

Leroy meets a kid named Stevie Hamilton in the parking lot at the new shopping center. While they pretend to be strangers meeting over a stalled car, Stevie tosses an ounce of marijuana under the front seat of Leroy's car. Stevie is wearing orange jogging shoes and a T-shirt that says CHATTAHOOCHEE SUPER-RAT. His father is a prominent doctor who lives in one of the expensive subdivisions in a new white-columned brick house that looks like a funeral parlor. In the phone book under his name there is a separate number, with the listing "Teenagers."

"Where do you get this stuff?" asks Leroy. "From your pappy?"

"That's for me to know and you to find out," Stevie says. He is slit-eyed and   20
skinny.

"What else you got?"

"What you interested in?"

"Nothing special. Just wondered."

Leroy used to take speed on the road. Now he has to go slowly. He needs to be mellow. He leans back against the car and says, "I'm aiming to build me a log house, soon as I get time. My wife, though, I don't think she likes the idea."

"Well, let me know when you want me again," Stevie says. He has a cigarette in   25
his cupped palm, as though sheltering it from the wind. He takes a long drag, then stomps it on the asphalt and slouches away.

Stevie's father was two years ahead of Leroy in high school. Leroy is thirty-four. He married Norma Jean when they were both eighteen, and their child Randy was born a few months later, but he died at the age of four months and three days. He would be about Stevie's age now. Norma Jean and Leroy were at the drive-in, watching a double feature (*Dr. Strangelove* and *Lover Come Back*), and the baby was sleeping in the back seat. When the first movie ended, the baby was dead. It was the sudden infant death syndrome. Leroy remembers handing Randy to a nurse at the emergency room, as though he were offering her a large doll as a present. A dead baby feels like a sack of flour. "It just happens sometimes," said the doctor, in what Leroy always recalls as a nonchalant tone. Leroy can hardly remember the child anymore, but he still sees vividly a scene from *Dr. Strangelove* in which the President of the United States was talking in a folksy voice on the hot line to the Soviet premier about the bomber accidentally headed toward Russia. He was in the War Room, and the world map was lit up. Leroy remembers Norma Jean standing catatonically beside him in the hospital and himself thinking: Who is this strange girl? He had forgotten who she was. Now scientists are saying that crib death is caused by a virus. Nobody knows anything, Leroy thinks. The answers are always changing.

When Leroy gets home from the shopping center, Norma Jean's mother, Mabel Beasley, is there. Until this year, Leroy has not realized how much time she spends with

Norma Jean. When she visits, she inspects the closets and then the plants, informing Norma Jean when a plant is droopy or yellow. Mabel calls the plants "flowers," although there are never any blooms. She always notices if Norma Jean's laundry is piling up. Mabel is a short, overweight woman whose tight, brown-dyed curls look more like a wig than the actual wig she sometimes wears. Today she has brought Norma Jean an off-white dust ruffle she made for the bed; Mabel works in a custom-upholstery shop.

"This is the tenth one I made this year," Mabel says. "I got started and couldn't stop."

"It's real pretty," says Norma Jean.

"Now we can hide things under the bed," says Leroy, who gets along with his   30
mother-in-law primarily by joking with her. Mabel has never really forgiven him for disgracing her by getting Norma Jean pregnant. When the baby died, she said that fate was mocking her.

"What's that thing?" Mabel says to Leroy in a loud voice, pointing to a tangle of yarn on a piece of canvas.

Leroy holds it up for Mabel to see. "It's my needlepoint," he explains. "This is a *Star Trek* pillow cover."

"That's what a woman would do," says Mabel. "Great day in the morning!"

"All the big football players on TV do it," he says.

"Why, Leroy, you're always trying to fool me. I don't believe you for one minute.   35
You don't know what to do with yourself—that's the whole trouble. Sewing!"

"I'm aiming to build a log house," says Leroy. "Soon as my plans come."

"Like *heck* you are," says Norma Jean. She takes Leroy's needlepoint and shoves it into a drawer. "You have to find a job first. Nobody can afford to build now anyway."

Mabel straightens her girdle and says, "I still think before you get tied down y'all ought to take a little run to Shiloh."

"One of these days, Mama," Norma Jean says impatiently.

Mabel is talking about Shiloh, Tennessee. For the past few years, she has been urg-   40
ing Leroy and Norma Jean to visit the Civil War battleground there. Mabel went there on her honeymoon—the only real trip she ever took. Her husband died of a perforated ulcer when Norma Jean was ten, but Mabel, who was accepted into the United Daughters of the Confederacy in 1975, is still preoccupied with going back to Shiloh.

"I've been to kingdom come and back in that truck out yonder," Leroy says to Mabel, "but we never yet set foot in that battleground. Ain't that something? How did I miss it?"

"It's not even that far," Mabel says.

After Mabel leaves, Norma Jean reads to Leroy from a list she has made. "Things you could do," she announces. "You could get a job as a guard at Union Carbide, where they'd let you set on a stool. You could get on at the lumberyard. You could do a little carpenter work, if you want to build so bad. You could—"

"I can't do something where I'd have to stand up all day."

"You ought to try standing up all day behind a cosmetics counter. It's amazing   45
that I have strong feet, coming from two parents that never had strong feet at all." At the moment Norma Jean is holding on to the kitchen counter, raising her knees one at a time as she talks. She is wearing two-pound ankle weights.

"Don't worry," says Leroy. "I'll do something."

"You could truck calves to slaughter for somebody. You wouldn't have to drive any big old truck for that."

"I'm going to build you this house," says Leroy. "I want to make you a real home."

"I don't want to live in any log cabin."

"It's not a cabin. It's a house."

"I don't care. It looks like a cabin."

"You and me together could lift those logs. It's just like lifting weights."

Norma Jean doesn't answer. Under her breath, she is counting. Now she is marching through the kitchen. She is doing goose steps.

Before his accident, when Leroy came home he used to stay in the house with Norma Jean, watching TV in bed and playing cards. She would cook fried chicken, picnic ham, chocolate pie—all his favorites. Now he is home alone much of the time. In the mornings, Norma Jean disappears, leaving a cooling place in the bed. She eats a cereal called Body Buddies, and she leaves the bowl on the table, with the soggy tan balls floating in a milk puddle. He sees things about Norma Jean that he never realized before. When she chops onions, she stares off into a corner, as if she can't bear to look. She puts on her house slippers almost precisely at nine o'clock every evening and nudges her jogging shoes under the couch. She saves bread heels for the birds. Leroy watches the birds at the feeder. He notices the peculiar way goldfinches fly past the window. They close their wings, then fall, then spread their wings to catch and lift themselves. He wonders if they close their eyes when they fall. Norma Jean closes her eyes when they are in bed. She wants the lights turned out. Even then, he is sure she closes her eyes.

He goes for long drives around town. He tends to drive a car rather carelessly.   55 Power steering and an automatic shift make a car feel so small and inconsequential that his body is hardly involved in the driving process. His injured leg stretches out comfortably. Once or twice he has almost hit something, but even the prospect of an accident seems minor in a car. He cruises the new subdivisions, feeling like a criminal rehearsing for a robbery. Norma Jean is probably right about a log house being inappropriate here in the new subdivisions. All the houses look grand and complicated. They depress him.

One day when Leroy comes home from a drive he finds Norma Jean in tears. She is in the kitchen making a potato and mushroom-soup casserole, with grated-cheese topping. She is crying because her mother caught her smoking.

"I didn't hear her coming. I was standing here puffing away pretty as you please," Norma Jean says, wiping her eyes.

"I knew it would happen sooner or later," says Leroy, putting his arm around her.

"She don't know the meaning of the word 'knock,'" says Norma Jean. "It's a wonder she hadn't caught me years ago."

"Think of it this way," Leroy says. "What if she caught me with a joint?"   60

"You better not let her!" Norma Jean shrieks. "I'm warning you, Leroy Moffitt!"

"I'm just kidding. Here, play me a tune. That'll help you relax."

Norma Jean puts the casserole in the oven and sets the timer. Then she plays a ragtime tune, with horns and banjo, as Leroy lights up a joint and lies on the couch, laughing to himself about Mabel's catching him at it. He thinks of Stevie Hamilton—a doctor's son pushing grass. Everything is funny. The whole town seems crazy and small. He is reminded of Virgil Mathis, a boastful policeman Leroy used to shoot pool with. Virgil recently led a drug bust in a back room at a bowling alley, where he seized ten thousand dollars' worth of marijuana. The newspaper had a picture of him holding up the bags of grass and grinning widely. Right now, Leroy can imagine Virgil breaking down the door and arresting him with a lungful of smoke. Virgil would probably have been alerted to the scene because of all the racket Norma Jean is making. Now she sounds like a hard-rock band. Norma Jean is terrific. When she switches to a Latin-rhythm version of "Sunshine Superman," Leroy hums along. Norma Jean's foot goes up and down, up and down.

"Well, what do you think?" Leroy says, when Norma Jean pauses to search through her music.

"What do I think about what?"

His mind has gone blank. Then he says, "I'll sell my rig and build a house." That wasn't what he wanted to say. He wanted to know what she thought—what she *really* thought—about them.

"Don't start in on that again," says Norma Jean. She begins playing "Who'll Be the Next in Line?"

Leroy used to tell hitchhikers his whole life story—about his travels, his hometown, the baby. He would end with a question: "Well, what do you think?" It was just a rhetorical question. In time, he had the feeling that he'd been telling the same story over and over to the same hitchhikers. He quit talking to hitchhikers when he realized how his voice sounded—whining and self-pitying, like some teenage-tragedy song. Now Leroy has the sudden impulse to tell Norma Jean about himself, as if he had just met her. They have known each other so long they have forgotten a lot about each other. They could become reacquainted. But when the oven timer goes off and she runs to the kitchen, he forgets why he wants to do this.

The next day, Mabel drops by. It is Saturday and Norma Jean is cleaning. Leroy is studying the plans of his log house, which have finally come in the mail. He has them spread out on the table—big sheets of stiff blue paper, with diagrams and numbers printed in white. While Norma Jean runs the vacuum, Mabel drinks coffee. She sets her coffee cup on a blueprint.

"I'm just waiting for time to pass," she says to Leroy, drumming her fingers on the table.

As soon as Norma Jean switches off the vacuum, Mabel says in a loud voice, "Did you hear about the datsun dog that killed the baby?"

Norma Jean says, "The word is 'dachshund.'"

"They put the dog on trial. It chewed the baby's legs off. The mother was in the next room all the time." She raises her voice. "They thought it was neglect."

Norma Jean is holding her ears. Leroy manages to open the refrigerator and get some Diet Pepsi to offer Mabel. Mabel still has some coffee and she waves away the Pepsi.

"Datsuns are like that," Mabel says. "They're jealous dogs. They'll tear a place to pieces if you don't keep an eye on them."

"You better watch out what you're saying, Mabel," says Leroy.

"Well, facts is facts."

Leroy looks out the window at his rig. It is like a huge piece of furniture gathering dust in the backyard. Pretty soon it will be an antique. He hears the vacuum cleaner. Norma Jean seems to be cleaning the living room rug again.

Later, she says to Leroy, "She just said that about the baby because she caught me smoking. She's trying to pay me back."

"What are you talking about?" Leroy says, nervously shuffling blueprints.

"You know good and well," Norma Jean says. She is sitting in a kitchen chair with her feet up and her arms wrapped around her knees. She looks small and helpless. She says, "The very idea, her bringing up a subject like that! Saying it was neglect."

"She didn't mean that," Leroy says.

"She might not have *thought* she meant it. She always says things like that. You don't know how she goes on."

"But she didn't really mean it. She was just talking."

Leroy opens a king-sized bottle of beer and pours it into two glasses, dividing it carefully. He hands a glass to Norma Jean and she takes it from him mechanically. For a long time, they sit by the kitchen window watching the birds at the feeder. 85

Something is happening. Norma Jean is going to night school. She has graduated from her six-week body-building course and now she is taking an adult-education course in composition at Paducah Community College. She spends her evenings outlining paragraphs.

"First you have a topic sentence," she explains to Leroy. "Then you divide it up. Your secondary topic has to be connected to your primary topic."

To Leroy, this sounds intimidating. "I never was any good in English," he says.

"It makes a lot of sense."

"What are you doing this for, anyhow?" 90

She shrugs. "It's something to do." She stands up and lifts her dumbbells a few times.

"Driving a rig, nobody cared about my English."

"I'm not criticizing your English."

Norma Jean used to say, "If I lose ten minutes' sleep, I just drag all day." Now she stays up late, writing compositions. She got a B on her first paper—a how-to theme on soup-based casseroles. Recently Norma Jean has been cooking unusual foods—tacos, lasagna, Bombay chicken. She doesn't play the organ anymore, though her second paper was called "Why Music Is Important to Me." She sits at the kitchen table, concentrating on her outlines, while Leroy plays with his log house plans, practicing with a set of Lincoln Logs. The thought of getting a truckload of notched, numbered logs scares him, and he wants to be prepared. As he and Norma Jean work together at the kitchen table, Leroy has the hopeful thought that they are sharing something, but he knows he is a fool to think this. Norma Jean is miles away. He knows he is going to lose her. Like Mabel, he is just waiting for time to pass.

One day, Mabel is there before Norma Jean gets home from work, and Leroy finds himself confiding in her. Mabel, he realizes, must know Norma Jean better than he does. 95

"I don't know what's got into that girl," Mabel says. "She used to go to bed with the chickens. Now you say she's up all hours. Plus her a-smoking. I like to died."

"I want to make her this beautiful home," Leroy says, indicating the Lincoln Logs. "I don't thinks she even wants it. Maybe she was happier with me gone."

"She don't know what to make of you, coming home like this."

"Is that it?"

Mabel takes the roof off his Lincoln Log cabin. "You couldn't get *me* in a log cabin," she says. "I was raised in one. It's no picnic, let me tell you." 100

"They're different now," says Leroy.

"I tell you what," Mabel says, smiling oddly at Leroy.

"What?"

"Take her on down to Shiloh. Y'all need to get out together, stir a little. Her brain's all balled up over them books."

Leroy can see traces of Norma Jean's features in her mother's face. Mabel's worn face has the texture of crinkled cotton, but suddenly she looks pretty. It occurs to Leroy that Mabel has been hinting all along that she wants them to take her with them to Shiloh. 105

"Let's all go to Shiloh," he says. "You and me and her. Some Sunday."

Mabel throws up her hands in protest. "Oh, no, not me. Young folks want to be by theirselves."

When Norma Jean comes in with groceries, Leroy says excitedly, "Your mama here's been dying to go to Shiloh for forty-five years. It's about time we went, don't you think?"

"I'm not going to butt in on anybody's second honeymoon," Mabel says.

"Who's going on a honeymoon, for Christ's sake?" Norma Jean says loudly. 110

"I never raised no daughter of mine to talk that-a-way," Mabel says.

"You ain't seen nothing yet," says Norma Jean. She starts putting away boxes and cans, slamming cabinet doors.

"There's a log cabin at Shiloh," Mabel says. "It was there during the battle. There's bullet holes in it."

"When are you going to *shut up* about Shiloh, Mama?" asks Norma Jean.

"I always thought Shiloh was the prettiest place, so full of history," Mabel goes on. 115 "I just hoped y'all could see it once before I die, so you could tell me about it." Later, she whispers to Leroy, "You do what I said. A little change is what she needs."

"Your name means 'the king,'" Norma Jean says to Leroy that evening. He is trying to get her to go to Shiloh, and she is reading a book about another century.

"Well, I reckon I ought to be right proud."

"I guess so."

"Am I still king around here?"

Norma Jean flexes her biceps and feels them for hardness. "I'm not fooling around 120 with anybody, if that's what you mean," she says.

"Would you tell me if you were?"

"I don't know."

"What does *your* name mean?"

"It was Marilyn Monroe's real name."

"No kidding!" 125

"Norma comes from the Normans. They were invaders," she says. She closes her book and looks hard at Leroy. "I'll go to Shiloh with you if you'll stop staring at me."

On Sunday, Norma Jean packs a picnic and they go to Shiloh. To Leroy's relief, Mabel says she does not want to come with them. Norma Jean drives, and Leroy, sitting beside her, feels like some boring hitchhiker she has picked up. He tries some conversation, but she answers him in monosyllables. At Shiloh, she drives aimlessly through the park, past bluffs and trails and steep ravines. Shiloh is an immense place, and Leroy cannot see it as a battleground. It is not what he expected. He thought it would look like a golf course. Monuments are everywhere, showing through the thick clusters of trees. Norma Jean passes the log cabin Mabel mentioned. It is surrounded by tourists looking for bullet holes.

"That's not the kind of log house I've got in mind," says Leroy apologetically.

"I know *that*."

"This is a pretty place. Your mama was right." 130

"It's O.K.," says Norma Jean. "Well, we've seen it. I hope she's satisfied."

They burst out laughing together.

At the park museum, a movie on Shiloh is shown every half hour, but they decide that they don't want to see it. They buy a souvenir Confederate flag for Mabel, and then they find a picnic spot near the cemetery. Norma Jean has brought a picnic cooler, with pimiento sandwiches, soft drinks, and Yodels. Leroy eats a sandwich and then smokes a joint, hiding it behind the picnic cooler. Norma Jean has quit smoking altogether. She is picking cake crumbs from the cellophane wrapper, like a fussy bird.

Leroy says, "So the boys in gray ended up in Corinth. The Union soldiers zapped 'em finally, April 7, 1862."

They both know that he doesn't know any history. He is just talking about some   135
of the historical plaques they have read. He feels awkward, like a boy on a date with an older girl. They are still just making conversation.

"Corinth is where Mama eloped to," says Norma Jean.

They sit in silence and stare at the cemetery for the Union dead and, beyond, at a tall cluster of trees. Campers are parked nearby, bumper to bumper, and small children in bright clothing are cavorting and squealing. Norma Jean wads up the cake wrapper and squeezes it tightly in her hand. Without looking at Leroy, she says, "I want to leave you."

Leroy takes a bottle of Coke out of the cooler and flips off the cap. He holds the bottle poised near his mouth but cannot remember to take a drink. Finally he says, "No, you don't."

"Yes, I do."

"I won't let you."   140

"You can't stop me."

"Don't do me that way."

Leroy knows Norma Jean will have her own way. "Didn't I promise to be home from now on?" he says.

"In some ways, a woman prefers a man who wanders," says Norma Jean. "That sounds crazy, I know."

"You're not crazy."   145

Leroy remembers to drink from his Coke. Then he says, "Yes, you *are* crazy. You and me could start all over again. Right back at the beginning."

"We *have* started all over again," says Norma Jean. "And this is how it turned out."

"What did I do wrong?"

"Nothing."

"Is this one of those women's lib things?" Leroy asks.   150

"Don't be funny."

The cemetery, a green slope dotted with white markers, looks like a subdivision site. Leroy is trying to comprehend that his marriage is breaking up, but for some reason he is wondering about white slabs in a graveyard.

"Everything was fine till Mama caught me smoking," says Norma Jean, standing up. "That set something off."

"What are you talking about?"

"She won't leave me alone—*you* won't leave me alone." Norma Jean seems to be   155
crying, but she is looking away from him. "I feel eighteen again. I can't face that all over again." She starts walking away. "No, it *wasn't* fine. I don't know what I'm saying. Forget it."

Leroy takes a lungful of smoke and closes his eyes as Norma Jean's words sink in. He tries to focus on the fact that thirty-five hundred soldiers died on the grounds around him. He can only think of that war as a board game with plastic soldiers. Leroy almost smiles, as he compares the Confederates' daring attack on the Union camps and Virgil Mathis's raid on the bowling alley. General Grant, drunk and furious, shoved the Southerners back to Corinth, where Mabel and Jet Beasley were married years later, when Mabel was still thin and good-looking. The next day, Mabel and Jet visited the battleground, and then Norma Jean was born, and then she married Leroy and they had a baby, which they lost, and now Leroy and Norma Jean are here at the same battleground. Leroy knows he is leaving out a lot. He is leaving out the insides of history.

History was always just names and dates to him. It occurs to him that building a house out of logs is similarly empty—too simple. And the real inner workings of a marriage, like most of history, have escaped him. Now he sees that building a log house is the dumbest idea he could have had. It was clumsy of him to think Norma Jean would want a log house. It was a crazy idea. He'll have to think of something else, quickly. He will wad the blueprints into tight balls and fling them into the lake. Then he'll get moving again. He opens his eyes. Norma Jean has moved away and is walking through the cemetery, following a serpentine brick path.

Leroy gets up to follow his wife, but his good leg is asleep and his bad leg still hurts him. Norma Jean is far away, walking rapidly toward the bluff by the river, and he tries to hobble toward her. Some children run past him, screaming noisily. Norma Jean has reached the bluff, and she is looking out over the Tennessee River. Now she turns toward Leroy and waves her arms. Is she beckoning to him? She seems to be doing an exercise for her chest muscles. The sky is unusually pale—the color of the dust ruffle Mabel made for their bed.

THE RECEPTIVE READER

1. This story takes us to a working-class *setting,* with such class markers as the characters' working-class language. Where does their language become most noticeable, or where does it become an issue, in the story? ◆ Attitudes toward the working class have traditionally ranged from snobbish contempt to solidarity for the aspirations of common people. What is the attitude of the author?

2. Some Southern readers feel particularly at home in this story. To you, what if anything is Southern about the setting and about this story as a whole?

3. Mason is a fanatic for apparently trivial *realistic detail*—about Leroy's job, his accident, his therapy; about Norma Jean's job at the drugstore, her body-building exercises, her classes at the college; about their trip to Shilo, and so forth. What to you are striking examples of these apparent trivia? What do they do for the story as a whole?

4. Mason makes the setting real with striking uses of *figurative language*—language using imaginative comparisons. What images and feelings does she bring into play when she says that Leroy's rig parked in the back was like a big bird come home to roost? What are other striking examples of imaginative comparisons?

5. How ordinary are the lives of these people? What are some of the ordinary everyday things that make their lives average? Do extraordinary things happen to them?

6. The *dialogue* in this story is very sparse. What are occasions in the story where you expect them to say more about their lives or their feelings than they do? Are their feelings "frozen," as one student reader said?

7. What role does Mabel, Leroy's mother-in-law, play as a *minor character* in the story? What is her relationship with Leroy? with her daughter? How does the author use her to develop or round out the setting of the story?

8. Readers are likely to detect *symbolic* meanings or overtones in details and incidents in this story. What are the possible symbolic meanings of the parked rig, the "nondescript" rented home, the electronic organ, the change in the cooking, Mabel's hair, the log cabin Leroy wants to build, the trip to the battlefield?

9. When did you first decide that the marriage was going to break up? For you, was the breakup a foregone conclusion? Who or what is to blame?

10. Both *major characters,* Leroy and Norma Jean, change or develop in the course of this story. How do they change or grow? Do they develop in the same direction or along parallel lines? Do they understand what is happening to them? (How much self-realization is there in this story?)

THE PERSONAL RESPONSE

Anne Tyler, a fellow writer reviewing Mason's stories for the *New Republic,* said that it was "heartening to find male characters portrayed sympathetically, with an appreciation for the fact that they can feel as confused and hurt and lonely as the female characters." What are your personal feelings toward the two major characters in "Shiloh?" Do you feel closer to Leroy or to Norma Jean? Why?

YUKIO MISHIMA   (1925–1970)

Yukio Mishima (pen name of Kimitake Hiraoka) was a prolific writer of novels, plays, and stories. He was a flamboyant media personality who became a cult figure in Japan and a legend in the West. Alienated from Westernized, materialistic modern Japan, he became obsessed with Japanese history and traditional Japanese values. He set out to revive and reenact the code and ritual of the Samurai warriors of Japan's feudal, aristocratic past, with traditions akin to the code of chivalry of the European Middle Ages. He studied the martial arts—boxing, karate, and sword fighting; he created the Shield Society, a private army of a hundred dedicated followers. In a final spectacular rejection of the decadent present, he committed *seppuku,* or public ritual suicide, in 1970.

Translations of Mishima's best-known works include *Confessions of a Mask* (1958), *The Sailor Who Fell from Grace with the Sea* (1965), and *Sun and Steel* (1970). In *The Sailor Who Fell from Grace,* a boy who disapproves of the lover of his widowed mother joins with a band of his fellows in an effort to terminate the love affair and the lover. Mishima's short stories were collected in *Death and Midsummer and Other Stories* (1966). Some of his best-known stories celebrate the ecstasy of married love, loyalty to the empire, and ceremonial suicide. He once spoke of "my heart's leaning toward Death, Night, and Blood." The following story will take you to a different world—not merely a different geographical setting but a different world of thought and feeling.

Swaddling Clothes   1966

TRANSLATED BY IVAN MORRIS

He was always busy, Toshiko's husband. Even tonight he had to dash off to an appointment, leaving her to go home alone by taxi. But what else could a woman expect when she married an actor—an attractive one? No doubt she had been foolish to hope that he would spend the evening with her. And yet he must have known how she dreaded going back to their house, unhomely with its Western-style furniture and with the bloodstains still showing on the floor.

Toshiko had been oversensitive since girlhood: that was her nature. As the result of constant worrying she never put on weight, and now, an adult woman, she looked more like a transparent picture than a creature of flesh and blood. Her delicacy of spirit was evident to her most casual acquaintance.

Earlier that evening, when she had joined her husband at a night club, she had been shocked to find him entertaining friends with an account of "the incident." Sitting there in his American-style suit, puffing at a cigarette, he had seemed to her almost a stranger.

"It's a fantastic story," he was saying, gesturing flamboyantly as if in an attempt to outweigh the attractions of the dance band. "Here this new nurse for our baby arrives from the employment agency, and the very first thing I notice about her is her stomach. It's enormous—as if she had a pillow stuck under her kimono! No wonder, I thought, for I soon saw that she could eat more than the rest of us put together. She polished off the contents of our rice bin like that. . . ." He snapped his fingers. "'Gastric dilation'—that's how she explained her girth and her appetite. Well, the day before yesterday we heard groans and moans coming from the nursery. We rushed in and found her squatting on the floor, holding her stomach in her two hands, and moaning like a cow. Next to her our baby lay in his cot, scared out of his wits and crying at the top of his lungs. A pretty scene, I can tell you!"

"So the cat was out of the bag?" suggested one of their friends, a film actor like   5
Toshiko's husband.

"Indeed it was! And it gave me the shock of my life. You see, I'd completely swallowed that story about 'gastric dilation.' Well, I didn't waste any time. I rescued our good rug from the floor and spread a blanket for her to lie on. The whole time the girl was yelling like a stuck pig. By the time the doctor from the maternity clinic arrived, the baby had already been born. But our sitting room was a pretty shambles!"

"Oh, that I'm sure of!" said another of their friends, and the whole company burst into laughter.

Toshiko was dumbfounded to hear her husband discussing the horrifying happening as though it were no more than an amusing incident which they chanced to have witnessed. She shut her eyes for a moment and all at once she saw the newborn baby lying before her: on the parquet floor the infant lay, and his frail body was wrapped in bloodstained newspapers.

Toshiko was sure that the doctor had done the whole thing out of spite. As if to emphasize his scorn for this mother who had given birth to a bastard under such sordid conditions, he had told his assistant to wrap the baby in some loose newspapers, rather than proper swaddling. This callous treatment of the newborn child had offended Toshiko. Overcoming her disgust at the entire scene, she had fetched a brand-new piece of flannel from her cupboard and, having swaddled the baby in it, had lain him carefully in an armchair.

This all had taken place in the evening after her husband had left the house.   10
Toshiko had told him nothing of it, fearing that he would think her oversoft, oversentimental; yet the scene had engraved itself deeply in her mind. Tonight she sat silently thinking back on it, while the jazz orchestra brayed and her husband chatted cheerfully with his friends. She knew that she would never forget the sight of the baby, wrapped in stained newspapers and lying on the floor—it was a scene fit for a butchershop. Toshiko, whose own life had been spent in solid comfort, poignantly felt the wretchedness of the illegitimate baby.

I am the only person to have witnessed its shame, the thought occurred to her. The mother never saw her child lying there in its newspaper wrappings, and the baby itself of course didn't know. I alone shall have to preserve that terrible scene in my memory. When the baby grows up and wants to find out about his birth, there will be no one to tell him, so long as I preserve silence. How strange that I should have this feeling of guilt! After all, it was I who took him up from the floor, swathed him properly in flannel, and laid him down to sleep in the armchair.

They left the night club and Toshiko stepped into the taxi that her husband had called for her. "Take this lady to Ushigomé," he told the driver and shut the door from the outside. Toshiko gazed through the window at her husband's smiling face and noticed his strong, white teeth. Then she leaned back in the seat, oppressed by the knowledge that their life together was in some way too easy, too painless. It would have been difficult for her to put her thoughts into words. Through the rear window of the taxi she took a last look at her husband. He was striding along the street toward his Nash car, and soon the back of his rather garish tweed coat had blended with the figures of the passers-by.

The taxi drove off, passed down a street dotted with bars and then by a theater, in front of which the throngs of people jostled each other on the pavement. Although the performance had only just ended, the lights had already been turned out and in the half dark outside it was depressingly obvious that the cherry blossoms decorating the front of the theater were merely scraps of white paper.

Even if that baby should grow up in ignorance of the secret of his birth, he can never become a respectable citizen, reflected Toshiko, pursuing the same train of thoughts. Those soiled newspaper swaddling clothes will be the symbol of his entire life. But why should I keep worrying about him so much? Is it because I feel uneasy about the future of my own child? Say twenty years from now, when our boy will have grown up into a fine, carefully educated young man, one day by a quirk of fate he meets the other boy, who then will also have turned twenty. And say that the other boy, who has been sinned against, savagely stabs him with a knife. . . .

It was a warm, overcast April night, but thoughts of the future made Toshiko feel   15
cold and miserable. She shivered on the back seat of the car.

No, when the time comes I shall take my son's place, she told herself suddenly. Twenty years from now I shall be forty-three. I shall go to that young man and tell him straight out about everything—about his newspaper swaddling clothes, and about how I went and wrapped him in flannel.

The taxi ran along the dark wide road that was bordered by the park and by the Imperial Palace moat. In the distance Toshiko noticed the pinpricks of light which came from the blocks of tall office buildings.

Twenty years from now that wretched child will be in utter misery. He will be living a desolate, hopeless, poverty-stricken existence—a lonely rat. What else could happen to a baby who has had such a birth? He'll be wandering through the streets by himself, cursing his father, loathing his mother.

No doubt Toshiko derived a certain satisfaction from her somber thoughts: she tortured herself with them without cease. The taxi approached Hanzomon and drove past the compound of the British Embassy. At that point the famous rows of cherry trees were spread out before Toshiko in all their purity. On the spur of the moment she decided to go and view the blossoms by herself in the dark night. It was a strange decision for a timid and unadventurous young woman, but then she was in a strange state of mind and she dreaded the return home. That evening all sorts of unsettling fancies had burst open in her mind.

She crossed the wide street—a slim, solitary figure in the darkness. As a rule when   20
she walked in the traffic Toshiko used to cling fearfully to her companion, but tonight she darted alone between the cars and a moment later had reached the long narrow park that borders the Palace moat. Chidorigafuchi, it is called—the Abyss of the Thousand Birds.

Tonight the whole park had become a grove of blossoming cherry trees. Under the calm cloudy sky the blossoms formed a mass of solid whiteness. The paper lanterns that hung from wires between the trees had been put out; in their place electric light bulbs, red, yellow, and green, shone dully beneath the blossoms. It was well past ten o'clock and most of the flower-viewers had gone home. As the occasional passers-by strolled through the park, they would automatically kick aside the empty bottles or crush the waste paper beneath their feet.

Newspapers, thought Toshiko, her mind going back once again to those happenings. Bloodstained newspapers. If a man were ever to hear of that piteous birth and know that it was he who had lain there, it would ruin his entire life. To think that I, a perfect stranger, should from now on have to keep such a secret—the secret of a man's whole existence. . . .

Lost in these thoughts, Toshiko walked on through the park. Most of the people still remaining there were quiet couples; no one paid her any attention. She noticed two people sitting on a stone bench beside the moat, not looking at the blossoms, but gazing silently at the water. Pitch black it was, and swathed in heavy shadows. Beyond the moat the somber forest of the Imperial Palace blocked her view. The trees reached up, to form a solid dark mass against the night sky. Toshiko walked slowly along the path beneath the blossoms hanging heavily overhead.

On a stone bench, slightly apart from the others, she noticed a pale object—not, as she had at first imagined, a pile of cherry blossoms, nor a garment forgotten by one of the visitors to the park. Only when she came closer did she see that it was a human form lying on the bench. Was it, she wondered, one of those miserable drunks often to be seen sleeping in public places? Obviously not, for the body had been systematically covered with newspapers, and it was the whiteness of those papers that had attracted Toshiko's attention. Standing by the bench, she gazed down at the sleeping figure.

It was a man in a brown jersey who lay there, curled up on layers of newspapers, other newspapers covering him. No doubt this had become his normal night residence now that spring had arrived. Toshiko gazed down at the man's dirty, unkempt hair, which in places had become hopelessly matted. As she observed the sleeping figure wrapped in its newspapers, she was inevitably reminded of the baby who had lain on the floor in its wretched swaddling clothes. The shoulder of the man's jersey rose and fell in the darkness in time with his heavy breathing.

It seemed to Toshiko that all her fears and premonitions had suddenly taken concrete form. In the darkness the man's pale forehead stood out, and it was a young forehead, though carved with the wrinkles of long poverty and hardship. His khaki trousers had been slightly pulled up; on his sockless feet he wore a pair of battered gym shoes. She could not see his face and suddenly had an overmastering desire to get one glimpse of it.

She walked to the head of the bench and looked down. The man's head was half buried in his arms, but Toshiko could see that he was surprisingly young. She noticed the thick eyebrows and the fine bridge of his nose. His slightly open mouth was alive with youth.

But Toshiko had approached too close. In the silent night the newspaper bedding rustled, and abruptly the man opened his eyes. Seeing the young woman standing directly beside him, he raised himself with a jerk, and his eyes lit up. A second later a powerful hand reached out and seized Toshiko by her slender wrist.

She did not feel in the least afraid and made no effort to free herself. In a flash the thought had struck her. Ah, so the twenty years have already gone by! The forest of the Imperial Palace was pitch dark and utterly silent.

THE RECEPTIVE READER

1. What is strange and what is familiar about the *setting*? What expectations (or what stereotypes) do you bring to the Japanese setting of the story? How much of an effort of the imagination is necessary for you to get into the spirit of this story?

2. The author makes a point of the Westernized or Americanized ways of Toshiko's husband. What are revealing details? What contrast is Mishima setting up between the husband and the wife as *key characters?* What role does that contrast play in the story as a whole? ✧ What is the author's attitude toward the husband?

3. What are Toshiko's feelings about the illegitimate child? Does she reflect the expected attitudes of her culture? Are there parallels in American culture or social mores to the attitude toward unwed mothers and children born out of wedlock that play a strong role in this story? (Are our attitudes more enlightened or just different?)

4. Is the ending a *surprise ending,* or has the author prepared you for it? Does the story as a whole lead up to it? How? Do you react to it as something that really happened or as a dream, a nightmare?

5. Some of the details in this story are not just mentioned in passing. They come up again, providing a kind of link or a continuing strand. What is the role of recurrent details like the cherry blossoms or newspapers in this story?

6. One editor said that "this fiercely condensed" story, focused on a "single, overpowering incident," "explodes in a burst of revelation or illumination" (Irving Howe). For you, what is that revelation? Does this story have a point? Does it have a *theme*— some key idea acted out or implied in the story as a whole?

THE PERSONAL RESPONSE

Does the story as a whole remain strange or alien for you? How do you relate to Toshiko as the central character? How do you relate to the story as a whole?

THE RANGE OF INTERPRETATION

Mishima's story invites a wide range of reactions. In your judgment, which of the following student responses best gets into the spirit of the story? How or why does the student writer seem to do justice to the author's intention? How are these responses different from your own interpretation of the story?

1. Since Mishima's story takes place in Japan, we might expect a setting where the standards of a different culture prevail. Instead, the interaction of conflicting cultures plays a central role in this story. At the beginning, Mishima sets up a contrast between the Westernized husband and the traditional Japanese wife. While her loud, insensitive husband goes to his important appointments, the wife is put in a taxicab to her home. His flashy, flamboyant ways and Westernized suits seem a corruption of the traditional Japanese lifestyle. (I would guess that the author despises the husband.) Toshiko in the story seems to be most strongly aware of the traditional values of her society. While her blasé husband seems to look at the horrifying birth of the baby as an "amusing incident," Toshiko is acutely aware of the shame and prejudice that attend illegitimate birth in the traditional culture. While some Americans still hold similar views toward children born out of wedlock, as Americans we have generally become more liberal. (We don't have to worry about shaming 10,000 years of ancestors.) But paradoxically Toshiko is also the one who rebels against the traditional treatment of the illegitimate child. She is the only one who seems to care. While her husband only apes Western ways, Toshiko seems closest to our own ideal of compassion for the unfortunate. Actually, she seems to care more than most people would in either culture.

2. This story is very disturbing. Although it is set in Japan, the story reflects stereotypical sex roles reminding me of many couples I know. The husband

is domineering and shallow, and Toshiko is the stereotypically passive, dependent "oversensitive" wife. Under the quiet stereotypical surface, Toshiko is a warm, caring person. But whereas she is a keen observer of her culture (her gloomy prediction for the baby reveals this), she lives her whole life in her fears and feelings. While the husband is vain and self-absorbed, Toshiko spends her life alone in the private world of her fears. She feels great warmth toward the child, but she knows that it will suffer greatly as the result of its dishonorable beginnings. What we see in Toshiko is the constant battle waged between the traditional role and the emergence of the more modern woman. She is alienated from her callous, self-centered husband, and she assumes responsibility for the harsh treatment that society has in store for the newborn child.

3. This story is very fatalistic. The child, because of its illegitimate birth, is doomed to "utter misery." I expected Toshiko to come to a tragic end. I could empathize with Toshiko somewhat because of her culture and beliefs, but I wanted to stop her from feeling so guilty and destroying her life. It is as if Toshiko created the ending in the park. She is determined to sacrifice herself. At times I wanted to reach into the story and stop her from being so guilt-ridden and oversensitive. As a woman, it made me angry that she would destroy herself.

4. On the literal level, this story leaves many questions unresolved. The abrupt, surprising ending leaves me wondering whether it is real—is it a dream? a nightmare? If the derelict in the park literally attacked the woman, was the result death? rape? Symbolically, in the context of the story as a whole, Toshiko is taking the place of her own son. She is sacrificing herself in his stead, so that she rather than he will be the target of the dispossessed child's anger and resentment when it returns to exact vengeance. In spite of the difference in cultures, the story made me hear echoes of my own Catholic upbringing. The incident where Toshiko wrapped the child in swaddling clothes mirrored the birth of Christ in a manger where Mary wrapped him in swaddling clothes. The ending where Toshiko is willing to give up her life so that her son may live parallels Christ's willingness to give up his life so that his people may have eternal life.

WRITING ABOUT LITERATURE

2. Exploring the Setting (The Structured Paper)

It still comes as a shock to me to realize that I don't write about what I know: I write in order to find out what I know.

PATRICIA HAMPL

The Writing Workshop As you write about setting, explore the major dimensions that together give shape to the characteristic world of a story. Location in city or country, the past history of a region, the ways people make a living there, local customs or traditions—all of these may help you understand the characters, the ways they live and think and feel, or the situations in which they find themselves.

As you develop a paper focused on setting, you will go through many of the same basic steps as in writing papers focused on other facets of the story-teller's art. The first step toward real writing is to build up a rich backlog of material. No one can write a full paper from an empty mind. To write good papers about literary topics, try to operate on the computer principle of "good input makes for good output." Build the habit of scribbling comments in the margins of what you read (not in library copies!). Make it a habit to take ample reading notes. Compare notes and impressions with classmates or friends.

However, the second major step is to bring your material under control. Early in the process of gathering the material, you will start thinking through the issues it raises. You may begin to focus on a key question you will want to answer, a key issue that you may want to explore. You will start formulating a strategy for presenting your findings to your reader. You will think about lay-ing out your evidence in a pattern that makes sense. Early in your reading, you will start pulling together quotations that bear on the same point; you will begin collating details that help you answer the same question. This process of sorting out, of pulling your material into shape, will provide the ground plan or working outline for your first draft. You then refine or adjust your plan as necessary as you revise your paper.

What are some basic requirements for the finished paper that will be the result of this process of focusing, shaping, and revising? Remember: Each paper is different. The following guidelines are meant to alert you to needs that arise again and again in student papers. In considering these guidelines, try not to look at them as a formula that fits all topics. Change or adapt what needs to be changed to suit your purpose.

✧ *Avoid generic titles.* Although you may not hit on the right title until late in the process of writing your paper, remember that the title will be the first thing to strike your reader. Titles should not be perfunctory and inter-changeable—good perhaps for filing the paper under the author's name or the name of the story, but not enough to hook the reader into reading your essay. A good title is informative (it helps map the territory), but it should also be beckoning. Your title should be specific and attractive enough to invite the reader. It need not be a "grabber," but it should be alive: It should suggest a topic, a point of view, a program, a tone, a style.

TOO INTERCHANGEABLE:	Joyce's "Araby"
INFORMAL (and perhaps too cute?):	A Boy and His Bubble
FORMAL:	The Dark Infatuation of Joyce's "Araby"

✧ *Take your reader into the world of the story.* Help your reader get into the spirit by starting with a revealing quotation or a crucial incident:

"Your name means 'the king,'" Norma Jean informs her husband Leroy in Bobbie Ann Mason's "Shiloh," but Leroy, a disabled truck driver, model-kit hobbyist, and occasional joint smoker, is more like the palace grounds-keeper than the king.

✧ *Bring your paper into focus.* The first page is crucial. What is your central focus? What is your overall plan? After a brief pointed introduction, use your opening paragraphs to set directions. Try to provide a preview or program. Sketch out or hint at your overall scheme. Avoid a program that is too general—too open and interchangeable:

> WEAK: In this story, certain elements of the setting underscore and highlight the problems of the main characters.
>
> (What certain elements? This is too vague: No one is going to say, "I am all excited—I am going to be told about certain elements!")

Instead, for a short paper, try to sketch out a three-point or four-point program that provides a road map for your reader. Create expectations that your paper as a whole is going to fulfill. For instance, in writing about Mason's "Shiloh," you might plan to show how three main characters relate differently to their setting:

> The characters in Mason's story relate differently to their Southern setting: Leroy, the husband, is stranded in the present; Mabel, the mother-in-law, is living in the past; Norma Jean, the wife, has a future.

This statement provides a **thesis,** summing up the central idea of the paper. However, it also implies an itinerary. It alerts the reader to how the thesis is going to be followed up as the writer looks at each of the major characters in turn.

✧ *Wean yourself from a mere plot summary.* Follow a logical rather than merely chronological order. Sometimes, especially for a story with a complicated plot, an initial tracing of the story line can help writer and reader get their bearings. But avoid a mere "read-along-with-me" effect—make sure your readers do not think your paper as a whole will merely retell the story. Show that you have tied things together, that you can bring together evidence from different parts of the story. Show that you can pull out relevant quotations or incidents that bear on a key question or key point. (If you follow the order of the story, look at each segment from the angle that is the issue. Use each stage in the story to make a point that is part of your overall argument.)

✧ *Weave in rich, authentic detail.* Remember that any point worth making is worth following up with examples and support. Provide ample telling detail and show its significance in the story. For instance, in "Shiloh," the organ is rich in electronic wizardry—and Norma Jean masters it "almost immediately" (a hint of her ability to adjust to what is new?). Early in your paper, start weaving in telling, revealing short quotations. For instance, you might use the following interchange between Leroy and Norma Jean when you try to show the reader how these two are "slowly drifting apart":

"We *have* started all over again," says Norma Jean. "And this is how it turned out."

"What did I do wrong?"

"Nothing."

Use specific details and apt quotations to show your command of the material. Build up a rich texture of supporting detail to counteract the thin, anemic, overgeneral effect of improvised, hastily written prose.

✧ *Strengthen logical connections.* Avoid lame **transitions** like *also* or *another*. When you find yourself writing "another important aspect of the setting is . . . , " ask yourself: How is this feature of the setting *related* to the others—how is it part of the whole picture?

Perhaps you have made a point of Leroy's inability to communicate. (He wants to talk about their marriage but instead lamely repeats that he will build his wife a house.) You now want to move on to a second point: "Leroy's anachronistic behavior is *another problem* in the Moffitt marriage." (His playing with the plans for model log houses points to the past, not the future.) What is the logical connection between the two points? What is the connection in the larger context of the story? Perhaps you could strengthen the connection by a transition like the following;

TRANSITION: Having no way to voice his feelings articulately with words, he builds model log houses because he has no other way to express himself. However, this preoccupation with symbols of the past only serves to widen the gap between him and his wife. . . .

✧ *Aim at a strong conclusion.* Revise a conclusion that is merely a lame recapitulation of points already clear. Try bringing your paper full circle by picking up an image, incident, or keynote from the beginning of the paper. Use the opportunity to drive home a key point. Or use the opportunity to branch out, showing larger implications, showing a personal connection. One student paper started: "'Shiloh' by Bobbie Ann Mason presents a dull yet strikingly real vision of America." The following conclusion drives home the central point and highlights the connection between the story and our own lives:

"Shiloh" is a perfect portrayal of life in the 1990s. It is realistic, poignant, and depressing. It is ordinary, sometimes dismal, but rarely extravagant. That is left for Oprah and Geraldo to display on television. We see ourselves in the couple—our drive to succeed and prosper in Norma Jean and our love of the couch in Leroy.

Study the following sample paper. What role does the setting of the story play in the paper? How well does the paper live up to the requirements sketched above?

SAMPLE STUDENT PAPER

Muscle Building in the New South

Bobbie Ann Mason's short story "Shiloh" is a bleak portrait of a marriage at the point of dissolution—a picture of two people poised at the brink of what for the woman is a new life of personal growth and freedom but what is for the man the loss of most in his life that he thought secure. Mason uses physical detail—the way the characters relate to their bodies and to their physical setting—to mirror the wife's upward spiral and the husband's decline. They both find themselves in a new world that is different from the old South represented by Leroy's mother-in-law. But for one of them this new world means disillusionment and stagnation; for the other it means opportunity.

Leroy Moffitt is a truck driver from Kentucky, who is at home recovering from an accident in which his leg was badly injured. It is the first time since the early days of his marriage that he has been at home for any length of time, and he begins to feel that he has missed much of his married life. He realizes "that in all the years he was on the road he never took time to examine anything. He was always flying past scenery." Now his years of flying past the scenery of his life are over, and he for the first time is experiencing what it is like to stay in one place. Having a chance to watch his wife for more than hurried intervals, he finds that she is a different person from the woman he married.

His injured leg symbolizes Leroy's new slowing down, his new lack of mobility. It was badly twisted in its socket when his truck jackknifed in the road, and he now has a steel pin in his hip. Although he is healing, he is scared to go back on the road; he has moved from an extremely fast-paced, always-moving lifestyle to one in which he can walk only with difficulty. His career and his marriage have shuddered painfully to a standstill. He finds himself in a setting where much of what he does merely helps to pass the time: building small-scale model log houses, expecting his wife to play old favorites on a state-of-the-art electronic piano.

Leroy's new immobility is reflected even in Leroy's drug of choice. Where before he took drugs that were suited to his fast, mobile lifestyle, he now uses drugs of a more mellow nature: "Leroy used to take speed on the road. Now he has to go slowly. He needs to be mellow." The weed he buys allows him to dull and slow down his perception of his surroundings. He buys his joints from a source who represents the downside of the New South—a son of a doctor, whose drug-dealing symbolizes the rejection of his goal-oriented doctor father.

While Leroy is slowing down, however, his wife Norma Jean is speeding up. After fifteen years of staying home while her husband traveled, she is physically and symbolically stepping out into a new world. She is trying to move beyond the drugstore job—beyond the feeling of going nowhere experienced by people who are trapped in an average existence. She is taking steps toward personal improvement and intellectual growth—steps which are reflected in her new attention to her body. Early in the story, we see her working out with dumbbells, improving her muscle tone and physical appearance: "I'd give anything if I could just get these muscles to where they're real hard," she says impatiently. Leroy, with some foreboding, sees the potential for improvement in her, thinking that as she stood with her legs apart she reminded him of "Wonder Woman." Norma Jean wears ankle weights, lifts barbells, and flexes her arm to test the size of her biceps—testing, symbolically, her emotional and intellectual strength as she nears the point of breaking away from Leroy.

As she is improving herself physically, she improves herself intellectually with night classes and reading. As Leroy notes, "she stays up late, writing compositions." Norma Jean breaks out of confining old habits: She quits smoking; she cooks unusual foods, walking around the kitchen with ankle weights attached. Although she is still living in their house, her mind and body are already in a different place.

The differences in Leroy's and Norma Jean's emotional and intellectual needs lead to the final breakup in a setting full of hints of forgotten conflicts, the Civil War battleground at Shiloh. When Norma Jean walks away from Leroy, he is physically unable to follow her, for "his good leg is asleep and his bad leg still hurts him." She moves quickly, widening the chasm where their marriage used to be. In our last glimpse of Leroy and Norma Jean, she is waving her arms in some sort of "exercise for her chest muscles," testing her wings, perhaps, before moving upward and away from her old life.

QUESTIONS

How well does the introduction get you into the spirit of the story? Where does the central idea or thesis come into focus? Where does the program or agenda for the paper as a whole become clear to the reader? Where does the writer do a good job of relating specific details to the concerns of the paper as a whole? What use does the paper make of quotations? What transitions effectively move the reader from point to point? How does the conclusion wrap up the paper? How does it hark back to earlier parts of the paper; what does it add that is new? Where do you agree and where would you take issue with the paper?

3 CHARACTER
The Buried Self

I don't invent characters because the Almighty has already invented millions, just as experts at fingerprints do not create fingerprints but learn how to read them.

ISAAC BASHEVIS SINGER

I am enormously interested in other people, other lives, and with the least provocation I could "go into" your personality and try to imagine it, try to find a way of dramatizing it. I am fascinated by people I meet, or don't meet, people I only correspond with, or read about. . . . It seems to me that there are so many people who are inarticulate but who suffer and doubt and love, nobly, who need to be explained.

JOYCE CAROL OATES

I live with the people I create, and it has always made my essential loneliness less keen.

CARSON McCULLERS

FOCUS ON CHARACTER

Storytellers strive to create believable characters and set them in motion. The writers appeal to an ancient curiosity: We are fascinated with the variety of people in our world. We are willing to hear about their quirks and ploys, their clever and dense ways, their ways of acting smart and outsmarting themselves. However, the more we learn about them, the harder it is for us to stay aloof. We begin to care; we take sides; we become involved.

In the following passage from Bobbie Ann Mason's "Shiloh," we begin to see character traits of the husband who was a truck driver but has been in a bad accident. What kind of a person is beginning to emerge?

. . . Leroy has been home in Kentucky for three months, and his leg is almost healed, but the accident frightened him and he does not want to drive any more long hauls. He is not sure what to do next. In the meantime, he makes things from craft kits. He started by building a miniature log cabin from notched Popsicle sticks. He varnished it and placed it on the TV set, where it remains. It reminds him of a rustic Nativity scene. Then he tried string art (sailing ships on black velvet), a macramé owl kit, a snap-together B-17 Flying Fortress, and a lamp made out of a model truck, with a light fixture screwed in the top of the cab. At first the kits were diversions, something to kill time, but now he is thinking about building a full-scale log house from a kit. It would be considerably cheaper than building a regular house, and besides, Leroy has grown to appreciate how things are put together.

What clues to the character does this description furnish the reader? The kind of person that emerges does not seem to feel the need to act macho, to prove something by going back to the dangerous job. Instead, he was spooked by the accident (as many ordinary people might have been). He does not seem to be making any grandiose plans but seems to have the patience for tasks that require careful plodding work—and not a great deal of imagination. He certainly has no high-flown tastes for avant-garde art; the projects he works on all seem in keeping with the most average popular taste. Like many average people, he seems to have a liking for tradition—the Nativity scene, the log cabin. He likes the idea of saving money and doing something with his hands by building an actual log cabin to live in. All in all, we seem to be look-ing at a quiet, unambitious, average person, with very average tastes. We prob-ably do not expect him to initiate any upheavals or make angry speeches. Perhaps he is going to be more passive than active in the story that is about to take shape.

Notice that the author here does not take shortcuts but lets the character build as you read. The author does not put *labels* on Leroy but lets you reach your own conclusions about how average and basically dull he apparently is. At the same time, he does not fit a simple *stereotype*—whether of a grumbling, re-sentful, unemployed individual or of the couch potato with no initiative at all (he *is* thinking about building a log house). Finally, the character is not static, set in cement. He is changing or developing in response to what he experi-ences (he has come to appreciate how things are put together).

THE RANGE OF CHARACTERIZATION

You would have me, when I describe horse thieves, say: "Stealing horses is evil." But that has been known for ages without my saying so. Let the jury judge them; it's my job simply to show what sort of people they are.

ANTON CHEKHOV

How do you come to understand the characters in a short story you read? An author may give you a capsule portrait as advance notice of what you may expect of a character. However, in much modern fiction, you read to see char-acter *unfold*. You see people act out (and hear them talk out) who they are. The author may choose to make you watch a character from outside, letting you draw your own conclusions. Or the author may take you inside the character's mind, letting you overhear private thoughts and share in feelings masked to the outside world.

When you pay close attention to character, you try to anwer questions like the following:

Who are these people?
How do you get to know them?
How does what they say reveal character?
How does what they do reveal character?
What incidents or challenges put them to the test?
What motives do you recognize?
How do the characters look to other people in the story?
Does what others say about them tend to inform you or mislead you?
How do they interact with other people?
Do they live up to your estimate of them, or do they surprise you?
Does the author directly or indirectly steer your reactions?

As you explore such questions, bear in mind features that will keep you from giving oversimple answers:

Action and Motivation As you study character in fiction, you will find yourself going from the *what* to the *why*—from people's words and actions to their motives. Why do people talk and act the way they do? Be prepared to ponder the byways of **motivation.** Characters who act spiteful or hostile may not be by temperament spiteful or hostile people. They may be venting pent-up frustrations; they may have been driven to the edge of their endurance by a series of adverse events. Apparent hostility may be a way to fend off unwanted sympathy. Be prepared to look for clues to behavior that may seem puzzling on the surface. Be ready to look at the real motives behind the rationalizations or alibis offered by a character.

Flat and Round Characters **Flat characters** are people with a one-track personality: The miser is always a Scrooge, the braggart is always the blowhard, the whiner always finds fault. Such one-dimensional characters are common in popular fiction and make for easy recognition (and, sometimes, the easy laugh). **Round characters** have the combination of traits that make real people complicated (and at times infuriating). They may be loyal to a person or a cause—with their loyalty tempered by serious private doubts. They may have been raised in an atmosphere of rah-rah patriotism but discover unsuspected sympathies for a prisoner of war—the "enemy." In your study of characters in fiction, be prepared to recognize divided loyalties, mixed emotions.

Static and Growing Characters In serious fiction, characters may prove capable of growth, development. Stories like Alice Munro's "Boys and Girls" are stories of **initiation.** They reenact rites of passage—from childhood to adolescence, from the happy protected childhood world to a realization of the limitations of the adult world.

Person and Persona   Many writers of modern fiction delight in going beyond the surface, beyond the stereotype. They probe for the hidden personality, the buried self, beneath the public **persona.** They love to explore the contrast between the image, the face we present to the outside world (perfect hostess, Mr. Personality), and our private insecurities, doubts, hang-ups, or vendettas.

The Interplay of Characters   Sometimes only a single character emerges from the background—giving, as it were, a solo performance. More typically, a character's personality is revealed in the interaction with others. We see characters as part of a web of relationships. In the Alice Munro story, the girl who is at the center of the story is influenced by two conflicting role models, her father and her mother.

Guard against predictable ways of short-circuiting your understanding of a character. Let the character develop—instead of saying prematurely, "I know the type!" Similarly, try not to judge or reject prematurely: Once you turn angry or judgmental, you may not be able to muster the empathy needed to sense how the mind of a character works. Try to understand before you judge.

JUXTAPOSITIONS

Capsule Portraits

In both of the following short shorts, a character takes shape before our eyes in a brief space. The first story was written by a writer who for a time was one of the most authentic voices of heartland America. The second was written by an immigrant from the West Indies whose candor and commitment gained her a large audience in her adopted country. What would you include in a capsule portrait of the central character in each story? Do you recognize or understand these people?

SHERWOOD ANDERSON   (1876–1941)

Sherwood Anderson grew up in the small country towns and factory towns of Ohio. He worked on farms, in livery stables, and on racetracks; and he eventually left his family and a job as a factory manager to become a full-time writer in Chicago. His *Winesburg, Ohio* (1919) went beyond the polite social surface to probe the emotional drives and frustrations of his characters. Anderson influenced and inspired critics and writers searching for a more vigorous, more experimental, more modern American literature, including H. L. Mencken, Ernest Hemingway, and William Faulkner. A fellow writer said of him that in his fiction "the uneventful and imprisoned life he saw around him became moving and tragic as though another dimension had been added when it passed through his passionate survey—like the same river flowing between deeper walls."

Paper Pills 1919

He was an old man with a white beard and huge nose and hands. Long before the time during which we will know him, he was a doctor and drove a jaded white horse from house to house through the streets of Winesburg. Later he married a girl who had money. She had been left a large fertile farm when her father died. The girl was quiet, tall, and dark, and to many people she seemed very beautiful. Everyone in Winesburg wondered why she married the doctor. Within a year after the marriage she died.

The knuckles of the doctor's hands were extraordinarily large. When the hands were closed they looked like clusters of unpainted wooden balls as large as walnuts fastened together by steel rods. He smoked a cob pipe and after his wife's death sat all day in his empty office close by a window that was covered with cobwebs. He never opened the window. Once on a hot day in August he tried but found it stuck fast and after that he forgot all about it.

Winesburg had forgotten the old man, but in Doctor Reefy there were the seeds of something very fine. Alone in his musty office in the Heffner Block above the Paris Dry Goods Company's store, he worked ceaselessly, building up something that he himself destroyed. Little pyramids of truth he erected and after erecting knocked them down again that he might have the truths to erect other pyramids.

Doctor Reefy was a tall man who had worn one suit of clothes for ten years. It was frayed at the sleeves and little holes had appeared at the knees and elbows. In the office he wore also a linen duster with huge pockets into which he continually stuffed scraps of paper. After some weeks the scraps of paper became little hard round balls, and when the pockets were filled he dumped them out upon the floor. For ten years he had but one friend, another old man named John Spaniard who owned a tree nursery. Sometimes, in a playful mood, old Doctor Reefy took from his pockets a handful of the paper balls and threw them at the nursery man. "That is to confound you, you blithering old sentimentalist," he cried, shaking with laughter.

The story of Doctor Reefy and his courtship of the tall dark girl who became his wife and left her money to him was a very curious story. It is delicious, like the twisted little apples that grow in the orchards of Winesburg. In the fall one walks in the orchards and the ground is hard with frost underfoot. The apples have been taken from the trees by the pickers. They have been put in barrels and shipped to the cities where they will be eaten in apartments that are filled with books, magazines, furniture, and people. On the trees are only a few gnarled apples that the pickers have rejected. They look like the knuckles of Doctor Reefy's hands. One nibbles at them and they are delicious. Into a little round place at the side of the apple has been gathered all of its sweetness. One runs from tree to tree over the frosted ground picking the gnarled, twisted apples and filling his pockets with them. Only the few know the sweetness of the twisted apples.

The girl and Doctor Reefy began their courtship on a summer afternoon. He was forty-five then and already he had begun the practice of filling his pockets with the scraps of paper that became hard balls and were thrown away. The habit had been formed as he sat in his buggy behind the jaded white horse and went slowly along country roads. On the papers were written thoughts, ends of thoughts, beginnings of thoughts.

One by one the mind of Doctor Reefy had made the thoughts. Out of many of them he formed a truth that arose gigantic in his mind. The truth clouded the world. It became terrible and then faded away and the little thoughts began again.

5

The tall dark girl came to see Doctor Reefy because she was in the family way and had become frightened. She was in that condition because of a series of circumstances also curious.

The death of her father and mother and the rich acres of land that had come down to her had set a train of suitors on her heels. For two years she saw suitors almost every evening. Except two they were all alike. They talked to her of passion and there was a strained eager quality in their voices and in their eyes when they looked at her. The two who were different were much unlike each other. One of them, a slender young man with white hands, the son of a jeweler in Winesburg, talked continually of virginity. When he was with her he was never off the subject. The other, a black-haired boy with large ears, said nothing at all but always managed to get her into the darkness, where he began to kiss her.

For a time the tall dark girl thought she would marry the jeweler's son. For hours   10
she sat in silence listening as he talked to her and then she began to be afraid of something. Beneath his talk of virginity she began to think there was a lust greater than in all the others. At times it seemed to her that as he talked he was holding her body in his hands. She imagined him turning it slowly about in the white hands and staring at it. At night she dreamed that he had bitten into her body and that his jaws were dripping. She had the dream three times, then she became in the family way to the one who said nothing at all but who in the moment of his passion actually did bite her shoulder so that for days the marks of his teeth showed.

After the tall dark girl came to know Doctor Reefy it seemed to her that she never wanted to leave him again. She went into his office one morning and without her saying anything he seemed to know what had happened to her.

In the office of the doctor there was a woman, the wife of the man who kept the bookstore in Winesburg. Like all old-fashioned country practitioners, Doctor Reefy pulled teeth, and the woman who waited held a handkerchief to her teeth and groaned. Her husband was with her and when the tooth was taken out they both screamed and blood ran down on the woman's white dress. The tall dark girl did not pay any attention. When the woman and the man had gone the doctor smiled. "I will take you driving into the country with me," he said.

For several weeks the tall dark girl and the doctor were together almost every day. The condition that had brought her to him passed in an illness, but she was like one who has discovered the sweetness of the twisted apples, she could not get her mind fixed again upon the round perfect fruit that is eaten in the city apartments. In the fall after the beginning of her acquaintanceship with him she married Doctor Reefy and in the following spring she died. During the winter he read to her all of the odds and ends of thoughts he had scribbled on the bits of paper. After he had read them he laughed and stuffed them away in his pockets to become round hard balls.

THE RECEPTIVE READER

1. Like other characters in Anderson's stories, the doctor as the *central character* is likely to seem an eccentric or outsider to the people around him. Do *you* think he is strange? What makes him seem strange or understandable to you? What is the author's attitude toward him, and how can you know?

2. What kind of person is the woman in the story? What picture do you form of the two men who are courting her? What determines her choices?

3. What might be the *symbolic* significance of the "twisted apples"?

THE PERSONAL RESPONSE

Would you call this story a love story? How is it different from what you might expect in a love story? How do you react to it?

JAMAICA KINCAID   (born 1941)

When people say you're charming you are in deep trouble.
                                          JAMAICA KINCAID

Jamaica Kincaid was born in Antigua in the West Indies and left home to come to the United States when she was sixteen. An interviewer said of her that she grew up "in the shadow of a loving but domineering mother while learning proper British etiquette at colonial schools" (Donna Perry). After she came to New York and shed her original name (Elaine Potter Richardson), she worked at odd jobs, took photography classes, and was eventually discovered by the *New Yorker*. Two novels, *Annie John* (1983) and *Lucy* (1990), grew out of her *New Yorker* stories. She says that she felt like an outsider even when she lived at home among people who were mostly black like her and many of whom were women like her. She has been praised for her honesty and criticized for her anger, which she directs both at the suffering brought by colonialism and at the shortsightedness of the new rulers of the Third World.

A few words in Kincaid's story go back to the local dialect of her childhood: *benna* is calypso-inspired popular music; *doukona* is a spicy pudding.

Girl   1978

Wash the white clothes on Monday and put them on the stone heap; wash the color clothes on Tuesday and put them on the clothesline to dry; don't walk barehead in the hot sun; cook pumpkin fritters in very hot sweet oil; soak your little cloths right after you take them off; when buying cotton to make yourself a nice blouse, be sure that it doesn't have gum on it, because that way it won't hold up well after a wash; soak salt fish overnight before you cook it; is it true that you sing benna in Sunday school?; always eat your food in such a way that it won't turn someone else's stomach; on Sundays try to walk like a lady and not like the slut you are so bent on becoming; don't sing benna in Sunday school; you mustn't speak to wharf-rat boys, not even to give directions; don't eat fruits on the street—flies will follow you; *but I don't sing benna on Sundays at all and never in Sunday school;* this is how to sew on a button; this is how to make a buttonhole for the button you have just sewed on; this is how to hem a dress when you see the hem coming down and so to prevent yourself from looking like the slut I know you are so bent on becoming; this is how you iron your father's khaki shirt so that it doesn't have a crease; this is how you iron your father's khaki pants so that they don't have a crease; this is how you grow okra—far from the house, because okra tree harbors red ants; when you are growing dasheen, make sure it gets plenty of water or else it makes your throat itch when you are eating it; this is how you sweep a corner;

this is how you sweep a whole house; this is how you sweep a yard; this is how you smile to someone you don't like too much; this is how you smile to someone you don't like at all; this is how you smile to someone you like completely; this is how you set a table for tea; this is how you set a table for dinner; this is how you set a table for dinner with an important guest; this is how you set a table for lunch; this is how you set a table for breakfast; this is how to behave in the presence of men who don't know you very well, and this way they won't recognize immediately the slut I have warned you against becoming; be sure to wash every day, even if it is with your own spit; don't squat down to play marbles—you are not a boy, you know; don't pick people's flowers—you might catch something; don't throw stones at blackbirds, because it might not be a blackbird at all; this is how to make a bread pudding; this is how to make doukona; this is how to make pepper pot; this is how to make a good medicine for a cold; this is how to make a good medicine to throw away a child before it even becomes a child; this is how to catch a fish; this is how to throw back a fish you don't like, and that way something bad won't fall on you; this is how to bully a man; this is how a man bullies you; this is how to love a man, and if this doesn't work there are other ways, and if they don't work don't feel too bad about giving up; this is how to spit up in the air if you feel like it, and this is how to move quick so that it doesn't fall on you; this is how to make ends meet; always squeeze bread to make sure it's fresh; *but what if the baker won't let me feel the bread?*; you mean to say that after all you are really going to be the kind of woman who the baker won't let near the bread?

THE RECEPTIVE READER

1. The central character in this short short takes shape entirely through *dialogue*. What kind of person do you hear talking? ✧ What is her range of favorite topics? (*Benna* in the story is a dialect word for popular music—calypso, rock and roll—that the speaker considers a bad influence.) ✧ What expressions or ways of talking do you recognize, and why?

2. As in many one-way conversations, the listener in this story does not have a chance to have her say. Do you nevertheless hear her thinking? What would she say if she had a chance?

THE PERSONAL RESPONSE

Do you find yourself siding with the girl? Does the older woman have a point?

THE CREATIVE DIMENSION

Write a last letter from Anderson's doctor to his wife, or from the wife to her husband. Or write a letter from the girl in Kincaid's story to the person lecturing her.

THE UNIQUENESS OF HUMAN BEINGS

Unlike social scientists, who make descriptive statements about the varying divorce rates between, say, middle-class blacks and blue-collar whites, short-story writers seek to strip away these labels and create characters whose lives are contradictory and unfinished and do not possess the coherence of a psychological theory. Writers reveal instead

the unpredictability of human beings, caught between the
lack of consciousness or conviction or certainty and the
need to make decisions and get on with their lives.

MICHAEL NAGLER AND WILLIAM SWANSON

In some stories, the characters stay pale. They may seem interchangeable with others of their time, their setting; they may be representative of their stage in life or of their class. In other stories, the mystery of personality seems at the center of the story. The story probes a character's motives, explores surface contradictions, or ponders a change of heart. To a large extent, the character is the story. In the stories that follow, character plays a central role.

R A Y M O N D   C A R V E R   (1939–1988)

Carver has an acute sense of the singularity, the endearing
oddity, of each human being; to each person he grants a
measure of dignity because, if nothing else at all, this
person has the sure distinction that no one else is exactly
like him—no human life can be replicated; therefore each,
however flawed, is precious.

JONATHAN YARDLEY

No one's brevity is as rich, as complete, as Raymond
Carver's.

PATRICIA HAMPL

Raymond Carver has been praised for his intentional "blue-collar realism and unsophistication" (John Barth). Carver had himself worked at blue-collar jobs in the towns of the Pacific Northwest that is the setting of many of his stories. He himself, like some of his characters, had done battle against alcoholism. His characters are often unskilled, unemployed, and unremarkable, yet of sufficient human interest to the author. He often gives a voice to the feelings or point of view of people of few words, "speaking the thoughts of those who cannot themselves speak" (John Clute). One reviewer thought of him as the kind of writer "who turned banality's pockets out and found all their contents beautiful" (Marilynne Robinson).

Carver is one of a group of contemporary writers tending toward a **minimalist** stance (though he himself disliked the fashionable label). Like other minimalist writers, he kept his stories to the essential minimum, writing on the theory that "less is more," being suspicious of all showy effects. He once said, "I cut my work to the marrow, not just the bone." Carver seems to enjoy teasing the reader with the puzzle of personality. His narrator, as in the following story, may be someone listening to another character, piecing together the pieces of the puzzle, wanting to say (as does Carver's reader) "Tell me more. "

The Third Thing That Killed My Father Off   1977

I'll tell you what did my father in. The third thing was Dummy, that Dummy died. The first thing was Pearl Harbor. And the second thing was moving to my grandfather's farm near Wenatchee. That's where my father finished out his days, except they were probably finished before that.

My father blamed Dummy's death on Dummy's wife. Then he blamed it on the fish. And finally he blamed himself—because he was the one that showed Dummy the ad in the back of *Field and Stream* for live black bass shipped anywhere in the U.S.

It was after he got the fish that Dummy started acting peculiar. The fish changed Dummy's whole personality. That's what my father said.

I never knew Dummy's real name. If anyone did, I never heard it. Dummy it was then, and it's Dummy I remember him by now. He was a little wrinkled man, bald-headed, short but very powerful in the arms and legs. If he grinned, which was seldom, his lips folded back over brown, broken teeth. It gave him a crafty expression. His watery eyes stayed fastened on your mouth when you were talking—and if you weren't, they'd go to someplace queer on your body.

I don't think he was really deaf. At least not as deaf as he made out. But he sure couldn't talk. That was for certain.

Deaf or no, Dummy'd been on as a common laborer out at the sawmill since the 1920s. This was the Cascade Lumber Company in Yakima, Washington. The years I knew him, Dummy was working as a cleanup man. And all those years I never saw him with anything different on. Meaning a felt hat, a khaki workshirt, a denim jacket over a pair of coveralls. In his top pockets he carried rolls of toilet paper, as one of his jobs was to clean and supply the toilets. It kept him busy, seeing as how the men on nights used to walk off after their tours with a roll or two in their lunchboxes.

Dummy carried a flashlight, even though he worked days. He also carried wrenches, pliers, screwdrivers, friction tape, all the same things the millwrights carried. Well, it made them kid Dummy, the way he was, always carrying everything. Carl Lowe, Ted Slade, Johnny Wait, they were the worst kidders of the ones that kidded Dummy. But Dummy took it all in stride. I think he'd gotten used to it.

My father never kidded Dummy. Not to my knowledge, anyway. Dad was a big, heavy-shouldered man with a crew-haircut, double chin, and a belly of real size. Dummy was always staring at that belly. He'd come to the filing room where my father worked, and he'd sit on a stool and watch my dad's belly while he used the big emery wheels on the saws.

Dummy had a house as good as anyone's.

It was a tarpaper-covered affair near the river, five or six miles from town. Half a mile behind the house, at the end of a pasture, there lay a big gravel pit that the state had dug when they were paving the roads around there. Three good-sized holes had been scooped out, and over the years they'd filled with water. By and by, the three ponds came together to make one.

It was deep. It had a darkish look to it.

Dummy had a wife as well as a house. She was a woman years younger and said to go around with Mexicans. Father said it was busybodies that said that, men like Lowe and Wait and Slade.

She was a small stout woman with glittery little eyes. The first time I saw her, I saw those eyes. It was when I was with Pete Jensen and we were on our bicycles and we stopped at Dummy's to get a glass of water.

When she opened the door, I told her I was Del Fraser's son. I said, "He works with—" And then I realized. "You know, your husband. We were on our bicycles and thought we could get a drink."

"Wait here," she said.

She came back with a little tin cup of water in each hand. I downed mine in a single gulp.

But she didn't offer us more. She watched us without saying anything. When we started to get on our bicycles, she came over to the edge of the porch.

"You little fellas had a car now, I might catch a ride with you."

She grinned. Her teeth looked too big for her mouth.

"Let's go," Pete said, and we went.

There weren't many places you could fish for bass in our part of the state. There was rainbow mostly, a few brook and Dolly Varden in some of the high mountain streams, and silvers in Blue Lake and Lake Rimrock. That was mostly it, except for the runs of steelhead and salmon in some of the freshwater rivers in late fall. But if you were a fisherman, it was enough to keep you busy. No one fished for bass. A lot of people I knew had never seen a bass except for pictures. But my father had seen plenty of them when he was growing up in Arkansas and Georgia, and he had high hopes to do with Dummy's bass, Dummy being a friend.

The day the fish arrived, I'd gone swimming at the city pool. I remember coming home and going out again to get them since Dad was going to give Dummy a hand—three tanks Parcel Post from Baton Rouge, Louisiana.

We went in Dummy's pickup, Dad and Dummy and me.

These tanks turned out to be barrels, really, the three of them crated in pine lath. They were standing in the shade out back of the train depot, and it took my dad and Dummy both to lift each crate into the truck.

Dummy drove very carefully through town and just as carefully all the way to his house. He went right through his yard without stopping. He went on down to within feet of the pond. By that time it was nearly dark, so he kept his headlights on and took out a hammer and a tire iron from under the seat, and then the two of them lugged the crates up close to the water and started tearing open the first one.

The barrel inside was wrapped in burlap, and there were these nickel-sized holes in the lid. They raised it off and Dummy aimed his flashlight in.

It looked like a million bass fingerlings were finning inside. It was the strangest sight, all those live things busy in there, like a little ocean that had come on the train.

Dummy scooted the barrel to the edge of the water and poured it out. He took his flashlight and shined it into the pond. But there was nothing to be seen anymore. You could hear the frogs going, but you could hear them going anytime it newly got dark.

"Let me get the other crates," my father said, and he reached over as if to take the hammer from Dummy's coveralls. But Dummy pulled back and shook his head.

He undid the other two crates himself, leaving dark drops of blood on the lath where he ripped his hand doing it.

From that night on, Dummy was different.

Dummy wouldn't let anyone come around now anymore. He put up fencing all around the pasture, and then he fenced off the pond with electrical barbed wire. They said it cost him all his savings for that fence.

Of course, my father wouldn't have anything to do with Dummy after that. Not since Dummy ran him off. Not from fishing, mind you, because the bass were just babies still. But even from trying to get a look.

One evening two years after, when Dad was working late and I took him his food and a jar of iced tea, I found him standing talking with Syd Glover, the millwright. Just as I came in, I heard Dad saying, "You'd reckon the fool was married to them fish, the way he acts."

"From what I hear," Syd said, "he'd do better to put that fence round his house."   35

My father saw me then, and I saw him signal Syd Glover with his eyes.

But a month later my dad finally made Dummy do it. What he did was, he told Dummy how you had to thin out the weak ones on account of keeping things fit for the rest of them. Dummy stood there pulling at his ear and staring at the floor. Dad said, Yeah, he'd be down to do it tomorrow because it had to be done. Dummy never said yes, actually. He just never said no, is all. All he did was pull on his ear some more.

When Dad got home that day, I was ready and waiting. I had his old bass plugs out and was testing the treble hooks with my finger.

"You set?" he called to me, jumping out of the car. "I'll go to the toilet, you put the stuff in. You can drive us out there if you want."

I'd stowed everything in the back seat and was trying out the wheel when he came   40
back out wearing his fishing hat and eating a wedge of cake with both hands.

Mother was standing in the door watching. She was a fair-skinned woman, her blonde hair pulled back in a tight bun and fastened down with a rhinestone clip. I wonder if she ever went around back in those happy days, or what she ever really did.

I let out the handbrake. Mother watched until I'd shifted gears, and then, still unsmiling, she went back inside.

It was a fine afternoon. We had all the windows down to let the air in. We crossed the Moxee Bridge and swung west onto Slater Road. Alfalfa fields stood off to either side, and farther on it was cornfields.

Dad had his hand out the window. He was letting the wind carry it back. He was restless, I could see.

It wasn't long before we pulled up at Dummy's. He came out of the house wear-   45
ing his hat. His wife was looking out the window.

"You got your frying pan ready?" Dad hollered out to Dummy, but Dummy just stood there eyeing the car. "Hey, Dummy!" Dad yelled. "Hey, Dummy, where's your pole, Dummy?"

Dummy jerked his head back and forth. He moved his weight from one leg to the other and looked at the ground and then at us. His tongue rested on his lower lip, and he began working his foot into the dirt.

I shouldered the creel. I handed Dad his pole and picked up my own.

"We set to go?" Dad said. "Hey, Dummy, we set to go?"

Dummy took off his hat and, with the same hand, he wiped his wrist over his head.   50
He turned abruptly, and we followed him across the spongy pasture. Every twenty feet or so a snipe sprang up from the clumps of grass at the edge of the old furrows.

At the end of the pasture, the ground sloped gently and became dry and rocky, nettle bushes and scrub oaks scattered here and there. We cut to the right, following an old set of car tracks, going through a field of milkweed that came up to our waists, the dry pods at the tops of the stalks rattling angrily as we pushed through. Presently, I saw the sheen of water over Dummy's shoulder, and I heard Dad shout, "Oh, Lord, look at that!"

But Dummy slowed down and kept bringing his hand up and moving his hat back and forth over his head, and then he just stopped flat.

Dad said, "Well, what do you think, Dummy? One place good as another? Where do you say we should come onto it?"

Dummy wet his lower lip.

"What's the matter with you, Dummy?" Dad said. "This your pond, ain't it?"   55

Dummy looked down and picked an ant off his coveralls.

"Well, hell," Dad said, letting out his breath. He took out his watch. "If it's all right with you, we'll get to it before it gets too dark."

Dummy stuck his hands in his pockets and turned back to the pond. He started walking again. We trailed along behind. We could see the whole pond now, the water dimpled with rising fish. Every so often a bass would leap clear and come down in a splash.

"Great God," I heard my father say.

We came up to the pond at an open place, a gravel beach kind of.   60

Dad motioned to me and dropped into a crouch. I dropped too. He was peering into the water in front of us, and when I looked, I saw what had taken him so.

"Honest to God," he whispered.

A school of bass was cruising, twenty, thirty, not one of them under two pounds. They veered off, and then they shifted and came back, so densely spaced they looked like they were bumping up against each other. I could see their big, heavy-lidded eyes watching us as they went by. They flashed away again, and again they came back.

They were asking for it. It didn't make any difference if we stayed squatted or stood up. The fish just didn't think a thing about us. I tell you, it was a sight to behold.

We sat there for quite a while, watching that school of bass go so innocently about   65 their business, Dummy the whole time pulling at his fingers and looking around as if he expected someone to show up. All over the pond the bass were coming up to nuzzle the water, or jumping clear and falling back, or coming up to the surface to swim along with their dorsals sticking out.

Dad signaled, and we got up to cast. I tell you, I was shaky with excitement. I could hardly get the plug loose from the cork handle of my pole. It was while I was trying to get the hooks out that I felt Dummy seize my shoulder with his big fingers. I looked, and in answer Dummy worked his chin in Dad's direction. What he wanted was clear enough, no more than one pole.

Dad took off his hat and then put it back on and then he moved over to where I stood.

"You go on, Jack" he said. "That's all right, son—you do it now."

I looked at Dummy just before I laid out my cast. His face had gone rigid, and there was a thin line of drool on his chin.

"Come back stout on the sucker when he strikes," Dad said. "Sons of bitches got   70 mouths hard as doorknobs."

I flipped off the drag lever and threw back my arm. I sent her out a good forty feet. The water was boiling even before I had time to take up the slack.

"Hit him!" Dad yelled. "Hit the son of a bitch! Hit him good!"

I came back hard, twice. I had him, all right. The rod bowed over and jerked back and forth. Dad kept yelling what to do.

"Let him go, let him go! Let him run! Give him more line! Now wind in! Wind in! No, let him run! Woo-ee! Will you look at that!"

The bass danced around the pond. Every time it came up out of the water, it shook its head so hard you could hear the plug rattle. And then he'd take off again. But by and by I wore him out and had him in up close. He looked enormous, six or seven pounds maybe. He lay on his side, whipped, mouth open, gills working. My knees felt so weak I could hardly stand. But I held the rod up, the line tight. 75

Dad waded out over his shoes. But when he reached for the fish, Dummy started sputtering, shaking his head, waving his arms.

"Now what the hell's the matter with you, Dummy? The boy's got hold of the biggest bass I ever seen, and he ain't going to throw him back, by God!"

Dummy kept carrying on and gesturing toward the pond.

"I ain't about to let this boy's fish go. You hear me, Dummy? You got another think coming if you think I'm going to do that."

Dummy reached for my line. Meanwhile, the bass had gained some strength back. He turned himself over and started swimming again. I yelled and then I lost my head and slammed down the brake on the reel and started winding. The bass made a last, furious run. 80

That was that. The line broke. I almost fell over on my back.

"Come on, Jack," Dad said, and I saw him grabbing up his pole. "Come on, god-damn the fool, before I knock the man down."

That February the river flooded.

It had snowed pretty heavy the first weeks of December, and turned real cold be-fore Christmas. The ground froze. The snow stayed where it was. But toward the end of January, the Chinook wind struck. I woke up one morning to hear the house getting buffeted and the steady drizzle of water running off the roof.

It blew for five days, and on the third day the river began to rise. 85

"She's up to fifteen feet," my father said one evening, looking over his newspaper. "Which is three feet over what you need to flood. Old Dummy going to lose his dar-lings."

I wanted to go down to the Moxee Bridge to see how high the water was running. But my dad wouldn't let me. He said a flood was nothing to see.

Two days later the river crested, and after that the water began to subside.

Orin Marshall and Danny Owens and I bicycled out to Dummy's one morning a week after. We parked our bicycles and walked across the pasture that bordered Dummy's property.

It was a wet, blustery day, the clouds dark and broken, moving fast across the sky. The ground was soppy wet and we kept coming to puddles in the thick grass. Danny was just learning how to cuss, and he filled the air with the best he had every time he stepped in over his shoes. We could see the swollen river at the end of the pasture. The water was still high and out of its channel, surging around the trunks of trees and eating away at the edge of the land. Out toward the middle, the current moved heavy and swift, and now and then a bush floated by, or a tree with its branches sticking up. 90

We came to Dummy's fence and found a cow wedged in up against the wire. She was bloated and her skin was shiny-looking and gray. It was the first dead thing of any size I'd ever seen. I remember Orin took a stick and touched the open eyes.

We moved on down the fence, toward the river. We were afraid to go near the wire because we thought it might still have electricity in it. But at the edge of what looked like a deep canal, the fence came to an end. The ground had simply dropped into the water here, and the fence along with it.

We crossed over and followed the new channel that cut directly into Dummy's land and headed straight for his pond, going into it lengthwise and forcing an outlet for itself at the other end, then twisting off until it joined up with the river farther on.

You didn't doubt that most of Dummy's fish had been carried off. But those that hadn't been were free to come and go.

Then I caught sight of Dummy. It scared me, seeing him. I motioned to the other 95
fellows, and we all got down.

Dummy was standing at the far side of the pond near where the water was rushing out. He was just standing there, the saddest man I ever saw.

"I sure do feel sorry for old Dummy, though," my father said at supper a few weeks after. "Mind, the poor devil brought it on himself. But you can't help but be troubled for him."

Dad went on to say George Laycock saw Dummy's wife sitting in the Sportsman's Club with a big Mexican fellow.

"And that ain't the half of it—"

Mother looked up at him sharply and then at me. But I just went on eating like I 100
hadn't heard a thing.

Dad said, "Damn it to hell, Bea, the boy's old enough!"

He'd changed a lot, Dummy had. He was never around any of the men anymore, not if he could help it. No one felt like joking with him either, not since he'd chased Carl Lowe with a two-by-four stud after Carl tipped Dummy's hat off. But the worst of it was that Dummy was missing from work a day or two a week on the average now, and there was some talk of his being laid off.

"The man's going off the deep end," Dad said. "Clear crazy if he don't watch out."

Then on a Sunday afternoon just before my birthday, Dad and I were cleaning the garage. It was a warm, drifty day. You could see the dust hanging in the air. Mother came to the back door and said, "Del, it's for you. I think it's Vern."

I followed Dad in to wash up. When he was through talking, he put the phone 105
down and turned to us.

"It's Dummy," he said. "Did in his wife with a hammer and drowned himself. Vern just heard it in town."

When we got out there, cars were parked all around. The gate to the pasture stood open, and I could see tire marks that led on to the pond.

The screen door was propped ajar with a box, and there was this lean, pock-faced man in slacks and sports shirt and wearing a shoulder holster. He watched Dad and me get out of the car.

"I was his friend," Dad said to the man.

The man shook his head. "Don't care who you are. Clear off unless you got busi- 110
ness here."

"Did they find him?" Dad said.

"They're dragging," the man said, and adjusted the fit of his gun.

"All right if we walk down? I knew him pretty well."

The man said, "Take your chances. They chase you off, don't say you wasn't warned."

We went on across the pasture, taking pretty much the same route we had the day 115
we tried fishing. There were motorboats going on the pond, dirty fluffs of exhaust hanging over it. You could see where the high water had cut away the ground and car-ried off trees and rocks. The two boats had uniformed men in them, and they were

going back and forth, one man steering and the other man handling the rope and hooks.

An ambulance waited on the gravel beach where we'd set ourselves to cast for Dummy's bass. Two men in white lounged against the back, smoking cigarettes.

One of the motorboats cut off. We all looked up. The man in back stood up and started heaving on his rope. After a time, an arm came out of the water. It looked like the hooks had gotten Dummy in the side. The arm went back down and then it came out again, along with a bundle of something.

It's not him, I thought. It's something else that has been in there for years.

The man in the front of the boat moved to the back, and together the two men hauled the dripping thing over the side.

I looked at Dad. His face was funny the way it was set.   120

"Women," he said. He said, "That's what the wrong kind of woman can do to you, Jack."

But I don't think Dad really believed it. I think he just didn't know who to blame or what to say.

It seemed to me everything took a bad turn for my father after that. Just like Dummy, he wasn't the same man anymore. That arm coming up and going back down in the water, it was like so long to good times and hello to bad. Because it was nothing but that all the years after Dummy drowned himself in that dark water.

Is that what happens when a friend dies? Bad luck for the pals he left behind?   125

But as I said, Pearl Harbor and having to move back to his dad's place didn't do my dad one bit of good, either.

THE RECEPTIVE READER

1. How do we learn what we come to know about Dummy? Who is the *narrator*—what kind of person tells us the story? What is his role in the story? Is he a major or a minor character? What is his vantage point? What are his limitations?

2. How does the author make Dummy come to life in the early sections of the story? What is Dummy's problem? Can you visualize his physical appearance? How much and what kind of *descriptive detail* do we get?

3. How do Dummy's coworkers treat him, and how are we expected to feel about them?

4. What is the relationship between the narrator's father and Dummy? Who is the true *central character* in the story? Does the story have a hero?

5. As the story unfolds, how much insight do we get into Dummy's personality or character? Do you understand the way Dummy acts about the fish, the pond, the flood? (How important are the fish in the story as a whole?)

6. What role does Dummy's wife play in the story? Is she playing a bit part? Is she expendable?

7. A central *irony* in the story is that Dummy is the character who seems to have urgent things to say to the others, but he is unable to communicate through language. How *does* he communicate? What is he trying to tell the others?

8. What is the role of humor in the story? What is the tone of the references to the father's death in the title, at the beginning, and in the conclusion? Do they color the story as a whole?

9. Do you think the author should have given the reader less of an outsider's and more of an insider's view of Dummy as a major character in the story? Would you have liked more insight into the workings of Dummy's mind?

10. What is the pattern of the narrative as a whole? Do you think its leisurely pace and straightforward development are part of the author's larger intentions or overall conception of the story?

THE PERSONAL RESPONSE

For you, is Dummy an eccentric—an isolated individual, a person with special personal problems all of his own? Is he someone "acting peculiar"? Or does his story have a more general human meaning?

THE CREATIVE DIMENSION

Assume Dummy could have been a more articulate or eloquent character. Write an extended suicide note that he might have written to explain himself to his friends.

ALICE MUNRO   (born 1931)

Alice Munro is one of several Canadian writers who became widely known in the United States in the 1970s and 1980s. She grew up in southwestern Ontario, and many of her stories take us to rural settings—the countryside and small towns of eastern Canada, where during the harsh winters snowdrifts would curl around the houses "like sleeping whales." Her father was a farmer, and when she writes in the first person as a girl growing up on a farm, it is tempting to equate the "I" telling the story with the author. However, she also uses the "I" when she has a small-town boy tell the story of his experimenting with liquor and first love on a Saturday night and finding both wanting. The "I" of her stories is fictitious—it is part of a vividly imagined world that blends autobiographical materials and sharp-eyed observation of fellow humanity.

Munro's first collection of short stories, *Dance of the Happy Shades,* was published in 1968 and received the Canadian Governor General's Literary Award. She published her second collection of stories, *Something I've Been Meaning to Tell You,* in 1972. Her novel *Lives of Girls and Women* appeared in 1971.

Munro has a special gift for creating a sense of place. In her story "Thanks for the Ride," she takes us to a town where the signs in Pop's Cafe (between fly-speckled and slightly yellowed cutouts of strawberry sundaes and tomato sandwiches) say things like "Don't ask for information—if we knew anything, we wouldn't be here." One of the boys in the story has a habit of reading signs out loud—"Mission Creek. Population 1700. Gateway to the Bruce. We love our children." The houses are likely to have linoleum on the floor; there is likely to be a glossy sofa "with a Niagara Falls and 'To Mother' cushion on it"; a big vase of paper apple blossoms may round out the decor.

In such settings, created in faithful and totally believable detail, she places characters who are often undergoing a rite of passage. (One editor said about Munro's stories that her "characters' lives and landscapes are inextricably intertwined.") They may be at a turning point in their lives, moving from childhood to adolescence, or from the confused passions of adolescence to the world of adult responsibilities. Her characters are often people who are still spontaneous and innocent but who encounter people more knowing, more experienced, and perhaps more defeated than they are. Such a story may become a story of **initiation,** as the hero or heroine discovers the limitations, the invisible walls, that mark his or her world.

In the following story, there is much nostalgic recreation of the golden world of childhood. But at the center of the story is a young woman at the crossroads. Who is this young woman? What are the contradictory influences that help shape her identity? Viewed as a rite of passage, her story is a passage from what to what? Where is she headed at the end of the story?

Boys and Girls   1968

> It is difficult to stand forth in one's growing if one is not permitted to live through the states of one's unripeness, clumsiness, unreadiness, as well as one's grace and aptitude.

M. C. RICHARDS

[The Ave referred to in a song mentioned early in the story is short for the Catholic prayer Ave Maria, or Hail Mary. Orangemen's Day (July 12) is a Protestant holiday dedicated to the memory of William of Orange, who replaced the Catholic James II as king of England in 1689. Judy Canova was a popular entertainer of the 1930s and 1940s.]

My father was a fox farmer. That is, he raised silver foxes, in pens; and in the fall and early winter, when their fur was prime, he killed them and skinned them and sold their pelts to the Hudson's Bay Company or the Montreal Fur Traders. These companies supplied us with heroic calendars to hang, one on each side of the kitchen door. Against a background of cold blue sky and black pine forests and treacherous northern rivers, plumed adventurers planted the flags of England or of France; magnificent savages bent their backs to the portage.

For several weeks before Christmas, my father worked after supper in the cellar of our house. The cellar was whitewashed, and lit by a hundred-watt bulb over the work-table. My brother Laird and I sat on the top step and watched. My father removed the pelt inside-out from the body of the fox, which looked surprisingly small, mean and rat-like, deprived of its arrogant weight of fur. The naked, slippery bodies were collected in a sack and buried at the dump. One time the hired man, Henry Bailey, had taken a swipe at me with this sack, saying, "Christmas present!" My mother thought that was not funny. In fact she disliked the whole pelting operation—that was what the killing, skinning, and preparation of the furs was called—and wished it did not have to take place in the house. There was the smell. After the pelt had been stretched inside-out on a long board my father scraped away delicately, removing the little clotted webs of blood vessels, the bubbles of fat; the smell of blood and animal fat, with the strong primitive odor of the fox itself, penetrated all parts of the house. I found it reassuringly seasonal, like the smell of oranges and pine needles.

Henry Bailey suffered from bronchial troubles. He would cough and cough until his narrow face turned scarlet, and his light blue, derisive eyes filled up with tears; then he took the lid off the stove, and, standing well back, shot out a great clot of phlegm—hsss— straight into the heart of the flames. We admired him for this performance and for his ability to make his stomach growl at will, and for his laughter, which was full of high whistlings and gurglings and involved the whole faulty machinery of his chest. It was sometimes hard to tell what he was laughing at, and always possible that it might be us.

After we had been sent to bed we could still smell fox and still hear Henry's laugh, but these things, reminders of the warm, safe, brightly lit downstairs world, seemed lost and diminished, floating on the stale cold air upstairs. We were afraid at night in the winter. We were not afraid of *outside* though this was the time of year when snowdrifts curled around our house like sleeping whales and the wind harassed us all night, coming up from the buried fields, the frozen swamp, with its old bugbear chorus of threats and misery. We were afraid of *inside,* the room where we slept. At this time the upstairs of our house was not finished. A brick chimney went up one wall. In the middle of the floor was a square hole, with a wooden railing around it; that was where the stairs came up. On the other side of the stairwell were the things that nobody had any use for any more—a soldiery roll of linoleum, standing on end, a wicker baby carriage, a fern basket, china jugs and basins with cracks in them, a picture of the Battle of Balaclava, very sad to look at. I had told Laird, as soon as he was old enough to understand such things, that bats and skeletons lived over there; whenever a man escaped from the county jail, twenty miles away, I imagined that he had somehow let himself in the window and was hiding behind the linoleum. But we had rules to keep us safe. When the light was on, we were safe as long as we did not step off the square of worn carpet which defined our bedroom-space; when the light was off no place was safe but the beds themselves. I had to turn out the light kneeling on the end of my bed, and stretching as far as I could to reach the cord.

In the dark we lay on our beds, our narrow life rafts, and fixed our eyes on the faint light coming up the stairwell, and sang songs. Laird sang "Jingle Bells," which he would sing any time, whether it was Christmas or not, and I sang "Danny Boy." I loved the sound of my own voice, frail and supplicating, rising in the dark. We could make out the tall frosted shapes of the windows now, gloomy and white. When I came to the part, *When I am dead, as dead I well may be*—a fit of shivering caused not by the cold sheets but by pleasurable emotion almost silenced me. *You'll kneel and say, and Ave there above me*—What was an Ave? Every day I forgot to find out.

Laird went straight from singing to sleep. I could hear his long, satisfied, bubbly breaths. Now for the time that remained to me, the most perfectly private and perhaps the best time of the whole day, I arranged myself tightly under the covers and went on with one of the stories I was telling myself from night to night. These stories were about myself, when I had grown a little older; they took place in a world that was recognizably mine, yet one that presented opportunities for courage, boldness and self-sacrifice, as mine never did. I rescued people from a bombed building (it discouraged me that the real war had gone on so far away from Jubilee). I shot two rabid wolves who were menacing the schoolyard (the teachers cowered terrified at my back). I rode a fine horse spiritedly down the main street of Jubilee, acknowledging the townspeople's gratitude for some yet-to-be-worked-out piece of heroism (nobody ever rode a horse there, except King Billy in the Orangemen's Day parade). There was always riding and shooting in these stories, though I had only been on a horse twice—bareback because we did not own a saddle—and the second time I had slid right around and dropped under the horse's feet; it had stepped placidly over me. I really was learning to shoot, but I could not hit anything yet, not even tin cans on fence posts.

5

Alive, the foxes inhabited a world my father made for them. It was surrounded by a high guard fence, like a medieval town, with a gate that was padlocked at night. Along the streets of this town were ranged large, sturdy pens. Each of them had a real door that a man could go through, a wooden ramp along the wire, for the foxes to run up and down on, and a kennel—something like a clothes chest with airholes— where they slept and stayed in winter and had their young. There were feeding and watering dishes attached to the wire in such a way that they could be emptied and cleaned from the outside. The dishes were made of old tin cans, and the ramps and kennels of odds and ends of old lumber. Everything was tidy and ingenious; my father was tirelessly inventive and his favorite book in the world was *Robinson Crusoe*. He had fitted a tin drum on a wheelbarrow, for bringing water down to the pens. This was my job in summer, when the foxes had to have water twice a day. Between nine and ten o'clock in the morning, and again after supper, I filled the drum at the pump and trundled it down through the barnyard to the pens, where I parked it, and filled my watering can and went along the streets. Laird came too, with his little cream and green gardening can, filled too full and knocking against his legs and slopping water on his canvas shoes. I had the real watering can, my father's, though I could only carry it three-quarters full.

The foxes all had names, which were printed on a tin plate and hung beside their doors. They were not named when they were born, but when they survived the first year's pelting and were added to the breeding stock. Those my father had named were called names like Prince, Bob, Wally and Betty. Those I had named were called Star or Turk, or Maureen or Diana. Laird named one Maud after a hired girl we had when he was little, one Harold after a boy at school, and one Mexico, he did not say why.

Naming them did not make pets out of them, or anything like it. Nobody but my father ever went into the pens, and he had twice had blood-poisoning from bites. When I was bringing them their water they prowled up and down on the paths they had made inside their pens, barking seldom—they saved that for nighttime, when they might get up a chorus of community frenzy—but always watching me, their eyes burning, clear gold, in their pointed, malevolent faces. They were beautiful for their delicate legs and heavy, aristocratic tails and the bright fur sprinkled on dark down their backs—which gave them their name—but especially for their faces, drawn exquisitely sharp in pure hostility, and their golden eyes.

Besides carrying water I helped my father when he cut the long grass, and the lamb's quarter and flowering money-musk, that grew between the pens. He cut with the scythe and I raked into piles. Then he took a pitchfork and threw fresh-cut grass all over the top of the pens, to keep the foxes cooler and shade their coats, which were browned by too much sun. My father did not talk to me unless it was about the job we were doing. In this he was quite different from my mother, who, if she was feeling cheerful, would tell me all sorts of things—the name of a dog she had had when she was a little girl, the names of boys she had gone out with later on when she was grown up, and what certain dresses of hers had looked like—she could not imagine now what had become of them. Whatever thoughts and stories my father had were private, and I was shy of him and would never ask him questions. Nevertheless I worked willingly under his eyes, and with a feeling of pride. One time a feed salesman came down into the pens to talk to him and my father said, "Like to have you meet my new hired man." I turned away and raked furiously, red in the face with pleasure.

"Could of fooled me," said the salesman. "I thought it was only a girl."

After the grass was cut, it seemed suddenly much later in the year. I walked on stubble in the earlier evening, aware of the reddening skies, the entering silences,

10

of fall. When I wheeled the tank out of the gate and put the padlock on, it was almost dark. One night at this time I saw my mother and father standing talking on the little rise of ground we called the gangway, in front of the barn. My father had just come from the meathouse; he had his stiff bloody apron on, and a pail of cut-up meat in his hand.

It was an odd thing to see my mother down at the barn. She did not often come out of the house unless it was to do something—hang out the wash or dig potatoes in the garden. She looked out of place, with her bare lumpy legs, not touched by the sun, her apron still on and damp across the stomach from the supper dishes. Her hair was tied up in a kerchief, wisps of it falling out. She would tie her hair up like this in the morning, saying she did not have time to do it properly, and it would stay tied up all day. It was true, too; she really did not have time. These days our back porch was piled with baskets of peaches and grapes and pears, bought in town, and onions and tomatoes and cucumbers grown at home, all waiting to be made into jelly and jam and preserves, pickles and chili sauce. In the kitchen there was a fire in the stove all day, jars clinked in boiling water, sometimes a cheesecloth bag was strung on a pole between two chairs straining blue-black grape pulp for jelly. I was given jobs to do and I would sit at the table peeling peaches that had been soaked in the hot water, or cutting up onions, my eyes smarting and streaming. As soon as I was done I ran out of the house, trying to get out of earshot before my mother thought of what she wanted me to do next. I hated the hot dark kitchen in summer, the green blinds and the flypapers, the same old oilcloth table and wavy mirror and bumpy linoleum. My mother was too tired and preoccupied to talk to me, she had no heart to tell about the Normal School Graduation Dance; sweat trickled over her face and she was always counting under her breath, pointing at jars, dumping cups of sugar. It seemed to me that work in the house was endless, dreary and peculiarly depressing; work done out of doors, and in my father's service, was ritualistically important.

I wheeled the tank up to the barn, where it was kept, and I heard my mother saying, "Wait till Laird gets a little bigger, then you'll have a real help."

What my father said I did not hear. I was pleased by the way he stood listening, politely as he would to a salesman or a stranger, but with an air of wanting to get on with his real work. I felt my mother had no business down here and I wanted him to feel the same way. What did she mean about Laird? He was no help to anybody. Where was he now? Swinging himself sick on the swing, going around in circles, or trying to catch caterpillars. He never once stayed with me till I was finished.

"And then I can use her more in the house," I heard my mother say. She had a dead-quiet, regretful way of talking about me that always made me uneasy. "I just get my back turned and she runs off. It's not like I had a girl in the family at all."

I went and sat on a feed bag in the corner of the barn, not wanting to appear when this conversation was going on. My mother, I felt, was not to be trusted. She was kinder than my father and more easily fooled, but you could not depend on her, and the real reasons for the things she said and did were not to be known. She loved me, and she sat up late at night making a dress of the difficult style I wanted, for me to wear when school started, but she was also my enemy. She was always plotting. She was plotting now to get me to stay in the house more, although she knew I hated it (*because* she knew I hated it) and keep me from working for my father. It seemed to me she would do this simply out of perversity, and to try her power. It did not occur to me that she could be lonely, or jealous. No grown-up could be; they were too fortunate. I sat and kicked my heels monotonously against a feed bag, raising dust, and did not come out till she was gone.

15

At any rate, I did not expect my father to pay any attention to what she said. Who could imagine Laird doing my work—Laird remembering the padlock and cleaning out the watering dishes with a leaf on the end of a stick, or even wheeling the tank without it tumbling over? It showed how little my mother knew about the way things really were.

I have forgotten to say what the foxes were fed. My father's bloody apron reminded me. They were fed horsemeat. At this time most farmers still kept horses, and when a horse got too old to work, or broke a leg or got down and would not get up, as they sometimes did, the owner would call my father, and he and Henry went out to the farm in the truck. Usually they shot and butchered the horse there, paying the farmer from five to twelve dollars. If they had already too much meat on hand, they would bring the horse back alive, and keep it for a few days or weeks in our stable, until the meat was needed. After the war the farmers were buying tractors and gradually getting rid of horses altogether, so it sometimes happened that we got a good healthy horse, that there was just no use for any more. If this happened in the winter we might keep the horse in our stable till spring, for we had plenty of hay and if there was a lot of snow— and the plow did not always get our road cleared—it was convenient to be able to go to town with a horse and cutter.

The winter I was eleven years old we had two horses in the stable. We did not know what names they had had before, so we called them Mack and Flora. Mack was an old black workhorse, sooty and indifferent. Flora was a sorrel mare, a driver. We took them both out in the cutter. Mack was slow and easy to handle. Flora was given to fits of violent alarm, veering at cars and even at other horses, but we loved her speed and high-stepping, her general air of gallantry and abandon. On Saturdays we went down to the stable and as soon as we opened the door on its cosy, animal-smelling darkness Flora threw up her head, rolled her eyes, whinnied despairingly and pulled herself through a crisis of nerves on the spot. It was not safe to go into her stall; she would kick.

This winter also I began to hear a great deal more on the theme my mother had sounded when she had been talking in front of the barn. I no longer felt safe. It seemed that in the minds of the people around me there was a steady undercurrent of thought, not to be deflected, on this one subject. The word *girl* had formerly seemed to be innocent and unburdened, like the word *child;* now it appeared that it was no such thing. A girl was not, as I had supposed, simply what I was; it was what I had to become. It was a definition, always touched with emphasis, with reproach and disappointment. Also it was a joke on me. Once Laird and I were fighting, and for the first time ever I had to use all my strength against him; even so, he caught and pinned my arm for a moment, really hurting me. Henry saw this, and laughed, saying, "Oh, that there Laird's gonna show you, one of these days!" Laird was getting a lot bigger. But I was getting bigger too.

My grandmother came to stay with us for a few weeks and I heard other things. "Girls don't slam doors like that." "Girls keep their knees together when they sit down." And worse still, when I asked some questions, "That's none of girls' business." I continued to slam the doors and sit as awkwardly as possible, thinking that by such measures I kept myself free.

When spring came, the horses were let out in the barnyard. Mack stood against the barn wall trying to scratch his neck and haunches, but Flora trotted up and down and reared at the fences, clattering her hooves against the rails. Snow drifts dwindled quickly, revealing the hard gray and brown earth, the familiar rise and fall of the ground, plain and bare after the fantastic landscape of winter. There was a great feeling of open-

20

ing-out, of release. We just wore rubbers now, over our shoes; our feet felt ridiculously light. One Saturday we went out to the stable and found all the doors open, letting in the unaccustomed sunlight and fresh air. Henry was there, just idling around looking at his collection of calendars which were tacked up behind the stalls in a part of the stable my mother had probably never seen.

"Come to say goodbye to your old friend Mack?" Henry said. "Here, you give him a taste of oats." He poured some oats into Laird's cupped hands and Laird went to feed Mack. Mack's teeth were in bad shape. He ate very slowly, patiently shifting the oats around in his mouth, trying to find a stump of a molar to grind it on. "Poor old Mack," said Henry mournfully. "When a horse's teeth's gone, he's gone. That's about the way."

"Are you going to shoot him today?" I said. Mack and Flora had been in the stable   25
so long I had almost forgotten they were going to be shot.

Henry didn't answer me. Instead he started to sing in a high, trembly, mocking-sorrowful voice, *Oh, there's no more work, for poor Uncle Ned, he's gone where the good darkies go.* Mack's thick, blackish tongue worked diligently at Laird's hand. I went out before the song was ended and sat down on the gangway.

I had never seen them shoot a horse, but I knew where it was done. Last summer Laird and I had come upon a horse's entrails before they were buried. We had thought it was a big black snake, coiled up in the sun. That was around in the field that ran up beside the barn. I thought that if we went inside the barn, and found a wide crack or a knothole to look through, we would be able to see them do it. It was not something I wanted to see; just the same, if a thing really happened, it was better to see it, and know.

My father came down from the house, carrying the gun.

"What are you doing here?" he said.

"Nothing."   30

"Go on up and play around the house."

He sent Laird out of the stable. I said to Laird, "Do you want to see them shoot Mack?" and without waiting for an answer led him around to the front door of the barn, opened it carefully, and went in. "Be quiet or they'll hear us," I said. We could hear Henry and my father talking in the stable, then the heavy, shuffling steps of Mack being backed out of his stall.

In the loft it was cold and dark. Thin, crisscrossed beams of sunlight fell through the cracks. The hay was low. It was a rolling country, hills and hollows, slipping under our feet. About four feet up was a beam going around the walls. We piled hay up in one corner and I boosted Laird up and hoisted myself. The beam was not very wide; we crept along it with our hands flat on the barn walls. There were plenty of knotholes, and I found one that gave me the view I wanted—a corner of the barnyard, the gate, part of the field. Laird did not have a knothole and began to complain.

I showed him a widened crack between two boards. "Be quiet and wait. If they hear you you'll get us in trouble."

My father came in sight carrying the gun. Henry was leading Mack by the halter.   35
He dropped it and took out his cigarette papers and tobacco; he rolled cigarettes for my father and himself. While this was going on Mack nosed around in the old, dead grass along the fence. Then my father opened the gate and they took Mack through. Henry led Mack way from the path to a patch of ground and they talked together, not loud enough for us to hear. Mack again began searching for a mouthful of fresh grass, which was not to be found. My father walked away in a straight line, and stopped short at a distance which seemed to suit him. Henry was walking away from Mack too, but

sideways, still negligently holding on to the halter. My father raised the gun and Mack looked up as if he had noticed something and my father shot him.

Mack did not collapse at once but swayed, lurched sideways and fell, first on his side; then he rolled over on his back and, amazingly, kicked his legs for a few seconds in the air. At this Henry laughed, as if Mack had done a trick for him. Laird, who had drawn a long, groaning breath of surprise when the shot was fired, said out loud, "He's not dead." And it seemed to me it might be true. But his legs stopped, he rolled on his side again, his muscles quivered and sank. The two men walked over and looked at him in a business-like way; they bent down and examined his forehead where the bullet had gone in, and now I saw his blood on the brown grass.

"Now they just skin him and cut him up," I said. "Let's go." My legs were a little shaky and I jumped gratefully down into the hay. "Now you've seen how they shoot a horse," I said in a congratulatory way, as if I had seen it many times before. "Let's see if any barn cat's had kittens in the hay." Laird jumped. He seemed young and obedient again. Suddenly I remembered how, when he was little, I had brought him into the barn and told him to climb the ladder to the top beam. That was in the spring, too, when the hay was low. I had done it out of a need for excitement, a desire for something to happen so that I could tell about it. He was wearing a little bulky brown and white checked coat, made down from one of mine. He went all the way up just as I told him, and sat down on the top beam with the hay far below him on one side, and the barn floor and some old machinery on the other. Then I ran screaming to my father, "Laird's up on the top beam!" My father came, my mother came, my father went up the ladder talking very quietly and brought Laird down under his arm, at which my mother leaned against the ladder and began to cry. They said to me, "Why weren't you watching him?" but nobody ever knew the truth. Laird did not know enough to tell. But whenever I saw the brown and white checked coat hanging in the closet, or at the bottom of the rag bag, which was where it ended up, I felt a weight in my stomach, the sadness of unexorcised guilt.

I looked at Laird, who did not even remember this, and I did not like the look on this thin, winter-pale face. His expression was not frightened or upset, but remote, concentrating. "Listen," I said, in an unusually bright and friendly voice, "you aren't going to tell, are you?"

"No," he said absently.

"Promise." 40

"Promise," he said. I grabbed the hand behind his back to make sure he was not crossing his fingers. Even so, he might have a nightmare; it might come out that way. I decided I had better work hard to get all thoughts of what he had seen out of his mind—which, it seemed to me, could not hold very many things at a time. I got some money I had saved and that afternoon we went into Jubilee and saw a show, with Judy Canova, at which we both laughed a great deal. After that I thought it would be all right.

Two weeks later I knew they were going to shoot Flora. I knew from the night before, when I heard my mother ask if the hay was holding out all right, and my father said, "Well, after tomorrow there'll just be the cow, and we should be able to put her out to grass in another week." So I knew it was Flora's turn in the morning.

This time I didn't think of watching it. That was something to see just one time. I had not thought about it very often since, but sometimes when I was busy, working at school, or standing in front of the mirror combing my hair and wondering if I would be pretty when I grew up, the whole scene would flash into my mind: I would see the easy, practiced way my father raised the gun, and hear Henry laughing when Mack kicked his legs in the air. I did not have any great feeling of horror and opposition, such as a city child might have had; I was too used to seeing the death of animals as a necessity by which we lived. Yet I felt a little ashamed, and there was a new wariness, a sense of holding-off, in my attitude to my father and his work.

It was a fine day, and we were going around the yard picking up tree branches that had been torn off in winter storms. This was something we had been told to do, and also we wanted to use them to make a teepee. We heard Flora whinny, and then my father's voice and Henry's shouting, and we ran down to the barnyard to see what was going on.

The stable door was open. Henry had just brought Flora out, and she had broken away from him. She was running free in the barnyard, from one end to the other. We climbed up on the fence. It was exciting to see her running, whinnying, going up on her hind legs, prancing and threatening like a horse in a Western movie, and unbroken ranch horse, though she was just an old driver, an old sorrel mare. My father and Henry ran after her and tried to grab the dangling halter. They tried to work her into a corner, and they had almost succeeded when she made a run between them, wild-eyed, and disappeared around the corner of the barn. We heard the rails clatter down as she got over the fence, and Henry yelled, "She's into the field now!"

That meant she was in the long L-shaped field that ran up by the house. If she got around the center, heading towards the lane, the gate was open; the truck had been driven into the field this morning. My father shouted to me, because I was on the other side of the fence, nearest the lane, "Go shut the gate!"

I could run very fast. I ran across the garden, past the tree where our swing was hung, and jumped across a ditch into the lane. There was the open gate. She had not got out, I could not see her up on the road; she must have run to the other end of the field. The gate was heavy. I lifted it out of the gravel and carried it across the roadway. I had it halfway across when she came in sight, galloping straight toward me. There was just time to get the chain on. Laird came scrambling through the ditch to help me.

Instead of shutting the gate, I opened it as wide as I could. I did not make any decision to do this, it was just what I did. Flora never slowed down; she galloped straight past me, and Laird jumped up and down, yelling, "Shut it, shut it!" even after it was too late. My father and Henry appeared in the field a moment too late to see what I had done. They only saw Flora heading for the township road. They would think I had not got there in time.

They did not waste any time asking about it. They went back to the barn and got the gun and the knives they used, and put these in the truck; then they turned the truck around and came bouncing up the field toward us. Laird called to them, "Let me go too, let me go too!" and Henry stopped the truck and they took him in. I shut the gate after they were all gone.

I supposed Laird would tell. I wondered what would happen to me. I had never disobeyed my father before, and I could not understand why I had done it. Flora would not really get away. They would catch up with her in the truck. Or if they did not catch her this morning somebody would see her and telephone us this afternoon or tomorrow. There was no wild country here for her to run to, only farms. What was more, my father had paid for her, we needed the meat to feed the foxes, we needed the foxes to make our living. All I had done was make more work for my father who worked hard enough already. And when my father found out about it he was not going to trust me any more; he would know that I was not entirely on his side. I was on Flora's side, and that made me no use to anybody, not even to her. Just the same, I did not regret it; when she came running at me and I held the gate open, that was the only thing I could do.

I went back to the house, and my mother said, "What's all the commotion?" I told her that Flora had kicked down the fence and got away. "Your poor father," she said, "now he'll have to go chasing over the countryside. Well, there isn't any use planning dinner before one." She put up the ironing board. I wanted to tell her, but thought better of it and went upstairs and sat on my bed.

Lately I had been trying to make my part of the room fancy, spreading the bed with old lace curtains, and fixing myself a dressing table with some leftovers of cretonne for a skirt. I planned to put up some kind of barricade between my bed and Laird's, to keep my section separate from his. In the sunlight, the lace curtains were just dusty rags. We did not sing at night any more. One night when I was singing Laird said, "You sound silly," and I went right on but the next night I did not start. There was not so much need to anyway, we were no longer afraid. We knew it was just old furniture over there, old jumble and confusion. We did not keep to the rules. I still stayed awake after Laird was asleep and told myself stories, but even in these stories something different was happening, mysterious alterations took place. A story might start off in the old way, with a spectacular danger, a fire or wild animals, and for a while I might rescue people; then things would change around, and instead, somebody would be rescuing me. It might be a boy from our class at school, or even Mr. Campbell, our teacher, who tickled girls under the arms. And at this point the story concerned itself at great length with what I looked like—how long my hair was, and what kind of dress I had on; by the time I had these details worked out the real excitement of the story was lost.

It was later than one o'clock when the truck came back. The tarpaulin was over the back, which meant there was meat in it. My mother had to heat dinner up all over again. Henry and my father had changed from their bloody overalls into ordinary working overalls in the barn, and they washed their arms and necks and faces at the sink, and splashed water on their hair and combed it. Laird lifted his arm to show off a streak of blood. "We shot old Flora," he said, "and cut her up in fifty pieces."

"Well I don't want to hear about it," my mother said. "And don't come to my table like that."

My father made him go and wash the blood off.   55

We sat down and my father said grace and Henry pasted his chewing gum on the end of his fork, the way he always did; when he took it off he would have us admire the pattern. We began to pass the bowls of steaming, overcooked vegetables. Laird looked across the table at me and said proudly, distinctly, "Anyway it was her fault Flora got away."

"What?" my father said.

"She could of shut the gate and she didn't. She just open' it up and Flora run out."

"Is that right?" my father said.

Everybody at the table was looking at me. I nodded, swallowing food with great   60
difficulty. To my shame, tears flooded my eyes.

My father made a curt sound of disgust. "What did you do that for?"

I did not answer. I put down my fork and waited to be sent from the table, still not looking up.

But this did not happen. For some time nobody said anything, then Laird said matter-of-factly, "She's crying."

"Never mind," my father said. He spoke with resignation, even good humor, the words which absolved and dismissed me for good. "She's only a girl," he said.

I didn't protest that, even in my heart. Maybe it was true.

THE RECEPTIVE READER

1. What about the physical *setting* of this story is most real? What striking images or imaginative comparisons help bring the setting to life? How would you expect the physical world of the story to influence a person's character? How do you think watching the work with the foxes and horses would affect a person's outlook?

2. Like many adolescents, the girl in this story faces a *conflict* between different models that she might choose to follow. What kind of role model is her father? How would you describe his kind of person or temperament? How does she feel about his work? What scenes or incidents do most to illuminate her relationship with her father?

3. What kind of role model is the mother? What is the girl's relationship with the mother and what she stands for? What makes the father and the mother in this story *polar opposites*? What details for you most strikingly bring the opposition between the father's and the mother's influence into focus?

4. The setting in which people grow up often set limits to what they can be or become. What are these limits in this story? How do we become aware of them? Can you point to a key phrase or to a *thematic passage*—spelling out a key idea acted out in the story as a whole?

5. The story reaches its *climax*, or high point, when Flora, the horse about to be shot, gets away. Why does the girl relate to Flora differently than she did to Mack, the other horse in the story? What is the girl's role in the climactic episode? Why does she do what she does? How does her behavior here change the way she thinks of her father and of herself?

6. What is the role of the *minor characters* in this story? What are the roles of Henry and of the grandmother? In this story of growing up, how does the role of Laird, the girl's younger brother, change? What facets of the girl's character are shown in her relationship with her brother?

7. If you read this story as a story of *initiation*, of passing from one stage to another, how would you sum up the girl's starting point and the stage she reaches at the end of the story?

THE PERSONAL RESPONSE

Do you think of the girl as defeated by the end of the story? What do you think are her prospects for the future? What facets of her character would you consider in making a prediction?

THE CREATIVE DIMENSION

Write a *monologue* (one person talking without interruption by others) in which you imagine yourself in the place of one of the characters in the story. From that person's point of view, look at one of the *other* characters in the story. For instance, look at
  ✧ the younger brother as seen through the eyes of the girl (or vice versa);
  ✧ the father as seen through the eyes of the girl;
  ✧ the girl as seen through the eyes of her mother;
  ✧ the mother as seen through the eyes of her daughter.

CROSS-REFERENCES—For Discussion or Writing

Compare and contrast Joyce's "Araby" and Munro's "Boys and Girls" as stories of initiation, or growing up.

ANN BEATTIE   (born 1947)

I don't think my characters are what they are because of interesting psychological complexities. They're not clinical studies to me. . . . I just seem to react to what is right in front of me. So that's usually the way I write.

ANN BEATTIE

Ann Beattie is often heard as a voice of the post-Vietnam generation. Her characters are often people who grew up with the love-ins and teach-ins and antiwar demonstrations of the sixties, who experienced the euphoria of the rock festivals and of the counterculture. As the passions and euphoria of the hippie era faded, many of her generation were left with a vague sense of betrayal; no energy seemed to remain for great enthusiasms or commitments. She often writes about no-longer-young urban malcontents who feel they have compromised their youthful ideals but who have no sense of where to go from here. As Beattie said about her novel *Chilly Scenes of Winter* (1976), she writes about people who feel let down—either "by not having involved themselves more" or by "having involved themselves to no avail."

Beattie, like other currently fashionable authors, writes in a **minimalist** mode, staying close to the boring surface of everyday life, avoiding flights of imagination or bursts of emotion. Some critics have faulted her for failing to live up to more conventional expectations: She seems to have an obsession with petty, disjointed detail—the lyrics of popular songs, recipes for junky food, reading matter like the *National Enquirer*. Her characters do not seem to have "an emotional core" or vital center; they do not seem to have "meaningful connections" with others; they do not seem to develop or grow. Her stories do not seem to work toward a resolution or conclusion. However, her admirers see in what she calls her "flat simple sentences" an "uncanny fidelity" to the ordinary and familiar (John Updike), a concern for "the integrity of things and people in themselves" (John Romano).

Of the two presidential candidates alluded to in the following story, Nixon talked about peace with honor and McGovern talked about peace, period.

Shifting   1979

The woman's name was Natalie, and the man's name was Larry. They had been childhood sweethearts; he had first kissed her at an ice-skating party when they were ten. She had been unlacing her skates and had not expected the kiss. He had not expected to do it, either—he had some notion of getting his face out of the wind that was blowing across the iced-over lake, and he found himself ducking his head toward her. Kissing her seemed the natural thing to do. When they graduated from high school he was named "class clown" in the yearbook, but Natalie didn't think of him as being particularly funny. He spent more time than she thought he needed to studying chemistry, and he never laughed when she joked. She really did not think of him as funny. They went to the same college, in their hometown, but he left after a year to go to a larger, more impressive university. She took the train to be with him on weekends, or he took the train to see her. When he graduated, his parents gave him a car. If they had given it to him when he was still in college, it would have made things much easier. They waited to give it to him until graduation day, forcing him into attending the graduation exercises. He thought his parents were wonderful people, and Natalie liked them in a way, too, but she resented their perfect timing, their careful smiles. They were afraid that he would marry her. Eventually, he did. He had gone on to graduate school after college, and he set a date six months ahead for their wedding so that it would take place after his first-semester final exams. That way he could devote his time to studying for the chemistry exams.

When she married him he had had the car for eight months. It still smelled like a brand-new car. There was never any clutter in the car. Even the ice scraper was kept in the glove compartment. There was not even a sweater or a lost glove in the back seat. He vacuumed the car every weekend, after washing it at the car wash. On Friday nights, on their way to some cheap restaurant and a dollar movie, he would stop at the car wash, and she would get out so he could vacuum all over the inside of the car. She would lean against the metal wall of the car wash and watch him clean it.

It was expected that she would not become pregnant. She did not. It had also been expected that she would keep their apartment clean, and keep out of the way as much as possible in such close quarters while he was studying. The apartment was messy, though, and when he was studying late at night she would interrupt him and try to talk him into going to sleep. He gave a chemistry-class lecture once a week, and she would often tell him that overpreparing was as bad as underpreparing. She did not know if she believed this, but it was a favorite line of hers. Sometimes he listened to her.

On Tuesdays, when he gave the lecture, she would drop him off at school and then drive to a supermarket to do the week's shopping. Usually she did not make a list before she went shopping, but when she got to the parking lot she would take a tablet out of her purse and write a few items on it, sitting in the car in the cold. Even having a few things written down would stop her from wandering aimlessly in the store and buying things that she would never use. Before this, she had bought several pans and cans of food that she had not used, or that she could have done without. She felt better when she had a list.

She would drop him at school again on Wednesdays, when he had two seminars that together took up all the afternoon. Sometimes she would drive out of town then, to the suburbs, and shop there if any shopping needed to be done. Otherwise, she would go to the art museum, which was not far away but hard to get to by bus. There was one piece of sculpture in there that she wanted very much to touch, but the guard was always nearby. She came so often that in time the guard began to nod hello. She wondered if she could ever persuade the man to turn his head for a few seconds—only that long—so she could stroke the sculpture. Of course she would never dare ask. After wandering through the museum and looking at least twice at the sculpture, she would go to the gift shop and buy a few postcards and then sit on one of the museum benches, padded with black vinyl, with a Calder mobile hanging overhead, and write notes to friends. (She never wrote letters.) She would tuck the postcards in her purse and mail them when she left the museum. But before she left, she often had coffee in the restaurant: she saw mothers and children struggling there, and women dressed in fancy clothes talking with their faces close together, as quietly as lovers.

On Thursdays he took the car. After his class he would drive to visit his parents and his friend Andy, who had been wounded in Vietnam. About once a month she would go with him, but she had to feel up to it. Being with Andy embarrassed her. She

5

had told him not to go to Vietnam—told him that he could prove his patriotism in some other way—and finally, after she and Larry had made a visit together and she had seen Andy in the motorized bed in his parents' house, Larry had agreed that she need not go again. Andy had apologized to her. It embarrassed her that this man, who had been blown sky-high by a land mine and had lost a leg and lost the full use of his arms, would smile up at her ironically and say, "You were right." She also felt as though he wanted to hear what she would say now, and that now he would listen. Now she had nothing to say. Andy would pull himself up, relying on his right arm, which was the stronger, gripping the rails at the side of the bed, and sometimes he would take her hand. His arms were still weak, but the doctors said he would regain complete use of his right arm with time. She had to make an effort not to squeeze his hand when he held hers because she found herself wanting to squeeze energy back into him. She had a morbid curiosity about what it felt like to be blown from the ground—and go up, and to come crashing down. During their visit Larry put on the class-clown act for Andy, telling funny stories and laughing uproariously.

Once or twice Larry had talked Andy into getting in his wheelchair and had loaded him into the car and taken him to a bar. Larry called her once, late, pretty drunk, to say that he would not be home that night—that he would sleep at his parents' house. "My God," she said. "Are you going to drive Andy home when you're drunk?" "What the hell else can happen to him?" he said.

Larry's parents blamed her for Larry's not being happy. His mother could only be pleasant with her for a short while, and then she would veil her criticisms by putting them as questions. "I know that one thing that helps enormously is good nutrition," his mother said. "He works so hard that he probably needs quite a few vitamins as well, don't you think?" Larry's father was the sort of man who found hobbies in order to avoid his wife. His hobbies were building model boats, repairing clocks, and photography. He took pictures of himself building the boats and fixing the clocks, and gave the pictures, in cardboard frames, to Natalie and Larry for Christmas and birthday presents. Larry's mother was very anxious to stay on close terms with her son, and she knew that Natalie did not like her very much. Once she had visited them during the week, and Natalie, not knowing what to do with her, had taken her to the museum. She had pointed out the sculpture, and his mother had glanced at it and then ignored it. Natalie hated her for her bad taste. She had bad taste in the sweaters she gave Larry, too, but he wore them. They made him look collegiate. That whole world made her sick.

When Natalie's uncle died and left her his 1965 Volvo, they immediately decided to sell it and use the money for a vacation. They put an ad in the paper, and there were several callers. There were some calls on Tuesday, when Larry was in class, and Natalie found herself putting the people off. She told one woman that the car had too much mileage on it, and mentioned body rust, which it did not have; she told another caller, who was very persistent, that the car was already sold. When Larry returned from school she explained that the phone was off the hook because so many people were calling about the car and she had decided not to sell it after all. They could take a little money from their savings account and go on the trip if he wanted. But she did not want to sell the car. "It's not an automatic shift," he said. "You don't know how to drive it." She told him that she could learn. "It will cost money to insure it," he said, "and it's old and probably not even dependable." She wanted to keep the car. "I know," he said, "but it doesn't make sense. When we have more money, you can have a car. You can have a newer, better car."

The next day she went out to the car, which was parked in the driveway of an old lady next door. Her name was Mrs. Larsen and she no longer drove a car, and she told 10

Natalie she could park their second car there. Natalie opened the car door and got behind the wheel and put her hands on it. The wheel was covered with a flaky yellow-and-
black plastic cover. She eased it off. A few pieces of foam rubber stuck to the wheel. She
picked them off. Underneath the cover, the wheel was a dull red. She ran her fingers
around and around the circle of the wheel. Her cousin Burt had delivered the car—a
young opportunist, sixteen years old, who said he would drive it the hundred miles
from his house to theirs for twenty dollars and a bus ticket home. She had not even invited him to stay for dinner, and Larry had driven him to the bus station. She wondered
if it was Burt's cigarette in the ashtray or her dead uncle's. She could not even remember if her uncle smoked. She was surprised that he had left her his car. The car was
much more comfortable than Larry's, and it had a nice smell inside. It smelled a little
the way a field smells after a spring rain. She rubbed the side of her head back and forth
against the window and then got out of the car and went in to see Mrs. Larsen. The
night before, she had suddenly thought of the boy who brought the old lady the
evening newspaper every night; he looked old enough to drive, and he would probably
know how to shift. Mrs. Larsen agreed with her—she was sure that he could teach her.
"Of course, everything has its price," the old lady said.

"I know that. I meant to offer him money," Natalie said, and was surprised, listening to her voice, that she sounded old too.

She took an inventory and made a list of things in their apartment. Larry had met
an insurance man one evening while playing basketball at the gym who told him that
they should have a list of their possessions, in case of theft. "What's worth anything?"
she said when he told her. It was their first argument in almost a year—the first time in
a year, anyway, that their voices were raised. He told her that several of the pieces of
furniture his grandparents gave them when they got married were antiques, and the
man at the gym said that if they weren't going to get them appraised every year, at least
they should take snapshots of them and keep the pictures in a safe-deposit box. Larry
told her to photograph the pie safe (which she used to store linen), the piano with an
inlaid mother-of-pearl decoration on the music rack (neither of them knew how to
play), and the table with hand-carved wooden handles and a marble top. He bought
her an Instamatic camera at the drugstore, with film and flash bulbs. "Why can't you do
it?" she said, and an argument began. He said that she had no respect for his profession
and no understanding of the amount of study that went into getting a master's degree
in chemistry.

That night he went out to meet two friends at the gym, to shoot baskets. She put
the little flashcube into the top of the camera, dropped in the film and closed the back.
She went first to the piano. She leaned forward so that she was close enough to see the
inlay clearly, but she found that when she was that close the whole piano wouldn't fit
into the picture. She decided to take two pictures. Then she photographed the pie safe,
with one door open, showing the towels and sheets stacked inside. She did not have a
reason for opening the door, except that she remembered a *Perry Mason* show in which
detectives photographed everything with the doors hanging open. She photographed
the table, lifting the lamp off it first. There were still eight pictures left. She went to the
mirror in their bedroom and held the camera above her head, pointing down at an
angle, and photographed her image in the mirror. She took off her slacks and sat on the
floor and leaned back, aiming the camera down at her legs. Then she stood up and
took a picture of her feet, leaning over and aiming down. She put on her favorite
record: Stevie Wonder singing "For Once in My Life." She found herself wondering
what it would be like to be blind, to have to feel things to see them. She thought about

the piece of sculpture in the museum—the two elongated mounds, intertwined, the smooth gray stone as shiny as sea pebbles. She photographed the kitchen, bathroom, bedroom and living room. There was one picture left. She put her left hand on her thigh, palm up, and with some difficulty—with the camera nestled into her neck like a violin—snapped a picture of it with her right hand. The next day would be her first driving lesson.

He came to her door at noon, as he had said he would. He had on a long maroon scarf, which made his deep-blue eyes very striking. She had only seen him from her window when he carried the paper in to the old lady. He was a little nervous. She hoped that it was just the anxiety of any teen-ager confronting an adult. She needed to have him like her. She did not learn about mechanical things easily (Larry had told her that he would have invested in a "real" camera, except that he did not have the time to teach her about it), so she wanted him to be patient. He sat on the footstool in her living room, still in coat and scarf, and told her how a stick shift operated. He moved his hand through the air. The motion he made reminded her of the salute spacemen gave to earthlings in a science-fiction picture she had recently watched on late-night television. She nodded. "How much—" she began, but he interrupted and said, "You can decide what it was worth when you've learned." She was surprised and wondered if he meant to charge a great deal. Would it be her fault and would she have to pay him if he named his price when the lessons were over? But he had an honest face. Perhaps he was just embarrassed to talk about money.

He drove for a few blocks, making her watch his hand on the stick shift. "Feel how the car is going?" he said. "Now you shift." He shifted. The car jumped a little, hummed, moved into gear. It was an old car and didn't shift too easily, he said. She had been sitting forward, so that when he shifted she rocked back hard against the seat—harder than she needed to. Almost unconsciously, she wanted to show him what a good teacher he was. When her turn came to drive, the car stalled. "Take it easy," he said. "Ease up on the clutch. Don't just raise your foot off of it like that." She tried it again. "That's it," he said. She looked at him when the car was in third. He sat in the seat, looking out the window. Snow was expected. It was Thursday. Although Larry was going to visit his parents and would not be back until late Friday afternoon, she decided she would wait until Tuesday for her next lesson. If he came home early, he would find out that she was taking lessons, and she didn't want him to know. She asked the boy, whose name was Michael, whether he thought she would forget all he had taught her in the time between lessons. "You'll remember," he said. 15

When they returned to the old lady's driveway, the car stalled going up the incline. She had trouble shifting. The boy put his hand over hers and kicked the heel of his hand forward. "You'll have to treat this car a little roughly, I'm afraid," he said. That afternoon, after he left, she made spaghetti sauce, chopping little pieces of pepper and onion and mushroom. When the sauce had cooked down, she called Mrs. Larsen and said that she would bring over dinner. She usually ate with the old lady once a week. The old lady often added a pinch of cinnamon to her food, saying that it brought out the flavor better than salt, and that since she was losing her sense of smell, food had to be strongly flavored for her to taste it. Once she had sprinkled cinnamon on a knockwurst. This time, as they ate, Natalie asked the old lady how much she paid the boy to bring the paper.

"I give him a dollar a week," the old lady said.

"Did he set the price, or did you?"

"He set the price. He told me he wouldn't take much because he has to walk this street to get to his apartment anyway."

"He taught me a lot about the car today," Natalie said.   20
"He's very handsome, isn't he?" the old lady said.

She asked Larry, "How were your parents?"
"Fine," he said. "But I spent almost all the time with Andy. It's almost his birthday, and he's depressed. We went to see Mose Allison."
"I think it stinks that hardly anyone else ever visits Andy," she said.
"He doesn't make it easy. He tells you everything that's on his mind, and there's   25
no way you can pretend that his troubles don't amount to much. You just have to sit
there and nod."
She remembered that Andy's room looked like a gymnasium. There were hand-
grips and weights scattered on the floor. There was even a psychedelic pink hula hoop
that he was to put inside his elbow and then move his arm in circles wide enough to
make the hoop spin. He couldn't do it. He would lie in bed with the hoop in back of
his neck, and holding the sides, lift his neck off the pillow. His arms were barely strong
enough to do that, really, but he could raise his neck with no trouble, so he just pretended that his arms pulling the loop were raising it. His parents thought that it was a
special exercise that he had mastered.
"What did you do today?" Larry said now.
"I made spaghetti," she said. She had made it the day before, but she thought that
since he was mysterious about the time he spent away from her ("in the lab" and "at
the gym" became interchangeable), she did not owe him a straight answer. That day
she had dropped off the film and then she had sat at the drugstore counter to have a
cup of coffee. She bought some cigarettes, though she had not smoked since high
school. She smoked one mentholated cigarette and then threw the pack away in a
garbage container outside the drugstore. Her mouth still felt cool inside.
He asked if she had planned anything for the weekend.
"No," she said.   30
"Let's do something you'd like to do. I'm a little ahead of myself in the lab right
now."
That night they ate spaghetti and made plans, and the next day they went for a
ride in the country, to a factory where wooden toys were made. In the showroom he
made a bear marionette shake and twist. She examined a small rocking horse, rhythmi-
cally pushing her finger up and down on the back rung of the rocker to make it rock.
When they left they took with them a catalogue of toys they could order. She knew that
they would never look at the catalogue again. On their way to the museum he stopped
to wash the car. Because it was the weekend there were quite a few cars lined up waiting to go in. They were behind a blue Cadillac that seemed to inch forward of its own
accord, without a driver. When the Cadillac moved into the washing area, a tiny man
hopped out. He stood on tiptoe to reach the coin box to start the washing machine.
She doubted if he was five feet tall.
"Look at that poor son of a bitch," he said.
The little man was washing his car.
"If Andy could get out more," Larry said. "If he could get rid of that feeling he   35
has that he's the only freak . . . I wonder if it wouldn't do him good to come spend a
week with us."
"Are you going to take him in the wheelchair to the lab with you?" she said. "I'm
not taking care of Andy all day."
His face changed. "Just for a week was all I meant," he said.
"I'm not doing it," she said. She was thinking of the boy, and of the car. She had
almost learned how to drive the car.

"Maybe in the warm weather," she said. "When we could go to the park or something."

He said nothing. The little man was rinsing his car. She sat inside when their turn came. She thought that Larry had no right to ask her to take care of Andy. Water flew out of the hose and battered the car. She thought of Andy, in the woods at night, stepping on the land mine, being blown into the air. She wondered if it threw him in an arc, so he ended up somewhere away from where he had been walking, or if it just blasted him straight up, if he went up the way an umbrella opens. Andy had been a wonderful ice skater. They all envied him his long sweeping turns, with his legs somehow neatly together and his body at the perfect angle. She never saw him have an accident on the ice. Never once. She had known Andy, and they had skated at Parker's pond, for eight years before he was drafted.

The night before, as she and Larry were finishing dinner, he had asked her if she intended to vote for Nixon or McGovern in the election. "McGovern," she said. How could he not have known that? She knew then that they were farther apart than she had thought. She hoped that on Election Day she could drive herself to the polls—not go with him and not walk. She planned not to ask the old lady if she wanted to come along because that would be one vote she could keep Nixon from getting.

At the museum she hesitated by the sculpture but did not point it out to him. He didn't look at it. He gazed to the side, above it, at a Francis Bacon painting. He could have shifted his eyes just a little and seen the sculpture, and her, standing and staring.

After three more lessons she could drive the car. The last two times, which were later in the afternoon than her first lesson, they stopped at the drugstore to get the old lady's paper, to save him from having to make the same trip back on foot. When he came out of the drugstore with the paper, after the final lesson, she asked him if he'd like to have a beer to celebrate.

"Sure," he said.

They walked down the street to a bar that was filled with college students. She wondered if Larry ever came to this bar. He had never said that he did.

She and Michael talked. She asked why he wasn't in high school. He told her that he had quit. He was living with his brother, and his brother was teaching him carpentry, which he had been interested in all along. On his napkin he drew a picture of the cabinets and bookshelves he and his brother had spent the last week constructing and installing in the house of two wealthy old sisters. He drummed the side of his thumb against the edge of the table in time with the music. They each drank beer, from heavy glass mugs.

"Mrs. Larsen said your husband was in school," the boy said. "What's he studying?"

She looked up, surprised. Michael had never mentioned her husband before. "Chemistry," she said.

"I liked chemistry pretty well," he said. "Some of it."

"My husband doesn't know you've been giving me lessons. I'm just going to tell him that I can drive the stick shift, and surprise him."

"Yeah?" the boy said. "What will he think about that?"

"I don't know," she said. "I don't think he'll like it."

"Why?" the boy said.

His question made her remember that he was sixteen. What she had said would never have provoked another question from an adult. The adult would have nodded or said, "I know."

She shrugged. The boy took a long drink of beer. "I thought it was funny that he didn't teach you himself, when Mrs. Larsen told me you were married," he said.

They had discussed her. She wondered why Mrs. Larsen wouldn't have told her that, because the night she ate dinner with her she had talked to Mrs. Larsen about whan an extraordinarily patient teacher Michael was. Had Mrs. Larsen told him that Natalie talked about him?

On the way back to the car she remembered the photographs and went back to the drugstore and picked up the prints. As she took money out of her wallet she remembered that today was the day she would have to pay him. She looked around at him, at the front of the store, where he was flipping through magazines. He was tall and he was wearing a very old black jacket. One end of his long thick maroon scarf was hanging down his back.

"What did you take pictures of?" he said when they were back in the car.

"Furniture. My husband wanted pictures of our furniture, in case it was stolen."

"Why?" he said.

"They say if you have proof that you had valuable things, the insurance company won't hassle you about reimbursing you."

"You have a lot of valuable stuff?" he said.

"My husband thinks so," she said.

A block from the driveway she said, "What do I owe you?"

"Four dollars," he said.

"That's nowhere near enough," she said and looked over at him. He had opened the envelope with the pictures in it while she was driving. He was staring at the picture of her legs. "What's this?" he said.

She turned into the driveway and shut off the engine. She looked at the picture. She could not think of what to tell him it was. Her hands and heart felt heavy.

"Wow," the boy said. He laughed. "Never mind. Sorry. I'm not looking at any more of them."

He put the pack of pictures back in the envelope and dropped it on the seat between them.

She tried to think what to say, of some way she could turn the pictures into a joke. She wanted to get out of the car and run. She wanted to stay, not to give him the money, so he would sit there with her. She reached into her purse and took out her wallet and removed four one-dollar bills.

"How many years have you been married?" he asked.

"One," she said. She held the money out to him. He said "Thank you" and leaned across the seat and put his right arm over her shoulder and kissed her. She felt his scarf bunched up against their cheeks. She was amazed at how warm his lips were in the cold car.

He moved his head away and said, "I didn't think you'd mind if I did that." She shook her head no. He unlocked the door and got out.

"I could drive you to your brother's apartment," she said. Her voice sounded hollow. She was extremely embarrassed, but she couldn't let him go.

He got back in the car. "You could drive me and come in for a drink," he said. "My brother's working."

When she got back to the car two hours later she saw a white parking ticket clamped under the windshield wiper, flapping in the wind. When she opened the car door and sank into the seat, she saw that he had left the money, neatly folded, on the floor mat on his side of the car. She did not pick up the money. In a while she started the car. She stalled it twice on the way home. When she had pulled into the driveway she looked at the money for a long time, then left it lying there. She left the car unlocked, hoping the money would be stolen. If it disappeared, she could tell herself that she had paid him. Otherwise she would not know how to deal with the situation.

When she got into the apartment, the phone rang. "I'm at the gym to play basketball," Larry said. "Be home in an hour."

"I was at the drugstore," she said. "See you then."

She examined the pictures. She sat on the sofa and laid them out, the twelve of them, in three rows on the cushion next to her. The picture of the piano was between the picture of her feet and the picture of herself that she had shot by aiming into the mirror. She picked up the four pictures of their furniture and put them on the table. She picked up the others and examined them closely. She began to understand why she had taken them. She had photographed parts of her body, fragments of it, to study the pieces. She had probably done it because she thought so much about Andy's body and the piece that was gone—the leg, below the knee, on his left side. She had had two bourbon-and-waters at the boy's apartment, and drinking always depressed her. She felt very depressed looking at the pictures, so she put them down and went into the bedroom. She undressed. She looked at her body—whole, not a bad figure—in the mirror. It was an automatic reaction with her to close the curtains when she was naked, so she turned quickly and went to the window and did that. She went back to the mirror; the room was darker now and her body looked better. She ran her hands down her sides, wondering if the feel of her skin was anything like the way the sculpture would feel. She was sure that the sculpture would be smoother—her hands would move more quickly down the slopes of it than she wanted—that it would be cool, and that somehow she could feel the grayness of it. Those things seemed preferable to her hands lingering on her body, the imperfection of her skin, the overheated apartment. If she were the piece of sculpture and if she could feel, she would like her sense of isolation.

This was in 1972, in Philadelphia.   80

THE RECEPTIVE READER

1. Beattie is a writer who patiently chronicles the uneventful events of the ordinary day. Which of the thoughts going through the main character's mind seem trivial? Which seem more significant, more likely to help you understand her character?

2. How does her relationship with her husband help define her as a person? What kind of person is he? How does he serve as a *foil?* How does she react to his attitude toward his studies? How does she interact with his parents? How does she relate to his car?

3. The Vietnam War and the disabled war veteran return in this story like a refrain. What is Natalie's involvement with or reaction to both? How has the experience with both helped shape her character?

4. To what in her makeup as a person does the dead uncle's car appeal? What are her dealings with the boy who teaches her to drive it? What side (or sides) of her character does the relationship reveal or bring into play?

THE PERSONAL RESPONSE

As a writer of the minimalist school, Beattie does not go out of her way to burden the reader with explanations, psychological theories, or background. How well do you come to know Natalie? What unanswered questions about the main character remain in your mind? How do you relate to her as a person? (Is it true, as one critic claimed, that Beattie is "unable to make us feel any empathy for most of the characters—perhaps because they are too self-absorbed to feel anything for each other"?)

WRITING ABOUT LITERATURE

3. Tracing Character (Focus on Prewriting)

The Writing Workshop   Our interest in a story often centers on a main character, or on the interaction of two or more main characters, in a story. A paper focused on a central character may show how a key trait, an overriding ambition, or a basic fear or trauma serves as the key unlocking the character's personality. Or a paper may trace the vital contradictions that make a character a complex human being rather than a cardboard cutout with simple predictable motives. Or a paper may trace the growth of a character in flux, still malleable, still subject to formative influences.

In working on this and on other papers, imagine yourself in a writing workshop situation. In a workshop format, no one expects a full-blown paper to materialize overnight. Instead, there is time for preliminaries, for tentative first attempts, for feedback, for revision and fine-tuning. In writing your paper on characterization, your basic task will be the same as in writing papers on other dimensions of fiction. You will need to immerse yourself in the story first—and then push toward general conclusions that you can present and support in a well-developed paper. You will need to take your paper through major (overlapping) stages in the writing process.

In particular, make time for three important **prewriting** activities that should precede your writing of your first draft: note taking, pushing toward a thesis, and structuring your paper.

Running Commentary   The following is part of a running commentary—on the Munro story—prepared by a reader with open eyes and alert ears, who is keeping an open mind about the possible general drift of the story. These reading notes seize on possibly meaningful striking details; they record verbatim quotations that could be useful in helping get a reader into the prevailing mood of the story. These notes already include much material related to the girl narrator's search for identity:

Senses predominate. Penetrating smell of foxes, dead flesh, blood. Beauty of live foxes contrasts with scraping particles of fat and blood from the inside of the dead skin. Naked slippery dead carcasses look "surprisingly small, mean and rat-like." When alive, foxes have faces "drawn exquisitely sharp in pure hostility" and "golden eyes."

Death and blood are taken rather casually by the men. There is something alarming about the coldness of the term "fox farm." There is a hierarchy of value? Horses are killed to feed foxes, who provide furs and money.

Children's unfinished bedroom in the loft is a place of childhood fears. Brother and sister sing "Jingle Bells" and "Danny Boy" to ward off fear of the dark.

Life is seen entirely through the eyes of the young girl telling the story, who is naturally inclined toward "male activities." The work done "in her father's service" was important like a ritual. Her little brother tags timidly along, obeying her.

The narrator is treated like a boy and acts like one, and she is introduced by her father as "my new hired man." The salesman responds that he thought it was "only a girl." The girl wants to possess the characteristic masculine strengths and virtues.

The mother is constantly invoking the female stereotype, implying that when her daughter helps the father with "male" duties, the help is not real. She is eager to get her daughter into the house to help with girl work. ("It's not like I had a girl in the family at all.") The girl "hated the hot dark kitchen in summer"; "work in the house was endless, dreary and peculiarly depressing."

The horses give an interesting twist to the gender issue, because there is a male and a female. The male, Mack, is slow and docile, while the female, Flora, is spirited, temperamental and rebellious . . .

Pushing toward a Thesis   Early in your note taking, the central question is likely to emerge: In the world of Munro's story, what does it mean to be a girl? What does it mean to be a boy? In your paper, you may want to focus on the key issue: Some people easily take to the role society has sketched out for them. They fit the mold. But the girl in this story is an independent, adventurous, imaginative spirit.

In the following paragraph, the student who prepared the reading notes sums up what might become the unifying overall idea of a paper:

> Children search for their identities and constantly run up against the wall of gender stereotypes to which they are made to conform. *The girl in the story reluctantly conforms to the stereotypes that will deny a part of her personality.* In her innocence, the girl in the story identifies with the outdoor work of her father, "red in the face with pleasure" when her father seems to praise and accept her as a co-worker. Her daydreams are about heroic rescues in which she plays the hero's part. However, her mother and grandmother conspire to drive home what is expected of a girl. It seems that after a last act of futile rebellion the invisible walls of the predestined gender roles will close in on her.

Structuring the Paper   How will your paper be laid out? Since this is a story of initiation, your paper as a whole might follow the pattern of a spiritual journey. In addition, a contrast of polar opposites (light/dark, male/female) may help structure the paper. For instance, in writing about the Munro story, you may move from the girl's innocent identification with the father's work and *male* values to the weight of traditional stereotypes about the *female* role. Early in your work with the paper, prepare a **scratch outline** like the one that guided the author of the reading notes in her first draft:

—spirited imaginative character—the prank played on kid brother, leadership etc. daydreams: "courage, boldness, and self-sacrifice"
—the lure of the father's job
—the mother and grandmother as voices of the stereotype
—the climactic rebellion
—pivotal role of younger brother—he will overtake her by virtue of the mere fact of being born male; he has the advantage

Look at the way the student's prewriting fed into a first draft of a paper. What use did the student make of her prewriting? How nearly finished is this paper? What suggestions or advice would you give the student writer when she is ready to prepare a final draft?

SAMPLE FIRST DRAFT

A Story of Initiation

Alice Munro's story "Boys and Girls" introduces us to a spirited, imaginative young girl. She plays scary pranks on her kid brother, making him climb to the top beam of the barn. She also experiences the fears of childhood, as she and the brother try to mark off a "safe" zone among the scary shadows of the unfinished loft where they sleep, singing "Jingle Bells" and "Danny Boy" to ward off fear of the dark. Above all, she admires her father, who runs a fox farm for the pelts of the animals. As her father's helper and Girl Friday, she is used to the penetrating smell of the foxes. She responds to the beauty of the live foxes who have faces "drawn exquisitely sharp in pure hostility" and "golden eyes." She is just as used to the naked slippery dead carcasses that look "surprisingly small, mean and rat-like." However, in the course of the story, the girl has to leave this world of her childhood behind, growing up to discover her true destined role in a "man's world."

Children search for their identities and constantly run up against the wall of gender stereotypes to which they are made to conform. The girl in the story reluctantly conforms to the stereotypes that will deny a part of her personality. In her innocence, the girl in the story identifies with the outdoor work of her father, "red in the face with pleasure" when her father seems to praise and accept her as a co-worker. Her daydreams are about heroic rescues in which she plays the hero's part. However, her mother and grandmother conspire to drive home what is expected of a girl. It seems that after a last act of futile rebellion the invisible walls of the predestined gender roles will close in on her.

Life is seen entirely through the eyes of the young girl telling the story. As a child, she seems naturally inclined toward "male activities." The work done "in her father's service" is important to her like a ritual. (Her little brother tags timidly along, obeying her.) The narrator is treated like a boy and acts like one, and she is introduced by her father as "my new hired man." The salesman he is talking to responds that he thought it was "only a girl," a hint of the disillusionment that lies ahead. In her innocence, the narrator values and espouses those traditionally male qualities admired by the world, and she strives to cultivate those strengths within herself, as yet unburdened by the weight of stereotypes.

However, the mother increasingly represents the weight of the adult world, invoking the female stereotype, implying that when her daughter helps the father with "male" duties, the help is not real. The mother is eager to get her daughter into the house to help with girl work. ("It's not like I had a girl in the family at all.") The girl "hated the hot dark kitchen in summer"; "work in the house was endless, dreary and peculiarly depressing."

The horses that are kept to provide meat for the foxes give an interesting twist to the gender issue, because there are a male and a female. The male, Mack, is slow and docile, while the female, Flora, is spirited, temperamental and rebellious. When Flora's turn comes to be killed and butchered to feed the foxes, the narrator, in a dramatic act of rebellion against the way things are, lets her escape through the open gate that her father asks her to close. In trying to free the horse, she is making a last symbolic attempt to free herself. But she fails, both literally and symbolically. Flora is free for only a few hours longer. And the narrator, who is "only a girl," cannot free herself from the stereotype society has imposed on her, except for a few brief childhood years.

QUESTIONS

What, to you, are the strengths and possible weaknesses of this paper? How clear is the overall pattern of the paper? In her final draft, what details or what features do you think the student should add to round out the character?

4 PLOT
The Chain of Events

There has to be a tension, a sense that something is imminent, that certain things are in relentless motion, or else, most often, there simply won't be a story.

RAYMOND CARVER

A narrative line is in its deeper sense the tracing out of a meaning, and the real continuity of a story lies in this probing forward.

EUDORA WELTY

Writing prose is like laying a mosaic.

KURT TUCHOLSKY

FOCUS ON PLOT

A traditional short story puts believable characters in a setting that becomes real and then sets them in motion. We focus on **plot** when we trace what happens as a result. The plot is the story line, the sequence of actions or events that gives direction to the story as a whole. When we study plot, we focus on what drives, motivates, shapes the story. Plot sets up the scaffolding that supports the rest of the narrative; it maps out the itinerary that takes the reader to the conclusion.

An effective plot pulls us into the story. It does not just activate our curiosity; it stirs our emotions. True, some stories leave us cold, or lukewarm at best; we read them to pass the time or to satisfy an assignment. But stories that come to mean something have a way of drawing us in; they make us live through rather than merely watch an experience.

Frank O'Connor's short story classic "Guests of the Nation" takes us to the Irish side in the war between the Irish and the English that led to the establishment of the Irish Free State in 1922, after centuries of English rule. We spend our time with two young soldiers in the Irish Republican Army. They are guarding two English prisoners—although security is lax, since with their English accents and khaki tunics the prisoners would not get very far, even if they had a mind to escape. The foursome pass the time playing cards, arguing about capitalism and communism, about priests and love of country. The Englishmen join in the occasional dances with the local young women; one of the Englishmen becomes a mainstay and helpmate to the lady of the house, doing chores and running errands for her. Inevitably, however, the grim realities of the war catch up with us: The English have executed Irish rebels, and the two English hostages will be shot in retaliation.

Where are we as readers in this story? Maybe we can keep cool and refuse to become involved. It's not *our* war; the hostages have long been dead and buried. More likely, however, we will be drawn into the story. We will be saying when word comes down from headquarters to execute the hostages: "No, you cannot do that!" We are likely to argue and agonize and prevaricate. The chances are we will finally do as told; we will feel sick about it afterwards; and, like the narrator in the story, we will never again be quite the same. We will not know what to say when the lady of the house asks: "What did ye do with them?"

PLOTTING THE STORY

Storytellers, in their speaking, allow us to see the narrative character of our lives. The stories they tell touch us. What we thought was an accidental sequence of experience suddenly takes the dramatic shape of an unresolved story.

J. P. CARSE

Order and form no more spring out of order and form than they come riding in to us upon seashells through the spray. In fiction they have to be made out of their very antithesis, life.

EUDORA WELTY

When you think about plot, you ask yourself: "How does the story take shape? What sets it in motion? What keeps it going? What brings it to a satisfying close?"

A well-plotted tale establishes a **situation** that has in it the seeds of a story. As you start reading a story, you need to be alert for signs of something unstable, some agenda to be attended to, some score to be settled. This initial setting up or **exposition** creates a situation that has the seed of further developments in it. You need to pay special attention here to see where the story might be headed. Perhaps a new element disturbs the status quo: A stranger arrives; an outsider marries into the family; a distant relative comes close.

The **characters** of a story are by definition capable of engaging in action, of precipitating events. Their motives—their motivation—is their potential for action: "what sets them in motion." An accident-prone character is, as we say, "an accident waiting to happen." A character with seething resentment is a time bomb waiting to go off. A desperately lonely character may take desperate steps to make human contact. As an attentive reader, you will be sizing up characters for what they might do.

As the lives of several characters intersect, there is a potential for **conflict.** Rivals in love or ambition may face off like the **protagonist** (the first or chief contender) and the **antagonist** (the worthy or formidable opponent) in ancient Greek drama. However, the conflict need not be dramatic but may be low-key. People may find themselves at cross-purposes without the will or ability to articulate loud grievances. Mason's "Shiloh" develops a conflict between the opposed, diverging needs of a couple; the conflict plays itself out without fireworks or fanfare.

The story line may involve **external** physical action—quarrels, journeys, acts of defiance, suicides. The characters may have mountains to scale or adversaries to confront. But much of the action may be **internal,** psychological. A character may experience a change in perspective, learning something about others. A character may reach a moment of self-realization, facing up to something important about himself or herself. Then again, characters may merely act out who they are.

The actual story line—the central action or progression of events—will vary greatly from story to story:

✧ There may be a **loose** narrative structure, with events coming to pass in leisurely, apparently artless fashion, in chronological order. Things just seem to happen—"and then" this, "and then" that. In Carver's "The Third Thing That Killed My Father Off," we see the central character develop an interest in a hobby that interferes with his performance at work. An apparent misunderstanding leads to the alienation of old friends. Unexpected natural events intervene. In other stories, there may be a **tight** narrative structure, with events marching on relentlessly from cause to effect. In John Steinbeck's story "Flight," a proud young boy is provoked into a fatal brawl and then is hunted down methodically by the friends of the man he killed. Some writers much prefer this kind of compact, tightly plotted story. They start close to a crisis, focusing on what Frank O'Connor has called "some glowing center of action."

✧ Many stories build to a **climax,** or high point. In Malamud's "The Magic Barrel," you are going to see a pattern of deliberate, purposeful repetition. You will find a repeated pattern of marriage prospects touted by the matchmaker and found to be disappointing—till the plot takes a turn that brings the search to a climactic conclusion.

✧ A more experimental narrative structure may break up the chronological sequence of events. **Flashbacks** may gradually fill in the missing pieces of a puzzle. In a Faulkner story like "A Rose for Emily" (included in this chapter), you may have to reconstruct the actual chain of events from partial clues, gradually letting the puzzle take shape.

Traditional stories tend to have a strong plot line that you can chart from beginning through middle to end. They may move from cause to effect, or from motive to action and reaction. At the other end of the spectrum, much modern fiction plays down plot, with little happening that would appear on a police blotter or make the evening news. However, whether played up or played down, plot serves a number of functions basic to the storyteller's art:

✧ *The plot of a story engages and holds our attention.* For the story to succeed, we have to keep turning the page to see how things will come out. Much traditional fiction concentrated on this function of plot (and much popular fiction still does). Many a well-plotted story aims at creating and maintaining **suspense.** We feel that we *have* to know whether an enterprise will prosper or falter, whether an escape will succeed or fail, whether or not a secret meant to be buried with the dead will be revealed.

A classic kind of science fiction story might show us a young man seated at a lifeline predictor machine. It is a little after nine o'clock. The man inserts a coin and pushes the predictor button. The message screen lights up, with the message reading: "You will die of a heart attack today at 10:05 A.M." Taken aback, the young man pushes a button for "death averted." The screen lights up with a clip showing him finishing his college education, getting a degree, taking a job. A year later he is killed by a hit-and-run car. Again the young man pushes "death averted." The next clip shows him getting a promotion to manager, getting married, having a child. He is killed in a plane accident as an airliner collides with a commuter plane. Again the young man pushes "death averted." He is watching his first grandchild being born when the wall clock shows 10:05 A.M. He drops dead of a heart attack.

This story sets up a pattern that keeps us moving in accordance with accepted premises: It repeats several times the pattern of a threat surfacing and the threat removed. It keeps us turning the pages leading up to the surprise ending—which, however, is not a total surprise. It was prepared for early, and it pulls all the pieces of the story together in a satisfying overall pattern.

✧ *The plot gives shape to the story as a whole.* A story like Bobbie Ann Mason's "Shiloh" is rich in leisurely surface detail, from Norma Jean's three-pound dumbbells to Leroy's "lamp made out of a model truck, with a light fixture screwed in the top of the cab." However, the story moves by slow stages to its final destination. The plot takes us from first signs of estrangement, through the husband's ineffectual yearning for a return to their happier past, to a last doomed try at picking up the pieces during the trip to the battlefield at Shiloh. At the end of the story, something has been settled; a chapter in their lives has been written. Although their lives will go on, their marriage seems to be over. The story leaves us with a satisfying sense of completion. It achieves **closure**—a satisfying wrapping up or pulling together.

Note: Writers of the serious modern short story became suspicious of the plot devices of **popular fiction.** Audiences used to love a story that ends with a twist: A husband sells his gold watch to buy an expensive comb for his wife's rich, full hair; the wife has her hair cut short and sells it to buy an expensive attachment for the husband's watch. Popular audiences now as always love a happy end: A last-minute rescue heads off disaster. A rich uncle leaves an inheritance. A miracle drug restores eyesight. Much serious modern fiction refuses to rely on such strokes of good luck (although an occasional story still does!). Much modern fiction appeals to our sense of **irony:** With a wry smile, we see good intentions defeated by naive bumbling. We see evil resulting not from fiendish malice but from well-meant efforts by people who do not know what they do.

EXPLORATIONS

Short Short

The following short short is by a novelist who was born in Persia (now Iran), grew up in a British colony in Africa (now Zimbabwe), and went to live in England. What happens in the story? What is the unifying thread? How do its characters interact? What leaves the reader with a gratifying sense of completion? (Isaac Babel was a Jewish writer who wrote about Jewish life in Russia. Do we need to know who he is or how he writes for the story to work?)

DORIS LESSING   (born 1919)

Homage for Isaac Babel   1958

The day I had promised to take Catherine down to visit my young friend Philip at his school in the country, we were to leave at eleven, but she arrived at nine. Her blue dress was new, and so were her fashionable shoes. Her hair had just been done. She looked more than ever like a pink-and-gold Renoir girl who expects everything from life.

Catherine lives in a white house overlooking the sweeping brown tides of the river. She helped me clean up my flat with a devotion which said that she felt small flats were altogether more romantic than large houses. We drank tea, and talked mainly about Philip, who, being fifteen, has pure stern tastes in everything from food to music. Catherine looked at the books lying around his room, and asked if she might borrow the stories of Isaac Babel to read on the train. Catherine is thirteen. I suggested she might find them difficult, but she said: "Philip reads them, doesn't he?"

During the journey I read newspapers and watched her pretty frowning face as she turned the pages of Babel, for she was determined to let nothing get between her and her ambition to be worthy of Philip.

At the school, which is charming, civilized, and expensive, the two children walked together across green fields, and I followed, seeing how the sun gilded their bright friendly heads turned toward each other as they talked. In Catherine's left hand she carried the stories of Isaac Babel.

After lunch we went to the pictures. Philip allowed it to be seen that he thought going to the pictures just for the fun of it was not worthy of intelligent people, but he made the concession, for our sakes. For his sake we chose the more serious of the two films that were showing in the little town. It was about a good priest who helped criminals in New York. His goodness, however, was not enough to prevent one of them from being sent to the gas chamber; and Philip and I waited with Catherine in the dark until she had stopped crying and could face the light of a golden evening.

At the entrance of the cinema the doorman was lying in wait for anyone who had red eyes. Grasping Catherine by her suffering arm, he said bitterly: "Yes, why are you crying? He had to be punished for his crime, didn't he?" Catherine stared at him, incredulous. Philip rescued her by saying with disdain: "Some people don't know right from wrong even when it's *demonstrated* to them." The doorman turned his attention to the next red-eyed emerger from the dark; and we went on together to the station, the children silent because of the cruelty of the world.

5

Finally Catherine said, her eyes wet again: "I think it's all absolutely beastly, and I can't bear to think about it." And Philip said: "But we've got to think about it, don't you see, because if we don't it'll just go on and *on*, don't you see?"

In the train going back to London I sat beside Catherine. She had the stories open in front of her, but she said: "Philip's awfully lucky. I wish I went to that school. Did you notice that girl who said hullo to him in the garden? They must be great friends. I wish my mother would let me have a dress like that, it's *not* fair."

"I thought it was too old for her."

"Oh, *did* you?"

Soon she bent her head again over the book, but almost at once lifted it to say: "Is he a very famous writer?"

"He's a marvellous writer, brilliant, one of the very best."

"Why?"

"Well, for one thing he's so simple. Look how few words he uses, and how strong his stories are."

"I see. Do you know him? Does he live in London?"

"Oh no, he's dead."

"Oh. Then why did you—I thought he was alive, the way you talked."

"I'm sorry, I suppose I wasn't thinking of him as dead."

"When did he die?"

"He was murdered. About twenty years ago, I suppose."

"Twenty years." Her hands began the movement of pushing the book over to me, but then relaxed. "I'll be fourteen in November," she stated, sounding threatened, while her eyes challenged me.

I found it hard to express my need to apologize, but before I could speak, she said, patiently attentive again: "You said he was murdered?"

"Yes."

"I expect the person who murdered him felt sorry when he discovered he had murdered a famous writer."

"Yes, I expect so."

"Was he old when he was murdered?"

"No, quite young really."

"Well, that was bad luck, wasn't it?"

"Yes, I suppose it was bad luck."

"Which do you think is the very best story here? I mean, in your honest opinion, the very very best one."

I chose the story about killing the goose. She read it slowly, while I sat waiting, wishing to take it from her, wishing to protect this charming little person from Isaac Babel.

When she had finished, she said: "Well, some of it I don't understand. He's got a funny way of looking at things. Why should a man's legs in boots look like *girls?*" She finally pushed the book over at me, and said: "I think it's all morbid."

"But you have to understand the kind of life he had. First, he was a Jew in Russia. That was bad enough. Then his experience was all revolution and civil war and. . . ."

But I could see these words bounding off the clear glass of her fiercely denying gaze; and I said: "Look, Catherine, why don't you try again when you're older? Perhaps you'll like him better then?"

She said gratefully: "Yes, perhaps that would be best. After all, Philip is two years older than me, isn't he?"

A week later I got a letter from Catherine.

Thank you very much for being kind enough to take me to visit Philip at his school. It was the most lovely day in my whole life. I am extremely grateful to you for taking me. I have been thinking about the Hoodlum Priest. That was a film which demonstrated to me beyond any shadow of doubt that Capital Punishment is a Wicked Thing, and I shall never forget what I learned that afternoon, and the lessons of it will be with me all my life. I have been meditating about what you said about Isaac Babel, the famed Russian short story writer, and I now see that the conscious simplicity of his style is what makes him, beyond the shadow of a doubt, the great writer that he is, and now in my school compositions I am endeavoring to emulate him so as to learn a conscious simplicity which is the only basis for a really brilliant writing style. Love, Catherine. P.S. Has Philip said anything about my party? I wrote but he hasn't answered. Please find out if he is coming or if he just forgot to answer my letter. I hope he comes, because sometimes I feel I shall die if he doesn't. P.P.S. Please don't tell him I said anything, because I should die if he knew. Love, Catherine.

THREE MASTER STORYTELLERS

A plot is a narrative of events, the emphasis falling on causality. "The king died and then the queen died" is a story. "The king died, and then the queen died of grief" is a plot.

E. M. FORSTER

The following three selections are by writers who know how to write gripping stories. They know how to entice readers into a story and then lock in their interest until the story reaches its satisfying conclusion. However, the three writers use very different techniques, ranging from the more traditional to the more modern. Try to chart the plot, the story line, as you read.

BERNARD MALAMUD   (1914–1986)

A bad reading of my work would indicate that I'm writing about losers. That would be a very bad reading. One of my most important themes is a man's hidden strength.

BERNARD MALAMUD

Bernard Malamud was born and went to school in Brooklyn; he continued his education at the College of the City of New York and Columbia University. He taught high school evening classes for years before he could make a living as a writer and university teacher. He knew the cultural heritage of the American Jewish community from close by, and he wrote about Jewish everyday life and Jewish history in novels like *The Assistant* (1956), about a struggling neighborhood grocer and the down-and-out stranger he befriends. *The Fixer* (1966) tells the story of a Jew accused of ritual murder in czarist Russia. Malamud's fiction is colored by the tragic view of life of a people who underwent centuries of persecution. (In the depths of loneliness and bitterness, Leo Finkle, the rabbinical student in Malamud's story "The Magic Barrel," reminds himself "that he was yet a Jew and that a Jew suffered.") However, intermeshing with this mournful strand is a zany sense of humor, as likely to target one's own shortcomings as those of others. Finally, even in defeat, Malamud's characters often seem to project a love of life and a solidarity with suffering humanity that defy adversity.

Malamud's "The Magic Barrel" has the kind of straightforward surface plot that delights lovers of unspoilt spontaneous storytelling. A young rabbinical student, shy and lonely, enlists the services of a traditional matchmaker or marriage broker in his search for a suitable wife. The young man's quest for happiness leads him through a series of tragicomic adventures that seem to doom him to disappointment. However, the story shows him overcoming the obstacles in his path and leads to a surprise ending that is a happy ending or not depending on the beholder's point of view.

What makes the story rich and complex is that it moves on more than one level. While the official plot is played out toward its conclusion, much of what the characters publicly say and do plays to a counterpoint of private thoughts and feelings. These are often betrayed by revealing gestures, hesitations, or slips of the tongue. The role each character plays—the matchmaker, the serious theology student, the teacher looking for a spouse—is a public **persona**; it is the personality they exhibit to the outside world, the face they wear in public. Much of the comedy is in the sad and funny contrast between their deliberate public pronouncements and their unacknowledged real selves.

Once you focus on the private feelings of the characters, you are likely to observe that parallel to the overt action—the search for a mate—a spiritual journey takes place. The main plot with its quest for happiness is the occasion for a parallel story line—a journey toward self-discovery. Leo learns things about himself that before he did not know or care to admit. He reexamines his life, his history, his vocation. What does he learn? How does his character develop or grow in the course of the story?

The Magic Barrel   1958

Not long ago there lived in uptown New York, in a small, almost meager room, though crowded with books, Leon Finkle, a rabbinical student in the Yeshivah University. Finkle, after six years of study, was to be ordained in June and had been advised by an acquaintance that he might find it easier to win himself a congregation if he were married. Since he had no present prospects of marriage, after two tormented days of turning it over in his mind, he called in Pinye Salzman, a marriage broker, whose two-line advertisement he had read in the *Forward*.

The matchmaker appeared one night out of the dark fourth-floor hallway of the graystone rooming house, grasping a black, strapped portfolio that had been worn thin with use. Salzman, who had been long in the business, was of slight but dignified build, wearing an old hat and an overcoat too short and tight for him. He smelled frankly of fish, which he loved to eat, and although he was missing a few teeth, his presence was not displeasing, because of an amiable manner curiously contrasted by mournful eyes. His voice, his lips, his wisp of beard, his bony fingers were animated, but give him a moment of repose, and his mild blue eyes soon revealed a depth of sadness, a characteristic that put Leo a little at ease although the situation, for him, was inherently tense.

He at once informed Salzman why he had asked him to come, explaining that his home was in Cleveland, and that but for his parents, who had married comparatively late in life, he was alone in the world. He had for six years devoted himself entirely to his studies, as a result of which, quite understandably, he had found himself without time for a social life and the company of young women. Therefore he thought it the better part of trial and error—of embarrassing fumbling—to call in an experienced person to advise him in these matters. He remarked in passing that the function of the marriage broker was ancient and honorable, highly approved in the Jewish community, because it made practical the necessary without hindering joy. Moreover, his own parents had been brought together by a matchmaker. They had made, if not a financially profitable marriage—since neither had possessed any worldly goods to speak of—at least a successful one in the sense of their everlasting devotion to one another. Salzman listened in embarrassed surprise, sensing a sort of apology. Later, however, he experienced a glow of pride in his work, an emotion that had left him years ago, and he heartily approved of Finkle.

The two men went to their business. Leo had led Salzman to the only clear place in the room, a table near a window that overlooked the lamplit city. He seated himself at the matchmaker's side but facing him, attempting by an act of will to suppress the unpleasant tickle in his throat. Salzman eagerly unstrapped his portfolio and removed a loose rubber band from a thin packet of much-handled cards. As he flipped through them, a gesture and sound that physically hurt Leo, the student pretended not to see and gazed steadfastly out the window. Although it was still February, winter was on its last legs, signs of which he had for the first time in years begun to notice. He now observed the round white moon, moving high in the sky through a cloud-menagerie, and watched with half-open mouth as it penetrated a huge hen and dropped out of her like an egg laying itself. Salzman, though pretending through eyeglasses he had just slipped on, to be engaged in scanning the writing on the cards, stole occasional glances at the young man's distinguished face, noting with pleasure the long, severe scholar's nose, brown eyes heavy with learning, sensitive yet ascetic lips, and a certain almost hollow quality of the dark cheeks. He gazed around at shelves upon shelves of books and let out a soft but happy sigh.

When Leo's eyes fell upon the cards, he counted six spread out in Salzman's hand.   5

"So few?" he said in disappointment.

"You wouldn't believe me how much cards I got in my office," Salzman replied. "The drawers are already filled to the top, so I keep them now in a barrel, but is every girl good for a new rabbi?"

Leo blushed at this, regretting all he had revealed of himself in a curriculum vitae he had sent to Salzman. He had thought it best to acquaint him with his strict standards and specifications, but in having done so now felt he had told the marriage broker more than was absolutely necessary.

He hesitantly inquired, "Do you keep photographs of your clients on file?"

"First comes family, amount of dowry, also what kind promises," Salzman replied,   10 unbuttoning his tight coat and settling himself in the chair. "After comes pictures, rabbi."

"Call me Mr. Finkle. I'm not a rabbi yet."

Salzman said he would, but instead called him doctor, which he changed to rabbi when Leo was not listening too attentively.

Salzman adjusted his horn-rimmed spectacles, gently cleared his throat and read in an eager voice the contents on the top card:

"Sophie P. Twenty-four years. Widow for one year. No children. Educated high school and two years college. Father promises eight thousand dollars. Has a wonderful wholesale business. Also real estate. On mother's side comes teachers, also one actor. Well known on Second Avenue."

Leo gazed up in surprise. "Did you say a widow?"   15

"A widow don't mean spoiled, rabbi. She lived with her husband maybe four months. He was a sick boy, she made a mistake to marry him."

"Marrying a widow has never entered my mind."

"This is because you have no experience. A widow, specially if she is young and healthy like this girl, is a wonderful person to marry. She will be thankful to you the rest of her life. Believe me, if I was looking now for a bride, I would marry a widow."

Leo reflected, then shook his head.

Salzman hunched his shoulders in an almost imperceptible gesture of disappoint-   20
ment. He placed the card down on the wooden table and began to read another:

"Lily H. High-school teacher. Regular. Not a substitute. Has savings and new Dodge car. Lived in Paris one year. Father is successful dentist thiry-five years. Interested in professional man. Well Americanized family. Wonderful opportunity.

"I know her personally," said Salzman. "I wish you could see this girl. She is a doll. Also very intelligent. All day you could talk to her about books and theater and what not. She also knows current events."

"I don't believe you mentioned her age?"

"Her age?" Salzman said, raising his brows in surprise. "Her age is thirty-two years."

Leo said after a while, "I'm afraid that seems a little too old."   25

Salzman let out a laugh. "So how old are you, rabbi?"

"Twenty-seven."

"So what is the difference, tell me, between twenty-seven and thirty-two? My own wife is seven years older than me. So what did I suffer?—Nothing. If Rothschild's daughter wants to marry you, would you say on account of her age, no?"

"Yes," Leo said dryly.

Salzman shook off the no in the yes. "Five years don't mean a thing. I give you my   30
word that when you will live with her for one week, you will forget her age. What does it mean five years—that she lived more and knows more than somebody who is younger? On this girl, God bless her, years are not wasted. Each one that it comes makes better the bargain."

"What subject does she teach in high school?"

"Languages. If you heard the way she reads French, you will think it is music. I am in the business twenty-five years, and I recommend her with my whole heart. Believe me, I know what I'm talking, rabbi."

"What's on the next card?" Leo said abruptly.

Salzman reluctantly turned up the third card:

"Ruth K. Nineteen years. Honor student. Father offers thirteen thousand dollars   35
cash to the right bridegroom. He is a medical doctor. Stomach specialist with marvelous practice. Brother-in-law owns own garment business. Particular people."

Salzman looked up as if he had read his trump card.

"Did you say nineteen?" Leo asked with interest.

"On the dot."

"Is she attractive?" He blushed. "Pretty?"

Salzman kissed his fingertips. "A little doll. On this I give you my word. Let me   40
call the father tonight and you will see what means pretty."

But Leo was troubled. "You're sure she's that young?"

"This I am positive. The father will show you the birth certificate."

"Are you positive there isn't something wrong with her?" Leo insisted.

"Who says there is wrong?"

"I don't understand why an American girl her age should go to a marriage   45
broker."

A smile spread over Salzman's face.

"So for the same reason you went, she comes."

Leo flushed. "I am pressed for time."

Salzman, realizing he had been tactless, quickly explained. "The father came,
not her. He wants she should have the best, so he looks around himself. When we
will locate the right boy, he will introduce him and encourage. This makes a better
marriage than if a young girl without experience takes for herself. I don't have to tell
you this."

"But don't you think this young girl believes in love?" Leo spoke uneasily.   50

Salzman was about to guffaw, but caught himself and said soberly, "Love comes
with the right person, not before."

Leo parted dry lips but did not speak. Noticing that Salzman had snatched a quick
glance at the next card, he cleverly asked, "How is her health?"

"Perfect," Salzman said, breathing with difficulty. "Of course, she is a little lame
on her right foot from an auto accident that it happened to her when she was twelve
years, but nobody notices on account she is so brilliant and also beautiful."

Leo got up heavily and went to the window. He felt curiously bitter and upbraided
himself for having called in the marriage broker. Finally, he shook his head.

"Why not?" Salzman persisted, the pitch of his voice rising.   55

"Because I hate stomach specialists."

"So what do you care what is his business? After you marry her, do you need him?
Who says he must come every Friday night to your house?"

Ashamed of the way the talk was going, Leo dismissed Salzman, who went home
with melancholy eyes.

Though he had felt only relief at the marriage broker's departure, Leo was in low
spirits the next day. He explained it as arising from Salzman's failure to produce a suitable bride for him. He did not care for his type of clientele. But when Leo found himself hesitating over whether to seek out another matchmaker, one more polished than
Pinye, he wondered if it could be—his protestations to the contrary, and although he
honored his father and mother—that he did not, in essence, care for the matchmaking
institution? This thought he quickly put out of his mind yet found himself still upset.
All day he ran around in a fog—missed an important appointment, forgot to give out
his laundry, walked out of a Broadway cafeteria without paying and had to run back
with the ticket in his hand; had even not recognized his landlady in the street when she
passed with a friend and courteously called out, "A good evening to you, Doctor Finkle." By nightfall, however, he had regained sufficient calm to sink his nose into a book
and there found peace from his thoughts.

Almost at once there came a knock on the door. Before Leo could say enter, Salz-   60
man, commercial cupid, was standing in the room. His face was gray and meager, his

expression hungry, and he looked as if he would expire on his feet. Yet the marriage broker managed, by some trick of the muscles, to display a broad smile.

"So good evening. I am invited?"

Leo nodded, disturbed to see him again, yet unwilling to ask him to leave.

Beaming still, Salzman laid his portfolio on the table. "Rabbi, I got for you tonight good news."

"I've asked you not to call me rabbi. I'm still a student."

"Your worries are finished. I have for you a first-class bride."   65

"Leave me in peace concerning this subject." Leo pretended lack of interest.

"The world will dance at your wedding."

"Please, Mr. Salzman, no more."

"But first must come back my strength," Salzman said weakly. He fumbled with the portfolio straps and took out of the leather case an oily paper bag, from which he extracted a hard seeded roll and a small smoked whitefish. With one motion of his hand he stripped the fish out of its skin and began ravenously to chew. "All day in a rush," he muttered.

Leo watched him eat.   70

"A sliced tomato you have maybe?" Salzman hesitantly inquired.

"No."

The marriage broker shut his eyes and ate. When he had finished, he carefully cleaned up the crumbs and rolled up the remains of the fish in the paper bag. His spectacled eyes roamed the room until he discovered, amid some piles of books, a one-burner gas stove. Lifting his hat, he humbly asked, "A glass of tea you got, rabbi?"

Conscience-stricken, Leo rose and brewed the tea. He served it with a chunk of lemon and two cubes of lump sugar, delighting Salzman.

After he had drunk his tea, Salzman's strength and good spirits were restored.   75

"So tell me, rabbi," he said amiably, "you considered any more the three clients I mentioned yesterday?"

"There was no need to consider."

"Why not?"

"None of them suits me."

"What, then, suits you?"   80

Leo let it pass because he could give only a confused answer.

Without waiting for a reply, Salzman asked, "You remember this girl I talked to you—the high-school teacher?"

"Age thirty-two?"

But, surprisingly, Salzman's face lit in a smile. "Age twenty-nine."

Leo shot him a look. "Reduced from thirty-two?"   85

"A mistake," Salzman avowed. "I talked today with the dentist. He took me to his safety deposit box and showed me the birth certificate. She was twenty-nine last August. They made her a party in the mountains where she went for her vacation. When her father spoke to me the first time, I forgot to write the age and I told you thirty-two, but now I remember this was a different client, a widow."

"The same one you told me about? I thought she was twenty-four?"

"A different. Am I responsible that the world is filled with widows?"

"No, but I'm not interested in them, nor for that matter, in schoolteachers."

Salzman passionately pulled his clasped hands to his breast. Looking at the ceiling   90
he exclaimed, "Jewish children, what can I say to somebody that he is not interested in high-school teachers? So what then you are interested?"

Leo flushed but controlled himself.

"In who else you will be interested," Salzman went on, "if you not interested in this fine girl that she speaks four languages and has personally in the bank ten thousand dollars? Also her father guarantees further twelve thousand. Also she has a new car, wonderful clothes, talks on all subjects, and she will give you a first-class home and children. How near do we come in our life to paradise?"

"If she's so wonderful, why wasn't she married ten years ago?"

"Why," said Salzman with a heavy laugh. "—Why? Because she is *partikler*. This is why. She wants only the *best*."

Leo was silent, amused at how he had trapped himself. But Salzman had aroused   95
his interest in Lily H., and he began seriously to consider calling on her. When the marriage broker observed how intently Leo's mind was at work on the facts he had supplied, he felt positive they would soon come to an agreement.

Late Saturday afternoon, conscious of Salzman, Leo Finkle walked with Lily Hirschorn along Riverside Drive. He walked briskly and erectly, wearing with distinction the black fedora he had that morning taken with trepidation out of the dusty hatbox on his closet shelf, and the heavy black Saturday coat he had thoroughly whisked clean. Leo also owned a walking stick, a present from a distant relative, but had decided not to use it. Lily, petite and not unpretty, had on something signifying the approach of spring. She was *au courant*, animatedly, with all subjects, and he weighed her words and found her surprisingly sound—score another for Salzman, whom he uneasily sensed to be somewhere around, hiding perhaps high in a tree along the street, flashing the lady signals; or perhaps a cloven-hoofed Pan, piping nuptial ditties as he danced his invisible way before them, strewing wild buds on the walk and purple summer grapes in their path, symbolizing fruit of a union, of which there was yet none.

Lily startled Leo by remarking, "I was thinking of Mr. Salzman, a curious figure, wouldn't you say?"

Not certain what to answer, he nodded.

She bravely went on, blushing, "I for one am grateful for his introducing us. Aren't you?"

He courteously replied, "I am."   100

"I mean," she said with a little laugh—and it was all in good taste, or at least gave the effect of being not in bad—"do you mind that we came together so?"

He was not afraid of her honesty, recognizing that she meant to set the relationship aright, and understanding that it took a certain amount of experience in life, and courage, to want to do it quite that way. One had to have some sort of past to make that kind of beginning.

He said that he did not mind. Salzman's function was traditional and honorable—valuable for what it might achieve, which, he pointed out, was frequently nothing.

Lily agreed with a sigh. They walked on for a while, and she said after a long silence, again with a nervous laugh, "Would you mind if I asked you something a little bit personal? Frankly, I find the subject fascinating." Although Leo shrugged, she went on half embarrassedly, "How was it that you came to your calling? I mean, was it a sudden passionate inspiration?"

Leo, after a time, slowly replied, "I was always interested in the Law."   105

"You saw revealed in it the presence of the Highest?"

He nodded and changed the subject. "I understand you spent a little time in Paris, Miss Hirschorn?"

"Oh, did Mr. Salzman tell you, Rabbi Finkle?" Leo winced, but she went on, "It was ages and ages ago and almost forgotten. I remember I had to return for my sister's wedding."

But Lily would not be put off. "When," she asked in a trembly voice, "did you become enamored of God?"

He stared at her. Then it came to him that she was talking not about Leo Finkle, but a total stranger, some mystical figure, perhaps even passionate prophet that Salzman had conjured up for her—no relation to the living or dead. Leo trembled with rage and weakness. The trickster had obviously sold her a bill of goods, just as he had him, who'd expected to become acquainted with a young lady of twenty-nine, only to behold, the moment he laid eyes upon her strained and anxious face, a woman past thirty-five and aging very rapidly. Only his self-control, he thought, had kept him this long in her presence. 110

"I am not," he said gravely, "a talented religious person," and in seeking words to go on, found himself possessed by fear and shame. "I think," he said in a strained manner, "that I came to God not because I love Him, but because I did not."

This confession he spoke harshly because its unexpectedness shook him.

Lily wilted. Leo saw a profusion of loaves of bread sailing like ducks high over his head, not unlike the loaves by which he had counted himself to sleep last night. Mercifully, then, it snowed, which he would not put past Salzman's machinations.

He was infuriated with the marriage broker and swore he would throw him out of the room the moment he reappeared. But Salzman did not come that night, and when Leo's anger had subsided, an unaccountable despair grew in its place. At first he thought this was caused by his disappointment in Lily, but before long it became evident that he had involved himself with Salzman without a true knowledge of his own intent. He gradually realized—with an emptiness that seized him with six hands—that he had called in the broker to find him a bride because he was incapable of doing it himself. This terrifying insight he had derived as a result of his meeting and conversation with Lily Hirschorn. Her probing questions had somehow irritated him into revealing—to himself more than her—the true nature of his relationship with God, and from that it had come upon him, with shocking force, that apart from his parents, he had never loved anyone. Or perhaps it went the other way, that he did not love God so well as he might, because he had not loved man. It seemed to Leo that his whole life stood starkly revealed and he saw himself, for the first time, as he truly was—unloved and loveless. This bitter but somehow not fully unexpected revelation brought him to a point of panic controlled only by extraordinary effort. He covered his face with his hands and wept.

The week that followed was the worst of his life. He did not eat, and lost weight. His beard darkened and grew ragged. He stopped attending lectures and seminars and almost never opened a book. He seriously considered leaving the Yeshivah, although he was deeply troubled at the thought of the loss of all his years of study—saw them like pages from a book strewn over the city—and at the devastating effect of this decision upon his parents. But he had lived without knowledge of himself, and never in the Five Books and all the Commentaries—mea culpa—had the truth been revealed to him. He did not know where to turn, and in all this desolating loneliness there was no to whom, although he often thought of Lily but not once could bring himself to go downstairs and make the call. He became touchy and irritable, especially with his landlady, who asked him all manner of questions; on the other hand, sensing his own disagreeableness, he waylaid her on the stairs and apologized abjectly, until mortified, she ran from him. Out of this, however, he drew the consolation that he was yet a Jew and that a 115

Jew suffered. But gradually, as the long and terrible week drew to a close, he regained his composure and some idea of purpose in life: to go on as planned. Although he was imperfect, the ideal was not. As for his quest of a bride, the thought of continuing afflicted him with anxiety and heartburn, yet perhaps with this new knowledge of himself he would be more successful than in the past. Perhaps love would now come to him and a bride to that love. And for this sanctified seeking who needed a Salzman?

The marriage broker, a skeleton with haunted eyes, returned that very night. He looked, withal, the picture of frustrated expectancy—as if he had steadfastly waited the week at Miss Lily Hirschorn's side for a telephone call that never came.

Casually coughing, Salzman came immediately to the point: "So how did you like her?"

Leo's anger rose and he could not refrain from chiding the matchmaker: "Why did you lie to me, Salzman?"

Salzman's pale face went dead white, as if the world had snowed on him.

"Did you not state that she was twenty-nine?" Leo insisted.   120

"I give you my word—"

"She was thirty-five. At *least* thirty-five."

"Of this I would not be too sure. Her father told me—"

"Never mind. The worst of it was that you lied to her."

"How did I lie to her, tell me?"   125

"You told her things about me that weren't true. You made me out to be more, consequently less than I am. She had in mind a totally different person, a sort of semi-mystical Wonder Rabbi."

"All I said, you was a religious man."

"I can imagine."

Salzman sighed. "This is my weakness that I have," he confessed. "My wife says to me I shouldn't be a salesman, but when I have two fine people that they would be wonderful to be married, I am so happy that I talk too much." He smiled wanly. "This is why Salzman is a poor man."

Leo's anger went. "Well, Salzman, I'm afraid that's all."   130

The marriage broker fastened hungry eyes on him.

"You don't want any more a bride?"

"I do," said Leo, "but I have decided to seek her in a different way. I am no longer interested in an arranged marriage. To be frank, I now admit the necessity of premarital love. That is, I want to be in love with the one I marry."

"Love?" said Salzman, astounded. After a moment he said, "For us, our love is our life, not for the ladies. In the ghetto they—"

"I know, I know," said Leo. "I've thought of it often. Love, I have said to myself,   135
should be a by-product of living and worship rather than its own end. Yet for myself I find it necessary to establish the level of my need and to fulfill it."

Salzman shrugged but answered, "Listen, rabbi, if you want love, this I can find for you also. I have such beautiful clients that you will love them the minute your eyes will see them."

Leo smiled unhappily. "I'm afraid you don't understand."

But Salzman hastily unstrapped his portfolio and withdrew a manila packet from it.

"Pictures," he said, quickly laying the envelope on the table.

Leo called after him to take the pictures away, but as if on the wings of the wind,   140
Salzman had disapeared.

March came. Leo had returned to his regular routine. Although he felt not quite himself yet—lacked energy—he was making plans for a more active social life. Of course it would cost something, but he was an expert in cutting corners; and when there were no corners left he could make circles rounder. All the while Salzman's pictures had lain on the table, gathering dust. Occasionally as Leo sat studying, or enjoying a cup of tea, his eyes fell on the manila envelope, but he never opened it.

The days went by, and no social life to speak of developed with a member of the opposite sex—it was difficult, given the circumstances of his situation. One morning Leo toiled up the stairs to his room and stared out the window at the city. Although the day was bright, his view of it was dark. For some time he watched the people in the street below hurrying along and then turned with a heavy heart to his little room. On the table was the packet. With a sudden relentless gesture he tore it open. For a half-hour he stood there, in a state of excitement, examining the photographs of the ladies Salzman had included. Finally, with a deep sigh he put them down. There were six, of varying degrees of attractiveness, but look at them long enough and they all became Lily Hirschorn: all past their prime, all starved behind bright smiles, not a true personality in the lot. Life, despite their anguished struggles and frantic yoohooings, had passed them by; they were photographs in a brief case that stank of fish. After a while, however, as Leo attempted to return the pictures into the envelope, he found another in it, a small snapshot of the type taken by a machine for a quarter. He gazed at it a moment and let out a cry.

Her face deeply moved him. Why, he could at first not say. It gave him the impression of youth—all spring flowers—yet age—a sense of having been used to the bone, wasted; this all came from the eyes, which were hauntingly familiar, yet absolutely strange. He had a strong impression that he had met her before, but try as he might he could not place her, although he could almost recall her name, as if he had read it written in her own handwriting. No, this couldn't be; he would have remembered her. It was not, he affirmed, that she had an extraordinary beauty—no, although her face was attractive enough; it was that *something* about her moved him. Feature for feature, even some of the ladies of the photographs could do better; but she leaped forth to the heart—had lived, or wanted to—more than just wanted, perhaps regretted it—had somehow deeply suffered: it could be seen in the depths of those reluctant eyes, and from the way the light enclosed and shone from her, and within her, opening whole realms of possibility: this was her own. Her he desired. His head ached and eyes narrowed with the intensity of his gazing, then, as if a black fog had blown up in the mind, he experienced fear of her and was aware that he had received an impression, somehow, of filth. He shuddered, saying softly, it is thus with us all. Leo brewed some tea in a small pot and sat sipping it, without sugar, to calm himself. But before he had finished drinking, again with excitement he examined the face and found it good: good for him. Only such a one could truly understand Leo Finkle and help him to seek whatever he was seeking. How she had come to be among the discards in Salzman's barrel he could never guess, but he knew he must urgently go find her.

Leo rushed downstairs, grabbed up the Bronx telephone book, and searched for Salzman's home address. He was not listed, nor was his office. Neither was he in the Manhattan book. But Leo remembered having written down the address on a slip of paper after he had read Salzman's advertisement in the "personals" column of the *Forward*. He ran up to his room and tore through his papers, without luck. It was exasperating. Just when he needed the matchmaker he was nowhere to be found. Fortunately Leo remembered to look in his wallet. There on a card he found his name written and a Bronx address. No phone number was listed, which, Leo now recalled, was the reason he had originally communicated with Salzman by letter. He got on his coat, put a hat on over his skull cap and hurried to the subway station. All the way to the far end of the

Bronx he sat on the edge of his seat. He was more than once tempted to take out the picture and see if the girl's face was as he remembered it, but he refrained, allowing the snapshot to remain in his inside coat pocket, content to have her so close. When the train pulled into the station, he was waiting at the door and bolted out. He quickly located the street Salzman had advertised.

The building he sought was less than a block from the subway, but it was not an office building, nor even a loft, nor a store in which one could rent office space. It was an old and grimy tenement. Leo found Salzman's name in pencil on a soiled tag under the bell and climbed three dark flights to his apartment. When he knocked, the door was opened by a thin, asthmatic, gray-haired woman, in felt slippers. 145

"Yes?" she said, expecting nothing. She listened without listening. He could have sworn he had seen her somewhere before but knew it was illusion.

"Salzman—does he live here? Pinye Salzman," he said, "the matchmaker?"

She stared at him a long time. "Of course."

He felt embarrassed. "Is he in?"

"No." Her mouth was open, but she offered nothing more. 150

"This is urgent. Can you tell me where his office is?"

"In the air." She pointed upward.

"You mean he has no office?" Leo said.

"In his socks."

He peered into the apartment. It was sunless and dingy, one large room divided by a half-open curtain, beyond which he could see a sagging metal bed. The nearer side of the room was crowded with rickety chairs, old bureaus, a three-legged table, racks of cooking utensils, and all the apparatus of a kitchen. But there was no sign of Salzman or his magic barrel, probably also a figment of his imagination. An odor of frying fish made Leo weak to the knees. 155

"Where is he?" he insisted, "I've got to see your husband."

At length she answered, "So who knows where he is? Every time he thinks a new thought he runs to a different place. Go home, he will find you."

"Tell him Leo Finkle."

She gave no sign that she had heard.

He went downstairs, deeply depressed. 160

But Salzman, breathless, stood waiting at his door.

Leo was overjoyed and astounded. "How did you get here before me?"

"I rushed."

"Come inside."

They entered. Leo fixed tea and a sardine sandwich for Salzman. 165

As they were drinking, he reached behind him for the packet of pictures and handed them to the marriage broker.

Salzman put down his glass and said expectantly, "You found maybe somebody you like?"

"Not among these."

The marriage broker turned sad eyes away.

"Here's the one I like." Leo held forth the snapshot. 170

Salzman slipped on his glasses and took the picture into his trembling hand. He turned ghastly and let out a miserable groan.

"What's the matter?" cried Leo.

"Excuse me. Was an accident this picture. She is not for you."

Salzman frantically shoved the manila packet into his portfolio. He thrust the snapshot into his pocket and fled down the stairs.

Leo, after momentary paralysis, gave chase and cornered the marriage broker in the   175
vestibule. The landlady made hysterical outcries, but neither of them listened.

"Give me back the picture, Salzman."

"No." The pain in his eyes was terrible.

"Tell me where she is then."

"This I can't tell you. Excuse me."

He made to depart, but Leo, forgetting himself, seized the matchmaker by his   180
tight coat and shook him frenziedly.

"Please," sighed Salzman. *"Please."*

Leo ashamedly let him go. "Tell me who she is," he begged. "It's very important
for me to know."

"She is not for you. She is a wild one—wild, without shame. This is not a bride for
a rabbi."

"What do you mean wild?"

"Like an animal. Like a dog. For her to be poor was a sin. This is why she is dead   185
now."

"In God's name, what do you mean?"

"Her I can't introduce to you," Salzman cried.

"Why are you so excited?"

"Why he asks," Salzman said, bursting into tears. "This is my baby, my Stella, she
should burn in hell."

Leo hurried up to bed and hid under the covers. Under the covers he thought his   190
whole life through. Although he soon fell asleep he could not sleep her out of his mind.
He woke, beating his breast. Though he prayed to be rid of her, his prayers went unanswered. Through days of torment he struggled endlessly not to love her; fearing success, he escaped it. He then concluded to convert her to goodness, himself to God. The
idea alternately nauseated and exalted him.

He perhaps did not know that he had come to a final decision until he encountered Salzman in a Broadway cafeteria. He was sitting alone at a rear table sucking the
bony remains of a fish. The marriage broker appeared haggard, and transparent to the
point of vanishing.

Salzman looked up at first without recognizing him. Leo had grown a pointed
beard, and his eyes were weighted with wisdom.

"Salzman," he said, "love has at last come to my heart."

"Who can love from a picture?" mocked the marriage broker.

"It is not impossible."   195

"If you can love her, then you can love anybody. Let me show you some new
clients that they just sent me their photographs. One is a little doll."

"Just her I want," Leo murmured.

"Don't be a fool, doctor. Don't bother with her."

"Put me in touch with her, Salzman," Leo said humbly. "Perhaps I can do her a
service."

Salzman had stopped chewing, and Leo understood with emotion that it was now   200
arranged.

Leaving the cafeteria, he was, however, afflicted by a tormenting suspicion that
Salzman had planned it all to happen this way.

Leo was informed by letter that she would meet him on a certain corner, and she
was there one spring night, waiting under a street lamp. He appeared, carrying a small
bouquet of violets and rosebuds. Stella stood by the lamppost, smoking. She wore

white with red shoes, which fitted his expectations, although in a troubled moment he had imagined the dress red, and only the shoes white. She waited uneasily and shyly. From afar he saw that her eyes—clearly her father's—were filled with desperate innocence. He pictured, in hers, his own redemption. Violins and lit candles revolved in the sky. Leo ran forward with the flowers outthrust.

Around the corner, Salzman, leaning against a wall, chanted prayers for the dead.

THE RECEPTIVE READER

1. What kind of story is this? What kind of story do the title and the *beginning* lead you to expect? Are your expectations fulfilled or disappointed by the rest of the story?

2. What is the *conflict* between the traditional view of love and romantic love in this story? How central is this conflict to the plot? How is the conflict resolved?

3. What are hints or touches that require you to read between the lines? Where are you most aware of the comic contrast between what the characters say and what they really think or know? What are striking examples of the contrast between make-believe and reality?

4. What role does Salzman play in the story as a whole? How essential is he to the plot? What are Finkle's mixed feelings about the "commercial cupid"?

5. What makes Salzman a *comic* figure? (What features do you recognize in his use of English?) How would you describe the kind of humor that pervades this story? What are striking examples?

6. Where in this story does Finkle experience *self-discovery* or self-revelation? What does he discover about himself? What role does this self-examination play in the story as a whole?

7. How believable is the *ending*?

THE PERSONAL RESPONSE

How essential is an understanding of Jewish culture or tradition to the reader's appreciation of this story? For you, does the author's ethnic background limit or enhance the appeal of the story? Why (or why not)?

CROSS-REFERENCES—For Discussion or Writing

Compare and contrast the plot of Malamud's story with the plot or narrative line of one or more of the stories by Joyce, Welty, or Mason printed earlier in this volume.

SHIRLEY JACKSON (1919–1965)

This story is about you—de te fabula.
FRANK O'CONNOR

*I hoped, by setting a particularly brutal ancient rite in the
present and in my own village, to shock the story's readers
with a graphic dramatization of the pointless violence and
general inhumanity in their own lives.*

SHIRLEY JACKSON

Shirley Jackson was a native of San Francisco who attended Syracuse University and settled in Vermont. She is a master of the modern horror story in which evil surfaces in ordinary everyday surroundings. Her story "The Lottery" is one of the great controversial stories of modern times. When first published in the *New Yorker* on June 28, 1948, it raised a tempest of protest. The story takes us to a village where we watch the preparations for a traditional ritual—in which one of the villagers is going to meet a terrible fate. The proceedings might remind us of accounts of ceremonial sacrifices to a vegetation god to ensure a rich harvest. ("Lottery in June, corn be heavy soon" is a folk saying in the village.)

Apparently two facets of the story were particularly disturbing to its original readers: First, the people in the story were not a prehistoric tribe whose primitive rituals they could have watched with detachment. This was a village that had a post office, a bank, and a school; the villagers talked about tractors and taxes. (Jackson once said she had in mind North Bennington, the town where she lived with her husband, who taught at Bennington College.) Second, the people selected to play the central role in the ritual were selected by lot—without the benefit of due process or trial by jury. They were chosen more simply and cheaply by a lottery.

Many of its original readers hated this story with a passion. The story generated "great batches" of mail, most of it critical and much of it abusive, making the author feel grateful that many in her own town did not know she was a writer. She said about the experience, "One of the most terrifying aspects of publishing stories is the realization they are going to be read, and read by strangers. . . . I had begun to perceive that I was very lucky indeed to be safely in Vermont, where no one in our small town had ever heard of the *New Yorker,* much less read my story. Millions of people, and my mother, had taken a pronounced dislike to me." Columnists in Chicago and New York reported gleefully that *New Yorker* subscriptions were being canceled left and right.

What explains the climate of fear in Jackson's story? We might try to see the story against the backdrop of its historical setting: Totalitarian regimes in Hitler's Germany and in Stalin's Russia had been persecuting artists, intellectuals, dissidents—a whole range of supposed "antisocial elements" and "enemies of the people." People whose families had lived in Germany for centuries, discovered—because their grandparents had been of the Jewish faith—that they were denied the right to live. In Stalinist Russia, young people whose family had owned a farm or a store found they were of the wrong social class—they had no right to go to school, to join the army, to make a living. Closer to home, during the Great Depression, families had been losing their farms or businesses and turned into hoboes. They were the random victims of an economic tailspin that threw millions out of work.

Here is the power of Jackson's story: What happens is irrational, but it seems inevitable. We see it coming but find it impossible to stop, like a freight train. The story has a concentrated impact created by a tightly crafted, linear plot. The author does not allow our attention to be distracted from her agenda. She once said about the writing of short stories, "no scene and no character can be allowed to wander off by itself; there must be some furthering of the story in every sentence."

At the same time, the characters remain fairly anonymous. They are part of the group, and they do what the community expects them to do. Perhaps this is what makes our identification with them possible—whether we identify with the victims or with the other townspeople, be they instigators or bystanders. As the Irish writer Frank O'Connor said about the secret of a powerful story, *"De te fabula"*—this fable, this story, is not about somebody else; it is about you.

The Lottery   1948

The morning of June 27th was clear and sunny, with the fresh warmth of a full-summer day; the flowers were blossoming profusely and the grass was richly green. The people of the village began to gather in the square, between the post office and the bank, around ten o'clock; in some towns there were so many people that the lottery took two days and had to be started on June 26th, but in this village, where there were only about three hundred people, the whole lottery took less than two hours, so it could begin at ten o'clock in the morning and still be through in time to allow the villagers to get home for noon dinner.

The children assembled first, of course. School was recently over for the summer, and the feeling of liberty sat uneasily on most of them; they tended to gather together quietly for a while before they broke into boisterous play, and their talk was still of the classroom and the teacher, of books and reprimands. Bobby Martin had already stuffed his pockets full of stones, and the other boys soon followed his example, selecting the smoothest and roundest stones; Bobby and Harry Jones and Dickie Delacroix—the villagers pronounced this name "Dellacroy"—eventually made a great pile of stones in one corner of the square and guarded it against the raids of the other boys. The girls stood aside, talking among themselves, looking over their shoulders at the boys, and the very small children rolled in the dust or clung to the hands of their older brothers or sisters.

Soon the men began to gather, surveying their own children, speaking of planting and rain, tractors and taxes. They stood together, away from the pile of stones in the corner, and their jokes were quiet and they smiled rather than laughed. The women, wearing faded house dresses and sweaters, came shortly after their menfolk. They greeted one another and exchanged bits of gossip as they went to join their husbands. Soon the women, standing by their husbands, began to call to their children, and the children came reluctantly, having to be called four or five times. Bobby Martin ducked under his mother's grasping hand and ran, laughing, back to the pile of stones. His father spoke up sharply, and Bobby came quickly and took his place between his father and his oldest brother.

The lottery was conducted—as were the square dances, the teenage club, the Halloween program—by Mr. Summers, who had time and energy to devote to civic activities. He was a round-faced, jovial man and he ran the coal business, and people were sorry for him, because he had no children and his wife was a scold. When he arrived in the square, carrying the black wooden box, there was a murmur of conversation among the villagers, and he waved and called, "Little late today, folks." The postmaster, Mr. Graves, followed him, carrying a three-legged stool, and the stool was put in the center of the square and Mr. Summers set the black box down on it. The villagers kept their distance, leaving a space between themselves and the stool, and when Mr. Summers said, "Some of you fellows want to give me a hand?" there was a hesitation before two men, Mr. Martin and his oldest son, Baxter, came forward to hold the box steady on the stool while Mr. Summers stirred up the papers inside it.

The original paraphernalia for the lottery had been lost long ago, and the black box now resting on the stool had been put into use even before Old Man Warner, the oldest man in town, was born. Mr. Summers spoke frequently to the villagers about making a new box, but no one liked to upset even as much tradition as was represented by the black box. There was a story that the present box had been made with some pieces of the box that had preceded it, the one that had been constructed when the first people settled down to make a village here. Every year, after the lottery, Mr. Summers began talking again about a new box, but every year the subject was allowed to fade off without anything's being done. The black box grew shabbier each year; by now it was no longer completely black but splintered badly along one side to show the original wood color, and in some places faded or stained.

Mr. Martin and his oldest son, Baxter, held the black box securely on the stool until Mr. Summers had stirred the papers thoroughly with his hand. Because so much of the ritual had been forgotten or discarded, Mr. Summers had been successful in having slips of paper substituted for the chips of wood that had been used for generations. Chips of wood, Mr. Summers had argued, had been all very well when the village was tiny, but now that the population was more than three hundred and likely to keep on growing, it was necessary to use something that would fit more easily into the black box. The night before the lottery, Mr. Summers and Mr. Graves made up the slips of paper and put them in the box, and it was then taken to the safe of Mr. Summers' coal company and locked up until Mr. Summers was ready to take it to the square next morning. The rest of the year, the box was put away, sometimes one place, sometimes another; it had spent one year in Mr. Graves's barn and another year underfoot in the post office, and sometimes it was set on a shelf in the Martin grocery and left there.

There was a great deal of fussing to be done before Mr. Summers declared the lottery open. There were the lists to make up—of heads of families, heads of households in each family, members of each household in each family. There was the proper swearing-in of Mr. Summers by the postmaster, as the official of the lottery; at one time, some people remembered, there had been a recital of some sort, performed by the official of the lottery, a perfunctory, tuneless chant that had been rattled off duly each year; some people believed that the official of the lottery used to stand just so when he said or sang it, others believed that he was supposed to walk among the people, but years and years ago this part of the ritual had been allowed to lapse. There had been, also, a ritual salute, which the official of the lottery had had to use in addressing each person who came up to draw from the box, but this also had changed with time, until now it was felt necessary only for the official to speak to each person approaching. Mr. Summers was very good at all this; in his clean white shirt and blue jeans, with one hand resting carelessly on the black box, he seemed very proper and important as he talked interminably to Mr. Graves and the Martins.

Just as Mr. Summers finally left off talking and turned to the assembled villagers, Mrs. Hutchinson came hurriedly along the path to the square, her sweater thrown over her shoulders, and slid into place in the back of the crowd. "Clean forgot what day it was," she said to Mrs. Delacroix, who stood next to her, and they both laughed softly. "Thought my old man was out back stacking wood," Mrs. Hutchinson went on, "and then I looked out the window and the kids was gone, and then I remembered it was

5

the twenty-seventh and came a-running." She dried her hands on her apron, and Mrs. Delacroix said, "You're in time, though. They're still talking away up there."

Mrs. Hutchinson craned her neck to see through the crowd and found her husband and children standing near the front. She tapped Mrs. Delacroix on the arm as a farewell and began to make her way through the crowd. The people separated good-humoredly to let her through; two or three people said, in voices just loud enough to be heard across the crowd, "Here comes your Missus, Hutchinson," and "Bill, she made it after all." Mrs. Hutchinson reached her husband, and Mr. Summers, who had been waiting, said cheerfully, "Thought we were going to have to get on without you, Tessie." Mrs. Hutchinson said, grinning, "Wouldn't have me leave m'dishes in the sink, now, would you, Joe?" and soft laughter ran through the crowd as the people stirred back into position after Mrs. Hutchinson's arrival.

"Well, now," Mr. Summers said soberly, "guess we better get started, get this over with, so's we can go back to work. Anybody ain't here?" 10

"Dunbar," several people said, "Dunbar, Dunbar."

Mr. Summers consulted his list. "Clyde Dunbar." he said. "That's right. He's broke his leg, hasn't he? Who's drawing for him?"

"Me, I guess," a woman said, and Mr. Summers turned to look at her. "Wife draws for her husband," Mr. Summers said. "Don't you have a grown boy to do it for you, Janey?" Although Mr. Summers and everyone else in the village knew the answer perfectly well, it was the business of the official of the lottery to ask such questions formally. Mr. Summers waited with an expression of polite interest while Mrs. Dunbar answered.

"Horace's not but sixteen yet," Mrs. Dunbar said regretfully. "Guess I gotta fill in for the old man this year."

"Right," Mr. Summers said. He made a note on the list he was holding. Then he asked, "Watson boy drawing this year?" 15

A tall boy in the crowd raised his hand. "Here," he said. "I'm drawing for m'mother and me." He blinked his eyes nervously and ducked his head as several voices in the crowd said things like "Good fellow, Jack," and "Glad to see your mother's got a man to do it."

"Well," Mr. Summers said, "guess that's everyone. Old Man Warner make it?"

"Here," a voice said, and Mr. Summers nodded.

A sudden hush fell on the crowd as Mr. Summers cleared his throat and looked at the list. "All ready?" he called. "Now, I'll read the names—heads of families first—and the men come up and take a paper out of the box. Keep the paper folded in your hand without looking at it until everyone has had a turn. Everything clear?"

The people had done it so many times that they only half listened to the directions; most of them were quiet, wetting their lips, not looking around. Then Mr. Summers raised one hand high and said, "Adams." A man disengaged himself from the crowd and came forward. "Hi, Steve," Mr. Summers said, and Mr. Adams said, "Hi, Joe." They grinned at one another humorlessly and nervously. Then Mr. Adams reached into the black box and took out a folded paper. He held it firmly by one corner as he turned and went hastily back to his place in the crowd, where he stood a little apart from his family, not looking down at his hand. 20

"Allen," Mr. Summers said. "Anderson. . . . Bentham."

"Seems like there's no time at all between lotteries any more," Mrs. Delacroix said to Mrs. Graves in the back row. "Seems like we got through with the last one only last week."

"Time sure goes fast," Mrs. Graves said.

"Clark. . . . Delacroix."

"There goes my old man," Mrs. Delacroix said. She held her breath while her hus-   25
band went forward.

"Dunbar," Mr. Summers said, and Mrs. Dunbar went steadily to the box while
one of the women said, "Go on, Janey," and another said, "There she goes."

"We're next," Mrs. Graves said. She watched while Mr. Graves came around from
the side of the box, greeted Mr. Summers gravely, and selected a slip of paper from the
box. By now, all through the crowd there were men holding the small folded papers in
their large hands, turning them over and over nervously. Mrs. Dunbar and her two sons
stood together, Mrs. Dunbar holding the slip of paper.

"Harburt. . . . Hutchinson."

"Get up there, Bill," Mrs. Hutchinson said, and the people near her laughed.

"Jones."   30

"They do say," Mrs. Adams said to Old Man Warner, who stood next to him,
"that over in the north village they're talking of giving up the lottery."

Old Man Warner snorted. "Pack of crazy fools," he said. "Listening to the young
folks, nothing's good enough for *them*. Next thing you know, they'll be wanted to go
back to living in caves, nobody work any more, live *that* way for a while. Used to be a
saying about 'Lottery in June, corn be heavy soon.' First thing you know, we'd all be
eating stewed chickweed and acorns. There's *always* been a lottery," he added petulant-
ly. "Bad enough to see young Joe Summers up there joking with everybody."

"Some places have already quit lotteries," Mrs. Adams said.

"Nothing but trouble in *that*," Old Man Warner said stoutly. "Pack of young
fools."

"Martin." And Bobby Martin watched his father go forward. "Overdyke. . . .   35
Percy."

"I wish they'd hurry," Mrs. Dunbar said to her older son. "I wish they'd hurry."

"They're almost through," her son said.

"You get ready to run tell Dad," Mrs. Dunbar said.

Mr. Summers called his own name and then stepped forward precisely and selected
a slip from the box. Then he called, "Warner."

"Seventy-seventh year I been in the lottery," Old Man Warner said as he went   40
through the crowd. "Seventy-seventh time."

"Watson." The tall boy came awkwardly through the crowd. Someone said,
"Don't be nervous, Jack," and Mr. Summers said, "Take your time, son."

"Zanini."

After that, there was a long pause, a breathless pause, until Mr. Summers, holding
his slip of paper in the air, said, "All right, fellows." For a minute, no one moved, and
then all the slips of paper were opened. Suddenly, all the women began to speak at
once, saying, "Who is it?," "Who's got it?," "Is it the Dunbars?," "Is it the Watsons?"
Then the voices began to say, "It's Hutchinson. It's Bill," "Bill Hutchinson's got it."

"Go tell your father," Mrs. Dunbar said to her older son.

People began to look around to see the Hutchinsons. Bill Hutchinson was stand-   45
ing quiet staring down at the paper in his hand. Suddenly, Tessie Hutchinson shouted
to Mr. Summers, "You didn't give him time enough to take any paper he wanted. I saw
you. It wasn't fair."

"Be a good sport, Tessie," Mrs. Delacroix called, and Mrs. Graves said, "All of us
took the same chance."

"Shut up, Tessie," Bill Hutchinson said.

"Well, everyone," Mr. Summers said, "that was done pretty fast, and now we've got to be hurrying a little more to get done in time." He consulted his next list. "Bill," he said, "you draw for the Hutchinson family. You got any other households in the Hutchinsons?"

"There's Don and Eva," Mrs. Hutchinson yelled. "Make *them* take their chance!"

"Daughters draw for their husbands' families, Tessie," Mr. Summers said gently. 50 "You know that as well as anyone else."

"It wasn't *fair*," Tessie said.

"I guess not, Joe," Bill Hutchinson said regretfully. "My daughter draws with her husband's family, that's only fair. And I've got no other family except the kids."

"Then, as far as drawing for families is concerned, it's you." Mr. Summers said in explanation, "and as far as drawing for households is concerned, that's you, too. Right?"

"Right," Bill Hutchinson said.

"How many kids, Bill?" Mr. Summers asked formally. 55

"Three," Bill Hutchinson said. "There's Bill, Jr., and Nancy, and little Dave. And Tessie and me."

"All right, then," Mr. Summers said. "Harry, you got their tickets back?"

Mr. Graves nodded and held up the slips of paper. "Put them in the box, then," Mr. Summers directed. "Take Bill's and put it in."

"I think we ought to start over," Mrs. Hutchinson said, as quietly as she could, "I tell you it wasn't *fair*. You didn't give him time enough to choose. *Every*body saw that."

Mr. Graves had selected the five slips and put them in the box, and he dropped all 60 the papers but those onto the ground, where the breeze caught them and lifted them off.

"Listen, everybody," Mrs. Hutchinson was saying to the people around her.

"Ready, Bill?" Mr. Summers asked, and Bill Hutchinson, with one quick glance around at his wife and children, nodded.

"Remember," Mr. Summers said, "take the slips and keep them folded until each person has taken one. Harry, you help little Dave." Mr. Graves took the hand of the little boy, who came willingly with him up to the box. "Take a paper out of the box, Davy," Mr. Summers said. Davy put his hand into the box and laughed. "Take just *one* paper," Mr. Summers said. "Harry, you hold it for him." Mr. Graves took the child's hand and removed the folded paper from the tight fist and held it while little Dave stood next to him and looked up at him wonderingly.

"Nancy next," Mr. Summers said. Nancy was twelve, and her school friends breathed heavily as she went forward, switching her skirt, and took a slip daintily from the box. "Bill, Jr.," Mr. Summers said, and Billy, his face red and his feet over-large, nearly knocked the box over as he got a paper out. "Tessie," Mr. Summers said. She hesitated for a minute, looking around defiantly, and then set her lips and went up to the box. She snatched a paper out and held it behind her.

"Bill," Mr. Summers said, and Bill Hutchinson reached into the box and felt 65 around, bringing his hand out at last with the slip of paper in it.

The crowd was quiet. A girl whispered, "I hope it's not Nancy," and the sound of the whisper reached the edges of the crowd.

"It's not the way it used to be," Old Man Warner said clearly. "People ain't the way they used to be."

"All right," Mr. Summers said. "Open the papers. Harry, you open little Dave's."

Mr. Graves opened the slip of paper and there was a general sigh through the crowd as he held it up and everyone could see that it was blank. Nancy and Bill, Jr.

opened theirs at the same time, and both beamed and laughed, turning around to the crowd and holding their slips of paper above their heads.

"Tessie," Mr. Summers said. There was a pause, and then Mr. Summers looked at   70
Bill Hutchinson, and Bill unfolded his paper and showed it. It was blank.

"It's Tessie," Mr. Summers said, and his voice was hushed. "Show us her paper, Bill."

Bill Hutchinson went over to his wife and forced the slip of paper out of her hand. It had a black spot on it, the black spot Mr. Summers had made the night before with the heavy pencil in the coal-company office. Bill Hutchinson held it up, and there was a stir in the crowd.

"All right, folks," Mr. Summers said. "Let's finish quickly."

Although the villagers had forgotten the ritual and lost the original black box, they still remembered to use stones. The pile of stones the boys had made earlier was ready; there were stones on the ground with the blowing scraps of paper that had come out of the box. Mrs. Delacroix selected a stone so large she had to pick it up with both hands and turned to Mrs. Dunbar. "Come on," she said. "Hurry up."

Mrs. Dunbar had small stones in both hands, and she said, gasping for breath, "I   75
can't run at all. You'll have to go ahead and I'll catch up with you."

The children had stones already, and someone gave little Davy Hutchinson a few pebbles.

Tessie Hutchinson was in the center of a cleared space by now, and she held her hands out desperately as the villagers moved in on her. "It isn't fair," she said. A stone hit her on the side of the head.

Old Man Warner was saying, "Come on, come on, everyone." Steve Adams was in the front of the crowd of villagers, with Mrs. Graves beside him.

"It isn't fair, it isn't right," Mrs. Hutchinson screamed, and then they were upon her.

THE RECEPTIVE READER

1. The story is told in apparently straightforward *chronological* fashion. As you read along, do you feel nevertheless that essential information is missing? What is being withheld and why? Why does the author tell the story the way she does?

2. Why do you think the author goes into such detail about the procedure, the preparations, the box used and its history? What possibly significant details stand out?

3. How did you expect the story to come out? When were you sure of the outcome? Does the author provide any *foreshadowing* or early hints of what is to come?

4. *Tradition* becomes a key force in this story. What role does it play in the story as a whole? What is its influence, its power? Who speaks up for it? Does anyone question it?

5. Jackson is a master of *irony*—of contradictions between what we might innocently expect and what happens in grim reality. What is ironic about the organizer, Mr. Summers—his other activities, his behavior during the ritual? Is there any humor in the way the author portrays him, and if so, what kind?

6. How does the author lead up the *climactic* event? How does she first introduce the victim and why? Why do you think the author puts in a second drawing—somewhat like a runoff election?

7. This story is often read as a study in mass psychology. What are the reactions of the crowd as the story approaches its climactic ending? Do they provide a comment on or insights into mob psychology?

8. How does the victim react? Is she right when she says the drawing was not fair? What are your feelings as you watch her reaction?

9. Where are you in this story? Do you identify with the victims? the instigators? the bystanders? Or do you stay aloof, like an observer from a distant planet? (How do your reactions compare with those of your classmates?)

10. Is there any division in the story along gender lines? Is it a coincidence that the lottery is run by men but that the victim in the story is a woman? Does the story show us a society in which the supporters of the lottery are male and potential resistance is female?

11. Do you object to or resent the story? How do you explain the reactions of hostile readers?

THE PERSONAL RESPONSE

What do you know about societies that used stoning as punishment? (What biblical reference comes to mind?) Can you think of any parallel situation from your own observation, experience, reading, or viewing? Does our society today have similar rituals? Are any of the psychological dynamics Jackson traces in this story at work in our society today?

THE CREATIVE DIMENSION

Have you ever felt unsatisfied at the end of a story? Have you felt unwilling to let the matter rest where the author concluded the story? Use your imagination—write a sequel to a story that left you wondering or unsatisfied. Study the following sequel as an example. How well does it get into the spirit of the original?

The Lottery, Part II

It is now twenty years later—June 27, 1968. It's the morning of the annual lottery. For a while, the lottery had taken two days to complete because there were so many townspeople, but in the last few years many of them moved out of the area and, too, there weren't many new people resettling there.

Bob and Harry Jones, Dave Hutchinson, Dick Delacroix, and their wives and children are the first villagers to arrive. In a short time, all the villagers are there, even Really Old Man Warner, who has just turned 97 but gets around in his wheelchair.

Suddenly a hush falls over the crowd as Mr. Summers, scoutmaster and conductor of the lottery, comes forward carrying a grey box (at one time it was black) and pronounces the lottery open. One by one, the head of each household comes up and draws a slip of paper from the grey box—Adams, Bowman, Carter, and so forth until Really Old Man Warner draws the last slip of paper.

After that, there's a sort of pause and then everyone opens up his or her slip of paper. Everyone begins talking at once. "Who is it?" "Who's got the dot?" Then the people begin to say, "It's Warner. It's Really Old Man Warner."

Everyone looks at Really Old Man Warner, who seems to be backpedalling in his wheelchair. "You know," he croaks, "some villages are talking about giving up the lottery."

CROSS-REFERENCES—For Discussion or Writing

Some years later, Shirley Jackson wrote *The Witchcraft of Salem Village,* a book for adolescents on the trial and execution of the Salem witches in seventeenth-century Massachusetts. (She had a private collection of over five hundred books on witchcraft and demonology from many countries.) This history of persecution and mass hysteria may already have been in Jackson's mind when she wrote "The Lottery." Research the Salem witchcraft trials. What are important parallels and differences between them and the events of this story?

EXPLORATIONS

The Critic's Voice

Lenemaja Friedman says in her book *Shirley Jackson* (1975),

> Jackson views man's nature as basically evil, and she indicates that, in his relationship with his fellow beings, man does not hesitate to lie, cheat, and steal—even to kill when it suits his purposes to do so. As in "The Lottery," he may be persuaded that the evil committed is for the common good; but he nevertheless has the herd instinct and does not oppose the harmful mores of his community. And, sadly enough, man does not improve with age; the grandmothers are as guilty of hypocrisy and wrongdoing as the younger members of society. (p. 76)

What evidence from the story would you cite when supporting or taking issue with this view?

WILLIAM FAULKNER   (1897–1962)

INTERVIEWER: Some people say they can't understand
your writing, even after they read it two or three times.
What approach would you suggest to them?
FAULKNER: Read it four times.

Faulkner was one of the great experimenters and innovators in early-twentieth-century fiction. In spite of his difficult, challenging prose (with many-layered sentences that may sprawl across paragraph breaks) and in spite of the broken-mirror effects of his narrative technique, he became one of the most widely read, translated, and discussed writers of modern times. His best-known novels—*As I Lay Dying* (1930), *Sanctuary* (1931), *Absalom, Absalom!* (1936), *Intruder in the Dust* (1948), *Requiem for a Nun* (1951)—have been read around the world. His first major critical success, *The Sound and the Fury* (1929), told the story of the same events as seen in turn by four different characters. He made readers look at characters and events as though seen through the different facets of a prism, with his readers left to form their own perception of the underlying story. All or part of a Faulkner story may use the technique of the **interior monologue,** transcribing the thoughts and feelings racing through a character's mind.

Faulkner's novels and short stories take us to a setting rich in the memories and traumas of the Old South. Many of his stories and novels were part of an ongoing saga of the people of his fictitious Yoknapatawpha County, modeled on Lafayette County in northern Mississippi, where he lived in Oxford, home of the University of Mississippi. As a child, Faulkner lived with a kindly but determined Scottish great-grandfather who made each child in the house recite a memorized Bible verse before breakfast (or else no breakfast). Faulkner served briefly in the Royal Canadian Flying Corps in World War I and lived in New Orleans for a time, working for a newspaper and trying to make a living as a writer. He returned to Mississippi in 1926 and eventually became a writer in residence at the university. He received the Nobel Prize for literature in 1950 and gave a much-reprinted acceptance speech in which he spoke of "the writer's duty" to champion personal values in an age of mass culture. As he once said in a interview, he believed in an individual code through which an individual "makes himself a better human being than his nature wants to be, if he followed his nature only."

Two sources of conflict tend to set events in motion in Faulkner's fiction:

✧ The first source of conflict is the meeting of the old world and the new. His characters are often embittered by seeing their values threatened in an uprooted modern world. They are often country people trying to live "off here to themselves"—to keep their distance from a new world of neon lights, easy quick money, and shiny automobiles traded in for a new model before the old one is paid for. Often the characters in his stories are fiercely, stubbornly independent—a thorn in the side to state officials, tax collectors, and government agents trying to "interfere with how a man farmed his own land, raised his own cotton."

✧ The second source of conflict derives from the traditional class structure of the South. Faulkner's own great-grandfather had become wealthy and famous in the Mississippi of before the Civil War. He became a colonel in the Confederate Army and was killed years later in a duel. Many of Faulkner's characters belong to clans—the Sartorises, the Compsons, the Sutpens, the McCaslins, the de Spains—that represent the old social aristocracy of the South. They belong to families that trace their origins back to the original settlers and that often still live in the antebellum, prewar mansions with their columned porticoes.

However, often the offspring of the old families are beset by debts and social upstarts—such as Flem Snopes, one of the "litter" of a family of poor white tenant farmers who never stay long in one place. In a story like "Spotted Horses" (1931), we see Flem at work—pushy, unscrupulous, dishonest, advancing his fortunes with dubious money-making schemes. In "Barn Burning" (1939), we look through the eyes of a boy named Colonel Sartoris Snopes at a vindictive, abusive father. The elder Snopes is a man with "wolflike independence" and "a ferocious conviction in the rightness of his own action." He spent years during or after the war hiding out with a string of captured (stolen) horses; he burnt down a neighbor's barn after a quarrel over a runaway hog; he first smears with his dirty boots and then ruins for good a precious white rug in the mansion of his new landlord, a Major de Spain. And always there are the black people of the Old South—often as servants, as observers, but at other times, as in the story "Dry September" (1931), caught up in the whirlpool of racial hatred and bigotry.

Faulkner broke up traditional plot structure. He told his stories in indirect, or oblique, ways, forcing us as readers to wonder at and puzzle out what is happening (the way we are often forced to in real life). Tense antagonisms, destructive passion, and raw violence erupt in the stories, but we tend to see the violent events only from a partial angle or in a confused rush, as we might in real life. The stories often lead up to a **climax**—a climactic event or revelation. However, they do so in a nonlinear way, through partial testimonies or through provocative details that yet seem to carry only incomplete information. Faulkner frequently uses **flashbacks**, in which glimpses of the past slowly begin to explain or illuminate the present. In the following famous Faulkner story, how does the truth, at first only hinted at, come slowly into focus? What makes a Faulkner story such as this one more haunting than straightforward storytelling?

A Rose for Emily   1931

When Miss Emily Grierson died, our whole town went to her funeral: the men through a sort of respectful affection for a fallen monument, the women mostly out of curiosity to see the inside of her house, which no one save an old manservant—a combined gardener and cook—had seen in at least ten years.

It was a big, squarish frame house that had once been white, decorated with cupolas and spires and scrolled balconies in the heavily lightsome style of the seventies, set on what had once been our most select street. But garages and cotton gins had encroached and obliterated even the august names of that neighborhood; only Miss Emily's house was left, lifting its stubborn and coquettish decay above the cotton wagons and the gasoline pumps—an eyesore among eyesores. And now Miss Emily had gone to join the representatives of those august names where they lay in the cedar-bemused cemetery among the ranked and anonymous graves of Union and Confederate soldiers who fell at the battle of Jefferson.

Alive, Miss Emily had been a tradition, a duty, and a care; a sort of hereditary obligation upon the town, dating from that day in 1894 when Colonel Sartoris, the mayor—he who fathered the edict that no Negro woman should appear on the streets without an apron—remitted her taxes, the dispensation dating from the death of her father on into perpetuity. Not that Miss Emily would have accepted charity. Colonel Sartoris invented an involved tale to the effect that Miss Emily's father had loaned money to the town, which the town, as a matter of business, preferred this way of repaying. Only a man of Colonel Sartoris' generation and thought could have invented it, and only a woman could have believed it.

When the next generation, with its more modern ideas, became mayors and aldermen, this arrangement created some little dissatisfaction. On the first of the year they mailed her a tax notice. February came, and there was no reply. They wrote her a formal letter, asking her to call at the sheriff's office at her convenience. A week later the mayor wrote her himself, offering to call or to send his car for her, and received in reply a note on paper of an archaic shape, in a thin, flowing calligraphy in faded ink, to the effect that she no longer went out at all. The tax notice was also enclosed, without comment.

They called a special meeting of the Board of Aldermen. A deputation waited upon   5
her, knocked at the door through which no visitor had passed since she ceased giving
china-painting lessons eight or ten years earlier. They were admitted by the old Negro
into a dim hall from which a stairway mounted into still more shadow. It smelled of
dust and disuse—a close, dank smell. The Negro led them into the parlor. It was furnished in heavy, leather-covered furniture. When the Negro opened the blinds of one
window, they could see that the leather was cracked; and when they sat down, a faint
dust rose sluggishly about their thighs, spinning with slow motes in the single sun-ray.
On a tarnished gilt easel before the fireplace stood a crayon portrait of Miss Emily's father.

They rose when she entered—a small, fat woman in black, with a thin gold chain
descending to her waist and vanishing into her belt, leaning on an ebony cane with a
tarnished gold head. Her skeleton was small and spare; perhaps that was why what
would have been merely plumpness in another was obesity in her. She looked bloated,
like a body long submerged in motionless water, and of that pallid hue. Her eyes, lost
in the fatty ridges of her face, looked like two small pieces of coal pressed into a lump
of dough as they moved from one face to another while the visitors stated their errand.

She did not ask them to sit. She just stood in the door and listened quietly until
the spokesman came to a stumbling halt. Then they could hear the invisible watch ticking at the end of the gold chain.

Her voice was dry and cold. "I have no taxes in Jefferson. Colonel Sartoris explained it to me. Perhaps one of you can gain access to the city records and satisfy yourselves."

"But we have. We are the city authorities, Miss Emily. Didn't you get a notice
from the sheriff, signed by him?"

"I received a paper, yes," Miss Emily said. "Perhaps he considers himself the sher-   10
iff. . . . I have no taxes in Jefferson."

"But there is nothing on the books to show that, you see. We must go by the—"

"See Colonel Sartoris. I have no taxes in Jefferson."

"But, Miss Emily—"

"See Colonel Sartoris." (Colonel Sartoris had been dead almost ten years.) "I have
no taxes in Jefferson. Tobe!" The Negro appeared. "Show these gentlemen out."

II

So she vanquished them, horse and foot, just as she had vanquished their fathers   15
thirty years before about the smell. That was two years after her father's death and a
short time after her sweetheart—the one we believed would marry her—had deserted
her. After her father's death she went out very little; after her sweetheart went away,
people hardly saw her at all. A few of the ladies had the temerity to call, but were not
received, and the only sign of life about the place was the Negro man—a young man
then—going in and out with a market basket.

"Just as if a man—any man—could keep a kitchen properly," the ladies said; so
they were not surprised when the smell developed. It was another link between the
gross, teeming world and the high and mighty Griersons.

A neighbor, a woman, complained to the mayor, Judge Stevens, eighty years old.

"But what will you have me do about it, madam?" he said.

"Why, send her word to stop it," the woman said. "Isn't there a law?"

"I'm sure that won't be necessary," Judge Stevens said. "It's probably just a snake   20
or a rat that nigger of hers killed in the yard. I'll speak to him about it."

The next day he received two more complaints, one from a man who came in diffident deprecation. "We really must do something about it, Judge. I'd be the last one in

the world to bother Miss Emily, but we've got to do something." That night the Board of Aldermen met—three graybeards and one younger man, a member of the rising generation.

"It's simple enough," he said. "Send her word to have her place cleaned up. Give her a certain time to do it in, and if she don't . . ."

"Dammit, sir," Judge Stevens said, "will you accuse a lady to her face of smelling bad?"

So the next night, after midnight, four men crossed Miss Emily's lawn and slunk about the house like burglars, sniffing along the base of the brickwork and at the cellar openings while one of them performed a regular sowing motion with his hand out of a sack slung from his shoulder. They broke open the cellar door and sprinkled lime there, and in all the outbuildings. As they recrossed the lawn, a window that had been dark was lighted and Miss Emily sat in it, the light behind her, and her upright torso motionless as that of an idol. They crept quietly across the lawn and into the shadow of the locusts that lined the street. After a week or two the smell went away.

That was when people had begun to feel really sorry for her. People in our town, remembering how old lady Wyatt, her great-aunt, had gone completely crazy at last, believed that the Griersons held themselves a little too high for what they really were. None of the young men were quite good enough for Miss Emily and such. We had long thought of them as a tableau, Miss Emily a slender figure in white in the background, her father a spraddled silhouette in the foreground, his back to her and clutching a horsewhip, the two of them framed by the back-flung front door. So when she got to be thirty and was still single, we were not pleased exactly, but vindicated; even with insanity in the family she wouldn't have turned down all of her chances if they had really materialized. 25

When her father died, it got about that the house was all that was left to her; and in a way, people were glad. At last they could pity Miss Emily. Being left alone, and a pauper, she had become humanized. Now she too would know the old thrill and the old despair of a penny more or less.

The day after his death all the ladies prepared to call at the house and offer condolence and aid, as is our custom. Miss Emily met them at the door, dressed as usual and with no trace of grief on her face. She told them that her father was not dead. She did that for three days, with the ministers calling on her, and the doctors, trying to persuade her to let them dispose of the body. Just as they were about to resort to law and force, she broke down, and they buried her father quickly.

We did not say she was crazy then. We believed she had to do that. We remembered all the young men her father had driven away, and we knew that with nothing left, she would have to cling to that which had robbed her, as people will.

III

She was sick for a long time. When we saw her again, her hair was cut short, making her look like a girl, with a vague resemblance to those angels in colored church windows—sort of tragic and serene.

The town had just let the contracts for paving the sidewalks, and in the summer after her father's death they began the work. The construction company came with niggers and mules and machinery, and a foreman named Homer Barron, a Yankee—a big, dark, ready man, with a big voice and eyes lighter than his face. The little boys would follow in groups to hear him cuss the niggers, and the niggers singing in time to the rise and fall of picks. Pretty soon he knew everybody in town. Whenever you heard a lot of laughing anywhere about the square, Homer Barron would be in the center of the 30 group. Presently we began to see him and Miss Emily on Sunday afternoons driving in the yellow-wheeled buggy and the matched team of bays from the livery stable.

At first we were glad that Miss Emily would have an interest, because the ladies all said, "Of course a Grierson would not think seriously of a Northerner, a day laborer." But there were still others, older people, who said that even grief could not cause a real lady to forget *noblesse oblige*—without calling it *noblesse oblige*. They just said, "Poor Emily. Her kinsfolk should come to her." She had some kin in Alabama; but years ago her father had fallen out with them over the estate of old lady Wyatt, the crazy woman, and there was no communication between the two families. They had not even been represented at the funeral.

And as soon as the old people said, "Poor Emily," the whispering began. "Do you suppose it's really so?" they said to one another. "Of course it is. What else could . . ." This behind their hands; rustling of craned silk and satin behind jalousies closed upon the sun of Sunday afternoon as the thin, swift clop-clop-clop of the matched team passed: "Poor Emily."

She carried her head high enough—even when we believed that she was fallen. It was as if she demanded more than ever the recognition of her dignity as the last Grierson; as if it had wanted that touch of earthiness to reaffirm her imperviousness. Like when she bought the rat poison, the arsenic. That was over a year after they had begun to say "Poor Emily," and while the two female cousins were visiting her.

"I want some poison," she said to the druggist. She was over thirty then, still a slight woman, though thinner than usual, with cold, haughty black eyes in a face the flesh of which was strained across the temples and about the eyesockets as you imagine a lighthouse-keeper's face ought to look. "I want some poison," she said.

"Yes, Miss Emily. What kind? For rats and such? I'd recom—"   35

"I want the best you have. I don't care what kind."

The druggist named several. "They'll kill anything up to an elephant. But what you want is—"

"Arsenic," Miss Emily said. "Is that a good one?"

"Is . . . arsenic? Yes, ma'am. But what you want—"

"I want arsenic."   40

The druggist looked down at her. She looked back at him, erect, her face like a strained flag. "Why, of course," the druggist said. "If that's what you want. But the law requires you to tell what you are going to use it for."

Miss Emily just stared at him, her head tilted back in order to look him eye for eye, until he looked away and went and got the arsenic and wrapped it up. The Negro delivery boy brought her the package; the druggist didn't come back. When she opened the package at home there was written on the box, under the skull and bones: "For rats."

IV

So the next day we all said, "She will kill herself"; and we said it would be the best thing. When she had first begun to be seen with Homer Barron, we had said, "She will marry him." Then we said, "She will persuade him yet," because Homer himself had remarked—he liked men, and it was known that he drank with the younger men in the Elks' Club—that he was not a marrying man. Later we said, "Poor Emily" behind the jalousies as they passed on Sunday afternoon in the glittering buggy, Miss Emily with her head high and Homer Barron with his hat cocked and a cigar in this teeth, reins and whip in a yellow glove.

Then some of the ladies began to say that it was a disgrace to the town and a bad example to the young peple. The men did not want to interfere, but at last the ladies forced the Baptist minister—Miss Emily's people were Episcopal—to call upon her. He would never divulge what happened during that interview, but he refused to go back again. The next Sunday they again drove about the streets, and the following day the minister's wife wrote to Miss Emily's relations in Alabama.

So she had blood-kin under her roof again and we sat back to watch develop-   45
ments. At first nothing happened. Then we were sure that they were to be married. We learned that Miss Emily had been to the jeweler's and ordered a man's toilet set in sil-ver, with the letters H.B. on each piece. Two days later we learned that she had bought a complete outfit of men's clothing, including a nightshirt, and we said, "They are mar-ried." We were really glad. We were glad because the two female cousins were even more Grierson than Miss Emily had ever been.

So we were not surprised when Homer Barron—the streets had been finished some time since—was gone. We were a little disappointed that there was not a public blowing-off, but we believed that he had gone on to prepare for Miss Emily's coming, or to give her a chance to get rid of the cousins. (By that time it was a cabal, and we were all Miss Emily's allies to help circumvent the cousins.) Sure enough, after another week they departed. And, as we had expected all along, within three days Homer Bar-ron was back in town. A neighbor saw the Negro man admit him at the kitchen door at dusk one evening.

And that was the last we saw of Homer Barron. And of Miss Emily for some time. The Negro man went in and out with the market basket, but the front door remained closed. Now and then we would see her at a window for a moment, as the men did that night when they sprinkled the lime, but for almost six months she did not appear on the streets. Then we knew that this was to be expected too; as if that quality of her fa-ther which had thwarted her woman's life so many times had been too virulent and too furious to die.

When we next saw Miss Emily, she had grown fat and her hair was turning gray. During the next few years it grew grayer and grayer until it attained an even pepper-and-salt iron-gray, when it ceased turning. Up to the day of her death at seventy-four it was still that vigorous iron-gray, like the hair of an active man.

From that time on her front door remained closed, save for a period of six or seven years, when she was about forty, during which she gave lessons in china-painting. She fitted up a studio in one of the downstairs rooms, where the daughters and grand-daughters of Colonel Sartoris' contemporaries were sent to her with the same regularity and in the same spirit that they were sent on Sundays with a twenty-five cent piece for the collection plate. Meanwhile her taxes had been remitted.

The newer generation became the backbone and the spirit of the town, and the   50
painting pupils grew up and fell away and did not send their children to her with boxes of color and tedious brushes and pictures cut from the ladies' magazines. The front door closed upon the last one and remained closed for good. When the town got free postal delivery, Miss Emily alone refused to let them fasten the metal numbers above her door and attach a mailbox to it. She would not listen to them.

Daily, monthly, yearly we watched the Negro grow grayer and more stooped, going in and out with the market basket. Each December we sent her a tax notice, which would be returned by the post office a week later, unclaimed. Now and then we would see her in one of the downstairs windows—she had evidently shut up the top floor of the house—like the carven torso of an idol in a niche, looking or not looking at us, we could never tell which. Thus she passed from generation to generation—dear, inescapable, impervious, tranquil, and perverse.

And so she died. Fell ill in the house filled with dust and shadows, with only a doddering Negro man to wait on her. We did not even know she was sick; we had long since given up trying to get any information from the Negro. He talked to no one, probably not even to her, for his voice had grown harsh and rusty, as if from disuse.

She died in one of the downstairs rooms, in a heavy walnut bed with a curtain, her gray head propped on a pillow yellow and moldy with age and lack of sunlight.

V

The Negro met the first of the ladies at the front door and let them in, with their hushed, sibilant voices and their quick, curious glances, and then he disappeared. He walked right through the house and out the back and was not seen again.

The two female cousins came at once. They held the funeral on the second day, with the town coming to look at Miss Emily beneath a mass of bought flowers, with the crayon face of her father musing profoundly above the bier and the ladies sibilant and macabre; and the very old men—some in their brushed Confederate uniforms—on the porch and the lawn, talking of Miss Emily as if she had been a contemporary of theirs, believing that they had danced with her and courted her perhaps, confusing time with its mathematical progression, as the old do, to whom all the past is not a diminishing road, but, instead, a huge meadow which no winter ever quite touches, divided from them now by the narrow bottleneck of the most recent decade of years.

Already we knew that there was one room in that region above stairs which no one had seen in forty years, and which would have to be forced. They waited until Miss Emily was decently in the ground before they opened it.

The violence of breaking down the door seemed to fill this room with pervading dust. A thin, acrid pall as of the tomb seemed to lie everywhere upon this room decked and furnished as for a bridal: upon the valance curtains of faded rose color, upon the rose-shaded lights, upon the dressing table, upon the delicate array of crystal and the man's toilet things backed with tarnished silver, silver so tarnished that the monogram was obscured. Among them lay a collar and tie, as if they had just been removed, which, lifted, left upon the surface a pale crescent in the dust. Upon the chair hung the suit, carefully folded; beneath it the two mute shoes and the discarded socks.

The man himself lay in the bed.

For a long while we just stood there, looking down at the profound and fleshless grin. The body had apparently once lain in the attitude of an embrace, but now the long sleep that outlasts love, that conquers even the grimace of love, had cuckolded him. What was left of him, rotted beneath what was left of the nightshirt, had become inextricable from the bed in which he lay; and upon him and upon the pillow beside him lay that even coating of the patient and biding dust.

Then we noticed that in the second pillow was the indentation of a head. One of us lifted something from it, and leaning forward, that faint and invisible dust dry and acrid in the nostrils, we saw a long strand of iron-gray hair.

THE RECEPTIVE READER

1. Faulkner said that the seed of this story was a picture in his mind "of the strand of hair on the pillow. . . . Simply a picture of a strand of hair on the pillow in the abandoned house." How does the strand of hair sum up what happened in this story or what is important in this story?

2. How and why does Faulkner's story depart from straightforward chronological storytelling? Where and how does Faulkner introduce the plot elements most essential to your understanding of the story? Can you reconstruct from the author's *flashbacks* a chronological sequence of events?

3. What is the keynote in Faulkner's treatment of the *setting*—Miss Emily's house, her street, the town?

4. How essential to the story is Faulkner's treatment of tradition and the Old South? What is Faulkner's attitude toward Colonel Sartoris' generation and the "next generation, with its more modern ideas"? What is the meaning of *noblesse oblige,* and what is the role of this concept in the story?

5. What picture emerges of Miss Emily as the *main character*? Is there a central clue to her personality? Is she a creature of her environment? What explains the attitude of the townspeople toward her?

6. Poetic justice is meted out to a character in poetry or fiction when he or she is justly punished for an offense, whether or not it was punishable according to law. Is Homer Barron the victim of poetic justice?

7. Faulkner is known for a *style* rich in unusual words, provocative images, and emotional overtones. What is the meaning of *coquettish, macabre, impervious, perverse*? How are these words related to the prevailing mood of the story? What is the effect on the reader of comparing Emily to a "carven torso of an idol in a niche"? What other striking imaginative comparisons play a role in the story?

8. The word *grotesque* describes literature or art that produces mixed reactions—emotions of terror or disgust mingling with dark or shuddery humor. Where do such mixed effects play a role in this story?

9. One student wrote : "Time does not pass in linear chronological fashion in this story; the plot does not move forward through the traditional build-up of tension to climax and denouement. However, in its indirect and apparently meandering way, the story leads to a much more startling climax than could have been possible in a classic short-story format." Can you show whether the student was right?

THE PERSONAL RESPONSE

As you read the story, do you feel you are expected to admire Miss Emily, condemn her, write her off as an eccentric? In what ways does the author steer your reactions about her? What are your feelings about her? Do you think you would feel different about her if Faulkner had told her story in a more traditional fashion? How or why?

CROSS-REFERENCES—For Discussion or Writing

✧ Compare and contrast the Old South of Faulkner's "A Rose for Emily" with the New South of Mason's "Shiloh." What is the relationship between the setting and the characters in each story?

✧ Compare and contrast plot structure in this story and in a more traditional story like Welty's "A Visit of Charity" or Malamud's "The Magic Barrel." How do differences in the story line affect the overall impact of each story?

✧ Compare and contrast Jackson's "The Lottery" and Faulkner's "A Rose for Emily" as modern horror stories. How does their use of horror differ from its use in popular entertainment? What use do the two authors make of the grotesque—a mixture of terror and dark humor?

WRITING ABOUT LITERATURE

4. Charting the Plot (Focus on Revision)

The Writing Workshop   In writing about plot, try to focus on the key question: How does the plot serve the story as a whole? Is it a mere scaffolding—a mere opportunity for characters to talk and act, to show who they are? Or does something important develop, take shape? Is the story perhaps headed toward some climactic event—some goal? Does it move toward a recognition or *epiphany*—some insight that strikes us forcibly, illuminating in a flash something that was previously obscure?

Do not just retell the story. Ask yourself: What am I going to do with this story? In the sequence of miscellaneous events, try to find a ground plan. Look for the pattern—the design in the carpet. (When you start writing in the "and-then," "and-then" mode, your paper is likely to be in trouble.) Consider guidelines like the following:

✧ *Avoid mere plot summaries.* Use them only if they are needed to help the readers find their bearings. (Summaries can be useful for giving an initial overview—they can make the reader see the overall line of development in a complex or multilayered story.)

✧ *Look at what sets a story in motion.* Look at key characters and their unmet needs, unfulfilled desires, or hidden agendas. Look at a situation that has in it potential sources of conflict: festering resentments, fatal misunderstandings.

✧ *Identify major stages.* Make sure your readers get a sense of the overall development of the story. Highlight turning points. Show how a story builds to a climactic event. Show how a conflict plays itself out and reaches a resolution.

✧ *Disentangle major threads.* Look for **polarities**—the possible play of polar opposites, such as the romantic and the realistic strands in Malamud's "The Magic Barrel."

✧ *Look for features that reinforce the overall pattern.* Look for examples of **foreshadowing**—for early hints of what is to come. Look for **recurrence** of key elements, for passages that echo earlier issues or concerns.

✧ *Take a second look at apparent detours or digressions.* See if you can relate apparently minor details to the larger pattern.

Instructor's Comments and Revision   Much revision of student writing used to be little more than retyping with a few cosmetic touches. With the coming of computers, changes in a previous draft have become much easier to make. Whether you use a typewriter or a word processor, take seriously editorial suggestions that ask you to do some real rewriting, some real rethinking.

Learn to respond to feedback from an instructor or editor as you revise a first draft. Study the samples of instructors' comments in the material that follows. Look at rewrites of passages in response to an instructor's comments.

◇ *Pay special attention to comments on your opening paragraphs.* Does the focus of your paper become clear enough? Does your reader get a preview of your overall approach? Should you spell out your main point or **thesis** more fully or more clearly early in your paper? (Remember that in real life many readers don't go on beyond the opening of an essay if they find it unfocused, murky, or confusing.)

◇ *Respond to suggestions for strengthening your overall plan.* Consider if reshuffling material might make for a stronger progression—for instance, from the fairly obvious to the controversial or new.

◇ *Respond to advice for improving the flow of material.* Respond to suggestions for building up a rich texture of comment, quotation, and interpretation.

ORIGINAL: After his first meeting with Salzman, the strange little matchmaker, Leo expresses doubts about the wisdom of having a bride chosen by someone else. Malamud writes,

> Leo was low in spirits. . . . He explained it as arising from Salzman's failure to produce a suitable bride for him. He did not care for his type of clientele. But when Leo found himself hesitating over whether to seek out another matchmaker, one more polished than Pinye, he wondered if it could be—his protestations to the contrary, and although he honored his father and mother—that he did not, in essence, care for the matchmaking institution? This thought he quickly put out of his mind.

COMMENT: You are probably using too many block quotations ("chunk quotations"—because they can make your paper seem chunky or lumpy). Save them to clinch an argument or highlight a major turning point. Try to work short, apt quotations into the flow of your argument.

REVISED: The first meeting with Salzman, the strange little matchmaker, does not go well. Leo is disheartened and expresses doubts about the wisdom of having a bride chosen by someone else. He entertains notions of hiring another matchmaker, someone "more polished than Pinye." But when Leo examines his deeper feelings, he wonders "if it could be—his protestations to the contrary, and although he honored his father and mother—that he did not, in essence, care for the matchmaking institution?" Although Leo has not yet realized it, this question is the beginning of the conflict between his traditional upbringing and his romantic nature. Although he "quickly put [this thought] out of his mind," it has planted a niggling suspicion that reaches full bloom as the story progresses.

◇ *Pay special attention to comments on weak transitions.* Where did the reader fail to see a logical connection that you thought was there? Be sure to respond to questions like "Why is this in here at this point? How are these two sections of your paper *related*? How does this fit into your overall plan?"

✧ *Respond to suggestions for strengthening your conclusion.*

ORIGINAL: Jackson's "The Lottery" showed how people will do all kinds of crazy things, even things they don't really want to do, in the name of tradition.

COMMENT: Perfunctory or lame conclusion? What *is* the force of tradition? Why does it seem to carry such weight?

REVISED: Jackson's "The Lottery" shows how tradition is like a subliminal force—because of it, people will do all kinds of crazy things, even things they don't really want to. We witness the peer pressure involved in tradition, forcing people to do something just because everyone else is doing it, and no one else is questioning it. As the story shows, human beings have a strong need to belong and be accepted by their society. This need causes them to want to conform, blindly and almost unconsciously, to the rules that their society has set up. Even stronger than tradition itself are the peer pressure and the human need for acceptance that fuel it.

Study the following sample student paper. Does it make you more conscious of the role of plot in giving shape to a story as a whole?

SAMPLE STUDENT PAPER

Magic and Reality

"The Magic Barrel." In its very title, Bernard Malamud hints at the paradoxical nature of his short story. "The Magic Barrel" prepares us, the readers, to expect a fairy tale; it asks us to enter imaginatively into a world where miracles are possible. On the other hand, "The Magic Barrel" also gives us pause. "The Magic Barrel?" A rounded wooden vessel used to store wine or fish, magical? Had Malamud chosen "The Magic Well" or "The Magic Chalice" as his title, we would have been less puzzled, less intrigued. Adept at creating dualities and contrasts, Malamud invests his plot with "magic" elements as well as with sobering, realistic ones, just as he does his title. Malamud's plot introduces us to the lonely young scholar and the eccentric, enigmatic matchmaker, both likely inhabitants of a fairy-tale world. However, it also reveals conditions all too familiar to many in their everyday reality: the desperate lovelessness of the scholar and the harsh poverty of the matchmaker. As the plot is unveiled, Bernard Malamud's story is both like and unlike a fairy tale, ultimately a story in which fantasy and reality blend.

As "The Magic Barrel" begins, we are introduced to a person who is well suited to the world of the fairy tale: Leo Finkle, a rabbinical student, lives in a room which is "small, almost meager . . . though crowded with books." Leo has been studying for six years and is about to be ordained. From the first words of the story, Leo appears to be the stereotypical poor, lonely scholar, possessing little in the way of worldly goods but rich in spirituality, a kind of inner prosperity. We would wish a devoted companion for such a worthy, lonely fellow, and we are not disappointed. Leo, the author tells us, has decided to enlist the services of Pinye Salzman, a professional matchmaker, or "commercial cupid" as Malamud calls him . Malamud prepares the reader for a traditional romantic story, and he does not disappoint. The plot follows Leo as he listens without satisfaction to the descriptions of Salzman's clients, and as he meets, without enthusiasm, one of the eligible women. It follows Leo after he decides he must have romantic love before marriage, and after he finds a small, displaced photograph in an envelope of snapshots loaned to him by Salzman to help him in his quest. In true romantic style, Leo chases around the city attempting to locate the matchmaker (and so the woman) as frantically as Prince Charming's courtiers tried to locate the owner of the lone glass slipper. In true romantic style, Leo finds he has fallen for the one woman he should not have, Stella, the "shameless" daughter Salzman considers dead, a woman whose picture found its way into the matchmaker's envelope only by mistake (a marvelous, unlikely coincidence). In true romantic style, Leo pursues her anyway, and, with the power of wishful thinking triumphing over probability fairy-tale style, he finds her. Leo's discovery of his need for romantic love and the actions he takes to fulfill that need are suited to the world of fairy tales.

However, Malamud's plot not only explores the romantic occurrences in Leo's life, it also explores the more mundane, realistic ones. If Leo is not Prince Charming, he is at least a close relative. He is, however, also very human. The plot takes him through experiences that belong in the potentially painful real world rather than in the fairy-tale world. Leo has been studying diligently to become a rabbi for six years, but we also learn that his motives were not particularly admirable. "I think," Leo confesses to Lily Hirschorn, startling himself as much as the reader, "that I came to God not because I love Him, but because I did not." After this revelation, Leo experiences the worst week of his life. "With shocking force," he realizes that apart from his parents, he had never loved anyone. "It seemed to Leo that his whole life stood starkly revealed and he saw himself, for the first time, as he truly was—unloved and loveless." This young student stops eating and begins to lose weight. As his health suffers, he stops attending class. Malamud eventually allows Leo to "regain his composure," but this section of the plot takes the student about as far down as a human can go. The romantic events in Leo's life may predominate in the story, but they do not create an unrealistic story. Leo earns his romance the hardest way possible.

Malamud's most ambiguous scene occurs at the end of "The Magic Barrel." On one hand, it is the most romantic moment. On the other, it is curious and ambiguous. In this scene, after he has extracted some cooperation from Salzman, Leo succeeds in meeting Stella, the love of his life. She seems a bit wild, but not in an incorrigible way. She stands by a lamppost, smoking, but she waits "uneasily and shyly," her eyes filled with "desperate innocence." Experiencing "violins and lit candles" revolving in the sky, Leo rushes toward her, a bouquet of flowers outstretched in his hands. This moment, the most romantic in the story, is love found. However, its ambiguity lies in Salzman's presence and actions. The matchmaker stands "around the corner . . . leaning against a wall," chanting "prayers for the dead." Salzman could be blessing the union in the only way he knows how while steadfastly opposing Stella's earlier lifestyle, thus contributing to a romantic ending. Conversely, he could be offering his last prayers to a daughter whom he is deserting. He could be saying a farewell to one who he thinks is making her biggest and final error in an already "wicked" life, contributing to a modern, realistic ending. Malamud's plot follows the fairy-tale romantic events in Leo's life as well as the soberingly realistic ones. In his ambiguous ending, the author illustrates both views in one stroke.

Bernard Malamud's "The Magic Barrel" navigates between fantasy and reality. Some of Leo's acts, such as finding the woman of his dreams in a displaced photograph, desperately searching for her, then finding her, are very romantic, befitting a fairy tale. Other events in Leo's life, such as his realization that he is "unloved and loveless" and his ensuing crisis, belong in the realm of reality, not the fairy tale. In choosing to craft his plot to encompass both realms, Malamud creates a story that satisfies both the romantic and the pragmatist in us, the readers. He reminds us that fairy tales were created by real people; they are based on real life, not separate from it. Romantic happenings and happy endings can be and should be a part of everyday reality.

QUESTIONS

Does this paper add something to your own reading and understanding of the story? What is the overall thesis of this paper? How well do you think it fits the story? How well does the student writer use evidence to support it? Where do you want to disagree or take issue? How do you react to the ending of the paper?

5 POINT OF VIEW
Windows on the World

The deepest quality of a work of art will always be the quality of the mind of the producer.

HENRY JAMES

The author is the central intelligence through whose eyes and mind we see the story.

MARTHA COX

FOCUS ON POINT OF VIEW

Whatever reality a story creates for us is always a selection. We look at the world through the eyes of the writer. We attend to what the author has brought into focus; we look at it from his or her angle of vision. No objective reality exists "out there" that is the same for everyone. What we call reality is our *perception* of reality, a picture we have constructed from input that is necessarily fragmentary, biased, incomplete. We read a story in part to share imaginatively in a writer's perception of reality, a writer's vision of the world. Often that vision, that perception, is as unmistakable as a signature.

Much modern fiction, like much critical discussion of fiction, takes this awareness of the angle of vision in a story an important step further. Quite apart from the author who is writing the story, who is telling the story *in the story?* Who is the **narrator** observing the events—observing them from what angle? In much nineteenth-century fiction, the **omniscient** author could pretend to be God—to know everything, to read the minds of all the different characters in a story, to be in several places at once to observe dispersed events. But this all-knowingness is unlike the way we take in reality in our own lives. We perceive reality according to our limited lights. We try to piece together the truth from partial and contradictory information.

Much modern fiction opts for a **limited** point of view. In Faulkner's "A Rose for Emily," we know of Miss Emily only through what the townspeople had a chance to observe. We share in what they had the opportunity to hear, to suspect, and to speculate. In a modern story, we are often aware of the **reflector**—a person inside or outside the story through whose eyes and ears we register details and events. We may take in only what a bystander or an observer at the scene would actually have witnessed. Or we may share in the private thoughts and feelings of only one of the characters, seeing the world through his or her eyes. We then become more conscious of the window that a story opens on the world.

THE LIMITED POINT OF VIEW

The effect of compactness and instantaneity sought in the short story is attained mainly by the observance of two "unities"—the old traditional one of time, and that other, more modern and complex, which requires that any rapidly enacted episode shall be seen through only one pair of eyes.

EDITH WHARTON

A short story condenses a particular vision of life. Much modern discussion of fiction is concerned with examining the angle of vision. From what vantage point does the person telling the story look at the world? Modern writers tend to be self-conscious, self-aware of the *how* as well of the *what* of their writing. They have generally moved away from traditional ways of envisioning the events of a story in order to limit the narrator's point of view. Here are some possible variations of narrative point of view. (At times, these may blend or overlap.)

The Omniscient Author   The traditional **omniscient,** all-knowing author had access to the private thoughts and feelings of everyone in a novel or a story. A nineteenth-century novelist like George Eliot (pen name of Marian Evans) knew what went on in the minds and hearts of her several characters. Of course, what the so-called omniscient author chose to tell the readers was a limited selection—the author merely acted as if she "knew all." The typical objection of her twentieth-century successors was that in our own reality we see the world from our particular window. A story should limit itself to what can be taken in by "one pair of eyes."

The Intruding Author   Some authors serve the reader as guides to their fictional world. The **intruding** author feels free to comment, to chat with us as the readers, to take us into his or her confidence. We are very much aware of the author's presence as the narrator. It is as if every so often the author stepped into the story from the outside, interrupting it to turn to us and offer asides, philosophical reflections, a personal view of life.

Third Person Objective   In many stories, there is no "I, the author" (or "I, the narrator") and no "You, the reader." The story talks about its characters in the "third person": *She* did so-and-so; *he* did such-and-such. What the characters think and feel is seen from the outside. In much early modern fiction, the stance of the author was: We are not mind readers; we can never enter totally into someone else's world of thinking and feeling. We *can* try to be impartial observers, faithful to what we see and hear. In a Hemingway story, for instance, the author often assumes the stance of the honest witness, the incorruptible reporter. It is as if the author were saying to us, "I tell you what I see—you draw your own conclusions." In such an **objective** narrative, there is little or no comment—a minimum of editorializing, judging, preaching. Our gain as readers is a sense of integrity—no one is trying to sell us a subjective interpretation. The limitation is that much of what we see and hear we can only speculate about; we never enter fully into the thoughts and emotions of the people in the story.

First Person Autobiographical   Much writing is at the opposite pole from the objective-observer stance of the Hemingway school. In many stories that seem deeply felt, we sense that the authors are speaking in thinly disguised form about their own childhood, their own families, their own conflicts or alienation. They are deeply involved, and their involvement, their commitment, shows. The "I" speaking in the story is talking about scenes and people from personal experience—perhaps with names and dates altered. Such writing may have a confessional tone; the writer may be unburdening his or her heart. Writing the story or novel may have been a way of coming to terms with traumatic happenings, with feelings of guilt. The act of writing may have been therapy or catharsis—a cleansing, a clearing of the slate. First-person narratives often have a special fascination; they create a special effect of intimacy. Someone is taking us into his or her confidence. We have a chance to look beyond the public façade.

However, even then, the **autobiographical** material is shaped by the creative imagination. Autobiographical fact shades over into fiction. The "I" speaking to us in the story then becomes a **persona**—an assumed identity. (A persona was originally the mask actors wore on the classical Greek stage; through it the sound of their voices came forth to reach the spectator—it "sounded through.") The distance between person and persona varies greatly from story to story, or from writer to writer. The persona of the narrator may have much in common with the author. Or else it may represent the author in disguise, as if wearing a mask. Finally, it may be a freely created imaginary identity, incorporating some elements or traits from the author's personality or experience.

First Person Observer   The fictionalized "I" will play different roles in different stories. We may see the story through the eyes of someone who is on the sidelines, who is not a major player. This person then becomes our scout, our reliable source, our "chosen interpreter." The person becomes our **reflector**—anything that happens in the story will reach us by way of his or her perceptions. Edith Wharton, in *The Writing of Fiction* (1925), spelled out a modern credo when she said that to create the "effect of probability" it was necessary never to let the character who serves as a reflector record anything not naturally within his register. It should be the storyteller's first care to choose this reflecting mind deliberately, as one would choose a building site, or decide upon the orientation of one's house, and when this is done, to live inside the mind chosen, trying to feel, see, and react exactly as the latter would, no more, no less, and, above all, no otherwise.

First Person Protagonist The **protagonist**—the main character, the hero or heroine—in a story may tell his or her story in the first person. This perspective places us at the center of the action. It is likely to draw us into the conflicts at the heart of the story; it may force us to take sides. In Alice Munro's "Boys and Girls," told in the first-person-protagonist mode, it is hard for us to look at the events from the point of view of the mother or of the younger brother. The feelings of the young girl telling the story are too strong, inevitably coloring our reactions.

The Naive Narrator A special kind of **irony** may make us react to the perspective of the narrator with a wry smile. We smile at the **naive narrator** who seems to know and understand less than an alert reader. Mark Twain's Huckleberry Finn in the classic of the same name watches the world with wide-open innocent eyes—recognizing human duplicity or vindictiveness long after the more knowing reader. Huck may be foolish to be more trusting than we are, but at the same time we may envy him the youthful innocence that makes him less bitter or cynical than we are.

Interior Monologue James Joyce and other early moderns experimented with the **stream-of-consciousness** technique. We enter into the mind of the narrator, sharing in a flow of thought and feeling. We listen in on the **interior monologue.** The narrative is not linear or logical but moves by leaps and bounds of association. We may be distracted by bodily sensations (like the feel of a wet bar of soap in a trouser pocket). We may be sent off on a tangent by a scent, or by a remark that rekindles a long-forgotten memory. However, like our own private thoughts and feelings, the narrator's flow of thought—trivial or pathetic much of the time—is likely to circle back sooner or later to the hopes, anxieties, or traumas that really matter.

However, many stories that take us into the mind of the narrator make us follow a more focused, more continuous interior monologue. We might call it an *edited* interior monologue. In Tillie Olsen's "I Stand Here Ironing," we share in the private thoughts of the narrator. However, her memories, thoughts, and feelings are focused on the hardships, struggles, and regrets related to the bringing up of her oldest child. No current distractions—thoughts of the next meal, worries about an appointment—interfere with the stock taking, the weighing of responsibilities, at the heart of the story.

When you look at how point of view shapes what you experience in a story, remember that critical categories tend to be neater than the realities of creative work. Different perspectives may blend or alternate. In Katherine Anne Porter's "The Jilting of Granny Weatherall," you follow an interior monologue in which the central character's blurred observations of events in the sickroom and her memories and regrets intersect. But this strand alternates with objectively recorded conversations that the central character no longer hears or understands.

JUXTAPOSITIONS

The Perspective of Youth

Stories of youth and adolescence often adopt a distinctive, limited point of view. They see the world through the eyes of people less experienced, less knowing than we are. Children and adolescents have an incomplete, unfinished view of the world. Much of what happens to them they experience for the first time. Both of the following stories, written a century apart, look at the world from the perspective of youth. How and how well does the author control the point of view in each story? What does the reader gain, and what does the reader lose, by looking at the world from a limited perspective?

ANTON CHEKHOV (1860–1904)

The first story is by Anton Chekhov, a nineteenth-century Russian writer from a lower-class family who became famous as a playwright and as a writer of short stories. He helped chart the directions for much short fiction in the twentieth century; his well-focused, tightly unified narratives departed from earlier, more leisurely forms of storytelling. His stories are self-contained—seizing on a pregnant moment and making it the center of a well-focused narrative.

Chekhov's family had only recently risen from the status of peasants and serfs, the lowest rung of nineteenth-century czarist Russia. After a rigidly religious upbringing, he tried to escape from poverty through work as a hack writer and journalist. He studied and practiced medicine but eventually devoted more and more of his time to writing. His plays—*Three Sisters, The Cherry Orchard*—are still part of the modern theatrical repertory. What features of the following story remind you that it takes its readers back to the prerevolutionary czarist past? What do you think might account for the appeal the story has for modern readers?

Vanka 1886

Vanka Zhukov, a nine-year-old boy, who had been apprenticed to Alyahin the shoemaker these three months, did not go to bed on Christmas Eve. After his master and mistress and the journeymen had gone to midnight Mass, he got an inkpot and a penholder with a rusty nib out of the master's cupboard and, having spread out a crumpled sheet of paper, began writing. Before he formed the first letter he looked fearfully at the doors and windows several times, shot a glance at the dark icon, at either side of which stretched shelves filled with lasts, and heaved a broken sigh. He was kneeling before a bench on which his paper lay.

"Dear Granddaddy, Konstantin Makarych," he wrote. "And I am writing you a letter. I wish you a merry Christmas and everything good from the Lord God. I have neither father nor mother, you alone are left me."

Vanka shifted his glance to the dark window on which flickered the reflection of his candle and vividly pictured his grandfather to himself. Employed as a watchman by the Zhivaryovs, he was a short, thin, but extraordinarily lively and nimble old man of about sixty-five whose face was always crinkled with laughter and who had a toper's eyes. By day he slept in the servants' kitchen or cracked jokes with the cook; at night, wrapped in an ample sheepskin coat, he made the rounds of the estate, shaking his clapper. The old bitch, Brownie, and the dog called Wriggles, who had a black coat and a long body like a weasel's, followed him with hanging heads. This Wriggles was extraordinarily deferential and demonstrative, looked with equally friendly eyes both at his masters and at strangers, but did not enjoy a good reputation. His deference and meekness concealed the most Jesuitical spite. No one knew better than he how to creep up behind you and suddenly snap at your leg, how to slip into the icehouse, or how to steal a hen from a peasant. More than once his hind legs had been all but broken, twice he had been hanged, every week he was whipped till he was half dead, but he always managed to revive.

At the moment Grandfather was sure to be standing at the gates, screwing up his eyes at the bright-red windows of the church stamping his felt boots, and cracking jokes with the servants. His clapper was tied to his belt. He was clapping his hands, shrugging with the cold, and, with a senile titter, pinching now the housemaid, now the cook.

"Shall we have a pinch of snuff?" he was saying, offering the women his snuffbox. 5

They each took a pinch and sneezed. Grandfather, indescribably delighted, went off into merry peals of laughter and shouted:

"Peel it off, it has frozen on!"

The dogs too are given a pinch of snuff. Brownie sneezes, wags her head, and walks away offended. Wriggles is too polite to sneeze and only wags his tail. And the weather is glorious. The air is still, clear, and fresh. The night is dark, but one can see the whole village with its white roofs and smoke streaming out of the chimneys, the trees silvery with hoarfrost, the snowdrifts. The entire sky is studded with gaily twinkling stars and the Milky Way is as distinctly visible as though it had been washed and rubbed with snow for the holiday. . . .

Vanka sighed, dipped his pen into the ink and went on writing:

"And yesterday I got it hot. The master pulled me out into the courtyard by the 10
hair and gave me a hiding with a knee-strap because I was rocking the baby in its cradle and happened to fall asleep. And last week the mistress ordered me to clean a herring and I began with the tail, and she took the herring and jabbed me in the mug with it. The helpers make fun of me, send me to the pothouse for vodka and tell me to steal pickles for them from the master, and the master hits me with anything that comes handy. And there is nothing to eat. In the morning they give me bread, for dinner porridge, and in the evening bread again. As for tea or cabbage soup, the master and mistress bolt it all themselves. And they tell me to sleep in the entry, and when the baby cries I don't sleep at all, but rock the cradle. Dear Granddaddy, for God's sake have pity on me, take me away from here, take me home to the village, it's more than I can bear. I bow down at your feet and I will pray to God for you forever, take me away from here or I'll die."

Vanka puckered his mouth, rubbed his eyes with his black fist, and gave a sob.

"I will grind your snuff for you," he continued, "I will pray to God for you, and if anything happens, you may thrash me all you like. And if you think there's no situation for me, I will beg the manager for Christ's sake to let me clean boots, or I will take Fedka's place as a shepherd boy. Dear Granddaddy, it's more than I can bear, it will simply be the death of me. I thought of running away to the village, but I have no boots and I am afraid of the frost. And in return for this when I grow big, I will feed you and won't let anybody do you any harm, and when you die I will pray for the repose of your soul, just as for my Mom's.

"Moscow is a big city. The houses are all the kind the gentry live in, and there are lots of horses, but no sheep, and the dogs are not fierce. The boys here don't go caroling, carrying the star at Christmas, and they don't let anyone sing in the choir, and once in a shop window I saw fishing-hooks for sale all fitted up with a line, for every kind of fish, very fine ones, there was even one hook that will hold a forty-pound sheat-fish. And I saw shops where there are all sorts of guns, like the master's at home, so maybe each one of them is a hundred rubles. And in butchers' shops there are woodcocks and partridge and hares, but where they shoot them the clerks won't tell.

"Dear Granddaddy, when they have a Christmas tree with presents at the master's, do get a gilt walnut and put it away in the little green chest. Ask the young lady, Olga Ignatyevna, for it, say it's for Vanka."

Vanka heaved a broken sigh and again stared at the window. He recalled that it   15 was his grandfather who always went to the forest to get the Christmas tree for the master's family and that he would take his grandson with him. It was a jolly time! Grandfather grunted, the frost crackled, and, not to be outdone, Vanka too made a cheerful noise in his throat. Before chopping down the Christmas tree, Grandfather would smoke a pipe, slowly take a pinch of snuff, and poke fun at Vanka who looked chilled to the bone. The young firs draped in hoarfrost stood still, waiting to see which of them was to die. Suddenly, coming out of nowhere, a hare would dart across the snowdrifts like an arrow. Grandfather could not keep from shouting: "Hold him, hold him, hold him! Ah, the bob-tailed devil!"

When he had cut down the fir tree, Grandfather would drag it to the master's house, and there they would set to work decorating it. The young lady, Olga Ignatyevna, Vanka's favorite, was the busiest of all. When Vanka's mother, Pelageya, was alive and a chambermaid in the master's house, the young lady used to give him goodies, and, having nothing with which to occupy herself, taught him to read and write, to count up to a hundred, and even to dance the quadrille. When Pelageya died, Vanka had been relegated to the servants' kitchen to stay with his grandfather, and from the kitchen to the shoemaker's.

"Do come, dear Granddaddy," Vanka went on. "For Christ's sake, I beg you, take me away from here. Have pity on me, an unhappy orphan, here everyone beats me, and I am terribly hungry, and I am so blue, I can't tell you how, I keep crying. And the other day the master hit me on the head with a last, so that I fell down and it was a long time before I came to. My life is miserable, worse than a dog's—I also send greetings to Alyona, one-eyed Yegorka and the coachman, and don't give my harmonica to anyone. I remain, your grandson, Ivan Zhukov, dear Granddaddy, do come."

Vanka twice folded the sheet covered with writing and put it into an envelope he had bought for a kopeck the previous day. He reflected a while, then dipped the pen into the ink and wrote the address:

To Grandfather in the village

Then he scratched himself, thought a little, and added: *Konstantin Makarych*. Glad that no one had interrupted him at his writing, he put on his cap and, without slipping on his coat, ran out into the street with nothing over his shirt.

The clerks at the butchers' whom he had questioned the day before had told him that letters were dropped into letter boxes and from the boxes they were carried all over the world in troikas with ringing bells and drunken drivers. Vanka ran to the nearest letter box and thrust the precious letter into the slit.

An hour later, lulled by sweet hopes, he was fast asleep. In his dream he saw the   20
stove. On the stove sat grandfather, his bare legs hanging down, and read the letter to the cooks. Near the stove was Wriggles, wagging his tail.

THE RECEPTIVE READER

1. What would you include in a *capsule portrait* of Vanka?

2. Why do you think Chekhov does not include any specific reference to the boy's mistreatment until we have read one-third of the story?

3. What details in the story keep reminding us of Vanka's limited *point of view*? (Does anything get into the story that should really be beyond the central character's ken?)

4. Where is the author in this story, and why does he adopt this limited perspective? What is the appeal for the reader—what do you gain (or lose) from looking at the world through Vanka's eyes?

THE PERSONAL RESPONSE

For you, does this story capture essential elements in a child's view of the world? (Does its picture of childhood seem dated or slanted in some way?)

THE CREATIVE DIMENSION

Write a letter that you might have written when you were nearer Vanka's age. Write about a topic that seemed important at the time; address your letter to someone who was then important in your life.

JOYCE CAROL OATES (born 1938)

Writers are always under attack, usually for not being "moral" enough. . . . There is insufficient recognition of the fact that one of the traditional roles of the writer is to bear witness—not simply to the presumably good things in life, the uplifting, life-enhancing, happy things, but to their polar opposites as well.

JOYCE CAROL OATES

The second story in this pairing is by Joyce Carol Oates, whose disturbing stories often make the reader look at familiar reality from a startling new perspective. Oates was thirty-one and one of the youngest writers so honored when she received the National Book Award for fiction in 1970. In the course of her career, she has published over twenty novels and over fifteen collections of short stories, not counting books of poems, essays, and literary criticism as well as plays and countless articles and reviews. Her best-known novel, *Them* (1961), is set in Detroit, where she taught. It takes place in a violent urban landscape that many Americans would prefer to ignore or block out. Her method is to activate a "brimming" memory not merely of images but also of the emotions connected with them—and to combine the results with systematic research of a topic (like boxing) or a period in history.

Oates has a gift for taking us into a reality that at first we may accept only reluctantly as part of our world. Her characters are often defined by what they are not; they often upset or annoy the reader by their failure to fit the reader's assumptions about what is normal, comforting, reassuring. Her characters tend to be "opaque, ungiving, uncharming; they have the taciturn qualities that come with the kind of people they are—heavy, hallucinated, outside the chatty middle class" (Alfred Kazin).

Oates' stories often call for a change in our usual perspective, making us try out a new and different point of view. Her story "Stalking" focuses on Gretchen, the central character, and takes us into her own private world. For the duration of the story, like it or not, we live in Gretchen's universe. We see what is in her field of vision. (What do we see?) We are tuned in to her ongoing daydream or fantasy. (What is it about? What role does it play in the story?) We return with her to her suburban home. (What is her connection with home and family?)

Stalking   1972

The Invisible Adversary is fleeing across a field.

Gretchen, walking slowly, deliberately, watches with her keen unblinking eyes the figure of the Invisible Adversary some distance ahead. The Adversary has run boldly in front of all the traffic—on long spiky legs brisk as colts' legs—and jumped up onto a curb of new concrete, and now is running across a vacant field. The Adversary glances over his shoulder at Gretchen.

Saturday afternoon. November. A cold gritty day. Gretchen is out stalking. She has hours for her game. Hours. She is dressed for the hunt, her solid legs crammed into old blue jeans, her big, square, strong feet jammed into white leather boots that cost her mother forty dollars not long ago, but are now scuffed and filthy with mud. Hopeless to get them clean again, Gretchen doesn't care. She is wearing a dark-green corduroy jacket that is worn out at the elbows and the rear, with a zipper that can be zipped up or down, attached to a fringed leather strip. On her head nothing, though it is windy today.

She has hours ahead.

Cars and trucks and buses from the city and enormous interstate trucks hauling automobiles pass by on the highway; Gretchen waits until the way is nearly clear, then starts out. A single car is approaching. *Slow down,* Gretchen thinks; and like magic he does.

Following the footprints of the Invisible Adversary. There is no sidewalk here yet, so she might as well cut right across the field. A gigantic sign announces the site of the new Pace & Fischbach Building, an office building of fifteen floors to be completed the

5

following year. The land around here is all dug up and muddy; she can see the Adversary's footsteps leading right past the gouged-up area . . . and there he is, smirking back at her, pretending panic.

I'll get you. Don't worry. Gretchen thinks carefully.

Because the Adversary is so light-footed and invisible, Gretchen doesn't make any effort to be that way. She plods along as she does at school, passing from classroom to classroom, unhurried and not even sullen, just unhurried. She knows she is very visible. She is thirteen years old and weighs one hundred and thirty-five pounds. She's only five feet three—stocky, muscular, squat in the torso and shoulders, with good strong legs and thighs. She could be good at gym, if she bothered; instead, she just stands around, her face empty, her arms crossed and her shoulders a little slumped. If forced, she takes part in the games of volleyball and basketball, but she runs heavily, without spirit, and sometimes bumps into other girls, hurting them. *Out of my way,* she thinks; at such times her face shows no expression.

And now? . . . The Adversary is peeking out at her from around the corner of a gas station. Something flickers in her brain. *I see you,* she thinks, with quiet excitement. The Adversary ducks back out of sight. Gretchen heads in the direction, plodding through a jumbled, bulldozed field of mud and thistles and debris that is mainly rocks and chunks of glass. The gas station is brand-new and not yet opened for business. It is all white tile, white concrete, perfect plate-glass windows with whitewashed X's on them, a large driveway and eight gasoline pumps, all proudly erect and ready for business. But the gas station has not opened since Gretchen and her family moved here—about six months ago. Something must have gone wrong. Gretchen fixes her eyes on the corner where the Adversary was last seen. He can't escape.

One wall of the gas station's white tile has been smeared with something like tar. 10
Dreamy, snakelike, thick twistings of black. Black tar. Several windows have been broken. Gretchen stands in the empty driveway, her hands jammed into her pockets. Traffic is moving slowly over here. A barricade has been set up that directs traffic out onto the shoulder of the highway, on a narrow, bumpy, muddy lane that loops out and back again onto the pavement. Cars move slowly, carefully. Their bottoms scrape against the road. The detour signs are great rectangular things, bright yellow with black zigzag lines. SLOW DETOUR. In the two center lanes of the highway are bulldozers not being used today, and gigantic concrete pipes to be used for storm sewers. Eight pipes. They are really enormous; Gretchen's eyes crinkle with awe, just to see them.

She remembers the Adversary.

There he is—headed for the shopping plaza. *He won't get away in the crowds,* Gretchen promises herself. She follows. Now she is approaching an area that is more completed, though there are still no sidewalks and some of the buildings are brand-new and yet unoccupied, vacant. She jumps over a concrete ditch that is stained with rust-colored water and heads up a slight incline to the service drive of the Federal Savings Bank. The drive-in tellers' windows are all dark today, behind their green-tinted glass. The whole bank is dark, closed. Is this the bank her parents go to now? It takes Gretchen a minute to recognize it.

Now a steady line of traffic, a single lane, turns onto the service drive that leads to the shopping plaza. BUCKINGHAM MALL. 101 STORES. Gretchen notices a few kids her own age, boys or girls, trudging in jeans and jackets ahead of her, through the mud. They might be classmates of hers. Her attention is captured again by the Invisible Adversary, who has run all the way up to the Mall and is hanging around the entrance of the Cunningham Drug Store, teasing her.

You'll be sorry for that, Gretchen thinks with a smile.

Automobiles pass her slowly. The parking lot for the Mall is enormous, many   15
acres. A city of cars on a Saturday afternoon. Gretchen sees a car that might be her
mother's, but she isn't sure. Cars are parked slanted here, in lanes marked LOT K, LANE
15; LOT K, LANE 16. The signs are spheres, bubbles, perched up on long slender poles.
At night they are illuminated.

Ten or twelve older kids are hanging around the drugstore entrance. One of them
is sitting on top of a mailbox, rocking it back and forth. Gretchen pushes past them—
they are kidding around, trying to block people—and inside the store her eye darts
rapidly up and down the aisles, looking for the Invisible Adversary.

Hiding here? Hiding?

She strolls along, cunning and patient. At the cosmetics counter a girl is showing
an older woman some liquid makeup. She smears a small oval onto the back of the
woman's hand, rubs it in gently. "That's Peach Pride," the girl says. She has shimmering blond hair and eyes that are penciled to show a permanent exclamatory interest. She
does not notice Gretchen, who lets a hand drift idly over a display of marked-down lip-
sticks, each only $1.59.

Gretchen slips the tube of lipstick into her pocket. Neatly. Nimbly. Ignoring the
Invisible Adversary, who is shaking a finger at her, she drifts over to the newsstand,
looks at the magazine covers without reading them, and edges over to another display.
Packages in a cardboard barrel, out in the aisle. Big bargains. Gretchen doesn't even
glance in the barrel to see what is being offered . . . she just slips one of the packages
in her pocket. No trouble.

She leaves by the other door, the side exit. A small smile tugs at her mouth.

The Adversary is trotting ahead of her. The Mall is divided into geometric   20
areas, each colored differently; the Adversary leaves the blue pavement and is now on
the green. Gretchen follows. She notices the Adversary going into a Franklin Joseph
store.

Gretchen enters the store, sniffs in the perfumy, overheated smell, sees nothing
that interests her on the counters or at the dress racks, and so walks right to the back of
the store, to the ladies' room. No one inside. She takes the tube of lipstick out of her
pocket, opens it, examines the lipstick. It has a tart, sweet smell. A very light pink:
Spring Blossom. Gretchen goes to the mirror and smears the lipstick onto it, at first
lightly, then coarsely; part of the lipstick breaks and falls into a sink littered with hair.
Gretchen goes into one of the toilet stalls and tosses the tube into the toilet bowl. She
takes handfuls of toilet paper and crumbles them into a ball and throws them into the
toilet. Remembering the package from the drugstore, she takes it out of her pocket—
just toothpaste. She throws it, cardboard package and all, into the toilet bowl, then, her
mind glimmering with an idea, she goes to the apparatus that holds the towel—a single
cloth towel on a roll—and tugs at it until it comes loose, then pulls it out hand over
hand, patiently, until the entire towel is out. She scoops it up and carries it to the toilet.
She pushes it in and flushes the toilet.

The stuff doesn't go down, so she tries again. This time it goes partway down before it gets stuck.

Gretchen leaves the rest room and strolls unhurried through the store. The Adversary is waiting for her outside—peeking through the window—wagging a finger at her.
Don't you wag no finger at me, she thinks, with a small tight smile. Outside, she follows
him at a distance. Loud music is blaring around her head. It is rock music, piped out
onto the colored squares and rectangles of the Mall, blown everywhere by the November wind, but Gretchen hardly hears it.

Some boys are fooling around in front of the record store. One of them bumps into Gretchen and they all laugh as she is pushed against a trash can. "Watch it, babe!" the boy sings out. Her leg hurts. Gretchen doesn't look at them but, with a cold, swift anger, her face averted, she knocks the trash can over onto the sidewalk. Junk falls out. The can rolls. Some women shoppers scurry to get out of the way and the boys laugh.

Gretchen walks away without looking back.

She wanders through Sampson Furniture, which has two entrances. In one door and out the other, as always, it is a ritual with her. Again she notices the sofa that is like the sofa in their family room at home—covered with black and white fur, real goatskin. All over the store there are sofas, chairs, tables, beds. A jumble of furnishings. People stroll around them, in and out of little displays, displays meant to be living rooms, dining rooms, bedrooms, family rooms. . . . It makes Gretchen's eyes squint to see so many displays: like seeing the inside of a hundred houses. She slows down, almost comes to a stop. Gazing at a living-room display on a raised platform. Only after a moment does she remember why she is here—whom she is following—and she turns to see the Adversary beckoning to her.

She follows him outside again. He goes into Dodi's Boutique and, with her head lowered so that her eyes seem to move to the bottom of her eyebrows, pressing up against her forehead, Gretchen follows him. *You'll regret this,* she thinks. Dodi's Boutique is decorated in silver and black. Metallic strips hang down from a dark ceiling, quivering. Salesgirls dressed in pants suits stand around with nothing to do except giggle with one another and nod their head in time to the music amplified throughout the store. It is music from a local radio station. Gretchen wanders over to the dress rack, for the hell of it. Size 14. "The time is now 2:35," a radio announcer says cheerfully. "The weather is 32 degrees with a chance of showers and possible sleet tonight. You're listening to WCKK, Radio Wonderful. . . ." Gretchen selects several dresses and a salesgirl shows her to a dressing room.

"Need any help?" the girl asks. She has long swinging hair and a high-shouldered, indifferent, bright manner.

"No," Gretchen mutters.

Alone, Gretchen takes off her jacket. She is wearing a navy blue sweater. She zips one of the dresses open and it falls off the flimsy plastic hanger before she can catch it. She steps on it, smearing mud onto the white wool. She lets it lie there and holds up another dress, gazing at herself in the mirror.

She has untidy, curly hair that looks like a wig set loosely on her head. Light brown curls spill out everywhere, bouncy, a little frizzy, a cascade, a tumbling of curls. Her eyes are deep set, her eyebrows heavy and dark. She has a stern, staring look, like an adult man. Her nose is perfectly formed, neat and noble. Her upper lip is long, as if it were stretched to close with difficulty over the front teeth. She wears no makeup, her lips are perfectly colorless, pale, a little chapped, and they are usually held tight, pursed tightly shut. She has a firm, rounded chin. Her facial structure is strong, pensive, its features stern and symmetrical as a statue's, blank, neutral, withdrawn. Her face is attractive. But there is a blunt, neutral stillness to it, as if she were detached from it and somewhere else, uninterested.

She holds the dress up to her body, smooths it down over her chest, staring at herself.

After a moment she hangs the dress up again, and runs down the zipper so roughly that it breaks. The other dress she doesn't bother with. She leaves the dressing room, putting on her jacket.

At the front of the store the salesgirl glances at her . . ."—Didn't fit?—"

"No," says Gretchen.

25

30

35

She wanders around for a while, in and out of Carmichael's, the Mall's big famous store, where she catches sight of her mother on an escalator going up. Her mother doesn't notice her. She pauses by a display of "winter homes." Her family owns a home like this, in the Upper Peninsula, except theirs is larger. This one comes complete for only $5330: PACKAGE ERECTED ON YOUR LOT—YEAR-ROUND HOME FIBER GLASS INSULA-TION—BEAUTIFUL ROUGH-SAWN VERTICAL B. C. CEDAR SIDING WITH DEEP SIMULATED SHADOW LINES FOR A RUGGED EXTERIOR.

Only 3:15. Gretchen goes into the Big Boy restaurant and orders a ground-round hamburger with French fries. Also a Coke. She sits at the crowded counter and eats slowly, her jaws grinding slowly, as she glances at her reflection in the mirror directly in front of her—her mop of hair moving almost imperceptibly with the grinding of her jaws—and occasionally she sees the Adversary waiting outside, coyly. *You'll get yours,* she thinks.

She leaves the Big Boy and wanders out into the parking lot, eating from a bag of potato chips. She wipes her greasy hands on her thighs. The afternoon has turned dark and cold. Shivering a little, she scans the maze of cars for the Adversary—yes, there he is—and starts after him. He runs ahead of her. He runs through the parking lot, waits teasingly at the edge of a field, and as she approaches he runs across the field, trotting along with a noisy crowd of four or five loose dogs that don't seem to notice him.

Gretchen follows him through that field, trudging in the mud, and through anoth-er muddy field, her eyes fixed on him. Now he is at the highway—hesitating there—now he is about to run across in front of traffic—now, now—now he darts out—

Now! He is struck by a car. His body knocked backward, spinning backward. Ah,   40 now, *now how does it feel?* Gretchen asks.

He picks himself up. Gets to his feet. Is he bleeding? Yes, bleeding! He stumbles across the highway to the other side, where there is a sidewalk. Gretchen follows him as soon as the traffic lets up. He is staggering now, like a drunken man. *How does it feel? Do you like it now?*

The Adversary staggers along the sidewalk. He turns onto a side street, beneath an archway, *Piney Woods.* He is leading Gretchen into the Piney Woods subdivision. Here the homes are quite large, on artificial hills that show them to good advantage. Most of the homes are white colonials with attached garages. There are no sidewalks here, so the Adversary has to walk in the street, limping like an old man, and Gretchen follows him in the street, with her eyes fixed on him.

Are you happy now? Does it hurt? Does it?

She giggles at the way he walks. He looks like a drunken man. He glances back at her, white-faced, and turns up a flagstone walk . . . goes right up to a big white colo-nial house. . . .

Gretchen follows him inside. She inspects the simulated brick of the foyer: yes,   45 there are blood spots. He is dripping blood. Entranced, she follows the splashes of blood into the hall, to the stairs . . . forgets her own boots, which are muddy . . . but she doesn't feel like going back to wipe her feet.

Nobody seems to be home. Her mother is probably still shopping, her father is out of town for the weekend. The house empty. Gretchen goes into the kitchen, opens the refrigerator, takes out a Coke, and wanders to the rear of the house, to the family room. It is two steps down from the rest of the house. She takes off her jacket and toss-es it somewhere. Turns on the television set. Sits on the goatskin sofa and stares at the screen: a return of a Shotgun Steve show, which she has already seen.

If the Adversary comes crawling behind her, groaning in pain, weeping, she won't even bother to glance at him.

THE RECEPTIVE READER

1. Oates is a master at noting in passing apparently random, mindless *detail* that we later suspect was planted deliberately in the story. What is the point of telling us about Gretchen's white leather boots—or about the car approaching when she crosses the highway? (What other details early in the story stuck in your mind?)

2. Gretchen is the kind of person who is popularly said to have an "attitude." What is her attitude toward school and gym? What is her attitude toward the school-mates she meets at the mall?

3. What are striking details about the suburban landscape through which Gretchen wanders? As you follow her through this *setting*, do you notice any connecting thread? Is there a keynote—a recurrent note struck more than once?

4. What kind of shoplifter is Gretchen? How does she do it? What are her *motives*—why does she do it? Do you feel you are getting an inside look at teenage vandalism in this story? How does she operate, and why?

5. Late in the story, Oates furnishes a fairly complete physical description of Gretchen. Do you learn anything from it? Does it include any clues to her character?

6. At a few points earlier in the story, we are reminded that Gretchen has a mother, a family, a home. What impression do these hints create? What kind of home, what kind of family, awaits Gretchen at the end of her excursion?

7. What is the role of the imaginary adversary in the story?

THE PERSONAL RESPONSE

The story presents Gretchen strictly on her own terms—with no comment. There is no editorializing, moralizing, or preaching by the author. For you, what is the point of the story? Is there a key to the central character—a unifying thread to her behavior and attitudes? How do you relate to her?

THE RANGE OF INTERPRETATION

How much depends on what you as a reader bring to Gretchen's story? Which of the following student-written responses is closest to your own? Why? Which to you seems least responsive to the story, and why?

1. Gretchen seems to me to be a very angry adolescent. Her anger is directed against her absent parents, her schoolmates who probably don't even notice her, but mostly against herself. Gretchen is an overweight, unattractive, thirteen-year-old. She is a loner. She can only express her anger through her game of stalking "the adversary." This make-believe character represents to Gretchen all the anger she hides inside herself. These stalking games are ritualistic to Gretchen; through them she can release her anger and best her adversary for a period of time.

2. I was able to feel empathy toward the character of Gretchen in Oates' story, despite her unpleasant personality. I thought both she and her surroundings epitomized the sterility and alienation of much modern suburban life; there is a rootlessness inherent in the setting that manifests itself in Gretchen's utter lack of interest or engagement. This lack of engagement with the world around her is central to explaining many of the things she does, such as her aimless shoplifting and careless muddying of her parents' home. She was not raised in an environment that would give her any cause for en-

thusiasm for anything. It is perhaps because Gretchen had no positive interests to draw her attention and enthusiasm outward that she became so carelessly destructive of herself and her environment.

3. Gretchen is pure isolation. She is an imaginative, creative person trapped in a suburban theater where the only stimuli are shopping malls and television. Her mother and father are not shown as bad people; they are just kept out of the picture. Her companion instead is the invisible adversary—playmate, lover, villain, whipping boy who never says no to any adventure she devises. Her relentless pursuit of him gives her day a purpose and a victory. In her conventional reality, the frustration and pain of failure in a social arena where only pretty girls are admitted would be too much to bear. Her destructive behavior is an acting out of her frustrated need to belong. If a lipstick or dress is not going to improve the problem, then they should be destroyed. And if there is no place to go, why hurry?

THE CREATIVE DIMENSION

What do you think you would see if you could be a mind reader looking into Gretchen's mind? Write a passage in which you change the point of view of the story. Imagine you can share in Gretchen's private thoughts and feelings instead of watching her much of the time from the outside. Write in the first person, as if she were talking confidentially to the reader.

WORLDS OF THOUGHT AND FEELING

Both of the following stories take us into a central character's personal world. They make us look at the world as seen through one character's eyes. Since the central characters in these stories are very different people, each takes us into a different universe of thought and feeling. However, in addition, the point of view from which the author chooses to tell the story varies, with the second story taking us a step closer to sharing fully in the character's most personal, most private thoughts and emotions.

TILLIE OLSEN   (born 1912)

The power and the need to create, over and beyond
reproduction, is native in both women and men. Where
the gifted among women (and men) have remained mute,
or have never attained full capacity, it is because of
circumstances, inner or outer, which oppose the needs of
creation.

TILLIE OLSEN

Tillie Olsen has come to be widely admired for giving voice to the story of the unheard, the silenced, in American society. Writing about the Great Depression of the thirties, she wrote with bitter eloquence about the working-class experience—poverty, illness, hunger, unemployment, soul-deadening jobs. Her novel *Yonnondio: From the Thirties* (1974) paid tribute to people thwarted, deprived of their chance to develop into full human beings "so that a few may languidly lie on couches and trill 'how exquisite' to paid dreamers." A native of Omaha, Nebraska, with only a high school education, she herself lived through grey poverty to write powerful stories shaking up our complacency, our euphemisms and alibis. Her story "Tell Me a Riddle" won the O. Henry Award as the best short story of the year in 1961. She has since received prestigious grants and honors and lectured at universities including Amherst and Stanford.

Women readers and women writers made her a revered figure in the women's movement. They identified with the heroic struggle of a "family wage earner at dull and time-sapping menial jobs" (Nolan Miller)—a woman who "held down a job, raised four children, and still somehow managed to become and remain a writer," surviving a "grueling obstacle race" that cost her "twenty years of her writing life" (Margaret Atwood). In her collection *Silences* (1978), Olsen collected and reprinted the testimony of writers, and especially women from Virginia Woolf to Katherine Mansfield, about the social and psychological forces that hobble the creative spirit, forcing many who are not white, male, or affluent into silence.

The following story is the kind of personally committed writing that stays close to personal experience but turns it into art by focusing it and interpreting it. We look through the eyes of a mother at a daughter who was "the child of anxious, not proud love." What world do we see through the narrator's eyes? (The WPA referred to in the story is the Works Progress Administration, begun in 1935 to provide federally funded jobs for the unemployed during the Great Depression.)

I Stand Here Ironing   1961

I stand here ironing, and what you asked me moves tormented back and forth with the iron.

"I wish you would manage the time to come in and talk with me about your daughter. I'm sure you can help me understand her. She's a youngster who needs help and whom I'm deeply interested in helping."

"Who needs help." . . . Even if I came, what good would it do? You think because I am her mother I have a key, or that in some way you could use me as a key? She has lived for nineteen years. There is all that life that has happened outside of me, beyond me.

And when is there time to remember, to sift, to weigh, to estimate, to total? I will start and there will be an interruption and I will have to gather it all together again. Or I will become engulfed with all I did or did not do, with what should have been and what cannot be helped.

She was a beautiful baby. The first and only one of our five that was beautiful at birth. You do not guess how new and uneasy her tenancy in her now-loveliness. You did not know her all those years she was thought homely, or see her poring over her baby pictures, making me tell her over and over how beautiful she had been—and would be, I would tell her—and was now, to the seeing eye. But the seeing eyes were few or nonexistent. Including mine.

I nursed her. They feel that's important nowadays. I nursed all the children, but with her, with all the fierce rigidity of first motherhood, I did like the books then said. Though her cries battered me to trembling and my breasts ached with swollenness, I waited till the clock decreed.

Why do I put that first? I do not even know if it matters, or if it explains anything.

She was a beautiful baby. She blew shining bubbles of sound. She loved motion, loved light, loved color and music and textures. She would lie on the floor in her blue overalls patting the surface so hard in ecstasy her hands and feet would blur. She was a miracle to me, but when she was eight months old I had to leave her daytimes with the woman downstairs to whom she was no miracle at all, for I worked or looked for work and for Emily's father, who "could no longer endure" (he wrote in his good-bye note) "sharing want with us."

I was nineteen. It was the pre-relief, pre-WPA world of the depression. I would start running as soon as I got off the streetcar, running up the stairs, the place smelling sour, and awake or asleep to startle awake, when she saw me she would break into a clogged weeping that could not be comforted, a weeping I can hear yet.

After a while I found a job hashing at night so I could be with her days, and it was better. But it came to where I had to bring her to his family and leave her. 10

It took a long time to raise the money for her fare back. Then she got chicken pox and I had to wait longer. When she finally came, I hardly knew her, walking quick and nervous like her father, looking like her father, thin, and dressed in a shoddy red that yellowed her skin and glared at the pockmarks. All the baby loveliness gone.

She was two. Old enough for nursery school they said, and I did not know then what I know now—the fatigue of the long day, and the lacerations of group life in the kinds of nurseries that are only parking places for children.

Except that it would have made no difference if I had known. It was the only place there was. It was the only way we could be together, the only way I could hold a job.

And even without knowing, I knew. I knew the teacher that was evil because all these years it has curdled into my memory, the little boy hunched in the corner, her rasp, "why aren't you outside, because Alvin hits you? that's no reason, go out, scaredy." I knew Emily hated it even if she did not clutch and implore "don't go Mommy" like the other children, mornings.

She always had a reason why we should stay home. Momma, you look sick. 15 Momma, I feel sick. Momma, the teachers aren't there today, they're sick. Momma, we can't go, there was a fire there last night. Momma, it's a holiday today, no school, they told me.

But never a direct protest, never rebellion. I think of our others in their three-, four-year-oldness—the explosions, the tempers, the denunciations, the demands—and I feel suddenly ill. I put the iron down. What in me demanded that goodness in her? And what was the cost, the cost to her of such goodness?

The old man living in the back once said in his gentle way: "You should smile at Emily more when you look at her." What *was* in my face when I looked at her? I loved her. There were all the acts of love.

It was only with the others I remembered what he said, and it was the face of joy, and not of care or tightness or worry I turned to them—too late for Emily. She does not smile easily, let alone almost always as her brothers and sisters do. Her face is closed and sombre, but when she wants, how fluid. You must have seen it in her pantomimes, you spoke of her rare gift for comedy on the stage that rouses laughter out of the audience so dear they applaud and applaud and do not want to let her go.

Where does it come from, that comedy? There was none of it in her when she came back to me that second time, after I had had to send her away again. She had a new daddy now to learn to love, and I think perhaps it was a better time.

Except when we left her alone nights, telling ourselves she was old enough.   20

"Can't you go some other time, Mommy, like tomorrow?" she would ask. "Will it be just a little while you'll be gone? Do you promise?"

The time we came back, the front door open, the clock on the floor in the hall. She rigid awake. "It wasn't just a little while. I didn't cry. Three times I called you, just three times, and then I ran downstairs to open the door so you could come faster. The clock talked loud. I threw it away, it scared me what it talked."

She said the clock talked loud again that night I went to the hospital to have Susan. She was delirious with the fever that comes before red measles, but she was fully conscious all the week I was gone and the week after we were home when she could not come near the new baby or me.

She did not get well. She stayed skeleton thin, not wanting to eat, and night after night she had nightmares. She would call for me, and I would rouse from exhaustion to sleepily call back: "You're all right, darling, go to sleep, it's just a dream," and if she still called, in a sterner voice, "now go to sleep, Emily, there's nothing to hurt you." Twice, only twice, when I had to get up for Susan anyhow, I went in to sit with her.

Now when it is too late (as if she would let me hold and comfort her like I do the   25
others) I get up and go to her at once at her moan or restless stirring. "Are you awake, Emily? Can I get you something?" And the answer is always the same: "No, I'm all right, go back to sleep, Mother."

They persuaded me at the clinic to send her away to a convalescent home in the country where "she can have the kind of food and care you can't manage for her, and you'll be free to concentrate on the new baby." They still send children to that place. I see pictures on the society page of sleek young women planning affairs to raise money for it, or dancing at the affairs, or decorating Easter eggs or filling Christmas stockings for the children.

They never have a picture of the children so I do not know if the girls still wear those gigantic red bows and the ravaged looks on the every other Sunday when parents can come to visit "unless otherwise notified"—as we were notified the first six weeks.

Oh it is a handsome place, green lawns and tall trees and fluted flower beds. High up on the balconies of each cottage the children stand, the girls in their red bows and white dresses, the boys in white suits and giant red ties. The parents stand below shrieking up to be heard and the children shriek down to be heard, and between them the invisible wall: "Not to Be Contaminated by Parental Germs or Physical Affection."

There was a tiny girl who always stood hand in hand with Emily. Her parents never came. One visit she was gone. "They moved her to Rose Cottage," Emily shouted in explanation. "They don't like you to love anybody here."

She wrote once a week, the labored writing of a seven-year-old. "I am fine. How is   30
the baby. If I write my leter nicly I will have a star. Love." There never was a star. We wrote every other day, letters she could never hold or keep but only hear read—once. "We simply do not have room for children to keep any personal possessions," they patiently explained when we pieced one Sunday's shrieking together to plead how much it would mean to Emily, who loved so to keep things, to be allowed to keep her letters and cards.

Each visit she looked frailer. "She isn't eating," they told us.

(They had runny eggs for breakfast or mush with lumps, Emily said later, I'd hold it in my mouth and not swallow. Nothing ever tasted good, just when they had chicken.)

It took us eight months to get her released home, and only the fact that she gained back so little of her seven lost pounds convinced the social worker.

I used to try to hold and love her after she came back, but her body would stay stiff, and after a while she'd push away. She ate little. Food sickened her, and I think much of life too. Oh she had physical lightness and brightness, twinkling by on skates, bouncing like a ball up and down up and down over the jump rope, skimming over the hill; but these were momentary.

She fretted about her appearance, thin and dark and foreign-looking at a time   35
when every little girl was supposed to look or thought she should look a chubby blonde replica of Shirley Temple. The doorbell sometimes rang for her, but no one seemed to come and play in the house or be a best friend. Maybe because we moved so much.

There was a boy she loved painfully through two school semesters. Months later she told me how she had taken pennies from my purse to buy him candy. "Licorice was his favorite and I brought him some every day, but he still liked Jennifer better'n me. Why, Mommy?" The kind of question for which there is no answer.

School was a worry to her. She was not glib or quick in a world where glibness and quickness were easily confused with ability to learn. To her overworked and exasperated teachers she was an overconscientious "slow learner" who kept trying to catch up and was absent entirely too often.

I let her be absent, though sometimes the illness was imaginary. How different from my now-strictness about attendance with the others. I wasn't working. We had a new baby, I was home anyhow. Sometimes, after Susan grew old enough, I would keep her home from school, too, to have them all together.

Mostly Emily had asthma, and her breathing, harsh and labored, would fill the house with a curiously tranquil sound. I would bring the two old dresser mirrors and her boxes of collections to her bed. She would select beads and single earrings, bottle tops and shells, dried flowers and pebbles, old postcards and scraps, all sorts of oddments; then she and Susan would play Kingdom, setting up landscapes and furniture, peopling them with action.

Those were the only times of peaceful companionship between her and Susan. I   40
have edged away from it, that poisonous feeling between them, that terrible balancing of hurts and needs I had to do between the two, and did so badly, those earlier years.

Oh there are conflicts between the others too, each one human, needing, demanding, hurting, taking—but only between Emily and Susan, no, Emily toward Susan that corroding resentment. It seems so obvious on the surface, yet it is not obvious. Susan, the second child, Susan, golden- and curly-haired and chubby, quick and articulate and assured, everything in appearance and manner Emily was not; Susan, not able to resist Emily's precious things, losing or sometimes clumsily breaking them; Susan telling jokes and riddles to company for applause while Emily sat silent (to say to me later: that was *my* riddle, Mother, I told it to Susan); Susan, who for all the five years' difference in age was just a year behind Emily in developing physically.

I am glad for that slow physical development that widened the difference between her and her contemporaries, though she suffered over it. She was too vulnerable for that terrible world of youthful competition, of preening and parading, of constant measuring of yourself against every other, of envy, "If I had that copper hair," "If I had that skin. . . ." She tormented herself enough about not looking like the others, there was enough of the unsureness, the having to be conscious of words before you speak, the constant caring—what are they thinking of me? without having it all magnified by the merciless physical drives.

Ronnie is calling. He is wet and I change him. It is rare there is such a cry now. That time of motherhood is almost behind me when the ear is not one's own but must always be racked and listening for the child cry, the child call. We sit for a while and I hold him, looking out over the city spread in charcoal with its soft aisles of light. "*Shoogily*," he breathes and curls closer. I carry him back to bed, asleep. *Shoogily*. A funny word, a family word, inherited from Emily, invented by her to say: *comfort*.

In this and other ways she leaves her seal, I say aloud. And startle at my saying it. What do I mean? What did I start to gather together, to try and make coherent? I was at the terrible, growing years. War years. I do not remember them well. I was working, there were four smaller ones now, there was not time for her. She had to help be a mother, and housekeeper, and shopper. She had to set her seal. Mornings of crisis and near hysteria trying to get lunches packed, hair combed, coats and shoes found, everyone to school or Child Care on time, the baby ready for transportation. And always the paper scribbled on by a smaller one, the book looked at by Susan then mislaid, the homework not done. Running out to that huge school where she was one, she was lost, she was a drop; suffering over the unpreparedness, stammering and unsure in her classes.

There was so little time left at night after the kids were bedded down. She would struggle over books, always eating (it was in those years she developed her enormous appetite that is legendary in our family) and I would be ironing, or preparing food for the next day, or writing V-mail to Bill, or tending the baby. Sometimes, to make me laugh, or out of her despair, she would imitate happenings or types at school.   45

I think I said once: "Why don't you do something like this in the school amateur show?" One morning she phoned me at work, hardly understandable through the weeping: "Mother, I did it. I won, I won; they gave me first prize; they clapped and clapped and wouldn't let me go."

Now suddenly she was Somebody, and as imprisoned in her difference as she had been in anonymity.

She began to be asked to perform at other high schools, even in colleges, than at city and statewide affairs. The first one we went to, I only recognized her that first moment when thin, shy, she almost drowned herself into the curtains. Then: Was this Emily? The control, the command, the convulsing and deadly clowning, the spell, then the roaring, stamping audience, unwilling to let this rare and precious laughter out of their lives.

Afterwards: You ought to do something about her with a gift like that—but without money or knowing how, what does one do? We have left it all to her, and the gift has as often eddied inside, clogged and clotted, as been used and growing.

She is coming. She runs up the stairs two at a time with her light graceful step, and I know she is happy tonight. Whatever it was that occasioned your call did not happen today.   50

"Aren't you ever going to finish the ironing, Mother? Whistler painted his mother in a rocker. I'd have to paint mine standing over an ironing board." This is one of her communicative nights and she tells me everything and nothing as she fixes herself a plate of food out of the icebox.

She is so lovely. Why did you want me to come in at all? Why were you concerned? She will find her way.

She starts up the stairs to bed. "Don't get me up with the rest in the morning." "But I thought you were having midterms." "Oh, those," she comes back in, kisses me, and says quite lightly, "in a couple of years when we'll all be atom-dead they won't matter a bit."

She has said it before. She *believes* it. But because I have been dredging the past, and all that compounds a human being is so heavy and meaningful in me, I cannot endure it tonight.

I will never total it all. I will never come in to say: She was a child seldom smiled   55
at. Her father left me before she was a year old. I had to work her first six years when there was work, or I sent her home and to his relatives. There were years she had care she hated. She was dark and thin and foreign-looking in a world where the prestige went to blondeness and curly hair and dimples, she was slow where glibness was prized. She was a child of anxious, not proud, love. We were poor and could not afford for her the soil of easy growth. I was a young mother, I was a distracted mother. There were other children pushing up, demanding. Her younger sister seemed all that she was not. There were years she did not want me to touch her. She kept too much in herself, her life was such she had to keep too much in herself. My wisdom came too late. She has much to her and probably little will come of it. She is a child of her age, of depression, of war, of fear.

Let her be. So all that is in her will not bloom—but in how many does it? There is still enough left to live by. Only help her to know—help make it so there is cause for her to know—that she is more than this dress on the ironing board, helpless before the iron.

THE RECEPTIVE READER

1. Who is the *you* addressed in the story?

2. How do the physical conditions, the circumstances of her life, shape the narrator's outlook? What physical details are especially telling or have a possible symbolic meaning?

3. Early in the story, we catch glimpes of the teacher, of Emily's father, and of the old man who lives in the back. What role do these people on the periphery of the story play in the narrator's world and her view of the world?

4. What is the narrator's attitude toward *institutions*? Why do they loom so large in the story? What are striking details? Is the narrator's attitude one-sided?

5. What picture of Emily as the oldest child emerges in this story? What are key points the narrator wants us to see or understand about Emily as a person? What makes the child—and the mother's relationship with her—*complex* rather than simple?

6. Although it is told in a low key, without melodrama or eloquent indictments, there are powerful undercurrents of *emotion* running in this story. What are they? Where are they harshest—or most frankly described?

7. What kind of summing up does the *ending* of the story provide? What attitude toward life or view of the world emerges here? Is it of one piece with the story as a whole?

8. Why do you think the author wrote this story? What do you think the act of writing did for her as the writer?

9. How do you think the situation or the child might have looked when seen from a *different* point of view? For instance, what might have been the perspective of a teacher or social worker? Does the narrator acknowledge different points of view?

THE PERSONAL RESPONSE

How do you relate to the narrator in the story? Do you think of her as a bitter person? an angry person? a defeated person? How do you relate to the daughter in the story? What do you think the future holds for her?

KATHERINE ANNE PORTER   (1890–1980)

The truth is, I have never written a story in my life that didn't have a very firm foundation in actual human experience—somebody else's experience quite often, but an experience that became my own by hearing the story, by witnessing the thing, by hearing just a word perhaps. It doesn't matter, it just takes a little—a tiny seed. Then it takes root, and it grows.

KATHERINE ANNE PORTER

In Katherine Anne Porter's stories, the effect has surely been never to diminish life but always to intensify life in the part significant to her story.

EUDORA WELTY

What her work celebrates is the toughness and integrity of the individual.

ROBERT PENN WARREN

Katherine Anne Porter became known as a writer more interested in a character's state of mind than in external action. She published *Flowering Judas,* her first collection of short stories, in 1930. Born in Texas, she drew on her experiences as a young girl growing up in the South and as an observer of revolutionary turmoil in Mexico. She is best known for her novellas (long short stories or short novels) "Noon Wine" (1937) and "Pale Horse, Pale Rider" (1939). She traveled widely, and she drew on her observations of Europe in the thirties and forties in her novel *Ship of Fools* (1962). This novel, made into a movie with José Ferrer, Oskar Werner, and Simone Signoret, followed a group of travelers on a voyage to Germany in 1931, when the Nazi movement was gathering strength, anti-Semitism was on the rise, and ominous signs pointed toward the Nazi takeover in 1933.

"The Jilting of Granny Weatherall" is a short story that takes us inside the consciousness of the main character, making us follow the stream of observations, memories, and rationalizations as they pass through the character's mind. Instead of following external action from cause to effect, or from action to reaction, we follow the **stream of consciousness.** In most of the story, we hear the main character thinking to herself; we listen to the **interior monologue.** Eudora Welty has said in *The Eye of the Story* (1965) that Porter is contemplating "the inner, secret faces" of her characters:

Often the revelation that pierces a character's mind and heart and shows him his life or his death comes in a dream, in retrospect, in illness or in utter defeat, the moment of vanishing hope, the moment of dying. What Porter makes us see are those subjective worlds of hallucination, obsession, fever, guilt. The presence of death hovering about Granny Weatherall she makes as real and brings as near as Granny's own familiar room that stands about her bed.

In this story, we move on two levels: We get glimpses of the outer, or surface, reality of the sickroom. But we also participate in the inner reality of the central character's observations, thoughts, and feelings. As often with the stream-of-consciousness technique, some of the stream of thoughts and emotions seems trivial or routine. But eventually the character's thinking circles back to what really matters.

The Jilting of Granny Weatherall   1929

She flicked her wrist neatly out of Doctor Harry's pudgy careful fingers and pulled the sheet up to her chin. The brat ought to be in knee breeches. Doctoring around the country with spectacles on his nose! "Get along now, take your schoolbooks and go. There's nothing wrong with me."

Doctor Harry spread a warm paw like a cushion on her forehead where the forked green vein danced and made her eyelids twitch. "Now, now, be a good girl, and we'll have you up in no time."

"That's no way to speak to a woman nearly eighty years old just because she's down. I'd have you respect your elders, young man."

"Well, Missy, excuse me." Doctor Harry patted her cheek. "But I've got to warn you, haven't I? You're a marvel, but you must be careful or you're going to be good and sorry."

"Don't tell me what I'm going to be. I'm on my feet now, morally speaking. It's   5
Cornelia. I had to go to bed to get rid of her."

Her bones felt loose, and floated around in her skin, and Doctor Harry floated like a balloon around the foot of the bed. He floated and pulled down his waistcoat and swung his glasses on a cord. "Well, stay where you are, it certainly can't hurt you."

"Get along and doctor your sick," said Granny Weatherall. "Leave a well woman alone. I'll call for you when I want you. . . . Where were you forty years ago when I pulled through milk-leg and double pneumonia? You weren't even born. Don't let Cornelia lead you on," she shouted, because Doctor Harry appeared to float up to the ceiling and out. "I pay my own bills, and I don't throw my money away on nonsense!"

She meant to wave good-by, but it was too much trouble. Her eyes closed of themselves, it was like a dark curtain drawn around the bed. The pillow rose and floated under her, pleasant as a hammock in a light wind. She listened to the leaves rustling outside the window. No, somebody was swishing newspapers: no, Cornelia and Doctor Harry were whispering together. She leaped broad awake, thinking they whispered in her ear.

"She was never like this, *never* like this!" "Well, what can we expect?" "Yes, eighty years old. . . ."

Well, and what if she was? She still had ears. It was like Cornelia to whisper around   10
doors. She always kept things secret in such a public way. She was always being tactful and kind. Cornelia was dutiful; that was the trouble with her. Dutiful and good: "So good and dutiful," said Granny, "that I'd like to spank her." She saw herself spanking Cornelia and making a fine job of it.

"What'd you say, Mother?"

Granny felt her face tying up in hard knots.

"Can't a body think, I'd like to know?"

"I thought you might want something."

"I do. I want a lot of things. First off, go away and don't whisper."   15

She lay and drowsed, hoping in her sleep that the children would keep out and let her rest a minute. It had been a long day. Not that she was tired. It was always pleasant to snatch a minute now and then. There was always so much to be done, let me see: to-morrow.

Tomorrow was far away and there was nothing to trouble about. Things were fin-ished somehow when the time came; thank God there was always a little margin over for peace: then a person could spread out the plan of life and tuck in the edges orderly. It was good to have everything clean and folded away, with the hair brushes and tonic bottles sitting straight on the white embroidered linen: the day started without fuss and the pantry shelves laid out with rows of jelly glasses and brown jugs and white stone-china jars with blue whirligigs and words painted on them: coffee, tea, sugar, ginger, cinnamon, allspice: and the bronze clock with the lion on top nicely dusted off. The dust that lion could collect in twenty-four hours! The box in the attic with all those let-ters tied up, well, she'd have to go through that tomorrow. All those letters—George's letters and John's letters and her letters to them both—lying around for the children to find afterwards made her uneasy. Yes, that would be tomorrow's business. No use to let them know how silly she had been once.

While she was rummaging around she found death in her mind and it felt clammy and unfamiliar. She had spent so much time preparing for death there was no need for bringing it up again. Let it take care of itself now. When she was sixty she had felt very old, finished, and went around making farewell trips to see her children and grandchil-dren, with a secret in her mind: This is the very last of your mother, children! Then she made her will and came down with a long fever. That was all just a notion like a lot of other things, but it was lucky too, for she had once for all got over the idea of dying for a long time. Now she couldn't be worried. She hoped she had better sense now. Her father had lived to be one hundred and two years old and had drunk a noggin of strong hot toddy on his last birthday. He told reporters it was his daily habit, and he owed his long life to that. He had made quite a scandal and was very pleased about it. She be-lieved she'd just plague Cornelia a little.

"Cornelia! Cornelia!" No footsteps, but a sudden hand on her cheek. "Bless you, where have you been?"

"Here, Mother."

"Well, Cornelia, I want a noggin of hot toddy."   20

"Are you cold, darling?"

"I'm chilly, Cornelia. Lying in bed stops the circulation. I must have told you that a thousand times."

Well, she could just hear Cornelia telling her husband that Mother was getting a little childish and they'd have to humor her. The thing that most annoyed her was that Cornelia thought she was deaf, dumb, and blind. Little hasty glances and tiny gestures tossed around her and over her head saying, "Don't cross her, let her have her way, she's eighty years old," and she sitting there as if she lived in a thin glass cage. Some-times Granny almost made up her mind to pack up and move back to her own house where nobody could remind her every minute that she was old. Wait, wait, Cornelia, till your own children whisper behind your back!

In her day she had kept a better house and had got more work done. She wasn't   25
too old yet for Lydia to be driving eighty miles for advice when one of the children jumped the track, and Jimmy still dropped in and talked things over: "Now, Mammy, you've a good business head, I want to know what you think of this? . . ." Old. Cor-nelia couldn't change the furniture around without asking. Little things, little things! They had been so sweet when they were little. Granny wished the old days were back again with the children young and everything to be done over. It had been a hard pull, but not too much for her. When she thought of all the food she had cooked, and all

the clothes she had cut and sewed, and all the gardens she had made—well, the children showed it. There they were, made out of her, and they couldn't get away from that. Sometimes she wanted to see John again and point to them and say, Well, I didn't do so badly, did I? But that would have to wait. That was for tomorrow. She used to think of him as a man, but now all the children were older than their father, and he would be a child beside her if she saw him now. It seemed strange and there was something wrong in the idea. Why, he couldn't possibly recognize her. She had fenced in a hundred acres once, digging the post holes herself and clamping the wires with just a negro boy to help. That changed a woman. John would be looking for a young woman with the peaked Spanish comb in her hair and the painted fan. Digging post holes changed a woman. Riding country roads in the winter when women had their babies was another thing: sitting up nights with sick horses and sick negroes and sick children and hardly ever losing one. John, I hardly ever lost one of them! John would see that in a minute, that would be something he could understand, she wouldn't have to explain anything!

It made her feel like rolling up her sleeves and putting the whole place to rights again. No matter if Cornelia was determined to be everywhere at once, there were a great many things left undone on this place. She would start tomorrow and do them. It was good to be strong enough for everything, even if all you made melted and changed and slipped under your hands, so that by the time you finished you almost forgot what you were working for. What was it I set out to do? she asked herself intently, but she could not remember. A fog rose over the valley, she saw it marching across the creek swallowing the trees and moving up the hill like an army of ghosts. Soon it would be at the near edge of the orchard, and then it was time to go in and light the lamps. Come in, children, don't stay out in the night air.

Lighting the lamps had been beautiful. The children huddled up to her and breathed like little calves waiting at the bars in the twilight. Their eyes followed the match and watched the flame rise and settle in a blue curve, then they moved away from her. The lamp was lit, they didn't have to be scared and hang on to mother any more. Never, never, never more. God, for all my life I thank Thee. Without Thee, my God, I could never have done it. Hail, Mary, full of grace.

I want you to pick all the fruit this year and see that nothing is wasted. There's always someone who can use it. Don't let good things rot for want of using. You waste life when you waste good food. Don't let things get lost. It's bitter to lose things. Now, don't let me get to thinking, not when I am tired and taking a little nap before supper. . . .

The pillow rose about her shoulders and pressed against her heart and the memory was being squeezed out of it: oh, push down the pillow, somebody: it would smother her if she tried to hold it. Such a fresh breeze blowing and such a green day with no threats in it. But he had not come, just the same. What does a woman do when she has put on the white veil and set out the white cake for a man and he doesn't come? She tried to remember. No, I swear he never harmed me but in that. He never harmed me but in that . . . and what if he did? There was the day, the day, but a whirl of dark smoke rose and covered it, crept up and over into the bright field where everything was planted so carefully in orderly rows. That was hell, she knew hell when she saw it. For sixty years she had prayed against remembering him and against losing her soul in the deep pit of hell, and now the two things were mingled in one and the thought of him was a smoky cloud from hell that moved and crept in her head when she had just got rid of Doctor Harry and was trying to rest a minute. Wounded vanity. Ellen, said a sharp voice in the top of her mind. Don't let your wounded vanity get the upper hand of you. Plenty of girls get jilted. You were jilted, weren't you? Then stand up to it. Her eyelids wavered and let in streamers of blue-gray light like tissue paper over her eyes. She must get up and pull the shades down or she'd never sleep. She was in bed again and the shades were not down. How could that happen? Better turn over, hide from the light, sleeping in the light gave you nightmares. "Mother, how do you feel now?" and a stinging wetness on her forehead. But I don't like having my face washed in cold water!

Hapsy? George? Lydia? Jimmy? No, Cornelia, and her features were swollen and 30 full of little puddles. "They're coming, darling, they'll all be here soon." Go wash your face, child, you look funny.

Instead of obeying, Cornelia knelt down and put her head on the pillow. She seemed to be talking but there was no sound. "Well, are you tongue-tied? Whose birthday is it? Are you going to give a party?"

Cornelia's mouth moved urgently in strange shapes. "Don't do that, you bother me, daughter."

"Oh, no, Mother. Oh, no. . . ."

Nonsense. It was strange about children. They disputed your every word. "No what, Cornelia?"

"Here's Doctor Harry." 35

"I won't see that boy again. He just left five minutes ago."

"That was this morning, Mother. It's night now. Here's the nurse."

"This is Doctor Harry, Mrs. Weatherall. I never saw you look so young and happy!"

"Ah, I'll never be young again—but I'd be happy if they'd let me lie in peace and get rested."

She thought she spoke up loudly, but no one answered. A warm weight on her 40 forehead, a warm bracelet on her wrist, and a breeze went on whispering, trying to tell her something. A shuffle of leaves in the everlasting hand of God, He blew on them and they danced and rattled. "Mother, don't mind, we're going to give you a little hypodermic." "Look here, daughter, how do ants get in this bed? I saw sugar ants yesterday." Did you send for Hapsy too?

It was Hapsy she really wanted. She had to go a long way back through a great many rooms to find Hapsy standing with a baby on her arm. She seemed to herself to be Hapsy also, and the baby on Hapsy's arm was Hapsy and himself and herself, all at once, and there was no surprise in the meeting. Then Hapsy melted from within and turned flimsy as gray gauze and the baby was a gauzy shadow, and Hapsy came up close and said, "I thought you'd never come," and looked at her very searchingly and said, "You haven't changed a bit!" They leaned forward to kiss, when Cornelia began whispering from a long way off, "Oh, is there anything you want to tell me? Is there anything I can do for you?"

Yes, she had changed her mind after sixty years and she would like to see George. I want you to find George. Find him and be sure to tell him I forgot him. I want him to know I had my husband just the same and my children and my house like any other woman. A good house too and a good husband that I loved and fine children out of him. Better than I hoped for even. Tell him I was given back everything he took away and more. Oh, no, oh, God, no, there was something else besides the house and the man and the children. Oh, surely they were not all? What was it? Something not given back. . . . Her breath crowded down under her ribs and grew into a monstrous frightening shape with cutting edges; it bored up into her head, and the agony was unbelievable: Yes, John, get the doctor now, no more talk, my time has come.

When this one was born it should be the last. The last. It should have been born first, for it was the one she had truly wanted. Everything came in good time. Nothing left out, left over. She was strong, in three days she would be as well as ever. Better. A woman needed milk in her to have her full health.

"Mother, do you hear me?"

"I've been telling you—"

"Mother, Father Connolly's here."

"I went to Holy Communion only last week. Tell him I'm not so sinful as all that."

"Father just wants to speak to you."

He could speak as much as he pleased. It was like him to drop in and inquire about her soul as if it were a teething baby, and then stay on for a cup of tea and a round of cards and gossip. He always had a funny story of some sort, usually about an Irishman who made his little mistakes and confessed them, and the point lay in some absurd thing he would blurt out in the confessional showing his struggles between native piety and original sin. Granny felt easy about her soul. Cornelia, where are your manners? Give Father Connolly a chair. She had her secret comfortable understanding with a few favorite saints who cleared a straight road to God for her. All as surely signed and sealed as the papers for the new Forty Acres. Forever . . . heirs and assigns forever. Since the day the wedding cake was not cut, but thrown out and wasted. The whole bottom dropped out of the world, and there she was blind and sweating with nothing under her feet and the walls falling away. His hand had caught her under the breast, she had not fallen, there was the freshly polished floor with the green rug on it, just as before. He had cursed like a sailor's parrot and said, "I'll kill him for you." Don't lay a hand on him, for my sake leave something to God. "Now, Ellen, you must believe what I tell you. . . ."

So there was nothing, nothing to worry about any more, except sometimes in the night one of the children screamed in a nightmare, and they both hustled out shaking and hunting for the matches and calling, "There, wait a minute, here we are!" John, get the doctor now, Hapsy's time has come. But there was Hapsy standing by the bed in a white cap. "Cornelia, tell Hapsy to take off her cap. I can't see her plain."

Her eyes opened very wide and the room stood out like a picture she had seen somewhere. Dark colors with the shadows rising toward the ceiling in long angles. The tall black dresser gleamed with nothing on it but John's picture, enlarged from a little one, with John's eyes very black when they should have been blue. You never saw him, so how do you know how he looked? But the man insisted the copy was perfect, it was very rich and handsome. For a picture, yes, but it's not my husband. The table by the bed had a linen cover and a candle and a crucifix. The light was blue from Cornelia's silk lampshades. No sort of light at all, just frippery. You had to live forty years with kerosene lamps to appreciate honest electricity. She felt very strong and she saw Doctor Harry with a rosy nimbus around him.

"You look like a saint, Doctor Harry, and I vow that's as near as you'll ever come to it."

"She's saying something."

"I heard you, Cornelia. What's all this carrying-on?"

"Father Connolly's saying—"

Cornelia's voice staggered and bumped like a cart in a bad road. It rounded corners and turned back again and arrived nowhere. Granny stepped up in the cart very lightly and reached for the reins, but a man sat beside her and she knew him by his hands, driving the cart. She did not look in his face, for she knew without seeing, but looked instead down the road where the trees leaned over and bowed to each other and a thousand birds were singing a Mass. She felt like singing too, but she put her hand in the bosom of her dress and pulled out a rosary, and Father Connolly murmured Latin in a very solemn voice and tickled her feet. My God, will you stop that nonsense? I'm a married woman. What if he did run away and leave me to face the priest by myself? I found another a whole world better. I wouldn't have exchanged my husband for anybody except Saint Michael himself, and you may tell him that for me with a thank you in the bargain.

Light flashed on her closed eyelids, and a deep roaring shook her. Cornelia, is that lightning? I hear thunder. There's going to be a storm. Close all the windows. Call the children in. . . . "Mother, here we are, all of us." "Is that you, Hapsy?" "Oh, no, I'm Lydia. We drove as fast as we could." Their faces drifted above her, drifted away. The rosary fell out of her hands and Lydia put it back. Jimmy tried to help, their hands fumbled together, and Granny closed two fingers around Jimmy's thumb. Beads wouldn't do, it must be something alive. She was so amazed her thoughts ran round and round. So, my dear Lord, this is my death and I wasn't even thinking about it. My children have come to see me die. But I can't, it's not time. Oh, I always hated surprises. I wanted to give Cornelia the amethyst set—Cornelia, you're to have the amethyst set, but Hapsy's to wear it when she wants, and, Doctor Harry, do shut up. Nobody sent for you. Oh, my dear Lord, do wait a minute. I meant to do something about the Forty Acres, Jimmy doesn't need it and Lydia will later on, with that worthless husband of hers. I meant to finish the altar cloth and send six bottles of wine to Sister Borgia for her dyspepsia. I want to send six bottles of wine to Sister Borgia, Father Connolly, now don't let me forget.

Cornelia's voice made short turns and tilted over and crashed. "Oh, Mother, oh, Mother, oh, Mother. . . ."

"I'm not going, Cornelia. I'm taken by surprise. I can't go."

You'll see Hapsy again. What about her? "I thought you'd never come." Granny made a long journey outward, looking for Hapsy. What if I don't find her? What then? Her heart sank down and down, there was no bottom to death, she couldn't come to the end of it. The blue light from Cornelia's lampshade drew into a tiny point in the center of her brain, it flickered and winked like an eye, quietly it fluttered and dwindled. Granny lay curled down within herself, amazed and watchful, staring at the point of light that was herself; her body was now only a deeper mass of shadow in an endless darkness and this darkness would curl around the light and swallow it up. God, give a sign!

For the second time there was no sign. Again no bridegroom and the priest in the house. She could not remember any other sorrow because this grief wiped them all away. Oh, no, there's nothing more cruel than this—I'll never forgive it. She stretched herself with a deep breath and blew out the light.

THE RECEPTIVE READER

1. In how much of this story do we look at the world from Granny Weatherall's *point of view*? How much is inner reality, or stream of consciousness? ◆ What is the alternative strand of things happening that the main character does not fully take in? How much of the story is the outer reality of the sickroom? ◆ What kind of rhythm does the alternation of the two points of view set up for the story as a whole?

2. What kinds of memories and concerns take up the early pages of the story? What are striking examples of the blending of present and past?

3. When does the narrative begin to close in on the events alluded to in the title? How are you able to piece together the story of what happened sixty years earlier? ✧ What is the central character's attitude toward those events from the distant past? What are her memories, emotions, thoughts, defenses? Is there a keynote—a recurrent thought or dominant feeling? What role did the jilting play in her life as a whole? ✧ Why do you think the author approaches this central topic in such a roundabout way?

4. What role does Cornelia play in the story? What role do Granny's husband and family play in the story as a whole? What role does Hapsy play in Granny's thoughts and feelings as the end approaches?

5. Does this story have a *plot*? Does any action or development take place parallel to the physical events of the sickroom? How does the ending tie major concerns of the story together?

6. How would you sum up in one sentence the attitude toward life implied in this story?

THE PERSONAL RESPONSE

How would you describe the central character in the story? What kind of person emerges from the story as a whole? What kind of life has she had? How do you relate to her as the reader? How do you think the author *expected* you to feel toward the central character? (Does she seem to steer the reader's feelings or reactions?)

CROSS-REFERENCES—For Discussion or Writing

✧ The technique of the interior monologue is designed to give you an intimate inside view of a character's thoughts and feelings. Does this story give you a fuller understanding of its central character than other stories you have read so far? Compare what and how you learn about the central character in this story and in a story like Alice Munro's "Boys and Girls."

✧ Feminist critics have praised in Porter's writing "the splendid portraits of women which fill her work"; her sympathy with "frustrated, maligned, unvalued, struggling, emotionally blocked, and intellectually undernourished women"; and her exasperation with "conventional social patterns, especially male-dominated marriage and the creed of domesticity" (Jane Flanders). How much of this description fits "The Jilting of Granny Weatherall"?

WRITING ABOUT LITERATURE

5. Sharing a Point of View (Focus on Peer Response)

The Writing Workshop How does point of view shape a story as a whole? What window does the story open on the world? Through whose eyes do we see the people and events, and what difference does it make? In writing a paper about point of view, ask yourself questions like the following:

✧ What is the narrator's relation to the events of the story? Are we listening to a casual observer? to a reliable impartial witness? to a person with an axe to grind? Does the story read like self-justification? like nostalgic reenactment of the past?

✧ How does the point of view limit your vision as the reader? (What is left out that you might want to know?) How does it steer your reactions? (Do you anywhere resist what the narrator apparently expects you to think or feel?)

✧ How might the events of the story look if seen from a different point of view? Try to imagine what the story would be like if told from the perspective of someone else in the story.

✧ Does the narrator take in more of what happens than someone else might—or less? Do you at times feel that you know (or suspect) more than the narrator does? Are you expected to question the perceptions of the narrator?

✧ Are there deliberate shifts in perspective or changes in point of view? Is part of the story seen through one pair of eyes, and another part through another? Does a more comprehensive overall view emerge from such a double perspective?

Focus on Peer Response

When you work on papers about the stories you read, bringing the topic into focus, gathering material, and pulling it into shape will absorb much of your attention. But sooner or later, you will begin to focus on what happens when your writing reaches the reader. In many writing classes, student writers have a chance to learn from **peer response.** When your writing is critiqued by your peers, you become more audience-conscious. You become more aware of how readers react. You become more conscious of what will help and what may hinder your reader.

When you in turn participate in peer response, you formulate your reactions to the writing of fellow students, trying to help them revise and strengthen their papers. Remember the golden rule of peer criticism: Respond unto others as you would have them respond unto you. Try to avoid mere faultfinding. Respond to both strengths and weaknesses, showing that you are basically on the writer's side. In responding to the paper of a fellow student, try to see details in the context of the paper as a whole. How do they affect the overall effectiveness of the paper? What can the writer do to make the paper more effective? Try to answer questions like the following:

✧ *What is the writer trying to do?* What seems to be the general purpose? How well has it been achieved?

✧ *Does the paper get off to a good start?* Do the title and the opening lines capture the attention of the reader? Do they channel it in the right direction?

✧ *Does the paper have a strong central idea or thesis?* Is it spelled out clearly enough—at the beginning or, sometimes, toward the end of the paper? Does the writer keep it in view or lose sight of it as the paper develops?

✧ *What is the general strategy or master plan?* Does it become clear enough to the reader? Or does the reader need more of a preview or program early in the paper? Does the reader run into apparent detours or digressions? Should the organization be streamlined? Should major sections of the paper be reshuffled?

✧ *Are key points well developed?* Is there a rich supporting texture of short quotable quotes and striking authentic detail? Where do you feel a lack of support or follow-through? Are any points merely mentioned in passing and then dropped?

✧ *How effective are the transitions from one point to the next?* Does the paper show the connection between major parts? Does it signal turning points or steps in an argument? Does the paper need stronger logical links?

✧ *Does the conclusion merely rehash points already made?* Or does it do a needed job of pulling together different parts of an argument? Does it add anything to show the larger meaning or implications of the author's points? Does it leave readers with a striking quotation or telling incident to remember?

✧ *How well does the paper communicate its points?* Where would you put in the margin "well put" or "well said" or "good touch"? Where are readers likely to stumble over garbled or incomplete sentences or over missing commas? Where are they likely to be confused by words that are near misses or just plain wrong? Where are big words or shifting, confusing terms used without definition? Where is the wording too disrespectful or slangy—and where too stiff or pretentious? Where do you hear clichés rather than the writer's own voice?

✧ *Does the paper show any personal involvement or commitment?* Does it sound too much like an "assignment"? Is there a personal connection?

Peer Responses to a Draft

Study the following sample student paper and the excerpts from peer responses that follow it. How carefully have the authors of the peer responses read the paper? How do these readers compare with your own vision of an ideal responsive reader for your own writing?

SAMPLE STUDENT PAPER

Creating an Empathetic Audience: A Skillful Use of Point of View

Point of view is a useful author's tool. If used skillfully, it can allow the reader to learn much about a character from a few carefully placed clues. This type of storytelling avoids preachy didacticism and allows the reader to form personal opinions about the character that are not influenced by other characters' thoughts or actions. Tillie Olsen's "I Stand Here Ironing" is an example of a first-person narrative in which the main character is speaking mostly about her nineteen-year-old daughter Emily, but the reader still learns much about the narrator herself. Also, by telling the story from the mother's point of view, Olsen allows the reader to feel empathy for a character who might otherwise inspire anger or disgust.

If this story were told from the troubled Emily's point of view, one can only imagine the vision of the mother that would emerge. A fly on the wall in the counselor's office who confronts Emily's mother at the beginning of the story might have heard Emily describe her mother in a negative light. Emily might tell the counselor, "My mother never smiled at me; she only smiled at my younger sister, Susan, who was prettier. She sent me away all the time—first to my father's family, then to a day school, then to an awful convalescent hospital. She never had time for me; she always worked. She was never there when I needed her." And so on, until all the mother's evils were categorized and the reader feels nothing but anger at the seemingly heartless mother and sympathy for Emily. But by telling the story from the mother's point of view, Olsen uncovers the flip side of the situation, allowing the woman to respond to her daughter's allegations and explain her actions, thus letting the reader empathize with her and gain a better understanding of her. In this way, Olsen also makes a point about the difficulties a single woman can face raising a child and how, oftentimes, innocent lives can be sacrificed and lost in the daily struggle to survive.

The narrator begins the story by describing how difficult it was for her in the early years after her husband left her, describing the hectic pace of her life as she tried to scrape up the daily necessities. "I would start running as soon as I got off the streetcar, running up the stairs, ..." She describes how she had to send her daughter away to her husband's family, and then later, once she was finally able to bring her back, how she had to send her to nursery school during the day. The narrator guiltily admits that she knew the nursery was evil, but "it was the only place there was." It was the only way we could be together, the only way I could hold a job." The first-person narrative of the story allows her readers this insight into the woman's actions. It allows them to learn that such actions, although they may seem cruel, were the only alternative the woman had as she desperately tried to support herself and her child.

Later in the story, the narrator explains how she had to send Emily away again—this time because she did not get well after a bout with the red measles. "They persuaded me at the clinic to send her away to a convalescent home in the country," she says. They told her Emily would receive "the kind of food and care you can't manage for her." The narrator discusses with heartwrenching guilt the "ravaged looks" of the girls in the home and how she desperately tried to get Emily back. If her readers did not have this insight into the woman's feelings, they might believe she was a careless or apathetic mother who found it easier to stick her child into a gruesome home rather than take proper care of her.

The narrator does admit, however, that she made many mistakes with Emily. She rarely smiled at Emily when she was a child, she never held and loved Emily as she did the other children, and she denied Emily the affection she showered on Susan, the second child. She knows these and other things made life harder on Emily than it was on the other children. The narrator admits her error, but knows in her heart that sometimes such happenings are inevitable. "I was at the terrible, growing years. War years. I do not remember them well. I was working, there were four smaller ones now, there was not time for her. She had to help be a mother, and housekeeper, and shopper." Through comments such as these, the reader learns that the narrator, very young herself, was also having a rough time making ends meet. And although it does seem a heavy burden to fall on Emily's small shoulders, placed in the context of an impoverished woman struggling to feed six mouths with one paycheck, Emily's burden becomes one of necessity, not of cruelty. The story's first-person point of view allows the reader the indulgence of pity for Emily and her difficult youth, yet also allows empathy for the mother. Because the reader is privy to the narrator's side of the situation, Emily's hardship is lessened in the face of the family's fierce struggle to survive.

Tillie Olsen's use of first-person narrative in "I Stand Here Ironing" permits the reader to step into the shoes of a poor working-class mother and her daily fight for survival. It permits those of us who have never experienced such hardship to ask ourselves "What would I do if . . . ?" The answer might shock us: we might do the exact thing the narrator was forced to do, which was to rely on a child to perform chores beyond her, in essence robbing that child of the playtime essential to healthy growth. The narrator Olsen creates is universal: a character struggling to survive despite overwhelming odds. And, although that character makes mistakes, these are forgiven in the face of the struggle. The situation Olsen creates is also universal, telling the often unavoidable fate of the children born into such conditions, whose own personalities are lost in the cycle of poverty and the fight for survival.

PEER RESPONSES

1. While reading this essay, I started on a very negative slant, but the author won me over. The paper starts slowly and actually somewhat awkwardly. To begin with, the title, for me, is too long and general. It gives no hint of what the major focus of the story is. Then the first three sentences are solely generalizations about point of view in general. Then, finally, the writer introduces the story that will be the major subject of the essay. So I stop to wonder—is the author writing about point of view, using this story as a convenient example, or is she writing about how point of view makes this story what it is? It is a subtle difference, but it significantly affects how one approaches the story. Both the title and the beginning talk about point of view in very general terms, and that hardly draws the reader in. However, once the author starts writing about Tillie Olsen and her story, she does an excellent job of following up and using quotes effectively to support her thesis: In this story, point of view creates a receptive, empathetic reader. She keeps this central idea in focus well throughout her essay.

2. The writer hints at her thesis in the title and then spells it out at the end of her first paragraph. The main point is that the first-person narrative—the point of view used in "I Stand Here Ironing"—lets the reader get inside the skin of the character and helps readers understand and empathize with her. The paper shows good use of counterpoint in the second paragraph: One key element that works well in this paper is that the writer balances the narrator's point of view with the projected point of view of the daughter. The reader is made to see how the story might have been completely different if told from the perspective of the daughter. The paper leads up effectively to an awareness of the universal nature of the narrator's predicament and her guilt. The ending shows great strength, making up for some of the mechanical quality of the beginning. As for the title, something more imaginative, perhaps drawn from the inner core of the story, would be better.

3. We get a good idea of the importance of point of view in this paper. The author gets right to the point and stays there. The purpose of the paper is to justify the mother's actions and decisions. I feel more attention could have been paid to how the mother actually felt about Emily. She may have resented ever having her. Often a parent will like one child and dislike another. Some phrases slip into clichés: "making ends meet"; "despite overwhelming odds."

QUESTIONS

1. Where are the student responses in substantial *agreement* on the strengths and weaknesses of this paper?

2. How do the responses *differ*? If you were the author of the paper, whose judgment would you be inclined to trust, and why?

3. What revised or improved *title* would you suggest that would be snappier and more informative at the same time?

4. What *opening quotation* chosen from the story might get the reader's attention and lead up effectively to the writer's thesis?

6 SYMBOL
The Eloquent Image

A symbol assumes two planes, two worlds of ideas and sensations, and a dictionary of correspondences between them.

ALBERT CAMUS

Symbolism adds a new value to an object or an act, without thereby violating its immediate or "historical" validity. . . . seen in this light the universe is no longer sealed off, nothing is isolated inside its own existence: everything is linked by a system of correspondences and assimilations.

MIRCEA ELIADE

FOCUS ON SYMBOLS

Symbols are images that have a meaning beyond themselves. In a short story, a symbol is a detail, a character, or an incident that has a meaning beyond its literal role in the narrative. When a flower, the moon, or a fountain is used as a symbol, it comes to mean more than the bloom of a plant, a source of light at night, or a device that recycles water. It is pregnant with a larger significance; it means something beyond itself. The "inconstant moon," for instance, may stand for change, uncertainty, lack of continuity. Or the pale moon may stand for the night side of our existence, for the hidden part of our character that shuns daylight.

Symbolic language gives expression to "the art of thinking in images" (Ananda Coomaraswamy). A symbol is an image that is not presented for its own sake. Imaginative literature involves us in sensory, sensuous experience that often seems richer than what our blunted senses take in from day to day. As we read, the mind's eye takes in images—vividly imagined details, shapes, textures. But often we sense that there is more there than meets the eye. Something tells us: "The sun in this story is not just a physical fact. It becomes overpowering, threatening. It leaves the landscape parched; it dries up the sources of life-giving water. It means something—it tells us something, if only we knew how to read between the lines."

When we reach the climactic incidents in Alice Munro's "Boys and Girls," we can read them on a literal level: On the fox farm where the story takes place, useless, discarded horses are needed as meat for the foxes. The young girl impulsively helps one of the horses escape—though only for a time. However, as we are watching her open the gate, we already sense that this is no routine incident. It is not just part of the day's work. This is the first time she has gone directly against the order of the father she admires. When we think about the girl and the horse, we discover strange parallels. They are both spirited. They are both rebelling against what seems to be their fate. The horse becomes a symbol: It is symbolic of the girl's rebellion, of her high-spiritedness that is doomed to be denied and defeated.

Symbols are concrete and tangible first. The literal-minded reader therefore may see only their physical surface. Not all readers may sense a larger symbolic significance, and different readers may read the same symbol differently. However, to respond fully to a story, you have to become sensitive to possible symbolic overtones and implications.

THE LANGUAGE OF SYMBOLS

In the short story the action is usually small, while the meanings are large.

THOMAS A. GULLERSON

Much of what imaginative literature tells you it does not say in so many words. Although symbols in fiction come to you through the medium of language, they are in a way a **nonverbal** language. Like the gestures of the actor, or the drumbeats of a Beethoven symphony, they do not put verbal labels on what they communicate. You as the reader have to decode, interpret, put into words what the images seem to tell you. Responding to symbols is a way of reading between (or behind) the lines.

As you interpret the language of symbols, keep points like the following in mind:

✧ Some symbols come into a story from *a shared language* of symbols. Much in human experience has traditional symbolic associations: the dawn with hope, the dark forest with evil, clay with death, water with fertility. Light is often the symbol for knowledge, for "enlightenment"—*fiat lux* ("let there be light") is the rallying cry of those fighting the darkness of ignorance.

✧ Some symbols have a *special personal meaning* for the writer, and their meaning may come into focus as they return again and again in the writer's work. Speaking of the Irish poet Seamus Heaney, a critic said that the source of his imaginative power lay in his rural childhood experience "that is centered and staked in the image of the pump. The pump, like his poetry, taps hidden springs to conduct what is sustaining and life-giving. The pump is a symbol of the nourishment which comes from knowing and belonging to a certain place and a certain mode of life" (Elmer Andrews).

✧ Literary symbols are *rich in associations*. They have more resonance, more reverberations than simple signs. The skull and bones that say "poison" have a clear, unequivocal message. But literary symbols do not simply signal "Danger" or "All Clear." One of the oldest symbols in the literature of Western culture is the garden. It brings with it a wealth of associations: The Garden of Eden was a scene of innocence and happiness, before the fall of Adam. The garden is a symbol of nature fruitful and life-sustaining. Like the Garden of Eden, it may be the cultivated spot in the surrounding wilderness. It may suggest the oasis in the desert. It may suggest a retreat from the intrigues of office or business—we retreat there to "cultivate our own garden." (It may also be a place where we struggle against pests and weeds.)

✧ Symbols *may be ambiguous*. In Melville's great American classic *Moby Dick*, the great mythic white whale seems paradoxically double-faced. To the obsessed Captain Ahab, the whale stands for everything that is destructive in nature—and the whale does in the end send his ship and his crew to the bottom of the sea. But at other times, the whale seems to stand for everything that is most serenely beautiful in nature—as it floats through the becalmed sea shedding "enticings."

✧ Symbols acquire their full meaning *in the context of a story*. In Nathaniel Hawthorne's novel *The Scarlet Letter*, the letter *A* for adultery, embroidered on the sinner's gown, may at first seem a matter of historical interest. We can say, "This is how the Puritans identified an adulteress; this is how it was done." But as we watch her and her innocent child, the scarlet letter begins to haunt us; it makes us think. The author used it as the title of the whole novel: *The Scarlet Letter*. As we finish the novel, that scarlet letter is likely to have been burned into our consciousness. It becomes a symbol of our consciousness of guilt, of our doubts about who is truly guilty. We begin to imagine it carried by others (like the Puritan minister Dimmesdale), who are implicated but not literally stigmatized.

✧ When symbols work together to act out a story, the result is **allegory.** In Le Guin's "The Ones Who Walk Away from Omelas," everything seems potentially symbolic. We are not in any place we could find on a map. The people who are happy in Le Guin's strange Utopia (Greek for "no-place" or neverland), the prisoner who is the dark secret of this beautiful place, and the people who "walk away"—all these play their role in a web of symbolic meaning.

The Range of Interpretation

Readers vary greatly in how responsive they are to symbolic overtones. The following excerpt is from an article by Danielle Schaub titled "Shirley Jackson's Use of Symbols in 'The Lottery.'" Her thesis: The story as a whole centers on the duality of a harmless-seeming everyday surface and the "horrendous" evil that will erupt. Similarly, much in the setting of the story has "ambivalent" symbolic overtones—benign when looked at from one point of view, ominous when looked at from another. Look at the polarities the critic traces in the story. Which to you seem well within the range of a shared language of symbols to which readers are likely to respond? Which to you seem most likely to be at work in the story?

DANIELLE SCHAUB
Symbols in "The Lottery"   1990

The author's recurrent use of symbols stresses the duality of things and beings, which paves the way for the final horrendous revelation. . . . Their ambivalence corroborates the message of the story, namely that first-hand impressions may well be deceptive; on the surface, things are smooth; deep down, reality is cruder. The usually positive value of any symbol needs to be counterbalanced by its hidden or less well-known negative value for us to have a clearer picture of the text. Its richness and quality result from the mixture of opposite values. Instead of a straightforward account of small-town life, the reader gets a fuller picture of Life with its inescapable conjunction of opposites.

Tension is already present in the description of the setting and in the atmosphere. Like a Janus figure [the two-faced god of Roman mythology], the sun is felt throughout as an ambiguous presence. Its generative heat, associated with youth, vitality, and fertility, heals and restores, but come midsummer and its scorching heat leads to the poisoning, burning madness of the solstice rite. The sun will provide better crops but only at the cost of the ritual murder of an innocent villager. Besides, the ambivalent character of the rite is stressed by the profusely blossoming flowers. By their very nature they symbolize beauty as well as point to the transitory stages of the vegetal cycle. They suggest not only virtue, goodness, and purity but also temptation and deceit. As such they are part of pleasant occasions but also of distressing functions—as a last tribute paid at a funeral, Tessie's for example. The green grass too reveals the discrepancy between the characters' appearance and deeds. Indeed, on the one hand, green suggests fertility, peace, balance, harmony, freshness, youth: these qualities, at first sight, seem to fit the description of the population. But, on the other hand, green implies ignorance, unripeness, inexperience—the very characteristics attributed to pagan sacrifices. Significantly too, prior to the insane murder of Tessie Hutchinson, the villagers gather in the square. As the square stands for firmness and stability, organization and construction, it is the source of order. No wonder then that traditions are perpetuated in the square.

From *Journal of the Short Story in English*, Spring 1990

A SHORT STORY CLASSIC: STEINBECK'S "CHRYSANTHEMUMS"

Literary classics, like public monuments in a park, become familiar. We have taken in whatever they have to offer; we feel that it is time to pass on to something new. However, the test of a true classic is that it surprises us by refusing to be passé. A new generation reads it from a fresh perspective, and rediscovers its power and its appeal.

JOHN STEINBECK (1902–1968)

Much of Steinbeck's fiction takes us to "Steinbeck Country"—California's agricultural Salinas Valley and scenic Monterey Bay, stretching south to the rugged coast of Big Sur. This area, where Steinbeck grew up and went to school, sets the scene for books like *Tortilla Flat* (1935), *Of Mice and Men* (1937), *Cannery Row* (1945), and *East of Eden* (1952). Many characters he places in this setting are social outcasts, poor people, derelicts, migrant workers—and the people who befriend them.

Steinbeck's work was part of the tradition of naturalistic fiction, represented earlier by Americans like Stephen Crane and Jack London. After decades of Victorian high-mindedness, **naturalism** (late in the nineteenth century) set out to correct the balance—to recognize the physical and instinctual nature of people. It tried to be more honest about their suppressed (or repressed) physical and emotional needs. Writers tried to strip life of its genteel pretenses, to look at it, if necessary, in the raw. Steinbeck represents the native tradition of naturalistic fiction in several ways: He has a special sympathy for unglamorous, unfashionable characters. He affectionately renders the coarse texture of common life. He chooses a few strong but simple symbols to carry his central themes.

Some of Steinbeck's best-known work was part of the literature of **social protest** of the thirties and forties. In the depths of the Great Depression, Steinbeck became famous with his novel *The Grapes of Wrath* (1939). Made into a movie starring Henry Fonda, Steinbeck's mythical novel proved to have a powerful hold on the imagination of millions around the world—more haunting and persuasive than the analyses and excuses prepared by historians and sociologists. Steinbeck told the story of the "Okies" (rural Americans from Oklahoma and other parts of the Dust Bowl of the thirties) who were driven from their farms by dust storms and *laissez-faire* (let-market-forces-do-their-work) economics. They were transformed from God-fearing, family-oriented, self-reliant Americans into homeless nomads looking desperately for work and a place to live. They were driven from migrant camp to migrant camp by sheriffs and politicians who were in the pay of those with power and money.

Feminist critics have in recent years taken a fresh look at the "strong women" in Steinbeck's fiction. These range from Ma Joad and Rose of Sharon, the "earth mother" figures in *The Grapes of Wrath,* to women like Elisa Allen in his short story "The Chrysanthemums." They may be women who have a strength of will missing in their husbands; they seem to have more energy and vitality than is needed for their tasks. They "must somehow express themselves meaningfully within the narrow possibilities open to women in a man's world" (Marilyn H. Mitchell).

Steinbeck wrote more than fifty short stories, including such classics as "Flight" and the stories that make up *The Red Pony* (1938). "The Chrysanthemums" has been called "Steinbeck's ultimate masterpiece in short fiction" (R. S. Hughes). Steinbeck said that this story was "designed to strike without the reader's knowledge." He meant that we may read the story casually but will feel after it is finished "that something profound has happened"—although we may "not know what nor how." Perhaps this is a key feature of fiction rich in symbolism—we finish reading with a sense that there is more to the story than meets the eye.

The Chrysanthemums   1937

The high grey-flannel fog of winter closed off the Salinas Valley from the sky and from all the rest of the world. On every side it sat like a lid on the mountains and made of the great valley a closed pot. On the broad, level land floor the gang plows bit deep and left the black earth shining like metal where the shares had cut. On the foothill ranches across the Salinas River, the yellow stubble fields seemed to be bathed in pale cold sunshine, but there was no sunshine in the valley now in December. The thick willow scrub along the river flamed with sharp and positive yellow leaves.

It was a time of quiet and of waiting. The air was cold and tender. A light wind blew up from the southwest so that the farmers were mildly hopeful of a good rain before long; but fog and rain do not go together.

Across the river, on Henry Allen's foothill ranch there was little work to be done, for the hay was cut and stored and the orchards were plowed up to receive the rain deeply when it should come. The cattle on the higher slopes were becoming shaggy and rough-coated.

Elisa Allen, working in her flower garden, looked down across the yard and saw Henry, her husband, talking to two men in business suits. The three of them stood by the tractor shed, each man with one foot on the side of the little Fordson. They smoked cigarettes and studied the machine as they talked.

Elisa watched them for a moment and then went back to her work. She was thirty-five. Her face was lean and strong and her eyes were as clear as water. Her figure looked blocked and heavy in her gardening costume, a man's black hat pulled low down over her eyes, clodhopper shoes, a figured print dress almost completely covered by a big corduroy apron with four big pockets to hold the snips, the trowel and scratcher, the seeds and the knife she worked with. She wore heavy leather gloves to protect her hands while she worked.

She was cutting down the old year's chrysanthemum stalks with a pair of short and powerful scissors. She looked down toward the men by the tractor shed now and then. Her face was eager and mature and handsome; even her work with the scissors was over-eager, over-powerful. The chrysanthemum stems seemed too small and easy for her energy.

She brushed a cloud of hair out of her eyes with the back of her glove, and left a smudge of earth on her cheek in doing it. Behind her stood the neat white farm house with red geraniums close-banked around it as high as the windows. It was a hard-swept looking little house, with hard-polished windows, and a clean mud-mat on the front steps.

Elisa cast another glance toward the tractor shed. The strangers were getting into their Ford coupe. She took off a glove and put her strong fingers down into the forest of new green chrysanthemum sprouts that were growing around the old roots. She spread the leaves and looked down among the close-growing stems. No aphids were there, no sowbugs or snails or cutworms. Her terrier fingers destroyed such pests before they could get started.

5

Elisa started at the sound of her husband's voice. He had come near quietly, and he leaned over the wire fence that protected her flower garden from cattle and dogs and chickens.

"At it again," he said. "You've got a strong new crop coming."   10

Elisa straightened her back and pulled on the gardening glove again. "Yes. They'll be strong this coming year." In her tone and on her face there was a little smugness.

"You've got a gift with things," Henry observed. "Some of those yellow chrysanthemums you had this year were ten inches across. I wish you'd work out in the orchard and raise some apples that big."

Her eyes sharpened. "Maybe I could do it, too. I've a gift with things, all right. My mother had it. She could stick anything in the ground and make it grow. She said it was having planters' hands that knew how to do it."

"Well, it sure works with flowers," he said.

"Henry, who were those men you were talking to?"   15

"Why, sure, that's what I came to tell you. They were from the Western Meat Company. I sold those thirty head of three-year-old steers. Got nearly my own price, too."

"Good," she said. "Good for you."

"And I thought," he continued, "I thought how it's Saturday afternoon, and we might go into Salinas for dinner at a restaurant, and then to a picture show—to celebrate, you see."

"Good," she repeated. "Oh, yes. That will be good."

Henry put on his joking tone. "There's fights tonight. How'd you like to go to the fights?"   20

"Oh, no," she said breathlessly. "No, I wouldn't like fights."

"Just fooling, Elisa. We'll go to a movie. Let's see. It's two now. I'm going to take Scotty and bring down those steers from the hill. It'll take us maybe two hours. We'll go in town about five and have dinner at the Cominos Hotel. Like that?"

"Of course I'll like it. It's good to eat away from home."

"All right, then. I'll go get up a couple of horses."

She said, "I'll have plenty of time to transplant some of these sets, I guess."   25

She heard her husband calling Scotty down by the barn. And a little later she saw the two men ride up the pale yellow hillside in search of the steers.

There was a little square sandy bed kept for rooting the chrysanthemums. With her trowel she turned the soil over and over, and smoothed it and patted it firm. Then she dug ten parallel trenches to receive the sets. Back at the chrysanthemum bed she pulled out the little crisp shoots, trimmed off the leaves of each one with her scissors and laid it on a small orderly pile.

A squeak of wheels and plod of hoofs came from the road. Elisa looked up. The country road ran along the dense bank of willows and cottonwoods that bordered the river, and up this road came a curious vehicle, curiously drawn. It was an old spring-wagon, with a round canvas top on it like the cover of a prairie schooner. It was drawn by an old bay horse and a little grey-and-white burro. A big stubble-bearded man sat between the cover flaps and drove the crawling team. Underneath the wagon, between the hind wheels, a lean and rangy mongrel dog walked sedately. Words were painted on the canvas, in clumsy, crooked letters. "Pots, pans, knives, sisors, lawn mores, Fixed." Two rows of articles, and the triumphantly definitive "Fixed" below. The black paint had run down in little sharp points beneath each letter.

Elisa, squatting on the ground, watched to see the crazy, loose-jointed wagon pass by. But it didn't pass. It turned into the farm road in front of her house, crooked old wheels skirling and squeaking. The rangy dog darted from between the wheels and ran ahead. Instantly the two ranch shepherds flew out at him. Then all three stopped, and with stiff and quivering tails, with taut straight legs, with ambassadorial dignity, they slowly circled, sniffing daintily. The caravan pulled up to Elisa's wire fence and stopped. Now the newcomer dog, feeling out-numbered, lowered his tail and retired under the wagon with raised hackles and bared teeth.

The man on the wagon seat called out, "That's a bad dog in a fight when he gets started."   30

Elisa laughed. "I see he is. How soon does he generally get started?"

The man caught up her laughter and echoed it heartily. "Sometimes not for weeks and weeks," he said. He climbly stiffly down, over the wheel. The horse and the donkey drooped like unwatered flowers.

Elisa saw that he was a very big man. Although his hair and beard were greying, he did not look old. His worn black suit was wrinkled and spotted with grease. The laughter had disappeared from his face and eyes the moment his laughing voice ceased. His eyes were dark, and they were full of the brooding that gets in the eyes of teamsters and of sailors. The calloused hands he rested on the wire fence were cracked, and every crack was a black line. He took off his battered hat.

"I'm off my general road, ma'am," he said. "Does this dirt road cut over across the river to the Los Angeles highway?"

Elisa stood up and shoved the thick scissors in her apron pocket. "Well, yes, it   35 does, but it winds around and then fords the river. I don't think your team could pull through the sand."

He replied with some asperity, "It might surprise you what them beasts can pull through."

"When they get started?" she asked.

He smiled for a second. "Yes. When they get started."

"Well," said Elisa, "I think you'll save time if you go back to the Salinas road and pick up the highway there."

He drew a big finger down the chicken wire and made it sing. "I ain't in any   40 hurry, ma'am. I go from Seattle to San Diego and back every year. Takes all my time. About six months each way. I aim to follow nice weather."

Elisa took off her gloves and stuffed them in the apron pocket with the scissors. She touched the under edge of her man's hat, searching for fugitive hairs. "That sounds like a nice kind of a way to live," she said.

He leaned confidentially over the fence. "Maybe you noticed the writing on my wagon. I mend pots and sharpen knives and scissors. You got any of them things to do?"

"Oh, no," she said quickly. "Nothing like that." Her eyes hardened with resistance.

"Scissors is the worst thing," he explained. "Most people just ruin scissors trying to sharpen 'em, but I know how. I got a special tool. It's a little bobbit kind of thing, and patented. But it sure does the trick."

"No. My scissors are all sharp."   45

"All right, then. Take a pot," he continued earnestly, "a bent pot, or a pot with a hole. I can make it like new so you don't have to buy no new ones. That's a saving for you."

"No," she said shortly. "I tell you I have nothing like that for you to do."

His face fell to an exaggerated sadness. His voice took on a whining undertone. "I ain't had a thing to do today. Maybe I won't have no supper tonight. You see I'm off my regular road. I know folks on the highway clear from Seattle to San Diego. They save their things for me to sharpen up because they know I do it so good and save them money."

"I'm sorry," Elisa said irritably. "I haven't anything for you to do."

His eyes left her face and fell to searching the ground. They roamed about until   50
they came to the chrysanthemum bed where she had been working. "What's them
plants, ma'am?"

The irritation and resistance melted from Elisa's face. "Oh, those are chrysanthemums, giant whites and yellows. I raise them every year, bigger than anybody
around here."

"Kind of a long-stemmed flower? Looks like a quick puff of colored smoke?" he
asked.

"That's it. What a nice way to describe them."

"They smell kind of nasty till you get used to them," he said.

"It's a good bitter smell," she retorted, "not nasty at all."   55

He changed his tone quickly. "I like the smell myself."

"I had ten-inch blooms this year," she said.

The man leaned farther over the fence. "Look. I know a lady down the road a
piece, has got the nicest garden you ever seen. Got nearly every kind of flower but no
chrysantheums. Last time I was mending a copper-bottom washtub for her (that's a
hard job but I do it good), she said to me, 'If you ever run acrost some nice chrysantheums I wish you'd try to get me a few seeds.' That's what she told me."

Elisa's eyes grew alert and eager. "She couldn't have known much about chrysanthemums. You *can* raise them from seed, but it's much easier to root the little sprouts
you see there."

"Oh," he said. "I s'pose I can't take none to her, then."   60

"Why yes you can," Elisa cried. "I can put some in damp sand, and you can carry
them right along with you. They'll take root in the pot if you keep them damp. And
then she can transplant them."

"She'd sure like to have some, ma'am. You say they're nice ones?"

"Beautiful," she said. "Oh, beautiful." Her eyes shone. She tore off the battered
hat and shook out her dark pretty hair. "I'll put them in a flower pot, and you can take
them right with you. Come into the yard."

While the man came through the picket gate Elisa ran excitedly along the gerani-
um-bordered path to the back of the house. And she returned carrying a big red flower
pot. The gloves were forgotten now. She kneeled on the ground by the starting bed and
dug up the sandy soil with her fingers and scooped it into the bright new flower pot.
Then she picked up the little pile of shoots she had prepared. With her strong fingers she
pressed them into the sand and tamped around them with her knuckles. The man stood
over her. "I'll tell you what to do," she said. "You remember so you can tell the lady."

"Yes, I'll try to remember."   65

"Well, look. These will take root in about a month. Then she must set them out,
about a foot apart in good rich earth like this, see?" She lifted a handful of dark soil for
him to look at. "They'll grow fast and tall. Now remember this: In July tell her to cut
them down, about eight inches from the ground."

"Before they bloom?" he asked.

"Yes, before they bloom." Her face was tight with eagerness. "They'll grow right
up again. About the last of September the buds will start."

She stopped and seemed perplexed. "It's the budding that takes the most care,"
she said hesitantly. "I don't know how to tell you." She looked deep into his eyes,
searchingly. Her mouth opened a little, and she seemed to be listening. "I'll try to tell
you," she said. "Did you ever hear of planting hands?"

"Can't say I have, ma'am."   70

"Well, I can only tell you what it feels like. It's when you're picking off the buds you don't want. Everything goes right down into your fingertips. You watch your fingers work. They do it themselves. You can feel how it is. They pick and pick the buds. They never make a mistake. They're with the plant. Do you see? Your fingers and the plant. You can feel that, right up your arm. They know. They never make a mistake. You can feel it. When you're like that you can't do anything wrong. Do you see that? Can you understand that?"

She was kneeling on the ground looking up at him. Her breast swelled passionately.

The man's eyes narrowed. He looked away self-consciously. "Maybe I know," he said. "Sometimes in the night in the wagon there——"

Elisa's voice grew husky. She broke in on him, "I've never lived as you do, but I know what you mean. When the night is dark—why, the stars are sharp-pointed, and there's quiet. Why, you rise up and up! Every pointed star gets driven into your body. It's like that. Hot and sharp and—lovely."

Kneeling there, her hand went out toward his legs in the greasy black trousers. Her hesitant fingers almost touched the cloth. Then her hand dropped to the ground. She crouched low like a fawning dog.   75

He said, "It's nice, just like you say. Only when you don't have no dinner, it ain't."

She stood up then, very straight, and her face was ashamed. She held the flower pot out to him and placed it gently in his arms. "Here. Put it in your wagon, on the seat, where you can watch it. Maybe I can find something for you to do."

At the back of the house she dug in the can pile and found two old and battered aluminum saucepans. She carried them back and gave them to him. "Here, maybe you can fix these."

His manner changed. He became professional. "Good as new I can fix them." At the back of his wagon he set a little anvil, and out of an oily tool box dug a small machine hammer. Elisa came through the gate to watch him while he pounded out the dents in the kettles. His mouth grew sure and knowing. At a difficult part of the work he sucked his under-lip.

"You sleep right in the wagon?" Elisa asked.   80

"Right in the wagon, ma'am. Rain or shine I'm dry as a cow in there."

"It must be nice," she said. "It must be very nice. I wish women could do such things."

"It ain't the right kind of a life for a woman."

Her upper lip raised a little, showing her teeth. "How do you know? How can you tell?" she said.

"I don't know, ma'am," he protested. "Of course I don't know. Now here's your   85 kettles, done. You don't have to buy no new ones."

"How much?"

"Oh, fifty cents'll do. I keep my prices down and my work good. That's why I have all them satisfied customers up and down the highway."

Elisa brought him a fifty-cent piece from the house and dropped it in his hand. "You might be surprised to have a rival some time. I can sharpen scissors, too. And I can beat the dents out of little pots. I could show you what a woman might do."

He put his hammer back in the oily box and shoved the little anvil out of sight. "It would be a lonely life for a woman, ma'am, and a scarey life, too, with animals creeping under the wagon all night." He climbed over the singletree, steadying himself with a hand on the burro's white rump. He settled himself in the seat, picked up the lines. "Thank you kindly, ma'am," he said. "I'll do like you told me; I'll go back and catch the Salinas road."

"Mind," she called, "if you're long in getting there, keep the sand damp."   90

"Sand, ma'am? . . . Sand? Oh, sure. You mean around the chrysanthemums. Sure

I will." He clucked his tongue. The beasts leaned luxuriously into their collars. The mongrel dog took his place between the back wheels. The wagon turned and crawled out the entrance road and back the way it had come, along the river.

Elisa stood in front of her wire fence watching the slow progress of the caravan. Her shoulders were straight, her head thrown back, her eyes half-closed, so that the scene came vaguely into them. Her lips moved silently, forming the words "Good-bye—good-bye." Then she whispered, "That's a bright direction. There's a glowing there." The sound of her whisper startled her. She shook herself free and looked about to see whether anyone had been listening. Only the dogs had heard. They lifted their heads toward her from their sleeping in the dust, and then stretched out their chins and settled asleep again. Elisa turned and ran hurriedly into the house.

In the kitchen she reached behind the stove and felt the water tank. It was full of hot water from the noonday cooking. In the bathroom she tore off her soiled clothes and flung them into the corner. And then she scrubbed herself with a little block of pumice, legs and thighs, loins and chest and arms, until her skin was scratched and red. When she had dried herself she stood in front of a mirror in her bedroom and looked at her body. She tightened her stomach and threw out her chest. She turned and looked over her shoulder at her back.

After a while she began to dress, slowly. She put on her newest underclothing and her nicest stockings and the dress which was the symbol of her prettiness. She worked carefully on her hair, penciled her eyebrows and rouged her lips.

Before she was finished she heard the little thunder of hoofs and the shouts of   95
Henry and his helper as they drove the red steers into the corral. She heard the gate bang shut and set herself for Henry's arrival.

His step sounded on the porch. He entered the house calling, "Elisa, where are you?"

"In my room, dressing. I'm not ready. There's hot water for your bath. Hurry up. It's getting late."

When she heard him splashing in the tub, Elisa laid his dark suit on the bed, and shirt and socks and tie beside it. She stood his polished shoes on the floor beside the bed. Then she went to the porch and sat primly and stiffly down. She looked toward the river road where the willow-line was still yellow with frosted leaves so that under the high grey fog they seemed a thin band of sunshine. This was the only color in the grey afternoon. She sat unmoving for a long time. Her eyes blinked rarely.

Henry came banging out of the door, shoving his tie inside his vest as he came. Elisa stiffened and her face grew tight. Henry stopped short and looked at her. "Why—why, Elisa. You look so nice!"

"Nice? You think I look nice? What do you mean by 'nice'?"   100

Henry blundered on. "I don't know. I mean you look different, strong and happy."

"I am strong? Yes, strong. What do you mean 'strong'?"

He looked bewildered. "You're playing some kind of a game," he said helplessly. "It's a kind of a play. You look strong enough to break a calf over your knee, happy enough to eat it like a watermelon."

For a second she lost her rigidity. "Henry! Don't talk like that. You didn't know what you said." She grew complete again. "I'm strong," she boasted. "I never knew before how strong."

Henry looked down toward the tractor shed, and when he brought his eyes back   105
to her, they were his own again. "I'll get out the car. You can put on your coat while I'm starting."

Elisa went into the house. She heard him drive to the gate and idle down his motor, and then she took a long time to put on her hat. She pulled it here and pressed it there. When Henry turned the motor off she slipped into her coat and went out.

The little roadster bounced along on the dirt road by the river, raising the birds and driving the rabbits into the brush. Two cranes flapped heavily over the willow-line and dropped into the river-bed.

Far ahead on the road Elisa saw a dark speck. She knew.

She tried not to look as they passed it, but her eyes would not obey. She whispered to herself sadly, "He might have thrown them off the road. That wouldn't have been much trouble, not very much. But he kept the pot," she explained. "He had to keep the pot. That's why he couldn't get them off the road."

The roadster turned a bend and she saw the caravan ahead. She swung full around 110 toward her husband so she could not see the little covered wagon and the mismatched team as the car passed them.

In a moment it was over. The thing was done. She did not look back.

She said loudly, to be heard above the motor, "It will be good, tonight, a good dinner."

"Now you're changed again," Henry complained. He took one hand from the wheel and patted her knee. "I ought to take you in to dinner oftener. It would be good for both of us. We get so heavy out on the ranch."

"Henry," she asked, "could we have wine at dinner?"

"Sure we could. Say! That will be fine." 115

She was silent for a while; then she said, "Henry, those prize fights, do the men hurt each other very much?"

"Sometimes a little, not often. Why?"

"Well, I've read how they break noses, and blood runs down their chests. I've read how the fighting gloves get heavy and soggy with blood."

He looked around at her. "What's the matter, Elisa? I didn't know you read things like that." He brought the car to a stop, then turned to the right over the Salinas River bridge.

"Do any women ever go to the fights?" she asked. 120

"Oh, sure, some. What's the matter, Elisa? Do you want to go? I don't think you'd like it, but I'll take you if you really want to go."

She relaxed limply in the seat. "Oh, no. No. I don't want to go. I'm sure I don't." Her face was turned away from him. "It will be enough if we can have wine. It will be plenty." She turned up her coat collar so he could not see that she was crying weakly— like an old woman.

THE RECEPTIVE READER

1. What is the meaning of the chrysanthemums as the central, gradually evolving *symbol* in the story? How much of a continuing thread do they provide for the story as a whole? What role do they play at the high point of the story? Were you surprised when you saw the flowers in the road?

2. When flowers are used as symbols, they activate a whole range of memories, associations, *connotations*. Cluster the word *flower*. What chains of association and patterns of thought does it bring to mind? Which of these do you think are especially relevant to this story?

3. What telling or revealing *details*—dress, the weather, features of the physical setting, the boxing, the wine—might be charged with symbolic significance?

4. Critics have found much sexual imagery, symbolism, or allusion in the encounter between Elisa and the tinker. What are striking examples? What is significant in the description of his arrival? What is strange or paradoxical about their relationship?

5. What is the role of the husband in this story? What kind of person is he? What kind of marriage do he and Elisa have? What are striking details or images that bring the nature of their relationship into focus?

6. What is the role of traditional assumptions about men's work and women's work, or about men's interests and women's interests, in this story? Do you see in the heroine an "ambiguous combination of feminine and masculine traits" (Marilyn H. Mitchell)?

7. Would you call the sight of the discarded flowers in the road the *climax*, or high point, of the story? Where does the story go afterwards? What impact have the developments of the story had on Elisa? How does the story end?

8. Critics have singled out Steinbeck as one of the few male authors of his time who went beyond stereotypical portraits of women. Do you think they are right? How might this story have been different if it had been written by a woman?

THE PERSONAL RESPONSE

How do you relate to Elisa as the *central character*? Do you find her sympathetic? strong? weak? strange? (Support your answer in detail.)

THE RANGE OF INTERPRETATION

In the following two critical excerpts, compare a traditional reading of the story by a male critic with a rereading of this and another story from a feminist point of view. Stanley Renner, in "The Real Woman inside the Fence in 'The Chrysanthemums,'" claims that "the story's evidence does not support the view that Elisa is a woman kept from fulfillment by male domination." For him, the story is shaped by traditional male complaints "against the sexual unresponsiveness of the female, against an ambivalent female sexuality that both invites and repels male admiration, against the sexual delicacy of the female, who, repelled by sexual reality, holds out for indulgences of her emotional and spiritual yearnings":

> Unlike men, women incline more toward romantic fantasies of sex than the act of love itself. Clearly Elisa romanticizes the tinker. In ironic mockery of Elisa's great and perverse capacity for romanticizing reality, Steinbeck makes everything about the tinker the utter antithesis of her fastidious tidiness, which symbolizes her delicate sexual sensibility. Unshaven, unwashed, his clothes "wrinkled and spotted with grease," he represents everything she furiously purges from her garden and scrubs out of her house. Yet she fantasizes sexual intercourse with him when he gratifies her hunger for romance because it is only a fantasy: he will presently climb back into his slovenly wagon and ride away into the romantic sunset. Henry, clean and reliable if a bit stodgy and clumsy, is reality pressing against Elisa's fence seeking an actual sexual relationship. But in rejecting reality, albeit unideal, as reality always is, for a patently falsified romantic fantasy, she defeats her own impulses toward a fuller life.

> From *Modern Fiction Studies*, Summer 1985

Contrasting with Renner's perspective focusing on male dissatisfaction and complaints, Marilyn H. Mitchell, in "Steinbeck's Strong Women: Feminine Identity in the Short Stories," claims that Steinbeck shows women who "are trapped between society's definition of the masculine and the feminine and are struggling against the limitations of the feminine." Steinbeck is using them "to refute outmoded conceptions of what a woman should be" and aims to show "the real human beauty beneath Elisa's rough and somewhat masculine exterior":

> Two of John Steinbeck's more intricate and memorable stories are "The Chrysanthemums" and "The White Quail." Both examine the psychology and sexuality of strong women who must somehow express themselves meaningfully within the narrow possibilities open to women in a man's world. In each case the woman chooses a traditional feminine activity, gardening, as a creative outlet. . . . Steinbeck reveals fundamental differences between the way women see themselves and the way they are viewed by men. For example, both husbands relate primarily to the physical attributes of their wives, making only meager attempts to comprehend their personalities. Consequently, a gulf of misunderstanding exists between the marriage partners, which creates verbal as well as sexual blocks to communication. In each marriage, at least one of the spouses is aware of some degree of sexual frustration, although dissatisfaction is never overtly articulated. Furthermore, the propensity of the men to see their wives as dependent inferiors, while the women perceive themselves as being equal if not superior partners, creates a strain within the marriage which is partially responsible for the isolation of each of the characters.
>
> Both Elisa Allen of "The Chrysanthemums" and Mary Teller in "The White Quail" display a strength of will usually identified with the male but which, in these cases, the husbands are not shown to have. . . . Elisa Allen demonstrates a very earthly sensuality in "The Chrysanthemums," though not in the presence of her husband, indicating that their failure as a couple may be as much his fault as hers.
>
> From R. S. Hughes, *Steinbeck: A Study of the Short Fiction*

Is there any common basis for these two approaches to the story? How and why do they disagree? Who do you think is more nearly right, and why?

CROSS-REFERENCES—For Discussion or Writing

Compare and contrast the treatment of unfulfilled desire in Katherine Anne Porter's "The Jilting of Granny Weatherall" and in John Steinbeck's "The Chrysanthemums." (Does it make a difference that one of the stories is by a female author and the other by a male author?)

THE CENTRAL SYMBOL

Often a **central symbol** becomes the focal point of a story. A central symbol focuses our attention. It provides a tangible object for our emotions—since many of us find it hard to anchor our feelings to disembodied ideas. A central symbol becomes the hub for meanings and associations. It may slowly evolve, acquiring its full meaning only as the story as a whole takes shape. In each of the following stories, a rich central symbol helps give shape to the story as a whole.

CHARLOTTE PERKINS GILMAN (1860–1935)

Gilman was a leading feminist and social activist at the turn of the century. She grew up in a family that included prominent suffragists (advocates of a woman's right to vote); one of her great-aunts was the abolitionist Harriet Beecher Stowe, author of *Uncle Tom's Cabin*. In her *Women and Economics* (1898) and other nonfiction works, Gilman argued that the traditional conception of women's roles was the result of social custom; it was culturally conditioned rather than anchored in biology. She proposed revolutionary rearrangements of domestic life to free women for work outside the home.

Born and raised in Connecticut, Gilman moved to California after separating from her first husband, and she edited and published feminist publications there. She helped organize the California Women's Congresses of 1894 and 1895 and was one of the founders of the Women's Peace Party. Besides writing nonfiction, she wrote novels and short stories that dramatized her belief in women's capacity for independence and self-realization.

Gilman's much-anthologized "The Yellow Wallpaper" chronicles a young woman's descent into insanity. The story has been read as a clinical study of the escalation of mental illness—as if we were watching the patient from the *outside*, somewhat the way the husband-physician does in the story. But the author makes us see everything in her story from the *inside*. We see everything from the point of view of the patient—including the limitations and condescending attitude of the doctor-husband. Gilman herself had suffered from severe postpartum depression after the birth of a daughter in 1884. She was treated by a specialist who prescribed a "rest cure"—bed rest and no physical exertion or intellectual stimulation. (This is the Weir Mitchell mentioned by the patient's husband in the story.) The treatment, Gilman said later, drove her "so near the borderline of mental ruin" that she "could see over."

The Yellow Wallpaper   1892

It is very seldom that mere ordinary people like John and myself secure ancestral halls for the summer.

A colonial mansion, a hereditary estate, I would say a haunted house, and reach the height of romantic felicity—but that would be asking too much of fate!

Still I will proudly declare that there is something queer about it.

Else, why should it be let so cheaply? And why have stood so long untenanted?

John laughs at me, of course, but one expects that in marriage.   5

John is practical in the extreme. He has no patience with faith, an intense horror of superstition, and he scoffs openly at any talk of things not to be felt and seen and put down in figures.

John is a physician, and *perhaps*—(I would not say it to a living soul, of course, but this is dead paper and a great relief to my mind—) *perhaps* that is one reason I do not get well faster.

You see he does not believe I am sick!

And what can one do?

If a physician of high standing, and one's own husband, assures friends and rela-   10
tives that there is really nothing the matter with one but temporary nervous depression—a slight hysterical tendency—what is one to do?

My brother is also a physician, and also of high standing, and he says the same
thing.

So I take phosphates or phosphites—whichever it is, and tonics, and journeys, and
air, and exercise, and am absolutely forbidden to "work" until I am well again.

Personally, I disagree with their ideas.

Personally, I believe that congenial work, with excitement and change, would do
me good.

But what is one to do?   15

I did write for a while in spite of them; but it *does* exhaust me a good deal—having
to be so sly about it, or else meet with heavy opposition.

I sometimes fancy that in my condition if I had less opposition and more society
and stimulus—but John says the very worst thing I can do is to think about my condition, and I confess it always makes me feel bad.

So I will let it alone and talk about the house.

The most beautiful place! It is quite alone, standing well back from the road, quite
three miles from the village. It makes me think of English places that you read about,
for there are hedges and walls and gates that lock, and lots of separate little houses for
the gardeners and people.

There is a *delicious* garden! I never saw such a garden—large and shady, full of   20
box-bordered paths, and lined with long grape-covered arbors with seats under them.

There were greenhouses, too, but they are all broken now.

There was some legal trouble, I believe, something about the heirs and coheirs;
anyhow, the place has been empty for years.

That spoils my ghostliness, I am afraid, but I don't care—there is something
strange about the house—I can feel it.

I even said so to John one moonlight evening, but he said what I felt was a
draught, and shut the window.

I get unreasonably angry with John sometimes. I'm sure I never used to be so sen-   25
sitive. I think it is due to this nervous condition.

But John says if I feel so, I shall neglect proper self-control; so I take pains to control myself—before him, at least, and that makes me very tired.

I don't like our room a bit. I wanted one downstairs that opened on the piazza
and had roses all over the window, and such pretty old-fashioned chintz hangings! but
John would not hear of it.

He said there was only one window and not room for two beds, and no near room
for him if he took another.

He is very careful and loving, and hardly lets me stir without special direction.

I have a schedule prescription for each hour in the day; he takes all care from me,   30
and so I feel basely ungrateful not to value it more.

He said we came here solely on my account, that I was to have perfect rest and all
the air I could get. "Your exercise depends on your strength, my dear," said he, "and
your food somewhat on your appetite; but air you can absorb all the time." So we took
the nursery at the top of the house.

It is a big, airy room, the whole floor nearly, with windows that look all ways, and
air and sunshine galore. It was nursery first and then playroom and gymnasium, I
should judge; for the windows are barred for little children, and there are rings and
things in the walls.

The paint and paper look as if a boys' school had used it. It is stripped off—the paper—in great patches all around the head of my bed, about as far as I can reach, and in a great place on the other side of the room low down. I never saw a worse paper in my life.

One of those sprawling flamboyant patterns committing every artistic sin.

It is dull enough to confuse the eye in following, pronounced enough to constant-ly irritate and provoke study, and when you follow the lame uncertain curves for a little distance they suddenly commit suicide—plunge off at outrageous angles, destroy them-selves in unheard of contradictions.

The color is repellent, almost revolting; a smouldering unclean yellow, strangely faded by the slow-turning sunlight.

It is a dull yet lurid orange in some places, a sickly sulphur tint in others.

No wonder the children hated it! I should hate it myself if I had to live in this room long.

There comes John, and I must put this away,—he hates to have me write a word.

I

We have been here two weeks, and I haven't felt like writing before, since that first day.

I am sitting by the window now, up in this atrocious nursery, and there is nothing to hinder my writing as much as I please, save lack of strength.

John is away all day, and even some nights when his cases are serious.

I am glad my case is not serious!

But these nervous troubles are dreadfully depressing.

John does not know how much I really suffer. He knows there is no *reason* to suf-fer, and that satisfies him.

Of course it is only nervousness. It does weigh on me so not to do my duty in any way!

I meant to be such a help to John, such a real rest and comfort, and here I am a comparative burden already!

Nobody would believe what an effort it is to do what little I am able,—to dress and entertain, and order things.

It is fortunate Mary is so good with the baby. Such a dear baby!

And yet I *cannot* be with him, it makes me so nervous.

I suppose John never was nervous in his life. He laughs at me so about this wall-paper!

At first he meant to repaper the room, but afterwards he said that I was letting it get the better of me, and that nothing was worse for a nervous patient than to give way to such fancies.

He said that after the wallpaper was changed it would be the heavy bedstead, and then the barred windows, and then that gate at the head of the stairs, and so on.

"You know the place is doing you good," he said, "and really, dear, I don't care to renovate the house just for a three months' rental."

"Then do let us go downstairs," I said, "there are such pretty rooms there."

Then he took me in his arms and called me a blessed little goose, and said he would go down cellar, if I wished, and have it whitewashed into the bargain.

But he is right enough about the beds and windows and things.

It is as airy and comfortable room as any one need wish, and, of course, I would not be so silly as to make him uncomfortable just for a whim.

I'm really getting quite fond of the big room, all but that horrid paper.

Out of one window I can see the garden, those mysterious deep-shaded arbors, the riotous old-fashioned flowers, and bushes and gnarly trees.

Out of another I get a lovely view of the bay and a little private wharf belonging to the estate. There is a beautiful shaded lane that runs down there from the house. I always fancy I see people walking in these numerous paths and arbors, but John has cautioned me not to give way to fancy in the least. He says that with my imaginative power and habit of story-making, a nervous weakness like mine is sure to lead to all manner of excited fancies, and that I ought to use my will and good sense to check the tendency. So I try.

I think sometimes that if I were only well enough to write a little it would relieve the press of ideas and rest me.

But I find I get pretty tired when I try.

It is so discouraging not to have any advice and companionship about my work. When I get really well, John says we will ask Cousin Henry and Julia down for a long visit; but he says he would as soon put fireworks in my pillow-case as to let me have those stimulating people about now.

I wish I could get well faster.   65

But I must not think about that. This paper looks to me as if it *knew* what a vicious influence it had!

There is a recurrent spot where the pattern lolls like a broken neck and two bulbous eyes stare at you upside down.

I get positively angry with the impertinence of it and the everlastingness. Up and down and sideways they crawl, and those absurd, unblinking eyes are everywhere. There is one place where two breadths didn't match, and the eyes go all up and down the line, one a little higher than the other.

I never saw so much expression in an inanimate thing before, and we all know how much expression they have! I used to lie awake as a child and get more entertainment and terror out of blank walls and plain furniture than most children could find in a toy-store.

I remember what a kindly wink the knobs of our big, old bureau used to have, and   70
there was one chair that always seemed like a strong friend.

I used to feel that if any of the other things looked too fierce I could always hop into that chair and be safe.

The furniture in this room is no worse than inharmonious, however, for we had to bring it all from downstairs. I suppose when this was used as a playroom they had to take the nursery things out, and no wonder! I never saw such ravages as the children have made here.

The wallpaper, as I said before, is torn off in spots, and it sticketh closer than a brother—they must have had perseverance as well as hatred.

Then the floor is scratched and gouged and splintered, the plaster itself is dug out here and there, and this great heavy bed which is all we found in the room, looks as if it had been through the wars.

But I don't mind it a bit—only the paper.   75

There comes John's sister. Such a dear girl as she is, and so careful of me! I must not let her find me writing.

She is a perfect and enthusiastic housekeeper, and hopes for no better profession. I verily believe she thinks it is the writing which made me sick!

But I can write when she is out, and see her a long way off from these windows.

There is one that commands the road, a lovely shaded winding road, and one that just looks off over the country. A lovely country, too, full of great elms and velvet meadows.

This wallpaper has a kind of subpattern in a different shade, a particularly irritating   80
one, for you can only see it in certain lights, and not clearly then.

But in the places where it isn't faded and where the sun is just so—I can see a strange, provoking, formless sort of figure, that seems to skulk about behind that silly and conspicuous front design.

There's sister on the stairs!

II

Well, the Fourth of July is over! The people are all gone and I am tired out. John thought it might do me good to see a little company, so we just had mother and Nellie and the children down for a week.

Of course I didn't do a thing. Jennie sees to everything now.

But it tired me all the same.   85

John says if I don't pick up faster he shall send me to Weir Mitchell in the fall.

But I don't want to go there at all. I had a friend who was in his hands once, and she says he is just like John and my brother, only more so!

Besides, it is such an undertaking to go so far.

I don't feel as if it was worth while to turn my hand over for anything, and I'm getting dreadfully fretful and querulous.

I cry at nothing, and cry most of the time.   90

Of course I don't when John is here, or anybody else, but when I am alone.

And I am alone a good deal just now. John is kept in town very often by serious cases, and Jennie is good and lets me alone when I want her to.

So I walk a little in the garden or down that lovely lane, sit on the porch under the roses, and lie down up here a good deal.

I'm getting really fond of the room in spite of the wallpaper. Perhaps *because* of the wallpaper.

It dwells in my mind so!   95

I lie here on this great immovable bed—it is nailed down, I believe—and follow that pattern about by the hour. It is as good as gymnastics, I assure you. I start, we'll say, at the bottom, down in the corner over there where it has not been touched, and I determine for the thousandth time that I *will* follow that pointless pattern to some sort of a conclusion.

I know a little of the principle of design, and I know this thing was not arranged on any laws of radiation, or alternation, or repetition, or symmetry, or anything else that I ever heard of.

It is repeated, of course, by the breadths, but not otherwise.

Looked at in one way each breadth stands alone, the bloated curves and flourishes—a kind of "debased Romanesque" with *delirium tremens* go waddling up and down in isolated columns of fatuity.

But, on the other hand, they connect diagonally, and the sprawling outlines run   100
off in great slanting waves of optic horror, like a lot of wallowing seaweeds in full chase.

The whole thing goes horizontally, too, at least it seems so, and I exhaust myself in trying to distinguish the order of its going in that direction.

They have used a horizontal breadth for a frieze, and that adds wonderfully to the confusion.

There is one end of the room where it is almost intact, and there, when the crosslights fade and the low sun shines directly upon it, I can almost fancy radiation after all,—the interminable grotesques seem to form around a common center and rush off in headlong plunges of equal distraction.

It makes me tired to follow it. I will take a nap I guess.

III

I don't know why I should write this.   105

I don't want to.

I don't feel able.

And I know John would think it absurd. But I *must* say what I feel and think in some way—it is such a relief!

But the effort is getting to be greater than the relief.

Half the time now I am awfully lazy, and lie down ever so much.   110

John says I mustn't lose my strength, and has me take cod liver oil and lots of tonics and things, to say nothing of ale and wine and rare meat.

Dear John! He loves me very dearly, and hates to have me sick. I tried to have a real earnest reasonable talk with him the other day, and tell him how I wish he would let me go and make a visit to Cousin Henry and Julia.

But he said I wasn't able to go, nor able to stand it after I got there; and I did not make out a very good case for myself, for I was crying before I had finished.

It is getting to be a great effort for me to think straight. Just this nervous weakness I suppose.

And dear John gathered me up in his arms, and just carried me upstairs and laid   115
me on the bed, and sat by me and read to me till it tired my head.

He said I was his darling and his comfort and all he had, and that I must take care of myself for his sake, and keep well.

He says no one but myself can help me out of it, that I must use my will and self-control and not let any silly fancies run away with me.

There's one comfort, the baby is well and happy, and does not have to occupy this nursery with the horrid wallpaper.

If we had not used it, that blessed child would have! What a fortunate escape! Why, I wouldn't have a child of mine, an impressionable little thing, live in such a room for worlds.

I never thought of it before, but it is lucky that John kept me here after all, I can   120
stand it so much easier than a baby, you see.

Of course I never mention it to them any more—I am too wise,—but I keep watch of it all the same.

There are things in that paper that nobody knows but me, or ever will.

Behind that outside pattern the dim shapes get clearer every day.

It is always the same shape, only very numerous.

And it is like a woman stooping down and creeping about behind that pattern. I   125
don't like it a bit. I wonder—I begin to think—I wish John would take me away from here!

IV

It is so hard to talk with John about my case, because he is so wise, and because he loves me so.

But I tried it last night.

It was moonlight. The moon shines in all around just as the sun does.

I hate to see it sometimes, it creeps so slowly, and always comes in by one window or another.

John was asleep and I hated to waken him, so I kept still and watched the moon-   130
light on that undulating wallpaper till I felt creepy.

The faint figure behind seemed to shake the pattern, just as if she wanted to get out.

I got up softly and went to feel and see if the paper *did* move, and when I came back John was awake.

"What is it, little girl?" he said. "Don't go walking about like that—you'll get cold."

I thought it was a good time to talk, so I told him that I really was not gaining here, and that I wished he would take me away.

"Why, darling!" said he, "our lease will be up in three weeks, and I can't see how to leave before.   135

"The repairs are not done at home, and I cannot possibly leave town just now. Of course if you were in any danger, I could and would, but you really are better, dear, whether you can see it or not. I am a doctor, dear, and I know. You are gaining flesh and color, your appetite is better, I feel really much easier about you."

"I don't weigh a bit more," said I, "nor as much; and my appetite may be better in the evening when you are here, but it is worse in the morning when you are away!"

"Bless her little heart!" said he with a big hug, "she shall be as sick as she pleases! But now let's improve the shining hours by going to sleep, and talk about it in the morning!"

"And you won't go away?" I asked gloomily.

"Why, how can I, dear? It is only three weeks more and then we will take a nice lit-   140
tle trip of a few days while Jennie is getting the house ready. Really dear you are better!"

"Better in body perhaps—" I began, and stopped short, for he sat up straight and looked at me with such a stern, reproachful look that I could not say another word.

"My darling," said he, "I beg of you, for my sake and for our child's sake, as well as for your own, that you will never for one instant let that idea enter your mind! There is nothing so dangerous, so fascinating, to a temperament like yours. It is a false and foolish fancy. Can you not trust me as a physician when I tell you so?"

So of course I said no more on that score, and we went to sleep before long. He thought I was asleep first, but I wasn't, and lay there for hours trying to decide whether that front pattern and the back pattern really did move together or separately.

V

On a pattern like this, by daylight, there is a lack of sequence, a defiance of law, that is a constant irritant to a normal mind.

The color is hideous enough, and unreliable enough, and infuriating enough, but   145
the pattern is torturing.

You think you have mastered it, but just as you get well underway in following, it turns a back-somersault and there you are. It slaps you in the face, knocks you down, and tramples upon you. It is like a bad dream.

The outside pattern is a florid arabesque, reminding one of a fungus. If you can imagine a toadstool in joints, an interminable string of toadstools, budding and sprouting in endless convolutions—why, that is something like it.

That is, sometimes!

There is one marked peculiarity about this paper, a thing nobody seems to notice but myself, and that is that it changes as the light changes.

When the sun shoots in through the east window—I always watch for that first   150
long, straight ray—it changes so quickly that I never can quite believe it.

That is why I watch it always.

By moonlight—the moon shines in all night when there is a moon—I wouldn't know it was the same paper.

At night in any kind of light, in twilight, candlelight, lamplight, and worst of all by moonlight, it becomes bars! The outside pattern I mean, and the woman behind it is as plain as can be.

I didn't realize for a long time what the thing was that showed behind, that dim subpattern, but now I am quite sure it is a woman.

By daylight she is subdued, quiet. I fancy it is the pattern that keeps her so still. It is so puzzling. It keeps me quiet by the hour. 155

I lie down ever so much now. John says it is good for me, and to sleep all I can.

Indeed he started the habit by making me lie down for an hour after each meal.

It is a very bad habit I am convinced, for you see I don't sleep.

And that cultivates deceit, for I don't tell them I'm awake—O no!

The fact is I am getting a little afraid of John. 160

He seems very queer sometimes, and even Jennie has an inexplicable look.

It strikes me occasionally, just as a scientific hypothesis,—that perhaps it is the paper!

I have watched John when he did not know I was looking, and come into the room suddenly on the most innocent excuses, and I've caught him several times *looking at the paper!* And Jennie too. I caught Jennie with her hand on it once.

She didn't know I was in the room, and when I asked her in a quiet, a very quiet voice, with the most restrained manner possible, what she was doing with the paper— she turned around as if she had been caught stealing, and looked quite angry—asked me why I should frighten her so!

Then she said that the paper stained everything it touched, that she had found yel- 165 low smooches on all my clothes and John's, and she wished we would be more careful!

Did not that sound innocent? But I know she was studying that pattern, and I am determined that nobody shall find it out but myself!

VI

Life is very much more exciting now than it used to be. You see I have something more to expect, to look forward to, to watch. I really do eat better, and am more quiet than I was.

John is so pleased to see me improve! He laughed a little the other day, and said I seemed to be flourishing in spite of my wallpaper.

I turned it off with a laugh. I had no intention of telling him it was *because* of the wallpaper—he would make fun of me. He might even want to take me away.

I don't want to leave now until I have found it out. There is a week more, and I 170 think that will be enough.

VII

I'm feeling ever so much better! I don't sleep much at night, for it is so interesting to watch developments; but I sleep a good deal in the daytime.

In the daytime it is tiresome and perplexing.

There are always new shoots on the fungus, and new shades of yellow all over it. I cannot keep count of them, though I have tried conscientiously.

It is the strangest yellow, that wallpaper! It makes me think of all the yellow things I ever saw—not beautiful ones like buttercups, but old foul, bad yellow things.

But there is something else about that paper—the smell! I noticed it the moment 175 we came into the room, but with so much air and sun it was not bad. Now we have had a week of fog and rain, and whether the windows are open or not, the smell is here.

It creeps all over the house.

I find it hovering in the dining-room, skulking in the parlor, hiding in the hall, lying in wait for me on the stairs.

It gets into my hair.

Even when I go to ride, if I turn my head suddenly and surprise it—there is that smell!

Such a peculiar odor, too! I have spent hours in trying to analyze it, to find what it smelled like.   180

It is not bad—at first, and very gentle, but quite the subtlest, most enduring odor I ever met.

In this damp weather it is awful, I wake up in the night and find it hanging over me.

It used to disturb me at first. I thought seriously of burning the house—to reach the smell.

But now I am used to it. The only thing I can think of that it is like is the *color* of the paper! A yellow smell.

There is a very funny mark on this wall, low down, near the mopboard. A streak   185
that runs round the room. It goes behind every piece of furniture, except the bed, a long, straight, even *smooch*, as if it had been rubbed over and over.

I wonder how it was done and who did it, and what they did it for. Round and round and round—round and round and round!—it makes me *dizzy!*

VIII

I really have discovered something at last.

Through watching so much at night, when it changes so, I have finally found out.

The front pattern *does* move—and no wonder! The woman behind shakes it!

Sometimes I think there are a great many women behind, and sometimes only one,   190
and she crawls around fast, and her crawling shakes it all over.

Then in the very bright spots she keeps still, and in the very shady spots she just takes hold of the bars and shakes them hard.

And she is all the time trying to climb through. But nobody could climb through that pattern—it strangles so; I think that is why it has so many heads.

They get through, and then the pattern strangles them off and turns them upside down, and makes their eyes white!

If those heads were covered or taken off it would not be half so bad.

IX

I think that woman gets out in the daytime!   195

And I'll tell you why—privately—I've seen her!

I can see her out of every one of my windows!

It is the same woman, I know, for she is always creeping, and most women do not creep by daylight.

I see her in that long shaded lane, creeping up and down. I see her in those dark grape arbors, creeping all around the garden.

I see her on that long road under the trees, creeping along, and when a carriage   200
comes she hides under the blackberry vines.

I don't blame her a bit. It must be very humiliating to be caught creeping by daylight!

I always lock the door when I creep by daylight. I can't do it at night, for I know John would suspect something at once.

And John is so queer now, that I don't want to irritate him. I wish he would take another room! Besides, I don't want anybody to get that woman out at night but myself.

I often wonder if I could see her out of all the windows at once.

But, turn as fast as I can, I can only see out of one at one time.

And though I always see her, she *may* be able to creep faster than I can turn!

I have watched her sometimes away off in the open country, creeping as fast as a cloud shadow in a high wind.

X

If only that top pattern could be gotten off from the under one! I mean to try it, little by little.

I have found out another funny thing, but I shan't tell it this time! It does not do to trust people too much.

There are only two more days to get this paper off, and I believe John is beginning to notice. I don't like the look in his eyes. 210

And I heard him ask Jennie a lot of professional questions about me. She had a very good report to give.

She said I slept a good deal in the daytime.

John knows I don't sleep very well at night, for all I'm so quiet!

He asked me all sorts of questions, too, and pretended to be very loving and kind.

As if I couldn't see through him! 215

Still, I don't wonder he acts so, sleeping under this paper for three months.

It only interests me, but I feel sure John and Jennie are secretly affected by it.

XI

Hurrah! This is the last day, but it is enough. John to stay in town over night, and won't be out until this evening.

Jennie wanted to sleep with me—the sly thing! but I told her I should undoubtedly rest better for a night all alone.

That was clever, for really I wasn't alone a bit! As soon as it was moonlight and that poor thing began to crawl and shake the pattern, I got up and ran to help her. 220

I pulled and she shook, I shook and she pulled, and before morning we had peeled off yards of that paper.

A strip about as high as my head and half around the room.

And then when the sun came and that awful pattern began to laugh at me, I declared I would finish it today!

We go away tomorrow, and they are moving all my furniture down again to leave things as they were before.

Jennie looked at the wall in amazement, but I told her merrily that I did it out of pure spite at the vicious thing. 225

She laughed and said she wouldn't mind doing it herself, but I must not get tired.

How she betrayed herself that time!

But I am here, and no person touches this paper but me,—not *alive!*

She tried to get me out of the room—it was too patent! But I said it was so quiet and empty and clean now that I believed I would lie down again and sleep all I could; and not to wake me even for dinner—I would call when I woke.

So now she is gone, and the servants are gone, and the things are gone, and there is nothing left but that great bedstead nailed down, with the canvas mattress we found on it. 230

We shall sleep downstairs tonight, and take the boat home tomorrow.

I quite enjoy the room, now it is bare again.

How those children did tear about here!

This bedstead is fairly gnawed!

235

But I must get to work.

I have locked the door and thrown the key down into the front path.

I don't want to go out, and I don't want to have anybody come in, till John comes.

I want to astonish him.

I've got a rope up here that even Jennie did not find. If that woman does get out, and tries to get away, I can tie her!

But I forgot I could not reach far without anything to stand on! 240

This bed will *not* move!

I tried to lift and push it until I was lame, and then I got so angry I bit off a little piece at one corner—but it hurt my teeth.

Then I peeled off all the paper I could reach standing on the floor. It sticks horribly and the pattern just enjoys it! All those strangled heads and bulbous eyes and waddling fungus growths just shriek with derision!

I am getting angry enough to do something desperate. To jump out of the window would be admirable exercise, but the bars are too strong even to try.

Besides I wouldn't do it. Of course not. I know well enough that a step like that is 245
improper and might be misconstrued.

I don't like to *look* out of the windows even—there are so many of those creeping women, and they creep so fast.

I wonder if they all come out of that wallpaper as I did?

But I am securely fastened now by my well-hidden rope—you don't get *me* out in the road there!

I suppose I shall have to get back behind the pattern when it comes night, and that is hard!

It is so pleasant to be out in this great room and creep around as I please! 250

I don't want to go outside. I won't, even if Jennie asks me to.

For outside you have to creep on the ground, and everything is green instead of yellow.

But here I can creep smoothly on the floor, and my shoulder just fits in that long smooch around the wall, so I cannot lose my way.

Why there's John at the door!

It is no use, young man, you can't open it! 255

How he does call and pound!

Now he's crying for an axe.

It would be a shame to break down that beautiful door!

"John dear!" said I in the gentlest voice, "the key is down by the front steps, under a plaintain leaf!"

That silenced him for a few moments. 260

Then he said—very quietly indeed, "Open the door, my darling!"

"I can't," said I. "The key is down by the front door under a plaintain leaf!"

And then I said it again, several times, very gently and slowly, and said it so often that he had to go and see, and he got it of course, and came in. He stopped short by the door.

"What is the matter?" he cried. "For God's sake, what are you doing!"

I kept on creeping just the same, but I looked at him over my shoulder. 265

"I've got out at last," said I, "in spite of you and Jennie! And I've pulled off most of the paper, so you can't put me back!"

Now why should that man have fainted? But he did, and right across my path by the wall, so that I had to creep over him every time!

THE RECEPTIVE READER

1. At the beginning, the narrator refers to her husband John and herself as "ordinary people." What makes the setting and the people at the beginning of the story seem ordinary? What kind of ordinary person does the narrator seem to be? When do you notice the first hints of something extraordinary?

2. What and how do you learn about the narrator's illness? What and how do you learn about the treatment proposed by the doctor-husband?

3. What is the husband-physician's attitude toward his wife? What is her attitude toward him? How does it change in the course of the story? (How is your attitude toward him different from hers?)

4. How does the wallpaper become an obsessive preoccupation in this story? How does its appearance slowly change and shift? How does its meaning change or evolve as the *central symbol* in the story? What are some major stages?

5. Who is the woman behind the wallpaper? How does your perception of her change and evolve? What is the significance of the smudge (running the length of the wallpaper) that the woman begins to perceive?

6. What is the symbolic contrast between the garden and the enclosed, confined room? (Why does the woman herself throw the key away?)

7. What, for you, is the symbolic meaning of the way the story ends? (Can the ending be read as a kind of liberation?)

8. Feminist critics have found a special significance in the fact that the narrator has to do her writing secretly, against the wishes of her husband. What symbolic significance do you think they find in his prohibition?

THE PERSONAL RESPONSE

For you, what does the story as a whole say about the author's view of mental illness and her view of the relation between women and male physicians? Is the story still thought-provoking to current readers, or have changes in the modern world made the questions it raises obsolete?

GABRIEL GARCÍA MÁRQUEZ (born 1928)

In García Márquez's world, love is the primordial power that reigns as an obscure, impersonal, and all-powerful presence.

OCTAVIO PAZ

It always amuses me that the biggest praise for my work comes for the imagination, while the truth is that there's not a single line in all my work that does not have a basis in reality. The problem is that Caribbean reality resembles the wildest imagination.

GABRIEL GARCÍA MÁRQUEZ

García Márquez is a Colombian writer who became internationally famous with his novel *One Hundred Years of Solitude* (1967). His work became part of a Latin American renaissance that made the writings of Octavio Paz, Pablo Neruda, Jorge Luis Borges, and Carlos Fuentes known around the world.

García Márquez' stories are often marked by a mixture of grim reality and the surreal that has been called "magic realism." His "A Very Old Man with Enormous Wings" (1968) is about a very old, moth-eaten angel—"a dirty, muttering, helpless old man with bedraggled wings" (John Updike)—who falls out of the sky and confounds the inhabitants of the town. García Márquez is a master at evoking mixed emotions. His tales mix wit and horror; his voice is "able to praise and curse, laugh and cry, fabulate and sing" (Thomas Pynchon).

García Márquez moved from Colombia to Mexico in 1954 and later went to live in Spain. He has written plays and film scripts as well as novels and stories; he was awarded the Nobel Prize in literature in 1982. He became famous when he was almost forty after years of struggle that made him feel "like an extra," thinking that "I did not count anywhere." In an interview, he said that he sees both his books and his work with films as helping "to create a Latin American identity," helping "Latin Americans to become more aware of their own culture." His novel *Love in the Time of Cholera*—about a man who maintains his unanswered, unfulfilled passion for the love of his youth for fifty-one years—appeared in 1987.

(Esteban is Spanish for Stephen. The Sir Walter Raleigh alluded to in the story lived from 1552 to 1618 and was an English explorer and pirate of the Elizabethan Age.)

The Handsomest Drowned Man in the World   1970
A Tale for Children

TRANSLATED BY GREGORY RABASSA

The first children who saw the dark and slinky bulge approaching through the sea let themselves think it was an empty ship. Then they saw it had no flags or masts and they thought it was a whale. But when it washed up on the beach, they removed the clumps of seaweed, the jellyfish tentacles, and the remains of fish and flotsam, and only then did they see that it was a drowned man.

They had been playing with him all afternoon, burying him in the sand and digging him up again, when someone chanced to see them and spread the alarm in the village. The men who carried him to the nearest house noticed that he weighed more than any dead man they had ever known, almost as much as a horse, and they said to each other that maybe he'd been floating too long and the water had got into his bones. When they laid him on the floor they said he'd been taller than all other men because there was barely enough room for him in the house, but they thought that maybe the ability to keep on growing after death was part of the nature of certain drowned men. He had the smell of the sea about him and only his shape gave one to suppose that it was the corpse of a human being, because the skin was covered with a crust of mud and scales.

They did not even have to clean off his face to know that the dead man was a stranger. The village was made up of only twenty-odd wooden houses that had stone courtyards with no flowers and which were spread about on the end of a desertlike cape. There was so little land that mothers always went about with the fear that the wind would carry off their children and the few dead that the years had caused among them had to be thrown off the cliffs. But the sea was calm and bountiful and all the men fit into seven boats. So when they found the drowned man they simply had to look at one another to see that they were all there. That night they did not go out to work at sea. While the men went to find out if anyone was missing in neighboring villages, the women stayed behind to care for the drowned man. They took the mud off with grass swabs, they removed the underwater stones entangled in his hair, and they scraped the crust off with tools used for scaling fish. As they were doing that they noticed that the vegetation on him came from faraway oceans and deep water and that his clothes were in tatters, as if he had sailed through labyrinths of coral. They noticed too that he bore his death with pride, for he did not have the lonely look of other drowned men who came out of the sea or that haggard, needy look of men who drowned in rivers. But only when they finished cleaning him off did they become aware of the kind of man he was and it left them breathless. Not only was he the tallest, strongest, most virile, and best built man they had ever seen, but even though they were looking at him there was no room for him in their imagination.

They could not find a bed in the village large enough to lay him on nor was there a table solid enough to use for his wake. The tallest men's holiday pants would not fit him, nor the fattest ones' Sunday shirts, nor the shoes of the one with the biggest feet. Fascinated by his huge size and his beauty, the women then decided to make him some pants from a large piece of sail and a shirt from some bridal brabant linen so that he could continue through his death with dignity. As they sewed, sitting in a circle and gazing at the corpse between stitches, it seemed to them that the wind had never been so steady nor the sea so restless as on that night and they supposed that the change had something to do with the dead man. They thought that if that magnificent man had lived in the village, his house would have had the widest doors, the highest ceiling, and the strongest floor, his bedstead would have been made from a midship frame held together by iron bolts, and his wife would have been the happiest woman. They thought that he would have had so much authority that he could have drawn fish out of the sea simply by calling their names and that he would have put so much work into his land that springs would have burst forth from among the rocks so that he would have been able to plant flowers on the cliffs. They secretly compared him to their own men, thinking that for all their lives theirs were incapable of doing what he could do in one night, and they ended up dismissing them deep in their hearts as the weakest, meanest, and most useless creatures on earth. They were wandering through that maze of fantasy when the oldest woman, who as the oldest had looked upon the drowned man with more compassion than passion, sighed:

"He has the face of someone called Esteban."   5

It was true. Most of them had only to take another look at him to see that he could not have any other name. The more stubborn among them, who were the youngest, still lived for a few hours with the illusion that when they put his clothes on and he lay among the flowers in patent leather shoes his name might be Lautaro. But it was a vain illusion. There had not been enough canvas, the poorly cut and worse sewn pants were too tight, and the hidden strength of his heart popped the buttons on his shirt. After midnight the whistling of the wind died down and the sea fell into its Wednesday drowsiness. The silence put an end to any last doubts: he was Esteban. The women who had dressed him, who had combed his hair, had cut his nails and shaved him were unable to hold back a shudder of pity when they had to resign themselves to his being dragged along the ground. It was then that they understood how unhappy he must have been with that huge body since it bothered him even after death. They could see him in life, condemned to going through doors sideways, cracking his head on cross-beams, remaining on his feet during visits, not knowing what to do with his soft, pink, sea lion hands while the lady of the house looked for her most resistant chair and begged him, frightened to death, sit here, Esteban, please, and he, leaning against the wall, smiling, don't bother, ma'am, I'm fine where I am, his heels raw and his back roasted from having done the same thing so many times whenever he paid a visit, don't bother, ma'am, I'm fine where I am, just to avoid the embarrassment of breaking up the chair, and never knowing perhaps that the ones who said don't go, Esteban, at least wait till the coffee's ready, were the ones who later on would whisper the big boob finally left, how nice, the handsome fool has gone. That was what the women were thinking beside the body a little before dawn. Later, when they covered his face with a handkerchief so that the light would not bother him, he looked so forever dead, so defenseless, so much like their men that the first furrows of tears opened in their hearts. It was one of the younger ones who began the weeping. The others, coming to, went from sighs to wails, and the more they sobbed the more they felt like weeping, because the drowned man was becoming all the more Esteban for them, and so they wept so much, for he was the most destitute, most peaceful, and most obliging man on earth, poor Esteban. So when the men returned with the news that the drowned man was not from the neighboring villages either, the women felt an opening of jubilation in the midst of their tears.

"Praise the Lord," they sighed, "he's ours!"

The men thought the fuss was only womanish frivolity. Fatigued because of the difficult nighttime inquiries, all they wanted was to get rid of the bother of the newcomer once and for all before the sun grew strong on that arid, windless day. They improvised a litter with the remains of foremasts and gaffs, tying it together with rigging so that it would bear the weight of the body until they reached the cliffs. They wanted to tie the anchor from a cargo ship to him so that he would sink easily into the deepest waves, where fish are blind and divers die of nostalgia, and bad currents would not bring him back to shore, as had happened with other bodies. But the more they hurried, the more the women thought of ways to waste time. They walked about like startled hens, pecking with the sea charms on their breasts, some interfering on one side to put a scapular of the good wind on the drowned man, some on the other side to put a wrist compass on him, and after a great deal of *get away from there, woman, stay out of the way, look, you almost made me fall on top of the dead man*, the men began to feel mistrust in their livers and started grumbling about why so many main-altar decorations for a stranger, because no matter how many nails and holy-water jars he had on him, the sharks would chew him all the same, but the women kept piling on their junk relics, running back and forth, stumbling, while they released in sighs what they did not in tears, so that the men finally exploded with *since when has there ever been such a fuss over a drifting corpse, a drowned nobody, a piece of cold Wednesday meat*. One of the women, mortified by so much lack of care, then removed the handkerchief from the dead man's face and the men were left breathless too.

He was Esteban. It was not necessary to repeat it for them to recognize him. If they had been told Sir Walter Raleigh, even they might have been impressed with his gringo accent, the macaw on his shoulder, his cannibal-killing blunderbuss, but there could be only one Esteban in the world and there he was, stretched out like a sperm whale, shoeless, wearing the pants of an undersized child, and with those stony nails that had to be cut with a knife. They only had to take the handkerchief off his face to see that he was ashamed, that it was not his fault that he was so big or so heavy or so handsome, and if he had known that this was going to happen, he would have looked for a more discreet place to drown in, seriously, I even would have tied the anchor off a galleon around my neck and staggered off a cliff like someone who doesn't like things in order not to be upsetting people now with this Wednesday dead body, as you people say, in order not to be bothering anyone with this filthy piece of cold meat that doesn't have anything to do with me. There was so much truth in his manner that even the most mistrustful men, the ones who felt the bitterness of endless nights at sea fearing that their women would tire of dreaming about them and begin to dream of drowned men, even they and others who were harder still shuddered in the marrow of their bones at Esteban's sincerity.

That was how they came to hold the most splendid funeral they could conceive of   10
for an abandoned drowned man. Some women who had gone to get flowers in the neighboring villages returned with other women who could not believe what they had been told, and those women went back for more flowers when they saw the dead man, and they brought more and more until there were so many flowers and so many people that it was hard to walk about. At the final moment it pained them to return him to the waters as an orphan and they chose a father and mother from among the best people, and aunts and uncles and cousins, so that through him all the inhabitants of the village became kinsmen. Some sailors who heard weeping from a distance went off course and people heard of one who had himself tied to the mainmast, remembering ancient fables about sirens. While they fought for the privilege of carrying him on their shoulders along the steep escarpment by the cliffs, men and women became aware for the first time of the desolation of their streets, the dryness of their courtyards, the narrowness of their dreams as they faced the splendor and beauty of their drowned man. They let him go without an anchor so that he could come back if he wished and whenever he wished, and they all held their breath for the fraction of centuries the body took to fall into the abyss. They did not need to look at one another to realize that they were no longer all present, that they would never be. But they also knew that everything would be different from then on, that their houses would have wider doors, higher ceilings, and stronger floors so that Esteban's memory could go everywhere without bumping into beams and so that no one in the future would dare whisper the big boob finally died, too bad, the handsome fool has finally died, because they were going to paint their house fronts gay colors to make Esteban's memory eternal and they were going to break their backs digging for springs among the stones and planting flowers on the cliffs so that in future years at dawn the passengers on great liners would awaken, suffocated by the smell of gardens on the high seas, and the captain would have to come down from the bridge in his dress uniform, with his astrolabe, his pole star, and his row of war medals and, pointing to the promontory of roses on the horizon, he would say in fourteen languages, look there, where the wind is so peaceful now that it's gone to sleep beneath the beds, over there, where the sun's so bright that the sunflowers don't know which way to turn, yes, that's Esteban's village.

THE RECEPTIVE READER

1. What are your reactions as the story develops in the opening paragraphs? What are striking or puzzling details that linger in the reader's mind?

2. Is it a coincidence that the corpse washed up on the beach is discovered by children? (What is it about children that makes them the right—or the wrong—audience for this tale?)

3. A reviewer said of Márquez' stories that the "arid, unyielding rock" on which the tales are built is a reality of "poverty, hopelessness, exploitation, despotic and demonic rulers" from which the tales "are an escape" (Charles Champlin). What harsh realities provide the "rock" on which this story is built?

4. The same reviewer said that the wellsprings of García's stories "are in the legends, folk tales, superstition, and indeed in the prevalence of miracles in the orthodox

faith of Latin America." What miracle happens in this story? Does the reader have to believe in miracles to respond to the story?

5. What does the corpse of the drowned man symbolize? Do other supporting *symbols* play a role in this story?

6. What is the significance of the way the story ends?

7. What is paradoxical about the role death plays in this story?

THE PERSONAL RESPONSE

The following is the conclusion of a student paper titled "The Most Vibrant Corpse in the World." How do you react to this reader's search for a real-life application of the symbolism in the story? What real-life parallel or application would *you* suggest? How would you explain it or defend it?

All that is beautiful, enriching, animating, and ultimately effective in life is symbolized—with no lack of strangeness or irony—by a corpse in "The Handsomest Drowned Man in the World." Márquez' attractive cadaver is dead, yet he is far from lifeless. This corpse named Esteban is so full of life, he transmits it to anyone who looks upon him. After finishing the story, Márquez' slightly startled reader may wonder, what in real life is inanimate and yet so stimulating? Márquez may be suggesting that the answer is his own medium, literature. A story is alive and vibrant when it is being written down, fresh from the imagination of the writer, but it is only a dead thing when lying between the covers of a book; it is only flat, black print on a page. When it finds its way into the hands of an inhabitant of the village of Earth, however, and is gazed upon and absorbed by this inhabitant, it lives again, in a completely new way. No reader is exactly the same after such an encounter. She too may be inspired to paint her "house front gay colors"; she too may be inspired to break her back "digging for springs among the stones and planting flowers on the cliffs."

CROSS-REFERENCES—For Discussion or Writing

Examine the role of the imagination in the stories by Steinbeck, Gilman, and Márquez. How does it mirror or reflect reality? How does it change or transform it?

URSULA K. LE GUIN (born 1929)

Ursula K. Le Guin once described herself as an "aging, angry woman laying mightily about me with my handbag, fighting hoodlums off." She was born in Berkeley and educated at Radcliffe and Columbia. She has written eloquently in defense of the environment, passenger trains, abortion rights, and the cultural traditions of native Americans. She is widely admired as an author of travel literature, essays on feminist and other social topics, and science fiction. Her essays about the real America—away from the trendmongers and media events of the big cities—bear witness to her love of the land, her ear for the way people talk, her quick sympathetic eye for their weaknesses and strengths. Her science fiction does not focus on space-age gadgets and monstrous aliens but instead raises questions about human nature and human destiny. The novels of her *Earthsea Trilogy* (1968–1972) and her later novels made her a favorite of thoughtful readers.

The basic question underlying much science fiction is "What if?" The writer assumes something far removed from ordinary reality—talking apes have evolved and taken over the planet, or colonists from earth discover on Mars haunting memories of a lost civilization. The author then rewrites our familiar reality in accordance with this premise. Much early science fiction sketched out a future utopia in which age-old human dreams—of unlimited power, of perpetual happiness—were coming true. But gradually the vision of an ideal future darkened and many wrote the opposite—*dystopias,* or future worlds that made our nightmares come true. Where on the spectrum ranging from utopia to dystopia would you place the following story? (The William James alluded to in the subtitle of the story lived from 1842 to 1910 and was a pioneering American psychologist who wrote a famous book on the range of religious experience.)

The Ones Who Walk Away from Omelas   1973

Variations on a Theme by William James

With a clamor of bells that set the swallows soaring, the Festival of Summer came to the city Omelas, bright-towered by the sea. The rigging of the boats in harbor sparkled with flags. In the streets between houses with red roofs and painted walls, between old moss-grown gardens and under avenues of trees, past great parks and public buildings, processions moved. Some were decorous: old people in long stiff robes of mauve and grey, grave master workmen, quiet, merry women carrying their babies and chatting as they walked. In other streets the music beat faster, a shimmering of gong and tambourine, and the people went dancing, the procession was a dance. Children dodged in and out, their high calls rising like the swallows' crossing flights over the music and the singing. All the processions wound toward the north side of the city, where on the great water-meadow called the Green Fields boys and girls, naked in the bright air, with mud-stained feet and ankles and long, lithe arms, exercised their restive horses before the race. The horses wore no gear at all but a halter without bit. Their manes were braided with streamers of silver, gold, and green. They flared their nostrils and pranced and boasted to one another; they were vastly excited, the horse being the only animal who has adopted our ceremonies as his own. Far off to the north and west the mountains stood up half encircling Omelas on her bay. The air of morning was so clear that the snow still crowning the Eighteen Peaks burned with white-gold fire across the miles of sunlit air, under the dark blue of the sky. There was just enough wind to make the banners that marked the racecourse snap and flutter now and then. In the silence of the broad green meadows one could hear the music winding through the city streets, farther and nearer and ever approaching, a cheerful faint sweetness of the air that from time to time trembled and gathered together and broke out into the great joyous clanging of the bells.

Joyous! How is one to tell about joy? How describe the citizens of Omelas?

They were not simple folk, you see, though they were happy. But we do not say the words of cheer much any more. All smiles have become archaic. Given a description such as this one tends to make certain assumptions. Given a description such as this one tends to look next for the King, mounted on a splendid stallion and surrounded by his noble knights, or perhaps in a golden litter borne by great-muscled slaves. But there was no king. They did not use swords, or keep slaves. They were not barbarians. I do not know the rules and laws of their society, but I suspect that they were singularly few. As they did without monarchy and slavery, so they also got on without the stock exchange, the advertisement, the secret police, and the bomb. Yet I repeat that these were not simple folk, not dulcet shepherds, noble savages, bland utopians. They were not less complex than us. The trouble is that we have a bad habit, encouraged by pedants and sophisticates, of considering happiness as something rather stupid. Only pain is intellectual, only evil interesting. This is the treason of the artist: a refusal to admit the banality of evil and the terrible boredom of pain. If you can't lick 'em, join 'em. If it hurts, repeat it. But to praise despair is to condemn delight, to embrace violence is to lose hold of everything else. We have almost lost hold, we can no longer describe a happy man, nor make any celebration of joy. How can I tell you about the people of Omelas? They were not naïve and happy children—though their children were, in fact, happy. They were mature, intelligent, passionate adults whose lives were not wretched. O miracle! but I wish I could describe it better. I wish I could convince you. Omelas sounds in my words like a city in a fairy tale, long ago and far away, once upon a time. Perhaps it would be best if you imagined it as your own fancy bids, assuming it will rise to the occasion, for certainly I cannot suit you all. For instance, how about technology? I think that there would be no cars or helicopters in and above the streets; this follows from the fact that the people of Omelas are happy people. Happiness is based on a just discrimination of what is necessary, what is neither necessary nor destructive, and what is destructive. In the middle category, however—that of the unnecessary but undestructive, that of comfort, luxury, exuberance, etc.—they could perfectly well have central heating, subway trains, washing machines, and all kinds of marvelous devices not yet invented here, floating light-sources, fuelless power, a cure for the common cold. Or they could have none of that: it doesn't matter. As you like it. I incline to think that people from towns up and down the coast have been coming in to Omelas during the last days before the Festival on very fast little trains and double-decked trams, and that the train station of Omelas is actually the handsomest building in town, though plainer than the magnificent Farmers' Market. But even granted trains, I fear that Omelas so far strikes some of you as goody-goody. Smiles, bells, parades, horses, bleh. If so, please add an orgy. If an orgy would help, don't hesitate. Let us not, however, have temples from which issue beautiful nude priests and priestesses already half in ecstasy and ready to copulate with any man or woman, lover or stranger, who desires union with the deep godhead of the blood, although that was my first idea. But really it would be better not to have any temples in Omelas—at least, not manned temples. Religion yes, clergy no. Surely the beautiful nudes can just wander about, offering themselves like divine soufflés to the hunger of the needy and the rapture of the flesh. Let them join the processions. Let tambourines be struck above the copulations, and the glory of desire be proclaimed upon the gongs, and (a not unimportant point) let the offspring of these delightful rituals be beloved and looked after by all. One thing I know there is none of in Omelas is guilt. But what else should there be? I thought at first there were no drugs, but that is puritanical. For those who like it, the faint insistent sweetness of *drooz* may perfume the ways of the city, *drooz* which first brings a great lightness and brilliance to the mind and limbs, and then after some hours a dreamy languor, and wonderful visions at last of the very arcana and inmost secrets of the Universe, as well as exciting the pleasure of sex beyond all belief; and it is not habit-forming. For more modest tastes I think there ought to be beer. What else, what else belongs in the joyous city? The sense of victory, surely, the celebration of courage. But as we did without clergy, let us do without soldiers. The joy built upon successful slaughter is not the right kind of joy; it will not do; it is fearful and it is trivial. A boundless and generous contentment, a magnanimous triumph felt not against some outer enemy but in communion with the finest and fairest in the souls of all men everywhere and the splendor of the world's summer: this is what swells the hearts of the people of Omelas, and the victory they celebrate is that of life. I really don't think many of them need to take *drooz*.

Most of the procession have reached the Green Fields by now. A marvelous smell of cooking goes forth from the red and blue tents of the provisioners. The faces of small children are amiably sticky; in the benign grey beard of a man a couple of crumbs of rich pastry are entangled. The youths and girls have mounted their horses and are beginning to group around the starting line of the course. An old woman, small, fat, and laughing, is passing out flowers from a basket, and tall young men wear her flowers in their shining hair. A child of nine or ten sits at the edge of the crowd, alone, playing on a wooden flute. People pause to listen, and they smile, but they do not speak to him, for he never ceases playing and never sees them, his dark eyes wholly rapt in the sweet, thin magic of the tune.

He finishes, and slowly lowers his hands holding the wooden flute.   5

As if that little private silence were the signal, all at once a trumpet sounds from the pavilion near the starting line: imperious, melancholy, piercing. The horses rear on their slender legs, and some of them neigh in answer. Sober-faced, the young riders stroke the horses' necks and soothe them, whispering, "Quiet, quiet, there my beauty, my hope. . . ." They begin to form in rank along the starting line. The crowds along the racecourse are like a field of grass and flowers in the wind. The Festival of Summer has begun.

Do you believe? Do you accept the festival, the city, the joy? No? Then let me describe one more thing.

In a basement under one of the beautiful public buildings of Omelas, or perhaps in the cellar of one of its more spacious private homes, there is a room. It has one locked door, and no window. A little light seeps in dustily between cracks in the boards, secondhand from a cobwebbed window somewhere across the cellar. In one corner of the little room a couple of mops, with stiff, clotted, foul-smelling heads, stand near a rusty bucket. The floor is dirt, a little damp to the touch, as cellar dirt usually is. The room is about three paces long and two wide: a mere broom closet or disused tool room. In the room a child is sitting. It could be a boy or a girl. It looks about six, but actually is nearly ten. It is feeble-minded. Perhaps it was born defective, or perhaps it has become imbecile through fear, malnutrition, and neglect. It picks its nose and occasionally fumbles vaguely with its toes or genitals, as it sits hunched in the corner farthest from the bucket and the two mops. It is afraid of the mops. It finds them horrible. It shuts its eyes, but it knows the mops are still standing there; and the door is locked; and nobody will come. The door is always locked; and nobody ever comes, except that sometimes— the child has no understanding of time or interval—sometimes the door rattles terribly and opens, and a person, or several people, are there. One of them may come in and kick the child to make it stand up. The others never come close, but peer in at it with frightened, disgusted eyes. The food bowl and the water jug are hastily filled, the door is locked, the eyes disappear. The people at the door never say anything, but the child, who has not always lived in the tool room, and can remember sunlight and its mother's voice, sometimes speaks. "I will be good," it says. "Please let me out. I will be good!" They never answer. The child used to scream for help at night, and cry a good deal, but now it only makes a kind of whining, "eh-haa, eh-haa," and it speaks less and less often.

It is so thin there are no calves to its legs; its belly protrudes; it lives on a half-bowl of corn meal and grease a day. It is naked. Its buttocks and thighs are a mass of festered sores, as it sits in its own excrement continually.

They all know it is there, all the people of Omelas. Some of them have come to see it, others are content merely to know it is there. They all know that it has to be there. Some of them understand why, and some do not, but they all understand that their happiness, the beauty of their city, the tenderness of their friendships, the health of their children, the wisdom of their scholars, the skill of their makers, even the abundance of their harvest and the kindly weathers of their skies, depend wholly on this child's abominable misery.

This is usually explained to children when they are between eight and twelve, whenever they seem capable of understanding; and most of those who come to see the child are young people, though often enough an adult comes, or comes back, to see the child. No matter how well the matter has been explained to them, these young spectators are always shocked and sickened at the sight. They feel disgust, which they had thought themselves superior to. They feel anger, outrage, impotence, despite all the explanations. They would like to do something for the child. But there is nothing they can do. If the child were brought up into the sunlight out of the vile place, if it were cleaned and fed and comforted, that would be a good thing, indeed; but if it were done, in that day and hour all the prosperity and beauty and delight of Omelas would wither and be destroyed. Those are the terms. To exchange all the goodness and grace of every life in Omelas for that single, small improvement: to throw away the happiness of thousands for the chance of the happiness of one: that would be to let guilt within the walls indeed.

The terms are strict and absolute; there may not even be a kind word spoken to the child.

Often the young people go home in tears, or in a tearless rage, when they have seen the child and faced this terrible paradox. They may brood over it for weeks or years. But as time goes on they begin to realize that even if the child could be released, it would not get much good of its freedom: a little vague pleasure of warmth and food, no doubt, but little more. It is too degraded and imbecile to know any real joy. It has been afraid too long ever to be free of fear. Its habits are too uncouth for it to respond to humane treatment. Indeed, after so long it would probably be wretched without walls about it to protect it, and darkness for its eyes, and its own excrement to sit in. Their tears at the bitter injustice dry when they begin to perceive the terrible justice of reality, and to accept it. Yet it is their tears and anger, the trying of their generosity and the acceptance of their helplessness, which are perhaps the true source of the splendor of their lives. Theirs is no vapid, irresponsible happiness. They know that they, like the child, are not free. They know compassion. It is the existence of the child, and their knowledge of its existence, that makes possible the nobility of their architecture, the poignancy of their music, the profundity of their science. It is because of the child that they are so gentle with children. They know that if the wretched one were not there snivelling in the dark, the other one, the flute-player, could make no joyful music as the young riders line up in their beauty for the race in the sunlight of the first morning of summer.

Now do you believe in them? Are they not more credible? But there is one more thing to tell, and this is quite incredible.

At times one of the adolescent girls or boys who go to see the child does not go home to weep or rage, does not, in fact, go home at all. Sometimes also a man or woman much older falls silent for a day or two, and then leaves home. These people go out into the street, and walk down the street alone. They keep walking, and walk

10

straight out of the city of Omelas, through the beautiful gates. They keep walking across the farmlands of Omelas. Each one goes alone, youth or girl, man or woman. Night falls; the traveler must pass down village streets, between the houses with yellow-lit windows, and on out into the darkness of the fields. Each alone, they go west or north, toward the mountains. They go on. They leave Omelas, they walk ahead into the darkness, and they do not come back. The place they go toward is a place even less imaginable to most of us than the city of happiness. I cannot describe it at all. It is possible that it does not exist. But they seem to know where they are going, the ones who walk away from Omelas.

THE RECEPTIVE READER

1. How does the author create the "joyous" setting of the opening paragraphs? What striking details help create a beckoning world? What words are especially rich in positive *connotations*—overtones and associations that convey pleasurable or pleasing emotions and attitudes?

2. Why do you think the author lets each reader fill in his or her own details to complete the description of Omelas?

3. In her own specifications, what does the author explicitly exclude from her imaginary world and why? (For instance, how much or how little technology is there?) What do you make of her discussion of pros and cons, or of her warding off of possible misunderstandings?

4. What is the relationship between the author's science fiction world and your own? How is the world she creates similar to and different from your own ordinary reality?

5. When do you first suspect that the joyous, happy surface of Omelas might be deceptive?

6. What is the role of the imprisoned child in the world of the people of Omelas? For what in their world or yours is the child a *symbol*? Are there parallels in your world for what the child represents?

7. Do you think the author meant to suggest that the world of Omelas was fatally flawed—or that it was nearly perfect except for one serious flaw?

THE PERSONAL RESPONSE

Do you think you would have been among those who "walked away from Omelas"? Or would you have been one of those who stayed behind? Justify your choice.

THE CREATIVE DIMENSION

Science fiction has a special way of stimulating the imagination. Does it stimulate yours? Write down what your *first impressions* would be if you suddenly found yourself walking the streets of Omelas (or the streets of another imaginary location in a story you have read). Would your impressions be similar to or different from those in the following student-written sample?

Walking in Omelas

I am walking down the crowded streets of Omelas. It would be a lovely day except that the sunlight is too bright, the weather is too warm, and the noise of the crowd is too loud. It is not easy walking down the street; people bump into me, and sometimes I have to disentangle myself from their welcoming embraces. This celebration of which I am a part reminds me of Mardi Gras in New Orleans, which suggests that I do have memories of a time before Omelas. The people of Omelas are all smiling, but their smiles are only on their lips and do not reach their eyes. Those smiling faces are too perfect, and they remind me of masks. I wonder what is behind those smiling faces. The people all talk to me, but although I understand their words, I do not understand their meaning. As the crowd presses against me, I feel as though I might suffocate. Will I ever be able to walk away from Omelas?

WRITING ABOUT LITERATURE

6. Decoding Symbols (Two Readings of a Story)

The Writing Workshop   Writing about symbols tests your ability to be a responsive reader—to respond fully to the way imaginative literature acts out or embodies meanings. You cannot be too literal-minded, since you may miss much of the meaning a symbol suggests or implies. You cannot be too clinical or detached if strong, richly charged symbols are to bring into play the emotions and attitudes they are likely to carry. Here is the kind of advice a writing teacher might give you after studying several sets of papers focused on the role symbols play in short fiction:

✧ *Explore the full range of possible associations of a symbol.* Literary symbols tend not to be one-track, one-dimensional signals that simply say "danger" or "evil lurks here." A serpent may symbolize danger. It may symbolize guile (the snake in the grass). It may stand for the alien or otherness (since reptiles represent a very different life from our own mammalian existence). It may represent danger that has a strange paradoxical attraction or beauty.

The cluster on the next page traces some of the possible associations of flowers as familiar recurrent symbols carrying rich traditional freight. Many of these associations may be activated by a story like Steinbeck's "The Chrysanthemums," where flowers play a central role at turning points in the story. (Which of these associations do you think are relevant to Steinbeck's story?)

✧ *Trace the full meaning of a gradually evolving central symbol.* A symbol is not likely to come into a story with its symbolic value ready-made, like the monetary value of a dollar bill. In Gilman's "The Yellow Wallpaper," we at first look at the twisted pattern of the paper the way an interior designer might wonder at its strange design. But gradually we—or rather the narrator through whose eyes we see everything in the story—read more and more human meaning into its strange shapes. They come to life, making the narrator participate in the struggle of whatever seems imprisoned behind its bars. It is as if each time we look at the paper we discover a new and frightening dimension, leading to an escalation of apprehension and terror. We have to read and ponder the story as a whole to sense what the wallpaper comes to stand for as the story heads for its frightening conclusion.

❖ *Look for secondary symbols that echo the major theme of a story.* In addition to the chrysanthemums in Steinbeck's story, readers have scrutinized the pots and pans in need of mending as a possible symbol; they have wondered about the symbolic meaning of the fog that closes off the valley:

> "The high grey-flannel fog of winter closed off the Salinas Valley from the sky and from all the rest of the world," Steinbeck begins. This introductory sentence points to one of the basic themes of the story. Something (in this case, the fog) is keeping something or someone "closed off"—held in, cut off. The fog covers the valley. Similarly, Elisa's situation closes in on her, keeps her trapped, holds her back. Neither her husband nor the itinerant tinker understands the energy and care she puts into the chrysanthemums, and her ability and potential go unrecognized and unappreciated; they are kept under wraps, "closed off." The fog is the lid that keeps the sun from penetrating; Elisa's circumstances put the "lid" on her vital energy and desires.

❖ *Look for contrasts or polarities.* Often the play of opposites helps organize a story. In Steinbeck's "Chrysanthemums," a key contrast juxtaposes the farm family that stays fogbound and the tinker who follows "the nice weather." The conventional cattle-tending chores of the predictable, unimaginative husband contrast with the mismatched team pulling the strange wagon of the unconventional traveler. In Gilman's "The Yellow Wallpaper," the central symbol is the wallpaper, but a major polarity that helps organize the narrative plays off the colors green and yellow and what they symbolize in the story.

❖ *Relate key terms* (as in other kinds of papers) *specifically to the story.* If you bring in a term from the outside, show how it applies to the story. For instance, if you say that the García Márquez story "is simply a fantasy," *what kind* of fantasy is acted out in the story? What are its workings or dynamics? (In the story, the corpse of the drowned man seems to become a kind of catalyst for the villagers' imagination. Fantasy here is not divorced from reality or an escape from it; it seems to be the kind of active imagination that makes the villagers *transform* their reality.)

❖ *Look for the personal connection.* How does the use of symbols in a story touch your own life, your own experience? What symbols have a special personal meaning for you—as the way Elisa dresses in the chrysanthemums story had for the student writer of the following passage?

> Steinbeck's story dealt with feminine emotions that can be very hard to understand. I was struck by the contrast between Elisa's mannish "working clothes" (her shapeless outfit, her heavy gloves) and the makeup and dress she puts on after her encounter with the tinker. Much of her thinking revolves around whether the men in her world would respect her work and desire her at the same time. Her change of clothes symbolizes the fact that in the male world the woman has to play a dual role. She has to be a man's equal to survive in the world of work, yet on the other hand she is expected to be feminine and seductive. Today a woman has to look more like a man by wearing a dark "power" suit and practically no makeup to compete with men, or she may not be taken seriously. In a recent sitcom episode, I watched a sterile-looking businesswoman teaching a fashionable female how to dress for business success. Her pupil donned a blue suit, a buttoned white shirt, and a bandage-type thing to hide her breasts. Steinbeck's story points up this unresolved conflict: It is a sad but honest account of how women are taken advantage of when they expose their feminine selves.

Two Readings of a Story

The language of symbols may be universal, but it also by its very nature fosters a range of interpretation. Writers relying heavily on symbols are the least likely to spell out the meaning or the moral of a story in so many words. Where do the two following readings of "The Yellow Wallpaper" seem to agree? Where do they differ in emphasis or interpretation? Which is closer to your own reading of the story? Which do you learn from the most?

SAMPLE STUDENT PAPER 1

"The Yellow Wallpaper": A Woman's Struggle with Madness

"I've got out at last. . . . And I've pulled off most of the paper, so you can't put me back!" declares the narrator of "The Yellow Wallpaper" at the end of her futile struggle with madness. By peeling off the yellow wallpaper and releasing the woman the narrator sees trapped behind its "conspicuous front design," the narrator peels off the façade of normalcy she is trapped behind and releases her own madness. This façade is created by a "very careful and loving" husband, who refuses to believe his wife is ill, and is perpetuated by the medical conventions of the time that dismiss her mental illness as "a slight hysterical tendency."

In his effort to help his wife get over her "temporary nervous depression," John takes her to a house in the country which is "quite alone, standing well back from the road, quite three miles from the village." He feels that this quiet atmosphere along with "perfect rest" is just what she needs. In fact, she is "absolutely forbidden to 'work'" and has "a scheduled prescription for each hour of the day." The narrator, on the other hand, feels "that congenial work, with excitement and change, would do me good." However, because her husband is "a physician of high standing," she feels he must know what is best for her. When they first move into the house, she wants a room "downstairs that opened on the piazza and had roses all over the window, and such pretty old-fashioned chintz hangings" but "John would not hear of it." He insists they take "the nursery at the top of the house" even though "the windows are barred." The floor "is scratched and gouged and splintered, the plaster itself is dug out here and there," and the room is covered in a "horrid paper"—"one of those sprawling flamboyant patterns committing every artistic sin" and colored "repellent, almost revolting . . . unclean yellow." He also insists that she stop writing, which she feels "would relieve the press of ideas and rest me." She does manage to write a bit "in spite of them," but it is too exhausting "having to be so sly about it."

Consequently, with no outlet for her "imaginative power and habit of story-making," she develops a grotesque fascination with the yellow wallpaper. At first the paper is just irritating, "dull enough to confuse the eye in following, pronounced enough to constantly irritate and provoke study." But, as the narrator studies the wallpaper more and more, she begins to see hideous images in the pattern. "The pattern lolls like a broken neck and two bulbous eyes. . . . those absurd, unblinking eyes are everywhere." She dwells on this pattern and soon sees "a kind of subpattern in a different shade . . . that seems to skulk about behind" the front design. The wallpaper so disturbs the narrator that she tries to have "a real earnest reasonable talk" with her husband about her condition. He tells her that she is getting better, but she replies, "Better in body perhaps." He dismisses her concern for her mental state as "a false and foolish fancy." He tells her that she must not give in to her feelings, and that only she can help herself get better. She must use her "will and self-control and not let any silly fancies run away with [her]."

It is at this point in the story, after the narrator tries, unsuccessfully, to share her fears for her sanity, that she can no longer control the madness she has been struggling to contain. This madness takes the form of the woman behind the wallpaper. "I didn't realize for a long time what the thing was that showed behind, that dim subpattern, but now I am quite sure it is a woman." The narrator describes the woman as "subdued, quiet," and the narrator believes "it is the pattern that keeps her so still." The narrator is, in fact, describing herself, so quiet and subdued, and the pattern keeping her that way is her life.

As the narrator's illness progresses, she begins to identify more and more with the woman behind the wallpaper. She sees the woman creeping around everywhere: "in that long shaded lane. . . . in those dark grape arbors. . . . on that long road under the trees, creeping along, and when a carriage comes she hides." The narrator sympathizes with this woman for she, too, is creeping around. "I always lock the door when I creep by daylight," the narrator writes.

Ultimately, her madness takes complete control and her one purpose in life is to help the woman escape from the wallpaper. Piece by piece, the narrator peels off the wallpaper as she peels away at her own sanity, until the woman is able to escape from behind the paper, and the narrator is able to escape into her own madness. The narrator wonders "if they all come out of the wallpaper as I did?"

No less obvious than the symbolism of the yellow wallpaper is the irony of the story. A loving husband, a physician no less, prescribes a treatment of rest and relaxation he feels will improve his wife's slightly depressed condition; however, instead of helping her, he unwittingly drives her to insanity. His mistake was in not taking her condition seriously, not accepting that she was, indeed, very ill. We want to say, "Poor woman, if she existed today, she could have been helped." Maybe, and maybe not. Situations similar to the narrator's do exist today. The modern term for John is "enabler." Just as John, by pretending nothing was seriously wrong, enabled his wife to succumb to her illness, many spouses and families of alcoholics enable them to continue being alcoholics by not admitting they have a problem. They, too, are trapped behind the facades of normalcy they create. This is only one example. We are all "enablers" in one way or another. By ignoring the problems that exist all around us, and refusing to admit they are real problems, we perpetuate those problems. Only by admitting a problem exists, whether in the family or in society, can we truly begin to find a solution.

SAMPLE STUDENT PAPER 2

Yellow Women

Gilman's "The Yellow Wallpaper" is a tragic story of a woman's attempt to recover from post-partum depression. This story represents through symbolism the characteristic attitude toward woman and of women during the late 1800's and early 1900's. Gilman writes honestly of the isolated and confused feelings women were feeling. The woman in "The Yellow Wallpaper" goes through three periods of change throughout the story. The story begins with the description of the woman as being sick, but there are no signs of mental illness, and she is aware of her environment and even believes she is not really sick. Then there is a curious change in her character, and she appears to be disillusioned and on the verge of becoming mentally insane. And in the end she does go over the edge, and her character is literally lost. There are factors which cause these changes; I will explore these three major changes in her life as well as the use of powerful symbolism.

The woman in this story is taken to a summer house to rest and recuperate. Her husband, John, who is also her doctor, treats her as a child, and she says that "perhaps that is one reason I do not get well faster." She is apparently suffering from the baby blues, which is a depression some women experience after giving birth to a child. However, her husband sticks her in an atrocious nursery with barred windows and a wallpaper that she describes as

> dull enough to confuse the eye in following, pronounced enough to constantly irritate and provoke study, and when you follow the lame uncertain curves for a little distance they suddenly commit suicide—plunge off at outrageous angles, destroy themselves in unheard of contradictions.

Her description of the wallpaper represents her feelings about the paper, but it also symbolizes the feelings she has about herself. This confusing pattern could be a typical categorization of women, whereas a typical pattern for men might be straight and neat lines that meet at edges and appear to have an overall meaning. I say this because, in the story, John apparently knows all and has prescribed his wife's life as he sees fit. In a description of John's sister, the woman says she is "a perfect and enthusiastic housekeeper, and hopes for no better profession." This heartless description lacks praise for her sister-in-law's profession; it also symbolizes the status of women in the time the story was written.

Her husband, who calls her "his little girl" and his "blessed goose," forbids her to work until she is well; she disagrees, believing "congenial work, with excitement and change," would do her good. She believes she could recover from her baby blues if only she were able to keep active and do other things than sit alone in a nursery and stare at the wallpaper. She even asks her husband to have company for companionship, but he tells her "he would as soon put fireworks in my pillow-case as to let me have those stimulating people about now." She might not even have progressed to her second stage if it were not for her husband, brother, and sister-in-law constantly reminding her of how tired and sick she is.

Her second stage begins when she becomes "fond" of the wallpaper. She is losing contact with the outside world, instead spending her time trying, in a painstaking effort, to understand the overall pattern of the wallpaper. She sees a figure that looks like a "woman stooping down and creeping about behind that pattern." She also goes on to say, "I don't like it a bit. . . . I wish John would take me away from here." She is herself the woman "creeping" through the wallpaper. The woman creeping symbolizes women who are not allowed to stand tall and free and speak their minds. She "creeps" at night when her husband is asleep and, when she is caught "creeping," her husband tells her to get back in bed. Her husband, who has good intentions, keeps on assuring her that she is getting better, and when she disagrees with him by saying, "Better in body perhaps," he looks at her with such a "stern, reproachful" stare that she does not dare say another word.

She is alone in her own little world with no real support from anyone. She cannot be blamed for her condition and eventually insanity takes over her body. Here is another example of how the wallpaper symbolizes women:

> The front pattern *does* move—and no wonder! The woman behind shakes it!
>
> Sometimes I think there are a great many women behind. . . . And she is all the time trying to climb through. But nobody could climb through that pattern—it strangles so; I think that is why it has so many heads.

She realizes she is not the only woman who is lost but also many other women. This realization pushes her to her mental limit, and she tries to peel all of the wallpaper off so that the "strangled heads" can be free. She feels secure and safe in the room "creeping" and she says, "I don't want to go outside. . . . For outside you have to creep on the ground, and everything is green instead of yellow." She has no desire to live in the "green" world, and she chooses the "yellow" familiar world instead. She even locks herself in the room and throws away the key. This act symbolizes an instance of control over her own life. Comfortable in her "creeping" role, she does not want anyone to bother her. She is now mentally insane.

The woman in "The Yellow Wallpaper" represents many women, even today, in the late 20th century. There are many women who do not take advantage of their freedom, many who are also servants in life. I have seen this to be so in my grandmother's as well as in my mother's marriage. However, the wallpaper women are hiding behind is slowly being peeled off by both men and women.

QUESTIONS

1. Do these two papers agree in their estimate of the relation between the woman and her physician-husband?

2. How do the two papers compare in their interpretation of key symbolic elements: the wallpaper pattern, the woman behind the paper, the creeping, the peeling off of the paper?

3. Do both papers interpret the symbolism of the colors green and yellow, and do they agree in their interpretation?

4. How do the two papers compare in their view of what the story means to today's women?

THE PERSONAL RESPONSE

After reading the second paper, one student reader wrote the following comment. Where do you agree or disagree with it, and why?

> I remember that when first reading the story I was totally overpowered by it. This is a fascinating, disturbing paper that has made me see this terrible story in a new way. The "yellow women" designated by this student writer are not just victims to her; they are also "yellow," i.e. chicken, afraid, able only to escape via insanity. There's a strange implication—and judgment of—learned helplessness. Without quite saying it, this writer attempts to say that the flight into insanity is as much a cop-out as it is the oppressor's unknowing way of forcing insanity on the female. I get an ambiguous picture: the male isn't being deliberately patronizing; he is just as much a victim of the cultural norm as the female is. Conversely, the female plays as big a part in her insanity as the male. She could "choose" the green way—partly because she knows where the "green way" is: downstairs, near the roses and the entrance to the garden—and in her writing. A key word in this paper is "choose." The implication is that she can't buck convention enough to stand up for herself, so she retreats into the "yellow" room on the second floor, giving up the organic living greenness and groundedness in earth and reality of the first floor where she could heal naturally from a natural disequilibrium. If this writer does what I think she's doing, she has become aware of a double tragedy often missed: the pathetic ignorance of men as well as women in roles they wear because they know no other.

7 THEME
The Search for Meaning

*Invention, not preaching, enchants the modern reader
and sustains the illusion of reality.*

ANN CHARTERS

*Instead of placing one body of knowledge against another,
storytellers invite us to return from knowledge to thinking,
from a bounded way of looking to an unbounded way of
seeing.*

JAMES P. CARSE

*If I never contradict myself, then I'm either not thinking
or I'm conciliating positions and, therefore, not growing.*

NIKKI GIOVANNI

FOCUS ON THEME

Imaginative literature has the power to make you think about life, about yourself and other human beings. It is true that at times you will read mainly for entertainment or in order to escape from the daily routine. Even when you read imaginative literature for its human meaning, it may speak as much to your feelings as to your intellect. A story may make you vividly imagine scenes and events; it may stir your emotions—sometimes making you discover a capacity for feeling that you didn't know was there. However, a story that has a strong impact on you is also likely to make you think. It is likely to raise questions to which the story as a whole suggests possible answers. It is likely to make you reexamine or rethink some facet of human life. When you try to put the human meaning of a story into your own words, you formulate its **theme.** You try to state the idea or ideas that the story as a whole seems to act out.

Writers of earlier generations felt free to spell out the meaning of a story in **thematic passages.** They might put these in the mouth (or in the mind) of an observer or of a key character. In "The Blue Hotel" (1898), a story set in Nebraska in the Old West, Stephen Crane traces the events leading up to a barroom brawl in which a man is killed. From the beginning, our attention centers on the strange behavior of a recent arrival, the Swede. He is subject to neurotic fears, he covers up his apprehensions with bluster and bravado, and he is a source of irritation to the small group of men spending the night in the hotel. A long evening of drinking and random quarreling comes to a head when the Swede accuses a callous, loudmouthed local boy of cheating at poker and batters him in a bloody fight. Flushed with liquor and his sense of victory, the Swede checks out of the hotel (to the great relief of the innkeeper) and stumbles on to a saloon. He there picks a fight with a gambler who refuses to drink with him, and the trouble-making Swede is killed in the ensuing brawl.

> There was a great tumult, and then was seen a long blade in the hand of the gambler. It shot forward, and a human body, this citadel of virtue, wisdom, power, was pierced as easily as if it had been a melon. The Swede fell with a cry of supreme astonishment.

There are different ways to read this story. First, Crane has a grim sense of **irony.** He dramatizes the laughable lack of fit between our expectations or explanations on the one hand and reality on the other. The Swede's paranoid fears were unjustified. No one was out to destroy him. The irony is that he was destroyed anyway. Secondly, the more callous and dense among the locals feel that the Swede only got what he deserved; he had it coming. But Crane wants us to learn something else from this story, and in case we missed it, he puts it in the mouth of one of his characters. The "Easterner" has been mostly a silent observer and at times a calming, moderating influence in the story. He finally says to a local cowboy who accuses the Swede of acting like a jackass:

> You're a bigger jackass than the Swede by a million majority. Now let me tell you one thing. . . . Johnnie *was* cheating. I saw him. . . . And I refused to stand up and be a man. I let the Swede fight it out alone. And you—you were simply puffing around the place and wanting to fight. . . . We are all in it! . . . Every sin is the result of collaboration. We, five of us, have collaborated in the murder of this Swede. . . . that fool of an unfortunate gambler came merely as the culmination . . . and gets all the punishment.

Evil is the result of collaboration. Crane's theme in this story is a generalization, but it is not a glib or secondhand generalization. It is an earned generalization—not brought into the story ready-made from the outside. It is fully anchored in the lived experience of the story.

Most twentieth-century writers have gone a step beyond Crane. Rather than have the gambler sum up the theme in so many words, they probably would have preferred to have the reader *think* about the role collaboration plays in causing evil. Even more so than Crane, later writers have harbored a suspicion of glib words—big words not anchored to lived realities, uplifting messages delivered with no attempt to make their promise come true. Katherine Anne Porter echoed a prevailing modern creed when she praised Katherine Mansfield, another short story writer, for her "fine objectivity." Porter said about her fellow writer that "she bares a moment of experience, real experience, in the life of some one human being; she states no belief, gives no motives, airs no theories, but simply presents to the reader a situation, a place, and a character, and there it is."

Because of the modern writer's reluctance to editorialize, the themes of modern fiction tend to be implied rather than spelled out. They are ideas organically embedded in image, action, and emotion. Although they have something to tell us about life or human nature or society, what they say comes to us in a language different from that of official guidelines, advice columns in the newspapers, or sayings that can be printed in an almanac.

Short Short: A Story with a Twist

The following short short is by a writer whose stories are known for their surreal quality and dark humor. Luisa Valenzuela was born in Argentina and worked with Jorge Luis Borges at the National Library in Buenos Aires before she was twenty. She went to live in Paris for a time, working for Argentine publications, writing for French television and radio, and becoming part of a circle of avant-garde writers and critics. She later came to the United States, where she has participated in programs for writers at Iowa and Columbia. Her collection titled *Strange Things Happen Here* was published in 1975; *The Lizard's Tail*, a later volume, in 1983.

The story that follows creates suspense and ends with a shuddery surprise twist. Does it have a larger meaning? What is its theme?

LUISA VALENZUELA   (born 1938)
The Censors   1988
TRANSLATED BY DAVID UNGER

Poor Juan! One day they caught him with his guard down before he could even realize that what he had taken as a stroke of luck was really one of fate's dirty tricks. These things happen the minute you're careless and you let down your guard, as one often does. Juancito let happiness—a feeling you can't trust—get the better of him when he received from a confidential source Mariana's new address in Paris and he knew that she hadn't forgotten him. Without thinking twice, he sat down at his table and wrote her a letter. *The* letter that keeps his mind off his job during the day and won't let him sleep at night (what had he scrawled, what had he put on that sheet of paper he sent to Mariana?).

Juan knows there won't be a problem with the letter's contents, that it's irreproachable, harmless. But what about the rest? He knows that they examine, sniff, feel, and read between the lines of each and every letter, and check its tiniest comma and most accidental stain. He knows that all letters pass from hand to hand and go through all sorts of tests in the huge censorship offices and that, in the end, very few continue on their way. Usually it takes months, even years, if there aren't any snags; all this time the freedom, maybe even the life, of both sender and receiver is in jeopardy. And that's why Juan's so down in the dumps: thinking that something might happen to Mariana because of his letters. Of all people, Mariana, who must finally feel safe there where she always dreamed she'd live. But he knows that the *Censor's Secret Command* operates all over the world and cashes in on the discount in air rates; there's nothing to stop them from going as far as that hidden Paris neighborhood, kidnapping Mariana, and returning to their cozy homes, certain of having fulfilled their noble mission.

Well, you've got to beat them to the punch, do what everyone tries to do: sabotage the machinery, throw sand in its gears, get to the bottom of the problem so as to stop it.

This was Juan's sound plan when he, like many others, applied for a censor's job— not because he had a calling or needed a job: no, he applied simply to intercept his own letter, a consoling but unoriginal idea. He was hired immediately, for each day more and more censors are needed and no one would bother to check on his references.

Ulterior motives couldn't be overlooked by the *Censorship Division,* but they 5
needn't be too strict with those who applied. They knew how hard it would be for those poor guys to find the letter they wanted and even if they did, what's a letter or two when the new censor would snap up so many others? That's how Juan managed to join the *Post Office's Censorship Division,* with a certain goal in mind.

The building had a festive air on the outside which contrasted with its inner staidness. Little by little, Juan was absorbed by his job and he felt at peace since he was doing everything he could to get his letter for Mariana. He didn't even worry when, in his first month, he was sent to *Section K* where envelopes are very carefully screened for explosives.

It's true that on the third day, a fellow worker had his right hand blown off by a letter, but the division chief claimed it was sheer negligence on the victim's part. Juan and the other employees were allowed to go back to their work, albeit feeling less secure. After work, one of them tried to organize a strike to demand higher wages for unhealthy work, but Juan didn't join in; after thinking it over, he reported him to his superiors and thus got promoted.

You don't form a habit by doing something once, he told himself as he left his boss's office. And when he was transferred to *Section J,* where letters are carefully checked for poison dust, he felt he had climbed a rung in the ladder.

By working hard, he quickly reached *Section E* where the work was more interesting, for he could now read and analyze the letters' contents. Here he could even hope to get hold of his letter which, judging by the time that had elapsed, had gone through the other sections and was probably floating around in this one.

Soon his work became so absorbing that his noble mission blurred in his mind. 10
Day after day he crossed out whole paragraphs in red ink, pitilessly chucking many letters into the censored basket. These were horrible days when he was shocked by the subtle and conniving ways employed by people to pass on subversive messages; his instincts were so sharp that he found behind a simple "the weather's unsettled" or "prices continue to soar" the wavering hand of someone secretly scheming to overthrow the Government.

His zeal brought him swift promotion. We don't know if this made him happy. Very few letters reached him in *Section B*—only a handful passed the other hurdles—so he read them over and over again, passed them under a magnifying glass, searched for microprint with an electronic microscope, and tuned his sense of smell so that he was beat by the time he made it home. He'd barely manage to warm up his soup, eat some fruit, and fall into bed, satisfied with having done his duty. Only his darling mother worried, but she couldn't get him back on the right road. She'd say, though it wasn't always true: Lola called, she's at the bar with the girls, they miss you, they're waiting for you. Or else she'd leave a bottle of red wine on the table. But Juan wouldn't overdo it: any distraction could make him lose his edge and the perfect censor had to be alert, keen, attentive, and sharp to nab cheats. He had a truly patriotic task, both self-denying and uplifting.

His basket for censored letters became the best fed as well as the most cunning basket in the whole *Censorship Division*. He was about to congratulate himself for having finally discovered his true mission, when his letter to Mariana reached his hands. Naturally, he censored it without regret. And just as naturally, he couldn't stop them from executing him the following morning, another victim of his devotion to his work.

THE RECEPTIVE READER

Does this story make a statement about censorship? about human nature? What does it say? Does it act out ideas about life? about society? How?

THE MAKING OF MEANING

Art shrinks from . . . every abstract thing, from all that is of the brain only, from all that is not a fountain jetting from the entire hopes, memories, and sensations of the body.
WILLIAM BUTLER YEATS

The truth about any subject only comes when all the sides of the story are put together, and all their different meanings make one new one.
ALICE WALKER

As you encounter references to literary themes, you may note two slightly different uses. Often *theme* simply means a focus of attention, an area of concern. In this sense, one great modern theme is alienation—the feeling of uprootedness, the loss of the sense of home. A related theme is loneliness—our inability to communicate truly with others, our difficulty in forging lasting bonds. Another modern theme is a runaway technology that has put us at odds with nature. In much of our modern world, these "are in the air"; we encounter them again and again, like the strain of a popular song that we hear over and over—on the radio, in the supermarket, in the elevator.

This meaning of *theme* shades over into its more specific meaning, which makes us go a step or two beyond identifying an issue or an area of concern. It makes us ask what a story as a whole might be saying *about* an issue or area of attention. In this sense, the theme of a story is not alienation but what the story as a whole says about alienation. The story as a whole may be making a statement about the roots of alienation, or about our ways of coping with it, or about how alienation explains the kind of people we are. It is this kind of implied statement that you will usually be exploring when talking or writing about theme.

When reading for theme or when trying to formulate the theme of a story, remember cautions like the following:

✧ *Beware of large abstractions.* Part of the modern temper has been a suspicion of big words, hasty generalizations, and premature abstractions. **Abstractions** (from a Latin word meaning "pulling away") draw us away from the nitty gritty of unsorted detail to the larger labels and categories that we need to find our way in a complex, multilayered world. But because they cover much (they are "umbrella" terms), abstract terms easily become foggy or misleading. Be prepared to ask: "freedom"—to do what? "discovery of the self"—focusing on what? "love of humanity"—what part or what features of it?

✧ *Beware of oversimplification.* Often the meaning of a story takes shape in the interplay of conflicting human commitments and emotions. If you were to look for a common denominator for stories by Faulkner, Jackson, and Hawthorne in this volume, you might start by saying their authors agree that "evil lurks in the human heart." But this much most readers probably are ready to grant *before* they read one of these stories. The questions each story raises and the possible answers it leads us to explore are more complex than that. Like other writers who have wrestled with the problem of how to explain evil, how to think of evil, in our world, each of these authors has arrived at a somewhat different answer.

✧ *Beware of clichés.* "All you need is love" makes a marvelous Beatles song. But it is too sweeping and inspirational (and too obviously untrue) to serve as a lasting insight that we carry away from a gripping story. If you bring a ready-made phrase to a story from outside, it is not going to carry the authentic stamp of honest feeling, of lived experience. Be wary of greeting-card phrases—phrases we take down ready-made from the rack when we find it hard to put our own honest feeling and thinking into words.

THE THINKING READER

The concepts of beauty and ugliness are mysterious to me.
Many people write about them. In mulling over them, I
try to get underneath them and see what they mean,
understand the impact they have on what people do. I also
write about love and death. The problem I face as a writer
is to make my stories mean something. You can have
wonderful, interesting people, a fascinating story, but it's
not about anything. It has no real substance.
TONI MORRISON

Serious readers have always turned to literature as not just entertainment but as an interpretation of life. They listen attentively to writers who help them make sense of experience. They remember writers who served them as guideposts or beacons in times of bewilderment and confusion. Each of the following three stories puts its characters into situations that make them ask themselves searching questions. What are these questions in each story? What answers does the story as a whole suggest? What ideas—about people, about human nature, about good and evil—are acted out or fleshed out in each story?

ALICE   WALKER   (born 1944)

*Her deepest concern is with individuals and how their
relationships are affected by their confrontations with
wider political and moral issues.*

CAROL RUMENS

Alice Walker's novel *The Color Purple* (1982) was a major publishing event
that established her as a dominant voice in the quest for a new black identity and
black pride. In her Pulitzer Prize–winning novel, as in some of her short stories,
her heroines are women in the black community struggling to emerge from a
history of oppression and abuse. They find strength in bonding with other
women, and they turn to the African past in the search for alternatives to our
rapacious technological civilization. A recurrent feature in her fiction are black
males representing a generation of men who "had failed women—and themselves." Walker's more recent novel, *The Temple of My Familiar* (1989), has
been called a book of "amazing, overwhelming" richness, with characters
"pushing one another toward self-knowledge, honesty, engagement" (Ursula
K. Le Guin).

Born in Eatonton, Georgia, Walker knew poverty and racism at close quarters as the child of sharecroppers in the Deep South. While a student at Spel-
man College in Atlanta, she joined in the rallies, sit-ins, and freedom marches
of the civil rights movement, which, she said later, "broke the pattern of black
servitude in this country." She worked as a caseworker for the New York City
Welfare Department and as an editor for *Ms.* magazine. She has written and
lectured widely on the relationship between black men and women, between
black and white women, and between her writing and the work of African
American writers—Jean Toomer, Zora Neale Hurston—who were her inspiration. She has taught creative writing and black literature at colleges including
Jackson State College, Wellesley, and Yale.

Many of Walker's essays, articles, and reviews were collected in her *In
Search of Our Mothers' Gardens* (1983). In the title essay, she paid tribute to
women of her mother's and grandmother's generations, who channeled the
creative and spiritual energies that were denied other outlets into their rich
gardens and into the "fanciful, inspired, and yet simple" quilts they fashioned
from "bits and pieces of worthless rags." In the following story, the older generation tries to hold on to its hard-won pride, while members of a younger
generation assert their independence from the past by adopting Muslim names
and African greetings.

Everyday Use   1973

For Your Grandmamma

I will wait for her in the yard that Maggie and I made so clean and wavy yesterday
afternoon. A yard like this is more comfortable than most people know. It is not just a
yard. It is like an extended living room. When the hard clay is swept clean as a floor and
the fine sand around the edges lined with tiny, irregular grooves, anyone can come and

sit and look up into the elm tree and wait for the breezes that never come inside the house.

Maggie will be nervous until after her sister goes: she will stand hopelessly in corners, homely and ashamed of the burn scars down her arms and legs, eying her sister with a mixture of envy and awe. She thinks her sister has held life always in the palm of one hand, that "no" is a word the world never learned to say to her.

You've no doubt seen those TV shows where the child who has "made it" is confronted, as a surprise, by her own mother and father, tottering in weakly from backstage. (A pleasant surprise, of course: What would they do if parent and child came on the show only to curse out and insult each other?) On TV mother and child embrace and smile into each other's faces. Sometimes the mother and father weep, the child wraps them in her arms and leans across the table to tell how she would not have made it without their help. I have seen these programs.

Sometimes I dream a dream in which Dee and I are suddenly brought together on a TV program of this sort. Out of a dark and soft-seated limousine I am ushered into a bright room filled with many people. There I meet a smiling, gray, sporty man like Johnny Carson who shakes my hand and tells me what a fine girl I have. Then we are on the stage and Dee is embracing me with tears in her eyes. She pins on my dress a large orchid, even though she has told me once that she thinks orchids are tacky flowers.

In real life I am a large, big-boned woman with rough, man-working hands. In the winter I wear flannel nightgowns to bed and overalls during the day. I can kill and clean a hog as mercilessly as a man. My fat keeps me hot in zero weather. I can work outside all day, breaking ice to get water for washing; I can eat pork liver cooked over the open fire minutes after it comes steaming from the hog. One winter I knocked a bull calf straight in the brain between the eyes with a sledge hammer and had the meat hung up to chill before nightfall. But of course all this does not show on television. I am the way my daughter would want me to be: a hundred pounds lighter, my skin like an uncooked barley pancake. My hair glistens in the hot bright lights. Johnny Carson has much to do to keep up with my quick and witty tongue. 5

But that is a mistake. I know even before I wake up. Who ever knew a Johnson with a quick tongue? Who can even imagine me looking a strange white man in the eye? It seems to me I have talked to them always with one foot raised in flight, with my head turned in whichever way is farthest from them. Dee, though. She would always look anyone in the eye. Hesitation was no part of her nature.

"How do I look, Mama?" Maggie says, showing just enough of her thin body enveloped in pink skirt and red blouse for me to know she's there, almost hidden by the door.

"Come out into the yard," I say.

Have you ever seen a lame animal, perhaps a dog run over by some careless person rich enough to own a car, sidle up to someone who is ignorant enough to be kind to them? That is the way my Maggie walks. She has been like this, chin on chest, eyes on ground, feet in shuffle, ever since the fire that burned the other house to the ground.

Dee is lighter than Maggie, with nicer hair and a fuller figure. She's a woman now, though sometimes I forget. How long ago was it that the other house burned? Ten, twelve years? Sometimes I can still hear the flames and feel Maggie's arms sticking to me, her hair smoking and her dress falling off her in little black papery flakes. Her eyes seemed stretched open, blazed open by the flames reflected in them. And Dee. I see her standing off under the sweet gum tree she used to dig gum out of; a look of concentra- 10 tion on her face as she watched the last dingy gray board of the house fall in toward the red-hot brick chimney. Why don't you do a dance around the ashes? I'd wanted to ask her. She had hated the house that much.

I used to think she hated Maggie, too. But that was before we raised the money, the church and me, to send her to Augusta to school. She used to read to us without pity; forcing words, lies, other folks' habits, whole lives upon us two, sitting trapped and ignorant underneath her voice. She washed us in a river of make-believe, burned us with a lot of knowledge we didn't necessarily need to know. Pressed us to her with the serious way she read, to shove us away at just the moment, like dimwits, we seemed about to understand.

Dee wanted nice things. A yellow organdy dress to wear to her graduation from high school; black pumps to match a green suit she'd made from an old suit somebody gave me. She was determined to stare down any disaster in her efforts. Her eyelids would not flicker for minutes at a time. Often I fought off the temptation to shake her. At sixteen she had a style of her own: and knew what style was.

I never had an education myself. After second grade the school was closed down. Don't ask me why: in 1927 colored asked fewer questions than they do now. Sometimes Maggie reads to me. She stumbles along good naturedly but can't see well. She knows she is not bright. Like good looks and money, quickness passed her by. She will marry John Thomas (who has mossy teeth in an earnest face) and then I'll be free to sit here and I guess just sing church songs to myself. Although I never was a good singer. Never could carry a tune. I was always better at a man's job. I used to love to milk till I was hooked in the side in '49. Cows are soothing and slow and don't bother you, unless you try to milk them the wrong way.

I have deliberately turned my back on the house. It is three rooms, just like the one that burned, except the roof is tin; they don't make shingle roofs any more. There are no real windows, just some holes cut in the sides, like the portholes in a ship, but not round and not square, with rawhide holding the shutters up on the outside. This house is in a pasture, too, like the other one. No doubt when Dee sees it she will want to tear it down. She wrote me once that no matter where we "choose" to live, she will manage to come see us. But she will never bring her friends. Maggie and I thought about this and Maggie asked me, "Mama, when did Dee ever *have* any friends?"

She had a few. Furtive boys in pink shirts hanging about on washday after school. 15 Nervous girls who never laughed. Impressed with her they worshiped the well-turned phrase, the cute shape, the scalding humor that erupted like bubbles in lye. She read to them.

When she was courting Jimmy T she didn't have much time to pay to us, but turned all her faultfinding power on him. He *flew* to marry a cheap city girl from a family of ignorant flashy people. She hardly had time to recompose herself.

When she comes I will meet—but there they are!

Maggie attempts to make a dash for the house, in her shuffling way, but I stay her with my hand. "Come back here," I say. And she stops and tries to dig a well in the sand with her toe.

It is hard to see them clearly through the strong sun. But even the first glimpse of leg out of the car tells me it is Dee. Her feet were always neat-looking, as if God himself had shaped them with a certain style. From the other side of the car comes a short, stocky man. Hair is all over his head a foot long and hanging from his chin like a kinky mule tail. I hear Maggie suck in her breath. "Uhnnnh," is what it sounds like. Like when you see the wriggling end of a snake just in front of your foot on the road. "Uhnnnh."

Dee next. A dress down to the ground, in this hot weather. A dress so loud it hurts   20
my eyes. There are yellows and oranges enough to throw back the light of the sun. I
feel my whole face warming from the heat waves it throws out. Earrings gold, too, and
hanging down to her shoulders. Bracelets dangling and making noises when she moves
her arm up to shake the folds of the dress out of her armpits. The dress is loose and
flows, and as she walks closer, I like it. I hear Maggie go "Uhnnnh" again. It is her sister's hair. It stands straight up like the wool on a sheep. It is black as night and around
the edges are two long pigtails that rope about like small lizards disappearing behind
her ears.

"Wa-su-zo-Tean-o!" she says, coming on in that gliding way the dress makes her
move. The short stocky fellow with the hair to his navel is all grinning and he follows
up with "Asalamalakim, my mother and sister!" He moves to hug Maggie but she falls
back, right up against the back of my chair. I feel her trembling there and when I look
up I see the perspiration falling off her chin.

"Don't get up," says Dee. Since I am stout it takes something of a push. You can
see me trying to move a second or two before I make it. She turns, showing white heels
through her sandals, and goes back to the car. Out she peeks next with a Polaroid. She
stoops down quickly and lines up picture after picture of me sitting there in front of the
house with Maggie cowering behind me. She never takes a shot without making sure
the house is included. When a cow comes nibbling around the edge of the yard she
snaps it and me and Maggie *and* the house. Then she puts the Polaroid in the back seat
of the car, and comes up and kisses me on the forehead.

Meanwhile Asalamalakim is going through motions with Maggie's hand. Maggie's
hand is as limp as a fish, and probably as cold, despite the sweat, and she keeps trying to pull it back. It looks like Asalamalakim wants to shake hands but wants to do it
fancy. Or maybe he don't know how people shake hands. Anyhow, he soon gives up on
Maggie.

"Well," I say. "Dee."

"No, Mama," she says. "Not 'Dee,' Wangero Leewanika Kemanjo!"   25

"What happened to 'Dee'?" I wanted to know.

"She's dead," Wangero said. "I couldn't bear it any longer, being named after the
people who oppress me."

"You know as well as me you was named after your aunt Dicie," I said. Dicie is my
sister. She named Dee. We called her "Big Dee" after Dee was born.

"But who was *she* named after?" asked Wangero.

"I guess after Grandma Dee," I said.   30

"And who was she named after?" asked Wangero.

"Her mother," I said, and saw Wangero was getting tired. "That's about as far
back as I can trace it," I said. Though, in fact, I probably could have carried it back beyond the Civil War through the branches.

"Well," said Asalamalakim, "there you are."

"Uhnnnh," I heard Maggie say.

"There I was not," I said, "before 'Dicie' cropped up in our family, so why should   35
I try to trace it that far back?"

He just stood there grinning, looking down on me like somebody inspecting a
Model A car. Every once in a while he and Wangero sent eye signals over my head.

"How do you pronounce this name?" I asked.

"You don't have to call me by it if you don't want to," said Wangero.

"Why shouldn't I?" I asked. "If that's what you want us to call you, we'll call
you."

"I know it might sound awkward at first," said Wangero.   40

"I'll get used to it," I said. "Ream it out again."

Well, soon we got the name out of the way. Asalamalakim had a name twice as long and three times as hard. After I tripped over it two or three times he told me to just call him Hakim-a-barber. I wanted to ask him was he a barber, but I didn't really think he was, so I didn't ask.

"You must belong to those beef-cattle peoples down the road," I said. They said "Asalamalakim" when they met you, too, but they didn't shake hands. Always too busy: feeding the cattle, fixing the fences, putting up salt-lick shelters, throwing down hay. When the white folks poisoned some of the herd the men stayed up all night with rifles in their hands. I walked a mile and a half just to see the sight.

Hakim-a-barber said, "I accept some of their doctrines, but farming and raising cattle is not my style." (They didn't tell me, and I didn't ask, whether Wangero (Dee) had really gone and married him.)

We sat down to eat and right away he said he didn't eat collards and pork was un-   45 clean. Wangero, though, went on through the chitlins and corn bread, the greens and everything else. She talked a blue streak over the sweet potatoes. Everything delighted her. Even the fact that we still used the benches her daddy made for the table when we couldn't afford to buy chairs.

"Oh, Mama!" she cried. Then turned to Hakim-a-barber. "I never knew how lovely these benches are. You can feel the rump prints," she said, running her hands underneath her and along the bench. Then she gave a sigh and her hand closed over Grandma Dee's butter dish. "That's it!" she said. "I knew there was something I wanted to ask you if I could have." She jumped up from the table and went over in the corner where the churn stood, the milk in it clabber by now. She looked at the churn and looked at it.

"This churn top is what I need," she said. "Didn't Uncle Buddy whittle it out of a tree you all used to have?"

"Yes," I said.

"Uh huh," she said happily. "And I want the dasher, too."

"Uncle Buddy whittle that, too?" asked the barber.   50

Dee (Wangero) looked up at me.

"Aunt Dee's first husband whittled the dash," said Maggie so low you almost couldn't hear her. "His name was Henry, but they called him Stash."

"Maggie's brain is like an elephant's," Wangero said, laughing. "I can use the churn top as a centerpiece for the alcove table," she said, sliding a plate over the churn, "and I'll think of something artistic to do with the dasher."

When she finished wrapping the dasher the handle stuck out. I took it for a moment in my hands. You didn't even have to look close to see where hands pushing the dasher up and down to make butter had left a kind of sink in the wood. In fact, there were a lot of small sinks; you could see where thumbs and fingers had sunk into the wood. It was beautiful light yellow wood, from a tree that grew in the yard where Big Dee and Stash had lived.

After dinner Dee (Wangero) went to the trunk at the foot of my bed and started   55 rifling through it. Maggie hung back in the kitchen over the dishpan. Out came Wangero with two quilts. They had been pieced by Grandma Dee and then Big Dee and me had hung them on the quilt frames on the front porch and quilted them. One was in the Lone Star pattern. The other was Walk Around the Mountain. In both of them were scraps of dresses Grandma Dee had worn fifty and more years ago. Bits and pieces of Grandpa Jarrell's Paisley shirts. And one teeny faded blue piece, about the size of a penny matchbox, that was from Great Grandpa Ezra's uniform that he wore in the Civil War.

"Mama," Wangero said sweet as a bird. "Can I have these old quilts?"

I heard something fall in the kitchen, and a minute later the kitchen door slammed.

"Why don't you take one or two of the others?" I asked. "These old things was just done by me and Big Dee from some tops your grandma pieced before she died."

"No," said Wangero. "I don't want those. They are stitched around the borders by machine."

"That'll make them last better," I said.   60

"That's not the point," said Wangero. "These are all pieces of dresses Grandma used to wear. She did all this stitching by hand. Imagine!" She held the quilts securely in her arms, stroking them.

"Some of the pieces, like those lavender ones, come from old clothes her mother handed down to her," I said, moving up to touch the quilts. Dee (Wangero) moved back just enough so that I couldn't reach the quilts. They already belonged to her.

"Imagine!" she breathed again, clutching them closely to her bosom.

"The truth is," I said, "I promised to give them quilts to Maggie, for when she marries John Thomas."

She gasped like a bee had stung her.   65

"Maggie can't appreciate these quilts!" she said. "She'd probably be backward enough to put them to everyday use."

"I reckon she would," I said. "God knows I been saving 'em for long enough with nobody using 'em. I hope she will!" I didn't want to bring up how I had offered Dee (Wangero) a quilt when she went away to college. Then she had told me they were old-fashioned, out of style.

"But they're *priceless!*" she was saying now, furiously; for she has a temper. "Maggie would put them on the bed and in five years they'd be in rags. Less than that!"

"She can always make some more," I said. "Maggie knows how to quilt."

Dee (Wangero) looked at me with hatred. "You just will not understand. The   70
point is these quilts, *these* quilts!"

"Well," I said, stumped. "What would *you* do with them?"

"Hang them," she said. As if that was the only thing you *could* do with quilts.

Maggie by now was standing in the door. I could almost hear the sound her feet made as they scraped over each other.

"She can have them, Mama," she said, like somebody used to never winning any-thing, or having anything reserved for her. "I can 'member Grandma Dee without the quilts."

I looked at her hard. She had filled her bottom lip with checkerberry snuff and it   75
gave her face a kind of dopey, hangdog look. It was Grandma Dee and Big Dee who taught her how to quilt herself. She stood there with her scarred hands hidden in the folds of her skirt. She looked at her sister with something like fear but she wasn't mad at her. This was Maggie's portion. This was the way she knew God to work.

When I looked at her like that something hit me in the top of my head and ran down to the soles of my feet. Just like when I'm in church and the spirit of God touch-es me and I get happy and shout. I did something I never had done before: hugged Maggie to me, then dragged her on into the room, snatched the quilts out of Miss Wangero's hands and dumped them into Maggie's lap. Maggie just sat there on my bed with her mouth open.

"Take one or two of the others," I said to Dee.

But she turned without a word and went out to Hakim-a-barber.

"You just don't understand," she said, as Maggie and I came out to the car.

"What don't I understand?" I wanted to know.   80

"Your heritage," she said. And then she turned to Maggie, kissed her, and said, "You ought to try to make something of yourself, too, Maggie. It's really a new day for us. But from the way you and Mama still live you'd never know it."

She put on some sunglasses that hid everything above the tip of her nose and her chin.

Maggie smiled; maybe at the sunglasses. But a real smile, not scared. After we watched the car dust settle I asked Maggie to bring me a dip of snuff. And then the two of us sat there just enjoying, until it was time to go in the house and go to bed.

THE RECEPTIVE READER

1. What is the self-image of the mother? How does her sense of her real self contrast with her daydreams? ◇ How does her initial self-portrait as the *narrator* and central character point forward to what happens later in the story?

2. What is the contrasting history of the two siblings? How does one serve as a *foil* to the other? What is most significant in their earlier history?

3. What is the mother's view of Dee and her companion? How would you spell out the mother's attitude implied at various points in the story? What touches seem satirical and why? ◇ Is everything in the story seen from the mother's *point of view*?

4. How does the confrontation over the quilts bring things to a head? What do the quilts symbolize? How does the climactic ending resolve the central conflict in this story? How does it turn the tables on Dee's use of terms like *backward* and *heritage*?

5. How would you spell out in so many words the *theme* of this story? (How does the title hint at the central theme?)

6. What in the story helps especially to bring the theme to life for you and keep it from becoming an abstract idea?

THE PERSONAL RESPONSE

Do you identify with the narrator in this story? Is there another side to the story? Could you say something in defense of Dee?

THE CREATIVE DIMENSION

Write a passage in which one or the other of the daughters tells her side of the story. Or rewrite the ending the way you would have preferred the story to come out.

STEPHEN CRANE (1871–1900)

Stephen Crane is an outstanding early representative of **naturalism** in American fiction. Naturalist writers did not shirk the task of looking at nature in the raw or of confronting unembellished human nature. Like other writers in that tradition, Crane preferred not to preach or editorialize but to let the grim facts speak for themselves. He was born in Newark, New Jersey, as the fourteenth child in the home of a Methodist minister. After his college years at Lafayette and Syracuse, he scraped together a living as a free-lance journalist, and much of his fiction looks at harsh realities with the impartial honesty of the reporter. His first novel, *Maggie: A Girl of the Streets* (1893), took an un-compromising look at a subject then not considered a fit topic for polite con-versation. He became famous with *The Red Badge of Courage* (1895), a novel about the Civil War. Anticipating modern war novels, Crane went beyond the flag-waving and heroic oratory of stay-at-home patriots to probe the psycho-logical realities of war: the fear of death, the horror of mass destruction, the sense of solidarity with one's doomed comrades.

Crane had the strongly developed sense of irony that was to become the hallmark of much twentieth-century literature. His stories and poems highlight the sad and laughable contrast between our naive hopes or rosy daydreams and the world in which we actually live. Driven into exile by gossip about his irreg-ular personal life, enmeshed in what one editor has called "a malignant tangle of debts," he died of tuberculosis after publishing fourteen books in his short lifetime.

The following short story classic, which he called a tale "after the fact," is based on his personal experience as the survivor of the shipwreck of the steam-er *Commodore*. He had earlier written a factual account of the experience for the New York *Press*, published on January 7, 1887. What is the theme (or are the themes) of this story? What does it say about the relationship between human beings and nature? What does it say about male bonding? What does it say about the survival of the fittest—or, for that matter, about the survival of the unfit?

The Open Boat   1897

I

None of them knew the color of the sky. Their eyes glanced level, and were fas-tened upon the waves that swept toward them. These waves were of the hue of slate, save for the tops, which were of foaming white, and all of the men knew the colors of the sea. The horizon narrowed and widened, and dipped and rose, and at all times its edge was jagged with waves that seemed thrust up in points like rocks.

Many a man ought to have a bathtub larger than the boat which here rode upon the sea. These waves were most wrongfully and barbarously abrupt and tall, and each froth-top was a problem in small-boat navigation.

The cook squatted in the bottom, and looked with both eyes at the six inches of gunwale which separated him from the ocean. His sleeves were rolled over his fat fore-arms, and the two flaps of his unbuttoned vest dangled as he bent to bail out the boat. Often he said, "Gawd! that was a narrow clip." As he remarked it he invariably gazed eastward over the broken sea.

The oiler, steering with one of the two oars in the boat, sometimes raised himself suddenly to keep clear of water that swirled in over the stern. It was a thin little oar, and it seemed often ready to snap.

The correspondent, pulling at the other oar, watched the waves and wondered   5
why he was there.

The injured captain, lying in the bow, was at this time buried in that profound de-jection and indifference which comes, temporarily at least, to even the bravest and most enduring when, willy-nilly, the firm fails, the army loses, the ship goes down. The mind of the master of a vessel is rooted deep in the timbers of her, though he command for a day or a decade; and this captain had on him the stern impression of a scene in the greys of dawn of seven turned faces, and later a stump of a topmast with a white ball on it, that slashed to and fro at the waves, went low and lower, and down. Thereafter there was something strange in his voice. Although steady, it was deep with mourning, and of a quality beyond oration or tears.

"Keep 'er a little more south, Billie," said he.

"A little more south, sir," said the oiler in the stern.

A seat in his boat was not unlike a seat upon a bucking broncho, and by the same token a broncho is not much smaller. The craft pranced and reared and plunged like an animal. As each wave came, and she rose for it, she seemed like a horse making at a fence outrageously high. The manner of her scramble over these walls of water is a mystic thing, and, moreover, at the top of them were ordinarily these problems in white water, the foam racing down from the summit of each wave requiring a new leap, and a leap from the air. Then, after scornfully bumping a crest, she would slide and race and splash down a long incline, and arrive bobbing and nodding in front of the next menace.

A singular disadvantage of the sea lies in the fact that after successfully surmount-   10
ing one wave you discover that there is another behind it just as important and just as nervously anxious to do something effective in the way of swamping boats. In a ten-foot dinghy one can get an idea of the resources of the sea in the line of waves that is not probable to the average experience which is never at sea in a dinghy. As each slaty wall of water approached, it shut all else from the view of the men in the boat, and it was not difficult to imagine that this particular wave was the final outburst of the ocean, the last effort of the grim water. There was a terrible grace in the move of the waves, and they came in silence, save for the snarling of the crests.

In the wan light the faces of the men must have been grey. Their eyes must have glinted in strange ways as they gazed steadily astern. Viewed from a balcony, the whole thing would doubtless have been weirdly picturesque. But the men in the boat had no time to see it, and if they had had leisure, there were other things to occupy their minds. The sun swung steadily up the sky, and they knew it was broad day because the color of the sea changed from slate to emerald green streaked with amber lights, and the foam was like tumbling snow. The process of the breaking day was unknown to them. They were aware only of this effect upon the color of the waves that rolled toward them.

In disjointed sentences the cook and the correspondent argued as to the difference between a life-saving station and a house of refuge. The cook had said: "There's a house of refuge just north of the Mosquito Inlet Light, and as soon as they see us they'll come off in their boat and pick us up."

"As soon as who see us?" said the correspondent.

"The crew," said the cook.

"Houses of refuge don't have crews," said the correspondent. "As I understand   15
them, they are only places where clothes and grub are stored for the benefit of ship-wrecked people. They don't carry crews."

"Oh, yes, they do," said the cook.

"No, they don't," said the correspondent.

"Well, we're not there yet, anyhow," said the oiler, in the stern.

"Well," said the cook, "perhaps it's not a house of refuge that I'm thinking of as being near Mosquito Inlet Light; perhaps it's a life-saving station."

"We're not there yet," said the oiler in the stern.   20

II

As the boat bounced from the top of each wave the wind tore through the hair of the hatless men, and as the craft plopped her stern down again the spray slashed past them. The crest of each of these waves was a hill, from the top of which the men sur-veyed for a moment a broad tumultuous expanse, shining and wind-riven. It was proba-bly splendid, it was probably glorious, this play of the free sea, wild with lights of emerald and white and amber.

"Bully good thing it's an on-shore wind," said the cook. "If not, where would we be? Wouldn't have a show."

"That's right," said the correspondent.

The busy oiler nodded his assent.

Then the captain, in the bow, chuckled in a way that expressed humor, contempt,   25
tragedy, all in one. "Do you think we've got much of a show now, boys?" said he.

Whereupon the three were silent, save for a trifle of hemming and hawing. To ex-press any particular optimism at this time they felt to be childish and stupid, but they all doubtless possessed this sense of the situation in their minds. A young man thinks doggedly at such times. On the other hand, the ethics of their condition was decidedly against any open suggestion of hopelessness. So they were silent.

"Oh, well," said the captain, soothing his children, "we'll get ashore all right."

But there was that in his tone which made them think; so the oiler quoth, "Yes! if this wind holds."

The cook was bailing. "Yes! if we don't catch hell in the surf."

Canton-flannel gulls flew near and far. Sometimes they sat down on the sea, near   30
patches of brown seaweed that rolled over the waves with a movement like carpets on a line in a gale. The birds sat comfortably in groups, and they were envied by some in the dinghy, for the wrath of the sea was no more to them than it was to a covey of prairie chickens a thousand miles inland. Often they came very close and stared at the men with black bead-like eyes. At these times they were uncanny and sinister in their un-blinking scrutiny, and the men hooted angrily at them, telling them to be gone. One came, and evidently decided to alight on the top of the captain's head. The bird flew parallel to the boat and did not circle, but made short sidelong jumps in the air in chicken-fashion. His black eyes were wistfully fixed upon the captain's head. "Ugly brute," said the oiler to the bird. "You look as if you were made with a jackknife." The cook and the correspondent swore darkly at the creature. The captain naturally wished to knock it away with the end of the heavy painter, but he did not dare do it, because anything resembling an emphatic gesture would have capsized this freighted boat; and so, with his open hand, the captain gently and carefully waved the gull away. After it had been discouraged from the pursuit the captain breathed easier on account of his hair, and others breathed easier because the bird struck their minds at this time as being somehow gruesome and ominous.

In the meantime the oiler and the correspondent rowed. And also they rowed. They sat together in the same seat, and each rowed an oar. Then the oiler took both oars; then the correspondent took both oars; then the oiler; then the correspondent. They rowed and they rowed. The very ticklish part of the business was when the time came for the reclining one in the stern to take his turn at the oars. By the very last star of truth, it is easier to steal eggs from under a hen than it was to change seats in the dinghy. First the man in the stern slid his hand along the thwart and moved with care, as if he were of Sèvres. Then the man in the rowing-seat slid his hand along the other thwart. It was all done with the most extraordinary care. As the two sidled past each other, the whole party kept watchful eyes on the coming wave, and the captain cried: "Look out, now! Steady, there!"

The brown mats of seaweed that appeared from time to time were like islands, bits of earth. They were travelling, apparently, neither one way nor the other. They were, to all intents, stationary. They informed the men in the boat that it was making progress slowly toward the land.

The captain, rearing cautiously in the bow after the dinghy soared on a great swell, said that he had seen the lighthouse at Mosquito Inlet. Presently the cook remarked that he had seen it. The correspondent was at the oars then, and for some reason he too wished to look at the lighthouse; but his back was toward the far shore, and the waves were important, and for some time he could not seize an opportunity to turn his head. But at last there came a wave more gentle than the others, and when at the crest of it he swiftly scoured the western horizon.

"See it?" said the captain.

"No," said the correspondent, slowly; "I didn't see anything." 35

"Look again," said the captain. He pointed. "It's exactly in that direction."

At the top of another wave the correspondent did as he was bid, and this time his eyes chanced on a small, still thing on the edge of the swaying horizon. It was precisely like the point of a pin. It took an anxious eye to find a lighthouse so tiny.

"Think we'll make it, Captain?"

"If this wind holds and the boat don't swamp, we can't do much else," said the captain.

The little boat, lifted by each towering sea and splashed viciously by the crests, 40 made progress that in the absence of seaweed was not apparent to those in her. She seemed just a wee thing wallowing, miraculously top up, at the mercy of five oceans. Occasionally a great spread of water, like white flames, swarmed into her.

"Bail her, cook," said the captain, serenely.

"All right, Captain," said the cheerful cook.

III

It would be difficult to describe the subtle brotherhood of men that was here established on the seas. No one said that it was so. No one mentioned it. But it dwelt in the boat, and each man felt it warm him. They were a captain, an oiler, a cook, and a correspondent, and they were friends—friends in a more curiously iron-bound degree than may be common. The hurt captain, lying against the water-jar in the bow, spoke always in a low voice and calmly; but he could never command a more ready and swiftly obedient crew than the motley three of the dinghy. It was more than a mere recognition of what was best for the common safety. There was surely in it a quality that was personal and heart-felt. And after this devotion to the commander of the boat, there was this comradeship, that the correspondent, for instance, who had been taught to be cynical of men, knew even at the time was the best experience of his life. But no one said that it was so. No one mentioned it.

"I wish we had a sail," remarked the captain. "We might try my overcoat on the end of an oar, and give you two boys a chance to rest." So the cook and the correspondent held the mast and spread wide the overcoat; the oiler steered; and the little boat made good way with her new rig. Sometimes the oiler had to scull sharply to keep a sea from breaking into the boat, but otherwise sailing was a success.

Meanwhile the lighthouse had been growing slowly larger. It had now almost assumed color, and appeared like a little grey shadow on the sky. The man at the oars could not be prevented from turning his head rather often to try for a glimpse of this little grey shadow. 45

At last, from the top of each wave, the men in the tossing boat could see land. Even as the lighthouse was an upright shadow on the sky, this land seemed but a long black shadow on the sea. It certainly was thinner than paper. "We must be about opposite

New Smyrna," said the cook, who had coasted this shore often in schooners. "Captain, by the way, I believe they abandoned that life-saving station there about a year ago."

"Did they?" said the captain.

The wind slowly died away. The cook and the correspondent were not now obliged to slave in order to hold high the oar. But the waves continued their old impetuous swooping at the dinghy, and the little craft, no longer under way, struggled woundily over them. The oiler or the correspondent took the oars again.

Shipwrecks are apropos of nothing. If men could only train for them and have them occur when the men had reached pink condition, there would be less drowning at sea. Of the four in the dinghy none had slept any time worth mentioning for two days and two nights previous to embarking in the dinghy, and in the excitement of clambering about the deck of a foundering ship they had also forgotten to eat heartily.

For these reasons, and for others, neither the oiler nor the correspondent was fond of rowing at this time. The correspondent wondered ingenuously how in the name of all that was sane could there be people who thought it amusing to row a boat. It was not an amusement; it was a diabolical punishment, and even a genius of mental aberrations could never conclude that it was anything but a horror to the muscles and a crime against the back. He mentioned to the boat in general how the amusement of rowing struck him, and the weary-faced oiler smiled in full sympathy. Previously to the foundering, by the way, the oiler had worked a double watch in the engine-room of the ship.   50

"Take her easy now, boys," said the captain. "Don't spend yourselves. If we have to run a surf you'll need all your strength, because we'll sure have to swim for it. Take your time."

Slowly the land arose from the sea. From a black line it became a line of black and a line of white—trees and sand. Finally the captain said that he could make out a house on the shore. "That's the house of refuge, sure," said the cook. "They'll see us before long, and come out after us."

The distant lighthouse reared high. "The keeper ought to be able to make us out now, if he's looking through a glass," said the captain. "He'll notify the life-saving people."

"None of those other boats could have got ashore to give word of this wreck," said the oiler, in a low voice, "else the life-boat would be out hunting us."

Slowly and beautifully the land loomed out of the sea. The wind came again. It had veered from the north-east to the south-east. Finally a new sound struck the ears of the men in the boat. It was the low thunder of the surf on the shore. "We'll never be able to make the lighthouse now," said the captain. "Swing her head a little more north, Billie."   55

"A little more north, sir," said the oiler.

Whereupon the little boat turned her nose once more down the wind, and all but the oarsman watched the shore grow. Under the influence of this expansion doubt and direful apprehension were leaving the minds of the men. The management of the boat was still most absorbing, but it could not prevent a quiet cheerfulness. In an hour, perhaps, they would be ashore.

Their backbones had become thoroughly used to balancing in the boat, and they now rode this wild colt of a dinghy like circus men. The correspondent thought that he had been drenched to the skin, but happening to feel in the top pocket of his coat, he found therein eight cigars. Four of them were soaked with sea-water; four were perfectly scatheless. After a search, somebody produced three dry matches; and thereupon the four waifs rode impudently in their little boat and, with an assurance of an impending rescue shining in their eyes, puffed at the big cigars, and judged well and ill of all men. Everybody took a drink of water.

IV

"Cook," remarked the captain, "there don't seem to be any signs of life about your house of refuge."

"No," replied the cook. "Funny they don't see us!" 60

A broad stretch of lowly coast lay before the eyes of the men. It was of low dunes topped with dark vegetation. The roar of the surf was plain, and sometimes they could see the white lip of a wave as it spun up the beach. A tiny house was blocked out black upon the sky. Southward, the slim lighthouse lifted its little grey length.

Tide, wind, and waves were swinging the dinghy northward. "Funny they don't see us," said the men.

The surf's roar was here dulled, but its tone was nevertheless thunderous and mighty. As the boat swam over the great rollers the men sat listening to this roar. "We'll swamp sure," said everybody.

It is fair to say here that there was not a life-saving station within twenty miles in either direction; but the men did not know this fact, and in consequence they made dark and opprobrious remarks concerning the eyesight of the nation's life-savers. Four scowling men sat in the dinghy and surpassed records in the invention of epithets.

"Funny they don't see us." 65

The light-heartedness of a former time had completely faded. To their sharpened minds it was easy to conjure pictures of all kinds of incompetency and blindness and, indeed, cowardice. There was the shore of the populous land, and it was bitter and bitter to them that from it came no sign.

"Well," said the captain, ultimately, "I suppose we'll have to make a try for ourselves. If we stay out here too long, we'll none of us have strength left to swim after the boat swamps."

And so the oiler, who was at the oars, turned the boat straight for the shore. There was a sudden tightening of muscles. There was some thinking.

"If we don't all get ashore," said the captain—"if we don't all get ashore, I suppose you fellows know where to send news of my finish?"

They then briefly exchanged some addresses and admonitions. As for the reflections of the men, there was a great deal of rage in them. Perchance they might be formulated thus: "If I am going to be drowned—if I am going to be drowned—if I am going to be drowned, why, in the name of the seven mad gods who rule the sea, was I allowed to come thus far and contemplate sand and trees? Was I brought here merely to have my nose dragged away as I was about to nibble the sacred cheese of life? It is preposterous. If this old ninny-woman, Fate, cannot do better than this, she should be deprived of the management of men's fortunes. She is an old hen who knows not her intention. If she has decided to drown me, why did she not do it in the beginning and save me all this trouble? The whole affair is absurd.—But no; she cannot mean to drown me. She dare not drown me. She cannot drown me. Not after all this work." Afterward the man might have had an impulse to shake his fist at the clouds. "Just you drown me, now, and then hear what I call you!"

The billows that came at this time were more formidable. They seemed always just about to break and roll over the little boat in a turmoil of foam. There was a preparatory and long growl in the speech of them. No mind unused to the sea would have concluded that the dinghy could ascend these sheer heights in time. The shore was still afar. The oiler was a wily surfman. "Boys," he said swiftly, "she won't live three minutes more, and we're too far out to swim. Shall I take her to sea again, Captain?"

"Yes; go ahead!" said the captain. 70

This oiler, by a series of quick miracles and fast and steady oarsmanship, turned the boat in the middle of the surf and took her safely to sea again.

There was a considerable silence as the boat bumped over the furrowed sea to deeper water. Then somebody in gloom spoke: "Well, anyhow, they must have seen us from the shore by now."

The gulls went in slanting flight up the wind toward the grey, desolate east. A squall, marked by dingy clouds and clouds brick-red like smoke from a burning building, appeared from the southeast. 75

"What do you think of those life-saving people? Ain't they peaches?"

"Funny they haven't seen us."

"Maybe they think we're out here for sport! Maybe they think we're fishin'. Maybe they think we're damned fools."

It was a long afternoon. A changed tide tried to force them southward, but wind and wave said northward. Far ahead, where coast-line, sea, and sky formed their mighty angle, there were little dots which seemed to indicate a city on the shore.

"St. Augustine?" 80

The captain shook his head. "Too near Mosquito Inlet."

And the oiler rowed, and then the correspondent rowed; then the oiler rowed. It was a weary business. The human back can become the seat of more aches and pains than are registered in books for the composite anatomy of a regiment. It is a limited area, but it can become the theatre of innumerable muscular conflicts, tangles, wrenches, knots, and other comforts.

"Did you ever like to row, Billie?" asked the correspondent.

"No," said the oiler; "hang it!"

When one exchanged the rowing-seat for a place in the bottom of the boat, he suffered a bodily depression that caused him to be careless of everything save an obligation to wiggle one finger. There was cold sea-water swashing to and fro in the boat, and he lay in it. His head, pillowed on a thwart, was within an inch of the swirl of a wave-crest, and sometimes a particularly obstreperous sea came inboard and drenched him once more. But these matters did not annoy him. It is almost certain that if the boat had capsized he would have tumbled comfortably out upon the ocean as if he felt sure that it was a great soft mattress. 85

"Look! There's a man on the shore!"

"Where?"

"There! See 'im? See 'im?"

"Yes, sure! He's walking along."

"Now he's stopped. Look! He's facing us!" 90

"He's waving at us!"

"So he is! By thunder!"

"Ah, now we're all right! Now we're all right! There'll be a boat out here for us in half an hour."

"He's going on. He's running. He's going up to that house there."

The remote beach seemed lower than the sea, and it required a searching glance to discern the little black figure. The captain saw a floating stick, and they rowed to it. A bath towel was by some weird chance in the boat, and, tying this on the stick, the captain waved it. The oarsman did not dare turn his head, so he was obliged to ask questions. 95

"What's he doing now?"

"He's standing still again. He's looking, I think.—There he goes again—toward the house.—Now he's stopped again."

"Is he waving at us?"

"No, not now; he was, though."

"Look! There comes another man!"   100

"He's running."

"Look at him go, would you!"

"Why, he's on a bicycle. Now he's met the other man. They're both waving at us. Look!"

"There comes something up the beach."

"What the devil is that thing?"   105

"Why, it looks like a boat."

"Why, certainly, it's a boat."

"No; it's on wheels."

"Yes, so it is. Well, that must be the life-boat. They drag them along shore on a wagon."

"That's the life-boat, sure."   110

"No, by God, it's—it's an omnibus."

"I tell you it's a life-boat."

"It is not! It's an omnibus. I can see it plain. See? One of these big hotel omnibuses."

"By thunder, you're right. It's an omnibus, sure as fate. What do you suppose they are doing with an omnibus? Maybe they are going around collecting the life-crew, hey?"

"That's it, likely. Look! There's a fellow waving a little black flag. He's standing on   115
the steps of the omnibus. There come those other two fellows. Now they're all talking together. Look at the fellow with the flag. Maybe he ain't waving it!"

"That ain't a flag, is it? That's his coat. Why, certainly, that's his coat."

"So it is; it's his coat. He's taken it off and is waving it around his head. But would you look at him swing it!"

"Oh, say, there isn't any life-saving station there. That's just a winter-resort hotel omnibus that has brought over some of the boarders to see us drown."

"What's that idiot with the coat mean? What's he signalling, anyhow?"

"It looks as if he were trying to tell us to go north. There must be a life-saving sta-   120
tion up there."

"No; he thinks we're fishing. Just giving us a merry hand. See? Ah, there, Willie!"

"Well, I wish I could make something out of those signals. What do you suppose he means?"

"He don't mean anything; he's just playing."

"Well, if he'd just signal us to try the surf again, or to go to sea and wait, or go north, or go south, or go to hell, there would be some reason in it. But look at him! He just stands there and keeps his coat revolving like a wheel. The ass!"

"There come more people."   125

"Now there's quite a mob. Look! Isn't that a boat?"

"Where? Oh, I see where you mean. No, that's no boat."

"That fellow is still waving his coat."

"He must think we like to see him do that. Why don't he quit it? It don't mean anything."

"I don't know. I think he is trying to make us go north. It must be that there's a   130
life-saving station there somewhere."

"Say, he ain't tired yet. Look at 'im wave!"

"Wonder how long he can keep that up. He's been revolving his coat ever since he caught sight of us. He's an idiot. Why aren't they getting men to bring a boat out? A fishing-boat—one of those big yawls—could come out here all right. Why don't he do something?"

"Oh, it's all right now."

"They'll have a boat out here for us in less than no time, now that they've seen us."

A faint yellow tone came into the sky over the low land. The shadows on the sea   135
slowly deepened. The wind bore coldness with it, and the men began to shiver.

"Holy smoke!" said one, allowing his voice to express his impious mood, "if we keep on monkeying out here! If we've got to flounder out here all night!"

"Oh, we'll never have to stay here all night! Don't you worry. They've seen us now, and it won't be long before they'll come chasing out after us."

The shore grew dusky. The man waving a coat blended gradually into this gloom, and it swallowed in the same manner the omnibus and the group of people. The spray, when it dashed uproariously over the side, made the voyagers shrink and swear like men who were being branded.

"I'd like to catch the chump who waved the coat. I feel like socking him one, just for luck."

"Why? What did he do?"   140

"Oh, nothing, but then he seemed so damned cheerful."

In the meantime the oiler rowed, and then the correspondent rowed, and then the oiler rowed. Grey-faced and bowed forward, they mechanically, turn by turn, plied the leaden oars. The form of the lighthouse had vanished from the southern horizon, but finally a pale star appeared, just lifting from the sea. The streaked saffron in the west passed before the all-merging darkness, and the sea to the east was black. The land had vanished, and was expressed only by the low and drear thunder of the surf.

"If I am going to be drowned—if I am going to be drowned—if I am going to be drowned, why, in the name of the seven mad gods who rule the sea, was I allowed to come thus far and contemplate sand and trees? Was I brought here merely to have my nose dragged away as I was about to nibble the sacred cheese of life?"

The patient captain, drooped over the water-jar, was sometimes obliged to speak to the oarsman.

"Keep her head up! Keep her head up!"   145

"Keep her head up, sir." The voices were weary and low.

This was surely a quiet evening. All save the oarsman lay heavily and listlessly in the boat's bottom. As for him, his eyes were just capable of noting the tall black waves that swept forward in a most sinister silence, save for an occasional subdued growl of a crest.

The cook's head was on a thwart, and he looked without interest at the water under his nose. He was deep in other scenes. Finally he spoke. "Billie," he murmured, dreamfully, "what kind of pie do you like best?"

V

"Pie!" said the oiler and the correspondent, agitatedly. "Don't talk about those things, blast you!"

"Well," said the cook, "I was just thinking about ham sandwiches and—"   150

A night on the sea in an open boat is a long night. As darkness settled finally, the shine of the light, lifting from the sea in the south, changed to full gold. On the northern horizon a new light appeared, a small bluish gleam on the edge of the waters. These two lights were the furniture of the world. Otherwise there was nothing but waves.

Two men huddled in the stern, and distances were so magnificent in the dinghy that the rower was enabled to keep his feet partly warm by thrusting them under his companions. Their legs indeed extended far under the rowing-seat until they touched the feet of the captain forward. Sometimes, despite the efforts of the tired oarsman, a wave came piling into the boat, an icy wave of the night, and the chilling water soaked them anew. They would twist their bodies for a moment and groan, and sleep the dead sleep once more, while the water in the boat gurgled about them as the craft rocked.

The plan of the oiler and the correspondent was for one to row until he lost the ability, and then arouse the other from his sea-water couch in the bottom of the boat.

The oiler plied the oars until his head drooped forward and the overpowering sleep blinded him; and he rowed yet afterward. Then he touched a man in the bottom of the boat, and called his name. "Will you spell me for a little while?" he said, meekly.

"Sure, Billie," said the correspondent, awaking and dragging himself to a sitting 155
position. They exchanged places carefully, and the oiler, cuddling down in the sea-water at the cook's side, seemed to go to sleep instantly.

The particular violence of the sea had ceased. The waves came without snarling. The obligation of the man at the oars was to keep the boat headed so that the tilt of the rollers would not capsize her, and to preserve her from filling when the crests rushed past. The black waves were silent and hard to be seen in the darkness. Often one was al-most upon the boat before the oarsman was aware.

In a low voice the correspondent addressed the captain. He was not sure that the captain was awake, although this iron man seemed to be always awake. "Captain, shall I keep her making for that light north, sir?"

The same steady voice answered him. "Yes. Keep it about two points off the port bow."

The cook had tied a life-belt around himself in order to get even the warmth which this clumsy cork contrivance could donate, and he seemed almost stove-like when a rower, whose teeth invariably chattered wildly as soon as he ceased his labor, dropped down to sleep.

The correspondent, as he rowed, looked down at the two men sleeping underfoot. 160
The cook's arm was around the oiler's shoulders, and, with their fragmentary clothing and haggard faces, they were the babes of the sea—a grotesque rendering of the old babes in the wood.

Later he must have grown stupid at his work, for suddenly there was a growling of water, and a crest came with a roar and a swash into the boat, and it was a wonder that it did not set the cook afloat in his life-belt. The cook continued to sleep, but the oiler sat up, blinking his eyes and shaking with the new cold.

"Oh, I'm awful sorry, Billie," said the correspondent, contritely.

"That's all right, old boy," said the oiler, and lay down again and was asleep.

Presently it seemed that even the captain dozed, and the correspondent thought that he was the one man afloat on all the oceans. The wind had a voice as it came over the waves, and it was sadder than the end.

There was a long, loud swishing astern of the boat, and a gleaming trail of phos- 165
phorescence, like blue flame, was furrowed on the black waters. It might have been made by a monstrous knife.

Then there came a stillness, while the correspondent breathed with open mouth and looked at the sea.

Suddenly there was another swish and another long flash of bluish light, and this time it was alongside the boat, and might almost been reached with an oar. The corre-spondent saw an enormous fin speed like a shadow through the water, hurling the crys-talline spray and leaving the long glowing trail.

The correspondent looked over his shoulder at the captain. His face was hidden, and he seemed to be asleep. He looked at the babes of the sea. They certainly were asleep. So, being bereft of sympathy, he leaned a little way to one side and swore softly into the sea.

But the thing did not then leave the vicinity of the boat. Ahead or astern, on one side or the other, at intervals long or short, fled the long sparkling streak, and there was to be heard the *whirroo* of the dark fin. The speed and power of the thing was greatly to be admired. It cut the water like a gigantic and keen projectile.

The presence of this biding thing did not affect the man with the same horror that it would if he had been a picnicker. He simply looked at the sea dully and swore in an undertone. 170

Nevertheless, it is true that he did not wish to be alone with the thing. He wished one of his companions to awake by chance and keep him company with it. But the captain hung motionless over the water-jar, and the oiler and the cook in the bottom of the boat were plunged in slumber.

VI

"If I am going to be drowned—if I am going to be drowned—if I am going to be drowned, why, in the name of the seven mad gods who rule the sea, was I allowed to come thus far and contemplate sand and trees?"

During this dismal night, it may be remarked that a man would conclude that it was really the intention of the seven mad gods to drown him, despite the abominable injustice of it. For it was certainly an abominable injustice to drown a man who had worked so hard, so hard. The man felt it would be a crime most unnatural. Other people had drowned at sea since galleys swarmed with painted sails, but still—

When it occurs to a man that nature does not regard him as important, and that she feels she would not maim the universe by disposing of him, he at first wishes to throw bricks at the temple, and he hates deeply the fact that there are no bricks and no temples. Any visible expression of nature would surely be pelleted with his jeers.

Then, if there be no tangible thing to hoot, he feels, perhaps, the desire to confront a personification and indulge in pleas, bowed to one knee, and with hands supplicant, saying, "Yes, but I love myself." 175

A high cold star on a winter's night is the word he feels that she says to him. Thereafter he knows the pathos of his situation.

The men in the dinghy had not discussed these matters, but each had, no doubt, reflected upon them in silence and according to his mind. There was seldom any expression upon their faces save the general one of complete weariness. Speech was devoted to the business of the boat.

To chime the notes of his emotion, a verse mysteriously entered the correspondent's head. He had even forgotten that he had forgotten this verse, but it suddenly was in his mind.

> *A soldier of the Legion lay dying in Algiers;*
> *There was lack of woman's nursing, there was dearth of woman's tears;*
> *But a comrade stood beside him, and he took that comrade's hand,*
> *And he said, "I never more shall see my own, my native land."*

In his childhood the correspondent had been made acquainted with the fact that a soldier of the Legion lay dying in Algiers, but he had never regarded the fact as important. Myriads of his schoolfellows had informed him of the soldier's plight, but the dinning had naturally ended by making him perfectly indifferent. He had never considered it his affair that a soldier of the Legion lay dying in Algiers, nor had it appeared to him as a matter for sorrow. It was less to him than the breaking of a pencil's point.

Now, however, it quaintly came to him as a human, living thing. It was no longer 180 merely a picture of a few throes in the breast of a poet, meanwhile drinking tea and warming his feet at the grate; it was an actuality—stern, mournful, and fine.

The correspondent plainly saw the soldier. He lay on the sand with his feet out straight and still. While his pale left hand was upon his chest in an attempt to thwart the going of his life, the blood came between his fingers. In the far Algerian distance, a city of low square forms was set against a sky that was faint with the last sunset hues. The correspondent, plying the oars and dreaming of the slow and slower movements of the lips of the soldier, was moved by a profound and perfectly impersonal comprehension. He was sorry for the soldier of the Legion who lay dying in Algiers.

The thing which had followed the boat and waited had evidently grown bored at the delay. There was no longer to be heard the slash of the cutwater, and there was no longer the flame of the long trail. The light in the north still glimmered, but it was apparently no nearer to the boat. Sometimes the boom of the surf rang in the correspondent's ears, and he turned the craft seaward then and rowed harder. Southward, some one had evidently built a watch-fire on the beach. It was too low and too far to be seen, but it made a shimmering, roseate reflection upon the bluff in back of it, and this could be discerned from the boat. The wind came stronger, and sometimes a wave suddenly raged out like a mountain cat, and there was to be seen the sheen and sparkle of a broken crest.

The captain, in the bow, moved on his water-jar and sat erect. "Pretty long night," he observed to the correspondent. He looked at the shore. "Those life-saving people take their time."

"Did you see that shark playing around?"

"Yes, I saw him. He was a big fellow, all right."   185

"Wish I had known you were awake."

Later the correspondent spoke into the bottom of the boat. "Billie!" There was a slow and gradual disentanglement. "Billie, will you spell me?"

"Sure," said the oiler.

As soon as the correspondent touched the cold, comfortable sea-water in the bottom of the boat and had huddled close to the cook's life-belt he was deep in sleep, despite the fact that his teeth played all the popular airs. This sleep was so good to him that it was but a moment before he heard a voice call his name in a tone that demonstrated the last stages of exhaustion. "Will you spell me?"

"Sure, Billie."   190

The light in the north had mysteriously vanished, but the correspondent took his course from the wide-awake captain.

Later in the night they took the boat farther out to sea, and the captain directed the cook to take one oar at the stern and keep the boat facing the seas. He was to call out if he should hear the thunder of the surf. This plan enabled the oiler and the correspondent to get respite together. "We'll give those boys a chance to get into shape again," said the captain. They curled down and, after a few preliminary chatterings and trembles, slept once more the dead sleep. Neither knew they had bequeathed to the cook the company of another shark, or perhaps the same shark.

As the boat caroused on the waves, spray occasionally bumped over the side and gave them a fresh soaking, but this had no power to break their repose. The ominous slash of the wind and the water affected them as it would have affected mummies.

"Boys," said the cook, with the notes of every reluctance in his voice, "she's drifted in pretty close. I guess one of you had better take her to sea again." The correspondent, aroused, heard the crash of the toppled crests.

As he was rowing, the captain gave him some whisky-and-water, and this steadied   195
the chills out of him. "If I ever get ashore and anybody shows me even a photograph of
an oar—"

At last there was a short conversation.

"Billie!—Billie, will you spell me?"

"Sure," said the oiler.

VII

When the correspondent again opened his eyes, the sea and the sky were each of
the grey hue of the dawning. Later, carmine and gold was painted upon the waters.
The morning appeared finally, in its splendor, with a sky of pure blue, and the sunlight
flamed on the tips of the waves.

On the distant dunes were set many little black cottages, and a tall white windmill   200
reared above them. No man, nor dog, nor bicycle appeared on the beach. The cottages
might have formed a deserted village.

The voyagers scanned the shore. A conference was held in the boat. "Well," said
the captain, "if no help is coming, we might better try a run through the surf right
away. If we stay out here much longer we will be too weak to do anything for ourselves
at all." The others silently acquiesced in this reasoning. The boat was headed for the
beach. The correspondent wondered if none ever ascended the tall wind-tower, and if
then they never looked seaward. This tower was a giant, standing with its back to the
plight of the ants. It represented in a degree, to the correspondent, the serenity of nature amid the struggles of the individual—nature in the wind, and nature in the vision
of men. She did not seem cruel to him then, nor beneficent, nor treacherous, nor wise.
But she was indifferent, flatly indifferent. It is, perhaps, plausible that a man in this situation, impressed with the unconcern of the universe, should see the innumerable flaws
of his life, and have them taste wickedly in his mind, and wish for another chance. A
distinction between right and wrong seems absurdly clear to him, then, in this new ignorance of the grave-edge, and he understands that if he were given another opportunity he would mend his conduct and his words, and be better and brighter during an
introduction or at a tea.

"Now, boys," said the captain, "she is going to swamp sure. All we can do is to
work her in as far as possible, and then when she swamps, pile out and scramble for the
beach. Keep cool now, and don't jump until she swamps sure."

The oiler took the oars. Over his shoulders he scanned the surf. "Captain," he said,
"I think I'd better bring her about and keep her head-on to the seas and back her in."

"All right, Billie," said the captain. "Back her in." The oiler swung the boat then,
and, seated in the stern, the cook and the correspondent were obliged to look over
their shoulders to contemplate the lonely and indifferent shore.

The monstrous inshore rollers heaved the boat high until the men were again en-   205
abled to see the white sheets of water scudding up the slanted beach. "We won't get in
very close," said the captain. Each time a man could wrest his attention from the
rollers, he turned his glance toward the shore, and in the expression of the eyes during
this contemplation there was a singular quality. The correspondent, observing the
others, knew that they were not afraid, but the full meaning of their glances were
shrouded.

As for himself, he was too tired to grapple fundamentally with the fact. He tried to
coerce his mind into thinking of it, but the mind was dominated at this time by the
muscles, and the muscles said they did not care. It merely occurred to him that if he
should drown it would be a shame.

There were no hurried words, no pallor, no plain agitation. The men simply looked at the shore. "Now, remember to get well clear of the boat when you jump," said the captain.

Seaward the crest of a roller suddenly fell with a thunderous crash, and the long white comber came roaring down upon the boat.

"Steady now," said the captain. The men were silent. They turned their eyes from the shore to the comber and waited. The boat slid up the incline, leaped at the furious top, bounced over it, and swung down the long back of the wave. Some water had been shipped, and the cook bailed it out.

But the next crest crashed also. The tumbling, boiling flood of white water caught   210
the boat and whirled it almost perpendicular. Water swarmed in from all sides. The correspondent had his hands on the gunwale at this time, and when the water entered at that place he swiftly withdrew his fingers, as if he objected to wetting them.

The little boat, drunken with this weight of water, reeled and snuggled deeper into the sea.

"Bail her out, cook! Bail her out!" said the captain.

"All right, Captain," said the cook.

"Now, boys, the next one will do for us sure," said the oiler. "Mind to jump clear of the boat."

The third wave moved forward, huge, furious, implacable. It fairly swallowed the   215
dinghy, and almost simultaneously the men tumbled into the sea. A piece of life-belt had lain in the bottom of the boat, and as the correspondent went overboard he held this to his chest with his left hand.

The January water was icy, and he reflected immediately that it was colder than he had expected to find it off the coast of Florida. This appeared to his dazed mind as a fact important enough to be noted at the time. The coldness of the water was sad; it was tragic. This fact was somehow mixed and confused with his opinion of his own situation, so that it seemed almost a proper reason for tears. The water was cold.

When he came to the surface he was conscious of little but the noisy water. Afterward he saw his companions in the sea. The oiler was ahead in the race. He was swimming strongly and rapidly. Off to the correspondent's left, the cook's great white and corked back bulged out of the water; and in the rear the captain was hanging with his one good hand to the keel of the overturned dinghy.

There is a certain immovable quality to a shore, and the correspondent wondered at it amid the confusion of the sea.

It seemed also very attractive; but the correspondent knew that it was a long journey, and he paddled leisurely. The piece of life-preserver lay under him, and sometimes he whirled down the incline of a wave as if he were on a hand-sled.

But finally he arrived at a place in the sea where travel was beset with difficulty. He   220
did not pause swimming to inquire what manner of current had caught him, but there his progress ceased. The shore was set before him like a bit of scenery on a stage, and he looked at it and understood with his eyes each detail of it.

As the cook passed, much farther to the left, the captain was calling to him, "Turn over on your back, cook! Turn over on your back and use the oar."

"All right, sir." The cook turned on his back, and, paddling with an oar, went ahead as if he were a canoe.

Presently the boat also passed to the left of the correspondent, with the captain clinging with one hand to the keel. He would have appeared like a man raising himself to look over a board fence if it were not for the extraordinary gymnastics of the boat. The correspondent marvelled that the captain could still hold to it.

They passed on nearer to shore—the oiler, the cook, the captain—and following them went the water-jar, bouncing gaily over the seas.

The correspondent remained in the grip of this strange new enemy—a current. 225 The shore, with its white slope of sand and its green bluff topped with little silent cottages, was spread like a picture before him. It was very near to him then, but he was impressed as one who, in a gallery, looks at a scene from Brittany or Algiers.

He thought: "I am going to drown? Can it be possible? Can it be possible? Can it be possible?" Perhaps an individual must consider his own death to be the final phenomenon of nature.

But later a wave perhaps whirled him out of this small deadly current, for he found suddenly that he could again make progress toward the shore. Later still he was aware that the captain, clinging with one hand to the keel of the dinghy, had his face turned away from the shore and toward him, and was calling his name. "Come to the boat! Come to the boat!"

In his struggle to reach the captain and the boat, he reflected that when one gets properly wearied drowning must really be a comfortable arrangement—a cessation of hostilities accompanied by a large degree of relief; and he was glad of it, for the main thing in his mind for some moments had been horror of the temporary agony. He did not wish to be hurt.

Presently he saw a man running along the shore. He was undressing with most remarkable speed. Coat, trousers, shirt, everything flew magically off him.

"Come to the boat!" called the captain. 230

"All right, Captain." As the correspondent paddled, he saw the captain let himself down to bottom and leave the boat. Then the correspondent performed his one little marvel of the voyage. A large wave caught him and flung him with ease and supreme speed completely over the boat and far beyond it. It struck him even then as an event in gymnastics and a true miracle of the sea. An overturned boat in the surf is not a plaything to a swimming man.

The correspondent arrived in water that reached only to his waist, but his condition did not enable him to stand for more than a moment. Each wave knocked him into a heap, and the undertow pulled at him.

Then he saw the man who had been running and undressing, and undressing and running, come bounding into the water. He dragged ashore the cook, and then waded toward the captain; but the captain waved him away and sent him to the correspondent. He was naked—naked as a tree in winter; but a halo was about his head, and he shone like a saint. He gave a strong pull, and a long drag, and a bully heave at the correspondent's hand. The correspondent, schooled in the minor formulae, said "Thanks, old man." But suddenly the man cried, "What's that?" He pointed a swift finger. The correspondent said, "Go."

In the shallows, face downward, lay the oiler. His forehead touched sand that was periodically, between each wave, clear of the sea.

The correspondent did not know all that transpired afterward. When he achieved 235 safe ground he fell, striking the sand with each particular part of his body. It was as if he had dropped from a roof, but the thud was grateful to him.

It seemed that instantly the beach was populated with men with blankets, clothes, and flasks, and women with coffee-pots and all the remedies sacred to their minds. The welcome of the land to the men from the sea was warm and generous; but a still and dripping shape was carried slowly up the beach; and the land's welcome for it could only be the different and sinister hospitality of the grave.

When it came night, the white waves paced to and fro in the moonlight, and the wind brought the sound of the great sea's voice to the men on the shore, and they felt that they could then be interpreters.

THE RECEPTIVE READER

1. In the naturalistic manner, Crane traces in patient *detail* the physical dimension of the men's ordeal. How does he make the grueling experience real for the reader? What are striking details? What are recurrent notes, struck again and again?

2. The *dialogue* of the men in the boat may at first seem trivial or inane (like many other conversations). Does it nevertheless circle back to major issues or concerns? What is the subject matter of these conversations? What is their tone?

3. When do you first conclude that there is something representative and symbolic about the men's experience? What *symbols* do you recognize? What do you think might be the symbolic meaning of the sea? of the boat? of the seabirds? of the shark? of the unmanned life-saving station? of the lighthouse? of the tourists on the beach?

4. How much commentary is there by the *intruding author*? What does Crane have to say about the captain of the ship? about the relationship developing among the men in the boat?

5. Much of the story centers on the men's reactions to their fate. Are there different *stages*? Do individuals react differently?

6. How did you expect the story to *end*? Does the ending seem unexpected? Does it make you think?

7. What is the *theme* of the story? What does the story as a whole say about human beings and nature? about male bonding? about survival? How are these three topics related in the story as a whole?

8. What are striking examples of *irony* in the story—of the sad and comical discrepancy between what should be and what is? What are some striking examples of the author's ironic tone?

THE PERSONAL RESPONSE

Much literature through the centuries has celebrated the beauty of nature. What role does the beauty of nature play in this story? What is your own personal view of the relationship between nature and humankind? How is it different from the view that seems to be dominant in this story?

NATHANIEL HAWTHORNE   (1804–1864)

A dreamer may dwell so long among fantasies that the things without him will seem as real as those within.
NATHANIEL HAWTHORNE

The mere doubt of the existence of good and the thought that other human beings are evil can become such a corrosive force that it can eat out the life of the heart.
STUDENT PAPER

Nathaniel Hawthorne was born in Salem in Massachusetts and lived there for many years at his mother's house after finishing college. One of his ancestors had been a member of the court that sentenced the witches at the Salem witch trials in 1692. As a student and at first little-read writer, Hawthorne immersed himself in the history of colonial New England. When he married after a brief stint at a socialistic commune (Brook Farm), he settled at Concord, in the heart of historical New England.

Until Hawthorne went abroad to serve as an American consul in Liverpool in England, he spent most of his life in a setting where Puritan ministers like Cotton Mather and Jonathan Edwards had preached the depravity of mankind, the ever-powerful temptation of sin, the fear and trembling of sinners in the hands of an angry God, and the ever-lurking presence of the devil. Having left England to escape persecution as dissenters from the established Anglican church, Hawthorne's Puritanical ancestors set up a religious commonwealth where prayer and attendance at church services were rigidly enforced and where Quakers and other independent spirits were persecuted in turn.

Much of Hawthorne's fiction made his readers rethink and reexamine their assumptions about the Puritan past. His novel *The Scarlet Letter* (1850) has left readers around the world with unforgettable images of Hester Prynne, wearing the scarlet A branding her as an adulteress; her child Pearl at play in the forest; and the Puritan minister Dimmesdale, who had fathered the child, in the spiritual agonies of guilt. (As feminist critics have pointed out, Hester Prynne was for a long time the only central female character in a tradition of American fiction whose protagonists were more likely to be scouts, whaling captains, or runaway boys.)

The following much-discussed story is set in Puritan New England at the time of King William III, who ruled in England from 1689 to 1702. Salem Village, established only forty years before, was on the edge of the wilderness, with heathen natives in the forests. (The King Philip mentioned in the story was Metacomet, leader of the last organized Indian resistance in southern New England.) The people in the story, too humble to be called gentlemen and ladies, are called Goodman Brown and Goody (short for Goodwife) Cloyse or Goody Cory. (These women were among the victims of the Salem witchhunt that took the lives of twenty men and women.) Much of the learning of the Puritan divines had been concerned with witchcraft, and especially with the devil's power to create delusions and apparitions. At a Witches' Sabbath, according to the lore of the times, the devil himself would often preside at rituals that were a blasphemous perversion of the rites of the church.

Young Goodman Brown   1835

Young Goodman Brown came forth at sunset into the street at Salem village; but put his head back, after crossing the threshold, to exchange a parting kiss with his young wife. And Faith, as the wife was aptly named, thrust her own pretty head into the street, letting the wind play with the pink ribbons of her cap while she called to Goodman Brown.

"Dearest heart," whispered she, softly and rather sadly, when her lips were close to his ear, "prithee put off your journey until sunrise and sleep in your own bed tonight. A lone woman is troubled with such dreams and such thoughts that she's afeard of herself sometimes. Pray tarry with me this night, dear husband, of all nights in the year."

"My love and my Faith," replied Goodman Brown, "of all nights in the year, this one night must I tarry away from thee. My journey, as thou callest it, forth and back again, must needs be done 'twixt now and sunrise. What, my sweet, pretty wife, dost thou doubt me already, and we but three months married?"

"Then God bless you!" said Faith, with the pink ribbons; "and may you find all well when you come back."

"Amen!" cried Goodman Brown. "Say thy prayers, dear Faith, and go to bed at   5
dusk, and no harm will come to thee."

So they parted; and the young man pursued his way until, being about to turn the corner by the meeting-house, he looked back and saw the head of Faith still peeping after him with a melancholy air, in spite of her pink ribbons.

"Poor little Faith!" thought he, for his heart smote him. "What a wretch am I to leave her on such an errand! She talks of dreams, too. Methought as she spoke there was trouble in her face, as if a dream had warned her what work is to be done tonight. But no, no; 'twould kill her to think it. Well, she's a blessed angel on earth; and after this one night I'll cling to her skirts and follow her to heaven."

With this excellent resolve for the future, Goodman Brown felt himself justified in making more haste on his present evil purpose. He had taken a dreary road, darkened by all the gloomiest trees of the forest, which barely stood aside to let the narrow path creep through, and closed immediately behind. It was all as lonely as could be; and there is this peculiarity in such a solitude, that the traveller knows not who may be concealed by the innumerable trunks and the thick boughs overhead; so that with lonely footsteps he may yet be passing through an unseen multitude.

"There may be a devilish Indian behind every tree," said Goodman Brown to himself; and he glanced fearfully behind him as he added, "What if the devil himself should be at my very elbow!"

His head being turned back, he passed a crook of the road, and, looking forward   10
again, beheld the figure of a man, in grave and decent attire, seated at the foot of an old tree. He arose at Goodman Brown's approach and walked onward side by side with him.

"You are late, Goodman Brown," said he. "The clock of the Old South was striking as I came through Boston, and that is full fifteen minutes agone."

"Faith kept me back a while," replied the young man, with a tremor in his voice, caused by the sudden appearance of his companion, though not wholly unexpected.

It was now deep dusk in the forest, and deepest in that part of it where these two were journeying. As nearly as could be discerned, the second traveller was about fifty years old, apparently in the same rank of life as Goodman Brown, and bearing a considerable resemblance to him, though perhaps more in expression than features. Still they might have been taken for father and son. And yet, though the elder person was as simply clad as the younger, and as simple in manner too, he had an indescribable air of one who knew the world, and who would not have felt abashed at the governor's dinner table or in King William's court, were it possible that his affairs should call him thither. But the only thing about him that could be fixed upon as remarkable was his staff, which bore the likeness of a great black snake, so curiously wrought that it might almost be seen to twist and wriggle itself like a living serpent. This, of course, must have been an ocular deception, assisted by the uncertain light.

"Come, Goodman Brown," cried his fellow-traveller, "this is a dull place for the beginning of a journey. Take my staff, if you are so soon weary."

"Friend," said the other, exchanging his slow pace for a full stop, "having kept covenant by meeting thee here, it is my purpose now to return whence I came. I have scruples touching the matter thou wot'st of."

"Sayest thou so?" replied he of the serpent, smiling apart. "Let us walk on, nevertheless, reasoning as we go; and if I convince thee not thou shalt turn back. We are but a little way in the forest yet."

"Too far! too far!" exclaimed the goodman, unconsciously resuming his walk. "My father never went into the woods on such an errand, nor his father before him. We have been a race of honest men and good Christians since the days of the martyrs; and shall I be the first of the name of Brown that ever took this path and kept—"

"Such company, thou wouldst say," observed the elder person, interpreting his pause. "Well said, Goodman Brown! I have been as well acquainted with your family as with ever a one among the Puritans; and that's no trifle to say. I helped your grandfather, the constable, when he lashed the Quaker woman so smartly through the streets of Salem; and it was I that brought your father a pitch-pine knot, kindled at my own hearth, to set fire to an Indian village, in King Philip's war. They were my good friends, both; and many a pleasant walk have we had along this path, and returned merrily after midnight. I would fain be friends with you for their sake."

"If it be as thou sayest," replied Goodman Brown, "I marvel they never spoke of these matters; or, verily, I marvel not, seeing that the least rumor of the sort would have driven them from New England. We are a people of prayer, and good works to boot, and abide no such wickedness."

"Wickedness or not," said the traveller with the twisted staff, "I have a very general acquaintance here in New England. The deacons of many a church have drunk the communion wine with me; the selectmen of divers towns make me their chairman; and a majority of the Great and General Court are firm supporters of my interest. The governor and I, too—But these are state secrets."

"Can this be so?" cried Goodman Brown, with a stare of amazement at his undisturbed companion. "Howbeit, I have nothing to do with the governor and council; they have their own ways, and are no rule for a simple husbandman like me. But, were I to go on with thee, how should I meet the eye of that good old man, our minister, at Salem village? Oh, his voice would make me tremble both Sabbath day and lecture day."

Thus far the elder traveller had listened with due gravity; but now burst into a fit of irrepressible mirth, shaking himself so violently that his snake-like staff actually seemed to wriggle in sympathy.

"Ha! ha! ha!" shouted he again and again; then composing himself, "Well, go on, Goodman Brown, go on; but, prithee, don't kill me with laughing."

"Well, then, to end the matter at once," said Goodman Brown, considerably nettled, "there is my wife, Faith. It would break her dear little heart; and I'd rather break my own."

"Nay, if that be the case," answered the other, "e'en go thy ways, Goodman Brown. I would not for twenty old women like the one hobbling before us that Faith should come to any harm."

As he spoke he pointed his staff at a female figure on the path, in whom Goodman Brown recognized a very pious and exemplary dame, who had taught him his catechism in youth, and was still his moral and spiritual adviser, jointly with the minister and Deacon Gookin.

"A marvel, truly, that Goody Cloyse should be so far in the wilderness at nightfall," said he. "But with your leave, friend, I shall take a cut through the woods until we have left this Christian woman behind. Being a stranger to you, she might ask whom I was consorting with and whither I was going."

"Be it so," said his fellow-traveller. "Betake you to the woods, and let me keep the path."

Accordingly the young man turned aside, but took care to watch his companion, who advanced softly along the road until he had come within a staff's length of the old dame. She, meanwhile, was making the best of her way, with singular speed for so aged a woman, and mumbling some indistinct words—a prayer, doubtless—as she went. The traveller put forth his staff and touched her withered neck with what seemed the serpent's tail.

"The devil!" screamed the pious old lady.   30

"Then Goody Cloyse knows her old friend?" observed the traveller, confronting her and leaning on his writhing stick.

"Ah, forsooth, and is it your worship indeed?" cried the good dame. "Yea, truly it is, and in the very image of my old gossip, Goodman Brown, the grandfather of the silly fellow that now is. But—would your worship believe it?—my broomstick hath strangely disappeared, stolen, as I suspect, by that unhanged witch, Goody Cory, and that, too, when I was all anointed with the juice of smallage, and cinquefoil, and wolf's bane—"

"Mingled with fine wheat and the fat of a new-born babe," said the shape of old Goodman Brown.

"Ah, your worship knows the recipe," cried the old lady, cackling aloud. "So, as I was saying, being all ready for the meeting, and no horse to ride on, I made up my mind to foot it; for they tell me there is a nice young man to be taken into communion tonight. But now your good worship will lend me your arm, and we shall be there in a twinkling."

"That can hardly be," answered her friend. "I may not spare you my arm, Goody   35
Cloyse; but here is my staff, if you will."

So saying, he threw it down at her feet, where, perhaps, it assumed life, being one of the rods which its owner had formerly lent to the Egyptian magi. Of this fact, however, Goodman Brown could not take cognizance. He had cast up his eyes in astonishment, and, looking down again, beheld neither Goody Cloyse nor the serpentine staff, but his fellow-traveller alone, who waited for him as calmly as if nothing had happened.

"That old woman taught me my catechism," said the young man; and there was a world of meaning in this simple comment.

They continued to walk onward, while the elder traveller exhorted his companion to make good speed and persevere in the path, discoursing so aptly that his arguments seemed rather to spring up in the bosom of his auditor than to be suggested by himself. As they went, he plucked a branch of maple to serve for a walking stick, and began to strip it of the twigs and little boughs, which were wet with evening dew. The moment his fingers touched them they became strangely withered and dried up as with a week's sunshine. Thus the pair proceeded, at a good free pace, until suddenly, in a gloomy hollow of the road, Goodman Brown sat himself down on the stump of a tree and refused to go any farther.

"Friend," said he, stubbornly, "my mind is made up. Not another step will I budge on this errand. What if a wretched old woman do choose to go to the devil when I thought she was going to heaven: is that any reason why I should quit my dear Faith and go after her?"

"You will think better of this by and by," said his acquaintance, composedly. "Sit   40
here and rest yourself a while; and when you feel like moving again, there is my staff to help you along."

Without more words, he threw his companion the maple stick, and was as speedily out of sight as if he had vanished into the deepening gloom. The young man sat a few moments by the roadside, applauding himself greatly, and thinking with how clear a conscience he should meet the minister in his morning walk, nor shrink from the eye of good old Deacon Gookin. And what calm sleep would be his that very night, which was to have been spent so wickedly, but so purely and sweetly now, in the arms of Faith! Amidst these pleasant and praiseworthy meditations, Goodman Brown heard the tramp of horses along the road, and deemed it advisable to conceal himself within the verge of the forest, conscious of the guilty purpose that had brought him thither, though now so happily turned from it.

On came the hoof tramps and the voices of the riders, two grave old voices, conversing soberly as they drew near. These mingled sounds appeared to pass along the road, within a few yards of the young man's hiding-place; but, owing doubtless to the depth of the gloom at that particular spot, neither the travellers nor their steeds were visible. Though their figures brushed the small boughs by the wayside, it could not be seen that they intercepted, even for a moment, the faint gleam from the strip of bright sky athwart which they must have passed. Goodman Brown alternately crouched and stood on tiptoe, pulling aside the branches and thrusting forth his head as far as he durst without discerning so much as a shadow. It vexed him the more, because he could have sworn, were such a thing possible, that he recognized the voices of the minister and Deacon Gookin, jogging along quietly, as they were wont to do, when bound to some ordination or ecclesiastical council. While yet within hearing, one of the riders stopped to pluck a switch.

"Of the two, reverend sir," said the voice like the deacon's, "I had rather miss an ordination dinner than tonight's meeting. They tell me that some of our community are to be here from Falmouth and beyond, and others from Connecticut and Rhode Island, besides several of the Indian powwows, who, after their fashion, know almost as much deviltry as the best of us. Moreover, there is a goodly young woman to be taken into communion."

"Mighty well, Deacon Gookin!" replied the solemn old tones of the minister. "Spur up, or we shall be late. Nothing can be done, you know, until I get on the ground."

The hoofs clattered again; and the voices, talking so strangely in the empty air, 45 passed on through the forest, where no church had ever been gathered or solitary Christian prayed. Whither, then, could these holy men be journeying so deep into the heathen wilderness? Young Goodman Brown caught hold of a tree for support, being ready to sink down on the ground, faint and overburdened with the heavy sickness of his heart. He looked up to the sky, doubting whether there really was a heaven above him. Yet there was the blue arch, and the stars brightening in it.

"With heaven above and Faith below, I will yet stand firm against the devil!" cried Goodman Brown.

While he still gazed upward into the deep arch of the firmament and had lifted his hands to pray, a cloud, though no wind was stirring, hurried across the zenith and hid the brightening stars. The blue sky was still visible, except directly overhead, where this black mass of cloud was sweeping swiftly northward. Aloft in the air, as if from the depths of the cloud, came a confused and doubtful sound of voices. Once the listener fancied that he could distinguish the accents of townspeople of his own, men, and women, both pious and ungodly, many of whom he had met at the communion table, and had seen others rioting at the tavern. The next moment, so indistinct were the sounds, he doubted whether he had heard aught but the murmur of the old forest, whispering without a wind. Then came a stronger swell of those familiar tones, heard daily in the sunshine at Salem village, but never until now from a cloud of night. There was one voice, of a young woman, uttering lamentations, yet with an uncertain sorrow, and entreating for some favor, which, perhaps, it would grieve her to obtain; and all the unseen multitude, both saints and sinners, seemed to encourage her onward.

"Faith!" shouted Goodman Brown, in a voice of agony and desperation; and the echoes of the forest mocked him, crying, "Faith! Faith!" as if bewildered wretches were seeking her all through the wilderness.

The cry of grief, rage, and terror was yet piercing the night, when the unhappy husband held his breath for a response. There was a scream, drowned immediately in a louder murmur of voices, fading into far-off laughter, as the dark cloud swept away, leaving the clear and silent sky above Goodman Brown. But something fluttered lightly down through the air and caught on the branch of a tree. The young man seized it, and beheld a pink ribbon.

"My Faith is gone!" cried he, after one stupefied moment. "There is no good on earth; and sin is but a name. Come, devil; for to thee is this world given."

And, maddened with despair, so that he laughed loud and long, did Goodman Brown grasp his staff and set forth again, at such a rate that he seemed to fly along the forest path rather than to walk or run. The road grew wilder and drearier and more faintly traced, and vanished at length, leaving him in the heart of the dark wilderness, still rushing onward with the instinct that guides mortal man to evil. The whole forest was peopled with frightful sounds—the creaking of the trees, the howling of wild beasts, and the yell of Indians; while sometimes the wind tolled like a distant church bell, and sometimes gave a broad roar around the traveller, as if all Nature were laughing him to scorn. But he was himself the chief horror of the scene, and shrank not from its other horrors.

"Ha! ha! ha!" roared Goodman Brown when the wind laughed at him. "Let us hear which will laugh loudest. Think not to frighten me with your deviltry. Come witch, come wizard, come Indian powwow, come devil himself, and here comes Goodman Brown. You may as well fear him as he fear you."

In truth, all through the haunted forest there could be nothing more frightful than the figure of Goodman Brown. On he flew among the black pines, brandishing his staff with frenzied gestures, now giving vent to an inspiration of horrid blasphemy, and now shouting forth such laughter as set all the echoes of the forest laughing like demons around him. The fiend in his own shape is less hideous than when he rages in the breast of man. Thus sped the demoniac on his course, until, quivering among the trees, he saw a red light before him, as when the felled trunks and branches of a clearing have been set on fire, and throw up their lurid blaze against the sky, at the hour of midnight. He paused, in a lull of the tempest that had driven him onward, and heard the swell of what seemed a hymn, rolling solemnly from a distance with the weight of many voices. He knew the tune; it was a familiar one in the choir of the village meeting-house. The verse died heavily away, and was lengthened by a chorus, not of human voices, but of all the sounds of the benighted wilderness pealing in awful harmony together. Goodman Brown cried out, and his cry was lost to his own ear by its unison with the cry of the desert.

In the interval of silence he stole forward until the light glared full upon his eyes. At one extremity of an open space, hemmed in by the dark wall of the forest, arose a rock, bearing some rude, natural resemblance either to an altar or a pulpit, and surrounded by four blazing pines, their tops aflame, their stems untouched, like candles at an evening meeting. The mass of foliage that had overgrown the summit of the rock was all on fire, blazing high into the night and fitfully illuminating the whole field. Each pendent twig and leafy festoon was in a blaze. As the red light arose and fell, a numerous congregation alternately shone forth, then disappeared in shadow, and again grew, as it were, out of the darkness, peopling the heart of the solitary woods at once.

"A grave and dark-clad company," quoth Goodman Brown.   55

In truth they were such. Among them, quivering to and fro between gloom and splendor, appeared faces that would be seen next day at the council board of the province, and others which, Sabbath after Sabbath, looked devoutly heavenward, and benignantly over the crowded pews, from the holiest pulpits in the land. Some affirm that the lady of the governor was there. At least there were high dames well known to her, and wives of honored husbands, and widows, a great multitude, and ancient maidens, all of excellent repute, and fair young girls, who trembled lest their mothers should espy them. Either the sudden gleams of light flashing over the obscure field bedazzled Goodman Brown, or he recognized a score of the church members of Salem village famous for their especial sanctity. Good old Deacon Gookin had arrived, and waited at the skirts of that venerable saint, his revered pastor. But, irreverently consorting with these grave, reputable, and pious people, these elders of the church, these chaste dames and dewy virgins, there were men of dissolute lives and women of spotted fame, wretches given over to all mean and filthy vice, and suspected even of horrid crimes. It was strange to see that the good shrank not from the wicked, nor were the sinners abashed by the saints. Scattered also among their pale-faced enemies were the Indian priests, or powwows, who had often scared their native forest with more hideous incantations than any known to English witchcraft.

"But where is Faith?" thought Goodman Brown; and, as hope came into his heart, he trembled.

Another verse of the hymn arose, a slow and mournful strain, such as the pious love, but joined to words which expressed all that our nature can conceive of sin, and darkly hinted at far more. Unfathomable to mere mortals is the lore of fiends. Verse after verse was sung; and still the chorus of the desert swelled between like the deepest tone of a mighty organ; and with the final peal of that dreadful anthem there came a sound, as if the roaring wind, the rushing streams, the howling beasts, and every other voice of the unconverted wilderness were mingling and according with the voice of guilty man in homage to the prince of all. The four blazing pines threw up a loftier flame, and obscurely discovered shapes and visages of horror on the smoke wreaths above the impious assembly. At the same moment the fire on the rock shot redly forth and formed a glowing arch above its base, where now appeared a figure. With reverence be it spoken, the figure bore no slight similitude, both in garb and manner, to some grave divine of the New England churches.

"Bring forth the converts!" cried a voice that echoed through the field and rolled into the forest.

At the word, Goodman Brown stepped forth from the shadow of the trees and ap-   60
proached the congregation, with whom he felt a loathful brotherhood by the sympathy of all that was wicked in his heart. He could have well-nigh sworn that the shape of his own dead father beckoned him to advance, looking downward from a smoke wreath, while a woman, with dim features of despair, threw out her hand to warn him back. Was it his mother? But he had no power to retreat one step, nor to resist, even in thought, when the minister and good old Deacon Gookin seized his arms and led him to the blazing rock. Thither came also the slender form of a veiled female, led between Goody Cloyse, that pious teacher of the catechism, and Martha Carrier, who had received the devil's promise to be queen of hell. A rampant hag was she. And there stood the proselytes beneath the canopy of fire.

"Welcome, my children," said the dark figure, "to the communion of your race. Ye have found thus young your nature and your destiny. My children, look behind you!"

They turned; and flashing forth, as it were, in a sheet of flame, the fiend worshippers were seen; the smile of welcome gleamed darkly on every visage.

"There," resumed the sable form, "are all whom ye have reverenced from youth. Ye deemed them holier than yourselves, and shrank from your own sin, contrasting it with their lives of righteousness and prayerful aspirations heavenward. Yet here are they all in my worshipping assembly. This night it shall be granted you to know their secret deeds: how hoary-bearded elders of the church have whispered wanton words to the young maids of their households; how many a woman, eager for widows' weeds, has given her husband a drink at bedtime and let him sleep his last sleep in her bosom; how beardless youths have made haste to inherit their fathers' wealth; and how fair damsels—blush not, sweet ones—have dug little graves in the garden, and bidden me, the sole guest, to an infant's funeral. By the sympathy of your human hearts for sin ye shall scent out all the places—whether in church, bedchamber, street, field, or forest—where crime has been committed, and shall exult to behold the whole earth one stain of guilt, one mighty blood spot. Far more than this. It shall be yours to penetrate, in every bosom, the deep mystery of sin, the fountain of all wicked arts, and which inexhaustibly supplies more evil impulses than human power—than my power at its utmost—can make manifest in deeds. And now, my children, look upon each other."

They did so; and, by the blaze of the hell-kindled torches, the wretched man beheld his Faith, and the wife her husband, trembling before that unhallowed altar.

"Lo, there ye stand, my children," said the figure, in a deep and solemn tone, al-   65
most sad with its despairing awfulness, as if his once angelic nature could yet mourn for our miserable race. "Depending upon one another's hearts, ye had still hoped that virtue were not all a dream. Now are ye undeceived. Evil is the nature of mankind. Evil must be your only happiness. Welcome again, my children, to the communion of your race."

"Welcome," repeated the fiend worshippers, in one cry of despair and triumph.

And there they stood, the only pair, as it seemed, who were yet hesitating on the verge of wickedness in this dark world. A basin was hollowed, naturally, in the rock. Did it contain water, reddened by the lurid light? or was it blood? or, perchance, a liquid flame? Herein did the shape of evil dip his hand and prepare to lay the mark of baptism upon their foreheads, that they might be partakers of the mystery of sin, more conscious of the secret guilt of others, both in deed and thought, than they could now be of their own. The husband cast one look at his pale wife, and Faith at him. What polluted wretches would the next glance show them to each other, shuddering alike at what they disclosed and what they saw!

"Faith! Faith!" cried the husband, "look up to heaven, and resist the wicked one."

Whether Faith obeyed he knew not. Hardly had he spoken when he found himself amid calm night and solitude, listening to a roar of the wind which died heavily away through the forest. He staggered against the rock, and felt it chill and damp; while a hanging twig, that had been all on fire, besprinkled his cheek with the coldest dew.

The next morning young Goodman Brown came slowly into the street of Salem   70
village, staring around him like a bewildered man. The good old minister was taking a walk along the graveyard to get an appetite for breakfast and meditate his sermon, and bestowed a blessing, as he passed, on Goodman Brown. He shrank from the venerable saint as if to avoid an anathema. Old Deacon Gookin was at domestic worship, and the holy words of his prayer were heard through the open window. "What God doth the wizard pray to?" quoth Goodman Brown. Goody Cloyse, that excellent old Christian, stood in the early sunshine at her own lattice, catechizing a little girl who had brought

her a pint of morning's milk. Goodman Brown snatched away the child as from the grasp of the fiend himself. Turning the corner by the meeting-house, he spied the head of Faith, with the pink ribbons, gazing anxiously forth, and bursting into such joy at the sight of him that she skipped along the street and almost kissed her husband before the whole village. But Goodman Brown looked sternly and sadly into her face, and passed on without a greeting.

Had Goodman Brown fallen asleep in the forest and only dreamed a wild dream of a witch-meeting?

Be it so if you will; but, alas! it was a dream of evil omen for young Goodman Brown. A stern, a sad, a darkly meditative, a distrustful, if not a desperate man did he become from the night of that fearful dream. On the Sabbath day, when the congregation were singing a holy psalm, he could not listen because an anthem of sin rushed loudly upon his ear and drowned all the blessed strain. When the minister spoke from the pulpit with power and fervid eloquence, and, with his hand on the open Bible, of the sacred truths of our religion, and of saint-like lives and triumphant deaths, and of future bliss or misery unutterable, then did Goodman Brown turn pale, dreading lest the roof should thunder down upon the gray blasphemer and his hearers. Often, waking suddenly at midnight, he shrank from the bosom of Faith; and at morning or eventide, when the family knelt down at prayer, he scowled and muttered to himself, and gazed sternly at his wife, and turned away. And when he had lived long, and was borne to his grave a hoary corpse, followed by Faith, an aged woman, and children and grandchildren, a goodly procession, besides neighbors not a few, they carved no hopeful verse upon his tombstone, for his dying hour was gloom.

THE RECEPTIVE READER

1. As the story opens, what are major steps and key details in young Goodman Brown's journey into the forest? What is strange, what is frightening, and what is funny about the journey? Where does it go counter to our naive expectations, creating the effect of *irony*?

2. Much critical discussion of this much-discussed story has focused on the exact role of Brown's "aptly named" wife, Faith. What is her role in the story? When is she real; when is she a *symbol*? Could she be both? (What is the role of the pink ribbon?)

3. What exactly happens at the Witches' Sabbath? How does it end? What question or questions does it leave open?

4. How are we as readers expected to react to Brown's transformation after his experience in the forest?

5. How would you sum up in a sentence or two what the story as a whole says about sin or about evil? How does your statement of the *theme* compare with statements of the theme by your classmates?

THE RANGE OF INTERPRETATION

Hawthorne has a reputation for *ambiguity*, intentionally leaving his stories ambiguous and open-ended. Which of the following interpretations is to you most convincing? What evidence from the story would support it?

✧ Is young Goodman Brown's journey into the forest an evil dream (perhaps inspired by the devil)?

✧ Is his journey a dream vision telling him the truth about human nature?

✧ Is his journey a symbolic acting out of his own paranoid fears and suspicions about others?

❖ Is his journey a symbolic acting out of his own sinful nature, his secret inclination toward evil?

❖ Is Hawthorne's vision of evil in this story a recreation of a historical cycle that his generation had left behind? Or is it his own view?

CROSS-REFERENCES—For Discussion or Writing

Two other stories about evil lurking behind a genteel or reassuring surface are Shirley Jackson's "The Lottery" and William Faulkner's "A Rose for Emily." What is similar, or what is different, about the vision of evil in these three stories? Which do you find most persuasive, which least?

WRITING ABOUT LITERATURE

7. Tracing a Recurrent Theme (Comparing and Contrasting)

The Writing Workshop A crucial part of your task as a writer is to make connections. When you compare the treatment of the same theme by two different writers, you become more aware of each author's distinct way of looking at the world. Try your hand at tracing the same or a similar theme in two stories by different authors. See what you can learn from such a paper about comparison and contrast as a major organizational strategy.

When you try to show the connections between several stories, the overall plan of your paper will be more complex than usual. (You won't be able to follow the developments of a single story from beginning to end.) How will you make your readers' eyes travel between the two stories to make them see the connections you want them to see? How will you go about highlighting similarities and differences? How are you going to lay out your material?

However you proceed, try not to let your paper break up into two mini-essays (one on each story)—with your readers left to establish the cross-references themselves.

Let us assume you are writing about the vision of evil in Hawthorne's "Young Goodman Brown" and Jackson's "The Lottery." You have tentatively mapped out three areas where the stories seem to converge in their vision of how evil enters our world. Both stories take us into a world that is superficially benign—people seem superficially dignified, harmless, friendly, or virtuous. But these apparently harmless or well-meaning people are observed to engage in strange rituals—puzzling, disturbing observances that seem like part of an ancient tribal religion. Finally, the community as a whole seems implicated—all seem in some way involved in evil.

What plan of organization will allow you to show these three features in both of the stories? Here are organizing strategies you might consider:

❖ You might try a **point-by-point** comparison. The first third of your paper might show that in both stories there is a reassuring façade of normalcy that hides evil from the casual observer (point A). Then the second third of your paper might show that in both stories we witness strange quasi-religious rituals—as if evil were not something that happens casually or almost by accident. It is built into the traditions of the community (point B). Finally, the last third of your paper might show that evil does not seem the work of isolated individuals—a "criminal element." The whole community seems implicated in one way or another (point C). With a point-by-point comparison there is little danger that your readers will miss the connections.

✧ You might feel that in a point-by-point comparison your readers would not get enough of a sense of the characteristic atmosphere of each story as a whole. You might then try a **parallel-order** comparison. You discuss each story separately, but each time you run through the three key points in the same order: first the reassuring benign surface, then the strange traditional rituals, and finally the involvement in evil of the whole community. As you go through the second story, you might nudge your reader into realizing that you are in fact lining up the major points in the same order for easy cross-reference.

✧ You might decide to start by showing *similarities* between the two stories first—especially if they are likely to be readily noticed by the reader. You might then go on to show a crucial *difference* your readers might have overlooked. (Conversely, you might point out differences first but then go on to important features that two superficially very different stories have in common.)

The following student paper compares and contrasts two short stories treating a similar or related theme. What is the writer's organizing strategy? Does it become clear to the reader? How successful is the writer in carrying it out?

SAMPLE STUDENT PAPER

Two Women's Passions

John Steinbeck's "The Chrysanthemums" and Alice Walker's "Everyday Use" explore obstacles that women, both white and black, have had to face. Women often find that they are taken for granted; their intelligence, creative abilities, even the hard labor that they do often go unappreciated. Facing this reality, women find themselves pulled in conflicting directions. On the one hand, there is the strong desire to be attractive to men. Yet by pursuing the traditional ideal of femininity, they may be stifling their true being: their true passions about independence and their struggle toward their own reality.

Elisa in "The Chrysanthemums" is a housewife who has a particular talent in working with flowers. Because this is normally considered "women's work," there is no one restricting her from becoming passionate about it, so she does. Perhaps she puts her energy into her garden only because of her discontent with the rest of her life, where there is little outlet for her energy and strength. Like Elisa's chrysanthemums, the handmade quilts in "Everyday Use" also represent a passion in a woman's life. These quilts were pieced together by the woman and other women in her family from scraps of old dresses, shirts, and even a "teeny faded blue piece . . . that was from Great Grandpa Ezra's uniform that he wore in the Civil War." More than Elisa's flowers, however, these quilts were objects of everyday life, in "everyday use" as bed covers and sources of warmth. They represent a tradition of making do with limited resources, making the best of what you have, in a setting where there is little room for waste or extravagance.

In both stories, the women struggle with the desire to be attractive to men and the harsh realities these longings produce. Elisa finds herself spilling her passions to an old, dirty tinker who shows some false interest in her flowers. She begins by telling him of the budding process and of how to plant the seeds, and his encouraging nods and grunts lead her to continue. She talks passionately of night-time and the stars— "driven into your body. . . . Hot and sharp and—lovely." Apparently even this poor excuse for a man holds her attention enough for Elisa to reach out to him, hoping to find some connection to make her less isolated and trapped in her restricted existence. Unfortunately, the encounter turns into a humbling experience for her, as in the end the tinker is only looking for some pots to mend and cares little for the passions of a sexually frustrated housewife.

The black woman in "Everyday Use" wishes to be attractive as well, although for her this attractiveness would be a way of gaining her daughter's approval. Ideally, she would be "the way my daughter would want me to be: a hundred pounds lighter, my skin like an uncooked barley pancake," giving the quick-witted Johnny Carson "much to do to keep up with my quick and witty tongue." She realizes, however, that this image is far from reality:

In real life I am a large, big-boned woman with rough, man-working hands. In the winter I wear flannel nightgowns to bed and overalls during the day. I can kill and clean a hog as mercilessly as a man.

She knows too that in reality she has trouble looking white men (let alone a famous white comedian) in the eye; instead she has "talked to them always with one foot raised in flight." This fear or lack or confidence is part of her nature even though this woman is surviving on her own, feeding and educating her children with no help from a man.

Both women are patronized by others who care little for their passions and want to use them only for their own ends. The tinker in Steinbeck's story seems to listen with strong interest when Elisa goes on about the stars while he is actually waiting for the appropriate moment to ask for work. The mother in Walker's story is patronized by her daughter Dee, who goes through her mother's house looking for black artifacts that would be interesting objects to exhibit in her own home.

Today's reader is waiting for these women to leave their humiliation behind or to express their anger, to turn on those who condescend to them. Elisa's rebellion is weak and indirect at best. After seeing the chrysanthemums the tinker has discarded lying in the road, Elisa turns to her husband and asks him about some boxing matches, imagining them bloody and gory. Her interest in going to one surprises her husband, but he invites her to go. But she almost immediately draws back:

She relaxed limply in the seat. "Oh, no. No. I don't want to go. I'm sure I don't. " Her face was turned away from him. "It will be enough if we can have wine. It will be plenty." She turned up her coat collar so he could not see that she was crying weakly—like an old woman.

The mother in "Everyday Use" is more assertive in regaining her pride. Despite her daughter Dee's claim that the mother knew nothing of her heritage, she did not give in to her daughter's request for the quilts. The mother had promised the quilts to Maggie, Dee's younger sister, and despite Dee's protest that Maggie would ruin them by using them every day, their mother "dragged" Maggie into the room, "snatched the quilts" out of Dee's hand, and "dumped them into Maggie's lap." In this seemingly insignificant incident, the mother stood up for what she believed in.

In these stories, we get glimpses of women's needs and passions but also of the strength and wisdom women have. Perhaps in the future they will be able to channel their passion into science, politics, art, and our changing world rather than into 10-inch chrysanthemums and patchwork quilts.

QUESTIONS

How does the writer set up an overall perspective for comparing the two stories? What is the organizing strategy? Does this paper tend to break up into two separate mini-essays? What does the writer do to make the reader see the connections between the two stories? How successful is the paper in tracing similarities? Does it do justice to how the stories are different?

8 STYLE
A Manner of Speaking

The language must be careful and must appear effortless.
It must not sweat. It must suggest and be provocative at
the same time.

TONI MORRISON

Technique alone is never enough. You have to have
passion. Technique alone is just an embroidered potholder.

RAYMOND CHANDLER

Writing is a struggle against silence.

CARLOS FUENTES

FOCUS ON STYLE

What is style? **Style** is the manner in which a writer uses language to create his or her reality. It is the writer's personal way of using words and sentences to help create a distinctive voice that we come to recognize. The following two passages come from short stories at opposite poles of the spectrum of prose style. The first is from Ernest Hemingway's "Big Two-Hearted River," a story about a camping trip to the Upper Peninsula in Michigan (a trout fisher's paradise).

> He came down a hillside covered with stumps into a meadow. At the edge of the meadow flowed the river. Nick was glad to get to the river. He walked upstream through the meadow. His trousers were soaked with the dew as he walked. After the hot day, the dew had come quickly and heavily. The river made no sound. It was too fast and too smooth. At the edge of the meadow, before he mounted to a piece of high ground to make camp, Nick looked down the river at the trout rising. They were rising to insects come from the swamp on the other side of the stream when the sun went down. The trout jumped out of the water to take them. While Nick walked through the little stretch of meadow along the stream, trout had jumped high out of the water. Now as he looked down the river, the insects must be settling on the surface, for the trout were feeding steadily all down the stream. As far down the long stretch as he could see, the trout were rising, making circles all down the surface of the water, as though it were starting to rain.

This passage shows an unadorned modern style that aims at doing justice to reality. It does without embellishment, without fanfare, without grand gestures, without excessive emoting. There are several examples of the bare-fact sentences that for many readers became the hallmark of the stripped-down Hemingway style: "At the edge of the meadow flowed the river. . . . The river made no sound. It was too fast and too smooth." The words are simple, direct—and exactly adequate to their task of making the scene real for us: *soaked, dew, jumped, feeding, stream*. We know there is a feeling and thinking observer of the scene, but he does not come between us and the outdoor setting. The sentences that tell us about his state of mind—averaging in the story about one sentence for every paragraph full of patiently observed firsthand detail—are like minimal bulletins: "Nick was glad to get to the river."

However, this style of deliberate **understatement** does not keep us as readers from responding to the fresh, startling beauty of the unspoilt natural scene. Perhaps it makes us more rather than less ready to respond to the lovely image of the trout rising from below to feed on the insects settled on the surface of the water and making circles everywhere "as though it were starting to rain."

Fifty or a hundred years before Hemingway, the dominant style was to express emotion much more freely. A master at arousing the emotions of the audience was Edgar Allan Poe, who wrote the following passage in his short story "The Black Cat":

> With my aversion to this cat, however, its partiality for myself seemed to increase. It followed my footsteps with a pertinacity which it would be difficult to make the reader comprehend. Whenever I sat, it would crouch beneath my chair or spring upon my knees, covering me with its loathsome caresses. If I arose to walk, it would get between my feet and thus nearly throw me down, or, fastening its long and sharp claws in my dress, clamber in this manner to my breast. At such time, although I longed to destroy it with a blow, I was yet withheld from so doing, partly by a memory of my former crime, but chiefly—let me confess it at once—by absolute *dread* of the beast.

There are no bare-bones sentences here. Several sentences start with preambles like "If I . . ." or "Whenever I . . ." and then work their way through layers of mixed or complicated emotions. (The narrator would love to strangle the cat but is held back by his guilt feelings about having done the same to an earlier specimen.) The language is elevated, **formal**—deliberately above the trivial talk of everyday: *partiality* for *kindness, pertinacity* for *stubbornness, comprehend* for *understand*. Does the language signal that the events of this story are more important, more momentous, more ominous than what ordinary cat fanciers are likely to experience? The whole passage builds up to a climax of "absolute *dread*." No reluctance here to use superlatives! (or to italicize for emphasis). Poe's style is one of **hyperbole**—he is willing to exaggerate, to enhance, to pull the stops. If Poe continues to be read, it may because the modern reader has a capacity for strong feelings that a dry understated modern style tends to leave unused.

THE ELEMENTS OF STYLE

Great writers leave their mark by the originality of their
style, stamping it with an imprint that imposes a new face
on the coins of language.

JEAN-JOSEPH GOUX

We are what we imagine.
N. SCOTT MOMADAY

Style is more than a matter of style. It makes a statement of its own. That statement, however, may not be simple but complex. When American colleges built quads and dorms in the Gothic style of medieval Oxford or Cambridge, they showed their desire to tread in the footsteps of these revered institutions. When modern architects built office towers of glass and steel, they asserted that the beauty of a building was in its basic design, not in embellishments stuck on to mask an ugly surface. When postmodern architects put frills and curlicues back on office towers, they suggested that the modern style had become too stark, too mechanical, too inhuman.

How can you become more sensitive to style in what you read? One way of becoming more aware of prose style is to place elements of a writer's style on a spectrum, or on a scale ranging from one extreme to the other. (The two poles do not necessarily represent good and bad, although writers and critics often have strong preferences one way or the other.)

Abstract and Concrete   Some prose remains general or **abstract,** whereas other prose becomes **concrete:** It engages in rich specific detail with the sensory surface of life—with what we can see, hear, smell, touch, feel. Hemingway, for instance, was a stickler for detail (like many of his characters, who are often perfectionists, sticklers for doing something exactly the right way). In the following pair, compare the thin passage that a writer in a hurry might have written with the texture of concrete detail in a Hemingway story:

GENERAL: He went down to the stream and got water for his coffee.

SPECIFIC: He had forgotten to get water for the coffee. Out of the pack he got a folding canvas bucket and walked down the hill, across the edge of the meadow, to the stream. The other bank was in the white mist. The grass was wet and cold as he knelt on the bank and dipped the canvas bucket into the stream. It bellied and pulled hard in the current. The water was ice cold. Nick rinsed the bucket and carried it full up to the camp. Up away from the stream it was not so cold.
From "Big Two-Hearted River"

Often Hemingway will choose words especially suited to do justice to the rich sensory texture of firsthand experience. Concrete words are graphic words that conjure up a more vivid image than common, averaged-out words might. Concrete words speak more vividly to our senses than more colorless substitutes. What does each of the following concrete words add that might be missing from a near synonym, a near equivalent? In the story about the camping trip, Hemingway makes us see the water *swirl* (rather than wash) around the logs of the bridge; he makes us see and hear the wings of grasshoppers *whirr*. The camper breaks off *sprigs* of the heathery fern; with his ax he cuts off a *slab* of pine; the current raises a mist of sand in *spurts* from the bottom of the creek.

Denotation and Connotation   Some words point and identify. The word *glass* simply points to an object that holds liquid for drinking. The word in itself says nothing about whether the person who used it was thirsty, or likes to drink, or prefers a glass to a mug or a stein. Other words, however, bring into play attitudes or emotions. When James Joyce, in his story "Araby," uses the word *chalice*, it calls up a range of feelings associated with religious ritual: otherworldliness, devotion, religious exaltation.

The objective, emotionally neutral meaning of a word is its **denotation;** the denotation of *knife* is simply an instrument for cutting. The range of attitudes or emotions a word brings into play is its **connotation.** The word *knife* may suggest menace, threat, treachery. Connotative words, words charged with emotion, help set the tone. Angry words, sweet words, wistful words, or judgmental words help shape the emotional coloring of a story.

Literal and Figurative   Figurative language uses imaginative comparisons to carry meanings that otherwise might be hard to put into words. **Metaphors** are imaginative comparisons that do not come with a sign that says: "This is a comparison!" There is no word such as *like* or *as if* to alert us that someone is speaking on an as-if basis. (**Similes** are figurative expressions that *do* provide the *like* or *as if* that signals the comparison. In Bobbie Ann Mason's "Shiloh," Norma Jean picks up "cake crumbs from the cellophane wrapper, *like a fussy bird*.")

In the work of an imaginative writer, metaphors are likely to be rich and provocative. They may reveal new dimensions as they develop their full implications. Patricia Hampl, talking about her own writing, said, "Our most ancient metaphor says life is a journey." Writing about her experience, she "is the traveler who goes on foot, living the journey, taking in mountains, enduring deserts, marveling at the lush green places." As she writes, she moves "through it all faithfully, not so much a survivor with a harrowing tale to tell as a pilgrim, seeking, wondering." The journey metaphor here is rich in meaning and visual content: It makes us think of life as something that is not disjointed but has continuity, a purpose, a destination. Specifying that the journey will be on foot slows us down: We will have a chance to take things in, responding to sights and sounds missed by the traveler in a speeding car or on a plane. The journey will be prolonged enough to take us through both deserts and green valleys. It will be not a hurried, absentminded kind of trip but a journey like a pilgrimage, undertaken in a serious mood, with a solemn purpose.

Formal and Informal   Formal language can make events seem important and characters dignified. (When overdone, it can make characters seem pompous.) Informal language can put the reader at ease, but when it shades over into slang it can easily become disrespectful or insulting. (There is a world of difference between "Will you *please* leave now" and "Beat it, bozo.") *Who uses* distinctly formal or informal language in a story makes considerable difference to the narrative voice. If the formal or informal way of talking appears in **dialogue,** it helps create character—dignified, stodgy, laid-back, tough, or whatever. If it is used by the narrator, it will color the tone of the story as a whole. ("Ain't nobody gonna beat me at nuthin" says the tough city-kid narrator at the end of Toni Cade Bambara's "The Lesson.")

Simple and Complex   Bare-bones sentences sound matter-of-fact. They often do in Hemingway's prose. However, varied sentence length (the short and the long of it) is a major source of sentence variety: An arresting short sentence after a series of long and involved sentences, full of ifs and buts, may focus our attention and highlight an important thought or detail. It catches us up short. Sentences with elaborate **parallelism**—repetition of grammatically similar elements—can create a strong rhythm, building up emotion, hammering home a point, leading up to a climactic finale. The following is the climactic final sentence of a story written in a florid nineteenth-century style, ending the story with a last rhetorical flourish:

> And pulseless and cold, with a Derringer by his side and a bullet in his heart, though still calm as in life, beneath the snow lay he who was at once the strongest and yet the weakest of the outcasts of Poker Flat. (Bret Harte)

Earnest and Ironic   Some writers, like Bret Harte, have a saving sense of humor; others take life and literature *very* seriously. A pervasive feature of style in much modern fiction is a lively sense of **irony**—of the sad and comic contrast between expectation and event, between ideal and reality. The ironic tone may range from amused tolerance and indulgence of human foibles to cutting, sardonic exposure of stupidity and greed.

JUXTAPOSITIONS ⟺

Playing the Role

Each of the two stories that follow was written by a writer with a sharp eye for how people act and a quick ear for how people talk. (Both authors are alert observers of someone's personal *style*.) Dorothy Parker, who got her start in the publishing world by working for *Vogue* and *Vanity Fair,* became legendary in the twenties and thirties for her devastating wit. One interviewer said about her, "Her sentences are punctuated with observations phrased with lethal force." Parker said about her stories that they "made themselves stories by telling themselves through what people say. I haven't got a visual mind. I hear things." Toni Cade Bambara became known in the seventies for making her readers listen to the language of tough, scrappy kids from the poor part of town.

In both stories, young people without money come downtown to the pricey avenues of Manhattan. They come into stores that they know are not for them. The focus is on their manner: their style of behavior, their style of talking. What is similar, what is different, about the point of view from which we see the events of each story? What do the young people in the stories have in common? What is similar or different about the way they act and talk? Is there any connection between the roles the two sets of characters play in public? Do the stories differ in theme—in what each story as a whole has to say?

DOROTHY PARKER (1893–1967)
The Standard of Living   1926

Annabel and Midge came out of the tea room with the arrogant slow gait of the leisured, for their Saturday afternoon stretched ahead of them. They had lunched, as was their wont, on sugar, starches, oils, and butter-fats. Usually they ate sandwiches of spongy new white bread greased with butter and mayonnaise; they ate thick wedges of cake lying wet beneath ice cream and whipped cream and melted chocolate gritty with nuts. As alternates, they ate patties, sweating beads of inferior oil, containing bits of bland meat bogged in pale, stiffening sauce; they ate pastries, limber under rigid icing, filled with an indeterminate yellow sweet stuff, not still solid, not yet liquid, like salve that has been left in the sun. They chose no other sort of food, nor did they consider it. And their skin was like the petals of wood anemones, and their bellies were as flat and their flanks as lean as those of young Indian braves.

Annabel and Midge had been best friends almost from the day that Midge had found a job as stenographer with the firm that employed Annabel. By now, Annabel, two years longer in the stenographic department, had worked up to the wages of eighteen dollars and fifty cents a week; Midge was still at sixteen dollars. Each girl lived at home with her family and paid half her salary to its support.

The girls sat side by side at their desks, they lunched together every noon, together they set out for home at the end of the day's work. Many of their evenings and most of their Sundays were passed in each other's company. Often they were joined by two young men, but there was no steadiness to any such quartet; the two young men would give place, unlamented, to two other young men, and lament would have been inappropriate, really, since the newcomers were scarcely distinguishable from their predecessors. Invariably the girls spent the fine idle hours of their hot-weather Saturday afternoons together. Constant use had not worn ragged the fabric of their friendship.

They looked alike, though the resemblance did not lie in their features. It was in the shape of their bodies, their movements, their style, and their adornments. Annabel and Midge did, and completely, all that young office workers are besought not to do. They painted their lips and their nails, they darkened their lashes and lightened their hair, and scent seemed to shimmer from them. They wore thin, bright dresses, tight over their breasts and high on their legs, and tilted slippers, fancifully strapped. They looked conspicuous and cheap and charming.

Now, as they walked across to Fifth Avenue with their skirts swirled by the hot   5 wind, they received audible admiration. Young men grouped lethargically about news-stands awarded them murmurs, exclamations, even—the ultimate tribute—whistles. Annabel and Midge passed without the condescension of hurrying their pace; they held their heads higher and set their feet with exquisite precision, as if they stepped over the necks of peasants.

Always the girls went to walk on Fifth Avenue on their free afternoons, for it was the ideal ground for their favorite game. The game could be played anywhere, and, in-deed, was, but the great shop windows stimulated the two players to their best form.

Annabel had invented the game; or rather she had evolved it from an old one. Ba-sically, it was no more than the ancient sport of what-would-you-do-if-you-had-a-mil-lion dollars? But Annabel had drawn a new set of rules for it, had narrowed it, pointed it, made it stricter. Like all games, it was the more absorbing for being more difficult.

Annabel's version went like this: You must suppose that somebody dies and leaves you a million dollars, cool. But there is a condition to the bequest. It is stated in the will that you must spend every nickel of the money on yourself.

There lay the hazard of the game. If, when playing it, you forgot, and listed among your expenditures the rental of a new apartment for your family, for example, you lost your turn to the other player. It was astonishing how many—and some of them among the experts, too—would forfeit all their innings by such slips.

It was essential, of course, that it be played in passionate seriousness. Each pur-chase must be carefully considered and, if necessary, supported by argument. There was no zest to playing wildly. Once Annabel had introduced the game to Sylvia, another girl who worked in the office. She explained the rules to Sylvia and then offered her the gambit "What would be the first thing you'd do?" Sylvia had not shown the decency of even a second of hesitation. "Well," she said, "the first thing I'd do, I'd go out and hire somebody to shoot Mrs. Gary Cooper, and then . . ." So it is to be seen that she was no fun. 10

But Annabel and Midge were surely born to be comrades, for Midge played the game like a master from the moment she learned it. It was she who added the touches that made the whole thing cozier. According to Midge's innovations, the eccentric who died and left you the money was not anybody you loved, or, for the matter of that, any-body you even knew. It was somebody who had seen you somewhere and had thought, "That girl ought to have lots of nice things. I'm going to leave her a million dollars when I die." And the death was to be neither untimely nor painful. Your benefactor, full of years and comfortably ready to depart, was to slip softly away during sleep and go right to heaven. These embroideries permitted Annabel and Midge to play their game in the luxury of peaceful consciences.

Midge played with a seriousness that was not only proper but extreme. The single strain on the girls' friendship had followed an announcement once made by Annabel that the first thing she would buy with her million dollars would be a silver-fox coat. It was as if she had struck Midge across the mouth. When Midge recovered her breath, she cried that she couldn't imagine how Annabel could do such a thing—silver-fox coats were common! Annabel defended her taste with the retort that they were not common, either. Midge then said that they were so. She added that everybody had a silver-fox coat. She went on, with perhaps a slight loss of head, to declare that she her-self wouldn't be caught dead in silver fox.

For the next few days, though the girls saw each other as constantly, their conver-sation was careful and infrequent, and they did not once play their game. Then one morning, as soon as Annabel entered the office, she came to Midge and said that she had changed her mind. She would not buy a silver-fox coat with any part of her million dollars. Immediately on receiving the legacy, she would select a coat of mink.

Midge smiled and her eyes shone. "I think," she said, "you're doing absolutely the right thing."

Now, as they walked along Fifth Avenue, they played the game anew. It was one of those days with which September is repeatedly cursed; hot and glaring, with slivers of dust in the wind. People drooped and shambled, but the girls carried themselves tall and walked a straight line, as befitted young heiresses on their afternoon promenade. There was no longer need for them to start the game at its formal opening. Annabel went direct to the heart of it. 15

"All right," she said. "So you've got this million dollars. So what would be the first thing you'd do?"

"Well, the first thing I'd do," Midge said, "I'd get a mink coat." But she said it mechanically, as if she were giving the memorized answer to an expected question.

"Yes," Annabel said, "I think you ought to. The terribly dark kind of mink." But she, too, spoke as if by rote. It was too hot; fur, no matter how dark and sleek and supple, was horrid to the thoughts.

They stepped along in silence for a while. Then Midge's eye was caught by a shop window. Cool, lovely gleamings were there set off by chaste and elegant darkness.

"No," Midge said, "I take it back. I wouldn't get a mink coat the first thing. Know what I'd do? I'd get a string of pearls. Real pearls." 20

Annabel's eyes turned to follow Midge's.

"Yes," she said, slowly. "I think that's kind of a good idea. And it would make sense, too. Because you can wear pearls with anything."

Together they went over to the shop window and stood pressed against it. It contained but one object—a double row of great, even pearls clasped by a deep emerald around a little pink velvet throat.

"What do you suppose they cost?" Annabel said.

"Gee, I don't know." Midge said. "Plenty, I guess." 25

"Like a thousand dollars?" Annabel said.

"Oh, I guess like more," Midge said. "On account of the emerald."

"Well, like ten thousand dollars?" Annabel said.

"Gee, I wouldn't even know," Midge said.

The devil nudged Annabel in the ribs. "Dare you to go in and price them," she said. 30

"Like fun!" Midge said.

"Dare you," Annabel said.

"Why, a store like this wouldn't even be open this afternoon," Midge said.

"Yes, it is so, too," Annabel said. "People just came out. And there's a doorman on. Dare you."

"Well," Midge said. "But you've got to come too." 35

They tendered thanks, icily, to the doorman for ushering them into the shop. It was cool and quiet, a broad, gracious room with paneled walls and soft carpet. But the girls wore expressions of bitter disdain, as if they stood in a sty.

A slim, immaculate clerk came to them and bowed. His neat face showed no astonishment at their appearance.

"Good afternoon," he said. He implied that he would never forget it if they would grant him the favor of accepting his soft-spoken greeting.

"Good afternoon," Annabel and Midge said together, and in like freezing accents.

"Is there something—?" the clerk said. 40

"Oh, we're just looking," Annabel said. It was as if she flung the words down from a dais.

The clerk bowed.

"My friend and myself merely happened to be passing," Midge said, and stopped, seeming to listen to the phrase. "My friend here and myself," she went on, "merely happened to be wondering how much are those pearls you've got in your window."

"Ah, yes," the clerk said. "The double rope. That is two hundred and fifty thousand dollars, Madam."

"I see," Midge said.   45

The clerk bowed. "An exceptionally beautiful necklace," he said. "Would you care to look at it?"

"No, thank you," Annabel said.

"My friend and myself merely happened to be passing," Midge said.

They turned to go; to go, from their manner, where the tumbrel awaited them. The clerk sprang ahead and opened the door. He bowed as they swept by him.

The girls went on along the Avenue and disdain was still on their faces.   50

"Honestly!" Annabel said. "Can you imagine a thing like that?"

"Two hundred and fifty thousand dollars!" Midge said. "That's a quarter of a million dollars right there!"

"He's got his nerve!" Annabel said.

They walked on. Slowly the disdain went, slowly and completely as if drained from them, and with it went the regal carriage and tread. Their shoulders dropped and they dragged their feet; they bumped against each other, without notice or apology, and caromed away again. They were silent and their eyes were cloudy.

Suddenly Midge straightened her back, flung her head high, and spoke, clear and   55
strong.

"Listen, Annabel," she said. "Look. Suppose there was this terribly rich person, see? You don't know this person, but this person has seen you somewhere and wants to do something for you. Well, it's a terribly old person, see? And so this person dies, just like going to sleep, and leaves you ten million dollars. Now, what would be the first thing you'd do?"

THE RECEPTIVE READER

1. How well do you come to know the young women? What is their style? How do they dress, act, and talk?

2. What does the game the two young women play tell you about them?

3. Parker was known for her sharp tongue and malicious *wit*. Do these show in the style of this story?

4. What is the author's attitude toward the two young women? How do you think she expects you to react to them?

THE PERSONAL RESPONSE

Does this story strike you as being based on real life? Do you think this story is out of date?

TONI CADE BAMBARA (born 1939)
The Lesson   1972

Back in the days when everyone was old and stupid or young and foolish and me and Sugar were the only ones just right, this lady moved on our block with nappy hair and proper speech and no makeup. And quite naturally we laughed at her, laughed the way we did at the junk man who went about his business like he was some big-time president and his sorry-ass horse his secretary. And we kinda hated her too, hated the way we did the winos who cluttered up our parks and pissed on our handball walls and stank up our hallways and stairs so you couldn't halfway play hide-and-seek without a goddamn gas mask. Miss Moore was her name. The only woman on the block with no first name. And she was black as hell, cept for her feet, which were fish-white and spooky. And she was always planning these boring-ass things for us to do, us being my cousin, mostly, who lived on the block cause we all moved North the same time and to the same apartment then spread out gradual to breathe. And our parents would yank our heads into some kinda shape and crisp up our clothes so we'd be presentable for travel with Miss Moore, who always looked like she was going to church, though she never did. Which is just one of the things the grownups talked about when they talked behind her back like a dog. But when she came calling with some sachet she'd sewed up or some gingerbread she'd made or some book, why then they'd all be too embarrassed to turn her down and we'd get handed over all spruced up. She'd been to college and said it was only right that she should take responsibility for the young ones' education, and she not even related by marriage or blood. So they'd go for it. Specially Aunt Gretchen. She was the main gofer in the family. You got some ole dumb shit foolishness you want somebody to go for, you send for Aunt Gretchen. She been screwed into the go-along for so long, it's a blood-deep natural thing with her. Which is how she got saddled with me and Sugar and Junior in the first place while our mothers were in a la-de-da apartment up the block having a good ole time.

So this one day Miss Moore rounds us all up at the mailbox and it's puredee hot and she's knockin herself out about arithmetic. And school suppose to let up in summer I heard, but she don't never let up. And the starch in my pinafore scratching the shit outta me and I'm really hating this nappy-head bitch and her goddamn college degree. I'd much rather go to the pool or to the show where it's cool. So me and Sugar leaning on the mailbox being surly, which is a Miss Moore word. And Flyboy checking out what everybody brought for lunch. And Fat Butt already wasting his peanut-butter-and-jelly sandwich like the pig he is. And Junebug punchin on Q.T.'s arm for potato chips. And Rosie Giraffe shifting from one hip to the other waiting for somebody to step on her foot or ask her if she from Georgia so she can kick ass, preferably Mercedes'. And Miss Moore asking us do we know what money is, like we a bunch of retards. I mean real money, she say, like it's only poker chips or monopoly papers we lay on the grocer. So right away I'm tired of this and say so. And would much rather snatch Sugar and go to the Sunset and terrorize the West Indian kids and take their hair ribbons and their money too. And Miss Moore files that remark away for next week's lesson on brotherhood, I can tell. And finally I say we oughta get to the subway cause it's cooler and besides we might meet some cute boys. Sugar done swiped her mama's lipstick, so we ready.

So we heading down the street and she's boring us silly about what things cost and what our parents make and how much goes for rent and how money ain't divided up right in this country. And then she gets to the part about we all poor and live in the slums, which I don't feature. And I'm ready to speak on that, but she steps out in the street and hails two cabs just like that. Then she hustles half the crew in with her and hands me a five-dollar bill and tells me to calculate 10 percent tip for the driver. And we're off. Me and Sugar and Junebug and Flyboy hangin out the window and hollering to everybody, putting lipstick on each other cause Flyboy a faggot anyway, and making farts with our sweaty armpits. But I'm mostly trying to figure how to spend this money. But they all fascinated with the meter ticking and Junebug starts laying bets as to how much it'll read when Flyboy can't hold his breath no more. Then Sugar lays bets as to how much it'll be when we get there. So I'm stuck. Don't nobody want to go for my plan, which is to jump out at the next light and run off to the first bar-b-que we can find. Then the driver tells us to get the hell out cause we there already. And the meter reads eighty-five cents. And I'm stalling to figure out the tip and Sugar say give him a dime. And I decide he don't need it bad as I do, so later for him. But then he tries to take off with Junebug foot still in the door so we talk about his mama something ferocious. Then we check out that we on Fifth Avenue and everybody dressed up in stockings. One lady in a fur coat, hot as it is. White folks crazy.

"This is the place," Miss Moore say, presenting it to us in the voice she uses at the museum. "Let's look in the windows before we go in."

"Can we steal?" Sugar asks very serious like she's getting the ground rules squared   5
away before she plays. "I beg your pardon," say Miss Moore, and we fall out. So she leads us around the windows of the toy store and me and Sugar screamin, "This is mine, that's mine, I gotta have that, that was made for me, I was born for that," till Big Butt drowns us out.

"Hey, I'm goin to buy that there."

"That there? You don't even know what it is, stupid."

"I do so," he say punchin on Rosie Giraffe. "It's a microscope."

"Whatcha gonna do with a microscope, fool?"

"Look at things."   10

"Like what, Ronald?" ask Miss Moore. And Big Butt ain't got the first notion. So here go Miss Moore gabbing about the thousands of bacteria in a drop of water and the somethinorother in a speck of blood and the million and one living things in the air around us is invisible to the naked eye. And what she say that for? Junebug go to town on that "naked" and we rolling. Then Miss Moore ask what it cost. So we all jam into the window smudgin it up and the price tag say $300. So then she ask how long'd take for Big Butt and Junebug to save up their allowances. "Too long," I say. "Yeh," adds Sugar, "outgrown it by that time." And Miss Moore say no, you never outgrow learning instruments. "Why, even medical students and interns and," blah, blah, blah. And we ready to choke Big Butt for bringing it up in the first damn place.

"This here costs four hundred eighty dollars," says Rosie Giraffe. So we pile up all over her to see what she pointin out. My eyes tell me it's a chunk of glass cracked with something heavy, and different-color inks dripped into the splits, then the whole thing put into a oven or something. But for $480 it don't make sense.

"That's a paperweight made of semi-precious stones fused together under tremendous pressure," she explains slowly, with her hands doing the mining and all the factory work.

"So what's a paperweight?" asks Rosie Giraffe.

"To weigh paper with, dumbbell," say Flyboy, the wise man from the East.   15

"Not exactly," say Miss Moore, which is what she say when you warm or way off too. "It's to weigh paper down so it won't scatter and make your desk untidy." So right away me and Sugar curtsy to each other and then to Mercedes who is more the tidy type.

"We don't keep paper on top of the desk in my class," say Junebug, figuring Miss Moore crazy or lyin one.

"At home, then," she say. "Don't you have a calendar and pencil case and a blotter and a letter-opener on your desk at home where you do your homework?" And she know damn well what our homes look like cause she nosys around in them every chance she gets.

"I don't even have a desk," say Junebug. "Do we?"

"No. And I don't get no homework neither," says Big Butt.   20

"And I don't even have a home," say Flyboy like he do at school to keep the white folks off his back and sorry for him. Send this poor kid to camp posters, is his specialty.

"I do," says Mercedes. "I have a box of stationery on my desk and a picture of my cat. My godmother bought the stationery and the desk. There's a big rose on each sheet and the envelopes smell like roses."

"Who wants to know about your smelly-ass stationery," say Rosie Giraffe fore I can get my two cents in.

"It's important to have a work area all your own so that . . ."

"Will you look at this sailboat, please," say Flyboy, cuttin her off and pointin to   25
the thing like it was his. So once again we tumble all over each other to gaze at this magnificent thing in the toy store which is just big enough to maybe sail two kittens across the pond if you strap them to the posts tight. We all start reciting the price tag like we in assembly. "Handcrafted sailboat of fiberglass at one thousand one hundred ninety-five dollars."

"Unbelievable," I hear myself say and am really stunned. I read it again for myself just in case the group recitation put me in a trance. Same thing. For some reason this pisses me off. We look at Miss Moore and she lookin at us, waiting for I dunno what.

"Who'd pay all that when you can buy a sailboat set for a quarter at Pop's, a tube of glue for a dime, and a ball of string for eight cents? It must have a motor and a whole lot else besides," I say. "My sailboat cost me about fifty cents."

"But will it take water?" say Mercedes with her smart ass.

"Took mine to Alley Pond Park once," say Flyboy. "String broke. Lost it. Pity."

"Sailed mine in Central Park and it keeled over and sank. Had to ask my father for   30
another dollar."

"And you got the strap," laugh Big Butt. "The jerk didn't even have a string on it. My old man wailed on his behind."

Little Q.T. was staring hard at the sailboat and you could see he wanted it bad. But he too little and somebody'd just take it from him. So what the hell. "This boat for kids, Miss Moore?"

"Parents silly to buy something like that just to get all broke up," say Rosie Giraffe.

"That much money it should last forever," I figure.

"My father'd buy it for me if I wanted it."   35

"Your father, my ass," say Rosie Giraffe getting a chance to finally push Mercedes.

"Must be rich people shop here," say Q.T.

"You are a very bright boy," say Flyboy. "What was your first clue?" And he rap him on the head with the back of his knuckles, since Q.T. the only one he could get away with. Though Q.T. liable to come up behind you years later and get his licks in when you half expect it.

"What I want to know is," I says to Miss Moore though I never talk to her, I wouldn't give the bitch that satisfaction, "is how much a real boat costs? I figure a thousand'd get you a yacht any day."

"Why don't you check that out," she says, "and report back to the group?" Which   40
really pains my ass. If you gonna mess up a perfectly good swim day least you could do is have some answers. "Let's go in," she say like she got something up her sleeve. Only she don't lead the way. So me and Sugar turn the corner to where the entrance is, but when we get there I kinda hang back. Not that I'm scared, what's there to be afraid of, just a toy store. But I feel funny, shame. But what I got to be shamed about? Got as much right to go in as anybody. But somehow I can't seem to get hold of the door, so

I step away from Sugar to lead. But she hangs back too. And I look at her and she looks at me and this is ridiculous. I mean, damn, I have never ever been shy about doing nothing or going nowhere. But then Mercedes steps up and then Rosie Giraffe and Big Butt crowd in behind and shove, and next thing we all stuffed into the doorway with only Mercedes squeezing past us, smoothing out her jumper and walking right down the aisle. Then the rest of us tumble in like a glued-together jigsaw done all wrong. And people lookin at us. And it's like the time me and Sugar crashed into the Catholic church on a dare. But once we got in there and everything so hushed and holy and the candles and the bowin and the handkerchiefs on all the drooping heads, I just couldn't go through with the plan. Which was for me to run up to the altar and do a tap dance while Sugar played the nose flute and messed around in the holy water. And Sugar kept givin me the elbow. Then later teased me so bad I tied her up in the shower and turned it on and locked her in. And she'd be there till this day if Aunt Gretchen hadn't finally figured I was lyin about the boarder takin a shower.

Same thing in the store. We all walkin on tiptoe and hardly touchin the games and puzzles and things. And I watched Miss Moore who is steady watchin us like she waitin for a sign. Like Mama Drewery watches the sky and sniffs the air and takes note of just how much slant is in the bird formation. Then me and Sugar bump smack into each other, so busy gazing at the toys, specially the sailboat. But we don't laugh and go into our fat-lady bump-stomach routine. We just stare at that price tag. Then Sugar run a finger over the whole boat. And I'm jealous and want to hit her. Maybe not her, but I sure want to punch somebody in the mouth.

"Watcha bring us here for, Miss Moore?"

"You sound angry, Sylvia. Are you mad about something?" Givin me one of them grins like she tellin a grown-up joke that never turns out to be funny. And she's lookin very closely at me like maybe she planning to do my portrait from memory. I'm mad, but I won't give her that satisfaction. So I slouch around the store bein very bored and say, "Let's go."

Me and Sugar at the back of the train watchin the tracks whizzin by large then small then getting gobbled up in the dark. I'm thinkin about this tricky toy I saw in the store. A clown that somersaults on a bar then does chin-ups just cause you yank lightly at his leg. Cost $35. I could see me askin my mother for a $35 birthday clown. "You wanna who that costs what?" she'd say, cocking her head to the side to get a better view of the hole in my head. Thirty-five dollars could buy new bunk beds for Junior and Gretchen's boy. Thirty-five dollars and the whole household could go visit Granddaddy Nelson in the country. Thirty-five dollars would pay for the rent and the piano bill too. Who are these people that spend that much for performing clowns and $1000 for toy sailboats? What kinda work they do and how they live and how come we ain't in on it? Where we are is who we are, Miss Moore always pointin out. But it don't necessarily have to be that way, she always adds then waits for somebody to say that poor people have to wake up and demand their share of the pie and don't none of us know what kind of pie she talking about in the first damn place. But she ain't so smart cause I still got her four dollars from the taxi and she sure ain't gettin it. Messin up my day with this shit. Sugar nudges me in my pocket and winks.

Miss Moore lines us up in front of the mailbox where we started from, seem like years ago, and I got a headache for thinkin so hard. And we lean all over each other so we can hold up under the draggy-ass lecture she always finishes us off with at the end before we thank her for borin us to tears. But she just looks at us like she readin tea leaves. Finally she say, "Well, what did you think of F.A.O. Schwarz?"

Rosie Giraffe mumbles, "White folks crazy."

"I'd like to go there again when I get my birthday money," says Mercedes, and we shove her out the pack so she has to lean on the mailbox by herself.

"I'd like a shower. Tiring day," say Flyboy.

Then Sugar surprises me by sayin, "You know, Miss Moore, I don't think all of us here put together eat in a year what that sailboat costs." And Miss Moore lights up like somebody goosed her. "And?" she say, urging Sugar on. Only I'm standin on her foot so she don't continue.

"Imagine for a minute what kind of society it is in which some people can spend   50
on a toy what it would cost to feed a family of six or seven. What do you think?"

"I think," say Sugar pushing me off her feet like she never done before, cause I whip her ass in a minute, "that this is not much of a democracy if you ask me. Equal chance to pursue happiness means an equal crack at the dough, don't it?" Miss Moore is besides herself and I am disgusted with Sugar's treachery. So I stand on her foot one more time to see if she'll shove me. She shuts up, and Miss Moore looks at me, sorrowfully I'm thinkin. And somethin weird is goin on, I can feel it in my chest.

"Anybody else learn anything today?" lookin dead at me. I walk away and Sugar has to run to catch up and don't even seem to notice when I shrug her arm off my shoulder.

"Well, we got four dollars anyway," she says.

"Uh hunh."

"We could go to Hascombs and get half a chocolate layer and then go to the Sun-   55
set and still have plenty money for potato chips and ice cream sodas."

"Un hunh."

"Race you to Hascombs," she say.

We start down the block and she gets ahead which is O.K. by me cause I'm going to the West End and then over to the Drive to think this day through. She can run if she want to and even run faster. But ain't nobody gonna beat me at nuthin.

THE RECEPTIVE READER

1. In this story we see the children from uptown through the eyes of one of their own. How does this *point of view* shape the story as a whole? What do we take in of their behavior, their thinking, their sense of humor? Do you recognize a pattern or a type?

2. How does the tough street language the narrator and her friends speak differ from the genteel middle-class language used by other authors? What distinctive features do you recognize? Do you find the language offensive? Why or why not?

3. How is Miss Moore introduced to the reader? How do you feel about her at the beginning? How does her role change in the story? Does your estimate of her change?

4. The story reaches a *turning point* when the group comes to the store. What theme becomes overt at this point? (What is "the lesson" promised in the title?) Does the story get too preachy for you?

5. Where does the story go after the climactic episode in the toy store? How does it *end*? What does the ending do for the story as a whole?

6. What do you think is the relationship between the author and the first-person narrator in the story? (What do you think is the distance between the author as a person and the *persona* speaking in the story?)

THE PERSONAL RESPONSE

People who talk tough may be playing a role. Do you think there is a different personality behind the narrator's public persona?

THE CREATIVE DIMENSION

Write about a situation, real or imagined, in which a central character plays a public role—different from what he or she is when not observed by strangers or outsiders. The central character could be an imaginary third party (as in the Parker story), or *you* could be speaking in the first person as the narrator (as in the Bambara story). Recreate for your readers a manner of behaving, a style of talking. (You may want to try your hand at an episode or vignette in which the punch line is "Ain't nobody gonna beat me at nuthin.")

THE WRITER'S VOICE

When a writer has a distinctive style, we may recognize a passage regardless of the setting, plot, or theme of a particular story. Each writer in this section has a distinctive personal voice. Bret Harte writes in a popular nineteenth-century style, old-fashioned and ornate like a grandfather clock, with grand rhetorical flourishes and frank appeals to emotion. John Cheever writes in an ironic recent "postmodern" style—allusive, detached, wryly amused.

BRET HARTE (1836–1902)

Bret Harte, a native of Albany, New York, was a journalist who had come to California in time for the gold rush and who became nationally famous for his stories about the West. The short story that follows is a classic of American popular literature, and it preserves features of a long-popular nineteenth-century style. Harte is a shrewd observer of human nature, and his humor makes readers chuckle at the shenanigans of both the sober townspeople and a drunkard like Uncle Billy. At the same time, the story caters to the readers' love of **sentimentality,** making them cry both at the undeserved sufferings of the innocent and at unsuspected evidence of goodness in the guilty. Harte's prose is replete with fancy, flowery language (which is, however, often facetiously used). Both the author and his main character love rhetorical flourishes in keeping with a tradition of speech making that often verged on windbag oratory. At times, the author indulges in historical or literary allusions: a "Parthian volley" is like a hail of arrows launched by legendary enemies of the Romans; the English poet Alexander Pope translated the *Iliad*, Homer's epic about the Trojan War, in the eighteenth-century style.

The Outcasts of Poker Flat   1869

As Mr. John Oakhurst, gambler, stepped into the main street of Poker Flat on the morning of the twenty-third of November, 1850, he was conscious of a change in its moral atmosphere since the preceding night. Two or three men, conversing earnestly together, ceased as he approached and exchanged significant glances. There was a Sabbath lull in the air, which, in a settlement unused to Sabbath influences, looked ominous.

Mr. Oakhurst's calm, handsome face betrayed small concern in these indications. Whether he was conscious of any predisposing cause was another question. "I reckon they're after somebody," he reflected; "likely it's me." He returned to his pocket the handkerchief with which he had been whipping away the red dust of Poker Flat from his neat boots, and quietly discharged his mind of any further conjecture.

In point of fact, Poker Flat was "after somebody." It had lately suffered the loss of several thousand dollars, two valuable horses, and a prominent citizen. It was experiencing a spasm of virtuous reactions, quite as lawless and ungovernable as any of the acts that had provoked it. A secret committee had determined to rid the town of all improper persons. This was done permanently in regard to two men who were then hanging from the boughs of a sycamore in the gulch, and temporarily in the banishment of certain other objectionable characters. I regret to say that some of these were ladies. It is but due to the sex, however, to state that their impropriety was professional, and it was only in such easily established standards of evil that Poker Flat ventured to sit in judgment.

Mr. Oakhurst was right in supposing that he was included in this category. A few of the committee had urged hanging him as a possible example and a sure method of reimbursing themselves from his pockets of the sums he had won from them. "It's agin justice," said Jim Wheeler, "to let this yer young man from Roaring Camp—an entire stranger—carry away our money." But a crude sentiment of equity residing in the breasts of those who had been fortunate enough to win from Mr. Oakhurst overruled this narrower local prejudice.

Mr. Oakhurst received his sentence with philosophic calmness, none the less coolly that he was aware of the hesitation of his judges. He was too much of a gambler not to accept fate. With him life was at best an uncertain game, and he recognized the usual percentage in favor of the dealer.   5

A body of armed men accompanied the deported wickedness of Poker Flat to the outskirts of the settlement. Besides Mr. Oakhurst, who was known to be a coolly desperate man, and for whose intimidation the armed escort was intended, the expatriated party consisted of a young woman familiarly known as "The Duchess"; another who had won the title of "Mother Shipton"; and "Uncle Billy," a suspected sluice robber and confirmed drunkard. The cavalcade provoked no comments from the spectators, nor was any word uttered by the escort. Only when the gulch which marked the uttermost limit of Poker Flat was reached, the leader spoke briefly and to the point. The exiles were forbidden to return at the peril of their lives.

As the escort disappeared, their pent-up feelings found vent in a few hysterical tears from the Duchess, some bad language from Mother Shipton, and a Parthian volley of expletives from Uncle Billy. The philosophic Oakhurst alone remained silent. He listened calmly to Mother Shipton's desire to cut somebody's heart out, to the repeated statements of the Duchess that she would die in the road, and to the alarming oaths that seemed to be bumped out of Uncle Billy as he rode forward. With the easy good humor characteristic of his class, he insisted upon exchanging his own riding horse, "Five-Spot," for the sorry mule which the Duchess rode. But even this act did not draw the party into any closer sympathy. The young woman adjusted her somewhat draggled plumes with a feeble, faded coquetry; Mother Shipton eyed the possessor of Five-Spot with malevolence, and Uncle Billy included the whole party in one sweeping anathema.

The road to Sandy Bar—a camp that, not having as yet experienced the regenerating influences of Poker Flat, consequently seemed to offer some invitation to the emigrants—lay over a steep mountain range. It was distant a day's severe travel. In that advanced season the party soon passed out of the moist, temperate regions of the foothills into the dry, cold, bracing air of the Sierras. The trail was narrow and difficult.

At noon the Duchess, rolling out of her saddle upon the ground, declared her intention of going no farther, and the party halted.

The spot was singularly wild and impressive. A wooded amphitheater, surrounded on three sides by precipitous cliffs of naked granite, sloped gently toward the crest of another precipice that overlooked the valley. It was, undoubtedly, the most suitable spot for a camp, had camping been advisable. But Mr. Oakhurst knew that scarcely half the journey to Sandy Bar was accomplished, and the party were not equipped or provisioned for delay. This fact he pointed out to his companions curtly, with a philosophic commentary on the folly of "throwing up their hand before the game was played out." But they were furnished with liquor, which in this emergency stood them in place of food, fuel, rest, and prescience. In spite of his remonstrances, it was not long before they were more or less under its influence. Uncle Billy passed rapidly from a bellicose state into one of stupor, the Duchess became maudlin, and Mother Shipton snored. Mr. Oakhurst alone remained erect, leaning against a rock, calmly surveying them.

Mr. Oakhurst did not drink. It interfered with a profession which required coolness, impassiveness, and presence of mind, and, in his own language, he "couldn't afford it." As he gazed at his recumbent fellow exiles, the loneliness begotten of his pariah trade, his habits of life, his very vices, for the first time seriously oppressed him. He bestirred himself in dusting his black clothes, washing his hands and face, and other acts characteristic of his studiously neat habits, and for a moment forgot his annoyance. The thought of deserting his weaker and more pitiable companions never perhaps occurred to him. Yet he could not help feeling the want of that excitement which, singularly enough, was most conducive to that calm equanimity for which he was notorious. He looked at the gloomy walls that rose a thousand feet sheer above the circling pines around him, at the sky ominously clouded, at the valley below, already deepening into shadow; and, doing so, suddenly he heard his own name called.

A horseman slowly ascended the trail. In the fresh, open face of the newcomer Mr. Oakhurst recognized Tom Simson, otherwise known as "The Innocent," of Sandy Bar. He had met him sometime before over a "little game" and had, with perfect equanimity, won the entire fortune—amounting to some forty dollars—of that guileless youth. After the game was finished, Mr. Oakhurst drew the youthful speculator behind the door and thus addressed him: "Tommy, you're a good little man, but you can't gamble worth a cent. Don't try it over again." He then handed him his money back, pushed him gently from the room, and so made a devoted slave of Tom Simson.

There was a remembrance of this in his boyish and enthusiastic greeting of Mr. Oakhurst. He had started, he said, to go to Poker Flat to seek his fortune. "Alone?" No, not exactly alone; in fact (a giggle), he had run away with Piney Woods. Didn't Mr. Oakhurst remember Piney? She that used to wait on the table at the Temperance House? They had been engaged a long time, but old Jake Woods had objected, and so they had run away, and were going to Poker Flat to be married, and here they were. And they were tired out, and how lucky it was they had found a place to camp, and company. All this the Innocent delivered rapidly, while Piney, a stout, comely damsel of fifteen, emerged from behind the pine tree, where she had been blushing unseen, and rode to the side of her lover.

Mr. Oakhurst seldom troubled himself with sentiment, still less with propriety; but he had a vague idea that the situation was not fortunate. He retained, however, his presence of mind sufficiently to kick Uncle Billy, who was about to say something, and Uncle Billy was sober enough to recognize in Mr. Oakhurst's kick a superior power that would not bear trifling. He then endeavored to dissuade Tom Simson from delaying further, but in vain. He even pointed out the fact that there was no provision, nor

10

means of making a camp. But, unluckily, the Innocent met this objection by assuring the party that he was provided with an extra mule loaded with provisions, and by the discovery of a rude attempt at a log house near the trail. "Piney can stay with Mrs. Oakhurst," said the Innocent, pointing to the Duchess, "and I can shift for myself."

Nothing but Mr. Oakhurst's admonishing foot saved Uncle Billy from bursting into a roar of laughter. As it was, he felt compelled to retire up the canyon until he could recover his gravity. There he confided the joke to the tall pine trees, with many slaps of his leg, contortions of his face, and the usual profanity. But when he returned to the party, he found them seated by a fire—for the air had grown strangely chill and the sky overcast—in apparently amicable conversation. Piney was actually talking in an impulsive girlish fashion to the Duchess, who was listening with an interest and animation she had not shown for many days. The Innocent was holding forth, apparently with equal effect, to Mr. Oakhurst and Mother Shipton, who was actually relaxing into amiability. "Is this yer a d——d picnic?" said Uncle Billy, with inward scorn, as he surveyed the sylvan group, the glancing firelight, and the tethered animals in the foreground. Suddenly an idea mingled with the alcoholic fumes that disturbed his brain. It was apparently of a jocular nature, for he felt impelled to slap his leg again and cram his fist into his mouth.

As the shadows crept slowly up the mountain, a slight breeze rocked the tops of   15
the pine trees and moaned through their long and gloomy aisles. The ruined cabin, patched and covered with pine boughs, was set apart for the ladies. As the lovers parted, they unaffectedly exchanged a kiss, so honest and sincere that it might have been heard above the swaying pines. The frail Duchess and the malevolent Mother Shipton were probably too stunned to remark upon this last evidence of simplicity, and so turned without a word to the hut. The fire was replenished, the men lay down before the door, and in a few minutes were asleep.

Mr. Oakhurst was a light sleeper. Toward morning he awoke benumbed and cold. As he stirred the dying fire, the wind, which was now blowing strongly, brought to his cheek that which caused the blood to leave it—snow!

He started to his feet with the intention of awakening the sleepers, for there was no time to lose. But, turning to where Uncle Billy had been lying, he found him gone. A suspicion leaped to his brain, and a curse to his lips. He ran to the spot where the mules had been tethered—they were no longer there. The tracks were already rapidly disappearing in the snow.

The momentary excitement brought Mr. Oakhurst back to the fire with his usual calm. He did not waken the sleepers. The Innocent slumbered peacefully, with a smile on his good-humored, freckled face; the virgin Piney slept beside her frailer sisters as sweetly as though attended by celestial guardians; and Mr. Oakhurst, drawing his blanket over his shoulders, stroked his mustaches and waited for the dawn. It came slowly in a whirly mist of snowflakes that dazzled and confused the eye. What could be seen of the landscape appeared magically changed. He looked over the valley and summed up the present and future in two words, "Snowed in!"

A careful inventory of the provisions, which, fortunately for the party, had been stored within the hut, and so escaped the felonious fingers of Uncle Billy, disclosed the fact that with care and prudence, they might last ten days longer. "That is," said Mr. Oakhurst *sotto voce* to the Innocent, "if you're willing to board us. If you ain't—and perhaps you'd better not—you can wait till Uncle Billy gets back with provisions." For some occult reason, Mr. Oakhurst could not bring himself to disclose Uncle Billy's rascality, and so offered the hypothesis that he had wandered from the camp and had accidentally stampeded the animals. He dropped a warning to the Duchess and Mother Shipton, who of course knew the facts of their associate's defection. "They'll find out the truth about us *all* when they find out anything," he added significantly, "and there's no good frightening them now."

Tom Simson not only put all his worldly store at the disposal of Mr. Oakhurst, but seemed to enjoy the prospect of their enforced seclusion. "We'll have a good camp for a week, and then the snow'll melt, and we'll all go back together." The cheerful gaiety of the young man and Mr. Oakhurst's calm infected the others. The Innocent, with the aid of pine boughs, extemporized a thatch for the roofless cabin, and the Duchess directed Piney in the rearrangement of the interior with a taste and tact that opened the blue eyes of that provincial maiden to their fullest extent. "I reckon now you're used to fine things at Poker Flat," said Piney. The Duchess turned away sharply to conceal something that reddened her cheeks through their professional tint, and Mother Shipton requested Piney not to "chatter." But when Mr. Oakhurst returned from a weary search for the trail, he heard the sound of happy laughter echoed from the rocks. He stopped in some alarm, and his thoughts first naturally reverted to the whisky, which he had prudently cached. "And yet it don't somehow sound like whisky," said the gambler. It was not until he caught sight of the blazing fire through the still blind storm, and the group around it, that he settled to the conviction that it was "square fun."

Whether Mr. Oakhurst had cached his cards with the whisky as something debarred the free access of the community, I cannot say. It was certain that, in Mother Shipton's words, he "didn't say 'cards' once" during that evening. Haply the time was beguiled by an accordion, produced somewhat ostentatiously by Tom Simson from his pack. Notwithstanding some difficulties attending the manipulation of this instrument, Piney Woods managed to pluck several reluctant melodies from its keys, to an accompaniment by the Innocent on a pair of bone castanets. But the crowning festivity of the evening was reached in a rude camp-meeting hymn, which the lovers, joining hands, sang with great earnestness and vociferation. I fear that a certain defiant tone and Covenanters' swing to its chorus, rather than any devotional quality, caused it speedily to infect the others, who at last joined in the refrain:

> "I'm proud to live in the service of the Lord,
> And I'm bound to die in His army."

The pines rocked, the storm eddied and whirled above the miserable group, and the flames of their altar leaped heavenward, as if in token of the vow.

At midnight the storm abated, the rolling clouds parted, and the stars glittered keenly above the sleeping camp. Mr. Oakhurst, whose professional habits had enabled him to live on the smallest possible amount of sleep, in dividing the watch with Tom Simson, somehow managed to take upon himself the greater part of that duty. He excused himself to the Innocent by saying that he had "often been a week without sleep." "Doing what?" asked Tom. "Poker!" replied Oakhurst sententiously. "When a man gets a streak of luck, he don't get tired. The luck gives in first. Luck," continued the gambler reflectively, "is a mighty queer thing. All you know about it for certain is that it's bound to change. And it's finding out when it's going to change that makes you. We've had a streak of bad luck since we left Poker Flat—you come along, and slap, you get into it, too. If you can hold your cards right along, you're all right. For," added the gambler, with cheerful irrelevance,

"I'm proud to live in the service of the Lord,
And I'm bound to die in His army."

The third day came, and the sun, looking through the white-curtained valley, saw the outcasts dividing their slowly decreasing store of provisions for the morning meal. It was one of the peculiarities of that mountain climate that its rays diffused a kindly warmth over the wintry landscape, as if in regretful commiseration of the past. But it revealed drift on drift of snow piled high around the hut—a hopeless, uncharted, trackless sea of white lying below the rocky shores to which the castaways still clung. Through the marvelously clear air the smoke of the pastoral village of Poker Flat rose miles away. Mother Shipton saw it and, from a remote pinnacle of her rocky fastness, hurled in that direction a final malediction. It was her last vituperative attempt and, perhaps for that reason, was invested with a certain degree of sublimity. It did her good, she privately informed the Duchess. "Just you go out there and cuss, and see." She then set herself to the task of amusing "the child," as she and the Duchess were pleased to call Piney. Piney was no chicken, but it was a soothing and original theory of the pair thus to account for the fact that she didn't swear and wasn't improper.

When night crept up again through the gorges, the reedy notes of the accordion rose and fell in fitful spasms and long-drawn gasps by the flickering campfire. But music failed to fill entirely the aching void left by insufficient food, and a new diversion was proposed by Piney—storytelling. Neither Mr. Oakhurst nor his female companions caring to relate their personal experiences, this plan would have failed too, but for the Innocent. Some months before he had chanced upon a stray copy of Mr. Pope's ingenious translation of the *Iliad*. He now proposed to narrate the principal incidents of that poem—having thoroughly mastered the argument and fairly forgotten the words—in the current vernacular of Sandy Bar. And so, for the rest of that night, the Homeric demigods again walked the earth. Trojan bully and wily Greek wrestled in the winds, and the great pines in the canyon seemed to bow to the wrath of the son of Peleus. Mr. Oakhurst listened with great satisfaction. Most especially was he interested in the fate of "Ashheels," as the Innocent persisted in denominating the "swift-footed Achilles."

So, with small food and much of Homer and the accordion, a week passed over   25
the heads of the outcasts. The sun again forsook them, and again from leaden skies the snowflakes were sifted over the land. Day by day closer around them drew the snowy circle, until at last they looked from their prison over drifted walls of dazzling white that towered twenty feet above their heads. It became more and more difficult to replenish their fires, even from the fallen trees beside them, now half-hidden in the drifts. And yet no one complained. The lovers turned from the dreary prospect and looked into each other's eyes, and were happy. Mr. Oakhurst settled himself coolly to the losing game before him. The Duchess, more cheerful than she had been, assumed the care of Piney. Only Mother Shipton—once the strongest of the party—seemed to sicken and fade. At midnight on the tenth day, she called Oakhurst to her side. "I'm going," she said, in a voice of querulous weakness, "but don't say anything about it. Don't waken the kids. Take the bundle from under my head, and open it." Mr. Oakhurst did so. It contained Mother Shipton's rations for the last week, untouched. "Give 'em to the child," she said, pointing to the sleeping Piney. "You've starved yourself," said the gambler. "That's what they call it," said the woman querulously, as she lay down again and, turning her face to the wall, passed quietly away.

The accordion and the bones were put aside that day, and Homer was forgotten. When the body of Mother Shipton had been committed to the snow, Mr. Oakhurst took the Innocent aside and showed him a pair of snowshoes, which he had fashioned from the old packsaddle. "There's one chance in a hundred to save her yet," he said, pointing to Piney: "but it's there," he added, pointing toward Poker Flat. "If you can reach there in two days, she's safe." "And you?" asked Tom Simson. "I'll stay here," was the curt reply.

The lovers parted with a long embrace. "You are not going, too?" said the Duchess, as she saw Mr. Oakhurst apparently waiting to accompany him. "As far as the canyon," he replied. He turned suddenly and kissed the Duchess, leaving her pallid face aflame and her trembling limbs rigid with amazement.

Night came, but not Mr. Oakhurst. It brought the storm again and the whirling snow. Then the Duchess, feeding the fire, found someone had quietly piled beside the hut enough fuel to last a few days longer. The tears rose to her eyes, but she hid them from Piney.

The women slept but little. In the morning, looking into each other's faces, they read their fate. Neither spoke, but Piney, accepting the position of the stronger, drew near and placed her arm around the Duchess's waist. They kept this attitude for the rest of the day. That night the storm reached its greatest fury and, rending asunder the protecting vines, invaded the very hut.

Toward morning they found themselves unable to feed the fire, which gradually died away. As the embers slowly blackened, the Duchess crept closer to Piney and broke the silence of many hours: "Piney, can you pray?" "No, dear," said Piney simply. The Duchess, without knowing exactly why, felt relieved and, putting her head upon Piney's shoulder, spoke no more. And so reclining, the younger and purer pillowing the head of her soiled sister upon her virgin breast, they fell asleep.   30

The wind lulled as if it feared to waken them. Feathery drifts of snow, shaken from the long pine boughs, flew like white-winged birds and settled about them as they slept. The moon through the rifted clouds looked down upon what had been the camp. But all human stain, all trace of earthly travail, was hidden beneath the spotless mantle mercifully flung from above.

They slept all that day and the next, nor did they waken when voices and footsteps broke the silence of the camp. And when pitying fingers brushed the snow from their wan faces, you could scarcely have told from the equal peace that dwelt upon them which was she that had sinned. Even the law of Poker Flat recognized this and turned away, leaving them still locked in each other's arms.

But at the head of the gulch, on one of the largest pine trees, they found the deuce of clubs pinned to the bark with a bowie knife. It bore the following, written in pencil in a firm hand:

BENEATH THIS TREE

LIES THE BODY

OF

JOHN OAKHURST,

WHO STRUCK A STREAK OF BAD LUCK

ON THE 23D OF NOVEMBER, 1850,

AND

HANDED IN HIS CHECKS

ON THE 7TH DECEMBER, 1850.

And pulseless and cold, with a Derringer by his side and a bullet in his heart, though still calm as in life, beneath the snow lay he who was at once the strongest and yet the weakest of the outcasts of Poker Flat.

THE RECEPTIVE READER

1. Study examples of *formal* word choice, or diction, in the first three paragraphs of the story. What makes Harte's vocabulary more elevated, more dignified, than ordinary informal speech? What would be informal equivalents of some striking formal expressions? ❖ Why does some of the elevated, dignified diction here have a humorous effect? What are striking examples of *euphemisms*—roundabout innocuous-sounding phrases that disguise harsh realities?

2. Bret Harte was one of the writers creating the mystique of the American West that gave people cooped up in cities a larger scope for their imagination. What features of the setting and of the plot do you recognize as part of the Western *genre*?

3. What are telling touches in Harte's *satirical portrait* of the moral majority in Poker Flat? How and how successfully does Harte steer your reactions?

4. What types do you recognize among Harte's ill-assorted cast of characters? How does Mother Shipton fit the *stereotype* of the prostitute with a heart of gold? What stereotype does the young couple live up to? What other examples are there of the sentimental stereotype that there is some good in everyone? ❖ What is the role of Uncle Billy in the story?

5. What is the gambler's style? What is his role in the story? Do you find his actions surprising or predictable?

6. What is distinctive about the final sentence of the story? How would it read if you were to break it up into Hemingway sentences?

THE PERSONAL RESPONSE

How obsolete is Harte's brand of sentimentality? Do any features of it survive in current popular entertainment? Why do you think modern critics have made sentimentality a prime target? Do you agree with them? Or can something be said in its defense?

JOHN CHEEVER (1912–1982)

Fiction is art and art is the triumph over chaos (no less) and we can accomplish this only by the most vigilant exercise of choice, but in a world that changes more swiftly than we can perceive there is always the danger that our powers of selection will be mistaken and that the vision we serve will come to nothing.

JOHN CHEEVER

John Cheever was born in Quincy, Massachusetts, and was expelled from a private New England academy at seventeen. He returned to academic life only for brief stints teaching at Barnard and in the prestigious creative writing program at the University of Iowa. (He also received an honorary doctorate from Harvard in 1978.) He was much honored—receiving a Guggenheim, a National Book Award, a Pulitzer Prize.

Cheever is among the outstanding practitioners of the modern short story for whom the *New Yorker* provided an ideal outlet. (The magazine published more than two hundred of his stories.) His fiction seemed well attuned to the self-image of the mythical sophisticated *New Yorker* reader—who has a taste for the uncommon and a tolerance for human eccentricity, who has the appropriate liberal political sympathies but has a horror of sensationalism and popular enthusiasm. A key to Cheever's style is irony—the witty exposure of the discrepancy between what people should be and what they are. His stories often reach a turning point where the sunny, reassuring surface wears thin and a chilling note is heard, similar to "that hour of a spring day. . . when the dark of the woods and the cold and damp from any nearby pond or brook are suddenly felt, when you realize that the world was lighted, until a minute ago . . . and that your clothes are thin" ("Just Tell Me Who It Was").

Cheever often seems to look at his characters with wry amusement from without—rather than getting embroiled in their inner turmoil, sharing in their confusions and frustrations. His own journals, published after his death, and a book by his daughter probing her parents' unhappy marriage (*Home before Dark,* 1984) have given readers a glimpse of the writer's own traumas, which he masked by the defensive armor of his witty, ironic style. His son, Benjamin Cheever, said about him, "He showed the world what he thought it wanted to see. The picture he presented was sharp, witty, cogent, and often false." Many of Cheever's journal entries focus on his gay life-style (which he calls his "contested sexuality") and his struggles with alcoholism. He wrote early in his journal, "I come back again and again to the image of a naked prisoner in an unlocked cell, and to tell the truth I don't know how he will escape."

Cheever's "The Enormous Radio" revolves around strange fragmentary messages heard on a radio. The story is thus an ideal vehicle for the kind of **allusion** and name-dropping that became fashionable as part of a late-twentieth-century (postmodern) style. An allusion is a brief mention that activates our memory. It brings to mind a range of associations; it makes us recall a story. When we first read about the upwardly mobile couple in this story, we are expected to recognize that Andover is a tony private boarding school on the New England preppie circuit (the husband is an alumnus). Westchester (where the couple eventually hope to live) is a suburban sanctuary for well-shod commuters to New York City. The couple love classical composers like Mozart, Schubert, and Chopin—great composers, but part of a safe repertory (often too much with us?) that avoids the challenges of a Bach or a Stravinsky.

The Enormous Radio   1947

Jim and Irene Westcott were the kind of people who seem to strike that satisfactory average of income, endeavor, and respectability that is reached by the statistical reports in college alumni bulletins. They were the parents of two young children, they had been married nine years, they lived on the twelfth floor of an apartment house near Sutton Place, they went to the theatre on an average of 10.3 times a year, and they hoped someday to live in Westchester. Irene Westcott was a pleasant, rather plain girl with soft brown hair and a wide, fine forehead upon which nothing at all had been written, and in the cold weather she wore a coat of fitch skins dyed to resemble mink. You could not say that Jim Westcott looked younger than he was, but you could at least say of him that he seemed to feel younger. He wore his graying hair cut very short, he dressed in the kind of clothes his class had worn at Andover, and his manner was earnest, vehement, and intentionally naïve. The Westcotts differed from their friends, their classmates, and their neighbors only in an interest they shared in serious music. They went to a great many concerts—although they seldom mentioned this to anyone—and they spent a good deal of time listening to music on the radio.

Their radio was an old instrument, sensitive, unpredictable, and beyond repair. Neither of them understood the mechanics of radio—or of any of the other appliances that surrounded them—and when the instrument faltered, Jim would strike the side of the cabinet with his hand. This sometimes helped. One Sunday afternoon, in the middle of a Schubert quartet, the music faded away altogether. Jim struck the cabinet repeatedly, but there was no response; the Schubert was lost to them forever. He promised to buy Irene a new radio, and on Monday when he came home from work he told her that he had got one. He refused to describe it, and said it would be a surprise for her when it came.

The radio was delivered at the kitchen door the following afternoon, and with the assistance of her maid and the handyman Irene uncrated it and brought it into the living room. She was struck at once with the physical ugliness of the large gumwood cabinet. Irene was proud of her living room, she had chosen its furnishings and colors as carefully as she chose her clothes, and now it seemed to her that the new radio stood among her intimate possessions like an aggressive intruder. She was confounded by the number of dials and switches on the instrument panel, and she studied them thoroughly before she put the plug into a wall socket and turned the radio on. The dials flooded with a malevolent green light, and in the distance she heard the music of a piano quintet. The quintet was in the distance for only an instant; it bore down upon her with a speed greater than light and filled the apartment with the noise of music amplified so mightily that it knocked a china ornament from a table to the floor. She rushed to the instrument and reduced the volume. The violent forces that were snared in the ugly gumwood cabinet made her uneasy. Her children came home from school then, and she took them to the Park. It was not until later in the afternoon that she was able to return to the radio.

The maid had given the children their suppers and was supervising their baths when Irene turned on the radio, reduced the volume, and sat down to listen to a Mozart quintet that she knew and enjoyed. The music came through clearly. The new instrument had a much purer tone, she thought, than the old one. She decided that tone was most important and that she could conceal the cabinet behind a sofa. But as soon as she had made her peace with the radio, the interference began. A crackling sound like the noise of a burning powder fuse began to accompany the singing of the strings. Beyond the music, there was a rustling that reminded Irene unpleasantly of the sea, and as the quintet progressed, these noises were joined by many others. She tried all the dials and switches but nothing dimmed the interference, and she sat down, disappointed and bewildered, and tried to trace the flight of the melody. The elevator shaft in her building ran beside the living-room wall, and it was the noise of the elevator that gave her a clue to the character of the static. The rattling of the elevator cables and the opening and closing of the elevator doors were reproduced in her loudspeaker, and, realizing that the radio was sensitive to electrical currents of all sorts, she began to discern through the Mozart the ringing of telephone bells, the dialing of phones, and the lamentation of a vacuum cleaner. By listening more carefully, she was able to distinguish doorbells, elevator bells, electric razors, and Waring mixers, whose sounds had been picked up from the apartments that surrounded hers and transmitted through her loudspeaker. The powerful and ugly instrument, with its mistaken sensitivity to discord, was more than she could hope to master, so she turned the thing off and went into the nursery to see her children.

When Jim Westcott came home that night, he went to the radio confidently and worked the controls. He had the same sort of experience Irene had had. A man was speaking on the station Jim had chosen, and his voice swung instantly from the distance into a force so powerful that it shook the apartment. Jim turned the volume control and reduced the voice. Then, a minute or two later, the interference began. The ringing of telephones and doorbells set in, joined by the rasp of the elevator doors and the whir of cooking appliances. The character of the noise had changed since Irene had tried the radio earlier; the last of the electric razors was being unplugged, the vacuum cleaners had all been returned to their closets, and the static reflected that change in pace that overtakes the city after the sun goes down. He fiddled with the knobs but couldn't get rid of the noises, so he turned the radio off and told Irene that in the morning he'd call the people who had sold it to him and give them hell.

The following afternoon, when Irene returned to the apartment from a luncheon date, the maid told her that a man had come and fixed the radio. Irene went into the living room before she took off her hat or her furs and tried the instrument. From the loudspeaker came a recording of the "Missouri Waltz." It reminded her of the thin, scratchy music from an old-fashioned phonograph that she sometimes heard across the lake where she spent her summers. She waited until the waltz had finished, expecting an explanation of the recording, but there was none. The music was followed by silence, and then the plaintive and scratchy record was repeated. She turned the dial and got a satisfactory burst of Caucasian music—the thump of bare feet in the dust and the rattle of coin jewelry—but in the background she could hear the ringing of bells and a confusion of voices. Her children came home from school then, and she turned off the radio and went to the nursery.

When Jim came home that night, he was tired, and he took a bath and changed his clothes. Then he joined Irene in the living room. He had just turned on the radio when the maid announced dinner, so he left it on, and he and Irene went to the table.

Jim was too tired to make even pretense of sociability, and there was nothing about the dinner to hold Irene's interest, so her attention wandered from the food to the deposits of silver polish on the candlesticks and from there to the music in the other room. She listened for a few minutes to a Chopin prelude and then was surprised to hear a man's voice break in. "For Christ's sake, Kathy," he said, "do you always have to play the piano when I get home?" The music stopped abruptly. "It's the only chance I have," a woman said. "I'm at the office all day." "So am I," the man said. He added something obscene about an upright piano, and slammed a door. The passionate and melancholy music began again.

"Did you hear that?" Irene asked.

"What?" Jim was eating his dessert.

"The radio. A man said something while the music was still going on—something dirty."

"It's probably a play."

"I don't think it *is* a play," Irene said.

They left the table and took their coffee into the living room. Irene asked Jim to try another station. He turned the knob. "Have you seen my garters?" a man asked. "Button me up," a woman said. "Have you seen my garters?" the man said again. "Just button me up and I'll find your garters," the woman said. Jim shifted to another station. "I wish you wouldn't leave apple cores in the ashtrays," a man said. "I hate the smell."

"This is strange," Jim said.

"Isn't it?" Irene said.

Jim turned the knob again. "'On the coast of Coromandel where the early pumpkins blow,'" a woman with a pronounced English accent said, "'in the middle of the woods lived the Yonghy-Bonghy-Bò. Two old chairs, and half a candle, one old jug without a handle . . .'"

"My God!" Irene cried. "That's the Sweeneys' nurse."

"'These were all his worldly goods,'" the British voice continued.

"Turn that thing off," Irene said. "Maybe they can hear *us*." Jim switched the radio off. "That was Miss Armstrong, the Sweeneys' nurse," Irene said. "She must be reading to the little girl. They live in 17-B. I've talked with Miss Armstrong in the Park. I know her voice very well. We must be getting other people's apartments."

"That's impossible," Jim said.

"Well, that was the Sweeneys' nurse," Irene said hotly. "I know her voice. I know it very well. I'm wondering if they can hear us."

Jim turned the switch. First from a distance and then nearer, nearer, as if borne on the wind, came the pure accents of the Sweeneys' nurse again: "*'Lady Jingly! Lady Jingly!'*" she said, "*'sitting where the pumpkins blow, will you come and be my wife? said the* Yonghy-Bonghy-Bò . . .'"

Jim went over to the radio and said "Hello" loudly into the speaker.

"*'I am tired of living singly,'*" the nurse went on, "*'on this coast so wild and shingly, I'm a-weary of my life; if you'll come and be my wife, quite serene would be my life . . .'*"

"I guess she can't hear us," Irene said. "Try something else."

Jim turned to another station, and the living room was filled with the uproar of a cocktail party that had overshot its mark. Someone was playing the piano and singing the "Whiffenpoof Song," and the voices that surrounded the piano were vehement and happy. "Eat some more sandwiches," a woman shrieked. There were screams of laughter and a dish of some sort crashed to the floor.

"Those must be the Fullers, in 11-E," Irene said. "I knew they were giving a party this afternoon. I saw her in the liquor store. Isn't this too divine? Try something else. See if you can get those people in 18-C."

The Westcotts overheard that evening a monologue on salmon fishing in Canada, a bridge game, running comments on home movies of what had apparently been a fortnight at Sea Island, and a bitter family quarrel about an overdraft at the bank. They turned off their radio at midnight and went to bed, weak with laughter. Sometime in the night, their son began to call for a glass of water and Irene got one and took it to his room. It was very early. All the lights in the neighborhood were extinguished, and from the boy's window she could see the empty street. She went into the living room and tried the radio. There was some faint coughing, a moan, and then a man spoke. "Are you all right, darling?" he asked. "Yes," a woman said wearily. "Yes, I'm all right, I guess," and then she added with great feeling, "But, you know, Charlie, I don't feel like myself anymore. Sometimes there are about fifteen or twenty minutes in the week when I feel like myself. I don't like to go to another doctor, because the doctor's bills are so awful already, but I just don't feel like myself, Charlie. I just never feel like myself." They were not young, Irene thought. She guessed from the timbre of their voices that they were middle-aged. The restrained melancholy of the dialogue and the draft from the bedroom window made her shiver, and she went back to bed.

The following morning, Irene cooked breakfast for the family—the maid didn't come up from her room in the basement until ten—braided her daughter's hair, and waited at the door until her children and her husband had been carried away in the elevator. Then she went into the living room and tried the radio. "I don't want to go to school," a child screamed. "I hate school. I won't go to school. I hate school." "You will

20

25

30

go to school," an enraged woman said. "We paid eight hundred dollars to get you into that school and you'll go if it kills you." The next number on the dial produced the worn record of the "Missouri Waltz." Irene shifted the control and invaded the privacy of several breakfast tables. She overheard demonstrations of indigestion, carnal love, abysmal vanity, faith, and despair. Irene's life was nearly as simple and sheltered as it appeared to be, and the forthright and sometimes brutal language that came from the loudspeaker that morning astonished and troubled her. She continued to listen until her maid came in. Then she turned off the radio quickly, since this insight, she realized, was a furtive one.

Irene had a luncheon date with a friend that day, and she left her apartment at a little after twelve. There were a number of women in the elevator when it stopped at her floor. She stared at their handsome and impassive faces, their furs, and the cloth flowers in their hats. Which one of them had been to Sea Island? she wondered. Which one had overdrawn her bank account. The elevator stopped at the tenth floor and a woman with a pair of Skye terriers joined them. Her hair was rigged high on her head and she wore a mink cape. She was humming the "Missouri Waltz."

Irene had two Martinis at lunch, and she looked searchingly at her friend and wondered what her secrets were. They had intended to go shopping after lunch, but Irene excused herself and went home. She told the maid that she was not to be disturbed; then she went into the living room, closed the doors, and switched on the radio. She heard, in the course of the afternoon, the halting conversation of a woman entertaining her aunt, the hysterical conclusion of a luncheon party, and a hostess briefing her maid about some cocktail guests. "Don't give the best Scotch to anyone who hasn't white hair," the hostess said. "See if you can get rid of that liver paste before you pass those hot things, and could you lend me five dollars? I want to tip the elevator man."

As the afternoon waned, the conversations increased in intensity. From where Irene sat, she could see the open sky above the East River. There were hundreds of clouds in the sky, as though the south wind had broken the winter into pieces and were blowing it north, and on her radio she could hear the arrival of cocktail guests and the return of children and businessmen from their schools and offices. "I found a good-sized diamond on the bathroom floor this morning," a woman said. "It must have fallen out of that bracelet Mrs. Dunston was wearing last night." "We'll sell it," a man said. "Take it down to the jeweler on Madison Avenue and sell it. Mrs. Dunston won't know the difference, and we could use a couple of hundred bucks . . ." "'Oranges and lemons, say the bells of St. Clement's,'" the Sweeneys' nurse sang. "'Halfpence and farthings, say the bells of St. Martin's. When will you pay me? say the bells at old Bailey . . .'" "It's not a hat," a woman cried, and at her back roared a cocktail party. "It's not a hat, it's a love affair. That's what Walter Florell said. He said it's not a hat, it's a love affair," and then, in a lower voice, the same woman added, "Talk to somebody, for Christ's sake, honey, talk to somebody. If she catches you standing here not talking to anybody, she'll take us off her invitation list, and I love these parties."

The Westcotts were going out for dinner that night, and when Jim came home, Irene was dressing. She seemed sad and vague, and he brought her a drink. They were dining with friends in the neighborhood, and they walked to where they were going. The sky was broad and filled with light. It was one of those splendid spring evenings that excite memory and desire, and the air that touched their hands and faces felt very soft. A Salvation Army band was on the corner playing "Jesus Is Sweeter." Irene drew on her husband's arm and held him there for a minute, to hear the music. "They're really such nice people, aren't they?" she said. "They have such nice faces. Actually, they're so much nicer than a lot of the people we know." She took a bill from her purse and walked over and dropped it into the tambourine. There was in her face, when she returned to her husband, a look of radiant melancholy that he was not familiar with. And her conduct at the dinner party that night seemed strange to him, too. She interrupted her hostess rudely and stared at the people across the table from her with an intensity for which she would have punished her children.

It was still mild when they walked home from the party, and Irene looked up at   35
the spring stars. "'How far that little candle throws its beams,'" she exclaimed. "'So shines a good deed in a naughty world.'" She waited that night until Jim had fallen asleep, and then went into the living room and turned on the radio.

Jim came home at about six the next night. Emma, the maid, let him in, and he had taken off his hat and was taking off his coat when Irene ran into the hall. Her face was shining with tears and her hair was disordered. "Go up to 16-C, Jim!" she screamed. "Don't take off your coat. Go up to 16-C. Mr. Osborn's beating his wife. They've been quarreling since four o'clock, and now he's hitting her. Go up there and stop him."

From the radio in the living room, Jim heards screams, obscenities, and thuds. "You know you don't have to listen to this sort of thing," he said. He strode into the living room and turned the switch. "It's indecent," he said. "It's like looking in windows. You know you don't have to listen to this sort of thing. You can turn it off."

"Oh, it's so horrible, it's so dreadful," Irene was sobbing. "I've been listening all day, and it's so depressing."

"Well, if it's so depressing, why do you listen to it? I bought this damned radio to give you some pleasure," he said. "I paid a great deal of money for it. I thought it might make you happy. I wanted to make you happy."

"Don't, don't, don't, don't quarrel with me," she moaned, and laid her head on   40
his shoulder. "All the others have been quarreling all day. Everybody's been quarreling. They're all worried about money. Mrs. Hutchinson's mother is dying of cancer in Florida and they don't have enough money to send her to the Mayo Clinic. At least, Mr. Hutchinson says they don't have enough money. And some woman in this building is having an affair with the handyman—with that hideous handyman. It's too disgusting. And Mrs. Melville has heart trouble, and Mr. Hendricks is going to lose his job in April and Mrs. Hendricks is horrid about the whole thing and that girl who plays the 'Missouri Waltz' is a whore, a common whore, and the elevator man has tuberculosis and Mr. Osborn has been beating Mrs. Osborn." She wailed, she trembled with grief and checked the stream of tears down her face with the heel of her palm.

"Well, why do you have to listen?" Jim asked again. "Why do you have to listen to this stuff if it makes you so miserable?"

"Oh, don't, don't, don't," she cried. "Life is too terrible, too sordid and awful. But we've never been like that, have we, darling? Have we? I mean, we've always been good and decent and loving to one another, haven't we? And we have two children, two beautiful children. Our lives aren't sordid, are they, darling? Are they?" She flung her arms around his neck and drew his face down to hers. "We're happy, aren't we, darling? We are happy, aren't we?"

"Of course we're happy," he said tiredly. He began to surrender his resentment. "Of course we're happy. I'll have that damned radio fixed or taken away tomorrow." He stroked her soft hair. "My poor girl," he said.

"You love me, don't you?" she asked. "And we're not hypercritical or worried about money or dishonest, are we?"

"No, darling," he said.   45

A man came in the morning and fixed the radio. Irene turned it on cautiously and was happy to hear a California-wine commercial and a recording of Beethoven's Ninth

Symphony, including Schiller's "Ode to Joy." She kept the radio on all day and nothing untoward came from the speaker.

A Spanish suite was being played when Jim came home. "Is everything all right?" he asked. His face was pale, she thought. They had some cocktails and went in to dinner to the "Anvil Chorus" from *Il Trovatore*. This was followed by Debussy's "La Mer."

"I paid the bill for the radio today," Jim said. "It cost four hundred dollars. I hope you'll get some enjoyment out of it."

"Oh, I'm sure I will," Irene said.

"Four hundred dollars is a good deal more than I can afford," he went on. "I wanted to get something that you'd enjoy. It's the last extravagance we'll be able to indulge in this year. I see that you haven't paid your clothing bills yet. I saw them on your dressing table." He looked directly at her. "Why did you tell me you'd paid them? Why did you lie to me?"   50

"I just didn't want you to worry, Jim," she said. She drank some water. "I'll be able to pay my bills out of this month's allowance. There were the slipcovers last month, and that party."

"You've got to learn to handle the money I give you a little more intelligently, Irene," he said. "You've got to understand that we don't have as much money this year as we had last. I had a very sobering talk with Mitchell today. No one is buying anything. We're spending all our time promoting new issues, and you know how long that takes. I'm not getting any younger, you know. I'm thirty-seven. My hair will be gray next year. I haven't done as well as I'd hoped to do. And I don't suppose things will get any better."

"Yes, dear," she said.

"We've got to start cutting down," Jim said. "We've got to think of the children. To be perfectly frank with you, I worry about money a great deal. I'm not at all sure of the future. No one is. If anything should happen to me, there's the insurance, but that wouldn't go very far today. I've worked awfully hard to give you and the children a comfortable life," he said bitterly. "I don't like to see all my energies, all of my youth, wasted in fur coats and radios and slipcovers and—"

"Please, Jim," she said. "Please. They'll hear us."   55

"*Who'll hear us?* Emma can't hear us."

"The radio."

"Oh, I'm sick!" he shouted. "I'm sick to death of your apprehensiveness. The radio can't hear us. Nobody can hear us. And what if they can hear us? Who cares?"

Irene got up from the table and went into the living room. Jim went to the door and shouted at her from there. "Why are you so Christly all of a sudden? What's turned you overnight into a convent girl? You stole your mother's jewelry before they probated her will. You never gave your sister a cent of that money that was intended for her— not even when she needed it. You made Grace Howland's life miserable, and where was all your piety and your virtue when you went to that abortionist? I'll never forget how cool you were. You packed your bag and went off to have that child murdered as if you were going to Nassau. If you'd had any reasons, if you'd had any good reasons—"

Irene stood for a minute before the hideous cabinet, disgraced and sickened, but   60
she held her hand on the switch before she extinguished the music and the voices, hoping that the instrument might speak to her kindly, that she might hear the Sweeneys' nurse. Jim continued to shout at her from the door. The voice on the radio was suave and noncommittal. "An early-morning railroad disaster in Tokyo," the loudspeaker said, "killed twenty-nine people. A fire in a Catholic hospital near Buffalo for the care of

blind children was extinguished early this morning by nuns. The temperature is forty-seven. The humidity is eighty-nine.'"

THE RECEPTIVE READER

1. What is the *keynote* in Cheever's description of his suburban couple? What are telling details? What is his attitude toward these people—how does it show?

2. Is there a *pattern*—a thread that connects the snatches of conversation or the fragments of people's lives that are heard on the strange radio?

3. On the subject of *allusions:* What is funny about the Whiffenpoof Song picked up by the radio being a college drinking song, or about the Missouri Waltz being a sentimental favorite that President Truman used to play on the piano? ❖ The snatches of humorous verse read by the "woman with the pronounced English accent" are from the work of Edward Lear, a cherished author of nonsense verse and a contemporary and kindred spirit of Lewis Carroll, the author of *Alice in Wonderland*. What touch do they lend to the story?

4. What has happened to the couple at the end? Why is what has happened to them *ironic* in the light of how the author described them at the beginning?

THE PERSONAL RESPONSE

For you, is the story as a whole amusing or serious, or both?

WRITING ABOUT LITERATURE

8. Responding to Style (Prewriting to Finished Paper)

The Writing Workshop Writing about an author's style requires you to pay close attention to word choice, sentence rhythms, key images, ways of expressing (or suppressing) emotion. However, as you read closely for detail, try to see how features of style serve the larger purposes of a story. When you write about style, you confront in especially urgent and hard-to-miss form a need that you also face with many other writing tasks: You need to start with close attention to detail—and to stay close to detail—but you have to go on to sort out and lay out your material in a pattern that makes sense.

From Prewriting to First Draft

Do you ever suffer from writer's block? Do you find yourself staring at a blank screen or blank sheet of paper? Go through some of the steps that other writers use to start the flow. Draw on the different prewriting techniques that help a substantial, purposeful paper take shape.

Brainstorming Brainstorming allows you to bring up from hidden corners of your memory material that might prove relevant to your topic. Let us assume you are going to write about Bret Harte's "The Outcasts of Poker Flat" as an example of the sentimentality that is a staple of American popular culture. Try to call up and jot down any phrases, catchwords, quotations, images, or incidents connected with your key word. Leave sifting and editing for later. Sample:

Sentimentality: The word brings to mind true love and romance, life lovingly and beautifully portrayed, with death only a momentary transition to a better place. Every cloud has a silver lining. Life may be harsh and cruel, but redemption and salvation are the eventual outcome. Everything is loaded with sympathy, empathy, compassion, caring. There is some good in everyone. "Life is real; life is earnest." Live is invigorating, challenging.

Death is softened, described almost tenderly. Mother holds the hand of darling child dying of tuberculosis. Dying soldier props himself up on elbow to remember loved ones. The gentle easing from sleep to death. Nothing gory, bloody, sickening.

Hearts, flowers, sunsets, baby shoes. Make the reader feel good. Life may be cruel, but there is justice and beauty. Hallmark greeting cards.

Reading Notes   Focus your reading notes on questions of tone or style. Look for possible connections; try to be open to a possible pattern that might emerge. Sample notes:

appeal to our sympathy: the heartless, self-righteous townspeople turn out the band of sinners in the dead of winter

(Holman and Harmon on sentimentality in *A Handbook of Literature:* "an optimistic overemphasis on the goodness of humanity")

finding goodness in unexpected places: Oakhurst, the gambler, gives up his horse to the Duchess, trading for her "sorry mule"; later, Oakhurst decides to stay with his "weaker and more pitiable companions"

the naive young "innocents": "they unaffectedly exchanged a kiss, so honest and sincere that it might have been heard above the swaying pines"; note: the naive purity of the innocents softens the hardened sinners

Mother Shipton, notorious for her coarse language and violent oaths, becomes the hooker with the heart of gold who starves herself so that the virginal Piney may eat an additional portion of the rations and so have a chance to live

final good deed: Oakhurst piles firewood by the cabin before he dies with a flourish, "handing in his checks"

softening of death: the Duchess and Piney (sin and innocence) die "locked in each other's arms," with the "younger and purer pillowing the head of her soiled sister upon her virgin breast"; they "fell asleep"; the fatal blizzard becomes a flurry of soft flakes—"feathery drifts of snow" cover the dead

saving touches of grim realism: Uncle Billy is a true rascal and hard-bitten cynic (and he survives when the others die); the hypocritical citizens of Poker Flat are satirized for their self-righteousness

Structuring Your Paper   Look at the way the following excerpted paper plays off two different facets of an author's style in an "on-the-one-hand" and "on-the-other-hand" pattern:

The Sentimental Sinners of Poker Flat

(introduction: defining the key term)

Driven out of town by the moral majority, "The Outcasts of Poker Flat" perish (with one exception) in an early snowstorm that traps them in the mountains. Two prostitutes, a gambler, and a drunk—these, along with two innocents, are the main characters of Bret Harte's sentimental tale. In sentimental writing, the tender emotions, such as love and pity, are superabundant, and evil exists mainly to stimulate our pity for the victims and our moral indignation. We feel tender pity for the innocent victims and we feel a warm glow of emotion when evildoers repent or show an unexpected noble side.

(thesis: a sentimental story saved from mawkishness)

Bret Harte's characters do indeed act their parts in a story that has most of the elements of nineteenth-century sentimentality. Nevertheless, somehow the story does not leave us with that sickeningly sweet, cloying sensation that a truly sentimental narrative often produces. Harte's skillful use of humor rescues "The Outcasts" from complete mawkishness.

(first major point: the sentimental side of the story)

The story is indeed sentimental. A group of characters who are extremely unlikely candidates for sainthood nevertheless exhibit heroic virtue and selflessness. Their ordeal, rather than demonstrating the baseness of human nature, shows humanity's basic goodness. The only appearance of anything less than virtuous is in Uncle Billy, the drunk. He steals away in the night with the mules, stranding the others in the snowstorm. The rest of the group are inspired to attain a saintly goodness. There is no fighting over food or shelter; each individual is concerned only for the others. . . .

(further follow-up of first point: clinching examples)

The real heroics, though, come from the greatest "sinners," in true sentimental fashion. The gambler, Oakhurst, although he is known to be "a coolly desperate man," never "thought of deserting his weaker and more pitiable companions." Mother Shipton, the legendary prostitute with a heart of gold, starves herself to save the young virgin. . . .

(turning point of the essay: Harte's saving humor)

However, Harte's story as a whole is more successful and more enjoyable than this description would suggest. Humor is the key to Harte's success. Harte's wry humor—a Western, often ironic brand—runs throughout the story, setting it apart from other sentimental writing and allowing a modern reader to appreciate it. The beginning of the story sets the tone: The community of Poker Flat, having lately suffered the loss of "several thousand dollars, two valuable horses," and (almost as an afterthought)" a prominent citizen," is experiencing "a spasm of virtuous reactions." The real reason the townspeople are after Oakhurst is not simply that he is a gambler but that he is a better one than they are—and they want their money back. Oakhurst himself is presented as a worldly-wise character who looks at life with dry ironic humor: "With him life was at best an uncertain game, and he recognized the usual percentage in favor of the dealer."

(conclusion: sentimental ending with a final humorous touch)

The ending of the story is the closest approach to cloying sentimentality. The virgin and the prostitute huddle together in the snow and freeze to death in each other's arms. However, the story does not end there but with a final touch of humor. Oakhurst has left his own epitaph, scribbled on the deuce of clubs and pinned to a tree with a knife. In keeping with his character, it reads: "Beneath this tree lies the body of John Oakhurst, who struck a streak of bad luck . . . and handed in his checks on the 7th December, 1850."

QUESTIONS

Where or how is the initial definition of sentimentality echoed later in the paper? How would you state the central thesis in your own words? How and how well is the program it implies implemented in the paper? Where do you agree and where do you disagree with the student author?

9 THE WRITER'S VOICE
Flannery O'Connor

No writer is a pessimist; the very act of writing is an optimistic act.

FLANNERY O'CONNOR

FOCUS ON THE WRITER'S VOICE

Critics admonish us to read a story on its own terms: We should read it without preconceptions. We should let it create its own world, its own context, its own version of reality. In practice, however, we often do not read an anonymous story; we read Joyce or Faulkner or O'Connor. As we come to know the author, we anticipate certain kinds of pleasures and rewards. When we start reading an unfamiliar story by a familiar writer, we may feel like a traveler recognizing landmarks: We find our bearings more easily than in reading a new and unknown author. We begin to recognize the writer's voice: a familiar solemn or ironic tone, a familiar mood of foreboding or expectation, a way of looking at places and people. We bring expectations to the story, and we take pleasure in seeing them fulfilled. At the same time, we need to expect the unexpected. We need to remain flexible enough to see a side of the author that we did not notice before.

FLANNERY O'CONNOR: AUTHOR AND WORK

The creator of our nature has also imparted to us the character of love. . . . If love is absent, all the elements of the image are deformed.

GREGORY OF NYSSA

With the serious writer, violence is never an end in itself. It is the extreme situation that best reveals what we are essentially, and I believe these are the times when writers are more interested in what we are essentially than in the tenor of our daily lives.

FLANNERY O'CONNOR

When Flannery O'Connor (1924–1964) was asked to name the most important influences on her life, she replied they were probably "being a Catholic and a Southerner and a writer." O'Connor was a devout Catholic in the Baptist South; she attended Catholic schools before she went to Georgia Women's College. Readers of her fiction encounter two sides of a central paradox: Her characters live in a violent world in which evil seems to triumph. But her stories are written by an author who believes in redemption, in divine grace, in the supremacy of God's mercy. She once said that a writer of fiction is "concerned with ultimate mystery as we find it embodied in the concrete world of sense experience."

O'Connor grew up in Savannah and Milledgeville, Georgia, in the segregated South, in a landscape dotted with sharecroppers' shacks. When a Southern novelist was asked why the South had produced so many of America's best writers, he pointed to the lost war that made the Southern experience different from that of the North. O'Connor commented on his reply that he

> didn't mean by that simply that a lost war makes good subject matter. What he was saying was that we had our Fall. We have gone into the modern world with an inburnt knowledge of human limitations and with a sense of mystery which could not have developed in our first state of innocence—as it has not sufficiently developed in the rest of the country.

O'Connor was a master of the grotesque—the freakish mixture of the frightening and the comic. She had a sharp eye for the laughable, for the absurd. ("It is not surprising that she first wanted to be a cartoonist, and sent off cartoons, week after week, to the *New Yorker,* where they were invariably rejected"—Joyce Carol Oates). But in her fiction, horror and comedy mingle, and laughter is muted by our sense of unease, fear, and puzzlement as we watch her strange parables of antagonism and violence unfold. It is as if she had some implied vision of humankind in harmony with God's purposes by which our imperfect, sinful human reality is judged and found wanting—and laughable. She said: "Whenever I am asked why Southern writers particularly have a penchant for writing about freaks, I say it is because we are still able to recognize one. To be able to recognize a freak, you have to have some conception of the whole man, and in the South the general conception of man is still, in the main, theological." Even the good, in O'Connor's view, had traits of the freakish, the grotesque, because "in us the good is something under construction."

O'Connor suffered from a debilitating hereditary illness (lupus), and she was on crutches during most of her writing life. Some of her best work was not published until after her early death at age thirty-nine. Joyce Carol Oates said of her, "We measure an artist by the quality and depth of interior vision, and by the magnitude of achievement, and by these standards Flannery O'Connor is one of our finest writers." Her work "is a deeply moving, deeply disturbing, and ultimately a very beautiful record of a highly complex woman artist whose art was, perhaps, too profound for even the critic in her to grasp."

A Good Man Is Hard to Find   1955

The grandmother didn't want to go to Florida. She wanted to visit some of her connections in east Tennessee and she was seizing every chance to change Bailey's mind. Bailey was the son she lived with, her only boy. He was sitting on the edge of his chair at the table, bent over the orange sports section of the *Journal.* "Now look here, Bailey," she said, "see here, read this," and she stood with one hand on her thin hip and the other rattling the newspaper at his bald head. "Here this fellow that calls himself The Misfit is aloose from the Federal Pen and headed toward Florida and you read here what it says he did to these people. Just you read it. I wouldn't take my children in any direction with a criminal like that aloose in it. I couldn't answer to my conscience if I did."

Bailey didn't look up from his reading so she wheeled around then and faced the children's mother; a young woman in slacks, whose face was as broad and innocent as a cabbage and was tied around with a green headkerchief that had two points on the top like rabbit's ears. She was sitting on the sofa, feeding the baby his apricots out of a jar. "The children have been to Florida before," the old lady said. "You all ought to take them somewhere else for a change so they would see different parts of the world and be broad. They never have been to east Tennessee."

The children's mother didn't seem to hear her, but the eight-year-old boy, John Wesley, a stocky child with glasses, said, "If you don't want to go to Florida, why dontcha stay at home?" He and the little girl, June Star, were reading the funny papers on the floor.

"She wouldn't stay at home to be queen for a day," June Star said without raising her yellow head.

"Yes, and what would you do if this fellow, The Misfit, caught you?" the grand-   5
mother asked.

"I'd smack his face," John Wesley said.

"She wouldn't stay at home for a million bucks," June Star said. "Afraid she'd miss something. She has to go everywhere we go."

"All right, Miss," the grandmother said. "Just remember that the next time you want me to curl your hair."

June Star said her hair was naturally curly.

The next morning the grandmother was the first one in the car, ready to go. She   10
had her big black valise that looked like the head of a hippopotamus in one corner, and underneath it she was hiding a basket with Pitty Sing, the cat, in it. She didn't intend for the cat to be left alone in the house for three days because he would miss her too much and she was afraid he might brush against one of the gas burners and accidentally asphyxiate himself. Her son, Bailey, didn't like to arrive at a motel with a cat.

She sat in the middle of the back seat with John Wesley and June Star on either side of her. Bailey and the children's mother and the baby sat in the front and they left Atlanta at eight forty-five with the mileage on the car at 55890. The grandmother wrote this down because she thought it would be interesting to say how many miles they had been when they got back. It took them twenty minutes to reach the outskirts of the city.

The old lady settled herself comfortably, removing her white cotton gloves and putting them up with her purse on the shelf in front of the back window. The children's mother still had on slacks and still had her head tied up in a green kerchief, but the grandmother had on a navy blue straw sailor hat with a bunch of white violets on the brim and a navy blue dress with a small white dot in the print. Her collar and cuffs were white organdy trimmed with lace and at her neckline she had pinned a purple spray of cloth violets containing a sachet. In case of an accident, anyone seeing her dead on the highway would know at once that she was a lady.

She said she thought it was going to be a good day for driving, neither too hot nor too cold, and she cautioned Bailey that the speed limit was fifty-five miles an hour and that the patrolmen hid themselves behind billboards and small clumps of trees and sped out after you before you had a chance to slow down. She pointed out interesting details of the scenery: Stone Mountain; the blue granite that in some places came up to both sides of the highway; the brilliant red clay banks slightly streaked with purple; and the various crops that made rows of green lace-work on the ground. The trees were full of silver-white sunlights and the meanest of them sparkled. The children were reading comic magazines and their mother had gone back to sleep.

"Let's go through Georgia fast so we won't have to look at it much," John Wesley said.

"If I were a little boy," said the grandmother, "I wouldn't talk about my native   15
state that way. Tennessee has the mountains and Georgia has the hills."

"Tennessee is just a hillbilly dumping ground," John Wesley said, "and Georgia is a lousy state too."

"You said it," June Star said.

"In my time," said the grandmother, folding her thin veined fingers, "children were more respectful of their native states and their parents and everything else. People did right then. Oh look at the cute little pickaninny!" she said and pointed to a Negro child standing in the door of a shack. "Wouldn't that make a picture, now?" she asked and they all turned and looked at the little Negro out of the back window. He waved.

"He didn't have any britches on," June Star said.

"He probably didn't have any," the grandmother explained. "Little niggers in the   20
country don't have things like we do. If I could paint, I'd paint that picture," she said.

The children exchanged comic books.

The grandmother offered to hold the baby and the children's mother passed him over the front seat to her. She set him on her knee and bounced him and told him about the things they were passing. She rolled her eyes and screwed up her mouth and stuck her leathery thin face into his smooth bland one. Occasionally he gave her a far-away smile. They passed a large cotton field with five or six graves fenced in the middle of it, like a small island. "Look at the graveyard!" the grandmother said, pointing it out. "That was the old family burying ground. That belonged to the plantation."

"Where's the plantation?" John Wesley asked.

"Gone With the Wind," said the grandmother. "Ha. Ha."

When the children finished all the comic books they had brought, they opened the   25
lunch and ate it. The grandmother ate a peanut butter sandwich and an olive and would not let the children throw the box and the paper napkins out the window. When there was nothing else to do they played a game by choosing a cloud and making the other two guess what shape it suggested. John Wesley took one the shape of a cow and June Star guessed a cow and John Wesley said, no, an automobile, and June Star said he didn't play fair, and they began to slap each other over the grandmother.

The grandmother said she would tell them a story if they would keep quiet. When she told a story, she rolled her eyes and waved her head and was very dramatic. She said once when she was a maiden lady she had been courted by a Mr. Edgar Atkins Teagarden from Jasper, Georgia. She said he was a very good-looking man and a gentleman and that he brought her a watermelon every Saturday afternoon with his initials cut in it, E.A.T. Well, one Saturday, she said, Mr. Teagarden brought the watermelon and there was nobody at home and he left it on the front porch and returned in his buggy to Jasper, but she never got the watermelon, she said, because a nigger boy ate it when he saw the initials, E.A.T.! This story tickled John Wesley's funny bone and he giggled and giggled but June Star didn't think it was any good. She said she wouldn't marry a man that just brought her a watermelon on Saturday. The grandmother said she would have done well to marry Mr. Teagarden because he was a gentleman and had bought Coca-Cola stock when it first came out and that he had died only a few years ago, a very wealthy man.

They stopped at The Tower for barbecued sandwiches. The Tower was a part-stucco and part-wood filling station and dance hall set in a clearing outside of Timothy. A fat man named Red Sammy Butts ran it and there were signs stuck here and there on the building and for miles up and down the highway saying, TRY RED SAMMY'S FAMOUS BARBECUE. NONE LIKE FAMOUS RED SAMMY'S! RED SAM! THE FAT BOY WITH THE HAPPY LAUGH. A VETERAN! RED SAMMY'S YOUR MAN!

Red Sammy was lying on the bare ground outside The Tower with his head under a truck while a gray monkey about a foot high, chained to a small chinaberry tree, chattered nearby. The monkey sprang back into the tree and got on the highest limb as soon as he saw the children jump out of the car and run toward him.

Inside, The Tower was a long dark room with a counter at one end and tables at the other and dancing space in the middle. They all sat down at a broad table next to the nickelodeon and Red Sam's wife, a tall burnt-brown woman with hair and eyes lighter than her skin, came and took their order. The children's mother put a dime in the machine and played "The Tennessee Waltz," and the grandmother said that tune always made her want to dance. She asked Bailey if he would like to dance but he only glared at her. He didn't have a naturally sunny disposition like she did and trips made him nervous. The grandmother's brown eyes were very bright. She swayed her head from side to side and pretended she was dancing in her chair. June Star said play something she could tap to so the children's mother put in another dime and played a fast number and June Star stepped out onto the dance floor and did her tap routine.

"Ain't she cute?" Red Sam's wife said, leaning over the counter. "Would you like   30
to come be my little girl?"

"No, I certainly wouldn't," June Star said. "I wouldn't live in a broken-down place like this for a million bucks!" and she ran back to the table.

"Ain't she cute?" the woman repeated, stretching her mouth politely.

"Aren't you ashamed?" hissed the grandmother.

Red Sam came in and told his wife to quit lounging on the counter and hurry up with these people's order. His khaki trousers reached just to his hip bones and his stomach hung over them like a sack of meal swaying under his shirt. He came over and sat down at a table nearby and let out a combination sigh and yodel. "You can't win," he said. "You can't win," and he wiped his sweating red face off with a gray handkerchief. "These days you don't know who to trust," he said. "Ain't that the truth?"

"People are certainly not nice like they used to be," said the grandmother.   35

"Two fellers come in here last week," Red Sammy said, "driving a Chrysler. It was an old beat-up car but it was a good one and these boys looked all right to me. Said they worked at the mill and you know I let them fellers charge the gas they bought? Now why did I do that?"

"Because you're a good man!" the grandmother said at once.

"Yes'm, I suppose so," Red Sam said as if he were struck with this answer.

His wife brought the orders, carrying the five plates all at once without a tray, two in each hand and one balanced on her arm. "It isn't a soul in this green world of God's that you can trust," she said. "And I don't count nobody out of that, not nobody," she repeated, looking at Red Sammy.

"Did you read about that criminal, The Misfit, that's escaped?" asked the grand-   40
mother.

"I wouldn't be a bit surprised if he didn't attack this place right here," said the woman. "If he hears about it being here, I wouldn't be none surprised to see him. If he hears it's two cent in the cash register, I wouldn't be a tall surprised if he . . ."

"That'll do," Red Sam said. "Go bring these people their Co'-Colas," and the woman went off to get the rest of the order.

"A good man is hard to find," Red Sammy said. "Everything is getting terrible. I remember the day you could go off and leave your screen door unlatched. Not no more."

He and the grandmother discussed better times. The old lady said that in her opinion Europe was entirely to blame for the way things were now. She said the way Europe acted you would think we were made of money and Red Sam said it was no use talking about it, she was exactly right. The children ran outside into the white sunlight and looked at the monkey in the lacy chinaberry tree. He was busy catching fleas on himself and biting each one carefully between his teeth as if it were a delicacy.

They drove off again into the hot afternoon. The grandmother took cat naps and   45
woke up every few minutes with her own snoring. Outside of Toombsboro she woke up and recalled an old plantation that she had visited in this neighborhood once when she was a young lady. She said the house had six white columns across the front and that there was an avenue of oaks leading up to it and two little wooden trellis arbors on either side in front where you sat down with your suitor after a stroll in the garden. She recalled exactly which road to turn off to get to it. She knew that Bailey would not be willing to lose any time looking at an old house, but the more she talked about it, the more she wanted to see it once again and find out if the little twin arbors were still standing. "There was a secret panel in this house," she said craftily, not telling the truth but wishing that she were, "and the story went that all the family silver was hidden in it when Sherman came through but it was never found . . ."

"Hey!" John Wesley said. "Let's go see it! We'll find it! We'll poke all the woodwork and find it! Who lives there? Where do you turn off at? Hey Pop, can't we turn off there?"

"We never have seen a house with a secret panel!" June Star shrieked. "Let's go to the house with the secret panel! Hey, Pop, can't we go see the house with the secret panel!"

"It's not far from here, I know," the grandmother said. "It wouldn't take over twenty minutes."

Bailey was looking straight ahead. His jaw was as rigid as a horseshoe. "No," he said.

The children began to yell and scream that they wanted to see the house with the   50
secret panel. John Wesley kicked the back of the front seat and June Star hung over her mother's shoulder and whined desperately into her ear that they never had any fun even on their vacation, that they could never do what THEY wanted to do. The baby began to scream and John Wesley kicked the back of the seat so hard that his father could feel the blows in his kidney.

"All right!" he shouted and drew the car to a stop at the side of the road. "Will you all shut up? Will you all just shut up for one second? If you don't shut up, we won't go anywhere."

"It would be very educational for them," the grandmother murmured.

"All right," Bailey said, "but get this. This is the only time we're going to stop for anything like this. This is the one and only time."

"The dirt road that you have to turn down is about a mile back," the grandmother directed. "I marked it when we passed."

"A dirt road," Bailey groaned.   55

After they had turned around and were headed toward the dirt road, the grandmother recalled other points about the house, the beautiful glass over the front doorway and the candle lamp in the hall. John Wesley said that the secret panel was probably in the fireplace.

"You can't go inside this house," Bailey said. "You don't know who lives there."

"While you all talk to the people in front, I'll run around behind and get in a window," John Wesley suggested.

"We'll all stay in the car," his mother said.

They turned onto the dirt road and the car raced roughly along in a swirl of pink   60
dust. The grandmother recalled the times when there were no paved roads and thirty miles was a day's journey. The dirt road was hilly and there were sudden washes in it and sharp curves on dangerous embankments. All at once they would be on a hill, looking down over the blue tops of trees for miles around, then the next minute, they would be in a red depression with the dust-coated trees looking down on them.

"This place had better turn up in a minute," Bailey said, "or I'm going to turn around."

The road looked as if no one had traveled on it in months.

"It's not much farther," the grandmother said and just as she said it, a horrible thought came to her. The thought was so embarrassing that she turned red in the face and her eyes dilated and her feet jumped up, upsetting her valise in the corner. The instant the valise moved, the newspaper top she had over the basket under it rose with a snarl and Pitty Sing, the cat, sprang onto Bailey's shoulder.

The children were thrown to the floor and their mother, clutching the baby, was thrown out the door onto the ground; the old lady was thrown into the front seat. The car turned over once and landed right-side-up in a gulch on the side of the road. Bailey remained in the driver's seat with the cat—gray-striped with a broad white face and an orange nose—clinging to his neck like a caterpillar.

As soon as the children saw they could move their arms and legs, they scrambled   65
out of the car, shouting, "We've had an ACCIDENT!" The grandmother was curled up under the dashboard, hoping she was injured so that Bailey's wrath would not come down on her all at once. The horrible thought she had had before the accident was that the house she had remembered so vividly was not in Georgia but in Tennessee.

Bailey removed the cat from his neck with both hands and flung it out the window against the side of a pine tree. Then he got out of the car and started looking for the children's mother. She was sitting against the side of the red gutted ditch, holding the screaming baby, but she only had a cut down her face and a broken shoulder. "We've had an ACCIDENT!" the children screamed in a frenzy of delight.

"But nobody's killed," June Star said with disappointment as the grandmother limped out of the car, her hat still pinned to her head but the broken front brim standing up at a jaunty angle and the violet spray hanging off the side. They all sat down in the ditch, except the children, to recover from the shock. They were all shaking.

"Maybe a car will come along," said the children's mother hoarsely.

"I believe I have injured an organ," said the grandmother, pressing her side, but no one answered her. Bailey's teeth were clattering. He had on a yellow sport shirt with bright blue parrots designed in it and his face was as yellow as the shirt. The grandmother decided that she would not mention that the house was in Tennessee.

The road was about ten feet above and they could see only the tops of the trees on   70
the other side of it. Behind the ditch they were sitting in there were more woods, tall
and dark and deep. In a few minutes they saw a car some distance away on top of a hill,
coming slowly as if the occupants were watching them. The grandmother stood up and
waved both arms dramatically to attract their attention. The car continued to come on
slowly, disappeared around a bend and appeared again, moving even slower, on top of
the hill they had gone over. It was a big black battered hearselike automobile. There
were three men in it.

It came to a stop over them and for some minutes, the driver looked down with a
steady expressionless gaze to where they were sitting, and didn't speak. Then he turned
his head and muttered something to the other two and they got out. One was a fat boy
in black trousers and a red sweat shirt with a silver stallion embossed on the front of it.
He moved around on the right side of them and stood staring, his mouth partly open
in a kind of loose grin. The other had on khaki pants and a blue striped coat and a gray
hat pulled down very low, hiding most of his face. He came around slowly on the left
side. Neither spoke.

The driver got out of the car and stood by the side of it, looking down at them.
He was an older man than the other two. His hair was just beginning to gray and he
wore silver-rimmed spectacles that gave him a scholarly look. He had a long creased
face and didn't have on any shirt or undershirt. He had on blue jeans that were too
tight for him and was holding a black hat and a gun. The two boys also had guns.

"We've had an ACCIDENT!" the children screamed.

The grandmother had the peculiar feeling that the bespectacled man was someone
she knew. His face was as familiar to her as if she had known him all her life but she
could not recall who he was. He moved away from the car and began to come down
the embankment, placing his feet carefully so that he wouldn't slip. He had on tan and
white shoes and no socks, and his ankles were red and thin. "Good afternoon," he said.
"I see you all had you a little spill."

"We turned over twice!" said the grandmother.   75

"Oncet," he corrected. "We seen it happen. Try their car and see will it run,
Hiram," he said quietly to the boy with the gray hat.

"What you got that gun for?" John Wesley asked. "Whatcha gonna do with
that gun?"

"Lady," the man said to the children's mother, "would you mind calling them
children to sit down by you? Children make me nervous. I want all you all to sit down
right together there were you're at."

"What are you telling us what to do for?" June Star asked.

Behind them the line of woods gaped like a dark open mouth. "Come here," said   80
their mother.

"Look here now," Bailey began suddenly, "we're in a predicament! We're in . . ."

The grandmother shrieked. She scrambled to her feet and stood staring.

"You're The Misfit!" she said. "I recognized you at once!"

"Yes'm," the man said, smiling slightly as if he were pleased in spite of himself to
be known, "but it would have been better for all of you, lady, if you hadn't of reck-
ernized me."

Bailey turned his head sharply and said something to his mother that shocked even   85
the children. The old lady began to cry and The Misfit reddened.

"Lady," he said, "don't you get upset. Sometimes a man says things he don't
mean. I don't reckon he meant to talk to you thataway."

"You wouldn't shoot a lady, would you?" the grandmother said and removed a
clean handkerchief from her cuff and began to slap at her eyes with it.

The Misfit pointed the toe of his shoe into the ground and made a little hole and then covered it up again. "I would hate to have to," he said.

"Listen," the grandmother almost screamed, "I know you're a good man. You don't look a bit like you have common blood. I know you must come from nice people!"

"Yes mam," he said, "finest people in the world." When he smiled he showed a row of strong white teeth. "God never made a finer woman than my mother and my daddy's heart was pure gold," he said. The boy with the red sweat shirt had come around behind them and was standing with his gun at his hip. The Misfit squatted down on the ground. "Watch them children, Bobby Lee," he said. "You know they make me nervous." He looked at the six of them huddled together in front of him and he seemed to be embarrassed as if he couldn't think of anything to say. "Ain't a cloud in the sky," he remarked, looking up at it. "Don't see no sun but don't see no cloud neither."

"Yes, it's a beautiful day," said the grandmother. "Listen," she said, "you shouldn't call yourself The Misfit because I know you're a good man at heart. I can just look at you and tell."

"Hush!" Bailey yelled. "Hush! Everybody shut up and let me handle this!" He was squatting in the position of a runner about to spring forward but he didn't move.

"I pre-chate that, lady," The Misfit said and drew a little circle in the ground with the butt of his gun.

"It'll take a half a hour to fix this here car," Hiram called, looking over the raised hood of it.

"Well, first you and Bobby Lee get him and that little boy to step over yonder with you," The Misfit said, pointing to Bailey and John Wesley. "The boys want to ask you something," he said to Bailey. "Would you mind stepping back in them woods there with them?"

"Listen," Bailey began, "we're in a terrible predicament! Nobody realizes what this is," and his voice cracked. His eyes were as blue and intense as the parrots in his shirt and he remained perfectly still.

The grandmother reached up to adjust her hat brim as if she were going to the woods with him but it came off in her hand. She stood staring at it and after a second she let it fall on the ground. Hiram pulled Bailey up by the arm as if he were assisting an old man. John Wesley caught hold of his father's hand and Bobby Lee followed. They went off toward the woods and just as they reached the dark edge, Bailey turned and supporting himself against a gray naked pine trunk, he shouted, "I'll be back in a minute, Mamma, wait on me!"

"Come back this instant!" his mother shrilled but they all disappeared into the woods.

"Bailey Boy!" the grandmother called in a tragic voice but she found she was looking at The Misfit squatting on the ground in front of her. "I just know you're a good man," she said desperately. "You're not a bit common!"

"Nome, I ain't a good man," The Misfit said after a second as if he had considered her statement carefully, "but I ain't the worst in the world neither. My daddy said I was a different breed of dog from my brothers and sisters. 'You know,' Daddy said, 'it's some that can live their whole life out without asking about it and it's others has to know why it is, and this boy is one of the latters. He's going to be into everything!'" He put on his black hat and looked up suddenly and then away deep into the woods as if he were embarrassed again. "I'm sorry I don't have on a shirt before you ladies," he said, hunching his shoulders slightly. "We buried our clothes that we had on when we escaped and we're just making do until we can get better. We borrowed these from some folks we met," he explained.

"That's perfectly all right," the grandmother said. "Maybe Bailey has an extra shirt in his suitcase."

"I'll look and see terrectly," The Misfit said.

"Where are they taking him?" the children's mother screamed.

"Daddy was a card himself," The Misfit said. "You couldn't put anything over on him. He never got in trouble with the Authorities though. Just had the knack of handling them."

"You could be honest too if you'd only try," said the grandmother. "Think how wonderful it would be to settle down and live a comfortable life and not have to think about somebody chasing you all the time." 105

The Misfit kept scratching in the ground with the butt of his gun as if he were thinking about it. "Yes'm, somebody is always after you," he murmured.

The grandmother noticed how thin his shoulder blades were just behind his hat because she was standing up looking down on him. "Do you ever pray?" she asked.

He shook his head. All she saw was the black hat wiggle between his shoulder blades. "Nome," he said.

There was a pistol shot from the woods, followed closely by another. Then silence. The old lady's head jerked around. She could hear the wind move through the tree tops like a long satisfied insuck of breath. "Bailey Boy!" she called.

"I was a gospel singer for a while," The Misfit said. "I been most everything. Been in the arm service, both land and sea, at home and abroad, been twict married, been an undertaker, been with the railroads, plowed Mother Earth, been in a tornado, seen a man burnt alive oncet," and he looked up at the children's mother and the little girl who were sitting close together, their faces white and their eyes glassy; "I even seen a woman flogged," he said. 110

"Pray, pray," the grandmother began, "pray, pray . . ."

"I never was a bad boy that I remember of," The Misfit said in an almost dreamy voice, "but somewheres along the line I done something wrong and got sent to the penitentiary. I was buried alive," and he looked up and held her attention to him by a steady stare.

"That's when you should have started to pray," she said. "What did you do to get sent to the penitentiary that first time?"

"Turn to the right, it was a wall," The Misfit said, looking up again at the cloudless sky. "Turn to the left, it was a wall. Look up it was a ceiling, look down it was a floor. I forget what I done, lady. I set there and set there, trying to remember what it was I done and I ain't recalled it to this day. Oncet in a while, I would think it was coming to me, but it never come."

"Maybe they put you in by mistake," the old lady said vaguely. 115

"Nome," he said. "It wasn't no mistake. They had the papers on me."

"You must have stolen something," she said.

The Misfit sneered slightly. "Nobody had nothing I wanted," he said. "It was a head-doctor at the penitentiary said what I had done was kill my daddy but I known that for a lie. My daddy died in nineteen ought nineteen of the epidemic flu and I never had a thing to do with it. He was buried in the Mount Hopewell Baptist churchyard and you can go there and see for yourself."

"If you would pray," the old lady said, "Jesus would help you."

"That's right," The Misfit said.   120

"Well then, why don't you pray?" she asked trembling with delight suddenly.

"I don't want no hep," he said. "I'm doing all right by myself."

Bobby Lee and Hiram came ambling back from the woods. Bobby Lee was dragging a yellow shirt with bright blue parrots in it.

"Throw me that shirt, Bobby Lee," The Misfit said. The shirt came flying at him
and landed on his shoulder and he put it on. The grandmother couldn't name what the
shirt reminded her of. "No, lady," The Misfit said while he was buttoning up, "I found
out the crime don't matter. You can do one thing or you can do another, kill a man or
take a tire off his car, because sooner or later you're going to forget what it was you
done and just be punished for it."

The children's mother had begun to make heaving noises as if she couldn't get her   125
breath. "Lady," he asked, "would you and that little girl like to step off yonder with
Bobby Lee and Hiram and join your husband?"

"Yes, thank you," the mother said faintly. Her left arm dangled helplessly and she
was holding the baby, who had gone to sleep, in the other. "Hep that lady up, Hiram,"
The Misfit said as she struggled to climb out of the ditch, "and Bobby Lee, you hold
onto that little girl's hand."

"I don't want to hold hands with him," June Star said. "He reminds me of a pig."

The fat boy blushed and laughed and caught her by the arm and pulled her off
into the woods after Hiram and her mother.

Alone with The Misfit, the grandmother found that she had lost her voice. There
was not a cloud in the sky nor any sun. There was nothing around her but woods. She
wanted to tell him that he must pray. She opened and closed her mouth several times
before anything came out. Finally she found herself saying, "Jesus, Jesus," meaning,
Jesus will help you, but the way she was saying it, it sounded as if she might be cursing.

"Yes'm," The Misfit said as if he agreed. "Jesus thrown everything off balance. It   130
was the same case with Him as with me except He hadn't committed any crime and
they could prove I had committed one because they had the papers on me. Of course,"
he said, "they never shown me my papers. That's why I sign myself now. I said long
ago, you get you a signature and sign everything you do and keep a copy of it. Then
you'll know what you done and you can hold up the crime to the punishment and see
do they match and in the end you'll have something to prove you ain't been treated
right. I call myself The Misfit," he said, "because I can't make what all I done wrong fit
what all I gone through in punishment."

There was a piercing scream from the woods, followed closely by a pistol report.
"Does it seem right to you, lady, that one is punished a heap and another ain't punished at all?"

"Jesus!" the old lady cried. "You've got good blood! I know you wouldn't shoot a
lady! I know you come from nice people! Pray! Jesus, you ought not to shoot a lady.
I'll give you all the money I've got!"

"Lady," The Misfit said, looking beyond her far into the woods, "there never was
a body that give the undertaker a tip."

There were two more pistol reports and the grandmother raised her head like a
parched old turkey hen crying for water and called, "Bailey Boy, Bailey Boy!" as if her
heart would break.

"Jesus was the only One that ever raised the dead," The Misfit continued, "and   135
He shouldn't have done it. He thrown everything off balance. If He did what He said,
then it's nothing for you to do but throw away everything and follow Him, and if He
didn't then it's nothing for you to do but enjoy the few minutes you got left the best way

you can—by killing somebody or burning down his house or doing some other mean-ness to him. No pleasure but meanness," he said and his voice had become almost a snarl.

"Maybe He didn't raise the dead," the old lady mumbled, not knowing what she was saying and feeling so dizzy that she sank down in the ditch with her legs twisted under her.

"I wasn't there so I can't say He didn't," The Misfit said. "I wisht I had of been there," he said, hitting the ground with his fist. "It ain't right I wasn't there because if I had of been there I would of known. Listen lady," he said in a high voice, "if I had of been there I would of known and I wouldn't be like I am now." His voice seemed about to crack and the grandmother's head cleared for an instant. She saw the man's face twisted close to her own as if he were going to cry and she murmured, "Why, you're one of my babies. You're one of my own children!" She reached out and touched him on the shoulder. The Misfit sprang back as if a snake had bitten him and shot her three times through the chest. Then he put his gun down on the ground and took off his glasses and began to clean them.

Hiram and Bobby Lee returned from the woods and stood over the ditch, looking down at the grandmother who half sat and half lay in a puddle of blood with her legs crossed under her like a child's and her face smiling up at the cloudless sky.

Without his glasses, The Misfit's eyes were red-rimmed and pale and defenseless-looking. "Take her off and throw her where you thrown the others," he said, picking up the cat that was rubbing itself against his leg.

"She was a talker, wasn't she?" Bobby Lee said, sliding down the ditch with a   140
yodel.

"She would of been a good woman," The Misfit said, "if it had been somebody there to shoot her every minute of her life."

"Some fun!" Bobby Lee said.

"Shut up, Bobby Lee," The Misfit said. "It's no real pleasure in life."

THE RECEPTIVE READER

1. What kind of person is the grandmother? What roles (or how many roles) does she play as a *central character* in the development of the story? At how many points in the story does she play a major or minor part? ✧ Does she symbolically represent the past—the "old South"? Is there a conflict between the generations?

2. What is your reaction to the other members of the family as *minor characters* in the story? Are they comical? strange? ordinary? repellent?

3. What role does the *episode*, or interlude, at the "fat man's" barbecue play in the story?

4. How or why did these characters meet their fate? (How would you summarize the *plot* or story line?)

5. Is there anything representative or *symbolic* about what happens to these people?

6. What is the Misfit's story (and how much of it do you believe)? ✧ What are his manners? (Do you find them surprising or *ironic*?) ✧ What is the gist of the cli-mactic conversation between the Misfit and the grandmother? Does it suggest a *theme*; does it have thematic implications?

7. Where would you draw the line between the comic and the tragic in this story? How does it illustrate the mixed genre critics call the *grotesque*?

8. Does this story change your idea about "senseless violence"? How?

THE PERSONAL RESPONSE

How true to the spirit of the story, or how far off, is the personal reaction in the following journal entry?

> Maybe the Misfit was like Lucifer, the misfit Angel. Lucifer didn't see things God's way, so God cast him out of heaven and punished him. Did Lucifer become evil because of the punishment not fitting the crime? Or was Lucifer just inherently evil? If he was inherently evil, he wouldn't have been an angel in the first place. I think those who jailed the Misfit turned him from just different to bad. I wasn't terribly sorry to see that family go, especially those rancid children. The mother was harmless, but I had real sympathy only for the Misfit, the baby, and the cat, Pitty Sing. Maybe O'Connor made the family so nasty and annoying to act as a foil for the Misfit, who really was a pitiful man.

THE CREATIVE DIMENSION

O'Connor's stories leave readers with haunting images or the memory of striking incidents. Critics puzzle over key phrases ("good country people"), provocative sentences ("a good man is hard to find"), symbolic gestures, climactic exchanges, violent confrontations. Focus on a haunting image, incident, gesture, or saying in O'Connor's stories. Re-create it, following the train of ideas, images, or associations it calls up in your mind.

As you start reading the following story by the same author, do you find yourself in familiar territory? Do its characters seem in some way akin to those in the preceding story? Does this second story raise issues or explore questions that seem related to those in the first?

Everything That Rises Must Converge   1965

Her doctor had told Julian's mother that she must lose twenty pounds on account of her blood pressure, so on Wednesday nights Julian had to take her downtown on the bus for a reducing class at the Y. The reducing class was designed for working girls over fifty, who weighed from 165 to 200 pounds. His mother was one of the slimmer ones, but she said ladies did not tell their age or weight. She would not ride the buses by herself at night since they had been integrated, and because the reducing class was one of her few pleasures, necessary for her health, and *free,* she said Julian could at least put himself out to take her, considering all she did for him. Julian did not like to consider all she did for him, but every Wednesday night he braced himself and took her.

She was almost ready to go, standing before the hall mirror, putting on her hat, while he, his hands behind him, appeared pinned to the door frame, waiting like Saint Sebastian for the arrows to begin piercing him. The hat was new and had cost her seven dollars and a half. She kept saying, "Maybe I shouldn't have paid that for it. No, I shouldn't have. I'll take it off and return it tomorrow. I shouldn't have bought it."

Julian raised his eyes to heaven. "Yes, you should have bought it," he said. "Put it on and let's go." It was a hideous hat. A purple velvet flap came down on one side of it and stood up on the other; the rest of it was green and looked like a cushion with the stuffing out. He decided it was less comical than jaunty and pathetic. Everything that gave her pleasure was small and depressed him.

She lifted the hat one more time and set it down slowly on top of her head. Two wings of gray hair protruded on either side of her florid face, but her eyes, sky-blue, were as innocent and untouched by experience as they must have been when she was ten. Were it not that she was a widow who had struggled fiercely to feed and clothe and put him through school and who was supporting him still, "until he got on his feet," she might have been a little girl that he had to take to town.

"It's all right, it's all right," he said. "Let's go." He opened the door himself and   5
started down the walk to get her going. The sky was a dying violet and the houses stood out darkly against it, bulbous liver-colored monstrosities of a uniform ugliness though no two were alike. Since this had been a fashionable neighborhood forty years ago, his mother persisted in thinking they did well to have an apartment in it. Each house had a narrow collar of dirt around it in which sat, usually, a grubby child. Julian walked with his hands in his pockets, his head down and thrust forward and his eyes glazed with the determination to make himself completely numb during the time he would be sacrificed to her pleasure.

The door closed and he turned to find the dumpy figure, surmounted by the atrocious hat, coming toward him. "Well," she said, "you only live once and paying a little more for it, I at least won't meet myself coming and going."

"Some day I'll start making money," Julian said gloomily—he knew he never would—"and you can have one of those jokes whenever you take the fit." But first they would move. He visualized a place where the nearest neighbors would be three miles away on either side.

"I think you're doing fine," she said, drawing on her gloves. "You've only been out of school a year. Rome wasn't built in a day."

She was one of the few members of the Y reducing class who arrived in hat and gloves and who had a son who had been to college. "It takes time," she said, "and the world is in such a mess. This hat looked better on me than any of the others, though when she brought it out I said, 'Take that thing back. I wouldn't have it on my head,' and she said, 'Now wait till you see it on,' and when she put it on me, I said, 'We-ull,' and she said, 'If you ask me, that hat does something for you and you do something for the hat, and besides,' she said, 'with that hat, you won't meet yourself coming and going.'"

Julian thought he could have stood his lot better if she had been selfish, if she had   10
been an old hag who drank and screamed at him. He walked along, saturated in depression, as if in the midst of his martyrdom he had lost his faith. Catching sight of his long, hopeless, irritated face, she stopped suddenly with a grief-stricken look, and pulled back on his arm. "Wait on me," she said. "I'm going back to the house and take this thing off and tomorrow I'm going to return it. I was out of my head. I can pay the gas bill with that seven-fifty."

He caught her arm in a vicious grip. "You are not going to take it back," he said. "I like it."

"Well," she said, "I don't think I ought . . ."

"Shut up and enjoy it," he muttered, more depressed than ever.

"With the world in the mess it's in," she said, "it's a wonder we can enjoy anything. I tell you, the bottom rail is on the top."

Julian sighed.   15

"Of course," she said, "if you know who you are, you can go anywhere." She said this every time he took her to the reducing class. "Most of them in it are not our kind of people," she said, "but I can be gracious to anybody. I know who I am."

"They don't give a damn for your graciousness," Julian said savagely. "Knowing who you are is good for one generation only. You haven't the foggiest idea where you stand now or who you are."

She stopped and allowed her eyes to flash at him. "I most certainly do know who I am," she said, "and if you don't know who you are, I'm ashamed of you."

"Oh hell," Julian said.

"Your great-grandfather was a former governor of this state," she said. "Your   20
grandfather was a prosperous land-owner. Your grandmother was a Godhigh."

"Will you look around you," he said tensely, "and see where you are now?" and he swept his arm jerkily out to indicate the neighborhood, which the growing darkness at least made less dingy.

"You remain what you are," she said. "Your great-grandfather had a plantation and two hundred slaves."

"There are no more slaves," he said irritably.

"They were better off when they were," she said. He groaned to see that she was off on that topic. She rolled onto it every few days like a train on an open track. He knew every stop, every junction, every swamp along the way, and knew the exact point at which her conclusion would roll majestically into the station: "It's ridiculous. It's simply not realistic. They should rise, yes, but on their own side of the fence."

"Let's skip it," Julian said.   25

"The ones I feel sorry for," she said, "are the ones that are half white. They're tragic."

"Will you skip it?"

"Suppose we were half white. We would certainly have mixed feelings."

"I have mixed feelings now," he groaned.

"Well let's talk about something pleasant," she said. "I remember going to Grand-   30
pa's when I was a little girl. Then the house had double stairways that went up to what was really the second floor—all the cooking was done on the first. I used to like to stay down in the kitchen on account of the way the walls smelled. I would sit with my nose pressed against the plaster and take deep breaths. Actually the place belonged to the Godhighs but your grandfather Chestny paid the mortgage and saved it for them. They were in reduced circumstances," she said, "but reduced or not, they never forgot who they were."

"Doubtless that decayed mansion reminded them," Julian muttered. He never spoke of it without contempt or thought of it without longing. He had seen it once when he was a child before it had been sold. The double stairways had rotted and been torn down. Negroes were living in it. But it remained in his mind as his mother had known it. It appeared in his dreams regularly. He would stand on the wide porch, listening to the rustle of oak leaves, then wander through the high-ceilinged hall into the parlor that opened onto it and gaze at the worn rugs and faded draperies. It occurred to him that it was he, not she, who could have appreciated it. He preferred its threadbare elegance to anything he could name and it was because of it that all the neighborhoods they had lived in had been a torment to him—whereas she had hardly known the difference. She called her insensitivity "being adjustable."

"And I remember the old darky who was my nurse, Caroline. There was no better person in the world. I've always had a great respect for my colored friends," she said. "I'd do anything in the world for them and they'd . . ."

"Will you for God's sake get off that subject?" Julian said. When he got on a bus by himself, he made it a point to sit down beside a Negro, in reparation as it were for his mother's sins.

"You're mighty touchy tonight," she said. "Do you feel all right?"

"Yes I feel all right," he said. "Now lay off."   35

She pursed her lips. "Well, you certainly are in a vile humor," she observed. "I just won't speak to you at all."

They had reached the bus stop. There was no bus in sight and Julian, his hands still jammed in his pockets and his head thrust forward, scowled down the empty street. The frustration of having to wait on the bus as well as ride on it began to creep up his neck like a hot hand. The presence of his mother was borne in upon him as she gave a pained sigh. He looked at her bleakly. She was holding herself very erect under the preposterous hat, wearing it like a banner of her imaginary dignity. There was in him an evil urge to break her spirit. He suddenly unloosened his tie and pulled it off and put it in his pocket.

She stiffened. "Why must you look like *that* when you take me to town?" she said. "Why must you deliberately embarrass me?"

"If you'll never learn where you are," he said, "you can at least learn where I am."

"You look like a—thug," she said.   40

"Then I must be one," he murmured.

"I'll just go home," she said. "I will not bother you. If you can't do a little thing like that for me . . ."

Rolling his eyes upward, he put his tie back on. "Restored to my class," he muttered. He thrust his face toward her and hissed, "True culture is in the mind, the *mind*," he said, and tapped his head, "the mind."

"It's in the heart," she said, "and in how you do things and how you do things is because of who you *are*."

"Nobody in the damn bus cares who you are."   45

"I care who I am," she said icily.

The lighted bus appeared on top of the next hill and as it approached, they moved out into the street to meet it. He put his hand under her elbow and hoisted her up on the creaking step. She entered with a little smile, as if she were going into a drawing room where everyone had been waiting for her. While he put in the tokens, she sat down on one of the broad front seats for three which faced the aisle. A thin woman with protruding teeth and long yellow hair was sitting on the end of it. His mother moved up beside her and left room for Julian beside herself. He sat down and looked at the floor across the aisle where a pair of thin feet in red and white canvas sandals were planted.

His mother immediately began a general conversation meant to attract anyone who felt like talking. "Can it get any hotter?" she said and removed from her purse a folding fan, black with a Japanese scene on it, which she began to flutter before her.

"I reckon it might could," the woman with the protruding teeth said, "but I know for a fact my apartment couldn't get no hotter."

"It must get the afternoon sun," his mother said. She sat forward and looked up   50
and down the bus. It was half filled. Everybody was white. "I see we have the bus to ourselves," she said. Julian cringed.

"For a change," said the woman across the aisle, the owner of the red and white canvas sandals. "I come on one the other day and they were thick as fleas—up front and all through."

"The world is in a mess everywhere," his mother said. "I don't know how we've let it get in this fix."

"What gets my goat is all those boys from good families stealing automobile tires," the woman with the protruding teeth said. "I told my boy, I said you may not be rich but you been raised right and if I ever catch you in any such mess, they can send you on to the reformatory. Be exactly where you belong."

"Training tells," his mother said. "Is your boy in high school?"

"Ninth grade," the woman said.   55

"My son just finished college last year. He wants to write but he's selling typewriters until he gets started," his mother said.

The woman leaned forward and peered at Julian. He threw her such a malevolent look that she subsided against the seat. On the floor across the aisle there was an abandoned newspaper. He got up and got it and opened it out in front of him. His mother discreetly continued the conversation in a lower tone but the woman across the aisle said in a loud voice, "Well that's nice. Selling typewriters is close to writing. He can go right from one to the other."

"I tell him," his mother said, "that Rome wasn't built in a day."

Behind the newspaper Julian was withdrawing into the inner compartment of his mind where he spent most of his time. This was a kind of mental bubble in which he established himself when he could not bear to be a part of what was going on around him. From it he could see out and judge but in it he was safe from any kind of penetration from without. It was the only place where he felt free of the general idiocy of his fellows. His mother had never entered it but from it he could see her with absolute clarity.

The old lady was clever enough and he thought that if she had started from any of   60
the right premises, more might have been expected of her. She lived according to the laws of her own fantasy world, outside of which he had never seen her set foot. The law of it was to sacrifice herself for him after she had first created the necessity to do so by making a mess of things. If he had permitted her sacrifices, it was only because her lack of foresight had made them necessary. All of her life had been a struggle to act like a Chestny without the Chestny goods, and to give him everything she thought a Chestny ought to have; but since, said she, it was fun to struggle, why complain? And when you had won, as she had won, what fun to look back on the hard times! He could not forgive her that she had enjoyed the struggle and that she thought *she* had won.

What she meant when she said she had won was that she had brought him up successfully and had sent him to college and that he had turned out so well—good looking (her teeth had gone unfilled so that his could be straightened), intelligent (he realized he was too intelligent to be a success), and with a future ahead of him (there was of course no future ahead of him). She excused his gloominess on the grounds that he was still growing up and his radical ideas on his lack of practical experience. She said he didn't yet know a thing about "life," that he hadn't even entered the real world—when already he was as disenchanted with it as a man of fifty.

The further irony of all this was that in spite of her, he had turned out so well. In spite of going to only a third-rate college, he had, on his own initiative, come out with a first-rate education; in spite of growing up dominated by a small mind, he had ended up with a large one; in spite of all her foolish views, he was free of prejudice and unafraid to face facts. Most miraculous of all, instead of being blinded by love for her as she was for him, he had cut himself emotionally free of her and could see her with complete objectivity. He was not dominated by his mother.

The bus stopped with a sudden jerk and shook him from his meditation. A woman from the back lurched forward with little steps and barely escaped falling in his newspaper as she righted herself. She got off and a large Negro got on. Julian kept his paper lowered to watch. It gave him a certain satisfaction to see injustice in daily operation. It confirmed his view that with a few exceptions there was no one worth knowing within a radius of three hundred miles. The Negro was well dressed and carried a briefcase. He looked around and then sat down on the other end of the seat where the woman with the red and white canvas sandals was sitting. He immediately unfolded a newspaper and obscured himself behind it. Julian's mother's elbow at once prodded insistently into his ribs. "Now you see why I won't ride on these buses by myself," she whispered.

The woman with the red and white canvas sandals had risen at the same time the Negro sat down and had gone further back in the bus and taken the seat of the woman who had got off. His mother leaned forward and cast her an approving look.

Julian rose, crossed the aisle, and sat down in the place of the woman with the can- 65
vas sandals. From this position, he looked serenely across at his mother. Her face had turned an angry red. He stared at her, making his eyes the eyes of a stranger. He felt his tension suddenly lift as if he had openly declared war on her.

He would have liked to get in conversation with the Negro and to talk with him about art or politics or any subject that would be above the comprehension of those around them, but the man remained entrenched behind his paper. He was either ignoring the change of seating or had never noticed it. There was no way for Julian to convey his sympathy.

His mother kept her eyes fixed reproachfully on his face. The woman with the protruding teeth was looking at him avidly as if he were a type of monster new to her.

"Do you have a light?" he asked the Negro.

Without looking away from his paper, the man reached in his pocket and handed him a packet of matches.

"Thanks," Julian said. For a moment he held the matches foolishly. A NO SMOKING 70
sign looked down upon him from over the door. This alone would not have deterred him; he had no cigarettes. He had quit smoking some months before because he could not afford it. "Sorry," he muttered and handed back the matches. The Negro lowered the paper and gave him an annoyed look. He took the matches and raised the paper again.

His mother continued to gaze at him but she did not take advantage of his momentary discomfort. Her eyes retained their battered look. Her face seemed to be unnaturally red, as if her blood pressure had risen. Julian allowed no glimmer of sympathy to show on his face. Having got the advantage, he wanted desperately to keep it and carry it through. He would have liked to teach her a lesson that would last her a while, but there seemed no way to continue the point. The Negro refused to come out from behind his paper.

Julian folded his arms and looked stolidly before him, facing her but as if he did not see her, as if he had ceased to recognize her existence. He visualized a scene in which, the bus having reached their stop, he would remain in his seat and when she said, "Aren't you going to get off?" he would look at her as a stranger who had rashly addressed him. The corner they got off on was usually deserted, but it was well lighted and it would not hurt her to walk by herself the four blocks to the Y. He decided to wait until the time came and then decide whether or not he would let her get off by herself. He would have to be at the Y at ten to bring her back, but he could leave her wondering if he was going to show up. There was no reason for her to think she could always depend on him.

He retired again into the high-ceilinged room sparsely settled with large pieces of antique furniture. His soul expanded momentarily but then he became aware of his mother across from him and the vision shriveled. He studied her coldly. Her feet in little pumps dangled like a child's and did not quite reach the floor. She was training on him an exaggerated look of reproach. He felt completely detached from her. At that moment he could with pleasure have slapped her as he would have slapped a particularly obnoxious child in his charge.

He began to imagine various unlikely ways by which he could teach her a lesson. He might make friends with some distinguished Negro professor or lawyer and bring him home to spend the evening. He would be entirely justified but her blood pressure would rise to 300. He could not push her to the extent of making her have a stroke, and moreover, he had never been successful at making any Negro friends. He had tried to strike up an acquaintance on the bus with some of the better types, with ones that looked like professors or ministers or lawyers. One morning he had sat down next to a distinguished-looking dark brown man who had answered his questions with a sonorous solemnity but who had turned out to be an undertaker. Another day he had sat down beside a cigar-smoking Negro with a diamond ring on his finger, but after a few stilted pleasantries, the Negro had rung the buzzer and risen, slipping two lottery tickets into Julian's hand as he climbed over him to leave.

He imagined his mother lying desperately ill and his being able to secure only a Negro doctor for her. He toyed with that idea for a few minutes and then dropped it for a momentary vision of himself participating as a sympathizer in a sit-in demonstration. This was possible but he did not linger with it. Instead, he approached the ultimate horror. He brought home a beautiful suspiciously Negroid woman. Prepare yourself, he said. There is nothing you can do about it. This is the woman I've chosen. She's intelligent, dignified, even good, and she's suffered and she hasn't thought it *fun*. Now persecute us, go ahead and persecute us. Drive her out of here, but remember, you're driving me too. His eyes were narrowed and through the indignation he had generated, he saw his mother across the aisle, purple-faced, shrunken to the dwarf-like proportions of her moral nature, sitting like a mummy beneath the ridiculous banner of her hat.

He was tilted out of his fantasy again as the bus stopped. The door opened with a sucking hiss and out of the dark a large, gaily dressed, sullen-looking colored woman got on with a little boy. The child, who might have been four, had on a short plaid suit and a Tyrolean hat with a blue feather in it. Julian hoped that he would sit down beside him and that the woman would push in beside his mother. He could think of no better arrangement.

As she waited for her tokens, the woman was surveying the seating possibilities— he hoped with the idea of sitting where she was least wanted. There was something familiar-looking about her but Julian could not place what it was. She was a giant of a woman. Her face was set not only to meet opposition but to seek it out. The downward tilt of her large lower lip was like a warning sign: DON'T TAMPER WITH ME. Her bulging figure was encased in a green crepe dress and her feet overflowed in red shoes. She had on a hideous hat. A purple velvet flap came down on one side of it and stood up on the other; the rest of it was green and looked like a cushion with the stuffing out. She carried a mammoth red pocketbook that bulged throughout as if it were stuffed with rocks.

To Julian's disappointment, the little boy climbed up on the empty seat beside his mother. His mother lumped all children, black and white, into the common category, "cute," and she thought little Negroes were on the whole cuter than little white children. She smiled at the little boy as he climbed on the seat.

Meanwhile the woman was bearing down upon the empty seat beside Julian. To his annoyance, she squeezed herself into it. He saw his mother's face change as the

75

woman settled herself next to him and he realized with satisfaction that this was more objectionable to her than it was to him. Her face seemed almost gray and there was a look of dull recognition in her eyes, as if suddenly she had sickened at some awful confrontation. Julian saw that it was because she and the woman had, in a sense, swapped sons. Though his mother would not realize the symbolic significance of this, she would feel it. His amusement showed plainly on his face.

The woman next to him muttered something unintelligible to herself. He was conscious of a kind of bristling next to him, a muted growling like that of an angry cat. He could not see anything but the red pocketbook upright on the bulging green thighs. He visualized the woman as she had stood waiting for her tokens—the ponderous figure, rising from the red shoes upward over the solid hips, the mammoth bosom, the haughty face, to the green and purple hat. 80

His eyes widened.

The vision of the two hats, identical, broke upon him with the radiance of a brilliant sunrise. His face was suddenly lit with joy. He could not believe that Fate had thrust upon his mother such a lesson. He gave a loud chuckle so that she would look at him and see that he saw. She turned her eyes on him slowly. The blue in them seemed to have turned a bruised purple. For a moment he had an uncomfortable sense of her innocence, but it lasted only a second before principle rescued him. Justice entitled him to laugh. His grin hardened until it said to her as plainly as if he were saying aloud: Your punishment exactly fits your pettiness. This should teach you a permanent lesson.

Her eyes shifted to the woman. She seemed unable to bear looking at him and to find the woman preferable. He became conscious again of the bristling presence at his side. The woman was rumbling like a volcano about to become active. His mother's mouth began to twitch slightly at one corner. With a sinking heart, he saw incipient signs of recovery on her face and realized that this was going to strike her suddenly as funny and was going to be no lesson at all. She kept her eyes on the woman and an amused smile came over her face. The little Negro was looking up at her with large fascinated eyes. He had been trying to attract her attention for some time.

"Carver!" the woman said suddenly. "Come heah!"

When he saw that the spotlight was on him at last, Carver drew his feet up and turned himself toward Julian's mother and giggled. 85

"Carver!" the woman said. "You heah me? Come heah!"

Carver slid down from the seat but remained squatting with his back against the base of it, his head turned slyly around toward Julian's mother, who was smiling at him. The woman reached a hand across the aisle and snatched him to her. He righted himself and hung backwards on her knees, grinning at Julian's mother. "Isn't he cute?" Julian's mother said to the woman with the protruding teeth.

"I reckon he is," the woman said without conviction.

His mother yanked him upright but he eased out of her grip and shot across the aisle and scrambled, giggling wildly, onto the seat beside his love.

"I think he likes me," Julian's mother said, and smiled at the woman. It was the smile she used when she was being particularly gracious to an inferior. Julian saw everything lost. The lesson had rolled off her like rain on a roof. 90

The woman stood up and yanked the little boy off the seat as if she were snatching him from contagion. Julian could feel the rage in her at having no weapon like his mother's smile. She gave the child a sharp slap across his leg. He howled once and then thrust his head into her stomach and kicked his feet against her shins. "Behave," she said vehemently.

The bus stopped and the Negro who had been reading the newspaper got off. The woman moved over and set the little boy down with a thump between herself and Julian. She held him firmly by the knee. In a moment he put his hands in front of his face and peeped at Julian's mother through his fingers.

"I see yoooooooo!" she said and put her hand in front of her face and peeped at him.

The woman slapped his hand down. "Quit yo' foolishness," she said, "before I knock the living Jesus out of you!"

Julian was thankful that the next stop was theirs. He reached up and pulled the   95
cord. The woman reached up and pulled it at the same time. Oh my God, he thought. He had the terrible intuition that when they got off the bus together, his mother would open her purse and give the little boy a nickel. The gesture would be as natural to her as breathing. The bus stopped and the woman got up and lunged to the front, dragging the child, who wished to stay on, after her. Julian and his mother got up and followed. As they neared the door, Julian tried to relieve her of her pocketbook.

"No," she murmured, "I want to give the little boy a nickel."

"No!" Julian hissed. "No!"

She smiled down at the child and opened her bag. The bus door opened and the woman picked him up by the arm and descended with him, hanging at her hip. Once in the street she set him down and shook him.

Julian's mother had to close her purse while she got down the bus step but as soon as her feet were on the ground, she opened it again and began to rummage inside. "I can't find but a penny," she whispered, "but it looks like a new one."

"Don't do it!" Julian said fiercely between his teeth. There was a streetlight on the   100
corner and she hurried to get under it so that she could better see into her pocketbook. The woman was heading off rapidly down the street with the child still hanging backward on her hand.

"Oh little boy!" Julian's mother called and took a few quick steps and caught up with them just beyond the lamppost. "Here's a bright new penny for you," and she held out the coin, which shone bronze in the dim light.

The huge woman turned and for a moment stood, her shoulders lifted and her face frozen with frustrated rage, and stared at Julian's mother. Then all at once she seemed to explode like a piece of machinery that had been given one ounce of pressure too much. Julian saw the black fist swing out with the red pocketbook. He shut his eyes and cringed as he heard the woman shout, "He don't take nobody's pennies!" When he opened his eyes, the woman was disappearing down the street with the little boy staring wide-eyed over her shoulder. Julian's mother was sitting on the sidewalk.

"I told you not to do that," Julian said angrily. "I told you not to do that!"

He stood over her for a minute, gritting his teeth. Her legs were stretched out in front of her and her hat was on her lap. He squatted down and looked her in the face. It was totally expressionless. "You got exactly what you deserved," he said. "Now get up."

He picked up her pocketbook and put what had fallen out back in it. He picked   105
the hat up off her lap. The penny caught his eye on the sidewalk and he picked that up and let it drop before her eyes into the purse. Then he stood up and leaned over and held his hands out to pull her up. She remained immobile. He sighed. Rising above them on either side were black apartment buildings, marked with irregular rectangles of light. At the end of the block a man came out of a door and walked off in the opposite direction. "All right," he said, "suppose somebody happens by and wants to know why you're sitting on the sidewalk?"

She took the hand and, breathing hard, pulled heavily up on it and then stood for a moment, swaying slightly as if the spots of light in the darkness were circling around her. Her eyes, shadowed and confused, finally settled on his face. He did not try to conceal his irritation. "I hope this teaches you a lesson," he said. She leaned forward and her eyes raked his face. She seemed trying to determine his identity. Then, as if she found nothing familiar about him, she started off with a headlong movement in the wrong direction.

"Aren't you going on to the Y?" he asked.

"Home," she muttered.

"Well, are we walking?"

For answer she kept going. Julian followed along, his hands behind him. He saw no reason to let the lesson she had had go without backing it up with an explanation of its meaning. She might as well be made to understand what had happened to her. "Don't think that was just an uppity Negro woman," he said. "That was the whole colored race which will no longer take your condescending pennies. That was your black double. She can wear the same hat as you, and to be sure," he added gratuitously (because he thought it was funny), "it looked better on her than it did on you. What all this means," he said, "is that the old world is gone. The old manners are obsolete and your graciousness is not worth a damn." He thought bitterly of the house that had been lost for him. "You aren't who you think you are," he said.

She continued to plow ahead, paying no attention to him. Her hair had come undone on one side. She dropped her pocketbook and took no notice. He stooped and picked it up and handed it to her but she did not take it.

"You needn't act as if the world had come to an end," he said, "because it hasn't. From now on you've got to live in a new world and face a few realities for a change. Buck up," he said, "it won't kill you."

She was breathing fast.

"Let's wait on the bus," he said.

"Home," she said thickly.

"I hate to see you behave like this," he said. "Just like a child. I should be able to expect more of you." He decided to stop where he was and make her stop and wait for a bus. "I'm not going any farther," he said, stopping. "We're going on the bus."

She continued to go on as if she had not heard him. He took a few steps and caught her arm and stopped her. He looked into her face and caught his breath. He was looking into a face he had never seen before. "Tell Grandpa to come get me," she said.

He stared, stricken.

"Tell Caroline to come get me," she said.

Stunned, he let her go and she lurched forward again, walking as if one leg were shorter than the other. A tide of darkness seemed to be sweeping her from him. "Mother!" he cried. "Darling, sweetheart, wait!" Crumpling, she fell to the pavement. He dashed forward and fell at her side, crying, "Mamma, Mamma!" He turned her over. Her face was fiercely distorted. One eye, large and staring, moved slightly to the left as if it had become unmoored. The other remained fixed on him, raked his face again, found nothing and closed.

"Wait here, wait here!" he cried and jumped up and began to run for help toward a cluster of lights he saw in the distance ahead of him. "Help, help!" he shouted, but his voice was thin, scarcely a thread of sound. The lights drifted farther away the faster he ran and his feet moved numbly as if they carried him nowhere. The tide of darkness seemed to sweep him back to her, postponing from moment to moment his entry into the world of guilt and sorrow.

THE RECEPTIVE READER

1. What kind of person is Julian's mother? What kind of attitudes and mental habits shape her personality? (How are they revealed in such telling details as the hat, the to-do about the seating in the bus, the coin for the black child?) ✧ What is her view of her son? What are her true feelings about him? ✧ Is there any one dominant trait that provides a clue to her character?

2. O'Connor is a master of mixed feelings and contradictory emotions. What kind of person is Julian? What is his basic conflict with his mother? What are the central themes of his mental monologues? Which incidents are most revealing of his character? ✧ What would you identify as his most characteristic trait or problem? Are there any contradictions in his personality? (Are we supposed to like him or identify with his point of view?)

3. This story takes us to the South in a period of *transition*. Blacks or African Americans are still called Negroes (or, more politely, "colored"). Buses have recently been integrated, with no more relegation of colored people to the back of the bus. What is the role of black people in this story? What kind of person is the mother of the little boy? Is the author's portrait of her unflattering or favorable?

4. Can you find any passages that would serve as *capsule portraits* of the major characters?

5. What is the significance of the *ending*?

6. Does this story reinforce or does it counteract stereotypes about Southerners and blacks?

THE PERSONAL RESPONSE

In this story, do you find yourself taking sides between Julian's mother and her son? What side are you on, and why? Do you think the author expects you to like Julian or identify with his point of view?

THE CREATIVE DIMENSION

Flannery O'Connor is a writer who keeps very tight control over her characters, with every detail meaningful and very little left to chance. Suppose one of the characters—Julian's mother, Julian, or the black woman (or maybe the child)—had a chance to have a last word, talking freely about what he or she felt deep down. Choose one of these, and write what you think he or she might say.

The following is a lesser-known story by O'Connor. Do you recognize in it her characteristic way of looking at the world? Do you recognize features of the O'Connor style?

Enoch and the Gorilla 1952

Enoch Emery had borrowed his landlady's umbrella and he discovered as he stood in the entrance of the drugstore, trying to open it, that it was at least as old as she was. When he finally got it hoisted, he pushed his dark glasses back on his eyes and reentered the downpour.

The umbrella was one his landlady had stopped using fifteen years before (which was the only reason she had lent it to him) and as soon as the rain touched the top of it, it came down with a shriek and stabbed him in the back of the neck. He ran a few feet with it over his head and then backed into another store entrance and removed it. Then to get it up again, he had to place the tip of it on the ground and ram it open with his foot. He ran out again, holding his hand up near the spokes to keep them open and this allowed the handle, which was carved to represent the head of a fox terrier, to jab him every few seconds in the stomach. He proceeded for another quarter of a block this way before the back half of the silk stood up off the spokes and allowed the storm to sweep down his collar. Then he ducked under the marquee of a movie house. It was Saturday and a lot of children were standing more or less in a line in front of the ticket box.

Enoch was not very fond of children, but children always seemed to like to look at him. The line turned and twenty or thirty eyes began to observe him with a steady interest. The umbrella had assumed an ugly position, half up and half down, and the half that was up was about to come down and spill more water under his collar. When this happened the children laughed and jumped up and down. Enoch glared at them and turned his back and lowered his dark glasses. He found himself facing a life-size four-color picture of a gorilla. Over the gorilla's head, written in red letters was "GONGA! Giant Jungle Monarch and a Great Star! HERE IN PERSON!!!" At the level of the gorilla's knee, there was more that said, "Gonga will appear in person in front of this theater at 12 A.M. *TODAY!* A free pass to the first ten brave enough to step up and shake his hand!"

Enoch was usually thinking of something else at the moment that Fate began drawing back her leg to kick him. When he was four years old, his father had brought him home a tin box from the penitentiary. It was orange and had a picture of some peanut brittle on the outside of it and green letters that said, "A NUTTY SURPRISE!" When Enoch had opened it, a coiled piece of steel had sprung out at him and broken off the ends of his two front teeth. His life was full of so many happenings like that that it would seem he should have been more sensitive to his times of danger. He stood there and read the poster twice through carefully. To his mind, an opportunity to insult a successful ape came from the hand of Providence.

He turned around and asked the nearest child what time it was. The child said it was twelve-ten and that Gonga was already ten minutes late. Another child said that maybe the rain had delayed him. Another said, no, not the rain, his director was taking a plane from Hollywood. Enoch gritted his teeth. The first child said that if he wanted to shake the star's hand, he would have to get in line like the rest of them and wait his turn. Enoch got into line. A child asked him how old he was. Another observed that he had funny-looking teeth. He ignored all this as best he could and began to straighten out the umbrella.

In a few minutes a black truck turned around the corner and came slowly up the street in the heavy rain. Enoch pushed the umbrella under his arm and began to squint through his dark glasses. As the truck approached, a phonograph inside it began to play "Tarara Boom Di Aye," but the music was almost drowned out by the rain. There was a large illustration of a blonde on the outside of the truck, advertising some picture other than the one with the gorilla.

The children held their line carefully as the truck stopped in front of the movie house. The back door of it was constructed like a paddy wagon, with a grate, but the ape was not at it. Two men in raincoats got out of the cab part, cursing, and ran around to the back and opened the door. One of them stuck his head in and said, "Okay, make it snappy, willya?" The other jerked his thumb at the children and said, "Get back willya, willya get back?"

5

A voice on the record inside the truck said, "Here's Gonga, folks, Roaring Gonga and a Great Star! Give Gonga a big hand, folks!" The voice was barely a mumble in the rain.

The man who was waiting by the door of the truck stuck his head in again. "Okay, willya get out?" he said.

There was a faint thump somewhere inside the van. After a second a dark furry arm   10
emerged just enough for the rain to touch it and then drew back inside.

The man who was under the marquee took off his raincoat and threw it to the man by the door, who threw it into the wagon. After two or three minutes more, the gorilla appeared at the door, with the raincoat buttoned up to his chin and the collar turned up. There was an iron chain hanging from around his neck; the man grabbed it and pulled him down and the two of them bounded under the marquee together. A motherly-looking woman was in the glass ticket box, getting the passes ready for the first ten children brave enough to step up and shake hands.

The gorilla ignored the children entirely and followed the man over to the other side of the entrance where there was a small platform raised about a foot off the ground. He stepped up on it and turned facing the children and began to growl. His growls were not so much loud as poisonous; they appeared to issue from a black heart. Enoch was terrified and if he had not been surrounded by the children, he would have run away.

"Who'll step up first?" the man said. "Come on, come on, who'll step up first? A free pass to the first kid stepping up."

There was no movement from the group of children. The man glared at them. "What's the matter with you kids?" he barked. "You yellow? He won't hurt you as long as I got him by this chain." He tightened his grip on the chain and jangled it at them to show he was holding it securely.

After a minute a little girl separated herself from the group. She had long wood-   15
shaving curls and a fierce triangular face. She moved up to within four feet of the star.

"Okay okay," the man said, rattling the chain, "make it snappy."

The ape reached out and gave her hand a quick shake. By this time there was another little girl ready and then two boys. The line re-formed and began to move up.

The gorilla kept his hand extended and turned his head away with a bored look at the rain. Enoch had got over his fear and was trying frantically to think of a remark that would be suitable to insult him with. Usually he didn't have any trouble with this kind of composition but nothing came to him now. His brain, both parts, was completely empty. He couldn't think even of the insulting phrase he used every day.

There were only two children in front of him by now. The first one shook hands and stepped aside. Enoch's heart was beating violently. The child in front of him finished and stepped aside and left him facing the ape, who took his hand with an automatic motion.

It was the first hand that had been extended to Enoch since he had come to the   20
city. It was warm and soft.

For a second he only stood there, clasping it. Then he began to stammer. "My name is Enoch Emery," he mumbled. "I attended the Rodemill Boys' Bible Academy. I work at the city zoo. I seen two of your pictures. I'm only eighteen years old but I already work for the city. My daddy made me come . . ." and his voice cracked.

The star leaned slightly forward and a change came in his eyes: an ugly pair of human ones moved closer and squinted at Enoch from behind the celluloid pair. "You go take a jump," a surly voice inside the ape-suit said, low but distinctly, and the hand was jerked away.

Enoch's humiliation was so sharp and painful that he turned around three times before he realized which direction he wanted to go in. Then he ran off into the rain as fast as he could.

In spite of himself, Enoch couldn't get over the expectation that something was going to happen to him. The virtue of hope, in Enoch, was made up of two parts suspicion and one part desire. It operated on him all the rest of the day. He had only a vague idea what he wanted, but he was not a boy without ambition: he wanted to become something. He wanted to better his condition. He wanted, some day, to see a line of people waiting to shake his hand.

All afternoon he fidgeted and fooled in his room, biting his nails and shredding   25 what was left of the silk off the landlady's umbrella. Finally he denuded it entirely and broke off the spokes. What was left was a black stick with a sharp steel point at one end and a dog's head at the other. It might have been an instrument for some specialized kind of torture that had gone out of fashion. Enoch walked up and down his room with it under his arm and realized that it would distinguish him on the sidewalk.

About seven o'clock in the evening he put on his coat and took the stick and headed for a little restaurant two blocks away. He had the sense that he was setting off to get some honor, but he was very nervous, as if he were afraid he might have to snatch it instead of receive it.

He never set out for anything without eating first. The restaurant was called the Paris Diner; it was a tunnel about six feet wide, located between a shoeshine parlor and a dry-cleaning establishment. Enoch slid in and climbed up on the far stool at the counter and said he would have a bowl of split-pea soup and a chocolate malted milkshake.

The waitress was a tall woman with a big yellow dental plate and the same color hair done up in a black hairnet. One hand never left her hip; she filled orders with the other one. Although Enoch came in nightly, she had never learned to like him.

Instead of filling his order, she began to fry bacon; there was only one other customer in the place and he had finished his meal and was reading a newspaper; there was no one to eat the bacon but her. Enoch reached over the counter and prodded her hip with the stick. "Listen here," he said, "I got to go. I'm in a hurry."

"Go then," she said. Her jaw began to work and she stared into the skillet with a   30 fixed attention.

"Lemme just have a piece of theter cake yonder," he said, pointing to a half of pink and yellow cake on a round glass stand. "I think I got something to do. I got to be going. Set it up there next to him," he said, indicating the customer reading the newspaper. He slid over the stools and began reading the outside sheet of the man's paper.

The man lowered the paper and looked at him. Enoch smiled. The man raised the paper again. "Could I borrow some part of your paper that you ain't studying?" Enoch asked. The man lowered it again and stared at him; he had muddy unflinching eyes. He leafed deliberately through the paper and shook out the sheet with the comic strips and handed it to Enoch. It was Enoch's favorite part. He read it every evening like an office. While he ate the cake that the waitress had torpedoed down the counter at him, he read and felt himself surge with kindness and courage and strength.

When he finished one side, he turned the sheet over and began to scan the advertisements for movies that filled the other side. His eye went over three columns without stopping; then it came to a box that advertised Gonga, Giant Jungle Monarch, and listed the theaters he would visit on his tour and the hours he would be at each one. In thirty minutes he would arrive at the Victory on 57th Street and that would be his last appearance in the city.

If anyone had watched Enoch read this, he would have seen a certain transformation in his countenance. It still shone with the inspiration he had absorbed from the comic strips, but something else had come over it: a look of awakening.

The waitress happened to turn around to see if he hadn't gone. "What's the matter   35
with you?" she said. "Did you swallow a seed?"

"I know what I want," Enoch murmured.

"I know what I want too," she said with a dark look.

Enoch felt for his stick and laid his change on the counter. "I got to be going now."

"Don't let me keep you," she said.

"You may not see me again," he said, "—the way I am."   40

"Any way I don't see you will be all right with me," she said.

Enoch left. It was a pleasant damp evening. The puddles on the sidewalk shone and the store windows were steamy and bright with junk. He disappeared down a side street and made his way rapidly along the darker passages of the city, pausing only once or twice at the end of an alley to dart a glance in each direction before he ran on. The Victory was a small theater, suited to the needs of the family, in one of the closer subdivisions; he passed through a succession of lighted areas and then on through more alleys and back streets until he came to the business section that surrounded it. Then he slowed up. He saw it about a block away, glittering in its darker setting. He didn't cross the street to the side it was on but kept on the far side, moving forward with his squint fixed on the glary spot. He stopped when he was directly across from it and hid himself in a narrow stair cavity dividing a building.

The truck that carried Gonga was parked across the street and the star was standing under the marquee, shaking hands with an elderly woman. She moved aside and a gentleman in a polo shirt stepped up and shook hands vigorously, like a sportsman. He was followed by a boy of about three who wore a tall Western hat that nearly covered his face; he had to be pushed ahead by the line. Enoch watched for some time, his face working with envy. The small boy was followed by a lady in shorts, she by an old man who tried to draw extra attention to himself by dancing up instead of walking in a dignified way. Enoch suddenly darted across the street and slipped noiselessly into the open back door of the truck.

The handshaking went on until the feature picture was ready to begin. Then the star got back in the van and the people filed into the theater. The driver and the man who was master of ceremonies climbed in the cab part and the truck rumbled off. It crossed the city rapidly and continued on the highway, going very fast.

There came from the van certain thumping noises, not those of the normal gorilla,   45
but they were drowned out by the drone of the motor and the steady sound of wheels against the road. The night was pale and quiet, with nothing to stir it but an occasional complaint from a hoot owl and the distant muted jarring of a freight train. The truck sped on until it slowed for a crossing, and as the van rattled over the tracks, a figure slipped from the door and almost fell, and then limped hurriedly off toward the woods.

Once in the darkness of a pine thicket, he laid down a pointed stick he had been clutching and something bulky and loose that he had been carrying under his arm, and began to undress. He folded each garment neatly after he had taken it off and then stacked it on top of the last thing he had removed. When all his clothes were in the pile, he took up the stick and carefully began making a hole in the ground with it.

The darkness of the pine grove was broken by paler moonlit spots that moved over him now and again and showed him to be Enoch. His natural appearance was marred by a gash that ran from the corner of his lip to his collarbone and by a lump under his eye that gave him a dulled insensitive look. Nothing could have been more deceptive for he was burning with the intensest kind of happiness.

He dug rapidly until he had made a trench about a foot long and a foot deep. Then he placed the stack of clothes in it and stood aside to rest a second. Burying his clothes was not a symbol to him of burying his former self; he only knew he wouldn't need them any more. As soon as he got his breath, he pushed the displaced dirt over the hole and stamped it down with his foot. He discovered while he did this that he still had his shoes on, and when he finished, he removed them and threw them from him. Then he picked up the loose bulky object and shook it vigorously.

In the uncertain light, one of his lean white legs could be seen to disappear and then the other, one arm and then the other: a black heavier shaggier figure replaced his. For an instant, it had two heads, one light and one dark, but after a second, it pulled the dark black head over the other and corrected this. It busied itself with certain hidden fastenings and what appeared to be minor adjustments of its hide.

For a time after this, it stood very still and didn't do anything. Then it began to growl and beat its chest; it jumped up and down and flung its arms and thrust its head forward. The growls were thin and uncertain at first but they grew louder after a second. They became low and poisonous, louder again, low and poisonous again; they stopped altogether. The figure extended its hand, clutched nothing, and shook its arm vigorously; it withdrew the arm, extended it again, clutched nothing, and shook. It repeated this four or five times. Then it picked up the pointed stick and placed it at a cocky angle under its arm and left the woods for the highway. No gorilla anywhere, Africa or California or New York, was happier than he.

A man and woman sitting close together on a rock just off the highway were looking across an open stretch of valley at a view of the city in the distance and they didn't see the shaggy figure approaching. The smokestacks and square tops of buildings made a black uneven wall against the lighter sky and here and there a steeple cut a sharp wedge out of a cloud. The young man turned his neck just in time to see the gorilla standing a few feet away, hideous and black, with its hand extended. He eased his arm from around the woman and disappeared silently into the woods. She, as soon as she turned her eyes, fled screaming down the highway. The gorilla stood as though surprised and presently its arm fell to its side. It sat down on the rock where they had been sitting and stared over the valley at the uneven skyline of the city.

THE RECEPTIVE READER

1. What features of this story might make a reader recognize it as the work of Flannery O'Connor? For instance, what makes Enoch an outsider or misfit?

2. What details introduce *grotesque* overtones—or undertones? (What, for instance, makes the umbrella a very nonordinary umbrella?) Where does the author's wicked sense of humor show, and what is its relation to the more serious aspects of the story?

3. What is the role of *violence*? Is it similar to or different from its role in other O'Connor stories?

4. What is the meaning or *theme* of Enoch's story? Does the story as a whole have a redeeming or humanizing quality?

THE PERSONAL RESPONSE

How do you personally react to the story? Does it seem too far removed from your own concerns or from the concerns of ordinary people?

JUXTAPOSITIONS ⟝⟞

A Range of Sources

With a puzzling, provocative author like Flannery O'Connor, readers may turn for help to a range of **secondary sources.** They may look for guidance in the author's own comments in conversations, lectures, or letters. They may look for helpful hints in tributes by fellow writers or in expert testimony by literary critics.

Author Testimony

O'Connor herself lectured and wrote extensively about the writing and teaching of literature. (She did, however, once say, "Asking me to lecture about story-writing is like asking a fish to lecture on swimming.") The following is her interpretation of one of her stories from a reading she presented to a college audience.

FLANNERY O'CONNOR

On "A Good Man Is Hard to Find" 1963

This is the story of a family of six which, on its way driving to Florida, gets wiped out by an escaped convict who calls himself the Misfit. The family is made up of the Grandmother and her son, Bailey, and his children, John Wesley and June Star and the baby, and there is also the cat and the children's mother. The cat is named Pitty Sing, and the Grandmother is taking him with them, hidden in a basket.

Now I think it behooves me to try to establish with you the basis on which reason operates in this story. Much of my fiction takes its character from a reasonable use of the unreasonable, though the reasonableness of my use of it may not always be apparent. The assumptions that underlie this use of it, however, are those of the central Christian mysteries. These are assumptions to which a large part of the modern audience takes exception. About this I can only say that there are perhaps other ways than my own in which this story could be read, but none other by which it could have been written. Belief, in my own case anyway, is the engine that makes perception operate.

The heroine of this story, the Grandmother, is in the most significant position life offers the Christian. She is facing death. And to all appearances she, like the rest of us, is not too well prepared for it. She would like to see the event postponed. Indefinitely.

I've talked to a number of teachers who use this story in class and who tell their students that the Grandmother is evil, that in fact, she's a witch, even down to the cat. One of these teachers told me that his students, and particularly his Southern students, resisted this interpretation with a certain bemused vigor, and he didn't understand why. I had to tell him that they resisted it because they all had grandmothers or great-aunts just like her at home, and they knew, from personal experience, that the old lady lacked comprehension, but that she had a good heart. The Southerner is usually tolerant of those weaknesses that proceed from innocence, and he knows that a taste for self-preservation can be readily combined with the missionary spirit.

This same teacher was telling his students that morally the Misfit was several cuts above the Grandmother. He had a really sentimental attachment to the Misfit. But then a prophet gone wrong is almost always more interesting than your grandmother, and you have to let people take their pleasures where they find them.

It is true that the old lady is a hypocritical old soul; her wits are no match for the Misfit's, nor is her capacity for grace equal to his; yet I think the unprejudiced reader will feel that the Grandmother has a special kind of triumph in this story which instinctively we do not allow to someone altogether bad.

I often ask myself what makes a story work, and what makes it hold up as a story, and I have decided that it is probably some action, some gesture of a character that is unlike any other in the story, one which indicates where the real heart of the story lies. This would have to be an action or a gesture which was both totally right and totally unexpected; it would have to be one that was both in character and beyond character; it would have to suggest both the world and eternity. The action or gesture I'm talking about would have to be on . . . the level which has to do with the Divine life and our participation in it. It would be a gesture that transcended any neat allegory that might have been intended or any pat moral categories a reader could make. It would be a gesture which somehow made contact with mystery.

There is a point in this story where such a gesture occurs. The Grandmother is at last alone, facing the Misfit. Her head clears for an instant and she realizes, even in her limited way, that she is responsible for the man before her and joined to him by ties of kinship which have their roots deep in the mystery she has been merely prattling about so far. And at this point, she does the right thing, she makes the right gesture. . . .

I don't want to equate the Misfit with the devil. I prefer to think that, however unlikely this may seem, the old lady's gesture, like the mustard seed, will grow to be a great crow-filled tree in the Misfit's heart, and will be enough of a pain to him there to turn him into the prophet he was meant to become. But that's another story.

From *Mystery and Manners*, edited by Sally and Robert Fitzgerald

QUESTION

Does this account by the author change your understanding of the story?

Author Correspondence

Readers often turn to an author's published **letters** for insights into the writer's personality and work. The following is an excerpt from a review by Joyce Carol Oates of a volume of O'Connor's letters. Oates said, "It will be no surprise to admirers of Flannery O'Connor's enigmatic, troubling, and highly idiosyncratic fiction to learn that there were, behind the near-perfect little rituals of violence and redemption she created, not one but several Flannery O'Connors."

JOYCE CAROL OATES
A Self-Portrait in Letters   1987

It must be said of the letters that they give life to a wonderfully warm, witty, generous, and complex personality, surely one of the most gifted of contemporary writers. At the same time they reveal a curiously girlish, childlike, touchingly timid personality. . . . The letters give voice, on one side, to a hilariously witty observer of the grotesque, the vulgar, and the merely silly in this society, and in the rather limited world of the Catholic imagination; and then they reveal a Catholic intellectual so conservative and docile that she will write to a priest-friend for permission to read Gide and Sartre (at that time on the Church's Index of forbidden writers). . . .

The first letter in the collection was written in 1948, when Flannery was "up north" at Yaddo, the writers' colony in Saratoga Springs. The last letter, a heartbreaking one, was written just before her death on August 3, 1964, when she knew she was dying of complications following an operation for the removal of a tumor. The years between 1948 and 1964 were rich, full ones, despite the fact that Flannery's debilitating condition (lupus) kept her at home, and frequently bedridden, for long periods of time. She was not at all a solitary, reclusive person; she had a wide circle of friends, and clearly loved seeing them, and writing to them often. . . .

She always knew that the process of creation was subjected to no rules, and that, as an artist, she "discovered" the truth of her stories in the writing of them. She enjoyed writing—perhaps it is not an exaggeration to say that she lived for it, and in it. Easily exhausted, she forced herself to work two or three hours every day, in the morning, and managed by this discipline to write about one story a year during the worst periods. During the final year of her life, 1964, when everything seemed to go wrong, she was completing the volume that would be her finest achievement, "Everything That Rises Must Converge," which would be published, to wide critical acclaim, after her death. One cannot imagine an ailing person less given to self-pity. When, as a fairly young woman, she learned she would probably be on crutches the rest of her life, she says merely, "So, so much for that. I will henceforth be a structure with flying buttresses. . . ." Writing to a friend in 1964, she says she must submit to an operation because "I have a large tumor and if they don't make haste and get rid of it, they will have to remove me and leave it." It is only near the very end of her life that she says, briefly, to the same friend: "Prayers requested. I am sick of being sick."

From "Flannery O'Connor: A Self-Portrait in Letters," in *Antaeus*, Autumn 1987

QUESTIONS

Which details or comments in this review do most to round out your mental picture of O'Connor? Which are most enlightening or thought provoking?

Tribute by a Fellow Writer

Alice Walker, author of *The Color Purple,* grew up in a sharecropper's shack a few miles from where O'Connor lived for a time in a house built by slaves. Walker discovered the "dazzling perfection" of O'Connor's writing while taking a course on Southern writers up North. Walker appreciated O'Connor's work because she wrote about Southern white women with "not a whiff of magnolia" hovering in the air and about "black folks without melons and superior racial patience." Walker says, "As a college student in the sixties I read her books endlessly, scarcely conscious of the difference between her racial and economic background and my own, but put them away in anger when I discovered that, while I was reading O'Connor—Southern, Catholic, and white—there were other women writers—some Southern, some religious, all black—I had not been allowed to know." Later, after discovering black writers like Zora Neale Hurston and Jean Toomer, Walker came to look at O'Connor's fiction from a new perspective.

ALICE WALKER
Beyond the Peacock 1975

Whether one "understands" her stories or not, one knows her characters are new and wondrous creations in the world and that none of her stories—not even the earliest ones in which her consciousness of racial matters had not evolved sufficiently to be interesting or to differ much from the insulting and ignorant racial stereotyping that preceded it—could have been written by anyone else. As one can tell . . . a Picasso from a Hallmark card, one can tell an O'Connor story from any story laid next to it. Her Catholicism did not in any way limit (by defining it) her art. After her great stories of sin, damnation, prophecy and revelation, the stories one reads casually in the average magazine seem to be about love and roast beef. . . .

She destroyed the last vestiges of sentimentality in white Southern writing; she caused white women to look ridiculous on pedestals, and she approached her black characters—as a mature artist—with unusual humility and restraint. She also cast spells and worked magic with the written word.

From In Search of Our Mothers' Gardens

QUESTIONS

How did you react to the references to black people in O'Connor's stories? Can you relate Walker's comments to the stories you have read?

The Critic's Voice

Many critics take their clue from O'Connor's Catholicism in looking in her "startling dramas" for hints of divine love or redemption—for religious overtones that are implied rather than spelled out. The critic who wrote the following excerpt said that love is "at the very core of Flannery O'Connor's fiction."

RICHARD GIANNONE
The Mystery of Love 1989

There is no reason to contest the fact that human dereliction sets O'Connor's narratives in motion and directs their course and outcome. What we need to look for is the gift of grace, the exultant salute to the eternal that she avows in her lectures and correspondence and that brings her anguished conflicts to a higher resolution. "It is a sign of maturity not to be scandalized and to try to find explanations in charity." O'Connor candidly challenges us to take a charitable view of her work, and scarcely anyone has met that challenge.

A shift in the locus of inquiry will bring about a change in our perception of O'Connor. She will emerge as more than an astute recorder of casual disasters. A quiet, patient smile of controlled abandonment to love shines through all of her fictional violence. And an unexpected contour will emerge from her art. . . . To the undiscerning or the psychologically oriented, O'Connor's unrelenting exposure of human fault might seem like obsession or preacherly harangue; for O'Connor, however, the sight of inner wretchedness precedes the experience of love. . . . The guilt and punishment that her characters bring upon themselves have no independent reality of their own, but are the dark shadows of the grace and life that O'Connor finds in existence. . . .

Her strange choices for heroes—nihilists, petty tyrants, and killers—turn out to be wanderers in love. Their encounter with the mystery of their existence, the adventurer of love whom O'Connor calls God, brings the quest to a close. All the endings take both protagonist and reader by surprise. O'Connor believes, and in powerful action shows, unfathomable reality to suggest the overwhelming boldness of divine love invading human life. Her fundamental understanding of this mysterious incursion is that love is not a human right or a mental deduction but a divine revelation, a gift of plenitude found within the human heart. "I believe love to be efficacious in the loooong run" she writes to a friend. O'Connor's fiction enacts her belief.

From *Flannery O'Connor and the Mystery of Love*

QUESTION

Does this critic make you reexamine the role of the author's religious convictions in her stories? How?

WRITING ABOUT LITERATURE

9. One Author in Depth (Integrating Sources)

The role autobiography plays in fiction is precisely the role that reality plays in a dream.
JOHN CHEEVER

The Writing Workshop   When you are puzzled, intrigued, or provoked by a story, you may turn to other stories by the same author to see if you can find a pattern. You try to see if you can detect clues to familiar preoccupations or a recurrent theme. In addition, you may want to turn to personal testimony by the author—in letters, in lectures, in conversations with friends. You may be able to get ideas or help from biographers and critics who focus on the relationship between the author and the work. Choose an author for the subject of a paper in which you look for the common thread or a recurrent issue in several stories. Draw on background materials that help you bring a common theme or central issue into focus.

Your task will be to write a unified paper while integrating diverse materials. It will be especially important to develop an agenda—an overall purpose or direction. Ask yourself: "What am I trying to do in this paper?" Here are accounts of what gave purpose and direction to some sample projects:

✧ A student writer was intrigued by the fact that both the talkative grandmother in "A Good Man Is Hard to Find" and the mother in "Everything That Rises Must Converge" seem to live in the past, holding on to genteel traditions and to concepts of good breeding that no longer fit the realities of the South. The student found a third O'Connor story that spells out the same underlying theme even more directly: In "A Late Encounter with the Enemy," a teacher has been taking summer classes for years to earn a belated teaching credential. She plans to have her grandfather present at her graduation. He is a Confederate general, 104 years old, and she wants him to shame the upstarts by having him there to represent the "old traditions! Dignity! Honor! Courage! My kin!" The irony of the story is that the supposed general was actually a foot soldier in the war, who was given his general's uniform by a movie company promoting *Gone with the Wind*.

✧ One student wrote about a recurrent pattern in three stories by John Cheever: We start out with people in a comfortable middle-class or upper-middle-class existence, but something happens to show that these people "are not quite who they appear to be at first, and by the end of the story, their true natures are revealed." The "fragile veneer of the characters' happy lives begins to crack." Their weaknesses, disguised by a smug façade, are shown. By the end of the story, they may, like the main character in "The Swimmer," find themselves "miserable, cold, tired, and bewildered," exposed to the ridicule of passing motorists. Drawing on revealing comments by both Cheever himself and by his son, the student writer showed that this fear of exposure was a haunting preoccupation in Cheever's own private life.

✧ In a paper discussing several stories by Flannery O'Connor, a student writer focused on the "moment of revelation" (the *epiphany*) when a character "suddenly accepts into his or her consciousness key facts or conditions of his or her life." For instance, at the end of "A Good Man Is Hard to Find," the Misfit rejects the grandmother's last frantic appeal to spare her life as she tells him, "I know you come from nice people." She urges him to pray and reaches out to touch him: "Why, you're one of my babies. You're one of my own children!" The student writer quoted O'Connor as explaining the ending to an audience to whom she was reading this story: The grandmother realizes, "even in her limited way, that she is responsible for the man before her and joined to him by ties of kinship which have their roots deep in the mystery she has been merely prattling about so far." The paper found a similar pattern of a climactic final insight or realization in two other stories.

Writing an Integrated Paper

A paper tracing a common thread in several stories by the same author tests your ability to integrate material. Keep your paper from seeming stitched together—with too many of the seams showing. Consider guidelines like the following:

✧ *Push toward a unifying thesis.* Note the weak *also* in the following opening paragraph of a first draft. (How are the two points raised there related?)

FIRST DRAFT: O'Connor's stories shock the reader because, as she herself says, "No matter how well we are able to soften the grotesque by humor or compassion, there is always an intensity about it that creates a general discomfort." O'Connor writes about the mixture of the frightening and the comical that we call the grotesque. The conflict between good and evil is also central to O'Connor's themes. These themes are evident in several of her stories . . .

A more integrated trial thesis might read like this:

SECOND DRAFT: O'Connor's stories shock the reader because, as she herself says, "No matter how well we are able to soften the grotesque by humor or compassion, there is always an intensity about it that creates a general discomfort." O'Connor's preoccupation with the grotesque is rooted in one of her most basic themes: the struggle between good and evil. *When evil erupts into our ordinary world, it is frightening, but it is also comical because it is so different from what we expect or what should be.*

✧ *Chart your overall strategy.* For instance, you may decide to explore the role of violence in each of three stories, tracing important continuities and key differences as you examine *each story* in turn. You then have to make sure to keep important connections in view as you leave one story behind and move on to the next. Instead, you might plot your essay to move not from story to story but from point to point. You might set up three or four key features of the archetypal Southern lady found in many of O'Connor's stories and take up *each feature* in turn. You might identify such common character traits as nostalgia for a more genteel past, outdated condescending views on race, and unrealistic expectations of the current crop of white people merely because they are white. You would then take each of these up in turn and show that each can be found in all three or four major characters you are examining.

✧ *Use brief characteristic quotations to take your reader into the author's world.* Suppose you are trying to show in a lesser-known story by O'Connor the familiar blend of the threatening and strange with the zany and comical. A web of specific references and short apt quotations will create the familiar atmosphere:

Enoch in "Enoch and the Gorilla" is isolated from others. When he had opened "a nutty surprise" that his father had brought for him from the penitentiary, a "coiled piece of steel had sprung out at him and broken off the ends of his two front teeth." The waitress who instead of filling his order begins to fry bacon for herself bids him farewell by saying "Any way I don't see you will be all right with me." When Enoch lines up with the children waiting to shake hands with a man in a gorilla suit promoting a gorilla movie, the gorilla's hand is "the first hand that had been extended to Enoch since he had come to the city." This handshake changes Enoch's life; he attacks the hapless gorilla to take over the suit so that he can "see people . . . waiting to shake his hand."

❖ *Test a critic's opinion against your own firsthand reading.* Do not just accept the critic's say-so as gospel. Show why the critic's comment is helpful; show why you agree or disagree. The following passage does a good job of working a critical quotation into the student writer's own text:

> Susanne M. Paulson, in *Flannery O'Connor: A Study of the Short Fiction*, says, "Both the Misfit and the grandmother derive from the same human family tainted by sin and suffering in the material world." O'Connor is indeed showing the reader that the Misfit is not an alien being but might be one of our neighbors or our own family. The Misfit himself says, "I been most everything. Been in the arm service . . . twict married, been an undertaker, been with the railroads." He says, "I was a gospel singer for a while." We could have encountered him anywhere in familiar everyday reality.

❖ *Pay special attention to transitions.* You will need strong ties and cross-references between the several different stories you are discussing. Suppose you are moving on from the story about the Misfit to the story about Enoch and the gorilla. Avoid a lame transition like "We see similar themes in another O'Connor story." Provide the missing link between the two sections of your paper. Show a strong thematic connection by highlighting a major shared element:

> TRANSITION: Like the Misfit in "A Good Man Is Hard to Find," Enoch in "Enoch and the Gorilla" is also a "misfit" in his world.

What is the focus of the following student paper? How successful is it in integrating material from several different stories? How successful is it in defining and making meaningful a key term in critical discussions of O'Connor's work?

SAMPLE STUDENT PAPER

Flannery O'Connor's Grotesques

> The grotesque: absurdly incongruous; departing markedly from the natural, the expected, or the typical . . . a combination of horror and humor.

This definition of the word *grotesque* perfectly describes the life of Flannery O'Connor. After all, isn't it absurd and unexpected that, as a young woman of twenty-five, her bones were so weak from lupus that she was forced to hobble around on crutches like a woman of eighty? Or ironic that she would eventually die from complications of an abdominal operation that was supposed to help improve her condition? And despite the horror O'Connor undoubtedly had to deal with during her illness, she still held a positive outlook on life, writing shortly before her relapse and death in 1964, "I intend to survive this." This absurdity, this incongruity, this grotesqueness that seemed to dominate the path of her life has carried over into O'Connor's writing, as can be seen in the short stories "A Good Man Is Hard to Find," "Everything That Rises Must Converge," and "Enoch and the Gorilla." In each of these stories lurk characteristics of the grotesque—descriptions and comparisons that seem unnatural or incongruous, ideas that are absurd or unexpected, and that same ironic combination of horror and positive humor that haunted O'Connor throughout her illness.

Perhaps it was her own physical illness that caused O'Connor's fascination with physical deformity. Many brief descriptions in her stories reflect this fascination, such as in "Everything That Rises Must Converge," when Julian turned his stricken mother over and saw that "her face was fiercely distorted. One eye, large and staring, moved slightly to the left as if it had become unmoored." This sense of grotesque distortion is also evident in the description of Enoch putting on the gorilla suit in "Enoch and the Gorilla." O'Connor portrays the act as a weird metamorphosis, as if the boy were actually turning into a gorilla:

> In the uncertain light, one of his lean white legs could be seen to disappear and then the other, one arm and then the other: a black heavier shaggier figure replaced his. For an instant, it had two heads, one light and one dark. . . .

Likewise, the comparisons O'Connor draws between two objects often seem unnatural or incongruous. In "A Good Man Is Hard to Find," the mother's face is described as "broad and innocent as a cabbage," which I found to be a peculiar comparison. Similarly, in "Enoch and the Gorilla," Enoch's broken umbrella is compared to "an instrument for some specialized kind of torture that had gone out of fashion," which I thought was a warped, distorted way of viewing a common household object.

The descriptions and comparisons were not the only hints of distortion or unnaturalness. In fact, some of O'Connor's main story ideas contain elements of the unnatural or the unexpected, sometimes to the point of absurdity. In "A Good Man Is Hard to Find," the whole idea of the grandmother trying to talk a hardened criminal out of killing her on the basis that she is "a good lady" and of "good blood" is absurd. The situation becomes even more ridiculous when the grandmother and the Misfit begin very nonchalantly to discuss the weather, or when the grandmother, showing her good breeding and southern hospitality, kindly offers him one of her own son's shirts to wear, despite the fact that he is just about to have her son killed and is planning to own the shirt the son had been wearing.

Also unexpected and absurd is the Misfit's exceedingly calm and polite manner. In fact, when he notices that the mother is getting very uneasy and anxious, he politely asks her, "Lady, would you and that little girl like to step off yonder with Bobby Lee and Hiram and join your husband?" to which the mother answers in obvious relief, "'Yes, thank you.'" Ever the gentleman, he orders his men to "hep that lady up."

Although the Misfit's gentlemanly mannerisms are very surprising, perhaps the most unexpected part of the story occurs when the grandmother has been talking to the Misfit for a while. Suddenly feeling as if she were beginning to understand him, she declares, "Why, you're one of my babies. You're one of my own children!" Ironically it is at this moment of understanding and intimacy that the Misfit chooses to kill her.

Despite the grim ending of this and the other two stories, there is evidence of an ironic blending of humor with horror. In "A Good Man Is Hard to Find," the images of the cat jumping onto Bailey's shoulder, "clinging . . . like a caterpillar," and the children scrambling out of the overturned car shouting, "'We've had an ACCIDENT!'" are humorous. In fact, even after we realize the mother has suffered serious injury, the accident still seems funny in a sick sort of way.

Similarly, in "Enoch and the Gorilla," Enoch's nervous introduction to Gonga the Gorilla is hilarious, although we know how hurt and humiliated Enoch must have felt afterwards:

> "My name is Enoch Emery," he mumbled. "I attended the Rodemill Boys' Bible Academy. I work at the city zoo. I seen two of your pictures. I'm only eighteen years old but I already work for the city. My daddy made me come. . . ." and his voice cracked. . . ."You go take a jump," a surly voice inside the ape-suit said.

In "Everything That Rises Must Converge," the humor found in Julian's rebellious fantasies in which he "brought home a beautiful suspiciously Negroid woman" or "imagined his mother lying desperately ill and his being able to secure only a Negro doctor for her" lies on the surface of a pain that lurks underneath, the pain of his and his mother's strained relationship. The humor is there, but the underlying pain and horror make it feel warped and distorted.

This warping of reality, this distortion of common things, this grotesqueness, is something O'Connor shows an affinity for and a talent in using. Through her manipulation of unnatural comparisons, unexpected and absurd ideas, and humor laced with horror, she shows how even her most self-righteous characters are not clean of the grotesque. Despite the grandmother's "good blood," she too was grotesque in her absurd conversation with the Misfit. Even bright, young, non-prejudiced, socially-aware Julian was tainted with the grotesque because of the delight he took in destroying his mother's comfortable little dreamworld in which she and her ancestors had a special identity. O'Connor has a knack for using distortion to create a confusing environment for her characters in which the line between the "good" and "evil" characters is very finely drawn. As one critic put it, "The real grotesques are the self-justified, the apparent grotesques may be the blessed."

QUESTIONS

How would you sum up the student writer's definition of the key term? What is the writer's strategy for structuring the paper? How adequate or convincing are the examples? What questions does the paper leave unanswered?

10 PERSPECTIVES
The Range of Interpretation

Writing disappears unless there is a response to it.
BARBARA CHRISTIAN

FOCUS ON CRITICISM

Critics are attracted to writers that present a challenge, that test their powers of interpretation. James Joyce, William Faulkner, and Flannery O'Connor are among writers whose fiction has drawn the attention of many commentators. Checking your college library for critical discussions of Nathaniel Hawthorne's "Young Goodman Brown," a richly symbolic and ambiguous story, you might find a hundred or more articles.

What accounts for differences in interpretation? For one thing, readers may focus on different corners of the familiar communication triangle: sender—message—receiver. An *author* (sender) writes a *text* (message) that will be read by a *reader* (receiver). Critics may focus attention on the author, on the internal workings of a story, or on what happens in the mind of the reader.

✧ Much traditional literary criticism focused on *the author*. **Author biography** aimed at a full accounting on the author's life and times. It studied the setting or *milieu* of the artist's work. It would place John Steinbeck, for instance, in the context of the California coastal and agricultural region that was his home. It would see his sympathy with the down-and-out against the background of the Great Depression. It would examine his ties with the Communist party, "in dubious battle" (the title of one of his books) against the capitalist system. It would probe his family life (marriages and children) for clues to what shaped his views of men and women. Modern biographers continue to look in depth at an author and his or her background. On the whole, they tend to be less genteel and discreet than their predecessors. Many modern biographers seem determined to go beyond an author's public image—the warmhearted storyteller, the loving parent—to probe the personal problems behind the public persona.

✧ In a reaction against the traditional focus on the author's life and times, the **New Criticism** (originally new in the forties and fifties) focused on *the* *work* itself. It focused on a story or poem as a finished artifact—self-contained, complete in itself. Rather than studying the background, the author, or the times, critics let the work speak for itself. The emphasis shifted to the close reading of the text itself. Instead of bringing preconceptions to a story from the outside, readers read *out of* the story what it had to say about contemporary politics, contemporary religion, or whatever. In practice, the newer approach often meant close study of matters of form and technique, which could be studied directly in the text. Critics paid detailed attention to image, symbol, irony, point of view. Critics paying close attention to form and technique are often called **formalists,** a label implying that *too much* attention is being paid to form (rather than to the larger meanings).

❖ In recent years, many critics have put renewed emphasis on *the reader.* The experience of literature is not complete until the reader responds as a thinking and feeling being. A story is just dead letters on a page until the reader's imagination brings it to life in the theater of the mind. Major schools of criticism stress the importance of what happens in the reader's mind:

Psychoanalytic critics, or critics influenced by psychoanalysis, early claimed that a story grips the readers' imagination when it engages with deep-seated concerns, agendas, or traumas in their own personal experience. The symbolic action of the story takes them through a process of recognizing their own psychological burdens and trying to cope with them. Often these prove to be rooted in traumatic early childhood experiences or family conflicts—repressed or thwarted love for the mother, rebellion against a domineering father, or sibling rivalry.

Myth critics looked for the echoes of myths and archetypes anchored in the collective racial memory of the human species. Stories that have a powerful hold on the reader activate unconscious memories of basic patterns of human life. Archetypes are "the psychic residue" of numberless experiences "deeply implanted in the memory of the race"; although they may seem strange on the surface, there is "that within us which leaps at the sight of them, a cry of the blood which tells us we have known them always" (Gilbert Murray). Patterns of initiation into adulthood, rituals of death and rebirth, find a profound echo in our "racial memory."

Critics stressing **reader response** focus on how the experience, expectations, and needs that readers bring to a story shape their reading of the text. Readers are not empty vessels into which the author's meanings are poured. They experience and reconstruct a story or a poem in accordance with their own vital concerns and interests. They provide the "missing bridges" between the world of the story and their own personal experience (Wolfgang Iser).

❖ Among recent critical approaches are other strong countertrends to the tendency to see a story or a poem as a finished, self-contained masterpiece that could be displayed like an ancient Greek vase:

Deconstructionists probe beyond the finished surface of a story. Having been written by a human being with unresolved conflicts and contradictory emotions, a story may disguise rather than reveal the underlying anxieties or perplexities of the author. Below the surface, unresolved tensions or contradictions may account for the true dynamics of the story. A story may have one message for the ordinary unsophisticated reader and another for a reader who responds to its subtext, its subsurface ironies. Readers who deconstruct a text will be "resistant" readers. They will not be taken in by what a story says on the surface but will try "to penetrate the disguises" of the text.

Marxist critics focus on how literature mirrors, distorts, or tries to change social and economic reality. They look at the way a writer's assumptions and loyalties are shaped by social class and economic status. They study the way the power structure of a society tries to use (and at times to suppress) literature for its own purposes.

Feminist critics focus on how literature reflects, and at times challenges, traditional gender roles. They have a special interest in female authors and their neglect or recognition in a male-dominated culture. They make us more conscious of the way male authors have traditionally shaped our assumptions about men and women. In the work of many current critics, these major trends and countertrends meet or interact in fascinating ways.

KAFKA AND HIS READERS

> We need the books that affect us like a disaster, that grieve us deeply, like the death of someone we loved more than ourselves, like being banished into forests far from everyone, like a suicide. A book must be the axe for the frozen sea within.
>
> FRANZ KAFKA

> Kafka's fictions all seem to be awakenings into an incomprehensible world, which he truly wants to understand.
>
> FREDERICK R. KARL

Franz Kafka, whose enigmatic, disturbing stories have intrigued readers around the world, provides a vivid demonstration of the range of critical interpretation. How critics read his work is strongly influenced by the assumptions and interests they bring to his stories. Using one of his best-known stories as a test case, you will be able to test your own reading of the text against critical approaches that have shaped the expectations of many readers.

FRANZ KAFKA   (1883–1924)

> The only thing for me to do now . . . is to keep my intelligence calm and discriminating to the end.
>
> FRANZ KAFKA, THE TRIAL

Kafka is one of the great prophetic voices of modern literature. His strange dreamlike stories and novels are parables that make us ponder the great twentieth-century themes. He was the prophet of alienation—homelessness, rootless-ness—and the anxiety it generates. He foresaw a totalitarian future in which the individual is helpless when struggling against a faceless all-pervading bu-reaucratic authority. Kafka made *angst*—a feverish, all-pervading anxiety—a household world.

Kafka was born as the son of wealthy Jewish parents in Prague when Czechoslovakia was still part of the Austrian empire. Though surrounded by people speaking Czech, Kafka and his friends spoke German; he studied first German literature and then law at the German university in Prague. He wrote his best-known works—"The Judgment," "Metamorphosis," *The Trial, The Castle, Amerika*—between 1912 and his death from tuberculosis in 1924. He worked in an insurance office, dealing with workmen's compensa-tion. However, he was channeling his vital energies into writing, which he pur-sued with intense seriousness and bouts of paralyzing self-doubt. Kafka published only his short stories during his lifetime, and even these only reluc-tantly. He instructed his friend Max Brod to burn all unpublished work (in-cluding the great novels) in case of Kafka's death. These instructions Brod decided he could not in good conscience carry out, thus saving for posterity what Thomas Mann called some of the "great mysterious fictions" of the twentieth century.

Kafka's narratives have been called "anti–fairy tales." In a fairy tale, the hero often sets out alone on a quest and overcomes obstacles in his search for good fortune. In a Kafka story, the hero is likely to get bogged down in the struggle. In his great mysterious novel *The Castle,* a homeless, nameless stranger—called K.—arrives in the village, claiming that he has been promised a job as a land surveyor. K. engages in an exhausting struggle to secure the most basic human needs: a place to live, a job to do, a minimum of privacy, some human contact and human warmth. K. moves among people who are cowed by a nameless fear of a faceless bureaucratic power, and he musters all his energy and ingenuity to make the bureaucracy recognize him as a human being. K.'s untiring efforts to accomplish his impossible mission are both sad and comical, reminding later readers of the sad clowns—Charles Chaplin, Buster Keaton—of the silent screen.

Kafka's blessing and bane were a tremendous hypersensitivity. The Ameri-can novelist (and writer of short fiction) John Updike said of him, "He had a sensation of anxiety and shame, a sensitivity acute beyond usefulness, as if the nervous system, flayed of its old hide of social usage, must record every touch of pain." Kafka had a kinesthetic imagination, with ideas instantly translated not merely into feelings but into intense bodily sensations.

Kafka once called his fiction "rays of light into an infinite confusion." Readers have found his stories gripping and perturbing—without being able to agree on the source of their fascination. Critics have differed widely on what these stories say about the human condition. Like Shakespeare's *Hamlet,* Kafka's enigmatic tales have been for critics more like a mirror than a window. Critics look into the mirror of these tales and see reflected there their own pre-occupations and perplexities.

The Country Doctor

1919

TRANSLATED BY WILLA MUIR AND EDWIN MUIR

I was in great perplexity; I had to start on an urgent journey; a seriously ill patient was waiting for me in a village ten miles off; a thick blizzard of snow filled all the wide spaces between him and me; I had a gig, a light gig with big wheels, exactly right for our country roads; muffled in furs, my bag of instruments in my hand, I was in the courtyard all ready for the journey; but there was no horse to be had, no horse. My own horse had died in the night, worn out by the fatigues of this icy winter; my servant girl was now running round the village trying to borrow a horse; but it was hopeless, I knew it, and I stood there forlornly, with the snow gathering more and more thickly upon me, more and more unable to move. In the gateway the girl appeared, alone, and waved the lantern; of course, who would lend a horse at this time for such a journey? I strode through the courtway once more; I could see no way out; in my confused distress I kicked at the dilapidated door of the yearlong uninhabited pigsty. It flew open and flapped to and fro on its hinges. A steam and smell as of horses came out of it. A dim stable lantern was swinging inside from a rope. A man, crouching on his hams in that low space, showed an open blue-eyed face. "Shall I yoke up?" he asked, crawling out on all fours. I did not know what to say and merely stooped down to see what else was in the sty. The servant girl was standing beside me. "You never know what you're going to find in your own house," she said, and we both laughed. "Hey there, Brother, hey there, Sister!" called the groom, and two horses, enormous creatures with powerful flanks, one after the other, their legs tucked close to their bodies, each well-shaped head lowered like a camel's, by sheer strength of buttocking squeezed out through the door hole which they filled entirely. But at once they were standing up, their legs long and their bodies steaming thickly. "Give him a hand," I said, and the willing girl hurried to help the groom with the harnessing. Yet hardly was she beside him when the groom clipped hold of her and pushed his face against hers. She screamed and fled back to me; on her cheek stood out in red the marks of two rows of teeth. "You brute," I yelled in fury, "do you want a whipping?" but in the same moment reflected that the man was a stranger; that I did not know where he came from, and that of his own free will he was helping me out when everyone else had failed me. As if he knew my thoughts he took no offense at my threat but, still busied with the horses, only turned round once toward me. "Get in," he said then, and indeed everything was ready. A magnificent pair of horses, I observed, such as I had never sat behind, and I climbed in happily. "But I'll drive, you don't know the way," I said. "Of course," said he, "I'm not coming with you anyway, I'm staying with Rose." "No," shrieked Rose, fleeing into the house with a justified presentiment that her fate was inescapable; I heard the door chain rattle as she put it up; I heard the key turn in the lock; I could see, moreover, how she put out the lights in the entrance hall and in further flight all through the rooms to keep herself from being discovered. "You're coming with me," I said to the groom, "or I won't go, urgent as my journey is. I'm not thinking of paying for it by handing the girl over to you." "Gee up!" he said; clapped his hands; the gig whirled off like a log in a freshet; I could just hear the door of my house splitting and bursting as the groom charged at it and then I was deafened and blinded by a storming rush that steadily buffeted all my senses. But this only for a moment, since, as if my patient's farmyard had opened out just before my courtyard gate, I was already there; the horses had come quietly to a standstill; the blizzard had stopped; moonlight all around; my patient's parents hurried out of the house, his sister behind them; I was almost lifted out of the gig; from their confused ejaculations I gathered not a word; in the sickroom the air was almost unbreathable; the neglected stove was smoking; I wanted to push open a window; but first I had to look at my patient. Gaunt, without any fever, not cold, not warm, with vacant eyes, without a shirt, the youngster heaved himself up from under the feather bedding, threw his arms around my neck, and whispered in my ear: "Doctor, let me die." I glanced round the room; no one had heard it; the parents were leaning forward in silence waiting for my verdict; the sister had set a chair for my hand-bag; I opened the bag and hunted among my instruments; the boy kept clutching at me from his bed to remind me of his entreaty; I picked up a pair of tweezers, examined them in the candlelight and laid them down again. "Yes," I thought blasphemously, "in cases like this the gods are helpful, send the missing horse, add to it a second because of the urgency, and to crown everything bestow even a groom—" And only now did I re-member Rose again; what was I to do, how could I rescue her, how could I pull her away from under that groom at ten miles' distance, with a team of horses I couldn't control. These horses, now, they had somehow slipped the reins loose, pushed the win-dows open from outside, I did not know how; each of them had stuck a head in at a window and, quite unmoved by the startled cries of the family, stood eyeing the pa-tient. "Better go back at once," I thought, as if the horses were summoning me to the return journey, yet I permitted the patient's sister, who fancied that I was dazed by the heat, to take my fur coat from me. A glass of rum was poured out for me, the old man clapped me on the shoulder, a familiarity justified by this offer of his treasure. I shook my head; in the narrow confines of the old man's thoughts I felt ill; that was my only reason for refusing the drink. The mother stood by the bedside and cajoled me toward it; I yielded, and, while one of the horses whinnied loudly to the ceiling, laid my head to the boy's breast, which shivered under my wet beard. I confirmed what I already knew; the boy was quite sound, something a little wrong with his circulation, saturated with coffee by his solicitous mother, but sound and best turned out of bed with one shove. I am no world reformer and so I let him lie. I was the district doctor and did my duty to the uttermost, to the point where it became almost too much. I was badly paid and yet generous and helpful to the poor. I had still to see that Rose was all right, and then the boy might have his way and I wanted to die too. What was I doing there in that endless winter! My horse was dead, and not a single person in the village would lend me another. I had to get my team out of the pigsty; if they hadn't chanced to be horses I should have had to travel with swine. That was how it was. And I nodded to the family. They knew nothing about it, and, had they known, would not have believed it. To write prescriptions is easy, but to come to an understanding with people is hard. Well, this should be the end of my visit, I had once more been called out needlessly, I was used to that, the whole district made my life a torment with my night bell, but that I should have to sacrifice Rose this time as well, the pretty girl who had lived in my house for years almost without my noticing her—that sacrifice was too much to ask, and I had somehow to get it reasoned out in my head with the help of what craft I could muster, in order not to let fly at this family, which with the best will in the world could not restore Rose to me. But as I shut my bag and put an arm out for my fur coat, the family meanwhile standing together, the father sniffing at the glass of rum in his hand, the mother, apparently disappointed in me—why, what do people expect?—bit-ing her lips with tears in her eyes, the sister fluttering a blood-soaked towel, I was somehow ready to admit conditionally that the boy might be ill after all. I went toward him, he welcomed me smiling as if I were bringing him the most nourishing invalid broth—ah, now both horses were whinnying together; the noise, I suppose, was or-dained by heaven to assist my examination of the patient—and this time I discovered that the boy was indeed ill. In his right side, near the hip, was an open wound as big as the palm of my hand. Rose-red, in many variations of shade, dark in the hollows, lighter at the edges, softly granulated, with irregular clots of blood, open as a surface mine to the daylight. That was how it looked from a distance. But on a closer inspection there was another complication. I could not help a low whistle of surprise. Worms, as thick and as long as my little finger, themselves rose-red and blood-spotted as well, were wriggling from their fastness in the interior of the wound toward the light, with small white heads and many little legs. Poor boy, you were past helping. I had discovered your great wound; this blossom in your side was destroying you. The family was pleased; they saw me busying myself; the sister told the mother, the mother the father, the father told several guests who were coming in, through the moonlight at the open door, walking on tiptoe, keeping their balance with outstretched arms. "Will you save me?" whispered the boy with a sob, quite blinded by the life within his wound. That is what people are like in my district. Always expecting the impossible from the doctor. They have lost their ancient beliefs; the parson sits at home and unravels his vestments, one after another; but the doctor is supposed to be omnipotent with his merciful surgeon's hand. Well, as it pleases them; I have not thrust my services on them; if they misuse me for sacred ends, I let that happen to me too; what better do I want, old country doctor that I am, bereft of my servant girl! And so they came, the family and the village elders, and stripped my clothes off me; a school choir with the teacher at the head of it stood before the house and sang these words to an utterly simple tune:

> Strip his clothes off, then he'll heal us,
> If he doesn't, kill him dead!
> Only a doctor, only a doctor.

Then my clothes were off and I looked at the people quietly, my fingers in my beard and my head cocked to one side. I was altogether composed and equal to the situation and remained so, although it was no help to me, since they now took me by the head and feet and carried me to the bed. They laid me down in it next to the wall, on the side of the wound. Then they all left the room; the door was shut; the singing stopped; clouds covered the moon; the bedding was warm around me; the horses' heads in the opened windows wavered like shadows. "Do you know," said a voice in my ear, "I have very little confidence in you. Why, you were only blown in here, you didn't come on your own feet. Instead of helping me, you're cramping me on my deathbed. What I'd like best is to scratch your eyes out." "Right," I said, "it is a shame. And yet I am a doctor. What am I to do? Believe me, it is not too easy for me either." "Am I supposed to be content with this apology? Oh, I must be, I can't help it. I always have to put up with things. A fine wound is all I brought into the world; that was my sole endowment." "My young friend," said I, "your mistake is: you have not a wide enough view. I have been in all the sickrooms, far and wide, and I tell you: your wound is not so bad. Done in a tight corner with two strokes of the ax. Many a one proffers his side and can hardly hear the ax in the forest, far less that it is coming nearer to him." "Is that really so, or are you deluding me in my fever?" "It is really so, take the word of honor of an official doctor." And he took it and lay still. But now it was time for me to think of escaping. The horses were still standing faithfully in their places. My clothes, my fur coat, my bag were quickly collected; I didn't want to waste time dressing; if the horses raced home as they had come, I should only be springing, as it were, out of this bed into my own. Obediently a horse backed away from the window; I threw my bundle into the gig; the fur coat missed its mark and was caught on a hook only by the sleeve. Good enough. I swung myself onto the horse. With the reins loosely trailing, one horse barely fastened to the other, the gig swaying behind, my fur coat last of all in the snow. "Gee up!" I said, but there was no galloping; slowly, like old men, we crawled through the snowy wastes; a long time echoed behind us the new but faulty song of the children:

O be joyful, all you patients,
The doctor's laid in bed beside you!

Never shall I reach home at this rate; my flourishing practice is done for; my successor is robbing me, but in vain, for he cannot take my place; in my house the disgusting groom is raging; Rose is the victim; I do not want to think about it any more. Naked, exposed to the frost of this most unhappy of ages, with an earthly vehicle, unearthly horses, old man that I am, I wander astray. My fur coat is hanging from the back of the gig, but I cannot reach it, and none of my limber pack of patients lifts a finger. Betrayed! Betrayed! A false alarm on the night bell once answered—it cannot be made good, not ever.

THE RECEPTIVE READER

As you read and reread the story, pay special attention to questions that come up again and again in critical interpretations:

1. How far into the story can you read while assuming it to be a realistic narrative of events? What are your first clues that this story is going to be *surreal*, like a dream?

2. What is the role of the *groom*? How is he different from the doctor, who is supposedly his employer? What is the doctor's attitude toward him?

3. What is the possible *symbolism* of the horses? the pigsty?

4. What is the role of *Rose*? (Could she be a "mother figure"? Could she be for the doctor an object of unacknowledged sexual desire?)

5. What do you make of the doctor's first declaring the patient healthy and then finding the incurable wound? (Could the wound be the wound in the side of Christ on the cross?)

6. What is the doctor's interaction with the patient's family? How do they treat him?

7. The doctor seems very inadequate as the modern physician-healer who is supposed to perform the miracles of modern medicine. Could he be a *satirical* portrait of the overreaching pride—or hubris—of modern science?

8. Why is the *parson* sitting at home unraveling his vestments?

9. Although the events of the story are surreal, the doctor often uses *trite sayings* that sound as if things were normal. Why? What are striking examples?

THE PERSONAL RESPONSE

Although many critics approach Kafka with deadly earnestness, other readers have marveled at the mixture of the sad and comic in his fiction. (Kafka read some of his stories to his friends with tears of laughter streaming down his face.) Does anything about this story strike you as comical?

CROSS-REFERENCES—For Discussion or Writing

Look at one or more stories that have been called Kafkaesque, such as Luisa Valenzuela's "The Censors" (included in this volume) or John Cheever's "The Swimmer" (not included). What is "Kafkaesque" about these stories?

THE RANGE OF INTERPRETATION

*Reading about Kafka, one is usually struck by the chaotic
variety of interpretations, in which each reader makes his
own associations.*

RONALD GRAY

*Kafka is often so obscure, his imagery so vague . . . and
his situations capable of being interpreted so variously,
that his work lends itself to endless speculation.*

H. S. REISS

The following discussions and excerpts sample major directions in Kafka
criticism. What assumptions, what expectations, does each school of critics
bring to a reading of his stories? Which of these approaches seem to you most
directly applicable to "The Country Doctor"? Which shed light on the story in
a more indirect way?

The Prophetic Kafka

*Art is a mirror that, like a clock running too fast, foretells
the future.*

FRANZ KAFKA

Many readers have seen Kafka's fiction, and especially his novels, as a
prophecy of modern totalitarian societies where the nameless, anonymous individual is at the mercy of an all-powerful bureaucratic authority. Innocent people find themselves hounded and judged, till they finally start to believe in
their guilt themselves. The Czech writer Milan Kundera, who lived in Kafka's
Prague under communist rule, found himself in a society like the one Kafka
had predicted: "a world," in Kundera's words, "that is nothing but a single
huge, labyrinthine institution" that Kafka's characters could not escape and
could not understand. This Kafkaesque society provides the context for Kundera's novel *The Incredible Lightness of Being*, which became a best-seller in the
West and was made into a movie centered on the suppression of the stirrings
of political and cultural independence called the "Prague Spring."

The following excerpt from an article by Kundera probes the psychological
roots of the modern totalitarian state. Kundera said, "Kafka made no prophe-
cies. All he did was see what was 'behind.' He did not know that his seeing
was also a fore-seeing. He did not intend to unmask a social system. He shed
light on the mechanisms he knew from private and microsocial human practice, not suspecting that later developments would put those mechanisms into
action on the great stage of History."

MILAN KUNDERA
Kafka and Modern History   1988

There are tendencies in modern history that produce the Kafkaesque quality in the broad social dimension: the progressive concentration of power, tending to deify itself [make itself godlike]; the bureaucratization of social activity that turns all institutions into boundless labyrinths; and the resulting depersonalization of the individual.

Totalitarian states, as extreme concentrations of these tendencies, have brought out the close relationship between Kafka's novels and real life. But . . . in fact, the society we call democratic is also familiar with the process that bureaucratizes and depersonalizes; the entire planet has become a theater of this process. . . .

Why was Kafka the first novelist to grasp these tendencies, which appeared on History's stage so clearly and brutally only after his death? Mystifications and legends aside, there is no significant trace anywhere of Franz Kafka's political interests; in that sense, he is different from all his Prague friends, from Max Brod, Franz Werfel, Egon Erwin Kisch, and from all the avantgardes that, claiming to know the direction of History, indulged in conjuring up the face of the future.

So how is it that not their works but those of their solitary, introverted companion, immersed in his own life and his art, are recognized today as a sociopolitical prophecy, and are for that very reason banned in a large part of the world?

I pondered this mystery one day after witnessing a little scene in the home of an old friend of mine. The woman in question had been arrested in 1951 during the Stalinist trials in Prague, and convicted of crimes she hadn't committed. Hundreds of Communists were in the same situation at the time. All their lives they had entirely identified themselves with their Party. When it suddenly became their prosecutor, they agreed, like Joseph K., "to examine their whole lives, their entire past, down to the smallest details" to find the hidden offense and, in the end, to confess to imaginary crimes. My friend managed to save her own life because she had the extraordinary courage to refuse to undertake—as her comrades did, as the poet A. did—the "search for her offense." Refusing to assist her persecutors, she became unusable for the final show trial. So instead of being hanged she got away with life imprisonment. After fourteen years, she was completely rehabilitated and released.

The woman had a one-year-old child when she was arrested. On release from prison, she thus rejoined her fifteen-year-old son and had the joy of sharing her humble solitude with him from then on. That she became passionately attached to the boy is entirely comprehensible. One day I went to see them—by then her son was twenty-five. The mother, hurt and angry, was crying. The cause was utterly trivial: the son had overslept or something like that. I asked the mother: "Why get so upset over such a trifle? Is it worth crying about? Aren't you overdoing it?"

It was the son who answered for his mother: "No, my mother's not overdoing it. My mother is a splendid, brave woman. She resisted when everyone else cracked. She wants me to become a real man. It's true, all I did was oversleep, but what my mother reproached me for is something much deeper. It's my attitude. My selfish attitude. I want to become what my mother wants me to be. And with you as a witness, I promise her I will."

What the party never managed to do to the mother, the mother had managed to do to her son. She had forced him to identify with an absurd accusation, to "seek his offense," to make a public confession. I looked on, dumbfounded, at this Stalinist minitrial, and I understood all at once that the psychological mechanisms that function in great (apparently incredible and inhuman) historical events are the same as those that regulate private (quite ordinary and very human) situations.

From *The Art of the Novel*

QUESTIONS

How is modern society like a labyrinth? Does it make sense to you that modern mass societies act out on a large scale patterns and motives that we can observe from close up in the family unit?

The Psychoanalytic Kafka

Psychoanalytic critics assume a basic similarity between the world of dreams and the world created by the imagination of a great artist. In both, according to Freud, repressed material beyond the grasp of the censorious conscious intellect rises from the unconscious to let us know things about ourselves that we did not suspect. With a writer like Kafka, the psychoanalytic critic has a head start: Many of Kafka's stories have the feverish, oppressive quality of a dream—of an anxiety dream, a nightmare that we find hard to shake off. For this psychoanalytic critic, "the Country Doctor's fantastic adventure points to an unrecognized, unadmitted sexual crisis on the part of a middle-aged bachelor professional."

JAMES M. MCGLATHERY
The Challenges of Desire   1981

The Country Doctor's experiences in answering a sick call in the middle of the night are best read as fantasy on the central figure's part. Also, just because it happens first, one should not assume that the night call brings on the crisis in the physician's relationship with his maid Rosa. On the contrary, the imaginary call to duty likely is the product of a developing crisis in his feelings about the live-in maid. And most important, his experiences with his patient cannot be divorced from his feelings—conscious and unconscious—regarding Rosa.

To some extent, at least, the physician must identify in his fantasy with the demonic figure of the stable boy, Rosa's would-be and presumably successful ravisher. Yet, on the conscious level, the doctor sees himself as quite the opposite, as Rosa's angel of rescue, as her only hope of escape from the rape attempt. This state of affairs suggests that his emotional crisis stems from unadmitted, unconscious sexual guilt. . . . Thus he blames his professional calling for the loss of his maid and of the opportunity to prove himself a hero in her eyes. Up to this time, however, he has not allowed himself to notice Rosa, much less to think of possessing her—a thought which even in his fantasy he cannot attribute to himself, and thus projects onto the stable boy.

The young man to whom the doctor is called to minister likely represents the latter's image of himself as a youth, when he was first reaching an age to marry. The patient's wish to die would then be a projection of the doctor's middle-aged bachelor guilt over his having fled as a young man from marriage into devotion to his calling. The doctor's failure at first to discover the wound may project his guilt over having suppressed awareness regarding the motivation for his complete dedication to his calling. And his subsequent discovery of the wound may reflect his dawning awareness of this guilt, even though he still cannot admit these feelings to himself.

The doctor's unadmitted shame and remorse over having escaped from the challenges of Desire into a career of healing may likewise express itself in the conclusion of his nightmarish fantasy, where he has given up the patient—that is, himself as a youth—for dead, and then finds himself condemned to be carried endlessly through the snowy wastes by an uncontrollable horse, bereft of his maid, his clothing, and likely also his practice.

From "Desire's Persecutions in Kafka's 'Judgement,' 'Metamorphosis,' and 'A Country Doctor,'" In *Perspectives on Contemporary Literature*, vol. 7

QUESTIONS

How much direct evidence is there in the story on the relations between the doctor, Rosa, and the groom? What details in the story suggest sexual overtones? What mechanisms of projection does the author of this excerpt describe? How believable are they?

The Marxist Kafka

Marxist critics look for the social and political implications of a writer's work. To what social class does the author belong? How does he relate to its political and economic interests? Does he accept or attack the existing class structure? Works of literature do not exist outside of society in an idyllic value-less sphere; they have inevitable social and political relevance. Some writers show their political commitments openly, others by implication. A writer who keeps quiet about the injustices of his society endorses and supports them by implication; artists and writers often allow themselves to be used to lend the prestige of "culture" to unjust social systems.

Marxist critics claimed early that the pervasive fear, the paralyzing anxiety, of Kafka's fiction was the result of living among the insecurities and injustices of a capitalistic, bourgeois society. Kafka's work found a tremendous echo among twentieth-century readers because of the all-pervasive sense of fear generated by political factors that were, to the Marxist, the logical outgrowth of the traditional capitalistic society: the rise of fascism and Hitlerism, the ever-present threat of nuclear war.

ERNST FISHER
"The Country Doctor" and Ideology   1981

Kafka's hero, always the same . . . is not a romantic hero, but a desperate petty bourgeois in the world of late capitalism. He would like to conform to society and applaud its everyday phenomena such as family, marriage, and job—but it doesn't work. The breach is unbridgeable: business success and private happiness, social career and humane personality have become irreconcilable. . . . In contrast to most writers of his generation, Kafka constantly dealt with the problem of work and profession, that is, with the great problems of the mechanized, industrialized, commercialized world. Horrified by the specialization, Taylorization [dehumanizing and speedup of labor], and fragmentation of work, Kafka senses the growing divergence between occupation and personality.

His heroes fail because of this division: they are not satisfied with an occupation they feel to be senseless; they are alienated by it; they are overwhelmed by the vanity of their efforts.

The country doctor, by nature an isolated person, is vulnerable to the tragicomic contradiction between the idea of being the helper in a wide area and the poverty of his means. He clings to the idea of being a helper, wards off resignation, is ready to sacrifice his private life for his professional ethics, and is forced in the most cruel way to recognize the vanity of his efforts. . . . one can recognize in the "unearthly horses" which emerge from the pigpen a fantastic and melancholy satire on ideals which have become ghosts, which are no longer appropriate to social conditions: . . . the bourgeois sense of duty, unconditional obedience when the signal sounds. Everything begins with a "false ringing of the night bell." . . . Not one word says: "Defend yourself, country doctor! You need a living horse, not ideological ghosts!" But when the ghost horses . . . so unwillingly drag themselves through the infinite snow after the death of the patient, we hear the lament, the protest:

> Naked, prey to the frost of this most unfortunate age, I, an old man, am driven around with an earthly coach and unearthly horses. My fur coat is hanging in the back of the coach; I can't reach it, and not one of the active churls among the patients lifts his finger. Deceived! Deceived!

It is the lament, the protest of him who has been cheated out of the dignity of his occupation; the sense of his life, the echo of a false alarm from the very beginning—not a call to revolution, but also not a recognition of the historically determined as an eternal *condition humaine* [human condition]; rather, a rebellion against the coldness, the frost of "this most unfortunate age."

From Kenneth Hughes, *Franz Kafka: An Anthology of Marxist Criticism*

QUESTIONS

How much direct evidence is there in the story of the doctor's view of his vocation or profession? How crucial is his inadequacy as a healer to the story as a whole?

The Feminist Kafka

*A radical critique of literature, feminist in its impulse,
would take the work first of all as a clue to how we live,
how we have been living, how we have been led to imagine
ourselves . . . how we can begin to see—and therefore
live—afresh.*

ADRIENNE RICH

Feminist critics have asked readers to reread and rethink literary classics from the perspective of the woman reader. How have traditional assumptions about what it means to be male or female shaped the literature of the past? How have these assumptions shaped the way scholars or critics have interpreted the classics of our literary heritage? The author of the following excerpt said that a feminist reading of Kafka must start by questioning his alleged "universality." Male critics finding universal themes in Kafka's prose were not necessarily speaking for women. "Kafka's fictional world is male." Where woman is not obscured, "she is seen as purely instrumental"; she is a pawn in the power struggles of a male world.

EVELYN TORTON BECK
Gender and Power in Kafka 1987

The essential power struggles in Kafka's texts are between the males. . . . Nowhere in Kafka does woman speak for herself. . . . Because it is his male heroes who organize the text's way of seeing, the angle of vision in Kafka's texts is necessarily androcentric—i.e., male centered. . . .

Throughout, Kafka's male characters think of women in the language of ownership. "I'm not thinking of handing the girl over to you," says the country doctor to his groom. . . . Woman exists only on the margins, entrapped in a power system in which she is never an actor, only acted upon. . . .

For women have been taught to see through an androcentric lens, it is a way of seeing we all have to un-learn. Such a paradigm shift is both exhilarating and disorienting, since it forces us to rethink our received truths about literary study and about the world. It challenges our codified values, especially about "old masters" and "eternal truths." It forces us to rethink and reconceptualize the values systems by which we live. Such disruptions are never comfortable, but to paraphrase a Kafka aphorism, a book should act on us like a sharp blow—it should serve as an ax for "frozen sea within us." Though I would prefer less violent language, this perception well describes the kind of awakening a feminist analysis of literature can catalyze. We ought to welcome it.

From "Kafka's Traffic in Women: Gender, Power, and Sexuality," in *The Dove and the Mole: Kafka's Journey into Darkness and Creativity,* edited by Moshe Lazar and Ronald Gottesman

QUESTIONS

How stereotypical is the treatment of Rose in the story? Do you think female readers can identify with the anxieties of the doctor? How or why?

CROSS-REFERENCE—For Discussion or Writing

Do you think there are "universals" that cut across gender divisions in the short stories by Flannery O'Connor and Franz Kafka? Or are there major differences in her female and his male perspective?

WRITING ABOUT LITERATURE
10. Quoting the Critics (Documented Paper)

The Writing Workshop For a paper based on library research, you may be asked to study in depth one important critical approach to a much-discussed story. Or, instead of studying one critical perspective in depth, you may be asked to compare two or more different critical approaches. Some sample projects:

 ✧ Hundreds of critical articles (and chapters in books) have been written on Nathaniel Hawthorne's richly symbolic and ambiguous "Young Goodman Brown." You might want to focus on critics' differing views of the relationship between Hawthorne's story and the role of sin and guilt in the Puritan tradition of New England. Was Hawthorne himself profoundly influenced by that tradition? Or was he critical of it, distancing himself from it?

 ✧ A classic short story like John Steinbeck's "The Chrysanthemums" or Charlotte Gilman's "The Yellow Wallpaper" will reveal new or unexpected depth when a new generation of critics looks at it from a fresh perspective. You might want to contrast a more traditional approach to such a story with a recent rereading from a feminist perspective.

 ✧ You may want to choose a Kafka story—like "A Country Doctor," "Metamorphosis," or "The Judgment." Your paper might focus on the definition of a key term. For example, you might focus on the "Jewish" Kafka, or on Kafka as the prophet of totalitarianism, or on the Freudian Kafka.

Finding Promising Leads   To work up material for your paper, you are likely to begin by checking in electronic or printed indexes for books, collections of critical articles, and individual articles in periodicals. For a writer like Kafka, Hawthorne, or O'Connor, most college libraries will have a wide range of critical and scholarly sources.

For instance, although Kafka's work was banned in Nazi Germany after 1935 and by the communists in his native Prague after 1945, he became one of the most widely known and discussed authors of the twentieth century. (In the words of the critic Susan Sontag, he attracted "armies of interpreters.") Books on Kafka by his friend Max Brod (who stressed the influence on Kafka of Jewish tradition), by Wilhelm Emrich (who examined Kafka's relation to existentialist thought), and by Heinz Politzer (who focused on Kafka's use of paradox and irony) are only the major milestones in a vast amount of critical explication and argument. Beginning with Angel Flores' *The Kafka Problem* (1946), there have been over fifty collections of critical articles on Kafka, including critical anthologies like the following:

> Ronald Gray, *Kafka: A Collection of Critical Essays*
> Heinz Politzer, *Franz Kafka*
> Angel Flores, *The Kafka Debate*
> J.P. Stern, *The World of Franz Kafka*
> Kenneth Hughes, *Kafka: An Anthology of Marxist Criticism*
> Ruth V. Gross, *Critical Essays on Franz Kafka*

In addition, by searching for sources with Kafka's name in the title, you might be able to locate books like Anthony Northey's *Kafka's Relatives* (with background material for a biographical perspective on Kafka's fiction) or recent articles like John Felstiner's "Looking for Kafka" (in *Stanford* for December 1991).

Taking Notes   During your exploratory reading, you need to look sources over quickly, deciding whether they will be helpful. But you also have to slow down and close in when you hit upon promising materials. Remember:

 ✧ *Be a stickler for accuracy.* Copy direct quotations accurately, word for word. Enclose all quoted material in quotation marks to show material copied verbatim. (Include the *closing* quotation mark to show where the quotation ends.)

 ✧ *Tag your notes.* Start your notes with a tag or **descriptor.** (Indicate the subtopic or section of your paper where a quotation or piece of information will be useful.)

 ✧ *Look ahead.* Include all the publishing information you will need later when you identify your sources in a documented paper. Include exact page numbers for your quotations. (Also note *inclusive* page numbers for a whole article or story.) Sample notes might look like this:

self-contained quotation

KAFKA THE WRITER

   "'A Country Doctor' reveals much about Kafka's attitude toward being a writer . . . what qualifies him to be a writer, what people expected of him as a writer, what he could accomplish, what would be his ultimate fate."

Peter Mailloux, *A Hesitation Before Birth: The Life of Franz Kafka* (Newark: U of Delaware P, 1989) 392.

partial quotation

SYMBOLS—horses

   Critic John Hibberd believes Kafka's "unearthly" horses "represent the power of inspiration that promised Kafka fulfillment but carried him away to a devastating reminder of his helplessness."

John Hibberd, *Kafka in Context* (New York: Studio Vista, 1975) 84.

Distinguish clearly between **paraphrase** and direct firsthand quotation. When you paraphrase, you put someone else's ideas in your own words. You can thus highlight what seems most important to you and condense other parts. Even when you paraphrase, be sure to use quotation marks for striking phrases that you keep in the exact wording of the author. (For instance, in summing up briefly a critic's view of Kafka's doctor, put in quotation marks a striking reference to the doctor himself as "the patient, the smitten victim.")

Note finer points: Use **single quotation marks** for a phrase that appears as a quote-within-a-quote: "Freudian critics are fascinated by Kafka's 'unearthly horses.'" Use the **ellipsis**—three spaced periods—to show an omission (see Mailloux quotation above). Use four periods when the periods include the period at the end of a sentence. **Square brackets** show that you have inserted material into the original quotation: "He became engaged [to Felice Bauer], broke off the engagement, became engaged again."

Pushing toward a Thesis   Your note taking becomes truly productive when you begin to follow up tentative patterns and promising connections that you discover in your reading. Even during your preliminary reading and note taking, you will be looking for a unifying thread, for a figure in the carpet. Avoid a stitched-together pattern that goes from "one critic said this" to "another critic said that." Look for recurrent issues; look for a note that in your materials is struck again and again. The following might be a tentative thesis:

TRIAL THESIS: Critics again and again find a connection between the hesitations and ineffectualness of the country doctor and Kafka's own hesitations and doubts as a writer.

Using a Working Outline   To give direction to your reading and writing, sketch out a **working outline** as soon as you have a rough idea how your material is shaping up. At first, your plan might be very tentative. A working outline is not a final blueprint; its purpose is to help you visualize a possible pattern and to help you refine it as you go along. Suppose you are moving toward a paper showing how different critical approaches make the reader notice and concentrate on different key images in a story. At an intermediate stage, your working outline might look like this:

WORKING OUTLINE: —Freudian emphasis on sexual overtones
the buttocking horses
the animalistic groom
Rose as victim
—Marxist emphasis on the doctor's social role
ineffectualness of the doctor
doctor vs. priest
immobilized doctor at the end
—religious critic's emphasis on religious symbols
wound in the side of the boy (allusion to Christ on
the cross?)
jeering, hostile patients (Christ reviled?)

Drafting and Revising   In your first draft, you are likely to concentrate on feeding into your paper the evidence you have collected. As always, feel free to work on later sections of the paper first—perhaps concentrating on key segments and filling in the connecting threads later. In your first draft, quotations are likely to be chunky, to be woven into the paper more tightly or more smoothly during revision. Often you will need to read a first draft back to yourself to see where major changes in strategy would be advisable. A reordering of major sections might be necessary to correct awkward backtrackings.

You might need to strengthen the evidence for major points and play down material that tends to distract from your major arguments.

Documenting the Paper When you draw on a range of sources—for instance, a range of critical interpretations of a story—you may be asked to provide **documentation.** In a documented paper, you fully identify your sources, furnishing complete publishing information and exact page numbers. Accurate documentation shows that your readers are welcome to go to the sources you have drawn on—to check your use of them and to get further information from them if they wish. Unless instructed otherwise, follow the current style of documentation of the Modern Language Association (MLA). This current style has done away with footnotes (though it still provides for **explanatory notes** at the end of a paper).

The current MLA style requires you to remember three simple principles:

❖ *Identify your sources briefly in your text.* Generally, introduce a quotation by saying something like "Lucy M. Freibert says in her article on Margaret Atwood's *The Handmaid's Tale.* . . ."

❖ *Give page references in parentheses in your text.* For instance, type (89) or (280–82). If you have not mentioned the author, this is the place to give his or her last name: (Freibert 280–82). If you are using more than one source by the same author, you may also have to specify briefly which one (Freibert, "Control" 280–82). Remember to tag author or title in parentheses only if you have not already given the information in your running text.

❖ *Describe each source fully in a final alphabetical listing of Works Cited.* This used to be the bibliography (literally the "book list"), but it now often includes *non*print sources—interviews, lectures, PBS broadcasts, videotapes, computer software. Here is a typical entry for an article in a critical journal. This entry includes volume number (a volume usually covers all issues for one year), date, and the complete page numbers for the whole article (not just the material you have quoted):

> Shumaker, Conrad. "'Too Terribly Good to Be Printed': Charlotte Gilman's 'The Yellow Wallpaper.'" *American Literature* 57 (1985): 588–99.

Study sample entries for your alphabetical listing of Works Cited. Remember a few pointers:

❖ Use *italics* (or <u>underlining</u> on a typewriter) for the title of a *whole* publication—whether a book-length study, a collection or anthology of stories or essays, a periodical that prints critical articles, or a newspaper that prints reviews. However, use quotation marks for titles of short stories or critical articles that are *part* of a collection.

❖ Leave two spaces after periods marking off chunks of information in the entry. Indent the second and following lines of each entry five spaces.

❖ Use *ed.* for editor, *trans.* for a translator.

❖ Abbreviate the names of publishing houses (Prentice for Prentice-Hall, Inc.; Southern Illinois UP for Southern Illinois University Press). Abbreviate the names of the months: Dec., Apr., Mar.

Primary sources: listing of short stories, letters, or interviews

Cheever, John. *The Stories of John Cheever.* New York: Knopf, 1978.
[Collected stories of the author. The publisher's name is short for Alfred A. Knopf.]

O'Connor, Flannery. *Everything That Rises Must Converge.* New York: Farrar, 1965.
[A selection of the author's stories, named after the title story. Name of publisher is short for Farrar, Straus and Giroux.]

Achebe, Chinua. "Dead Men's Path." *The Story and Its Writer: An Introduction to Short Fiction.* Ed. Ann Charters. 3rd ed. Boston: Bedford, 1991. 10–12.
[A story reprinted in an anthology, with editor's name and number of edition and with inclusive page numbers for the story.]

Cheever, Benjamin, ed. *The Letters of John Cheever.* New York: Simon, 1988.
[Author's correspondence, edited by his son.]

Faulkner, William. Interview. *Writers at Work: The* Paris Review *Interviews.* Ed. Malcolm Cowley. New York: Viking-Compass, 1959. 122–41.
[Compass was an imprint, or special line of books, of Viking Press. The title of the *Paris Review* is roman—straight type—to set it off from italicized book title.]

Tan, Amy. Lecture. Visiting Author Series. Santa Clara, 12 Jan. 1992.
[Talk by an author as part of a lecture series.]

Secondary sources: listing of critical studies, articles, or reviews

Abel, Darrel. *The Moral Picturesque: Studies in Hawthorne's Fiction.* West Lafayette, IN: Purdue UP, 1988.
[Book with subtitle, published by a university press.]

Emrich, Wilhelm. *Franz Kafka: A Critical Study of His Writings.* Trans. Sheema Zeben Buehne. New York: Ungar, 1968.
[Book with translator's name.]

Cady, Edwin H., and Louis J. Budd, eds. Introduction. *On Hawthorne: The Best from* American Literature. Durham: Duke UP, 1990. vi–x.
[Introduction to a collection with two editors— only the first typed with last name first. Page numbers for prefaces and the like are given in small roman numerals. Use roman type (not italics) for title within title.]

Freibert, Lucy M. "Control and Creativity: The Politics of Risk in Margaret Atwood's *The Handmaid's Tale.*" *Critical Essays on Margaret Atwood.* Ed. Judith McCombs. Boston: Hall, 1988. 280–91.
[Article in a collection, with inclusive page numbers. Note "Ed." for the editor who assembled the collection.]

Davenport, Mary. "Today's Minimalist Fiction." *New York Times* 15 May 1991, late ed., sec. 2: 1+.
[Newspaper article, with edition and section specified. Article starts on page 1 and continues later in the newspaper.]

Shumaker, Conrad. "'Too Terribly Good to Be Printed': Charlotte Gilman's 'The Yellow Wallpaper.'" *American Literature* 57 (1985): 588–99.
[Journal article, with volume number and inclusive page numbers. Note quotation in title—single quotation marks; note that title of story is

quoted in title of article—single quotation marks. Sometimes number of volume *and* issue may be needed when pages are not numbered consecutively throughout a single volume: *Fiction Review* 14.3 (1992): 17–21.]

The Art of the Story. Narr. Pat Evans. Writ. and prod. Jeremiah Phelps. KCBM, San Benito. 17 Nov. 1991.
[A television program with names of narrator and writer-producer. Should be listed alphabetically under "Art."]

Study the following example of a documented paper. How successful was the student author in finding contemporary sources? How well does the paper support its main points? How clear or adequate are parenthetical documentation and the entries in the Works Cited? Are there unusual situations or entries?

SAMPLE DOCUMENTED PAPER

The Psychoanalytic Kafka: Dream and Reality

Once, when Kafka was visiting his good friend Max Brod, he accidentally woke up Brod's father, who was sleeping on the couch. Instead of just simply apologizing, Kafka slowly tiptoed out of the room, whispering, "Please consider me a dream" (Baumer 2). When we look at Kafka the writer, this incident acquires symbolic meaning. Dreams fascinated Kafka, and he was obsessed with chronicling his "dreamlike inner existence," which threatened to crowd out ordinary daylight reality. He said in a diary entry for August 6, 1914:

> The taste for describing my dreamlike inner existence has pushed everything else in the background, where it has atrophied in a terrifying way and does not cease to atrophy. Nothing else can satisfy me. (qtd. in Baumer 3)

In a letter to Max Brod in 1922, Kafka called this exploration of the inner self "this descent to the dark powers, this unleashing . . . of dubious embraces and everything else that may be happening below." He said that a writer who "writes stories in the sunlight" above "no longer knows anything" about this hidden subconscious reality (qtd. in Baumer 7). For Kafka, "the dream reveals the reality" while "conception"—our ability to understand—"lags behind" (qtd. in Hamalian 12). It is this search for a deeper truth buried in our subconscious and revealed in dreams that made Franz Kafka, in the words of Peter Dow Webster, "the psychologist's perfect dreamer" (118). The psychoanalytical theory concerning dreams, first introduced by Freud, assumes that dreams tell us the real truth about ourselves, especially about our subconscious fears and desires. Our dreams keep coming back to our innermost preoccupations and dilemmas. In Kafka's case, in the words of Ruth Gross, these include "power and impotence," "marriage versus bachelorhood," and "success versus failure" (577).

Kafka's "A Country Doctor" has a typical dreamlike sequence of events, with time and space distorted in such a way that the events cannot be literally happening. The story reveals Kafka's innermost struggle with a choice he made in his own life and the subconscious feelings surrounding that choice. In a letter to Brod, Kafka wrote that "in order to devote himself to literature, the writer must sacrifice fulfillment in life" (qtd. in Sokel 1158). Kafka had a strong desire for marriage and family, but because of his fears and hesitancies—and because of his exclusive devotion to his mission as a writer—his various engagements and romantic involvements ended in failure. In his own words, "The price to pay for this 'life as a writer' is rigid, uncompromising aloneness, a radical isolation from the outside world, from other people and—most painfully—from his beloved" (qtd. in Beug 125).

The dreamlike images and plot of "A Country Doctor" encourage us to see the story as an exploration of Kafka's own ambivalent feelings toward major choices in his own life. As suggested in one critical interpretation, when the country doctor heeds "the call of the 'nightbell' summoning him to the bedside of a patient," the call of the bell "can be understood as a translation into sensory terms of Kafka's call to literature, which he understood as an art of healing and self-preservation, a 'doctor's' art" (Sokel 1158).

However, when the doctor tries to respond to the call, he finds out his horse has died from overexertion. Rose, the servant girl he has just begun to notice, is unable to borrow a horse—"no horse to be had, no horse." In his dilemma, the doctor turns "absentmindedly" to his forgotten pigsty and in doing so releases the animal-like groom and a team of unearthly horses (Kafka 137). He allows the groom to take Rose; contrary to what the doctor says, he does in fact leave Rose behind. She is the price for the groom's aid. "The 'unearthly horses' transport the doctor away from life, woman, and home" (Sokel 1158). This scene seems to mirror Kafka's continual withdrawal from the various women in his life when they would press him for a commitment. Whenever a relationship became too serious, he would back away, claiming that his fanatical dedication to his writing "would condemn his spouse to monastic loneliness" (Sokel 1153).

As Kafka writes about the journey between the two houses, the doctor's and the patient's, he mirrors his own ambivalence toward his writer's art and the sacrifices he has made on behalf of that art. In the story, the two houses graphically represent the two poles of the doctor's existence. In his own house, the doctor abandons the possibility of fulfillment through love; in the other house, the house of the patient, he dedicates himself to his art, exploring "the congenital wound of mortality"—the wound in the young patient's side (Sokel 1158).

The doctor's ambivalence is such that he cannot be content at either pole. At home, he sacrifices the young woman to his mission, but at his destination he regrets the price he has paid and wants to return. Thoughts of Rose begin to haunt him: "And only now did I remember Rose again: what was I to do, how could I rescue her, how could I pull her away from under that groom at ten miles distance, with a team of horses I couldn't control?" (Kafka 139). This pull in contradictory directions mirrors Kafka's own problem. He would make every effort to discourage a woman's hope for the future. However, in the case of Felice Bauer, for instance, the moment she showed signs of heeding his warning, he would return to the role of ardent wooer. As much as Kafka desired marriage and family, he was also fearful and would become "oppressed by the actual prospect of marriage" (Sokel 1154).

At the end of the story, the doctor is seen escaping the patient's house. While it took the doctor only seconds to arrive at the house of the sick boy, now it is taking him forever to get home: "Never shall I reach home at this rate; my flourishing practice is done for; my successor is robbing me . . ." (Kafka 143). The doctor is shown riding aimlessly between the houses—the distance between them has become immeasurable, and he cannot stay at either place.

Kafka's tendency to explore the subconscious in a dreamlike fashion is strongly evident in "The Country Doctor." As readers, we cannot be quite sure whether, in fact, his story is an actual dream (where the subconscious is revealed and dominates) or whether it is based on actual events with subconcious thoughts quickly intruding on the conscious mind. Kafka has chosen a country doctor to portray his own inner struggles as an author who must deal with the choices he has made. In this sense, we are all country doctors and have to deal with our own internal voices speaking to our consciousness. Kafka is not alone. What career mother leaving home and a sick child does not experience a twinge of guilt as her guilt feelings about her choices rise to the surface? What student working late into the night does not have visions of responsibilities denied or postponed—the dinner not cooked, the phone calls not returned?

Works Cited

Baumer, Franz. *Franz Kafka.* New York: Unger, 1971.

Beug, Joachim. "The Cunning of a Writer." *The World of Franz Kafka.* Ed. J. P. Stern. New York: Holt, 1980. 122–33.

Gross, Ruth V. "Fallen Bridge, Fallen Women, Fallen Text." *The Literary Review* 26.4 (1983): 577–87.

Hamalian, Leo. Introduction. *Franz Kafka: A Collection of Criticism.* Ed. Leo Hamalian. New York: McGraw, 1981. 1–17.

Kafka, Franz. *The Metamorphosis, the Penal Colony, and Other Stories.* Trans. Willa and Edwin Muir. New York: Schocken, 1975.

Sokel, Walter H. "Franz Kafka." *European Writers: The Twentieth Century.* Ed. George Stade. Vol. 9. New York: Scribner's, 1989. 1151–77.

Webster, Peter Dow. "'Dies Irae' in the Unconscious, or the Significance of Franz Kafka." *Franz Kafka: A Collection of Criticism.* Ed. Leo Hamalian. New York: McGraw, 1981. 118–25.

QUESTIONS

How convincing is the parallel between the doctor as healer and the writer who provides spiritual comfort and healing? In addition to the lines quoted in this paper, are there other references to Rose while the doctor is in the patient's house?

OTHER VOICES/OTHER VISIONS
Stories for Further Reading

MARGARET ATWOOD   (born 1939)

Rape Fantasies   1977

[In this story, we find ourselves in a company lunchroom where a group of women workers congregate to eat, play bridge, and talk. The speaker—a file clerk—comments on her colleagues while making many references to contemporary life, such as the detergent Mr. Clean, and the cold medicine NeoCitran. Women's magazines become the catalyst for the lunch group's discussion; in them questionnaires are common, the narrator notes, such as ones that help readers discover their body type, like *endomorph* or *ectomorph*. Rape has become one of the most popular topics in these magazines. Although the narrator would rather see sentimentalized love movies starring June Allyson than discuss rape with her peers, she finds herself pulled away from her card game and into the discussion of women's rape fantasies. A *Cossack number* refers to a Russian folk dance called the *kazatzka*.]

The way they're going on about it in the magazines you'd think it was just invented, and not only that but it's something terrific, like a vaccine for cancer. They put it in capital letters on the front cover, and inside they have these questionnaires like the ones they used to have about whether you were a good enough wife or an endomorph or an ectomorph, remember that? with the scoring upside down on page 73, and then these numbered do-it-yourself dealies, you know? RAPE, TEN THINGS TO DO ABOUT IT, like it was ten new hairdos or something. I mean, what's so new about it?

So at work they all have to talk about it because no matter what magazine you open, there it is, staring you right between the eyes, and they're beginning to have it on the television, too. Personally I'd prefer a June Allyson movie anytime but they don't make them anymore and they don't even have them that much on the Late Show. For instance, day before yesterday, that would be Wednesday, thank god it's Friday as they say, we were sitting around in the women's lunch room—the *lunch* room, I mean you'd think you could get some peace and quiet in there—and Chrissy closes up the magazine she's been reading and says, "How about it, girls, do you have rape fantasies?"

The four of us were having our game of bridge the way we always do, and I had a bare twelve points counting the singleton with not that much of a bid in anything. So I said one club, hoping Sondra would remember about the one club convention, because the time before when I used that she thought I really meant clubs and she bid us up to three, and all I had was four little ones with nothing higher than a six, and we went down two and on top of that we were vulnerable. She is not the world's best bridge player. I mean, neither am I but there's a limit.

Darlene passed but the damage was done, Sondra's head went round like it was on ball bearings and she said, "*What* fantasies?"

"Rape fantasies," Chrissy said. She's a receptionist and she looks like one; she's   5 pretty but cool as a cucumber, like she's been painted all over with nail polish, if you know what I mean. Varnished. "It says here all women have rape fantasies."

"For Chrissake, I'm eating an egg sandwich," I said, "and I bid one club and Dar-lene passed."

"You mean, like some guy jumping you in an alley or something," Sondra said. She was eating her lunch, we all eat our lunches during the game, and she bit into a piece of that celery she always brings and started to chew away on it with this thought-ful expression in her eyes and I knew we might as well pack it in as far as the game was concerned.

"Yeah, sort of like that," Chrissy said. She was blushing a little, you could see it even under her makeup.

"I don't think you should go out alone at night," Darlene said, "you put yourself in a position," and I may have been mistaken but she was looking at me. She's the old-est, she's forty-one though you wouldn't know it and neither does she, but I looked it up in the employees' file. I like to guess a person's age and then look it up to see if I'm right. I let myself have an extra pack of cigarettes if I am, though I'm trying to cut down. I figure it's harmless as long as you don't tell. I mean, not everyone has access to that file, it's more or less confidential. But it's all right if I tell you, I don't expect you'll ever meet her, though you never know, it's a small world. Anyway.

"For *heaven's* sake, it's only *Toronto,*" Greta said. She worked in Detroit for three   10 years and she never lets you forget it, it's like she thinks she's a war hero or something, we should all admire her just for the fact that she's still walking this earth, though she was really living in Windsor the whole time, she just worked in Detroit. Which for me doesn't really count. It's where you sleep, right?

"Well, do you?" Chrissy said. She was obviously trying to tell us about hers but she wasn't about to go first, she's cautious, that one.

"I certainly don't," Darlene said, and she wrinkled up her nose, like this, and I had to laugh. "I think it's disgusting." She's divorced, I read that in the file too, she never talks about it. It must've been years ago anyway. She got up and went over to the cof-fee machine and turned her back on us as though she wasn't going to have anything more to do with it.

"Well," Greta said. I could see it was going to be between her and Chrissy. They're both blondes, I don't mean that in a bitchy way but they do try to outdress each other. Greta would like to get out of Filing, she'd like to be a receptionist too so she could meet more people. You don't meet much of anyone in Filing except other people in Filing. Me, I don't mind it so much, I have outside interests.

"Well," Greta said, "I sometimes think about, you know my apartment? It's got this little balcony, I like to sit out there in the summer and I have a few plants out there. I never bother that much about locking the door to the balcony, it's one of those sliding glass ones, I'm on the eighteenth floor for heaven's sake, I've got a good view of the lake and the CN Tower and all. But I'm sitting around one night in my house-coat, watching TV with my shoes off, you know how you do, and I see this guy's feet, coming down past the window, and the next thing you know he's standing on the balcony, he's let himself down by a rope with a hook on the end of it from the floor above, that's the nineteenth, and before I can even get up off the chesterfield he's inside the apartment. He's all dressed in black with black gloves on"—I knew right away what show she got the black gloves off because I saw the same one—"and then he, well, you know."

"You know what?" Chrissy said, but Greta said, "And afterwards he tells me that he goes all over the outside of the apartment building like that, from one floor to another, with his rope and his hook . . . and then he goes out to the balcony and tosses his rope, and he climbs up it and disappears."

"Just like Tarzan," I said, but nobody laughed.

"Is that all?" Chrissy said. "Don't you ever think about, well, I think about being in the bathtub, with no clothes on . . ."

"So who takes a bath in their clothes?" I said, you have to admit it's stupid when you come to think of it, but she just went on, ". . . with lots of bubbles, what I use is Vitabath, it's more expensive but it's so relaxing, and my hair pinned up, and the door opens and this fellow's standing there. . . ."

"How'd he get in?" Greta said.

"Oh, I don't know, through a window or something. Well, I can't very well get out of the bathtub, the bathroom's too small and besides he's blocking the doorway, so I just *lie* there, and he starts to very slowly take his own clothes off, and then he gets into the bathtub with me."

"Don't you scream or anything?" said Darlene. She'd come back with her cup of coffee, she was getting really interested. "I'd scream like bloody murder."

"Who'd hear me?" Chrissy said. "Besides, all the articles say it's better not to resist, that way you don't get hurt."

"Anyway you might get bubbles up your nose," I said, "from the deep breathing," and I swear all four of them looked at me like I was in bad taste, like I'd insulted the Virgin Mary or something. I mean, I don't see what's wrong with a little joke now and then. Life's too short, right?

"Listen," I said, "those aren't *rape* fantasies. I mean, you aren't getting *raped,* it's just some guy you haven't met formally who happens to be more attractive than Derek Cummins"—he's the Assistant Manager, he wears elevator shoes or at any rate they have these thick soles and he has this funny way of talking, we call him Derek Duck—"and you have a good time. Rape is when they've got a knife or something and you don't want to."

"So what about you, Estelle," Chrissy said, she was miffed because I laughed at her fantasy, she thought I was putting her down. Sondra was miffed too, by this time she'd finished her celery and she wanted to tell about hers, but she hadn't got in fast enough.

"All right, let me tell you one," I said. "I'm walking down this dark street at night and this fellow comes up and grabs my arm. Now it so happens that I have a plastic lemon in my purse, you know how it always says you should carry a plastic lemon in your purse? I don't really do it, I tried it once but the darn thing leaked all over my checkbook, but in this fantasy I have one, and I say to him, "You're intending to rape me, right?" and he nods, so I open my purse to get the plastic lemon, and I can't find it! My purse is full of all this junk, Kleenex and cigarettes and my change purse and my lipstick and my driver's licence, you know the kind of stuff; so I ask him to hold out his hands, like this, and I pile all this junk into them and down at the bottom there's the plastic lemon, and I can't get the top off. So I hand it to him and he's very obliging, he twists the top off and hands it back to me, and I squirt him in the eye."

15

20

25

I hope you don't think that's too vicious. Come to think of it, it is a bit mean, especially when he was so polite and all.

"*That's* your rape fantasy?" Chrissy says. "I don't believe it."

"She's a card," Darlene says, she and I are the ones that've been here the longest and she never will forget the time I got drunk at the office party and insisted I was going to dance under the table instead of on top of it, I did a sort of Cossack number but then I hit my head on the bottom of the table—actually it was a desk—when I went to get up, and I knocked myself out cold. She's decided that's the mark of an original mind and she tells everyone new about it and I'm not sure that's fair. Though I did do it.

"I'm being totally honest," I say. I always am and they know it. There's no point in being anything else, is the way I look at it, and sooner or later the truth will out so you might as well not waste the time, right? "You should hear the one about the Easy-Off Oven Cleaner."   30

But that was the end of the lunch hour, with one bridge game shot to hell, and the next day we spent most of the time arguing over whether to start a new game or play out the hands we had left over from the day before, so Sondra never did get a chance to tell about her rape fantasy.

It started me thinking though, about my own rape fantasies. Maybe I'm abnormal or something, I mean I have fantasies about handsome strangers coming in through the window too, like Mr. Clean, I wish one would, please god somebody without flat feet and big sweat marks on his shirt, and over five feet five, believe me being tall is a handicap though it's getting better, tall guys are starting to like someone whose nose reaches higher than their belly button. But if you're being totally honest you can't count those as rape fantasies. In a real rape fantasy, what you should feel is this anxiety, like when you think about your apartment building catching on fire and whether you should use the elevator or the stairs or maybe just stick your head under a wet towel, and you try to remember everything you've read about what to do but you can't decide.

For instance, I'm walking along this dark street at night and this short, ugly fellow comes up and grabs my arm, and not only is he ugly, you know, with a sort of puffy nothing face, like those fellows you have to talk to in the bank when your account's overdrawn—of course I don't mean they're all like that—but he's absolutely covered in pimples. So he gets me pinned against the wall, he's short but he's heavy, and he starts to undo himself and the zipper gets stuck. I mean, one of the most significant moments in a girl's life, it's almost like getting married or having a baby or something, and he sticks the zipper.

So I say, kind of disgusted, "Oh for Chrissake," and he starts to cry. He tells me he's never been able to get anything right in his entire life, and this is the last straw, he's going to go jump off a bridge.

"Look," I say, I feel so sorry for him, in my rape fantasies I always end up feeling   35 sorry for the guy, I mean there has to be something *wrong* with them, if it was Clint Eastwood it'd be different but worse luck it never is. I was the kind of little girl who buried dead robins, know what I mean? It used to drive my mother nuts, she didn't like me touching them, because of the germs I guess. So I say, "Listen, I know how you feel. You really should do something about those pimples, if you got rid of them you'd be quite good looking, honest; then you wouldn't have to go around doing stuff like this. I had them myself once," I say, to comfort him, but in fact I did, and it ends up I give him the name of my old dermatologist, the one I had in high school, that was back in Leamington, except I used to go to St. Catharine's for the dermatologist. I'm telling you, I was really lonely when I first came here; I thought it was going to be such a big adventure and all, but it's a lot harder to meet people in a city. But I guess it's different for a guy.

Or I'm lying in bed with this terrible cold, my face is all swollen up, my eyes are red and my nose is dripping like a leaky tap, and this fellow comes in through the window and *he* has a terrible cold too, it's a new kind of flu that's been going around. So he says, "I'b goig do rabe you"—I hope you don't mind me holding my nose like this but that's the way I imagine it—and he lets out this terrific sneeze, which slows him down a bit, also I'm no object of beauty myself, you'd have to be some kind of pervert to want to rape someone with a cold like mine, it'd be like raping a bottle of LePage's mucilage the way my nose is running. He's looking wildly around the room, and I realize it's because he doesn't have a piece of Kleenex! "Id's ride here," I say, and I pass him the Kleenex, god knows why he even bothered to get out of bed, you'd think if you were going to go around climbing in windows you'd wait till you were healthier, right? I mean, that takes a certain amount of energy. So I ask him why doesn't he let me fix him a NeoCitran and scotch, that's what I always take, you still have the cold but you don't feel it, so I do and we end up watching the Late Show together. I mean, they aren't all sex maniacs, the rest of the time they must lead a normal life. I figure they enjoy watching the Late Show just like anybody else.

I do have a scarier one though . . . where the fellow says he's hearing angel voices that're telling him he's got to kill me, you know, you read about things like that all the time in the papers. In this one I'm not in the apartment where I live now, I'm back in my mother's house in Leamington and the fellow's been hiding in the cellar, he grabs my arm when I go downstairs to get a jar of jam and he's got hold of the axe too, out of the garage, that one is really scary. I mean, what do you say to a nut like that?

So I start to shake but after a minute I get control of myself and I say, is he sure the angel voices have got the right person, because I hear the same angel voices and they've been telling me for some time that I'm going to give birth to the reincarnation of St. Anne who in turn has the Virgin Mary and right after that comes Jesus Christ and the end of the world, and he wouldn't want to interfere with that, would he? So he gets confused and listens some more, and then he asks for a sign and I show him my vaccination mark, you can see it's sort of an odd-shaped one, it got infected because I scratched the top off, and that does it, he apologizes and climbs out the coal chute again, which is how he got in in the first place, and I say to myself there's some advantage in having been brought up a Catholic even though I haven't been to church since they changed the service into English, it just isn't the same, you might as well be a Protestant. I must write to Mother and tell her to nail up that coal chute, it always has bothered me. Funny, I couldn't tell you at all what this man looks like but I know exactly what kind of shoes he's wearing, because that's the last I see of him, his shoes going up the coal chute, and they're the old-fashioned kind that lace up the ankles, even though he's a young fellow. That's strange, isn't it?

Let me tell you though I really sweat until I see him safely out of there and I go upstairs right away and make myself a cup of tea. I don't think about that one much. My mother always said you shouldn't dwell on unpleasant things and I generally agree with that, I mean, dwelling on them doesn't make them go away. Though not dwelling on them doesn't make them go away either, when you come to think of it.

Sometimes I have these short ones where the fellow grabs my arm but I'm really a Kung-Fu expert, can you believe it, in real life I'm sure it would just be a conk on the head and that's that, like getting your tonsils out, you'd wake up and it would be all over except for the sore places, and you'd be lucky if your neck wasn't broken or something, I could never even hit the volleyball in gym and a volleyball is fairly large, you know?—and I just go *zap* with my fingers into his eyes and that's it, he falls over, or

40

I flip him against a wall or something. But I could never really stick my fingers in anyone's eyes, could you? It would feel like hot jello and I don't even like cold jello, just thinking about it gives me the creeps. I feel a bit guilty about that one, I mean how would you like walking around knowing someone's been blinded for life because of you?

But maybe it's different for a guy.

The most touching one I have is when the fellow grabs my arm and I say, sad and kind of dignified, "You'd be raping a corpse." That pulls him up short and I explain that I've just found out I have leukemia and the doctors have only given me a few months to live. That's why I'm out pacing the streets alone at night, I need to think, you know, come to terms with myself. I don't really have leukemia but in the fantasy I do, I guess I chose that particular disease because a girl in my grade four class died of it, the whole class sent her flowers when she was in the hospital. I didn't understand then that she was going to die and I wanted to have leukemia too so I could get flowers. Kids are funny, aren't they? Well, it turns out that he has leukemia himself, and *he* only has a few months to live, that's why he's going around raping people, he's very bitter because he's so young and his life is being taken from him before he's really lived it. So we walk along gently under the street lights, it's spring and sort of misty, and we end up going for coffee, we're happy we've found the only other person in the world who can understand what we're going through, it's almost like fate, and after a while we just sort of look at each other and our hands touch, and he comes back with me and moves into my apartment and we spend our last months together before we die, we just sort of don't wake up in the morning, though I've never decided which one of us gets to die first. If it's him I have to go on and fantasize about the funeral, if it's me I don't have to worry about that, so it just about depends on how tired I am at the time. You may not believe this but sometimes I even start crying. I cry at the ends of movies, even the ones that aren't all that sad, so I guess it's the same thing. My mother's like that too.

The funny thing about these fantasies is that the man is always someone I don't know, and the statistics in the magazines, well, most of them anyway, they say it's often someone you do know, at least a little bit, like your boss or something—I mean, it wouldn't be *my* boss, he's over sixty and I'm sure he couldn't rape his way out of a paper bag, poor old thing, but it might be someone like Derek Duck, in his elevator shoes, perish the thought—or someone you just met, who invites you up for a drink, it's getting so you can hardly be sociable anymore, and how are you supposed to meet people if you can't trust them even that basic amount? You can't spend your whole life in the Filing Department or cooped up in your own apartment with all the doors and windows locked and the shades down. I'm not what you would call a drinker but I like to go out now and then for a drink or two in a nice place, even if I am by myself, I'm with Women's Lib on that even though I can't agree with a lot of the other things they say. Like here for instance, the waiters all know me and if anyone, you know, bothers me . . . I don't know why I'm telling you all this, except I think it helps you get to know a person, especially at first, hearing some of the things they think about. At work they call me the office worry wart, but it isn't so much like worrying, it's more like figuring out what you should do in an emergency, like I said before.

Anyway, another thing about it is that there's a lot of conversation, in fact I spend most of my time, in the fantasy that is, wondering what I'm going to say and what he's going to say, I think it would be better if you could get a conversation going. Like, how could a fellow do that to a person he's just had a long conversation with, once you let them know you're human, you have a life too, I don't see how they could go ahead with it, right? I mean, I know it happens but I just don't understand it, that's the part I really don't understand.

ISAAC BABEL (1894–1939)

My First Goose   1925

[This story, taking place during the period of instability after the Bolshevik Revolution of 1917, focuses on the rite of passage of a young intellectual who must step from the world of theory into the world of brute reality. Ironically, Isaac Babel himself, one of the intellectual supporters of the revolution, became one of its victims. A *standard* is a flag or emblem of an army; St. Petersburg University is a famous university in a czarist Russian city which became Leningrad after the revolution but was renamed St. Petersburg in 1991 after the failure of communism; a *Cossack* is an elite horseman from any of various tribes in czarist Russia; *Ryazan* refers to one of those tribes of Slavic warriors; *Pravda* was the leading communist newspaper; *billet* refers to lodging; *purblind*, to dimsightedness.]

Savitsky, Commander of the VI Division, rose when he saw me, and I wondered at the beauty of his giant's body. He rose, the purple of his riding breeches and the crimson of his little tilted cap and the decorations stuck on his chest cleaving the hut as a standard cleaves the sky. A smell of scent and the sickly sweet freshness of soap emanated from him. His long legs were like girls sheathed to the neck in shining riding boots.

He smiled at me, struck his riding whip on the table, and drew toward him an order that the Chief of Staff had just finished dictating. It was an order for Ivan Chesnokov to advance on Chugunov-Dobryvodka with the regiment entrusted to him, to make contact with the enemy and destroy the same.

"For which destruction," the Commander began to write, smearing the whole sheet, "I make this same Chesnokov entirely responsible, up to and including the supreme penalty, and will if necessary strike him down on the spot; which you, Chesnokov, who have been working with me at the front for some months now, cannot doubt."

The Commander signed the order with a flourish, tossed it to his orderlies and turned upon me gray eyes that danced with merriment.

I handed him a paper with my appointment to the Staff of the Division.   5

"Put it down in the Order of the Day," said the Commander. "Put him down for every satisfaction save the front one. Can you read and write?"

"Yes, I can read and write," I replied, envying the flower and iron of that youthfulness. "I graduated in law from St. Petersburg University."

"Oh, are you one of those grinds?" he laughed. "Specs on your nose, too! What a nasty little object! They've sent you along without making any enquiries; and this is a hot place for specs. Think you'll get on with us?"

"I'll get on all right," I answered, and went off to the village with the quartermaster to find a billet for the night.

The quartermaster carried my trunk on his shoulder. Before us stretched the village   10
street. The dying sun, round and yellow as a pumpkin, was giving up its roseate ghost to the skies.

We went up to a hut painted over with garlands. The quartermaster stopped, and said suddenly, with a guilty smile:

"Nuisance with specs. Can't do anything to stop it, either. Not a life for the brainy type here. But you go and mess up a lady, and a good lady too, and you'll have the boys patting you on the back."

He hesitated, my little trunk on his shoulder; then he came quite close to me, only to dart away again despairingly and run to the nearest yard. Cossacks were sitting there, shaving one another.

"Here, you soldiers," said the quartermaster, setting my little trunk down on the ground. "Comrade Savitsky's orders are that you're to take this chap in your billets, so no nonsense about it, because the chap's been through a lot in the learning line."

The quartermaster, purple in the face, left us without looking back. I raised my hand to my cap and saluted the Cossacks. A lad with long straight flaxen hair and the handsome face of the Ryazan Cossacks went over to my little trunk and tossed it out at the gate. Then he turned his back on me and with remarkable skill emitted a series of shameful noises. 15

"To your guns—number double-zero!" an older Cossack shouted at him, and burst out laughing. "Running fire!"

His guileless art exhausted, the lad made off. Then, crawling over the ground, I began to gather together the manuscript and tattered garments that had fallen out of the trunk. I gathered them up and carried them to the other end of the yard. Near the hut, on a brick stove, stood a cauldron in which pork was cooking. The steam that rose from it was like the far-off smoke of home in the village, and it mingled hunger with desperate loneliness in my head. Then I covered my little broken trunk with hay, turning it into a pillow, and lay down on the ground to read in *Pravda* Lenin's speech at the Second Congress of the Comintern. The sun fell upon me from behind the toothed hillocks, the Cossacks trod on my feet, the lad made fun of me untiringly, the beloved lines came toward me along a thorny path and could not reach me. Then I put aside the paper and went out to the landlady, who was spinning on the porch.

"Landlady," I said, "I've got to eat."

The old woman raised to me the diffused whites of her purblind eyes and lowered them again.

"Comrade," she said, after a pause, "what with all this going on, I want to go and hang myself." 20

"Christ!" I muttered, and pushed the old woman in the chest with my fist. "You don't suppose I'm going to go into explanations with you, do you?"

And turning around I saw somebody's sword lying within reach. A severe-looking goose was waddling about the yard, inoffensively preening its feathers. I overtook it and pressed it to the ground. Its head cracked beneath my boot, cracked and emptied itself. The white neck lay stretched out in the dung, the wings twitched.

"Christ!" I said, digging into the goose with my sword. "Go and cook it for me, landlady."

Her blind eyes and glasses glistening, the old woman picked up the slaughtered bird, wrapped it in her apron, and started to bear it off toward the kitchen.

"Comrade," she said to me, after a while, "I want to go and hang myself." And she closed the door behind her. 25

The Cossacks in the yard were already sitting around their cauldron. They sat motionless, stiff as heathen priests at a sacrifice, and had not looked at the goose.

"The lad's all right," one of them said, winking and scooping up the cabbage soup with his spoon.

The Cossacks commenced their supper with all the elegance and restraint of peasants who respect one another. And I wiped the sword with sand, went out at the gate, and came in again, depressed. Already the moon hung above the yard like a cheap earring.

"Hey, you," suddenly said Surovkov, an older Cossack. "Sit down and feed with us till your goose is done."

He produced a spare spoon from his boot and handed it to me. We supped up the-   30
cabbage soup they had made, and ate the pork.

"What's in the newspaper?" asked the flaxen-haired lad, making room for me.

"Lenin writes in the paper," I said, pulling out *Pravda* . "Lenin writes that there's
a shortage of everything."

And loudly, like a triumphant man hard of hearing, I read Lenin's speech out to
the Cossacks.

Evening wrapped about me the quickening moisture of its twilight sheets; evening
laid a mother's hand upon my burning forehead. I read on and rejoiced, spying out ex-
ultingly the secret curve of Lenin's straight line.

"Truth tickles everyone's nostrils," said Surovkov, when I had come to the end.   35
"The question is, how's it to be pulled from the heap. But he goes and strikes at it
straight off like a hen pecking at a grain!"

This remark about Lenin was made by Surovkov, platoon commander of the Staff
Squadron; after which we lay down to sleep in the hayloft. We slept, all six of us, beneath a wooden roof that let in the stars, warming one another, our legs intermingled.
I dreamed: and in my dreams saw women. But my heart, stained with bloodshed, grat-
ed and brimmed over.

DONALD   BARTHELME   (1931–1989)
The Balloon   1967

The balloon, beginning at a point on Fourteenth Street, the exact location of
which I cannot reveal, expanded northward all one night, while people were sleeping,
until it reached the Park. There, I stopped it; at dawn the northernmost edges lay over
the Plaza; the free-hanging motion was frivolous and gentle. But experiencing a faint irritation at stopping, even to protect the trees, and seeing no reason the balloon should
not be allowed to expand upward, over the parts of the city it was already covering, into
the "air space" to be found there, I asked the engineers to see to it. This expansion
took place throughout the morning, soft imperceptible sighing of gas through the
valves. The balloon then covered forty-five blocks north-south on either side of the Avenue in some places. That was the situation, then.

But it is wrong to speak of "situations," implying sets of circumstances leading to
some resolution, some escape of tension; there were no situations, simply the balloon
hanging there—muted heavy grays and browns for the most part, contrasting with walnut and soft yellows. A deliberate lack of finish, enhanced by skillful installation, gave
the surface a rough, forgotten quality; sliding weights on the inside, carefully adjusted,
anchored the great, vari-shaped mass at a number of points. Now we have had a flood
of original ideas in all media, works of singular beauty as well as significant milestones
in the history of inflation, but at that moment there was only *this balloon,* concrete particular, hanging there.

There were reactions. Some people found the balloon "interesting." As a response
this seemed inadequate to the immensity of the balloon, the suddenness of its appearance over the city; on the other hand, in the absence of hysteria or other societally induced anxiety, it must be judged a calm, "mature" one. There was a certain amount of
initial argumentation about the "meaning" of the balloon; this subsided, because we
have learned not to insist on meanings, and they are rarely even looked for now, except
in cases involving the simplest, safest phenomena. It was agreed that since the meaning

of the balloon could never be known absolutely, extended discussion was pointless, or at least less purposeful than the activities of those who, for example, hung green and blue paper lanterns from the warm gray underside, in certain streets, or seized the occasion to write messages on the surface, announcing their availability for the performance of unnatural acts, or the availability of acquaintances.

Daring children jumped, especially at those points where the balloon hovered close to a building, so that the gap between balloon and building was a matter of a few inches, or points where the balloon actually made contact, exerting an ever-so-slight pressure against the side of a building, so that balloon and building seemed a unity. The upper surface was so structured that a "landscape" was presented, small valleys as well as slight knolls, or mounds; once atop the balloon, a stroll was possible, or even a trip, from one place to another. There was pleasure in being able to run down an incline, then up the opposing slope, both gently graded, or in making a leap from one side to the other. Bouncing was possible, because of the pneumaticity of the surface, and even falling, if that was your wish. That all these varied motions, as well as others, were within one's possibilities, in experiencing the "up" side of the balloon, was extremely exciting for children, accustomed to the city's flat, hard skin. But the purpose of the balloon was not to amuse children.

Too, the number of people, children and adults, who took advantage of the opportunities described was not so large as it might have been: a certain timidity, lack of trust in the balloon, was seen. There was, furthermore, some hostility. Because we had hidden the pumps, which fed helium to the interior, and because the surface was so vast that the authorities could not determine the point of entry—that is, the point at which the gas was injected—a degree of frustration was evidenced by those city officers into whose province such manifestations normally fell. The apparent purposelessness of the balloon was vexing (as was the fact that it was "there" at all). Had we painted, in great letters, "LABORATORY TESTS PROVE" or "18% MORE EFFECTIVE!" on the sides of the balloon, this difficulty would have been circumvented. But I could not bear to do so. On the whole, these officers were remarkably tolerant, considering the dimensions of the anomaly, this tolerance being the result of, first, secret tests conducted by night that convinced them that little or nothing could be done in the way of removing or destroying the balloon, and, secondly, a public warmth that arose (not uncolored by touches of the aforementioned hostility) toward the balloon, from ordinary citizens.

As a single balloon must stand for a lifetime of thinking about balloons, so each citizen expressed, in the attitude he chose, a complex of attitudes. One man might consider that the balloon had to do with the notion *sullied*, as in the sentence *The big balloon sullied the otherwise clear and radiant Manhattan sky.* That is, the balloon was, in this man's view, an imposture, something inferior to the sky that had formerly been there, something interposed between the people and their "sky." But in fact it was January, the sky was dark and ugly; it was not a sky you could look up into, lying on your back in the street, with pleasure, unless pleasure, for you, proceeded from having been threatened, from having been misused. And the underside of the balloon was a pleasure to look up into, we had seen to that, muted grays and browns for the most part, contrasted with walnut and soft, forgotten yellows. And so, while this man was thinking *sullied*, still there was an admixture of pleasurable cognition in his thinking, struggling with the original perception.

Another man, on the other hand, might view the balloon as if it were part of a system of unanticipated rewards, as when one's employer walks in and says, "Here, Henry, take this package of money I have wrapped for you, because we have been doing so well in the business here, and I admire the way you bruise the tulips, without which bruising your department would not be a success, or at least not the success that it is."

5

For this man the balloon might be a brilliantly heroic "muscle and pluck" experience, even if an experience poorly understood.

Another man might say, "Without the example of——, it is doubtful that—— would exist today in its present form," and find many to agree with him, or to argue with him. Ideas of "bloat" and "float" were introduced, as well as concepts of dream and responsibility. Others engaged in remarkably detailed fantasies having to do with a wish either to lose themselves in the balloon, or to engorge it. The private character of these wishes, of their origins, deeply buried and unknown, was such that they were not much spoken of; yet there is evidence that they were widespread. It was also argued that what was important was what you felt when you stood under the balloon; some people claimed that they felt sheltered, warmed, as never before, while enemies of the balloon felt, or reported feeling, constrained, a "heavy" feeling.

Critical opinion was divided:

"monstrous pourings"

                                              "harp"

XXXXXXX *"certain contrasts with darker portions"*

                                  "inner joy"

"large, square corners"

"conservative eclecticism that has so far governed modern balloon design"

  :::::: *"abnormal vigor"*

"warm, soft, lazy passages"

The Balloon

"Has unity been sacrificed for a sprawling quality?"

"Quelle catastrophe!"

"munching"

People began, in a curious way, to locate themselves in relation to aspects of the balloon: "I'll be at that place where it dips down into Forty-seventh Street almost to the sidewalk, near the Alamo Chile House," or, "Why don't we go stand on top, and take the air, and maybe walk about a bit, where it forms a tight, curving line with the façade of the Gallery of Modern Art—" Marginal intersections offered entrances with a given time duration, as well as "warm, soft, lazy passages" in which . . . But it is wrong to speak of "marginal intersections," each intersection was crucial, none could be ignored (as if, walking there, you might not find someone capable of turning your attention, in a flash, from old exercises to new exercises, risks and escalations). Each intersection was crucial, meeting of balloon and building, meeting of balloon and man, meeting of balloon and balloon.

It was suggested that what was admired about the balloon was finally this: that it was not limited, or defined. Sometimes a bulge, blister, or sub-section would carry all the way east to the river on its own initiative, in the manner of an army's movements on a map, as seen in a headquarters remote from the fighting. Then that part would be, as it were, thrown back again, or would withdraw into new dispositions; the next morning, that part would have made another sortie, or disappeared altogether. This ability of the balloon to shift its shape, to change, was very pleasing, especially to people whose lives were rather rigidly patterned, persons to whom change, although desired, was not available. The balloon, for the twenty-two days of its existence, offered the possibility, in its randomness, of mislocation of the self, in contradistinction to the grid of precise, rectangular pathways under our feet. The amount of specialized training currently

    10

needed, and the consequent desirability of long-term commitments, has been occasioned by the steadily growing importance of complex machinery, in virtually all kinds of operations; as this tendency increases, more and more people will turn, in bewildered inadequacy, to solutions for which the balloon may stand as a prototype, or "rough draft."

I met you under the balloon, on the occasion of your return from Norway; you asked if it was mine; I said it was. The balloon, I said, is a spontaneous autobiographical disclosure, having to do with the unease I felt at your absence, and with sexual deprivation, but now that your visit to Bergen has been terminated, it is no longer necessary or appropriate. Removal of the balloon was easy; trailer trucks carried away the depleted fabric, which is now stored in West Virginia, awaiting some other time of unhappiness, sometime, perhaps, when we are angry with one another.

AMBROSE BIERCE (1842–1913)
An Occurrence at Owl Creek Bridge 1891

[At the opening of this story, a man is about to be hanged—another casualty of the United States Civil War. Bierce refers to the fall of Corinth, the site of a battle between Federal (Union) forces and the Confederate army in 1862. War terminology peppers the story, such as Bierce's reference to *grapeshot*, a cluster of small pellets fired from a cannon, similar to shrapnel. *Diminuendo* is a musical term for fading out.]

1

A man stood upon a railroad bridge in Northern Alabama, looking down into the swift waters twenty feet below. The man's hands were behind his back, the wrists bound with a cord. A rope loosely encircled his neck. It was attached to a stout crosstimber above his head, and the slack fell to the level of his knees. Some loose boards laid upon the sleepers supporting the metals of the railway supplied a footing for him and his executioners—two private soldiers of the Federal army, directed by a sergeant, who in civil life may have been a deputy sheriff. At a short remove upon the same temporary platform was an officer in the uniform of his rank, armed. He was a captain. A sentinel at each end of the bridge stood with his rifle in the position known as "support," that is to say, vertical in front of the left shoulder, the hammer resting on the forearm thrown straight across the chest—a formal and unnatural position, enforcing an erect carriage of the body. It did not appear to be the duty of these two men to know what was occurring at the center of the bridge; they merely blockaded the two ends of the foot plank which traversed it.

Beyond one of the sentinels nobody was in sight; the railroad ran straight away into a forest for a hundred yards, then, curving, was lost to view. Doubtless there was an outpost further along. The other bank of the stream was open ground—a gentle acclivity crowned with a stockade of vertical tree trunks, loop-holed for rifles, with a single embrasure through which protruded the muzzle of a brass cannon commanding the bridge. Midway of the slope between bridge and fort were the spectators—a single company of infantry in line, at "parade rest," the butts of the rifles on the ground, the barrels inclining slightly backward against the right shoulder, the hands crossed upon the stock. A lieutenant stood at the right of the line, the point of his sword upon the ground, his left hand resting upon his right. Excepting the group of four at the center of the bridge not a man moved. The company faced the bridge, staring stonily, motionless. The sentinels, facing the banks of the stream, might have been statues to adorn the bridge. The captain stood with folded arms, silent, observing the work of his subordinates but making no sign. Death is a dignitary who, when he comes announced, is to be received with formal manifestations of respect, even by those most familiar with him. In the code of military etiquette silence and fixity are forms of deference.

The man who was engaged in being hanged was apparently about thirty-five years of age. He was a civilian, if one might judge from his dress, which was that of a planter. His features were good—a straight nose, firm mouth, broad forehead, from which his long, dark hair was combed straight back, falling behind his ears to the collar of his well-fitting frock coat. He wore a moustache and pointed beard, but no whiskers; his eyes were large and dark grey and had a kindly expression which one would hardly have expected in one whose neck was in the hemp. Evidently this was no vulgar assassin. The liberal military code makes provision for hanging many kinds of people, and gentlemen are not excluded.

The preparations being complete, the two private soldiers stepped aside and each drew away the plank upon which he had been standing. The sergeant turned to the captain, saluted and placed himself immediately behind that officer, who in turn moved apart one pace. These movements left the condemned man and the sergeant standing on the two ends of the same plank, which spanned three of the cross-ties of the bridge. The end upon which the civilian stood almost, but not quite, reached a fourth. This plank had been held in place by the weight of the captain; it was now held by that of the sergeant. At a signal from the former, the latter would step aside, the plank would tilt and the condemned man go down between two ties. The arrangement commended itself to his judgment as simple and effective. His face had not been covered nor his eyes bandaged. He looked a moment at his "unsteadfast footing," then let his gaze wander to the swirling water of the stream racing madly beneath his feet. A piece of dancing driftwood caught his attention and his eyes followed it down the current. How slowly it appeared to move! What a sluggish stream!

He closed his eyes in order to fix his last thoughts upon his wife and children. The water, touched to gold by the early sun, the brooding mists under the banks at some distance down the stream, the fort, the soldiers, the piece of drift—all had distracted him. And now he became conscious of a new disturbance. Striking through the thought of his dear ones was a sound which he could neither ignore nor understand, a sharp, distinct, metallic percussion like the stroke of a blacksmith's hammer upon the anvil; it had the same ringing quality. He wondered what it was, and whether immeasurably distant or nearby—it seemed both. Its recurrence was regular, but as slow as the tolling of a death knell. He awaited each stroke with impatience and—he knew not why—apprehension. The intervals of silence grew progressively longer, the delays became maddening. With their greater infrequency the sounds increased in strength and sharpness. They hurt his ear like the thrust of a knife; he feared he would shriek. What he heard was the ticking of his watch.

He unclosed his eyes and saw again the water below him. "If I could free my hands," he thought, "I might throw off the noose and spring into the stream. By diving I could evade the bullets, and, swimming vigorously, reach the bank, take to the woods, and get away home. My home, thank God, is as yet outside their lines; my wife and little ones are still beyond the invader's farthest advance."

As these thoughts, which have here to be set down in words, were flashed into the doomed man's brain rather than evolved from it, the captain nodded to the sergeant. The sergeant stepped aside.

5

2

Peyton Farquhar was a well-to-do planter, of an old and highly-respected Alabama family. Being a slave owner, and, like other slave owners, a politician, he was naturally an original secessionist and ardently devoted to the Southern cause. Circumstances of an imperious nature which it is unnecessary to relate here, had prevented him from taking service with the gallant army which had fought the disastrous campaigns ending with the fall of Corinth, and he chafed under the inglorious restraint, longing for the release of his energies, the larger life of the soldier, the opportunity for distinction. That opportunity, he felt, would come, as it comes to all in war time. Meanwhile he did what he could. No service was too humble for him to perform in aid of the South, no adventure too perilous for him to undertake if consistent with the character of a civilian who was at heart a soldier, and who in good faith and without too much qualification assented to at least a part of the frankly villainous dictum that all is fair in love and war.

One evening while Farquhar and his wife were sitting on a rustic bench near the entrance to his grounds, a grey-clad soldier rode up to the gate and asked for a drink of water. Mrs. Farquhar was only too happy to serve him with her own white hands. While she was gone to fetch the water, her husband approached the dusty horseman and inquired eagerly for news from the front.

"The Yanks are repairing the railroads," said the man, "and are getting ready for   10
another advance. They have reached the Owl Creek bridge, put it in order, and built a stockade on the other bank. The commandant has issued an order, which is posted everywhere, declaring that any civilian caught interfering with the railroad, its bridges, tunnels, or trains, will be summarily hanged. I saw the order."

"How far is it to the Owl Creek bridge?" Farquhar asked.

"About thirty miles."

"Is there no force on this side the creek?"

"Only a picket post half a mile out, on the railroad, and a single sentinel at this end of the bridge."

"Suppose a man—a civilian and student of hanging—should elude the picket post   15
and perhaps get the better of the sentinel," said Farquhar, smiling, "what could he accomplish?"

The soldier reflected. "I was there a month ago," he replied. "I observed that the flood of last winter had lodged a great quantity of driftwood against the wooden pier at this end of the bridge. It is now dry and would burn like tow."

The lady had now brought the water, which the soldier drank. He thanked her ceremoniously, bowed to her husband, and rode away. An hour later, after nightfall, he repassed the plantation, going northward in the direction from which he had come. He was a Federal scout.

3

As Peyton Farquhar fell straight downward through the bridge, he lost consciousness and was as one already dead. From this state he was awakened—ages later, it seemed to him—by the pain of a sharp pressure upon his throat, followed by a sense of suffocation. Keen, poignant agonies seemed to shoot from his neck downward through every fibre of his body and limbs. These pains appeared to flash along well-defined lines of ramification, and to beat with an inconceivably rapid periodicity. They seemed like streams of pulsating fire heating him to an intolerable temperature. As to his head, he was conscious of nothing but a feeling of fullness—of congestion. These sensations were unaccompanied by thought. The intellectual part of his nature was already effaced; he had power only to feel, and feeling was torment. He was conscious of motion. Encompassed in a luminous cloud, of which he was now merely the fiery heart, without material substance, he swung through unthinkable arcs of oscillation, like a vast pendulum. Then all at once, with terrible suddenness, the light about him shot upward with the noise of a loud plash; a frightful roaring was in his ears, and all was cold and dark. The power of thought was restored; he knew that the rope had broken and he had fallen into the stream. There was no additional strangulation; the noose about his neck was already suffocating him, and kept the water from his lungs. To die of hanging at the bottom of a river!—the idea seemed to him ludicrous. He opened his eyes in the blackness and saw above him a gleam of light, but how distant, how inaccessible! He was still sinking, for the light became fainter and fainter until it was a mere glimmer. Then it began to grow and brighten, and he knew that he was rising toward the surface—knew it with reluctance, for he was now very comfortable. "To be hanged and drowned," he thought, "that is not so bad; but I do not wish to be shot. No; I will not be shot; that is not fair."

He was not conscious of an effort, but a sharp pain in his wrist apprised him that he was trying to free his hands. He gave the struggle his attention, as an idler might observe the feat of a juggler, without interest in the outcome. What splendid effort!—what magnificent, what superhuman strength! Ah, that was a fine endeavor! Bravo! The cord fell away; his arms parted and floated upward, the hands dimly seen on each side in the growing light. He watched them with a new interest as first one and then the other pounced upon the noose at his neck. They tore it away and thrust it fiercely aside, its undulations resembling those of a water-snake. "Put it back, put it back!" He thought he shouted these words to his hands, for the undoing of the noose had been succeeded by the direst pang which he had yet experienced. His neck ached horribly; his brain was on fire; his heart, which had been fluttering faintly, gave a great leap, trying to force itself out at his mouth. His whole body was racked and wrenched with an insupportable anguish! But his disobedient hands gave no heed to the command. They beat the water vigorously with quick, downward strokes, forcing him to the surface. He felt his head emerge; his eyes were blinded by the sunlight; his chest expanded convulsively, and with a supreme and crowning agony his lungs engulfed a great draught of air, which instantly he expelled in a shriek!

He was now in full possession of his physical senses. They were, indeed, preternaturally keen and alert. Something in the awful disturbance of his organic system had so exalted and refined them that they made record of things never before perceived. He felt the ripples upon his face and heard their separate sounds as they struck. He looked at the forest on the bank of the stream, saw the individual trees, the leaves and the veining of each leaf—the very insects upon them, the locusts, the brilliant-bodied flies, the grey spiders stretching their webs from twig to twig. He noted the prismatic colors in all the dewdrops upon a million blades of grass. The humming of the gnats that danced above the eddies of the stream, the beating of the dragonflies' wings, the strokes of the water spiders' legs, like oars which had lifted their boat—all these made audible music. A fish slid along beneath his eyes and he heard the rush of its body parting the water.

He had come to the surface facing down the stream; in a moment the visible world seemed to wheel slowly round, himself the pivotal point, and he saw the bridge, the fort, the soldiers upon the bridge, the captain, the sergeant, the two privates, his executioners. They were in silhouette against the blue sky. They shouted and gesticulated, pointing at him; the captain had drawn his pistol, but did not fire; the others were unarmed. Their movements were grotesque and horrible, their forms gigantic.

Suddenly he heard a sharp report and something struck the water smartly within a few inches of his head, spattering his face with spray. He heard a second report, and

20

saw one of the sentinels with his rifle at his shoulder, a light cloud of blue smoke rising from the muzzle. The man in the water saw the eye of the man on the bridge gazing into his own through the sights of the rifle. He observed that it was a grey eye, and remembered having read that grey eyes were keenest and that all famous marksmen had them. Nevertheless, this one had missed.

A counter swirl had caught Farquhar and turned him half round; he was again looking into the forest on the bank opposite the fort. The sound of a clear, high voice in a monotonous singsong now rang out behind him and came across the water with a distinctness that pierced and subdued all other sounds, even the beating of the ripples in his ears. Although no soldier, he had frequented camps enough to know the dread significance of that deliberate, drawling, aspirated chant; the lieutenant on shore was taking a part in the morning's work. How coldly and pitilessly—with what an even, calm intonation, presaging and enforcing tranquillity in the men—with what accurately-measured intervals fell those cruel words:

"Attention, company. . . . Shoulder arms. . . . Ready. . . . Aim. . . . Fire."

Farquhar dived—dived as deeply as he could. The water roared in his ears like the voice of Niagara, yet he heard the dulled thunder of the volley, and rising again toward the surface, met shining bits of metal, singularly flattened, oscillating slowly downward. Some of them touched him on the face and hands, then fell away, continuing their descent. One lodged between his collar and neck; it was uncomfortably warm, and he snatched it out.

As he rose to the surface, gasping for breath, he saw that he had been a long time under water; he was perceptibly farther down stream—nearer to safety. The soldiers had almost finished reloading; the metal ramrods flashed all at once in the sunshine as they were drawn from the barrels, turned in the air, and thrust into their sockets. The two sentinels fired again, independently and ineffectually.

The hunted man saw all this over his shoulder; he was now swimming vigorously with the current. His brain was as energetic as his arms and legs; he thought with the rapidity of lightning.

"The officer," he reasoned, "will not make that martinet's error a second time. It is as easy to dodge a volley as a single shot. He has probably already given the command to fire at will. God help me, I cannot dodge them all!"

An appalling plash within two yards of him, followed by a loud rushing sound, *diminuendo*, which seemed to travel back through the air to the fort and died in an explosion which stirred the very river to its deeps! A rising sheet of water, which curved over him, fell down upon him, blinded him, strangled him! The cannon had taken a hand in the game. As he shook his head free from the commotion of the smitten water, he heard the deflected shot humming through the air ahead, and in an instant it was cracking and smashing the branches in the forest beyond.

"They will not do that again," he thought; "the next time they will use a charge of grape. I must keep my eye upon the gun; the smoke will apprise me—the report arrives too late; it lags behind the missile. It is a good gun."

Suddenly he felt himself whirled round and round—spinning like a top. The water, the banks, the forest, the now distant bridge, fort and men—all were commingled and blurred. Objects were represented by their colors only; circular horizontal streaks of color—that was all he saw. He had been caught in a vortex and was being whirled on with a velocity of advance and gyration which made him giddy and sick. In a few moments he was flung upon the gravel at the foot of the left bank of the stream—the southern bank—and behind a projecting point which concealed him from his enemies. The sudden arrest of his motion, the abrasion of one of his hands on the gravel, restored him and he wept with delight. He dug his fingers into the sand, threw it over himself in handfuls and audibly blessed it. It looked like gold, like diamonds, rubies, emeralds; he could think of nothing beautiful which it did not resemble. The trees upon the bank were giant garden plants; he noted a definite order in their arrangement, inhaled the fragrance of their blooms. A strange, roseate light shone through the spaces among their trunks, and the wind made in their branches the music of æolian harps. He had no wish to perfect his escape, was content to remain in that enchanting spot until retaken.

A whizz and rattle of grapeshot among the branches high above his head roused him from his dream. The baffled cannoneer had fired him a random farewell. He sprang to his feet, rushed up the sloping bank, and plunged into the forest.

All that day he travelled, laying his course by the rounding sun. The forest seemed interminable; nowhere did he discover a break in it, not even a woodman's road. He had not known that he lived in so wild a region. There was something uncanny in the revelation.

By nightfall he was fatigued, footsore, famishing. The thought of his wife and children urged him on. At last he found a road which led him in what he knew to be the right direction. It was as wide and straight as a city street, yet it seemed untravelled. No fields bordered it, no dwelling anywhere. Not so much as the barking of a dog suggested human habitation. The black bodies of the great trees formed a straight wall on both sides, terminating on the horizon in a point, like a diagram in a lesson in perspective. Overhead, as he looked up through this rift in the wood, shone great golden stars looking unfamiliar and grouped in strange constellations. He was sure they were arranged in some order which had a secret and malign significance. The wood on either side was full of singular noises, among which—once, twice, and again—he distinctly heard whispers in an unknown tongue.

His neck was in pain, and, lifting his hand to it, he found it horribly swollen. He   35
knew that it had a circle of black where the rope had bruised it. His eyes felt congested; he could no longer close them. His tongue was swollen with thirst; he relieved its fever by thrusting it forward from between his teeth into the cool air. How softly the turf had carpeted the untravelled avenue! He could no longer feel the roadway beneath his feet!

Doubtless, despite his suffering, he fell asleep while walking, for now he sees another scene—perhaps he has merely recovered from a delirium. He stands at the gate of his own home. All is as he left it, and all bright and beautiful in the morning sunshine. He must have travelled the entire night. As he pushes open the gate and passes up the wide white walk, he sees a flutter of female garments; his wife, looking fresh and cool and sweet, steps down from the verandah to meet him. At the bottom of the steps she stands waiting, with a smile of ineffable joy, an attitude of matchless grace and dignity. Ah, how beautiful she is! He springs forward with extended arms. As he is about to clasp her, he feels a stunning blow upon the back of the neck; a blinding white light blazes all about him, with a sound like the shock of a cannon—then all is darkness and silence!

Peyton Farquhar was dead; his body, with a broken neck, swung gently from side to side beneath the timbers of the Owl Creek bridge.

RAY BRADBURY   (born 1920)
There Will Come Soft Rains   1948

[The incinerator in this story is compared to the biblical Baal, or Beelzebub, one of the false gods of idol-worshipers. The title of the story is borrowed from a poem the American poet Sara Teasdale wrote after the end of the carnage of World War I. The artworks consumed by the fire in this story are priceless paintings by the Spanish Pablo Picasso and the French Henri Matisse, two of the great early moderns.]

In the living room the voice-clock sang, *Tick-tock, seven o'clock, time to get up, time to get up, seven o'clock!* as if it were afraid that nobody would. The morning house lay empty. The clock ticked on, repeating and repeating its sounds into the emptiness. *Seven-nine, breakfast time, seven-nine!*

In the kitchen the breakfast stove gave a hissing sigh and ejected from its warm interior eight pieces of perfectly browned toast, eight eggs sunnyside up, sixteen slices of bacon, two coffees, and two cool glasses of milk.

"Today is August 4, 2026," said a second voice from the kitchen ceiling, "in the city of Allendale, California." It repeated the date three times for memory's sake. "Today is Mr. Featherstone's birthday. Today is the anniversary of Tilita's marriage. Insurance is payable, as are the water, gas, and light bills."

Somewhere in the walls, relays clicked, memory tapes glided under electric eyes.

Eight-one, tick-tock, eight-one o'clock, off to school, off to work, run, run, eight-one!   5
But no doors slammed, no carpets took the soft tread of rubber heels. It was raining outside. The weather box on the front door sang quietly: "Rain, rain, go away; rubbers, raincoats for today . . ." And the rain tapped on the empty house, echoing.

Outside, the garage chimed and lifted its door to reveal the waiting car. After a long wait the door swung down again.

At eight-thirty the eggs were shriveled and the toast was like stone. An aluminum wedge scraped them into the sink, where hot water whirled them down a metal throat which digested and flushed them away to the distant sea. The dirty dishes were dropped into a hot washer and emerged twinkling dry.

Nine-fifteen, sang the clock, *time to clean.*

Out of warrens in the wall, tiny robot mice darted. The rooms were acrawl with the small cleaning animals, all rubber and metal. They thudded against chairs, whirling their mustached runners, kneading the rug nap, sucking gently at hidden dust. Then, like mysterious invaders, they popped into their burrows. Their pink electric eyes faded. The house was clean.

Ten o'clock. The sun came out from behind the rain. The house stood alone in a   10
city of rubble and ashes. This was the one house left standing. At night the ruined city gave off a radioactive glow which could be seen for miles.

Ten-fifteen. The garden sprinklers whirled up in golden founts, filling the soft morning air with scatterings of brightness. The water pelted windowpanes, running down the charred west side where the house had been burned evenly free of its white paint. The entire west face of the house was black, save for five places. Here the silhouette in paint of a man mowing a lawn. Here, as in a photograph, a woman bent to pick flowers. Still farther over, their images burned on wood in one titanic instant, a small boy, hands flung into the air; higher up, the image of a thrown ball, and opposite him a girl, hands raised to catch a ball which never came down.

The five spots of paint—the man, the woman, the children, the ball—remained. The rest was a thin charcoaled layer.

The gentle sprinkler rain filled the garden with falling light.

Until this day, how well the house had kept its peace. How carefully it had inquired, "Who goes there? What's the password?" and, getting no answer from lonely foxes and whining cats, it had shut up its windows and drawn shades in an old-maidenly preoccupation with self-protection which bordered on a mechanical paranoia.

It quivered at each sound, the house did. If a sparrow brushed a window, the   15
shade snapped up. The bird, startled, flew off! No, not even a bird must touch the house!

The house was an altar with ten thousand attendants, big, small, servicing, attending, in choirs. But the gods had gone away, and the ritual of the religion continued senselessly, uselessly.

Twelve noon.

A dog whined, shivering, on the front porch.

The front door recognized the dog voice and opened. The dog, once huge and fleshy, but now gone to bone and covered with sores, moved in and through the house, tracking mud. Behind it whirred angry mice, angry at having to pick up mud, angry at inconvenience.

For not a leaf fragment blew under the door but what the wall panels flipped open   20
and the copper scrap rats flashed swiftly out. The offending dust, hair, or paper, seized in miniature steel jaws, was raced back to the burrows. There, down tubes which fed into the cellar, it was dropped into the sighing vent of an incinerator which sat like evil Baal in a dark corner.

The dog ran upstairs, hysterically yelping to each door, at last realizing, as the house realized, that only silence was here.

It sniffed the air and scratched the kitchen door. Behind the door, the stove was making pancakes which filled the house with a rich baked odor and the scent of maple syrup.

The dog frothed at the mouth, lying at the door, sniffing, its eyes turned to fire. It ran wildly in circles, biting at its tail, spun in a frenzy, and died. It lay in the parlor for an hour.

Two o'clock, sang a voice.

Delicately sensing decay at last, the regiments of mice hummed out as softly as   25
blown gray leaves in an electrical wind.

Two-fifteen.

The dog was gone.

In the cellar, the incinerator glowed suddenly and a whirl of sparks leaped up the chimney.

Two thirty-five.

Bridge tables sprouted from patio walls. Playing cards fluttered onto pads in a   30
shower of pips. Martinis manifested on an oaken bench with egg-salad sandwiches. Music played.

But the tables were silent and the cards untouched.

At four o'clock the tables folded like great butterflies back through the paneled walls.

Four-thirty.

The nursery walls glowed.

Animals took shape: yellow giraffes, blue lions, pink antelopes, lilac panthers ca-   35
vorting in crystal substance. The walls were glass. They looked out upon color and fan-

tasy. Hidden films clocked through well-oiled sprockets, and the walls lived. The nursery floor was woven to resemble a crisp, cereal meadow. Over this ran aluminum roaches and iron crickets, and in the hot still air butterflies of delicate red tissue wavered among the sharp aroma of animal spoors! There was the sound like a great matted yellow hive of bees within a dark bellows, the lazy bumble of a purring lion. And there was the patter of okapi feet and the murmur of a fresh jungle rain, like other hoofs, falling upon the summer-starched grass. Now the walls dissolved into distances of parched weed, mile on mile, and warm endless sky. The animals drew away into thorn brakes and water holes.

It was the children's hour.

Five o'clock. The bath filled with clear hot water.
Six, seven, eight o'clock. The dinner dishes manipulated like magic tricks, and in the study a *click*. In the metal stand opposite the hearth where a fire now blazed up warmly, a cigar popped out, half an inch of soft gray ash on it, smoking, waiting.
Nine o'clock. The beds warmed their hidden circuits, for nights were cool here.
Nine-five. A voice spoke from the study ceiling: 40
"Mrs. McClellan, which poem would you like this evening?"
The house was silent.
The voice said at last, "Since you express no preference, I shall select a poem at random." Quiet music rose to back the voice. "Sara Teasdale. As I recall, your favorite. . . .

"There will come soft rains and the smell of the ground,
And swallows circling with their shimmering sound;

And frogs in the pools singing at night,
And wild plum-trees in tremulous white;

Robins will wear their feathery fire
Whistling their whims on a low fence-wire;

And not one will know of the war, not one
Will care at last when it is done.

Not one would mind, either bird nor tree
If mankind perished utterly;

And Spring herself, when she woke at dawn,
Would scarcely know that we were gone."

The fire burned on the stone hearth and the cigar fell away into a mound of quiet ash on its tray. The empty chairs faced each other between the silent walls, and the music played.

At ten o'clock the house began to die.   45
The wind blew. A falling tree bough crashed through the kitchen window. Cleaning solvent, bottled, shattered over the stove. The room was ablaze in an instant!
"Fire!" screamed a voice. The house lights flashed, water pumps shot water from the ceilings. But the solvent spread on the linoleum, licking, eating under the kitchen door, while the voices took it up in chorus: "Fire, fire, fire!"
The house tried to save itself. Doors sprang tightly shut, but the windows were broken by the heat and the wind blew and sucked upon the fire.

The house gave ground as the fire in ten billion angry sparks moved with flaming ease from room to room and then up the stairs. While scurrying water rats squeaked from the walls, pistoled their water, and ran for more. And the wall sprays let down showers of mechanical rain.

But too late. Somewhere, sighing, a pump shrugged to a stop. The quenching rain ceased. The reserve water supply which had filled baths and washed dishes for many quiet days was gone.

The fire crackled up the stairs. It fed upon Picassos and Matisses in the upper halls, like delicacies, baking off the oily flesh, tenderly crisping the canvases into black shavings.

Now the fire lay in beds, stood in windows, changed the colors of drapes!

And then, reinforcements.

From attic trapdoors, blind robot faces peered down with faucet mouths gushing green chemical.

The fire backed off, as even an elephant must at the sight of a dead snake. Now there were twenty snakes whipping over the floor, killing the fire with a clear cold venom of green froth.

But the fire was clever. It had sent flame outside the house, up through the attic to the pumps there. An explosion! The attic brain which directed the pumps was shattered into bronze shrapnel on the beams.

The fire rushed back into every closet and felt of the clothes hung there.

The house shuddered, oak bone on bone, its bared skeleton cringing from the heat, its wire, its nerves revealed as if a surgeon had torn the skin off to let the red veins and capillaries quiver in the scalded air. Help, help! Fire! Run, run! Heat snapped mirrors like the first brittle winter ice. And the voices wailed Fire, fire, run, run, like a tragic nursery rhyme, a dozen voices, high, low, like children dying in a forest, alone, alone. And the voices fading as the wires popped their sheathings like hot chestnuts. One, two, three, four, five voices died.

In the nursery the jungle burned. Blue lions roared, purple giraffes bounded off. The panthers ran in circles, changing color, and ten million animals, running before the fire, vanished off toward a distant steaming river. . . .

Ten more voices died. In the last instant under the fire avalanche, other choruses, oblivious, could be heard announcing the time, playing music, cutting the lawn by remote-control mower, or setting an umbrella frantically out and in the slamming and opening front door, a thousand things happening, like a clock shop when each clock strikes the hour insanely before or after the other, a scene of maniac confusion, yet unity; singing, screaming, a few last cleaning mice darting bravely out to carry the horrid ashes away! And one voice, with sublime disregard for the situation, read poetry aloud in the fiery study, until all the film spools burned, until all the wires withered and the circuits cracked.

The fire burst the house and let it slam flat down, puffing out skirts of spark and smoke.

In the kitchen, an instant before the rain of fire and timber, the stove could be seen making breakfasts at a psychopathic rate, ten dozen eggs, six loaves of toast, twenty dozen bacon strips, which, eaten by fire, started the stove working again, hysterically hissing!

The crash. The attic smashing into kitchen and parlor. The parlor into cellar, cellar into sub-cellar. Deep freeze, armchair, film tapes, circuits, beds, and all like skeletons thrown in a cluttered mound deep under.

Smoke and silence. A great quantity of smoke.

Dawn showed faintly in the east. Among the ruins, one wall stood alone. Within   65
the wall, a last voice said, over and over again and again, even as the sun rose to shine
upon the heaped rubble and steam:

"Today is August 5, 2026, today is August 5, 2026, today is . . . ."

WILLA CATHER (1876–1947)

Paul's Case   1905

[Paul in this story wants more than his dull life can offer. He seeks attention and excitement in the world of Carnegie Hall—its music, and its glamour.
Among the music lover's favorites mentioned in the story are Giuseppe Verdi's
opera *Rigoletto* and Johann Strauss' *Blue Danube* waltz. *Auf Wiedersehen* is
German for good-bye; *hauteur* is French for a haughty attitude.]

It was Paul's afternoon to appear before the faculty of the Pittsburgh High School
to account for his various misdemeanors. He had been suspended a week ago, and his
father had called at the Principal's office and confessed his perplexity about his son.
Paul entered the faculty room suave and smiling. His clothes were a trifle out-grown,
and the tan velvet on the collar of his open overcoat was frayed and worn; but for all
that there was something of the dandy about him, and he wore an opal pin in his neatly
knotted black four-in-hand, and a red carnation in his button-hole. This latter adorn-
ment the faculty somehow felt was not properly significant of the contrite spirit befitting a boy under the ban of suspension.

Paul was tall for his age and very thin, with high, cramped shoulders and a narrow
chest. His eyes were remarkable for a certain hysterical brilliancy, and he continually
used them in a conscious, theatrical sort of way, peculiarly offensive in a boy. The
pupils were abnormally large, as though he were addicted to belladonna, but there was
a glassy glitter about them which that drug does not produce.

When questioned by the Principal as to why he was there, Paul stated, politely
enough, that he wanted to come back to school. This was a lie, but Paul was quite
accustomed to lying; found it, indeed, indispensable for overcoming friction. His
teachers were asked to state their respective charges against him, which they did
with such a rancor and aggrievedness as evinced that this was not a usual case. Disorder and impertinence were among the offenses named, yet each of his instructors
felt that it was scarcely possible to put into words the real cause of the trouble, which
lay in a sort of hysterically defiant manner of the boy's; in the contempt which they
all knew he felt for them, and which he seemingly made not the least effort to
conceal. Once, when he had been making a synopsis of a paragraph at the black-
board, his English teacher had stepped to his side and attempted to guide his
hand. Paul had started back with a shudder and thrust his hands violently behind him.
The astonished woman could scarcely have been more hurt and embarrassed had he
struck at her. The insult was so involuntary and definitely personal as to be unforgettable. In one way and another, he had made all his teachers, men and women alike,
conscious of the same feeling of physical aversion. In one class he habitually sat with his
hand shading his eyes; in another he always looked out of the window during the
recitation; in another he made a running commentary on the lecture, with humorous
intent.

His teachers felt this afternoon that his whole attitude was symbolized by his shrug and his flippantly red carnation flower, and they fell upon him without mercy, his English teacher leading the pack. He stood through it smiling, his pale lips parted over his white teeth. (His lips were continually twitching, and he had a habit of raising his eyebrows that was contemptuous and irritating to the last degree.) Older boys than Paul had broken down and shed tears under that ordeal, but his set smile did not once desert him, and his only sign of discomfort was the nervous trembling of the fingers that toyed with the buttons of his overcoat, and an occasional jerking of the other hand which held his hat. Paul was always smiling, always glancing about him, seeming to feel that people might be watching him and trying to detect something. This conscious expression, since it was as far as possible from boyish mirthfulness, was usually attributed to insolence or "smartness."

As the inquisition proceeded, one of his instructors repeated an impertinent remark of the boy's, and the Principal asked him whether he thought that a courteous speech to make to a woman. Paul shrugged his shoulders slightly and his eyebrows twitched.   5

"I don't know," he replied. "I didn't mean to be polite or impolite, either. I guess it's a sort of way I have, of saying things regardless."

The Principal asked him whether he didn't think that a way it would be well to get rid of. Paul grinned and said he guessed so. When he was told that he could go, he bowed gracefully and went out. His bow was like a repetition of the scandalous red carnation.

His teachers were in despair, and his drawing master voiced the feeling of them all when he declared there was something about the boy which none of them understood. He added: "I don't really believe that smile of his comes altogether from insolence; there's something sort of haunted about it. The boy is not strong, for one thing. There is something wrong about the fellow."

The drawing master had come to realize that, in looking at Paul, one saw only his white teeth and the forced animation of his eyes. One warm afternoon the boy had gone to sleep at his drawing-board, and his master had noted with amazement what a white, blue-veined face it was; drawn and wrinkled like an old man's about the eyes, the lips twitching even in his sleep.

His teachers left the building dissatisfied and unhappy; humiliated to have felt   10
so vindictive toward a mere boy, to have uttered this feeling in cutting terms, and to have set each other on, as it were, in the gruesome game of intemperate reproach. One of them remembered having seen a miserable street cat set at bay by a ring of tormentors.

As for Paul, he ran down the hill whistling the Soldiers' Chorus from *Faust,* looking wildly behind him now and then to see whether some of his teachers were not there to witness his lightheartedness. As it was now late in the afternoon and Paul was on duty that evening as usher at Carnegie Hall, he decided that he would not go home to supper.

When he reached the concert hall the doors were not yet open. It was chilly outside, and he decided to go up into the picture gallery—always deserted at this hour— where there were some of Raffelli's gay studies of Paris streets and an airy blue Venetian scene or two that always exhilarated him. He was delighted to find no one in the gallery but the old guard, who sat in the corner, a newspaper on his knee, a black patch over one eye and the other closed. Paul possessed himself of the place and walked confidently up and down, whistling under his breath. After a while he sat down before a blue Rico and lost himself. When he bethought him to look at his watch, it was after seven o'clock, and he rose with a start and ran downstairs, making a face at Augustus Cæsar, peering out from the cast-room, and an evil gesture at the Venus of Milo as he passed her on the stairway.

When Paul reached the ushers' dressing-room half-a-dozen boys were there already, and he began excitedly to tumble into his uniform. It was one of the few that at all approached fitting, and Paul thought it very becoming—though he knew the tight, straight coat accentuated his narrow chest, about which he was exceedingly sensitive. He was always excited while he dressed, twanging all over to the tuning of the strings and the preliminary flourishes of the horns in the music room; but tonight he seemed quite beside himself, and he teased and plagued the boys until, telling him that he was crazy, they put him down on the floor and sat on him.

Somewhat calmed by his suppression, Paul dashed out to the front of the house to seat the early comers. He was a model usher. Gracious and smiling he ran up and down the aisles. Nothing was too much trouble for him; he carried messages and brought programs as though it were his greatest pleasure in life, and all the people in his section thought him a charming boy, feeling that he remembered and admired them. As the house filled, he grew more and more vivacious and animated, and the color came to his cheeks and lips. It was very much as though this were a great reception and Paul were the host. Just as the musicians came out to take their places, his English teacher arrived with checks for the seats which a prominent manufacturer had taken for the season. She betrayed some embarrassment when she handed Paul the tickets, and a *hauteur* which subsequently made her feel very foolish. Paul was startled for a moment, and had the feeling of wanting to put her out; what business had she here among all these fine people and gay colors? He looked her over and decided that she was not appropriately dressed and must be a fool to sit downstairs in such togs. The tickets had probably been sent her out of kindness, he reflected, as he put down a seat for her, and she had about as much right to sit there as he had.

When the symphony began Paul sank into one of the rear seats with a long sigh of relief, and lost himself as he had done before the Rico. It was not that symphonies, as such, meant anything in particular to Paul, but the first sigh of the instruments seemed to free some hilarious spirit within him; something that struggled there like the Genius in the bottle found by the Arab fisherman. He felt a sudden zest of life; the lights danced before his eyes and the concert hall blazed into unimaginable splendor. When the soprano soloist came on, Paul forgot even the nastiness of his teacher's being there, and gave himself up to the peculiar intoxication such personages always had for him. The soloist chanced to be a German woman, by no means in her first youth, and the mother of many children; but she wore a satin gown and a tiara, and she had that indefinable air of achievement, that world-shine upon her, which always blinded Paul to any possible defects.

After a concert was over, Paul was often irritable and wretched until he got to sleep,—and tonight he was even more than usually restless. He had the feeling of not being able to let down; of its being impossible to give up this delicious excitement which was the only thing that could be called living at all. During the last number he withdrew and, after hastily changing his clothes in the dressing-room, slipped out to the side door where the singer's carriage stood. Here he began pacing rapidly up and down the walk, waiting to see her come out.

Over yonder the Schenley, in its vacant stretch, loomed big and square through the fine rain, the windows of its twelve stories glowing like those of a lighted cardboard house under a Christmas tree. All the actors and singers of any importance stayed there when they were in the city, and a number of the big manufacturers of the place

15

lived there in the winter. Paul had often hung about the hotel, watching the people go in and out, longing to enter and leave schoolmasters and dull care behind him for ever.

At last the singer came out, accompanied by the conductor, who helped her into her carriage and closed the door with a cordial *auf wiedersehen,*—which set Paul to wondering whether she were not an old sweetheart of his. Paul followed the carriage over to the hotel, walking so rapidly as not to be far from the entrance when the singer alighted and disappeared behind the swinging glass doors which were opened by a negro in a tall hat and a long coat. In the moment that the door was ajar, it seemed to Paul that he, too, entered. He seemed to feel himself go after her up the steps, into the warm, lighted building, into an exotic, a tropical world of shiny, glistening surfaces and basking ease. He reflected upon the mysterious dishes that were brought into the dining-room, the green bottles in buckets of ice, as he had seen them in the supper party pictures of the Sunday supplement. A quick gust of wind brought the rain down with sudden vehemence, and Paul was startled to find that he was still outside in the slush of the gravel driveway; that his boots were letting in the water and his scanty overcoat was clinging wet about him; that the lights in front of the concert hall were out, and that the rain was driving in sheets between him and the orange glow of the windows above him. There it was, what he wanted—tangibly before him, like the fairy world of a Christmas pantomime; as the rain beat in his face, Paul wondered whether he were destined always to shiver in the black night outside, looking up at it.

He turned and walked reluctantly toward the car tracks. The end had to come sometime; his father in his night-clothes at the top of the stairs, explanations that did not explain, hastily improvised fictions that were forever tripping him up, his upstairs room and its horrible yellow wallpaper, the creaking bureau with the greasy plush collarbox, and over his painted wooden bed the pictures of George Washington and John Calvin, and the framed motto, "Feed my Lambs," which had been worked in red worsted by his mother, whom Paul could not remember.

Half an hour later, Paul alighted from the Negley Avenue car and went slowly   20
down one of the side streets off the main thoroughfare. It was a highly respectable street, where all the houses were exactly alike, and where business men of moderate means begot and reared large families of children, all of whom went to Sabbath-school and learned the shorter catechism, and were interested in arithmetic; all of whom were as exactly alike as their homes, and of a piece with the monotony in which they lived. Paul never went up Cordelia Street without a shudder of loathing. His home was next the house of the Cumberland minister. He approached it tonight with the nerveless sense of defeat, the hopeless feeling of sinking back forever into ugliness and commonness that he had always had when he came home. The moment he turned into Cordelia Street he felt the waters close above his head. After each of these orgies of living, he experienced all the physical depression which follows a debauch; the loathing of respectable beds, of common food, of a house permeated by kitchen odors; a shuddering repulsion for the flavorless, colorless mass of everyday existence; a morbid desire for cool things and soft lights and fresh flowers.

The nearer he approached the house, the more absolutely unequal Paul felt to the sight of it all; his ugly sleeping chamber; the cold bathroom with the grimy zinc tub, the cracked mirror, the dripping spiggots; his father, at the top of the stairs, his hairy legs sticking out from his night-shirt, his feet thrust into carpet slippers. He was so much later than usual that there would certainly be inquiries and reproaches. Paul stopped short before the door. He felt that he could not be accosted by his father tonight; that he could not toss again on that miserable bed. He would not go in. He would tell his father that he had no carfare, and it was raining so hard he had gone home with one of the boys and stayed all night.

Meanwhile, he was wet and cold. He went around to the back of the house and tried one of the basement windows, found it open, raised it cautiously, and scrambled down the cellar wall to the floor. There he stood, holding his breath, terrified by the noise he had made; but the floor above him was silent, and there was no creak on the stairs. He found a soap-box, and carried it over to the soft ring of light that streamed from the furnace door, and sat down. He was horribly afraid of rats, so he did not try to sleep, but sat looking distrustfully at the dark, still terrified lest he might have awakened his father. In such reactions, after one of the experiences which made days and nights out of the dreary blanks of the calendar, when his senses were deadened, Paul's head was always singularly clear. Suppose his father had heard him getting in at the window and had come down and shot him for a burglar? Then, again, suppose his father had come down, pistol in hand, and he had cried out in time to save himself, and his father had been horrified to think how nearly he had killed him? Then, again, suppose a day should come when his father would remember that night, and wish there had been no warning cry to stay his hand? With this last supposition Paul entertained himself until daybreak.

The following Sunday was fine; the sodden November chill was broken by the last flash of autumnal summer. In the morning Paul had to go to church and Sabbath-school, as always. On seasonable Sunday afternoons the burghers of Cordelia Street usually sat out on their front "stoops," and talked to their neighbours on the next stoop, or called to those across the street in neighborly fashion. The men sat placidly on gay cushions placed upon the steps that led down to the sidewalk, while the women, in their Sunday "waists," sat in rockers on the cramped porches, pretending to be greatly at their ease. The children played in the streets; there were so many of them that the place resembled the recreation grounds of a kindergarten. The men on the steps—all in their shirt sleeves, their vests unbuttoned—sat with their legs well apart, their stomachs comfortably protruding, and talked of the prices of things, or told anecdotes of the sagacity of their various chiefs and overlords. They occasionally looked over the multitude of squabbling children, listened affectionately to their high-pitched, nasal voices, smiling to see their own proclivities reproduced in their offspring, and interspersed their legends of the iron kings with remarks about their sons' progress at school, their grades in arithmetic, and the amounts they had saved in their toy banks.

On this last Sunday of November, Paul sat all the afternoon on the lowest step of his "stoop," staring into the street, while his sisters, in their rockers, were talking to the minister's daughters next door about how many shirt-waists they had made in the last week, and how many waffles someone had eaten at the last church supper. When the weather was warm, and his father was in a particularly jovial frame of mind, the girls made lemonade, which was always brought out in a red-glass pitcher, ornamented with forget-me-nots in blue enamel. This the girls thought very fine, and the neighbors joked about the suspicious color of the pitcher.

Today Paul's father, on the top step, was talking to a young man who shifted a restless baby from knee to knee. He happened to be the young man who was daily held up to Paul as a model, and after whom it was his father's dearest hope that he would pattern. This young man was of a ruddy complexion, with a compressed, red mouth, and faded, near-sighted eyes, over which he wore thick spectacles, with gold bows that curved about his ears. He was clerk to one of the magnates of a great steel corporation, and was looked upon in Cordelia Street as a young man with a future. There was a story that, some five years ago—he was now barely twenty-six—he had been a trifle "dissipated," but in order to curb his appetites and save the loss of time and strength that a sowing of wild oats might have entailed, he had taken his chief's advice, oft reiterated to his employés, and at twenty-one had married the first woman whom he could

25

persuade to share his fortunes. She happened to be an angular school-mistress, much older than he, who also wore thick glasses, and who had now borne him four children, all near-sighted, like herself.

The young man was relating how his chief, now cruising in the Mediterranean, kept in touch with all the details of the business, arranging his office hours on his yacht just as though he were at home, and "knocking off work enough to keep two stenographers busy." His father told, in turn, the plan his corporation was considering, of putting in an electric railway plant at Cairo. Paul snapped his teeth; he had an awful apprehension that they might spoil it all before he got there. Yet he rather liked to hear these legends of the iron kings, that were told and retold on Sundays and holidays; these stories of palaces in Venice, yachts on the Mediterranean, and high play at Monte Carlo appealed to his fancy, and he was interested in the triumphs of cash boys who had become famous, though he had no mind for the cash-boy stage.

After supper was over, and he had helped to dry the dishes, Paul nervously asked his father whether he could go to George's to get some help in his geometry, and still more nervously asked for carfare. This latter request he had to repeat, as his father, on principle, did not like to hear requests for money, whether much or little. He asked Paul whether he could not go to some boy who lived nearer, and told him that he ought not to leave his school work until Sunday; but he gave him the dime. He was not a poor man, but he had a worthy ambition to come up in the world. His only reason for allowing Paul to usher was that he thought a boy ought to be earning a little.

Paul bounded upstairs, scrubbed the greasy odor of the dishwater from his hands with the ill-smelling soap he hated, and then shook over his fingers a few drops of violet water from the bottle he kept hidden in his drawer. He left the house with his geometry conspicuously under his arm, and the moment he got out of Cordelia Street and boarded a downtown car, he shook off the lethargy of two deadening days, and began to live again.

The leading juvenile of the permanent stock company which played at one of the downtown theatres was an acquaintance of Paul's, and the boy had been invited to drop in at the Sunday-night rehearsals whenever he could. For more than a year Paul had spent every available moment loitering about Charley Edwards's dressing-room. He had won a place among Edwards's following not only because the young actor, who could not afford to employ a dresser, often found him useful, but because he recognized in Paul something akin to what churchmen term "vocation."

It was at the theatre and at Carnegie Hall that Paul really lived; the rest was but a   30
sleep and a forgetting. This was Paul's fairy tale, and it had for him all the allurement of a secret love. The moment he inhaled the gassy, painty, dusty odor behind the scenes, he breathed like a prisoner set free, and felt within him the possibility of doing or saying splendid, brilliant things. The moment the cracked orchestra beat out the overture from *Martha*, or jerked at the serenade from *Rigoletto*, all stupid and ugly things slid from him, and his senses were deliciously, yet delicately fired.

Perhaps it was because, in Paul's world, the natural nearly always wore the guise of ugliness, that a certain element of artificiality seemed to him necessary in beauty. Perhaps it was because his experience of life elsewhere was so full of Sabbath-school picnics, petty economies, wholesome advice as to how to succeed in life, and the unescapable odors of cooking, that he found this existence so alluring, these smartly-clad men and women so attractive, that he was so moved by these starry apple orchards that bloomed perennially under the lime-light.

It would be difficult to put it strongly enough how convincingly the stage entrance of that theatre was for Paul the actual portal of Romance. Certainly none of the company ever suspected it, least of all Charley Edwards. It was very like the old stories that used to float about London of fabulously rich Jews, who had subterranean halls, with palms, and fountains, and soft lamps and richly apparelled women who never saw the disenchanting light of London day. So, in the midst of that smoke-palled city, enamored of figures and grimy toil, Paul had his secret temple, his wishing-carpet, his bit of blue-and-white Mediterranean shore bathed in perpetual sunshine.

Several of Paul's teachers had a theory that his imagination had been perverted by garish fiction; but the truth was, he scarcely ever read at all. The books at home were not such as would either tempt or corrupt a youthful mind, and as for reading the novels that some of his friends urged upon him—well, he got what he wanted much more quickly from music; any sort of music, from an orchestra to a barrel organ. He needed only the spark, the indescribable thrill that made his imagination master of his senses, and he could make plots and pictures enough of his own. It was equally true that he was not stage-struck—not, at any rate, in the usual acceptation of that expression. He had no desire to become an actor, any more than he had to become a musician. He felt no necessity to do any of these things; what he wanted was to see, to be in the atmosphere, float on the wave of it, to be carried out, blue league after blue league, away from everything.

After a night behind the scenes, Paul found the school-room more than ever repulsive; the bare floors and naked walls; the prosy men who never wore frock coats, or violets in their button-holes; the women with their dull gowns, shrill voices, and pitiful seriousness about prepositions that govern the dative. He could not bear to have the other pupils think, for a moment, that he took these people seriously; he must convey to them that he considered it all trivial, and was there only by way of a joke, anyway. He had autograph pictures of all the members of the stock company which he showed his classmates, telling them the most incredible stories of his familiarity with these people, of his acquaintance with the soloists who came to Carnegie Hall, his suppers with them and the flowers he sent them. When these stories lost their effect, and his audience grew listless, he would bid all the boys good-bye, announcing that he was going to travel for awhile; going to Naples, to California, to Egypt. Then, next Monday, he would slip back, conscious and nervously smiling; his sister was ill, and he would have to defer his voyage until spring.

Matters went steadily worse with Paul at school. In the itch to let his instructors know how heartily he despised them, and how thoroughly he was appreciated elsewhere, he mentioned once or twice that he had no time to fool with theorems; adding—with a twitch of the eyebrows and a touch of that nervous bravado which so perplexed them—that he was helping the people down at the stock company; they were old friends of his.

The upshot of the matter was, that the Principal went to Paul's father, and Paul was taken out of school and put to work. The manager at Carnegie Hall was told to get another usher in his stead; the doorkeeper at the theatre was warned not to admit him to the house; and Charley Edwards remorsefully promised the boy's father not to see him again.

The members of the stock company were vastly amused when some of Paul's stories reached them—especially the women. They were hard-working women, most of them supporting indolent husbands or brothers, and they laughed rather bitterly at having stirred the boy to such fervid and florid inventions. They agreed with the faculty and with his father, that Paul's was a bad case.

The east-bound train was plowing through a January snowstorm; the dull dawn was beginning to show grey when the engine whistled a mile out of Newark. Paul started up from the seat where he had lain curled in uneasy slumber, rubbed the breath-misted window glass with his hand, and peered out. The snow was whirling in curling eddies above the white bottom lands, and the drifts lay already deep in the fields and along the fences, while here and there the long dead grass and dried weed stalks protruded black above it. Lights shone from the scattered houses, and a gang of laborers who stood beside the track waved their lanterns.

Paul had slept very little, and he felt grimy and uncomfortable. He had made the all-night journey in a day coach because he was afraid if he took a Pullman he might be seen by some Pittsburgh business man who had noticed him in Denny & Carson's office. When the whistle woke him, he clutched quickly at his breast pocket, glancing about him with an uncertain smile. But the little, clay-bespattered Italians were still sleeping, the slatternly women across the aisle were in open-mouthed oblivion, and even the crumby, crying babies were for the nonce stilled. Paul settled back to struggle with his impatience as best he could.

When he arrived at the Jersey City station, he hurried through his breakfast, manifestly ill at ease and keeping a sharp eye about him. After he reached the Twenty-third Street station, he consulted a cabman, and had himself driven to a men's furnishing establishment which was just opening for the day. He spent upward of two hours there, buying with endless reconsidering and great care. His new street suit he put on in the fitting-room; the frock coat and dress clothes he had bundled into the cab with his new shirts. Then he drove to a hatter's and a shoe house. His next errand was at Tiffany's, where he selected silver mounted brushes and a scarf-pin. He would not wait to have his silver marked, he said. Lastly, he stopped at a trunk shop on Broadway, and had his purchases packed into various travelling bags. 40

It was a little after one o'clock when he drove up to the Waldorf, and, after settling with the cabman, went into the office. He registered from Washington; said his mother and father had been abroad, and that he had come down to await the arrival of their steamer. He told his story plausibly and had no trouble, since he offered to pay for them in advance, in engaging his rooms; a sleeping-room, sitting-room and bath.

Not once, but a hundred times Paul had planned this entry into New York. He had gone over every detail of it with Charley Edwards, and in his scrap book at home there were pages of description about New York hotels, cut from the Sunday papers.

When he was shown to his sitting-room on the eighth floor, he saw at a glance that everything was as it should be; there was but one detail in his mental picture that the place did not realize, so he rang for the bell boy and sent him down for flowers. He moved about nervously until the boy returned, putting away his new linen and fingering it delightedly as he did so. When the flowers came, he put them hastily into water, and then tumbled into a hot bath. Presently he came out of his white bath-room, resplendent in his new silk underwear, and playing with the tassels of his red robe. The snow was whirling so fiercely outside his windows that he could scarcely see across the street; but within, the air was deliciously soft and fragrant. He put the violets and jonquils on the tabouret beside the couch, and threw himself down with a long sigh, covering himself with a Roman blanket. He was thoroughly tired; he had been in such haste, he had stood up to such a strain, covered so much ground in the last twenty-four hours, that he wanted to think how it had all come about. Lulled by the sound of the wind, the warm air, and the cool fragrance of the flowers, he sank into deep, drowsy retrospection.

It had been wonderfully simple; when they had shut him out of the theatre and concert hall, when they had taken away his bone, the whole thing was virtually determined. The rest was a mere matter of opportunity. The only thing that at all surprised him was his own courage—for he realized well enough that he had always been tormented by fear, a sort of apprehensive dread that, of late years, as the meshes of the lies he had told closed about him, had been pulling the muscles of his body tighter and tighter. Until now, he could not remember a time when he had not been dreading something. Even when he was a little boy, it was always there—behind him, or before, or on either side. There had always been the shadowed corner, the dark place into which he dared not look, but from which something seemed always to be watching him—and Paul had done things that were not pretty to watch, he knew.

But now he had a curious sense of relief, as though he had at last thrown down the gauntlet to the thing in the corner.   45

Yet it was but a day since he had been sulking in the traces; but yesterday afternoon that he had been sent to the bank with Denny & Carson's deposit as usual—but this time he was instructed to leave the book to be balanced. There was above two thousand dollars in checks, and nearly a thousand in the bank notes which he had taken from the book and quietly transferred to his pocket. At the bank he had made out a new deposit slip. His nerves had been steady enough to permit of his returning to the office, where he had finished his work and asked for a full day's holiday tomorrow, Saturday, giving a perfectly reasonable pretext. The bank book, he knew, would not be returned before Monday or Tuesday, and his father would be out of town for the next week. From the time he slipped the bank notes into his pocket until he boarded the night train for New York, he had not known a moment's hesitation.

How astonishingly easy it had all been; here he was, the thing done; and this time there would be no awakening, no figure at the top of the stairs. He watched the snow flakes whirling by his window until he fell asleep.

When he awoke, it was four o'clock in the afternoon. He bounded up with a start; one of his precious days gone already! He spent nearly an hour in dressing, watching every stage of his toilet carefully in the mirror. Everything was quite perfect; he was exactly the kind of boy he had always wanted to be.

When he went downstairs, Paul took a carriage and drove up Fifth Avenue toward the Park. The snow had somewhat abated; carriages and tradesmen's wagons were hurrying soundlessly to and fro in the winter twilight; boys in woollen mufflers were shovelling off the doorsteps; the avenue stages made fine spots of color against the white street. Here and there on the corners whole flower gardens blooming behind glass windows, against which the snow flakes stuck and melted; violets, roses, carnations, lilies of the valley—somehow vastly more lovely and alluring that they blossomed thus unnaturally in the snow. The Park itself was a wonderful stage winter-piece.

When he returned, the pause of the twilight had ceased, and the tune of the streets   50 had changed. The snow was falling faster, lights streamed from the hotels that reared their many stories fearlessly up into the storm, defying the raging Atlantic winds. A long, black stream of carriages poured down the avenue, intersected here and there by other streams, tending horizontally. There were a score of cabs about the entrance of his hotel, and his driver had to wait. Boys in livery were running in and out of the awning stretched across the sidewalk, up and down the red velvet carpet laid from the door to the street. Above, about, within it all, was the rumble and roar, the hurry and toss of thousands of human beings as hot for pleasure as himself, and on every side of him towered the glaring affirmation of the omnipotence of wealth.

The boy set his teeth and drew his shoulders together in a spasm of realization; the plot of all dramas, the text of all romances, the nerve-stuff of all sensations was whirling about him like the snow flakes. He burnt like a faggot in a tempest.

When Paul came down to dinner, the music of the orchestra floated up the elevator shaft to greet him. As he stepped into the thronged corridor, he sank back into one of the chairs against the wall to get his breath. The lights, the chatter, the perfumes, the bewildering medley of color—he had, for a moment, the feeling of not being able to stand it. But only for a moment; these were his own people, he told himself. He went slowly about the corridors, through the writing-rooms, smoking-rooms, reception-rooms, as though he were exploring the chambers of an enchanted palace, built and peopled for him alone.

When he reached the dining-room he sat down at a table near a window. The flowers, the white linen, the many-colored wine glasses, the gay toilettes of the women, the low popping of corks, the undulating repetitions of the *Blue Danube* from the orchestra, all flooded Paul's dream with bewildering radiance. When the roseate tinge of his champagne was added—that cold, precious, bubbling stuff that creamed and foamed in his glass—Paul wondered that there were honest men in the world at all. This was what all the world was fighting for, he reflected; this was what all the struggle was about. He doubted the reality of his past. Had he ever known a place called Cordelia Street, a place where fagged looking business men boarded the early car? Mere rivets in a machine they seemed to Paul,—sickening men, with combings of children's hair always hanging to their coats, and the smell of cooking in their clothes. Cordelia Street—Ah, that belonged to another time and country! Had he not always been thus, had he not sat here night after night, from as far back as he could remember, looking pensively over just such shimmering textures, and slowly twirling the stem of a glass like this one between his thumb and middle finger? He rather thought he had.

He was not in the least abashed or lonely. He had no especial desire to meet or to know any of these people; all he demanded was the right to look on and conjecture, to watch the pageant. The mere stage properties were all he contended for. Nor was he lonely later in the evening, in his loge at the Opera. He was entirely rid of his nervous misgivings, of his forced aggressiveness, of the imperative desire to show himself different from his surroundings. He felt now that his surroundings explained him. Nobody questioned the purple; he had only to wear it passively. He had only to glance down at his dress coat to reassure himself that here it would be impossible for anyone to humiliate him.

He found it hard to leave his beautiful sitting-room to go to bed that night, and sat long watching the raging storm from his turret window. When he went to sleep, it was with the lights turned on in his bedroom; partly because of his old timidity, and partly so that, if he should wake in the night, there would be no wretched moment of doubt, no horrible suspicion of yellow wall-paper, or of Washington and Calvin above his bed.   55

On Sunday morning the city was practically snow-bound. Paul breakfasted late, and in the afternoon he fell in with a wild San Francisco boy, a freshman at Yale, who said he had run down for a "little flyer" over Sunday. The young man offered to show Paul the night side of the town, and the two boys went off together after dinner, not returning to the hotel until seven o'clock the next morning. They had started out in the confiding warmth of a champagne friendship, but their parting in the elevator was singularly cool. The freshman pulled himself together to make his train, and Paul went to bed. He awoke at two o'clock in the afternoon, very thirsty and dizzy, and rang for ice-water, coffee, and the Pittsburgh papers.

On the part of the hotel management, Paul excited no suspicion. There was this to be said for him, that he wore his spoils with dignity and in no way made himself conspicuous. His chief greediness lay in his ears and eyes, and his excesses were not offensive ones. His dearest pleasures were the grey winter twilights in his sitting-room; his quiet enjoyment of his flowers, his clothes, his wide divan, his cigarette and his sense of power. He could not remember a time when he had felt so at peace with himself. The mere release from the necessity of petty lying, lying every day and every day, restored

his self-respect. He had never lied for pleasure, even at school; but to make himself noticed and admired, to assert his difference from other Cordelia Street boys; and he felt a
good deal more manly, more honest, even, now that he had no need for boastful pre-
tensions, now that he could, as his actor friends used to say, "dress the part." It was
characteristic that remorse did not occur to him. His golden days went by without a
shadow, and he made each as perfect as he could.

On the eighth day after his arrival in New York, he found the whole affair exploited in the Pittsburgh papers, exploited with a wealth of detail which indicated that local
news of a sensational nature was at a low ebb. The firm of Denny & Carson announced
that the boy's father had refunded the full amount of his theft, and that they had no intention of prosecuting. The Cumberland minister had been interviewed, and expressed
his hope of yet reclaiming the motherless lad, and Paul's Sabbath-school teacher declared that she would spare no effort to that end. The rumor had reached Pittsburgh
that the boy had been seen in a New York hotel, and his father had gone East to find
him and bring him home.

Paul had just come in to dress for dinner; he sank into a chair, weak in the knees,
and clasped his head in his hands. It was to be worse than jail, even; the tepid waters of
Cordelia Street were to close over him finally and forever. The gray monotony
stretched before him in hopeless, unrelieved years; Sabbath-school, Young People's
Meeting, the yellow-papered room, the damp dish-towels; it all rushed back upon him
with sickening vividness. He had the old feeling that the orchestra had suddenly
stopped, the sinking sensation that the play was over. The sweat broke out on his face,
and he sprang to his feet, looked about him with his white, conscious smile, and
winked at himself in the mirror. With something of the childish belief in miracles with
which he had so often gone to class, all his lessons unlearned, Paul dressed and dashed
whistling down the corridor to the elevator.

He had no sooner entered the dining-room and caught the measure of the music,   60
than his remembrance was lightened by his old elastic power of claiming the moment,
mounting with it, and finding it all sufficient. The glare and glitter about him, the mere
scenic accessories had again, and for the last time, their old potency. He would show
himself that he was game, he would finish the thing splendidly. He doubted, more than
ever, the existence of Cordelia Street, and for the first time he drank his wine recklessly.
Was he not, after all, one of these fortunate beings? Was he not still himself, and in his
own place? He drummed a nervous accompaniment to the music and looked about
him, telling himself over and over that it had paid.

He reflected drowsily, to the swell of the violin and the chill sweetness of his wine,
that he might have done it more wisely. He might have caught an outbound steamer
and been well out of their clutches before now. But the other side of the world had
seemed too far away and too uncertain then; he could not have waited for it; his need
had been too sharp. If he had to choose over again, he would do the same thing tomorrow. He looked affectionately about the dining-room, now gilded with a soft mist.
Ah, it had paid indeed!

Paul was awakened next morning by a painful throbbing in his head and feet. He
had thrown himself across the bed without undressing, and had slept with his shoes on.
His limbs and hands were lead heavy, and his tongue and throat were parched. There
came upon him one of those fateful attacks of clear-headedness that never occurred except when he was physically exhausted and his nerves hung loose. He lay still and
closed his eyes and let the tide of realities wash over him.

His father was in New York; "stopping at some joint or other," he told himself.
The memory of successive summers on the front stoop fell upon him like a weight of
black water. He had not a hundred dollars left; and he knew now, more than ever, that

money was everything, the wall that stood between all he loathed and all he wanted. The thing was winding itself up; he had thought of that on his first glorious day in New York, and had even provided a way to snap the thread. It lay on his dressing-table now; he had got it out last night when he came blindly up from dinner,—but the shiny metal hurt his eyes, and he disliked the look of it, anyway.

He rose and moved about with a painful effort, succumbing now and again to attacks of nausea. It was the old depression exaggerated; all the world had become Cordelia Street. Yet somehow he was not afraid of anything, was absolutely calm; perhaps because he had looked into the dark corner at last, and knew. It was bad enough, what he saw there; but somehow not so bad as his long fear of it had been. He saw everything clearly now. He had a feeling that he had made the best of it, that he had lived the sort of life he was meant to live, and for half an hour he sat staring at the revolver. But he told himself that was not the way, so he went downstairs and took a cab to the ferry.

When Paul arrived at Newark, he got off the train and took another cab, directing the driver to follow the Pennsylvania tracks out of the town. The snow lay heavy on the roadways and had drifted deep in the open fields. Only here and there the dead grass or dried weed stalks projected, singularly black, above it. Once well into the country, Paul dismissed the carriage and walked, floundering along the tracks, his mind a medley of irrelevant things. He seemed to hold in his brain an actual picture of everything he had seen that morning. He remembered every feature of both his drivers, the toothless old woman from whom he had bought the red flowers in his coat, the agent from whom he had got his ticket, and all of his fellow-passengers on the ferry. His mind, unable to cope with vital matters near at hand, worked feverishly and deftly at sorting and grouping these images. They made for him a part of the ugliness of the world, of the ache in his head, and the bitter burning on his tongue. He stooped and put a handful of snow into his mouth as he walked, but that, too, seemed hot. When he reached a little hillside, where the tracks ran through a cut some twenty feet below him, he stopped and sat down.

The carnations in his coat were drooping with the cold, he noticed; all their red glory over. It occurred to him that all the flowers he had seen in the show windows that first night must have gone the same way, long before this. It was only one splendid breath they had, in spite of their brave mockery at the winter outside the glass. It was a losing game in the end, it seemed, this revolt against the homilies by which the world is run. Paul took one of the blossoms carefully from his coat and scooped a little hole in the snow, where he covered it up. Then he dozed a while, from his weak condition, seeming insensible to the cold.

The sound of an approaching train woke him, and he started to his feet, remembering only his resolution, and afraid lest he should be too late. He stood watching the approaching locomotive, his teeth chattering, his lips drawn away from them in a frightened smile; once or twice he glanced nervously sidewise, as though he were being watched. When the right moment came, he jumped. As he fell, the folly of his haste occurred to him with merciless clearness, the vastness of what he had left undone. There flashed through his brain, clearer than ever before, the blue of Adriatic water, the yellow of Algerian sands.

He felt something strike his chest,—his body was being thrown swiftly through the air, on and on, immeasurably far and fast, while his limbs gently relaxed. Then, because the picture making mechanism was crushed, the disturbing visions flashed into black, and Paul dropped back into the immense design of things.

ANTON CHEKHOV (1860–1904)
Gooseberries 1898

[Chekhov was not only a writer but also a medical doctor, exercising a profession that allowed him to learn much about every class of Russian society. In this story within a story, the storyteller wants us to understand something about the difference between happiness and a purpose in life. Gooseberries, the symbol around which the story revolves, are small, sour fruits which grow on prickly shrubs in unfavorable soil. Other words and references are *winnowing*—a process which separates chaff from grain, *gubernia*—a province, *Zemstvo*—the elected council charged with the local administration of a province, and Alexander Pushkin (1799–1837)—a Russian poet, short story writer, and dramatist.]

The sky had been covered with rain-clouds ever since the early morning, it was a still day, cool and dull, one of those misty days when the clouds have long been lowering overhead and you keep thinking it is just going to rain, and the rain holds off. Ivan Ivanich, the veterinary surgeon, and Burkin, the high-school teacher, had walked till they were tired, and the way over the fields seemed endless to them. Far ahead they could just make out the windmill of the village of Mironositskoye, and what looked like a range of low hills at the right extending well beyond the village, and they both knew that this range was really the bank of the river, and that further on were meadows, green willow-trees, country-estates; if they were on top of these hills, they knew they would see the same boundless fields and telegraph-posts, and the train, like a crawling caterpillar in the distance, while in fine weather even the town would be visible. On this still day, when the whole of nature seemed kindly and pensive, Ivan Ivanich and Burkin felt a surge of love for this plain, and thought how vast and beautiful their country was.

"The last time we stayed in Elder Prokofy's hut," said Burkin, "you said you had a story to tell me."

"Yes. I wanted to tell you the story of my brother."

Ivan Ivanich took a deep breath and lighted his pipe as a preliminary to his narrative, but just then the rain came. Five minutes later it was coming down in torrents and nobody could say when it would stop. Ivan Ivanich and Burkin stood still, lost in thought. The dogs, already soaked, stood with drooping tails, gazing at them wistfully.

"We must try and find shelter," said Burkin. "Let's go to Alekhin's. It's quite near." 5

"Come on, then."

They turned aside and walked straight across the newly reaped field, veering to the right till they came to a road. Very soon poplars, an orchard, and the red roofs of barns came into sight. The surface of a river gleamed, and they had a view of an extensive reach of water, a windmill and a whitewashed bathing-shed. This was Sofyino, where Alekhin lived.

The mill was working, and the noise made by its sails drowned the sound of the rain; the whole dam trembled. Horses, soaking wet, were standing near some carts, their heads drooping, and people were moving about with sacks over their heads and shoulders. It was wet, muddy, bleak, and the water looked cold and sinister. Ivan Ivanich and Burkin were already experiencing the misery of dampness, dirt, physical discomfort, their boots were caked with mud, and when, having passed the mill-dam, they took the upward path to the landowner's barns, they fell silent, as if vexed with one another.

The sound of winnowing came from one of the barns; the door was open, and clouds of dust issued from it. Standing in the doorway was Alekhin himself, a stout man of some forty years, with longish hair, looking more like a professor or an artist than a landed proprietor. He was wearing a white shirt, greatly in need of washing, belted with a piece of string, and long drawers with no trousers over them. His boots, too, were caked with mud and straw. His eyes and nose were ringed with dust. He recognized Ivan Ivanich and Burkin, and seemed glad to see them.

"Go up to the house, gentlemen," he said, smiling. "I'll be with you in a minute."   10

It was a large two-story house. Alekhin occupied the ground floor, two rooms with vaulted ceilings and tiny windows, where the stewards had lived formerly. They were poorly furnished, and smelled of rye-bread, cheap vodka, and harness. He hardly ever went into the upstairs rooms, excepting when he had guests. Ivan Ivanich and Burkin were met by a maid-servant, a young woman of such beauty that they stood still involuntarily and exchanged glances.

"You have no idea how glad I am to see you here, dear friends," said Alekhin, overtaking them in the hall. "It's quite a surprise! Pelageya," he said, turning to the maid, "find the gentlemen a change of clothes. And I might as well change, myself. But I must have a wash first, for I don't believe I've had a bath since the spring. Wouldn't you like to go and have a bathe while they get things ready here?"

The beauteous Pelageya, looking very soft and delicate, brought them towels and soap, and Alekhin and his guests set off for the bathing-house.

"Yes, it's a long time since I had a wash," he said, taking off his clothes. "As you see I have a nice bathing-place, my father had it built, but somehow I never seem to get time to wash."

He sat on the step, soaping his long locks and his neck, and all round him the   15 water was brown.

"Yes, you certainly . . ." remarked Ivan Ivanich, with a significant glance at his host's head.

"It's a long time since I had a wash . . ." repeated Alekhin, somewhat abashed, and he soaped himself again, and now the water was dark-blue, like ink.

Ivan Ivanich emerged from the shed, splashed noisily into the water, and began swimming beneath the rain, spreading his arms wide, making waves all round him, and the white water-lilies rocked on the waves he made. He swam into the very middle of the river and then dived, a moment later came up at another place and swam further, diving constantly, and trying to touch the bottom. "Ah, my God," he kept exclaiming in his enjoyment. "Ah, my God. . . ." He swam up to the mill, had a little talk with some peasants there and turned back, but when he got to the middle of the river, he floated, holding his face up to the rain. Burkin and Alekhin were dressed and ready to go, but he went on swimming and diving.

"God! God!" he kept exclaiming. "Dear God!"

"Come out!" Burkin shouted to him.   20

They went back to the house. And only after the lamp was lit in the great drawing-room on the upper floor, and Burkin and Ivan Ivanich, in silk dressing-gowns and warm slippers, were seated in arm-chairs, while Alekhin, washed and combed, paced the room in his new frock-coat, enjoying the warmth, the cleanliness, his dry clothes and comfortable slippers, while the fair Pelageya, smiling benevolently, stepped noiselessly over the carpet with her tray of tea and preserves, did Ivan Ivanich embark upon his yarn, the ancient dames, young ladies, and military gentlemen looking down at them severely from the gilded frames, as if they, too, were listening.

"There were two of us brothers," he began. "Ivan Ivanich (me), and my brother Nikolai Ivanich, two years younger than myself. I went in for learning and became a veterinary surgeon, but Nikolai started working in a government office when he was only nineteen. Our father, Chimsha-Himalaisky, was educated in a school for the sons of private soldiers, but was later promoted to officer's rank, and was made a hereditary nobleman and given a small estate. After his death the estate had to be sold for debts, but at least our childhood was passed in the freedom of the country-side, where we roamed the fields and the woods like peasant children, taking the horses to graze, peeling bark from the trunks of lime-trees, fishing, and all that sort of thing. And anyone who has once in his life fished for perch, or watched the thrushes fly south in the autumn, rising high over the village on clear, cool days, is spoilt for town life, and will long for the country-side for the rest of his days. My brother pined in his government office. The years passed and he sat in the same place every day, writing out the same documents and thinking all the time of the same thing—how to get back to the country. And these longings of his gradually turned into a definite desire, into a dream of purchasing a little estate somewhere on the bank of a river or the shore of a lake.

"He was a meek, good-natured chap, I was fond of him, but could feel no sympathy with the desire to lock oneself up for life in an estate of one's own. They say man only needs six feet of earth. But it is a corpse, and not man, which needs these six feet. And now people are actually saying that it is a good sign for our intellectuals to yearn for the land and try to obtain country-dwellings. And yet these estates are nothing but those same six feet of earth. To escape from the town, from the struggle, from the noise of life, to escape and hide one's head on a country-estate, is not life, but egoism, idleness, it is a sort of renunciation, but renunciation without faith. It is not six feet of earth, not a country-estate, that man needs, but the whole globe, the whole of nature, room to display his qualities and the individual characteristics of his soul.

"My brother Nikolai sat at his office-desk, dreaming of eating soup made from his own cabbages, which would spread a delicious smell all over his own yard, of eating out of doors, on the green grass, of sleeping in the sun, sitting for hours on a bench outside his gate, and gazing at the fields and woods. Books on agriculture, and all those hints printed on calendars were his delight, his favorite spiritual nourishment. He was fond of reading newspapers, too, but all he read in them was advertisements of the sale of so many acres of arable and meadowland, with residence attached, a river, an orchard, a mill, and ponds fed by springs. His head was full of visions of garden paths, flowers, fruit, nesting-boxes, carp-ponds, and all that sort of thing. These visions differed according to the advertisements he came across, but for some reason gooseberry bushes invariably figured in them. He could not picture to himself a single estate or picturesque nook that did not have gooseberry bushes in it.

"'Country life has its conveniences,' he would say. 'You sit on the verandah, drinking tea, with your own ducks floating on the pond, and everything smells so nice, and . . . and the gooseberries ripen on the bushes.'

"He drew up plans for his estate, and every plan showed the same features: a) the main residence, b) the servant's wing, c) the kitchen-garden, d) gooseberry bushes. He lived thriftily, never ate or drank his fill, dressed anyhow, like a beggar, and saved up all his money in the bank. He became terribly stingy. I could hardly bear to look at him, and whenever I gave him a little money, or sent him a present on some holiday, he put that away, too. Once a man gets an idea into his head, there's no doing anything with him.

"The years passed, he was sent to another gubernia, he was over forty, and was still reading advertisements in the papers, and saving up. At last I heard he had married. All for the same purpose, to buy himself an estate with gooseberry bushes on it, he married an ugly elderly widow, for whom he had not the slightest affection, just because she had some money. After his marriage he went on living as thriftily as ever, half-starving his wife, and putting her money in his own bank account. Her first husband had been a postmaster, and she was used to pies and cordials, but with her second husband she did not even get enough black bread to eat. She began to languish under such a regime, and three years later yielded up her soul to God. Of course my brother did not for a moment consider himself guilty of her death. Money, like vodka, makes a man eccentric. There was a merchant in our town who asked for a plate of honey on his deathbed and ate up all his bank-notes and lottery tickets with the honey, so that no one else should get it. And one day when I was examining a consignment of cattle at a railway station, a drover fell under the engine and his leg was severed from his body. We carried him all bloody into the waiting-room, a terrible sight, and he did nothing but beg us to look for his leg, worrying all the time—there were twenty rubles in the boot, and he was afraid they would be lost."

"You're losing the thread," put in Burkin.

Ivan Ivanich paused for a moment, and went on: "After his wife's death my brother began to look about for an estate. You can search for five years, of course, and in the end make a mistake and buy something quite different from what you dreamed of. My brother Nikolai bought three hundred acres, complete with gentleman's house, servants' quarters, and a park, as well as a mortgage to be paid through an agent, but there were neither an orchard, gooseberry bushes, nor a pond with ducks on it. There was a river, but it was as dark as coffee, owing to the fact that there was a brick-works on one side of the estate, and bone-kilns on the other. Nothing daunted, however, my brother Nikolai Ivanich ordered two dozen gooseberry bushes and settled down as a landed proprietor.

"Last year I paid him a visit. I thought I would go and see how he was getting on   30 there. In his letters my brother gave his address as Chumbaroklova Pustosh or Himalaiskoye. I arrived at Himalaiskoye in the afternoon. It was very hot. Everywhere were ditches, fences, hedges, rows of fir-trees, and it was hard to drive into the yard and find a place to leave one's carriage. As I went a fat ginger-colored dog, remarkably like a pig, came out to meet me. It looked as if it would have barked if it were not so lazy. The cook, who was also fat and like a pig, came out of the kitchen, barefoot, and said her master was having his after-dinner rest. I made my way to my brother's room, and found him sitting up in bed, his knees covered by a blanket. He had aged, and grown stout and flabby. His cheeks, nose and lips protruded—I almost expected him to grunt into the blanket.

"We embraced and wept—tears of joy, mingled with melancholy—because we had once been young and were now both grey-haired and approaching the grave. He put on his clothes and went out to show me over his estate.

"'Well, how are you getting on here?' I asked.

"'All right, thanks be, I'm enjoying myself.'"

"He was no longer the poor, timid clerk, but a true proprietor, a gentleman. He had settled down, and was entering with zest into country life. He ate a lot, washed in the bath-house, and put on flesh. He had already got into litigation with the village commune, the brick-works and the bone-kilns, and took offence if the peasants failed to call him 'Your Honor.' He went in for religion in a solid, gentlemanly way, and there was nothing casual about his pretentious good works. And what were these good works? He treated all the diseases of the peasants with bicarbonate of soda and castor-oil, and had a special thanksgiving service held on his name-day, after which he provided half a pail of vodka, supposing that this was the right thing to do. Oh, those terrible half pails! Today the fat landlord hauls the peasants before the Zemstvo representative for letting their sheep graze on his land, tomorrow, on the day of rejoicing, he treats them to half a pail of vodka, and they drink and sing and shout hurrah, prostrating themselves before him when they are drunk. Any improvement in his conditions, anything like satiety or idleness, develops the most insolent complacency in a Russian. Nikolai Ivanich, who had been afraid of having an opinion of his own when he was in the government service, was now continually coming out with axioms, in the most ministerial manner: 'Education is essential, but the people are not ready for it yet,' 'corporal punishment is an evil, but in certain cases it is beneficial and indispensable.'

"'I know the people and I know how to treat them,' he said. 'The people love me. I only have to lift my little finger, and the people will do whatever I want.' 35

"And all this, mark you, with a wise, indulgent smile. Over and over again he repeated: 'We the gentry,' or 'speaking as a gentleman,' and seemed to have quite forgotten that our grandfather was a peasant, and our father a common soldier. Our very surname—Chimsha-Himalaisky—in reality so absurd, now seemed to him a resounding, distinguished, and euphonious name.

"But it is of myself, and not of him, that I wish to speak. I should like to describe to you the change which came over me in those few hours I spent on my brother's estate. As we were drinking tea in the evening, the cook brought us a full plate of gooseberries. These were not gooseberries bought for money, they came from his own garden, and were the first fruits of the bushes he had planted. Nikolai Ivanich broke into a laugh and gazed at the gooseberries, in tearful silence for at least five minutes. Speechless with emotion, he popped a single gooseberry into his mouth, darted at me the triumphant glance of a child who has at last gained possession of a longed-for toy, and said:

"'Delicious!'

"And he ate them greedily, repeating over and over again:

"'Simply delicious! You try them.' 40

"They were hard and sour, but, as Pushkin says: 'The lie which elates us is dearer than a thousand sober truths.' I saw before me a really happy man, one whose dearest wish had come true, who had achieved his aim in life, got what he wanted, and was content with his lot and with himself. There had always been a tinge of melancholy in my conception of human happiness, and now, confronted by a happy man, I was overcome by a feeling of sadness bordering on desperation. This feeling grew strongest of all in the night. A bed was made up for me in the room next to my brother's bedroom, and I could hear him moving about restlessly, every now and then getting up to take a gooseberry from a plate. How many happy, satisfied people there are, after all, I said to myself! What an overwhelming force! Just consider this life—the insolence and idleness of the strong, the ignorance and bestiality of the weak, all around intolerable poverty, cramped dwellings, degeneracy, drunkenness, hypocrisy, lying. . . . And yet peace and order apparently prevail in all those homes and in the streets. Of the fifty thousand inhabitants of a town, not one will be found to cry out, to proclaim his indignation aloud. We see those who go to the market to buy food, who eat in the day-time and sleep at night, who prattle away, marry, grow old, carry their dead to the cemeteries. But we neither hear nor see those who suffer, and the terrible things in life are played out behind the scenes. All is calm and quiet, only statistics, which are dumb, protest: so many have gone mad, so many barrels of drink have been consumed, so many children died of malnutrition. . . . And apparently this is as it should be. Apparently those who are happy can only enjoy themselves because the unhappy bear their burdens in silence, and but for this silence happiness would be impossible. It is a kind of universal hypnosis. There ought to be a man with a hammer behind the door of every happy man, to remind him by his constant knocks that there are unhappy people, and that happy as he himself may be, life will sooner or later show him its claws, catastrophe will overtake him—sickness, poverty, loss—and nobody will see it, just as he now neither sees nor hears the misfortunes of others. But there is no man with a hammer, the happy man goes on living and the petty vicissitudes of life touch him lightly, like the wind in an aspen-tree, and all is well.

"That night I understood that I, too, was happy and content," continued Ivan Ivanich, getting up. "I, too, while out hunting, or at the dinner table, have held forth on the right way to live, to worship, to manage the people. I, too, have declared that without knowledge there can be no light, that education is essential, but that bare literacy is sufficient for the common people. Freedom is a blessing, I have said, one can't get on without it, any more than without air, but we must wait. Yes, that is what I said, and now I ask: In the name of what must we wait?" Here Ivan Ivanich looked angrily at Burkin. "In the name of what must we wait, I ask you. What is there to be considered? Don't be in such a hurry, they tell me, every idea materializes gradually, in its own time. But who are they who say this? What is the proof that it is just? You refer to the natural order of things, to the logic of facts, but according to what order, what logic do I, a living, thinking individual, stand on the edge of a ditch and wait for it to be gradually filled up, or choked with silt, when I might leap across it or build a bridge over it? And again, in the name of what must we wait? Wait, when we have not the strength to live, though live we must and to live we desire!

"I left my brother early the next morning, and ever since I have found town life intolerable. The peace and order weigh on my spirits, and I am afraid to look into windows, because there is now no sadder spectacle for me than a happy family seated around the tea-table. I am old and unfit for the struggle, I am even incapable of feeling hatred. I can only suffer inwardly, and give way to irritation and annoyance, at night my head burns from the rush of thoughts, and I am unable to sleep. . . . Oh, if only I were young!"

Ivan Ivanich began pacing backwards and forwards, repeating:

"If only I were young still!"   45

Suddenly he went up to Alekhin and began pressing first one of his hands, and then the other.

"Pavel Konstantinich," he said in imploring accents. "Don't *you* fall into apathy, don't *you* let your conscience be lulled to sleep! While you are still young, strong, active, do not be weary of well-doing. There is no such thing as happiness, nor ought there to be, but if there is any sense or purpose in life, this sense and purpose are to be found not in our own happiness, but in something greater and more rational. Do good!"

Ivan Ivanich said all this with a piteous, imploring smile, as if he were asking for something for himself.

Then they all three sat in their armchairs a long way apart from one another, and said nothing. Ivan Ivanich's story satisfied neither Burkin or Alekhin. It was not interesting to listen to the story of a poor clerk who ate gooseberries, when from the walls generals and fine ladies, who seemed to come to life in the dark, were looking down from their gilded frames. It would have been much more interesting to hear about elegant people, lovely women. And the fact that they were sitting in a drawing-room in which everything—the swathed chandeliers, the arm-chairs, the carpet on the floor, proved that the people now looking out of the frames had once moved about here, sat in the chairs, drunk tea, where the fair Pelageya was now going noiselessly to and fro, was better than any story.

Alekhin was desperately sleepy. He had got up early, at three o'clock in the morn-   50
ing, to go about his work on the estate, and could now hardly keep his eyes open. But he would not go to bed, for fear one of his guests would relate something interesting

after he was gone. He could not be sure whether what Ivan Ivanich had just told them was wise or just, but his visitors talked of other things besides grain, hay, or tar, of things which had no direct bearing on his daily life, and he liked this, and wanted them to go on. . . .

"Well, time to go to bed," said Burkin, getting up. "Allow me to wish you a good night."

Alekhin said good night and went downstairs to his own room, the visitors remaining on the upper floor. They were allotted a big room for the night, in which were two ancient bedsteads of carved wood, and an ivory crucifix in one corner. There was a pleasant smell of freshly laundered sheets from the wide, cool beds which the fair Pelageya made up for them.

Ivan Ivanich undressed in silence and lay down.

"Lord have mercy on us, sinners," he said, and covered his head with the sheet.

There was a strong smell of stale tobacco from his pipe, which he put on the table, 55 and Burkin lay awake a long time, wondering where the stifling smell came from.

The rain tapped on the window-panes all night.

KATE CHOPIN (1851–1904)

The Story of an Hour   1891

Knowing that Mrs. Mallard was afflicted with a heart trouble, great care was taken to break to her as gently as possible the news of her husband's death.

It was her sister Josephine who told her, in broken sentences, veiled hints that revealed in half concealing. Her husband's friend Richards was there, too, near her. It was he who had been in the newspaper office when intelligence of the railroad disaster was received, with Brently Mallard's name leading the list of "killed." He had only taken the time to assure himself of its truth by a second telegram, and had hastened to forestall any less careful, less tender friend in bearing the sad message.

She did not hear the story as many women have heard the same, with a paralyzed inability to accept its significance. She wept at once, with sudden, wild abandonment, in her sister's arms. When the storm of grief had spent itself she went away to her room alone. She would have no one follow her.

There stood, facing the open window, a comfortable, roomy armchair. Into this she sank, pressed down by a physical exhaustion that haunted her body and seemed to reach into her soul.

She could see in the open square before her house the tops of trees that were all 5 aquiver with the new spring life. The delicious breath of rain was in the air. In the street below a peddler was crying his wares. The notes of a distant song which some one was singing reached her faintly, and countless sparrows were twittering in the eaves.

There were patches of blue sky showing here and there through the clouds that had met and piled above the other in the west facing her window.

She sat with her head thrown back upon the cushion of the chair quite motionless, except when a sob came up into her throat and shook her, as a child who has cried itself to sleep continues to sob in its dreams.

She was young, with a fair, calm face, whose lines bespoke repression and even a certain strength. But now there was a dull stare in her eyes, whose gaze was fixed away off yonder on one of those patches of blue sky. It was not a glance of reflection, but rather indicated a suspension of intelligent thought.

There was something coming to her and she was waiting for it, fearfully. What was it? She did not know; it was too subtle and elusive to name. But she felt it, creeping out of the sky, reaching toward her through the sounds, the scents, the color that filled the air.

Now her bosom rose and fell tumultuously. She was beginning to recognize this thing that was approaching to possess her, and she was striving to beat it back with her will—as powerless as her two white slender hands would have been. 10

When she abandoned herself a little whispered word escaped her slightly parted lips. She said it over and over under her breath: "Free, free, free!" The vacant stare and the look of terror that had followed it went from her eyes. They stayed keen and bright. Her pulses beat fast, and the coursing blood warmed and relaxed every inch of her body.

She did not stop to ask if it were not a monstrous joy that held her. A clear and exalted perception enabled her to dismiss the suggestion as trivial.

She knew that she would weep again when she saw the kind, tender hands folded in death; the face that had never looked save with love upon her, fixed and gray and dead. But she saw beyond that bitter moment a long procession of years to come that would belong to her absolutely. And she opened and spread her arms out to them in welcome.

There would be no one to live for during those coming years; she would live for herself. There would be no powerful will bending her in that blind persistence with which men and women believe they have a right to impose a private will upon a fellow creature. A kind intention or a cruel intention made the act seem no less a crime as she looked upon it in that brief moment of illumination.

And yet she had loved him—sometimes. Often she had not. What did it matter! What could love, the unsolved mystery, count for in face of this possession of self-assertion which she suddenly recognized as the strongest impulse of her being. 15

"Free! Body and soul free!" she kept whispering.

Josephine was kneeling before the closed door with her lips to the keyhole, imploring for admission. "Louise, open the door! I beg; open the door—you will make yourself ill. What are you doing, Louise? For heaven's sake open the door."

"Go away. I am not making myself ill." No; she was drinking in a very elixir of life through that open window.

Her fancy was running riot along those days ahead of her. Spring days, and summer days, and all sorts of days that would be her own. She breathed a quick prayer that life might be long. It was only yesterday she had thought with a shudder that life might be long.

She arose at length and opened the door to her sister's importunities. There was a feverish triumph in her eyes, and she carried herself unwittingly like a goddess of Victory. She clasped her sister's waist, and together they descended the stairs. Richards stood waiting for them at the bottom. 20

Some one was opening the front door with a latchkey. It was Brently Mallard who entered, a little travel-stained, composedly carrying his grip-sack and umbrella. He had been far from the scene of accident, and did not even know there had been one. He stood amazed at Josephine's piercing cry; at Richards' quick motion to screen him from the view of his wife.

But Richards was too late.

When the doctors came they said she had died of heart disease—of joy that kills.

JOSEPH CONRAD
The Secret Sharer   1911

[This rich and complex story can be read on several levels: action, psychology, myth, morality, even allegory. Nautical terms include *deadened in stays*— stopped in the water, *mainsail haul*— changing the sail to catch the wind better, *hard alee*— command to change direction of boat, and *sail locker*— a compartment into which the sails are stowed. Koh-ring is a fictionalized version of Koh-rong, an island in the Indian Ocean near the Gulf of Siam.]

1

On my right hand there were lines of fishing-stakes resembling a mysterious system of half-submerged bamboo fences, incomprehensible in its division of the domain of tropical fishes, and crazy of aspect as if abandoned forever by some nomad tribe of fishermen now gone to the other end of the ocean; for there was no sign of human habitation as far as the eye could reach. To the left a group of barren islets, suggesting ruins of stone walls, towers, and blockhouses, had its foundations set in a blue sea that itself looked solid, so still and stable did it lie below my feet; even the track of light from the westering sun shone smoothly, without that animated glitter which tells of an imperceptible ripple. And when I turned my head to take a parting glance at the tug which had just left us anchored outside the bar, I saw the straight line of the flat shore joined to the stable sea, edge to edge, with a perfect and unmarked closeness, in one levelled floor half brown, half blue under the enormous dome of the sky. Corresponding in their insignificance to the islets of the sea, two small clumps of trees, one on each side of the only fault in the impeccable joint, marked the mouth of the river Meinam we had just left on the first preparatory stage of our homeward journey; and, far back on the inland level, a larger and loftier mass, the grove surrounding the great Paknam pagoda, was the only thing on which the eye could rest from the vain task of exploring the monotonous sweep of the horizon. Here and there gleams as of a few scattered pieces of silver marked the windings of the great river; and on the nearest of them, just within the bar, the tug steaming right into the land became lost to my sight, hull and funnel and masts, as though the impassive earth had swallowed her up without an effort, without a tremor. My eye followed the light cloud of her smoke, now here, now there, above the plain, according to the devious curves of the stream, but always fainter and farther away, till I lost it at last behind the mitre-shaped hill of the great pagoda. And then I was left alone with my ship, anchored at the head of the Gulf of Siam.

She floated at the starting-point of a long journey, very still in an immense stillness, the shadows of her spars flung far to the eastward by the setting sun. At that moment I was alone on her decks. There was not a sound in her—and around us nothing moved, nothing lived, not a canoe on the water, not a bird in the air, not a cloud in the sky. In this breathless pause at the threshold of a long passage we seemed to be measuring our fitness for a long and arduous enterprise, the appointed task of both our existences to be carried out, far from all human eyes, with only sky and sea for spectators and for judges.

There must have been some glare in the air to interfere with one's sight, because it was only just before the sun left us that my roaming eyes made out beyond the highest ridge of the principal islet of the group something which did away with the solemnity of perfect solitude. The tide of darkness flowed on swiftly; and with tropical suddenness a swarm of stars came out above the shadowy earth, while I lingered yet, my hand resting lightly on my ship's rail as if on the shoulder of a trusted friend. But, with all that multitude of celestial bodies staring down at one, the comfort of quiet communion with her was gone for good. And there were also disturbing sounds by this time— voices, footsteps forward; the steward flitted along the main deck, a busily ministering spirit; a hand-bell tinkled urgently under the poop deck. . . .

I found my two officers waiting for me near the supper table, in the lighted cuddy. We sat down at once, and as I helped the chief mate, I said:

"Are you aware that there is a ship anchored inside the islands? I saw her mast-   5
heads above the ridge as the sun went down."

He raised sharply his simple face, overcharged by a terrible growth of whisker, and emitted his usual ejaculations, "Bless my soul, sir! You don't say so!"

My second mate was a round-cheeked, silent young man, grave beyond his years, I thought; but as our eyes happened to meet I detected a slight quiver on his lips. I looked down at once. It was not my part to encourage sneering on board my ship. It must be said, too, that I knew very little of my officers. In consequence of certain events of no particular significance, except to myself, I had been appointed to the com- mand only a fortnight before. Neither did I know much of the hands forward. All these people had been together for eighteen months or so, and my position was that of the only stranger on board. I mention this because it has some bearing on what is to fol- low. But what I felt most was my being a stranger to the ship; and if all the truth must be told, I was somewhat of a stranger to myself. The youngest man on board (barring the second mate), and untried as yet by a position of the fullest responsibility, I was willing to take the adequacy of the others for granted. They had simply to be equal to their tasks; but I wondered how far I should turn out faithful to that ideal conception of one's own personality every man sets up for himself secretly.

Meantime the chief mate, with an almost visible effect of collaboration on the part of his round eyes and frightful whiskers, was trying to evolve a theory of the anchored ship. His dominant trait was to take all things into earnest consideration. He was of a painstaking turn of mind. As he used to say, he "liked to account to himself" for practi- cally everything that came in his way, down to a miserable scorpion he had found in his cabin a week before. The why and the wherefore of that scorpion—how it got on board and came to select his room rather than the pantry (which was a dark place and more what a scorpion would be partial to), and how on earth it managed to drown itself in the inkwell of his writing-desk—had exercised him infinitely. The ship within the is- lands was much more easily accounted for; and just as we were about to rise from table he made his pronouncement. She was, he doubted not, a ship from home lately arrived. Probably she drew too much water to cross the bar except at the top of spring tides. Therefore she went into that natural harbor to wait for a few days in preference to re- maining in an open roadstead.

"That's so," confirmed the second mate suddenly, in his slightly hoarse voice. "She draws over twenty feet. She's the Liverpool ship *Sephora* with a cargo of coal. Hundred and twenty-three days from Cardiff."

We looked at him in surprise.   10

"The tugboat skipper told me when he come on board for your letters, sir," ex- plained the young man. "He expects to take her up the river the day after tomorrow."

After thus overwhelming us with the extent of his information he slipped out of the cabin. The mate observed regretfully that he "could not account for that young fel- low's whims." What prevented him telling us all about it at once, he wanted to know.

I detained him as he was making a move. For the last two days the crew had had plenty of hard work, and the night before they had very little sleep. I felt painfully that I—a stranger—was doing something unusual when I directed him to let all hands turn in without setting an anchor-watch. I proposed to keep on deck myself till one o'clock or thereabouts. I would get the second mate to relieve me at that hour.

"He will turn out the cook and the steward at four," I concluded, "and then give you a call. Of course at the slightest sign of any sort of wind we'll have the hands up and make a start at once."

He concealed his astonishment. "Very well, sir." Outside the cuddy he put his head in the second mate's door to inform him of my unheard-of caprice to take a five hours' anchor-watch on myself. I heard the other raise his voice incredulously—"What? The captain himself?" Then a few more murmurs, a door closed, then another. A few moments later I went on deck.   15

My strangeness, which had made me sleepless, had prompted that unconventional arrangement, as if I had expected in those solitary hours of the night to get on terms with the ship of which I knew nothing, manned by men of whom I knew very little more. Fast alongside a wharf, littered like any ship in port with a tangle of unrelated things, invaded by unrelated shore people, I had hardly seen her yet properly. Now, as she lay cleared for sea, the stretch of her main deck seemed to me very fine under the stars. Very fine, very roomy for her size, and very inviting. I descended the poop and paced the waist, my mind picturing to myself the coming passage through the Malay Archipelago, down the Indian Ocean, and up the Atlantic. All its phases were familiar enough to me, every characteristic, all the alternatives which were likely to face me on the high seas—everything! . . . except the novel responsibility of command. But I took heart from the reasonable thought that the ship was like other ships, the men like other men, and that the sea was not likely to keep any special surprises expressly for my discomfiture.

Arrived at that comforting conclusion, I bethought myself of a cigar and went below to get it. All was still down there. Everybody at the after end of the ship was sleeping profoundly. I came out again on the quarter-deck, agreeably at ease in my sleeping suit on that warm, breathless night, barefooted, a glowing cigar in my teeth, and, going forward, I was met by the profound silence of the fore end of the ship. Only as I passed the door of the forecastle I heard a deep, quiet, trustful sigh of some sleeper inside. And suddenly I rejoiced in the great security of the sea as compared with the unrest of the land, in my choice of that untempted life presenting no disquieting problems, invested with an elementary moral beauty by the absolute straightforwardness of its appeal and by the singleness of its purpose.

The riding-light in the fore-rigging burned with a clear, untroubled, as if symbolic, flame, confident and bright in the mysterious shades of the night. Passing on my way aft along the other side of the ship, I observed that the rope side-ladder, put over, no doubt, for the master of the tug when he came to fetch away our letters, had not been hauled in as it should have been. I became annoyed at this, for exactitude in small matters is the very soul of discipline. Then I reflected that I had myself peremptorily dismissed my officers from duty, and by my own act had prevented the anchor-watch being formally set and things properly attended to. I asked myself whether it was wise ever to interfere with the established routine of duties even from the kindest of motives. My action might have made me appear eccentric. Goodness only knew how that absurdly whiskered mate would "account" for my conduct, and what the whole ship thought of that informality of their new captain. I was vexed with myself.

Not from compunction certainly, but, as it were mechanically, I proceeded to get the ladder in myself. Now a side-ladder of that sort is a light affair and comes in easily, yet my vigorous tug, which should have brought it flying on board, merely recoiled upon my body in a totally unexpected jerk. What the devil! . . . I was so astounded by the immovableness of that ladder that I remained stock-still, trying to account for it to myself like that imbecile mate of mine. In the end, of course, I put my head over the rail.

The side of the ship made an opaque belt of shadow on the darkling glassy shim-   20
mer of the sea. But I saw at once something elongated and pale floating very close to the ladder. Before I could form a guess a faint flash of phosphorescent light, which seemed to issue suddenly from the naked body of a man, flickered in the sleeping water with the elusive, silent play of summer lightning in a night sky. With a gasp I saw re-vealed to my stare a pair of feet, the long legs, a broad livid back immersed right up to the neck in a greenish cadaverous glow. One hand, awash, clutched the bottom rung of the ladder. He was complete but for the head. A headless corpse! The cigar dropped out of my gaping mouth with a tiny plop and a short hiss quite audible in the absolute stillness of all things under heaven. At that I suppose he raised up his face, a dimly pale oval in the shadow of the ship's side. But even then I could only barely make out down there the shape of his black-haired head. However, it was enough for the horrid, frost-bound sensation which had gripped me about the chest to pass off. The moment of vain exclamations was past too. I only climbed on the spare spar and leaned over the rail as far as I could, to bring my eyes nearer to that mystery floating alongside.

As he hung by the ladder, like a resting swimmer, the sea-lightning played about his limbs at every stir; and he appeared in it ghastly, silvery, fish-like. He remained as mute as a fish, too. He made no motion to get out of the water, either. It was incon-ceivable that he should not attempt to come on board, and strangely troubling to sus-pect that perhaps he did not want to. And my first words were prompted by just that troubled incertitude.

"What's the matter?" I asked in my ordinary tone, speaking down to the face up-turned exactly under mine.

"Cramp," it answered, no louder. Then slightly anxious, "I say, no need to call any one."

"I was not going to," I said.

"Are you alone on deck?"   25

"Yes."

I had somehow the impression that he was on the point of letting go the ladder to swim away beyond my ken—mysterious as he came. But, for the moment, this being appearing as if he had risen from the bottom of the sea (it was certainly the nearest land to the ship) wanted only to know the time. I told him. And he, down there, tentatively:

"I suppose your captain's turned in?"

"I am sure he isn't," I said.

He seemed to struggle with himself, for I heard something like the low, bitter mur-   30
mur of doubt. "What's the good?" His next words came out with a hesitating effort.

"Look here, my man. Could you call him out quietly?"

I thought the time had come to declare myself.

"*I* am the captain."

I heard a "By Jove!" whispered at the level of the water. The phosphorescence flashed in the swirl of the water all about his limbs, his other hand seized the ladder.

"My name's Leggatt."   35

The voice was calm and resolute. A good voice. The self-possession of that man had somehow induced a corresponding state in myself. It was very quietly that I re-marked:

"You must be a good swimmer."

"Yes. I've been in the water practically since nine o'clock. The question for me now is whether I am to let go this ladder and go on swimming till I sink from exhaustion, or—to come on board here."

I felt this was no mere formula of desperate speech, but a real alternative in the view of a strong soul. I should have gathered from this that he was young; indeed, it is only the young who are ever confronted by such clear issues. But at the time it was pure intuition on my part. A mysterious communication was established already between us two—in the face of that silent, darkened tropical sea. I was young, too; young enough to make no comment. The man in the water began suddenly to climb up the ladder, and I hastened away from the rail to fetch some clothes.

Before entering the cabin I stood still, listening in the lobby at the foot of the stairs. A faint snore came through the closed door of the chief mate's room. The second mate's door was on the hook, but the darkness in there was absolutely soundless. He, too, was young and could sleep like a stone. Remained the steward, but he was not likely to wake up before he was called. I got a sleeping suit out of my room, and, coming back on deck, saw the naked man from the sea sitting on the main-hatch, glimmering white in the darkness, his elbows on his knees and his head in his hands. In a moment he had concealed his damp body in a sleeping suit of the same grey-stripe pattern as the one I was wearing, and followed me like my double on the poop. Together we moved right aft, barefooted, silent.

"What is it?" I asked in a deadened voice, taking the lighted lamp out of the binnacle, and raising it to his face.

"An ugly business."

He had rather regular features; a good mouth; light eyes under somewhat heavy, dark eyebrows; a smooth, square forehead; no growth on his cheeks; a small, brown moustache, and a well-shaped, round chin. His expression was concentrated, meditative, under the inspecting light of the lamp I held up to his face; such as a man thinking hard in solitude might wear. My sleeping suit was just right for his size. A well-knit young fellow of twenty-five at most. He caught his lower lip with the edge of white, even teeth.

"Yes," I said, replacing the lamp in the binnacle. The warm, heavy tropical night closed upon his head again.

"There's a ship over there," he murmured.

"Yes, I know. The *Sephora*. Did you know of us?"

"Hadn't the slightest idea. I am the mate of her——" He paused and corrected himself. "I should say I *was*."

"Aha! Something wrong?"

"Yes. Very wrong indeed. I've killed a man."

"What do you mean? Just now?"

"No, on the passage. Weeks ago. Thirty-nine south. When I say a man——"

"Fit of temper," I suggested confidently.

The shadowy, dark head, like mine, seemed to nod imperceptibly above the ghostly grey of my sleeping suit. It was, in the night, as though I had been faced by my own reflection in the depths of a somber and immense mirror.

"A pretty thing to have to own up to for a Conway boy," murmured my double distinctly.

"You're a Conway boy?"

"I am," he said, as if startled. Then, slowly . . . "Perhaps you too. . . ."

It was so; but being a couple of years older I had left before he joined. After a quick interchange of dates a silence fell; and I thought suddenly of my absurd mate with his terrific whiskers and the "Bless my soul—you don't say so" type of intellect. My double gave me an inkling of his thoughts by saying:

"My father's a parson in Norfolk. Do you see me before a judge and jury on that charge? For myself I can't see the necessity. There are fellows that an angel from heaven——And I am not that. He was one of those creatures that are just simmering all the time with a silly sort of wickedness. Miserable devils that have no business to live at all. He wouldn't do his duty and wouldn't let anybody else do theirs. But what's the good of talking! You know well enough the sort of ill-conditioned snarling cur. . . ."

He appealed to me as if our experiences had been as identical as our clothes. And I knew well enough the pestiferous danger of such a character where there are no means of legal repression. And I knew well enough also that my double there was no homicidal ruffian. I did not think of asking him for details, and he told me the story roughly in brusque, disconnected sentences. I needed no more. I saw it all going on as though I were myself inside that other sleeping suit.

"It happened while we were setting a reefed foresail, at dusk. Reefed foresail! You 60 understand the sort of weather. The only sail we had left to keep the ship running; so you may guess what it had been like for days. Anxious sort of job, that. He gave me some of his cursed insolence at the sheet. I tell you I was overdone with this terrific weather that seemed to have no end to it. Terrific, I tell you—and a deep ship. I believe the fellow himself was half crazed with funk. It was no time for gentlemanly reproof, so I turned round and felled him like an ox. He up and at me. We closed just as an awful sea made for the ship. All hands saw it coming and took to the rigging, but I had him by the throat, and went on shaking him like a rat, the men above us yelling. 'Look out! Look out!' Then a crash as if the sky had fallen on my head. They say that for over ten minutes hardly anything was to be seen of the ship—just the three masts and a bit of the forecastle head and of the poop all awash driving along in a smother of foam. It was a miracle that they found us, jammed together behind the forebits. It's clear that I meant business, because I was holding him by the throat still when they picked us up. He was black in the face. It was too much for them. It seems they rushed us aft together, gripped as we were, screaming 'Murder!' like a lot of lunatics, and broke into the cuddy. And the ship running for her life, touch and go all the time, any minute her last in a sea fit to turn your hair grey only a-looking at it. I understand that the skipper, too, started raving like the rest of them. The man had been deprived of sleep for more than a week, and to have this sprung on him at the height of a furious gale nearly drove him out of his mind. I wonder they didn't fling me overboard after getting the carcass of their precious shipmate out of my fingers. They had rather a job to separate us, I've been told. A sufficiently fierce story to make an old judge and a respectable jury sit up a bit. The first thing I heard when I came to myself was the maddening howling of that endless gale, and on that the voice of the old man. He was hanging on to my bunk, staring into my face out of his sou'wester.

"'Mr. Leggatt, you have killed a man. You can act no longer as chief mate of this ship.'"

His care to subdue his voice made it sound monotonous. He rested a hand on the end of the skylight to steady himself with, and all that time did not stir a limb, so far as I could see. "Nice little tale for a quiet tea-party," he concluded in the same tone.

One of my hands, too, rested on the end of the skylight; neither did I stir a limb, so far as I knew. We stood less than a foot from each other. It occurred to me that if old "Bless my soul—you don't say so" were to put his head up the companion and catch sight of us, he would think he was seeing double, or imagine himself come upon a scene of weird witchcraft: the strange captain having a quiet confabulation by the wheel with his own grey ghost. I became very much concerned to prevent anything of the sort. I heard the other's soothing undertone:

"My father's a parson in Norfolk," it said. Evidently he had forgotten he had told me this important fact before. Truly a nice little tale.

"You had better slip down into my stateroom now," I said, moving off stealthily. My double followed my movements; our bare feet made no sound; I let him in, closed the door with care, and, after giving a call to the second mate, returned on deck for my relief.

"Not much sign of any wind yet," I remarked when he approached.

"No, sir. Not much," he assented sleepily in his hoarse voice, with just enough deference, no more, and barely suppressing a yawn.

"Well, that's all you have to look out for. You have got your orders."

"Yes, sir."

I paced a turn or two on the poop and saw him take up his position face forward with his elbow in the ratlines of the mizzen-rigging before I went below. The mate's faint snoring was still going on peacefully. The cuddy lamp was burning over the table on which stood a vase with flowers, a polite attention from the ship's provision merchant—the last flowers we should see for the next three months at the very least. Two bunches of bananas hung from the beam symmetrically, one on each side of the rudder-casing. Everything was as before in the ship—except that two of her captain's sleeping suits were simultaneously in use, one motionless in the cuddy, the other keeping very still in the captain's stateroom.

It must be explained here that my cabin had the form of the capital letter L, the door being within the angle and opening into the short part of the letter. A couch was to the left, the bedplace to the right; my writing-desk and the chronometers' table faced the door. But any one opening it, unless he stepped right inside, had no view of what I call the long (or vertical) part of the letter. It contained some lockers surmounted by a bookcase; and a few clothes, a thick jacket or two, caps, oilskin coat, and such-like, hung on hooks. There was at the bottom of that part a door opening into my bathroom, which could be entered also directly from the saloon. But that way was never used.

The mysterious arrival had discovered the advantage of this particular shape. Entering my room, lighted strongly by a big bulkhead lamp swung on gimbals above my writing-desk, I did not see him anywhere till he stepped out quietly from behind the coats hung in the recessed part.

"I heard somebody moving about, and went in there at once," he whispered.

I, too, spoke under my breath.

"Nobody is likely to come in here without knocking and getting permission."

He nodded. His face was thin and the sunburn faded, as though he had been ill. And no wonder. He had been, I heard presently, kept under arrest in his cabin for nearly nine weeks. But there was nothing sickly in his eyes or in his expression. He was not a bit like me, really; yet, as we stood leaning over my bedplace, whispering side by side, with our dark heads together and our backs to the door, anybody bold enough to open it stealthily would have been treated to the uncanny sight of a double captain busy talking in whispers with his other self.

"But all this doesn't tell me how you came to hang on to our side-ladder," I inquired, in the hardly audible murmurs we used, after he had told me something more of the proceedings on board the *Sephora* once the bad weather was over.

"When we sighted Java Head I had had time to think all those matters out several times over. I had six weeks of doing nothing else, and with only an hour or so every evening for a tramp on the quarter-deck."

He whispered, his arms folded on the side of my bedplace, staring through the open port. And I could imagine perfectly the manner of this thinking out—a stubborn if not a steadfast operation; something of which I should have been perfectly incapable.

"I reckoned it would be dark before we closed with the land," he continued, so low that I had to strain my hearing, near as we were to each other, shoulder touching shoulder almost. "So I asked to speak to the old man. He always seemed very sick when he came to see me—as if he could not look me in the face. You know, that foresail saved the ship. She was too deep to have run long under bare poles. And it was I that managed to set it for him. Anyway, he came. When I had him in my cabin—he stood by the door looking at me as if I had the halter round my neck already—I asked him right away to leave my cabin door unlocked at night while the ship was going through Sunda Straits. There would be the Java coast within two or three miles, off Anjer Point. I wanted nothing more. I've had a prize for swimming my second year in the Conway."

"I can believe it," I breathed out.

"God only knows why they locked me in every night. To see some of their faces you'd have thought they were afraid I'd go about at night strangling people. Am I a murdering brute? Do I look it? By Jove! if I had been he wouldn't have trusted himself like that into my room. You'll say I might have chucked him aside and bolted out, there and then—it was dark already. Well, no. And for the same reason I wouldn't think of trying to smash the door. There would have been a rush to stop me at the noise, and I did not mean to get into a confounded scrimmage. Somebody else might have got killed—for I would not have broken out only to get chucked back, and I did not want any more of that work. He refused, looking more sick than ever. He was afraid of the men, and also of that old second mate of his who had been sailing with him for years—a grey-headed old humbug; and his steward, too, had been with him devil knows how long—seventeen years or more—a dogmatic sort of loafer who hated me like poison, just because I was the chief mate. No chief mate ever made more than one voyage in the *Sephora*, you know. Those two old chaps ran the ship. Devil only knows what the skipper wasn't afraid of (all his nerve went to pieces altogether in that hellish spell of bad weather we had)—of what the law would do to him—of his wife, perhaps. Oh yes! she's on board. Though I don't think she would have meddled. She would have been only too glad to have me out of the ship in any way. The 'brand of Cain' business, don't you see? That's all right. I was ready enough to go off wandering on the face of the earth—and that was price enough to pay for an Abel of that sort. Anyhow, he wouldn't listen to me. 'This thing must take its course. I represent the law here.' He was shaking like a leaf. 'So you won't?' 'No!' 'Then I hope you will be able to sleep on that,' I said, and turned my back on him. 'I wonder that *you* can,' cries he, and locks the door.

"Well, after that, I couldn't. Not very well. That was three weeks ago. We have had a slow passage through the Java Sea; drifted about Carimata for ten days. When we anchored here they thought, I suppose, it was all right. The nearest land (and that's five miles) is the ship's destination; the consul would soon set about catching me; and there would have been no object in bolting to these islets there. I don't suppose there's a drop of water on them. I don't know how it was, but tonight that steward, after bringing me my supper, went out to let me eat it, and left the door unlocked. And I ate it—all there was, too. After I had finished I strolled out on the quarter-deck. I don't know that I meant to do anything. A breath of fresh air was all I wanted, I believe. Then a sudden temptation came over me. I kicked off my slippers and was in the water before I had made up my mind fairly. Somebody heard the splash and they raised on awful hullabaloo. 'He's gone! Lower the boats! He's committed suicide! No, he's swimming.'

Certainly I was swimming. It's not so easy for a swimmer like me to commit suicide by drowning. I landed on the nearest islet before the boat left the ship's side. I heard them pulling about in the dark, hailing, and so on, but after a bit they gave up. Everything quieted down and the anchorage became as still as death. I sat down on a stone and began to think. I felt certain they would start searching for me at daylight. There was no place to hide on those stony things—and if there had been, what would have been the good? But now I was clear of that ship, I was not going back. So after a while I took off all my clothes, tied them up in a bundle with a stone inside, and dropped them in the deep water on the outer side of that islet. That was suicide enough for me. Let them think what they liked, but I didn't mean to drown myself. I meant to swim till I sank—but that's not the same thing. I struck out for another of these little islands, and it was from that one that I first saw your riding-light. Something to swim for. I went on easily, and on the way I came upon a flat rock a foot or two above water. In the day-time, I dare say, you might make it out with a glass from your poop. I scrambled up on it and rested myself for a bit. Then I made another start. That last spell must have been over a mile."

His whisper was getting fainter and fainter, and all the time he stared straight out through the porthole, in which there was not even a star to be seen. I had not inter-rupted him. There was something that made comment impossible, in his narrative, or perhaps in himself; a sort of feeling, a quality, which I can't find a name for. And when he ceased, all I found was a futile whisper, "So you swam for our light?"

"Yes—straight for it. It was something to swim for. I couldn't see any stars low   85
down because the coast was in the way, and I couldn't see the land, either. The water was like glass. One might have been swimming in a confounded thousand feet deep cis-tern with no place for scrambling out anywhere; but what I didn't like was the notion of swimming round and round like a crazed bullock before I gave out; and as I didn't mean to go back . . . No. Do you see me being hauled back, stark naked, off one of these little islands by the scruff of the neck and fighting like a wild beast? Somebody would have got killed for certain, and I did not want any of that. So I went on. Then your ladder——"

"Why didn't you hail the ship?" I asked, a little louder.

He touched my shoulder lightly. Lazy footsteps came right over our heads and stopped. The second mate had crossed from the other side of the poop and might have been hanging over the rail, for all we knew.

"He couldn't hear us talking—could he?" My double breathed into my very ear anxiously.

His anxiety was an answer, a sufficient answer, to the question I had put to him. An answer containing all the difficulty of that situation. I closed the porthole quietly, to make sure. A louder word might have been overheard.

"Who's that?" he whispered then.   90

"My second mate. But I don't know much more of the fellow than you do."

And I told him a little about myself. I had been appointed to take charge while I least expected anything of the sort, not quite a fortnight ago. I didn't know either the ship or the people. Hadn't had the time in port to look about me or size anybody up. And as to the crew, all they knew was that I was appointed to take the ship home. For the rest, I was almost as much of a stranger on board as himself, I said. And at the mo-ment I felt it most acutely. I felt that it would take very little to make me a suspect per-son in the the the eyes of the ship's company.

He had turned about meantime; and we, the two strangers in the ship, faced each other in identical attitudes.

"Your ladder——" he murmured, after a silence. "Who'd have thought of finding a ladder hanging over at night in a ship anchored out here! I felt just then a very unpleasant faintness. After the life I've been leading for nine weeks, anybody would have got out of condition. I wasn't capable of swimming round as far as your rudder-chains. And, lo and behold! there was a ladder to get hold of. After I gripped it I said to myself, 'What's the good?' When I saw a man's head looking over I thought I would swim away presently and leave him shouting—in whatever language it was. I didn't mind being looked at. I—I liked it. And then you speaking to me so quietly—as if you had expected me—made me hold on a little longer. It had been a confounded lonely time—I don't mean while swimming. I was glad to talk a little to somebody that didn't belong to the *Sephora*. As to asking for the captain, that was a mere impulse. It could have been no use, with all the ship knowing about me and the other people pretty certain to be round here in the morning. I don't know—I wanted to be seen, to talk with somebody, before I went on. I don't know what I would have said. . . . 'Fine night, isn't it?' or something of the sort."

"Do you think they will be round here presently?" I asked, with some incredulity.   95

"Quite likely," he said faintly.

He looked extremely haggard all of a sudden. His head rolled on his shoulders.

"H'm. We shall see then. Meantime get into that bed," I whispered. "Want help? There."

It was a rather high bedplace with a set of drawers underneath. This amazing swimmer really needed the lift I gave him by seizing his leg. He tumbled in, rolled over on his back, and flung one arm across his eyes. And then, with his face nearly hidden, he must have looked exactly as I used to look in that bed. I gazed upon my other self for a while before drawing across carefully the two green serge curtains which ran on a brass rod. I thought for a moment of pinning them together for greater safety, but I sat down on the couch, and once there I felt unwilling to rise and hunt for a pin. I would do it in a moment. I was extremely tired, in a peculiarly intimate way, by the strain of stealthiness, by the effort of whispering, and the general secrecy of this excitement. It was three o'clock by now, and I had been on my feet since nine, but I was not sleepy; I could not have gone to sleep. I sat there, fagged out, looking at the curtains, trying to clear my mind of the confused sensation of being in two places at once, and greatly bothered by an exasperating knocking in my head. It was a relief to discover suddenly that it was not in my head at all, but on the outside of the door. Before I could collect myself, the words "Come in" were out of my mouth, and the steward entered with a tray, bringing in my morning coffee. I had slept, after all, and I was so frightened that I shouted, "This way! I am here, steward," as though he had been miles away. He put down the tray on the table next the couch and only then said, very quietly, "I can see you are here, sir." I felt him give me a keen look, but I dared not meet his eyes just then. He must have wondered why I had drawn the curtains of my bed before going to sleep on the couch. He went out, hooking the door open as usual.

I heard the crew washing decks above me. I knew I would have been told at once   100
if there had been any wind. Calm, I thought, and I was doubly vexed. Indeed, I felt dual more than ever. The steward reappeared suddenly in the doorway. I jumped up from the couch so quickly that he gave a start.

"What do you want here?"

"Close your port, sir—they are washing decks."

"It is closed," I said, reddening.

"Very well, sir." But he did not move from the doorway and returned my stare in an extraordinary, equivocal manner for a time. Then his eyes wavered, all his expression changed, and in a voice unusually gentle, almost coaxingly:

"May I come in to take the empty cup away, sir?"

105

"Of course!" I turned my back on him while he popped in and out. Then I unhooked and closed the door and even pushed the bolt. This sort of thing could not go on very long. The cabin was as hot as an oven, too. I took a peep at my double, and discovered that he had not moved; his arm was still over his eyes; but his chest heaved, his hair was wet, his chin glistened with perspiration. I reached over him and opened the port.

"I must show myself on deck," I reflected.

Of course, theoretically, I could do what I liked, with no one to say nay to me within the whole circle of the horizon; but to lock my cabin door and take the key away I did not dare. Directly I put my head out of the companion I saw the group of my two officers, the second mate barefooted, the chief mate in long indiarubber boots, near the break of the poop, and the steward half-way down the poop ladder talking to them eagerly. He happened to catch sight of me and dived, the second ran down on the main deck shouting some order or other, and the chief mate came to meet me, touching his cap.

There was a sort of curiosity in his eye that I did not like. I don't know whether the steward had told them that I was "queer" only, or downright drunk, but I know the man meant to have a good look at me. I watched him coming with a smile which, as he got into point-blank range, took effect and froze his very whiskers. I did not give him time to open his lips.

"Square the yards by lifts and braces before the hands go to breakfast."

110

It was the first particular order I had given on board that ship; and I stayed on deck to see it executed too. I had felt the need of asserting myself without loss of time. That sneering young cub got taken down a peg or two on that occasion, and I also seized the opportunity of having a good look at the face of every foremast man as they filed past me to go to the after braces. At breakfast time, eating nothing myself, I presided with such frigid dignity that the two mates were only too glad to escape from the cabin as soon as decency permitted; and all the time the dual working of my mind distracted me almost to the point of insanity. I was constantly watching myself, my secret self, as dependent on my actions as my own personality, sleeping in that bed, behind that door which faced me as I sat at the head of the table. It was very much like being mad, only it was worse, because one was aware of it.

I had to shake him for a solid minute, but when at last he opened his eyes it was in the full possession of his senses, with an inquiring look.

"All's well so far," I whispered. "Now you must vanish into the bathroom."

He did so, as noiseless as a ghost, and I then rang for the steward, and facing him boldly, directed him to tidy up my stateroom while I was having my bath— "and be quick about it." As my tone admitted of no excuses, he said, "Yes, sir," and ran off to fetch his dust-pan and brushes. I took a bath and did most of my dressing, splashing, and whistling softly for the steward's edification, while the secret sharer of my life stood drawn bolt upright in that little space, his face looking very sunken in daylight, his eyelids lowered under the stern, dark line of his eyebrows drawn together by a slight frown.

When I left him there to go back to my room the steward was finishing dusting. I

115

sent for the mate and engaged him in some insignificant conversation. It was, as it were, trifling with the terrific character of his whiskers; but my object was to give him an opportunity for a good look at my cabin. And then I could at last shut, with a clear conscience, the door of my stateroom and get my double back into the recessed part. There was nothing else for it. He had to sit still on a small folding stool, half smothered by the heavy coats hanging there. We listened to the steward going into the bathroom out of the saloon, filling the water-bottles there, scrubbing the bath, setting things to rights, whisk, bang, clatter—out again into the saloon—turn the key—click. Such was my scheme for keeping my second self invisible. Nothing better could be contrived under the circumstances. And there we sat: I at my writing-desk ready to appear busy with some papers, he behind me, out of sight of the door. It would not have been prudent to talk in daytime; and I could not have stood the excitement of that queer sense of whispering to myself. Now and then, glancing over my shoulder, I saw him far back there, sitting rigidly on the low stool, his bare feet close together, his arms folded, his head hanging on his breast—and perfectly still. Anybody would have taken him for me.

I was fascinated by it myself. Every moment I had to glance over my shoulder. I was looking at him when a voice outside the door said:

"Beg pardon, sir."

"Well!" . . . I kept my eyes on him, and so when the voice outside the door announced, "There's a ship's boat coming our way, sir," I saw him give a start—the first movement he had made for hours. But he did not raise his bowed head.

"All right. Get the ladder over."

I hesitated. Should I whisper something to him? But what? His immobility seemed   120
to have been never disturbed. What could I tell him he did not know already? . . . Finally I went on deck.

2

The skipper of the *Sephora* had a thin, red whisker all round his face, and the sort of complexion that goes with hair of that color; also the particular, rather smeary shade of blue in the eyes. He was not exactly a showy figure; his shoulders were high, his stature but middling—one leg slightly more bandy than the other. He shook hands, looking vaguely around. A spiritless tenacity was his main characteristic, I judged. I behaved with a politeness which seemed to disconcert him. Perhaps he was shy. He mumbled to me as if he were ashamed of what he was saying; gave his name (it was something like Archbold—but at this distance of years I hardly am sure), his ship's name, and a few other particulars of that sort, in the manner of a criminal making a reluctant and doleful confession. He had had terrible weather on the passage out—terrible—terrible—wife aboard, too.

By this time we were seated in the cabin and the steward brought in a tray with a bottle and glasses. "Thanks! No." Never took liquor. Would have some water, though. He drank two tumblerfuls. Terrible thirsty work. Ever since daylight had been exploring the islands round his ship.

"What was that for—fun?" I asked, with an appearance of polite interest.

"No!" He sighed. "Painful duty."

As he persisted in his mumbling and I wanted my double to hear every word, I hit   125
upon the notion of informing him that I regretted to say I was hard of hearing.

"Such a young man, too!" he nodded, keeping his smeary, blue, unintelligent eyes fastened upon me. "What was the cause of it—some disease?" he inquired, without the least sympathy and as if he thought that, if so, I'd got no more than I deserved.

"Yes; disease," I admitted in a cheerful tone which seemed to shock him. But my point was gained, because he had to raise his voice to give me his tale. It is not worth while to record that version. It was just over two months since all this had happened, and he had thought so much about it that he seemed completely muddled as to its bearings, but still immensely impressed.

"What would you think of such a thing happening on board your own ship? I've had the *Sephora* for these fifteen years. I am a well-known shipmaster."

He was densely distressed—and perhaps I should have sympathized with him if I had been able to detach my mental vision from the unsuspected sharer of my cabin as though he were my second self. There he was on the other side of the bulkhead, four or five feet from us, no more, as we sat in the saloon. I looked politely at Captain Archbold (if that was his name), but it was the other I saw, in a grey sleeping suit, seated on a low stool, his bare feet close together, his arms folded, and every word said between us falling into the ears of his dark head bowed on his chest.

"I have been at sea now, man and boy, for seven and thirty years, and I've never   130
heard of such a thing happening in an English ship. And that it should be my ship. Wife on board, too."

I was hardly listening to him.

"Don't you think," I said, "that the heavy sea which, you told me, came aboard just then might have killed the man? I have seen the sheer weight of a sea kill a man very neatly, by simply breaking his neck."

"Good God!" he uttered impressively, fixing his smeary blue eyes on me. "The sea! No man killed by the sea ever looked like that." He seemed positively scandalized at my suggestion. And as I gazed at him, certainly not prepared for anything original on his part, he advanced his head close to mine and thrust his tongue out at me so suddenly that I couldn't help starting back.

After scoring over my calmness in this graphic way he nodded wisely. If I had seen the sight, he assured me, I would never forget it as long as I lived. The weather was too bad to give the corpse a proper sea burial. So next day at dawn they took it up on the poop, covering its face with a bit of bunting; he read a short prayer, and then, just as it was, in its oilskins and long boots, they launched it amongst those mountainous seas that seemed ready every moment to swallow up the ship herself and the terrified lives on board of her.

"That reefed foresail saved you," I threw in.   135

"Under God—it did," he exclaimed fervently. "It was by a special mercy, I firmly believe, that it stood some of those hurricane squalls."

"It was the setting of that sail which——" I began.

"God's own hand in it," he interrupted me. "Nothing less could have done it. I don't mind telling you that I hardly dared give the order. It seemed impossible that we could touch anything without losing it, and then our last hope would have been gone."

The terror of that gale was on him yet. I let him go on for a bit, then said casually—as if returning to a minor subject:

"You were very anxious to give up your mate to the shore people, I believe?"   140

He was. To the law. His obscure tenacity on that point had in it something incomprehensible and a little awful; something, as it were, mystical, quite apart from his anxiety that he should not be suspected of "countenancing any doings of that sort." Seven and thirty virtuous years at sea, of which over twenty of immaculate command, and the last fifteen in the *Sephora*, seemed to have laid him under some pitiless obligation.

"And you know," he went on, groping shamefacedly amongst his feelings, "I did not engage that young fellow. His people had some interest with my owners. I was in a way forced to take him on. He looked very smart, very gentlemanly, and all that. But do you know—I never liked him, somehow. I am a plain man. You see, he wasn't exactly the sort for the chief mate of a ship like the *Sephora*."

I had become so connected in thoughts and impressions with the secret sharer of my cabin that I felt as if I, personally, were being given to understand that I, too, was not the sort that would have done for the chief mate of a ship like the *Sephora*. I had no doubt of it in my mind.

"Not at all the style of man. You understand," he insisted superfluously, looking hard at me.

I smiled urbanely. He seemed at a loss for a while.   145

"I suppose I must report a suicide."

"Beg pardon?"

"Sui—cide! That's what I'll have to write to my owners directly I get in."

"Unless you manage to recover him before tomorrow," I assented dispassionately.
. . . "I mean, alive."

He mumbled something which I really did not catch, and I turned my ear to him   150
in a puzzled manner. He fairly bawled:

"The land—I say, the mainland is at least seven miles off my anchorage."

"About that."

My lack of excitement, of curiosity, of surprise, of any sort of pronounced interest, began to arouse his distrust. But except for the felicitous pretence of deafness I had not tried to pretend anything. I had felt utterly incapable of playing the part of ignorance properly, and therefore was afraid to try. It is also certain that he had brought some ready-made suspicions with him, and that he viewed my politeness as a strange and un-natural phenomenon. And yet how else could I have received him? Not heartily! That was impossible for psychological reasons, which I need not state here. My only object was to keep off his inquiries. Surlily? Yes, but surliness might have provoked a point-blank question. From its novelty to him and from its nature, punctilious courtesy was the manner best calculated to restrain the man. But there was the danger of his break-ing through my defense bluntly. I could not, I think, have met him by a direct lie, also for psychological (not moral) reasons. If he had only known how afraid I was of his putting my feeling of identity with the other to the test! But, strangely enough (I thought of it only afterward), I believe that he was not a little disconcerted by the re-verse side of that weird situation, by something in me that reminded him of the man he was seeking—suggested a mysterious similitude to the young fellow he had distrusted and disliked from the first.

However that might have been, the silence was not very prolonged. He took an-other oblique step.

"I reckon I had no more than a two-mile pull to your ship. Not a bit more."   155

"And quite enough, too, in this awful heat," I said.

Another pause full of mistrust followed. Necessity, they say, is mother of inven-tion, but fear, too, is not barren of ingenious suggestions. And I was afraid he would ask me point-blank for news of my other self.

"Nice little saloon, isn't it?" I remarked, as if noticing for the first time the way his eyes roamed from one closed door to the other. "And very well fitted out, too. Here, for instance," I continued, reaching over the back of my seat negligently and flinging the door open, "is my bathroom."

He made an eager movement, but hardly gave it a glance. I got up, shut the door of the bathroom, and invited him to have a look round, as if I were very proud of my accommodation. He had to rise and be shown round, but he went through the busi-ness without any raptures whatever.

"And now we'll have a look at my stateroom," I declared, in a voice as loud as I   160
dared to make it, crossing the cabin to the starboard side with purposely heavy steps.

He followed me in and gazed around. My intelligent double had vanished. I played my part.

"Very convenient—isn't it?"

"Very nice. Very comf . . ." He didn't finish, and went out brusquely as if to es-cape from some unrighteous wiles of mine. But it was not to be. I had been too frightened not to feel vengeful; I felt I had him on the run, and I meant to keep him on the run. My polite insistence must have had something menacing in it, because he gave in suddenly. And I did not let him off a single item: mates' rooms, pantry, storerooms, the very sail-locker, which was also under the poop—he had to look into them all. When at last I showed him out on the quarter-deck he drew a long, spiritless sigh, and mumbled dismally that he must really be going back to his ship now. I desired my mate, who had joined us, to see to the captain's boat.

The man of whiskers gave a blast on the whistle which he used to wear hanging round his neck, and yelled, *"Sephora's* away!" My double down there in my cabin must have heard, and certainly could not feel more relieved than I. Four fellows came running out from somewhere forward and went over the side, while my own men, appearing on deck too, lined the rail. I escorted my visitor to the gangway ceremoniously, and nearly overdid it. He was a tenacious beast. On the very ladder he lingered, and in that unique, guiltily conscientious manner of sticking to the point:

"I say . . . you . . . you don't think that——"   165

I covered his voice loudly:

"Certainly not. . . . I am delighted. Goodbye."

I had an idea of what he meant to say, and just saved myself by the privilege of defective hearing. He was too shaken generally to insist, but my mate, close witness of that parting, looked mystified and his face took on a thoughtful cast. As I did not want to appear as if I wished to avoid all communication with my officers, he had the opportunity to address me.

"Seems a very nice man. His boat's crew told our chaps a very extraordinary story, if what I am told by the steward is true. I suppose you had it from the captain, sir?"

"Yes. I had a story from the captain."   170

"A very horrible affair—isn't it, sir?"

"It is."

"Beats all these tales we hear about murders in Yankee ships."

"I don't think it beats them. I don't think it resembles them in the least."

"Bless my soul—you don't say so! But of course I've no acquaintance whatever   175
with American ships, not I, so I couldn't go against your knowledge. It's horrible enough for me. . . . But the queerest part is that those fellows seemed to have some idea the man was hidden aboard here. They had really. Did you ever hear of such a thing?"

"Preposterous—isn't it?"

We were walking to and fro athwart the quarter-deck. No one of the crew forward could be seen (the day was Sunday), and the mate pursued:

"There was some little dispute about it. Our chaps took offense. 'As if we would harbor a thing like that,' they said. 'Wouldn't you like to look for him in our coalhole?' Quite a tiff. But they made it up in the end. I suppose he did drown himself. Don't you, sir?"

"I don't suppose anything."

"You have no doubt in the matter, sir?"   180

"None whatever."

I left him suddenly. I felt I was producing a bad impression, but with my double down there it was most trying to be on deck. And it was almost as trying to be below. Altogether a nerve-trying situation. But on the whole I felt less torn in two when I was with him. There was no one in the whole ship whom I dared take into my confidence. Since the hands had got to know his story, it would have been impossible to pass him off for any one else, and an accidental discovery was to be dreaded now more than ever. . . .

The steward being engaged in laying the table for dinner, we could talk only with our eyes when I first went down. Later in the afternoon we had a cautious try at whispering. The Sunday quietness of the ship was against us; the stillness of air and water around her was against us; the elements, the men were against us—everything was against us in our secret partnership; time itself—for this could not go on forever. The very trust in Providence was, I supposed, denied to his guilt. Shall I confess that this thought cast me down very much? And as to the chapter of accidents which counts for so much in the book of success, I could only hope that it was closed. For what favorable accident could be expected?

"Did you hear everything?" were my first words as soon as we took up our position side by side, leaning over my bedplace.

He had. And the proof of it was his earnest whisper, "The man told you he hardly   185
dared to give the order."

I understood the reference to be to that saving foresail.

"Yes. He was afraid of it being lost in the setting."

"I assure you he never gave the order. He may think he did, but he never gave it. He stood there with me on the break of the poop after the maintopsail blew away, and whimpered about our last hope—positively whimpered about it and nothing else—and the night coming on! To hear one's skipper go on like that in such weather was enough to drive any fellow out of his mind. It worked me up into a sort of desperation. I just took it into my own hands and went away from him, boiling, and—— But what's the use telling you? *You* know! . . . Do you think that if I had not been pretty fierce with them I should have got the men to do anything? Not it! The boss'en perhaps? Perhaps! It wasn't a heavy sea—it was a sea gone mad! I suppose the end of the world will be something like that; and a man may have the heart to see it coming once and be done with it—but to have to face it day after day . . . I don't blame anybody. I was precious little better than the rest. Only—I was an officer of that old coal-waggon, anyhow. . . ."

"I quite understand," I conveyed that sincere assurance into his ear. He was out of breath with whispering; I could hear him pant slightly. It was all very simple. The same strung-up force which had given twenty-four men a chance, at least, for their lives had, in a sort of recoil, crushed an unworthy mutinous existence.

But I had no leisure to weigh the merits of the matter—footsteps in the saloon, a   190
heavy knock. "There's enough wind to get under way with, sir." Here was the call of a new claim upon my thoughts and even upon my feelings.

"Turn the hands up," I cried through the door. "I'll be on deck directly."

I was going out to make the acquaintance of my ship. Before I left the cabin our eyes met—the eyes of the only two strangers on board. I pointed to the recessed part where the little camp-stool awaited him and, laid my finger on my lips. He made a gesture—somewhat vague—a little mysterious, accompanied by a faint smile, as if of regret.

This is not the place to enlarge upon the sensations of a man who feels for the first time a ship move under his feet to his own independent word. In my case they were not unalloyed. I was not wholly alone with my command; for there was that stranger in my cabin. Or, rather, I was not completely and wholly with her. Part of me was absent. That mental feeling of being in two places at once affected me physically as if the mood of secrecy had penetrated my very soul. Before an hour had elapsed since the ship had begun to move, having occasion to ask the mate (he stood by my side) to take a compass bearing of the Pagoda, I caught myself reaching up to his ear in whispers. I say I caught myself, but enough had escaped to startle the man. I can't describe it otherwise than by saying that he shied. A grave, preoccupied manner, as though he were in possession of some perplexing intelligence, did not leave him henceforth. A little later I moved away from the rail to look at the compass with such a stealthy gait that the helmsman noticed it—and I could not help noticing the unusual roundness of his eyes. These are trifling instances, though it's to no commander's advantage to be suspected of ludicrous eccentricities. But I was also more seriously affected. There are to a seaman certain words, gestures, that should in given conditions come as naturally, as instinctively, as the winking of a menaced eye. A certain order should spring on to his lips without thinking; a certain sign should get itself made, so to speak, without reflection. But all unconscious alertness had abandoned me. I had to make an effort of will to recall myself back (from the cabin) to the conditions of the moment. I felt that I was appearing an irresolute commander to those people who were watching me more or less critically.

And, besides, there were the scares. On the second day out, for instance, coming off the deck in the afternoon (I had straw slippers on my bare feet) I stopped at the open pantry door and spoke to the steward. He was doing something there with his back to me. At the sound of my voice he nearly jumped out of his skin, as the saying is, and incidentally broke a cup.

"What on earth's the matter with you?" I asked, astonished.   195

He was extremely confused. "Beg your pardon, sir. I made sure you were in your cabin."

"You see I wasn't."

"No, sir. I could have sworn I had heard you moving in there not a moment ago. It's most extraordinary . . . very sorry, sir."

I passed on with an inward shudder. I was so identified with my secret double that I did not even mention the fact in those scanty, fearful whispers we exchanged. I suppose he had made some slight noise of some kind or other. It would have been miraculous if he hadn't at one time or another. And yet, haggard as he appeared, he looked always perfectly self-controlled, more than calm—almost invulnerable. On my suggestion he remained almost entirely in the bathroom, which, upon the whole, was the safest place. There could be really no shadow of an excuse for any one ever wanting to go in there, once the steward had done with it. It was a very tiny place. Sometimes he reclined on the floor, his legs bent, his head sustained on one elbow. At others I would find him on the camp-stool, sitting in his grey sleeping suit and with his cropped dark hair like a patient, unmoved convict. At night I would smuggle him into my bedplace, and we would whisper together, with the regular footfalls of the officer of the watch passing and repassing over our heads. It was an infinitely miserable time. It was lucky that some tins of fine preserves were stowed in a locker in my stateroom; hard bread I could always get hold of; and so he lived on stewed chicken, pâté de foie gras, asparagus, cooked oysters, sardines—on all sorts of abominable sham-delicacies out of tins. My early morning coffee he always drank; and it was all I dared do for him in that respect.

Every day there was the horrible maneuvering to go through so that my room and   200
then the bathroom should be done in the usual way. I came to hate the sight of the steward, to abhor the voice of that harmless man. I felt that it was he who would bring on the disaster of discovery. It hung like a sword over our heads.

The fourth day out, I think (we were then working down the east side of the Gulf of Siam, tack for tack, in light winds and smooth water)—the fourth day, I say, of this miserable juggling with the unavoidable, as we sat at our evening meal, that man, whose slightest movement I dreaded, after putting down the dishes ran up on deck busily. This could not be dangerous. Presently he came down again; and then it appeared that he had remembered a coat of mine which I had thrown over a rail to dry after having been wetted in a shower which had passed over the ship in the afternoon. Sitting stolidly at the head of the table I became terrified at the sight of the garment on his arm. Of course he made for my door. There was no time to lose.

"Steward!" I thundered. My nerves were so shaken that I could not govern my voice and conceal my agitation. This was the sort of thing that made my terrifically whiskered mate tap his forehead with his forefinger. I had detected him using that gesture while talking on deck with a confidential air to the carpenter. It was too far to hear a word, but I had no doubt that this pantomime could only refer to the strange new captain.

"Yes, sir," the pale-faced steward turned resignedly to me. It was this maddening course of being shouted at, checked without rhyme or reason, arbitrarily chased out of my cabin, suddenly called into it, sent flying out of his pantry on incomprehensible errands, that accounted for the growing wretchedness of his expression.

"Where are you going with that coat?"

"To your room, sir."   205

"Is there another shower coming?"

"I'm sure I don't know, sir. Shall I go up again and see, sir?"

"No! never mind."

My object was attained, as of course my other self in there would have heard everything that passed. During this interlude my two officers never raised their eyes off their respective plates; but the lip of that confounded cub, the second mate, quivered visibly.

I expected the steward to hook my coat on and come out at once. He was very   210
slow about it; but I dominated my nervousness sufficiently not to shout after him. Suddenly I became aware (it could be heard plainly enough) that the fellow for some reason or other was opening the door of the bathroom. It was the end. The place was literally not big enough to swing a cat in. My voice died in my throat and I went stony all over. I expected to hear a yell of surprise and terror, and made a movement, but had not the strength to get on my legs. Everything remained still. Had my second self taken the poor wretch by the throat? I don't know what I could have done next moment if I had not seen the steward come out of my room, close the door, and then stand quietly by the sideboard.

"Saved," I thought. "But, no! Lost! Gone! He was gone!"

I laid my knife and fork down and leaned back in my chair. My head swam. After a while, when sufficiently recovered to speak in a steady voice, I instructed my mate to put the ship round at eight o'clock himself.

"I won't come on deck," I went on. "I think I'll turn in, and unless the wind shifts I don't want to be disturbed before midnight. I feel a bit seedy."

"You did look middling bad a little while ago," the chief mate remarked without showing any great concern.

They both went out, and I stared at the steward clearing the table. There was   215
nothing to be read on that wretched man's face. But why did he avoid my eyes? I asked myself. Then I thought I should like to hear the sound of his voice.

"Steward!"

"Sir!" Startled as usual.

"Where did you hang up that coat?"

"In the bathroom, sir." The usual anxious tone. "It's not quite dry yet, sir."

For some time longer I sat in the cuddy. Had my double vanished as he had come?   220
But of his coming there was an explanation, whereas his disappearance would be inex-

plicable. . . . I went slowly into my dark room, shut the door, lighted the lamp, and for a time dared not turn round. When at last I did I saw him standing bolt upright in the narrow recessed part. It would not be true to say I had a shock, but an irresistible doubt of his bodily existence flitted through my mind. Can it be, I asked myself, that he is not visible to other eyes than mine? It was like being haunted. Motionless, with a grave face, he raised his hands slightly at me in a gesture which meant clearly, "Heavens! what a narrow escape!" Narrow indeed. I think I had come creeping quietly as near insanity as any man who has not actually gone over the border. That gesture restrained me, so to speak.

The mate with the terrific whiskers was now putting the ship on the other tack. In the moment of profound silence which follows upon the hands going to their stations I heard on the poop his raised voice: "Hard alee!" and the distant shout of the order repeated on the main deck. The sails, in that light breeze, made but a faint fluttering noise. It ceased. The ship was coming round slowly; I held my breath in the renewed stillness of expectation; one wouldn't have thought that there was a single living soul on her decks. A sudden brisk shout, "Mainsail haul!" broke the spell, and in the noisy cries and rush overhead of the men running away with the main brace we two, down in my cabin, came together in our usual position by the bedplace.

He did not wait for my question. "I heard him fumbling here and just managed to squat myself down in the bath," he whispered to me. "The fellow only opened the door and put his arm in to hang the coat up. All the same. . . ."

"I never thought of that," I whispered back, even more appalled than before at the closeness of the shave, and marvelling at that something unyielding in his character which was carrying him through so finely. There was no agitation in his whisper. Whoever was being driven distracted, it was not he. He was sane. And the proof of his sanity was continued when he took up the whispering again.

"It would never do for me to come to life again."

It was something that a ghost might have said. But what he was alluding to was his 225
old captain's reluctant admission of the theory of suicide. It would obviously serve his turn—if I had understood at all the view which seemed to govern the unalterable purpose of his action.

"You must maroon me as soon as ever you can get amongst these islands off the Cambodje shore," he went on.

"Maroon you! We are not living in a boy's adventure tale," I protested. His scornful whispering took me up.

"We aren't indeed! There's nothing of a boy's tale in this. But there's nothing else for it. I want no more. You don't suppose I am afraid of what can be done to me? Prison or gallows or whatever they may please. But you don't see me coming back to explain such things to an old fellow in a wig and twelve respectable tradesmen, do you? What can they know whether I am guilty or not—or of *what* I am guilty, either? That's my affair. What does the Bible say? 'Driven off the face of the earth.' Very well. I am off the face of the earth now. As I came at night so I shall go."

"Impossible!" I murmured. "You can't."

"Can't? . . . Not naked like a soul on the Day of Judgement. I shall freeze on to 230
this sleeping suit. The Last Day is not yet—and . . . you have understood thoroughly. Didn't you?"

I felt suddenly ashamed of myself. I may say truly that I understood—and my hesitation in letting that man swim away from my ship's side had been a mere sham sentiment, a sort of cowardice.

"It can't be done now till next night," I breathed out. "The ship is on the offshore tack and the wind may fail us."

"As long as I know that you understand," he whispered. "But of course you do. It's a great satisfaction to have got somebody to understand. You seem to have been there on purpose." And in the same whisper, as if we two whenever we talked had to say things to each other which were not fit for the world to hear, he added, "It's very wonderful."

We remained side by side talking in our secret way—but sometimes silent or just exchanging a whispered word or two at long intervals. And as usual he stared through the port. A breath of wind came now and again into our faces. The ship might have been moored in dock, so gently and on an even keel she slipped through the water, that did not murmur even at our passage, shadowy and silent like a phantom sea.

At midnight I went on deck, and to my mate's great surprise put the ship round 235 on the other tack. His terrible whiskers flitted round me in silent criticism. I certainly should not have done it if it had been only a question of getting out of that sleepy gulf as quickly as possible. I believe he told the second mate, who relieved him, that it was a great want of judgement. The other only yawned. That intolerable cub shuffled about so sleepily and lolled against the rails in such a slack, improper fashion that I came down on him sharply.

"Aren't you properly awake yet?"

"Yes, sir! I am awake."

"Well, then, be good enough to hold yourself as if you were. And keep a look out. If there's any current we'll be closing with some islands long before daylight."

The east side of the gulf is fringed with islands, some solitary, others in groups. On the blue background of the high coast they seem to float on silvery patches of calm water, arid and grey, or dark green and rounded like clumps of evergreen bushes, with the larger ones, a mile or two long, showing the outlines of ridges, ribs of grey rock under the dank mantle of matted leafage. Unknown to trade, to travel, almost to geography, the manner of life they harbor is an unsolved secret. There must be villages—settlements of fishermen at least—on the largest of them, and some communication with the world is probably kept up by native craft. But all that forenoon, as we headed for them, fanned along by the faintest of breezes, I saw no sign of man or canoe in the field of the telescope I kept on pointing at the scattered group.

At noon I gave no orders for a change of course, and the mate's whiskers became 240 much concerned and seemed to be offering themselves unduly to my notice. At last I said:

"I am going to stand right in. Quite in—as far as I can take her."

The stare of extreme surprise imparted an air of ferocity also to his eyes, and he looked truly terrific for a moment.

"We're not doing well in the middle of the gulf," I continued casually. "I am going to look for the land breezes tonight."

"Bless my soul! Do you mean, sir, in the dark amongst the lot of all them islands and reefs and shoals?"

"Well, if there are any regular land breezes at all on this coast one must get close 245 inshore to find them—mustn't one?"

"Bless my soul!" he exclaimed again under his breath. All that afternoon he wore a dreamy, comtemplative appearance which in him was a mark of perplexity. After dinner I went into my stateroom as if I meant to take some rest. There we two bent our dark heads over a half-unrolled chart lying on my bed.

"There," I said. "It's got to be Koh-ring. I've been looking at it ever since sunrise. It has got two hills and a low point. It must be inhabited. And on the coast opposite there is what looks like the mouth of a biggish river—with some town, no doubt, not far up. It's the best chance for you that I can see."

"Anything. Koh-ring let it be."

He looked thoughtfully at the chart as if surveying chances and distances from a lofty height—and following with his eyes his own figure wandering on the blank land of Cochin-China, and then passing off that piece of paper clean out of sight into uncharted regions. And it was as if the ship had two captains to plan her course for her. I had been so worried and restless running up and down that I had not had the patience to dress that day. I had remained in my sleeping suit, with straw slippers and a soft floppy hat. The closeness of the heat in the gulf had been most oppressive, and the crew were used to see me wandering in that airy attire.

"She will clear the south point as she heads now," I whispered into his ear. "Goodness only knows when, though—but certainly after dark. I'll edge her in to half a mile, as far as I may be able to judge in the dark. . . . "   250

"Be careful," he murmured warningly—and I realized suddenly that all my future, the only future for which I was fit, would perhaps go irretrievably to pieces in any mishap to my first command.

I could not stop a moment longer in the room. I motioned him to get out of sight and made my way on the poop. That unplayful cub had the watch. I walked up and down for a while thinking things out, then beckoned him over.

"Send a couple of hands to open the two quarter-deck ports," I said mildly.

He actually had the impudence, or else so forgot himself in his wonder at such an incomprehensible order, as to repeat:

"Open the quarter-deck ports! What for, sir?"   255

"The only reason you need concern yourself about is because I tell you to do so. Have them opened wide and fastened properly."

He reddened and went off, but I believe made some jeering remark to the carpenter as to the sensible practice of ventilating a ship's quarter-deck. I know he popped into the mate's cabin to impart the fact to him, because the whiskers came on deck, as it were by chance, and stole glances at me from below—for signs of lunacy or drunkenness, I suppose.

A little before supper, feeling more restless than ever, I rejoined, for a moment, my second self. And to find him sitting so quietly was surprising, like something against nature, inhuman.

I developed my plan in a hurried whisper.

"I shall stand in as close as I dare and then put her round. I shall presently find   260 means to smuggle you out of here into the sail-locker, which communicates with the lobby. But there is an opening, a sort of square for hauling the sails out, which gives straight on the quarter-deck and which is never closed in fine weather, so as to give air to the sails. When the ship's way is deadened in stays and all the hands are aft at the main braces you shall have a clear road to slip out and get overboard through the open quarter-deck port. I've had them both fastened up. Use a rope's end to lower yourself into the water so as to avoid a splash—you know. It could be heard and cause some beastly complication."

He kept silent for a while, then whispered, "I understand."

"I won't be there to see you go," I began with an effort. "The rest . . . I only hope I have understood too."

"You have. From first to last"—and for the first time there seemed to be a faltering, something strained in his whisper. He caught hold of my arm, but the ringing of the supper bell made me start. He didn't, though; he only released his grip.

After supper I didn't come below again till well past eight o'clock. The faint, steady breeze was loaded with dew; and the wet, darkened sails held all there was of propelling power in it. The night, clear and starry, sparkled darkly, and the opaque, lightless patches shifting slowly amongst the low stars were the drifting islets. On the port bow there was a big one more distant and shadowily imposing by the great space of sky it eclipsed.

On opening the door I had a back view of my very own self looking at a chart. He   265
had come out of the recess and was standing near the table.

"Quite dark enough," I whispered.

He stepped back and leaned against my bed with a level, quiet glance. I sat on the couch. We had nothing to say to each other. Over our heads the officer of the watch moved here and there. Then I heard him move quickly. I knew what that meant. He was making for the companion; and presently his voice was outside my door.

"We are drawing in pretty fast, sir. Land looks rather close."

"Very well," I answered. "I am coming on deck directly."

I waited till he was gone out of the cuddy, then rose. My double moved too. The   270
time had come to exchange our last whispers, for neither of us was ever to hear each other's natural voice.

"Look here!" I opened a drawer and took out three sovereigns. "Take this, any-how. I've got six and I'd give you the lot, only I must keep a little money to buy some fruit and vegetables for the crew from native boats as we go through Sunda Straits."

He shook his head.

"Take it," I urged him, whispering desperately. "No one can tell what . . . "

He smiled and slapped meaningly the only pocket of the sleeping jacket. It was not safe, certainly. But I produced a large old silk handkerchief of mine, and tying the three pieces of gold in a corner, pressed it on him. He was touched, I suppose, because he took it at last and tied it quickly round his waist under the jacket, on his bare skin.

Our eyes met; several seconds elapsed, till, our glances still mingled, I extended my   275
hand and turned the lamp out. Then I passed through the cuddy, leaving the door of my room wide open. . . . "Steward!"

He was still lingering in the pantry in the greatness of his zeal, giving a rub-up to a plated cruet stand the last thing before going to bed. Being careful not to wake up the mate, whose room was opposite, I spoke in an undertone.

He looked round anxiously. "Sir!"

"Can you get me a little hot water from the galley?"

"I am afraid, sir, the galley fire's been out for some time now."

"Go and see."   280

He fled up the stairs.

"Now," I whispered loudly into the saloon—too loudly, perhaps, but I was afraid I couldn't make a sound. He was by my side in an instant—the double captain slipped past the stairs—through a tiny dark passage . . . a sliding door. We were in the sail-locker, scrambling on our knees over the sails. A sudden thought struck me. I saw my-self wandering barefooted, bareheaded, the sun beating on my dark poll. I snatched off my floppy hat and tried hurriedly in the dark to ram it on my other self. He dodged and fended off silently. I wonder what he thought had come to me before he under-stood and suddenly desisted. Our hands met gropingly, lingered united in a steady, motionless clasp for a second. . . . No word was breathed by either of us when they separated.

I was standing quietly by the pantry door when the steward returned.

"Sorry, sir. Kettle barely warm. Shall I light the spirit-lamp?"

"Never mind."   285

I came out on deck slowly. It was now a matter of conscience to shave the land as close as possible—for now he must go overboard whenever the ship was put in stays.

Must! There could be no going back for him. After a moment I walked over to leeward and my heart flew into my mouth at the nearness of the land on the bow. Under any other circumstances I would not have held on a minute longer. The second mate had followed me anxiously.

I looked on till I felt I could command my voice.

"She will weather," I said then in a quiet tone.

"Are you going to try that, sir?" he stammered out incredulously.

I took no notice of him and raised my tone just enough to be heard by the 290
helmsman.

"Keep her good full."

"Good full, sir."

The wind fanned my cheek, the sails slept, the world was silent. The strain of watching the dark loom of the land grow bigger and denser was too much for me. I had to shut my eyes—because the ship must go closer. She must! The stillness was intolerable. Were we standing still?

When I opened my eyes the second view started my heart with a thump. The black southern hill of Koh-ring seemed to hang right over the ship like a towering fragment of the everlasting night. On that enormous mass of blackness there was not a gleam to be seen, not a sound to be heard. It was gliding irresistibly towards us and yet seemed already within reach of the hand. I saw the vague figures of the watch grouped in the waist, gazing in awed silence.

"Are you going on, sir?" inquired an unsteady voice at my elbow. 295

I ignored it. I had to go on.

"Keep her full. Don't check her way. That won't do now," I said warningly.

"I can't see the sails very well," the helmsman answered me, in strange, quavering tones.

Was she close enough? Already she was, I won't say in the shadow of the land, but in the very blackness of it, already swallowed up as it were, gone too close to be recalled, gone from me altogether.

"Give the mate a call," I said to the young man who stood at my elbow as still as 300
death. "And turn all hands up."

My tone had a borrowed loudness reverberated from the height of the land. Several voices cried out together, "We are all on deck, sir."

Then stillness again, with the great shadow gliding closer, towering higher, without a light, without a sound. Such a hush had fallen on the ship that she might have been a bark of the dead floating in slowly under the very gate of Erebus.

"My God! Where are we?"

It was the mate moaning at my elbow. He was thunderstruck, and as it were deprived of the moral support of his whiskers. He clapped his hands and absolutely cried out, "Lost!"

"Be quiet," I said sternly. 305

He lowered his tone, but I saw the shadowy gesture of his despair. "What are we doing here?"

"Looking for the land wind."

He made as if to tear his hair, and addressed me recklessly.

"She will never get out. You have done it, sir. I knew it'd end in something like this. She will never weather, and you are too close now to stay. She'll drift ashore before she's round. O my God!"

I caught his arm as he was raising it to batter his poor devoted head, and shook it 310
violently.

"She's ashore already," he wailed, trying to tear himself away.

"Is she? . . . Keep good full there!"

"Good full, sir," cried the helmsman in a frightened, thin, child-like voice.

I hadn't let go the mate's arm and went on shaking it. "Ready about, do you hear? You go forward"—shake—"and stop there"—shake—"and hold your noise"—shake—"and see these head-sheets properly overhauled"—shake, shake—shake.

And all the time I dared not look towards the land lest my heart should fail me. I released my grip at last and he ran forward as if fleeing for dear life.   315

I wondered what my double there in the sail-locker thought of this commotion. He was able to hear everything—and perhaps he was able to understand why, on my conscience, it had to be thus close—no less. My first order "Hard alee!" re-echoed ominously under the towering shadow of Koh-ring as if I had shouted in a mountain gorge. And then I watched the land intently. In that smooth water and light wind it was impossible to feel the ship coming-to. No! I could not feel her. And my second self was making now ready to slip out and lower himself overboard. Perhaps he was gone already . . . ?

The great black mass brooding over our very mast-heads began to pivot away from the ship's side silently. And now I forgot the secret stranger ready to depart, and remembered only that I was a total stranger to the ship. I did not know her. Would she do it? How was she to be handled?

I swung the mainyard and waited helplessly. She was perhaps stopped, and her very fate hung in the balance, with the black mass of Koh-ring like the gate of the everlasting night towering over her taffrail. What would she do now? Had she way on her yet? I stepped to the side swiftly, and on the shadowy water I could see nothing except a faint phosphorescent flash revealing the glassy smoothness of the sleeping surface. It was impossible to tell—and I had not learned yet the feel of my ship. Was she moving? What I needed was something easily seen, a piece of paper, which I could throw overboard and watch. I had nothing on me. To run down for it I didn't dare. There was no time. All at once my strained, yearning stare distinguished a white object floating within a yard of the ship's side—white, on the black water. A phosphorescent flash passed under it. What was that thing? . . . I recognized my own floppy hat. It must have fallen off his head . . . and he didn't bother. Now I had what I wanted—the saving mark for my eyes. But I hardly thought of my other self, now gone from the ship, to be hidden forever from all friendly faces, to be a fugitive and a vagabond on the earth, with no brand of the curse on his sane forehead to stay a slaying hand . . . too proud to explain.

And I watched the hat—the expression of my sudden pity for his mere flesh. It had been meant to save his homeless head from the dangers of the sun. And now—behold—it was saving the ship, by serving me for a mark to help out the ignorance of my strangeness. Ha! It was drifting forward, warning me just in time that the ship had gathered sternway.

"Shift the helm," I said in a low voice to the seaman standing still like a statue.   320

The man's eyes glistened wildly in the binnacle light as he jumped round to the other side and spun round the wheel.

I walked to the break of the poop. On the overshadowed deck all hands stood by the forebraces waiting for my order. The stars ahead seemed to be gliding from right to left. And all was so still in the world that I heard the quiet remark, "She's round," passed in a tone of intense relief between two seamen.

"Let go and haul."

The foreyards ran round with a great noise, amidst cheery cries. And now the frightful whiskers made themselves heard giving various orders. Already the ship was drawing ahead. And I was alone with her. Nothing! no one in the world should stand now between us, throwing a shadow on the way of silent knowledge and mute affection; the perfect communion of a seaman with his first command.

Walking to the taffrail, I was in time to make out, on the very edge of a darkness thrown by a towering black mass like the very gateway of Erebus—yes, I was in time to catch an evanescent glimpse of my white hat left behind to mark the spot where the secret sharer of my cabin and of my thoughts, as though he were my second self, had lowered himself into the water to take his punishment: a free man, a proud swimmer striking out for a new destiny.   325

RALPH ELLISON   (born 1914)

Mister Toussan   1941

Once upon a time
The goose drink wine
Monkey chew tobacco
And he spit white lime.
RHYME USED AS A PROLOGUE TO NEGRO SLAVE STORIES

"I hope they all gits rotten and the worms git in 'em," the first boy said.

"I hopes a big windstorm comes and blows down all the trees," said the second boy.

"Me too," the first boy said. "And when old Rogan comes out to see what happened I hope a tree falls on his head and kills him."

"Now jus' look a-yonder at them birds," the second boy said, "they eating all they want and when we asked him to let us git some off the ground he had to come calling us names and chasing us home!"

"Doggonit," said the second boy, "I hope them birds got poison in they feet!"   5

The two small boys, Riley and Buster, sat on the floor of the porch, their bare feet resting upon the cool earth as they stared past the line on the paving where the sun consumed the shade, to a yard directly across the street. The grass in the yard was very green and a house stood against it, neat and white in the morning sun. A double row of trees stood alongside the house, heavy with cherries that showed deep red against the dark green of the leaves and dull dark brown of the branches. They were watching an old man who rocked himself in a chair as he stared back at them across the street.

"Just look at him," said Buster. "Ole Rogan's so scared we gonna git some of his ole cherries he ain't even got sense enough to go in outa the sun!"

"Well, them birds is gitting theirs," said Riley.

"They mockingbirds."

"I don't care what kinda birds they is, they sho in them trees."   10

"Yeah, old Rogan don't see *them*. Man, white folks ain't got no sense."

They were silent now, watching the darting flight of the birds into the trees. Behind them they could hear the clatter of a sewing machine: Riley's mother was sewing for the white folks. It was quiet and, as the woman worked, her voice rose above the whirring machine in song.

"Your mamma sho can sing, man," said Buster.

"She sings in the choir," said Riley, "and she sings all the leads in church."

"Shucks, I know it," said Buster. "You tryin' to brag?"   15

As they listened they heard the voice rise clear and liquid to float upon the morning air:

> I got wings, you got wings,
> All God's chillun got a-wings
> When I git to heaven gonna put on my wings
> Gonna shout all ovah God's heaven.
> Heab'n, heab'n
> Everybody talkin' bout heab'n ain't going there
> Heab'n, heab'n, Ah'm gonna fly all ovah God's heab'n. . . .

She sang as though the words possessed a deep and throbbing meaning for her, and the boys stared blankly at the earth, feeling the somber, mysterious calm of church. The street was quiet and even old Rogan had stopped rocking to listen. Finally the voice trailed off to a hum and became lost in the clatter of the busy machine.

"Sure wish I could sing like that," said Buster.

Riley was silent, looking down to the end of the porch where the sun had eaten a bright square into the shade, fixing a flitting butterfly in its brilliance.

"What would you do if you had wings?" he said.   20

"Shucks, I'd outfly an eagle, I wouldn't stop flying till I was a million, billion, trillion, zillion miles away from this ole town."

"Where'd you go, man?"

"Up north, maybe to Chicago."

"Man, if I had wings I wouldn't never settle down."

"Me neither. With wings you could go anywhere, even up to the sun if it wasn't   25
too hot. . . ."

". . . I'd go to New York. . . ."

"Even around the stars. . ."

"Or Dee-troit, Michigan . . ."

"You could git some cheese off the moon and some milk from the Milky Way. . . ."

"Or anywhere else colored is free. . . ."   30

"I bet I'd loop-the-loop. . . ."

"And parachute. . . ."

"I'd land in Africa and git me some diamonds. . . ."

"Yeah, and them cannibals would eat you too," said Riley.

"The heck they would, not fast as I'd fly away. . . ."   35

"Man, they'd catch you and stick soma them long spears in you!" said Riley.

Buster laughed as Riley shook his head gravely: "Boy, you'd look like a black pincushion when they got through with you," said Riley.

"Shucks, man, they couldn't catch me, them suckers is too lazy. The geography book says they 'bout the most lazy folks in the whole world," said Buster with disgust, "just black and lazy!"

"Aw naw, they ain't neither," exploded Riley.

"They is too! The geography book says they is!"   40

"Well, my ole man says they ain't!"

"How come they ain't then?"

"'Cause my ole man says that over there they got kings and diamonds and gold and ivory, and if they got all them things, all of 'em cain't be lazy," said Riley. "Ain't many colored folks over here got them things."

"Sho ain't, man. The white folks won't let 'em," said Buster.

It was good to think that all the Africans were not lazy. He tried to remember   45
all he had heard of Africa as he watched a purple pigeon sail down into the street
and scratch where a horse had passed. Then, as he remembered a story his teacher
had told him, he saw a car rolling swiftly up the street and the pigeon stretching its
wings and lifting easily into the air, skimming the top of the car in its slow, rocking
flight. He watched it rise and disappear where the taut telephone wires cut the sky
above the curb. Buster felt good. Riley scratched his initials in the soft earth with his
big toe.

"Riley, you know all them African guys ain't really that lazy," he said.

"I know they ain't," said Riley, "I just tole you so."

"Yeah, but my teacher tole me, too. She tole us 'bout one of them African guys
named Toussan what she said whipped Napoleon!"

Riley stopped scratching the earth and looked up, his eyes rolling in disgust:

"Now how come you have to start lying?"   50

"Thass what she said."

"Boy, you oughta quit telling them things."

"I hope God may kill me."

"She said he was a *African*?"

"Cross my heart, man. . . ."   55

"Really?"

"Really, man. She said he come from a place named Hayti."

Riley looked hard at Buster and seeing the seriousness of the face felt the excitement of a story rise up within him.

"Buster, I'll bet a fat man you lyin'. What'd that teacher say?"

"Really, man, she said that Toussan and his men got up on one of them   60
African mountains and shot down them peckerwood soldiers fass as they'd try to come
up. . . ."

"Why good-a-mighty!" yelled Riley.

"Oh boy, they shot 'em down!" chanted Buster.

"Tell me about it, man!"

"And they throwed 'em all off the mountain. . . ."

". . . Goool-leee! . . ."   65

". . . And Toussan drove 'em cross the sand. . . ."

". . . Yeah! And what was they wearing, Buster? . . ."

"Man, they had on red uniforms and blue hats all trimmed with gold, and they
had some swords, all shining what they called sweet blades of Damascus. . . ."

"Sweet blades of Damascus! . . ."

". . . They really had 'em," chanted Buster.   70

"And what kinda guns?"

"Big, black cannon!"

"And where did ole what-you-call-'im run them guys? . . ."

"His name was Toussan."

"Toussan! Just like Tarzan. . ."   75

"Not *Taar*-zan, dummy, *Toou*-zan!"

"Toussan! And where'd ole Toussan run 'em?"

"Down to the water, man. . ."

". . . To the river water. . ."

". . . Where some great big ole boats was waiting for 'em. . ."   80

". . . Go on, Buster!"

"An' Toussan shot into them boats. . . ."

". . . He shot into 'em. . . ."

"With his great big cannons. . ."

". . . Yeah! . . ."   85

". . . Made a-brass. . ."

". . . Brass. . ."

". . . An' his big black cannonballs started killin' them peckerwoods. . . ."

". . . Lawd, Lawd. . ."

". . . Boy, till them peckerwoods hollered *'Please, please, Mister Toussan, we'll*   90
be good!'"

"An' what'd Toussan tell 'em, Buster?"

"'Boy,' he said in his big deep voice, *'I oughta drown all a-you.'"*

"An' what'd the peckerwoods say?"

"They said, 'Please, Please, *Please, Mister Toussan.* . .'"

". . . 'We'll be good,'" broke in Riley.   95

"Thass right, man," said Buster excitedly. He clapped his hands and kicked his
heels against the earth, his black face glowing in a burst of rhythmic joy.

"Boy!"

"And what'd ole Toussan say then?"

"He said in his big deep voice: 'You all peckerwoods better be good, *'cause this is*
sweet Papa Toussan talking and my men is crazy 'bout white meat!'"

"Ho, ho, ho!" Riley bent double with laughter. The rhythm still throbbed within   100
him and he wanted the story to go on and on. . . .

"Buster, you know didn't no teacher tell you that lie," he said.

"Yes she did, man."

"That teacher said there was really a guy like that what called hisself Sweet Papa
Toussan?"

Riley's voice was unbelieving and there was a wistful expression in his eyes which
Buster could not understand. Finally he dropped his head and grinned.

"Well," he said, "I bet thass what ole Toussan said. You know how grown folks is,   105
they cain't tell a story right, 'cepting real old folks like grandma."

"They sho cain't," said Riley. "They don't know how to put the right stuff to it."

Riley stood, his legs spread wide, and stuck his thumbs in the top of his trousers,
swaggering sinisterly.

"Come on, watch me do it now, Buster. Now I bet ole Toussan looked down at
them white folks standing just about like this and said in a soft easy voice: 'Ain't I done
begged you white folks to quit messin' with me? . . .'"

"Thass right, quit messing with 'im," chanted Buster.

"'But naw, you-all had to come on anyway. . . .'"   110

". . . Jus' 'cause they was black. . ."

"Thass right," said Riley. "Then ole Toussan felt so bad and mad the tears come a-
trickling down. . . ."

". . . He was really mad."

"And then, man, he said in his big bass voice: 'white folks, how come you-all cain't
let us colored alone?'"

". . . An' he was crying. . . ."   115

". . . An' Toussan tole them peckerwoods: 'I been beggin' you-all to quit bothering us. . . .'"

". . . Beggin' on his bended knees! . . ."

"Then, man, Toussan got real mad and snatched off his hat and started stompin'
up and down on it and the tears was tricklin' down and he said: 'You-all come tellin'
me about Napoleon. . . .'"

"They was tryin' to make him scared, man. . . ."

"Toussan said: 'I don't care about no Napoleon. . . .'"   120

". . . Wasn't studyin' 'bout him. . . ."

". . . Toussan said: 'Napoleon ain't nothing but a man!' Then Toussan pulled back his shining sword like this, and twirled it at them peckerwoods' throats so hard it z-z-z-zinged in the air!"

"Now keep on, finish it, man," said Buster. "What'd Toussan do then?"

"Then you know what he did, he said: 'I oughta beat you peckerwoods!'"

"Thass right, and he did it too," said Buster. He jumped to his feet and fenced vi-   125
olently with five desperate imaginary soldiers, running each through with his imaginary sword. Buster watched from the porch, grinning.

"Toussan musta scared them white folks almost to death!"

"Yeah, thass 'bout the way it was," said Buster. The rhythm was dying now and he sat back upon the porch, breathing tiredly.

"It sho is a good story," said Riley.

"Hecks, man, all the stories my teacher tells us is good. She's a good ole teacher— but you know one thing?"

"Naw; what?"   130

"Ain't none of them stories in the books! Wonder why?"

"You know why, ole Toussan was too hard on them white folks, thass why."

"Oh, he was a hard man!"

"He was mean. . . ."

"But a good mean!"   135

"Toussan was clean. . . ."

". . . He was a good, clean mean," said Riley.

"Aw, man, he was sooo-preme," said Buster.

"Riiiley!!"

The boys stopped short in their word play, their mouths wide.   140

"Riley I say!" It was Riley's mother's voice.

"Ma'am?"

"She musta heard us cussin'," whispered Buster.

"Shut up, man. . . . What you want, Ma?"

"I says I wants you-all to go around in the backyard and play, you keeping up too   145
much fuss out there. White folks says we tear up a neighborhood when we move in it and you-all out there jus' provin' them out true. Now git on round in the back."

"Aw, ma, we was jus' playing, ma. . . ."

"Boy, I said for you-all to go on."

"But, ma. . ."

"You hear me, boy!"

"Yessum, we going," said Riley. "Come on, Buster."   150

Buster followed slowly behind, feeling the dew upon his feet as he walked upon the shaded grass.

"What else did he do, man?" Buster said.

"Huh? Rogan?"

"Heck, naw! I mean Toussan."

"Doggone if I know, man—but I'm gonna ask that teacher."   155

"He was a fightin' son-of-a-gun, wasn't he, man?"

"He didn't stand for no foolishness," said Riley reservedly. He thought of other things now, and as he moved along he slid his feet easily over the short-cut grass, dancing as he chanted

Iron is iron,
And tin is tin,
And that's the way
The story . . .

"Aw come on man," interrupted Buster. "Let's go play in the alley. . . ."

And that's the way . . .

"Maybe we can slip around and git some cherries," Buster went on.

". . . the story ends," chanted Riley.

WILLIAM FAULKNER   (1897–1962)
Barn Burning   1939

[The boy in this story, Colonel Sartoris, is named for Faulkner's character Colonel John Sartoris, a plantation owner and Civil War hero. Because this story is set in the rural South, Faulkner uses dialects, idioms, and terminology of rural Southern people. Words such as *hame* and *logger-head*, for instance, refer to parts of a harness; *straight stock* and *middle buster* refer to ploughs; a *shoat* is a young pig. Other mostly regional words include *suspiration*—sighing, *rifeness*—fullness or abundance, *hermetic meat*—canned meat, a *Confederate provost's man*—a military policeman, *lye*—a caustic, alkaline solution, *cypress bolt*—a bar of a gate, and *tulle*—a silk dress. Faulkner makes two literary allusions: one to the six-inch-tall Lilliputians of Jonathan Swift's *Gulliver's Travels* (1726), the other to a popular eighteenth-century French nursery rhyme about a war hero, Malbrouck.]

The store in which the Justice of the Peace's court was sitting smelled of cheese. The boy, crouched on his nail keg at the back of the crowded room, knew he smelled cheese, and more: from where he sat he could see the ranked shelves close-packed with the solid, squat, dynamic shapes of tin cans whose labels his stomach read, not from the lettering which meant nothing to his mind but from the scarlet devils and the silver curve of fish—this, the cheese which he knew he smelled and the hermetic meat which his intestines believed he smelled coming in intermittent gusts momentary and brief between the other constant one, the smell and sense just a little of fear because mostly of despair and grief, the old fierce pull of blood. He could not see the table where the Justice sat and before which his father and his father's enemy (*our enemy* he thought in that despair; *ourn! mine and hisn both! He's my father!*) stood, but he could hear them, the two of them that is, because his father had said no word yet:
"But what proof have you, Mr. Harris?"
"I told you. The hog got into my corn. I caught it up and sent it back to him. He had no fence that would hold it. I told him so, warned him. The next time I put the hog in my pen. When he came to get it I gave him enough wire to patch up his pen. The next time I put the hog up and kept it. I rode down to his house and saw the wire

I gave him still rolled on to the spool in his yard. I told him he could have the hog when he paid me a dollar pound fee. That evening a nigger came with the dollar and got the hog. He was a strange nigger. He said, 'He say to tell you wood and hay kin burn.' I said, 'What?' 'That whut he say to tell you,' the nigger said. 'Wood and hay kin burn.' That night my barn burned. I got the stock out but I lost the barn."

"Where is the nigger? Have you got him?"

"He was a strange nigger, I tell you. I don't know what became of him." 5

"But that's not proof. Don't you see that's not proof?"

"Get that boy up here. He knows." For a moment the boy thought too that the man meant his older brother until Harris said, "Not him. The little one. The boy," and, crouching, small for his age, small and wiry like his father, in patched and faded jeans even too small for him, with straight, uncombed, brown hair and eyes gray and wild as storm scud, he saw the men between himself and the table part and become a lane of grim faces, at the end of which he saw the Justice, a shabby, collarless, graying man in spectacles, beckoning him. He felt no floor under his bare feet; he seemed to walk beneath the palpable weight of the grim turning faces. His father, stiff in his black Sunday coat donned not for the trial but for the moving, did not even look at him. *He aims for me to lie,* he thought, again with that frantic grief and despair. *And I will have to do hit.*

"What's your name, boy?" the Justice said.

"Colonel Sartoris Snopes," the boy whispered.

"Hey?" the Justice said. "Talk louder. Colonel Sartoris? I reckon anybody named 10 for Colonel Sartoris in this country can't help but tell the truth, can they?" The boy said nothing. *Enemy! Enemy!* he thought; for a moment he could not even see, could not see that the Justice's face was kindly nor discern that his voice was troubled when he spoke to the man named Harris: "Do you want me to question this boy?" But he could hear, and during those subsequent long seconds while there was absolutely no sound in the crowded little room save that of quiet and intent breathing it was as if he had swung outward at the end of a grape vine, over a ravine, and at the top of the swing had been caught in a prolonged instant of mesmerized gravity, weightless in time.

"No!" Harris said violently, explosively. "Damnation! Send him out of here!" Now time, the fluid world, rushed beneath him again, the voices coming to him again through the smell of cheese and sealed meat, the fear and despair and the old grief of blood:

"This case is closed. I can't find against you, Snopes, but I can give you advice. Leave this country and don't come back to it."

His father spoke for the first time, his voice cold and harsh, level, without emphasis: "I aim to. I don't figure to stay in a country among people who . . ." he said something unprintable and vile, addressed to no one.

"That'll do," the Justice said. "Take your wagon and get out of this country before dark. Case dismissed."

His father turned, and he followed the stiff black coat, the wiry figure walking a lit- 15 tle stiffly from where a Confederate provost's man's musket ball had taken him in the heel on a stolen horse thirty years ago, followed the two backs now, since his older brother had appeared from somewhere in the crowd, no taller than the father but thicker, chewing tobacco steadily, between the two lines of grim-faced men and out of the store and across the worn gallery and down the sagging steps and among the dogs and half-grown boys in the mild May dust, where as he passed a voice hissed:

"Barn burner!"

Again he could not see, whirling; there was a face in a red haze, moonlike, bigger than the full moon, the owner of it half again his size, he leaping in the red haze toward the face, feeling no blow, feeling no shock when his head struck the earth, scrabbling up and leaping again, feeling no blow this time either and tasting no blood, scrabbling up to see the other boy in full flight and himself already leaping into pursuit as his father's hand jerked him back, the harsh, cold voice speaking above him: "Go get in the wagon."

It stood in a grove of locusts and mulberries across the road. His two hulking sisters in their Sunday dresses and his mother and her sister in calico and sunbonnets were already in it, sitting on and among the sorry residue of the dozen and more movings which even the boy could remember—the battered stove, the broken beds and chairs, the clock inlaid with mother-of-pearl, which would not run, stopped at some fourteen minutes past two o'clock of a dead and forgotten day and time, which had been his mother's dowry. She was crying, though when she saw him she drew her sleeve across her face and began to descend from the wagon. "Get back," the father said.

"He's hurt. I got to get some water and wash his . . ."

"Get back in the wagon," his father said. He got in too, over the tail-gate. His father mounted to the seat where the older brother already sat and struck the gaunt mules two savage blows with the peeled willow, but without heat. It was not even sadistic; it was exactly that same quality which in later years would cause his descendants to over-run the engine before putting a motor car into motion, striking and reining back in the same movement. The wagon went on, the store with its quiet crowd of grimly watching men dropped behind; a curve in the road hid it. *Forever* he thought. *Maybe he's done satisfied now, now that he has . . .* stopping himself, not to say it aloud even to himself. His mother's hand touched his shoulder. 20

"Does hit hurt?" she said.

"Naw," he said. "Hit don't hurt. Lemme be."

"Can't you wipe some of the blood off before hit dries?"

"I'll wash to-night," he said. "Lemme be, I tell you."

The wagon went on. He did not know where they were going. None of them ever did or ever asked, because it was always somewhere, always a house of sorts waiting for them a day or two days or even three days away. Likely his father had already arranged to make a crop on another farm before he . . . Again he had to stop himself. He (the father) always did. There was something about his wolflike independence and even courage when the advantage was at least neutral which impressed strangers, as if they got from his latent ravening ferocity not so much a sense of dependability as a feeling that his ferocious conviction in the rightness of his own actions would be of advantage to all whose interest lay with his. 25

That night they camped, in a grove of oaks and beeches where a spring ran. The nights were still cool and they had a fire against it, of a rail lifted from a nearby fence and cut into lengths—a small fire, neat, niggard almost, a shrewd fire; such fires were his father's habit and custom always, even in freezing weather. Older, the boy might have remarked this and wondered why not a big one; why should not a man who had not only seen the waste and extravagance of war, but who had in his blood an inherent voracious prodigality with material not his own, have burned everything in sight? Then he might have gone a step farther and thought that that was the reason: that niggard blaze was the living fruit of nights passed during those four years in the woods hiding from all men, blue or gray, with his strings of horses (captured horses, he called them). And older still, he might have divined the true reason: that the element of fire spoke to some deep mainspring of his father's being, as the element of steel or of powder spoke to other men, as the one weapon for the preservation of integrity, else breath were not worth the breathing, and hence to be regarded with respect and used with discretion.

But he did not think this now and he had seen those same niggard blazes all his life. He merely ate his supper beside it and was already half asleep over his iron plate when his father called him, and once more he followed the stiff back, the stiff and ruthless limp, up the slope and on to the starlit road where, turning, he could see his father against the stars but without face or depth—a shape black, flat, and bloodless as though cut from tin in the iron folds of the frockcoat which had not been made for him, the voice harsh like tin and without heat like tin:

"You were fixing to tell them. You would have told him." He didn't answer. His father struck him with the flat of his hand on the side of the head, hard but without heat, exactly as he had struck the two mules at the store, exactly as he would strike either of them with any stick in order to kill a horse fly, his voice still without heat or anger: "You're getting to be a man. You got to learn. You got to learn to stick to your own blood or you ain't going to have any blood to stick to you. Do you think either of them, any man there this morning, would? Don't you know all they wanted was a chance to get at me because they knew I had them beat? Eh?" Later, twenty years later, he was to tell himself, "If I had said they wanted only truth, justice, he would have hit me again." But now he said nothing. He was not crying. He just stood there. "Answer me," his father said.

"Yes," he whispered. His father turned.

"Get on to bed. We'll be there tomorrow."   30

Tomorrow they were there. In the early afternoon the wagon stopped before a paintless two-room house identical almost with the dozen others it had stopped before even in the boy's ten years, and again, as on the other dozen occasions, his mother and aunt got down and began to unload the wagon, although his two sisters and his father and brother had not moved.

"Likely hit ain't fitten for hawgs," one of the sisters said.

"Nevertheless, fit it will and you'll hog it and like it," his father said. "Get out of them chairs and help your Ma unload."

The two sisters got down, big, bovine, in a flutter of cheap ribbons; one of them drew from the jumbled wagon bed a battered lantern, the other a worn broom. His father handed the reins to the older son and began to climb stiffly over the wheel. "When they get unloaded, take the team to the barn and feed them." Then he said, and at first the boy thought he was still speaking to his brother: "Come with me."

"Me?" he said.   35

"Yes," his father said. "You."

"Abner," his mother said. His father paused and looked back—the harsh level stare beneath the shaggy, graying, irascible brows.

"I reckon I'll have a word with the man that aims to begin to-morrow owning me body and soul for the next eight months."

They went back up the road. A week ago—or before last night, that is—he would have asked where they were going, but not now. His father had struck him before last night but never before had he paused afterward to explain why; it was as if the blow and the following calm, outrageous voice still rang, repercussed, divulging nothing to him save the terrible handicap of being young, the light weight of his few years, just heavy enough to prevent his soaring free of the world as it seemed to be ordered but not heavy enough to keep him footed solid in it, to resist it and try to change the course of its events.

Presently he could see the grove of oaks and cedars and the other flowering trees   40
and shrubs where the house would be, though not the house yet. They walked beside a

fence massed with honeysuckle and Cherokee roses and came to a gate swinging open between two brick pillars, and now, beyond a sweep of drive, he saw the house for the first time and at that instant he forgot his father and the terror and despair both, and even when he remembered his father again (who had not stopped) the terror and despair did not return. Because, for all the twelve movings, they had sojourned until now in a poor country, a land of small farms and fields and houses, and he had never seen a house like this before. *Hit's big as a courthouse* he thought quietly, with a surge of peace and joy whose reason he could not have thought into words, being too young for that: *They are safe from him. People whose lives are a part of this peace and dignity are beyond his touch, he no more to them than a buzzing wasp: capable of stinging for a little moment but that's all; the spell of this peace and dignity rendering even the barns and stable and cribs which belong to it impervious to the puny flames he might contrive* . . . this, the peace and joy, ebbing for an instant as he looked again at the stiff black back, the stiff and implacable limp of the figure which was not dwarfed by the house, for the reason that it had never looked big anywhere and which now, against the serene columned backdrop, had more than ever that impervious quality of something cut ruthlessly from tin, depthless, as though, sidewise to the sun, it would cast no shadow. Watching him, the boy remarked the absolutely undeviating course which his father held and saw the stiff foot come squarely down in a pile of fresh droppings where a horse had stood in the drive and which his father could have avoided by a simple change of stride. But it ebbed only for a moment, though he could not have thought this into words either, walking on in the spell of the house, which he could even want but without envy, without sorrow, certainly never with that ravening and jealous rage which unknown to him walked in the ironlike black coat before him: *Maybe he will feel it too. Maybe it will even change him now from what maybe he couldn't help but be.*

They crossed the portico. Now he could hear his father's stiff foot as it came down on the boards with clocklike finality, a sound out of all proportion to the displacement of the body it bore and which was not dwarfed either by the white door before it, as though it had attained to a sort of vicious and ravening minimum not to be dwarfed by anything—the flat, wide, black hat, the formal coat of broadcloth which had once been black but which had now that friction-glazed greenish cast of the bodies of old house flies, the lifted sleeve which was too large, the lifted hand like a curled claw. The door opened so promptly that the boy knew the Negro must have been watching them all the time, an old man with neat grizzled hair, in a linen jacket, who stood barring the door with his body, saying, "Wipe yo foots, white man, fo you come in here. Major ain't home nohow."

"Get out of my way, nigger," his father said, without heat too, flinging the door back and the Negro also and entering, his hat still on his head. And now the boy saw the prints of the stiff foot on the doorjamb and saw them appear on the pale rug behind the machinelike deliberation of the foot which seemed to bear (or transmit) twice the weight which the body compassed. The Negro was shouting "Miss Lula! Miss Lula!" somewhere behind them, then the boy, deluged as though by a warm wave by a suave turn of carpeted stair and a pendant glitter of chandeliers and a mute gleam of gold frames, heard the swift feet and saw her too, a lady—perhaps he had never seen her like before either—in a gray, smooth gown with lace at the throat and an apron tied at the waist and the sleeves turned back, wiping cake or biscuit dough from her hands with a towel as she came up the hall, looking not at his father at all but at the tracks on the blond rug with an expression of incredulous amazement.

"I tried," the Negro cried. "I tole him to . . ."

"Will you please go away?" she said in a shaking voice. "Major de Spain is not at home. Will you please go away?"

His father had not spoken again. He did not speak again. He did not even look at   45
her. He just stood stiff in the center of the rug, in his hat, the shaggy iron-gray brows
twitching slightly above the pebble-colored eyes as he appeared to examine the house
with brief deliberation. Then with the same deliberation he turned; the boy watched
him pivot on the good leg and saw the stiff foot drag round the arc of the turning, leaving a final long and fading smear. His father never looked at it, he never once looked
down at the rug. The Negro held the door. It closed behind them, upon the hysteric
and indistinguishable woman-wail. His father stopped at the top of the steps and
scraped his boot clean on the edge of it. At the gate he stopped again. He stood for a
moment, planted stiffly on the stiff foot, looking back at the house. "Pretty and white,
ain't it?" he said. "That's sweat. Nigger sweat. Maybe it ain't white enough yet to suit
him. Maybe he wants to mix some white sweat with it."

Two hours later the boy was chopping wood behind the house within which his
mother and aunt and the two sisters (the mother and aunt, not the two girls, he knew
that; even at this distance and muffled by walls the flat loud voices of the two girls emanated an incorrigible idle inertia) were setting up the stove to prepare a meal, when he
heard the hooves and saw the linen-clad man on a fine sorrel mare, whom he recognized even before he saw the rolled rug in front of the Negro youth following on a fat
bay carriage horse—a suffused, angry face vanishing, still at full gallop, beyond the corner of the house where his father and brother were sitting in the two tilted chairs; and a
moment later, almost before he could have put the axe down, he heard the hooves
again and watched the sorrel mare go back out of the yard, already galloping again.
Then his father began to shout one of the sisters' names, who presently emerged backward from the kitchen door dragging the rolled rug along the ground by one end while
the other sister walked behind it.

"If you ain't going to tote, go on and set up the wash pot," the first said.

"You, Sarty!" the second shouted. "Set up the wash pot!" His father appeared at
the door, framed against that shabbiness, as he had been against that other bland perfection, impervious to either, the mother's anxious face at his shoulder.

"Go on," the father said. "Pick it up." The two sisters stooped, broad, lethargic;
stooping, they presented an incredible expanse of pale cloth and a flutter of tawdry
ribbons.

"If I thought enough of a rug to have to git hit all the way from France I wouldn't   50
keep hit where folks coming in would have to tromp on hit," the first said. They raised
the rug.

"Abner," the mother said. "Let me do it."

"You go back and git dinner," his father said. "I'll tend to this."

From the woodpile through the rest of the afternoon the boy watched them, the
rug spread flat in the dust beside the bubbling wash-pot, the two sisters stooping over
it with that profound and lethargic reluctance, while the father stood over them in turn,
implacable and grim, driving them though never raising his voice again. He could smell
the harsh homemade lye they were using; he saw his mother come to the door once
and look toward them with an expression not anxious now but very like despair; he saw
his father turn, and he fell to with the axe and saw from the corner of his eye his father
raise from the ground a flattish fragment of field stone and examine it and return to the
pot, and this time his mother actually spoke: "Abner. Abner. Please don't. Please,
Abner."

Then he was done too. It was dusk; the whippoorwills had already begun. He
could smell coffee from the room where they would presently eat the cold food remaining from the mid-afternoon meal, though when he entered the house he realized they
were having coffee again probably because there was a fire on the hearth, before which

the rug now lay spread over the backs of the two chairs. The tracks of his father's foot were gone. Where they had been were now long, water-cloudy scoriations resembling the sporadic course of a lilliputian mowing machine.

It still hung there while they ate the cold food and then went to bed, scattered without order or claim up and down the two rooms, his mother in one bed, where his father would later lie, the older brother in the other, himself, the aunt, and the two sisters on pallets on the floor. But his father was not in bed yet. The last thing the boy remembered was the depthless, harsh silhouette of the hat and coat bending over the rug and it seemed to him that he had not even closed his eyes when the silhouette was standing over him, the fire almost dead behind it, the stiff foot prodding him awake. "Catch up the mule," his father said.

When he returned with the mule his father was standing in the black door, the rolled rug over his shoulder. "Ain't you going to ride?" he said.

"No. Give me your foot."

He bent his knee into his father's hand, the wiry, surprising power flowed smoothly, rising, he rising with it, on to the mule's bare back (they had owned a saddle once; the boy could remember it though not when or where) and with the same effortlessness his father swung the rug up in front of him. Now in the starlight they retraced the afternoon's path, up the dusty road rife with honeysuckle, through the gate and up the black tunnel of the drive to the lightless house, where he sat on the mule and felt the rough warp of the rug drag across his thighs and vanish.

"Don't you want me to help?" he whispered. His father did not answer and now he heard again that stiff foot striking the hollow portico with that wooden and clocklike deliberation, that outrageous overstatement of the weight it carried. The rug, hunched, not flung (the boy could tell that even in the darkness) from his father's shoulder struck the angle of wall and floor with a sound unbelievably loud, thunderous, then the foot again, unhurried and enormous; a light came on in the house and the boy sat, tense, breathing steadily and quietly and just a little fast, though the foot itself did not increase its beat at all, descending the steps now; now the boy could see him.

"Don't you want to ride now?" he whispered. "We kin both ride now," the light within the house altering now, flaring up and sinking. *He's coming down the stairs now,* he thought. He had already ridden the mule up beside the horse block; presently his father was up behind him and he doubled the reins over and slashed the mule across the neck, but before the animal could begin to trot the hard, thin arm came round him, the hard, knotted hand jerking the mule back to a walk.

In the first red rays of the sun they were in the lot, putting plow gear on the mules. This time the sorrel mare was in the lot before he heard it at all, the rider collarless and even bareheaded, trembling, speaking in a shaking voice as the woman in the house had done, his father merely looking up once before stooping again to the hame he was buckling, so that the man on the mare spoke to his stooping back:

"You must realize you have ruined that rug. Wasn't there anybody here, any of your women . . ." he ceased, shaking, the boy watching him, the older brother leaning now in the stable door, chewing, blinking slowly and steadily at nothing apparently. "It cost a hundred dollars. But you never had a hundred dollars. You never will. So I'm going to charge you twenty bushels of corn against your crop. I'll add it in your contract and when you come to the commissary you can sign it. That won't keep Mrs. de Spain quiet but maybe it will teach you to wipe your feet off before you enter her house again."

Then he was gone. The boy looked at his father, who still had not spoken or even looked up again, who was now adjusting the logger-head in the hame.

55

60

"Pap," he said. His father looked at him—the inscrutable face, the shaggy brows beneath which the gray eyes glinted coldly. Suddenly the boy went toward him, fast, stopping as suddenly. "You done the best you could!" he cried. "If he wanted hit done different why didn't he wait and tell you how? He won't git no twenty bushels! He won't git none! We'll gether hit and hide hit! I kin watch . . ."

"Did you put the cutter back in that straight stock like I told you?" 65

"No, sir," he said.

"Then go do it."

That was Wednesday. During the rest of that week he worked steadily, at what was within his scope and some which was beyond it, with an industry that did not need to be driven nor even commanded twice; he had this from his mother, with the difference that some at least of what he did he liked to do, such as splitting wood with the half-size axe which his mother and aunt had earned, or saved money somehow, to present him with at Christmas. In company with the two older women (and on one afternoon, even one of the sisters), he built pens for the shoat and the cow which were a part of his father's contract with the landlord, and one afternoon, his father being absent, gone somewhere on one of the mules, he went to the field.

They were running a middle buster now, his brother holding the plow straight while he handled the reins, and walking beside the straining mule, the rich black soil shearing cool and damp against his bare ankles, he thought *Maybe this is the end of it. Maybe even that twenty bushels that seems hard to have to pay for just a rug will be a cheap price for him to stop forever and always from being what he used to be*; thinking, dreaming now, so that his brother had to speak sharply to him to mind the mule: *Maybe he even won't collect the twenty bushels. Maybe it will all add up and balance and vanish—corn, rug, fire; the terror and grief, the being pulled two ways like between two teams of horses— gone, done with for ever and ever.*

Then it was Saturday; he looked up from beneath the mule he was harnessing and 70 saw his father in the black coat and hat. "Not that," his father said. "The wagon gear." And then, two hours later, sitting in the wagon bed behind his father and brother on the seat, the wagon accomplished a final curve, and he saw the weathered paintless store with its tattered tobacco- and patent-medicine posters and the tethered wagons and saddle animals below the gallery. He mounted the gnawed steps behind his father and brother, and there again was the lane of quiet, watching faces for the three of them to walk through. He saw the man in spectacles sitting at the plank table and he did not need to be told this was a Justice of the Peace; he sent one glare of fierce, exultant, partisan defiance at the man in collar and cravat now, whom he had seen but twice before in his life, and that on a galloping horse, who now wore on his face an expression not of rage but of amazed unbelief which the boy could not have known was at the incredible circumstance of being sued by one of his own tenants, and came and stood against his father and cried at the Justice: "He ain't done it! He ain't burnt . . ."

"Go back to the wagon," his father said.

"Burnt?" the Justice said. "Do I understand this rug was burned too?"

"Does anybody here claim it was?" his father said. "Go back to the wagon." But he did not, he merely retreated to the rear of the room, crowded as that other had been, but not to sit down this time, instead, to stand pressing among the motionless bodies, listening to the voices:

"And you claim twenty bushels of corn is too high for the damage you did to the rug?"

"He brought the rug to me and said he wanted the tracks washed out of it. I 75 washed the tracks out and took the rug back to him."

"But you didn't carry the rug back to him in the same condition it was in before you made the tracks on it."

His father did not answer, and now for perhaps half a minute there was no sound at all save that of breathing, the faint, steady suspiration of complete and intent listening.

"You decline to answer that, Mr. Snopes?" Again his father did not answer. "I'm going to find against you, Mr. Snopes. I'm going to find that you were responsible for the injury to Major de Spain's rug and hold you liable for it. But twenty bushels of corn seems a little high for a man in your circumstances to have to pay. Major de Spain claims it cost a hundred dollars. October corn will be worth about fifty cents. I figure that if Major de Spain can stand a ninety-five dollar loss on something he paid cash for, you can stand a five-dollar loss you haven't earned yet. I hold you in damages to Major de Spain to the amount of ten bushels of corn over and above your contract with him, to be paid to him out of your crop at gathering time. Court adjourned."

It had taken no time hardly, the morning was but half begun. He thought they would return home and perhaps back to the field, since they were late, far behind all other farmers. But instead his father passed on behind the wagon, merely indicating with his hand for the older brother to follow with it, and crossed the road toward the blacksmith shop opposite, pressing on after his father, overtaking him, speaking, whispering up at the harsh, calm face beneath the weathered hat: "He won't git no ten bushels neither. He won't git one. We'll . . ." until his father glanced for an instant down at him, the face absolutely calm, the grizzled eyebrows tangled above the cold eyes, the voice almost pleasant, almost gentle:

"You think so? Well, we'll wait till October anyway."   80

The matter of the wagon—the setting of a spoke or two and the tightening of the tires—did not take long either, the business of the tires accomplished by driving the wagon into the spring branch behind the shop and letting it stand there, the mules nuzzling into the water from time to time, and the boy on the seat with the idle reins, looking up the slope and through the sooty tunnel of the shed where the slow hammer rang and where his father sat on an upended cypress bolt, easily, either talking or listening, still sitting there when the boy brought the dripping wagon up out of the branch and halted it before the door.

"Take them on to the shade and hitch," his father said. He did so and returned. His father and the smith and a third man squatting on his heels inside the door were talking, about crops and animals; the boy, squatting too in the ammoniac dust and hoof-parings and scales of rust, heard his father tell a long and unhurried story out of the time before the birth of the older brother even when he had been a professional horsetrader. And then his father came up beside him where he stood before a tattered last year's circus poster on the other side of the store, gazing rapt and quiet at the scarlet horses, the incredible poisings and convolutions of tulle and tights and the painted leers of comedians, and said, "It's time to eat."

But not at home. Squatting beside his brother against the front wall, he watched his father emerge from the store and produce from a paper sack a segment of cheese and divide it carefully and deliberately into three with his pocket knife and produce crackers from the same sack. They all three squatted on the gallery and ate, slowly, without talking; then in the store again, they drank from a tin dipper tepid water smelling of the cedar bucket and of living beech trees. And still they did not go home. It was a horse lot this time, a tall rail fence upon and along which men stood and sat and out of which one by one horses were led, to be walked and trotted and then cantered back and forth along the road while the slow swapping and buying went on and the sun began to slant westward, they—the three of them—watching and listening, the older brother with his muddy eyes and his steady, inevitable to-bacco, the father commenting now and then on certain of the animals, to no one in particular.

It was after sundown when they reached home. They ate supper by lamplight, then, sitting on the doorstep, the boy watched the night fully accomplish, listening to the whippoorwills and the frogs, when he heard his mother's voice: "Abner! No! No! Oh, God. Oh, God. Abner!" and he rose, whirled, and saw the altered light through the door where a candle stub now burned in a bottle neck on the table and his father, still in the hat and coat, at once formal and burlesque as though dressed carefully for some shabby and ceremonial violence, emptying the reservoir of the lamp back into the five-gallon kerosene can from which it had been filled, while the mother tugged at his arm until he shifted the lamp to the other hand and flung her back, not savagely or vi-ciously, just hard, into the wall, her hands flung out against the wall for balance, her mouth open and in her face the same quality of hopeless despair as had been in her voice. Then his father saw him standing in the door.

"Go to the barn and get that can of oil we were oiling the wagon with," he said.   85
The boy did not move. Then he could speak.

"What . . ." he cried. "What are you . . ."

"Go get that oil," his father said. "Go."

Then he was moving, running, outside the house, toward the stable: this the old habit, the old blood which he had not been permitted to choose for himself, which had been bequeathed him willy nilly and which had run for so long (and who knew where, battening on what of outrage and savagery and lust) before it came to him. *I could keep on*, he thought. *I could run on and on and never look back, never need to see his face again. Only I can't. I can't*, the rusted can in his hand now, the liquid sploshing in it as he ran back to the house and into it, into the sound of his mother's weeping in the next room, and handed the can to his father.

"Ain't you going to even send a nigger?" he cried. "At least you sent a nigger before!"

This time his father didn't strike him. The hand came even faster than the blow   90
had, the same hand which had set the can on the table with almost excruciating care flashing from the can toward him too quick for him to follow it, gripping him by the back of his shirt and on to tiptoe before he had seen it quit the can, the face stooping at him in breathless and frozen ferocity, the cold, dead voice speaking over him to the older brother who leaned against the table, chewing with that steady, curious, sidewise motion of cows:

"Empty the can into the big one and go on. I'll catch up with you."

"Better tie him up to the bedpost," the brother said.

"Do like I told you," the father said. Then the boy was moving, his bunched shirt and the hard, bony hand between his shoulder-blades, his toes just touching the floor, across the room and into the other one, past the sisters sitting with spread heavy thighs in the two chairs over the cold hearth, and to where his mother and aunt sat side by side on the bed, the aunt's arms about his mother's shoulders.

"Hold him," the father said. The aunt made a startled movement. "Not you," the father said. "Lennie. Take hold of him. I want to see you do it." His mother took him by the wrist. "You'll hold him better than that. If he gets loose don't you know what he is going to do? He will go up yonder." He jerked his head toward the road. "Maybe I'd better tie him."

"I'll hold him," his mother whispered.   95

"See you do then." Then his father was gone, the stiff foot heavy and measured upon the boards, ceasing at last.

Then he began to struggle. His mother caught him in both arms, he jerking and wrenching at them. He would be stronger in the end, he knew that. But he had no time to wait for it. "Lemme go!" he cried. "I don't want to have to hit you!"

"Let him go!" the aunt said. "If he don't go, before God, I am going up there myself!"

"Don't you see I can't?" his mother cried. "Sarty! Sarty! No! No! Help me, Lizzie!"

Then he was free. His aunt grasped at him but it was too late. He whirled, running, his mother stumbled forward on to her knees behind him, crying to the nearer sister: "Catch him, Net! Catch him!" But that was too late too, the sister (the sisters were twins, born at the same time, yet either of them now gave the impression of being, encompassing as much living meat and volume and weight as any other two of the family) not yet having begun to rise from the chair, her head, face, alone merely turned, presenting to him in the flying instant an astonishing expanse of young female features untroubled by any surprise even, wearing only an expression of bovine interest. Then he was out of the room, out of the house, in the mild dust of the starlit road and the heavy rifeness of honeysuckle, the pale ribbon unspooling with terrific slowness under his running feet, reaching the gate at last and turning in, running, his heart and lungs drumming, on up the drive toward the lighted house, the lighted door. He did not knock, he burst in, sobbing for breath, incapable for the moment of speech; he saw the astonished face of the Negro in the linen jacket without knowing when the Negro had appeared.

"De Spain!" he cried, panted. "Where's . . ." then he saw the white man too emerging from a white door down the hall. "Barn!" he cried. "Barn!"

"What?" the white man said. "Barn?"

"Yes!" the boy cried. "Barn!"

"Catch him!" the white man shouted.

But it was too late this time too. The Negro grasped his shirt, but the entire sleeve, rotten with washing, carried away, and he was out that door too and in the drive again, and had actually never ceased to run even while he was screaming into the white man's face.

Behind him the white man was shouting. "My horse! Fetch my horse!" and he thought for an instant of cutting across the park and climbing the fence into the road, but he did not know the park nor how high the vine-massed fence might be and he dared not risk it. So he ran on down the drive, blood and breath roaring; presently he was in the road again though he could not see it. He could not hear either: the galloping mare was almost upon him before he heard her, and even then he held his course, as if the very urgency of his wild grief and need must in a moment more find him wings, waiting until the ultimate instant to hurl himself aside and into the weed-choked roadside ditch as the horse thundered past and on, for an instant in furious silhouette against the stars, the tranquil early summer night sky which, even before the shape of the horse and rider vanished, stained abruptly and violently upward: a long, swirling roar incredible and soundless, blotting the stars, and he springing up and into the road again, running again, knowing it was too late yet still running even after he heard the shot and, an instant later, two shots, pausing now without knowing he had ceased to run, crying "Pap! Pap!", running again before he knew he had begun to run, stumbling, tripping over something and scrabbling up again without ceasing to run, looking backward over his shoulder at the glare as he got up, running on among the invisible trees, panting, sobbing, "Father! Father!"

At midnight he was sitting on the crest of a hill. He did not know it was midnight and he did not know how far he had come. But there was no glare behind him now and he sat now, his back toward what he had called home for four days anyhow, his face toward the dark woods which he would enter when breath was strong again, small, shaking steadily in the chill darkness, hugging himself into the remainder of his thin, rotten shirt, the grief and despair now no longer terror and fear but just grief and despair. *Father. My father*, he thought. "He was brave!" he cried suddenly, aloud but not loud, no more than a whisper: "He was! He was in the war! He was in Colonel Sartoris' cav'ry!" not knowing that his father had gone to that war a private in the fine old European sense, wearing no uniform, admitting the authority of and giving fidelity to no man or army or flag, going to war as Malbrouck himself did: for booty—it meant nothing and less than nothing to him if it were enemy booty or his own.

The slow constellations wheeled on. It would be dawn and then sun-up after a while and he would be hungry. But that would be tomorrow and now he was only cold, and walking would cure that. His breathing was easier now and he decided to get up and go on, and then he found that he had been asleep because he knew it was almost dawn, the night almost over. He could tell that from the whippoorwills. They were everywhere now among the dark trees below him, constant and inflectioned and ceaseless, so that, as the instant for giving over to the day birds drew nearer and nearer, there was no interval at all between them. He got up. He was a little stiff, but walking would cure that too as it would the cold, and soon there would be the sun. He went on down the hill, toward the dark woods within which the liquid silver voices of the birds called unceasing—the rapid and urgent beating of the urgent and quiring heart of the late spring night. He did not look back.

NADINE GORDIMER (born 1923)

Amnesty 1991

[Told from a young country woman's point of view, this story provides a provocative perspective on the struggle for rights in South Africa. Her husband-to-be has been imprisoned for five years on the Island, a well-known prison similar to Alcatraz in the San Francisco Bay. *Standard 8* refers to the eighth grade of school, an education the narrator is proud of; *veld* is grassland with few trees; Cape Town is the capital of South Africa and a major seaport; a *doek* is a scarf; a *combi* is a van; the *Boer* (or *Afrikaner*) are South Africans of Dutch or Huguenot descent.]

When we heard he was released I ran all over the farm and through the fence to our people on the next farm to tell everybody. I only saw afterwards I'd torn my dress on the barbed wire, and there was a scratch, with blood, on my shoulder.

He went away from this place nine years ago, signed up to work in town with what they call a construction company—building glass walls up to the sky. For the first two years he came home for the weekend once a month and two weeks at Christmas; that was when he asked my father for me. And he began to pay. He and I thought that in three years he would have paid enough for us to get married. But then he started wearing that T-shirt, he told us he'd joined the union, he told us about the strike, how he was one of the men who went to talk to the bosses because some others had been laid off after the strike. He's always been good at talking, even in English—he was the best at the farm school, he used to read the newspapers the Indian wraps soap and sugar in when you buy at the store.

There was trouble at the hostel where he had a bed, and riots over paying rent in the townships and he told me—just me, not the old ones—that wherever people were fighting against the way we are treated they were doing it for all of us, on the farms as well as the towns, and the unions were with them, he was with them, making speeches, marching. The third year, we heard he was in prison. Instead of getting married. We didn't know where to find him, until he went on trial. The case was heard in a town far away. I couldn't go often to the court because by that time I had passed my Standard 8 and I was working in the farm school. Also my parents were short of money. Two of my brothers who had gone away to work in town didn't send home; I suppose they lived with girl-friends and had to buy things for them. My father and other brother work here for the Boer and the pay is very small, we have two goats, a few cows we're allowed to graze, and a patch of land where my mother can grow vegetables. No cash from that.

When I saw him in the court he looked beautiful in a blue suit with a striped shirt and brown tie. All the accused—his comrades, he said—were well-dressed. The union bought the clothes so that the judge and the prosecutor would know they weren't dealing with stupid *yes-baas* black men who didn't know their rights. These things and everything else about the court and trial he explained to me when I was allowed to visit him in jail. Our little girl was born while the trial went on and when I brought the baby to court the first time to show him, his comrades hugged him and then hugged me across the barrier of the prisoners' dock and they had clubbed together to give me some money as a present for the baby. He chose the name for her, Inkululeko.

Then the trial was over and he got six years. He was sent to the Island. We all   5
knew about the Island. Our leaders had been there so long. But I have never seen the sea except to color it in blue at school, and I couldn't imagine a piece of earth surrounded by it. I could only think of a cake of dung, dropped by the cattle, floating in a pool of rain-water they'd crossed, the water showing the sky like a looking-glass, blue. I was ashamed only to think that. He had told me how the glass walls showed the pavement trees and the other buildings in the street and the colors of the cars and the clouds as the crane lifted him on a platform higher and higher through the sky to work at the top of a building.

He was allowed one letter a month. It was my letter because his parents didn't know how to write. I used to go to them where they worked on another farm to ask what message they wanted to send. The mother always cried and put her hands on her head and said nothing, and the old man, who preached to us in the veld every Sunday, said tell my son we are praying, God will make everything all right for him. Once he wrote back, That's the trouble—our people on the farms, they're told God will decide what's good for them so that they won't find the force to do anything to change their lives.

After two years had passed, we—his parents and I—had saved up enough money to go to Cape Town to visit him. We went by train and slept on the floor at the station and asked the way, next day, to the ferry. People were kind; they all knew that if you wanted the ferry it was because you had somebody of yours on the Island.

And there it was—there was the sea. It was green *and* blue, climbing and falling, bursting white, all the way to the sky. A terrible wind was slapping it this way and that; it hid the Island, but people like us, also waiting for the ferry, pointed where the Island must be, far out in the sea that I never thought would be like it really was.

There were other boats, and ships as big as buildings that go to other places, all over the world, but the ferry is only for the Island, it doesn't go anywhere else in the world, only to the Island. So everybody waiting there was waiting for the Island, there could be no mistake we were not in the right place. We had sweets and biscuits, trousers and a warm coat for him (a woman standing with us said we wouldn't be allowed to give him the clothes) and I wasn't wearing, anymore, the old beret pulled down over my head that farm girls wear, I had bought relaxer cream from the man who comes round the farms selling things out of a box on his bicycle, and my hair was combed up thick under a flowered scarf that didn't cover the gold-colored rings in my ears. His mother had her blanket tied round her waist over her dress, a farm woman, but I looked just as good as any of the other girls there. When the ferry was ready to take us, we stood all pressed together and quiet like the cattle waiting to be let through a gate. One man kept looking round with his chin moving up and down, he was counting, he must have been afraid there were too many to get on and he didn't want to be left behind. We all moved up to the policeman in charge and everyone ahead of us went onto the boat. But when our turn came and he put out his hand for something, I didn't know what.

We didn't have a permit. We didn't know that before you come to Cape Town, 10 before you come to the ferry for the Island, you have to have a police permit to visit a prisoner on the Island. I tried to ask him nicely. The wind blew the voice out of my mouth.

We were turned away. We saw the ferry rock, bumping the landing where we stood, moving, lifted and dropped by all that water, getting smaller and smaller until we didn't know if we were really seeing it or one of the birds that looked black, dipping up and down, out there.

The only good thing was one of the other people took the sweets and biscuits for him. He wrote and said he got them. But it wasn't a good letter. Of course not. He was cross with me; I should have found out, I should have known about the permit. He was right—I bought the train tickets, I asked where to go for the ferry, I should have known about the permit. I have passed Standard 8. There was an advice office to go to in town, the churches ran it, he wrote. But the farm is so far from town, we on the farms don't know about these things. It was as he said; our ignorance is the way we are kept down, this ignorance must go.

We took the train back and we never went to the Island—never saw him in the three more years he was there. Not once. We couldn't find the money for the train. His father died and I had to help his mother from my pay. For our people the worry is always money, I wrote. When will we ever have money? Then he sent such a good letter. That's what I'm on the Island for, far away from you, I'm here so that one day our people will have the things they need, land, food, the end of ignorance. There was something else—I could just read the word "power" the prison had blacked out. All his letters were not just for me; the prison officer read them before I could.

He was coming home after only five years!

That's what it seemed to me, when I heard—the five years were suddenly disap- 15 peared—nothing!—there was no whole year still to wait. I showed my—our—little girl his photo again. That's your daddy, he's coming, you're going to see him. She told the other children at school, I've got a daddy, just as she showed off about the kid goat she had at home.

We wanted him to come at once, and at the same time we wanted time to prepare. His mother lived with one of his uncles; now that his father was dead there was no house of his father for him to take me to as soon as we married. If there had been time, my father would have cut poles, my mother and I would have baked bricks, cut thatch, and built a house for him and me and the child.

We were not sure what day he would arrive. We only heard on my radio his name and the names of some others who were released. Then at the Indian's store I noticed the newspaper, *The Nation,* written by black people, and on the front a picture of a lot of people dancing and waving—I saw at once it was at that ferry. Some men were being carried on other men's shoulders. I couldn't see which one was him. We were waiting. The ferry had brought him from the Island but we remembered Cape Town is a long way from us. Then he did come. On a Saturday, no school, so I was working with my mother, hoeing and weeding round the pumpkins and mealies, my hair, that I meant to keep nice, tied in an old *doek*. A combi came over the veld and his comrades had brought him. I wanted to run away and wash but he stood there stretching his legs, calling, hey! hey! with his comrades making a noise around him, and my mother started shrieking in the old style aie! aie! and my father was clapping and stamping towards him. He held his arms open to us, this big man in town clothes, polished shoes, and all the time while he hugged me I was holding my dirty hands, full of mud, away from him behind his back. His teeth hit me hard through his lips, he grabbed at my mother and she struggled to hold the child up to him. I thought we would all fall down! Then everyone was quiet. The child hid behind my mother. He picked her up but she turned her head away to her shoulder. He spoke to her gently but she wouldn't speak to him. She's nearly six years old! I told her not to be a baby. She said, That's not him.

The comrades all laughed, we laughed, she ran off and he said, She has to have time to get used to me.

He has put on weight, yes; a lot. You couldn't believe it. He used to be so thin his feet looked too big for him. I used to feel his bones but now—that night—when he lay on me he was so heavy, I didn't remember it was like that. Such a long time. It's strange to get stronger in prison; I thought he wouldn't have enough to eat and would come out weak. Everyone said, Look at him!—he's a man, now. He laughed and banged his fist on his chest, told them how the comrades exercised in their cells, he would run three miles a day, stepping up and down on one place on the floor of that small cell where he was kept. After we were together at night we used to whisper a long time but now I can feel he's thinking of some things I don't know and I can't worry him with talk. Also I don't know what to say. To ask him what it was like, five years shut away there; or to tell him something about school or about the child. What else has happened, here? Nothing. Just waiting. Sometimes in the daytime I do try to tell him what it was like for me, here at home on the farm, five years. He listens, he's interested, just like he's interested when people from the other farms come to visit and talk to him about little things that happened to them while he was away all that time on the Island. He smiles and nods, asks a couple of questions and then stands up and stretches. I see it's to show them it's enough, his mind is going back to something he was busy with before they came. And we farm people are very slow; we tell things slowly, he used to, too.

He hasn't signed on for another job. But he can't stay at home with us; we   20
thought, after five years over there in the middle of that green and blue sea, so far, he would rest with us a little while. The combi or some car comes to fetch him and he says don't worry, I don't know what day I'll be back. At first I asked, what week, next week? He tried to explain to me: in the Movement it's not like it was in the union, where you do your work every day and after that you are busy with meetings; in the Movement you never know where you will have to go and what is going to come up next. And the same with money. In the Movement, it's not like a job, with regular pay—I know that, he doesn't have to tell me—it's like it was going to the Island, you do it for all our people who suffer because we haven't got money, we haven't got land—look, he said,

speaking of my parents', my home, the home that has been waiting for him, with his child: look at this place where the white man owns the ground and lets you squat in mud and tin huts here only as long as you work for him—*Baba* and your brother planting his crops and looking after his cattle, Mama cleaning his house and you in the school without even having the chance to train properly as a teacher. The farmer owns us, he says.

I've been thinking we haven't got a home because there wasn't time to build a house before he came from the Island; but we haven't got a home at all. Now I've understood that.

I'm not stupid. When the comrades come to this place in the combi to talk to him here I don't go away with my mother after we've brought them tea or (if she's made it for the weekend) beer. They like her beer, they talk about our culture and there's one of them who makes a point of putting his arm around my mother, calling her the mama of all of them, the mama of Africa. Sometimes they please her very much by telling her how they used to sing on the Island and getting her to sing an old song we all know from our grandmothers. Then they join in with their strong voices. My father doesn't like this noise travelling across the veld; he's afraid that if the Boer finds out my man is a political, from the Island, and he's holding meetings on the Boer's land, he'll tell my father to go, and take his family with him. But my brother says if the Boer asks anything just tell him it's a prayer meeting. Then the singing is over; my mother knows she must go away into the house.

I stay, and listen. He forgets I'm there when he's talking and arguing about something I can see is important, more important than anything we could ever have to say to each other when we're alone. But now and then, when one of the other comrades is speaking I see him look at me for a moment the way I will look up at one of my favorite children in school to encourage the child to understand. The men don't speak to me and I don't speak. One of the things they talk about is organizing the people on the farms—the workers, like my father and brother, and like his parents used to be. I learn what all these things are: minimum wage, limitation of working hours, the right to strike, annual leave, accident compensation, pensions, sick and even maternity leave. I am pregnant, at last I have another child inside me, but that's women's business. When they talk about the Big Man, the Old Men, I know who these are: our leaders are also back from prison. I told him about the child coming; he said, And this one belongs to a new country, he'll build the freedom we've fought for! I know he wants to get married but there's no time for that at present. There was hardly time for him to make the child. He comes to me just like he comes here to eat a meal or put on clean clothes. Then he picks up the little girl and swings her round and there!—it's done, he's getting into the combi, he's already turning to his comrade that face of his that knows only what's inside his head, those eyes that move quickly as if he's chasing something you can't see. The little girl hasn't had time to get used to this man. But I know she'll be proud of him, one day!

How can you tell that to a child six years old. But I tell her about the Big Man and the Old Men, our leaders, so she'll know that her father was with them on the Island, this man is a great man, too.

On Saturday, no school and I plant and weed with my mother, she sings but I don't; I think. On Sunday there's no work, only prayer meetings out of the farmer's way under the trees, and beer drinks at the mud and tin huts where the farmers allow us to squat on their land. I go off on my own as I used to do when I was a child, making up games and talking to myself where no one would hear me or look for me. I sit on a warm stone in the late afternoon, high up, and the whole valley is a path between the hills, leading away from my feet. It's the Boer's farm but that's not true, it belongs to nobody. The cattle don't know that anyone says he owns it, the sheep—they are grey stones, and then they become a thick grey snake moving—don't know. Our huts and the old mulberry tree and the little brown mat of earth that my mother dug over yesterday, way down there, and way over there the clump of trees round the chimneys and the shiny thing that is the TV mast of the farmhouse—they are nothing, on the back of this earth. It could twitch them away like a dog does a fly.

I am up with the clouds. The sun behind me is changing the colors of the sky and the clouds are changing themselves, slowly, slowly. Some are pink, some are white, swelling like bubbles. Underneath is a bar of grey, not enough to make rain. It gets longer and darker, it grows a thin snout and long body and then the end of it is a tail. There's a huge grey rat moving across the sky, eating the sky.

The child remembered the photo; she said *That's not him*. I'm sitting here where I came often when he was on the Island. I came to get away from the others, to wait by myself.

I'm watching the rat, it's losing itself, its shape, eating the sky, and I'm waiting. Waiting for him to come back.

Waiting.

I'm waiting to come back home.   30

Z O R A   N E A L E   H U R S T O N   (1901–1960)
Sweat   1926

[This story re-creates black Southern dialect of the twenties. Dialect words include *biggety* for conceited and *tote* for carry. A *buckboard* is an open horse-drawn wagon; a *Mogul* is a big or important person; *epizootic* stands for sickness or epidemic. Biblical allusions include Gethsemane (the garden where Christ was betrayed to the Roman soldiers), Calvary (the hill where Christ was crucified), and Jordan (the river the Jews had to cross on the way to the Promised Land).]

It was eleven o'clock of a Spring night in Florida. It was Sunday. Any other night, Delia Jones would have been in bed for two hours by this time. But she was a washwoman, and Monday morning meant a great deal to her. So she collected the soiled clothes on Saturday when she returned the clean things. Sunday night after church, she sorted them and put the white things to soak. It saved her almost a half day's start. A great hamper in the bedroom held the clothes that she brought home. It was so much neater than a number of bundles lying around.

She squatted in the kitchen floor beside the great pile of clothes, sorting them into small heaps according to color, and humming a song in a mournful key, but wondering through it all where Sykes, her husband, had gone with her horse and buckboard.

Just then something long, round, limp and black fell upon her shoulders and slithered to the floor beside her. A great terror took hold of her. It softened her knees and dried her mouth so that it was a full minute before she could cry out or move. Then she saw that it was the big bull whip her husband liked to carry when he drove.

She lifted her eyes to the door and saw him standing there bent over with laughter at her fright. She screamed at him.

"Sykes, what you throw dat whip on me like dat? You know it would skeer me—   5
looks just like a snake, an' you knows how skeered Ah is of snakes."

"Course Ah knowed it! That's how come Ah done it." He slapped his leg with his
hand and almost rolled on the ground in his mirth. "If you such a big fool dat you got
to have a fit over a earth worm or a string, Ah don't keer how bad Ah skeer you."

"You aint got no business doing it. Gawd knows it's a sin. Some day Ah'm gointuh drop dead from some of yo' foolishness. 'Nother thing, where you been wid mah
rig? Ah feeds dat pony. He aint fuh you to be drivin' wid no bull whip."

"You sho is one aggravatin' nigger woman!" he declared and stepped into the
room. She resumed her work and did not answer him at once. "Ah done tole you time
and again to keep them white folks' clothes outa dis house."

He picked up the whip and glared down at her. Delia went on with her work. She
went out into the yard and returned with a galvanized tub and set it on the washbench.
She saw that Sykes had kicked all of the clothes together again, and now stood in her
way truculently, his whole manner hoping, *praying,* for an argument. But she walked
calmly around him and commenced to re-sort the things.

"Next time, Ah'm gointer kick'em outdoors," he threatened as he struck a match   10
along the leg of his corduroy breeches.

Delia never looked up from her work, and her thin, stooped shoulders sagged
further.

"Ah aint for no fuss t'night Sykes. Ah just come from taking sacrament at the
church house."

He snorted scornfully. "Yeah, you just come from de church house on a Sunday
night, but heah you is gone to work on them clothes. You ain't nothing but a hyp-
ocrite. One of them amen-corner Christians—sing, whoop, and shout, then come
home and wash white folks clothes on the Sabbath."

He stepped roughly upon the whitest pile of things, kicking them helter-skelter as
he crossed the room. His wife gave a little scream of dismay, and quickly gathered them
together again.

"Sykes, you quit grindin' dirt into these clothes! How can Ah git through by   15
Sat'day if Ah don't start on Sunday?"

"Ah don't keer if you never git through. Anyhow, Ah done promised Gawd and a
couple of other men, Ah aint gointer have it in mah house. Don't gimme no lip neither, else Ah'll throw 'em out and put mah fist up side yo' head to boot."

Delia's habitual meekness seemed to slip from her shoulders like a blown scarf. She
was on her feet; her poor little body, her bare knuckly hands bravely defying the strap-
ping hulk before her.

"Looka heah, Sykes, you done gone too fur. Ah been married to you fur fifteen
years, and Ah been takin' in washin' fur fifteen years. Sweat, sweat, sweat! Work and
sweat, cry and sweat, pray and sweat!"

"What's that got to do with me?" he asked brutally.

"What's it got to do with you, Sykes? Mah tub of suds is filled yo' belly with vittles   20
more times than yo' hands is filled it. Mah sweat is done paid for this house and Ah
reckon Ah kin keep on sweatin' in it."

She seized the iron skillet from the stove and struck a defensive pose, which act
surprised him greatly, coming from her. It cowed him and he did not strike her as he
usually did.

"Naw you won't," she panted, "that ole snaggle-toothed black woman you
runnin' with aint comin' heah to pile up on *mah* sweat and blood. You aint paid for
nothin' on this place, and Ah'm gointer stay right heah till Ah'm toted out foot
foremost."

"Well, you better quit gittin' me riled up, else they'll be totin' you out sooner than you expect. Ah'm so tired of you Ah don't know whut to do. Gawd! how Ah hates skinny wimmen!"

A little awed by this new Delia, he sidled out of the door and slammed the back gate after him. He did not say where he had gone, but she knew too well. She knew very well that he would not return until nearly daybreak also. Her work over, she went on to bed but not to sleep at once. Things had come to a pretty pass!

She lay awake, gazing upon the debris that cluttered their matrimonial trail. Not an image left standing along the way. Anything like flowers had long ago been drowned in the salty stream that had been pressed from her heart. Her tears, her sweat, her blood. She had brought love to the union and he had brought a longing after the flesh. Two months after the wedding, he had given her the first brutal beating. She had the memory of his numerous trips to Orlando with all of his wages when he had returned to her penniless, even before the first year had passed. She was young and soft then, but now she thought of her knotty, muscled limbs, her harsh knuckly hands, and drew herself up into an unhappy little ball in the middle of the big feather bed. Too late now to hope for love, even if it were not Bertha it would be someone else. This case differed from the others only in that she was bolder than the others. Too late for everything except her little home. She had built it for her old days, and planted one by one the trees and flowers there. It was lovely to her, lovely.

Somehow, before sleep came, she found herself saying aloud: "Oh well, whatever goes over the Devil's back, is got to come under his belly. Sometime or ruther, Sykes, like everybody else, is gointer reap his sowing." After that she was able to build a spiritual earthworks against her husband. His shells could no longer reach her. *Amen*. She went to sleep and slept until he announced his presence in bed by kicking her feet and rudely snatching the covers away.

"Gimme some kivah heah, an' git yo' damn foots over on yo' own side! Ah oughter mash you in yo' mouf fuh drawing dat skillet on me."

Delia went clear to the rail without answering him. A triumphant indifference to all that he was or did.

The week was as full of work for Delia as all other weeks, and Saturday found her behind her little pony, collecting and delivering clothes.

It was a hot, hot day near the end of July. The village men on Joe Clarke's porch even chewed cane listlessly. They did not hurl the caneknots as usual. They let them dribble over the edge of the porch. Even conversation had collapsed under the heat.

"Heah come Delia Jones," Jim Merchant said, as the shaggy pony came 'round the bend of the road toward them. The rusty buckboard was heaped with baskets of crisp, clean laundry.

"Yep," Joe Lindsay agreed. "Hot or col', rain or shine, jes ez reg'lar ez de weeks roll roun' Delia carries 'em an' fetches 'em on Sat'day."

"She better if she wanter eat," said Moss. "Syke Jones aint wuth de shot an' powder hit would tek tuh kill 'em. Not to *huh* he aint."

"He sho' aint," Walter Thomas chimed in. "It's too bad, too, cause she wuz a right pritty lil trick when he got huh. Ah'd uh mah'ied huh mahseff if he hadnter beat me to it."

Delia nodded briefly at the men as she drove past.

"Too much knockin' will ruin *any* 'oman. He done beat huh 'nough tuh kill three women, let 'lone change they looks," said Elijah Moseley. "How Syke kin stommuck dat big black greasy Mogul he's layin' roun' wid, gits me. Ah swear dat eight-rock couldn't kiss a sardine can Ah done thowed out de back do' 'way las' yeah."

25

30

35

"Aw, she's fat, thass how come. He's allus been crazy 'bout fat women," put in Merchant. "He'd a' been tied up wid one long time ago if he could a' found one tuh have him. Did Ah tell yuh 'bout him come sidlin' roun' *mah* wife—bringin' her a basket uh peecans outa his yard fuh a present? Yessir, mah wife! She tol' him tuh take 'em right straight back home, cause Delia works so hard ovah dat washtub she reckon everything on de place taste lak sweat an' soapsuds. Ah jus' wisht Ah'd a' caught 'im 'roun' dere! Ah'd a' made his hips ketch on fiah down dat shell road."

"Ah know he done it, too. Ah sees 'im grinnin' at every 'oman dat passes," Walter Thomas said. "But even so, he useter eat some mighty big hunks uh humble pie tuh git dat lil' 'oman he got. She wuz ez pritty ez a speckled pup! Dat wuz fifteen yeahs ago. He useter be so skeered uh losin' huh, she could make him do some parts of a husband's duty. Dey never wuz de same in de mind."

"There oughter be a law about him," said Lindsay. "He aint fit tuh carry guts tuh a bear."

Clarke spoke for the first time. "Taint no law on earth dat kin make a man be decent if it aint in 'im. There's plenty men dat takes a wife lak dey do a joint uh sugarcane. It's round, juicy an' sweet when dey gits it. But dey squeeze an' grind, squeeze an' grind an' wring tell dey wring every drop uh pleasure dat's in 'em out. When dey's satisfied dat dey is wrung dry, dey treats 'em jes lak dey do a cane-chew. Dey throws 'em away. Dey knows whut dey is doin' while dey is at it, an' hates theirselves fuh it but they keeps on hangin' after huh tell she's empty. Den dey hates huh fuh bein' a cane-chew an' in de way." [40]

"We oughter take Syke an' dat stray 'oman uh his'n down in Lake Howell swamp an' lay on de rawhide till they cain't say Lawd a' mussy. He allus wuz uh ovahbearin' niggah, but since dat white 'oman from up north done teached 'im how to run a automobile, he done got too biggety to live—an' we oughter kill 'im," Old Man Anderson advised.

A grunt of approval went around the porch. But the heat was melting their civic virtue and Elijah Moseley began to bait Joe Clarke.

"Come on, Joe, git a melon outa dere an' slice it up for yo' customers. We'se all sufferin' wid de heat. De bear's done got *me!*"

"Thass right, Joe, a watermelon is jes' whut Ah needs tuh cure de eppizudicks," Walter Thomas joined forces with Moseley. "Come on dere, Joe. We all is steady customers an' you aint set us up in a long time. Ah chooses dat long, bowlegged Floridy favorite."

"A god, an' be dough. You all gimme twenty cents and slice way," Clarke retorted. [45] "Ah needs a col' slice m'self. Heah, everybody chip in. Ah'll lend y'll mah meat knife."

The money was quickly subscribed and the huge melon brought forth. At that moment, Sykes and Bertha arrived. A determined silence fell on the porch and the melon was put away again.

Merchant snapped down the blade of his jackknife and moved toward the store door.

"Come on in, Joe, an' gimme a slab uh sow belly an' uh pound uh coffee—almost fuhgot 'twas Sat'day. Got to git on home." Most of the men left also.

Just then Delia drove past on her way home, as Sykes was ordering magnificently for Bertha. It pleased him for Delia to see.

"Git whutsoever yo' heart desires, Honey. Wait a minute, Joe. Give huh two [50] bottles uh strawberry soda-water, uh quart uh parched groundpeas, an' a block uh chewin' gum."

With all this they left the store, with Sykes reminding Bertha that this was his town and she could have it if she wanted it.

The men returned soon after they left, and held their watermelon feast.

"Where did Syke Jones git da 'oman from nohow?" Lindsay asked.

"Ovah Apopka. Guess dey musta been cleanin' out de town when she lef'. She don't look lak a thing but a hunk uh liver wid hair on it."

"Well, she sho' kin squall," Dave Carter contributed. "When she gits ready tuh laff, she jes' opens huh mouf an' latches it back tuh de las' notch. No ole grandpa alligator down in Lake Bell ain't got nothin' on huh." 55

Bertha had been in town three months now. Sykes was still paying her room rent at Della Lewis'—the only house in town that would have taken her in. Sykes took her frequently to Winter Park to "stomps." He still assured her that he was the swellest man in the state.

"Sho' you kin have dat lil' ole house soon's Ah kin git dat 'oman outa dere. Everything b'longs tuh me an' you sho' kin have it. Ah sho' 'bominates uh skinny 'oman. Lawdy, you sho' is got one portly shape on you! You kin git *anything* you wants. Dis is *mah* town an' you sho' kin have it."

Delia's work-worn knees crawled over the earth in Gethsemane and up the rocks of Calvary many, many times during these months. She avoided the villagers and meeting places in her efforts to be blind and deaf. But Bertha nullified this to a degree, by coming to Delia's house to call Sykes out to her at the gate.

Delia and Sykes fought all the time now with no peaceful interludes. They slept and ate in silence. Two or three times Delia had attempted a timid friendliness, but she was repulsed each time. It was plain that the breaches must remain agape.

The sun had burned July to August. The heat streamed down like a million hot arrows, smiting all things living upon the earth. Grass withered, leaves browned, snakes went blind in shedding and men and dogs went mad. Dog days! 60

Delia came home one day and found Sykes there before her. She wondered, but started to go on into the house without speaking, even though he was standing in the kitchen door and she must either stoop under his arm or ask him to move. He made no room for her. She noticed a soap box beside the steps, but paid no particular attention to it, knowing that he must have brought it there. As she was stooping to pass under his outstretched arm, he suddenly pushed her backward, laughingly.

"Look in de box dere Delia, Ah done brung yuh somethin'!"

She nearly fell upon the box in her stumbling, and when she saw what it held, she all but fainted outright.

"Syke! Syke, mah Gawd! You take dat rattlesnake 'way from heah! You *gottuh*, Oh, Jesus, have mussy!"

"Ah aint gut tuh do nuthin' uh de kin'—fact is Ah aint got tuh do nothin' but die. Taint no use uh you puttin' on airs makin' out lak you skeered uh dat snake—he's gointer stay right heah tell he die. He wouldn't bite me cause Ah knows how tuh handle 'im. Nohow he wouldn't risk breakin' out his fangs 'gin *yo'* skinny laigs." 65

"Naw, now Syke, don't keep dat thing 'roun' heah tuh skeer me tuh death. You knows Ah'm even feared uh earth worms. Thass de biggest snake Ah evah did see. Kill 'im Syke, please."

"Doan ast me tuh do nothin' fuh yuh. Goin' 'roun' tryin' tuh be so damn asterperious. Naw, Ah aint gonna kill it. Ah think uh damn sight mo' uh him dan you! Dat's a nice snake an' anybody doan lak 'im kin jes' hit de grit."

The village soon heard that Sykes had the snake, and came to see and ask questions.

"How de hen-fire did you ketch dat six-foot rattler, Syke?" Thomas asked.

"He's full uh frogs so he caint hardly move, thass how Ah eased up on 'm. But   70
Ah'm a snake charmer an' knows how tuh handle 'em. Shux, dat aint nothin'. Ah could
ketch one eve'y day if Ah so wanted tuh."

"Whut he needs is a heavy hick'ry club leaned real heavy on his head. Dat's de bes
'way tuh charm a rattlesnake."

"Naw, Walt, y'll jes' don't understand dese diamon' backs lak Ah do," said Sykes
in a superior tone of voice.

The village agreed with Walter, but the snake stayed on. His box remained by
the kitchen door with its screen wire covering. Two or three days later it had digested its meal of frogs and literally came to life. It rattled at every movement in the
kitchen or the yard. One day as Delia came down the kitchen steps she saw his
chalky-white fangs curved like scimitars hung in the wire meshes. This time she did not
run away with averted eyes as usual. She stood for a long time in the doorway in a red
fury that grew bloodier for every second that she regarded the creature that was her
torment.

That night she broached the subject as soon as Sykes sat down to the table.

"Syke, Ah wants you tuh take dat snake 'way fum heah. You done starved me an'   75
Ah put up widcher, you done beat me an' Ah took dat, but you done kilt all mah insides bringin' dat varmint heah."

Sykes poured out a saucer full of coffee and drank it deliberately before he answered her.

"A whole lot Ah keer 'bout how you feels inside uh out. Dat snake aint goin' no
damn wheah till Ah gits ready fuh 'im tuh go. So fur as beatin' is concerned, yuh aint
took near all dat you gointer take ef yuh stay 'roun' *me*."

Delia pushed back her plate and got up from the table. "Ah hates you, Sykes," she
said calmly. "Ah hates you tuh de same degree dat Ah useter love yuh. Ah done took
an' took till mah belly is full up tuh mah neck. Dat's de reason Ah got mah letter fum
de church an' moved mah membership tuh Woodbridge—so Ah don't haftuh take
no sacrament wid yuh. Ah don't wantuh see yuh 'roun' me atall. Lay 'roun' wid dat
'oman all yuh wants tuh, but gwan 'way fum me an' mah house. Ah hates yuh lak uh
suck-egg dog."

Sykes almost let the huge wad of corn bread and collard greens he was chewing fall
out of his mouth in amazement. He had a hard time whipping himself up to the proper
fury to try to answer Delia.

"Well, Ah'm glad you does hate me. Ah'm sho' tiahed uh you hangin' ontuh me.   80
Ah don't want yuh. Look at yuh stringey ole neck! Yo' rawbony laigs an' arms is
enough tuh cut uh man tuh death. You looks jes' lak de devvul's doll-baby tuh *me*. You
cain't hate me no worse dan Ah hates you. Ah been hatin' *you* fuh years."

"Yo' ole black hide don't look lak nothin' tuh me, but uh passle uh wrinkled up
rubber, wid yo' big ole yeahs flappin' on each side lak uh paih uh buzzard wings. Don't
think Ah'm gointuh be run 'way fum mah house neither. Ah'm goin' tuh de white folks
bout *you*, mah young man, de very nex' time you lay yo' han's on me. Mah cup is done
run ovah." Delia said this with no signs of fear and Sykes departed from the house,
threatening her, but made not the slightest move to carry out any of them.

That night he did not return at all, and the next day being Sunday, Delia was glad
she did not have to quarrel before she hitched up her pony and drove the four miles to
Woodbridge.

She stayed to the night service—"love feast"—which was very warm and full of
spirit. In the emotional winds her domestic trials were borne far and wide so that she
sang as she drove homeward,

"Jurden water, black an' col'
Chills de body, not de soul
An' Ah wantah cross Jurden in uh calm time."

She came from the barn to the kitchen door and stopped.

"Whut's de mattah, ol' satan, you aint kickin' up yo' racket?" She addressed the   85
snake's box. Complete silence. She went on into the house with a new hope in its birth
struggles. Perhaps her threat to go to the white folks had frightened Sykes! Perhaps
he was sorry! Fifteen years of misery and suppression had brought Delia to the place
where she would hope *anything* that looked toward a way over or through her wall of
inhibitions.

She felt in the match safe behind the stove at once for a match. There was only one
there.

"Dat niggah wouldn't fetch nothin' heah tuh save his rotten neck, but he kin run
thew whut Ah brings quick enough. Now he done toted off nigh on tuh haff uh box
uh matches. He done had dat 'oman heah in mah house, too."

Nobody but a woman could tell how she knew this even before she struck the
match. But she did and it put her into a new fury.

Presently she brought in the tubs to put the white things to soak. This time she
decided she need not bring the hamper out of the bedroom; she would go in there and
do the sorting. She picked up the pot-bellied lamp and went in. The room was small
and the hamper stood hard by the foot of the white iron bed. She could sit and reach
through the bedposts—resting as she worked.

"Ah wantah cross Jurden in uh calm time." She was singing again. The mood of   90
the "love feast" had returned. She threw back the lid of the basket almost gaily. Then,
moved by both horror and terror, she sprang back toward the door. *There lay the snake
in the basket!* He moved sluggishly at first, but even as she turned round and round,
jumped up and down in an insanity of fear, he began to stir vigorously. She saw him
pouring his awful beauty from the basket upon the bed, then she seized the lamp and
ran as fast as she could to the kitchen. The wind from the open door blew out the light
and the darkness added to her terror. She sped to the darkness of the yard, slamming
the door after her before she thought to set down the lamp. She did not feel safe even
on the ground, so she climbed up in the hay barn.

There for an hour or more she lay sprawled upon the hay a gibbering wreck.

Finally she grew quiet, and after that, coherent thought. With this, stalked through
her a cold, bloody rage. Hours of this. A period of introspection, a space of retrospection, then a mixture of both. Out of this an awful calm.

"Well, Ah done de bes' Ah could. If things aint right, Gawd knows taint mah
fault."

She went to sleep—a twitch sleep—and woke up to a faint gray sky. There was a
loud hollow sound below. She peered out. Sykes was at the woodpile, demolishing a
wire-covered box.

He hurried to the kitchen door, but hung outside there some minutes before he   95
entered, and stood some minutes more inside before he closed it after him.

The gray in the sky was spreading. Delia descended without fear now, and
crouched beneath the low bedroom window. The drawn shade shut out the dawn, shut
in the night. But the thin walls held back no sound.

"Dat ol' scratch is woke up now!" She mused at the tremendous whirr inside,
which every woodsman knows, is one of the sound illusions. The rattler is a ven-
triloquist. His whirr sounds to the right, to the left, straight ahead, behind, close

under foot—everywhere but where it is. Woe to him who guesses wrong unless he is prepared to hold up his end of the argument! Sometimes he strikes without rattling at all.

Inside, Sykes heard nothing until he knocked a pot lid off the stove while trying to reach the match safe in the dark. He had emptied his pockets at Bertha's.

The snake seemed to wake up under the stove and Sykes made a quick leap into the bedroom. In spite of the gin he had had, his head was clearing now.

"Mah Gawd!" he chattered, "ef Ah could on'y strack uh light!"   100

The rattling ceased for a moment as he stood paralyzed. He waited. It seemed that the snake waited also.

"Oh, fuh de light! Ah thought he'd be too sick"—Sykes was muttering to himself when the whirr began again, closer, right underfoot this time. Long before this, Sykes' ability to think had been flattened down to primitive instinct and he leaped—onto the bed.

Outside Delia heard a cry that might have come from a maddened chimpanzee, a stricken gorilla. All the terror, all the horror, all the rage that man possibly could express, without a recognizable human sound.

A tremendous stir inside there, another series of animal screams, the intermittent whirr of the reptile. The shade torn violently down from the window, letting in the red dawn, a huge brown hand seizing the window stick, great dull blows upon the wooden floor punctuating the gibberish of sound long after the rattle of the snake had abruptly subsided. All this Delia could see and hear from her place beneath the window, and it made her ill. She crept over to the four o'clocks and stretched herself on the cool earth to recover.

She lay there. "Delia, Delia!" She could hear Sykes calling in a most despairing   105
tone as one who expected no answer. The sun crept on up, and he called. Delia could not move—her legs were gone flabby. She never moved, he called, and the sun kept rising.

"Mah Gawd!" She heard him moan, "Mah Gawd fum Heben!" She heard him stumbling about and got up from her flower-bed. The sun was growing warm. As she approached the door she heard him call out hopefully, "Delia, is dat you Ah heah?"

She saw him on his hands and knees as soon as she reached the door. He crept an inch or two toward her—all that he was able, and she saw his horribly swollen neck and his one open eye shining with hope. A surge of pity too strong to support bore her away from that eye that must, could not, fail to see the tubs. He would see the lamp. Orlando with its doctors was too far. She could scarcely reach the Chinaberry tree, where she waited in the growing heat while inside she knew the cold river was creeping up and up to extinguish that eye which must know by now that she knew.

KAZUO ISHIGURO   (born 1954)

A Family Supper   1990

[This story focuses on a perplexing generational conflict filled with unexplained feelings. About his fiction Ishiguro has said, "I try to put in as little plot as possible." Chou En-lai was a Chinese communist leader who became premier in 1949; Osaka is a large city in southern Japan.]

Fugu is a fish caught off the Pacific shores of Japan. The fish has held a special significance for me ever since my mother died after eating one. The poison resides in the sex glands of the fish, inside two fragile bags. These bags must be removed with caution when preparing the fish, for any clumsiness will result in the poison leaking into the veins. Regrettably, it is not easy to tell whether or not this operation has been carried out successfully. The proof is, as it were, in the eating.

Fugu poisoning is hideously painful and almost always fatal. If the fish has been eaten during the evening, the victim is usually overtaken by pain during his sleep. He rolls about in agony for a few hours and is dead by morning. The fish became extremely popular in Japan after the war. Until stricter regulations were imposed, it was all the rage to perform the hazardous gutting operation in one's own kitchen, then to invite neighbors and friends round for the feast.

At the time of my mother's death, I was living in California. My relationship with my parents had become somewhat strained around that period and consequently I did not learn of the circumstances of her death until I returned to Tokyo two years later. Apparently, my mother had always refused to eat fugu, but on this particular occasion she had made an exception, having been invited by an old school friend whom she was anxious not to offend. It was my father who supplied me with the details as we drove from the airport to his house in the Kamakura district. When we finally arrived, it was nearing the end of a sunny autumn day.

"Did you eat on the plane?" my father asked. We were sitting on the tatami floor of his tearoom.

"They gave me a light snack." 5

"You must be hungry. We'll eat as soon as Kikuko arrives."

My father was a formidable-looking man with a large stony jaw and furious black eyebrows. I think now, in retrospect, that he much resembled Chou En-lai, although he would not have cherished such a comparison, being particularly proud of the pure samurai blood that ran in the family. His general presence was not one that encouraged relaxed conversation; neither were things helped much by his odd way of stating each remark as if it were the concluding one. In fact, as I sat opposite him that afternoon, a boyhood memory came back to me of the time he had struck me several times around the head for "chattering like an old woman." Inevitably, our conversation since my arrival at the airport had been punctuated by long pauses.

"I'm sorry to hear about the firm," I said when neither of us had spoken for some time. He nodded gravely.

"In fact, the story didn't end there," he said. "After the firm's collapse, Watanabe killed himself. He didn't wish to live with the disgrace."

"I see." 10

"We were partners for seventeen years. A man of principle and honor. I respected him very much."

"Will you go into business again?" I asked.

"I am . . . in retirement. I'm too old to involve myself in new ventures now. Business these days has become so different. Dealing with foreigners. Doing things their way. I don't understand how we've come to this. Neither did Watanabe." He sighed. "A fine man. A man of principle."

The tearoom looked out over the garden. From where I sat I could make out the ancient well that as a child I had believed to be haunted. It was just visible now through the thick foliage. The sun had sunk low and much of the garden had fallen into shadow.

"I'm glad in any case that you've decided to come back," my father said. "More than a short visit, I hope." 15

"I'm not sure what my plans will be."

"I, for one, am prepared to forget the past. Your mother, too, was always ready to welcome you back—upset as she was by your behavior."

"I appreciate your sympathy. As I say, I'm not sure what my plans are."

"I've come to believe now that there were no evil intentions in your mind," my father continued. "You were swayed by certain . . . influences. Like so many others."

"Perhaps we should forget it, as you suggest." 20

"As you will. More tea?"

Just then a girl's voice came echoing through the house.

"At last." My father rose to his feet. "Kikuko has arrived."

Despite our difference in years, my sister and I had always been close. Seeing me again seemed to make her excessively excited, and for a while she did nothing but giggle nervously. But she calmed down somewhat when my father started to question her about Osaka and her university. She answered him with short, formal replies. She in turn asked me a few questions, but she seemed inhibited by the fear that her question might lead to awkward topics. After a while, the conversation had become even sparser than prior to Kikuko's arrival. Then my father stood up, saying: "I must attend to the supper. Please excuse me for being burdened by such matters. Kikuko will look after you."

My sister relaxed quite visibly once he had left the room. Within a few minutes, 25 she was chatting freely about her friends in Osaka and about her classes at university. Then quite suddenly she decided we should walk in the garden and went striding out onto the veranda. We put on some straw sandals that had been left along the veranda rail and stepped out into the garden. The light in the garden had grown very dim.

"I've been dying for a smoke for the last half hour," she said, lighting a cigarette.

"Then why didn't you smoke?"

She made a furtive gesture back toward the house, then grinned mischievously.

"Oh, I see," I said.

"Guess what? I've got a boyfriend now." 30

"Oh, yes?"

"Except I'm wondering what to do. I haven't made up my mind yet."

"Quite understandable."

"You see, he's making plans to go to America. He wants me to go with him as soon as I finish studying."

"I see. And you want to go to America?" 35

"If we go, we're going to hitchhike." Kikuko waved a thumb in front of my face. "People say it's dangerous, but I've done it in Osaka and it's fine."

"I see. So what is it you're unsure about?"

We were following a narrow path that wound through the shrubs and finished by the old well. As we walked, Kikuko persisted in taking unnecessarily theatrical puffs on her cigarette.

"Well, I've got lots of friends now in Osaka. I like it there. I'm not sure I want to leave them all behind just yet. And Suichi . . . I like him, but I'm not sure I want to spend so much time with him. Do you understand?"

"Oh, perfectly." 40

She grinned again, then skipped on ahead of me until she had reached the well. "Do you remember," she said as I came walking up to her, "how you used to say this well was haunted?"

"Yes, I remember."

We both peered over the side.

"Mother always told me it was the old woman from the vegetable store you'd seen that night," she said. "But I never believed her and never came out here alone."

"Mother used to tell me that too. She even told me once the old woman had con-   45
fessed to being the ghost. Apparently, she'd been taking a shortcut through our garden. I imagine she had some trouble clambering over these walls."

Kikuko gave a giggle. She then turned her back to the well, casting her gaze about the garden.

"Mother never really blamed you, you know," she said, in a new voice. I remained silent. "She always used to say to me how it was their fault, hers and Father's, for not bringing you up correctly. She used to tell me how much more careful they'd been with me, and that's why I was so good." She looked up and the mischievous grin had returned to her face. "Poor Mother," she said.

"Yes. Poor Mother."

"Are you going back to California?"

"I don't know. I'll have to see."   50

"What happened to . . . to her? To Vicki?"

"That's all finished with," I said. "There's nothing much left for me now in California."

"Do you think I ought to go there?"

"Why not? I don't know. You'll probably like it." I glanced toward the house. "Perhaps we'd better go in soon. Father might need a hand with the supper."

But my sister was once more peering down into the well. "I can't see any ghosts,"   55
she said. Her voice echoed a little.

"Is Father very upset about his firm collapsing?"

"Don't know. You never can tell with Father." Then suddenly she straightened up and turned to me. "Did he tell you about old Watanabe? What he did?"

"I heard he committed suicide."

"Well, that wasn't all. He took his whole family with him. His wife and his two little girls."

"Oh, yes?"   60

"Those two beautiful little girls. He turned on the gas while they were all asleep. Then he cut his stomach with a meat knife."

"Yes, Father was just telling me how Watanabe was a man of principle."

"Sick." My sister turned back to the well.

"Careful. You'll fall right in."

"I can't see any ghost," she said. "You were lying to me all that time."   65

"But I never said it lived down the well."

"Where is it then?"

We both looked around at the trees and shrubs. The daylight had almost gone. Eventually I pointed to a small clearing some ten yards away.

"Just there I saw it. Just there."

We stared at the spot.   70

"What did it look like?"

"I couldn't see very well. It was dark."

"But you must have seen something."

"It was an old woman. She was just standing there, watching me."

We kept staring at the spot as if mesmerized.   75

"She was wearing a white kimono," I said. "Some of her hair came undone. It was blowing around a little."

Kikuko pushed her elbow against my arm. "Oh, be quiet. You're trying to frighten me all over again." She trod on the remains of her cigarette, then for a brief moment stood regarding it with a perplexed expression. She kicked some pine needles over it, then once more displayed her grin. "Let's see if supper's ready," she said.

We found my father in the kitchen. He gave us a quick glance, then carried on with what he was doing.

"Father's become quite a chef since he's had to manage on his own," Kikuko said with a laugh.

He turned and looked at my sister coldly. "Hardly a skill I'm proud of," he said.   80
"Kikuko, come here and help."

For some moments my sister did not move. Then she stepped forward and took an apron hanging from a drawer.

"Just these vegetables need cooking now," he said to her. "The rest just needs watching." Then he looked up and regarded me strangely for some seconds. "I expect you want to look around the house," he said eventually. He put down the chopsticks he had been holding. "It's a long time since you've seen it."

As we left the kitchen I glanced toward Kikuko, but her back was turned.

"She's a good girl," my father said.

I followed my father from room to room. I had forgotten how large the house   85
was. A panel would slide open and another room would appear. But the rooms were all startlingly empty. In one of the rooms the lights did not come on, and we stared at the stark walls and tatami in the pale light that came from the windows.

"This house is too large for a man to live in alone," my father said. "I don't have much use for most of these rooms now."

But eventually my father opened the door to a room packed full of books and papers. There were flowers in vases and pictures on the walls. Then I noticed something on a low table in the corner of the room. I came nearer and saw it was a plastic model of a battleship, the kind constructed by children. It had been placed on some newspaper; scattered around it were assorted pieces of gray plastic.

My father gave a laugh. He came up to the table and picked up the model.

"Since the firm folded," he said, "I have a little more time on my hands." He laughed again, rather strangely. For a moment his face looked almost gentle. "A little more time."

"That seems odd," I said. "You were always so busy."   90

"Too busy, perhaps." He looked at me with a small smile. "Perhaps I should have been a more attentive father."

I laughed. He went on contemplating his battleship. Then he looked up. "I hadn't meant to tell you this, but perhaps it's best that I do. It's my belief that your mother's death was no accident. She had many worries. And some disappointments."

We both gazed at the plastic battleship.

"Surely," I said eventually, "my mother didn't expect me to live here forever."

"Obviously you don't see. You don't see how it is for some parents. Not only must   95
they lose their children, they must lose them to things they don't understand." He spun the battleship in his fingers. "These little gunboats here could have been better glued, don't you think?"

"Perhaps. I think it looks fine."

"During the war I spent some time on a ship rather like this. But my ambition was always the air force. I figured it like this: If your ship was struck by the enemy, all you could do was struggle in the water hoping for a lifeline. But in an airplane—well, there was always the final weapon." He put the model back onto the table. "I don't suppose you believe in war."

"Not particularly."

He cast an eye around the room. "Supper should be ready by now," he said. "You must be hungry."

Supper was waiting in a dimly lit room next to the kitchen. The only source of   100
light was a big lantern that hung over the table, casting the rest of the room in shadow. We bowed to each other before starting the meal.

There was little conversation. When I made some polite comment about the food, Kikuko giggled a little. Her earlier nervousness seemed to have returned to her. My father did not speak for several minutes. Finally he said:

"It must feel strange for you, being back in Japan."

"Yes, it is a little strange."

"Already, perhaps, you regret leaving America."

"A little. Not so much. I didn't leave behind much. Just some empty rooms."   105

"I see."

I glanced across the table. My father's face looked stony and forbidding in the half-light. We ate on in silence.

Then my eye caught something at the back of the room. At first I continued eating, then my hands became still. The others noticed and looked at me. I went on gazing into the darkness past my father's shoulder.

"Who is that? In that photograph there?"

"Which photograph?" My father turned slightly, trying to follow my gaze.   110

"The lowest one. The old woman in the white kimono."

My father put down his chopsticks. He looked first at the photograph, then at me.

"Your mother." His voice had become very hard. "Can't you recognize your own mother?"

"My mother. You see, it's dark. I can't see it very well."

No one spoke for a few seconds, then Kikuko rose to her feet. She took the photo-   115
graph down from the wall, came back to the table, and gave it to me.

"She looks a lot older," I said.

"It was taken shortly before her death," said my father.

"It was the dark. I couldn't see very well."

I looked up and noticed my father holding out a hand. I gave him the photograph. He looked at it intently, then held it toward Kikuko. Obediently, my sister rose to her feet once more and returned the picture to the wall.

There was a large pot left unopened at the center of the table. When Kikuko had   120
seated herself again, my father reached forward and lifted the lid. A cloud of steam rose up and curled toward the lantern. He pushed the pot a little toward me.

"You must be hungry," he said. One side of his face had fallen into shadow.

"Thank you." I reached forward with my chopsticks. The steam was almost scalding. "What is it?"

"Fish."

"It smells very good."

In the soup were strips of fish that had curled almost into balls. I picked one out   125
and brought it to my bowl.

"Help yourself. There's plenty."

"Thank you." I took a little more, then pushed the pot toward my father. I watched him take several pieces to his bowl. Then we both watched as Kikuko served herself.

My father bowed slightly. "You must be hungry," he said again. He took some fish to his mouth and started to eat. Then I, too, chose a piece and put it in my mouth. It felt soft, quite fleshy against my tongue.

The three of us ate in silence. Several minutes went by. My father lifted the lid and once more steam rose up. We all reached forward and helped ourselves.

"Here," I said to my father, "you have this last piece." 130

"Thank you."

When we had finished the meal, my father stretched out his arms and yawned with an air of satisfaction. "Kikuko," he said, "prepare a pot of tea, please."

My sister looked at him, then left the room without comment. My father stood up.

"Let's retire to the other room. It's rather warm in here."

I got to my feet and followed him into the tearoom. The large sliding win- 135 dows had been left open, bringing in a breeze from the garden. For a while we sat in silence.

"Father," I said, finally.

"Yes?"

"Kikuko tells me Watanabe-san took his whole family with him."

My father lowered his eyes and nodded. For some moments he seemed deep in thought. "Watanabe was very devoted to his work," he said at last. "The collapse of the firm was a great blow to him. I fear it must have weakened his judgment."

"You think what he did . . . it was a mistake?" 140

"Why, of course. Do you see it otherwise?"

"No, no. Of course not."

"There are other things besides work," my father said.

"Yes."

We fell silent again. The sound of locusts came in from the garden. I looked out 145 into the darkness. The well was no longer visible.

"What do you think you will do now?" my father asked. "Will you stay in Japan for a while?"

"To be honest, I hadn't thought that far ahead."

"If you wish to stay here, I mean here in this house, you would be very welcome. That is, if you don't mind living with an old man."

"Thank you. I'll have to think about it."

I gazed out once more into the darkness. 150

"But of course," said my father, "this house is so dreary now. You'll no doubt return to America before long."

"Perhaps. I don't know yet."

"No doubt you will."

For some time my father seemed to be studying the back of his hands. Then he looked up and sighed.

"Kikuko is due to complete her studies next spring," he said. "Perhaps she will 155 want to come home then. She's a good girl."

"Perhaps she will."

"Things will improve then."

"Yes, I'm sure they will."

We fell silent once more, waiting for Kikuko to bring the tea.

HENRY JAMES   (1843–1916)
The Real Thing   1892

[The painter-narrator's vocabulary in this story reflects his lifelong interest in the arts and his knowledge of French and Italian. A *sunk piece* refers to a painting losing its brilliance because the paint has dried and sunk in; *covers* are flocks of game birds. Some French words are *quoi*—whatever, *table d'hôte*—restaurant serving one standard meal, *bêtement*—foolishly, *profils perdus*—a profile showing more of the back of the head than the face, *sentiment de la pose*—an instinct for striking poses, and *Ce sont des gens qu'il faut mettre à la porte*—This kind of person should be shown the door. *Lazzarone* is Italian for a beggar. *Coloro che sanno* is Italian for "those in the know." "Having no respect for the *h*" refers to the cockney accent of working-class Londoners who drop h's, as in *'ere*. *The City* refers to the financial center of London. References to famous artists and poets are Raffaello Sanzio (1483–1520), an Italian Renaissance painter; Leonardo da Vinci (1452–1519), another Italian Renaissance painter, creator of the *Mona Lisa* and *The Last Supper;* and Dante Alighieri (1265–1321), author of *The Divine Comedy*.]

1

When the porter's wife, who used to answer the housebell, announced "A gentleman and a lady, sir," I had, as I often had in those days—the wish being father to the thought—an immediate vision of sitters. Sitters my visitors in this case proved to be; but not in the sense I should have preferred. There was nothing at first however to indicate that they mightn't have come for a portrait. The gentleman, a man of fifty, very high and very straight, with a moustache slightly grizzled and a dark gray walking-coat admirably fitted, both of which I noted professionally—I don't mean as a barber or yet as a tailor—would have struck me as a celebrity if celebrities often were striking. It was a truth of which I had for some time been conscious that a figure with a good deal of frontage was, as one might say, almost never a public institution. A glance at the lady helped to remind me of this paradoxical law: she also looked too distinguished to be a "personality." Moreover one would scarcely come across two variations together.

Neither of the pair immediately spoke—they only prolonged the preliminary gaze suggesting that each wished to give the other a chance. They were visibly shy; they stood there letting me take them in—which, as I afterwards perceived, was the most practical thing they could have done. In this way their embarrassment served their cause. I had seen people painfully reluctant to mention that they desired anything so gross as to be represented on canvas; but the scruples of my new friends appeared almost insurmountable. Yet the gentleman might have said "I should like a portrait of my wife," and the lady might have said "I should like a portrait of my husband." Perhaps they weren't husband and wife—this naturally would make the matter more delicate. Perhaps they wished to be done together—in which case they ought to have brought a third person to break the news.

"We come from Mr. Rivet," the lady finally said with a dim smile that had the effect of a moist sponge passed over a "sunk" piece of painting, as well as of a vague allusion to vanished beauty. She was as tall and straight, in her degree, as her companion, and with ten years less to carry. She looked as sad as a woman could look whose face was not charged with expression; that is her tinted oval mask showed waste as an exposed surface shows friction. The hand of time had played over her freely, but to an effect of elimination. She was slim and stiff, and so well-dressed, in dark blue cloth, with lappets and pockets and buttons, that it was clear she employed the same tailor as her husband. The couple had an indefinable air of prosperous thrift—they evidently got a good deal of luxury for their money. If I was to be one of their luxuries it would behove me to consider my terms.

"Ah, Claude Rivet recommended me?" I echoed; and I added that it was very kind of him, though I could reflect that, as he only painted landscape, this wasn't a sacrifice.

The lady looked very hard at the gentleman, and the gentleman looked round the room. Then staring at the floor a moment and stroking his moustache, he rested his pleasant eyes on me with the remark: "He said you were the right one." [5]

"I try to be, when people want to sit."

"Yes, we should like to," said the lady anxiously.

"Do you mean together?"

My visitors exchanged a glance. "If you could do anything with *me* I suppose it would be double," the gentleman stammered.

"Oh yes, there's naturally a higher charge for two figures than for one." [10]

"We should like to make it pay," the husband confessed.

"That's very good of you," I returned, appreciating so unwonted a sympathy—for I supposed he meant pay the artist.

A sense of strangeness seemed to draw on the lady.

"We mean for the illustrations—Mr. Rivet said you might put one in."

"Put in—an illustration?" I was equally confused. [15]

"Sketch her off, you know," said the gentleman, coloring.

It was only then that I understood the service Claude Rivet had rendered me; he had told them how I worked in black-and-white, for magazines, for storybooks, for sketches of contemporary life, and consequently had copious employment for models. These things were true, but it was not less true—I may confess it now; whether because the aspiration was to lead to everything or to nothing I leave the reader to guess—that I couldn't get the honors, to say nothing of the emoluments, of a great painter of portraits out of my head. My "illustrations" were my pot-boilers; I looked to a different branch of art—far and away the most interesting it had always seemed to me—to perpetuate my fame. There was no shame in looking to it also to make my fortune; but that fortune was by so much further from being made from the moment my visitors wished to be "done" for nothing. I was disappointed; for in the pictorial sense I had immediately *seen* them. I had seized their type—I had already settled what I would do with it. Something that wouldn't absolutely have pleased them, I afterwards reflected.

"Ah you're—you're—a—?" I began as soon as I had mastered my surprise. I couldn't bring out the dingy word "models": it seemed so little to fit the case.

"We haven't had much practice," said the lady.

"We've got to *do* something, and we've thought that an artist in your line might perhaps make something of us," her husband threw off. He further mentioned that they didn't know many artists and that they had gone first, on the off-chance—he painted views of course, but sometimes put in figures; perhaps I remembered—to Mr. Rivet, whom they had met a few years before at a place in Norfolk where he was sketching. [20]

"We used to sketch a little ourselves," the lady hinted.

"It's very awkward, but we absolutely *must* do something," her husband went on.

"Of course we're not so *very* young," she admitted with a wan smile.

With the remark that I might as well know something more about them the husband had handed me a card extracted from a neat new pocket-book—their appurtenances were all of the freshest—and inscribed with the words "Major Monarch." Impressive as these words were they didn't carry my knowledge much further; but my visitor presently added: "I've left the army and we've had the misfortune to lose our money. In fact our means are dreadfully small."

"It's awfully trying—a regular strain," said Mrs. Monarch.   25

They evidently wished to be discreet—to take care not to swagger because they were gentlefolk. I felt them willing to recognize this as something of a drawback, at the same time that I guessed at an underlying sense—their consolation in adversity—that they *had* their points. They certainly had; but these advantages struck me as preponderantly social; such for instance as would help to make a drawing-room look well. However, a drawing-room was always, or ought to be, a picture.

In consequence of his wife's allusion to their age Major Monarch observed: "Naturally it's more for the figure that we thought of going in. We can still hold ourselves up." On the instant I saw that the figure was indeed their strong point. His "naturally" didn't sound vain, but it lighted up the question. "*She* has the best one," he continued, nodding at his wife with a pleasant after-dinner absence of circumlocution. I could only reply, as if we were in fact sitting over our wine, that this didn't prevent his own from being very good; which led him in turn to make answer: "We thought that if you ever have to do people like us we might be something like it. *She* particularly—for a lady in a book, you know."

I was so amused by them that, to get more of it, I did my best to take their point of view; and though it was an embarrassment to find myself appraising physically, as if they were animals on hire or useful blacks, a pair whom I should have expected to meet only in one of the relations in which criticism is tacit, I looked at Mrs. Monarch judicially enough to be able to exclaim after a moment with conviction: "Oh yes, a lady in a book!" She was singularly like a bad illustration.

"We'll stand up, if you like," said the Major; and he raised himself before me with a really grand air.

I could take his measure at a glance—he was six feet two and a perfect gentleman.   30
It would have paid any club in process of formation and in want of a stamp to engage him at a salary to stand in the principal window. What struck me at once was that in coming to me they had rather missed their vocation; they could surely have been turned to better account for advertising purposes. I couldn't of course see the thing in detail, but I could see them make somebody's fortune—I don't mean their own. There was something in them for a waistcoat-maker, an hotel-keeper or a soap-vendor. I could imagine "We always use it" pinned on their bosoms with the greatest effect; I had a vision of the brilliancy with which they would launch a table d'hôte.

Mrs. Monarch sat still, not from pride but from shyness, and presently her husband said to her; "Get up, my dear, and show how smart you are." She obeyed, but she had no need to get up to show it. She walked to the end of the studio and then came back blushing, her fluttered eyes on the partner of her appeal. I was reminded of an incident I had accidentally had a glimpse of in Paris being with a friend there, a dramatist about to produce a play, when an actress came to him to ask to be entrusted with a part. She went through her paces before him, walked up and down as Mrs. Monarch was doing. Mrs. Monarch did it quite as well, but I abstained from applauding. It was very odd to see such people apply for such poor pay. She looked as if she had ten thousand a year. Her husband had used the word that described her: she was in the London current jargon essentially and typically "smart." Her figure was, in the same order of ideas, conspicuously and irreproachably "good." For a woman of her age her waist was surprisingly small; her elbow moreover had the orthodox crook. She held her head at the conventional angle, but why did she come to *me*? She ought to have tried on jackets at a big shop. I feared my visitors were not only destitute but "artistic"—which would be a great complication. When she sat down again I thanked her, observing that what a draughtsman most valued in his model was the faculty of keeping quiet.

"Oh *she* can keep quiet," said Major Monarch. Then he added jocosely: "I've always kept her quiet."

"I'm not a nasty fidget, am I?" It was going to wring tears from me, I felt, the way she hid her head, ostrich-like, in the other's broad bosom.

The owner of this expanse addressed his answer to me. "Perhaps it isn't out of place to mention—because we ought to be quite business-like, oughtn't we?—that when I married her she was known as the Beautiful Statue."

"Oh dear!" said Mrs. Monarch ruefully.   35

"Of course I should want a certain amount of expression," I rejoined.

"Of *course!*"—and I had never heard such unanimity.

"And then I suppose you know that you'll get awfully tired."

"Oh we *never* get tired!" they eagerly cried.

"Have you had any kind of practice?"   40

They hesitated—they looked at each other. "We've been photographed—*immensely*," said Mrs. Monarch.

"She means the fellows have asked us themselves," added the Major.

"I see—because you're so good-looking."

"I don't know what they thought, but they were always after us."

"We always got our photographs for nothing," smiled Mrs. Monarch.   45

"We might have brought some, my dear," her husband remarked.

"I'm not sure we have any left. We've given quantities away," she explained to me.

"With our autographs and that sort of thing." said the Major.

"Are they to be got in the shops?" I enquired as a harmless pleasantry.

"Oh yes, *hers*—they used to be."   50

"Not now," said Mrs. Monarch with her eyes on the floor.

2

I could fancy the "sort of thing" they put on the presentation copies of their photographs, and I was sure they wrote a beautiful hand. It was odd how quickly I was sure of everything that concerned them. If they were now so poor as to have to earn shillings and pence they could never have had much of a margin. Their good looks had been their capital, and they had good-humoredly made the most of the career that this resource marked out for them. It was in their faces, the blankness, the deep intellectual repose of the twenty years of country-house visiting that had given them pleasant intonations. I could see the sunny drawing-rooms, sprinkled with periodicals she didn't read, in which Mrs. Monarch had continuously sat; I could see the wet shrubberies in which she had walked, equipped to admiration for either exercise. I could see the rich covers the Major had helped to shoot and the wonderful garments in which, late at night, he repaired to the smoking-room to talk about them. I could imagine their leggings and waterproofs, their knowing tweeds and rugs, their rolls of sticks and cases of tackle and neat umbrellas; and I could evoke the exact appearance of their servants and the compact variety of their luggage on the platforms of country stations.

They gave small tips, but they were liked; they didn't do anything themselves, but they were welcome. They looked so well everywhere; they gratified the general relish for stature, complexion and "form." They knew it without fatuity or vulgarity, and they respected themselves in consequence. They weren't superficial; they were thorough and kept themselves up—it had been their line. People with such a taste for activity had to have some line. I could feel how even in a dull house they could have been counted on for the joy of life. At present something had happened—it didn't matter what, their little income had grown less, it had grown least—and they had to do something for pocket-money. Their friends could like them, I made out, without liking to support them. There was something about them that represented credit—their clothes, their manners, their type; but if credit is a large empty pocket in which an occasional chink reverberates, the chink at least must be audible. What they wanted of me was to help to make it so. Fortunately they had no children—I soon divined that. They would also perhaps wish our relations to be kept secret: this was why it was "for the figure"—the reproduction of the face would betray them.

I liked them—I felt, quite as their friends must have done—they were so simple; and I had no objection to them if they would suit. But somehow with all their perfections I didn't easily believe in them. After all they were amateurs, and the ruling passion of my life was the detestation of the amateur. Combined with this was another perversity—an innate preference for the represented subject over the real one: the defect of the real one was so apt to be a lack of representation. I liked things that appeared; then one was sure. Whether they *were* or not was a subordinate and almost always a profitless question. There were other considerations, the first of which was that I already had two or three recruits in use, notably a young person with big feet, in alpaca, from Kilburn, who for a couple of years had come to me regularly for my illustrations and with whom I was still—perhaps ignobly—satisfied. I frankly explained to my visitors how the case stood, but they had taken more precautions than I supposed. They had reasoned out their opportunity, for Claude Rivet had told them of the projected *édition de luxe* of one of the writers of our day—the rarest of the novelists—who, long neglected by the multitudinous vulgar and dearly prized by the attentive (need I mention Philip Vincent?) had had the happy fortune of seeing, late in life, the dawn and then the full light of a higher criticism; an estimate in which on the part of the public there was something really of expiation. The edition preparing, planned by a publisher of taste, was practically an act of high reparation; the wood-cuts with which it was to be enriched were the homage of English art to one of the most independent representatives of English letters. Major and Mrs. Monarch confessed to me they had hoped I might be able to work *them* into my branch of the enterprise. They knew I was to do the first of the books, "Rutland Ramsay," but I had to make clear to them that my participation in the rest of the affair—this first book was to be a test—must depend on the satisfaction I should give. If this should be limited my employers would drop me with scarce common forms. It was therefore a crisis for me, and naturally I was making special preparations, looking about for new people, should they be necessary, and securing the best types. I admitted however that I should like to settle down to two or three good models who would do for everything.

"Should we have often to—a—put on special clothes?" Mrs. Monarch timidly demanded.   55

"Dear yes—that's half the business."

"And should we be expected to supply our own costumes?"

"Oh no; I've got a lot of things. A painter's models put on—or put off—anything he likes."

"And you mean—a—the same?"

"The same?"   60

Mrs. Monarch looked at her husband again.

"Oh she was just wondering," he explained, "if the costumes are in *general* use." I had to confess that they were, and I mentioned further that some of them—I had a lot of genuine greasy last-century things—had served their time, a hundred years ago, on living world-stained men and women; on figures not perhaps so far removed, in that vanished world, from *their* type, the Monarchs', *quoi!* of a breeched and bewigged age. "We'll put on anything that *fits*," said the Major.

"Oh I arrange that—they fit in the pictures."

"I'm afraid I should do better for the modern books. I'd come as you like," said Mrs. Monarch.

"She has got a lot of clothes at home: they might do for contemporary life," her   65
husband continued.

"Oh I can fancy scenes in which you'd be quite natural." And indeed I could see the slipshod rearrangements of stale properties—the stories I tried to produce pictures for without the exasperation of reading them—whose sandy tracts the good lady might help to people. But I had to return to the fact that for this sort of work—the daily mechanical grind—I was already equipped: the people I was working with were fully adequate.

"We only thought we might be more like *some* characters," said Mrs. Monarch mildly, getting up.

Her husband also rose; he stood looking at me with a dim wistfulness that was touching in so fine a man.

"Wouldn't it be rather a pull sometimes to have—a—to have—?" He hung fire; he wanted me to help him by phrasing what he meant. But I couldn't—I didn't know. So he brought it out awkwardly: "The *real* thing; a gentleman, you know, or a lady." I was quite ready to give a general assent—I admitted that there was a great deal in that. This encouraged Major Monarch to say, following up his appeal with an unacted gulp: "It's awfully hard—we've tried everything." The gulp was communicative; it proved too much for his wife. Before I knew it Mrs. Monarch had dropped again upon a divan and burst into tears. Her husband sat down beside her, holding one of her hands; whereupon she quickly dried her eyes with the other, while I felt embarrassed as she looked up at me. "There isn't a confounded job I haven't applied for—waited for—prayed for. You can fancy we'd be pretty bad first. Secretaryships and that sort of thing? You might as well ask for a peerage. I'd be *anything*—I'm strong; a messenger or a coalheaver. I'd put on a gold-laced cap and open carriage-doors in front of the haberdasher's; I'd hang about a station to carry portmanteaux; I'd be a postman. But they won't *look* at you; there are thousands as good as yourself already on the ground. *Gentlemen*, poor beggars, who've drunk their wine, who've kept their hunters!"

I was as reassuring as I knew how to be, and my visitors were presently on their   70
feet again while, for the experiment, we agreed on an hour. We were discussing it when the door opened and Miss Churm came in with a wet umbrella. Miss Churm had to take the omnibus to Maida Vale and then walk half a mile. She looked a trifle blowsy and slightly splashed. I scarcely ever saw her come in without thinking fresh how odd it was that, being so little in herself, she should yet be so much in others. She was a meager little Miss Churm, but was such an ample heroine of romance. She was only a freckled cockney, but she could represent everything, from a fine lady to a shepherdess; she had the faculty as she might have had a fine voice or long hair. She couldn't spell and she loved beer, but she had two or three "points," and practice, and a knack, and mother-wit, and a whimsical sensibility, and a love of the theatre, and seven sisters, and not an ounce of respect, especially for the *h*. The first thing my visitors saw was that her umbrella was wet, and in their spotless perfection they visibly winced at it. The rain had come on since their arrival.

"I'm all in a soak; there *was* a mess of people in the 'bus. I wish you lived near a styation," said Miss Churm. I requested her to get ready as quickly as possible, and she passed into the room in which she always changed her dress. But before going out she asked me what she was to get into this time.

"It's the Russian princess, don't you know?" I answered; "the one with the 'golden eyes,' in black velvet, for the long thing in the *Cheapside*."

"Golden eyes? I *say!*" cried Miss Churm, while my companions watched her with intensity as she withdrew. She always arranged herself, when she was late, before I could turn around; and I kept my visitors a little on purpose, so that they might get an idea, from seeing her, what would be expected of themselves. I mentioned that she was quite my notion of an excellent model—she was really very clever.

"Do you think she looks like a Russian princess?" Major Monarch asked with lurking alarm.

"When I make her, yes."   75

"Oh if you have to *make* her—!" he reasoned, not without point.

"That's the most you can ask. There are so many who are not makeable."

"Well now, *here's* a lady"—and with a persuasive smile he passed his arm into his wife's—"who's already made!"

"Oh I'm not a Russian princess," Mrs. Monarch protested a little coldly. I could see she had known some and didn't like them. There at once was a complication of a kind I never had to fear with Miss Churm.

This young lady came back in black velvet—the gown was rather rusty and very   80
low on her lean shoulders—and with a Japanese fan in her red hands. I reminded her that in the scene I was doing she had to look over someone's head. "I forget whose it is; but it doesn't matter. Just look over a head."

"I'd rather look over a stove," said Miss Churm; and she took her station near the fire. She fell into position, settled herself into a tall attitude, gave a certain backward inclination to her head and a certain forward droop to her fan, and looked, at least to my prejudiced sense, distinguished and charming, foreign and dangerous. We left her looking so while I went downstairs with Major and Mrs. Monarch.

"I believe I could come about as near it as that," said Mrs. Monarch.

"Oh, you think she's shabby, but you must allow for the alchemy of art."

However, they went off with an evident increase of comfort founded on their demonstrable advantage in being the real thing. I could fancy them shuddering over Miss Churm. She was very droll about them when I went back, for I told her what they wanted.

"Well, if *she* can sit I'll tyke to bookkeeping," said my model.   85

"She's very ladylike," I replied as an innocent form of aggravation.

"So much the worse for *you*. That means she can't turn round."

"She'll do for the fashionable novels."

"Oh yes, she'll *do* for them!" my model humorously declared. "Ain't they bad enough without her?" I had often sociably denounced them to Miss Churm.

3

It was for the elucidation of a mystery in one of these works that I first tried Mrs.   90
Monarch. Her husband came with her, to be useful if necessary—it was sufficiently clear that as a general thing he would prefer to come with her. At first I wondered if this were for "propriety's" sake—if he were going to be jealous and meddling. The idea was too tiresome, and if it had been confirmed it would speedily have brought our acquaintance to a close. But I soon saw there was nothing in it and that if he accompanied Mrs. Monarch it was—in addition to the chance of being wanted—simply because he had nothing else to do. When they were separate his occupation was gone and they never

had been separate. I judged rightly that in their awkward situation their close union was their main comfort and that this union had no weak spot. It was a real marriage, an encouragement to the hesitating, a nut for pessimists to crack. Their address was humble—I remember afterwards thinking it had been the only thing about them that was really professional—and I could fancy the lamentable lodgings in which the Major would have been left alone. He could sit there more or less grimly with his wife—he couldn't sit there anyhow without her.

He had too much tact to try and make himself agreeable when he couldn't be useful; so when I was too absorbed in my work to talk he simply sat and waited. But I liked to hear him talk—it made my work, when not interrupting it, less mechanical, less special. To listen to him was to combine the excitement of going out with the economy of staying at home. There was only one hindrance—that I seemed not to know any of the people this brilliant couple had known. I think he wondered extremely, during the term of our intercourse, whom the deuce I *did* know. He hadn't a stray sixpence of an idea to fumble for, so we didn't spin it very fine; we confined ourselves to questions of leather and even of liquor—saddlers and breeches-makers and how to get excellent claret cheap—and matters like "good trains" and the habits of small game. His lore on these last subjects was astonishing—he managed to interweave the station-master with the ornithologist. When he couldn't talk about greater things he could talk cheerfully about smaller, and since I couldn't accompany him into reminiscences of the fashionable world he could lower the conversation without a visible effort to my level.

So earnest a desire to please was touching in a man who could so easily have knocked one down. He looked after the fire and had an opinion on the draught of the stove without my asking him, and I could see that he thought many of my arrangements not half knowing. I remember telling him that if I were only rich I'd offer him a salary to come and teach me how to live. Sometimes he gave a random sigh of which the essence might have been: "Give me even such a bare old barrack as *this,* and I'd do something with it!" When I wanted to use him he came alone; which was an illustration of the superior courage of women. His wife could bear her solitary second floor, and she was in general more discreet; showing by various small reserves that she was alive to the propriety of keeping our relations markedly professional—not letting them slide into sociability. She wished it to remain clear that she and the Major were employed, not cultivated, and if she approved of me as a superior, who could be kept in his place, she never thought me quite good enough for an equal.

She sat with great intensity, giving the whole of her mind to it, and was capable of remaining for an hour almost as motionless as before a photographer's lens. I could see she had been photographed often, but somehow the very habit that made her good for that purpose unfitted her for mine. At first I was extremely pleased with her ladylike air, and it was a satisfaction, on coming to follow her lines, to see how good they were and how far they could lead the pencil. But after a little skirmishing I began to find her too insurmountably stiff; do what I would with it my drawing looked like a photograph or a copy of a photograph. Her figure had no variety of expression—she herself had no sense of variety. You may say that this was my business and was only a question of placing her. Yet I placed her in every conceivable position and she managed to obliterate their differences. She was always a lady certainly, and into the bargain was always the same lady. She was the real thing, but always the same thing. There were moments when I rather writhed under the serenity of her confidence that she *was* the real thing. All her dealings with me and all her husband's were an implication that this was lucky for *me*. Meanwhile I found myself trying to invent types that approached her own, instead of making her own transform itself—in the clever way that was not impossible for instance to poor Miss Churm. Arrange as I would and take the precautions I would, she always came out, in my pictures, too tall—landing me in the dilemma of having represented a fascinating woman as seven feet high, which (out of respect perhaps to my own very much scantier inches) was far from my idea of such personage.

The case was worse with the Major—nothing I could do would keep *him* down, so that he became useful only for representation of brawny giants. I adored variety and range, I cherished human accidents, the illustrative note; I wanted to characterize closely, and the thing in the world I most hated was the danger of being ridden by a type. I had quarrelled with some of my friends about it; I had parted company with them for maintaining that one *had* to be, and that if the type was beautiful—witness Raphael and Leonardo—the servitude was only a gain. I was neither Leonardo nor Raphael—I might only be a presumptuous young modern searcher; but I held that everything was to be sacrificed sooner than character. When they claimed that the obsessional form could easily *be* character I retorted, perhaps superficially, "Whose?" It couldn't be everybody's—it might end in being nobody's.

After I had drawn Mrs. Monarch a dozen times I felt surer even than before that the value of such a model as Miss Churm resided precisely in the fact that she had no positive stamp, combined of course with the other fact that what she did have was a curious and inexplicable talent for imitation. Her usual appearance was like a curtain which she could draw up at request for a capital performance. This performance was simply suggestive; but it was a word to the wise—it was vivid and pretty. Sometimes even I thought it, though she was plain herself, too insipidly pretty; I made it a reproach to her that the figures drawn from her were monotonously (*bêtement*, as we used to say) graceful. Nothing made her more angry: it was so much of her pride to feel she could sit for characters that had nothing in common with each other. She would accuse me at such moments of taking away her "reputytion."

It suffered a certain shrinkage, this queer quantity, from the repeated visits of my new friends. Miss Churm was greatly in demand, never in want of employment, so I had no scruple in putting her off occasionally, to try them more at my ease. It was certainly amusing at first to do the real thing—it was amusing to do Major Monarch's trousers. They *were* the real thing, even if he did come out colossal. It was amusing to do his wife's back hair—it was so mathematically neat—and the particular "smart" tension of her tight stays. She lent herself especially to positions in which the face was somewhat averted or blurred; she abounded in ladylike back views and *profils perdus*. When she stood erect she took naturally one of the attitudes in which court-painters represent queens and princesses; so that I found myself wondering whether, to draw out this accomplishment, I couldn't get the editor of the *Cheapside* to publish a really royal romance, "A Tale of Buckingham Palace." Sometimes however the real thing and the make-believe came into contact; by which I mean that Miss Churm, keeping an appointment or coming to make one on days when I had much work in hand, encountered her invidious rivals. The encounter was not on their part, for they noticed her no more than if she had been the housemaid; not from intentional loftiness, but simply because as yet, professionally, they didn't know how to fraternize, as I could imagine they would have liked—or at least that the Major would. They couldn't talk about the omnibus—they always walked; and they didn't know what else to try—she wasn't interested in good trains or cheap claret. Besides, they must have felt—in the air—that she was amused at them, secretly derisive of their ever knowing how. She wasn't a person to conceal the limits of her faith if she had had a chance to show them. On the other hand Mrs. Monarch didn't think her tidy; for why else did she take pains to say to me—it was going out of the way, for Mrs. Monarch—that she didn't like dirty women?

One day when my young lady happened to be present with my other sitters—she even dropped in, when it was convenient, for a chat—I asked her to be so good as to

95

lend a hand in getting tea, a service with which she was familiar and which was one of a class that, living as I did in a small way, with slender domestic resources, I often appealed to my models to render. They liked to lay hands on my property, to break the sitting, and sometimes the china—it made them feel Bohemian. The next time I saw Miss Churm after this incident she surprised me greatly by making a scene about it—she accused me of having wished to humiliate her. She hadn't resented the outrage at the time, but had seemed obliging and amused, enjoying the comedy of asking Mrs. Monarch, who sat vague and silent, whether she would have cream and sugar, and putting an exaggerated simper into the question. She had tried intonations—as if she too wished to pass for the real thing—till I was afraid my other visitors would take offense.

Oh they were determined not to do this, and their touching patience was the measure of their great need. They would sit by the hour, uncomplaining, till I was ready to use them; they would come back on the chance of being wanted and would walk away cheerfully if it failed. I used to go to the door with them to see in what magnificent order they retreated. I tried to find other employment for them—I introduced them to several artists. But they didn't "take," for reasons I could appreciate, and I became rather anxiously aware that after such disappointments they fell back upon me with a heavier weight. They did me the honor to think me most *their* form. They weren't romantic enough for the painters, and in those days there were few serious workers in black-and-white. Besides, they had an eye to the great job I had mentioned to them—they had secretly set their hearts on supplying the right essence for my pictorial vindication of our fine novelist. They knew that for this undertaking I should want no costume-effects, none of the frippery of past ages—that it was a case in which everything would be contemporary and satirical and presumably genteel. If I could work them into it their future would be assured, for the labor would of course be long and the occupation steady.

One day Mrs. Monarch came without her husband—she explained his absence by his having had to go to the City. While she sat there in her usual relaxed majesty there came at the door a knock which I immediately recognized as the subdued appeal of a model out of work. It was followed by the entrance of a young man whom I at once saw to be a foreigner and who proved in fact an Italian acquainted with no English word but my name, which he uttered in a way that made it seem to include all others. I hadn't then visited his country, nor was I proficient in his tongue; but as he was not so meanly constituted—what Italian is?—as to depend only on that member for expression he conveyed to me, in familiar but graceful mimicry, that he was in search of exactly the employment in which the lady before me was engaged. I was not struck with him at first, and while I continued to draw I dropped few signs of interest or encouragement. He stood his ground however—not importunately, but with a dumb dog-like fidelity in his eyes that amounted to innocent impudence, the manner of a devoted servant—he might have been in the house for years—unjustly suspected. Suddenly it struck me that this very attitude and expression made a picture; whereupon I told him to sit down and wait till I should be free. There was another picture in the way he obeyed me, and I observed as I worked that there were others still in the way he looked wonderingly, with his head thrown back, about the high studio. He might have been crossing himself in Saint Peter's. Before I finished I said to myself "The fellow's a bankrupt orange-monger, but a treasure."

When Mrs. Monarch withdrew he passed across the room like a flash to open the door for her, standing there with the rapt pure gaze of the young Dante spellbound by the young Beatrice. As I never insisted, in such situations, on the blankness of the British domestic, I reflected that he had the making of a servant—and I needed one, but couldn't pay him to be only that—as well as of a model; in short I resolved to adopt my bright adventurer if he would agree to officiate in the double capacity. He jumped at my offer, and in the event my rashness—for I had really known nothing about him—wasn't brought home to me. He proved a sympathetic though a desultory ministrant, and had in a wonderful degree the *sentiment de la pose*. It was uncultivated, instinctive, a part of the happy instinct that had guided him to my door and helped him to spell out my name on the card nailed to it. He had had no other introduction to me than a guess, from the shape of my high north window, seen outside, that my place was a studio and that as a studio it would contain an artist. He had wandered to England in search of fortune, like other itinerants, and had embarked, with a partner and a small green hand-cart, on the sale of penny ices. The ices had melted away and the partner had dissolved in their train. My young man wore tight yellow trousers with reddish stripes and his name was Oronte. He was sallow but fair, and when I put him into some old clothes of my own he looked like an Englishman. He was as good as Miss Churm, who could look, when requested, like an Italian.

4

I thought Mrs. Monarch's face slightly convulsed when, on her coming back with her husband, she found Oronte installed. It was strange to have to recognize in a scrap of a lazzarone a competitor to her magnificent Major. It was she who scented danger first, for the Major was anecdotically unconscious. But Oronte gave us tea, with a hundred eager confusions—he had never been concerned in so queer a process—and I think she thought better of me for having at last an "establishment." They saw a couple of drawings that I had made of the establishment, and Mrs. Monarch hinted that it never would have struck her he had sat for them. "Now the drawings you make from *us*, they look exactly like us," she reminded me, smiling in triumph; and I recognized that this was indeed just their defect. When I drew the Monarchs I couldn't anyhow get away from them—get into the character I wanted to represent; and I hadn't the least desire my model should be discoverable in my picture. Miss Churm never was, and Mrs. Monarch thought I hid her, very properly, because she was vulgar; whereas if she was lost it was only as the dead who go to heaven are lost—in the gain of an angel the more.

By this time I had got a certain start with "Rutland Ramsay," the first novel in the great projected series; that is I had produced a dozen drawings, several with the help of the Major and his wife, and I had sent them in for approval. My understanding with the publishers, as I have already hinted, had been that I was to be left to do my work, in this particular case, as I liked, with the whole book committed to me; but my connection with the rest of the series was only contingent. There were moments when, frankly, it *was* a comfort to have the real thing under one's hand; for there were characters in "Rutland Ramsay" that were very much like it. There were people presumably as erect as the Major and women of as good a fashion as Mrs. Monarch. There was a great deal of country-house life—treated, it is true, in a fine fanciful ironical generalized way—and there was a considerable implication of knickerbockers and kilts. There were certain things I had to settle at the outset; such things for instance as the exact appearance of the hero and the particular bloom and figure of the heroine. The author of course gave me a lead, but there was a margin for interpretation. I took the Monarchs into my confidence, I told them frankly what I was about, I mentioned my embarrassments and alternatives. "Oh take *him!*" Mrs. Monarch murmured sweetly, looking at her husband; and "What could you want better than my wife?" the Major enquired with the comfortable candor that now prevailed between us.

I wasn't obliged to answer these remarks—I was only obliged to place my sitters. I wasn't easy in mind, and I postponed a little timidly perhaps the solving of my question. The book was a large canvas, the other figures were numerous, and I worked off at first some of the episodes in which the hero and the heroine were not concerned. When once I had set *them* up I should have to stick to them—I couldn't make my young man seven feet high in one place and five feet nine in another. I inclined on the whole to the latter measurement, though the Major more than once reminded me that *he* looked about as young as any one. It was indeed quite possible to arrange him, for the figure, so that it would have been difficult to detect his age. After the spontaneous Oronte had been with me a month, and after I had given him to understand several times over that his native exuberance would presently constitute an insurmountable barrier to our further intercourse, I waked to a sense of his heroic capacity. He was only five feet seven, but the remaining inches were latent. I tried him almost secretly at first, for I was really rather afraid of the judgment my other models would pass on such a choice. If they regarded Miss Churm as little better than a snare what would they think of the representation by a person so little the real thing as an Italian street-vendor of a protagonist formed by a public school?

If I went a little in fear of them it wasn't because they bullied me, because they had got an oppressive foothold, but because in their really pathetic decorum and mysteriously permanent newness they counted on me so intensely. I was therefore very glad when Jack Hawley came home: he was always of such good counsel. He painted badly himself, but there was no one like him for putting his finger on the place. He had been absent from England for a year; he had been somewhere—I don't remember where—to get a fresh eye. I was in a good deal of dread of any such organ, but we were old friends; he had been away for months and a sense of emptiness was creeping into my life. I hadn't dodged a missile for a year.

He came back with a fresh eye, but with the same old black velvet blouse, and the first evening he spent in my studio we smoked cigarettes till the small hours. He had done no work himself, he had only got the eye; so the field was clear for the production of my little things. He wanted to see what I had produced for the *Cheapside,* but he was disappointed in the exhibition. That at least seemed the meaning of two or three comprehensive groans which, as he lounged on my big divan, his leg folded under him, looking at my latest drawings, issued from his lips with the smoke of the cigarette. 105

"What's the matter with you?" I asked.

"What's the matter with *you?*"

"Nothing save that I'm mystified."

"You are indeed. You're quite off the hinge. What's the meaning of this new fad?" And he tossed me, with visible irreverence, a drawing in which I happened to have depicted both my elegant models. I asked if he didn't think it good, and he replied that it struck him as execrable, given the sort of thing I had always represented myself to him as wishing to arrive at; but I let that pass—I was so anxious to see exactly what he meant. The two figures in the picture looked colossal, but I supposed this was *not* what he meant, inasmuch as, for aught he knew the contrary, I might have been trying for some such effect. I maintained that I was working exactly in the same way as when he last had done me the honor to tell me I might do something some day. "Well, there's a screw loose somewhere," he answered; "wait a bit and I'll discover it." I depended upon him to do so: where else was the fresh eye? But he produced at last nothing more luminous than "I don't know—I don't like your types." This was lame for a critic who had never consented to discuss with me anything but the question of execution, the direction of strokes and the mystery of values.

"In the drawings you've been looking at I think my types are very handsome."   110
"Oh they won't do!"
"I've been working with new models."
"I see you have. *They* won't do."
"Are you very sure of that?"
"Absolutely—they're stupid."   115
"You mean *I* am—for I ought to get round that."
"You *can't*—with such people. Who are they?"

I told him, so far as was necessary, and he concluded heartlessly: "Ce sont des gens qu'il faut mettre à la porte."

"You've never seen them; they're awfully good"—I flew to their defence.

"Not seen them? Why all this recent work of yours drops to pieces with them. It's   120
all I want to see of them."

"No one else has said anything against it—the *Cheapside* people are pleased."

"Everyone else is an ass, and the *Cheapside* people the biggest asses of all. Come, don't pretend at this time of day to have pretty illusions about the public, especially about publishers and editors. It's not for *such* animals you work—it's for those who know, *coloro che sanno;* so keep straight for *me* if you can't keep straight for yourself. There was a certain sort of thing you used to try for—and a very good thing it was. But this twaddle isn't *in* it." When I talked with Hawley later about "Rutland Ramsay" and its possible successors he declared that I must get back into my boat again or I should go to the bottom. His voice in short was the voice of warning.

I noted the warning, but I didn't turn my friends out of doors. They bored me a good deal; but the very fact that they bored me admonished me not to sacrifice them— if there was anything to be done with them—simply to irritation. As I look back at this phase they seem to me to have pervaded my life not a little. I have a vision of them as most of the time in my studio, seated against the wall on an old velvet bench to be out of the way, and resembling the while a pair of patient courtiers in a royal ante-chamber. I'm convinced that during the coldest weeks of the winter they held their ground be- cause it saved them fire. Their newness was losing its gloss, and it was impossible not to feel them objects of charity. Whenever Miss Churm arrived they went away, and after I was fairly launched in "Rutland Ramsay" Miss Churm arrived pretty often. They man- aged to express to me tacitly that they supposed I wanted her for the low life of the book, and I let them suppose it, since they had attempted to study the work—it was lying about the studio—without discovering that it dealt only with the highest circles. They had dipped into the most brilliant of our novelists without deciphering many pas- sages. I still took an hour from them, now and again, in spite of Jack Hawley's warning: it would be time enough to dismiss them, if dismissal should be necessary, when the rigor of the season was over. Hawley had made their acquaintance—he had met them at my fireside—and thought them a ridiculous pair. Learning that he was a painter they tried to approach him, to show him too that they were the real thing; but he looked at them, across the big room, as if they were miles away: they were a compendium of everything he most objected to in the social system of his country. Such people as that, all convention and patent-leather, with ejaculations that stopped conversation, had no business in a studio. A studio was a place to learn to see, and how could you see through a pair of feather-beds?

The main inconvenience I suffered at their hands was that at first I was shy of let- ting it break upon them that my artful little servant had begun to sit to me for "Rut- land Ramsay." They knew I had been odd enough—they were prepared by this time to allow oddity to artists—to pick a foreign vagabond out of the streets when I might have had a person with whiskers and credentials, but it was some time before they learned how high I rated his accomplishments. They found him in an attitude more than once, but they never doubted I was doing him as an organ-grinder. There were several things they never guessed, and one of them was that for a striking scene in the novel, in which a footman briefly figured, it occurred to me to make use of Major Monarch as the menial. I kept putting this off, I didn't like to ask him to don the livery—besides the difficulty of finding a livery to fit him. At last, one day late in the winter, when I was at work on the despised Oronte, who caught one's idea on the wing, and was in the glow of feeling myself go very straight, they came in, the Major and his wife, with their society laugh about nothing (there was less and less to laugh at); came in like country-callers—they always reminded me of that—who have walked across the park after church and are presently persuaded to stay to luncheon. Luncheon was over, but they could stay to tea—I knew they wanted it. The fit was on me, however, and I couldn't let my ardour cool and my work wait, with the fading daylight, while my model prepared it. So I asked Mrs. Monarch if she would mind laying it out—a request which for an instant brought all the blood to her face. Her eyes were on her husband's for a second, and some mute telegraphy passed between them. Their folly was over the next instant; his cheerful shrewdness put an end to it. So far from pitying their wounded pride, I must add, I was moved to give it as complete a lesson as I could. They bustled about together and got out the cups and saucers and made the kettle boil. I know they felt as if they were waiting on my servant, and when the tea was prepared I said: "He'll have a cup, please—he's tired." Mrs. Monarch brought him one where he stood, and he took it from her as if he had been a gentleman at a party squeezing a crush-hat with an elbow.

Then it came over me that she had made a great effort for me—made it with a kind of nobleness—and that I owed her a compensation. Each time I saw her after this I wondered what the compensation could be. I couldn't go on doing the wrong thing to oblige them. Oh it *was* the wrong thing, the stamp of the work for which they sat—Hawley was not the only person to say it now. I sent in a large number of the drawings I had made for "Rutland Ramsay," and I received a warning that was more to the point than Hawley's. The artistic adviser of the house for which I was working was of opinion that many of my illustrations were not what had been looked for. Most of these illustrations were the subjects in which the Monarchs had figured. Without going into the question of what *had* been looked for, I had to face the fact that at this rate I shouldn't get the other books to do. I hurled myself in despair on Miss Churm—I put her through all her paces. I not only adopted Oronte publicly as my hero, but one morning when the Major looked in to see if I didn't require him to finish a *Cheapside* figure for which he had begun to sit the week before, I told him I had changed my mind—I'd do the drawing from my man. At this my visitor turned pale and stood looking at me. "Is *he* your idea of an English gentleman?" he asked.

I was disappointed, I was nervous, I wanted to get on with my work; so I replied with irritation: "Oh my dear Major—I can't be ruined for *you!*"

It was a horrid speech, but he stood another moment—after which, without a word, he quitted the studio. I drew a long breath, for I said to myself that I shouldn't see him again. I hadn't told him definitely that I was in danger of having my work rejected, but I was vexed at his not having felt the catastrophe in the air, read with me the moral of our fruitless collaboration, the lesson that in the deceptive atmosphere of art even the highest respectability may fail of being plastic.

I didn't owe my friends money, but I did see them again. They reappeared together three days later, and, given all the other facts, there was something tragic in that one.

125

It was a clear proof they could find nothing else in life to do. They had threshed the matter out in a dismal conference—they had digested the bad news that they were not in for the series. If they weren't useful to me even for the *Cheapside* their function seemed difficult to determine, and I could only judge at first that they had come, forgivingly, decorously, to take a last leave. This made me rejoice in secret that I had little leisure for a scene; for I had placed both my other models in position together and I was pegging away at a drawing from which I hoped to derive glory. It had been suggested by the passage in which Rutland Ramsay, drawing up a chair to Artemisia's piano-stool, says extraordinary things to her while she ostensibly fingers out a difficult piece of music. I had done Miss Churm at the piano before—it was an attitude in which she knew how to take on an absolutely poetic grace. I wished the two figures to "compose" together with intensity, and my little Italian had entered perfectly into my conception. The pair were vividly before me, the piano had been pulled out; it was a charming show of blended youth and murmured love, which I had only to catch and keep. My visitors stood and looked at it, and I was friendly to them over my shoulder.

They made no response, but I was used to silent company and went on with my work, only a little disconcerted—even though exhilarated by the sense that *this* was at least the ideal thing—at not having got rid of them after all. Presently I heard Mrs. Monarch's sweet voice beside or rather above me: "I wish her hair were a little better done." I looked up and she was staring with a strange fixedness at Miss Churm, whose back was turned to her. "Do you mind my just touching it?" she went on—a question which made me spring up for an instant as with the instinctive fear that she might do the young lady a harm. But she quieted me with a glance I shall never forget—I confess I should like to have been able to paint *that*—and went for a moment to my model. She spoke to her softly, laying a hand on her shoulder and bending over her; and as the girl, understanding, gratefully assented, she disposed her rough curls, with a few quick passes, in such a way as to make Miss Churm's head twice as charming. It was one of the most heroic personal services I've ever seen rendered. Then Mrs. Monarch turned away with a low sigh and, looking about her as if for something to do, stooped to the floor with a noble humility and picked up a dirty rag that had dropped out of my paint-box.

The Major meanwhile had also been looking for something to do, and, wandering to the other end of the studio, saw before him my breakfast-things neglected, unremoved. "I say, can't I be useful *here*?" he called out to me with an irrepressible quaver. I assented with a laugh that I fear was awkward, and for the next ten minutes, while I worked, I heard the light clatter of china and the tinkle of spoons and glass. Mrs. Monarch assisted her husband—they washed up my crockery, they put it away. They wandered off into my little scullery, and I afterwards found that they had cleaned my knives and that my slender stock of plate had an unprecedented surface. When it came over me, the latent eloquence of what they were doing, I confess that my drawing was blurred for a moment—the picture swam. They had accepted their failure, but they couldn't accept their fate. They had bowed their heads in bewilderment to the perverse and cruel law in virtue of which the real thing could be so much less precious than the unreal; but they didn't want to starve. If my servants were my models; then my models might be my servants. They would reverse the parts—the others would sit for the ladies and gentlemen and *they* would do the work. They would still be in the studio—it was an intense dumb appeal to me not to turn them out. "Take us on," they wanted to say—"we'll do *anything*."

My pencil dropped from my hand; my sitting was spoiled and I got rid of my sitters, who were also evidently rather mystified and awestruck. Then, alone with the

130

Major and his wife I had a most uncomfortable moment. He put their prayer into a single sentence: "I say, you know—just let *us* do for you, can't you?" I couldn't—it was dreadful to see them emptying my slops; but I pretended I could, to oblige them, for about a week. Then I gave them a sum of money to go away, and I never saw them again. I obtained the remaining books, but my friend Hawley repeats that Major and Mrs. Monarch did me a permanent harm, got me into false ways. If it be true I'm content to have paid the price—for the memory.

D. H. LAWRENCE   (1885–1930)

The Rocking-Horse Winner   1932

[This story takes place in post–World War I England and uses such British expressions as *bonny,* meaning pretty, healthy, cheerful, and *pram,* meaning a baby carriage. The Ascot, the Lincolnshire Handicap, the St. Leger Stakes, the Grand National Steeplechase, and the Derby are all English horse races; a *perfect blade of the "turf"* is a dashing young person seen at the track. Nat Gould (1857–1919) was a novelist and journalist who wrote about horse racing. A *batman* is a British officer's orderly. Eton, an exclusive preparatory school for boys, was founded in 1440 by Henry VI.]

There was a woman who was beautiful, who started with all the advantages, yet she had no luck. She married for love, and the love turned to dust. She had bonny children, yet she felt they had been thrust upon her, and she could not love them. They looked at her coldly, as if they were finding fault with her. And hurriedly she felt she must cover up some fault in herself. Yet what it was that she must cover up she never knew. Nevertheless, when her children were present, she always felt the center of her heart go hard. This troubled her, and in her manner she was all the more gentle and anxious for her children, as if she loved them very much. Only she herself knew that at the center of her heart was a hard little place that could not feel love, no, not for anybody. Everybody else said of her: "She is such a good mother. She adores her children." Only she herself, and her children themselves, knew it was not so. They read it in each other's eyes.

There were a boy and two little girls. They lived in a pleasant house, with a garden, and they had discreet servants, and felt themselves superior to anyone in the neighborhood.

Although they lived in style, they felt always an anxiety in the house. There was never enough money. The mother had a small income, and the father had a small income, but not nearly enough for the social position which they had to keep up. The father went in to town to some office. But though he had good prospects, these prospects never materialized. There was always the grinding sense of the shortage of money, though the style was always kept up.

At last the mother said: "I will see if *I* can't make something." But she did not know where to begin. She racked her brains, and tried this thing and the other, but could not find anything successful. The failure made deep lines come into her face. Her children were growing up, they would have to go to school. There must be more money, there must be more money. The father, who was always very handsome and expensive in his tastes, seemed as if he never *would* be able to do anything worth doing.

And the mother, who had a great belief in herself, did not succeed any better, and her tastes were just as expensive.

And so the house came to be haunted by the unspoken phrase: *There must be more* 5
money! There must be more money! The children could hear it all the time, though nobody said it aloud. They heard it at Christmas, when the expensive and splendid toys filled the nursery. Behind the shining modern rocking-horse, behind the smart doll's-house, a voice would start whispering: "There *must* be more money! There *must* be more money!" And the children would stop playing, to listen for a moment. They would look into each other's eyes, to see if they had all heard. And each one saw in the eyes of the other two that they too had heard. "There *must* be more money! There *must* be more money!"

It came whispering from the springs of the still-swaying rocking-horse, and even the horse, bending his wooden, champing head, heard it. The big doll, sitting so pink and smirking in her new pram, could hear it quite plainly, and seemed to be smirking all the more self-consciously because of it. The foolish puppy, too, that took the place of the teddy-bear, he was looking so extraordinarily foolish for no other reason but that he heard the secret whisper all over the house: "There *must* be more money!"

Yet nobody ever said it aloud. The whisper was everywhere, and therefore no one spoke it. Just as no one ever says: "We are breathing!" in spite of the fact that breath is coming and going all the time.

"Mother," said the boy Paul one day, "why don't we keep a car of our own? Why do we always use uncle's, or else a taxi?"

"Because we're the poor members of the family," said the mother.

"But why *are* we, mother?" 10

"Well—I suppose," she said slowly and bitterly, "it's because your father has no luck."

The boy was silent for some time.

"Is luck money, mother?" he asked rather timidly.

"No, Paul. Not quite. It's what causes you to have money."

"Oh!" said Paul vaguely. "I thought when Uncle Oscar said *filthy lucker*, it meant 15
money."

"*Filthy lucre* does mean money," said the mother. "But it's lucre, not luck."

"Oh!" said the boy. "Then what *is* luck, mother?"

"It's what causes you to have money. If you're lucky you have money. That's why it's better to be born lucky than rich. If you're rich, you may lose your money. But if you're lucky, you will always get more money."

"Oh! Will you? And is father not lucky?"

"Very unlucky, I should say," she said bitterly. 20

The boy watched her with unsure eyes.

"Why?" he asked.

"I don't know. Nobody ever knows why one person is lucky and another unlucky."

"Don't they? Nobody at all? Does *nobody* know?"

"Perhaps God. But He never tells." 25

"He ought to, then. And aren't you lucky either, mother?"

"I can't be, if I married an unlucky husband."

"But by yourself, aren't you?"

"I used to think I was, before I married. Now I think I am very unlucky indeed."

"Why?" 30

"Well—never mind! Perhaps I'm not really," she said.

The child looked at her, to see if she meant it. But he saw, by the lines of her mouth, that she was only trying to hide something from him.

"Well, anyhow," he said stoutly, "I'm a lucky person."

"Why?" said his mother, with a sudden laugh.

He stared at her. He didn't even know why he had said it.   35

"God told me," he asserted, brazening it out.

"I hope He did, dear!" she said, again with a laugh, but rather bitter.

"He did, mother!"

"Excellent!" said the mother, using one of her husband's exclamations.

The boy saw she did not believe him; or, rather, that she paid no attention to his   40
assertion. This angered him somewhat, and made him want to compel her attention.

He went off by himself, vaguely, in a childish way, seeking for the clue to "luck." Absorbed, taking no heed of other people, he went about with a sort of stealth, seeking inwardly for luck. He wanted luck, he wanted it, he wanted it. When the two girls were playing dolls in the nursery, he would sit on his big rocking-horse, charging madly into space, with a frenzy that made the little girls peer at him uneasily. Wildly the horse careered, the waving dark hair of the boy tossed, his eyes had a strange glare in them. The little girls dared not speak to him.

When he had ridden to the end of his mad little journey, he climbed down and stood in front of his rocking-horse, staring fixedly into its lowered face. Its red mouth was slightly open, its big eye was wide and glassy-bright.

"Now!" he would silently command the snorting steed. "Now, take me to where there is luck! Now take me!"

And he would slash the horse on the neck with the little whip he had asked Uncle Oscar for. He *knew* the horse could take him to where there was luck, if only he forced it. So he would mount again, and start on his furious ride, hoping at last to get there. He knew he could get there.

"You'll break your horse, Paul!" said the nurse.   45

"He's always riding like that! I wish he'd leave off!" said his elder sister Joan.

But he only glared down on them in silence. Nurse gave him up. She could make nothing of him. Anyhow he was growing beyond her.

One day his mother and his Uncle Oscar came in when he was on one of his furious rides. He did not speak to them.

"Hallo, you young jockey! Riding a winner?" said his uncle.

"Aren't you growing too big for a rocking-horse? You're not a very little boy any   50
longer, you know," said his mother.

But Paul only gave a blue glare from his big, rather close-set eyes. He would speak to nobody when he was in full tilt. His mother watched him with an anxious expression on her face.

At last he suddenly stopped forcing his horse into the mechanical gallop, and slid down.

"Well, I got there!" he announced fiercely, his blue eyes still flaring, and his sturdy long legs straddling apart.

"Where did you get to?" asked his mother.

"Where I wanted to go," he flared back at her.   55

"That's right, son!" said Uncle Oscar. "Don't you stop till you get there. What's the horse's name?"

"He doesn't have a name," said the boy.

"Gets on without all right?" asked the uncle.

"Well, he has different names. He was called Sansovino last week."

"Sansovino, eh? Won the Ascot. How did you know his name?"   60

"He always talks about horse-races with Bassett," said Joan.

The uncle was delighted to find that his small nephew was posted with all the racing news. Bassett, the young gardener, who had been wounded in the left foot in the
war and had got his present job through Oscar Cresswell, whose batman he had been,
was a perfect blade of the "turf." He lived in the racing events, and the small boy lived
with him.

Oscar Cresswell got it all from Bassett.

"Master Paul comes and asks me, so I can't do more than tell him, sir," said Bassett, his face terribly serious, as if he were speaking of religious matters.

"And does he ever put anything on a horse he fancies?"   65

"Well—I don't want to give him away—he's a young sport, a fine sport, sir. Would
you mind asking him himself? He sort of takes a pleasure in it, and perhaps he'd feel I
was giving him away, sir, if you don't mind."

Bassett was serious as a church.

The uncle went back to his nephew and took him off for a ride in the car.

"Say, Paul, old man, do you ever put anything on a horse?" the uncle asked.

The boy watched the handsome man closely.   70

"Why, do you think I oughtn't to?" he parried.

"Not a bit of it! I thought perhaps you might give me a tip for the Lincoln."

The car sped on into the country, going down to Uncle Oscar's place in Hamp-
shire.

"Honor bright?" said the nephew.

"Honor bright, son!" said the uncle.   75

"Well, then, Daffodil."

"Daffodil! I doubt it, sonny. What about Mirza?"

"I only know the winner," said the boy. "That's Daffodil."

"Daffodil, eh?"

There was a pause. Daffodil was an obscure horse comparatively.   80

"Uncle!"

"Yes, son?"

"You won't let it go any further, will you? I promised Bassett."

"Bassett be damned, old man! What's he got to do with it?"

"We're partners. We've been partners from the first. Uncle, he lent me my first five   85
shillings, which I lost. I promised him, honor bright, it was only between me and him;
only you gave me that ten-shilling note I started winning with, so I thought you were
lucky. You won't let it go any further, will you?"

The boy gazed at his uncle from those big, hot, blue eyes, set rather close together. The uncle stirred and laughed uneasily.

"Right you are, son! I'll keep your tip private. Daffodil, eh? How much are you
putting on him?"

"All except twenty pounds," said the boy. "I keep that in reserve."

The uncle thought it a good joke.

"You keep twenty pounds in reserve, do you, you young romancer? What are you   90
betting, then?"

"I'm betting three hundred," said the boy, gravely. "But it's between you and me,
Uncle Oscar! Honor bright?"

The uncle burst into a roar of laughter.

"It's between you and me all right, you young Nat Gould," he said, laughing.
"But where's your three hundred?"

"Bassett keeps it for me. We're partners."

"You are, are you! And what is Bassett putting on Daffodil?"   95

"He won't go quite as high as I do, I expect. Perhaps he'll go a hundred and fifty."

"What, pennies?" laughed the uncle.

"Pounds," said the child, with a surprised look at his uncle. "Bassett keeps a bigger reserve than I do."

Between wonder and amusement Uncle Oscar was silent. He pursued the matter no further, but he determined to take his nephew with him to the Lincoln races.

"Now, son," he said, "I'm putting twenty on Mirza, and I'll put five for you on   100
any horse you fancy. What's your pick?"

"Daffodil, uncle."

"No, not the fiver on Daffodil!"

"I should if it was my own fiver," said the child.

"Good! Good! Right you are! A fiver for me and a fiver for you on Daffodil."

The child had never been to a race-meeting before, and his eyes were blue fire. He   105
pursed his mouth tight, and watched. A Frenchman just in front had put his money on Lancelot. Wild with excitement, he flayed his arms up and down, yelling "*Lancelot! Lancelot!*" in his French accent.

Daffodil came in first, Lancelot second, Mirza third. The child, flushed and with eyes blazing, was curiously serene. His uncle brought him four five-pound notes, four to one.

"What am I to do with these?" he cried, waving them before the boy's eyes.

"I suppose we'll talk to Bassett," said the boy. "I expect I have fifteen hundred now; and twenty in reserve; and this twenty."

His uncle studied him for some moments.

"Look here, son!" he said. "You're not serious about Bassett and that fifteen hun-   110
dred, are you?"

"Yes, I am. But it's between you and me, uncle. Honor bright!"

"Honor bright all right, son! But I must talk to Bassett."

"If you'd like to be a partner, uncle, with Bassett and me, we could all be partners. Only, you'd have to promise, honor bright, uncle, not to let it go beyond us three. Bassett and I are lucky, and you must be lucky, because it was your ten shillings I started winning with. . . ."

Uncle Oscar took both Bassett and Paul into Richmond Park for an afternoon, and there they talked.

"It's like this, you see, sir," Bassett said. "Master Paul would get me talking about   115
racing events, spinning yarns, you know, sir. And he was always keen on knowing if I'd made or if I'd lost. It's about a year since, now, that I put five shillings on Blush of Dawn for him—and we lost. Then the luck turned, with the ten shillings he had from you, that we put on Singhalese. And since that time, it's been pretty steady, all things considering. What do you say, Master Paul?"

"We're all right when we're sure," said Paul. "It's when we're not quite sure that we go down."

"Oh, but we're careful then," said Bassett.

"But when are you *sure?*" smiled Uncle Oscar.

"It's Master Paul, sir," said Bassett, in a secret, religious voice. "It's as if he had it from heaven. Like Daffodil, now, for the Lincoln. That was as sure as eggs."

"Did you put anything on Daffodil?" asked Oscar Cresswell.   120

"Yes, sir. I made my bit."

"And my nephew?"

Bassett was obstinately silent, looking at Paul.

"I made twelve hundred, didn't I, Bassett? I told uncle I was putting three hundred on Daffodil."

"That's right," said Bassett, nodding.   125

"But where's the money?" asked the uncle.

"I keep it safe locked up, sir. Master Paul he can have it any minute he likes to ask for it."

"What, fifteen hundred pounds?"

"And twenty! And *forty*, that is, with the twenty he made on the course."

"It's amazing!" said the uncle.   130

"If Master Paul offers you to be partners, sir, I would, if I were you; if you'll excuse me," said Bassett.

Oscar Cresswell thought about it.

"I'll see the money," he said.

They drove home again, and sure enough, Bassett came round to the garden-house with fifteen hundred pounds in notes. The twenty pounds reserve was left with Joe Glee, in the Turf Commission deposit.

"You see, it's all right, uncle, when I'm *sure!* Then we go strong, for all we're   135
worth. Don't we, Bassett?"

"We do that, Master Paul"

"And when are you sure?" said the uncle, laughing.

"Oh, well, sometimes I'm *absolutely* sure, like about Daffodil," said the boy; "and sometimes I have an idea; and sometimes I haven't even an idea, have I, Bassett? Then we're careful, because we mostly go down."

"You do, do you! And when you're sure, like about Daffodil, what makes you sure, sonny?"

"Oh, well, I don't know," said the boy uneasily. "I'm sure, you know, uncle; that's   140
all."

"It's as if he had it from heaven, sir," Bassett reiterated.

"I should say so!" said the uncle.

But he became a partner. And when the Leger was coming on, Paul was "sure" about Lively Spark, which was a quite inconsiderable horse. The boy insisted on putting a thousand on the horse, Bassett went for five hundred, and Oscar Cresswell two hundred. Lively Spark came in first, and the betting had been ten to one against him. Paul had made ten thousand.

"You see," he said, "I was absolutely sure of him."

Even Oscar Cresswell had cleared two thousand.   145

"Look here, son," he said, "this sort of thing makes me nervous."

"It needn't, uncle! Perhaps I shan't be sure again for a long time."

"But what are you going to do with your money?" asked the uncle.

"Of course," said the boy, "I started it for mother. She said she had no luck, because father is unlucky, so I thought if *I* was lucky, it might stop whispering."

"What might stop whispering?"   150

"Our house. I *hate* our house for whispering."

"What does it whisper?"

"Why—why"—the boy fidgeted—"why, I don't know. But it's always short of money, you know, uncle."

"I know it, son, I know it."

"You know people send mother writs, don't you, uncle?"   155

"I'm afraid I do," said the uncle.

"And then the house whispers, like people laughing at you behind your back. It's awful, that is! I thought if I was lucky . . ."

"You might stop it," added the uncle.

The boy watched him with big blue eyes, that had an uncanny cold fire in them, and he said never a word.

"Well, then!" said the uncle. "What are we doing?"   160

"I shouldn't like mother to know I was lucky," said the boy.

"Why not, son?"

"She'd stop me."

"I don't think she would."

"Oh!"—and the boy writhed in an odd way—"I *don't* want her to know, uncle."   165

"All right, son! We'll manage it without her knowing."

They managed it very easily. Paul, at the other's suggestion, handed over five thousand pounds to his uncle, who deposited it with the family lawyer, who was then to inform Paul's mother that a relative had put five thousand pounds into his hands, which sum was to be paid out a thousand pounds at a time, on the mother's birthday, for the next five years.

"So she'll have a birthday present of a thousand pounds for five successive years," said Uncle Oscar. "I hope it won't make it all the harder for her later."

Paul's mother had her birthday in November. The house had been "whispering" worse than ever lately, and, even in spite of his luck, Paul could not bear up against it. He was very anxious to see the effect of the birthday letter, telling his mother about the thousand pounds.

When there were no visitors, Paul now took his meals with his parents, as he was   170
beyond the nursery control. His mother went into town nearly every day. She had discovered that she had an odd knack of sketching furs and dress materials, so she worked secretly in the studio of a friend who was the chief "artist" for the leading drapers. She drew the figures of ladies in furs and ladies in silk and sequins for the newspaper advertisements. This young woman artist earned several thousand pounds a year, but Paul's mother only made several hundreds, and she was again dissatisfied. She so wanted to be first in something, and she did not succeed, even in making sketches for drapery advertisements.

She was down to breakfast on the morning of her birthday. Paul watched her face as she read her letters. He knew the lawyer's letter. As his mother read it, her face hardened and became more expressionless. Than a cold, determined look came on her mouth. She hid the letter under the pile of others, and said not a word about it.

"Didn't you have anything nice in the post for your birthday, mother?" said Paul.

"Quite moderately nice," she said, her voice cold and absent.

She went away to town without saying more.

But in the afternoon Uncle Oscar appeared. He said Paul's mother had had a long   175
interview with the lawyer, asking if the whole five thousand could not be advanced at once, as she was in debt.

"What do you think, uncle?" said the boy.

"I leave it to you, son."

"Oh, let her have it, then! We can get some more with the other," said the boy.

"A bird in the hand is worth two in the bush, laddie!" said Uncle Oscar.

"But I'm sure to *know* for the Grand National; or the Lincolnshire; or else the   180
Derby. I'm sure to know for *one* of them," said Paul.

So Uncle Oscar signed the agreement, and Paul's mother touched the whole five thousand. Then something very curious happened. The voices in the house suddenly went mad, like a chorus of frogs on a spring evening. There were certain new furnishings, and Paul had a tutor. He was *really* going to Eton, his father's school, in the following autumn. There were flowers in the winter, and a blossoming of the luxury Paul's mother had been used to. And yet the voices in the house, behind the sprays of mimosa and almond blossom, and from under the piles of iridescent cushions, simply trilled and screamed in a sort of ecstasy: "There *must* be more money! Oh-h-h; there *must* be more money Oh, now, now-w! Now-w-w—there *must* be more money!—more than ever! More than ever!"

It frightened Paul terribly. He studied away at his Latin and Greek with his tutors. But his intense hours were spent with Bassett. The Grand National had gone by: he had not "known," and had lost a hundred pounds. Summer was at hand. He was in agony for the Lincoln. But even for the Lincoln he didn't "know," and he lost fifty pounds. He became wild-eyed and strange, as if something were going to explode in him.

"Let it alone, son! Don't you bother about it!" urged Uncle Oscar. But it was as if the boy couldn't really hear what his uncle was saying.

"I've got to know for the Derby! I've got to know for the Derby!" the child reiterated, his big blue eyes blazing with a sort of madness.

His mother noticed how overwrought he was.   185

"You'd better go to the seaside. Wouldn't you like to go now to the seaside, instead of waiting? I think you'd better," she said, looking down at him anxiously, her heart curiously heavy because of him.

But the child lifted his uncanny blue eyes.

"I couldn't possibly go before the Derby, mother!" he said. "I couldn't possibly!"

"Why not?" she said, her voice becoming heavy when she was opposed. "Why not? You can still go from the seaside to see the Derby with your Uncle Oscar, if that's what you wish. No need for you to wait here. Besides, I think you care too much about these races. It's a bad sign. My family has been a gambling family, and you won't know till you grow up how much damage it has done. But it has done damage. I shall have to send Bassett away, and ask Uncle Oscar not to talk racing to you, unless you promise to be reasonable about it; go away to the seaside and forget it. You're all nerves!"

"I'll do what you like, mother, so long as you don't send me away till after the   190
Derby," the boy said.

"Send you away from where? Just from this house?"

"Yes," he said, gazing at her.

"Why, you curious child, what makes you care about this house so much, suddenly? I never knew you loved it."

He gazed at her without speaking. He had a secret within a secret, something he had not divulged, even to Bassett or to his Uncle Oscar.

But his mother, after standing undecided and a little bit sullen for some mo-   195
ments, said:

"Very well, then! Don't go to the seaside till after the Derby, if you don't wish it. But promise me you won't let your nerves go to pieces. Promise you won't think so much about horse-racing and events, as you call them!"

"Oh, no," said the boy casually. "I won't think much about them, mother. You needn't worry. I wouldn't worry, mother, if I were you."

"If you were me and I were you," said his mother, "I wonder what we *should* do!"

"But you know you needn't worry, mother, don't you?" the boy repeated.

"I should be awfully glad to know it," she said wearily.   200

"Oh, well, you *can*, you know. I mean, you *ought* to know you needn't worry," he insisted.

"Ought I? Then I'll see about it," she said.

Paul's secret of secrets was his wooden horse, that which had no name. Since he was emancipated from a nurse and a nursery-governess, he had had his rocking-horse removed to his own bedroom at the top of the house.

"Surely, you're too big for a rocking-horse!" his mother had remonstrated.

"Well, you see, mother, till I can have a *real* horse, I like to have *some* sort of ani-   205
mal about," had been his quaint answer.

"Do you feel he keeps you company?" she laughed.

"Oh, yes! He's very good, he always keeps me company, when I'm there," said Paul.

So the horse, rather shabby, stood in an arrested prance in the boy's bedroom.

The Derby was drawing near, and the boy grew more and more tense. He hardly heard what was spoken to him, he was very frail, and his eyes were really uncanny. His mother had sudden strange seizures of uneasiness about him. Sometimes, for half-an-hour, she would feel a sudden anxiety about him that was almost anguish. She wanted to rush to him at once, and know he was safe.

Two nights before the Derby, she was at a big party in town, when one of her   210
rushes of anxiety about her boy, her first-born, gripped her heart till she could hardly speak. She fought with the feeling, might and main, for she believed in common-sense. But it was too strong. She had to leave the dance and go downstairs to telephone to the country. The children's nursery-governess was terribly surprised and startled at being rung up in the night.

"Are the children all right, Miss Wilmot?"

"Oh, yes, they are quite all right."

"Master Paul? Is he all right?"

"He went to bed as right as a trivet. Shall I run up and look at him?"

"No," said Paul's mother reluctantly. "No! Don't trouble. It's all right. Don't sit   215
up. We shall be home fairly soon." She did not want her son's privacy intruded upon.

"Very good," said the governess.

It was about one o'clock when Paul's mother and father drove up to their house. All was still. Paul's mother went to her room and slipped off her white fur cloak. She had told her maid not to wait up for her. She heard her husband downstairs, mixing a whisky-and-soda.

And then, because of the strange anxiety at her heart, she stole upstairs to her son's room. Noiselessly she went along the upper corridor. Was there a faint noise? What was it?

She stood, with arrested muscles, outside his door, listening. There was a strange, heavy, and yet not loud noise. Her heart stood still. It was a soundless noise, yet rushing and powerful. Something huge, in violent, hushed motion. What was it? What in God's name was it? She ought to know. She felt that she knew the noise. She knew what it was.

Yet she could not place it. She couldn't say what it was. And on and on it went,   220
like a madness.

Softly, frozen with anxiety and fear, she turned the door-handle.

The room was dark. Yet in the space near the window, she heard and saw something plunging to and fro. She gazed in fear and amazement.

Then suddenly she switched on the light, and saw her son, in his green pyjamas, madly surging on the rocking-horse. The blaze of light suddenly lit him up, as he urged the wooden horse, and lit her up, as she stood, blonde, in her dress of pale green and crystal, in the doorway.

"Paul!" she cried. "Whatever are you doing?"

"It's Malabar!" he screamed, in a powerful, strange voice. "It's Malabar!"   225

His eyes blazed at her for one strange and senseless second, as he ceased urging his wooden horse. Then he fell with a crash to the ground, and she, all her tormented motherhood flooding upon her, rushed to gather him up.

But he was unconscious, and unconscious he remained, with some brain-fever. He talked and tossed, and his mother sat stonily by his side.

"Malabar! It's Malabar! Bassett, Bassett, I *know!* It's Malabar!"

So the child cried, trying to get up and urge the rocking-horse that gave him his inspiration.

"What does he mean by Malabar?" asked the heart-frozen mother.   230

"I don't know," said the father stonily.

"What does he mean by Malabar?" she asked her brother Oscar.

"It's one of the horses running for the Derby," was the answer.

And, in spite of himself, Oscar Cresswell spoke to Bassett, and himself put a thousand on Malabar: at fourteen to one.

The third day of the illness was critical: they were waiting for a change. The boy,   235
with his rather long, curly hair, was tossing ceaselessly on the pillow. He neither slept nor regained consciousness, and his eyes were like blue stones. His mother sat, feeling her heart had gone, turned actually into a stone.

In the evening, Oscar Cresswell did not come, but Bassett sent a message, saying could he come up for one moment, just one moment? Paul's mother was very angry at the intrusion, but on second thought she agreed. The boy was the same. Perhaps Bassett might bring him to consciousness.

The gardener, a shortish fellow with a little brown moustache, and sharp little brown eyes, tip-toed into the room, touched his imaginary cap to Paul's mother, and stole to the bedside, staring with glittering, smallish eyes, at the tossing, dying child.

"Master Paul!" he whispered. "Master Paul! Malabar came in first all right, a clean win. I did as you told me. You've made over seventy thousand pounds, you have; you've got over eighty thousand. Malabar came in all right, Master Paul."

"Malabar! Malabar! Did I say Malabar, mother? Did I say Malabar? Do you think I'm lucky, mother? I knew Malabar, didn't I? Over eighty thousand pounds! I call that lucky, don't you, mother? Over eighty thousand pounds! I knew, didn't I know I knew! Malabar came in all right. If I ride my horse till I'm sure, then I tell you, Bassett, you can go as high as you like. Did you go for all you were worth, Bassett?"

"I went a thousand on it, Master Paul."   240

"I never told you, mother, that if I can ride my horse, and *get there,* then I'm absolutely sure—oh absolutely! Mother, did I ever tell you? I *am* lucky!"

"No, you never did," said the mother.

But the boy died in the night.

And even as he lay dead, his mother heard her brother's voice saying to her: "My God, Hester, you're eighty-odd thousand to the good, and a poor devil of a son to the bad. But, poor devil, poor devil, he's best gone out of a life where he rides his rocking-horse to find a winner."

DORIS LESSING   (born 1919)

Wine   1957

[In a Paris café, a man and a woman sit together, thinking and talking. The man uses one French word: *pâtisserie,* which means bakery.]

A man and woman walked toward the boulevard from a little hotel in a side street.

The trees were still leafless, black, cold; but the fine twigs were swelling toward spring, so that looking upward it was with an expectation of the first glimmering greenness. Yet everything was calm, and the sky was a calm, classic blue.

The couple drifted slowly along. Effort, after days of laziness, seemed impossible; and almost at once they turned into a café and sank down, as if exhausted, in the glass-walled space that was thrust forward into the street.

The place was empty. People were seeking the midday meal in the restaurants. Not all: that morning crowds had been demonstrating, a procession had just passed, and its straggling end could still be seen. The sounds of violence, shouted slogans and singing, no longer absorbed the din of Paris traffic; but it was these sounds that had roused the couple from sleep.

A waiter leaned at the door, looking after the crowds, and he reluctantly took an order for coffee.   5

The man yawned; the woman caught the infection; and they laughed with an affectation of guilt and exchanged glances before their eyes, without regret, parted. When the coffee came, it remained untouched. Neither spoke. After some time the woman yawned again; and this time the man turned and looked at her critically, and she looked back. Desire asleep, they looked. This remained; that while everything which drove them slept, they accepted from each other a sad irony; they could look at each other without illusion, steady-eyed.

And then, inevitably, the sadness deepened in her till she consciously resisted it; and into him came the flicker of cruelty.

"Your nose needs powdering," he said.

"You need a whipping boy."

But always he refused to feel sad. She shrugged, and leaving him to it, turned to look out. So did he. At the far end of the boulevard there was a faint agitation, like stirred ants, and she heard him mutter, "Yes, and it still goes on. . . ."   10

Mocking, she said, "Nothing changes, everything is always the same. . . ."

But he had flushed. "I remember," he began, in a different voice. He stopped, and she did not press him, for he was gazing at the distant demonstrators with a bitterly nostalgic face.

Outside drifted the lovers, the married couples, the students, the old people. There the stark trees; there the blue, quiet sky. In a month the trees would be vivid green; the sun would pour down heat; the people would be brown, laughing, bare-limbed. No, no, she said to herself, at this vision of activity. Better the static sadness. And, all at once, unhappiness welled up in her, catching her throat, and she was back fifteen years in another country. She stood in blazing tropical moonlight, stretching her arms to a landscape that offered her nothing but silence; and then she was running down a path where small stones glinted sharp underfoot, till at last she fell spent in a swathe of glistening grass. Fifteen years.

It was at this moment that the man turned abruptly and called the waiter and ordered wine.

"What," she said humorously, "already?"   15

"Why not?"

For the moment she loved him completely and maternally, till she suppressed the counterfeit and watched him wait, fidgeting, for the wine, pour it, and then set the two glasses before them beside the still-brimming coffee cups. But she was again remembering that night, envying the girl ecstatic with moonlight, who ran crazily through the trees in an unsharable desire for—but that was the point.

"What are you thinking of?" he asked, still a little cruel.

"Ohhh," she protested humorously.

"That's the trouble, that's the trouble." He lifted his glass, glanced at her, and set 20
it down. "Don't you want to drink?"

"Not yet."

He left his glass untouched and began to smoke.

These moments demanded some kind of gesture—something slight, even casual, but still an acknowledgment of the separateness of those two people in each of them; the one seen, perhaps, as a soft-staring never-closing eye, observing, always observing, with a tired compassion; the other, a shape of violence that struggled on in the cycle of desire and rest, creation and achievement.

He gave it to her. Again their eyes met in the grave irony, before he turned away, flickering his fingers irritably against the table; and she turned also, to note the black branches where the sap was tingling.

"I remember," he began; and again she said, in protest, "Ohhh!" 25

He checked himself. "Darling," he said drily, "you're the only woman I've ever loved." They laughed.

"It must have been this street. Perhaps this café—only they change so. When I went back yesterday to see the place where I came every summer, it was a *pâtisserie,* and the woman had forgotten me. There was a whole crowd of us—we used to go around together—and I met a girl here, I think, for the first time. There were recognized places for contacts; people coming from Vienna or Prague, or wherever it was, knew the places—it couldn't be this café, unless they've smartened it up. We didn't have the money for all this leather and chromium."

"Well, go on."

"I keep remembering her, for some reason. Haven't thought of her for years. She was about sixteen, I suppose. Very pretty—no, you're quite wrong. We used to study together. She used to bring her books to my room. I liked her, but I had my own girl, only she was studying something else, I forget what." He paused again, and again his face was twisted with nostalgia, and involuntarily she glanced over her shoulder down the street. The procession had completely disappeared, not even the sounds of singing and shouting remained.

"I remember her because. . . ." And, after a preoccupied silence: "Perhaps it is 30
always the fate of the virgin who comes and offers herself, naked, to be refused."

"What!" she exclaimed, startled. Also, anger stirred in her. She noted it, and sighed. "Go on."

"I never made love to her. We studied together all that summer. Then, one week-end, we all went off in a bunch. None of us had any money, of course, and we used to stand on the pavements and beg lifts, and meet up again in some village. I was with my own girl, but that night we were helping the farmer get in his fruit, in payment for using his barn to sleep in, and I found this girl Marie was beside me. It was moonlight, a lovely night, and we were all singing and making love. I kissed her, but that was all. That night she came to me. I was sleeping up in the loft with another lad. He was asleep. I sent her back down to the others. They were all together down in the hay. I told her she was too young. But she was no younger than my own girl." He stopped; and after all these years his face was rueful and puzzled. "I don't know," he said. "I don't know why I sent her back." Then he laughed. "Not that it matters, I suppose."

"Shameless hussy," she said. The anger was strong now. "You had kissed her, hadn't you?"

He shrugged. "But we were all playing the fool. It was a glorious night—gathering apples, the farmer shouting and swearing at us because we were making love more than working, and singing and drinking wine. Besides, it was that time: the youth movement. We regarded faithfulness and jealousy and all that sort of thing as remnants of bourgeois morality." He laughed again, rather painfully. "I kissed her. There she was, beside me, and she knew my girl was with me that weekend."

"You kissed her," she said accusingly.   35

He fingered the stem of his wineglass, looking over at her and grinnig. "Yes, darling," he almost crooned at her. "I kissed her."

She snapped over into anger. "There's a girl all ready for love. You make use of her for working. Then you kiss her. You know quite well. . . ."

"What do I know quite well?"

"It was a cruel thing to do."

"I was a kid myself. . . ."   40

"Doesn't matter." She noted, with discomfort, that she was almost crying. "Working with her! Working with a girl of sixteen, all summer!"

"But we all studied very seriously. She was a doctor afterward, in Vienna. She managed to get out when the Nazis came in, but. . . ."

She said impatiently, "Then you kissed her, on *that* night. Imagine her, waiting till the others were asleep, then she climbed up the ladder to the loft, terrified the other man might wake up, then she stood watching you sleep, and she slowly took off her dress and. . . ."

"Oh, I wasn't asleep. I pretended to be. She came up dressed. Shorts and sweater—our girls didn't wear dresses and lipstick—more bourgeois morality. I watched her strip. The loft was full of moonlight. She put her hand over my mouth and came down beside me." Again, his face was filled with rueful amazement. "God knows, I can't understand it myself. She was a beautiful creature. I don't know why I remember it. It's been coming into my mind the last few days." After a pause, slowly twirling the wineglass: "I've been a failure in many things, but not with. . . ." He quickly lifted her hand, kissed it, and said sincerely: "I don't know why I remember it now, when. . . ." Their eyes met, and they sighed.

She said slowly, her hand lying on his: "And so you turned her away."   45

He laughed. "Next morning she wouldn't speak to me. She started a love affair with my best friend—the man who'd been beside me that night in the loft, as a matter of fact. She hated my guts, and I suppose she was right."

"Think of her. Think of her at that moment. She picked up her clothes, hardly daring to look at you. . . ."

"As a matter of fact, she was furious. She called me all the names she could think of; I had to keep telling her to shut up, she'd wake the whole crowd."

"She climbed down the ladder and dressed again in the dark. Then she went out of the barn, unable to go back to the others. She went into the orchard. It was still brilliant moonlight. Everything was silent and deserted, and she remembered how you'd all been singing and laughing and making love. She went to the tree where you'd kissed her. The moon was shining on the apples. She'll never forget it, never, never!"

He looked at her curiously. The tears were pouring down her face.   50

"It's terrible," she said. "Terrible. Nothing could ever make up to her for that. Nothing, as long as she lived. Just when everything was most perfect, all her life, she'd suddenly remember that night, standing alone, not a soul anywhere, miles of damned empty moonlight. . . ."

He looked at her shrewdly. Then with a sort of humorous, deprecating grimace, he bent over and kissed her and said: "Darling, it's not my fault; it just isn't my fault."

"No," she said.

He put the wineglass into her hands; and she lifted it, looked at the small crimson globule of warming liquid, and drank with him.

KATHERINE MANSFIELD   (1888–1923)

The Doll's House   1920

When dear old Mrs. Hay went back to town after staying with the Burnells she sent the children a doll's house. It was so big that the carter and Pat carried it into the courtyard, and there it stayed, propped up on two wooden boxes beside the feed-room door. No harm could come of it; it was summer. And perhaps the smell of paint would have gone off by the time it had to be taken in. For, really, the smell of paint coming from that doll's house ("Sweet of old Mrs. Hay, of course; most sweet and generous!")—but the smell of paint was quite enough to make any one seriously ill, in Aunt Beryl's opinion. Even before the sacking was taken off. And when it was. . . .

There stood the doll's house, a dark, oily, spinach green, picked out with bright yellow. Its two solid little chimneys, glued on to the roof, were painted red and white, and the door, gleaming with yellow varnish, was like a little slab of toffee. Four windows, real windows, were divided into panes by a broad streak of green. There was actually a tiny porch, too, painted yellow, with big lumps of congealed paint hanging along the edge.

But perfect, perfect little house! Who could possibly mind the smell? It was part of the joy, part of the newness.

"Open it quickly, some one!"

The hook at the side was stuck fast. Pat pried it open with his penknife, and the whole house-front swung back, and—there you were, gazing at one and the same moment into the drawing-room and dining-room, the kitchen and two bedrooms. That is the way for a house to open! Why don't all houses open like that? How much more exciting than peering through the slit of a door into a mean little hall with a hatstand and two umbrellas! That is—isn't it?—what you long to know about a house when you put your hand on the knocker. Perhaps it is the way God opens houses at dead of night when He is taking a quiet turn with an angel. . . .

"O-oh!" The Burnell children sounded as though they were in despair. It was too marvellous; it was too much for them. They had never seen anything like it in their lives. All the rooms were papered. There were pictures on the walls, painted on the paper, with gold frames complete. Red carpet covered all the floors except the kitchen; red plush chairs in the drawing-room, green in the dining-room; tables, beds with real bedclothes, a cradle, a stove, a dresser with tiny plates and one big jug. But what Kezia liked more than anything, what she liked frightfully, was the lamp. It stood in the middle of the dining-room table, an exquisite little amber lamp with a white globe. It was even filled all ready for lighting, though, of course, you couldn't light it. But there was something inside that looked like oil, and that moved when you shook it.

The father and mother dolls, who sprawled very stiff as though they had fainted in the drawing-room, and their two little children asleep upstairs, were really too big for the doll's house. They didn't look as though they belonged. But the lamp was perfect. It seemed to smile at Kezia, to say, "I live here." The lamp was real.

The Burnell children could hardly walk to school fast enough the next morning. They burned to tell everybody, to describe, to—well—to boast about their doll's house before the school-bell rang.

"I'm to tell," said Isabel, "because I'm the eldest. And you two can join in after. But I'm to tell first."

5

There was nothing to answer. Isabel was bossy, but she was always right, and Lot tie and Kezia knew too well the powers that went with being eldest. They brushed through the thick buttercups at the road edge and said nothing.

"And I'm to choose who's to come and see it first. Mother said I might."

For it had been arranged that while the doll's house stood in the courtyard they might ask the girls at school, two at a time, to come and look. Not to stay to tea, of course, or to come traipsing through the house. But just to stand quietly in the court-yard while Isabel pointed out the beauties, and Lottie and Kezia looked pleased. . . .

But hurry as they might, by the time they had reached the tarred palings of the boys' playground the bell had begun to jangle. They only just had time to whip off their hats and fall into line before the roll was called. Never mind. Isabel tried to make up for it by looking very important and mysterious and by whispering behind her hand to the girls near her, "Got something to tell you at playtime."

Playtime came and Isabel was surrounded. The girls of her class nearly fought to put their arms around her, to walk away with her, to beam flatteringly, to be her special friend. She held quite a court under the huge pine trees at the side of the playground. Nudging, giggling together, the little girls pressed up close. And the only two who stayed outside the ring were the two who were always outside, the little Kelveys. They knew better than to come anywhere near the Burnells.

For the fact was, the school the Burnell children went to was not at all the kind of place their parents would have chosen if there had been any choice. But there was none. It was the only school for miles. And the consequence was all the children in the neighborhood, the Judge's little girls, the doctor's daughters, the store-keeper's chil-dren, the milkman's, were forced to mix together. Not to speak of there being an equal number of rude, rough little boys as well. But the line had to be drawn somewhere. It was drawn at the Kelveys. Many of the children, including the Burnells, were not al-lowed even to speak to them. They walked past the Kelveys with their heads in the air, and as they set the fashion in all matters of behavior, the Kelveys were shunned by everybody. Even the teacher had a special voice for them, and a special smile for the other children when Lil Kelvey came up to her desk with a bunch of dreadfully com-mon-looking flowers.

They were the daughters of a spry, hardworking little washerwoman, who went about from house to house by the day. This was awful enough. But where was Mr. Kelvey? Nobody knew for certain. But everybody said he was in prison. So they were the daughters of a washerwoman and a jailbird. Very nice company for other people's children! And they looked it. Why Mrs. Kelvey made them so conspicuous was hard to understand. The truth was they were dressed in "bits" given to her by the people for whom she worked. Lil, for instance, who was a stout, plain child, with big freckles, came to school in a dress made from a green art-serge table-cloth of the Burnells', with red plush sleeves from the Logans' curtains. Her hat, perched on top of her high fore-head, was a grown-up woman's hat, once the property of Miss Lecky, the postmistress. It was turned up at the back and trimmed with a large scarlet quill. What a little guy she looked! It was impossible not to laugh. And her little sister, our Else, wore a long white dress, rather like a nightgown, and a pair of little boy's boots. But whatever our Else wore she would have looked strange. She was a tiny wishbone of a child, with cropped hair and enormous solemn eyes—a little white owl. Nobody had ever seen her smile; she scarcely ever spoke. She went through life holding on to Lil, with a piece of Lil's skirt screwed up in her hand. Where Lil went our Else followed. In the playground, on the road going to and from school, there was Lil marching in front and our Else hold-ing on behind. Only when she wanted anything, or when she was out of breath, our

Else gave Lil a tug, a twitch, and Lil stopped and turned round. The Kelveys never failed to understand each other.

Now they hovered at the edge; you couldn't stop them listening. When the little girls turned round and sneered, Lil, as usual, gave her silly, shamefaced smile, but our Else only looked.

And Isabel's voice, so very proud, went on telling. The carpet made a great sensation, but so did the beds with real bedclothes, and the stove with an oven door.

When she finished Kezia broke in. "You've forgotten the lamp, Isabel."

"Oh, yes," said Isabel, "and there's a teeny little lamp, all made of yellow glass,   20
with a white globe that stands on the dining room table. You couldn't tell it from a real one."

"The lamp's best of all," cried Kezia. She thought Isabel wasn't making half enough of the little lamp. But nobody paid any attention. Isabel was choosing the two who were to come back with them that afternoon and see it. She chose Emmie Cole and Lena Logan. But when the others knew they were all to have a chance, they couldn't be nice enough to Isabel. One by one they put their arms round Isabel's waist and walked her off. They had something to whisper to her, a secret. "Isabel's *my* friend."

Only the little Kelveys moved away forgotten; there was nothing more for them to hear.

Days passed, and as more children saw the doll's house, the fame of it spread. It became the one subject, the rage. The one question was, "Have you seen Burnells' doll's house? Oh, ain't it lovely!" "Haven't you seen it? Oh, I say!"

Even the dinner hour was given up to talking about it. The little girls sat under the pines eating their thick mutton sandwiches and big slabs of johnny cake spread with butter. While always, as near as they could get, sat the Kelveys, our Else holding on to Lil, listening too, while they chewed their jam sandwiches out of a newspaper soaked with large red blobs. . . .

"Mother," said Kezia, "can't I ask the Kelveys just once?"   25

"Certainly not, Kezia."

"But why not?"

"Run away, Kezia; you know quite well why not."

At last everybody had seen it except them. On that day the subject rather flagged. It was the dinner hour. The children stood together under the pine trees, and suddenly, as they looked at the Kelveys eating out of their paper, always by themselves, always listening, they wanted to be horrid to them. Emmie Cole started the whisper.

"Lil Kelvey's going to be a servant when she grows up."   30

"O-oh, how awful!" said Isabel Burnell, and she made eyes at Emmie.

Emmie swallowed in a very meaning way and nodded to Isabel as she'd seen her mother do on those occasions.

"It's true—it's true—it's true," she said.

Then Lena Logan's little eyes snapped. "Shall I ask her?" she whispered.

"Bet you don't," said Jessie May.   35

"Pooh, I'm not frightened," said Lena. Suddenly she gave a little squeal and danced in front of the other girls. "Watch! Watch me! Watch me now!" said Lena. And sliding, gliding, dragging one foot, giggling behind her hand, Lena went over to the Kelveys.

Lil looked up from her dinner. She wrapped the rest quickly away. Our Else stopped chewing. What was coming now?

"Is it true you're going to be a servant when you grow up, Lil Kelvey?" shrilled Lena.

Dead silence. But instead of answering, Lil only gave her silly, shamefaced smile. She didn't seem to mind the question at all. What a sell for Lena! The girls began to titter.

Lena couldn't stand that. She put her hands on her hips; she shot forward. "Yah,   40 yer father's in prison!" she hissed, spitefully.

This was such a marvellous thing to have said that the little girls rushed away in a body, deeply, deeply excited, wild with joy. Someone found a long rope, and they began skipping. And never did they skip so high, run in and out so fast, or do such daring things as on that morning.

In the afternoon Pat called for the Burnell children with the buggy and they drove home. There were visitors. Isabel and Lottie, who liked visitors, went upstairs to change their pinafores. But Kezia thieved out at the back. Nobody was about; she began to swing on the big white gates of the courtyard. Presently, looking along the road, she saw two little dots. They grew bigger, they were coming toward her. Now she could see that one was in front and one close behind. Now she could see that they were the Kelveys. Kezia stopped swinging. She slipped off the gate as if she was going to run away. Then she hesitated. The Kelveys came nearer, and beside them walked their shadows, very long, stretching right across the road with their heads in the buttercups. Kezia clambered back on the gate; she had made up her mind; she swung out.

"Hullo," she said to the passing Kelveys.

They were so astounded that they stopped. Lil gave her silly smile. Our Else stared.

"You can come and see our doll's house if you want to," said Kezia, and she   45 dragged one toe on the ground. But at that Lil turned red and shook her head quickly.

"Why not?" asked Kezia.

Lil gasped, then she said, "Your ma told our ma you wasn't to speak to us."

"Oh, well," said Kezia. She didn't know what to reply. "It doesn't matter. You can come and see our doll's house all the same. Come on. Nobody's looking."

But Lil shook her head still harder.

"Don't you want to?" asked Kezia.   50

Suddenly there was a twitch, a tug at Lil's skirt. She turned round. Our Else was looking at her with big, imploring eyes; she was frowning; she wanted to go. For a moment Lil looked at our Else very doubtfully. But then our Else twitched her skirt again. She started forward. Kezia led the way. Like two little stray cats they followed across the courtyard to where the doll's house stood.

"There it is," said Kezia.

There was a pause. Lil breathed loudly, almost snorted; our Else was still as a stone.

"I'll open it for you," said Kezia kindly. She undid the hook and they looked inside.

"There's the drawing-room and the dining-room, and that's the—"   55

"Kezia!"

Oh, what a start they gave!

"Kezia!"

It was Aunt Beryl's voice. They turned round. At the back door stood Aunt Beryl, staring as if she couldn't believe what she saw.

"How dare you ask the little Kelveys into the courtyard?" said her cold, furious   60 voice. "You know as well as I do, you're not allowed to talk to them. Run away, children, run away at once. And don't come back again," said Aunt Beryl. And she stepped into the yard and shooed them out as if they were chickens.

"Off you go immediately!" she called, cold and proud.

They did not need telling twice. Burning with shame, shrinking together, Lil huddling along like her mother, our Else dazed, somehow they crossed the big courtyard and squeezed through the white gate.

"Wicked, disobedient little girl!" said Aunt Beryl bitterly to Kezia, and she slammed the doll's house to.

The afternoon had been awful. A letter had come from Willie Brent, a terrifying, threatening letter, saying if she did not meet him that evening in Pulman's Bush, he'd come to the front door and ask the reason why! But now that she had frightened those little rats of Kelveys and given Kezia a good scolding, her heart felt lighter. That ghastly pressure was gone. She went back to the house humming.

When the Kelveys were well out of sight of Burnells', they sat down to rest on a   65
big red drain-pipe by the side of the road. Lil's cheeks were still burning; she took off the hat with the quill and held it on her knee. Dreamily they looked over the hay paddocks, past the creek, to the group of wattles where Logan's cows stood waiting to be milked. What were their thoughts?

Presently our Else nudged up close to her sister. But now she had forgotten the cross lady. She put out a finger and stroked her sister's quill; she smiled her rare smile.

"I seen the little lamp," she said, softly.

Then both were silent once more.

GUY DE MAUPASSANT (1850–1893)

The Necklace   1884

[The couple in this story, by a strange coincidence, live in Paris in the *Rue des Martyrs*—the street of the Martyrs. A *louis* is a gold coin worth twenty francs. The *Champs-Élysées* is a famous boulevard of fashionable stores in the heart of Paris.]

She was one of those pretty and charming girls born, as though fate had blundered over her, into a family of artisans. She had no marriage portion, no expectations, no means of getting known, understood, loved, and wedded by a man of wealth and distinction; and she let herself be married off to a little clerk in the Ministry of Education.

Her tastes were simple because she had never been able to afford any other, but she was as unhappy as though she had married beneath her; for women have no caste or class, their beauty, grace, and charm serving them for birth or family. Their natural delicacy, their instinctive elegance, their nimbleness of wit, are their only mark of rank, and put the slum girl on a level with the highest lady in the land.

She suffered endlessly, feeling herself born for every delicacy and luxury. She suffered from the poorness of her house, from its mean walls, worn chairs, and ugly curtains. All these things, of which other women of her class would not even have been aware, tormented and insulted her. The sight of the little Breton girl who came to do the work in her little house aroused heart-broken regrets and hopeless dreams in her mind. She imagined silent antechambers, heavy with Oriental tapestries, lit by torches in lofty bronze sockets, with two tall footmen in knee-breeches sleeping in large armchairs, overcome by the heavy warmth of the stove. She imagined vast saloons hung with antique silks, exquisite pieces of furniture supporting priceless ornaments, and small, charming, perfumed rooms, created just for little parties of intimate friends, men who were famous and sought after, whose homage roused every other woman's envious longings.

When she sat down for dinner at the round table covered with a three-days-old cloth, opposite her husband, who took the cover off the soup-tureen, exclaiming delightedly: "Aha! Scotch broth! What could be better?" she imagined delicate meals, gleaming silver, tapestries peopling the walls with folk of a past age and strange birds in faery forests; she imagined delicate food served in marvelous dishes, murmured gallantries, listened to with an inscrutable smile as one trifled with the rosy flesh of trout or wings of asparagus chicken.

She had no clothes, no jewels, nothing. And these were the only things she loved; she felt that she was made for them. She had longed so eagerly to charm, to be desired, to be wildly attractive and sought after.   5

She had a rich friend, an old school friend whom she refused to visit, because she suffered so keenly when she returned home. She would weep whole days, with grief, regret, despair, and misery.

One evening her husband came home with an exultant air, holding a large envelope in his hand.

"Here's something for you," he said.

Swiftly she tore the paper and drew out a printed card on which were these words:

"The Minister of Education and Madame Ramponneau request the pleasure of the company of Monsieur and Madame Loisel at the Ministry on the evening of Monday, January the 18th."

Instead of being delighted, as her husband hoped, she flung the invitation petu-   10
lantly across the table, murmuring:

"What do you want me to do with this?"

"Why, darling, I thought you'd be pleased. You never go out, and this is a great occasion. I had tremendous trouble to get it. Every one wants one; it's very select, and very few go to the clerks. You'll see all the really big people there."

She looked at him out of furious eyes, and said impatiently:

"And what do you suppose I am to wear to such an affair?"

He had not thought about it; he stammered: 15

"Why, the dress you go to the theatre in. It looks very nice, to me. . . ."

He stopped, stupefied and utterly at a loss when he saw that his wife was beginning to cry. Two large tears ran slowly down from the corners of her eyes toward the corners of her mouth.

"What's the matter with you? What's the matter with you?" he faltered.

But with a violent effort she overcame her grief and replied in a calm voice, wiping her wet cheeks:

"Nothing. Only I haven't a dress and so I can't go to this party. Give your invita-   20
tion to some friend of yours whose wife will be turned out better than I shall."

He was heart-broken.

"Look here, Mathilde," he persisted. "What would be the cost of a suitable dress, which you could use on other occasions as well, something very simple?"

She thought for several seconds, reckoning up prices and also wondering for how large a sum she could ask without bringing upon herself an immediate refusal and an exclamation of horror from the careful-minded clerk.

At last she replied with some hestitation:

"I don't know exactly, but I think I could do it on four hundred francs."   25

He grew slightly pale, for this was exactly the amount he had been saving for a gun, intending to get a little shooting next summer on the plain of Nanterre with some friends who went lark-shooting there on Sundays.

Nevertheless he said: "Very well. I'll give you four hundred francs. But try and get a really nice dress with the money."

The day of the party drew near, and Madame Loisel seemed sad, uneasy and anxious. Her dress was ready, however. One evening her husband said to her:

"What's the matter with you? You've been very odd for the last three days."

"I'm utterly miserable at not having any jewels, not a single stone, to wear," she   30
replied. "I shall look like a total nobody. I would almost rather not go to the party."

"Wear flowers," he said. "They're very smart at this time of the year. For ten francs you could get two or three gorgeous roses."

She was not convinced.

"No . . . there's nothing so humiliating as looking poor in the middle of a lot of rich women."

"How stupid you are!" exclaimed her husband. "Go and see Madame Forestier and ask her to lend you some jewels. You know her quite well enough for that."

She uttered a cry of delight.   35

"That's true. I never thought of it."

Next day she went to see her friend and told her trouble.

Madame Forestier went to her dressing-table, took up a large box, brought it to Madame Loisel, opened it, and said:

"Choose, my dear."

First she saw some bracelets, then a pearl necklace, then a Venetian cross in gold   40
and gems, of exquisite workmanship. She tried the effect of the jewels before the mirror, hesitating, unable to make her mind to leave them, to give them up. She kept on asking:

"Haven't you anything else?"

"Yes. Look for yourself. I don't know what you would like best."

Suddenly she discovered, in a black satin case, a superb diamond necklace; her heart began to beat covetously. Her hands trembled as she lifted it. She fastened it round her neck, upon her high dress, and remained in ecstasy at sight of herself.

Then, with hesitation, she asked in anguish:

"Could you lend me this, just this alone?"   45

"Yes, of course."

She flung herself on her friend's breast, embraced her frenziedly, and went away with her treasure.

The day of the party arrived. Madame Loisel was a success. She was the prettiest woman present, elegant, graceful, smiling, and quite above herself with happiness. All the men stared at her, inquired her name, and asked to be introduced to her. All the Under-Secretaries of State were eager to waltz with her. The Minister noticed her.

She danced madly, ecstatically, drunk with pleasure, with no thought for anything, in the triumph of her beauty, in the pride of her success, in a cloud of happiness made up of this universal homage and admiration, of the desires she had aroused, of the completeness of a victory so dear to her feminine heart.

She left about four o'clock in the morning. Since midnight her husband had been   50
dozing in a deserted little room, in company with three other men whose wives were having a good time.

He threw over her shoulders the garments he had brought for them to go home in, modest everyday clothes, whose poverty clashed with the beauty of the ball-dress. She was conscious of this and was anxious to hurry away, so that she should not be noticed by the other women putting on their costly furs.

Loisel restrained her.

"Wait a little. You'll catch cold in the open. I'm going to fetch a cab."

But she did not listen to him and rapidly descended the staircase. When they were out in the street they could not find a cab; they began to look for one, shouting at the drivers whom they saw passing in the distance.

They walked down toward the Seine, desperate and shivering. At last they found   55 on the quay one of those old night-prowling carriages which are only to be seen in Paris after dark, as though they were ashamed of their shabbiness in the daylight.

It brought them to their door in the Rue des Martyrs, and sadly they walked up to their own apartment. It was the end, for her. As for him, he was thinking that he must be at the office at ten.

She took off the garments in which she had wrapped her shoulders, so as to see herself in all her glory before the mirror. But suddenly she uttered a cry. The necklace was no longer round her neck!

"What's the matter with you?" asked her husband, already half undressed.

She turned toward him in the utmost distress.

"I . . . I . . . I've no longer got Madame Forestier's necklace. . . ."   60

He started with astonishment.

"What! . . . Impossible!"

They searched in the folds of her dress, in the folds of the coat, in the pockets, everywhere. They could not find it.

"Are you sure that you still had it on when you came away from the ball?" he asked.

"Yes, I touched it in the hall at the Ministry."   65

"But if you had lost it in the street, we should have heard it fall."

"Yes. Probably we should. Did you take the number of the cab?"

"No. You didn't notice it, did you?"

"No."

They stared at one another, dumbfounded. At last Loisel put on his clothes again.   70

"I'll go over all the ground we walked," he said, "and see if I can't find it."

And he went out. She remained in her evening clothes, lacking strength to get into bed, huddled on a chair, without volition or power of thought.

Her husband returned about seven. He found nothing.

He went to the police station, to the newspapers, to offer a reward, to the cab companies, everywhere that a ray of hope impelled him.

She waited all day long, in the same state of bewilderment at this fearful cata-   75 strophe.

Loisel came home at night, his face lined and pale; he had discovered nothing.

"You must write to your friend," he said, "and tell her that you've broken the clasp of her necklace and are getting it mended. That will give us time to look about us."

She wrote at his dictation.

By the end of a week they had lost all hope.

Loisel, who had aged five years, declared: 80

"We must see about replacing the diamonds."

Next day they took the box which had held the necklace and went to the jewellers whose name was inside. He consulted his books.

"It was not I who sold this necklace, Madame; I must have merely supplied the clasp."

Then they went from jeweller to jeweller, searching for another necklace like the first, consulting their memories, both ill with remorse and anguish of mind.

In a shop at the Palais-Royal they found a string of diamonds which seemed to them exactly like the one they were looking for. It was worth forty thousand francs. They were allowed to have it for thirty-six thousand.

They begged the jeweller not to sell it for three days. And they arranged matters on the understanding that it would be taken back for thirty-four thousand francs, if the first one were found before the end of February.

Loisel possessed eighteen thousand francs left to him by his father. He intended to borrow the rest.

He did borrow it, getting a thousand from one man, five hundred from another, five louis here, three louis there. He gave notes of hand, entered into ruinous agreements, did business with usurers and the whole tribe of money-lenders. He mortgaged the whole remaining years of his existence, risked his signature without even knowing if he could honor it and, appalled at the agonizing face of the future, at the black misery about to fall upon him, at the prospect of every possible physical privation and moral torture, he went to get the new necklace and put down upon the jeweller's counter thirty-six thousand francs.

When Madame Loisel took back the necklace to Madame Forestier, the latter said to her in a chilly voice:

"You ought to have brought it back sooner; I might have needed it."

She did not, as her friend had feared, open the case. If she had noticed the substitution, what would she have thought? What would she have said? Would she not have taken her for a thief?

Madame Loisel came to know the ghastly life of abject poverty. From the very first she played her part heroically. This fearful debt must be paid off. She would pay it. The servant was dismissed. They changed their flat; they took a garret under the roof.

She came to know the heavy work of the house, the hateful duties of the kitchen. She washed the plates, wearing out her pink nails on the coarse pottery and the bottoms of pans. She washed the dirty linen, the shirts and dish-clothes, and hung them out to dry on a string; every morning she took the dustbin down into the street and carried up the water, stopping on each landing to get her breath. And, clad like a poor woman, she went to the fruiterer, to the grocer, to the butcher, a basket on her arm, haggling, insulted, fighting for every wretched penny of her money.

Every month notes had to be paid off, others renewed, time gained.

Her husband worked in the evenings at putting straight a merchant's accounts, and often at night he did copying at pennies a page.

And this life lasted ten years.

At the end of ten years everything was paid off, everything, the usurer's charges, the accumulation of superimposed interest.

Madame Loisel looked old now. She had become like all the other strong, hard, coarse women of poor households. Her hair was badly done, her skirts were awry, her hands were red. She spoke in a shrill voice, and the water slopped all over the floor when she scrubbed it. But sometimes, when her husband was at the office, she sat down by the window and thought of that evening long ago, of the ball at which she had been so beautiful and so much admired.

What would have happened if she had never lost those jewels. Who knows? Who knows? How strange life is, how fickle! How little is needed to ruin or to save!

One Sunday, as she had gone for a walk along the Champs-Élysées to freshen   100
herself after the labors of the week, she caught sight suddenly of a woman who was taking a child out for a walk. It was Madame Forestier, still young, still beautiful, still attractive.

Madame Loisel was conscious of some emotion. Should she speak to her? Yes, certainly. And now that she had paid, she would tell her all. Why not?

She went up to her.

"Good morning, Jeanne."

The other did not recognize her, and was surprised at being thus familiarly addressed by a poor woman.

"But . . . Madame . . . " she stammered. "I don't know . . . you must be   105
making a mistake."

"No . . . I am Mathilde Loisel."

Her friend uttered a cry.

"Oh! . . . my poor Mathilde, how you have changed! . . . "

"Yes, I've had some hard times since I saw you last; and many sorrows . . . and
all on your account."

"On my account! . . . How was that?"   110

"You remember the diamond necklace you lent me for the ball at the Ministry?"

"Yes. Well?"

"Well, I lost it."

"How could you? Why, you brought it back."

"I brought you another one just like it. And for the last ten years we have been   115
paying for it. You realize it wasn't easy for me; we had no money. . . . Well, it's paid
for at last, and I'm glad indeed."

Madame Forestier had halted.

"You say you bought a diamond necklace to replace mine?"

"Yes. You hadn't noticed it? They were very much alike."

And she smiled in proud and innocent happiness.

Madame Forestier, deeply moved, took her two hands.   120

"Oh, my poor Mathilde! But mine was imitation. It was worth at the very most
five hundred francs! . . . "

HERMAN MELVILLE   (1819–1891)

Bartleby the Scrivener   1853

[Melville's story takes us into the world of legal offices in nineteenth-century New York. The narrator is a conveyancer, engaged in title searches and
transfer of titles to property. He has had himself appointed as Master in
Chancery—a judge involved in the settlement of contract disputes. He has
scriveners working for him, who—with pen and ink—make necessary copies of
legal documents. Duns are bill collectors; the Tombs is a prison in New York
City; a reference is a meeting between lawyers. The story refers to a fatal quarrel in which the actor John Colt killed the printer Samuel Adams. The narrator
expects the reader to recognize biblical and classical allusions: Lot's wife was
turned into a pillar of salt when she turned to look back at the destruction of
Sodom. The Roman general and consul Marius, after he was driven from of-

fice, sought refuge in Carthage, an enemy city that he had destroyed. Petra is a deserted, ruined ancient city in Jordan. A few features of everyday life in Melville's day are no longer familiar to modern readers: For instance, Spitzenbergs are apples; anthracite is used for fuel; a blacking box has shoe polish in it.]

I am a rather elderly man. The nature of my avocations, for the last thirty years, has brought me into more than ordinary contact with what would seem an interesting and somewhat singular set of men, of whom, as yet, nothing, that I know of, has ever been written—I mean, the law-copyists, or scriveners. I have known very many of them, professionally and privately, and, if I pleased, could relate divers histories, at which good-natured gentlemen might smile, and sentimental souls might weep. But I waive the biographies of all other scriveners, for a few passages in the life of Bartleby, who was a scrivener, the strangest I ever saw, or heard of. While, of other law-copyists, I might write the complete life, of Bartleby nothing of that sort can be done. I believe that no materials exist, for a full and satisfactory biography of this man. It is an irreparable loss to literature. Bartleby was one of those beings of whom nothing is ascertainable, except from the original sources, and, in his case, those are very small. What my own astonished eyes saw of Bartleby, *that* is all I know of him, except, indeed, one vague report, which will appear in the sequel.

Ere introducing the scrivener, as he first appeared to me, it is fit I make some mention of myself, my *employés,* my business, my chambers, and general surroundings; because some such description is indispensable to an adequate understanding of the chief character about to be presented. Imprimis: I am a man who, from his youth upwards, has been filled with a profound conviction that the easiest way of life is the best. Hence, though I belong to a profession proverbially energetic and nervous, even to turbulence, at times, yet nothing of that sort have I ever suffered to invade my peace. I am one of those unambitious lawyers who never addresses a jury, or in any way draws down public applause; but, in the cool tranquillity of a snug retreat, do a snug business among rich men's bonds, and mortgages, and title-deeds. All who know me, consider me an eminently *safe* man. The late John Jacob Astor, a personage little given to poetic enthusiasm, had no hesitation in pronouncing my first grand point to be prudence; my next, method. I do not speak it in vanity, but simply record the fact, that I was not unemployed in my profession by the late John Jacob Astor; a name which, I admit, I love to repeat; for it hath a rounded and orbicular sound to it, and rings like unto bullion. I will freely add, that I was not insensible to the late John Jacob Astor's good opinion.

Some time prior to the period at which this little history begins, my avocations had been largely increased. The good old office, now extinct in the State of New York, of a Master in Chancery, had been conferred upon me. It was not a very arduous office, but very pleasantly remunerative. I seldom lose my temper; much more seldom indulge in dangerous indignation at wrongs and outrages; but I must be permitted to be rash here and declare, that I consider the sudden and violent abrogation of the office of Master in Chancery, by the new Constitution, as a——premature act; inasmuch as I had counted upon a life-lease of the profits, whereas I only received those of a few short years. But this is by the way.

My chambers were up stairs, at No.—Wall Street. At one end, they looked upon the white wall of the interior of a spacious sky-light shaft, penetrating the building from top to bottom.

This view might have been considered rather tame than otherwise, deficient in what landscape painters call "life." But, if so, the view from the other end of my cham-

5

bers offered, at least, a contrast, if nothing more. In that direction, my windows commanded an unobstructed view of a lofty brick wall, black by age and everlasting shade; which wall required no spy-glass to bring out its lurking beauties, but, for the benefit of all near-sighted spectators, was pushed up to within ten feet of my window panes. Owing to the great height of the surrounding buildings, and my chambers being on the second floor, the interval between this wall and mine not a little resembled a huge square cistern.

At the period just preceding the advent of Bartleby, I had two persons as copyists in my employment, and a promising lad as an office-boy. First, Turkey; second, Nippers; third, Ginger Nut. These may seem names, the like of which are not usually found in the Directory. In truth, they were nicknames, mutually conferred upon each other by my three clerks, and were deemed expressive of their respective persons or characters. Turkey was a short, pursy Englishman, of about my age—that is, somewhere not far from sixty. In the morning, one might say, his face was of a fine florid hue, but after twelve o'clock, meridian—his dinner hour—it blazed like a grate full of Christmas coals; and continued blazing—but, as it were, with a gradual wane—till six o'clock, P.M., or thereabouts; after which, I saw no more of the proprietor of the face, which, gaining its meridian with the sun, seemed to set with it, to rise, culminate, and decline the following day, with the like regularity and undiminished glory. There are many singular coincidences I have known in the course of my life, not the least among which was the fact, that, exactly when Turkey displayed his fullest beams from his red and radiant countenance, just then, too, at that critical moment, began the daily period when I considered his business capacities as seriously disturbed for the remainder of the twenty-four hours. Not that he was absolutely idle, or averse to business, then; far from it. The difficulty was, he was apt to be altogether too energetic. There was a strange, inflamed, flurried, flighty recklessness of activity about him. He would be incautious in dipping his pen into his inkstand. All his blots upon my documents were dropped there after twelve o'clock, meridian. Indeed, not only would he be reckless, and sadly given to making blots in the afternoon, but, some days, he went further, and was rather noisy. At such times, too, his face flamed with augmented blazonry, as if cannel coal had been heaped on anthracite. He made an unpleasant racket with his chair; spilled his sand-box; in mending his pens, impatiently split them all to pieces, and threw them on the floor in a sudden passion; stood up, and leaned over his table, boxing his papers about in a most indecorous manner, very sad to behold in an elderly man like him. Nevertheless, as he was in many ways a most valuable person to me, and all the time before twelve o'clock meridian, was the quickest, steadiest creature, too, accomplishing a great deal of work in a style not easily to be matched—for these reasons, I was willing to overlook his eccentricities, though, indeed, occasionally, I remonstrated with him. I did this very gently, however, because, though the civilest, nay, the blandest and most reverential of men in the morning, yet, in the afternoon, he was disposed, upon provocation, to be slightly rash with his tongue—in fact, insolent. Now, valuing his morning services as I did, and resolved not to lose them—yet, at the same time, made uncomfortable by his inflamed ways after twelve o'clock—and being a man of peace, unwilling by my admonitions to call forth unseemly retorts from him, I took upon me, one Saturday noon (he was always worse on Saturdays) to hint to him, very kindly, that, perhaps, now that he was growing old, it might be well to abridge his labors; in short, he need not come to my chambers after twelve o'clock, but, dinner over, had best go home to his lodgings, and rest himself till tea-time. But no; he insisted upon his afternoon devotions. His countenance became intolerably fervid, as he oratorically assured me—gesticulating with a long ruler at the other end of the room—that if his services in the morning were useful, how indispensable, then, in the afternoon?

"With submission, sir," said Turkey, on this occasion, "I consider myself your right-hand man. In the morning I but marshal and deploy my columns; but in the afternoon I put myself at their head, and gallantly charge the foe, thus"—and he made a violent thrust with the ruler.

"But the blots, Turkey," intimated I.

"True; but, with submission, sir, behold these hairs! I am getting old. Surely, sir, a blot or two of a warm afternoon is not to be severely urged against gray hairs. Old age—even if it blot the page—is honorable. With submission, sir, we *both* are getting old."

This appeal to my fellow-feeling was hardly to be resisted. At all events, I saw that go he would not. So, I made up my mind to let him stay, resolving, nevertheless, to see to it that, during the afternoon, he had to do with my less important papers.

Nippers, the second on my list, was a whiskered, sallow, and, upon the whole, rather piratical-looking young man, of about five-and-twenty. I always deemed him the victim of two evil powers—ambition and indigestion. The ambition was evinced by a certain impatience of the duties of a mere copyist, an unwarrantable usurpation of strictly professional affairs, such as the original drawing up of legal documents. The indigestion seemed betokened in an occasional nervous testiness and grinning irritability, causing the teeth to audibly grind together over mistakes committed in copying; unnecessary maledictions, hissed, rather than spoken, in the heat of business; and especially by a continual discontent with the height of the table where he worked. Though of a very ingenious mechanical turn, Nippers could never get this table to suit him. He put chips under it, blocks of various sorts, bits of pasteboard, and at last went so far as to attempt an exquisite adjustment, by final pieces of folded blotting-paper. But no invention would answer. If, for the sake of easing his back, he brought the table-lid at a sharp angle well up towards his chin, and wrote there like a man using the steep roof of a Dutch house for his desk, then he declared that it stopped the circulation in his arms. If now he lowered the table to his waistbands, and stooped over it in writing, then there was a sore aching in his back. In short, the truth of the matter was, Nippers knew not what he wanted. Or, if he wanted anything, it was to be rid of a scrivener's table altogether. Among the manifestations of his diseased ambition was a fondness he had for receiving visits from certain ambiguous-looking fellows in seedy coats, whom he called his clients. Indeed, I was aware that not only was he, at times, considerable of a ward-politician, but he occasionally did a little business at the Justices' courts, and was not unknown on the steps of the Tombs. I have good reason to believe, however, that one individual who called upon him at my chambers, and who, with a grand air, he insisted was his client, was no other than a dun, and the alleged title-deed, a bill. But, with all his failings, and the annoyances he caused me, Nippers, like his compatriot Turkey, was a very useful man to me; wrote a neat, swift hand; and, when he chose, was not deficient in a gentlemanly sort of deportment. Added to this he always dressed in a gentlemanly sort of way; and so, incidentally, reflected credit upon my chambers. Whereas, with respect to Turkey, I had much ado to keep him from being a reproach to me. His clothes were apt to look oily, and smell of eating-houses. He wore his pantaloons very loose and baggy in summer. His coats were execrable; his hat not to be handled. But while the hat was a thing of indifference to me, inasmuch as his natural civility and deference, as a dependent Englishman, always led him to doff it the moment he entered the room, yet his coat was another matter. Concerning his coats, I reasoned with him; but with no effect. The truth was, I suppose, that a man with so small an income could not afford to sport such a lustrous face and a lustrous coat at one and the same time. As Nippers once observed, Turkey's money went chiefly for red ink. One winter day, I presented Turkey with a highly respectable-looking coat of my own—a padded gray coat,

10

of a most comfortable warmth, and which buttoned straight up from the knee to the neck. I thought Turkey would appreciate the favor, and abate his rashness and obstreperousness of afternoons. But no; I verily believe that buttoning himself up in so downy and blanket-like a coat had a pernicious effect upon him—upon the same principle that too much oats are bad for horses. In fact, precisely as a rash, restive horse is said to feel his oats, so Turkey felt his coat. It made him insolent. He was a man whom prosperity harmed.

Though, concerning the self-indulgent habits of Turkey, I had my own private surmises, yet, touching Nippers, I was well persuaded that, whatever might be his faults in other respects, he was, at least, a temperate young man. But, indeed, nature herself seemed to have been his vintner, and, at his birth, charged him so thoroughly with an irritable, brandy-like disposition, that all subsequent potations were needless. When I consider how, amid the stillness of my chambers, Nippers would sometimes impatiently rise from his seat, and stooping over his table, spread his arms wide apart, seize the whole desk, and move it, and jerk it, with a grim, grinding motion on the floor, as if the table were a perverse voluntary agent, intent on thwarting and vexing him, I plainly perceive that, for Nippers, brandy-and-water were altogether superfluous.

It was fortunate for me that, owing to its peculiar cause—indigestion—the irritability and consequent nervousness of Nippers were mainly observable in the morning, while in the afternoon he was comparatively mild. So that, Turkey's paroxysms only coming on about twelve o'clock, I never had to do with their eccentricities at one time. Their fits relieved each other, like guards. When Nippers's was on, Turkey's was off; and *vice versa*. This was a good natural arrangement, under the circumstances.

Ginger Nut, the third on my list, was a lad, some twelve years old. His father was a carman, ambitious of seeing his son on the bench instead of a cart, before he died. So he sent him to my office, as student at law, errand-boy, cleaner and sweeper, at the rate of one dollar a week. He had a little desk to himself, but he did not use it much. Upon inspection, the drawer exhibited a great array of the shells of various sorts of nuts. Indeed, to this quick-witted youth, the whole noble science of the law was contained in a nut-shell. Not the least among the employments of Ginger Nut, as well as one which he discharged with the most alacrity, was his duty as cake and apple purveyor for Turkey and Nippers. Copying lawpapers being proverbially a dry, husky sort of business, my two scriveners were fain to moisten their mouths very often with Spitzenbergs, to be had at the numerous stalls nigh the Custom House and Post Office. Also, they sent Ginger Nut very frequently for that peculiar cake—small, flat, round, and very spicy—after which he had been named by them. Of a cold morning, when business was but dull, Turkey would gobble up scores of these cakes, as if they were mere wafers—indeed, they sell them at the rate of six or eight for a penny—the scrape of his pen blending with the crunching of the crisp particles in his mouth. Rashest of all the fiery afternoon blunders and flurried rashnesses of Turkey, was his once moistening a ginger-cake between his lips, and clapping it on to a mortgage, for a seal. I came within an ace of dismissing him then. But he mollified me by making an oriental bow, and saying—

"With submission, sir, it was generous of me to find you in stationery on my own account."   15

Now my original business—that of a conveyancer and title hunter, and drawer-up of recondite documents of all sorts—was considerably increased by receiving the master's office. There was now great work for scriveners. Not only must I push the clerks already with me, but I must have additional help.

In answer to my advertisement, a motionless young man one morning stood upon my office threshold, the door being open, for it was summer. I can see that figure now—pallidly neat, pitiably respectable, incurably forlorn! It was Bartleby.

After a few words touching his qualifications, I engaged him, glad to have among my corps of copyists a man of so singularly sedate an aspect, which I thought might operate beneficially upon the flighty temper of Turkey, and the fiery one of Nippers.

I should have stated before that ground-glass folding-doors divided my premises into two parts, one of which was occupied by my scriveners, the other by myself. According to my humor, I threw open these doors, or closed them. I resolved to assign Bartleby a corner by the folding-doors, but on my side of them, so as to have this quiet man within easy call, in case any trifling thing was to be done. I placed his desk close up to a small side-window in that part of the room, a window which originally had afforded a lateral view of certain grimy backyards and bricks, but which, owing to subsequent erections, commanded at present no view at all, though it gave some light. Within three feet of the panes was a wall, and the light came down from far above, between two lofty buildings, as from a very small opening in a dome. Still further to a satisfactory arrangement, I procured a high green folding screen, which might entirely isolate Bartleby from my sight, though not remove him from my voice. And thus, in a manner, privacy and society were conjoined.

At first, Bartleby did an extraordinary quantity of writing. As if long famishing for   20
something to copy, he seemed to gorge himself on my documents. There was no pause for digestion. He ran a day and night line, copying by sun-light and by candle-light. I should have been quite delighted with his application, had he been cheerfully industrious. But he wrote on silently, palely, mechanically.

It is, of course, an indispensable part of a scrivener's business to verify the accuracy of his copy, word by word. Where there are two or more scriveners in an office, they assist each other in this examination, one reading from the copy, the other holding the original. It is a very dull, wearisome, and lethargic affair. I can readily imagine that, to some sanguine temperaments, it would be altogether intolerable. For example, I cannot credit that the mettlesome poet, Byron, would have contentedly sat down with Bartleby to examine a law document of, say five hundred pages, closely written in a crimpy hand.

Now and then, in the haste of business, it had been my habit to assist in comparing some brief document myself, calling Turkey or Nippers for this purpose. One object I had, in placing Bartleby so handy to me behind the screen, was, to avail myself of his services on such trivial occasions. It was on the third day, I think, of his being with me, and before any necessity had arisen for having his own writing examined, that, being much hurried to complete a small affair I had in hand, I abruptly called to Bartleby. In my haste and natural expectancy of instant compliance, I sat with my head bent over the original on my desk, and my right hand sideways, and somewhat nervously extended with the copy, so that, immediately upon emerging from his retreat, Bartleby might snatch it and proceed to business without the least delay.

In this very attitude did I sit when I called to him, rapidly stating what it was I wanted him to do—namely, to examine a small paper with me. Imagine my surprise, nay, my consternation, when, without moving from his privacy, Bartleby, in a singularly mild, firm voice, replied, "I would prefer not to."

I sat awhile in perfect silence, rallying my stunned faculties. Immediately it occurred to me that my ears had deceived me, or Bartleby had entirely misunderstood my meaning. I repeated my request in the clearest tone I could assume; but in quite as clear a one came the previous reply, "I would prefer not to."

"Prefer not to," echoed I, rising in high excitement, and crossing the room with a   25
stride. "What do you mean? Are you moon-struck? I want you to help me compare this sheet here—take it," and I thrust it towards him.

"I would prefer not to," said he.

I looked at him steadfastly. His face was leanly composed; his gray eye dimly calm. Not a wrinkle of agitation rippled him. Had there been the least uneasiness, anger, impatience or impertinence in his manner; in other words, had there been anything ordinarily human about him, doubtless I should have violently dismissed him from the premises. But as it was, I should have as soon thought of turning my pale plaster-of-paris bust of Cicero out of doors. I stood gazing at him awhile, as he went on with his own writing, and then reseated myself at my desk. This is very strange, thought I. What had one best do? But my business hurried me. I concluded to forget the matter for the present, reserving it for my future leisure. So, calling Nippers from the other room, the paper was speedily examined.

A few days after this, Bartleby concluded four lengthy documents, being quadruplicates of a week's testimony taken before me in my High Court of Chancery. It became necessary to examine them. It was an important suit, and great accuracy was imperative. Having all things arranged, I called Turkey, Nippers and Ginger Nut, from the next room, meaning to place the four copies in the hands of my four clerks, while I should read from the original. Accordingly, Turkey, Nippers, and Ginger Nut had taken their seats in a row, each with his document in his hand, when I called to Bartleby to join this interesting group.

"Bartleby! quick, I am waiting."

I heard a slow scrape of his chair legs on the uncarpeted floor, and soon he appeared standing at the entrance of his hermitage.   30

"What is wanted?" said he, mildly.

"The copies, the copies," said I, hurriedly. "We are going to examine them. There"—and I held toward him the fourth quadruplicate.

"I would prefer not to," he said, and gently disappeared behind the screen.

For a few moments I was turned into a pillar of salt, standing at the head of my seated column of clerks. Recovering myself, I advanced towards the screen, and demanded the reason for such extraordinary conduct.

"*Why* do you refuse?"   35

"I would prefer not to."

With any other man I should have flown outright into a dreadful passion, scorned all further words, and thrust him ignominiously from my presence. But there was something about Bartleby that not only strangely disarmed me, but, in a wonderful manner, touched and disconcerted me. I began to reason with him.

"These are your own copies we are about to examine. It is labor saving to you, because one examination will answer for your four papers. It is common usage. Every copyist is bound to help examine his copy. Is it not so? Will you not speak? Answer!"

"I prefer not to," he replied in a flute-like tone. It seemed to me that, while I had been addressing him, he carefully revolved every statement that I made; fully comprehended the meaning; could not gainsay the irresistible conclusion; but, at the same time, some paramount consideration prevailed with him to reply as he did.

"You are decided, then, not to comply with my request—a request made according to common usage and common sense?"   40

He briefly gave me to understand, that on that point my judgment was sound. Yes: his decision was irreversible.

It is not seldom the case that, when a man is browbeaten in some unprecedented and violently unreasonable way, he begins to stagger in his own plainest faith. He begins, as it were, vaguely to surmise that, wonderful as it may be, all the justice and all the reason is on the other side. Accordingly, if any disinterested persons are present, he turns to them for some reinforcement for his own faltering mind.

"Turkey," said I, "what do you think of this? Am I not right?"

"With submission, sir," said Turkey, in his blandest tone, "I think that you are."

"Nippers," said I, "what do *you* think of it?"   45

"I think I should kick him out of the office."

(The reader of nice perceptions will here perceive that, it being morning, Turkey's answer is couched in polite and tranquil terms, but Nippers replies in ill-tempered ones. Or, to repeat a previous sentence, Nippers's ugly mood was on duty, and Turkey's off.)

"Ginger Nut," said I, willing to enlist the smallest suffrage in my behalf, "what do *you* think of it?"

"I think, sir, he's a little *luny*," replied Ginger Nut, with a grin.

"You hear what they say," said I, turning towards the screen, "come forth and do   50 your duty."

But he vouchsafed no reply. I pondered a moment in sore perplexity. But once more business hurried me. I determined again to postpone the consideration of this dilemma to my future leisure. With a little trouble we made out to examine the papers without Bartleby, though at every page or two Turkey deferentially dropped his opinion, that this proceeding was quite out of the common; while Nippers, twitching in his chair with a dyspeptic nervousness, ground out, between his set teeth, occasional hissing maledictions against the stubborn oaf behind the screen. And for his (Nippers's) part, this was the first and the last time he would do another man's business without pay.

Meanwhile Bartleby sat in his hermitage, oblivious to everything but his own peculiar business there.

Some days passed, the scrivener being employed upon another lengthy work. His late remarkable conduct led me to regard his ways narrowly. I observed that he never went to dinner; indeed, that he never went anywhere. As yet I had never, of my personal knowledge, known him to be outside of my office. He was a perpetual sentry in the corner. At about eleven o'clock though, in the morning, I noticed that Ginger Nut would advance toward the opening in Bartleby's screen, as if silently beckoned thither by a gesture invisible to me where I sat. The boy would then leave the office, jingling a few pence, and reappear with a handful of ginger-nuts, which he delivered in the hermitage, receiving two of the cakes for his trouble.

He lives, then, on ginger-nuts, thought I; never eats a dinner, properly speaking; he must be a vegetarian, then, but no; he never eats even vegetables, he eats nothing but ginger-nuts. My mind then ran on in reveries concerning the probable effects upon the human constitution of living entirely on ginger-nuts. Ginger-nuts are so called, because they contain ginger as one of their peculiar constituents, and the final flavoring one. Now, what was ginger? A hot, spicy thing. Was Bartleby hot and spicy? Not at all. Ginger, then, had no effect upon Bartleby. Probably he preferred it should have none.

Nothing so aggravates an earnest person as a passive resistance. If the individual so   55 resisted be of a not inhumane temper, and the resisting one perfectly harmless in his passivity, then, in the better moods of the former, he will endeavor charitably to construe to his imagination what proves impossible to be solved by his judgment. Even so, for the most part, I regarded Bartleby and his ways. Poor fellow! thought I, he means no mischief; it is plain he intends no insolence; his aspect sufficiently evinces that his eccentricities are involuntary. He is useful to me. I can get along with him. If I turn him away, the chances are he will fall in with some less-indulgent employer, and then he will be rudely treated, and perhaps driven forth miserably to starve. Yes. Here I can cheaply purchase a delicious self-approval. To befriend Bartleby; to humor him in his strange willfulness, will cost me little or nothing, while I lay up in my soul what will eventually prove a sweet morsel for my conscience. But this mood was not invariable with me. The passiveness of Bartleby sometimes irritated me. I felt strangely goaded on to encounter him in new opposition—to elicit some angry spark from him answerable to my own. But, indeed, I might as well have essayed to strike fire with my knuckles against a bit of Windsor soap. But one afternoon the evil impulse in me mastered me, and the following little scene ensued:

"Bartleby," said I, "when those papers are all copied, I will compare them with you."

"I would prefer not to."

"How? Surely you do not mean to persist in that mulish vagary?"

No answer.

I threw open the folding-doors near by, and, turning upon Turkey and Nippers, exclaimed: 60

"Bartleby a second time says, he won't examine his papers. What do you think of it, Turkey?"

It was afternoon, be it remembered. Turkey sat glowing like a brass boiler; his bald head steaming; his hands reeling among his blotted papers.

"Think of it?" roared Turkey. "I think I'll just step behind his screen, and black his eyes for him!"

So saying, Turkey rose to his feet and threw his arms into a pugilistic position. He was hurrying away to make good his promise, when I detained him, alarmed at the effect of incautiously rousing Turkey's combativeness after dinner.

"Sit down, Turkey," said I, "and hear what Nippers has to say. What do you think   65
of it, Nippers? Would I not be justified in immediately dismissing Bartleby?"

"Excuse me, that is for you to decide, sir. I think his conduct quite unusual, and, indeed, unjust, as regards Turkey and myself. But it may only be a passing whim."

"Ah," exclaimed I, "you have strangely changed your mind, then—you speak very gently of him now."

"All beer," cried Turkey; "gentleness is effects of beer—Nippers and I dined together to-day. You see how gentle *I* am, sir. Shall I go and black his eyes?"

"You refer to Bartleby, I suppose. No, not today, Turkey," I replied; "pray, put up your fists."

I closed the doors, and again advanced towards Bartleby. I felt additional incen-   70
tives tempting me to my fate. I burned to be rebelled against again. I remembered that Bartleby never left the office.

"Bartleby," said I, "Ginger Nut is away; just step around to the Post Office, won't you?" (it was but a three minutes' walk) "and see if there is anything for me."

"I would prefer not to."

"You *will* not?"

"I *prefer* not."

I staggered to my desk, and sat there in a deep study. My blind inveteracy re-   75
turned. Was there any other thing in which I could procure myself to be ignominiously repulsed by this lean, penniless wight?—my hired clerk? What added thing is there, perfectly reasonable, that he will be sure to refuse to do?

"Bartleby!"

No answer.

"Bartleby," in a louder tone.

No answer.

"Bartleby," I roared.   80

Like a very ghost, agreeably to the laws of magical invocation, at the third summons, he appeared at the entrance of his hermitage.

"Go to the next room, and tell Nippers to come to me."

"I prefer not to," he respectfully and slowly said, and mildly disappeared.

"Very good, Bartleby," said I, in a quiet sort of serenely-severe self-possessed tone, intimating the unalterable purpose of some terrible retribution very close at hand. At the moment I half intended something of the kind. But upon the whole, as it was drawing towards my dinner-hour, I thought it best to put on my hat and walk home for the day, suffering much from perplexity and distress of mind.

Shall I acknowledge it? The conclusion of this whole business was, that it soon became a fixed fact of my chambers, that a pale young scirvener, by the name of Bartleby, had a desk there; that he copied for me at the usual rate of four cents a folio (one hundred words); but he was permanently exempt from examining the work done by him, that duty being transferred to Turkey and Nippers, out of compliment, doubtless, to their superior acuteness; moreover, said Bartleby was never, on any account, to be dispatched on the most trivial errand of any sort; and that even if entreated to take upon him such a matter, it was generally understood that he would "prefer not to"—in other words, that he would refuse point-blank.

85

As days passed on, I became considerably reconciled to Bartleby. His steadiness, his freedom from all dissipation, his incessant industry (except when he chose to throw himself into a standing revery behind his screen), his great stillness, his unalterableness of demeanor under all circumstances, made him a valuable acquisition. One prime thing was this—*he was always there*—first in the morning, continually through the day, and the last at night. I had a singular confidence in his honesty. I felt my most precious papers perfectly safe in his hands. Sometimes, to be sure, I could not, for the very soul of me, avoid falling into sudden spasmodic passions with him. For it was exceeding difficult to bear in mind all the time those strange peculiarities, privileges, and unheard-of exemptions, forming the tacit stipulations on Bartleby's part under which he remained in my office. Now and then, in the eagerness of dispatching pressing business, I would inadvertently summon Bartleby, in a short, rapid tone, to put his finger, say, on the incipient tie of a bit of red tape with which I was about compressing some papers. Of course, from behind the screen the usual answer, "I prefer not to," was sure to come; and then, how could a human creature, with the common infirmities of our nature, refrain from bitterly exclaiming upon such perverseness—such unreasonableness? However, every added repulse of this sort which I received only tended to lessen the probability of my repeating the inadvertence.

Here it must be said, that, according to the custom of most legal gentlemen occupying chambers in densely-populated law buildings, there were several keys to my door. One was kept by a woman residing in the attic, which person weekly scrubbed and daily swept and dusted my apartments. Another was kept by Turkey for convenience sake. The third I sometimes carried in my own pocket. The fourth I knew not who had.

Now, one Sunday morning I happened to go to Trinity Church, to hear a celebrated preacher, and finding myself rather early on the ground I thought I would walk round to my chambers for a while. Luckily I had my key with me; but upon applying it to the lock, I found it resisted by something inserted from the inside. Quite surprised, I called out; when to my consternation a key was turned from within; and thrusting his lean visage at me, and holding the door ajar, the apparition of Bartleby appeared, in his shirtsleeves, and otherwise in a strangely tattered *déshabillé,* saying quietly that he was sorry, but he was deeply engaged just then, and—preferred not admitting me at present. In a brief word or two, he moreover added, that perhaps I had better walk round the block two or three times, and by that time he would probably have concluded his affairs.

Now, the utterly unsurmised appearance of Bartleby, tenanting my law-chambers of a Sunday morning, with his cadaverously gentlemanly *nonchalance*, yet withal firm and self-possessed, had such a strange effect upon me, that incontinently I slunk away from my own door, and did as desired. But not without sundry twinges of impotent rebellion against the mild effrontery of this unaccountable scrivener. Indeed, it was his wonderful mildness chiefly, which not only disarmed me, but unmanned me as it were. For I consider that one, for the time, is sort of unmanned when he tranquilly permits his hired clerk to dictate to him, and order him away from his own premises. Furthermore, I was full of uneasiness as to what Bartleby could possibly be doing in my office in his shirt sleeves, and in an otherwise dismantled condition of a Sunday morning. Was anything amiss going on? Nay, that was out of the question. It was not to be thought of for a moment that Bartleby was an immoral person. But what could he be doing there?—copying? Nay again, whatever might be his eccentricities, Bartleby was an eminently decorous person. He would be the last man to sit down to his desk in any state approaching to nudity. Besides, it was Sunday; and there was something about Bartleby that forbade the supposition that he would by any secular occupation violate the proprieties of the day.

Nevertheless, my mind was not pacified; and full of a restless curiosity, at last I returned to the door. Without hindrance I inserted my key, opened it, and entered. Bartleby was not to be seen. I looked round anxiously, peeped behind his screen; but it was very plain that he was gone. Upon more closely examining the place, I surmised that for an indefinite period Bartleby must have eaten, dressed, and slept in my office, and that too without plate, mirror, or bed. The cushioned seat of a ricketty old sofa in one corner bore the faint impress of a lean, reclining form. Rolled away under his desk, I found a blanket; under the empty grate, a blacking box and brush; on a chair, a tin basin, with soap and a ragged towel; in a newspaper a few crumbs of ginger-nuts and a morsel of cheese. Yes, thought I, it is evident enough that Bartleby has been making his home here, keeping bachelor's hall all by himself. Immediately then the thought came sweeping across me, what miserable friendlessness and loneliness are here revealed! His poverty is great; but his solitude, how horrible! Think of it. Of a Sunday, Wall Street is deserted as Petra; and every night of every day it is an emptiness. This building, too, which of week-days hums with industry and life, at nightfall echoes with sheer vacancy, and all through Sunday is forlorn. And here Bartleby makes his home; sole spectator of a solitude which he has seen all populous—a sort of innocent and transformed Marius brooding among the ruins of Carthage!

For the first time in my life a feeling of overpowering stinging melancholy seized me. Before, I had never experienced aught but a not unpleasing sadness. The bond of a common humanity now drew me irresistibly to gloom. A fraternal melancholy! For both I and Bartleby were sons of Adam. I remembered the bright silks and sparkling faces I had seen that day, in gala trim, swan-like sailing down the Mississippi of Broadway; and I contrasted them with the pallid copyist, and thought to myself, Ah, happiness courts the light, so we deem the world is gay; but misery hides aloof, so we deem that misery there is none. These sad fancyings—chimeras, doubtless, of a sick and silly brain—led on to other and more special thoughts, concerning the eccentricities of Bartleby. Presentiments of strange discoveries hovered round me. The scrivener's pale form appeared to me laid out, among uncaring strangers, in its shivering winding-sheet.

Suddenly I was attracted by Bartleby's closed desk, the key in open sight left in the lock.

I mean no mischief, seek the gratification of no heartless curiosity, thought I; besides, the desk is mine, and its contents, too, so I will make bold to look within. Every-

90

thing was methodically arranged, the papers smoothly placed. The pigeon holes were deep, and removing the files of documents, I groped into their recesses. Presently I felt something there, and dragged it out. It was an old bandana handkerchief, heavy and knotted. I opened it, and saw it was a savings's bank.

I now recalled all the quiet mysteries which I had noted in the man. I remembered that he never spoke but to answer; that, though at intervals he had considerable time to himself, yet I had never seen him reading—no, not even a newspaper; that for long periods he would stand looking out, at his pale window behind the screen, upon the dead brick wall; I was quite sure he never visited any refectory or eating house; while his pale face clearly indicated that he never drank beer like Turkey, or tea and coffee even, like other men; that he never went anywhere in particular that I could learn; never went out for a walk, unless, indeed, that was the case at present; that he had declined telling who he was, or whence he came, or whether he had any relatives in the world; that though so thin and pale, he never complained of ill health. And more than all, I remembered a certain unconscious air of pallid—how shall I call it?—of pallid haughtiness, say, or rather an austere reserve about him, which had positively awed me into my tame compliance with his eccentricities, when I had feared to ask him to do the slightest incidental thing for me, even though I might know, from his long-continued motionlessness, that behind his screen he must be standing in one of those dead-wall reveries of his.

Revolving all these things, and coupling them with the recently discovered fact, that he made my office his constant abiding place and home, and not forgetful of his morbid moodiness; revolving all these things, a prudential feeling began to steal over me. My first emotions had been those of pure melancholy and sincerest pity; but just in proportion as the forlornness of Bartleby grew and grew to my imagination, did that same melancholy merge into fear, that pity into repulsion. So true it is, and so terrible, too, that up to a certain point the thought or sight of misery enlists our best affections; but, in certain special cases, beyond that point it does not. They err who would assert that invariably this is owing to the inherent selfishness of the human heart. It rather proceeds from a certain hopelessness of remedying excessive and organic ill. To a sensitive being, pity is not seldom pain. And when at last it is perceived that such pity cannot lead to effectual succor, common sense bids the soul be rid of it. What I saw that morning persuaded me that the scrivener was the victim of innate and incurable disorder. I might give alms to his body; but his body did not pain him; it was his soul that suffered, and his soul I could not reach.

I did not accomplish the purpose of going to Trinity Church that morning. Somehow, the things I had seen disqualified me for the time from church-going. I walked homeward, thinking what I would do with Bartleby. Finally, I resolved upon this—I would put certain calm questions to him the next morning, touching his history, etc., and if he declined to answer them openly and unreservedly (and I supposed he would prefer not), then to give him a twenty dollar bill over and above whatever I might owe him, and tell him his services were no longer required; but that if in any other way I could assist him, I would be happy to do so, especially if he desired to return to his native place, wherever that might be, I would willingly help to defray the expenses. Moreover, if, after reaching home, he found himself at any time in want of aid, a letter from him would be sure of a reply.

The next morning came.

"Bartleby," said I, gently calling to him behind his screen.

No reply.

"Bartleby," said, in a still gentler tone, "come here; I am not going to ask you to do anything you would prefer not to do—I simply wish to speak to you."

Upon this he noiselessly slid into view.

"Will you tell me, Bartleby, where you were born?"

"I would prefer not to."

"Will you tell me *anything* about yourself?"

"I would prefer not to." 105

"But what reasonable objection can you have to speak to me? I feel friendly towards you."

He did not look at me while I spoke, but kept his glance fixed upon my bust of Cicero, which, as I then sat, was directly behind me, some six inches above my head.

"What is your answer, Bartleby?" said I, after waiting a considerable time for a reply, during which his countenance remained immovable, only there was the faintest conceivable tremor of the white attenuated mouth.

"At present I prefer to give no answer," he said, and retired into his hermitage.

It was rather weak in me I confess, but his manner, on this occasion, nettled me. 110
Not only did there seem to lurk in it a certain calm disdain, but his perverseness seemed ungrateful, considering the undeniable good usage and indulgence he had received from me.

Again I sat ruminating what I should do. Mortified as I was at his behavior, and resolved as I had been to dismiss him when I entered my office, nevertheless I strangely felt something superstitious knocking at my heart, and forbidding me to carry out my purpose, and denouncing me for a villain if I dared to breathe one bitter word against this forlornest of mankind. At last, familiarly drawing my chair behind his screen, I sat down and said: "Bartleby, never mind, then, about revealing your history; but let me entreat you, as a friend, to comply as far as may be with the usages of this office. Say now, you will help to examine papers tomorrow or next day: in short, say now, that in a day or two you will begin to be a little reasonable:—say so, Bartleby."

"At present I would prefer not to be a little reasonable," was his mildly cadaverous reply.

Just then the folding-doors opened, and Nippers approached. He seemed suffering from an unusually bad night's rest, induced by severer indigestion than common. He overheard those final words of Bartleby.

"*Prefer not*, eh?" gritted Nippers—"I'd *prefer* him, if I were you, sir," addressing me—"I'd *prefer* him; I'd give him preferences, the stubborn mule! What is it, sir, pray, that he *prefers* not to do now?"

Bartleby moved not a limb. 115

"Mr. Nippers," said I, "I'd prefer that you would withdraw for the present."

Somehow, of late, I had got into the way of involuntarily using this word "prefer" upon all sorts of not exactly suitable occasions. And I trembled to think that my contact with the scrivener had already and seriously affected me in a mental way. And what further and deeper aberration might it not yet produce? This apprehension had not been without efficacy in determining me to summary measures.

As Nippers, looking very sour and sulky, was departing, Turkey blandly and deferentially approached.

"With submission, sir," said he, "yesterday I was thinking about Bartleby here, and I think that if he would but prefer to take a quart of good ale every day, it would do much towards mending him, and enabling him to assist in examining his papers."

"So you have got the word, too," said I, slightly excited. 120

"With submission, what word, sir?" asked Turkey, respectfully crowding himself into the contracted space behind the screen, and by so doing, making me jostle the scrivener. "What word, sir?"

"I would prefer to be left alone here," said Bartleby, as if offended at being mobbed in his privacy.

"*That's* the word, Turkey," said I—"*that's* it."

"Oh, *prefer?* oh yes—queer word. I never use it myself. But, sir, as I was saying, if he would but prefer—"

"Turkey," interrupted I, "you will please withdraw."   125

"Oh certainly, sir, if you *prefer* that I should."

As he opened the folding-door to retire, Nippers at his desk caught a glimpse of me, and asked whether I would prefer to have a certain paper copied on blue paper or white. He did not in the least roguishly accent the word "prefer." It was plain that it involuntarily rolled from his tongue. I thought to myself, surely I must get rid of a demented man, who already has in some degree turned the tongues, if not the heads of myself and clerks. But I thought it prudent not to break the dismission at once.

The next day I noticed that Bartleby did nothing but stand at his window in his dead-wall revery. Upon asking him why he did not write, he said that he had decided upon doing no more writing.

"Why, how now? what next?" exclaimed I, "do no more writing?"

"No more."   130

"And what is the reason?"

"Do you not see the reason for yourself?" he indifferently replied.

I looked steadfastly at him, and perceived that his eyes looked dull and glazed. Instantly it occurred to me, that his unexampled diligence in copying by his dim window for the first few weeks of his stay with me might have temporarily impaired his vision.

I was touched. I said something in condolence with him. I hinted that of course he did wisely in abstaining from writing for a while; and urged him to embrace that opportunity of taking wholesome exercise in the open air. This, however, he did not do. A few days after this, my other clerks being absent, and being in a great hurry to dispatch certain letters by the mail, I thought that, having nothing else earthly to do, Bartleby would surely be less inflexible than usual, and carry these letters to the Post Office. But he blankly declined. So, much to my inconvenience, I went myself.

Still added days went by. Whether Bartleby's eyes improved or not, I could not   135
say. To all appearance, I thought they did. But when I asked him if they did, he vouchsafed no answer. At all events, he would do no copying. At last, in reply to my urgings, he informed me that he had permanently given up copying.

"What!" exclaimed I; "suppose your eyes should get entirely well—better than ever before—would you not copy then?"

"I have given up copying," he answered, and slid aside.

He remained as ever, a fixture in my chamber. Nay—if that were possible—he became still more of a fixture than before. What was to be done? He would do nothing in the office; why should he stay there? In plain fact, he had now become a millstone to me, not only useless as a necklace, but afflictive to bear. Yet I was sorry for him. I speak less than truth when I say that, on his own account, he occasioned me uneasiness. If he would but have named a single relative or friend, I would instantly have written, and urged their taking the poor fellow away to some convenient retreat. But he seemed alone, absolutely alone in the universe. A bit of wreck in the mid-Atlantic. At length, necessities connected with my business tyrannized over all other considerations. Decently as I could, I told Bartleby that in six days' time he must unconditionally leave the office. I warned him to take measures, in the interval, for procuring some other abode. I offered to assist him in this endeavor, if he himself would but take the first step towards a removal. "And when you finally quit me, Bartleby," added I, "I shall see that you go not away entirely unprovided. Six days from this hour, remember."

At the expiration of that period, I peeped behind the screen, and lo! Bartleby was there.

I buttoned up my coat, balanced myself; advanced slowly towards him, touched his 140 shoulder, and said, "The time has come; you must quit this place; I am sorry for you; here is money; but you must go."

"I would prefer not," he replied, with his back still towards me.

"You *must*."

He remained silent.

Now I had an unbounded confidence in this man's common honesty. He had frequently restored to me sixpences and shillings carelessly dropped upon the floor, for I am apt to be very reckless in such shirt-button affairs. The proceeding, then, which followed will not be deemed extraordinary.

"Bartleby," said I, "I owe you twelve dollars on account; here are thirty-two; the 145 odd twenty are yours—Will you take it?" and I handed the bills towards him.

But he made no motion.

"I will leave them here, then," putting them under a weight on the table. Then taking my hat and cane and going to the door, I tranquilly turned and added—"After you have removed your things from these offices, Bartleby, you will of course lock the door—since every one is now gone for the day but you—and if you please, slip your key underneath the mat, so that I may have it in the morning. I shall not see you again; so good-by to you. If, hereafter, in your new place of abode, I can be of any service to you, do not fail to advise me by letter. Good-by, Bartleby, and fare you well."

But he answered not a word; like the last column of some ruined temple, he remained standing mute and solitary in the middle of the otherwise deserted room.

As I walked home in a pensive mood, my vanity got the better of my pity. I could not but highly plume myself on my masterly management in getting rid of Bartleby. Masterly I call it, and such it must appear to any dispassionate thinker. The beauty of my procedure seemed to consist in its perfect quietness. There was no vulgar bullying, no bravado of any sort, no choleric hectoring, and striding to and fro across the apartment, jerking out vehement commands for Bartleby to bundle himself off with his beggarly traps. Nothing of the kind. Without loudly bidding Bartleby depart—as an inferior genius might have done—I *assumed* the ground that depart he must; and upon that assumption built all I had to say. The more I thought over my procedure, the more I was charmed with it. Nevertheless, next morning, upon awakening, I had my doubts—I had somehow slept off the fumes of vanity. One of the coolest and wisest hours a man has, is just after he awakes in the morning. My procedure seemed as sagacious as ever—but only in theory. How it would prove in practice—there was the rub. It was truly a beautiful thought to have assumed Bartleby's departure; but, after all, that assumption was simply my own, and none of Bartleby's. The great point was, not whether I had assumed that he would quit me, but whether he would prefer so to do. He was more a man of preferences than assumptions.

After breakfast, I walked down town, arguing the probabilities *pro* and *con*. One 150 moment I thought it would prove a miserable failure, and Bartleby would be found all alive at my office as usual; the next moment it seemed certain that I should find his chair empty. And so I kept veering about. At the corner of Broadway and Canal Street, I saw quite an excited group of people standing in earnest conversation.

"I'll take odds he doesn't," said a voice as I passed.

"Doesn't go?—done!" said I, "put up your money."

I was instinctively putting my hand in my pocket to produce my own, when I remembered that this was an election day. The words I had overheard bore no reference to Bartleby, but to the success or non-success of some candidate for the mayoralty. In my intent frame of mind, I had, as it were, imagined that all Broadway shared in my excitement, and were debating the same question with me. I passed on, very thankful that the uproar of the street screened my momentary absent-mindedness.

As I had intended, I was earlier than usual at my office door. I stood listening for a moment. All was still. He must be gone. I tried the knob. The door was locked. Yes, my procedure had worked to a charm; he indeed must be vanished. Yet a certain melancholy mixed with this: I was almost sorry for my brilliant success. I was fumbling under the door mat for the key, which Bartleby was to have left there for me, when accidentally my knee knocked against a panel, producing a summoning sound, and in response a voice came to me from within—"Not yet; I am occupied."

It was Bartleby.   155

I was thunderstruck. For an instant I stood like the man who, pipe in mouth, was killed one cloudless afternoon long ago in Virginia, by summer lightning; at his own warm open window he was killed, and remained leaning out there upon the dreamy afternoon, till some one touched him, when he fell.

"Not gone!" I murmured at last. But again obeying that wondrous ascendancy which the inscrutable scrivener had over me, and from which ascendancy, for all my chafing, I could not completely escape, I slowly went down stairs and out into the street, and while walking round the block, considered what I should next do in this unheard-of perplexity. Turn the man out by an actual thrusting I could not; to drive him away by calling him hard names would not do; calling in the police was an unpleasant idea; and yet, permit him to enjoy his cadaverous triumph over me—this, too, I could not think of. What was to be done? or, if nothing could be done, was there anything further that I could *assume* in the matter? Yes, as before I had prospectively assumed that Bartleby would depart, so now I might retrospectively assume that departed he was. In the legitimate carrying out of this assumption, I might enter my office in a great hurry, and pretending not to see Bartleby at all, walk straight against him as if he were air. Such a proceeding would in a singular degree have the appearance of a homethrust. It was hardly possible that Bartleby could withstand such an application of the doctrine of assumptions. But upon second thoughts the success of the plan seemed rather dubious. I resolved to argue the matter over with him again.

"Bartleby," said I, entering the office, with a quietly severe expression, "I am seriously displeased. I am pained, Bartleby. I had thought better of you. I had imagine you of such a gentlemanly organization, that in any delicate dilemma a slight hint would suffice—in short, an assumption. But it appears I am deceived. Why," I added, unaffectedly starting, "you have not even touched that money yet," pointing to it, just where I had left it the evening previous.

He answered nothing.

"Will you, or will you not, quit me?" I now demanded in a sudden passion, ad-   160
vancing close to him.

"I would prefer *not* to quit you," he replied, gently emphasizing the *not*.

"What earthly right have you to stay here? Do you pay any rent? Do you pay my taxes? Or is this property yours?"

He answered nothing.

"Are you ready to go on and write now? Are your eyes recovered? Could you copy a small paper for me this morning? or help examine a few lines? or step round to the Post Office? In a word, will you do anything at all, to give a coloring to your refusal to depart the premises?"

He silently retired into his hermitage.   165

I was now in such a state of nervous resentment that I thought it but prudent to check myself at present from further demonstrations. Bartleby and I were alone. I remembered the tragedy of the unfortunate Adams and the still more unfortunate Colt in the solitary office of the latter; and how poor Colt, being dreadfully incensed by Adams, and imprudently permitted himself to get wildly excited, was at unawares hurried into his fatal act—an act which certainly no man could possibly deplore more than the actor himself. Often it had occurred to me in my ponderings upon the subject that had that altercation taken place in the public street, or at a private residence, it would not have terminated as it did. It was the circumstance of being alone in a solitary office, up stairs, of a building entirely unhallowed by humanizing domestic associations—an uncarpeted office, doubtless, of a dusty, haggard sort of appearance—this it must have been, which greatly helped to enhance the irritable desperation of the hapless Colt.

But when this old Adam of resentment rose in me and tempted me concerning Bartleby, I grappled him and threw him. How? Why, simply by recalling the divine injunction: "A new commandment give I unto you, that ye love one another." Yes, this it was that saved me. Aside from higher considerations, charity often operates as a vastly wise and prudent principle—a great safeguard to its possessor. Men have committed murder for jealousy's sake, and anger's sake, and hatred's sake, and selfishness' sake, and spiritual pride's sake; but no man, that ever I heard of, ever committed a diabolical murder for sweet charity's sake. Mere self-interest, then, if no better motive can be enlisted, should, especially with high-tempered men, prompt all beings to charity and philanthropy. At any rate, upon the occasion in question, I strove to drown my exasperated feelings towards the scrivener by benevolently construing his conduct. Poor fellow, poor fellow! thought I, he don't mean anything; and besides, he has seen hard times, and ought to be indulged.

I endeavored, also, immediately to occupy myself, and at the same time to comfort my despondency. I tried to fancy, that in the course of the morning, at such time as might prove agreeable to him, Bartleby, of his own free accord, would emerge from his hermitage and take up some decided line of march in the direction of the door. But no. Half-past twelve o'clock came; Turkey began to glow in the face, overturn his inkstand, and become generally obstreperous; Nippers abated down into quietude and courtesy; Ginger Nut munched his noon apple; and Bartleby remained standing at his window in one of his profoundest dead-wall reveries. Will it be credited? Ought I to acknowledge it? That afternoon I left the office without saying one further word to him.

Some days now passed, during which, at leisure intervals I looked a little into "Edwards on the Will," and "Priestley on Necessity." Under the circumstances, those books induced a salutary feeling. Gradually I slid into the persuasion that these troubles of mine, touching the scrivener, had been all predestinated from eternity, and Bartleby was billeted upon me for some mysterious purpose of an all-wise Providence, which it was not for a mere mortal like me to fathom. Yes, Bartleby, stay there behind your screen, thought I; I shall persecute you no more; you are harmless and noiseless as any of these old chairs; in short, I never feel so private as when I know you are here. At last I see it, I feel it; I penetrate to the predestinated purpose of my life. I am content. Others may have loftier parts to enact; but my mission in this world, Bartleby, is to furnish you with office-room for such period as you may see fit to remain.

I believe that this wise and blessed frame of mind would have continued with me, had it not been for the unsolicited and uncharitable remarks obtruded upon me by my professional friends who visited the rooms. But thus it often is, that the constant friction of illiberal minds wears out at last the best resolves of the more generous. Though to be sure, when I reflected upon it, it was not strange that people entering my office should be struck by the peculiar aspect of the unaccountable Bartleby, and so be tempted to throw out some sinister observations concerning him. Sometimes an attorney, having business with me, and calling at my office, and finding no one but the scrivener

170

OTHER VOICES/OTHER VISIONS

there, would undertake to obtain some sort of precise information from him touching my whereabouts; but without heeding his idle talk, Bartleby would remain standing immovable in the middle of the room. So after contemplating him in that position for a time, the attorney would depart, no wiser than he came.

Also, when a reference was going on, and the room full of lawyers and witnesses, and business driving fast, some deeply-occupied legal gentleman present, seeing Bartleby wholly unemployed, would request him to run round to his (the legal gentleman's) office and fetch some papers for him. Thereupon, Bartleby would tranquilly decline, and yet remain idle as before. Then the lawyer would give a great stare, and turn to me. And what could I say? At last I was made aware that all through the circle of my professional acquaintance, a whisper of wonder was running round, having reference to the strange creature I kept at my office. This worried me very much. And as the idea came upon me of his possibly turning out a long-lived man, and keep occupying my chambers, and denying my authority; and perplexing my visitors; and scandalizing my professional reputation; and casting a general gloom over the premises; keeping soul and body together to the last upon his savings (for doubtless he spent but half a dime a day), and in the end perhaps outlive me, and claim possession of my office by right of his perpetual occupancy: as all these dark anticipations crowded upon me more and more, and my friends continually intruded their relentless remarks upon the apparition in my room; a great change was wrought in me. I resolved to gather all my faculties together, and forever rid me of this intolerable incubus.

Ere revolving any complicated project, however, adapted to this end, I first simply suggested to Bartleby the propriety of his permanent departure. In a calm and serious tone, I commended the idea to his careful and mature consideration. But, having taken three days to meditate upon it, he apprised me, that his original determination remained the same; in short, that he still preferred to abide with me.

What shall I do? I now said to myself, buttoning up my coat to the last button. What shall I do? what ought I to do? what does conscience say I *should* do with this man, or, rather, ghost. Rid myself of him, I must; go, he shall. But how? You will not thrust him, the poor, pale, passive mortal—you will not thrust such a helpless creature out of your door? you will not dishonor yourself by such cruelty? No, I will not, I cannot do that. Rather would I let him live and die here, and then mason up his remains in the wall. What, then, will you do? For all your coaxing, he will not budge. Bribes he leaves under your own paperweight on your table; in short, it is quite plain that he prefers to cling to you.

Then something severe, something unusual must be done. What! surely you will not have him collared by a constable, and commit his innocent pallor to the common jail? And upon what ground could you procure such a thing to be done?—a vagrant, is he? What! he a vagrant, a wanderer, who refuses to budge? It is because he will *not* be a vagrant, then, that you seek to count him *as* a vagrant. That is too absurd. No visible means of support: there I have him. Wrong again: for indubitably he *does* support himself, and that is the only unanswerable proof that any man can show of his possessing the means so to do. No more, then. Since he will not quit me, I must quit him. I will change my offices; I will move elsewhere, and give him fair notice, that if I find him on my new premises I will then proceed against him as a common trespasser.

Acting accordingly, next day I thus addressed him: "I find these chambers too far from the City Hall; the air is unwholesome. In a word, I propose to remove my offices next week, and shall no longer require your services. I tell you this now, in order that you may seek another place."

He made no reply, and nothing more was said.

On the appointed day I engaged carts and men, proceeded to my chambers, and, having but little furniture, everything was removed in a few hours. Throughout, the scrivener remained standing behind the screen, which I directed to be removed the last thing. It was withdrawn; and, being folded up like a huge folio, left him the motionless occupant of a naked room. I stood in the entry watching him a moment, while something from within me upbraided me.

I re-entered, with my hand in my pocket—and—and my heart in my mouth.

"Good-by, Bartleby; I am going—good-by, and God some way bless you; and take that," slipping something in his hand. But it dropped upon the floor, and then—strange to say—I tore myself from him whom I had so longed to be rid of.

Established in my new quarters, for a day or two I kept the door locked, and start- 180 ed at every footfall in the passages. When I returned to my rooms, after any little absence, I would pause at the threshold for an instant, and attentively listen, ere applying my key. But these fears were needless. Bartleby never came nigh me.

I thought all was going well, when a perturbed-looking stranger visited me, inquiring whether I was the person who had recently occupied rooms at No. — Wall Street.

Full of forebodings, I replied that I was.

"Then, sir," said the stranger, who proved a lawyer, "you are responsible for the man you left there. He refuses to do any copying; he refuses to do anything; he says he prefers not to; and he refuses to quit the premises."

"I am very sorry, sir," said I, with assumed tranquillity, but an inward tremor, "but, really, the man you allude to is nothing to me—he is no relation or apprentice of mine, that you should hold me responsible for him."

"In mercy's name, who is he?" 185

"I certainly cannot inform you. I know nothing about him. Formerly I employed him as a copyist; but he has done nothing for me now for some time past."

"I shall settle him, then—good morning, sir."

Several days passed, and I heard nothing more; and, though I often felt a charitable prompting to call at the place and see poor Bartleby, yet a certain squeamishness, of I know not what, withheld me.

All is over with him, by this time, thought I, at last, when, through another week, no further intelligence reached me. But, coming to my room the day after, I found several persons waiting at my door in a high state of nervous excitement.

"That's the man—here he comes," cried the foremost one, whom I recognized as 190 the lawyer who had previously called upon me alone.

"You must take him away, sir, at once," cried a portly person among them, advancing upon me, and whom I knew to be the landlord of No. — Wall Street. "These gentlemen, my tenants, cannot stand it any longer; Mr. B——," pointing to the lawyer, "has turned him out of his room, and he now persists in haunting the building generally, sitting upon the banisters of the stairs by day, and sleeping in the entry by night. Everybody is concerned; clients are leaving the offices; some fears are entertained of a mob; something you must do, and that without delay."

Aghast at this torrent, I fell back before it, and would fain have locked myself in my new quarters. In vain I persisted that Bartleby was nothing to me—no more than to any one else. In vain—I was the last person known to have anything to do with him, and they held me to the terrible account. Fearful, then, of being exposed in the papers (as one person present obscurely threatened), I considered the matter, and, at length, said, that if the lawyer would give me a confidential interview with the scrivener, in his (the lawyer's) own room, I would, that afternoon, strive my best to rid them of the nuisance they complained of.

516 OTHER VOICES/OTHER VISIONS

Going up stairs to my old haunt, there was Bartleby silently sitting upon the banister at the landing.

"What are you doing here, Bartleby?" said I.

"Sitting upon the banister," he mildly replied.   195

I motioned him into the lawyer's room, who then left us.

"Bartleby," said I, "are you aware that you are the cause of great tribulation to me, by persisting in occupying the entry after being dismissed from the office?"

No answer.

"Now one of two things must take place. Either you must do something, or something must be done to you. Now what sort of business would you like to engage in? Would you like to re-engage in copying for some one?"

"No; I would prefer not to make any change."   200

"Would you like a clerkship in a dry-goods store?"

"There is too much confinement about that. No, I would not like a clerkship; but I am not particular."

"Too much confinement," I cried, "why, you keep yourself confined all the time!"

"I would prefer not to take a clerkship," he rejoined, as if to settle that little item at once.

"How would a bar-tender's business suit you? There is no trying of the eye-sight   205
in that."

"I would not like it at all; though, as I said before, I am not particular."

His unwonted wordiness inspirited me. I returned to the charge.

"Well, then, would you like to travel through the country collecting bills for the merchants? That would improve your health."

"No, I would prefer to be doing something else."

"How, then, would going as a companion to Europe, to entertain some young   210
gentleman with your conversation—how would that suit you?"

"Not at all. It does not strike me that there is anything definite about that. I like to be stationary. But I am not particular."

"Stationary you shall be, then," I cried, now losing all patience, and, for the first time in all my exasperating connection with him, fairly flying into a passion. "If you do not go away from these premises before night, I shall feel bound—indeed, I *am* bound—to—to—to quit the premises myself!" I rather absurdly concluded, knowing not with what possible threat to try to frighten his immobility into compliance. Despairing of all further efforts, I was precipitately leaving him, when a final thought occurred to me—one which had not been wholly unindulged before.

"Bartleby," said I, in the kindest tone I could assume under such exciting circumstances, "will you go home with me now—not to my office, but my dwelling—and remain there till we can conclude upon some convenient arrangement for you at our leisure? Come, let us start now, right away."

"No: at present I would prefer not to make any change at all."

I answered nothing; but, effectually dodging every one by the suddenness and ra-   215
pidity of my flight, rushed from the building, ran up Wall Street towards Broadway, and, jumping into the first omnibus, was soon removed from pursuit. As soon as tranquillity returned, I distinctly perceived that I had now done all that I possibly could, both in respect to the demands of the landlord and his tenants, and with regard to my own desire and sense of duty, to benefit Bartleby, and shield him from rude persecution. I now strove to be entirely care-free and quiescent; and my conscience justified me in the attempt; though, indeed, it was not so successful as I could have wished. So fearful was I of being again hunted out by the incensed landlord and his exasperated ten-

ants, that, surrendering my business to Nippers, for a few days, I drove about the upper part of the town and through the suburbs, in my rockaway; crossed over to Jersey City and Hoboken, and paid fugitive visits to Manhattanville and Astoria. In fact, I almost lived in my rockaway for the time.

When again I entered my office, lo, a note from the landlord lay upon the desk. I opened it with trembling hands. It informed me that the writer had sent to the police, and had Bartleby removed to the Tombs as a vagrant. Moreover, since I knew more about him than any one else, he wished me to appear at that place, and make a suitable statement of the facts. These tidings had a conflicting effect upon me. At first I was indignant; but, at last, almost approved. The landlord's energetic, summary disposition, had led him to adopt a procedure which I do not think I would have decided upon myself; and yet, as a last resort, under such peculiar circumstances, it seemed the only plan.

As I afterwards learned, the poor scrivener, when told that he must be conducted to the Tombs, offered not the slightest obstacle, but, in his pale, unmoving way, silently acquiesced.

Some of the compassionate and curious bystanders joined the party; and headed by one of the constables arm-in-arm with Bartleby, the silent procession filed its way through all the noise, and heat, and joy of the roaring thoroughfares at noon.

The same day I received the note, I went to the Tombs, or, to speak more properly, the Halls of Justice. Seeking the right officer, I stated the purpose of my call, and was informed that the individual I described was, indeed, within. I then assured the functionary that Bartleby was a perfectly honest man, and greatly to be compassionated, however unaccountably eccentric. I narrated all I knew, and closed by suggesting the idea of letting him remain in as indulgent confinement as possible, till something less harsh might be done—though, indeed, I hardly knew what. At all events, if nothing else could be decided upon, the alms-house must receive him. I then begged to have an interview.

Being under no disgraceful charge, and quite serene and harmless in all his ways,   220
they had permitted him freely to wander about the prison, and, especially, in the inclosed grass-platted yards thereof. And so I found him there, standing all alone in the quietest of the yards, his face towards a high wall, while all around, from the narrow slits of the jail windows, I thought I saw peering out upon him the eyes of murderers and thieves.

"Bartleby!"

"I know you," he said, without looking round—"and I want nothing to say to you."

"It was not I that brought you here, Bartleby," said I, keenly pained at his implied suspicion. "And to you, this should not be so vile a place. Nothing reproachful attaches to you by being here. And see, it is not so sad a place as one might think. Look, there is the sky, and here is the grass."

"I know where I am," he replied, but would say nothing more, and so I left him.

As I entered the corridor again, a broad meat-like man, in an apron, accosted me,   225
and, jerking his thumb over his shoulder, said—"Is that your friend?"

"Yes."

"Does he want to starve? If he does, let him live on the prison fare, that's all."

"Who are you?" asked I, not knowing what to make of such an unofficially speaking person in such a place.

"I am the grub-man. Such gentlemen as have friends here, hire me to provide them with something good to eat."

"Is this so?" said I, turning to the turnkey.   230

He said it was.

"Well, then," said I, slipping some silver into the grub-man's hands (for so they called him), "I want you to give particular attention to my friend there; let him have the best dinner you can get. And you must be as polite to him as possible."

"Introduce me, will you?" said the grub-man, looking at me with an expression which seemed to say he was all impatience for an opportunity to give a specimen of his breeding.

Thinking it would prove of benefit to the scrivener, I acquiesced; and, asking the grub-man his name, went up with him to Bartleby.

"Bartleby, this is a friend; you will find him very useful to you."   235

"Your savrant, sir, your sarvant," said the grub-man, making a low salutation behind his apron. "Hope you find it pleasant here, sir; nice grounds—cool apartments— hope you'll stay with us some time—try to make it agreeable. What will you have for dinner today?"

"I prefer not to dine today," said Bartleby, turning away. "It would disagree with me; I am unused to dinners." So saying, he slowly moved to the other side of the inclosure, and took up a position fronting the dead-wall.

"How's this?" said the grub-man, addressing me with a stare of astonishment. "He's odd, ain't he?"

"I think he is a little deranged," said I, sadly.

"Deranged? deranged is it? Well, now, upon my word, I thought that friend of   240 yourn was a gentleman forger; they are always pale and genteel-like, them forgers. I can't help pity 'em—can't help it, sir. Did you know Monroe Edwards?" he added, touchingly, and paused. Then, laying his hand piteously on my shoulder, sighed, "he died of consumption at Sing-Sing. So you weren't acquainted with Monroe?"

"No, I was never socially acquainted with any forgers. But I cannot stop longer. Look to my friend yonder. You will not lose by it. I will see you again."

Some few days after this, I again obtained admission to the Tombs, and went through the corridors in quest of Bartleby; but without finding him.

"I saw him coming from his cell not long ago," said a turnkey, "may be he's gone to loiter in the yards."

So I went in that direction.

"Are you looking for the silent man?" said another turnkey, passing me. "Yonder   245 he lies—sleeping in the yard there. 'Tis not twenty minutes since I saw him lie down."

The yard was entirely quiet. It was not accessible to the common prisoners. The surrounding walls, of amazing thickness, kept off all sounds behind them. The Egyptian character of the masonry weighed upon me with its gloom. But a soft imprisoned turf grew under foot. The heart of the eternal pyramids, it seemed, wherein, by some strange magic, through the clefts, grass-seed, dropped by birds, had sprung.

Strangely huddled at the base of the wall, his knees drawn up, and lying on his side, his head touching the cold stones, I saw the wasted Bartleby. But nothing stirred. I paused; then went close up to him; stooped over, and saw that his dim eyes were open; otherwise he seemed profoundly sleeping. Something prompted me to touch him. I felt his hand, when a tingling shiver ran up my arm and down my spine to my feet.

The round face of the grub-man peered upon me now. "His dinner is ready. Won't he dine today, either? Or does he live without dining?"

"Lives without dining," said I, and closed the eyes.

"Eh!—He's asleep, ain't he?"   250

"With kings and counselors," murmured I.

There would seem little need for proceeding further in this history. Imagination will readily supply the meagre recital of poor Bartleby's interment. But, ere parting with the reader, let me say, that if this little narrative has sufficiently interested him, to awaken curiosity as to who Bartleby was, and what manner of life he led prior to the present narrator's making his acquaintance, I can only reply, that in such curiosity I fully share, but am wholly unable to gratify it. Yet here I hardly know whether I should divulge one little item of rumor, which came to my ear a few months after the scrivener's decease. Upon what basis it rested, I could never ascertain; and hence, how true it is I cannot now tell. But, inasmuch as this vague report has not been without a certain suggestive interest to me, however sad, it may prove the same with some others; and so I will briefly mention it. The report was this: that Bartleby had been a subordinate clerk in the Dead Letter Office at Washington, from which he had been suddenly removed by a change in the administration. When I think over this rumor, hardly can I express the emotions which seize me. Dead letters! does it not sound like dead men? Conceive a man by nature and misfortune prone to a pallid hopelessness, can any business seem more fitted to heighten it than that of continually handling these dead letters, and assorting them for the flames? For by the cartload they are annually burned. Sometimes from out the folded paper the pale clerk takes a ring—the finger it was meant for, perhaps, moulders in the grave; a bank-note sent in swiftest charity—he whom it would relieve, nor eats nor hungers any more; pardon for those who died despairing; hope for those who died unhoping; good tidings for those who died stifled by unrelieved calamities. On errands of life, these letters speed to death.

Ah, Bartleby! Ah, humanity!

COMMENTARY

In a letter he wrote to Hawthorne in 1851, Melville, speaking of his friend in the third person, offered him this praise: "There is the grand truth about Nathaniel Hawthorne. He says NO! in thunder; but the Devil himself cannot make him say *yes*. For all men who say *yes*, lie. . . ." Melville was referring to Hawthorne's relation to the moral order of the universe as it is conventionally imagined, but his statement, which has become famous, is often read as Melville's own call to resist the conformity that society seeks to impose. It was taken in this way by one of the notable students of Melville, Richard Chase, who quotes it at the beginning of an account of Melville's attitude toward the American life of his time and goes on to say that "although Melville was not exclusively a nay-sayer, his experiences and his reflections upon the quality of American civilization had taught him to utter the powerful 'no' he attributes to Hawthorne. He learned to say 'no' to the boundlessly optimistic commercialized creed of most Americans, with its superficial and mean conception of the possibilities of human life, its denial of all the genuinely creative or heroic capacities of man, and its fear and dislike of any but the mildest truths. Melville's 'no' finds expression in the tragic-comic tale of 'Bartleby the Scrivener.' . . ."

But although this great story tells of a nay-saying of a quite ultimate kind, perhaps the first thing we notice about Bartleby's "no" is how far it is from being uttered "in thunder." And exactly its distance from thunder makes the negation as momentous as it is; the contrast between the extent of Bartleby's refusal and the minimal way in which he expresses it accounts for the story's strange force, its mythic impressiveness. Whether he is being asked to accommodate himself to the routine of his job in the law office or to the simplest requirements of life itself, Bartleby makes the same answer, "'I prefer not to'"—the phrase is prim, genteel, rather finicking; the negative volition it expresses seems to be of a very low intensity. Melville is at pains to point up the odd inadequacy of that word *prefer* by the passage in which he tells how it was unconsciously adopted into the speech of the narrator and his office staff, and with what comic effect.

Actually, of course, the small, muted phrase that Bartleby chooses for his negation is the measure of his intransigence. A "NO! in thunder" implies that the person who utters it is involved with and has strong feelings about whatever it is that he rejects or opposes. The louder his thunder, the greater is his (and our) belief in the power, the interest, the real existence of what he negates. Bartleby's colorless formula of refusal has the opposite effect—in refusing to display articulate anger against the social order he rejects, our poor taciturn nay-sayer denies its interest and any claim it may have on his attention and reason. "'I prefer not to'" implies that reason is not in point; the choice that is being made does not need the substantiation of reason: it is, as it were, a matter of "taste," even of whim, an act of pure volition, having reference to nothing but the nature of the agent. Or the muted minimal phrase might be read as an expression of the extremest possible arrogance—this Bartleby detaches himself from all human need or desire and acts at no behest other than that of his own unconditioned will.

It is possible that Melville never heard of Karl Marx, although the two men were contemporaries, but Melville's "story of Wall Street" exemplifies in a very striking way the concept of human alienation which plays an important part in Marx's early philosophical writings and has had considerable influence on later sociological thought. Alienation is the condition in which one acts as if at the behest not of one's own will but of some will other (Latin: *alius*) than one's own. For Marx its most important manifestation is in what he called "alienated labor," although he suggested that the phrase was redundant, since all labor is an alienated activity. In Latin *labor* has the meaning of pain and weariness as well as of work that causes pain and weariness, and we use the word to denote work that is in some degree enforced and that goes against the grain of human nature: a culprit is sentenced to a term of "hard labor," not of "hard work." By the same token, not all work is alienated; Marx cites the work of the artist as an example of free activity, happily willed, gratifying and dignifying those who perform it.

In undertaking to explain the reason for the alienated condition of man, Marx refused to accept the idea that it is brought about by the necessities of survival. Man, he said, can meet these necessities with the consciousness of free will, with the sense that he is at one with himself; it is society that alienates man from himself. And Marx held that alienation is at its extreme in those societies which are governed by money-values. In a spirited passage, he describes the process of accumulating capital in terms of the sacrifice of the free human activities that it entails: "The less you eat, drink, and read books; the less you go to the theatre, the dance hall, the public-house; the less you think, love, theorize, sing, paint, fence, etc., and the more you *save*—the greater becomes your treasure which neither moth nor dust will devour—your *capital*. The less you *are*, the more you *have*; the less you express your own life, the greater is your *externalized* life—the greater is the store of your alienated being." This describes the program for success in a money society; it was followed, we may note, in his early days by John Jacob Astor, who commands the ironized respect of the narrator of "Bartleby the Scrivener," and no doubt to some extent by the narrator himself. Those members of a money society who do not consent to submit to the program are, of course, no less alienated, and they do not have the comforting illusion of freedom that the power of money can give.

It can be said of Bartleby that he behaves quite as if he were devoting himself to capitalist accumulation. He withdraws from one free human activity after another. If

5

"the theater, the dance hall, the public-house" had ever been within his ken, they are now far beyond it. If there had ever been a time when he delighted to "think, love, theorize, sing, paint, fence, etc.," it has long gone by. He never drinks. He eats less and less, eventually not at all. But of course nothing is further from his intention than accumulation—the self-denial he practices has been instituted in the interests of his freedom, a sad, abstract, metaphysical freedom but the only one he can aspire to. In the degree that he diminishes his self, he is the less an alienated self: his will is free, he cannot be compelled. A theory of suicide advanced by Sigmund Freud is in point here. It proposes the idea that the suicide's chief although unconscious purpose is to destroy not himself but some other person whom he has incorporated into his psychic fabric and whom he conceives to have great malign authority over him. Bartleby, by his gradual self-annihilation, annihilates the social order as it exists within himself.

An important complication is added to the story of Bartleby's fate by the character and the plight of the nameless narrator. No one could have behaved in a more forebearing and compassionate way than this good-tempered gentleman. He suffers long and is kind; he finds it hard, almost impossible, to do what common sense has long dictated he should do—have Bartleby expelled from the office by force—and he goes so far in charity as to offer to take Bartleby into his own home. Yet he feels that he has incurred guilt by eventually separating himself from Bartleby, and we think it appropriate that he should feel so, even while we sympathize with him; and in making this judgment we share his guilt. It is to him that Bartleby's only moment of anger is directed: "'I know you,'" says Bartleby in the prison yard, "' and I want nothing to say to you.'" The narrator is "keenly pained at his implied suspicion" that it was through his agency that Bartleby had been imprisoned, and we are pained for him, knowing the suspicion to be unfounded and unjust. Yet we know why it was uttered.

Bartleby's "I prefer not to" is spoken always in response to an order or request having to do with business utility. We may speculate about what would have happened if the narrator or one of Bartleby's fellow-copyists, alone with him in the office, had had occasion to say, "Bartleby, I feel sick and faint. Would you help me to the couch and fetch me a glass of water?" Perhaps the answer would have been given: "'I prefer not to.'" But perhaps not.

TONI MORRISON (born 1931)
1920 1973

[This section of Toni Morrison's novel *Sula* focuses on Nel Wright's family and its past. As the title indicates, the story takes place in November 1920, the second anniversary of the armistice ending World War I. The setting is the segregated South, where white men stand like *wrecked Dorics,* or heavy Greek columns, eyeing the movements of black Americans. In New Orleans some people speak Creole, a form of French. The Creole terms in the story include *Vrai?* (Is that true?), *chère* (dear), *Comment t'appelle?* (What's your name?), *oui* (yes), and *'Voir* (short for *Au revoir*—see you again). The *Frenchified shotgun house* is a house in which all the rooms are in line front to back. Elysian Fields is a major street running through the poor section of New Orleans; the name is ironic, since in Greek mythology the Elysian Fields are the abode of the blessed after death, thus any place or state of perfect bliss.]

It had to be as far away from the Sundown House as possible. And her grandmother's middle-aged nephew who lived in a Northern town called Medallion was the one chance she had to make sure it would be. The red shutters had haunted both Helene Sabat and her grandmother for sixteen years. Helene was born behind those shutters, daughter of a Creole whore who worked there. The grandmother took Helene away from the soft lights and flowered carpets of the Sundown House and raised her under the dolesome eyes of a multicolored Virgin Mary, counseling her to be constantly on guard for any sign of her mother's wild blood.

So when Wiley Wright came to visit his Great Aunt Cecile in New Orleans, his enchantment with the pretty Helene became a marriage proposal—under the pressure of both women. He was a seaman (or rather a lakeman, for he was a ship's cook on one of the Great Lakes lines), in port only three days out of every sixteen.

He took his bride to his home in Medallion and put her in a lovely house with a brick porch and real lace curtains at the window. His long absences were quite bearable for Helene Wright, especially when, after some nine years of marriage, her daughter was born.

Her daughter was more comfort and purpose than she had ever hoped to find in this life. She rose grandly to the occasion of motherhood—grateful, deep down in her heart, that the child had not inherited the great beauty that was hers: that her skin had dusk in it, that her lashes were substantial but not undignified in their length, that she had taken the broad flat nose of Wiley (although Helene expected to improve it somewhat) and his generous lips.

Under Helene's hand the girl became obedient and polite. Any enthusiasms that little Nel showed were calmed by the mother until she drove her daughter's imagination underground. 5

Helene Wright was an impressive woman, at least in Medallion she was. Heavy hair in a bun, dark eyes arched in a perpetual query about other people's manners. A woman who won all social battles with presence and a conviction of the legitimacy of her authority. Since there was no Catholic church in Medallion then, she joined the most conservative black church. And held sway. It was Helene who never turned her head in church when latecomers arrived; Helene who established the practice of seasonal altar flowers; Helene who introduced the giving of banquets of welcome to returning Negro veterans. She lost only one battle—the pronunciation of her name. The people in the Bottom refused to say Helene. They called her Helen Wright and left it at that.

All in all her life was a satisfactory one. She loved her house and enjoyed manipulating her daughter and her husband. She would sigh sometimes just before falling asleep, thinking that she had indeed come far enough away from the Sundown House.

So it was with extremely mixed emotions that she read a letter from Mr. Henri Martin describing the illness of her grandmother, and suggesting she come down right away. She didn't want to go, but could not bring herself to ignore the silent plea of the woman who had rescued her.

It was November. November, 1920. Even in Medallion there was a victorious swagger in the legs of white men and a dull-eyed excitement in the eyes of colored veterans.

Helene thought about the trip South with heavy misgiving but decided that she 10 had the best protection: her manner and her bearing, to which she would add a beautiful dress. She bought some deep-brown wool and three-fourths of a yard of matching velvet. Out of this she made herself a heavy but elegant dress with velvet collar and pockets.

Nel watched her mother cutting the pattern from newspapers and moving her eyes rapidly from a magazine model to her own hands. She watched her turn up the kerosene lamp at sunset to sew far into the night.

The day they were ready, Helene cooked a smoked ham, left a note for her lake-bound husband, in case he docked early, and walked head high and arms stiff with luggage ahead of her daughter to the train depot.

It was a longer walk than she remembered, and they saw the train steaming up just as they turned the corner. They ran along the track looking for the coach pointed out to them by the colored porter. Even at that they made a mistake. Helene and her daughter entered a coach peopled by some twenty white men and women. Rather than go back and down the three wooden steps again, Helene decided to spare herself some embarrassment and walk on through to the colored car. She carried two pieces of luggage and a string purse; her daughter carried a covered basket of food.

As they opened the door marked COLORED ONLY, they saw a white conductor coming toward them. It was a chilly day but a light skim of sweat glistened on the woman's face as she and the little girl struggled to hold the door open, hang on to their luggage and enter all at once. The conductor let his eyes travel over the pale yellow woman and then stuck his little finger into his ear, jiggling it free of wax. "What you think you doin', gal?"

Helene looked up at him.   15

So soon. So soon. She hadn't even begun the trip back. Back to her grandmother's house in the city where the red shutters glowed, and already she had been called "gal." All the old vulnerabilities, all the old fears of being somehow flawed gathered in her stomach and made her hands tremble. She had heard only that one word; it dangled above her wide-brimmed hat, which had slipped, in her exertion, from its carefully leveled placement and was now tilted in a bit of a jaunt over her eye.

Thinking he wanted her tickets, she quickly dropped both the cowhide suitcase and the straw one in order to search for them in her purse. An eagerness to please and an apology for living met in her voice. "I have them. Right here somewhere, sir . . ."

The conductor looked at the bit of wax his fingernail had retrieved. "What was you doin' back in there? What was you doin' in that coach yonder?"

Helene licked her lips. "Oh . . . I . . ." Her glance moved beyond the white man's face to the passengers seated behind him. Four or five black faces were watching, two belonging to soldiers still in their shit-colored uniforms and peaked caps. She saw their closed faces, their locked eyes, and turned for compassion to the gray eyes of the conductor.

"We made a mistake, sir. You see, there wasn't no sign. We just got in the wrong   20
car, that's all. Sir."

"We don't 'low no mistakes on this train. Now git your butt on in there."

He stood there staring at her until she realized that he wanted her to move aside. Pulling Nel by the arm, she pressed herself and her daughter into the foot space in front of a wooden seat. Then, for no earthly reason, at least no reason that anybody could understand, certainly no reason that Nel understood then or later, she smiled. Like a street pup that wags its tail at the very doorjamb of the butcher shop he has been kicked away from only moments before, Helene smiled. Smiled dazzlingly and coquettishly at the salmon-colored face of the conductor.

Nel looked away from the flash of pretty teeth to the other passengers. The two black soldiers, who had been watching the scene with what appeared to be indifference, now looked stricken. Behind Nel was the bright and blazing light of her mother's smile; before her the midnight eyes of the soldiers. She saw the muscles of their faces tighten, a movement under the skin from blood to marble. No change in the expression of the eyes, but a hard wetness that veiled them as they looked at the stretch of her mother's foolish smile.

As the door slammed on the conductor's exit, Helene walked down the aisle to a seat. She looked about for a second to see whether any of the men would help her put the suitcases in the overhead rack. Not a man moved. Helene sat down, fussily, her back toward the men. Nel sat opposite, facing both her mother and the soldiers, neither of whom she could look at. She felt both pleased and ashamed to sense that these men, unlike her father, who worshiped his graceful, beautiful wife, were bubbling with a hatred for her mother that had not been there in the beginning but had been born with the dazzling smile. In the silence that preceded the train's heave, she looked deeply at the folds of her mother's dress. There in the fall of the heavy brown wool she held her eyes. She could not risk letting them travel upward for fear of seeing that the hooks and eyes in the placket of the dress had come undone and exposed the custard-colored skin underneath. She stared at the hem, wanting to believe in its weight but knowing that custard was all that it hid. If this tall, proud woman, this woman who was very particular about her friends, who slipped into church with unequaled elegance, who could quell a roustabout with a look, if *she* were really custard, then there was a chance that Nel was too.

It was on that train, shuffling toward Cincinnati, that she resolved to be on guard—always. She wanted to make certain that no man ever looked at her that way. That no midnight eyes or marbled flesh would ever accost her and turn her into jelly. 25

For two days they rode; two days of watching sleet turn to rain, turn to purple sunsets, and one night knotted on the wooden seats (their heads on folded coats), trying not to hear the snoring soldiers. When they changed trains in Birmingham for the last leg of the trip, they discovered what luxury they had been in through Kentucky and Tennessee, where the rest stops had all had colored toilets. After Birmingham there were none. Helene's face was drawn with the need to relieve herself, and so intense was her distress she finally brought herself to speak about her problem to a black woman with four children who had got on in Tuscaloosa.

"Is there somewhere we can go to use the restroom?"

The woman looked up at her and seemed not to understand. "Ma'am?" Her eyes fastened on the thick velvet collar, the fair skin, the high-tone voice.

"The restroom," Helene repeated. Then, in a whisper, "The toilet."

The woman pointed out the window and said, "Yes, ma'am. Yonder." 30

Helene looked out of the window halfway expecting to see a comfort station in the distance; instead she saw gray-green trees leaning over tangled grass. "Where?"

"Yonder," the woman said. "Meridian. We be pullin' in direc'lin." Then she smiled sympathetically and asked, "Kin you make it?"

Helene nodded and went back to her seat trying to think of other things—for the surest way to have an accident would be to remember her full bladder.

At Meridian the women got out with their children. While Helene looked about the tiny stationhouse for a door that said COLORED WOMEN, the other woman stalked off to a field of high grass on the far side of the track. Some white men were leaning on the railing in front of the stationhouse. It was not only their tongues curling around toothpicks that kept Helene from asking information of them. She looked around for the other woman and, seeing just the top of her head rag in the grass, slowly realized where "yonder" was. All of them, the fat woman and her four children, three boys and a girl, Helene and her daughter, squatted there in the four o'clock Meridian sun. They did it again in Ellisville, again in Hattiesburg, and by the time they reached Slidell, not too far from Lake Pontchartrain, Helene could not only fold leaves as well as the fat woman, she never felt a stir as she passed the muddy eyes of the men who stood like wrecked Dorics under the station roofs of those towns.

The lift in spirit that such an accomplishment produced in her quickly disappeared 35 when the train finally pulled into New Orleans.

Cecile Sabat's house leaned between two others just like it on Elysian Fields. A Frenchified shotgun house, it sported a magnificent garden in the back and a tiny wrought-iron fence in the front. On the door hung a black crepe wreath with purple ribbon. They were too late. Helene reached up to touch the ribbon, hesitated, and knocked. A man in a collarless shirt opened the door. Helene identified herself and he said he was Henri Martin and that he was there for the settin'-up. They stepped into the house. The Virgin Mary clasped her hands in front of her neck three times in the front room and once in the bedroom where Cecile's body lay. The old woman had died without seeing or blessing her granddaughter.

No one other than Mr. Martin seemed to be in the house, but a sweet odor as of gardenias told them that someone else had been. Blotting her lashes with a white handkerchief, Helene walked through the kitchen to the back bedroom where she had slept for sixteen years. Nel trotted along behind, enchanted with the smell, the candles and the strangeness. When Helene bent to loosen the ribbons of Nel's hat, a woman in a yellow dress came out of the garden and onto the back porch that opened into the bedroom. The two women looked at each other. There was no recognition in the eyes of either. Then Helene said, "This is your . . . grandmother, Nel." Nel looked at her mother and then quickly back at the door they had just come out of.

"No. That was your great-grandmother. This is your grandmother. My mother . . ."

Before the child could think, her words were hanging in the gardenia air. "But she looks so young."

The woman in the canary-yellow dress laughed and said she was forty-eight, "an 40 old forty-eight."

Then it was she who carried the gardenia smell. This tiny woman with the softness and glare of a canary. In that somber house that held four Virgin Marys, where death sighed in every corner and candles sputtered, the gardenia smell and canary-yellow dress emphasized the funeral atmosphere surrounding them.

The woman smiled, glanced in the mirror and said, throwing her voice toward Helene, "That your only one?"

"Yes," said Helene.

"Pretty. A lot like you."

"Yes. Well. She's ten now." 45

"Ten? Vrai? Small for her age, no?"

Helene shrugged and looked at her daughter's questioning eyes. The woman in the yellow dress leaned forward. "Come. Come, chère."

Helene interrupted. "We have to get cleaned up. We been three days on the train with no chance to wash or . . ."

"Comment t'appelle?"

"She doesn't talk Creole." 50

"Then you ask her."

"She wants to know your name, honey."

With her head pressed into her mother's heavy brown dress, Nel told her and then asked, "What's yours?"

"Mine's Rochelle. Well. I must be going on." She moved closer to the mirror and stood there sweeping hair up from her neck back into its halo-like roll, and wetting with spit the ringlets that fell over her ears. "I been here, you know, most of the day. She pass on yesterday. The funeral tomorrow. Henri takin' care." She struck a match, blew it out and darkened her eyebrows with the burnt head. All the while Helene and Nel watched her. The one in a rage at the folded leaves she had endured, the wooden benches she had slept on, all to miss seeing her grandmother and seeing instead that painted canary who never said a word of greeting or affection or . . .

Rochelle continued, "I don't know what happen to de house. Long time paid for. You be thinkin' on it? Oui?" Her newly darkened eyebrows queried Helene.   55

"Oui." Helene's voice was chilly. "I be thinkin' on it."

"Oh, well. Not for me to say . . ."

Suddenly she swept around and hugged Nel—a quick embrace tighter and harder than one would have imagined her thin soft arms capable of.

"'Voir! 'Voir!" and she was gone.

In the kitchen, being soaped head to toe by her mother, Nel ventured an observa-   60
tion. "She smelled so nice. And her skin was so soft."

Helene rinsed the cloth. "Much handled things are always soft."

"What does 'vwah' mean?"

"I don't know," her mother said. "I don't talk Creole." She gazed at her daughter's wet buttocks. "And neither do you."

When they got back to Medallion and into the quiet house they saw the note exactly where they had left it and the ham dried out in the icebox.

"Lord, I've never been so glad to see this place. But look at the dust. Get the rags,   65
Nel. Oh, never mind. Let's breathe awhile first. Lord, I never thought I'd get back here safe and sound. Whoo. Well it's over. Good and over. Praise His name. Look at that. I told that old fool not to deliver any milk and there's the can curdled to beat all. What gets into people? I told him not to. Well, I got other things to worry 'bout. Got to get a fire started. I left it ready so I wouldn't have to do nothin' but light it. Lord, it's cold. Don't just sit there, honey. You could be pulling your nose . . ."

Nel sat on the red-velvet sofa listening to her mother but remembering the smell and the tight, tight hug of the woman in yellow who rubbed burned matches over her eyes.

Late that night after the fire was made, the cold supper eaten, the surface dust removed, Nel lay in bed thinking of her trip. She remembered clearly the urine running down and into her stockings until she learned how to squat properly; the disgust on the face of the dead woman and the sound of the funeral drums. It had been an exhilarating trip but a fearful one. She had been frightened of the soldiers' eyes on the train, the black wreath on the door, the custard pudding she believed lurked under her mother's heavy dress, the feel of unknown streets and unknown people. But she had gone on a real trip, and now she was different. She got out of bed and lit the lamp to look in the mirror. There was her face, plain brown eyes, three braids and the nose her mother hated. She looked for a long time and suddenly a shiver ran through her.

"I'm me," she whispered. "Me."

Nel didn't know quite what she meant, but on the other hand she knew exactly what she meant.

"I'm me. I'm not their daughter. I'm not Nel. I'm me. Me."   70

Each time she said the word *me* there was a gathering in her like power, like joy, like fear. Back in bed with her discovery, she stared out the window at the dark leaves of the horse chestnut.

"Me," she murmured. And then, sinking deeper into the quilts, "I want . . . I want to be . . . wonderful. Oh, Jesus, make me wonderful."

The many experiences of her trip crowded in on her. She slept. It was the last as well as the first time she was ever to leave Medallion.

For days afterward she imagined other trips she would take, alone though, to far-away places. Contemplating them was delicious. Leaving Medallion would be her goal. But that was before she met Sula, the girl she had seen for five years at Garfield Primary but never played with, never knew, because her mother said Sula's mother was sooty. The trip, perhaps, or her new found me-ness, gave her the strength to cultivate a friend in spite of her mother.

When Sula first visited the Wright house, Helene's curdled scorn turned to butter.   75
Her daughter's friend seemed to have none of the mother's slackness. Nel, who regarded the oppressive neatness of her home with dread, felt comfortable in it with Sula, who loved it and would sit on the red-velvet sofa for ten to twenty minutes at a time—still as dawn. As for Nel, she preferred Sula's woolly house, where a pot of something was always cooking on the stove; where the mother, Hannah, never scolded or gave directions; where all sorts of people dropped in; where newspapers were stacked in the hallway, and dirty dishes left for hours at a time in the sink, and where a one-legged grandmother named Eva handed you goobers from deep inside her pockets or read you a dream.

FARLEY MOWAT   (born 1921)
The Snow Walker   1975

After death carried the noose to Angutna and Kipmik, their memory lived on with the people of the Great Plains. But death was not satisfied and, one by one, he took the lives of the people until none was left to remember. Before the last of them died, the story was told to a stranger and so it is that Angutna and Kipmik may cheat oblivion a little while longer.

It begins on a summer day when Angutna was only a boy. He had taken his father's kayak and paddled over the still depths of the lake called Big Hungry until he entered a narrow strait called Muskox Thing. Here he grounded the kayak beneath a wall of looming cliffs and climbed cautiously upward under a cloud-shadowed sky. He was hunting for *Tuktu*, the caribou, which was the source of being for those who lived in the heart of the tundra. Those people knew of the sea only as a legend. For them seals, walrus and whales were mythical beasts. For them the broad-antlered caribou was the giver of life.

Angutna was lucky. Peering over a ledge he saw three caribou bucks resting their rumbling bellies on a broad step in the cliffs. They were not sleeping, and one or other of them kept raising his head to shake off the black hordes of flies that clung to nostrils and ears, so Angutna was forced to crawl forward an inch or two at a time. It took him an hour to move twenty yards, but he moved with such infinite caution that the bucks remained unaware of his presence. He had only a few more yards to crawl before he could drive an arrow from his short bow with enough power to kill.

Sunlight burst suddenly down through the yielding grey scud and struck hot on the crouched back of the boy and the thick coats of the deer. The warmth roused the bucks and one by one they got to their feet. Now they were restless, alert, and ready to move. In an agony of uncertainty Angutna lay still as a rock. This was the first time he had tried to stalk Tuktu all by himself, and if he failed in his first hunt he believed it would bode ill for his luck in the years ahead.

But the burst of sunlight had touched more than the deer and the boy. It had   5
beamed into a cleft in the cliffs overhanging the ledge where it had wakened two sleeping fox pups. Now their catlike grey faces peered short-sightedly over the brilliant roll of the lake and the land. Cloudy black eyes took in the tableau of the deer and the boy; but in their desire to see more, the pups forgot the first precept of all wild things—to see and hear but not to be seen or heard. They skittered to the edge of the cleft, shrilling a mockery of the dog fox's challenge at the strange beasts below.

The bucks turned their heavy heads and their ears flopped anxiously until their eyes found the pups scampering back and forth far over their heads. They continued to watch the young foxes, and so they did not see the boy move rapidly closer.

The hard twang of the bow and the heavy thud of an arrow striking into flesh came almost together. The deer leapt for the precipitous slope leading to the lake, but one of them stumbled, fell to his knees, and went sliding down on his side. In a moment Angutna was on him. The boy's copper knife slipped smoothly between the vertebrae in the deer's neck, and the buck lay dead.

The curiosity of the pups had now passed all bounds. One of them hung so far out over the ledge that he lost his balance. His hind legs scrabbled furiously at the smooth face of the rocks while his front feet pushed against air. The rocks thrust him away and he came tumbling in a steep arc to pitch into the moss almost at Angutna's feet.

The pup was too stunned to resist as the boy picked him up by the tail. Angutna put a tentative finger on the small beast's head, and when it failed to snap at him he laughed aloud. His laughter rang over the hills to the ears of the mother fox far from her den; it speeded the flight of the two surviving bucks, and rose to the ears of a high-soaring raven.

Then the boy spoke to the fox: 10

"*Ayee!* Kipmik—Little Dog—we have made a good hunt, you and I. Let it be always this way, for surely you must be one of the Spirits-Who-Help."

That night in his father's skin tent Angutna told the tale of the hunting. Elder men smiled as they listened and agreed that the fox must indeed be a good token sent to the boy. Tethered to a tent pole, the pup lay in a little grey ball with his ears flat to his head and his eyes tightly shut, hoping with all his small heart that this was only a dream from which he would wake to find solace at the teats of his mother.

Such was the coming of the white fox into the habitations of men. In the days that followed, Angutna shared most of his waking hours with Kipmik who soon forgot his fears; for it is in the nature of the white fox to be so filled with curiosity that fear can be only a passing thing.

While the pup was still young enough to risk falling into the lean jaws of the dogs that prowled about the camp, he was kept tethered at night; but during the days, fox and boy travelled the land and explored the world that was theirs. On these expeditions the pup ran freely ahead of the boy over the rolling plains and hills, or he squatted motionless on the precarious deck of a kayak as Angutna drove the slim craft across the shining lakes.

Boy and fox lived together as one, and their thoughts were almost as one. The   15
bond was strong between them for Angutna believed the fox was more than a fox, being also the embodiment of the Spirit-Who-Helps which had attached itself to him. As for Kipmik, perhaps he saw in the boy the shape of his own guardian spirit.

The first snows of the year came in late September and soon after that Kipmik shed the sombre grey fur of youth and donned the white mantle of the dog fox. His long hair was as fine as down and the white ruff that bordered his face framed glistening black eyes and the black spot of his nose. His tail was nearly as long and as round as his body. He was small compared to the red foxes who live in the forests, but he was twice as fleet and his courage was boundless.

During the second winter they spent together, Angutna came of age. He was fifteen and of a strength and awareness to accept manhood. In the time when the nights were so long they were almost unbroken, Angutna's father spoke to the father of a young girl named Epeetna. Then this girl moved into the snowhouse of Angutna's family and the boy who was now a man took her to wife.

During the winters life was lived without much exertion in the camps of the barrenland people for the deer were far to the south and men lived on the fat and meat they had stored up from the fall slaughter. But with the return of the snowbirds, spring and the deer came back to the plains around the Big Hungry and the camps woke to new and vigorous life.

In the spring of the first year of his marriage, Angutna went to the deer-hunting places as a full-fledged hunter. With him went the white fox. The two would walk over the softening drifts to reach rocky defiles that channelled the north-flowing deer. Angutna would hide in one of the ravines while the fox ran high up on the ridges to a place where he could overlook the land and see the dark skeins of caribou approaching the ambush. When the old doe leading a skein approached the defile, she would look carefully around and see the little white shadow watching from above. Kipmik would bark a short greeting to Tuktu, and the herd would move fearlessly forward believing that, if danger lurked, the fox would have barked a cry of alarm. But Kipmik's welcoming bark was meant for the ears of Angutna, who drew back the arrow on the bent bow and waited.

Angutna made good hunts during that spring and as a result he was sung about at   20
the drum dances held in the evenings. The fox was not forgotten either, and in some of the songs the boy and the fox were called the Two Who Were One, and that name became theirs.

In the summer, when the deer had passed on to the fawning grounds far to the north, the fox and the boy sought other food. The Two Who Were One took the kayak down the roaring rivers that debouched over the scarred face of the plains, seeking the hiding places of the geese that nested in that land. After midsummer the adult geese lost their flight quills and had to stay on the water, and at such times they became very shy. The kayak sought out the backwaters where the earthbound geese waited in furtive seclusion for the gift of flight to return.

While Angutna concealed himself behind rocks near the shore, Kipmik would dance on the open beach, barking and squealing like a young pup. He would roll on his back or leap into the air. As he played, the geese would emerge from their hiding places and swim slowly toward him, fascinated by this peculiar behavior in an animal they all knew so well. They had no fear of the fox for they knew he would not try to swim. The geese would come closer, cackling to one another with necks outstretched in amazement. Then Angutna's sling would whir and a stone would fly with an angry hiss. A goose would flap its wings on the water and die.

It was an old trick Kipmik played on the geese, one used by foxes since time began . . . but only Kipmik played that game for the benefit of man.

So the years passed until there were two children in the summer tent of Angutna— a boy and a girl who spent long hours playing with the soft tail of the fox. They were not the only young to play with that white brush. Every spring, when the ptarmigan mated on the hills and the wild dog foxes barked their challenges as an overtone to the sonorous singing of the wolves, unrest would come into the heart of the fox that lived in the houses of men.

On a night he would slip away from the camp and be gone many days. When he returned, lean and hungry, Angutna would feed him special tidbits and smilingly wish good luck to the vixen secreted in some newly dug den not far away. The vixen never ventured into the camp, but Kipmik saw to it that she and her pups were well fed, for Angutna did not begrudge the fox and his family a fair share of the meat that was killed. Sometimes Angutna followed the fox into the hills to the burrow. Then Angutna might leave a fresh fish at its mouth, and he would speak kindly to the unseen vixen cowering within. "Eat well, little sister," he would say.

As the years slipped by, stories of the Two Who Were One spread through the land. One of them told of a time when Angutna and his family were camped alone by the lake called Lamp of the Woman. It was a very bad year. In midwinter there was an unbroken month of great storms and the people used up all the meat stored near the camp but the weather was too savage to permit the men to travel to their more distant caches. The people grew hungry and cold, for there was no more fat for the lamps.

Finally there came a day without wind. Angutna hitched up his team and set out for a big cache lying two days' travel to the west. The dogs pulled as hard as their starved muscles would let them while the fox, like a white wraith, flitted ahead, choosing the easiest road for the team. The sled runners rasped as if they were being hauled over dry sand, for the temperature stood at fifty or sixty degrees below freezing.

On the second day of the journey the sun failed to show itself and there was only a pallid grey light on the horizon. After a while the fox stopped and stared hard into the north, his short ears cocked forward. Then Angutna too began to hear a distant keening in the dark sky. He tried to speed up the dogs, hoping to reach the cache, which lay sheltered in a deep valley, before the storm broke. But the blizzard exploded soon after, and darkness fell with terrible swiftness as this great gale, which had swept a thousand miles south from the ice sea, scoured the frozen face of the plains. It drove snow before it like fragments of glass. The drifting granules swirled higher and higher, obscuring the plodding figures of man, fox and dogs.

Kipmik still moved at the head of the team but he was invisible to Angutna's straining, snowcaked eyes, and many times the anxious white shadow had to return to the sled so that the dogs would not lose their way. Finally the wind screamed to such a pitch that Angutna knew it would be madness to drive on. He tried to find a drift whose snow was firm enough for the making of a snowhouse, but there was none at hand and there was no time to search. Turning the sled on its side facing the gale, he dug a trench behind it with his snowknife—just big enough for his body. Wrapping himself in his robes he rolled into the trench and pulled the sled over the top of the hole.

The dogs curled abjectly nearby, noses under their tails, the snow drifting over them, while Kipmik ran among them snapping at their shoulders in his anxiety to make them continue on until some shelter was found. He gave up when the dogs were transformed into white, inanimate mushrooms. Then the fox ran to the sled and burrowed under it. He wormed in close, and Angutna made room so that he might share the warmth from the little body beside him.

For a day and a night nothing moved on the white face of the dark plains except the snow ghosts whirling before the blast of the gale. On the second day the wind died away. A smooth, curling drift shattered from within as Angutna fought free of the smothering snows. With all the haste his numbed body could muster, he began probing the nearby drifts seeking the dogs who were sealed into white tombs from which they could no longer escape by themselves.

He had little need of the probe. Kipmik ran to and fro, unerringly sniffing out the snow crypts of the dogs. They were all uncovered at last, and all were alive but so weak they could barely pull at the sled.

Angutna pressed on. He knew that if no food was found soon, the dogs would be finished. And if the dogs died, then all was lost, for there would be no way to carry the meat from the cache back to the camp. Mercilessly Angutna whipped the team on, and when the dogs could no longer muster the strength to keep the sled moving, he harnessed himself into the traces beside them.

Just before noon the sun slipped over the horizon and blazed red on a desolate world. The long sequence of blizzards had smoothed it into an immense and shapeless undulation of white. Angutna could see no landmarks. He was lost in that snow desert, and his heart sank within him.

Kipmik still ran ahead but for some little while he had been trying to swing the team to a northerly course. Time after time he ran back to Angutna and barked in his face when the man persisted in trudging into the west. So they straggled over that frozen world until the dogs could go no farther. Angutna killed one of the dogs and fed it to the others. He let them rest only briefly, for he was afraid a new storm would begin. 35

The sun was long since gone and there were no stars in the sky when they moved on; therefore, Angutna did not notice as, imperceptibly, Kipmik turned the team northward. He did not notice until late the next morning when the dawn glow showed him that all through the long night they had been travelling into the north.

Then Angutna, who was a man not given to rage, was filled with a terrible anger. He believed it was all finished for him and his family. He seized his snowknife from the sled and with a great shout leapt at the fox, his companion of so many years.

The blow would have sliced Kipmik in two but, even as he struck, Angutna stumbled. The blade hissed into the snow and the fox leapt aside. Angutna stayed on his knees until the anger went from him. When he rose to his feet he was steadfast once more.

"*Ayorama!*" he said to the fox who watched him without fear. "It cannot be helped. So, Little Pup, you will lead us your way? It is a small matter. Death awaits in all directions. If you wish, we will seek death to the north."

It is told how they staggered northward for half a day, then the fox abandoned the man and the dogs and ran on ahead. When Angutna caught up to Kipmik it was to find he had already tunnelled down through the snow to the rocks Angutna had heaped over a fine cache of meat and fat in the fall. 40

A year or so later a great change came to the world of the plains dwellers. One winter day a sled drove into the camps by the Big Hungry and a man of the sea people came into the snowhouses. Through many long nights the people listened to his wondrous tales of life by the salt water. They were particularly fascinated by his accounts of the wonders that had been brought to that distant land by a white man come out of the south. Their visitor had been commissioned by the white man to acquaint the plains people with the presence of a trading post on the eastern edge of the plains, and to persuade them to move close to that post and to trap furs for trade.

The idea was much talked about and there were some who thought it would be a good thing to go east for a winter, but most of the people were opposed. By reason of his renown as a hunter, Angutna's opinions carried weight and one night he spoke what was in his mind.

"I think it is to be remembered that we have lived good lives in this land, knowing little evil. Is it not true that *Tuktoriak* has fed and clothed us from before the time of the father's fathers? *Eeee!* It is so. And if we turn from the Deer Spirit now to seek other gifts, who can say what he may do? Perhaps he will be angry and speak to his children, the deer, and bid them abandon our people. And then of what value would be the promises made by this man on behalf of the Kablunait? . . . Those promises would be dead sticks in our hands."

So spoke Angutna, and most agreed with him. Still, when the stranger departed, there were two families who went with him. These returned before the snows thawed in the spring and they brought such wealth as a man could hardly credit: rifles, steel knives, copper kettles and many such things.

But they also brought something they did not know they were bringing.   45

It was a sickness that came into men's lungs and squeezed the life from their bodies. It was called the Great Pain and it flung itself on the plains people like a blazing wind. In one season it killed more than half of those who lived in that land.

Panic struck many of the survivors who, believing the land was now cursed, fled to the east to seek help from the white man. From him they learned a new way of life, becoming trappers of fur and eaters of white man's food. And, instead of Tuktu, the beast they now pursued was Terriganiak—the white fox. During all time that had been, the plains people had known the white fox as a friend in a land so vast and so empty that the bark of the fox was often the only welcoming sound. Since time began, foxes and men had shared that land and there had been no conflict between them. Now men turned on Terriganiak and lived by the sale of his skin.

For a time Angutna and a few other men and their families tried to continue living the old life in the old places, but hunger came more often upon them and one autumn the deer failed to appear at all. Some said this was because of the great slaughter of deer resulting from the new rifles in the hands of all northern people, Indian and Innuit; but Angutna believed it was due to the anger of Tuktoriak. In any event, the last few people living on the inland plains were forced to follow those who had already fled to the east and become trappers of fox.

When the survivors of that long trek came to the snowhouses which stood a few miles away from the house of the trader at the mouth of the River of Seals, they expected to be greeted with warmth and with food, for it had always been the law of the land that those who have food and shelter will share with those who have not.

Disappointment was theirs. White foxes, too, were scarce that winter and many   50
traps stood empty. Those people who had chosen to live by the fox were nearly as hungry as the people who journeyed out of the west.

Angutna built a small snowhouse for his family, but it was a dark place filled with dark thoughts. There was no fuel for the lamps and almost no fuel for the belly. Angutna, who had once been such a great hunter, was now forced to live on the labors of others because, even if he had so wished, he could not have trapped foxes. He could not have done so because Terriganiak was his Spirit-Who-Helps and, for him, the lives of all foxes were sacred. Other men went to their traps and, when they were lucky, caught foxes whose pelts they bartered for food. Sometimes a portion of that food was given to Angutna's wife; but Angutna had nothing to give in return.

The new way of life was as hard for Kipmik as for Angutna. The fox who had always been free now lay, day and night, tethered to a stick driven into the floor of the snowhouse. All around that place steel traps yawned for his kind and there were many men with rifles who, to help feed their families, would not have hesitated to put a bullet through him, for although Kipmik was growing old, his pelt was still thicker, softer and longer than that of any fox that had ever been seen before.

As the winter drew on, the remaining foxes deserted that part of the country and then hunger was the lot of all who had tried to live by the fox. There were no more gifts to the family of Angutna, who had himself become so emaciated that he could do little but sit like a statue in his cold house, dreaming of other times, other days. Sometimes his gaze would fix on the curled ball of white fur that was Kipmik, and his lips would move, but silently, for he was addressing a plea to the Spirit-Who-Helps. Sometimes the fox would raise its head and stare back into the eyes of the man, and perhaps he too was pleading . . . for the freedom that once had been his.

The trader heard about the fabulous fox who lived in the houses of men and one day he drove his dogs to the camps of the people to see for himself whether the stories were true. He entered Angutna's snowhouse, and as soon as he saw Kipmik curled up on the floor he wished to possess that magnificent pelt.

It distressed him to see the big, staring eyes and the swollen bellies of Angutna's   55
children. He felt pity for the people who were starving that winter. But what could he do? He did not own the food that lay in his storehouse. It belonged to the company that employed him, and he could not part with a pound unless there was payment in fur.

Angutna greeted the visitor with a smile that tautened the skin that was already stretched too tightly over the broad bones of his face. Even though he be in despair, a man must give a good greeting to those who visit his house. It was otherwise with the fox. Perhaps he smelled the death stink from the skins of so many of his kind this stranger had handled. He pulled away to the side of the snowhouse as far as his tether would reach and crouched there like a cat facing a hound.

The white man spoke of the hard times that lay on the people; of the shortage of foxes and the absence of deer. Then he turned to look at Kipmik again.

"That is a fine fox you have there. I have never seen better. If you will sell it to me, I can pay . . . as much as three sacks of flour and, yes, this I can do, ten, no, fifteen pounds of fat."

Angutna still smiled, and none knew the thoughts that swirled behind the masked face. He did not answer the white man directly, but spoke instead of trivial things while he wrestled with himself in his mind: food . . . food enough to ensure that his wife and children would live until spring. Perhaps he even believed his Spirit-Who-Helps had something to do with the miraculous hope the white man extended. Who will know what he thought?

The trader knew better than to say anything more about Kipmik, but when he   60
went outside to his waiting sled he ordered his Eskimo helper to take a small bag of flour into Angutna's snowhouse. Then he returned to his trading post at the mouth of the River of Seals.

That night the woman, Epeetna, made a small fire of willow twigs in the tunnel entrance and she and her children ate unleavened bread made of flour and water. She passed a cake of it to Angutna where he sat unmoving on the sleeping ledge, but he did not taste it. Instead he threw it to the fox. Kipmik bolted it down, for he too was starving. Then Angutna spoke, as it seemed, to himself.

"This is the way it must be."

Epeetna understood. The woman let her hair loose so that it hung down over her face. The acrid smoke from the fire clouded the four figures sitting on the high ledge. The small flames gave hardly enough light for Angutna to see what he was doing, but his fingers needed no light as he carefully plaited the Noose of Release.

When it was finished, Angutna slipped Kipmik's tether, and the fox leapt up to the ledge and stood with its paws braced against the chest of the man—free once again. The black eyes were fixed on the eyes of the man, in wonder perhaps, for the fox had never seen tears in those eyes before. Kipmik made no move when the noose fell over his neck. He made no move until Angutna spoke.

"Now, Little Pup, it is time. You will go out onto the plains where the deer wait   65
our coming."

And so Kipmik passed into that country from which nothing returns.

Next morning when the trader opened his door he found the frozen pelt of the fox suspended from the ridge of his porch by a strangely plaited noose. The pelt swayed and spun in the breath of the wind. The trader was delighted, but he was uneasy too. He had lived in that land long enough to know how little he knew. He wasted no time ordering his helper to load the promised food on a sled and take it to the snowhouse of Angutna.

The payment was received by Epeetna. Angutna could not receive it, for the Noose of Release was drawn tight at his throat. He had gone to join the one he had lost.

His grave still stands on the bank of the River of Seals. It is no more than a grey cairn of rocks with the decayed weapons of a hunter scattered among the quiet stones. Inside the grave lies Angutna, and beside him lies the fox who once lived in the houses of men.

The two are still one.   70

BHARATI MUKHERJEE   (born 1940)
A Wife's Story   1987

Imre says forget it, but I'm going to write David Mamet. So Patels are hard to sell real estate to. You buy them a beer, whisper Glengarry Glen Ross, and they smell swamp instead of sun and surf. They work hard, eat cheap, live ten to a room, stash their savings under futons in Queens, and before you know it they own half of Hoboken. You say, where's the sweet gullibility that made this nation great?

Polish jokes, Patel jokes: that's not why I want to write Mamet:

Seen their women?

Everybody laughs. Imre laughs. The dozing fat man with the Barnes & Noble sack between his legs, the woman next to him, the usher, everybody. The theater isn't so dark that they can't see me. In my red silk sari I'm conspicuous. Plump, gold paisleys sparkle on my chest.

The actor is just warming up. *Seen their women?* He plays a salesman, he's had   5
a bad day and now he's in a Chinese restaurant trying to loosen up. His face is pink. His wool-blend slacks are creased at the crotch. We bought our tickets at half-price, we're sitting in the front row, but at the edge, and we see things we shouldn't be seeing. At least I do, or think I do. Spittle, actors goosing each other, little winks, streaks of makeup.

Maybe they're improvising dialogue too. Maybe Mamet's provided them with insult kits, Thursdays for Chinese, Wednesdays for Hispanics, today for Indians. Maybe they get together before curtain time, see an Indian woman settling in the front row off to the side, and say to each other: "Hey, forget Friday. Let's get *her* today. See if she cries. See if she walks out." Maybe, like the salesmen they play, they have a little bet on.

Maybe I shouldn't feel betrayed.

Their women, he goes again. *They look like they've just been fucked by a dead cat.*

The fat man hoots so hard he nudges my elbow off our shared armrest.

"Imre. I'm going home." But Imre's hunched so far forward he doesn't hear.   10
English isn't his best language. A refugee from Budapest, he has to listen hard. "I didn't pay eighteen dollars to be insulted."

I don't hate Mamet. It's the tyranny of the American dream that scares me. First, you don't exist. Then you're invisible. Then you're funny. Then you're disgusting. Insult, my American friends will tell me, is a kind of acceptance. No instant dignity here. A play like this, back home, would cause riots. Communal, racist, and antisocial. The actors wouldn't make it off stage. This play, and all these awful feelings, would be safely locked up.

I long, at times, for clear-cut answers. Offer me instant dignity, today, and I'll take it.

"What?" Imre moves toward me without taking his eyes off the actor. "Come again?"

Tears come. I want to stand, scream, make an awful scene. I long for ugly, nasty rage.

The actor is ranting, flinging spittle. *Give me a chance. I'm not finished, I can get* 15
back on the board. I tell that asshole, give me a real lead. And what does that asshole give
me? Patels. Nothing but Patels.

This time Imre works an arm around my shoulders. "Panna, what is Patel? Why are you taking it all so personally?"

I shrink from his touch, but I don't walk out. Expensive girls' schools in Lausanne and Bombay have trained me to behave well. My manners are exquisite, my feelings are delicate, my gestures refined, my moods undetectable. They have seen me through riots, uprootings, separation, my son's death.

"I'm not taking it personally."

The fat man looks at us. The woman looks too, and shushes.

I stare back at the two of them. Then I stare, mean and cool, at the man's elbow. 20
Under the bright blue polyester Hawaiian shirt sleeve, the elbow looks soft and runny.
"Excuse me," I say. My voice has the effortless meanness of well-bred displaced Third
World women, though my rhetoric has been learned elsewhere. "You're exploiting my space."

Startled, the man snatches his arm away from me. He cradles it against his breast. By the time he's ready with comebacks, I've turned my back on him. I've probably ruined the first act for him. I know I've ruined it for Imre.

It's not my fault; it's the *situation*. Old colonies wear down. Patels—the new pioneers—have to be suspicious. Idi Amin's lesson is permanent. AT&T wires move good advice from continent to continent. Keep all assets liquid. Get into 7–11s, get out of condos and motels. I know how both sides feel, that's the trouble. The Patel sniffing out scams, the sad salesmen on the stage: postcolonialism has made me their referee. It's hate I long for; simple, brutish, partisan hate.

After the show Imre and I make our way toward Broadway. Sometimes he holds my hand; it doesn't mean anything more than that crazies and drunks are crouched in doorways. Imre's been here over two years, but he's stayed very old-world, very courtly, openly protective of women. I met him in a seminar on special ed. last semester. His wife is a nurse somewhere in the Hungarian countryside. There are two sons, and miles of petitions for their emigration. My husband manages a mill two hundred miles north of Bombay. There are no children.

"You make things tough on yourself," Imre says. He assumed Patel was a Jewish name or maybe Hispanic; everything makes equal sense to him. He found the play tasteless, he worried about the effect of vulgar language on my sensitive ears. "You have to let go a bit." And as though to show me how to let go, he breaks away from me, bounds ahead with his head ducked tight, then dances on amazingly jerky legs. He's a Magyar, he often tells me, and deep down, he's an Asian too. I catch glimpses of it, knife-blade Attila cheekbones, despite the blondish hair. In his faded jeans and leather jacket, he's a rock video star. I watch MTV for hours in the apartment when Charity's working the evening shift at Macy's. I listen to WPLJ on Charity's earphones. Why should I be ashamed? Television in India is so uplifting.

Imre stops as suddenly as he'd started. People walk around us. The summer side-walk is full of theatergoers in seersucker suits; Imre's year-round jacket is out of place. European. Cops in twos and threes huddle, lightly tap their thighs with night sticks and smile at me with benevolence. I want to wink at them, get us all in trouble, tell them the crazy dancing man is from the Warsaw Pact. I'm too shy to break into dance on Broadway. So I hug Imre instead.

The hug takes him by surprise. He wants me to let go, but he doesn't really expect me to let go. He staggers, though I weigh no more than 104 pounds, and with him, I pitch forward slightly. Then he catches me, and we walk arm in arm to the bus stop. My husband would never dance or hug a woman on Broadway. Nor would my broth-ers. They aren't stuffy people, but they went to Anglican boarding schools and they have a well-developed sense of what's silly.

"Imre." I squeeze his big, rough hand. "I'm sorry I ruined the evening for you."

"You did nothing of the kind." He sounds tired. "Let's not wait for the bus. Let's splurge and take a cab instead."

Imre always has unexpected funds. The Network, he calls it, Class of '56.

In the back of the cab, without even trying, I feel light, almost free. Memories of Indian destitutes mix with the hordes of New York street people, and they float free, like astronauts, inside my head. I've made it. I'm making something of my life. I've left home, my husband, to get a Ph.D. in special ed. I have a multiple-entry visa and a small scholarship for two years. After that, we'll see. My mother was beaten by her mother-in-law, my grandmother, when she'd registered for French lessons at the Alliance Française. My grandmother, the eldest daughter of a rich zamindar, was illiterate.

Imre and the cabdriver talk away in Russian. I keep my eyes closed. That way I can feel the floaters better. I'll write Mamet tonight. I feel strong, reckless. Maybe I'll write Steven Spielberg too; tell him that Indians don't eat monkey brains.

We've made it. Patels must have made it. Mamet, Spielberg: they're not conde-scending to us. Maybe they're a little bit afraid.

Charity Chin, my roommate, is sitting on the floor drinking Chablis out of a plas-tic wineglass. She is five foot six, three inches taller than me, but weighs a kilo and a half less than I do. She is a "hands" model. Orientals are supposed to have a monopoly in the hands-modelling business, she says. She had her eyes fixed eight or nine months ago and out of gratitude sleeps with her plastic surgeon every third Wednesday.

"Oh, good," Charity says. "I'm glad you're back early. I need to talk."

She's been writing checks. MCI, Con Ed, Bonwit Teller. Envelopes, already stamped and sealed, form a pyramid between her shapely, knee-socked legs. The check-book's cover is brown plastic, grained to look like cowhide. Each time Charity flips back the cover, white geese fly over sky-colored checks. She makes good money, but she's extravagant. The difference adds up to this shared, rent-controlled Chelsea one-bedroom.

"All right. Talk."

When I first moved in, she was seeing an analyst. Now she sees a nutritionist.

"Eric called. From Oregon."

"What did he want?"

25

30

35

"He wants me to pay half the rent on his loft for last spring. He asked me to move   40
back, remember? He *begged* me."

Eric is Charity's estranged husband.

"What does your nutritionist say?" Eric now wears a red jumpsuit and tills the soil
in Rajneeshpuram.

"You think Phil's a creep too, don't you? What else can he be when creeps are all I
attract?"

Phil is a flutist with thinning hair. He's very touchy on the subject of *flautists*
versus *flutists*. He's touchy on every subject, from music to books to foods to clothes.
He teaches at a small college upstate, and Charity bought a used blue Datsun
("Nissan," Phil insists) last month so she could spend weekends with him. She returns every Sunday night, exhausted and exasperated. Phil and I don't have much to
say to each other—he's the only musician I know; the men in my family are lawyers,
engineers, or in business—but I like him. Around me, he loosens up. When he visits,
he bakes us loaves of pumpernickel bread. He waxes our kitchen floor. Like many
men in this country, he seems to me a displaced child, or even a woman, looking for
something that passed him by, or for something that he can never have. If he thinks
I'm not looking, he sneaks his hands under Charity's sweater, but there isn't too
much there. Here, she's a model with high ambitions. In India, she'd be a flat-chested
old maid.

I'm shy in front of the lovers. A darkness comes over me when I see them horsing   45
around.

"It isn't the money," Charity says. Oh? I think. "He says he still loves me. Then he
turns around and asks me for five hundred."

What's so strange about that, I want to ask. She still loves Eric, and Eric, red jump
suit and all, is smart enough to know it. Love is a commodity, hoarded like any other.
Mamet knows. But I say, "I'm not the person to ask about love." Charity knows that
mine was a traditional Hindu marriage. My parents, with the help of a marriage broker,
who was my mother's cousin, picked out a groom. All I had to do was get to know his
taste in food.

It'll be a long evening, I'm afraid. Charity likes to confess. I unpleat my silk sari—
it no longer looks too showy—wrap it in muslin cloth and put it away in a dresser drawer. Saris are hard to have laundered in Manhattan, though there's a good man in
Jackson Heights. My next step will be to brew us a pot of chrysanthemum tea. It's a
very special tea from the mainland. Charity's uncle gave it to us. I like him. He's a
humpbacked, awkward, terrified man. He runs a gift store on Mott Street, and though
he doesn't speak much English, he seems to have done well. Once upon a time he
worked for the railways in Chengdu, Szechwan Province, and during the Wuchang Uprising, he was shot at. When I'm down, when I'm lonely for my husband, when I think
of our son, or when I need to be held, I think of Charity's uncle. If I hadn't left home,
I'd never have heard of the Wuchang Uprising. I've broadened my horizons.

Very late that night my husband calls me from Ahmadabad, a town of textile mills
north of Bombay. My husband is a vice president at Lakshmi Cotton Mills. Lakshmi is
the goddess of wealth, but LCM (Priv.), Ltd., is doing poorly. Lockouts, strikes, rock-
throwings. My husband lives on digitalis, which he calls the food for our *yuga* of discontent.

"We had a bad mishap at the mill today." Then he says nothing for seconds.   50

The operator comes on. "Do you have the right party, sir? We're trying to reach
Mrs. Butt."

"Bhatt," I insist. "*B* for Bombay, *H* for Haryana, *A* for Ahmadabad, double *T* for Tamil Nadu." It's a litany. "This is she."

"One of our lorries was firebombed today. Resulting in three deaths. The driver, old Karamchand, and his two children."

I know how my husband's eyes look this minute, how the eye rims sag and the yellow corneas shine and bulge with pain. He is not an emotional man—the Ahmadabad Institute of Management has trained him to cut losses, to look on the bright side of economic catastrophes—but tonight he's feeling low. I try to remember a driver named Karamchand, but can't. That part of my life is over, the way *trucks* have replaced *lorries* in my vocabulary, the way Charity Chin and her lurid love life have replaced inherited notions of marital duty. Tomorrow he'll come out of it. Soon he'll be eating again. He'll sleep like a baby. He's been trained to believe in turnovers. Every morning he rubs his scalp with cantharidine oil so his hair will grow back again.

"It could be your car next." Affection, love. Who can tell the difference in a traditional marriage in which a wife still doesn't call her husband by his first name?   55

"No. They know I'm a flunky, just like them. Well paid, maybe. No need for undue anxiety, please."

Then his voice breaks. He says he needs me, he misses me, he wants me to come to him damp from my evening shower, smelling of sandalwood soap, my braid decorated with jasmines.

"I need you too."

"Not to worry, please," he says. "I am coming in a fortnight's time. I have already made arrangements."

Outside my window, fire trucks whine, up Eighth Avenue. I wonder if he can hear   60 them, what he thinks of a life like mine, led amid disorder.

"I am thinking it'll be like a honeymoon. More or less."

When I was in college, waiting to be married, I imagined honeymoons were only for the more fashionable girls, the girls who came from slightly racy families, smoked Sobranies in the dorm lavatories and put up posters of Kabir Bedi, who was supposed to have made it as a big star in the West. My husband wants us to go to Niagara. I'm not to worry about foreign exchange. He's arranged for extra dollars through the Gujarati Network, with a cousin in San Jose. And he's bought four hundred more on the black market. "Tell me you need me. Panna, please tell me again."

I change out of the cotton pants and shirt I've been wearing all day and put on a sari to meet my husband at JFK. I don't forget the jewelry; the marriage necklace of *mangalsutra,* gold drop earrings, heavy gold bangles. I don't wear them every day. In this borough of vice and greed, who knows when, or whom, desire will overwhelm.

My husband spots me in the crowd and waves. He has lost weight, and changed his glasses. The arm, uplifted in a cheery wave, is bony, frail, almost opalescent.

In the Carey Coach, we hold hands. He strokes my fingers one by one. "How   65 come you aren't wearing my mother's ring?"

"Because muggers know about Indian women," I say. They know with us it's 24-karat. His mother's ring is showy, in ghastly taste anywhere but India: a blood-red Burma ruby set in a gold frame of floral sprays. My mother-in-law got her guru to bless the ring before I left for the States.

He looks disconcerted. He's used to a different role. He's the knowing, suspicious one in the family. He seems to be sulking, and finally he comes out with it. "You've said nothing about my new glasses." I compliment him on the glasses, how chic and

Western-executive they make him look. But I can't help the other things, necessities until he learns the ropes. I handle the money, buy the tickets. I don't know if this makes me unhappy.

Charity drives her Nissan upstate, so for two weeks we are to have the apartment to ourselves. This is more privacy than we ever had in India. No parents, no servants, to keep us modest. We play at housekeeping. Imre has lent us a hibachi, and I grill saffron chicken breasts. My husband marvels at the size of the Perdue hens. "They're big like peacocks, no? These Americans, they're really something!" He tries out pizzas, burgers, McNuggets. He chews. He explores. He judges. He loves it all, fears nothing, feels at home in the summer odors, the clutter of Manhattan streets. Since he thinks that the American palate is bland, he carries a bottle of red peppers in his pocket. I wheel a shopping cart down the aisles of the neighborhood Grand Union, and he follows, swift-ly, greedily. He picks up hair rinses and high-protein diet powders. There's so much I already take for granted.

One night, Imre stops by. He wants us to go with him to a movie. In his work shirt and red leather tie, he looks arty or strung out. It's only been a week, but I feel as though I am really seeing him for the first time. The yellow hair worn very short at the sides, the wide, narrow lips. He's a good-looking man, but self-conscious, almost arro-gant. He's picked the movie we should see. He always tells me what to see, what to read. He buys the *Voice*. He's a natural avant-gardist. For tonight he's chosen *Numéro Deux*.

"Is it a musical?" my husband asks. The Radio City Music Hall is on his list of sights to see. He's read up on the history of the Rockettes. He doesn't catch Imre's sympathetic wink. 70

Guilt, shame, loyalty. I long to be ungracious, not ingratiate myself with both men.

That night my husband calculates in rupees the money we've wasted on Godard. "That refugee fellow, Nagy, must have a screw loose in his head. I paid very steep price for dollars on the black market."

Some afternoons we go shopping. Back home we hated shopping, but now it is a lovers' project. My husband's shopping list startles me. I feel I am just getting to know him. Maybe, like Imre, freed from the dignities of old-world culture, he too could get drunk and squirt Cheez Whiz on a guest. I watch him dart into stores in his gleaming leather shoes. Jockey shorts on sale in outdoor bins on Broadway entrance him. White tube socks with different bands of color delight him. He looks for microcassettes, for anything small and electronic and smuggleable. He needs a garment bag. He calls it a "wardrobe," and I have to translate.

"All of New York is having sales, no?"

My heart speeds watching him this happy. It's the third week in August, almost the end of summer, and the city smells ripe, it cannot bear more heat, more money, more energy. 75

"This is so smashing! The prices are so excellent!" Recklessly, my prudent husband signs away traveller's checks. How he intends to smuggle it all back I don't dare ask. With a microwave, he calculates, we could get rid of our cook.

This has to be love, I think. Charity, Eric, Phil: they may be experts on sex. My husband doesn't chase me around the sofa, but he pushes me down on Charity's bat-tered cushions, and the man who has never entered the kitchen of our Ahmadabad house now comes toward me with a dish tub of steamy water to massage away the pavement heat.

Ten days into his vacation my husband checks out brochures for sightseeing tours. Shortline, Grayline, Crossroads: his new vinyl briefcase is full of schedules and pamphlets. While I make pancakes out of a mix, he comparison-shops. Tour number one costs $10.95 and will give us the World Trade Center, Chinatown, and the United Nations. Tour number three would take us both uptown *and* downtown for $14.95, but my husband is absolutely sure he doesn't want to see Harlem. We settle for tour number four: Downtown and the Dame. It's offered by a new tour company with a small, dirty office at Eighth and Forty-eighth.

The sidewalk outside the office is colorful with tourists. My husband sends me in to buy the tickets because he has come to feel Americans don't understand his accent.

The dark man, Lebanese probably, behind the counter comes on too friendly. "Come on, doll, make my day!" He won't say which tour is his. "Number four? Honey, no! Look, you've wrecked me! Say you'll change your mind." He takes two twenties and gives back change. He holds the tickets, forcing me to pull. He leans closer. "I'm off after lunch."

My husband must have been watching me from the sidewalk. "What was the chap saying?" he demands. "I told you not to wear pants. He thinks you are Puerto Rican. He thinks he can treat you with disrespect."

The bus is crowded and we have to sit across the aisle from each other. The tour guide begins his patter on Forty-sixth. He looks like an actor, his hair bleached and blow-dried. Up close he must look middle-aged, but from where I sit his skin is smooth and his cheeks faintly red.

"Welcome to the Big Apple, folks." The guide uses a microphone. "Big Apple. That's what we native Manhattan degenerates call our city. Today we have guests from fifteen foreign countries and six states from this U.S. of A. That makes the Tourist Bureau real happy. And let me assure you that while we may be the richest city in the richest country in the world, it's okay to tip your charming and talented attendant." He laughs. Then he swings his hip out into the aisle and sings a song.

"And it's mighty fancy on old Delancey Street, you know. . . ."

My husband looks irritable. The guide is, as expected, a good singer. "The bloody man should be giving us histories of buildings we are passing, no?" I pat his hand, the mood passes. He cranes his neck. Our window seats have both gone to Japanese. It's the tour of his life. Next to this, the quick business trips to Manchester and Glasgow pale.

"And tell me what street compares to Mott Street, in July. . . ."

The guide wants applause. He manages a derisive laugh from the Americans up front. He's working the aisles now. "I coulda been somebody, right? I coulda been a star!" Two or three of us smile, those of us who recognize the parody. He catches my smile. The sun is on his harsh, bleached hair. "Right, your highness? Look, we gotta maharani with us! Couldn't I have been a star?"

"Right!" I say, my voice coming out a squeal. I've been trained to adapt; what else can I say?

We drive through traffic past landmark office buildings and churches. The guide flips his hands. "Art deco," he keeps saying. I hear him confide to one of the Americans: "Beats me. I went to a cheap guide's school." My husband wants to know more about this Art Deco, but the guide sings another song.

"We made a foolish choice," my husband grumbles. "We are sitting in the bus only. We're not going into famous buildings." He scrutinizes the pamphlets in his jacket pocket. I think, at least it's air-conditioned in here. I could sit here in the cool shadows of the city forever.

Only five of us appear to have opted for the "Downtown and the Dame" tour. The others will ride back uptown past the United Nations after we've been dropped off at the pier for the ferry to the Statue of Liberty.

An elderly European pulls a camera out of his wife's designer tote bag. He takes pictures of the boats in the harbor, the Japanese in kimonos eating popcorn, scavenging pigeons, me. Then, pushing his wife ahead of him, he climbs back on the bus and waves to us. For a second I feel terribly lost. I wish we were on the bus going back to the apartment. I know I'll not be able to describe any of this to Charity, or to Imre. I'm too proud to admit I went on a guided tour.

The view of the city from the Circle Line ferry is seductive, unreal. The skyline wavers out of reach, but never quite vanishes. The summer sun pushes through fluffy clouds and dapples the glass of office towers. My husband looks thrilled, even more than he had on the shopping trips down Broadway. Tourists and dreamers, we have spent our life's savings to see this skyline, this statue.

"Quick, take a picture of me!" my husband yells as he moves toward a gap of railings. A Japanese matron has given up her position in order to change film. "Before the Twin Towers disappear!"

I focus, I wait for a large Oriental family to walk out of my range. My husband   95
holds his pose tight against the railing. He wants to look relaxed, an international businessman at home in all the financial markets.

A bearded man slides across the bench toward me. "Like this," he says and helps me get my husband in focus. "You want me to take the photo for you?" His name, he says, is Goran. He is Goran from Yugoslavia, as though that were enough for tracking him down. Imre from Hungary. Panna from India. He pulls the old Leica out of my hand, signaling the Orientals to beat it, and clicks away. "I'm a photographer," he says. He could have been a camera thief. That's what my husband would have assumed. Somehow, I trusted. "Get you a beer?" he asks.

"I don't. Drink, I mean. Thank you very much." I say those last words very loud, for everyone's benefit. The odd bottles of Soave with Imre don't count.

"Too bad." Goran gives back the camera.

"Take one more!" my husband shouts from the railing. "Just to be sure!"

The island itself disappoints. The Lady has brutal scaffolding holding her in. The   100
museum is closed. The snack bar is dirty and expensive. My husband reads out the prices to me. He orders two french fries and two Cokes. We sit at picnic tables and wait for the ferry to take us back.

"What was that hippie chap saying?"

As if I could say. A day-care center has brought its kids, at least forty of them, to the island for the day. The kids, all wearing name tags, run around us. I can't help noticing how many are Indian. Even a Patel, probably a Bhatt if I looked hard enough. They toss hamburger bits at pigeons. They kick styrofoam cups. The pigeons are slow, greedy, persistent. I have to shoo one off the table top. I don't think my husband thinks about our son.

"What hippie?"

"The one on the boat. With the beard and the hair."

My husband doesn't look at me. He shakes out his paper napkin and tries to pro-   105
tect his french fries from pigeon feathers.

"Oh, him. He said he was from Dubrovnik." It isn't true, but I don't want trouble.

"What did he say about Dubrovnik?"

I know enough about Dubrovnik to get by. Imre's told me about it. And about Mostar and Zagreb. In Mostar white Muslims sing the call to prayer. I would like to see that before I die: white Muslims. Whole peoples have moved before me; they've adapted. The night Imre told me about Mostar was also the night I saw my first snow in Manhattan. We'd walked down to Chelsea from Columbia. We'd walked and talked and I hadn't felt tired at all.

"You're too innocent," my husband says. He reaches for my hand. "Panna," he cries with pain in his voice, and I am brought back from perfect, floating memories of snow, "I've come to take you back. I have seen how men watch you."

"What?"   110

"Come back, now. I have tickets. We have all the things we will ever need. I can't live without you."

A little girl with wiry braids kicks a bottle cap at his shoes. The pigeons wheel and scuttle around us. My husband covers his fries with spread-out fingers. "No kicking," he tells the girl. Her name, Beulah, is printed in green ink on a heart-shaped name tag. He forces a smile, and Beulah smiles back. Then she starts to flap her arms. She flaps, she hops. The pigeons go crazy for fries and scraps.

"Special ed. course is two years," I remind him. "I can't go back."

My husband picks up our trays and throws them into the garbage before I can stop him. He's carried disposability a little too far. "We've been taken," he says, moving toward the dock, though the ferry will not arrive for another twenty minutes. "The ferry costs only two dollars round-trip per person. We should have chosen tour number one for $10.95 instead of tour number four for $14.95."

With my Lebanese friend, I think. "But this way we don't have to worry about   115
cabs. The bus will pick us up at the pier and take us back to midtown. Then we can walk home."

"New York is full of cheats and whatnot. Just like Bombay." He is not accusing me of infidelity. I feel dread all the same.

That night, after we've gone to bed, the phone rings. My husband listens, then hands the phone to me. "What is this woman saying?" He turns on the pink Macy's lamp by the bed. "I am not understanding these Negro people's accents."

The operator repeats the message. It's a cable from one of the directors of Lakshmi Cotton Mills. "Massive violent labor confrontation anticipated. Stop. Return posthaste. Stop. Cable flight details. Signed Kantilal Shah."

"It's not your factory," I say. "You're supposed to be on vacation."

"So, you are worrying about me? Yes? You reject my heartfelt wishes but you   120
worry about me?" He pulls me close, slips the straps of my nightdress off my shoulder. "Wait a minute."

I wait, unclothed, for my husband to come back to me. The water is running in the bathroom. In the ten days he has been here he has learned American rites: deodorants, fragrances. Tomorrow morning he'll call Air India; tomorrow evening he'll be on his way back to Bombay. Tonight I should make up to him for my years away, the gutted trucks, the degree I'll never use in India. I want to pretend with him that nothing has changed.

In the mirror that hangs on the bathroom door, I watch my naked body turn, the breasts, the thighs glow. The body's beauty amazes. I stand here shameless, in ways he has never seen me. I am free, afloat, watching somebody else.

CARMEN   NARANJO   (born 1931)

Walls

TRANSLATED BY BARBARA PASCHKE

I wonder why I was given this assignment? A response is a response, he says to himself as he watches the flight of a dark bird against the background of the clear blue sky, as they say in national anthems.

The meeting's to be here. He found it a natural place. A little town on hills of eucalyptus and pine, spread out to where the plains begin, with five blocks crowded with houses and the rest scattered among the streams and the lazy river bordered by stones and huge rocks where ferns grew and where lizards lay almost immobile.

In the hotel, a large old house with hallways all going toward the cobbled patio in the center full of tangled vines with meaty leaves and reddish flowers, they ask him how many days he's planning to stay. He says three. "Are you sure?" "Very sure, because I have other plans."

The room is dark and he finds it narrow and oppressive, the walls humid and spotted with mushrooms, which appear to be moving around on a badly drawn map. He leaves his small suitcase and goes out to look for the plaza and the church.

Bells are tolling for a funeral. Would this make it difficult to find the man? Fifth row on the side aisle, counting from the pulpit. White shirt, gray pants, and a black hat on his knees.

Old women in mourning are hurrying toward the plaza. A package tomorrow. Another on Tuesday in front of the altar. The last on Wednesday near the Chapel of the Poor Souls. Some children holding flowers are waiting at the corner. A family, all in black, crosses the street.

The Church is neglected but beautiful, with thick columns on which vines and grape branches climb and which on one side have images of the Holy Family, St. Joseph, the Virgin Mary, Baby Jesus, and on the other side, a fat and smiling saint, completely unknown but obviously the town's patron.

The bells toll, lacking the seriousness of the occasion, having instead a cheerful ring. Or else the bell ringer doesn't know what he's doing or suffers in happiness for other people's sorrow.

Over on a hill a tall pine is going up in flames, collapsing with crackling and hissing and frightening the neighbors. Perhaps it was struck by unexpected lightning.

When he goes up the stairway, a dead bird falls near his feet. Perhaps it died in flight.

In the vestibule near the door, one of the beggars shows him a bloody empty hole that looks as though he had just pulled out his eye.

The church smells of incense and freshly cut lilies. It's full. From the back he counts the pews and in the fifth one there are six men wearing white shirts.

He waits while he listens to the lapidary requiem for the pine coffin. At the end four men carry it off. Solemn faces, carved in sadness. Further back a group walking arm in arm weep with their faces hidden. The funeral procession is a mix of peasants and workers.

When he sees the empty pew, the fifth, he sinks down in the middle of it and waits. He hears footsteps behind him and waits for the tap on his shoulder. He remembers the password. During the night the walls walk.

An hour goes by. Nothing, no one. Another hour goes by. Nothing, no one, not even a devout old woman. Another hour. Better to come back tomorrow.

5

10

15

Lonely streets that seem even narrower lead him back to the hotel, and a lonely hallway takes him to his room. There he's surprised by how narrow it is. It looks like a cell. Moreover, he remembers that he left his suitcase in the middle of the room and now it's up against the wall, which, under careful inspection, looks as if it's become even blacker with mushrooms and feels as if it's grown thicker.

He sleeps badly because he thinks he feels the walls closing in and the mushrooms growing. It's hot in the room. It occurs to him to note the distance between the walls: eight feet wide by twelve feet long. More than a room, it's a niche, he says to himself, while he notices there are other spots of mushrooms, and maybe there's no mystery— maybe it's just that the paint is peeling because of the heat and the humidity. Several times he steps out the door in search of some open space to find out if it's dawn; his watch stopped when he arrived in town. But dawn is still a long way off, and each time he looks the darkness deepens. A heavy sleep envelops him in the early morning, and noon catches him in bed sweating, with bad breath. "Damn! I missed the nine o'clock appointment this morning and if he's not there at four, I'm taking the first flight out tomorrow."

At exactly four o'clock, passing through streets that are now really alleys, he finds the church empty, and empty he leaves it at seven, when the sacristan tells him he has to close up. What's going on, he wonders, maybe he didn't get the package, but he could have let me know, losing time like this and going back with nothing; the clients are really going to raise a stink.

In the hotel he's told that there won't be a plane until the airport is repaired; his flight was the last to land. And by road? Yes, that will be possible when the washed-out bridge is rebuilt. This can't be happening.

He walks through streets that seem like hallways. What am I going to do? Return   20
to that room? Never! The night's getting cold. Returning to the hotel, he asks if there isn't another room; his is too small. They're all the same, sir, and they're all occupied.

The room seems even smaller and the walls are almost completely black with mushrooms. He measures seven feet wide by twelve feet long. It could be that during the night, half asleep, he didn't count correctly. Besides, he has to figure out how to get out, how the hell to get out of this damned town.

He puts his suitcase in order, without knowing why. He tries to remember and re-members only yesterday's funeral, the sound of the bells, the pine tree writhing amidst the flames, the dead bird falling at his feet, the beggar's bloody empty eye socket, the men's faces, the coffin, the procession. Yesterday's corpse, could that have been who he's waiting for?

Luck had always accompanied him. Always. In the worst times, when everything was against him, luck was there, on his side, saving him time and again. It wasn't fair to think it had left him now; that would be challenging luck. But they say luck gives out, changes, and things become different. He whistles and looks for a deck of cards to play a game of solitaire on the bed. If he wins, luck is with him, and if he loses, well, it's gone. The room shakes, yes, shakes. Violently! He opens the door and runs. In the hallway, no one, in the alley, no one. Those alleys, more and more shrunken, laby-rinthine, almost mere passageways. A dead bird falls between his feet.

He returns to his room, and as he goes through the door he senses that the walls have moved. He counts again: five feet wide by ten feet long. It seems like a nightmare. It could have been the tremor. The best thing would be for the sun to come up soon. He gathers up the cards, feels it's better not to challenge luck. He tries to sleep and forget.

He hears a storm approaching; the distant thunder comes closer and a torrent of   25
water falls on the roof. The roar inundates the room. It rains hard. The storm moves

further away. It's time to rest, and the lullaby of the rain brings sleep. He moves the bed to get it away from the walls so he'll be able to know if this rare phenomenon is real, that here the walls walk, as the password says. Really, what a strange coincidence! Everything in this town is strange, even its name, Walls. Sleep closes his eyes as he debates with himself about staying awake, because strange things happen here, and sleeping, because the road will be long; he had planned to walk to the nearest town and there look for a way to get to the capital.

Around midnight, perhaps (time is so imprecise when one's watch doesn't work and the only reference point is darkness with no window), he wakes up, startled. Using his hands he confirms that there's no distance between his bed and the walls, both at the sides of the mattress, and at the ends of the bed. He looks for the door and doesn't find it; he's locked in, he's in prison. Yes, the kind of punishment he deserves has now been discovered and he knows it. It's all been a trap. The message to come to Walls, the transfer of the package, the hotel, the last plane flight, the destroyed bridge, the rain of dead birds, the funeral. What a subtle form of entrapment! Too subtle for him, an ordinary anonymous dealer. Why so elaborate and so complicated? Without a doubt, it would have been easier to detain him, interrogate him, and put him in some prison, just as he deserved. He did things with care, but there are always loose ends which only luck succeeds in tying up in favor of innocence, his innocence of appearing to be an anonymous being, a peaceful good citizen, an insignificant person no one pays any attention to. But underneath, an undesirable, and no one likes undesirables; they always want to capture them, torture them, and leave them to rot as they deserve.

The bed cracks, the walls are advancing. Another tremor, strong. The tremor hurls him down on the bed, which collapses on the floor.

A piece of plaster, hostile and sharp, falls on top of him. The end of the world. Yes, the end of the world, just as his grandmother said it would happen, December 31 at twelve midnight.

And the walls come together over the consciousness of someone who has been abandoned by luck for the first time.

He was found several days later. By then, swollen and foul smelling, his eyes open in terror. Indolence and bad service prevailed in the hotel. The cashier said the guy in room 21 had already been there a week and he figured he'd probably run out because there were no signs of life. There on top of the bed, half naked, he completely lost all sense of time and obligation to pay his debts. Later, the police searched thoroughly and found nothing to confirm the name and information he gave when he registered at the hotel. They called the number he'd given as his home phone, but a laundry answered and didn't know him. The town nurse, the only one who, along with the pharmacist, officially gave vaccinations and prescribed medicine, said it was a heart attack, judging from the terror on his face, as if something sudden and unexpected had come over him.

With nothing to do, no one to notify, they buried him in a corner of some public land, with no more formality than wrapping him in a sheet and putting him in a box that was inexpensive because the lid was made of a different wood and didn't fit very well.

The beggar with the bloody empty socket, master of all the dead birds, said to the other beggar, "Have you noticed that death is carrying away all the visitors to Walls?" "Really," answered the other, "I wonder why . . . ?"

FRANK O'CONNOR   (1903–1966)
Guests of the Nation   1931

[Many Irish writers of the twentieth century were passionately involved in the events leading up to and following Irish independence from Great Britain. Their literature reflects the turmoil and divided loyalties of the Irish struggle: the resentment of British rule that culminated in the Easter Rebellion of 1916; the division between the fiercely Catholic Irish majority and the Protestants loyal to the Crown; the civil war of 1922 between the new Irish Free State and die-hard Republicans refusing to settle for partial victory in their struggle with England. The Smith and Wesson, like the Webley, is a pistol.]

1

At dusk the big Englishman, Belcher, would shift his long legs out of the ashes and say "Well, chums, what about it?" and Noble or me would say "All right, chum" (for we had picked up some of their curious expressions), and the little Englishman, Hawkins, would light the lamp and bring out the cards. Sometimes Jeremiah Donovan would come up and supervise the game and get excited over Hawkins's cards, which he always played badly, and shout at him as if he was one of our own, "Ah, you divil, you, why didn't you play the tray?"

But ordinarily Jeremiah was a sober and contented poor devil like the big Englishman, Belcher, and was looked up to only because he was a fair hand at documents, though he was slow enough even with them. He wore a small cloth hat and big gaiters over his long pants, and you seldom saw him with his hands out of his pockets. He reddened when you talked to him, tilting from toe to heel and back, and looking down all the time at his big farmer's feet. Noble and me used to make fun of his broad accent, because we were from the town.

I couldn't at the time see the point of me and Noble guarding Belcher and Hawkins at all, for it was my belief that you could have planted that pair down anywhere from this to Claregalway and they'd have taken root there like a native weed. I never in my short experience seen two men to take to the country as they did.

They were handed on to us by the Second Battalion when the search for them became too hot, and Noble and myself, being young, took over with a natural feeling of responsibility, but Hawkins made us look like fools when he showed that he knew the country better than we did.

"You're the bloke they calls Bonaparte," he says to me. "Mary Brigid O'Connell   5
told me to ask you what you done with the pair of her brother's socks you borrowed."

For it seemed, as they explained it, that the Second used to have little evenings, and some of the girls of the neighborhood turned in, and, seeing they were such decent chaps, our fellows couldn't leave the two Englishmen out of them. Hawkins learned to dance "The Walls of Limerick," "The Siege of Ennis," and "The Waves of Tory" as well as any of them, though, naturally, we couldn't return the compliment, because our lads at that time did not dance foreign dances on principle.

So whatever privileges Belcher and Hawkins had with the Second they just naturally took with us, and after the first day or two we gave up all pretense of keeping a close eye on them. Not that they could have got far, for they had accents you could cut with a knife and wore khaki tunics and overcoats with civilian pants and boots. But it's my belief that they never had any idea of escaping and were quite content to be where they were.

It was a treat to see how Belcher got off with the old woman of the house where we were staying. She was a great warrant to scold, and cranky even with us, but before ever she had a chance of giving our guests, as I may call them, a lick of her tongue, Belcher had made her his friend for life. She was breaking sticks, and Belcher, who hadn't been more than ten minutes in the house, jumped up from his seat and went over to her.

"Allow me, madam," he says, smiling his queer little smile, "please allow me"; and he takes the bloody hatchet. She was struck too paralytic to speak, and after that, Belcher would be at her heels, carrying a bucket, a basket, or a load of turf, as the case might be. As Noble said, he got into looking before she leapt, and hot water, or any little thing she wanted, Belcher would have it ready for her. For such a huge man (and though I am five foot ten myself I had to look up at him) he had an uncommon shortness—or should I say lack?—of speech. It took us some time to get used to him, walking in and out, like a ghost, without a word. Especially because Hawkins talked enough for a platoon, it was strange to hear big Belcher with his toes in the ashes come out with a solitary "Excuse me, chum," or "That's right, chum." His one and only passion was cards, and I will say for him that he was a good cardplayer. He could have fleeced myself and Noble, but whatever we lost to him Hawkins lost to us, and Hawkins played with the money Belcher gave him.

Hawkins lost to us because he had too much old gab, and we probably lost to   10
Belcher for the same reason. Hawkins and Noble would spit at one another about religion into the early hours of the morning, and Hawkins worried the soul out of Noble, whose brother was a priest, with a string of questions that would puzzle a cardinal. To make it worse, even in treating of holy subjects, Hawkins had a deplorable tongue. I never in all my career met a man who could mix such a variety of cursing and bad language into an argument. He was a terrible man, and a fright to argue. He never did a stroke of work, and when he had no one else to talk to, he got stuck in the old woman.

He met his match in her, for one day when he tried to get her to complain profanely of the drought, she gave him a great come-down by blaming it entirely on Jupiter Pluvius (a deity neither Hawkins nor I had ever heard of, though Noble said that among the pagans it was believed that he had something to do with the rain). Another day he was swearing at the capitalists for starting the German war when the old lady laid down her iron, puckered up her little crab's mouth, and said: "Mr. Hawkins, you can say what you like about the war, and think you'll deceive me because I'm only a simple poor countrywoman, but I know what started the war. It was the Italian Count that stole the heathen divinity out of the temple in Japan. Believe me, Mr. Hawkins, nothing but sorrow and want can follow the people that disturb the hidden powers."

A queer old girl, all right.

2

We had our tea one evening, and Hawkins lit the lamp and we all sat into cards. Jeremiah Donovan came in too, and sat down and watched us for a while, and it suddenly struck me that he had no great love for the two Englishmen. It came as a great surprise to me, because I hadn't noticed anything about him before.

Late in the evening a really terrible argument blew up between Hawkins and Noble, about capitalists and priests and love of your country.

"The capitalists," says Hawkins with an angry gulp, "pays the priests to tell you   15
about the next world so as you won't notice what the bastards are up to in this."

"Nonsense, man!" says Noble, losing his temper. "Before ever a capitalist was thought of, people believed in the next world."

Hawkins stood up as though he was preaching a sermon.

"Oh, they did, did they?" he says with a sneer. "They believed all the things you believe, isn't that what you mean? And you believe that God created Adam, and Adam created Shem, and Shem created Jehoshaphat. You believe all that silly old fairytale about Eve and Eden and the apple. Well, listen to me, chum. If you're entitled to hold a silly belief like that, I'm entitled to hold my silly belief—which is that the first thing your God created was a bleeding capitalist, with morality and Rolls-Royce complete. Am I right, chum?" he says to Belcher.

"You're right, chum," says Belcher with his amused smile, and got up from the table to stretch his long legs into the fire and stroke his moustache. So, seeing that Jeremiah Donovan was going, and that there was no knowing when the argument about religion would be over, I went out with him. We strolled down to the village together, and then he stopped and started blushing and mumbling and saying I ought to be behind, keeping guard on the prisoners. I didn't like the tone he took with me, and anyway I was bored with life in the cottage, so I replied by asking him what the hell we wanted guarding them at all for. I told him I'd talked it over with Noble, and that we'd both rather be out with a fighting column.

"What use are those fellows to us?" says I.   20

He looked at me in surprise and said: "I thought you knew we were keeping them as hostages."

"Hostages?" I said.

"The enemy have prisoners belonging to us," he says, "and now they're talking of shooting them. If they shoot our prisoners, we'll shoot theirs."

"Shoot them?" I said.

"What else did you think we were keeping them for?" he says.   25

"Wasn't it very unforeseen of you not to warn Noble and myself of that in the beginning?" I said.

"How was it?" says he. "You might have known it."

"We couldn't know it, Jeremiah Donovan," says I. "How could we when they were on our hands so long?"

"The enemy have our prisoners as long and longer," says he.

"That's not the same thing at all," says I.   30

"What difference is there?" says he.

I couldn't tell him, because I knew he wouldn't understand. If it was only an old dog that was going to the vet's, you'd try and not get too fond of him, but Jeremiah Donovan wasn't a man that would ever be in danger of that.

"And when is this thing going to be decided?" says I.

"We might hear tonight," he says. "Or tomorrow or the next day at latest. So if it's only hanging round here that's a trouble to you, you'll be free soon enough."

It wasn't the hanging round that was a trouble to me at all by this time. I had   35
worse things to worry about. When I got back to the cottage the argument was still on. Hawkins was holding forth in his best style, maintaining that there was no next world, and Noble was maintaining that there was; but I could see that Hawkins had had the best of it.

"Do you know what, chum?" he was saying with a saucy smile. "I think you're just as big a bleeding unbeliever as I am. You say you believe in the next world, and you know just as much about the next world as I do, which is sweet damn-all. What's heaven? You don't know. Where's heaven? You don't know. You know sweet damn-all! I ask you again, do they wear wings?"

"Very well, then," says Noble, "they do. Is that enough for you? They do wear wings."

"Where do they get them, then? Who makes them? Have they a factory for wings? Have they a sort of store where you hands in your chit and takes your bleeding wings?"

"You're an impossible man to argue with," says Noble. "Now, listen to me—" And they were off again.

It was long after midnight when we locked up and went to bed. As I blew out the candle I told Noble what Jeremiah Donovan was after telling me. Noble took it very quietly. When we'd been in bed about an hour he asked me did I think we ought to tell the Englishmen. I didn't think we should, because it was more than likely that the English wouldn't shoot our men, and even if they did, the brigade officers, who were always up and down with the Second Battalion and knew the Englishmen well, wouldn't be likely to want them plugged. "I think so too," says Noble. "It would be great cruelty to put the wind up them now."

"It was very unforeseen of Jeremiah Donovan anyhow," says I.

It was next morning that we found it so hard to face Belcher and Hawkins. We went about the house all day scarcely saying a word. Belcher didn't seem to notice; he was stretched into the ashes as usual, with his usual look of waiting in quietness for something unforeseen to happen, but Hawkins noticed and put it down to Noble's being beaten in the argument of the night before.

"Why can't you take a discussion in the proper spirit?" he says severely. "You and your Adam and Eve! I'm a Communist, that's what I am. Communist or anarchist, it all comes to much the same thing." And for hours he went round the house, muttering when the fit took him. "Adam and Eve! Adam and Eve! Nothing better to do with their time than picking bleeding apples!"

3

I don't know how we got through that day, but I was very glad when it was over, the tea things were cleared away, and Belcher said in his peaceable way: "Well, chums, what about it?" We sat round the table and Hawkins took out the cards, and just then I heard Jeremiah Donovan's footstep on the path and a dark presentiment crossed my mind. I rose from the table and caught him before he reached the door.

"What do you want?" I asked.

"I want those two soldier friends of yours," he says, getting red.

"Is that the way, Jeremiah Donovan?" I asked.

"That's the way. There were four of our lads shot this morning, one of them a boy of sixteen."

"That's bad," I said.

At that moment Noble followed me out, and the three of us walked down the path together, talking in whispers. Feeney, the local intelligence officer, was standing by the gate.

"What are you going to do about it?" I asked Jeremiah Donovan.

"I want you and Noble to get them out; tell them they're being shifted again; that'll be the quietest way."

"Leave me out of that," says Noble under his breath.

Jeremiah Donovan looks at him hard.

"All right," he says. "You and Feeney get a few tools from the shed and dig a hole by the far end of the bog. Bonaparte and myself will be after you. Don't let anyone see you with the tools. I wouldn't like it to go beyond ourselves."

We saw Feeney and Noble go round to the shed and went in ourselves. I left Jeremiah Donovan to do the explanations. He told them that he had orders to send them back to the Second Battalion. Hawkins let out a mouthful of curses, and you could see that though Belcher didn't say anything, he was a bit upset too. The old woman was for having them stay in spite of us, and she didn't stop advising them until Jeremiah Donovan lost his temper and turned on her. He had a nasty temper, I noticed. It was pitch-dark in the cottage by this time, but no one thought of lighting the lamp, and in the darkness the two Englishmen fetched their topcoats and said good-bye to the old woman.

"Just as a man makes a home of a bleeding place, some bastard at headquarters thinks you're too cushy and shunts you off," says Hawkins, shaking her hand.

"A thousand thanks, madam," says Belcher. "A thousand thanks for everything"— as though he'd made it up.

We went round to the back of the house and down toward the bog. It was only then that Jeremiah Donovan told them. He was shaking with excitement.

"There were four of our fellows shot in Cork this morning and now you're to be shot as a reprisal." 60

"What are you talking about?" snaps Hawkins. "It's bad enough being mucked about as we are without having to put up with your funny jokes."

"It isn't a joke," says Donovan. "I'm sorry, Hawkins, but it's true," and begins on the usual rigmarole about duty and how unpleasant it is.

I never noticed that people who talk a lot about duty find it much of a trouble to them.

"Oh, cut it out!" says Hawkins.

"Ask Bonaparte," says Donovan, seeing that Hawkins isn't taking him seriously. 65 "Isn't it true, Bonaparte?"

"It is," I say, and Hawkins stops.

"Ah, for Christ's sake, chum."

"I mean it, chum," I say.

"You don't sound as if you meant it."

"If he doesn't mean it, I do," says Donovan, working himself up. 70

"What have you against me, Jeremiah Donovan?"

"I never said I had anything against you. But why did your people take our four of our prisoners and shoot them in cold blood?"

He took Hawkins by the arm and dragged him on, but it was impossible to make him understand that we were in earnest. I had the Smith and Wesson in my pocket and I kept fingering it and wondering what I'd do if they put up a fight for it or ran, and wishing to God they'd do one or the other. I knew if they did run for it, that I'd never fire on them. Hawkins wanted to know was Noble in it, and when we said yes, he asked us why Noble wanted to plug him. Why did any of us want to plug him? What had he done to us? Weren't we all chums? Didn't we understand him and didn't he understand us? Did we imagine for an instant that he'd shoot us for all the so-and-so officers in the so-and-so British Army?

By this time we'd reached the bog, and I was so sick I couldn't even answer him. We walked along the edge of it in the darkness, and every now and then Hawkins would call a halt and begin all over again, as if he was wound up, about our being chums, and I knew that nothing but the sight of the grave would convince him that we had to do it. And all the time I was hoping that something would happen; that they'd run for it or that Noble would take over the responsibility from me. I had the feeling that it was worse on Noble than on me.

4

At last we saw the lantern in the distance and made towards it. Noble was carrying 75 it, and Feeney was standing somewhere in the darkness behind him, and the picture of them so still and silent in the bogland brought it home to me that we were in earnest, and banished the last bit of hope I had.

Belcher, on recognizing Noble, said: "Hallo, chum," in his quiet way, but Hawkins flew at him at once, and the argument began all over again, only this time Noble had nothing to say for himself and stood with his head down, holding the lantern between his legs.

It was Jeremiah Donovan who did the answering. For the twentieth time, as though it was haunting his mind, Hawkins asked if anybody thought he'd shoot Noble.

"Yes, you would," says Jeremiah Donovan.

"No, I wouldn't, damn you!"

"You would, because you'd know you'd be shot for not doing it."   80

"I wouldn't, not if I was to be shot twenty times over. I wouldn't shoot a pal. And Belcher wouldn't—isn't that right, Belcher?"

"That's right, chum," Belcher said, but more by way of answering the question than of joining in the argument. Belcher sounded as though whatever unforeseen thing he'd always been waiting for had come at last.

"Anyway, who says Noble would be shot if I wasn't? What do you think I'd do if I was in his place, out in the middle of a blasted bog?"

"What would you do?" asks Donovan.

"I'd go with him wherever he was going, of course. Share my last bob with him   85
and stick by him through thick and thin. No one can ever say of me that I let down a pal."

"We had enough of this," says Jeremiah Donovan, cocking his revolver. "Is there any message you want to send?"

"No, there isn't."

"Do you want to say your prayers?"

Hawkins came out with a cold-blooded remark that even shocked me and turned on Noble again.

"Listen to me, Noble," he says. "You and me are chums. You can't come over to   90
my side, so I'll come over to your side. That show you I mean what I say? Give me a rifle and I'll go along with you and the other lads."

Nobody answered him. We knew that was no way out.

"Hear what I'm saying?" he says. "I'm through with it. I'm a deserter or anything else you like. I don't believe in your stuff, but it's no worse than mine. That satisfy you?"

Noble raised his head, but Donovan began to speak and he lowered it again without replying.

"For the last time, have you any messages to send?" says Donovan in a cold, excited sort of voice.

"Shut up, Donovan! You don't understand me, but these lads do. They're not the   95
sort to make a pal and kill a pal. They're not the tools of any capitalist."

I alone of the crowd saw Donovan raise his Webley to the back of Hawkins's neck, and as he did so I shut my eyes and tried to pray. Hawkins had begun to say something else when Donovan fired, and as I opened my eyes at the bang, I saw Hawkins stagger at the knees and lie out flat at Noble's feet, slowly and as quiet as a kid falling asleep, with the lantern-light on his lean legs and bright farmer's boots. We all stood very still, watching him settle out in the last agony.

Then Belcher took out a handkerchief and began to tie it about his own eyes (in our excitement we'd forgotten to do the same for Hawkins) and, seeing it wasn't big enough, turned and asked for the loan of mine. I gave it to him and he knotted the two together and pointed with his foot at Hawkins.

"He's not quite dead," he says. "Better give him another."

Sure enough, Hawkins's left knee is beginning to rise. I bend down and put my gun to his head; then, recollecting myself, I get up again. Belcher understands what's in my mind.

"Give him his first," he says. "I don't mind. Poor bastard, we don't know what's   100
happening to him now."

I knelt and fired. By this time I didn't seem to know what I was doing. Belcher, who was fumbling a bit awkwardly with the handkerchiefs, came out with a laugh as he heard the shot. It was the first time I heard him laugh and it sent a shudder down my back; it sounded so unnatural.

"Poor bugger!" he said quietly. "And last night he was so curious about it all. It's very queer, chums, I always think. Now he knows as much about it as they'll ever let him know, and last night he was all in the dark."

Donovan helped him to tie the handkerchiefs about his eyes. "Thanks, chum," he said. Donovan asked if there were any messages he wanted sent.

"No, chum," he says. "Not for me. If any of you would like to write to Hawkins's mother, you'll find a letter from her in his pocket. He and his mother were great chums. But my missus left me eight years ago. Went away with another fellow and took the kid with her. I like the feeling of a home, as you may have noticed, but I couldn't start again after that."

It was an extraordinary thing, but in those few minutes Belcher said more than in   105
all the weeks before. It was just as if the sound of the shot had started a flood of talk in him and he could go on the whole night like that, quite happily, talking about himself. We stood round like fools now that he couldn't see us any longer. Donovan looked at Noble, and Noble shook his head. Then Donovan raised his Webley, and at that moment Belcher gives his queer laugh again. He may have thought we were talking about him, or perhaps he noticed the same thing I'd noticed and couldn't understand it.

"Excuse me, chums," he says. "I feel I'm talking the hell of a lot, and so silly, about my being so handy about a house and things like that. But this thing came on me suddenly. You'll forgive me, I'm sure."

"You don't want to say a prayer?" asked Donovan.

"No, chum," he says. "I don't think it would help. I'm ready, and you boys want to get it over."

"You understand that we're only doing our duty?" says Donovan.

Belcher's head was raised like a blind man's, so that you could only see his chin   110
and the tip of his nose in the lantern-light.

"I never could make out what duty was myself," he said. "I think you're all good lads, if that's what you mean. I'm not complaining."

Noble, just as if he couldn't bear any more of it, raised his fist at Donovan, and in a flash Donovan raised his gun and fired. The big man went over like a sack of meal, and this time there was no need of a second shot.

I don't remember much about the burying, but that it was worse than all the rest because we had to carry them to the grave. It was all mad lonely with nothing but a patch of lantern-light between ourselves and the dark, and birds hooting and screeching all round, disturbed by the guns. Noble went through Hawkins's belongings to find the letter from his mother, and then joined his hands together. He did the same with Belcher. Then, when we'd filled in the grave, we separated from Jeremiah Donovan and Feeney and took our tools back to the shed. All the way we didn't speak a word. The kitchen was dark and cold as we'd left it, and the old woman was sitting over the hearth, saying her beads. We walked past her into the room, and Noble struck a match to light the lamp. She rose quietly and came to the doorway with all her cantankerousness gone.

"What did ye do with them?" she asked in a whisper, and Noble started so that the match went out in his hand.

"What's that?" he asked without turning round.   115

"I heard ye," she said.

"What did you hear?" asked Noble.

"I heard ye. Do ye think I didn't hear ye, putting the spade back in the houseen?"

Noble struck another match and this time the lamp lit for him.

"Was that what ye did to them?" she asked.   120

Then, by God, in the very doorway, she fell on her knees and began praying, and after looking at her for a minute or two Noble did the same by the fireplace. I pushed my way out past her and left them at it. I stood at the door, watching the stars and listening to the shrieking of the birds dying out over the bogs. It is so strange what you feel at times like that you can't describe it. Noble says he saw everything ten times the size, as though there were nothing in the whole world but that little patch of bog with the two Englishmen stiffening into it, but with me it was as if the patch of bog where the Englishmen were was a million miles away, and even Noble and the old woman, mumbling behind me, and the birds and the bloody stars were all far away, and I was somehow very small and very lost and lonely like a child astray in the snow. And anything that happened me afterwards, I never felt the same about again.

CYNTHIA OZICK (born 1928)

The Shawl   1980

[The following story takes us to a prison camp where women and children are starving to death and are subject to unspeakable brutality and degradation. In hallucinatory detail, the story takes us to a nightmare world familiar from photographs and testimonies documenting the Nazi death camps of World War II: the lice-ridden, rat-infested overcrowded barracks; the open spaces for the endless roll calls; the fences electrocuting those who touch them.]

Stella, cold, cold the coldness of hell. How they walked on the roads together. Rosa with Magda curled up between sore breasts, Magda wound up in the shawl. Sometimes Stella carried Magda. But she was jealous of Magda. A thin girl of fourteen, too small, with thin breasts of her own, Stella wanted to be wrapped in a shawl, hidden away, asleep, rocked by the march, a baby, a round infant in arms. Magda took Rosa's nipple, and Rosa never stopped walking, a walking cradle. There was not enough milk; sometimes Magda sucked air; then she screamed. Stella was ravenous. Her knees were tumors on sticks, her elbows chicken bones.

Rosa did not feel hunger; she felt light, not like someone walking but like someone in a faint, in trance, arrested in a fit, someone who is already a floating angel, alert and seeing everything, but in the air, not there, not touching the road. As if teetering on the tips of her fingernails. She looked into Magda's face through a gap in the shawl: a squirrel in a nest, safe, no one could reach her inside the little house of the shawl's windings. The face, very round, a pocket mirror of a face: but it was not Rosa's bleak complexion, dark like cholera, it was another kind of face altogether, eyes blue as air, smooth feathers of hair nearly as yellow as the Star sewn into Rosa's coat. You could think she was one of *their* babies.

Rosa, floating, dreamed of giving Magda away in one of the villages. She could leave the line for a minute and push Magda into the hands of any woman on the side of the road. But if she moved out of line they might shoot. And even if she fled the line for half a second and pushed the shawl-bundle at a stranger, would the woman take it? She might be surprised, or afraid; she might drop the shawl, and Magda would fall out and strike her head and die. The little round head. Such a good child, she gave up screaming, and sucked now only for the taste of the drying nipple itself. The neat grip of the tiny gums. One mite of a tooth tip sticking up in the bottom gum, how shining, an elfin tombstone of white marble gleaming there. Without complaining, Magda relinquished Rosa's teats, first the left, then the right; both were cracked, not a sniff of milk. The duct crevice extinct, a dead volcano, blind eye, chill hole, so Magda took the corner of the shawl and milked it instead. She sucked and sucked, flooding the threads with wetness. The shawl's good flavor, milk of linen.

It was a magic shawl, it could nourish an infant for three days and three nights. Magda did not die, she stayed alive, although very quiet. A peculiar smell, of cinnamon and almonds, lifted out of her mouth. She held her eyes open every moment, forgetting how to blink or nap, and Rosa and sometimes Stella studied their blueness. On the road they raised one burden of a leg after another and studied Magda's face. "Aryan," Stella said, in a voice grown as thin as a string; and Rosa thought how Stella gazed at Magda like a young cannibal. And the time that Stella said "Aryan," it sounded to Rosa as if Stella had really said "Let us devour her."

But Magda lived to walk. She lived that long, but she did not walk very well, partly because she was only fifteen months old, and partly because the spindles of her legs could not hold up her fat belly. It was fat with air, full and round. Rosa gave almost all her food to Magda, Stella gave nothing; Stella was ravenous, a growing child herself, but not growing much. Stella did not menstruate. Rosa did not menstruate. Rosa was ravenous, but also not; she learned from Magda how to drink the taste of a finger in one's mouth. They were in a place without pity, all pity was annihilated in Rosa, she looked at Stella's bones without pity. She was sure that Stella was waiting for Magda to die so she could put her teeth into the little thighs.

Rosa knew Magda was going to die very soon; she should have been dead already, but she had been buried away deep inside the magic shawl, mistaken there for the shivering mound of Rosa's breasts; Rosa clung to the shawl as if it covered only herself. No one took it away from her. Magda was mute. She never cried. Rosa hid her in the barracks, under the shawl, but she knew that one day someone would inform; or one day someone, not even Stella, would steal Magda to eat her. When Magda began to walk Rosa knew that Magda was going to die very soon, something would happen. She was afraid to fall asleep; she slept with the weight of her thigh on Magda's body; she was afraid she would smother Magda under her thigh. The weight of Rosa was becoming less and less; Rosa and Stella were slowly turning into air.

Magda was quiet, but her eyes were horribly alive, like blue tigers. She watched. Sometimes she laughed—it seemed a laugh, but how could it be? Magda had never seen anyone laugh. Still, Magda laughed at her shawl when the wind blew its corners, the bad wind with pieces of black in it, that made Stella's and Rosa's eyes tear. Magda's eyes were always clear and tearless. She watched like a tiger. She guarded her shawl. No one could touch it; only Rosa could touch it. Stella was not allowed. The shawl was Magda's own baby, her pet, her little sister. She tangled herself up in it and sucked on one of the corners when she wanted to be very still.

5

Then Stella took the shawl away and made Magda die.

Afterward Stella said: "I was cold."

And afterward she was always cold, always. The cold went into her heart: Rosa saw   10
that Stella's heart was cold. Magda flopped onward with her little pencil legs scribbling
this way and that, in search of the shawl; the pencils faltered at the barracks opening,
where the light began. Rosa saw and pursued. But already Magda was in the square
outside the barracks, in the jolly light. It was the roll-call arena. Every morning Rosa
had to conceal Magda under the shawl against a wall of the barracks and go out and
stand in the arena with Stella and hundreds of others, sometimes for hours, and Magda,
deserted, was quiet under the shawl, sucking on her corner. Every day Magda was
silent, and so she did not die. Rosa saw that today Magda was going to die, and at the
same time a fearful joy ran into Rosa's two palms, her fingers were on fire, she was astonished, febrile: Magda, in the sunlight, swaying on her pencil legs, was howling. Ever
since the drying up of Rosa's nipples, ever since Magda's last scream on the road,
Magda had been devoid of any syllable; Magda was a mute. Rosa believed that something had gone wrong with her vocal cords, with her windpipe, with the cave of her lar-
ynx; Magda was defective, without a voice; perhaps she was deaf; there might be
something amiss with her intelligence; Magda was dumb. Even the laugh that came
when the ash-stippled wind made a clown out of Magda's shawl was only the air-blown
showing of her teeth. Even when the lice, head lice and body lice, crazed her so that
she became as wild as one of the big rats that plundered the barracks at daybreak looking for carrion, she rubbed and scratched and kicked and bit and rolled without a
whimper. But now Magda's mouth was spilling a long viscous rope of clamor.

"Maaaa—"

It was the first noise Magda had ever sent out from her throat since the drying up
of Rosa's nipples.

"Maaaa . . . aaa!"

Again! Magda was wavering in the perilous sunlight of the arena, scrabbling on
such pitiful little bent shins. Rosa saw. She saw that Magda was grieving for the loss of
her shawl, she saw that Magda was going to die. A tide of commands hammered in
Rosa's nipples: Fetch, get, bring! But she did not know which to go after first, Magda
or the shawl. If she jumped out into the arena to snatch Magda up, the howling would
not stop, because Magda would still not have the shawl; but if she ran back into the
barracks to find the shawl, and if she found it, and if she came after Magda holding it
and shaking it, then she would get Magda back. Magda would put the shawl in her
mouth and turn dumb again.

Rosa entered the dark. It was easy to discover the shawl. Stella was heaped under   15
it, asleep in her thin bones. Rosa tore the shawl free and flew—she could fly, she was
only air—into the arena. The sunheat murmured of another life, of butterflies in summer. The light was placid, mellow. On the other side of the steel fence, far away, there
were green meadows speckled with dandelions and deep-colored violets; beyond them,
even farther, innocent tiger lilies, tall, lifting their orange bonnets. In the barracks they
spoke of "flowers," of "rain": excrement, thick turd-braids, and the slow stinking maroon waterfall that slunk down from the upper bunks, the stink mixed with a bitter fatty
floating smoke that greased Rosa's skin. She stood for an instant at the margin of the
arena. Sometimes the electricity inside the fence would seem to hum; even Stella said it
was only an imagining, but Rosa heard real sounds in the wire: grainy sad voices. The
farther she was from the fence, the more clearly the voices crowded at her. The lament-
ing voices strummed so convincingly, so passionately, it was impossible to suspect them
of being phantoms. The voices told her to hold up the shawl, high; the voices told her
to shake it, to whip with it, to unfurl it like a flag. Rosa lifted, shook, whipped, un-

furled. Far off, very far, Magda leaned across her air-fed belly, reaching out with the rods of her arms. She was high up, elevated, riding someone's shoulder. But the shoulder that carried Magda was not coming toward Rosa and the shawl, it was drifting away, the speck of Magda was moving more and more into the smoky distance. Above the shoulder a helmet glinted. The light tapped the helmet and sparkled it into a goblet. Below the helmet a black body like a domino and a pair of black boots hurled themselves in the direction of the electrified fence. The electric voices began to chatter wildly. "Maa-maa, maaamaaa," they all hummed together. How far Magda was from Rosa now, across the whole square, past a dozen barracks, all the way on the other side! She was no bigger than a moth.

All at once Magda was swimming through the air. The whole of Magda traveled through loftiness. She looked like a butterfly touching a silver vine. And the moment Magda's feathered round head and her pencil legs and balloonish belly and zigzag arms splashed against the fence, the steel voices went mad in their growling, urging Rosa to run and run to the spot where Magda had fallen from her flight against the electrified fence; but of course Rosa did not obey them. She only stood, because if she ran they would shoot, and if she tried to pick up the sticks of Magda's body they would shoot, and if she let the wolf's screech ascending now through the ladder of her skeleton break out, they would shoot; so she took Magda's shawl and filled her own mouth with it, stuffed it in and stuffed it in, until she was swallowing up the wolf's screech and tasting the cinnamon and almond depth of Magda's saliva; and Rosa drank Magda's shawl until it dried.

EDGAR ALLAN POE   (1809–1849)

The Cask of Amontillado   1846

The thousand injuries of Fortunato I had borne as I best could, but when he ventured upon insult I vowed revenge. You, who so well know the nature of my soul, will not suppose, however, that I gave utterance to a threat. *At length* I would be avenged; this was a point definitely settled—but the very definitiveness with which it was resolved precluded the idea of risk. I must not only punish but punish with impunity. A wrong is unredressed when retribution overtakes its redresser. It is equally unredressed when the avenger fails to make himself felt as such to him who has done the wrong.

It must be understood that neither by word nor deed had I given Fortunato cause to doubt my good will. I continued, as was my wont, to smile in his face, and he did not perceive that my smile *now* was at the thought of his immolation.

He had a weak point—this Fortunato—although in other regards he was a man to be respected and even feared. He prided himself on his connoisseurship in wine. Few Italians have the true virtuoso spirit. For the most part their enthusiasm is adopted to suit the time and opportunity, to practise imposture upon the British and Austrian *millionaires*. In painting and gemmary, Fortunato, like his countrymen, was a quack, but in the matter of old wines he was sincere. In this respect I did not differ from him materially;—I was skillful in the Italian vintages myself, and bought largely whenever I could.

It was about dusk, one evening during the supreme madness of the carnival season, that I encountered my friend. He accosted me with excessive warmth, for he had been drinking much. The man wore motley. He had on a tight-fitting parti-striped dress, and his head was surmounted by the conical cap and bells. I was so pleased to see him that I thought I should never have done wringing his hand.

I said to him—"My dear Fortunato, you are luckily met. How remarkably well you   5
are looking to-day. But I have received a pipe of what passes for Amontillado, and I
have my doubts."

"How?" said he. "Amontillado? A pipe? Impossible! And in the middle of the carnival!"

"I have my doubts," I replied; "and I was silly enough to pay the full Amontillado
price without consulting you in the matter. You were not to be found, and I was fearful
of losing a bargain."

"Amontillado!"

"I have my doubts."

"Amontillado!"   10

"And I must satisfy them."

"Amontillado!"

"As you are engaged, I am on my way to Luchresi. If any one has a critical turn it
is he. He will tell me—"

"Luchresi cannot tell Amontillado from Sherry."

"And yet some fools will have it that his taste is a match for your own."   15

"Come, let us go."

"Whither?"

"To your vaults."

"My friend, no; I will not impose upon your good nature. I perceive you have an
engagement. Luchresi—"

"I have no engagement;—come."   20

"My friend, no. It is not the engagement, but the severe cold with which I perceive you are afflicted. The vaults are insufferably damp. They are encrusted with nitre."

"Let us go, nevertheless. The cold is merely nothing. Amontillado! You have been
imposed upon. And as for Luchresi, he cannot distinguish Sherry from Amontillado."

Thus speaking, Fortunato possessed himself of my arm; and putting on a mask of
black silk and drawing a *roquelaire* closely about my person, I suffered him to hurry me
to my palazzo.

There were no attendants at home; they had absconded to make merry in honor of
the time. I had told them that I should not return until the morning, and had given
them explicit orders not to stir from the house. These orders were sufficient, I well
knew, to insure their immediate disappearance, one and all, as soon as my back was
turned.

I took from their sconces two flambeaux, and giving one to Fortunato, bowed him   25
through several suites of rooms to the archway that led into the vaults. I passed down a
long and winding staircase, requesting him to be cautious as he followed. We came at
length to the foot of the descent, and stood together upon the damp ground of the
catacombs of the Montresors.

The gait of my friend was unsteady, and the bells upon his cap jingled as he strode.

"The pipe," he said.

"It is farther on," said I; "but observe the white web-work which gleams from
these cavern walls."

He turned toward me, and looked into my eyes with two filmy orbs that distilled
the rheum of intoxication.

"Nitre?" he asked at length.   30

"Nitre," I replied. "How long have you had that cough?"

"Ugh! ugh! ugh!—ugh! ugh! ugh!—ugh! ugh! ugh!—ugh! ugh! ugh!—
ugh! ugh! ugh!"

My poor friend found it impossible to reply for many minutes.

"It is nothing," he said at last.

"Come," I said, with decision, "we will go back; your health is precious. You are   35
rich, respected, admired, beloved; you are happy, as once I was. You are a man to be
missed. For me it is no matter. We will go back; you will be ill, and I cannot be responsible. Besides, there is Luchresi—"

"Enough," he said; "the cough is a mere nothing; it will not kill me. I shall not die
of a cough."

"True—true," I replied; "and, indeed, I had no intention of alarming you unnecessarily—but you should use all proper caution. A draught of this Medoc will defend us
from the damps."

Here I knocked off the neck of a bottle which I drew from a long row of its fellows
that lay upon the mould.

"Drink," I said, presenting him the wine.

He raised it to his lips with a leer. He paused and nodded to me familiarly, while   40
his bells jingled.

"I drink," he said, "to the buried that repose around us."

"And I to your long life."

He again took my arm, and we proceeded.

"These vaults," he said, "are extensive."

"The Montresors," I replied, "were a great and numerous family."   45

"I forget your arms."

"A huge human foot d'or, in a field azure; the foot crushes a serpent rampant
whose fangs are imbedded in the heel."

"And the motto?"

"Nemo me impune lacessit."

"Good!" he said.   50

The wine sparkled in his eyes and the bells jingled. My own fancy grew warm with
the Medoc. We had passed through long walls of piled skeletons, with casks and pun-
cheons intermingling, into the inmost recesses of the catacombs. I paused again, and
this time I made bold to seize Fortunato by an arm above the elbow.

"The nitre!" I said; "see, it increases. It hangs like moss upon the vaults. We are
below the river's bed. The drops of moisture trickle among the bones. Come, we will
go back ere it is too late. Your cough—"

"It is nothing," he said; "let us go on. But first, another draught of the Medoc."

I broke and reached him a flagon of De Grâve. He emptied it at a breath. His eyes
flashed with a fierce light. He laughed and threw the bottle upwards with a gesticula-
tion I did not understand.

I looked at him in surprise. He repeated the movement—a grotesque one.   55

"You do not comprehend?" he said.

"Not I," I replied.

"Then you are not of the brotherhood."

"How?"

"You are not of the masons."   60

"Yes, yes," I said; "yes, yes."

"You? Impossible! A mason?"

"A mason," I replied.

"A sign," he said, "a sign."

"It is this," I answered, producing from beneath the folds of my *roquelaire* a   65
trowel.

"You jest," he exclaimed, recoiling a few paces. "But let us proceed to the Amontillado."

"Be it so," I said, replacing the tool beneath the cloak and again offering him my arm. He leaned upon it heavily. We continued our route in search of the Amontillado. We passed through a range of low arches, descended, passed on, and descending again, arrived at a deep crypt, in which the foulness of the air caused our flambeaux rather to glow than flame.

At the most remote end of the crypt there appeared another less spacious. Its walls had been lined with human remains, piled to the vault overhead, in the fashion of the great catacombs of Paris. Three sides of this interior crypt were still ornamented in this manner. From the fourth side the bones had been thrown down, and lay promiscuously upon the earth, forming at one point a mound of some size. Within the wall thus exposed by the displacing of the bones, we perceived a still interior crypt or recess, in depth about four feet, in width three, in height six or seven. It seemed to have been constructed for no especial use within itself, but formed merely the interval between two of the colossal supports of the roof of the catacombs, and was backed by one of their circumscribing walls of solid granite.

It was in vain that Fortunato, uplifting his dull torch, endeavored to pry into the depth of the recess. Its termination the feeble light did not enable us to see.

"Proceed," I said; "herein is the Amontillado. As for Luchresi—"   70

"He is an ignoramus," interrupted my friend, as he stepped unsteadily forward, while I followed immediately at his heels. In an instant he had reached the extremity of the niche, and finding his progress arrested by the rock, stood stupidly bewildered. A moment more and I had fettered him to the granite. In its surface were two iron staples, distant from each other about two feet, horizontally. From one of these depended a short chain, from the other a padlock. Throwing the links about his waist, it was but the work of a few seconds to secure it. He was too much astounded to resist. Withdrawing the key I stepped back from the recess.

"Pass your hand," I said, "over the wall; you cannot help feeling the nitre. Indeed, it is *very* damp. Once more let me *implore* you to return. No? Then I must positively leave you. But I must first render you all the little attentions in my power."

"The Amontillado!" ejaculated my friend, not yet recovered from his astonishment.

"True," I replied; "the Amontillado."

As I said these words I busied myself among the pile of bones of which I have before spoken. Throwing them aside, I soon uncovered a quantity of building stone and mortar. With these materials and with the aid of my trowel, I began vigorously to wall up the entrance of the niche.   75

I had scarcely laid the first tier of the masonry when I discovered that the intoxication of Fortunato had in a great measure worn off. The earliest indication I had of this was a low moaning cry from the depth of the recess. It was *not* the cry of a drunken man. There was a long and obstinate silence. I laid the second tier, and the third, and the fourth; and then I heard the furious vibrations of the chain. The noise lasted for several minutes, during which, that I might hearken to it with the more satisfaction, I ceased my labors and sat down upon the bones. When at last the clanking subsided, I resumed the trowel, and finished without interruption the fifth, the sixth, and the seventh tier. The wall was now nearly upon a level with my breast. I again paused, and holding the flambeaux over the mason-work, threw a few feeble rays upon the figure within.

A succession of loud and shrill screams, bursting suddenly from the throat of the chained form, seemed to thrust me violently back. For a brief moment I hesitated, I trembled. Unsheathing my rapier, I began to grope with it about the recess; but the thought of an instant reassured me. I placed my hand upon the solid fabric of the catacombs, and felt satisfied. I reapproached the wall; I replied to the yells of him who clamored. I re-echoed, I aided, I surpassed them in volume and in strength. I did this, and the clamorer grew still.

It was now midnight, and my task was drawing to a close. I had completed the eighth, the ninth and the tenth tier. I had finished a portion of the last and the eleventh; there remained but a single stone to be fitted and plastered in. I struggled with its weight; I placed it partially in its destined position. But now there came from out the niche a low laugh that erected the hairs upon my head. It was succeeded by a sad voice, which I had difficulty in recognizing as that of the noble Fortunato. The voice said—

"Ha! ha! ha!—he! he! he!—a very good joke, indeed—an excellent jest. We will have many a rich laugh about it at the palazzo—he! he! he!—over our wine—he! he! he!"

"The Amontillado!" I said.   80

"He! he! he!—he! he! he!—yes, the Amontillado. But is it not getting late? Will not they be awaiting us at the palazzo, the Lady Fortunato and the rest? Let us be gone."

"Yes," I said, "let us be gone."

"For the love of God, Montresor!"

"Yes," I said, "for the love of God."

But to these words I hearkened in vain for a reply. I grew impatient. I called   85
aloud—

"Fortunato!"

No answer. I called again—

"Fortunato!"

No answer still. I thrust a torch through the remaining aperture and let it fall within. There came forth in return only a jingling of the bells. My heart grew sick; it was the dampness of the catacombs that made it so. I hastened to make an end of my labor. I forced the last stone into its position; I plastered it up. Against the new masonry I re-erected the old rampart of bones. For the half of a century no mortal has disturbed them. *In pace requiescat!*

CRAIG STRETE   (born 1950)
Lives Far Child   1988

[This story, part Indian lore, part fantasy, has a surreal quality. The Latin American writer Jorge Luis Borges said about Native American writer Craig Strete that he is "one who can construct a universe within the skull, to rival the real. . . ." Like the stepmother's name, "Winter Gatherer," Indian names often have symbolic overtones; "Lives Far" suggests "She lives far away from this time, this place."]

"It was the beatings," was all Lives Far would say, and she knelt down by the bed with the red and blue Navaho blanket and wept.

"Seems to me, you married a hard one," said Navana, her father. He sat cross-legged by the door of the hogan. His hands were busy carving a small whistle out of elk bone.

"I don't mind the beatings so much," said Lives Far, "but it is not good for my children to see. It shows them the wrong path in life."

Navana watched her with vague unease. Lives Far was five years old, just five, but she was a strange, strange child.

Navana blew the bone scrapings off the whistle and put it to his lips. He blew gently on it and it made a pleasing birdlike trill.

Lives Far turned and looked in his direction, her eyes brightening in spite of the tears.

He held it out to her. "I made this for you, little one."

She came toward him eagerly and took it from his hands. Her face was still wet with tears.

"Make it sing, Lives Far," said Navana and his face lit with a brief hope.

She started to put it to her lips, delight in her eyes, but something stopped the delight and she became solemn and her hands closed in a fist over the whistle.

"I'll keep it and give it to my children," she said. "They are waiting for me outside."

Navana's second wife, Winter Gatherer, stood in the doorway. She was of another tribe and her ways were sometimes hard.

"That child must be punished!" she said bitterly. "We have heard enough of her lies."

Navana put his hand over the small child fist that held the elk bone whistle.

He smiled down at the child with sadness in his eyes.

"My people teach that lies are blackhearted and a child would be beaten if it talked like . . ." Winter Gatherer started again.

Navana turned on her angrily.

"I have heard enough about your people and your ways! We do not beat our little ones! Always gentleness, always respect and understanding, so I have been raised and so I will raise my children! Our way is better."

"A stupid way to raise children," she said. "But something will have to be done about her, if you're too cowardly to beat her."

"Go outside and play," Navana told the child.

"Yes. I've got washing to do and corn to weed and hoe," said Lives Far. "And I better see to fixing supper for Thomas or he'll beat me again."

She went outside, moving slowly, like an old woman bent under the burdens of a lifetime.

At birth, Lives Far was a child unlike other children. Her mother, Navana's first wife, slowly bleeding to death under the birth blankets, had looked into the tiny red face and feared greatly what she saw. Her own death, red and inevitable beneath the Pendleton blanket, did not scare her.

Death was an old friend but the things she saw in her child's eyes were older than anything that ever moved in her world.

When Navana had come at last into the quickening room, he saw the obscene birds of birth and death perched on the same withered branch of his living tree. His wife took his face in her hands when he bent down over her. Gently she turned him away so that he might not look upon the face of the child at her breast. For children at birth cannot hide themselves from the world until life is strong in their bodies.

And she feared that seeing the child for what it might be, he might wish to destroy it.

"I call this child, Lives Far," she said speaking prophecy, and she kept Navana busy with her own death until the child had taken enough of the world's wind into its body, enough living strength to hide its true self. The old ones say such a happening is an evil birth, evil when the greedy child sucks the life out of its own mother. But the child came into the world, evil or not, and was loved and grew under Navana's nurturing wing.

Navana knew Lives Far never played as other children played. She just sat in the sun and talked to people who were not there.

Lives Far, so she said, was married to a white man and had two children by him. His name was Thomas Morgan and he drank and beat her and was evil. Yes, that was what she said. And she described him in great detail, in a way no child of five could possibly know.

"Thomas burns with drink and it burns his head inside, burns someplace deep   30
until his hair no longer feels like hair, but like a scalp of ashes.

"Poor Thomas," she said and her child's voice seemed to forgive him everything. "The drink burns his tongue in the roof of his mouth so the words of his war night-mares can't escape as he sleeps. It started not just with his liking it, but his needing it, the drink, always the drink, because it is the water of war and it made one forget to be afraid and promised other kinds of forgetfulness."

Navana had felt like screaming in the face of such solemn, straight-faced gibberish, if a part of him had not been a little shocked by it, and a little frightened of it as well.

For though Navana did not heed the words of the old ones, who would have seen this child, Lives Far, who took her own mother out of this world, destroyed as an evil thing, still Navana was disturbed and uneasy sometimes when the child was acting this way. He loved her with all his heart but his mind sometimes saw shadows lurking all about her, and a darkness he could not fathom.

"But the forgetfulness must have been too deep or not deep enough. The Thomas Morgan that I married never came back from the war."

Her face was full of sorrow. "He doesn't sleep with me anymore," she confided in   35
a childish whisper. "I've begged him, pleaded with him, but he won't touch me now. He just drinks now and sometimes beats me and always, always, has nightmares. He used to be so sweet when he made love to me. Now he's a stranger to my bed."

Coming from the lips of a five-year-old, it was a tiny, almost mad horror.

Navana brushed the elk bone shavings off his lap.

Winter Gatherer remained in the doorway, looking out at the squash garden. Her beauty was like a weapon, her sharp tongue the point of her spear.

"She's just sitting there like always, Navana, talking to her invisible family. She's head-sick," said Winter Gatherer, fingering a beaded choker around her neck.

"She was always a big-eyed child. Always in a dream," remembered Navana. "The   40
sky is full of rabbits, yellow and brown ones, she would tell me. Or fish are swimming in my ears, Father, make them stop."

"Childish dreams are one thing," said Winter Gatherer. "But these strange dreams have grown to truth in her mind. She is like one possessed."

"Many were the strange dreams I myself had as a child, but as time moved me down the path of life, those dreams left me and new and proper ones came to take their place. So it will be with her, if we give her time," said Navana, but there was very little hope in his voice as much as he wanted to believe it.

Lives Far screamed.

Navana and Winter Gatherer ran outside.

They expected danger but saw none.   45

Just Lives Far alone, her eyes red with weeping, sprawled in a heap in the dust.

"What's wrong, little one? Spider bite you? See a snake?" asked Navana with loving concern, suddenly conscious of clenched fists and relaxing them.

"He's dead," she said.

"Who's dead?" said Winter Gatherer suspiciously, her eyes flashing darkly.

"My husband, Thomas," said Lives Far. "Mostly it's the drink I blame. It's what caused most of our trouble too. I always said it would be the death of him. And now it's taken him away forever. But he wouldn't listen to me. He just wouldn't listen, so he got into a fight in a bar and another white man stabbed him. Left me and the children all alone."

Navana wiped his face with his hand, anxiety plain in his face.

"Now I have to ask you if we can go bring the children to stay with us. It isn't right that the children should be home alone when I work. I know I'll have to work. Thomas fed us at least, but with him gone, it'll be up to me," said Lives Far solemnly, regarding each of them gravely.

"I'm sorry to hear he's dead," said Navana, not sure if he liked this sudden turn of events. If this meant an end to her strange make-believe and a return to being his little five-year-old girl, then Navana was all for it. But he had little real hope.

"We have to go get the children," insisted Lives Far.

"You don't have a husband and you don't have any damn children!" said Winter Gatherer, arms thrust out angrily at her side. She was like an angry snake, coiled to strike.

Navana looked at his wife, shaking his head no. "I'll handle this."

He bent down and put his arm around the frail child. He gently wiped the tears from her eyes.

"Listen to me, Lives Far. If we go to find your children, and there are no children, no Thomas, dead or otherwise, will you put aside this dream once and for all?"

"What dream?" asked Lives Far. "Please, Father, they are blood of your blood. You have to go with me to pick them up."

Navana decided to take the challenge.

"All right, little one, do you know the road to take?"

"West," said Lives Far. "Until we reach the great rock shaped like a turtle, there we turn left and then follow the stream bed. That's where they buried Thomas this morning. And my children will be just down the road from there."

Navana stood up, looked to the west and then nodded once, having come to a decision.

"Then west we shall go."

"Leave me out of the we," said Winter Gatherer. "I'm sick of the whole business."

Navana looked at her for a moment as if seeing her for the first time, and not exactly liking what he saw.

"No need for you to come," said Navana. "I'll saddle up just the one horse for me and Lives Far."

"Eat supper first. Man's going to be a damn fool, he ought to at least have a full belly first."

"I've got a full belly of something already," he said and he took Lives Far by the hand and led her to the barn.

While they were saddling up the horse, they heard the back door of the house slam.

"Isn't Winter Gatherer coming to see her grandchildren?" asked Lives Far.

"No," said Navana grimly, tightening the cinch strap under the belly of the horse. "I figure she's heading into the trading post. Probably to visit a couple relatives of hers that live in bottles. We don't need her anyway."

"How far do you reckon this place is?" said Navana, leading the horse out of the barn.

Lives Far trotted along at his side. "Years and years in Indian time," said Lives Far. "It's not far at all."

Navana swung up easily into the saddle. He bent down, reached for the child and swung her up gracefully behind him on the horse.   75

They trotted down the long dusty road to the west. The sun walked across the sky. The air was as dry as dust under a dead snake and the heat rose off the road in waves. Sweat soaked them both and they swayed dizzily in the saddle with the heat.

As the afternoon moved toward evening, Navana noticed that Lives Far was blood-red with the sun and the heat. She was barely conscious, her arms, loosening moment by moment around his waist.

"I've been down this road a thousand times, little one, as far west as it goes and I've never seen a rock shaped like a turtle."

With an effort the child opened her eyes, and moved her head so that she could see past him.

"There!" she cried. "There it is! Just like I said."   80

Navana turned and his eyes widened in horror.

A landslide had dumped a pile of rocks across one side of the road as it entered Devil's Canyon. Seen from a distance, the tumbled heap of stones did indeed look very much like a turtle.

"Funny nobody ever told me about that landslide," said Navana, shaking his head in bewilderment. "I was through here just last week and there was nothing like this."

"This is where we turn," said Lives Far. "Hurry, Father. We're almost there."

Reluctantly, with no sense of the make-believe coming to an end, Navana turned   85
the horse and they moved on.

The horse almost stumbled as it moved down into the bed of a long-dry stream.

"Now just follow the stream bed and we'll be there soon," said Lives Far. "I can't wait to see my children!"

Heartsick and feeling a growing uneasiness, Navana let the horse follow the stream bed at a walk.

The light of day was beginning to fade. The long shadows of night began marching across the sky. Now the stream bed seemed to melt under their feet and the sky was vanishing into darkness.

"Child, in all my years, I don't recall a stream being here. It's near dark and get-   90
ting hard to see the way. We ought to be home. Maybe we better turn back now."

"But we're almost there," cried Lives Far. "See over there, that's the graveyard!"

She was pointing off to the right.

Navana turned in horror and saw a small area of ground, fenced off with wrought iron. It was the kind of fence the white men used around their burying places. Navana felt raw pulsing terror rising in him.

Lives Far let go of his waist and slid off the horse. She hit hard, overbalanced and fell forward on her face. She bounced to her feet, ignoring her injuries, and began running toward the graveyard.

"Thomas!" she cried.   95

"Wait!" screamed Navana. "Come back!"

Lives Far ran through the front gate and dashed through the rows of tombstones, thrusting up into the night like the pale white stone fingers of dead men.

Navana jumped down off the horse and ran after her, screaming for her to stop.

She was lost to sight from him somewhere in the cold gray rows of stone.

He stumbled through the growing dark, calling out her name.   100

He couldn't find her anywhere.

His terror and panic grew. Each step seemed to take him deeper into darkness. He passed by a group of small tombstones at the far end of the graveyard and then he heard her voice.

"Poor Thomas. I loved you once." That was Lives Far's voice coming eerily from somewhere off to the right.

He staggered toward her.

"Lives Far!" he screamed.   105

A cloud passed overhead and the new moon cast a gray light on the graveyard.

In the distance he thought he saw her hunched over a small tombstone, her back to him.

"Lives Far, come away from there! You are disturbing the dead and doing them a dishonor! None of our people are buried here. Come away, child. I know you are sick in your mind. Very sick, Lives Far, and I am going to take you home now!"

Resolutely, he moved toward her, past the ice palaces of cold speechless stone.

"Don't you want to pay your respects to Thomas, Father?"   110

He came and stood over her, like a sad shadow in the moonlight.

"My poor little one," he said and he bent down to take her in his arms. But as he stooped over, the moon plainly illuminated the lettering on the gravestone.

HERE LIES THOMAS MORGAN
BELOVED HUSBAND OF LIVES FAR MORGAN
1830–1873

Navana backed away in terror.

"Where am I? Where is this place?"

"Father," said Lives Far. "We have to go now. My children are just down the   115
way."

"No, child," said Navana, his voice high with fear. "We must go back the way we came!"

"But I don't want to go back," said Lives Far. "I don't want to be a child back there. I belong here."

"Where is here?" asked Navana.

"Why, 1873 of course," said Lives Far. "The year I lost my husband, Thomas."

"We have to go back!" he cried, terror etching the lines of his face. He turned and   120
looked at the lettering on the gravestone. He knew that the date had to be right, but it could not be! When he had gotten up that morning, it was as the white men had numbered it, 1845, not 1873!

"I can't leave my children," said Lives Far. "You can't make me go back! I won't go! You're dead anyway now."

Lives Far started to back away from him.

"Wait! Listen to me!" he cried but she turned and began to run from him. "Go back!" she said. "You're dead here. And my children need me."

Navana wanted to run after her but terror held him like a dark mother embracing a night child.

She seemed to grow as she ran away from him. Gone were the short little legs of a   125
child, coltish and awkward. Now she ran with the grace of a young girl, as if now seeking the first ground-devouring strides of womanhood.

And then as she passed finally into the distance, she seemed to run with the full-legged gait of a woman.

"LIVES FAR!" His anguished cry chased her all through the moonlit night.

The child was gone.

As much as he wanted to run after her, a certainty as black as night itself, held him back.

He knew that on the other side of that graveyard, somewhere in 1873, his child   130
was a woman grown with children of her own and he was a tree of nothing but bones, shaking no more wind in its white branches.

Navana stood there like a lost deer in the night wind.

He looked back the way he had come and thought now of the childless house back there waiting for him, the empty maternal rooms, the dust gathering on soon-to-be-forgotten toys.

Could a life be lived in that house now? His thoughts turned unhappily to Winter Gatherer and to the rest of their journey of days together.

What did he have to go back to, with Lives Far gone from him?

A man without children was no better than a wind in the grave.   135

He squared his shoulders and began to walk in the direction Lives Far had gone. If the living can see the dead, then the dead can see the living, this was in his mind.

He stepped outside the back gate of the cemetery and his feet began to sink into the ground.

So this is what death is like, he thought.

Then he made a great effort to straighten his shoulders once more and again walk in the direction Lives Far had gone. With each step, he sank deeper as the dark earth reached up to pull the white bones down through his skin. His skin seemed to run away like water into the thirsty earth, seeking its own level.

He did not die as he left the cemetery. He could not die.   140

In Lives Far Woman's world, for five cold long years, he had already been dead.

AMY TAN   (born 1952)

Two Kinds   1989

My mother believed you could be anything you wanted to be in America. You could open a restaurant. You could work for the government and get good retirement. You could buy a house with almost no money down. You could become rich. You could become instantly famous.

"Of course you can be prodigy, too," my mother told me when I was nine. "You can be best anything. What does Auntie Lindo know? Her daughter, she is only best tricky."

America was where all my mother's hopes lay. She had come here in 1949 after losing everything in China: her mother and father, her family home, her first husband, and two daughters, twin baby girls. But she never looked back with regret. There were so many ways for things to get better.

We didn't immediately pick the right kind of prodigy. At first my mother thought I could be a Chinese Shirley Temple. We'd watch Shirley's old movies on TV as though they were training films. My mother would poke my arm and say, *"Ni kan"* —You watch. And I would see Shirley tapping her feet, or singing a sailor song, or pursing her lips into a very round O while saying, "Oh my goodness."

"Ni kan," said my mother as Shirley's eyes flooded with tears. "You already know   5
how. Don't need talent for crying!"

Soon after my mother got this idea about Shirley Temple, she took me to a beauty training school in the Mission district and put me in the hands of a student who could barely hold the scissors without shaking. Instead of getting big fat curls, I emerged with an uneven mass of crinkly black fuzz. My mother dragged me off to the bathroom and tried to wet down my hair.

"You look like Negro Chinese," she lamented, as if I had done this on purpose.

The instructor of the beauty training school had to lop off these soggy clumps to make my hair even again. "Peter Pan is very popular these days," the instructor assured my mother. I now had hair the length of a boy's, with straight-across bangs that hung at a slant two inches above my eyebrows. I liked the haircut and it made me actually look forward to my future fame.

In fact, in the beginning, I was just as excited as my mother, maybe even more so. I pictured this prodigy part of me as many different images, trying each one on for size. I was a dainty ballerina girl standing by the curtains, waiting to hear the right music that would send me floating on my tiptoes. I was like the Christ child lifted out of the straw manger, crying with holy indignity. I was Cinderella stepping from her pumpkin carriage with sparkly cartoon music filling the air.

In all of my imaginings, I was filled with a sense that I would soon become *perfect*. 10
My mother and father would adore me. I would be beyond reproach. I would never feel the need to sulk for anything.

But sometimes the prodigy in me became impatient. "If you don't hurry up and get me out of here, I'm disappearing for good," it warned. "And then you'll always be nothing."

Every night after dinner, my mother and I would sit at the Formica kitchen table. She would present new tests, taking her examples from stories of amazing children she had read in *Ripley's Believe It or Not*, or *Good Housekeeping*, *Reader's Digest*, and a dozen other magazines she kept in a pile in our bathroom. My mother got these magazines from people whose houses she cleaned. And since she cleaned many houses each week, we had a great assortment. She would look through them all, searching for stories about remarkable children.

The first night she brought out a story about a three-year-old boy who knew the capitals of all the states and even most of the European countries. A teacher was quoted as saying the little boy could also pronounce the names of the foreign cities correctly.

"What's the capital of Finland?" my mother asked me, looking at the magazine story.

All I knew was the capital of California, because Sacramento was the name of the 15
street we lived on in Chinatown. "Nairobi!" I guessed, saying the most foreign word I could think of. She checked to see if that was possibly one way to pronounce "Helsin-ki" before showing me the answer.

The tests got harder—multiplying numbers in my head, finding the queen of hearts in a deck of cards, trying to stand on my head without using my hands, predicting the daily temperatures in Los Angeles, New York, and London.

One night I had to look at a page from the Bible for three minutes and then report everything I could remember. "Now Jehoshaphat had riches and honor in abundance and . . . that's all I remember, Ma," I said.

And after seeing my mother's disappointed face once again, something inside of me began to die. I hated the tests, the raised hopes and failed expectations. Before going to bed that night, I looked in the mirror above the bathroom sink and when I saw only my face staring back—and that it would always be this ordinary face—I began to cry. Such a sad, ugly girl! I made high-pitched noises like a crazed animal, trying to scratch out the face in the mirror.

And then I saw what seemed to be the prodigy side of me—because I had never seen that face before. I looked at my reflection, blinking so I could see more clearly. The girl staring back at me was angry, powerful. This girl and I were the same. I had new thoughts, willful thoughts, or rather thoughts filled with lots of won'ts. I won't let her change me, I promised myself. I won't be what I'm not.

So now on nights when my mother presented her tests, I performed listlessly, my head propped on one arm. I pretended to be bored. And I was. I got so bored I started counting the bellows of the foghorns out on the bay while my mother drilled me in other areas. The sound was comforting and reminded me of the cow jumping over the moon. And the next day, I played a game with myself, seeing if my mother would give up on me before eight bellows. After a while I usually counted only one, maybe two bellows at most. At last she was beginning to give up hope.

Two or three months had gone by without any mention of my being a prodigy again. And then one day my mother was watching *The Ed Sullivan Show* on TV. The TV was old and the sound kept shorting out. Every time my mother got halfway up from the sofa to adjust the set, the sound would go back on and Ed would be talking. As soon as she sat down, Ed would go silent again. She got up, the TV broke into loud piano music. She sat down. Silence. Up and down, back and forth, quiet and loud. It was like a stiff embraceless dance between her and the TV set. Finally she stood by the set with her hand on the sound dial.

She seemed entranced by the music, a little frenzied piano piece with this mesmerizing quality, sort of quick passages and then teasing lilting ones before it returned to the quick playful parts.

"*Ni kan,*" my mother said, calling me over with hurried hand gestures. "Look here."

I could see why my mother was fascinated by the music. It was being pounded out by a little Chinese girl, about nine years old, with a Peter Pan haircut. The girl had the sauciness of a Shirley Temple. She was proudly modest like a proper Chinese child. And she also did this fancy sweep of a curtsy, so that the fluffy skirt of her white dress cascaded slowly to the floor like the petals of a large carnation.

In spite of these warning signs, I wasn't worried. Our family had no piano and we couldn't afford to buy one, let alone reams of sheet music and piano lessons. So I could be generous in my comments when my mother bad-mouthed the little girl on TV.

"Play note right, but doesn't sound good! No singing sound," complained my mother.

"What are you picking on her for?" I said carelessly.

"She's pretty good. Maybe she's not the best, but she's trying hard." I knew almost immediately I would be sorry I said that.

"Just like you," she said. "Not the best. Because you not trying." She gave a little huff as she let go of the sound dial and sat down on the sofa.

The little Chinese girl sat down also to play an encore of "Anitra's Dance" by Grieg. I remember the song, because later on I had to learn how to play it.

Three days after watching *The Ed Sullivan Show,* my mother told me what my schedule would be for piano lessons and piano practice. She had talked to Mr. Chong, who lived on the first floor of our apartment building. Mr. Chong was a retired piano teacher and my mother had traded housecleaning services for weekly lessons and a piano for me to practice on every day, two hours a day, from four until six.

When my mother told me this, I felt as though I had been sent to hell. I whined and then kicked my foot a little when I couldn't stand it anymore.

"Why don't you like me the way I am? I'm *not* a genius! I can't play the piano. And even if I could, I wouldn't go on TV if you paid me a million dollars!" I cried.

My mother slapped me. "Who ask you be genius?" she shouted. "Only ask you be your best. For you sake. You think I want you be genius? Hnnh! What for! Who ask you!"

"So ungrateful," I heard her mutter in Chinese. "If she had as much talent as she has temper, she would be famous now."   35

Mr. Chong, whom I secretly nicknamed Old Chong, was very strange, always tapping his fingers to the silent music of an invisible orchestra. He looked ancient in my eyes. He had lost most of the hair on top of his head and he wore thick glasses and had eyes that always looked tired and sleepy. But he must have been younger than I thought, since he lived with his mother and was not yet married.

I met Old Lady Chong once and that was enough. She had this peculiar smell like a baby that had done something in its pants. And her fingers felt like a dead person's, like an old peach I once found in the back of the refrigerator; the skin just slid off the meat when I picked it up.

I soon found out why Old Chong had retired from teaching piano. He was deaf. "Like Beethoven!" he shouted to me. "We're both listening only in our head!" And he would start to conduct his frantic silent sonatas.

Our lessons went like this. He would open the book and point to different things, explaining their purpose: "Key! Treble! Bass! No sharps or flats! So this is C major! Listen now and play after me!"

And then he would play the C scale a few times, a simple chord, and then, as if inspired by an old, unreachable itch, he gradually added more notes and running trills and a pounding bass until the music was really something quite grand.   40

I would play after him, the simple scale, the simple chord, and then I just played some nonsense that sounded like a cat running up and down on top of garbage cans. Old Chong smiled and applauded and then said, "Very good! But now you must learn to keep time!"

So that's how I discovered that Old Chong's eyes were too slow to keep up with the wrong notes I was playing. He went through the motions in half-time. To help me keep rhythm, he stood behind me, pushing down on my right shoulder for every beat. He balanced pennies on top of my wrists so I would keep them still as I slowly played scales and arpeggios. He had me curve my hand around an apple and keep that shape when playing chords. He marched stiffly to show me how to make each finger dance up and down, staccato like an obedient little soldier.

He taught me all these things, and that was how I also learned I could be lazy and get away with mistakes, lots of mistakes. If I hit the wrong notes because I hadn't practiced enough, I never corrected myself. I just kept playing in rhythm. And Old Chong kept conducting his own private reverie.

So maybe I never really gave myself a fair chance. I did pick up the basics pretty quickly, and I might have become a good pianist at that young age. But I was so determined not to try, not to be anybody different that I learned to play only the most ear-splitting preludes, the most discordant hymns.

Over the next year, I practiced like this, dutifully in my own way. And then one   45
day I heard my mother and her friend Lindo Jong both talking in a loud bragging tone of voice so others could hear. It was after church, and I was leaning against the brick wall wearing a dress with stiff white petticoats. Auntie Lindo's daughter, Waverly, who was about my age, was standing farther down the wall about five feet away. We had

grown up together and shared all the closeness of two sisters squabbling over crayons and dolls. In other words, for the most part, we hated each other. I thought she was snotty. Waverly Jong had gained a certain amount of fame as "Chinatown's Littlest Chinese Chess Champion."

"She bring home too many trophy," lamented Auntie Lindo that Sunday. "All day she play chess. All day I have no time do nothing but dust off her winnings." She threw a scolding look at Waverly, who pretended not to see her.

"You lucky you don't have this problem," said Auntie Lindo with a sigh to my mother.

And my mother squared her shoulders and bragged: "Our problem worser than yours. If we ask Jing-mei wash dish, she hear nothing but music. It's like you can't stop this natural talent."

And right then, I was determined to put a stop to her foolish pride.

A few weeks later, Old Chong and my mother conspired to have me play in a tal-   50
ent show which would be held in the church hall. By then, my parents had saved up enough to buy me a secondhand piano, a black Wurlitzer spinet with a scarred bench. It was the showpiece of our living room.

For the talent show, I was to play a piece called "Pleading Child" from Schumann's *Scenes from Childhood*. It was a simple, moody piece that sounded more difficult than it was. I was supposed to memorize the whole thing, playing the repeat parts twice to make the piece sound longer. But I dawdled over it, playing a few bars and then cheating, looking up to see what notes followed, I never really listened to what I was playing. I daydreamed about being somewhere else, about being someone else.

The part I liked to practice best was the fancy curtsy: right foot out, touch the rose on the carpet with a pointed foot, sweep to the side, left leg bends, look up and smile.

My parents invited all the couples from the Joy Luck Club to witness my debut. Auntie Lindo and Uncle Tin were there. Waverly and her two older brothers had also come. The first two rows were filled with children both younger and older than I was. The littlest ones got to go first. They recited simple nursery rhymes, squawked out tunes on miniature violins, twirled Hula Hoops, pranced in pink ballet tutus, and when they bowed or curtsied, the audience would sigh in unison, "Awww," and then clap enthusiastically.

When my turn came, I was very confident. I remember my childish excitement. It was as if I knew, without a doubt, that the prodigy side of me really did exist. I had no fear whatsoever, no nervousness. I remember thinking to myself, This is it! This is it! I looked out over the audience, at my mother's blank face, my father's yawn, Auntie Lindo's stiff-lipped smile, Waverly's sulky expression. I had on a white dress layered with sheets of lace, and a pink bow in my Peter Pan haircut. As I sat down I envisioned people jumping to their feet and Ed Sullivan rushing up to introduce me to everyone on TV.

And I started to play. It was so beautiful. I was so caught up in how lovely I   55
looked that at first I didn't worry how I would sound: So it was a surprise to me when I hit the first wrong note and I realized something didn't sound quite right. And then I hit another and another followed that. A chill started at the top of my head and began to trickle down. Yet I couldn't stop playing, as though my hands were bewitched. I kept thinking my fingers would adjust themselves back, like a train switching to the right track. I played this strange jumble through two repeats, the sour notes staying with me all the way to the end.

When I stood up, I discovered my legs were shaking. Maybe I had just been nervous and the audience, like Old Chong, had seen me go through the right motions and had not heard anything wrong at all. I swept my right foot out, went down on my knee, looked up and smiled. The room was quiet, except for Old Chong, who was beaming and shouting, "Bravo! Bravo! Well done!" But then I saw my mother's face, her stricken face. The audience clapped weakly, and as I walked back to my chair, with my whole face quivering as I tried not to cry, I heard a little boy whisper loudly to his mother, "That was awful," and the mother whispered back, "Well, she certainly tried."

And now I realized how many people were in the audience, the whole world it seemed. I was aware of eyes burning into my back. I felt the shame of my mother and father as they sat stiffly throughout the rest of the show.

We could have escaped during intermission. Pride and some strange sense of honor must have anchored my parents to their chairs. And so we watched it all: the eighteen-year-old boy with a fake mustache who did a magic show and juggled flaming hoops while riding a unicycle. The breasted girl with white makeup who sang from *Madama Butterfly* and got honorable mention. And the eleven-year-old boy who won first prize playing a tricky violin song that sounded like a busy bee.

After the show, the Hsus, the Jongs, and the St. Clairs from the Joy Luck Club came up to my mother and father.

"Lots of talented kids," Auntie Lindo said vaguely, smiling broadly.   60

"That was somethin' else," said my father, and I wondered if he was referring to me in a humorous way, or whether he even remembered what I had done.

Waverly looked at me and shrugged her shoulders. "You aren't a genius like me," she said matter-of-factly. And if I hadn't felt so bad, I would have pulled her braids and punched her stomach.

But my mother's expression was what devastated me: a quiet, blank look that said she had lost everything. I felt the same way, and it seemed as if everybody were now coming up, like gawkers at the scene of an accident, to see what parts were actually missing. When we got on the bus to go home, my father was humming the busy-bee tune and my mother was silent. I kept thinking she wanted to wait until we got home before shouting at me. But when my father unlocked the door to our apartment, my mother walked in and then went to the back, into the bedroom. No accusations. No blame. And in a way, I felt disappointed. I had been waiting for her to start shouting, so I could shout back and cry and blame her for all my misery.

I assumed my talent-show fiasco meant I never had to play the piano again. But two days later, after school, my mother came out of the kitchen and saw me watching TV.

"Four clock," she reminded me as if it were any other day. I was stunned, as   65
though she were asking me to go through the talent-show torture again. I wedged myself more tightly in front of the TV.

"Turn off TV," she called from the kitchen five minutes later.

I didn't budge. And then I decided. I didn't have to do what my mother said anymore. I wasn't her slave. This wasn't China. I had listened to her before and look what happened. She was the stupid one.

She came out from the kitchen and stood in the arched entryway of the living room. "Four clock," she said once again, louder.

"I'm not going to play anymore," I said nonchalantly. "Why should I? I'm not a genius."

She walked over and stood in front of the TV. I saw her chest was heaving up and   70
down in an angry way.

"No!" I said, and I now felt stronger, as if my true self had finally emerged. So this was what had been inside me all along.

"No! I won't!" I screamed.

She yanked me by the arm, pulled me off the floor, snapped off the TV. She was frighteningly strong, half pulling, half carrying me toward the piano as I kicked the throw rugs under my feet. She lifted me up and onto the hard bench. I was sobbing by now, looking at her bitterly. Her chest was heaving even more and her mouth was open, smiling crazily as if she were pleased I was crying.

"You want me to be someone that I'm not!" I sobbed. "I'll never be the kind of daughter you want me to be!"

"Only two kinds of daughters," she shouted in Chinese. "Those who are obedient and those who follow their own mind! Only one kind of daughter can live in this house. Obedient daughter!"

"Then I wish I wasn't your daughter. I wish you weren't my mother," I shouted. As I said these things I got scared. I felt like worms and toads and slimy things were crawling out of my chest, but it also felt good, as if this awful side of me had surfaced, at last.

"Too late change this," said my mother shrilly.

And I could sense her anger rising to its breaking point. I wanted to see it spill over. And that's when I remembered the babies she had lost in China, the ones we never talked about. "Then I wish I'd never been born!" I shouted. "I wish I were dead! Like them."

It was as if I had said the magic words. Alakazam!—and her face went blank, her mouth closed, her arms went slack, and she backed out of the room, stunned, as if she were blowing away like a small brown leaf, thin, brittle, lifeless.

It was not the only disappointment my mother felt in me. In the years that followed, I failed her so many times, each time asserting my own will, my right to fall short of expectations. I didn't get straight As. I didn't become class president. I didn't get into Stanford. I dropped out of college.

For unlike my mother, I did not believe I could be anything I wanted to be. I could only be me.

And for all those years, we never talked about the disaster at the recital or my terrible accusations afterward at the piano bench. All that remained unchecked, like a betrayal that was now unspeakable. So I never found a way to ask her why she had hoped for something so large that failure was inevitable.

And even worse, I never asked her what frightened me the most: Why had she given up hope?

For after our struggle at the piano, she never mentioned my playing again. The lessons stopped. The lid to the piano was closed, shutting out the dust, my misery, and her dreams.

So she surprised me. A few years ago, she offered to give me the piano, for my thirtieth birthday. I had not played in all those years. I saw the offer as a sign of forgiveness, a tremendous burden removed.

"Are you sure?" I asked shyly. "I mean, won't you and Dad miss it?"

"No, this your piano," she said firmly. "Always your piano. You only one can play."

"Well, I probably can't play anymore," I said. "It's been years."

"You pick up fast," said my mother, as if she knew this was certain. "You have natural talent. You could been genius if you want to."

"No I couldn't."

"You just not trying," said my mother. And she was neither angry nor sad. She said it as if to announce a fact that could never be disproved. "Take it," she said.

But I didn't at first. It was enough that she had offered it to me. And after that, every time I saw it in my parents' living room, standing in front of the bay windows, it made me feel proud, as if it were a shiny trophy I had won back.

Last week I sent a tuner over to my parents' apartment and had the piano reconditioned, for purely sentimental reasons. My mother had died a few months before and I had been getting things in order for my father, a little bit at a time. I put the jewelry in special silk pouches. The sweaters she had knitted in yellow, pink, bright orange—all the colors I hated—I put those in moth-proof boxes. I found some old Chinese silk dresses, the kind with little slits up the sides. I rubbed the old silk against my skin, then wrapped them in tissue and decided to take them home with me.

After I had the piano tuned, I opened the lid and touched the keys. It sounded even richer than I remembered. Really, it was a very good piano. Inside the bench were the same exercise notes with handwritten scales, the same secondhand music books with their covers held together with yellow tape.

I opened up the Schumann book to the dark little piece I had played at the recital. It was on the left-hand side of the page, "Pleading Child." It looked more difficult than I remembered. I played a few bars, surprised at how easily the notes came back to me.

And for the first time, or so it seemed, I noticed the piece on the right-hand side. It was called "Perfectly Contented." I tried to play this one as well. It had a lighter melody but the same flowing rhythm and turned out to be quite easy. "Pleading Child" was shorter but slower; "Perfectly Contented" was longer but faster. And after I played them both a few times, I realized they were two halves of the same song.

JAMES THURBER (1894–1961)
The Secret Life of Walter Mitty   1942

[In this much-reprinted story, Thurber's Walter Mitty spends much of his time in a fantasy world of daring exploits. He might imagine himself as a World War I bomber pilot braving the *archies*—anti-aircraft guns—on the way to another encounter with *von Richtman's circus*—a group of German fighter planes (the name is reminiscent of von Richthofen, famous German air ace). Or he might see himself as a crack surgeon dealing with imaginary medical emergencies like *obstreosis* and *coreopsis*.]

"We're going through!" The Commander's voice was like thin ice breaking. He wore his full-dress uniform, with the heavily braided white cap pulled down rakishly over one cold gray eye. "We can't make it, sir. It's spoiling for a hurricane, if you ask me." "I'm not asking you, Lieutenant Berg," said the Commander. "Throw on the power lights! Rev her up to 8,500! We're going through!" The pounding of the cylinders increased: ta-pocketa-pocketa-pocketa-*pocketa-pocketa*. The Commander stared at the ice forming on the pilot window. He walked over and twisted a row of complicated dials. "Switch on No. 8 auxiliary!" he shouted. "Switch on No. 8 auxiliary!" repeated Lieutenant Berg. "Full strength in No. 3 turret!" shouted the Commander. "Full strength in No. 3 turret!" The crew, bending to their various tasks in the huge, hurtling eight-engined Navy hydroplane, looked at each other and grinned. "The Old Man'll get us through," they said to one another. "The Old Man ain't afraid of Hell!" . . .

"Not so fast! You're driving too fast!" said Mrs. Mitty. "What are you driving so fast for?"

"Hmm?" said Walter Mitty. He looked at his wife, in the seat beside him, with shocked astonishment. She seemed grossly unfamiliar, like a strange woman who had yelled at him in a crowd. "You were up to fifty-five," she said. "You know I don't like to go more than forty. You were up to fifty-five." Walter Mitty drove on toward Waterbury in silence, the roaring of the SN202 through the worst storm in twenty years of Navy flying fading in the remote, intimate airways of his mind. "You're tensed up again," said Mrs. Mitty. "It's one of your days. I wish you'd let Dr. Renshaw look you over."

Walter Mitty stopped the car in front of the building where his wife went to have her hair done. "Remember to get those overshoes while I'm having my hair done," she said. "I don't need overshoes," said Mitty. She put her mirror back into her bag. "We've been all through that," she said, getting out of the car. "You're not a young man any longer." He raced the engine a little. "Why don't you wear your gloves? Have you lost your gloves?" Walter Mitty reached in a pocket and brought out the gloves. He put them on, but after she had turned and gone into the building and he had driven on to a red light, he took them off again. "Pick it up, brother!" snapped a cop as the light changed, and Mitty hastily pulled on his gloves and lurched ahead. He drove around the streets aimlessly for a time, and then he drove past the hospital on his way to the parking lot.

. . . "It's the millionaire banker, Wellington McMillan," said the pretty nurse. "Yes?" said Walter Mitty, removing his gloves slowly. "Who has the case?" "Dr. Renshaw and Dr. Benbow, but there are two specialists here, Dr. Remington from New York and Mr. Pritchard-Mitford from London. He flew over." A door opened down a long, cool corridor and Dr. Renshaw came out. He looked distraught and haggard. "Hello, Mitty," he said. "We're having the devil's own time with McMillan, the millionaire banker and close personal friend of Roosevelt. Obstreosis of the ductal tract. Tertiary. Wish you'd take a look at him." "Glad to," said Mitty.

In the operating room there were whispered introductions: "Dr. Remington, Dr. Mitty, Mr. Pritchard-Mitford, Dr. Mitty." "I've read your book on streptothricosis," said Pritchard-Mitford, shaking hands. "A brilliant performance, sir." "Thank you," said Walter Mitty. "Didn't know you were in the States, Mitty," grumbled Remington. "Coals to Newcastle, bringing Mitford and me up here for a tertiary." "You are very kind," said Mitty. A huge, complicated machine, connected to the operating table, with many tubes and wires, began at this moment to go pocketa-pocketa-pocketa. "The new anesthetizer is giving way!" shouted an interne. "There is no one in the East who knows how to fix it!" "Quiet, man!" said Mitty, in a low, cool voice. He sprang to the machine, which was now going pocketa-pocketa-queep-pocketa-queep. He began fingering delicately a row of glistening dials: "Give me a fountain pen!" he snapped. Someone handed him a fountain pen. He pulled a faulty piston out of the machine and inserted the pen in its place. "That will hold for ten minutes," he said. "Get on with the operation." A nurse hurried over and whispered to Renshaw, and Mitty saw the man turn pale. "Coreopsis has set in," said Renshaw nervously. "If you would take over, Mitty?" Mitty looked at him and at the craven figure of Benbow, who drank, and at the grave uncertain faces of the two great specialists. "If you wish," he said. They slipped a white gown on him; he adjusted a mask and drew on thin gloves; nurses handed him shining . . .

"Back it up, Mac! Look out for that Buick!" Walter Mitty jammed on the brakes. "Wrong lane, Mac," said the parking-lot attendant, looking at Mitty closely. "Gee. Yeh," muttered Mitty. He began cautiously to back out of the lane marked "Exit

5

Only." "Leave her sit there," said the attendant: "I'll put her away." Mitty got out of the car. "Hey, better leave the key." "Oh," said Mitty, handing the man the ignition key. The attendant vaulted into the car, backed it up with insolent skill, and put it where it belonged.

They're so damn cocky, thought Walter Mitty, walking along Main Street; they think they know everything. Once he had tried to take his chains off, outside New Milford, and he had got them wound around the axles. A man had had to come out in a wrecking car and unwind them, a young, grinning garageman. Since then Mrs. Mitty always made him drive to a garage to have the chains taken off. The next time, he thought, I'll wear my right arm in a sling; they won't grin at me then. I'll have my right arm in a sling and they'll see I couldn't possibly take the chains off myself. He kicked at the slush on the sidewalk. "Overshoes," he said to himself, and he began looking for a shoe store.

When he came out into the street again, with the overshoes in a box under his arm, Walter Mitty began to wonder what the other thing was his wife had told him to get. She had told him, twice, before they set out from their house for Waterbury. In a way he hated these weekly trips to town—he was always getting something wrong. Kleenex, he thought, Squibb's, razor blades? No. Toothpaste, toothbrush, bicarbonate, carborundum, initiative and referendum? He gave it up. But she would remember it. "Where's the what's-its-name?" she would ask. "Don't tell me you forgot the what's-its-name." A newsboy went by shouting something about the Waterbury trial.

. . . "Perhaps this will refresh your memory." The District Attorney suddenly thrust a heavy automatic at the quiet figure on the witness stand. "Have you ever seen this before?" Walter Mitty took the gun and examined it expertly. "This is my Webley-Vickers 50.80," he said calmly. An excited buzz ran around the courtroom. The Judge rapped for order. "You are a crack shot with any sort of firearms, I believe?" said the District Attorney, insinuatingly. "Objection!" shouted Mitty's attorney. "We have shown that the defendant could not have fired the shot. We have shown that he wore his right arm in a sling on the night of the fourteenth of July." Walter Mitty raised his hand briefly and the bickering attorneys were stilled. "With any known make of gun," he said evenly, "I could have killed Gregory Fitzhurst at three hundred feet *with my left hand*." Pandemonium broke loose in the courtroom. A woman's scream rose above the bedlam and suddenly a lovely, dark-haired girl was in Walter Mitty's arms. The District Attorney struck at her savagely. Without rising from his chair, Mitty let the man have it on the point of the chin. "You miserable cur!" . . .

"Puppy biscuit," said Walter Mitty. He stopped walking and the buildings of Waterbury rose up out of the misty courtroom and surrounded him again. A woman who was passing laughed. "He said 'Puppy biscuit,'" she said to her companion. "That man said 'Puppy biscuit' to himself." Walter Mitty hurried on. He went into an A & P, not the first one he came to but a smaller one farther up the street. "I want some biscuit for small, young dogs," he said to the clerk. "Any special brand, sir?" The greatest pistol shot in the world thought a moment. "It says 'Puppies Bark for It' on the box," said Walter Mitty.

His wife would be through at the hairdresser's in fifteen minutes, Mitty saw in looking at his watch, unless they had trouble drying it; sometimes they had trouble drying it. She didn't like to get to the hotel first; she would want him to be there waiting for her as usual. He found a big leather chair in the lobby, facing a window, and he put the overshoes and the puppy biscuit on the floor beside it. He picked up an old copy of *Liberty* and sank down into the chair. "Can Germany Conquer the World Through the Air?" Walter Mitty looked at the pictures of bombing planes and of ruined streets.

. . . "The cannonading has got the wind up in young Raleigh, sir," said the sergeant. Captain Mitty looked up at him through tousled hair. "Get him to bed," he said wearily. "With the others. I'll fly alone." "But you can't sir," said the sergeant anxiously. "It takes two men to handle that bomber and the Archies are pounding hell out of the air. Von Richtman's circus is between here and Saulier." "Somebody's got to get that ammunition dump," said Mitty. "I'm going over. Spot of brandy?" He poured a drink for the sergeant and one for himself. War thundered and whined around the dugout and battered at the door. There was a rending of wood and splinters flew through the room. "A bit of a near thing," said Captain Mitty carelessly. "The box barrage is closing in," said the sergeant. "We only live once, Sergeant," said Mitty, with his faint, fleeting smile. "Or do we?" He poured another brandy and tossed it off. "I never see a man could hold his brandy like you, sir," said the sergeant. "Begging your pardon, sir." Captain Mitty stood up and strapped on his huge Webley-Vickers automatic. "It's forty kilometers through hell, sir," said the sergeant. Mitty finished one last brandy. "After all," he said softly, "what isn't?" The pounding of the cannon increased; there was the rat-tat-tatting of machine guns, and from somewhere came the menacing pocketa-pocketa-pocketa of the new flame-throwers. Walter Mitty walked to the door of the dugout humming "Auprès de Ma Blonde." He turned and waved to the sergeant. "Cheerio!" he said. . . .

Something struck his shoulder. "I've been looking all over this hotel for you," said Mrs. Mitty. "Why do you have to hide in this old chair? How did you expect me to find you?" "Things close in," said Walter Mitty vaguely. "What?" Mrs. Mitty said. "Did you get the what's-its-name? The puppy biscuit? What's in that box?" "Overshoes," said Mitty. "Couldn't you have put them on in the store?" "I was thinking," said Walter Mitty. "Does it ever occur to you that I am sometimes thinking?" She looked at him. "I'm going to take your temperature when I get you home," she said.

They went out through the revolving doors that made a faintly derisive whistling sound when you pushed them. It was two blocks to the parking lot. At the drugstore on the corner she said, "Wait here for me. I forgot something. I won't be a minute." She was more than a minute. Walter Mitty lighted a cigarette. It began to rain, rain with sleet in it. He stood up against the wall of the drugstore, smoking. . . . He put his shoulders back and his heels together. "To hell with the handkerchief," said Walter Mitty scornfully. He took one last drag on his cigarette and snapped it away. Then, with that faint, fleeting smile playing about his lips, he faced the firing squad; erect and motionless, proud and disdainful, Walter Mitty the Undefeated, inscrutable to the last.

15

LEO TOLSTOY (1828–1910)
How Much Land Does a Man Need?

1886

TRANSLATED BY BARBARA MAKANOWITSKY

[At the start of this story, a Russian peasant named Pakhom declares that his life is good, but he wants just one thing: more land. Russian words that may be unfamiliar to you are *versts* (equaling two-thirds of a mile); *kopecks,* small Russian coins; and *kumiss,* a fermented drink made from mare's milk. *Bast* is a woody fiber used in making rope and mats; the *steppe* is a vast arid and treeless plain; a *hillock* is a small hill; *flax* is a plant from which linen thread and linseed oil are made. Bashkir is an area between the Volga River and the Ural Mountains, inhabited by a Turkish people.]

1

An older sister from town came to visit her younger sister in the country. The elder had married a merchant in town; the younger a peasant in the country. Drinking tea, the sisters chatted. The elder began to brag—to boast of her life in town; how spaciously and comfortably she lived, how well she dressed the children, how nicely she ate and drank, and how she went for drives, excursions, and to the theater.

The younger sister became offended and began disparaging the merchant's life and exalting her peasant life.

"I wouldn't trade my life for yours," she said. "Our life is rough, I grant you, but we haven't a worry. You may live more neatly, and, perhaps, earn a lot at your trade, but you may lose it all. Remember the proverb: loss is gain's big brother. It often goes like that: one day you're rich and the day after, you're begging in the streets. But our peasant life is more stable: a meager life, but a long one. We won't be rich, but we'll always eat."

The old sister began to speak:

"Eat—like the pigs and calves! No elegance, no manners! No matter how hard   5
your man works, you'll live and die in manure and so will your children!"

"What of it," said the younger; "that's our way. Our life may be hard, but we bow to no one, are afraid of no one, while you in town are surrounded by temptations. It's all right now, but tomorrow it may turn ugly—suddenly you'll find your man tempted by cards, or wine, or some young charmer, and everything will turn to ashes. That's what often happens, doesn't it?"

Pakhom, lying on top the stove, listened to the women babbling.

"It's the absolute truth," he said. "We're so busy tilling mother earth from infancy, we don't get such nonsense in our heads. There's just one trouble—too little land! If I had all the land I wanted, I wouldn't fear the Devil himself!"

The women finished their tea, chatted some more about dresses, cleared the dishes, and went to bed. But the Devil sitting behind the stove had heard everything. He was delighted that the peasant wife had induced her husband to boast and, particularly, to boast that if he had enough land even the Devil could not get him.

"All right," he thought, "we'll have a tussle, you and I; I'll give you plenty of land.   10
And then I'll get you through your land."

2

Next to the peasants there lived a small landowner. She had three hundred and twenty-five acres of land. And she had always lived in peace with the peasants—never abusing them. Then she hired as overseer a retired soldier who began to harass the peasants with fines. No matter how careful Pakhom was, either his horses wandered into her oats, or his cattle got into her garden, or his calves strayed onto her meadow—and there was a fine for everything.

Pakhom would pay up and then curse and beat his family. Many were the difficulties Pakhom suffered all summer because of that overseer. Come winter, he was glad to stable the cattle—he begrudged them the fodder, but at least he was free from worry.

It was rumored that winter that the lady was selling her land, and that the innkeeper on the main road was arranging to buy it. The peasants heard this and groaned.

"Well," they thought, "if the innkeeper gets the land, he'll pester us with worse fines than the lady. We can't get along without this land; we live too close."

A delegation of peasants representing the commune came to ask the lady not to sell the land to the innkeeper, but to give it to them. They promised to pay more. The lady agreed. The peasants started making arrangements for the commune to buy the land; they held one meeting and another meeting—but the matter was still unsettled. The Evil One divided them, and they were completely unable to agree. Then the peasants decided that each would buy individually as much as he could. To this, also, the lady agreed. Pakhom heard that his neighbor had bought fifty-five acres from the lady, and that she had loaned him half the money for a year. Pakhom became envious. "They're buying up all the land," he thought, "and I'll be left with nothing." He consulted his wife.

"People are buying," he said, "so we must buy about twenty-five acres, too. Otherwise we can't exist—the overseer is crushing us with fines."   15

They figured out how they could buy. They had one hundred rubles put aside, and they sold the colt and half the bee swarm, hired out their son as a worker, borrowed from their brother-in-law, and raised half the money.

Pakhom gathered up the money, chose his land—forty acres including a little woods—and went to bargain with the lady. He drove a bargain for his forty acres, and sealed it with his hand and a deposit. They went to town and signed the deed with half the money paid down and the rest due in two years.

So Pakhom had his own land. He borrowed seed, sowed the land he had bought: it produced well. In a year, he had settled his debts with both the lady and his brother-in-law. And so Pakhom became a landowner: he plowed and sowed his own land, mowed hay on his own land, cut timber from his own land, and pastured his herd on his own land. When Pakhom went out to plow the land which he now owned forever, or when he happened to glance over the sprouting fields and meadows, he could not rejoice enough. It seemed to him that the grass grew and the flowers flowered in a new way. When he had walked across this land before, it had been land like any land; now it had become completely exceptional.

3

So Pakhom lived and was pleased. Everything would have been fine, had the peasants not begun trespassing on his fields and meadows. He begged them politely to stop, but the trespassing continued. Either the cowherds let the cattle into the meadows, or the horses got into the wheat while grazing at night. Time after time, Pakhom chased them out and forgave without pressing charges; then he became tired of it and started to complain to the district court. And he knew the peasants did not do these things deliberately, but only because they were crowded, yet he thought: "One still mustn't let them or they'll ravage everything. They must be taught."

To teach them, he sued once, and then again; one was fined, then another.   20 Pakhom's neighbors began to hold a grudge against him; they started to trespass on purpose from time to time. One went to the grove at night and cut down a dozen linden trees for bast. When Pakhom walked through the woods, he looked and saw a white glimmer. He approached—there lay the discarded peelings, and there stood the little stumps. If the villain had only cut the edges of the bush, or left one standing, but he had razed them all, one after the other. Pakhom was enraged. He thought and thought: "It must be Semon," he thought. He went to search Semon's farm, found nothing, and quarreled with him. And Pakhom was even more certain Semon had done it. He filed a petition. Semon was called into court. The case dragged on and on; the peasant was acquitted for lack of evidence. Pakhom felt even more wronged, and abused the elder and the judges.

"You're hand and hand with thieves," he said. "If you led honest lives, you wouldn't let thieves go free."

Pakhom quarreled with both the judges and his neighbors. The peasants started threatening to set fire to his place. Although Pakhom had more land than before, his neighbors were closing in on him.

Just then, there was a rumor that people were moving to new places. And Pakhom thought: "I have no reason to leave my land, but if some of us go, there'll be more space. I could take their land, add it to my place; life would be better. It's too crowded now."

Once when Pakhom was sitting at home, a peasant passing through dropped in. Pakhom put him up for the night, fed him, talked to him, and asked him where, pray, he came from. The peasant said he came from below, beyond the Volga, where he had been working. One thing led to another and the peasant gradually started telling how people were going there to settle. He told how his own people had gone there, joined the community, and divided off twenty-five acres a man.

"And the land is so good," he said, "that they sowed rye, and you couldn't see a horse in the stalks, it was so high; and so thick, that five handfuls make a sheaf. One peasant," he said, "who hadn't a thing but his bare hands, came there and now has six horses, two cows." 25

Pakhom's heart took fire. He was thinking: "Why be poor and crowded here if one can live well there? We'll sell the house and land here; with this money, I'll build myself a house there and set up a whole establishment. There's only trouble in this crowded place. But I had better make the trip and look into it myself."

That summer he got ready and went. He sailed down the Volga to Samara in a steamer, then walked four hundred versts on foot. When he arrived, everything was just as described. The peasants were living amply on twenty-five acres per head, and they participated willingly in the activities of the community. And whoever had money could buy, in addition to his share, as much of the very best land as he wanted at a ruble an acre; you could buy as much as you wanted!

After finding out everything, Pakhom returned home and began selling all he owned. He sold the land at a profit, sold his own farm, sold his entire herd, resigned from the community, waited for spring, and set off with his family for the new place.

4

Pakhom arrived at the settlement with his family, and joined the community. He stood the elders drinks and put all the papers in order. They accepted Pakhom, divided off one hundred and twenty-five acres of land in various fields as his portion for his family of five—in addition to the use of the pasture. Pakhom built himself a farm and acquired a herd. His part of the common land alone was three times as large as before. And the land was fertile. He lived ten times better than in the past. You had arable land and fodder at will. And you could keep as many cattle as you wanted.

At first, while he was busy building and settling himself, he was content; but after he became used to it, he felt crowded on this land, too. The first year, Pakhom sowed wheat on his share of the common land—it grew well. He wanted to sow wheat again, but there was not enough common land. And what there was, was not suitable. In that region, wheat is sown only on grassland or wasteland. They sow the land for a year or two, then leave it fallow until the grass grows back again. And there are many wanting that kind of land, and not enough of it for all. There were disputes over it, too; the 30 richer peasants wanted to sow it themselves, while the poor people wanted to rent it to dealers to raise tax money. Pakhom wanted to sow more. The following year, he went to a dealer and rented land from him for a year. He sowed more—it grew well; but it was far from the village—you had to cart it about fifteen versts. He saw the peasant-dealers living in farmhouses and growing rich. "That's the thing," thought Pakhom; "if only I could buy land permanently for myself and build a farmhouse on my land. Everything would be at hand." And Pakhom began pondering over how he could buy freehold land.

So Pakhom lived for three years. He rented land and sowed wheat on it. The years were good ones, and the wheat grew well, and the surplus money accumulated. But Pakhom found it annoying to rent land from people every year and to have to move from place to place. Whenever there was a good piece of land, the peasants immediately rushed to divide up everything; if Pakhom did not hurry to buy, he had no land to sow. The third year, he and a dealer rented part of the common pasture from some peasants; he had already plowed when the peasants sued and the work was wasted. "If it had been my own land," he thought, "I'd bow to no one and there'd be no trouble."

And Pakhom began to inquire where land could be bought permanently. And he came across a peasant. The peasant had bought one thousand three hundred and fifty acres, then gone bankrupt, and was selling cheaply. Pakhom began talking terms with him. They haggled and haggled and agreed on fifteen hundred rubles, half of it payable later. They had just reached an agreement when a traveling merchant stopped at the farm for something to eat. They drank and talked. The merchant said he was returning from the far-off Bashkir country. There, he said, he bought thirteen thousand five hundred acres of land from the Bashkirs. And all for one thousand rubles. Pakhom began asking questions. The merchant recounted.

"You just have to be nice to the old men," he said. "I distributed about a hundred rubles' worth of oriental robes and carpets and a case of tea, and gave wine to whoever wanted it. And I got the land for less than ten kopecks an acre." He showed Pakhom the deed. "The land," it read, "lies along a river, and the steppe is all grassland."

Pakhom began asking him how, where, and what.

"The land there—" said the merchant, "you couldn't walk around it in a year. The Bashkirs own it all. And the people are as silly as sheep. You can almost get it free." 35

"Well," Pakhom thought, "why should I buy thirteen hundred and fifty acres for my thousand rubles and saddle myself with a debt as well, when I can really get something for a thousand rubles."

5

Pakhom asked the way to the Bashkirs and as soon as he had escorted the merchant to the door, he began getting ready to go himself. He left the house in his wife's charge, made preparations, and set off with his hired hand. They went to town, bought a case of tea, gifts, wine—everything just as the merchant had said. They traveled and traveled, traversing five hundred versts. The seventh fortnight, they arrived at a Bashkir camp. Everything was just as the merchant had said. They all lived in felt tents on the steppe near a stream. They themselves neither plowed nor ate bread, but their cattle and horses wandered over the steppes in herds. Twice a day they drove the mares to the colts tethered behind the huts; they milked the mares and made kumiss out of it. The women beat the kumiss and made cheese, while all the men did was drink tea and kumiss and eat mutton and play reed pipes. They were all polite and jolly and they made merry all summer. A completely backward people, with no knowledge of Russian, but friendly.

As soon as the Bashkirs saw Pakhom, they came out of their tents and surrounded their guest. An interpreter was found; Pakhom told him he had come for land. The Bashkirs were delighted, seized Pakhom, conducted him to one of the best tents, placed him on a carpet, put feather pillows under him, sat down in a circle around him, and began serving him tea and kumiss. They slaughtered a sheep and fed him mutton. Pakhom fetched his gifts from the wagon and began distributing them among the Bashkirs. When Pakhom finished presenting his gifts to them, he divided up the tea. The Bashkirs were delighted. They jabbered and jabbered among themselves, then asked the interpreter to speak.

"They ask me to tell you that they like you," said the interpreter, "and that it is our custom to give a guest every satisfaction, and to render gifts in kind. You have presented us with gifts; now tell us what we have that you like, so we can give a gift to you."

"What I like most of all," said Pakhom, "is your land. Our land is crowded, and, furthermore, all of it has been tilled, while your land is plentiful and good. I've never seen the like." 40

The interpreter translated. The Bashkirs talked and talked among themselves. Pakhom did not understand what they were saying, but he saw that they were merry, were shouting something, and laughing. Then they became silent, turned to Pakhom, and the interpreter said, "They asked me to tell you that in return for your kindness they will be glad to give you as much land as you want. Just point it out and it will be yours."

They started to talk again and began to quarrel about something. Pakhom asked what the quarrel was about. And the interpreter said, "Some say the elder must be consulted about the land, that it can't be done without him. But others say it can be done."

6

The Bashkirs were still quarreling when, suddenly, out came a man in a fox fur cap. Everyone fell silent and stood up. And the interpreter said:

"That's the elder himself."

Pakhom immediately fetched the best robe and brought it to the elder along with five pounds of tea. The elder accepted and sat down in a seat of honor. And the Bashkirs immediately started telling him something. The elder listened and listened, requested silence with a nod, and said to Pakhom in Russian: 45

"Well," he said. "It can be done. Choose whatever you like. Land's plentiful."

"What does that mean: take what I want," thought Pakhom. "It has to be secured somehow. Or they'll say it's yours, then take it away."

"Thank you," he said, "for your kind words. You do have a lot of land, and I need only a little. But I'd like to know which is mine. It must be measured off somehow, and secured as mine. Our lives and deaths are in God's hands. What you, good people, are giving, your children may take back."

"You're right," said the elder; "it can be secured."

Pakhom said: 50

"I heard there was a merchant here. You gave him a little piece of land too, and made a deed. I should have the same thing."

The elder understood.

"It can all be done," he said. "We have a scribe, and we'll go to the town to affix the seals."

"And what is the price?" said Pakhom.

"We've only one price: a thousand rubles a day." 55

Pakhom did not understand.

"What kind of measure is that—a day? How many acres does it have?"

"That," he said, "we don't know. But we sell by the day; as much as you can walk around in a day is yours, and the price is a thousand rubles a day."

Pakhom was astonished.

"But look," he said, "a day's walking is a lot of land." 60

The elder laughed.

"It's all yours!" he said. "There's just one condition: if you're not back where you started in a day, your money is lost."

"And how," Pakhom said, "will you mark where I go?"

"Well, we'll stand on the spot you choose, and stay there while you walk off a circle; and you'll take a spade with you and, where convenient, dig holes to mark your path and pile the dirt up high; then we'll drive a plow from pit to pit. Make your circle wherever you want. What you walk around is all yours, as long as you're back where you started by sundown."

Pakhom was delighted. They decided to start off early. They chatted, drank more 65 kumiss, ate mutton, drank tea again; night came on. They laid down a feather bed for Pakhom, and the Bashkirs dispersed, promising to assemble the next day at dawn to set out for the starting point before sunrise.

7

Pakhom lay on the feather bed, unable to sleep for thinking about the land. "I'll grab off a big piece of my own," he thought. "I can walk fifty versts in a day. The days are long now; there'll be quite a bit of land in fifty versts. What's poorest, I'll sell or let to the peasants, and I'll pick out the best to settle on myself. I'll get a plow and two oxen, and hire two laborers; I'll plow over a hundred acres and put cattle to graze on the rest."

All night Pakhom lay awake, drifting off to sleep only just before dawn. No sooner had he fallen asleep than he started to dream. He saw himself lying in the same hut and heard someone chuckling outside. And he wanted to see who was laughing, got up, went out of the hut, and there sat the Bashkir elder himself in front of the hut with both hands holding his sides, rocking back and forth, laughing at something.

Pakhom approached him and asked: "What are you laughing at?" Then he saw that it was not the Bashkir elder, but the merchant of the other day who had come to him and told him about the land. And he had barely asked the merchant, "Have you been here long?"—when it was no longer the merchant, but the peasant who had come on foot from the south long ago. Then Pakhom saw that it was not the peasant, but the Devil himself, laughing, horns, hoofs, and all; and in front of him lay a barefoot man in shirt and trousers. And Pakhom looked closer to see what sort of man he was. He saw it was a corpse and that it was—he himself. Horrified, Pakhom woke up. "The things one dreams," he thought. He looked around; through the open door he saw the dawn; it was already turning white. "Must rouse the people," he thought; "time to go." Pakhom got up, woke his hired hand who was asleep in the wagon, ordered the horses harnessed, and went to wake the Bashkirs.

"It's time," he said, "to go to the steppe to measure off the land."

The Bashkirs got up, assembled everything, and the elder arrived. The Bashkirs 70 began drinking kumiss again, and offered Pakhom tea, but he did not want to linger.

"If we're going, let's go," he said. "It's time."

8

The Bashkirs assembled, climbed on horseback and in wagons and set off. Meanwhile, Pakhom took a spade and set off with his laborer in his own wagon. They arrived at the steppe just as day was breaking. They went up a hillock (known as a *shikhan* in Bashkir). The Bashkirs climbed out of their wagons, slid down from their horses, and gathered in a group. The elder went to Pakhom and pointed.

"There," he said; "everything the eye encompasses is ours. Take your pick."

Pakhom's eyes glowed. It was all grassland, level as the palm of the hand, black as a poppy seed, and wherever there was a hollow, there was grass growing chest-high.

The elder took off his fox cap and put it on the ground.   75

"That," he said, "will be the marker. Leave from here; return here. Whatever you walk around will be yours."

Pakhom drew out his money, placed it on the cap, unfastened his belt, took off his outer coat, girded his belt tightly over his stomach again, put a bag of bread inside his jacket, tied a flask of water to his belt, drew his bootlegs tight, took the spade from his laborer, and got set to go. He pondered and pondered over which direction to take—it was good everywhere. He was thinking: "It's all the same: I'll head toward the sunrise." He turned to face the sun and paced restlessly, waiting for it to appear over the horizon. He was thinking: "I must lose no time. And walking's easier while it's still cold." As soon as the sun's rays spurted over the horizon, Pakhom flung the spade over his shoulder and started off across the steppe.

He walked neither quickly nor slowly. He covered a verst; stopped, dug out a hole, and piled the turf up so it could be seen. He walked further. He loosened up and lengthened his stride. He covered still more ground; dug still another pit.

Pakhom glanced back. The *shikhan* was clearly visible in the sun, and the people stood there, and the hoops of the cart wheels glittered. Pakhom guessed that he had covered about five versts. It was getting warmer; he took off his jacket, flung it over his shoulder, and went on. He covered another five versts. It was warm. He glanced at the sun—already breakfast time.

"One lap finished," thought Pakhom. "But there are four in a day; it's too early to   80
turn around yet. I'll just take my boots off." He sat down, took them off, stuck them in his belt, and went on. Walking became easier. He thought, "I'll just cover about five more versts, then start veering left. This is a very nice spot, too good to leave out. The farther away it is, the better it gets." He walked straight on. When he glanced around, the *shikhan* was barely visible, the people looked like black ants, and there was something faintly glistening on it.

"Well," thought Pakhom, "I've taken enough on this side; I must turn. Besides, I've been sweating—I'm thirsty." He stopped, dug a bigger hole, stacked the turf, untied his flask, and drank. Then he veered sharply to the left. On and on he went; the grass grew taller and it became hot.

Pakhom began to feel tired; he glanced at the sun—it was already lunch time. He stopped; sat on the ground; ate bread and drank water, but did not lie down. "Lie down and you'll fall asleep," he thought. After a while, he walked on. Walking was easy at first. Eating had increased his strength. But it had gotten very hot and he was becoming sleepy. Still he pressed on, thinking—an hour of suffering for a lifetime of living.

He walked a long way in this direction too, and when he was about to turn left, he came to a damp hollow, too nice to overlook. "Flax will grow well there," he thought. Again he went straight on. He took possession of the hollow, dug a hole beyond it, and turned the second corner. Pakhom glanced back at the *shikhan:* it was hazy from the heat, something seemed to be wavering in the air, and through the haze the people barely visible on top of the *shikhan*—fifteen versts away. "Well," thought Pakhom, "I've taken long sides, I must take this one shorter." As he walked the third side, he increased his stride. He looked at the sun—it was already approaching teatime, and he had only covered two versts on the third side. And it was still fifteen versts to the starting point. "No," he thought, "I'll have a lopsided place, but I must go straight back so I'll arrive in time. And not take any more. There's lots of land already." Pakhom shoveled out a hole as quickly as he could and turned straight toward the *shikhan*.

9

As Pakhom walked straight toward the *shikhan*, he began having difficulties. He was perspiring, and his bare legs were cut and bruised and were beginning to fail him. He wanted to rest but could not—otherwise he would not arrive before sunset. The sun would not wait; it continued sinking, sinking. "Ah," he thought, "if only I haven't made a mistake and taken too much! What if I don't make it?" He glanced ahead at the *shikhan*, looked at the sun: the starting point was far away, and the sun was nearing the horizon.

So Pakhom went on with difficulty; he kept increasing and increasing his stride. He walked, walked—and was still far away; he broke into a trot. He threw off his jacket, dropped his boots and flask; he threw off his cap, keeping only his spade to lean on. "Ah," he thought, "I've been too greedy, I've ruined the whole thing, I won't get there by sundown." And fear shortened his breath even more. Pakhom ran; his shirt and trousers clung to his body with sweat; his mouth was parched. His chest felt as though it had been inflated by the blacksmith's bellows; a hammer beat in his heart; and his legs no longer seemed to belong to his body—they were collapsing under him. Pakhom began to worry about dying of strain.

He was afraid of dying, but unable to stop. "I've run so far," he thought. "I'd be a fool to stop now." He ran and ran, and was very close when he heard a screeching—the Bashkirs shrieking at him—and his heart became even more inflamed by their cries. Pakhom pressed forward with his remaining strength, but the sun was already reaching the horizon; and, slipping behind a cloud, it became large, red, and bloody. Now it was beginning to go down. Although the sun was close to setting, Pakhom was no longer far from the starting point either. He could already see the people on the *shikhan* waving their arms at him, urging him on. He saw the fox cap on the ground and the money on it; and he saw the elder sitting on the ground, holding his sides with his hands. And Pakhom remembered his dream. "There is plenty of land," he thought, "if it please God to let me live on it. Oh, I've ruined myself," he thought. "I won't make it."

Pakhom glanced at the sun, but it had touched the earth and had already begun to slip behind the horizon which cut it into an arc. Pakhom overreached his remaining strength, driving his body forward so that his legs could barely move fast enough to keep him from falling. Just as Pakhom ran up to the base of the *shikhan*, it suddenly became dark. He glanced around—the sun had already set. Pakhom sighed. "My work has fallen through," he thought. He was about to stop when he heard the Bashkirs still shrieking. And he remembered that though it seemed below that the sun had set, it would still be shining on the top of the *shikhan*. Pakhom took a deep breath and ran up the *shikhan*. It was still light there. As Pakhom reached the top, he saw the elder sitting in front of the cap, chuckling, holding his sides with his hands. Pakhom remembered his dream and groaned; his legs gave way, and he fell forward, his hands touching the cap.

"Aiee, good man!" cried the elder. "You have acquired plenty of land!"

85

Pakhom's laborer ran to lift him, but the blood was flowing from his mouth and he lay dead.

The Bashkirs clicked their tongues in commiseration.   90

The laborer took up the spade, dug Pakhom a grave just long enough to reach from his feet to his head—six feet in all—and buried him.

JOHN UPDIKE   (born 1932)

A & P   1961

[The narrator in this story, nineteen-year-old Sammy, works at the A & P—The Great Atlantic and Pacific Tea Company, a large grocery chain. Three girls in bathing suits come into the store, triggering the chain of events that Sammy narrates. His narration is filled with humorous details, such as saying that in thirty years the store may be called the Great Alexandrov and Petrooshki Tea Company—a reference to a possible Russian takeover of the United States, a Cold War concern of many in the 1960s. But the concern of the people at the A & P this day is the three girls in bathing suits. As the narrator says, "It's not as if we're on the Cape," referring to Massachusetts' Cape Cod, a beach resort area.]

In walks these three girls in nothing but bathing suits. I'm in the third checkout slot, with my back to the door, so I don't see them until they're over by the bread. The one that caught my eye first was the one in the plaid green two-piece. She was a chunky kid, with a good tan and a sweet broad soft-looking can with those two crescents of white just under it, where the sun never seems to hit, at the top of the backs of her legs. I stood there with my hand on a box of HiHo crackers trying to remember if I rang it up or not. I ring it up again and the customer starts giving me hell. She's one of these cash-register-watchers, a witch about fifty with rouge on her cheekbones and no eyebrows, and I know it made her day to trip me up. She'd been watching cash registers for fifty years and probably never seen a mistake before.

By the time I got her feathers smoothed and her goodies into a bag—she gives me a little snort in passing, if she'd been born at the right time they would have burned her over in Salem—by the time I get her on her way the girls had circled around the bread and were coming back, without a pushcart, back my way along the counters, in the aisle between the checkouts and the Special bins. They didn't even have shoes on. There was this chunky one, with the two-piece—it was bright green and the seams on the bra were still sharp and her belly was still pretty pale so I guessed she just got it (the suit)— there was this one, with one of those chubby berry-faces, the lips all bunched together under her nose, this one, and a tall one, with black hair that hadn't quite frizzed right, and one of these sunburns right across under the eyes, and a chin that was too long— you know, the kind of girl other girls think is very "striking" and "attractive" but never quite makes it, as they very well know, which is why they like her so much—and then the third one, that wasn't quite so tall. She was the queen. She kind of led them, the other two peeking around and making their shoulders round. She didn't look around, not this queen, she just walked straight on slowly, on these long white primadonna legs. She came down a little hard on her heels, as if she didn't walk in her bare feet that much, putting down her heels and then letting the weight move along to her toes as if she was testing the floor with every step, putting a little deliberate extra action into it. You never know for sure how girls' minds work (do you really think it's a mind in there or just a little buzz like a bee in a glass jar?) but you got the idea she had talked the other two into coming in here with her, and now she was showing them how to do it, walk slow and hold yourself straight.

She had on a kind of dirty-pink—beige, maybe, I don't know—bathing suit with a little nubble all over it and, what got me, the straps were down. They were off her shoulders looped loose around the cool tops of her arms, and I guess as a result the suit had slipped a little on her, so all around the top of the cloth there was this shining rim. If it hadn't been there you wouldn't have known there could have been anything whiter than those shoulders. With the straps pushed off, there was nothing between the top of the suit and the top of her head except just *her,* this clean bare plane of the top of her chest down from the shoulder bones like a dented sheet of metal tilted in the light. I mean, it was more than pretty.

She had sort of oaky hair that the sun and salt had bleached, done up in a bun that was unraveling, and a kind of prim face. Walking into the A & P with your straps down, I suppose it's the only kind of face you *can* have. She held her head so high her neck, coming up out of those white shoulders, looked kind of stretched, but I didn't mind. The longer her neck was, the more of her there was.

She must have felt in the corner of her eye me and over my shoulder Stokesie in the second slot watching, but she didn't tip. Not this queen. She kept her eyes moving across the racks, and stopped, and turned so slow it made my stomach rub the inside of my apron, and buzzed to the other two, who kind of huddled against her for relief, and then they all three of them went up the cat-and-dog-food-breakfast-cereal-macaroni-rice-raisins-seasonings-spreads-spaghetti-soft-drinks-crackers-and-cookies aisle. From the third slot I look straight up this aisle to the meat counter, and I watched them all the way. The fat one with the tan sort of fumbled with the cookies, but on second thought she put the package back. The sheep pushing their carts down the aisle—the girls were walking against the usual traffic (not that we have one-way signs or anything)—were pretty hilarious. You could see them, when Queenie's white shoulders dawned on them, kind of jerk, or hop, or hiccup, but their eyes snapped back to their own baskets and on they pushed. I bet you could set off dynamite in an A & P and the people would by and large keep reaching and checking oatmeal off their lists and muttering "Let me see, there was a third thing, began with A, asparagus, no ah, yes, applesauce!" or whatever it is they do mutter. But there was no doubt, this jiggled them. A few houseslaves in pin curlers even looked around after pushing their carts past to make sure what they had seen was correct.

You know, it's one thing to have a girl in a bathing suit down on the beach, where what with the glare nobody can look at each other much anyway, and another thing in the cool of the A & P, under the fluorescent lights, against all those stacked packages, with her feet paddling along naked over our checkerboard green-and-cream rubber-tile floor.

"Oh Daddy," Stokesie said beside me. "I feel so faint."

"Darling," I said. "Hold me tight." Stokesie's married, with two babies chalked up on his fuselage already, but as far as I can tell that's the only difference. He's twenty-two, and I was nineteen this April.

"Is it done?" he asks, the responsible married man finding his voice. I forgot to say he thinks he's going to be manager some sunny day, maybe in 1990 when it's called the Great Alexandrov and Petrooshki Tea Company or something.

What he meant was, our town is five miles from the beach, with a big summer colony out on the Point, but we're right in the middle of town, and the women generally put on a shirt or shorts or something before they get out of the car into the street. And anyway these are usually women with six children and varicose veins mapping their legs and nobody, including them, could care less. As I say, we're right in the middle of town, and if you stand at our front doors you can see two banks and the Congregational church and the newspaper store and three real-estate offices and about twenty-seven old freeloaders tearing up Central Street because the sewer broke again. It's not as if we're on the Cape, we're north of Boston and there's people in this town haven't seen the ocean for twenty years.

The girls had reached the meat counter and were asking McMahon something. He pointed, they pointed, and they shuffled out of sight behind a pyramid of Diet Delight peaches. All that was left for us to see was old McMahon patting his mouth and looking after them sizing up their joints. Poor kids, I began to feel sorry for them, they couldn't help it.

Now here comes the sad part of the story, at least my family says it's sad, but I don't think it's so sad myself. The store's pretty empty, it being Thursday afternoon, so there was nothing much to do except lean on the register and wait for the girls to show up again. The whole store was like a pinball machine and I didn't know which tunnel they'd come out of. After a while they come around out of the far aisle, around the light bulbs, records at discount of the Caribbean Six or Tony Martin Sings or some such gunk you wonder they waste the wax on, sixpacks of candy bars, and plastic toys done up in cellophane that fall apart when a kid looks at them anyway. Around they come, Queenie still leading the way; and holding a little gray jar in her hand. Slots Three through Seven are unmanned and I could see her wondering between Stokes and me, but Stokesie with his usual luck draws an old party in baggy gray pants who stumbles up with four giant cans of pineapple juice (what do these bums *do* with all that pineapple juice? I've often asked myself) so the girls come to me. Queenie puts down the jar and I take it into my fingers icy cold. Kingfish Fancy Herring Snacks in Pure Sour Cream: 49¢. Now her hands are empty, not a ring or a bracelet, bare as God made them, and I wonder where the money's coming from. Still with that prim look she lifts a folded dollar bill out of the hollow at the center of her nubbed pink top. The jar went heavy in my hand. Really, I thought that was so cute.

Then everybody's luck begins to run out. Lengel comes in from haggling with a truck full of cabbages on the lot and is about to scuttle into that door marked MANAGER behind which he hides all day when the girls touch his eye. Lengel's pretty dreary, teaches Sunday school and the rest, but he doesn't miss that much. He comes over and says, "Girls, this isn't the beach."

Queenie blushes, though maybe it's just a brush of sunburn I was noticing for the first time, now that she was so close. "My mother asked me to pick up a jar of herring snacks." Her voice kind of startled me, the way voices do when you see the people first, coming out so flat and dumb yet kind of tony, too, the way it ticked over "pick up" and "snacks." All of a sudden I slid right down her voice into her living room. Her father and the other men were standing around in ice-cream coats and bow ties and the women were in sandals picking up herring snacks on toothpicks off a big glass plate and they were all holding drinks the color of water with olives and sprigs of mint in them. When my parents have somebody over they get lemonade and if it's a real racy affair Schlitz in tall glasses with "They'll Do It Every Time" cartoons stenciled on.

"That's all right," Lengel said. "But this isn't the beach." His repeating this struck me as funny, as if it had just occurred to him, and he had been thinking all these years the A & P was a great big dune and he was the head lifeguard. He didn't like my smil- 15 ing—as I say he doesn't miss much—but he concentrates on giving the girls that sad Sunday-school-superintendent stare.

Queenie's blush is no sunburn now, and the plump one in plaid, that I liked better from the back—a really sweet can—pipes up. "We weren't doing any shopping. We just came in for the one thing."

"That makes no difference," Lengel tells her, and I could see from the way his eyes went that he hadn't noticed she was wearing a two-piece before. "We want you decently dressed when you come in here."

"We *are* decent," Queenie says suddenly, her lower lip pushing, getting sore now that she remembers her place, a place from which the crowd that runs the A & P must look pretty crummy. Fancy Herring Snacks flashed in her very blue eyes.

"Girls, I don't want to argue with you. After this come in here with your shoulders covered. It's our policy." He turns his back. That's policy for you. Policy is what the kingpins want. What the others want is juvenile delinquency.

All this while, the customers had been showing up with their carts but, you know,   20
sheep, seeing a scene, they had all bunched up on Stokesie, who shook open a paper bag as gently as peeling a peach, not wanting to miss a word. I could feel in the silence everybody getting nervous, most of all Lengel, who asks me, "Sammy, have you rung up their purchase?"

I thought and said "No" but it wasn't about that I was thinking. I go through the punches, 4, 9, GROC. TOT—it's more complicated than you think, and after you do it often enough, it begins to make a little song, that you hear words to, in my case "Hello (*bing*) there, you (*gung*) hap-py *pee*-pul (*splat*)!"—the *splat* being the drawer flying out. I uncrease the bill, tenderly as you may imagine, it just having come from between the two smoothest scoops of vanilla I had ever known were there, and pass a half and a penny into her narrow pink palm, and nestle the herrings in a bag and twist its neck and hand it over, all the time thinking.

The girls, and who'd blame them, are in a hurry to get out, so I say "I quit" to Lengel quick enough for them to hear, hoping they'll stop and watch me, their unsuspected hero. They keep right on going, into the electric eye; the door flies open and they flicker across the lot to their car, Queenie and Plaid and Big Tall Goony-Goony (not that as raw material she was so bad), leaving me with Lengel and a kink in his eyebrow.

"Did you say something, Sammy?"

"I said I quit."

"I thought you did."   25

"You didn't have to embarrass them."

"It was they who were embarrassing us."

I started to say something that came out "Fiddle-de-doo." It's a saying of my grandmother's, and I know she would have been pleased.

"I don't think you know what you're saying," Lengel said.

"I know you don't," I said. "But I do." I pull the bow at the back of my apron   30
and start shrugging it off my shoulders. A couple customers that had been heading for my slot begin to knock against each other, like scared pigs in a chute.

Lengel sighs and begins to look very patient and old and gray. He's been a friend of my parents for years. "Sammy, you don't want to do this to your Mom and Dad," he tells me. It's true, I don't. But it seems to me that once you begin a gesture it's fatal not to go through with it. I fold the apron, "Sammy" stitched in red on the pocket, and put it on the counter, and drop the bow tie on top of it. The bow tie is theirs, if you've ever wondered. "You'll feel this for the rest of your life," Lengel says, and I know that's true, too, but remembering how he made that pretty girl blush makes me so scrunchy inside I punch the No Sale tab and the machine whirs "pee-pul" and the drawer splats out. One advantage to this scene taking place in summer, I can follow this up with a clean exit, there's no fumbling around getting your coat and galoshes. I just saunter into the electric eye in my white shirt that my mother ironed the night before, and the door heaves itself open, and outside the sunshine is skating around on the asphalt.

I look around for my girls, but they're gone, of course. There wasn't anybody but some young married screaming with her children about some candy they didn't get by the door of a powder-blue Falcon station wagon. Looking back in the big windows, over the bags of peat moss and aluminum lawn furniture stacked on the pavement, I could see Lengel in my place in the slot, checking the sheep through. His face was dark gray and his back stiff, as if he'd just had an injection of iron, and my stomach kind of fell as I felt how hard the world was going to be to me hereafter.

HELENA MARÍA VIRAMONTES (Born 1954)
The Moths 1985

[In this story, a fourteen-year-old girl has been asked to help *Abuelita*, her dying grandmother. Other Spanish names and phrases in the story are *Tío* (Uncle), *Amá* (Mother, as in *Y mi Amá?*—And my mother?); and *Apá* (Father). The *menudo* is a traditional soup made with tripe and red chili sauce; a *molcajete* is a grinding stone.

I was fourteen years old when Abuelita requested my help. And it seemed only fair. Abuelita had pulled me through the rages of scarlet fever by placing, removing, and replacing potato slices on the temples of my forehead; she had seen me through several whippings, an arm broken by a dare jump off Tío Enrique's toolshed, puberty, and my first lie. Really, I told Amá, it was only fair.

Not that I was her favorite granddaughter or anything special. I wasn't even pretty or nice like my older sisters and I just couldn't do the girl things they could do. My hands were too big to handle the fineries of crocheting or embroidery and I always pricked my fingers or knotted my colored threads time and time again while my sisters laughed and called me bull hands with their cute waterlike voices. So I began keeping a piece of jagged brick in my sock to bash my sisters or anyone who called me bull hands. Once, while we all sat in the bedroom, I hit Teresa on the forehead, right above her eyebrow and she ran to Amá with her mouth open, her hand over her eye while blood seeped between her fingers. I was used to the whippings by then.

I wasn't respectful either. I even went so far as to doubt the power of Abuelita's slices, the slices she said absorbed my fever. "You're still alive, aren't you?" Abuelita snapped back, her pasty gray eye beaming at me and burning holes in my suspicions. Regretful that I had let secret questions drop out of my mouth, I couldn't look into her eyes. My hands began to fan out, grow like a liar's nose until they hung by my side like low weights. Abuelita made a balm out of dried moth wings and Vicks and rubbed my hands, shaped them back to size and it was the strangest feeling. Like bones melting. Like sun shining through the darkness of your eyelids. I didn't mind helping Abuelita after that, so Amá would always send me over to her.

In the early afternoon Amá would push her hair back, hand me my sweater and shoes, and tell me to go to Mama Luna's. This was to avoid another fight and another whipping, I knew. I would deliver one last direct shot on Marisela's arm and jump out of our house, the slam of the screen door burying her cries of anger, and I'd gladly go help Abuelita plant her wild lilies or jasmine or heliotrope or cilantro or hierbabuena in red Hills Brothers coffee cans. Abuelita would wait for me at the top step of her porch holding a hammer and nail and empty coffee cans. And although we hardly spoke, hardly looked at each other as we worked over root transplants, I always felt her gray eye on me. It made me feel, in a strange sort of way, safe and guarded and not alone. Like God was supposed to make you feel.

On Abuelita's porch, I would puncture holes in the bottom of the coffee cans with   5
a nail and a precise hit of a hammer. This completed, my job was to fill them with red clay mud from beneath her rose bushes, packing it softly, then making a perfect hole, four fingers round, to nest a sprouting avocado pit, or the spidery sweet potatoes that Abuelita rooted in mayonnaise jars with toothpicks and daily water, or prickly chayotes that produced vines that twisted and wound all over her porch pillars, crawling to the roof, up and over the roof, and down the other side, making her small brick house look like it was cradled within the vines that grew pear-shaped squashes ready for the pick, ready to be steamed with onions and cheese and butter. The roots would burst out of the rusted coffee cans and search for a place to connect. I would then feed the seedlings with water.

But this was a different kind of help, Amá said, because Abuelita was dying. Looking into her gray eye, then into her brown one, the doctor said it was just a matter of days. And so it seemed only fair that these hands she had melted and formed found use in rubbing her caving body with alcohol and marihuana, rubbing her arms and legs, turning her face to the window so that she could watch the Bird of Paradise blooming or smell the scent of clove in the air. I toweled her face frequently and held her hand for hours. Her gray wiry hair hung over the mattress. Since I could remember, she'd kept her long hair in braids. Her mouth was vacant and when she slept, her eyelids never closed all the way. Up close, you could see her gray eye beaming out the window, staring hard as if to remember everything. I never kissed her. I left the window open when I went to the market.

Across the street from Jay's Market there was a chapel. I never knew its denomination, but I went in just the same to search for candles. I sat down on one of the pews because there were none. After I cleaned my fingernails, I looked up at the high ceiling. I had forgotten the vastness of these places, the coolness of the marble pillars and the frozen statues with blank eyes. I was alone. I knew why I had never returned.

That was one of Apá's biggest complaints. He would pound his hands on the table, rocking the sugar dish or spilling a cup of coffee, and scream that if I didn't go to mass every Sunday to save my goddamn sinning soul, then I had no reason to go out of the house, period. Punto final. He would grab my arm and dig his nails into me to make sure I understood the importance of catechism. Did he make himself clear? Then he strategically directed his anger at Amá for her lousy ways of bringing up daughters, being disrespectful and unbelieving, and my older sisters would pull me aside and tell me if I didn't get to mass right this minute, they were all going to kick the holy shit out of me. Why am I so selfish? Can't you see what it's doing to Amá, you idiot? So I would wash my feet and stuff them in my black Easter shoes that shone with Vaseline, grab a missal and veil, and wave good-bye to Amá.

I would walk slowly down Lorena to First to Evergreen, counting the cracks on the cement. On Evergreen I would turn left and walk to Abuelita's. I liked her porch because it was shielded by the vines of the chayotes and I could get a good look at the people and car traffic on Evergreen without them knowing. I would jump up the porch steps, knock on the screen door as I wiped my feet, and call Abuelita? mi Abuelita? As I opened the door and stuck my head in, I would catch the gagging scent of toasting chile on the placa. When I entered the sala, she would greet me from the kitchen, wringing her hands in her apron. I'd sit at the corner of the table to keep from being in her way. The chiles made my eyes water. Am I crying? No, Mama Luna, I'm sure not crying. I don't like going to mass, but my eyes watered anyway, the tears dropping on the tablecloth like candle wax. Abuelita lifted the burnt chiles from the fire and sprinkled water on them until the skins began to separate. Placing them in front of me, she turned to check the menudo. I peeled the skins off and put the flimsy, limp-looking green and yellow chiles in the molcajete and began to crush and crush and twist and crush the heart out of the tomato, the clove of garlic, the stupid chiles that made me cry, crushed them until they turned into liquid under my bull hand. With a wooden spoon, I scraped hard to destroy the guilt, and my tears were gone. I put the bowl of chile next to a vase filled with freshly cut roses. Abuelita touched my hand and pointed to the bowl of menudo that steamed in front of me. I spooned some chile into the menudo and rolled a corn tortilla thin with the palms of my hands. As I ate, a fine Sunday breeze entered the kitchen and a rose petal calmly feathered down to the table.

I left the chapel without blessing myself and walked to Jay's. Most of the time Jay didn't have much of anything. The tomatoes were always soft and the cans of Campbell soups had rusted spots on them. There was dust on the tops of cereal boxes. I picked up what I needed: rubbing alcohol, five cans of chicken broth, a big bottle of Pine Sol. At first Jay got mad because I thought I had forgotten the money. But it was there all the time, in my back pocket.

When I returned from the market, I heard Amá crying in Abuelita's kitchen. She looked up at me with puffy eyes. I placed the bags of groceries on the table and began putting the cans of soup away. Amá sobbed quietly. I never kissed her. After a while, I patted her on the back for comfort. Finally: "¿Y mi Amá?" she asked in a whisper, then choked again and cried into her apron.

Abuelita fell off the bed twice yesterday, I said, knowing that I shouldn't have said it and wondering why I wanted to say it because it only made Amá cry harder. I guess I became angry and just so tired of the quarrels and beatings and unanswered prayers and my hands just there hanging helplessly by my side. Amá looked at me again, confused, angry, and her eyes were filled with sorrow. I went outside and sat on the porch swing and watched the people pass. I sat there until she left. I dozed off repeating the words to myself like rosary prayers: when do you stop giving when do you start giving when do you . . . and when my hands fell from my lap, I awoke to catch them. The sun was setting, an orange glow, and I knew Abuelita was hungry.

There comes a time when the sun is defiant. Just about the time when moods change, inevitable seasons of a day, transitions from one color to another, that hour or minute or second when the sun is finally defeated, finally sinks into the realization that it cannot with all its power to heal or burn, exist forever, there comes an illumination where the sun and earth meet, a final burst of burning red orange fury reminding us that although endings are inevitable, they are necessary for rebirths, and when that time came, just when I switched on the light in the kitchen to open Abuelita's can of soup, it was probably then that she died.

The room smelled of Pine Sol and vomit and Abuelita had defecated the remains of her cancerous stomach. She had turned to the window and tried to speak, but her mouth remained open and speechless. I heard you, Abuelita, I said, stroking her cheek, I heard you. I opened the windows of the house and let the soup simmer and overboil on the stove. I turned the stove off and poured the soup down the sink. From the cabinet I got a tin basin, filled it with lukewarm water and carried it carefully to the room. I went to the linen closet and took out some modest bleached white towels. With the sacredness of a priest preparing his vestments, I unfolded the towels one by one on my shoulders. I removed the sheets and blankets from her bed and peeled off her thick flannel nightgown. I toweled her puzzled face, stretching out the wrinkles, removing the coils of her neck, toweled her shoulders and breasts. Then I changed the water. I returned to towel the creases of her stretch-marked stomach, her sporadic vaginal hairs, and her sagging thighs. I removed the lint from between her toes and noticed a mapped birthmark on the fold of her buttock. The scars on her back which were as thin as the life lines on the palms of her hands made me realize how little I really knew of Abuelita. I covered her with a thin blanket and went into the bathroom. I washed my hands, and turned on the tub faucets and watched the water pour into the tub with vitality and steam. When it was full, I turned off the water and undressed. Then, I went to get Abuelita.

She was not as heavy as I thought and when I carried her in my arms, her body fell   15
into a V, and yet my legs were tired, shaky, and I felt as if the distance between the bedroom and bathroom was miles and years away. Amá, where are you?

I stepped into the bathtub one leg first, then the other. I bent my knees slowly to descend into the water slowly so I wouldn't scald her skin. There, there, Abuelita, I said, cradling her, smoothing her as we descended, I heard you. Her hair fell back and spread across the water like eagle's wings. The water in the tub overflowed and poured onto the tile of the floor. Then the moths came. Small, gray ones that came from her soul and out through her mouth fluttering to light, circling the single dull light bulb of the bathroom. Dying is lonely and I wanted to go to where the moths were, stay with her and plant chayotes whose vines would crawl up her fingers and into the clouds; I wanted to rest my head on her chest with her stroking my hair, telling me about the moths that lay within the soul and slowly eat the spirit up; I wanted to return to the waters of the womb with her so that we would never be alone again. I wanted. I wanted my Amá. I removed a few strands of hair from Abuelita's face and held her small light head within the hollow of my neck. The bathroom was filled with moths, and for the first time in a long time I cried, rocking us, crying for her, for me, for Amá, the sobs emerging from the depths of anguish, the misery of feeling half born, sobbing until finally the sobs rippled into circles and circles of sadness and relief. There, there, I said to Abuelita, rocking us gently, there, there.

JEROME WEIDMAN   (born 1913)

My Father Sits in the Dark   1934

[In this story about a Jewish immigrant father, some terms that help us participate in the world of the characters are *borscht*—beet soup, a favorite food among Jewish immigrants from Eastern Europe; and *kretchma*—kretscham, an Austrian dialect word for a village tavern. Other references that may need explanation: The second section of the *Times* is the financial pages of the *New York Times;* Debs is Eugene Debs (1855–1926), legendary labor leader, 1900–1920; T. R. is Theodore Roosevelt (1858–1919), swashbuckling U. S. president, 1901–1909.]

My father has a peculiar habit. He is fond of sitting in the dark, alone. Sometimes I come home very late. The house is dark. I let myself in quietly because I do not want to disturb my mother. She is a light sleeper. I tiptoe into my room and undress in the dark. I go to the kitchen for a drink of water. My bare feet make no noise. I step into the room and almost trip over my father. He is sitting in a kitchen chair, in his pajamas, smoking his pipe.

"Hello, Pop," I say.

"Hello, son."

"Why don't you go to bed, Pa?"

"I will," he says.   5

But he remains there. Long after I am asleep I feel sure that he is still sitting there, smoking.

Many times I am reading in my room. I hear my mother get the house ready for the night. I hear my kid brother go to bed. I hear my sister come in. I hear her do things with jars and combs until she, too, is quiet. I know she has gone to sleep. In a little while I hear my mother say good night to my father. I continue to read. Soon I become thirsty. (I drink a lot of water.) I go to the kitchen for a drink. Again I almost stumble across my father. Many times it startles me. I forget about him. And there he is—smoking, sitting, thinking.

"Why don't you go to bed, Pop?"

"I will, son."

But he doesn't. He just sits there and smokes and thinks. It worries me. I can't un-   10
derstand it. What can he be thinking about? Once I asked him.

"What are you thinking about, Pa?"

"Nothing," he said.

Once I left him there and went to bed. I awoke several hours later. I was thirsty. I went to the kitchen. There he was. His pipe was out. But he sat there, staring into a corner of the kitchen. After a moment I became accustomed to the darkness. I took my drink. He still sat and stared. His eyes did not blink. I thought he was not even aware of me. I was afraid.

"Why don't you go to bed, Pop?"

"I will, son," he said. "Don't wait up for me."   15

"But," I said, "you've been sitting here for hours. What's wrong? What are you thinking about?"

"Nothing, son," he said. "Nothing. It's just restful. That's all."

The way he said it was convincing. He did not seem worried. His voice was even and pleasant. It always is. But I could not understand it. How could it be restful to sit alone in an uncomfortable chair far into the night, in darkness?

What can it be?

I review all the possibilities. It can't be money. I know that. We haven't much, but   20
when he is worried about money he makes no secret of it. It can't be his health. He is not reticent about that either. It can't be the health of anyone in the family. We are a bit short on money, but we are long on health. (Knock wood, my mother would say.) What can it be? I am afraid I do not know. But that does not stop me from worrying.

Maybe he is thinking of his brothers in the old country. Or of his mother and two step-mothers. Or of his father. But they are all dead. And he would not brood about them like that. I say brood, but it is not really true. He does not brood. He does not even seem to be thinking. He looks too peaceful, too, well not contented, just too peaceful, to be brooding. Perhaps it is as he says. Perhaps it is restful. But it does not seem possible. It worries me.

If I only knew what he thinks about. If I only knew that he thinks at all. I might not be able to help him. He might not even need help. It may be as he says. It may be restful. But at least I would not worry about it.

Why does he just sit there, in the dark? Is his mind failing? No, it can't be. He is only fifty-three. And he is just as keen-witted as ever. In fact, he is the same in every respect. He still likes beet soup. He still reads the second section of the *Times* first. He still wears wing collars. He still believes that Debs could have saved the country and that T.R. was a tool of the moneyed interests. He is the same in every way. He does not even look older than he did five years ago. Everybody remarks about that. Well-preserved, they say. But he sits in the dark, alone, smoking, staring straight ahead of him, unblinking, into the small hours of the night.

If it is as he says, if it is restful, I will let it go at that. But suppose it is not. Suppose it is something I cannot fathom. Perhaps he needs help. Why doesn't he speak? Why doesn't he frown or laugh or cry? Why doesn't he do something? Why does he just sit there?

Finally I become angry. Maybe it is just my unsatisfied curiosity. Maybe I *am* a bit   25
worried. Anyway, I become angry.

"Is something wrong, Pop?"

"Nothing, son. Nothing at all."

But this time I am determined not to be put off. I am angry.

"Then why do you sit here all alone, thinking, till late?"

"It's restful, son. I like it."   30

I am getting nowhere. Tomorrow he will be sitting there again. I will be puzzled. I will be worried. I will not stop now. I am angry.

"Well, what do you *think* about, Pa? Why do you just sit here? What's worrying you? What do you think about?"

"Nothing's worrying me, son. I'm all right. It's just restful. That's all. Go to bed, son."

My anger has left me. But the feeling of worry is still there. I must get an answer. It seems so silly. Why doesn't he tell me? I have a funny feeling that unless I get an answer I will go crazy. I am insistent.

"But what do you *think* about, Pa? What is it?"   35

"Nothing, son. Just things in general. Nothing special. Just things."

I can get no answer.

It is very late. The street is quiet and the house is dark. I climb the steps softly, skipping the ones that creak. I let myself in with my key and tiptoe into my room. I remove my clothes and remember that I am thirsty. In my bare feet I walk to the kitchen. Before I reach it I know he is there.

I can see the deeper darkness of his hunched shape. He is sitting in the same chair, his elbows on his knees, his cold pipe in his teeth, his unblinking eyes staring straight ahead. He does not seem to know I am there. He did not hear me come in. I stand quietly in the doorway and watch him.

Everything is quiet, but the night is full of little sounds. As I stand there motion-   40
less I begin to notice them. The ticking of the alarm clock on the icebox. The low hum of an automobile passing many blocks away. The swish of papers moved along the street by the breeze. A whispering rise and fall of sound, like low breathing. It is strangely pleasant.

The dryness in my throat reminds me. I step briskly into the kitchen.

"Hello, Pop," I say.

"Hello, son," he says. His voice is low and dreamlike. He does not change his position or shift his gaze.

I cannot find the faucet. The dim shadow of light that comes through the window from the street lamp only makes the room seem darker. I reach for the short chain in the center of the room. I snap on the light.

He straightens up with a jerk, as though he has been struck. "What's the matter,   45 Pop?" I ask.

"Nothing," he says. "I don't like the light."

"What's the matter with the light?" I say. "What's wrong?"

"Nothing," he says. "I don't like the light."

I snap the light off. I drink my water slowly. I must take it easy, I say to myself. I must get to the bottom of this.

"Why don't you go to bed? Why do you sit here so late in the dark?"   50

"It's nice," he says. "I can't get used to lights. We didn't have lights when I was a boy in Europe."

My heart skips a beat and I catch my breath happily. I begin to think I understand. I remember the stories of his boyhood in Austria. I see the wide-beamed *kretchma,* with my grandfather behind the bar. It is late, the customers are gone, and he is dozing. I see the bed of glowing coals, the last of the roaring fire. The room is already dark, and grows darker. I see a small boy, crouched on a pile of twigs at one side of the huge fireplace, his starry gaze fixed on the dull remains of the dead flames. The boy is my father.

I remember the pleasure of those few moments while I stood quietly in the doorway watching him.

"You mean there's nothing wrong? You just sit in the dark because you like it, Pop?" I find it hard to keep my voice from rising in a happy shout.

"Sure," he says. "I can't think with the light on."   55

I set my glass down and turn to go back to my room. "Good night, Pop," I say.

"Good night," he says.

Then I remember. I turn back. "What do you think about, Pop?" I ask.

His voice seems to come from far away. It is quiet and even again. "Nothing," he says softly. "Nothing special."

EDITH WHARTON   (1862–1937)

Roman Fever   1934

[The setting is Rome; the characters are privileged American women. The author portrays the negative effects of a patriarchal culture on the tedious lives of well-educated women of the early twentieth century. Long considered to be a novelist of manners, Wharton's works have recently been reevaluated as grappling with feminist issues, such as marriage and divorce. The Seven Hills are the famous hills on and around which the ancient city of Rome was built, with the Palatine the name of one of those seven hills; the Forum was a public place where people gathered on special occasions. Tarquinia is a Roman city named after the Roman king Tarquininius Superbus ("the Proud"), 534–510 B.C. A Baedeker is a famous nineteenth-century guidebook to Europe.]

1

From the table at which they had been lunching two American ladies of ripe but well-cared-for middle age moved across the lofty terrace of the Roman restaurant and, leaning on its parapet, looked first at each other, and then down on the outspread glories of the Palatine and the Forum, with the same expression of vague but benevolent approval.

As they leaned there a girlish voice echoed up gaily from the stairs leading to the court below. "Well, come along, then," it cried, not to them but to an invisible companion, "and let's leave the young things to their knitting"; and a voice as fresh laughed back: "Oh, look here, Babs, not actually *knitting*—" "Well, I mean figuratively," rejoined the first. "After all, we haven't left our poor parents much else to do. . . ." and at that point the turn of the stairs engulfed the dialogue.

The two ladies looked at each other again, this time with a tingle of smiling embarrassment, and the smaller and paler one shook her head and colored slightly.

"Barbara!" she murmured, sending an unheard rebuke after the mocking voice in the stairway.

The other lady, who was fuller, and higher in color, with a small determined nose   5
supported by vigorous black eyebrows, gave a good-humored laugh. "That's what our daughters think of us!"

Her companion replied by a deprecating gesture. "Not of us individually. We must remember that. It's just the collective modern idea of Mothers. And you see—" Half-guiltily she drew from her handsomely mounted black handbag a twist of crimson silk run through by two fine knitting needles. "One never knows," she murmured. "The new system has certainly given us a good deal of time to kill; and sometimes I get tired just looking—even at this." Her gesture was now addressed to the stupendous scene at their feet.

The dark lady laughed again, and they both relapsed upon the view, contemplating it in silence, with a sort of diffused serenity which might have been borrowed from the spring effulgence of the Roman skies. The luncheon hour was long past, and the two had their end of the vast terrace to themselves. At its opposite extremity a few groups, detained by a lingering look at the outspread city, were gathering up guidebooks and fumbling for tips. The last of them scattered, and the two ladies were alone on the air-washed height.

"Well, I don't see why we shouldn't just stay here," said Mrs. Slade, the lady of the high color and energetic brows. Two derelict basket chairs stood near, and she pushed them into the angle of the parapet, and settled herself in one, her gaze upon the Palatine. "After all, it's still the most beautiful view in the world."

"It always will be, to me," assented her friend Mrs. Ansley, with so slight a stress on the "me" that Mrs. Slade, though she noticed it, wondered if it were not merely accidental, like the random underlinings of old-fashioned letter writers.

"Grace Ansley was always old-fashioned," she thought; and added aloud, with a   10
retrospective smile: "It's a view we've both been familiar with for a good many years. When we first met here we were younger than our girls are now. You remember?"

"Oh, yes, I remember," murmured Mrs. Ansley, with the same undefinable stress. "There's that headwaiter wondering," she interpolated. She was evidently far less sure than her companion of herself and of her rights in the world.

"I'll cure him of wondering," said Mrs. Slade, stretching her hand toward a bag as discreetly opulent-looking as Mrs. Ansley's. Signing to the headwaiter, she explained that she and her friend were old lovers of Rome, and would like to spend the end of the afternoon looking down on the view—that is, if it did not disturb the service? The headwaiter, bowing over her gratuity, assured her that the ladies were most welcome, and would be still more so if they would condescend to remain for dinner. A full-moon night, they would remember. . . .

Mrs. Slade's black brows drew together, as though references to the moon were out of place and even unwelcome. But she smiled away her frown as the headwaiter retreated. "Well, why not? We might do worse. There's no knowing, I suppose, when the girls will be back. Do you even know back from *where*? I don't!"

Mrs. Ansley again colored slightly. "I think those young Italian aviators we met at the Embassy invited them to fly to Tarquinia for tea. I suppose they'll want to wait and fly back by moonlight."

"Moonlight—moonlight! What a part it still plays. Do you suppose they're as sentimental as we were?"

"I've come to the conclusion that I don't in the least know what they are," said Mrs. Ansley. "And perhaps we didn't know much more about each other."

"No; perhaps we didn't."

Her friend gave her a shy glance. "I never should have supposed you were sentimental, Alida."

"Well, perhaps I wasn't." Mrs. Slade drew her lids together in retrospect; and for a few moments the two ladies, who had been intimate since childhood, reflected how little they knew each other. Each one, of course, had a label ready to attach to the other's name; Mrs. Delphin Slade, for instance, would have told herself, or anyone who asked her, that Mrs. Horace Ansley, twenty-five years ago, had been exquisitely lovely—no, you wouldn't believe it, would you? . . . though, of course, still charming, distinguished. . . . Well, as a girl she had been exquisite; far more beautiful than her daughter Barbara, though certainly Babs, according to the new standards at any rate, was more effective—had more *edge*, as they say. Funny where she got it, with those two nullities as parents. Yes; Horace Ansley was—well, just the duplicate of his wife. Museum specimens of old New York. Good-looking, irreproachable, exemplary. Mrs. Slade and Mrs. Ansley had lived opposite each other—actually as well as figuratively—for years. When the drawing-room curtains in No. 20 East 73rd Street were renewed, No. 23, across the way, was always aware of it. And of all the movings, buyings, travels, anniversaries, illnesses—the tame chronicle of an estimable pair. Little of it escaped Mrs. Slade. But she had grown bored with it by the time her husband made his big *coup* in Wall Street, and when they bought in upper Park Avenue had already begun to think: "I'd rather live opposite a speakeasy for a change; at least one might see it raided." The idea of seeing Grace raided was so amusing that (before the move) she launched it at a woman's lunch. It made a hit, and went the rounds—she sometimes wondered if it had crossed the street, and reached Mrs. Ansley. She hoped not, but didn't much mind. Those were the days when respectability was at a discount, and it did the irreproachable no harm to laugh at them a little.

A few years later, and not many months apart, both ladies lost their husbands. There was an appropriate exchange of wreaths and condolences, and a brief renewal of intimacy in the half-shadow of their mourning; and now, after another interval, they had run across each other in Rome, at the same hotel, each of them the modest appendage of a salient daughter. The similarity of their lot had again drawn them together, lending itself to mild jokes, and the mutual confession that, if in old days it must have been tiring to "keep up" with daughters, it was now, at times, a little dull not to.

No doubt, Mrs. Slade reflected, she felt her unemployment more than poor Grace ever would. It was a big drop from being the wife of Delphin Slade to being his widow. She had always regarded herself (with a certain conjugal pride) as his equal in social gifts, as contributing her full share to the making of the exceptional couple they were: but the difference after his death was irremediable. As the wife of the famous corporation lawyer, always with an international case or two on hand, every day brought its ex-

15

20

citing and unexpected obligation: the impromptu entertaining of eminent colleagues from abroad, the hurried dashes on legal business to London, Paris or Rome, where the entertaining was so handsomely reciprocated; the amusement of hearing in her wake: "What, that handsome woman with the good clothes and the eyes is Mrs. Slade—*the* Slade's wife? Really? Generally the wives of celebrities are such frumps."

Yes; being *the* Slade's widow was a dullish business after that. In living up to such a husband all her faculties had been engaged; now she had only her daughter to live up to, for the son who seemed to have inherited his father's gifts had died suddenly in boyhood. She had fought through that agony because her husband was there, to be helped and to help; now, after the father's death, the thought of the boy had become unbearable. There was nothing left but to mother her daughter; and dear Jenny was such a perfect daughter that she needed no excessive mothering. "Now with Babs Ansley I don't know that I *should* be so quiet," Mrs. Slade sometimes half-enviously reflected; but Jenny, who was younger than her brilliant friend, was that rare accident, an extremely pretty girl who somehow made youth and prettiness seem as safe as their absence. It was all perplexing—and to Mrs. Slade a little boring. She wished that Jenny would fall in love—with the wrong man, even; that she might have to be watched, outmaneuvered, rescued. And instead, it was Jenny who watched her mother, kept her out of drafts, made sure that she had taken her tonic. . . .

Mrs. Ansley was much less articulate than her friend, and her mental portrait of Mrs. Slade was slighter, and drawn with fainter touches. "Alida Slade's awfully brilliant; but not as brilliant as she thinks," would have summed it up; though she would have added, for the enlightenment of strangers, that Mrs. Slade had been an extremely dashing girl; much more so than her daughter, who was pretty, of course, and clever in a way, but had none of her mother's—well, "vividness," someone had once called it. Mrs. Ansley would take up current words like this, and cite them in quotation marks, as unheard-of audacities. No; Jenny was not like her mother. Sometimes Mrs. Ansley thought Alida Slade was disappointed; on the whole she had had a sad life. Full of failures and mistakes; Mrs. Ansley had always been rather sorry for her. . . .

So these two ladies visualized each other, each through the wrong end of her little telescope.

2

For a long time they continued to sit side by side without speaking. It seemed as though, to both, there was a relief in laying down their somewhat futile activities in the presence of the vast Memento Mori which faced them. Mrs. Slade sat quite still, her eyes fixed on the golden slope of the Palace of the Caesars, and after a while Mrs. Ansley ceased to fidget with her bag, and she too sank into meditation. Like many intimate friends, the two ladies had never before had occasion to be silent together, and Mrs. Ansley was slightly embarrassed by what seemed, after so many years, a new stage in their intimacy, and one with which she did not yet know how to deal.

Suddenly the air was full of that deep clangor of bells which periodically covers Rome with a roof of silver. Mrs. Slade glanced at her wristwatch. "Five o'clock already," she said, as though surprised.

Mrs. Ansley suggested interrogatively: "There's bridge at the Embassy at five." For a long time Mrs. Slade did not answer. She appeared to be lost in contemplation, and Mrs. Ansley thought the remark had escaped her. But after a while she said, as if speaking out of a dream: "Bridge, did you say? Not unless you want to. . . . But I don't think I will, you know."

"Oh, no," Mrs. Ansley hastened to assure her. "I don't care to at all. It's so lovely here; and so full of old memories, as you say." She settled herself in her chair, and almost furtively drew forth her knitting. Mrs. Slade took sideway note of this activity, but her own beautifully cared-for hands remained motionless on her knee.

"I was just thinking," she said slowly, "what different things Rome stands for to each generation of travelers. To our grandmothers, Roman fever; to our mothers, sentimental dangers—how we used to be guarded!—to our daughters, no more dangers than the middle of Main Street. They don't know it—but how much they're missing!"

The long golden light was beginning to pale, and Mrs. Ansley lifted her knitting a little closer to her eyes. "Yes; how we were guarded!"   30

"I always used to think," Mrs. Slade continued, "that our mothers had a much more difficult job than our grandmothers. When Roman fever stalked the streets it must have been comparatively easy to gather in the girls at the danger hour; but when you and I were young, with such beauty calling us, and the spice of disobedience thrown in, and no worse risk than catching cold during the cool hour after sunset, the mothers used to be put to it to keep us in—didn't they?"

She turned again toward Mrs. Ansley, but the latter had reached a delicate point in her knitting. "One, two, three—slip two; yes, they must have been," she assented, without looking up.

Mrs. Slade's eyes rested on her with a deepened attention. "She can knit—in the face of *this!* How like her. . . ."

Mrs. Slade leaned back, brooding, her eyes ranging from the ruins which faced her to the long green hollow of the Forum, the fading glow of the church fronts beyond it, and the outlying immensity of the Colosseum. Suddenly she thought: "It's all very well to say that our girls have done away with sentiment and moonlight. But if Babs Ansley isn't out to catch that young aviator—the one who's a Marchese—then I don't know anything. And Jenny has no chance beside her. I know that too. I wonder if that's why Grace Ansley likes the two girls to go everywhere together? My poor Jenny as a foil—!" Mrs. Slade gave a hardly audible laugh, and at the sound Mrs. Ansley dropped her knitting.

"Yes—?"   35

"I—oh, nothing. I was only thinking how your Babs carries everything before her. That Campolieri boy is one of the best matches in Rome. Don't look so innocent, my dear—you know he is. And I was wondering, ever so respectfully, you understand . . . wondering how two such exemplary characters as you and Horace had managed to produce anything quite so dynamic." Mrs. Slade laughed again, with a touch of asperity.

Mrs. Ansley's hands lay inert across her needles. She looked straight out at the great accumulated wreckage of passion and splendor at her feet. But her small profile was almost expressionless. At length she said: "I think you overrate Babs, my dear."

Mrs. Slade's tone grew easier. "No; I don't. I appreciate her. And perhaps envy you. Oh, my girl's perfect; if I were a chronic invalid I'd—well, I think I'd rather be in Jenny's hands. There must be times . . . but there! I always wanted a brilliant daughter . . . and never quite understood why I got an angel instead."

Mrs. Ansley echoed her laugh in a faint murmur. "Babs is an angel too."

"Of course—of course! But she's got rainbow wings. Well, they're wandering by the sea with their young men; and here we sit . . . and it all brings back the past a little too acutely."   40

Mrs. Ansley had resumed her knitting. One might almost have imagined (if one had known her less well, Mrs. Slade reflected) that, for her also, too many memories rose from the lengthening shadows of those august ruins. But no; she was simply absorbed in her work. What was there for her to worry about? She knew that Babs would almost certainly come back engaged to the extremely eligible Campolieri. "And she'll sell the New York house, and settle down near them in Rome, and never be in their way . . . she's much too tactful. But she'll have an excellent cook, and just the right people in for bridge and cocktails . . . and a perfectly peaceful old age among her grandchildren."

Mrs. Slade broke off this prophetic flight with a recoil of self-disgust. There was no one of whom she had less right to think unkindly than of Grace Ansley. Would she never cure herself of envying her? Perhaps she had begun too long ago.

She stood up and leaned against the parapet, filling her troubled eyes with the tranquilizing magic of the hour. But instead of tranquilizing her the sight seemed to increase her exasperation. Her gaze turned toward the Colosseum. Already its golden flank was drowned in purple shadow, and above it the sky curved crystal clear, without light or color. It was the moment when afternoon and evening hang balanced in mid-heaven.

Mrs. Slade turned back and laid her hand on her friend's arm. The gesture was so abrupt that Mrs. Ansley looked up, startled.

"The sun's set. You're not afraid, my dear?"   45

"Afraid—?"

"Of Roman fever or pneumonia? I remember how ill you were that winter. As a girl you had a very delicate throat, hadn't you?"

"Oh, we're all right up here. Down below, in the Forum, it does get deathly cold, all of a sudden . . . but not here."

"Ah, of course you know because you had to be so careful." Mrs. Slade turned back to the parapet. She thought: "I must make one more effort not to hate her." Aloud she said: "Whenever I look at the Forum from up here, I remember that story about a great-aunt of yours, wasn't she? A dreadfully wicked great-aunt?"

"Oh, yes; great-aunt Harriet. The one who was supposed to have sent her young   50
sister out to the Forum after sunset to gather a night-blooming flower for her album. All our great-aunts and grandmothers used to have albums of dried flowers."

Mrs. Slade nodded. "But she really sent her because they were in love with the same man—"

"Well, that was the family tradition. They said Aunt Harriet confessed it years afterward. At any rate, the poor little sister caught the fever and died. Mother used to frighten us with the story when we were children."

"And you frightened *me* with it, that winter when you and I were here as girls. The winter I was engaged to Delphin."

Mrs. Ansley gave a faint laugh. "Oh, did I? Really frightened you? I don't believe you're easily frightened."

"Not often; but I was then. I was easily frightened because I was too happy. I   55
wonder if you know what that means?"

"I—yes . . ." Mrs. Ansley faltered.

"Well, I suppose that was why the story of your wicked aunt made such an impression on me. And I thought: 'There's no more Roman fever, but the Forum is deathly cold after sunset—especially after a hot day. And the Colosseum's even colder and damper.'"

"The Colosseum—?"

"Yes. It wasn't easy to get in, after the gates were locked for the night. Far from easy. Still, in those days it could be managed; it *was* managed, often. Lovers met there who couldn't meet elsewhere. You knew that?"

"I—I dare say. I don't remember."   60

"You don't remember? You don't remember going to visit some ruins or other one evening, just after dark, and catching a bad chill? You were supposed to have gone to see the moon rise. People always said that expedition was what caused your illness."

There was a moment's silence; then Mrs. Ansley rejoined: "Did they? It was all so long ago."

"Yes. And you got well again—so it didn't matter. But I suppose it struck your friends—the reason given for your illness, I mean—because everybody knew you were so prudent on account of your throat, and your mother took such care of you. . . . You *had* been out late sight-seeing, hadn't you, that night?"

"Perhaps I had. The most prudent girls aren't always prudent. What made you think of it now?"

Mrs. Slade seemed to have no answer ready. But after a moment she broke out: 65 "Because I simply can't bear it any longer—!"

Mrs. Ansley lifted her head quickly. Her eyes were wide and very pale. "Can't bear what?"

"Why—your not knowing that I've always known why you went."

"Why I went—?"

"Yes. You think I'm bluffing, don't you? Well, you went to meet the man I was engaged to—and I can repeat every word of the letter that took you there."

While Mrs. Slade spoke Mrs. Ansley had risen unsteadily to her feet. Her bag, her 70 knitting and gloves, slid in a panic-stricken heap to the ground. She looked at Mrs. Slade as though she were looking at a ghost.

"No, no—don't," she faltered out.

"Why not? Listen, if you don't believe me. 'My one darling, things can't go on like this. I must see you alone. Come to the Colosseum immediately after dark tomorrow. There will be somebody to let you in. No one whom you need fear will suspect'—but perhaps you've forgotten what the letter said?"

Mrs. Ansley met the challenge with an unexpected composure. Steadying herself against the chair she looked at her friend, and replied: "No; I know it by heart too."

"And the signature? 'Only *your* D.S.' Was that it? I'm right, am I? That was the letter that took you out that evening after dark?"

Mrs. Ansley was still looking at her. It seemed to Mrs. Slade that a slow struggle 75 was going on behind the voluntarily controlled mask of her small quiet face. "I shouldn't have thought she had herself so well in hand," Mrs. Slade reflected, almost resentfully. But at this moment Mrs. Ansley spoke. "I don't know how you knew. I burnt that letter at once."

"Yes; you would, naturally—you're so prudent!" The sneer was open now. "And if you burnt the letter you're wondering how on earth I know what was in it. That's it, isn't it?"

Mrs. Slade waited, but Mrs. Ansley did not speak.

"Well, my dear, I know what was in the letter because I wrote it!"

"You wrote it?"

"Yes." 80

The two women stood for a minute staring at each other in the last golden light. Then Mrs. Ansley dropped back into her chair. "Oh," she murmured, and covered her face with her hands.

Mrs. Slade waited nervously for another word or movement. None came, and at length she broke out: "I horrify you."

Mrs. Ansley's hands dropped to her knee. The face they uncovered was streaked with tears. "I wasn't thinking of you. I was thinking—it was the only letter I ever had from him!"

"And I wrote it. Yes; I wrote it! But I was the girl he was engaged to. Did you happen to remember that?"

Mrs. Ansley's head drooped again. "I'm not trying to excuse myself . . . I re- 85
membered. . . ."

"And still you went?"

"Still I went."

Mrs. Slade stood looking down on the small bowed figure at her side. The flame of her wrath had already sunk, and she wondered why she had ever thought there would be any satisfaction in inflicting so purposeless a wound on her friend. But she had to justify herself.

"You do understand? I'd found out—and I hated you, hated you. I knew you were in love with Delphin—and I was afraid; afraid of you, of your quiet ways, your sweetness . . . your . . . well, I wanted you out of the way, that's all. Just for a few weeks; just till I was sure of him. So in a blind fury I wrote that letter. . . . I don't know why I'm telling you now."

"I suppose," said Mrs. Ansley slowly, "it's because you've always gone on hating 90
me."

"Perhaps. Or because I wanted to get the whole thing off my mind." She paused. "I'm glad you destroyed the letter. Of course I never thought you'd die."

Mrs. Ansley relapsed into silence, and Mrs. Slade, leaning above her, was conscious of a strange sense of isolation, of being cut off from the warm current of human communion. "You think me a monster!"

"I don't know. . . . It was the only letter I had, and you say he didn't write it?"

"Ah, how you care for him still!"

"I cared for that memory," said Mrs. Ansley. 95

Mrs. Slade continued to look down on her. She seemed physically reduced by the blow—as if, when she got up, the wind might scatter her like a puff of dust. Mrs. Slade's jealousy suddenly leapt up again at the sight. All these years the woman had been living on that letter. How she must have loved him, to treasure the mere memory of its ashes! The letter of the man her friend was engaged to. Wasn't it she who was the monster?

"You tried your best to get him away from me, didn't you? But you failed; and I kept him. That's all."

"Yes. That's all."

"I wish now I hadn't told you. I'd no idea you'd feel about it as you do; I thought you'd be amused. It all happened so long ago, as you say; and you must do me the justice to remember that I had no reason to think you'd ever taken it seriously. How could I, when you were married to Horace Ansley two months afterward? As soon as you could get out of bed your mother rushed you off to Florence and married you. People were rather surprised—they wondered at its being done so quickly; but I thought I knew. I had an idea you did it out of *pique*—to be able to say you'd got ahead of Delphin and me. Girls have such silly reasons for doing the most serious things. And your marrying so soon convinced me that you'd never really cared."

"Yes. I suppose it would," Mrs. Ansley assented. 100

The clear heaven overhead was emptied of all its gold. Dusk spread over it, abruptly darkening the Seven Hills. Here and there lights began to twinkle through the foliage at their feet. Steps were coming and going on the deserted terrace—waiters looking out of the doorway at the head of the stairs, then reappearing with trays and napkins and flasks of wine. Tables were moved, chairs straightened. A feeble string of electric lights flickered out. Some vases of faded flowers were carried away, and brought back replenished. A stout lady in a dust coat suddenly appeared, asking in broken Italian if anyone had seen the elastic band which held together her tattered Baedeker. She poked with her stick under the table at which she had lunched, the waiters assisting.

The corner where Mrs. Slade and Mrs. Ansley sat was still shadowy and deserted. For a long time neither of them spoke. At length Mrs. Slade began again: "I suppose I did it as a sort of joke—"

"A joke?"

"Well, girls are ferocious sometimes, you know. Girls in love especially. And I remember laughing to myself all that evening at the idea that you were waiting around there in the dark, dodging out of sight, listening for every sound, trying to get in—Of course I was upset when I heard you were so ill afterward."

Mrs. Ansley had not moved for a long time. But now she turned slowly toward her   105 companion. "But I didn't wait. He'd arranged everything. He was there. We were let in at once," she said.

Mrs. Slade sprang up from her leaning position. "Delphin there? They let you in?—Ah, now you're lying!" she burst out with violence.

Mrs. Ansley's voice grew clearer, and full of surprise. "But of course he was there. Naturally he came—"

"Came? How did he know he'd find you there? You must be raving!"

Mrs. Ansley hesitated, as though reflecting. "But I answered the letter. I told him I'd be there. So he came."

Mrs. Slade flung her hands up to her face. "Oh, God—you answered! I never   110 thought of your answering. . . ."

"It's odd you never thought of it, if you wrote the letter."

"Yes. I was blind with rage."

Mrs. Ansley rose, and drew her fur scarf about her. "It is cold here. We'd better go. . . . I'm sorry for you," she said, as she clasped the fur about her throat.

The unexpected words sent a pang through Mrs. Slade. "Yes; we'd better go." She gathered up her bag and cloak. "I don't know why you should be sorry for me," she muttered.

Mrs. Ansley stood looking away from her toward the dusky secret mass of the   115 Colosseum. "Well—because I didn't have to wait that night."

Mrs. Slade gave an unquiet laugh. "Yes; I was beaten there. But I oughtn't to begrudge it to you, I suppose. At the end of all these years. After all, I had everything; I had him for twenty-five years. And you had nothing but that one letter that he didn't write."

Mrs. Ansley was again silent. At length she turned toward the door of the terrace. She took a step, and turned back, facing her companion.

"I had Barbara," she said, and began to move ahead of Mrs. Slade toward the stairway.

JEANETTE WINTERSON (born 1959)

The World and Other Places 1990

[The archetypal journey, real or imagined, is at the heart of this story. Note that the author, a woman, writes in the first person through a male narrator. Key words and phrases you may not be familiar with are *tarmac*—a road, airport runway, or parking area paved with a special binder; *midges*—tiny insects resembling a mosquito; *frangipani*—the flower of a tree or shrub from which perfume is made; *tundra*—one of the vast, nearly level, treeless plains of the arctic regions of Europe, Asia, and North America; *skirting board*—a baseboard; and *sari*—a long piece of material worn by Indian women with one end draped over the head or shoulders. Sopwith Camel, Spitfire, Tiger Moth, and Red Devil are legendary fighter planes of World War I or II fame; Bombay is a major city in western India on the Arabian Sea; Cairo is the capital of Egypt. R. D. Laing was a British psychiatrist who urged people to accept themselves as they were, arguing that whatever you are, is right; Jacques Lacan was a French analyst who argued that the ego, which we consider our most personal selves, is something we only acquire from the outside world when we learn language. A Stetson is a fancy, expensive cowboy hat.]

When I was a boy, I made model airplanes. We didn't have the money to go anywhere; sometimes we didn't have the money to go to the shop. There were six of us at night in the living room, six people and six carpet tiles. Usually the tiles were laid two by three in a dismal rectangle, but on Saturday, Airplane Night, we took one each and sat cross-legged with all the expectation of an Arabian prince. We were going to fly away—and we held on to the greasy underside of our mats, waiting for the magic word to lift us. Bombay, Cairo, Paris, Chicago: We took it in turns to say the word, and the one whose turn it was took my model airplane and spun it where it hung from the ceiling, round and round our huge blow-up globe. We'd saved cereal tokens for the globe, and it had been punctured twice. Iceland was covered in cellotape, and Great Britain was only a rubber bicycle patch on the panoply of the world.

I had memorized all the flight times from London Heathrow to anywhere you could mention. It was my job to announce them and to wish the passengers a pleasant flight. Sometimes I pointed out landmarks on the way, and we would lean over into the fireplace and have a look at Mont Blanc or crane our necks round the back of the sofa just to get a glimpse of the Rockies.

About halfway through our trip, Mum, who was Chief Steward, swayed down the aisle with cups of tea and toast and Marmite. After that, Dad came forward with next week's jobs around the house written on bits of paper and put in a hat. We took out our share, and somebody, the lucky one, would just get "Duty Free" on theirs and they didn't have to do a thing.

When we reached our destination, we were glad to get up and stretch our legs, and then my sister gave us each a blindfold. We put it on and sat quietly while one of us started talking about this strange place we were visiting . . .

How hot it is getting off the plane. Hot and stale like opening the door of a tumble dryer. There are no lights to show us where to go. Death will be this way. A rough passage with people we have never met and a hasty run across the tarmac to the terminal building. Inside, in the day-for-night illumination, a group of Indians are playing the cello. Where are they from, these orchestral refugees? Can it be part of the service? Beyond them, urchins in bare feet leap up and down with ragged cardboard signs, each bearing the name of someone more important than us. These are the people who will be whisked away in closed cars to comfortable beds. The rest of us will get on the bus.

Luggage. Heaven or Hell in the afterlife will be luggage or the lack of it. The virtuous ones, the ones who knew that love is enough and that possessions are only pastimes, will float free through the exit sign, their arms ready to hug their friends, their toothbrush in their pocket. The greedy ones, who stayed up late gathering and gathering like demented bees, will find that you can take it with you. The joke is that you have to carry it yourself.

Here's the bus. It has three, maybe four wheels, and the only part noisier than the engine is the horn. All human life is here. There is something to be said for not being in a closed car. I am traveling between a crate of chickens and a fortune-teller. The chickens peck at my leg and the fortune-teller suddenly grabs my palm. She laughs in my face. "When you grow up, you'll learn to fly."

For the rest of the journey I am bitten by midges.

At last we have reached the Hotel Cockroach. Dusty mats cover the mud floor and the clerk on reception has an open wound in his cheek. He tells me he was stabbed but I am not to worry. Then he gives me some lukewarm tea and shows me my room. It has a view over the incinerator and is farthest from the bathroom. At least I will not learn to think highly of myself.

In the darkness and the silence I can hear, far below, the matter of life going on   10
without me. The night shift. What are they doing, the people who come and go? What are their lives? Whom do they love, and why? What will they eat? Where will they sleep? How many of them will see the morning? Will I?

Dreams. The smell of incense and frangipani. The moon sailing on her back makes white passages on a dun-colored floor. The moon and the clouds white at the window. How many times have I seen it? How many times do I stop and look as though I've never seen it before? Perhaps it's true that every day is the world made new again but for our habits of mind. Frozen in thought, fossilized in what we have built, how dark is the tundra of our soul. During the night a mouse gives birth behind the skirting board.

At the end of the story, my family and I swapped anecdotes and exchanged souvenirs. Later we retired to bed with all the weariness of a travelers' reunion. We had done what the astronauts do: belted the world in a few hours and still found breath to talk about it.

I knew I would get away, better myself. Not because I despised who I was, but because I didn't know who I was. I was waiting to be invented.

We went up in an airplane, the pilot and I. It was a Cessna, modern and beautiful, off-white with a blue stripe right round it and a nose as finely balanced as a pedigree muzzle. I wanted to cup it in both hands and say, "Well done, boy."

In spite of the air-conditioned cockpit, overwarm and muzzy in an unexpected   15
economy-class way, the pilot had a battered flying jacket stuffed behind his seat. It was a real one, grubby sheepskin and a steel zip. I asked him why he bothered. "Romance," he said. "Flying is romantic. Even now, even so."

We were under a 747 at the time and I thought of its orange seats crammed three abreast on either side and all the odds and ends of families struggling with their beach mats and headphones. "Is that romantic?" I said, pointing upward.

He glanced out of the window. "That's not flying. That's following the road."

For a while we continued in silence. He didn't look at me, but sometimes I looked at him: strong jaw with a bit of stubble, brown eyes that never left the sky. He was pretending to be the only man in the air. His dream was the first dream when men in plus fours and motorcycle goggles pedaled with all the single-mindedness of a circus chimp to get their wooden frames and canvas wings upward and upward and upward. It was a solo experience, even when there were two of you. What did Amy Johnson say? "If the whole world were flying beside me, I would still be flying alone." Rhetoric, you think. Frontier talk. Then you reach your own frontier and it's not rhetoric anymore.

My parents were so proud of me when I joined the air force. I stood in our cluttered living room in my new uniform and I felt like an angel on a visit. I felt like
Gabriel coming to tell the shepherds the good news.

"Soon you'll have your wings," said my mother, and my father got out the scotch.   20

In my bedroom, the model airplanes had been dusted. Sopwith Camel, Spitfire,
Tiger Moth. I picked them up one by one and turned over their balsa-wood frames and
rice-paper wings. I never used a kit. What hopes they carried! More than the altar at
church, more than a good school report. In the secret places—under the fuselage, stuck
to the tail fin—I had hidden my hopes.

My mother came in. "You won't be taking them with you?"

I shook my head. I'd be laughed at, made fun of. And yet each of us in our silent
bunks at lights-out would be thinking of model airplanes and the things at home we
couldn't talk about anymore.

She said, "I gave them a wipe anyway."

Bombay. Cairo. Paris. Chicago. I've been to those places now. I've been almost   25
everywhere, and the curious thing is that after a while they begin to look the same. I
don't mean the buildings or the scenery, I mean the people. We're all preoccupied with
the same things: how to live, whom to love, and where we go when it's over. Pressing
needs—the need to eat, the need to make money, both forcing the same hungry expression into the face—sometimes distract us from our mortality. Those needs met,
however temporarily, we can't stop ourselves reviewing again and again how short is
the space between day and night.

I saw three things that made this clear to me.

The first was a beggar in New York. He was sitting, feet apart, head in hands, on a
low wall outside an all-night garage. As I went past him he whispered, "Do you have
two dollars?"

I got out the change and gave it to him. He said, "Will you sit with me a minute?"

His name was Bill, and he was a compulsive gambler trying to go straight. He
thought he might get a job on Monday morning if only he could have two nights in a
hostel to sleep well and keep clean. For a week he had been sleeping by the steam duct
of the garage. I gave him the hostel money and some extra for food, and the clenched
fist of his body unfolded. He was talkative, gentle. Already, in his mind, he had the job
and was making a success of it and had met a sweet woman in a snack bar. He got up to
hurry over to the hostel before it closed. He shook my hand. "You know, the worst
thing about being on the street, it's not that you're hungry and cold, it's that nobody
sees you. They don't look at you, or they look through you. It's like being a ghost. If
you're already dead, what's the point of trying to live?"

The second was a dress designer I met in Milan. She was at the very top of her   30
profession, and she worked long after the others had gone home. Anyone passing could
see the light in her window. It was the only one. I never had time to talk to her over a
meal or even a cup of coffee. She had food brought into her studio, and she ate like an
urchin, pencil in one hand, in the other a palmful of olives. She spat the stones at her
models.

"I never take holidays," she said. "My models, they are always taking holidays.
They don't care."

"Perhaps you should rest," I said. "Go to one of your houses." She had five houses, but she lived in a rented flat above her studio.

"And what would I do all day, Mr. Pilot? Stare at the sky?" She went to her work-
table and picked up a pair of shears. "You start thinking, you cut your own throat.
What is there to think about? I've tried it, and it ends up the same way. In your mind

there is a bolted door. You spend your life trying to avoid that door. You go to parties, work hard, have babies, have lovers—it doesn't make any difference what way you choose. But when you are on your own, quiet, nothing to do, or sometimes just walking up the stairs, you see the door again, waiting for you. Then you have to hurry, you have to stop yourself pulling the bolt and turning the handle. On the other side of the door is a mirror, and you will see yourself for the first time. You will see what you are and, worse than that, what you are not."

The third was a woman in the park with her dog. The dog was young, the woman was old. She carried a shopping bag and every so often took out a bottle and a bowl and gave the dog a drink of water.

"Come on, Sandy," she'd say when he'd finished. Then she'd disappear into the bushes, the dog's tail bobbing behind.   35

She fascinated me because she was everything I'm not. Put us together, side by side, and what do we look like? I'm six feet tall, in an airman's uniform, and I have a strong grip and steady eyes. She's about five feet high and threadbare. I could lift her with one hand. But if she met my gaze, I'd drop my eyes and blush like a teenager. She's got the edge on me. She's not waiting to be invented; she's done it herself.

How do I know? I don't know, but increasingly I'm looking at people to see who's a fake and who's genuine. Most of us are fakes, surrounded by gilded toys and fat address books and important offices, anything to keep away from that bolted door.

For some years, the early years of my air force days, I stopped worrying about such questions. I was happy and adventurous and it was obvious that I was a man because I was doing a man's job. That's how we define ourselves, isn't it? Then one day I woke up with the curious sensation that I wasn't myself. I hadn't turned into a beetle or a werewolf. My friends treated me as they usually did. I put on my favorite well-worn clothes, bought newspapers and eggs, walked in the park. At last I went to see a doctor. I said, "Doctor, I'm not myself these days." He asked me about my sex life and gave me a course of antidepressants.

I went to the library and took out books from the philosophy and psychology sections. I read R. D. Laing, who urged me to make myself whole. Then Lacan, who wants me to accept that I'm not. And all the time I thought, "If this isn't me, then I must be somewhere." That's when I started traveling so much. I left the air force and bought my own plane. Mostly I teach; sometimes I take out families who've won the first prize in a soup-packet competition. It doesn't matter. I have plenty of free time and I do what I need to do, which is look for myself. I know that if I fly long enough, wide enough, and far enough, I'll get a signal that tells me there's another aircraft on my wing. I'll glance out of my window, and it won't be a friendly Red Devil. It'll be me I see in the cockpit of that other plane.

I went home to see my mother and father. I flew over their village, taxied down their road, and left the nose of my plane pushed up against their front door. The tail was just a little on the pavement, and I was worried that some traffic warden might give me a ticket for causing an obstruction. I hung a sign on the back saying "Flying Doctor."   40

I'm always nervous about going home, just as I'm nervous about rereading books that have meant a lot to me. My parents want me to tell them about the places I've been and what I've seen. Their eyes are eager and full of love. Bombay, Cairo, Paris, Chicago: We've invented them so many times that to tell the truth can only be a disappointment. The blow-up globe still hangs over the mantelpiece, its faded plastic crinkly and torn. The countries of the Common Market are held together by red tape.

We go through my postcards one by one, and I give them presents: a sari for my mother, a Stetson for my father. They are the children now. We have a cup of tea and at evening they come outside to wave me off. "It's a lovely plane," says my mother. "Does it give you much trouble?"

I rev the engine, and the neighbors stand astonished in their doorways as the plane gathers speed down on our quiet road. A moment before the muzzle breaks through the apostles' window in our little church, I take off, rising higher and higher and disappearing into a bank of cloud.

GLOSSARY OF LITERARY TERMS

Abstraction A generic, broad label that describes a large category—such as happiness, freedom, or honor. See *concrete*.

Allegory A symbolic work in which characters, events, or settings represent moral qualities. The characters of an allegory are often *abstractions* personified. The meaning existing below the surface in an allegorical work may be religiously, morally, politically, or personally significant. Some famous allegories include Spenser's *The Faerie Queene* and Bunyan's *The Pilgrim's Progress.*

Alliteration The repetition of the same sound at the beginning of words, as in "He clasps the crag with crooked hands."

Allusion A reference in a literary work to a historical or literary character, event, idea, or place outside the work. Allusion serves to tap indirectly into an association already existing in the reader's mind. Greek mythology has been a major source of allusion over the ages, and Biblical allusions also are frequent in English literature.

Ambiguity A quality of certain words and phrases whereby the meaning is left unclear. Authors often use ambiguity deliberately to create multiple layers of meaning.

Antagonist The character or force that is the rival, opponent, or enemy of the principle character, or *protagonist,* in a work.

Antithesis A playing off of opposites or a balancing of one term against another, as in the point/counterpoint statement, "Man proposes, God disposes." "Thesis" and "antithesis" in the original Greek mean "statement" and "counterstatement."

Antonym A word with the opposite or nearly the opposite meaning of another word. See *synonym*.

Archaic language Language that is no longer in common use. Unlike *obsolete language,* archaic words and phrases have survived but have an old-fashioned flavor. Used intentionally, archaisms can be useful in re-creating a past style.

Archetype An image, character, or event recurrent in the literature and life of diverse cultures, suggestive of universal patterns of experience. According to psychologist Carl Jung, archetypes link common human experiences. Jung held that within the human race exists a "collective unconscious" formed by the repeated experience of our ancestors. The collective unconscious is expressed in myths, religion, dreams, fantasies, and literature.

Author biography criticism   See *criticism.*

Caricature   A comic distortion exaggerating key traits to make them ridiculous. From the Italian for "exaggeration," a caricature usually focuses on personal, physical qualities. Although caricature is most often associated with drawing, it can also refer to writing.

Character   The representation of a person in a story. A character who has a one-track personality, or who represents a stereotype, is often referred to as **flat**. A character who displays a realistically complex combination of traits—including mixed emotions, conflicting motivations, and divided loyalties—is often called **round**.

Characterization   The way in which an author portrays a character to the reader. Characterization can occur through author exposition about a character as well as through the character's actions, speech, and thoughts.

Circumlocution   Indirect, roundabout phrasing, such as calling a "home" a "primary residence." A *euphemism* can be a form of circumlocution.

Cliché   A term that has lost its freshness due to overuse, such as "strong as an ox," "tip of the iceberg," and "American as apple pie." Overused situations and plots in written works also can be regarded as clichés.

Climax   The highest point of interest or intensity in a literary work, reached after a series of preparatory steps. The climax is usually the point in a story where the fortunes of the protagonist take an important turn.

Closure   A satisfying conclusion or sense of completion at the end of a work.

Comic relief   A moment of humor in a serious work. Comic relief provides a temporary break from emotional intensity and often, paradoxically, heightens the seriousness of the story.

Concrete   Vivid, graphic images that appeal strongly to the senses, as opposed to generalized *abstractions.*

Conflict   An essential element of a literary work that creates interest and suspense and leads to resolution. Four different types of conflicts are the *protagonist's* struggle against: (1) nature, (2) another person (the *antagonist*), (3) society, or (4) himself or herself (in other words, a struggle between two contradictory elements within one person).

Connotation   The associations and attitudes called up by a word, as opposed to its *denotation* or straight, literal definition. For instance, the words "aroma" and "odor" both denote a "scent," but each word has a different connotation: "aroma" connotes a rich, pleasing scent, whereas "odor" suggests something pungent and foul-smelling.

Context   The information surrounding a particular word or expression that often determines its meaning.

Conventional symbol   A symbol with familiar, agreed-upon uses. For example, a rose conventionally symbolizes love.

Counterpoint   A contrasting but parallel element or statement. See *antithesis*.

Criticism   The study, analysis, and evaluation of works of art. Traditionally, literary critics employed **author biography criticism**, looking for the meaning of the work by examining the writer's background and historical milieu. The **New Critics** of the 1940s and 1950s moved away from this stress on context. Instead, they paid close attention to the intrinsic features of a work (such as imagery, symbolism, and point of view) and to how these contribute to meaning. Any such critical position focusing on the form and technique of a work is termed **formalist criticism**. In recent decades, many critics have once again widened their scope to consider the historical, personal, or sociological context of literary works.

Contemporary critics vary greatly in their approaches to literature. **Feminist criticism** examines representations of the feminine in all literature and often focuses on works written by women. **Marxist criticism** examines the political content of a work; it often examines how works either depict or contribute to the power struggle between the classes. **Language-centered** criticism looks closely at the characteristic or changing patterns of language in a work. **Reader response criticism** focuses on how the reader contributes to the meaning of a text. **Psychoanalytic criticism** traces in literary works the typical patterns of human development and consciousness first theorized by psychoanalists such as Freud and Jung. **Myth criticism** examines the archetypal echoes and recurrent mythical allusions or themes in literary works.

Dark humor   A paradoxical humor that often uses irony to find a comic angle on catastrophe, illness, and other events that usually defeat people.

Denotation   The literal definition of a word; its stripped-down meaning devoid of *connotation*.

Dénouement   French for "untying," the plot's unraveling, clarification, or solution. The term implies an ingenious, satisfying outcome of the main dilemma, as well as an explanation of the minor plot complications.

Deus ex machina   Latin for "god from a machine." In the ancient Greek theater a contraption lowered a god or goddess onto the stage to intervene in the action and to work a last-minute solution. Thus, the phrase refers to any device, character, or event introduced suddenly to resolve a conflict in a literary work.

Dialects   The regional variations of a common language that are still mutually intelligible, although some actually border on becoming separate languages.

Dialectic   The playing off of opposing forces or points of view.

Dialogue   Conversation between two or more people. In a literary work, dialogue advances plot and reveals characterization and can provide relief from expository or descriptive passages. See *monologue*.

Diction   The writer's choice and use of words.

Didacticism   In a literary work, the presentation of ideas intended to instruct or improve the reader.

Empathy   Identifying deeply with the experience, situation, feelings, or motives of another.

Epigram   A concise, cleverly worded remark making a pointed, witty statement. From the Greek for "inscription," an epigram often contains an antithesis, as in "Man proposes, God disposes."

Epiphany   A sudden flash of intuitive understanding in which the true meaning of things and events is revealed. The term was coined by James Joyce, and epiphanies appear at the end of many of his stories, including "Araby."

Euphemism   From the Greek for "good saying," the substitution of an indirect statement for a direct statement, often with the intention of sounding less offensive or more refined. Examples of euphemisms are calling a "janitor" a "sanitation engineer" or calling "death" "passing away."

Existentialism   A twentieth-century philosophy that denies the existence of a transcendent meaning to life and the universe and places the burden of justifying existence on individual human beings. Playwrights like Beckett, Ionesco, and Sartre helped to develop existentialism, which then influenced their drama (frequently called the *theater of the absurd*); Albert Camus called Kafka an existentialist novelist.

Explication   The line-by-line explanation of a literary text. Explication differs from interpretation in that it usually refers to a literal, step-by-step scrutiny of the language of a work, as opposed to a broader, more subjective look at its overall significance.

Exposition   The part of a story that establishes setting and situation and that often introduces important characters and themes.

Extended (or sustained) metaphor   A metaphor traced throughout a work.

External evidence   Evidence outside a piece of literature itself, examined in an attempt to understand a work's meaning. Characteristic themes in the author's other works or information found in the author's letters or interviews are common forms of external evidence.

Feminist criticism   See *criticism*.

Figurative language   Language in which the writer means something more than what is literally stated. See *allegory, hyperbole, metaphor,* and *simile*.

Flashback   A narrative structure whereby the chronological order between two or more scenes is reversed. A flashback presents a scene which took place before the time in which the story is taking place.

Foil   A character that, by contrast, underscores or enhances the distinctive characteristics of another.

Folklore   Traditional stories reflecting the customs and beliefs of a particular culture. Folklore can include superstitions, proverbs, myths, legends, riddles, charms, spells, omens, ballads, nursery rhymes, and songs.

Foreshadowing   Hints in a literary work concerning a future development. Foreshadowing can be achieved through establishment of a certain mood or atmosphere in the setting or through more concrete means such as objects, narration, or a character's speech or traits.

Formalist criticism   See *criticism.*

Frame story   A narrative which frames the main series of events of a story, and tends to be separated either in space or time, or both, from that main story.

Grotesque   Literature or art characterized by bizarre, fantastic, or ominous characters or events.

Hyperbole   A figure of speech using extreme exaggeration. From the Greek for "excess," hyperbole is often expressed as a simile, as in "he's as strong as an ox."

Idiom   The characteristic language style of a person or group of people. From the Greek for "peculiarity," idiom can refer to a regional speech or dialect or to the specialized vocabulary or jargon of a group such as doctors, lawyers, or scientists.

Image   A literal or concrete detail that speaks to the physical senses of sight, hearing, smell, taste, or touch. See *concrete.*

Incongruity   The quality of being composed of inconsistent, discordant parts. The *metaphysical poets* focused on incongruity in their works. See *irony, paradox,* and *polarity.*

Interpretation   Moving beyond line-by-line *explication* of a text and examining its major themes in order to see its larger human significance.

Intruding author   A narrative device whereby the author, or a persona representing the author, interrupts the story and addresses the reader directly, offering asides, philosophical reflections, or comments upon the plot of the story. The reader thus becomes aware of the author's presence outside the story.

Inversion   The reversal of normal word order in a sentence.

Irony   An effect produced when there is a discrepancy between two levels of meaning. **Irony of situation** refers to a contrast between what we expect to happen and what really happens. **Verbal irony** refers to a deliberate contrast between what is said and what is meant. See *paradox* and *hyperbole.*

Language-centered criticism   See *criticism.*

Malaproprism   An often humorous misuse of a word. The term is derived from the character Mrs. Malaprop, in Sheridan's play *The Rivals,* who voiced such expressions as "illiterate him . . . from your memory."

Marxist criticism   See *criticism.*

Melodrama   A story characterized by an overly dramatic, sensationalized romantic plot. Traditional melodramas present good and evil stock characters and have a happy ending, although tragedies that use similar techniques are also sometimes called melodramatic.

Metaphor   A comparison between two essentially unlike things. With metaphor, the speaker treats one thing as if it were another, without the use of "like" or "as," as in these Emily Dickinson lines: "Hope is the thing with feathers / That perches in the soul." See *extended metaphor* and *simile.*

Metonymy A figure of speech in which a term closely related to something serves as its substitute. For instance, the word "sword" means "military career" in the line "He abandoned the sword." See *synechdoche.*

Minimalism A contemporary style of writing that tries to eliminate all rhetoric and emotion or at least to reduce these elements to bare essentials. Minimalist writers include Anne Beattie and Raymond Carver.

Modernism A movement of the early twentieth century against the conventions of Romantic literary representation. In their search for new modes of expression, the modernists rejected the flowery and artificial language of Victorian literature and began using techniques such as *stream of consciousness* in fiction and *free verse* in poetry. Famous modernists include James Joyce, Virginia Woolf, and Ernest Hemingway.

Mood The emotional or psychological cast of a work, generally produced by literary devices such as *tone, imagery,* and *setting.*

Myth criticism See *criticism.*

Narrator The person who relates the story. See *speaker, point of view,* and *reflector.*

Naturalism A literary movement in the late nineteenth and early twentieth centuries characterized by frank, unidealized portrayals of life's raw elements. Naturalism strives toward objective portrayal, often resulting in a neutral portrayal of nature and a recognition of humanity's physical and emotional needs. Some notable writers of this period include John Steinbeck, Stephen Crane, and Guy de Maupassant.

Neoclassicism The eighteenth-century revival of interest in classical Greek and Roman works. Neoclassical writers believed that sound judgment should guide and restrain the poetic imagination. They prized order, concentration, economy, logic, restrained emotion, correctness, and decorum. Notable writers of this period include Milton, Pope, and Johnson.

New Critics See *criticism.*

Novel A work of narrative prose fiction, generally considerably longer and more complex than a short story, with a central character or group of characters whose experiences, actions, and feelings make up the plot.

Novella A pointed story shorter than a full-length novel but longer than a traditional short story.

Obsolete language Words and phrases that are no longer in use. See *archaic language.*

Onomatopoeia The use of a word that sounds like its meaning, such as *pop, hiss,* or *buzz.*

Oral history A cultural tradition of passing spoken stories from one generation to the next, often combining myth, history, and current events.

Paradox An apparent contradiction that, on second thought, illuminates a truth. See *incongruity, irony,* and *polarity.*

Parallelism The repetition of similar or identical structures within phrases or sentences.

Paraphrase Stating someone else's ideas in your own words.

Parody   A humorous, mocking imitation of a serious piece.

Pathos   A quality in literature or art that arouses pity, sympathy, tenderness, or sorrow. From the Greek for "suffering" and "passion," pathos usually applies to a helpless character who suffers passively.

Peripety   A sudden reversal of fortune for a protagonist brought on by an unexpected discovery. From the Greek for "to change suddenly."

Personification   Figurative language that endows something nonhuman with human qualities, as in "the trees whispered in the wind."

Plot   The pattern of events in a story. See *subplot.*

Point of view   The angle from which a story is told. In **first-person** point of view, one of the characters narrates the story. In **third-person omniscient** point of view, the writer may write as an "all-seeing" author, revealing actions and mental activities of the characters. In **third-person limited** point of view, the writer reveals the actions and thoughts of only some of the characters. In **third-person objective,** the writer offers little or no comment on the action.

Polarity   The play of two opposites on a spectrum. See *incongruity, irony,* and *paradox.*

Protagonist   The leading or principle figure in a work. The protagonist and the antagonist, the second most important character, are generally rivals, enemies, or foils. See *antagonist.*

Psychoanalytical criticism   See *criticism.*

Pun   A type of *word play,* sometimes on the similar sense or sound of two words and sometimes on different meanings of the same word.

Reader response criticism   See *criticism.*

Realism   A literary movement which lasted from roughly the mid-nineteenth century to the early twentieth century in America, England, and France. Realism is characterized by the attempt to truthfully depict the lives of ordinary men and women through the accurate description of details and psychologically realistic characters. Some famous writers of the period include Thomas Hardy, and Honoré de Balzac.

Recurrence   The reappearance of themes or key elements that serves to echo issues and concerns introduced earlier.

Reflector   A person through whom the reader experiences the story. Although this is often the narrator, it can also be a character within the story if important information is communicated through his or her perceptions or thoughts.

Reiteration   Purposeful, insistent repetition in poetry or prose that reinforces a basic point.

Repartee   A quick exchange of pointed, witty remarks.

Repetition   Recurrence of the same word or phrase used to highlight or emphasize something in a story.

Rhetoric   The study of the content, structure, and style of literature, with particular attention paid to the effective or persuasive use of language.

Romanticism   An artistic revolt of the late eighteenth and early nineteenth centuries against the traditional, formal, and orderly *Neoclassicism.* Whereas Neoclassicism stressed the "order in beauty," Romanticism stresses the "strangeness in beauty" (Walter Pater). The writers of this time dropped conventional poetic diction and forms in favor of freer forms and bolder language, and explored nature, "organic unity," mysticism, the grotesque, and emotional psychology in their art. Some famous writers of this period include Blake, Keats, and Shelley.

Sarcasm   A bitter or cutting remark that moves beyond verbal irony.

Satire   An ironic, witty literary work that criticizes human misconduct and ridicules stupidity, vice, and folly. Offenders are measured against an implied standard of humane behavior.

Sentimentality   An oversimplified, emotional quality of a literary work.

Setting   The location and time in which the action of a story takes place.

Simile   A comparison between two essentially unlike things, using "as" or "like" or "as if": "My love is like a red, red rose." Unlike the implied comparison of a *metaphor*, a simile says outright that something is like something else.

Slang   Colloquial, informal language not acceptable for highly formal usage.

Speaker   The voice speaking in a poem or story, as distinct from the author as a person. Also called the *narrator*.

Stream of consciousness   A narrative technique that reflects the mental world of a shifting sequence of sensations, thought, and feelings—a kaleidoscopic mix of fleeting images, bodily sensations, memories, half-finished trains of thought.

Stock character   A conventional character; a stereotype. Stock characters people literary works as the allegorical personifications in ancient morality plays to immediately recognizable characters in modern drama, such as the meddling in-laws or the studious "nerd."

Style   An author's unmistakable personal choice of words, sentence construction, diction, imagery, tone, and ideas.

Subplot   Story lines or conflicts parallel to the main plot that reinforce a work's central theme. See *plot*.

Symbol   An object or action that has acquired a meaning beyond itself. Symbols are often used to articulate the themes of a literary work. See *conventional symbol*.

Synechdoche   A figure of speech that uses the part to stand for the whole, or the whole to stand for the part: "wheels" to mean "car" and "hired hands" to mean "hired people." See *metonymy*.

Synonym   A word that has the same or nearly the same meaning as another word. See *antonym*.

Theme   A recurring, unifying subject, idea, or motif; the primary idea being explored or general statement being made by a literary work.

Thesis statement   A concise, memorable statement of what a written work is attempting to prove. The thesis statement often appears toward the beginning of the work but can also appear at the end. A thesis statement can be explicit, meaning it is stated outright, or implicit, meaning the work's theme is implied.

Tone   The implied attitude of a writer toward the subject, material, and reader.

Tragedy   A work that dramatizes traditional stories about lethal conflicts and fateful choices. The traditional tragedy recounts the fall of heroes or persons of high degree.

Tragicomedy   A mixed genre in which the tragic and comedic elements contend. A tragicomedy, for instance, can employ a tragic plot but end happily, like a comedy.

Transition   A link that smoothly moves the reader from one paragraph or idea to the next.

Understatement   Lack of emphasis on the undercurrents or implications of what is being talked about. See *tone*.

Vignette   A sketch or brief narrative that concisely captures a moment in time. It may be a separate whole or a portion of a larger work.

Word play   Witty or clever use of words. See *pun*.

ACKNOWLEDGMENTS

Chinua Achebe. "Why the Turtle's Shell Is Not Smooth" from *Things Fall Apart*. Copyright © 1959 by Chinua Achebe. Reprinted by permission of William Heinemann Limited.

Sherwood Anderson. "Paper Pills," from *Winesburg, Ohio* by Sherwood Anderson, Introduction, Malcolm Cowley. Copyright 1919 by B. W. Huebsch. Copyright 1947 by Eleanor Copenhaver Anderson. Used by permission of Viking Penguin, a division of Penguin Books USA Inc.

Margaret Atwood. "Rape Fantasies" from *Dancing Girls and Other Stories*. Copyright © 1977 by Margaret Atwood. Reprinted by permission of the Canadian Publishers, McClelland & Stewart Ltd. First appeared in *Chatelaine* Magazine.

Isaac Babel. "My First Goose." Reprinted by permission of S. G. Phillips, Inc. from *The Collected Stories of Isaac Babel*. Copyright © 1955 by S. G. Phillips, Inc.

Toni Cade Bambara. "The Lesson." From *Gorilla, My Love* by Toni Cade Bambara. Copyright © 1972 by Toni Cade Bambara. Reprinted by permission of Random House, Inc.

Donald Barthelme. "The Balloon" from *Unspeakable Practices, Unnatural Acts*. Copyright 1968 by Donald Barthelme, reprinted with the permission of Wylie, Aitken & Stone, Inc.

Ann Beattie. "Shifting." From *Secrets and Surprises* by Ann Beattie. Copyright © 1976, 1977, 1978 by Ann Beattie. Reprinted by permission of Random House, Inc.

Ray Bradbury. "There Will Come Soft Rains." Reprinted by permission of Don Congdon Associates, Inc. Copyright 1950, renewed © 1977 by Ray Bradbury. Originally published in *Collier's* Magazine. Sara Teasdale poem "There Will Come Soft Rains" reprinted with permission of Macmillan Publishing Company from *Collected Poems of Sara Teasdale*. Copyright 1920 by Macmillan Publishing Company, renewed 1948 by Mamie T. Wheless.

Raymond Carver. "The Third Thing That Killed My Father Off" from *Furious Seasons* (in which it appeared entitled "Dummy"), copyright © 1977 by Raymond Carver. Reprinted by permission of Capra Press, Santa Barbara.

John Cheever. "The Enormous Radio." From *The Stories of John Cheever* by John Cheever. Copyright 1947 by John Cheever. Reprinted by permission of Alfred A. Knopf, Inc.

Anton Chekhov. "Gooseberries" and "Vanka" by Anton Chekhov and translated by Avrahm Yarmolinsky, from *The Portable Chekhov* by Avrahm Yarmolinsky, editor. Copyright 1947, 1968 by Viking Penguin, Inc. Renewed copyright © 1975 by Avrahm Yarmolinsky. Used by permission of Viking Penguin, a division of Penguin Books USA Inc.

Rick DeMarinis. Excerpt from *The Coming Triumph of the Free World* by Rick DeMarinis. Copyright © 1988 by Rick DeMarinis. Used by permission of Viking Penguin, a division of Penguin Books USA Inc.

Ralph Ellison. "Mister Toussan," *New Masses, 41* (November 4, 1941). Reprinted by permission of the William Morris Agency, Inc.

William Faulkner. "A Rose for Emily" (copyright 1930 and renewed 1958 by William Faulkner) and "Barn Burning" (copyright 1950 by Random House, Inc. and renewed 1977 by Jill Faulkner Summers) from *Collected Stories of William Faulkner* by William Faulkner. Reprinted by permission of Random House, Inc.

Ernst Fisher. "'The Country Doctor' and Ideology." From "Kafka-Konference" in *Franz Kafka aus Prager Sicht 1963* (Prague 1965), pp. 157–168.

Gabriel García Márquez. "The Handsomest Drowned Man in the World" from *Leaf Storm and Other Stories* by Gabriel García Márquez, translated by Gregory Rabassa. English translation © 1970 by Gabriel García Márquez. Reprinted by permission of HarperCollins Publishers.

Richard Giannone. "The Mystery of Love." Excerpted from *Flannery O'Connor and the Mystery of Love* by Richard Giannone, © 1989. Reprinted by permission of the University of Illinois Press.

Nadine Gordimer. "Amnesty" from *Jump* by Nadine Gordimer. Copyright © 1991 by Felix Licensing, B. V. Reprinted by permission of Farrar, Straus & Giroux, Inc.

Ernest Hemingway. "Hills Like White Elephants." Reprinted with permission of Charles Scribner's Sons, an imprint of Macmillan Publishing Company, from *Men Without Women* by Ernest Hemingway. Copyright 1927 by Charles Scribner's Sons; renewal copyright 1955 by Ernest Hemingway.

Zora Neale Hurston. "Sweat" from *Their Eyes Were Watching God* by Zora Neale Hurston. Copyright 1937 by Harper & Row, Publishers, Inc. Copyright renewed 1965 by John C. Hurston and Joel Hurston. Reprinted by permission of HarperCollins Publishers.

Kazuo Ishiguro. "A Family Supper," copyright © 1990 by Kazuo Ishiguro. First appeared in *Esquire* Magazine. Reprinted by permission of the author.

Shirley Jackson. "The Lottery" from *The Lottery and Other Stories* by Shirley Jackson. Copyright 1948, 1949 by Shirley Jackson. Copyright renewed © 1976, 1977 by Laurence Hyman, Barry Hyman, Mrs. Sarah Webster and Mrs. Joanne Schnurer. Reprinted by permission of Farrar, Straus & Giroux, Inc.

Franz Kafka. "The Country Doctor." From *The Penal Colony* by Franz Kafka, translated by Willa and Edwin Muir. Translation copyright 1948 and renewed 1976 by Schocken Books, Inc. Reprinted by permission of Schocken Books, published by Pantheon Books, a division of Random House, Inc.

Jamaica Kincaid. "Girl" from *At the Bottom of the River* by Jamaica Kincaid. Copyright © 1978, 1983 by Jamaica Kincaid. Reprinted by permission of Farrar, Straus & Giroux, Inc.

Milan Kundera. "Kafka and Modern History" from *The Art of the Novel* by Milan Kundera, translated by Linda Asher and David Bellos. Copyright © 1988 by Grove Press, Inc. Used by permission of Grove Press, Inc.

D. H. Lawrence. "The Rocking Horse Winner" by D. H. Lawrence, copyright 1933 by the Estate of D. H. Lawrence, renewed © 1961 by Angelo Ravagli and C. M. Weekley, Executors of the Estate of Frieda Lawrence, from *Complete Short Stories of D. H. Lawrence* by D. H. Lawrence. Used by permission of Viking Penguin, a division of Penguin Books USA Inc.

Ursula K. Le Guin. "Those Who Walk Away from Omelas." Copyright © 1973 by Ursula K. Le Guin; first appeared in *New Dimensions 3;* reprinted by permission of the author and the author's agent, Virginia Kidd.

Doris Lessing. "Homage for Isaac Babel." From *A Man and Two Women* by Doris Lessing. Copyright © 1958, 1962, 1963 by Doris Lessing. Reprinted by permission of Simon & Schuster, Inc. "Wine" from *The Habit of Loving* by Doris Lessing. Copyright © 1957 by Doris Lessing. Reprinted by permission of HarperCollins Publishers.

James M. McGlathery. "The Challenges of Desire." From "Desire's Persecutions in Kafka's 'Judgement,' 'Metamorphosis,' and 'A Country Doctor,'" *Perspectives on Contemporary Literature*, Vol. 7. Reprinted by permission of the University of Kentucky Press.

Bernard Malamud. "The Magic Barrel" from *The Magic Barrel* by Bernard Malamud. Copyright 1954, renewal copyright © 1982 by Bernard Malamud. Reprinted by permission of Farrar, Straus & Giroux, Inc.

Katherine Mansfield. "The Doll's House." From *The Short Stories of Katherine Mansfield* by Katherine Mansfield. Copyright 1923 by Alfred A. Knopf, Inc. and renewed 1951 by John Middleton Murry. Reprinted by permission of the publisher.

Bobbie Ann Mason. "Shiloh" from *Shiloh and Other Stories* by Bobbie Ann Mason. Copyright © 1982 by Bobbie Ann Mason. Reprinted by permission of HarperCollins Publishers.

Yukio Mishima. "Swaddling Clothes." From Yukio Mishima: *Death in Midsummer.* Copyright © 1966 by New Directions Publishing Corporation. Reprinted by permission of New Directions Publishing Corporation.

Toni Morrison. "1920" from *Sula.* Copyright © 1973 by Toni Morrison. Reprinted by permission of the author.

Farley Mowat. "The Snow Walker." From *The Snow Walker* by Farley Mowat. Copyright © 1975 by McClelland and Stewart Limited. By permission of Little, Brown and Company and Farley Mowat Limited.

Bharati Mukherjee. "A Wife's Story" from *The Middleman and Other Stories* by Bharati Mukherjee. Copyright © 1988 by Bharati Mukherjee. Used by permission of Grove Press, Inc.

Alice Munro. "Boys and Girls" from *Dance of the Happy Shades.* Copyright © 1968 by Alice Munro. Originally published by McGraw-Hill Ryerson Limited. Reprinted by arrangement with Virginia Barber Literary Agency. All rights reserved.

Carmen Naranjo. "Walls," translated by Barbara Paschke. From Barbara Paschke and David Volpendesta, eds., *Clamor of Innocence: Central American Short Stories.* Copyright © 1988 by Barbara Paschke. Reprinted by permission of City Lights Books.

Joyce Carol Oates. "Stalking." From *Marriages and Infidelities* by Joyce Carol Oates. Copyright © 1968, 1969, 1970, 1971, 1972 by Joyce Carol Oates. Reprinted by permission of Vanguard Press, a division of Random House, Inc.

Flannery O'Connor. "Everything That Rises Must Converge" and "Enoch and the Gorilla" from *The Complete Stories* by Flannery O'Connor. Copyright © 1961, 1965, 1971 by the Estate of Mary Flannery O'Connor. Reprinted by permission of Farrar, Straus & Giroux, Inc. "A Good Man Is Hard to Find" from *A Good Man Is Hard to Find and Other Stories,* copyright 1953 by Flannery O'Connor and renewed 1981 by Regina O'Connor, reprinted by permission of Harcourt Brace Jovanovich, Inc. "On 'A Good Man Is Hard to Find,'" excerpt from *Mystery and Manners* by Flannery O'Connor. Copyright © 1969 by the Estate of Flannery O'Connor. Reprinted by permission of Farrar, Straus & Giroux, Inc.

Frank O'Connor. "Guests of the Nation." From *Collected Stories* by Frank O'Connor. Copyright © 1981 by Harriet O'Donovan Sheehy, Executrix of the Estate of Frank O'Connor. Reprinted by permission of Alfred A. Knopf, Inc. and Joan Daves Agency.

Tillie Olsen. "I Stand Here Ironing" from *Tell Me a Riddle* by Tillie Olsen. Copyright © 1956, 1957, 1960, 1961 by Tillie Olsen. Used by permission of Delacorte Press/Seymour Lawrence, a division of Bantam Doubleday Dell Publishing Group, Inc.

Cynthia Ozick. "The Shawl." From *The Shawl* by Cynthia Ozick. Copyright © 1980, 1983 by Cynthia Ozick. Reprinted by permission of Alfred A. Knopf, Inc.

Grace Paley. "Wants" from *Enormous Changes at the Last Minute* by Grace Paley. Copyright © 1971, 1974 by Grace Paley. Reprinted by permission of Farrar, Straus & Giroux, Inc.

Dorothy Parker. "The Standard of Living," copyright 1941 by Dorothy Parker, renewed © 1969 by Lillian Hellman, from *The Portable Dorothy Parker* by Dorothy Parker, Introduction by Brendan Gill. Used by permission of Viking Penguin, a division of Penguin Books USA Inc.

Katherine Anne Porter. "The Jilting of Granny Weatherall" from *Flowering Judas and Other Stories,* copyright 1930 and renewed 1958 by Katherine Anne Porter, reprinted by permission of Harcourt Brace Jovanovich, Inc.

Mary Robison. "Yours." From *An Amateur's Guide to the Night* by Mary Robison. Copyright © 1981, 1982, 1983 by Mary Robison. Reprinted by permission of Alfred A. Knopf, Inc.

John Steinbeck. "The Chrysanthemums," copyright 1937, renewed © 1965 by John Steinbeck, from *The Long Valley* by John Steinbeck. Used by permission of Viking Penguin, a division of Penguin Books USA Inc.

Craig Key Strete. "Lives Far Child" from *Death Chants* by Craig Key Strete (New York: Doubleday, 1988), copyright © 1988 by Craig Key Strete. Reprinted by permission of the author.

Amy Tan. "Two Kinds." Reprinted by permission of The Putnam Publishing Group from *The Joy Luck Club* by Amy Tan. Copyright © 1989 by Amy Tan.

James Thurber. "The Secret Life of Walter Mitty." Copyright 1942 James Thurber. Copyright © 1970 Helen Thurber and Rosemary A. Thurber. From *My World—and Welcome to It,* published by Harcourt Brace Jovanovich, Inc. Reprinted by permission.

Leo Tolstoy. "How Much Land Does a Man Need?" translated by Barbara Makanowitzky from *The Short Stories of Leo Tolstoy.* (Bantam Books, 1960), where it appears with the title "Land Enough for a Man." Translation copyright © 1960 by Barbara Makanowitzky. Reprinted by permission.

John Updike. "A & P." From *Pigeon Feathers and Other Stories* by John Updike. Copyright © 1962 by John Updike. Reprinted by permission of Alfred A. Knopf, Inc. Originally appeared in *The New Yorker.*

Luisa Valenzuela. "The Censors," translated by David Unger. Copyright © 1982 by David Unger. First appeared in *Short Shorts,* edited by Irving Howe (David Godine, 1982). Reprinted by permission of Susan Berholz Literary Services, New York, and by permission of Harold Ober Associates Inc. on behalf of Luisa Valenzuela.

Helena María Viramontes. "The Moths" from *The Moths and Other Stories* by Helena Maria Viramontes. Copyright © 1985 by Helena Maria Viramontes. Reprinted by permission of Arte Publico Press.

Alice Walker. "Everyday Use" from *In Love and Trouble,* copyright © 1973 by Alice Walker, reprinted by permission of Harcourt Brace Jovanovich, Inc.

Jerome Weidman. "My Father Sits in the Dark." From: *My Father Sits in the Dark and Other Stories.* Copyright 1934 by Jerome Weidman. Copyright renewed © 1961 by Jerome Weidman. Reprinted by permission of Brandt & Brandt Literary Agents, Inc.

Eudora Welty. "A Visit of Charity" from *A Curtain of Green and Other Stories,* copyright 1941 and renewed 1969 by Eudora Welty, reprinted by permission of Harcourt Brace Jovanovich, Inc.

Edith Wharton. "Roman Fever." Reprinted with the permission of Charles Scribner's Sons, an imprint of Macmillan Publishing Company, from *Roman Fever and Other Stories* by Edith Wharton. Copyright 1934 *Liberty* Magazine, renewed © 1962 by William R. Tyler.

Jeanette Winterson. "The World and Other Places." Reprinted by permission of International Creative Management, Inc. Copyright © 1990 by Jeanette Winterson. Originally appeared in *Grand Street* Magazine.

Tobias Wolff. "Say Yes" from *Back in the World* by Tobias Wolff. Copyright © 1985 by Tobias Wolff. Reprinted by permission of Houghton Mifflin Co. All rights reserved.

INDEX OF AUTHORS AND TITLES

INDEX OF LITERARY
AND RHETORICAL TERMS